Baseball America
2022
PROSPECT
HANDBOOK

BASEBALL AMERICA INC. DURHAM, N.C.

Baseball America

2022
PROSPECT
HANDBOOK

Editors
J.J. COOPER, MATT EDDY,
KYLE GLASER, CHRIS HILBURN-TRENKLE,
JOSH NORRIS AND GEOFF PONTES

Assistant Editors
BEN BADLER, TEDDY CAHILL,
MARK CHIARELLI, CARLOS COLLAZO,
JOE HEALY AND SAVANNAH MCCANN

Database and Application Development
BRENT LEWIS

Contributing Writers
MIKE DIGIOVANNA, JON MEOLI, BILL MITCHELL,
KYLE NEWMAN, NICK PIECORO, CHANDELR ROME,
JEFF SANDERS, ALEX SPEIER AND EMILY WALDON

Design & Production
JAMES ALWORTH

Cover Photo
BOBBY WITT JR.
BY BRACE HEMMELGARN/FOUR SEAM IMAGES

FOR ADDITIONAL COPIES
VISIT OUR WEBSITE AT BASEBALLAMERICA.COM OR
CALL 1-800-845-2726 TO ORDER.

US $34.95, PLUS SHIPPING AND HANDLING PER ORDER.
EXPEDITED SHIPPING AVAILABLE.

DISTRIBUTED BY SIMON & SCHUSTER
ISBN: 978-1-7355482-6-5

STATISTICS PROVIDED BY MAJOR LEAGUE BASEBALL
ADVANCED MEDIA AND COMPILED BY
BASEBALL AMERICA.

Baseball America

ESTABLISHED 1981 • P.O. Box 12877, Durham, NC 27709 • Phone (919) 682-9635

PRESIDENT	Tom Dondero
EDITOR IN CHIEF	J.J. Cooper @jjcoop36
EXECUTIVE EDITOR	Matt Eddy @MattEddyBA
CHIEF INNOVATION OFFICER	Ben Badler @benbadler
DIRECTOR OF DIGITAL STRATEGY	Mark Chiarelli @Mark_Chiarelli
CHIEF FINANCIAL OFFICER	Dan Curvelo

EDITORIAL

SENIOR EDITOR	Josh Norris @jnorris427
NATIONAL WRITERS	Teddy Cahill @tedcahill
	Carlos Collazo @CarlosACollazo
	Kyle Glaser @KyleAGlaser
PROSPECT WRITER	Geoff Pontes @GeoffPontesBA
ASSOCIATE EDITOR	Chris Hilburn-Trenkle @ChrisTrenkle
STAFF WRITER	Joe Healy @JoeHealyBA
WEB EDITOR	Kayla Lombardo @KaylaLombardo11
SPECIAL CONTRIBUTOR	Tim Newcomb @tdnewcomb

PRODUCTION

CREATIVE DIRECTOR	James Alworth

BUSINESS

TECHNOLOGY MANAGER	Brent Lewis
MARKETING/ OPERATIONS COORDINATOR	Angela Lewis
CUSTOMER SERVICE	Melissa Sunderman

STATISTICAL SERVICE
MAJOR LEAGUE BASEBALL ADVANCED MEDIA

BASEBALL AMERICA ENTERPRISES

Alliance
>>>> BASEBALL <<<<

CHAIRMAN & CEO	Gary Green
PRESIDENT	Larry Botel
GENERAL COUNSEL	Matthew Pace
DIRECTOR OF MARKETING	Amy Heart
INVESTOR RELATIONS	Michele Balfour
DIRECTOR OF OPERATIONS	Joan Disalvo
PARTNERS	Stephen Alepa
	Craig Amazeen
	Jon Ashley
	Martie Cordaro
	Andrew Fox
	Robert Hernreich
	Glenn Isaacson
	Sonny Kalsi
	Peter G. Riguardi
	Ian Ritchie
	Brian Rothschild
	Peter Ruprecht
	Beryl Snyder
	Tom Steiglehner
	Dan Waldman

INTRODUCTION

We are thrilled that you are holding in your hand a book that reflects the results, the stats and the evaluations that came from a full season of baseball games.

Before the 2021 Prospect Handbook, such a statement would seem somewhat puzzling and incredibly redundant. Of course a book of scouting reports would be heavily influenced by all the information gathered during the previous season.

Oh how naive we were.

If you own the 2021 Prospect Handbook, you know how that book was built through gathering the best information we could from the limited information coming out of alternate training sites and instructional leagues.

This year is a return to semi-normal. We sent this 2022 Prospect Handbook to the printer almost two years into the coronavirus pandemic, but once more there were complete high school, college and minor league seasons to analyze, mull over, attend and evaluate.

That's what we love to do. It's what you love to read about as well. So here we are with the best Prospect Handbook we could produce for you in 2022. It's full of as much detail as we could gather, and as we raced to complete it and send it to the printer, it was glorious to see stat line after stat line that read something other than "did not play."

J.J. COOPER
EDITOR IN CHIEF, BASEBALL AMERICA

A NOTE ABOUT THIS EDITION

Baseball America introduced BA Grades in the 2012 edition of the Prospect Handbook. We also grade all tools for the 300 players who rank as Top 10 Prospects, providing an quick overview of each player's strengths and weaknesses. All grades are projected future grades.

We grade players' tools on the 20-80 scouting scale, where 50 is average. A key to the abbreviations:

Players		Pitchers	
Hitting	Ability to hit for average	**FB**	Fastball
Power	Power	**CB**	Curveball
Run	Speed	**SL**	Slider
Field	Fielding ability	**CHG**	Changeup
Arm	Throwing arm	**CTL**	Control

ABOUT THE 2022 EDITION:

■ The transaction deadline for this book was Dec. 2, 2021, the date that MLB owners locked out the players, effectively freezing all transactions involving players on 40-man rosters.

■ To bring you more detailed scouting reports and more information about players' future outlooks, we reduced the statistical display for all prospects to include 2021 statistics and career totals only. The age displayed with each season is the player's baseball age—or age as of June 30, 2021.

■ Players are listed with their primary 2021 positions in the rankings but may be moved to a projected future position on the depth chart or in our overall position rankings.

■ Baseball America determines prospect eligibility based on major league playing time, without regard to MLB service time. Players lose prospect status for BA when they exceed 130 at-bats, 50 innings or 30 relief appearances in the big leagues. Notable players who appear in this book but are not eligible for MLB Rookie of the Year awards in 2022—because they have more than 45 days of big league service—include Reds shortstop Jose Barrero, Nationals catcher Keibert Ruiz and Cardinals outfielder Lars Nootbaar.

■ The creation of new minor league identities in 2021 necessitated the creation of new listings. The new abbreviations are derived from the following:

Triple-A: East and West

High-A: Central (Cent), East and West

Rookie: Arizona Complex (ACL), Florida Complex (FCL) and Dominican Summer (DSL) leagues

Double-A: Central (Cent), Northeast (NEast) and South

Low-A: East, Southeast (SEast) and West

TABLE OF CONTENTS

CHICAGO WHITE SOX
STARTS ON PAGE 98

No.Player, Pos.	Grade/Risk	No.Player, Pos.	Grade/Risk	No.Player, Pos.	Grade/Risk
1. Colson Montgomery, SS	55/X	11. Bryan Ramos, 3B	50/X	21. Blake Rutherford, OF	40/M
2. Yoelqui Cespedes, OF	50/H	12. Jimmy Lambert, RHP	40/M	22. Caleb Freeman, RHP	45/H
3. Norge Vera, RHP	55/X	13. Jonathan Stiever, RHP	45/H	23. Luis Mieses, OF	40/H
4. Wes Kath, 3B	55/X	14. Jason Bilous, RHP	45/H	24. Wilber Sanchez, SS	45/X
5. Jose Rodriguez, SS	50/H	15. Romy Gonzalez, SS	45/H	25. Yoelvin Silven, RHP	40/H
6. Andrew Dalquist, RHP	50/H	16. Yolbert Sanchez, 2B/SS	45/H	26. Bennett Sousa, LHP	40/H
7. Jake Burger, RHP	45/M	17. Lenyn Sosa, SS/2B	45/H	27. Brooks Gosswein, LHP	40/H
8. Jared Kelley, RHP	50/X	18. Micker Adolfo, OF	45/H	28. Gil Luna, LHP	40/H
9. Sean Burke, RHP	45/H	19. Tanner McDougal, RHP	50/X	29. Wilfred Veras, 3B/1B	45/X
10. Matthew Thompson, RHP	50/X	20. Cristian Mena, RHP	50/X	30. Adam Hackenberg, C	40/H

CINCINNATI REDS
STARTS ON PAGE 114

No.Player, Pos.	Grade/Risk	No.Player, Pos.	Grade/Risk	No.Player, Pos.	Grade/Risk
1. Jose Barrero, SS	55/M	11. Mat Nelson, C	50/H	21. Ariel Almonte, OF	50/X
2. Hunter Greene, RHP	55/H	12. Jose Torres, SS	50/H	22. Andrew Abbott, LHP	45/H
3. Nick Lodolo, LHP	55/H	13. Carson Spiers, RHP	50/H	23. Alexis Diaz, RHP	45/H
4. Elly de la Cruz, SS/3B	60/X	14. Allan Cerda, OF	55/X	24. Alejo Lopez, 2B	40/M
5. Matt McLain, SS	55/H	15. Dauri Moreta, RHP	45/M	25. Carlos Jorge, SS	50/X
6. Austin Hendrick, OF	50/H	16. Christian Roa, RHP	50/H	26. Mark Kolozsvary, C	45/H
7. Jay Allen, OF	55/X	17. Tyler Callihan, 2B	45/H	27. Leonardo Balcazar, SS	50/X
8. Rece Hinds, 3B	55/X	18. Ivan Johnson, 2B	45/H	28. Reiver Sanmartin, RHP	40/M
9. Graham Ashcraft, RHP	50/H	19. Daniel Vellojin, C	45/H	29. Yerlin Confidan, OF	50/X
10. Bryce Bonnin, RHP	50/H	20. TJ Friedl, OF	40/M	30. Mike Siani, OF	45/H

CLEVELAND GUARDIANS
STARTS ON PAGE 130

No.Player, Pos.	Grade/Risk	No.Player, Pos.	Grade/Risk	No.Player, Pos.	Grade/Risk
1. Tyler Freeman, SS	55/H	11. Jose Tena, SS/2B	50/V	21. Doug Nikhazy, LHP	45/H
2. Daniel Espino, RHP	55/H	12. Tanner Burns, RHP	45/H	22. Petey Halpin, OF	45/H
3. Brayan Rocchio, SS	55/H	13. Richie Palacios, 2B/OF	45/H	23. Tobias Myers, RHP	45/H
4. George Valera, OF	55/H	14. Peyton Battenfield, RHP	45/H	24. Ernie Clement, 2B/3B	40/M
5. Gabriel Arias, SS	55/H	15. Cody Morris, RHP	50/X	25. Aaron Bracho, 2B	45/H
6. Nolan Jones, 3B	50/M	16. Bryan Lavastida, C	45/H	26. Carlos Vargas, RHP	50/X
7. Bo Naylor, C	55/V	17. Carson Tucker, SS	50/X	27. Steven Kwan, OF	45/H
8. Gavin Williams, RHP	55/V	18. Gabriel Rodriguez, 3B/SS	50/X	28. Xzavion Curry, RHP	45/H
9. Logan Allen, LHP	50/H	19. Ethan Hankins, RHP	50/X	29. Tommy Mace, RHP	45/H
10. Angel Martinez, SS	50/V	20. Jhonkensy Noel, 3B/1B	50/X	30. Konnor Pilkington, LHP	45/H

COLORADO ROCKIES
STARTS ON PAGE 146

No.Player, Pos.	Grade/Risk	No.Player, Pos.	Grade/Risk	No.Player, Pos.	Grade/Risk
1. Zac Veen, OF	60/H	11. Jaden Hill, RHP	55/X	21. Noah Davis, RHP	45/H
2. Michael Toglia, 1B	50/H	12. Aaron Schunk, 3B	50/H	22. Joe Rock, LHP	45/H
3. Drew Romo, C	50/H	13. Chris McMahon, RHP	50/H	23. Karl Kauffmann, RHP	45/H
4. Ryan Rolison, LHP	45/M	14. Colton Welker, 3B/1B	45/M	24. Bladimir Restituyo, OF	40/H
5. Benny Montgomery, OF	55/X	15. Helcris Olivarez, LHP	50/X	25. Grant Lavigne, 1B	40/H
6. Ryan Vilade, OF	45/M	16. Warming Bernabel, 3B	50/X	26. Jameson Hannah, OF	40/H
7. Brenton Doyle, OF	50/H	17. Sam Weatherly, LHP	45/H	27. Yoan Aybar, LHP	45/X
8. Elehuris Montero, 3B/1B	50/H	18. Yanquiel Fernandez, OF	50/X	28. Reagan Todd, LHP	40/H
9. Ezequiel Tovar, SS	50/H	19. Adrian Pinto, SS/2B	50/X	29. Justin Lawrence, RHP	45/X
10. Adael Amador, SS/3B	55/X	20. Julian Fernandez, RHP	45/H	30. Gavin Hollowell, RHP	40/H

DETROIT TIGERS
STARTS ON PAGE 162

No.Player, Pos.	Grade/Risk	No.Player, Pos.	Grade/Risk	No.Player, Pos.	Grade/Risk
1. Riley Greene, OF	65/M	11. Cristian Santana, SS	50/X	21. Jason Foley, RHP	40/H
2. Spencer Torkelson, 1B	65/M	12. Manuel Sequera, SS	50/X	22. Wilmer Flores, RHP	45/V
3. Jackson Jobe, RHP	60/X	13. Colt Keith, 3B	50/X	23. Jose de la Cruz, OF	45/X
4. Dillon Dingler, C	50/H	14. Dylan Smith, RHP	45/H	24. Adinso Reyes, SS	45/X
5. Gage Workman, RHP	50/H	15. Reese Olson, RHP	45/H	25. Eliezer Alfonzo, C	40/H
6. Ty Madden, RHP	50/H	16. Daniel Cabrera, OF	45/H	26. Parker Meadows, OF	40/H
7. Ryan Kreidler, SS	50/H	17. Kody Clemens, 2B	40/H	27. Abel Bastidas, SS	45/X
8. Roberto Campos, OF	55/X	18. Beau Brieske, RHP	40/H	28. Bryant Packard, OF	40/H
9. Joey Wentz, LHP	50/H	19. Tyler Mattison, RHP	40/H	29. Paul Richan, RHP	40/H
10. Izaac Pacheco, 3B	55/X	20. Alex Faedo, RHP	40/H	30. Andre Lipcius, 3B	40/H

TABLE OF CONTENTS

MILWAUKEE BREWERS

STARTS ON PAGE 258

No. Player, Pos.	Grade/Risk	No. Player, Pos.	Grade/Risk	No. Player, Pos.	Grade/Risk
1. Aaron Ashby, LHP	60/H	11. Hendry Mendez, OF	50/X	21. Felix Valerio, 2B/SS/3B	45/V
2. Brice Turang, SS	50/M	12. Joe Gray Jr., OF	45/V	22. Jheremy Vargas, SS/3B/2B	45/V
3. Sal Frelick, OF	55/V	13. Antoine Kelly, LHP	50/X	23. Carlos Rodriguez, OF	40/H
4. Garrett Mitchell, OF	55/V	14. Russell Smith, LHP	45/H	24. Alec Bettinger, RHP	40/H
5. Tyler Black, 2B	50/H	15. Eduardo Garcia, SS	45/H	25. Victor Castaneda, RHP	40/H
6. Hedbert Perez, OF	55/X	16. Freddy Zamora, SS	45/H	26. Gregory Barrios, SS	45/X
7. Jeferson Quero, C	55/X	17. Zavier Warren, 3B/C	45/H	27. Daniel Guilarte, SS	45/X
8. Joey Wiemer, OF	50/V	18. Mario Feliciano, C	45/H	28. Dylan File, RHP	40/H
9. Ethan Small, LHP	45/H	19. Logan Henderson, RHP	50/X	29. Korry Howell, OF/3B/SS	40/H
10. Jackson Chourio, OF	50/X	20. Abner Uribe, RHP	45/V	30. Ethan Murray, SS	40/H

MINNESOTA TWINS

STARTS ON PAGE 274

No. Player, Pos.	Grade/Risk	No. Player, Pos.	Grade/Risk	No. Player, Pos.	Grade/Risk
1. Austin Martin, OF/SS	60/H	11. Emmanuel Rodriguez, OF	50/X	21. Danny De Andrade, SS/3B	50/X
2. Royce Lewis, SS	60/X	12. Louie Varland, RHP	45/H	22. Keoni Cavaco, SS	50/X
3. Jordan Balazovic, RHP	55/H	13. Steven Hajjar, LHP	45/H	23. Jovani Moran, LHP	40/M
4. Joe Ryan, RHP	50/M	14. Noah Miller, SS	50/X	24. Chris Vallimont, RHP	45/H
5. Jose Miranda, 3B/2B	50/M	15. Spencer Steer, 2B/3B	45/H	25. Matt Wallner, OF	45/V
6. Josh Winder, RHP	55/H	16. Cole Sands, RHP	45/H	26. Edouard Julien, 2B/3B/OF	45/X
7. Chase Petty, RHP	55/X	17. Drew Strotman, RHP	45/H	27. Kala'i Rosario, OF	45/X
8. Simeon Woods Richardson, RHP	50/H	18. Blayne Enlow, RHP	50/X	28. Misael Urbina, OF	45/X
9. Matt Canterino, RHP	55/X	19. Aaron Sabato, 1B	45/H	29. Jermaine Palacios, SS	40/H
10. Jhoan Duran, RHP	50/H	20. Gilberto Celestino, OF	40/M	30. Marco Raya, RHP	45/X

NEW YORK METS

STARTS ON PAGE 290

No. Player, Pos.	Grade/Risk	No. Player, Pos.	Grade/Risk	No. Player, Pos.	Grade/Risk
1. Francisco Alvarez, C	65/H	11. Jose Butto, RHP	45/H	21. Jose Peroza, 3B/2B	45/H
2. Brett Baty, 3B	60/H	12. Dominic Hamel, RHP	45/H	22. Robert Dominguez, RHP	50/X
3. Ronny Mauricio, SS `	55/H	13. Nick Plummer, OF	45/H	23. Hayden Senger, C	45/H
4. Mark Vientos, 3B	55/H	14. Mike Vasil, RHP	50/X	24. Javier Atencio, LHP	50/X
5. Matt Allan, RHP	60/X	15. Jaylen Palmer, 3B/OF	45/H	25. Vincent Perozo, C	50/X
6. J.T. Ginn, RHP	55/H	16. Carlos Cortes, OF	45/H	26. JT Schwartz, 1B	45/V
7. Alex Ramirez, OF	55/V	17. Luis Rodriguez, LHP	50/X	27. Kevin Kendall, SS/2B	45/V
8. Khalil Lee, OF	45/M	18. Junior Santos, RHP	50/X	28. Jake Mangum, OF	40/H
9. Joel Diaz, RHP	50/X	19. Jordany Ventura, RHP	50/X	29. Luke Ritter, 2B/1B	40/H
10. Calvin Ziegler, RHP	50/X	20. Adam Oller, RHP	45/H	30. Joander Suarez, RHP	40/V

NEW YORK YANKEES

STARTS ON PAGE 306

No. Player, Pos.	Grade/Risk	No. Player, Pos.	Grade/Risk	No. Player, Pos.	Grade/Risk
1. Anthony Volpe, SS	65/H	11. Everson Pereira, OF	50/H	21. Ron Marinaccio, RHP	40/M
2. Oswald Peraza, SS	55/H	12. Randy Vasquez, RHP	50/H	22. Antonio Gomez, C	50/X
3. Jasson Dominguez, OF	60/X	13. Clarke Schmidt, RHP	45/M	23. Brandon Lockridge, OF	45/H
4. Luis Gil, RHP	55/H	14. Deivi Garcia, RHP	45/M	24. Stephen Ridings, RHP	40/M
5. Austin Wells, C	50/H	15. Estevan Florial, OF	45/M	25. Beck Way, RHP	40/H
6. Hayden Wesneski, RHP	50/H	16. Brendan Beck, RHP	50/H	26. J.P. Sears, LHP	40/H
7. Trey Sweeney, SS	50/H	17. Brock Selvidge, LHP	50/X	27. Anthony Garcia, 1B/OF	45/X
8. Oswaldo Cabrera, 2B/3B	50/H	18. Elijah Dunham, OF	45/H	28. Alexander Vargas, SS	45/X
9. Luis Medina, RHP	50/H	19. Yoendrys Gomez, RHP	50/X	29. Hans Montero, SS	45/X
10. Ken Waldichuk, LHP	50/H	20. Josh Breaux, C	45/H	30. Greg Weissert, RHP	40/H

OAKLAND ATHLETICS

STARTS ON PAGE 322

No. Player, Pos.	Grade/Risk	No. Player, Pos.	Grade/Risk	No. Player, Pos.	Grade/Risk
1. Tyler Soderstrom, C	60/H	11. Jeff Criswell, RHP	45/H	21. Michael Guldberg, OF	45/H
2. Zack Gelof, 3B	55/H	12. Brent Honeywell, RHP	45/H	22. Jonah Bride, 1B/3B	40/M
3. Nick Allen, SS	45/H	13. Denzel Clarke, OF	50/X	23. Brady Feigl, RHP	40/M
4. Max Muncy, SS	55/X	14. Jordan Diaz, 1B/3B	45/H	24. Hogan Harris, LHP	45/H
5. Pedro Pineda, OF	55/X	15. Logan Davidson, SS	45/H	25. Brady Basso, LHP	45/H
6. A.J. Puk, LHP	50/H	16. Mason Miller, RHP	50/X	26. Mickey McDonald, OF	40/M
7. Daulton Jefferies, RHP	45/M	17. Robert Puason, SS	50/X	27. Max Schuemann, SS/2B	40/M
8. Brayan Buelvas, OF	50/H	18. Luis Barrera, OF	40/M	28. Junior Perez, OF	45/V
9. Lawrence Butler, 1B/OF	45/H	19. Jorge Juan, RHP	50/X	29. Angel Arevalo, SS/OF	45/X
10. Colin Peluse, RHP	45/H	20. Cody Thomas, OF	45/H	30. Brett Harris, 3B	40/H

TABLE OF CONTENTS

SEATTLE MARINERS
STARTS ON PAGE 418

No. Player, Pos.	Grade/Risk	No. Player, Pos.	Grade/Risk	No. Player, Pos.	Grade/Risk
1. Julio Rodriguez, OF	75/M	11. Andres Muñoz, RHP	55/X	21. Victor Labrada, OF	45/H
2. George Kirby, RHP	70/H	12. Zach DeLoach, OF	50/H	22. Bryce Miller, RHP	45/H
3. Noelvi Marte, SS	60/H	13. Connor Phillips, RHP	50/V	23. George Feliz, OF	50/X
4. Matt Brash, RHP	60/H	14. Alberto Rodriguez, OF	50/V	24. Kevin Padlo, 3B	40/M
5. Brandon Williamson, LHP	55/H	15. Edwin Arroyo, SS	50/X	25. Wyatt Mills, RHP	40/M
6. Emerson Hancock, RHP	55/V	16. Milkar Perez, 3B	50/X	26. Jonatan Clase, OF	50/X
7. Harry Ford, C	55/X	17. Juan Then, RHP	45/H	27. Devin Sweet, RHP	45/H
8. Levi Stoudt, RHP	50/H	18. Michael Morales, RHP	50/X	28. Cade Marlowe, OF	45/H
9. Adam Macko, LHP	55/X	19. Starlin Aguilar, 3B	50/X	29. Kaden Polcovich, 2B/OF	40/H
10. Gabriel Gonzalez, OF	55/X	20. Taylor Dollard, RHP	45/H	30. Penn Murfee, RHP	40/H

TAMPA BAY RAYS
STARTS ON PAGE 434

No. Player, Pos.	Grade/Risk	No. Player, Pos.	Grade/Risk	No. Player, Pos.	Grade/Risk
1. Shane Baz, RHP	65/M	11. Carlos Colmenarez, SS	55/X	21. Tommy Romero, RHP	45/M
2. Josh Lowe, OF	55/M	12. Seth Johnson, RHP	50/H	22. Rene Pinto, C	45/M
3. Vidal Bruján, 2B/OF	50/M	13. Sandy Gaston, RHP	55/X	23. Kameron Misner, OF	45/H
4. Taj Bradley, RHP	55/H	14. Ian Seymour, LHP	50/H	24. Calvin Faucher, RHP	45/H
5. Curtis Mead, 3B/1B	55/H	15. Colby White, RHP	45/M	25. Osleivis Basabe, 2B/SS	45/H
6. Greg Jones, SS	55/H	16. Cooper Kinney, 2B/3B	50/V	26. Ford Proctor, C/SS	45/H
7. Carson Williams, SS	55/X	17. JJ Goss, RHP	55/X	27. Blake Hunt, C	45/H
8. Xavier Edwards, 2B	50/H	18. Nick Bitsko, RHP	55/X	28. Heriberto Hernandez, OF	50/X
9. Cole Wilcox, RHP	55/X	19. Austin Shenton, 3B	45/M	29. Alika Williams, SS	45/H
10. Willy Vasquez, SS	55/X	20. Jonathan Aranda, 2B/1B	45/M	30. Jayden Murray, RHP	45/H

TEXAS RANGERS
STARTS ON PAGE 450

No. Player, Pos.	Grade/Risk	No. Player, Pos.	Grade/Risk	No. Player, Pos.	Grade/Risk
1. Jack Leiter, RHP	60/H	11. Sam Huff, C	50/H	21. Maximo Acosta, SS	50/X
2. Josh Jung, 3B	55/M	12. Aaron Zavala, OF	50/H	22. Trevor Hauver, 2B/OF	45/H
3. Cole Winn, RHP	55/H	13. Ricky Vanasco, RHP	55/X	23. Cody Bradford, LHP	45/H
4. Ezequiel Duran, 2B/SS	50/H	14. Tekoah Roby, RHP	55/X	24. Cole Ragans, LHP	45/H
5. Dustin Harris, 1B/OF	50/H	15. Glenn Otto, RHP	45/H	25. Cameron Cauley, SS	50/X
6. Justin Foscue, 2B	50/H	16. Yeison Morrobel, OF	50/X	26. Dane Acker, RHP	50/X
7. Owen White, RHP	50/H	17. Zak Kent, RHP	45/H	27. A.J. Alexy, RHP	40/M
8. Evan Carter, OF	55/X	18. Avery Weems, LHP	45/H	28. Yohel Pozo, C	40/M
9. Josh Smith, SS	50/H	19. Bayron Lora, OF	50/X	29. Ronny Henriquez, RHP	40/H
10. Luisangel Acuña, SS	50/H	20. Mitchell Bratt, LHP	50/X	30. Danyer Cueva, SS	45/X

TORONTO BLUE JAYS
STARTS ON PAGE 466

No. Player, Pos.	Grade/Risk	No. Player, Pos.	Grade/Risk	No. Player, Pos.	Grade/Risk
1. Gabriel Moreno, C	65/M	11. Samad Taylor, 2B/3B/OF	45/H	21. Miguel Hiraldo, 2B/3B	45/V
2. Nate Pearson, RHP	55/M	12. Estiven Machado, SS	50/X	22. Dahian Santos, RHP	45/X
3. Orelvis Martinez, SS/3B	55/H	13. Sem Robberse, RHP	45/H	23. Yhoangel Aponte, OF	45/X
4. Jordan Groshans, SS/3B	55/H	14. Irv Carter, RHP	50/X	24. Zach Logue, LHP	40/M
5. Gunnar Hoglund, RHP	55/X	15. Spencer Horwitz, 1B/OF	45/H	25. Eric Pardinho, RHP	45/X
6. Otto Lopez, 2B/OF/SS	50/H	16. C.J. Van Eyk, RHP	45/H	26. Kendry Rojas, LHP	45/X
7. Kevin Smith, SS/3B	45/M	17. Adam Kloffenstein, RHP	45/H	27. Hagen Danner, RHP	40/H
8. Manuel Beltre, SS	50/X	18. Thomas Hatch, RHP	40/M	28. Rikelvin de Castro, SS	45/X
9. Ricky Tiedemann, LHP	50/X	19. Tanner Morris, 2B/3B/SS	45/H	29. Luis Garcia, SS	45/X
10. Leonardo Jimenez, SS	45/H	20. Chad Dallas, RHP	45/V	30. Josh Palacios, OF	40/H

WASHINGTON NATIONALS
STARTS ON PAGE 482

No. Player, Pos.	Grade/Risk	No. Player, Pos.	Grade/Risk	No. Player, Pos.	Grade/Risk
1. Keibert Ruiz, C	60/M	11. Mason Thompson, RHP	40/M	21. Mitchell Parker, LHP	40/H
2. Cade Cavalli, RHP	60/H	12. Riley Adams, C	40/M	22. Evan Lee, RHP	40/H
3. Brady House, SS	60/H	13. Aldo Ramirez, RHP	50/H	23. Israel Pineda, C	40/H
4. Yasel Antuna, OF	55/X	14. Jeremy de la Rosa, OF	45/V	24. Daniel Marte, OF	45/X
5. Andry Lara, RHP	55/X	15. Matt Cronin, LHP	40/H	25. Roismar Quintana, OF	45/X
6. Cole Henry, RHP	50/H	16. Jackson Cluff, SS	40/H	26. Tres Barrera, C	40/H
7. Joan Adon, RHP	45/M	17. Donovan Casey, OF	40/H	27. Seth Romero, LHP	40/H
8. Gerardo Carrillo, RHP	50/V	18. Daylen Lile, OF	45/X	28. Mason Denaburg, RHP	45/X
9. Jackson Rutledge, RHP	50/V	19. Tim Cate, LHP	40/H	29. Jordy Barley, SS	40/V
10. Armando Cruz, SS	50/X	20. Sammy Infante, SS	45/X	30. Drew Millas, C	40/V

For the 11th year, Baseball America has assigned BA Grades and risk factors for each of the 900 prospects in the Prospect Handbook. For the BA Grade, we used a 20-to-80 scale, similar to the scale scouts use, to keep it familiar. However, most major league clubs put an overall numerical grade on players, called the Overall Future Potential or OFP. Often the OFP is merely an average of the player's tools.

The BA Grade is not an OFP. It's a measure of a prospect's value, and it attempts to gauge the player's realistic ceiling. We've continued to adjust our grades to try to be more realistic, and less optimistic, and keep refining the grade vetting process. The majority of the players in this book rest in the 50/High to 45/Medium range, because the vast majority of worthwhile prospects in the minors are players who either have a chance to be everyday regulars but are far from that possibility, or

BA GRADE

50 Risk: High

players who are closer to the majors but who are likely to be role players and useful contributors. Few future franchise players or perennial all-stars graduate from the minors in any given year. The goal of the Grade/Risk system is to allow readers to take a quick look at how strong their team's farm system is, and how much immediate help the big league club can expect from its prospect. Got a minor leaguer who was traded from one organization to the other after the book went to press? Use the player's BA Grade/Risk and see where he would rank in his new system.

It also helps with our organization talent rankings, but those will not simply flow, in formulaic fashion, from the Grade/Risk results, because we incorporate a lot of factors into our talent rankings, including the differences in risk between pitchers and hitters. Hitters have a lower injury risk and therefore are safer bets.

BA Grade Scale

GRADE	HITTER ROLE	PITCHER ROLE	EXAMPLES
75-80	Franchise Player	No. 1 starter	Mike Trout, Jacob deGrom, Juan Soto
65-70	Perennial All-Star	No. 2 starter	Jose Ramirez, George Springer, Brandon Woodruff
60	Occasional All-Star	No. 3 starter, Game's best reliever	Starling Marte, Brandon Crawford, Josh Hader
55	First-Division Regular	No. 3/No. 4 starter, Closer	Mitch Haniger, Dansby Swanson, Raisel Iglesias
50	Solid-Average Regular	No. 4 starter, Setup reliever	Avisail Garcia, Wade Miley, Blake Treinen
45	Second-Division Regular/Platoon	No. 5 starter, Middle reliever	Freddy Galvis, Jordan Lyles, Tyler Duffey
40	Reserve	Fill-in starter, Low-leverage reliever	Erik Gonzalez, Tom Eshelman, Wander Suero

RISK FACTORS

LOW: Likely to reach realistic ceiling, certain big league career barring injury.

MEDIUM: Some work left to refine their tools, but a polished player.

HIGH: Most top draft picks in their first seasons, players with plenty of projection left, players with a significant flaw left to correct or players whose injury history is worrisome.

VERY HIGH: Recent draft picks with a limited track record of success or injury issues.

EXTREME: Teenagers in Rookie ball, players with significant injury histories or players whose struggle with a key skill, especially control for pitchers or strikeout rate for hitters.

Explaining The 20-80 Scouting Scale

None of the authors of this book is a scout, but we speak extensively to scouts to report on the prospects and scouting reports enclosed in the Prospect Handbook. So we use their lingo, including the 20-80 scouting scale. Many of these grades are measurable data such as fastball velocity and speed (usually timed from home to first base or in workouts over 60 yards). A fastball grade doesn't stem solely from its velocity—command and life are crucial elements as well—but throwing 100 mph usually earns a player an 80 grade. Secondary pitches are graded in a similar fashion. The more swings and misses a pitch induces from hitters and the sharper the bite of the movement, the higher the grade.

Velocity steadily has increased over the past decade. Not all that long ago an 88-91 mph fastball was considered major league average, but current data shows it is now below-average. Big league starting pitchers now sit 92-94 mph on average. You can reduce the scale by 1 mph for lefthanders because they typically throw with slightly less velocity. Fastballs earn their grades based on their average velocity over the course of a typical outing, not their peak velocity.

A move to the bullpen complicates in another direction. Pitchers airing it out for one inning should throw harder than someone trying to last six or seven innings, so add 1-2 mph for relievers. Yes, nowadays, an 80 fastball for a reliever needs to sit 99-100 mph with movement and command.

Hitting ability is as much a skill as it is a tool, but the physical elements—hand-eye coordination, swing mechanics, bat speed—are key factors in the hit tool grade. Raw power generally is measured by how far a player can hit the ball, but game power is graded by how many home runs the hitter projects to hit in the majors, preferably an average over the course of a career. We have adjusted our power grades to reflect the recent rise in home run rates.

Arm strength can be evaluated by observing the velocity and carry of throws, measured in workouts with radar guns or measured in games for catchers with pop times—the time it takes from the pop of the ball in the catcher's mitt to the pop of the ball in the fielder's glove at second base. Defense takes different factors into account by position but starts with proper footwork and technique, incorporates physical attributes such as hands, short-area quickness and fluid actions, then adds subtle skills such as instincts and anticipation as a last layer.

Not every team uses the wording below. Some use a 20-to-80 scale without half-grades, and others use above-average and plus synonymously. But for the Handbook, consider this BA's 20-80 scale.

20: As bad as it gets for a big leaguer. Think Billy Hamilton's power or Albert Pujols' speed.

30: Poor, but not unplayable, such as Miguel Sano's hitting ability.

40: Below-average, such as Rafael Devers' defense or Blake Snell's control.

45: Fringe-average. Kyle Freeland's fastball and Kurt Suzuki's arm qualify.

50: Major league average. Eddie Rosario's speed.

55: Above-average. Xander Bogaerts' power.

60: Plus. Starling Marte's speed or Lance Lynn's control.

70: Plus-Plus. Among the best tools in the game, such as Manny Machado's arm, Adam Wainwright's curveball or Francisco Lindor's defense.

80: Top of the scale. Some scouts consider only one player's tool in all of the major leagues to be 80. Think of Aaron Judge's power, Byron Buxton's speed or Shohei Ohtani's splitter.

20-80 Measurables

HIT	POWER	SPEED		FASTBALL	ARM STRENGTH
Grade Batting Avg	**Grade Home Runs**	**Home-First (In Secs.)**		**Velocity (Starters)**	**Catcher: Pop**
		RHH—LHH		**Grade Velocity**	**Times To Second**
80 . . . . .315+	80 . . . . .40+			80 . . . . . 98+ mph	**Base (In Seconds)**
70 . . . . . .295-.314	70 34-39	80 . . . .4.00—3.90		70 97	80 . . . . < 1.90
60 . . . . . .275-.294	60 28-33	70 . . . .4.10—4.00		65 96	70 . . . . . .1.90-1.94
55 . . . . . .265-.274	55 23-27	65 . . . .4.15—4.05		60 95	60 . . . . . .1.95-1.99
50 . . . . . .255-.264	50 19-22	60 . . . .4.20—4.10		55 94	50 . . . . . .2.00-2.04
45 . . . . . .245-.254	45 14-18	55 . . . .4.25—4.15		50 93	40 . . . . . .2.05-2.09
40 . . . . . .235-.244	40 10-13	50 . . . .4.30—4.20		45 92	30 . . . . . .2.10-2.14
30 . . . . . .215-.234	30 5-9	45 . . . .4.35—4.25		40 90-91	20 . . . . > 2.15
20 . . . .<.215	20 0-4	40 . . . .4.40—4.30		30 88-89	
		30 . . . .4.50—4.40		20 . . . . .87 or less	
		20 . . . .4.60—4.50			

AN OVERVIEW

Another feature of the Prospect Handbook is a depth chart of every organization's minor league talent. This shows you at a glance what kind of talent a system has and provides even more prospects beyond the Top 30.

Players are usually listed on the depth charts where we think they'll ultimately end up. To help you better understand why players are slotted at particular positions, we show you here what scouts look for in the ideal candidate at each spot, with individual tools ranked in descending order.

LF
Power
Hitting
Fielding
Arm Strength
Speed

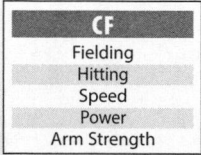

CF
Fielding
Hitting
Speed
Power
Arm Strength

RF
Power
Hitting
Arm Strength
Fielding
Speed

3B
Power
Hitting
Fielding
Arm Strength
Speed

SS
Fielding
Arm Strength
Hitting
Power
Speed

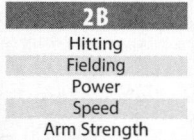

2B
Hitting
Fielding
Power
Speed
Arm Strength

1B
Power
Hitting
Fielding
Arm Strength
Speed

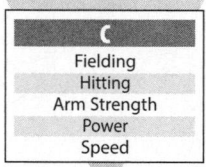

C
Fielding
Hitting
Arm Strength
Power
Speed

STARTING PITCHERS

No. 1 starter	No. 2 starter	No. 3 starter	No. 4-5 starters
• Two plus pitches	• Two plus pitches	• One plus pitch	• Command of two major league pitches
• Average third pitch	• Average third pitch	• Two average pitches	• Average velocity
• Plus-plus command	• Average command	• Average command	• Consistent breaking ball
• Plus makeup	• Average makeup	• Average makeup	• Decent changeup

CLOSER
• One dominant pitch
• Second plus pitch
• Plus command
• Plus-plus makeup

SETUP MAN
• Plus fastball
• Second above-average pitch
• Average command

Context is crucial to prospect evaluations. So to provide yet another layer of context, we rank prospects at all eight field positions plus righthanded and lefthanded starting pitchers. The rankings go deeper at the glamour positions, i.e. shortstop, center field and righthanded starter.

We grade players' tools on the 20-80 scouting scale, where 50 is average. The tools listed for position players are ability to hit for average (HIT), hit for power (POW), speed (SPD), fielding ability (FLD) and throwing arm (ARM). The tools listed for pitchers are fastball (FB), curveball (CB), slider (SL), changeup (CHG), other (OTH) and control (CTL). The "other" category can be a splitter, cutter or screwball.

Included as the final categories are BA Grades and Risk levels on a scale ranging from low to extreme.

CATCHER

No	Player	Org	HIT	POW	SPD	FLD	ARM	BA Grade	Risk
1.	Adley Rutschman	Orioles	70	65	40	60	70	75	Medium
2.	Gabriel Moreno	Blue Jays	70	50	40	55	60	65	Medium
3.	Francisco Alvarez	Mets	60	60	30	50	55	65	High
4.	Keibert Ruiz	Nationals	60	45	30	55	45	60	Medium
5.	Diego Cartaya	Dodgers	55	60	30	60	70	65	Very High
6.	Tyler Soderstrom	Athletics	60	60	40	40	55	60	High
7.	Henry Davis	Pirates	60	55	45	45	70	60	High
8.	MJ Melendez	Royals	45	60	45	60	70	55	Medium
9.	Luis Campusano	Padres	50	55	30	50	55	55	Medium
10.	Shea Langeliers	Braves	45	55	40	60	70	55	High

FIRST BASE

No	Player	Org	HIT	POW	SPD	FLD	ARM	BA Grade	Risk
1.	Spencer Torkelson	Tigers	60	70	45	50	50	65	Medium
2.	Triston Casas	Red Sox	55	65	40	55	50	60	Medium
3.	Nick Pratto	Royals	55	60	45	60	55	55	Medium
4.	Michael Toglia	Rockies	50	60	45	65	45	50	High
5.	Dustin Harris	Rangers	60	55	55	60	60	50	High
6.	Vinnie Pasquantino	Royals	60	60	30	50	45	50	High
7.	Juan Yepez	Cardinals	55	50	30	40	50	45	Medium
8.	Alex Binelas	Red Sox	45	65	40	45	50	45	High
9.	Seth Beer	D-backs	60	50	40	30	40	40	Medium
10.	Aaron Sabato	Twins	40	65	20	40	40	45	High

SECOND BASE

No	Player	Org	HIT	POW	SPD	FLD	ARM	BA Grade	Risk
1.	Nick Yorke	Red Sox	70	50	45	45	50	60	High
2.	Nick Gonzales	Pirates	65	50	55	50	50	55	Medium
3.	Michael Busch	Dodgers	55	55	45	45	40	55	High
4.	Vidal Bruján	Rays	60	40	70	55	60	50	Medium
5.	Ezequiel Duran	Rangers	55	60	50	45	50	50	High
6.	Justin Foscue	Rangers	45	55	40	45	45	50	High
7.	James Triantos	Cubs	60	50	50	40	50	55	Extreme
8.	Connor Norby	Orioles	55	45	55	50	45	50	High
9.	Xavier Edwards	Rays	70	20	70	55	45	50	High
10.	Eddys Leonard	Dodgers	55	50	50	40	50	50	High

THIRD BASE

No	Player	Org	HIT	POW	SPD	FLD	ARM	BA Grade	Risk
1.	Josh Jung	Rangers	60	40	40	45	55	55	Medium
2.	Miguel Vargas	Dodgers	65	55	45	45	50	60	High
3.	Jordan Walker	Cardinals	50	70	45	45	55	60	High
4.	Nolan Gorman	Cardinals	45	70	40	45	60	60	High
5.	Brett Baty	Mets	60	55	50	50	60	60	High
6.	Jose Miranda	Twins	55	55	30	40	55	50	Medium
7.	Curtis Mead	Rays	60	60	40	45	40	55	High
8.	Mark Vientos	Mets	45	60	30	45	60	55	High
9.	Coby Mayo	Orioles	50	60	45	50	60	50	High
10.	Elehuris Montero	Rockies	50	55	40	45	60	50	High

SHORTSTOP

No	Player	Org	HIT	POW	SPD	FLD	ARM	BA Grade	Risk
1.	Bobby Witt Jr.	Royals	60	70	70	60	60	75	Medium
2.	Oneil Cruz	Pirates	50	70	60	50	60	65	Medium
3.	Anthony Volpe	Yankees	60	60	55	50	45	65	High
4.	Marcelo Mayer	Red Sox	65	55	40	60	60	65	Very High
5.	CJ Abrams	Padres	70	50	80	60	55	65	High
6.	Marco Luciano	Giants	60	60	40	50	60	65	Very High
7.	Jordan Lawlar	D-backs	60	55	60	50	65	65	Extreme
8.	Noelvi Marte	Mariners	55	65	50	50	55	60	High
9.	Jose Barrero	Reds	50	55	60	55	60	55	Medium
10.	Bryson Stott	Phillies	55	50	55	55	55	55	High
11.	Tyler Freeman	Guardians	60	45	50	50	50	55	High
12.	Brayan Rocchio	Guardians	55	40	60	55	50	55	High
13.	Brady House	Nationals	50	65	50	55	60	60	Extreme
14.	Kahlil Watson	Marlins	60	55	60	55	55	60	Extreme
15.	Cristian Hernandez	Cubs	55	60	55	50	60	60	Extreme
16.	Orelvis Martinez	Blue Jays	50	60	40	45	60	55	High
17.	Gunnar Henderson	Orioles	50	60	55	55	60	55	High
18.	Gabriel Arias	Guardians	45	55	40	60	70	55	High
19.	Jeremy Peña	Astros	50	45	55	60	60	55	High
20.	Geraldo Perdomo	D-backs	50	45	55	60	55	50	Medium
21.	Royce Lewis	Twins	45	55	70	55	55	60	Extreme
22.	Elly de la Cruz	Reds	50	60	70	55	70	60	Extreme
23.	Jordan Westburg	Orioles	55	50	60	55	60	55	High
24.	Oswald Peraza	Yankees	60	50	55	55	55	55	High
25.	Liover Peguero	Pirates	55	50	55	50	55	55	High
26.	Brice Turang	Brewers	55	40	60	50	50	55	High
27.	Ronny Mauricio	Mets	40	60	40	55	60	55	High
28.	Jordan Groshans	Blue Jays	55	50	40	45	60	55	High
29.	Greg Jones	Rays	45	55	70	55	60	55	High
30.	Matt McLain	Reds	60	40	60	50	55	50	High

CENTER FIELD

No	Player	Org	HIT	POW	SPD	FLD	ARM	BA Grade	Risk
1.	Riley Greene	Tigers	60	60	55	60	55	65	Medium
2.	Brennen Davis	Cubs	50	60	60	55	60	60	Medium
3.	Corbin Carroll	D-backs	60	55	70	60	45	60	High
4.	Josh Lowe	Rays	45	60	70	60	60	55	Medium
5.	Alek Thomas	D-backs	60	45	60	60	45	55	Medium
6.	Michael Harris II	Braves	60	55	55	60	60	60	High
7.	Robert Hassell III	Padres	60	45	55	55	55	60	High
8.	Austin Martin	Twins	65	50	55	50	50	60	High
9.	Luis Matos	Giants	60	55	55	55	55	55	High
10.	Colton Cowser	Orioles	60	50	55	50	55	55	High
11.	Cristian Pache	Braves	40	50	70	80	70	55	High
12.	Jarren Duran	Red Sox	50	50	70	50	40	55	High
13.	Jasson Dominguez	Yankees	55	60	50	50	50	60	Extreme
14.	Sal Frelick	Brewers	60	40	70	55	45	55	Very High
15.	Garrett Mitchell	Brewers	50	50	80	60	60	55	Very High

CORNER OUTFIELD

No	Player	Org	HIT	POW	SPD	FLD	ARM	BA Grade	Risk
1.	Julio Rodriguez	Mariners	65	70	55	55	60	75	Medium
2.	Zac Veen	Rockies	60	60	50	60	50	60	High
3.	George Valera	Guardians	55	55	50	50	50	55	High
4.	Heliot Ramos	Giants	50	55	50	55	55	55	High
5.	Andy Pages	Dodgers	45	60	40	50	70	55	Very High
6.	Owen Caissie	Cubs	50	65	50	40	55	55	Extreme
7.	Kyle Isbel	Royals	55	45	60	60	55	45	Medium
8.	James Wood	Padres	45	65	55	50	50	55	Extreme
9.	Lars Nootbaar	Cardinals	55	45	40	50	50	45	Medium
10.	Kyle Stowers	Orioles	50	60	55	50	60	45	Medium

RIGHTHANDER

No	Pitcher	Team	FB	CB	SL	CHG	CTL	OTH	BA Grade	Risk
1.	Grayson Rodriguez	Orioles	70	55	70	65	60	—	70	High
2.	Shane Baz	Rays	80	45	60	50	60	—	65	Medium
3.	George Kirby	Mariners	70	55	60	50	80	—	70	High
4.	Cade Cavalli	Nationals	70	55	60	55	50	—	60	High
5.	Jack Leiter	Rangers	70	60	55	55	50	—	60	High
6.	Bobby Miller	Dodgers	70	60	50	60	50	—	60	High
7.	Mick Abel	Phillies	65	50	60	60	55	—	60	High
8.	Matt Brash	Mariners	70	50	70	55	45	—	60	High
9.	Nate Pearson	Blue Jays	65	50	60	50	45	—	55	Medium
10.	Taj Bradley	Rays	60	40	60	50	55	—	55	High
11.	Hunter Greene	Reds	70	—	60	45	55	—	55	High
12.	Eury Perez	Marlins	70	50	—	60	60	—	60	Extreme
13.	Roansy Contreras	Pirates	60	55	55	50	50	—	55	High
14.	Cole Winn	Rangers	60	60	55	50	50	—	55	High
15.	Jackson Jobe	Tigers	60	55	70	60	55	—	60	Extreme
16.	Daniel Espino	Guardians	70	50	60	50	50	—	55	High
17.	Sixto Sanchez	Marlins	80	55	55	70	60	—	60	Extreme
18.	Edward Cabrera	Marlins	70	60	—	50	45	—	55	High
19.	Jordan Balazovic	Twins	55	55	—	50	55	—	55	High
20.	Joe Ryan	Twins	65	40	50	50	55	—	50	Medium
21.	Quinn Priester	Pirates	60	60	50	45	55	—	55	High
22.	Max Meyer	Marlins	60	—	60	45	60	—	55	High
23.	Ryan Pepiot	Dodgers	70	50	45	80	40	—	55	High
24.	Hunter Brown	Astros	70	60	50	50	40	—	55	High
25.	Sam Bachman	Angels	70	—	70	50	50	—	55	High
26.	Ryne Nelson	D-backs	70	50	50	45	50	—	55	High
27.	Andrew Painter	Phillies	60	50	60	50	60	—	60	Extreme
28.	Brayan Bello	Red Sox	55	—	55	60	50	—	55	High
29.	Matt Allan	Mets	60	60	—	50	50	—	60	Extreme
30.	Michael McGreevy	Cardinals	55	60	50	50	70	—	55	High
31.	J.T. Ginn	Mets	55	—	60	50	60	—	55	High
32.	Jackson Kowar	Royals	60	55	—	70	50	—	50	Medium
33.	Josh Winder	Twins	55	50	60	60	55	—	55	High
34.	Luis Gil	Yankees	60	—	60	50	45	—	55	High
35.	Gavin Williams	Guardians	70	60	55	50	50	—	55	Very High
36.	Jared Jones	Pirates	60	55	60	50	45	—	55	Very High
37.	Emerson Hancock	Mariners	55	—	55	60	50	—	55	Very High
38.	Owen White	Rangers	70	55	55	50	60	—	50	High
39.	Caleb Kilian	Cubs	55	55		50	60	50†	50	High
40.	Will Bednar	Giants	60	—	60	50	50	—	50	High

LEFTHANDER

No	Pitcher	Team	FB	CB	SL	CHG	CTL	OTH	BA Grade	Risk
1.	Aaron Ashby	Brewers	60	50	65	55	45	—	60	High
2.	Reid Detmers	Angels	55	65	60	50	50	—	55	Medium
3.	Matthew Liberatore	Cardinals	55	55	55	55	55	—	55	Medium
4.	Asa Lacy	Royals	70	55	60	60	50	—	60	High
5.	Nick Lodolo	Reds	50	40	60	50	60	50†	55	High
6.	DL Hall	Orioles	70	55	60	55	45	—	60	Extreme
7.	Brandon Williamson	Mariners	60	65	50	50	50	—	55	High
8.	Blake Walston	D-backs	55	55	60	50	55	—	55	High
9.	Kyle Harrison	Giants	60	—	60	50	40	—	55	Very High
10.	Jake Eder	Marlins	60	—	60	50	60	—	55	Extreme
11.	Logan T. Allen	Guardians	50	—	50	60	60	—	50	High
12.	Kyle Muller	Braves	70	55	60	50	40	—	50	High
13.	Brailyn Marquez	Cubs	80	40	60	50	45	—	55	Extreme
14.	Jordan Wicks	Cubs	55	45	55	70	60	—	50	High
15.	DJ Herz	Cubs	60	50	—	65	45	—	50	High

* Splitter. ^ Screwball. † Cutter.

Organization	2021	2020	2019	2018	2017
1. Seattle Mariners	2	5	17	30	21

Julio Rodriguez is arguably the best position prospect in baseball and George Kirby is arguably the best pitching prospect in baseball. Combined with a standout group of upper-level pitchers and an intriguing group of lower-level position players, the Mariners have a lot of impact talent en route to Seattle.

2. Tampa Bay Rays	1	1	2	5	11

The Rays may no longer have the best prospect in baseball like they did in each of the past two seasons with Wander Franco, but they still have one of the deepest farm systems. Not only do the Rays have excellent home-grown talent, but they do as good a job of anyone at acquiring prospects in trades.

3. Pittsburgh Pirates	15	24	18	16	7

After consecutive drafts were executed with clockwork-like precision, the Pirates boast an embarrassment of riches at the top and impressive depth stretching 40 players deep. A balance of positional and pitching talent, close-to-the-majors players and high-upside youngsters herald a new era approaching in the Steel City.

4. Baltimore Orioles	7	12	22	17	27

Baltimore's depth is not yet on par with some of the other teams in the top five, but picking at the top of the draft has worked out very well. In catcher Adley Rutschman and righthander Grayson Rodriguez, the Orioles have two of the best prospects in the game.

5. Kansas City Royals	13	18	27	29	26

Bobby Witt Jr. is the clear headliner in the Royals' farm system, but the bounceback seasons by MJ Melendez and Nick Pratto in 2021, plus the emergence of prospects like Vinnie Pasquantino, have given the Royals a more well-rounded system than it had a year or two ago.

6. Detroit Tigers	5	11	14	20	25

Buoyed by elite-level talents at the top in Riley Greene and Spencer Torkelson, Detroit boasts a solid top 10, but the talent drops off precipitously from there. The two most recent drafts have yielded strong results for the Tigers, with six total picks from 2020 and 2021 ranking among their top 10.

7. Cincinnati Reds	18	29	7	10	13

Cincinnati has three prospects at the top of its system—Jose Barrero, Hunter Greene and Nick Lodolo—who should contribute in the majors in 2022. Beyond that, it has a long list of high-upside position players in the lower levels of the minors mixed with a number of close-to-the-majors bullpen arms.

8. Los Angeles Dodgers	9	3	10	9	2

The Dodgers' player development machine continues to hum along. Even after a copious number of recent prospect graduations and trades, the Dodgers still have a deep, balanced system featuring impact talent in the lineup (Diego Cartaya, Miguel Vargas, Michael Busch) and on the mound (Bobby Miller, Ryan Pepiot, Landon Knack).

9. Texas Rangers	24	20	24	22	23

The Rangers' system is topped by the excellent trio of Jack Leiter, Josh Jung and Cole Winn—their draft top picks in 2021, 2019 and 2018. The system also got a boost from midseason trades that netted them a bevy of middle infield prospects and an impressive return from righthander Owen White.

10. Arizona Diamondbacks	17	10	21	26	28

Arizona's top two prospects, Corbin Carroll and Jordan Lawlar, tore labrums in their shoulders, tamping the system's outlook down somewhat. Still, outfielder Alek Thomas and shortstop Geraldo Perdomo are impressive and righthander Ryne Nelson ranked among the minor league leaders in strikeouts last year.

11. Boston Red Sox	21	22	30	23	14

Boston's system isn't the deepest, but its opening trio of shortstop Marcelo Mayer, first baseman Triston Casas and second baseman Nick Yorke is one of the most enticing. Righthander Brayan Bello took steps forward in 2021, including an appearance in Denver at the Futures Game.

12. Cleveland Guardians	11	19	15	21	18

One can argue the Guardians' prospect depth is among the best in the game, but a lack of high-end talent at the top drags the system down. The next wave of major league talent is on the cusp of reaching Cleveland, most notably Tyler Freeman, Brayan Rocchio and George Valera.

13. New York Yankees	16	17	20	2	3

The Yankees' system is anchored by a pair of promising shortstops in Anthony Volpe and Oswald Peraza, both of whom had breakthrough 2021 seasons. Few organizations win like the Yankees in the minor leagues, and they do it with position talent and pitching talent, as exemplified by Luis Gil, Hayden Wesneski and Luis Medina.

14. Minnesota Twins	8	7	8	12	22

The deadline acquisition of Austin Martin provided Minnesota a top-of-the-system talent it sorely lacked. The group behind Martin includes 2017 top overall pick Royce Lewis but is notable for begin rich in pitching, with seven arms ranking in the top 10.

15. Chicago Cubs	22	21	29	28	16

The Cubs' teardown at the trade deadline brought back an abundance of talented players in the lower levels, such as outfielders Pete Crow-Armstrong and Kevin Alcantara. Many are years away from the majors and carry a lot of risk, but they are talented enough to potentially form the core of the next competitive Cubs team.

Organization	2021	2020	2019	2018	2017
16. New York Mets	19	25	19	27	15

Francisco Alvarez and Brett Baty took giant steps forward while making their full-season debuts, while Ronny Mauricio and Mark Vientos hit in the upper minors. The Mets don't have as much proximity pitching, but they have a number of lower-level arms that intrigue, mostly acquired internationally or in the 2021 draft.

Organization	2021	2020	2019	2018	2017
17. San Francisco Giants	14	13	28	25	24

San Francisco's lower levels featured breakout seasons from some of its best prospects, including outfielders Luis Matos and Jairo Pomares and lefty Kyle Harrison. Top prospect Marco Luciano mostly performed at Low-A before spinning his wheels a bit at High-A. Buster Posey's retirement means Joey Bart has a path to the majors.

Organization	2021	2020	2019	2018	2017
18. St. Louis Cardinals	12	14	11	13	12

Jordan Walker's smashing pro debut and the continued ascent of Nolan Gorman and Matthew Liberatore combine to give the Cardinals three premium prospects. The depth of the system falls off quickly, but breakouts from older, Triple-A players like Lars Nootbaar and Juan Yepez help mitigate some of that.

Organization	2021	2020	2019	2018	2017
19. Toronto Blue Jays	4	6	3	8	20

While major league acquisitions have thinned Toronto's farm system, breakout seasons by catcher Gabriel Moreno and shortstops Orelvis Martinez and Otto Lopez softened the blow. The Blue Jays feature a young prospect group, with a majority of their best talent having never played above High-A.

Organization	2021	2020	2019	2018	2017
20. Miami Marlins	10	9	25	24	29

The Marlins' system is as pitching-rich as any in the game. It is led by 6-foot-8 righthander Eury Perez, who reached High-A at 18 years old. Behind Perez is a line of talented pitchers, including major leaguers Sixto Sanchez and Edward Cabrera as well as near-ready righthander Max Meyer and breakout lefty Jake Eder.

Organization	2021	2020	2019	2018	2017
21. San Diego Padres	3	2	1	3	9

The Padres have either graduated or traded most of the prospects that made them the No. 1 farm system in baseball in 2019. CJ Abrams and Robert Hassell III give them two headliner prospects, but getting MacKenzie Gore back on track is critical for both a farm system and a franchise that now lacks depth.

Organization	2021	2020	2019	2018	2017
22. Atlanta Braves	6	4	4	1	1

The Braves had the No. 1 farm system in 2018, and that young talent helped the Braves win the 2021 World Series. The system still has some excellent top-end prospects like Michael Harris II and Shea Langeliers, but the depth is almost gone. That is partly because of the international amateur spending penalties the team faced.

Organization	2021	2020	2019	2018	2017
23. Philadelphia Phillies	27	26	12	7	6

After years of underwhelming talent coming through the pipeline, Philadelphia has gambled on prep pitching in the first round of consecutive drafts. Mick Abel and Andrew Painter rank Nos. 1 and 2 in the system, but outside of shortstop Bryson Stott, the Phillies have very little coming in the short term.

Organization	2021	2020	2019	2018	2017
24. Colorado Rockies	25	28	23	19	10

The Rockies' success in the complex leagues and at the Class A levels is indicative of the young talent lurking in the lower levels of their system. At the same time, those players are many years away and the upper levels of are largely barren.

Organization	2021	2020	2019	2018	2017
25. Milwaukee Brewers	28	30	26	6	8

Few organizations have developed homegrown pitching like the Brewers in recent years, with lefthander Aaron Ashby possibly the next in line. The rest of the Brewers system is less inspiring, with a host of high-upside question marks throughout the top half of their talent base.

Organization	2021	2020	2019	2018	2017
26. Washington Nationals	30	23	16	15	19

The Nationals looked headed to the basement of the organization talent rankings early last year, but trading for Keibert Ruiz and drafting Brady House helped significantly. Righthander Cade Cavalli gives the system a potential frontline starter, as well.

Organization	2021	2020	2019	2018	2017
27. Oakland Athletics	29	15	9	18	17

Tyler Soderstrom is a good place to start a farm system. But after that, the Athletics' system reflects a combination of struggling in the first round of the draft (Kyler Murray and Austin Beck), injuries (A.J. Puk) and trades (Jesus Luzardo). Help could be on the way if the A's trade Matt Olson and Matt Chapman for prospects.

Organization	2021	2020	2019	2018	2017
28. Houston Astros	26	27	5	11	4

Houston has built much of its perennial playoff team through excellent player development. Korey Lee and Jeremy Peña could help before long, but the rest of this system just isn't what it's been. The Astros don't have the onslaught of power arms that were a fixture of the system a few years ago.

Organization	2021	2020	2019	2018	2017
29. Los Angeles Angels	23	16	13	14	30

The help Mike Trout and Shohei Ohtani need to get to the playoffs isn't going to come from this farm system, which falls off sharply after the top three players. The Angels will have to rely on health from their stars and greater contributions from recent prospect graduates Jo Adell, Brandon Marsh, Griffin Canning and Patrick Sandoval.

Organization	2021	2020	2019	2018	2017
30. Chicago White Sox	20	8	6	4	5

The White Sox graduated a tremendous group of talent to the majors and reached back-to-back postseasons because of it. What's left is a thin system that was worsened by poor 2021 performances from their three top pitching prospects—righthanders Jared Kelley, Matthew Thompson and Andrew Dalquist.

Arizona Diamondbacks

BY NICK PIECORO

At times during the 2021 season, it was hard to find positives with the D-backs. Not only was the major league team a disaster of almost unfathomable proportions as they crashed to a 52-110 record, their young players weren't performing and their farm system was springing leaks. It felt like an organization in full collapse.

By the end of the year, that perception had shifted. Several players who went sideways early corrected themselves, others emerged from nowhere and the organization added more frontline talent to its pipeline.

The D-backs might still be years away from contending for the postseason, but there exists at least a theoretical core of their next good team. Early in the year, that wasn't so easy to envision. Top prospect Corbin Carroll went down with a shoulder injury. Outfielder Kristian Robinson was in legal limbo and missed a second consecutive season. Shortstop Geraldo Perdomo was hitting under .200 at Double-A. And in the big leagues, catcher/outfielder Daulton Varsho was struggling to find his footing. Other well-regarded prospects, including pitchers Slade Cecconi, Conor Grammes and Justin Martinez, were either underperforming or injured—or both.

Fast-forward to the end of the year and the D-backs appear far healthier—not like they're firing on all cylinders, but better.

Of course, Carroll's injury remains a concern—and will until he gets back on the field and shows he still has the same dynamic potential. But several other developments look more encouraging.

Robinson could be nearing a return. Perdomo retreated to the Arizona complex to rework his swing, and when he returned to Double-A he looked like he might be a better prospect than ever. Varsho turned in an impressive second half and was, at times, the team's most exciting player.

The club added one of the highest-upside players in the draft in Texas high school shortstop Jordan Lawlar and two college hitters in Ryan Bliss and Adrian Del Castillo who could be everyday regulars. Lawlar was the top ranked draft prospect on the BA board. He fell to Arizona at sixth overall and played in two games before succumbing to left shoulder surgery.

And then there was the pitching. A cavalcade of arms stormed through the system, including Ryne Nelson, Drey Jameson, Blake Walston and Brandon Pfaadt, among others. Not since the early 2010 have the D-backs possessed a crop of potential starters with so much upside.

Rookie Daulton Varsho hit .290/.349/.530 in the second half with more extensive playing time.

PROJECTED 2025 LINEUP

Catcher	Daulton Varsho	28
First Base	Deyvison de los Santos	22
Second Base	Josh Rojas	31
Third Base	Jordan Lawlar	22
Shortstop	Geraldo Perdomo	25
Left Field	Corbin Carroll	24
Center Field	Alek Thomas	25
Right Field	Pavin Smith	29
Designated Hitter	A.J. Vukovich	23
No. 1 Starter	Zac Gallen	29
No. 2 Starter	Blake Walston	24
No. 3 Starter	Luke Weaver	31
No. 4 Starter	Ryne Nelson	27
No. 5 Starter	Brandon Pfaadt	26
Closer	Drey Jameson	27

It lines up to make 2022 an interesting year from a developmental perspective. Even if the D-backs don't have the firepower to compete in the NL West, they figure to have several prominent prospects matriculate to the big leagues for extended looks, including Perdomo, outfielder Alek Thomas and any number of pitchers who reached Double-A last year. Plus, with the No. 2 overall pick in the 2022 draft, they figure to add another player with huge upside.

What the coming year holds remains to be seen. It could be that the D-backs are closer to contending than they might appear. It could be that they're even farther away, as difficult as that may be to fathom. ∎

ARIZONA DIAMONDBACKS

TOP 2022 ROOKIES	RANK
Alek Thomas, OF	3
Geraldo Perdomo, SS	4
Seth Beer, 1B/DH	21
BREAKOUT PROSPECTS	**RANK**
Bryce Jarvis, RHP	11
Joe Elbis, RHP	22
Tim Tawa, IF/OF	26

SOURCE OF TOP 30 TALENT

Homegrown	28	**Acquired**	2
College	12	Trade	2
Junior college	0	Rule 5 draft	0
High school	5	Independent league	0
Nondrafted free agent	0	Free agent/waivers	0
International	11		

LF
Dominic Canzone (16)
Cooper Hummel
Junior Franco
Eduardo Diaz

CF
Corbin Carroll (1)
Alek Thomas (3)
Jake McCarthy (15)
Alvin Guzman (25)
Jeferson Espinal (27)
Jorge Barrosa
Dominic Fletcher

RF
Kristian Robinson (13)
Wilderd Patino (28)
Stuart Fairchild

3B
Deyvison De Los Santos (8)
A.J. Vukovich (9)
Manuel Pena (30)
Buddy Kennedy
Alberto Ciprian

SS
Jordan Lawlar (2)
Geraldo Perdomo (4)
Jose Fernandez (29)
Juan Corniel

2B
Ryan Bliss (14)
Tim Tawa (26)
Blaze Alexander

1B
Seth Beer (21)
Neyfy Castillo

C
Adrian Del Castillo (19)
Jose Herrera
Kenny Castillo

LHP

LHSP	LHRP
Blake Walston (5)	Miguel Aguilar
Tommy Henry (20)	Mack Lemieux
Tyler Holton	Junior Garcia
Liam Norris	Jake Rice

RHP

RHSP	RHRP
Ryne Nelson (6)	Conor Grammes (24)
Drey Jameson (7)	Mitchell Stumpo
Brandon Pfaadt (10)	Ryan Weiss
Bryce Jarvis (11)	Levi Kelly
Slade Cecconi (12)	Josh Green
Luis Frias (17)	Jhosmer Alvarez
Corbin Martin (18)	Blake Workman
Joe Elbis (22)	Josh Swales
Justin Martinez (23)	Keegan Curtis
Jacob Steinmetz	

1 CORBIN CARROLL, OF

Born: Aug. 21, 2000. **B-T:** L-L. **HT:** 5-10. **WT:** 165.
Drafted: HS—Seattle, 2019 (1st round).
Signed by: Dan Ramsay.

BILL MITCHELL

TRACK RECORD: Carroll emerged early as one of the most talented players in the 2019 draft class, but concerns about his small stature caused him to fall to the 16th overall pick, where the D-backs were thrilled to scoop him up. He signed for $3.75 million to pass up a UCLA commitment and quickly went about justifying the D-backs' excitement. Carroll performed well in his pro debut while advancing out of the complex leagues after only 31 games and excelled at the alternate training site in 2020. He got off to a fast start at High-A Hillsboro in 2021 with 10 hits in his first 23 at-bats, but he hurt himself on a home-run swing in his seventh game of the season, tearing his labrum and capsule in his right, non-throwing shoulder. After having season-ending surgery in mid May, Carroll tried to make the most of his downtime by taking college classes and attending D-backs games at Chase Field, where he sat behind the plate with the team's advance scout, Jeff Gardner, asking questions and talking baseball.

SCOUTING REPORT: Carroll is a dynamic, multi-talented player who projects to fit at or near the top of a major league lineup. He has a fluid lefthanded swing, an all-fields approach and a propensity for finding the barrel, all of which helps him project to be a plus hitter. He produces impressive slugging numbers despite his 5-foot-10, 165-pound stature by shooting balls into the gaps and down the lines for extra bases. He has the sort of effortless swing in which he simplifies his movements to generate high exit velocities with relative ease. He is able to add loft while avoiding too steep of an angle in his swing, resulting in consistent hard contact in the air without a corresponding increase in swings and misses. Beyond his physical skills, Carroll has a mature approach and an advanced feel for the game. He makes quick adjustments at the plate and is sound fundamentally in the outfield and on the bases. He projects to be a plus defensive center fielder with his speed and instincts and should have no problem sticking at the position. If he ends up in a corner, he would profile better in left field, where his fringe-average arm fits best. How Carroll's tools will play after his injury remains a question. Not only did surgery cost him a year of development, but the procedure was anything but minor, meaning he will have to prove he can get back to being the impact player he was. He has

BA GRADE	SCOUTING GRADES
60 Risk: High	Hit: 60. Power: 55. Run: 70. Field: 60. Arm: 45.

Projected future grades on 20-80 scouting scale

BEST TOOLS

Best Hitter for Average	Corbin Carroll
Best Power Hitter	Deyvison De Los Santos
Best Strike-Zone Discipline	Cooper Hummel
Fastest Baserunner	Corbin Carroll
Best Athlete	Drey Jameson
Best Fastball	Ryne Nelson
Best Curveball	Luis Frias
Best Slider	Drey Jameson
Best Changeup	Bryce Jarvis
Best Control	Joe Elbis
Best Defensive Catcher	Jose Herrera
Best Defensive Infielder	Geraldo Perdomo
Best Infield Arm	Jordan Lawlar
Best Defensive Outfielder	Alek Thomas
Best Outfield Arm	Dominic Fletcher

shown upside in limited action but has just 215 career plate appearances in parts of three professional seasons.

THE FUTURE: The D-backs still view Carroll as a special talent and the best prospect in their system. Before the injury, he drew comparisons to the likes of Johnny Damon and Jacoby Ellsbury. He hopes to be fully healthy for the start of the 2022 season and is aiming to show he can be that type of potential all-star again. As long as he is healthy, he should see Double-A at some point in 2022 and has a chance to reach the majors by 2023. ∎

Year	Age	Club (Level)	Lge	AVG	G	AB	R	H	2B	3B	HR	RBI	BB	SO	SB	OBP	SLG
2021	20	Hillsboro (HiA)	West	.435	7	23	9	10	1	2	2	5	6	7	3	.552	.913
Minor League Totals (3 years)				.316	49	177	45	56	10	9	4	25	35	48	21	.428	.542

2 JORDAN LAWLAR, SS

Born: July 17, 2002. **B-T:** R-R. **HT:** 6-2. **WT:** 190. **Drafted:** HS—Dallas, 2021 (1st round). **Signed by:** J.R. Salinas.

TRACK RECORD: An accomplished prep player, Lawlar stood out on the showcase circuit as arguably the top player in the 2021 draft class and was named Gatorade's Texas player of the year in the spring. The D-backs eagerly selected him with the sixth overall pick and signed him for an above-slot $6.7 million to buy him out of a Vanderbilt commitment. Lawlar made his pro debut in the Arizona Complex League after signing, but he appeared in only two games before he suffered a labrum tear in his left shoulder that required season-ending surgery.

BA GRADE

65 Risk: Extreme

SCOUTING REPORT: Before his injury, Lawlar stood out as a tooled-up prospect with the potential to hit in the middle of the lineup and stick at one of the game's most demanding positions. He has terrific bat speed that allows him to handle velocity, controls the strike zone and battles through at-bats. He swings and misses a bit too much at times, but he generally self-corrects. Lawlar has plus raw power that occasionally shows up in games and could improve as he matures and adds strength to his athletic frame. For now, his power more safely projects in the form of doubles and triples given his easy plus speed. Defensively, Lawlar is a surefire shortstop with good hands, range and footwork. He has a nearly plus-plus, accurate arm and the ability to make difficult plays look easy.

THE FUTURE: Lawlar is expected to be fully healthy by the start of the 2022 season. He might have the most upside of any player in the D-backs organization and draws comparisons to a young Carlos Correa.

SCOUTING GRADES:	Hitting: 60	Power: 55	Running: 60	Fielding: 60	Arm: 65

Year	Age	Club (Level)	Lge	AVG	G	AB	R	H	2B	3B	HR	RBI	BB	SO	SB	OBP	SLG
2021	18	D-backs (R)	ACL	.400	2	5	0	2	1	0	0	1	1	1	1	.500	.600
Minor League Totals (1 year)				.400	2	5	0	2	1	0	0	1	1	1	1	.500	.600

3 ALEK THOMAS, OF

Born: April 28, 2000. **B-T:** L-L. **HT:** 5-11. **WT:** 175. **Drafted:** HS—Chicago, 2018 (2nd round). **Signed by:** Nate Birtwell.

TRACK RECORD: Thomas is the son of White Sox strength coach Allen Thomas and grew up around the game, spending time at Guaranteed Rate Field shagging fly balls and picking the brains of big leaguers. The D-backs drafted Thomas in the second round in 2018 and signed him away from a Texas Christian commitment for $1.2 million. Thomas has rocketed through the system since and climbed from Double-A to Triple-A in 2021 while amassing eye-popping numbers. He set new career highs in doubles (29), home runs (18), RBIs (59) and OPS (.953), all in his age-21 season at the minors' highest levels.

BA GRADE

55 Risk: Medium

SCOUTING REPORT: Thomas' career .312/.388/.495 batting line supports the notion of him being a pure hitter. He has quick, strong hands and that allows him to manipulate the barrel. He isn't physically imposing but he regularly hits balls hard. Though the D-backs say he has tightened up his approach, Thomas remains an aggressive hitter who is looking to swing the bat and do damage. That said, he also owns a solid 10% walk rate in his career. Thomas' swing has a lot of moving parts, including a pronounced leg kick. Defensively, Thomas uses his plus speed to cover wide swaths of ground in center field and gets good reads off the bat to project as a plus defender. His fringe-average arm is somewhat limiting but is fine in center.

THE FUTURE: Thomas is expected to come to big league camp pushing for a spot on the Opening Day roster. Whether it's right away or not, he figures to impact the big league team at some point early in 2022.

SCOUTING GRADES:	Hitting: 60	Power: 45	Running: 60	Fielding: 60	Arm: 45

Year	Age	Club (Level)	Lge	AVG	G	AB	R	H	2B	3B	HR	RBI	BB	SO	SB	OBP	SLG
2021	21	Amarillo (AA)	Cent	.283	72	286	54	81	18	8	10	41	37	65	8	.374	.507
	21	Reno (AAA)	West	.369	34	149	32	55	11	4	8	18	15	34	5	.434	.658
Minor League Totals (4 years)				.312	276	1128	212	352	66	25	30	141	128	241	40	.388	.495

4 GERALDO PERDOMO, SS

Born: Oct. 22, 1999. **B-T:** B-R. **HT:** 6-3. **WT:** 184. **Signed:** Dominican Republic, 2016. **Signed by:** Junior Noboa/Elvis Cruz.

TRACK RECORD: Signed for $70,000 in 2016 out of the Dominican Republic, Perdomo raced up the minors and was brought up for his major league debut early in the 2021 season with Nick Ahmed battling knee problems. Perdomo struggled in limited duty and carried those struggles with him when he was sent back to Double-A, prompting the D-backs to place him on the development list and send him back to Arizona at midseason to rebuild his swing and regain his confidence. It appeared to work as Perdomo hit .329/.415/.527 across three levels after he returned, including a strong showing in the majors in late September.

SCOUTING REPORT: Perdomo is a no-doubt shortstop, with easy, rhythmic movements, good hands and an above-average, dependable arm. He is tougher to evaluate at the plate, particularly after his night-and-day season. He has a discerning eye and the ability to put the bat on the ball, but he has long made soft contact and shown limited ability to drive the ball. After his development list stint, his mentality changed at the plate to where he appeared intent on crushing balls instead of simply making contact. Whether he can maintain those adjustments will determine if he reaches his potential as an average hitter with fringy power.

THE FUTURE: Perdomo provides an intriguing alternative to Ahmed, even if his production is heavily weighted toward on-base ability. If Perdomo can slug like he showed late in 2021, he may force his way into the lineup.

BA GRADE
50 Risk: Medium

SCOUTING GRADES:	Hitting: 50	Power: 45	Running: 55	Fielding: 60	Arm: 55

Year	Age	Club (Level)	Lge	AVG	G	AB	R	H	2B	3B	HR	RBI	BB	SO	SB	OBP	SLG
2021	21	Amarillo (AA)	Cent	.231	82	286	51	66	8	5	6	32	47	81	8	.351	.357
	21	Reno (AAA)	West	.417	3	12	1	5	0	0	0	3	2	1	0	.500	.417
	21	Arizona (MLB)	NL	.258	11	31	5	8	3	1	0	1	6	6	0	.378	.419
Major League Totals (1 year)				.258	11	31	5	8	3	1	0	1	6	6	0	.378	.419
Minor League Totals (5 years)				.267	321	1130	200	302	39	15	14	117	218	230	74	.397	.365

5 BLAKE WALSTON, LHP

Born: June 28, 2001. **B-T:** L-L. **HT:** 6-5. **WT:** 195. **Drafted:** HS—Wilmington, N.C., 2019 (1st round). **Signed by:** George Swain.

TRACK RECORD: The D-backs selected Walston, a former high school quarterback in addition to ace lefthander, with the second of their two first-round picks in 2019 and signed him away from a North Carolina State commitment for $2.45 million. After the coronavirus pandemic delayed his first full season, Walston turned in a solid 2021 across both Class A levels, showing glimpses of the frontline starter the D-backs hope he becomes while also exposing some areas that still need refinement.

SCOUTING REPORT: Walston has nearly everything scouts look for in a frontline starter, including command, velocity, ability to spin the ball and feel to pitch. He still has a thin frame, giving him room for more physical maturity but also affecting his present ability to hold his velocity. At his best, Walston

BA GRADE
55 Risk: High

sits in the low 90s and touches 94-95 mph. His velocity tends to decrease as games wear on, and his average velocity dropped from close to 92 mph in June to a tick under 90 mph in September. Walston's potentially plus curveball is his most advanced secondary pitch but remains inconsistent. His slider and changeup have improved to be above-average and average, respectively, and he is gaining trust in his changeup in particular. Walston throws everything for strikes with above-average control. He still has maturing to do when it comes to the consistency of his between-starts routine.

THE FUTURE: Walston has the most upside of any starter in the system. He took strides with his preparation, and coaches are excited to see what happens as his improved work ethic translates into further development.

SCOUTING GRADES:	Fastball: 55	Slider: 55	Curveball: 60	Changeup: 50	Control: 55

Year	Age	Club (Level)	Lge	W	L	ERA	G	GS	IP	H	HR	BB	SO	BB/9	SO/9	WHIP	AVG
2021	20	Visalia (LoA)	West	2	2	3.32	8	8	43	34	4	17	60	3.5	12.5	1.18	.209
	20	Hillsboro (HiA)	West	2	3	4.13	11	11	52	52	12	16	57	2.8	9.8	1.30	.252
Minor League Totals (3 years)				4	5	3.63	25	24	107	94	16	35	134	3.0	11.3	1.21	.230

6 RYNE NELSON, RHP

Born: Feb. 1, 1998. **B-T:** R-R. **HT:** 6-4. **WT:** 190. **Drafted:** Oregon, 2019 (2nd round). **Signed by:** Dan Ramsay.

TRACK RECORD: After years as a two-way player, Nelson began focusing solely on pitching at Oregon in 2019. The D-backs liked what they saw and selected him with the 56th overall pick after that season. Nelson was more projection than performance when he was drafted, but he showed up at instructional league in 2020 looking more refined and continued that progression through a breakout 2021 season. He went 7-4, 3.17 in 22 starts as he rose from High-A to Double-A and finished tied for fourth in the minors with 163 strikeouts.

SCOUTING REPORT: Nelson has a slow, methodical delivery, then overwhelms hitters with a fastball that averages 94 mph with high spin rates. He produces rise and carry on his fastball and learned to better locate the pitch up in the zone last year. He also cleaned up his delivery, getting himself more on line and making it more repeatable. Nelson's average curveball and slider alternate as his best secondary offering, but his curveball might pair best with his fastball. After years of tinkering, he found a changeup grip he likes—he calls it a hybrid circle change—and the pitch took significant strides to become fringy. After years of below-average control, Nelson finally started throwing strikes consistently in 2021, the biggest difference-maker in his season.

THE FUTURE: Given Nelson's relative newness to solely pitching, he could still have significant growth ahead. His control improvements have started to quiet concerns about a future move to the bullpen, with more observers now envisioning a potential mid-rotation starter.

BA GRADE

55 Risk: High

EDDIE KELLY/PROLOOK PHOTOS

SCOUTING GRADES:	Fastball: 70	Slider: 50	Curveball: 50	Changeup: 45	Control: 50

Year	Age	Club (Level)	Lge	W	L	ERA	G	GS	IP	H	HR	BB	SO	BB/9	SO/9	WHIP	AVG
2021	23	Hillsboro (HiA)	West	4	1	2.52	8	8	39	21	3	14	59	3.2	13.5	0.89	.153
2021	23	Amarillo (AA)	Cent	3	3	3.51	14	14	77	66	13	26	104	3.0	12.2	1.19	.232
Minor League Totals (3 years)				7	5	3.13	32	29	135	102	17	50	189	3.3	12.6	1.13	.209

7 DREY JAMESON, RHP

Born: Aug. 17, 1997. **B-T:** R-R. **HT:** 6-0. **WT:** 165. **Drafted:** Ball State, 2019 (1st round). **Signed by:** Jeremy Kehrt.

TRACK RECORD: The D-backs placed a bet on the undersized Jameson's athleticism when they selected him with the 34th overall pick in 2019 out of Ball State. Already, the gamble looks like it may pay off. Jameson turned in a solid first full season as a pro in 2021, posting a 3,98 ERA with 145 strikeouts in 110.2 innings as he rose from High-A to Double-A. Most importantly, he also provided reasons to believe he could stick as a starter in the majors.

SCOUTING REPORT: Jameson has perhaps the most electric stuff in the D-backs' system. His four-seam fastball averages 96 mph, occasionally touching 98-100, and he holds it deep into games and throughout the season. His four-seamer pairs well with a two-seamer that sits in the 91-93 mph range and his slider, which he can throw both for strikes and chase swings, is a dominant pitch that earns plus-plus grades at its best. Jameson's curveball rates as at least an average offering, as does his changeup, which behaves like a splitter when it's on. He has eased some durability concerns by toning down his delivery and looks more like a pitcher than a pure thrower, although his 6-foot, 165-pound size remains a question. Hitters at times see the ball well against him and his fastball doesn't play quite as well as his velocity would suggest.

THE FUTURE: Given his size, Jameson is the sort of prospect who can't dispel reliever risk until he succeeds as a starter in the majors. He will come to big league camp in 2022 and has a chance to break into the majors during the season.

BA GRADE

50 Risk: High

ZACHARY LUCY/FOUR SEAM IMAGES

SCOUTING GRADES:	Fastball: 65	Slider: 70	Curveball: 55	Changeup: 55	Control: 50

Year	Age	Club (Level)	Lge	W	L	ERA	G	GS	IP	H	HR	BB	SO	BB/9	SO/9	WHIP	AVG
2021	23	Hillsboro (HiA)	West	2	4	3.92	13	12	64	60	9	18	77	2.5	10.8	1.21	.246
	23	Amarillo (AA)	Cent	3	2	4.08	8	8	46	38	6	18	68	3.5	13.2	1.21	.225
Minor League Totals (3 years)				5	6	4.19	29	28	122	112	16	45	157	3.3	11.6	1.28	.243

8 DEYVISON DE LOS SANTOS, 3B

Born: June 21, 2003. **B-T:** R-R. **HT:** 6-1. **WT:** 210. **Signed:** Dominican Republic, 2019. **Signed by:** Cesar Geronimo/Wil Tejada.

TRACK RECORD: De los Santos is a hulking prospect whose ability to impact the baseball has been his calling card since he signed out of the Dominican Republic for $200,000 in 2019. The D-backs pushed de los Santos aggressively in 2021 and watched him post strong numbers in his pro debut in the Arizona Complex League before more than holding his own after a late promotion to Low-A Visalia.

SCOUTING REPORT: De los Santos possesses proverbial "light-tower power" and crushes balls to all fields with apparent ease. There is, and probably always will be, a good bit of swing-and-miss to his game, but the power he is capable of producing projects to be worth the tradeoff. De los Santos logged a solid 10 percent walk rate but his approach remains unrefined. He puts up impressive batted-ball data but needs to learn to hit fewer balls on the ground. De los Santos might eventually shift across the diamond to first base. For now, there is some optimism he could stick at third, where he showed improved footwork and reads on balls off the bat. He has enough arm strength for the hot corner, but his throwing accuracy needs to improve.

THE FUTURE: For someone getting his first taste of pro ball, de los Santos did not disappoint. He fits the profile of a middle-of-the-lineup run-producer and figures to open the 2022 season back in Low-A.

BA GRADE
55 Risk: Extreme

SCOUTING GRADES:	Hitting: 50	Power: 70	Running: 45	Fielding: 45	Arm: 50

Year	Age	Club (Level)	Lge	AVG	G	AB	R	H	2B	3B	HR	RBI	BB	SO	SB	OBP	SLG
2021	18	D-backs (R)	ACL	.329	25	82	19	27	4	2	5	17	13	24	1	.421	.610
2021	18	Visalia (LoA)	West	.276	37	145	26	40	12	0	3	20	13	43	2	.340	.421
Minor League Totals (1 year)				.295	62	227	45	67	16	2	8	37	26	67	3	.370	.489

9 A.J. VUKOVICH, 3B

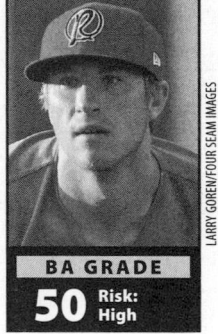

LARRY GOREN/FOUR SEAM IMAGES

Born: July 20, 2001. **B-T:** R-R. **HT:** 6-5. **WT:** 230. **Drafted:** HS—East Troy, Wis., 2020 (4th round). **Signed by:** Nate Birtwell.

TRACK RECORD: A multisport athlete in high school, Vukovich signed with the D-backs for an above-slot $1.25 million as a fourth-round pick in 2020 rather than stick with his commitment to Louisville. After a strong showing at instructional league in 2020, he skipped over the complex levels and went straight to Low-A Visalia for his pro debut in 2021. Vukovich got off to a rough start on both sides of the ball but righted the ship, earning a promotion to High-A and finishing with a solid .272/.323/.446 line.

SCOUTING REPORT: Vukovich has a long-levered, athletic frame. He has a closed off stance at the plate, an unusual setup for a modern hitter, but he manages to hit balls hard to all fields and has one of the better better-batted ball profiles of anyone in the D-backs system. Vukovich's pure contact skills are good and he has above-average power potential, but his plate discipline needs work. His chase rate spiked when he got to High-A, and he struggles with offspeed and breaking stuff in particular. Defensively, Vukovich showed below-average hands and throwing accuracy at third base during the opening weeks of the season but improved as the year progressed. He still widely projects to move to a corner outfield spot, where he should cover plenty of ground with his average speed.

THE FUTURE: Vukovich draws mixed reviews from rival scouts, but the D-backs are more bullish. They expect his swing decisions will improve and believe he'll become a middle-of-the-order power hitter with the ability to steal 10-15 bases. Even if he has to move positions, that is enough profile in an outfield corner.

BA GRADE
50 Risk: High

SCOUTING GRADES:	Hitting: 55	Power: 55	Running: 50	Fielding: 40	Arm: 50

Year	Age	Club (Level)	Lge	AVG	G	AB	R	H	2B	3B	HR	RBI	BB	SO	SB	OBP	SLG
2021	19	Visalia (LoA)	West	.259	62	247	42	64	15	1	10	42	19	77	10	.322	.449
	19	Hillsboro (HiA)	West	.298	30	121	13	36	4	2	3	20	3	28	6	.315	.438
Minor League Totals (2 years)				.272	92	368	55	100	19	3	13	62	22	105	16	.320	.446

10 BRANDON PFAADT, RHP

Born: Oct. 15, 1998. **B-T:** R-R. **HT:** 6-4. **WT:** 230. **Drafted:** Bellarmine (Ky.), 2020 (5th round). **Signed by:** Jeremy Kehrt.

TRACK RECORD: After splitting time between starting and relieving at Division II Bellarmine (Ky.), Pfaadt had a solid showing in the Cape Cod League after his sophomore season and hasn't looked back. He posted impressive numbers in five starts in his pandemic-shortened junior year, leading the D-backs to draft him in the fifth round, and he zipped up three levels to Double-A in his first season as a pro in 2021. He logged a 3.21 ERA across 22 starts and finished seventh in the minors with 160 strikeouts.

SCOUTING REPORT: Pfaadt is big and physical with a 6-foot-4, 230-pound frame built for logging innings and relentlessly pounds the strike zone with a four-pitch mix. His fastball sits comfortably in the 93-94 mph range, touches 97, and plays up with high spin rates and his aggressiveness using it. It sometimes displays good rise and other times good cutting action. His above-average slider with sharp downward action is his best secondary offering and his average changeup induces ground balls and the occasional swing and miss, although he needs to incorporate the pitch more regularly. Pfaadt throws his fastball for strikes in all for quadrants of the strike zone and commands his secondaries. He works hard, studies the game and is eager to improve.

THE FUTURE: Pfaadt quickly has gone from relative unknown to someone many expect to be a major leaguer. His debut may come in 2022 and he has a chance to settle into the middle or back of a rotation.

BRIAN WESTERHOLT/FOUR SEAM IMAGES

BA GRADE

50 Risk: High

SCOUTING GRADES:	Fastball: 55	Slider: 55	Curveball: 45	Changeup: 50	Control: 60

Year	Age	Club (Level)	Lge	W	L	ERA	G	GS	IP	H	HR	BB	SO	BB/9	SO/9	WHIP	AVG
2021	22	Hillsboro (HiA)	West	5	4	2.48	9	9	58	39	5	14	67	2.2	10.4	0.91	.186
	22	Visalia (LoA)	West	2	2	3.12	7	7	40	29	5	7	57	1.6	12.7	0.89	.191
	22	Amarillo (AA)	Cent	1	1	4.59	6	6	33	37	12	7	36	1.9	9.7	1.32	.276
Minor League Totals (2 years)				8	7	3.21	22	22	132	105	22	28	160	1.91	10.94	1.01	.212

11 BRYCE JARVIS, RHP

BA GRADE

45 Risk: High

Born: Dec. 26, 1997. **B-T:** L-R. **HT:** 6-2. **WT:** 195. **Drafted:** Duke, 2020 (1st round). **Signed by:** George Swain.

TRACK RECORD: Jarvis opened eyes with an impressive four-start, pre-quarantine stretch at Duke, giving the D-backs enough reason to snag him with the 18th overall pick and sign him to a $2.65 million deal in 2020. He touched two levels during his first full pro season, generally holding his own despite being sidelined for six weeks by an oblique injury.

SCOUTING REPORT: Jarvis has the components of a future rotation piece. His repertoire is four pitches deep, starting with a fastball that averages 94 mph. His best secondary offering is his changeup, a plus pitch that gets good action because of his ability to pronate. His curveball and slider can sometimes blend together but both are considered at least average pitches. Coaches say he still is learning to best utilize his stuff, noting he sometimes throws too many strikes and still needs to refine his ability to get hitters to chase.

THE FUTURE: The D-backs remain high on Jarvis' potential. They see a pitcher with four distinct pitches and the aptitude and commitment to improve and see no reason why he won't put things together, seeing him as a future mid-rotation starter. He likely will open this season back in Double-A.

Year	Age	Club (Level)	Lge	W	L	ERA	G	GS	IP	H	HR	BB	SO	BB/9	SO/9	WHIP	AVG
2021	23	D-backs (R)	ACL	0	0	0.00	1	1	3	1	0	0	7	0.0	21.0	0.33	.100
	23	Hillsboro (HiA)	West	1	2	3.62	7	7	37	30	4	13	42	3.1	10.1	1.15	.217
	23	Amarillo (AA)	Cent	1	2	5.66	8	8	35	32	8	17	40	4.4	10.3	1.40	.242
Minor League Totals (2 years)				2	4	4.42	16	16	75	63	12	30	89	3.6	10.6	1.23	.225

12 SLADE CECCONI, RHP

BA GRADE

45 Risk: High

Born: June 24, 1999. **B-T:** R-R. **HT:** 6-4. **WT:** 224. **Drafted:** Miami, 2020 (1st round supplemental). **Signed by:** Eric Cruz.

TRACK RECORD: After the D-backs selected Cecconi as a draft-eligible sophomore with the 33rd overall pick in 2020, he wasted little time opening eyes inside and outside the organization, showing overwhelming stuff during his time at the alternate site and instructional league.

Slowed by injuries during his first full season as a professional, Cecconi couldn't quite rediscover his high-end form, but he finished 2021 with a solid performance in the Arizona Fall League.

SCOUTING REPORT: During the year, Cecconi dealt with both left wrist and right elbow issues. The elbow problem brought an early end to his regular season but wasn't too serious since he returned a couple months later for the Fall League. Coaches say his delivery got out of whack during the year. In 2020, he featured a fastball that sat around 95 mph and touched the upper 90s with a wipeout slider. Last year, the fastball sat at 93, with the rest of his repertoire a tick down, as well. He has room to add strength to his frame, which should help his stuff tick back up.

THE FUTURE: Coaches believe that electric stuff is still in there; the hope is that with a fully healthy season he can tap into it the way he did in the past. He likely opens the year back in High-A with a chance to move quickly.

Year	Age	Club (Level)	Lge	W	L	ERA	G	GS	IP	H	HR	BB	SO	BB/9	SO/9	WHIP	AVG
2021	22	Hillsboro (HiA)	West	4	2	4.12	12	12	59	53	5	20	63	3.1	9.6	1.24	.240
Minor League Totals (2 years)				4	2	4.12	12	12	59	53	5	20	63	3.05	9.61	1.24	.240

13 KRISTIAN ROBINSON, OF

BA GRADE
50 Risk: Extreme

Born: Dec. 11, 2000. **B-T:** R-R. **HT:** 6-3. **WT:** 215. **Signed:** Bahamas, 2017.
Signed by: Cesar Geronimo/Craig Shipley.

TRACK RECORD: Robinson was viewed as perhaps the highest-upside position player in the D-backs system entering 2021, but it turned out to be a lost year due to legal issues stemming from a confrontation with a law enforcement officer in April 2020. Robinson pled to a felony assault charge in August 2021 and was sentenced to 18 months' probation and 150 hours community service. With a felony on his record, his visa status was up in the air, putting him in limbo.

SCOUTING REPORT: Robinson once was viewed as a potential five-tool player, with gobs of athleticism creating reason to dream on a massive upside despite some lack of refinement around his game. With the pandemic and his legal problems costing him two years' development, his future is harder to predict than ever. Other than instructional league in 2020, when he swung and missed an alarming amount, he has been limited mostly to informal workouts at the team's training facilities.

THE FUTURE: The D-backs were hopeful he would get back on the field in 2022 and added him to the 40-man roster in November. He will be on the restricted list until he is cleared to resume his career.

Year	Age	Club (Level)	Lge	AVG	G	AB	R	H	2B	3B	HR	RBI	BB	SO	SB	OBP	SLG
2021	20	Did not play															
Minor League Totals (3 years)				.281	126	477	91	134	25	2	21	92	58	144	29	.366	.474

14 RYAN BLISS, SS/2B

BA GRADE
45 Risk: High

Born: Dec. 13, 1999. **B-T:** R-R. **HT:** 5-9. **WT:** 165. **Drafted:** Auburn, 2021 (2nd round). **Signed by:** Kerry Jenkins.

TRACK RECORD: An undersized infielder without especially loud tools, Bliss raised his stock with an impressive junior year at Auburn, connecting for 15 homers while maintaining the bat-to-ball skills for which he always has been known. The D-backs' scouting department was won over by his consistency, his feel for the game, his ability to hit and his makeup.

SCOUTING REPORT: Bliss set out to hit for more power last year, doing so by using a more refined approach to pull certain pitches with authority. He has an aggressive mentality at the plate, a feel for finding the barrel and the ability to shoot line drives to all fields. He answered questions about how his new-found power would translate from aluminum to wood bat by slugging a solid .443 in Low-A. Defensively, he has good hands, range and footwork, making up for a fringe-average arm with a good game clock. He opened eyes with his play at shortstop but some still think the arm could force a move to second.

THE FUTURE: The D-backs see a player able to get more out of his ability than meets the eye, and they hope the power continues to play as he advances. If it does, they could have an above-average regular up the middle. If not, he could profile best in a utility role.

Year	Age	Club (Level)	Lge	AVG	G	AB	R	H	2B	3B	HR	RBI	BB	SO	SB	OBP	SLG
2021	21	D-backs (R)	ACL	.429	2	7	1	3	1	0	0	1	0	2	2	.429	.571
	21	Visalia (LoA)	West	.259	37	158	22	41	9	1	6	23	13	40	11	.322	.443
Minor League Totals (1 year)				.267	39	165	23	44	10	1	6	24	13	42	13	.326	.448

15 JAKE McCARTHY, OF

BA GRADE	
40	Risk: Medium

Born: July 30, 1997. **B-T:** L-L. **HT:** 6-3. **WT:** 215. **Drafted:** Virginia, 2018 (1st round supplemental). **Signed by:** Rick Matsko.

TRACK RECORD: McCarthy's career seemed stalled, first by injuries in 2019 and then by the pandemic in 2020, but after retooling his swing during quarantine, he opened eyes at instructional league that fall and carried his momentum into the 2021 season. McCarthy played well at both Double-A and Triple-A, earning a late-season promotion to the majors, where he held his own across 24 games.

SCOUTING REPORT: McCarthy's best tools remain his defense in center field and his speed. He gets good reads and takes accurate routes in center and likely was the D-backs' best defender in the majors at the position all season. In addition to his blazing speed—Statcast rated him among the Top 10 fastest players in baseball—McCarthy also is a smart, aggressive baserunner who looks to take the extra base. He tapped into more power than before thanks to his reworked swing; his 17 homers in 2021 were more than his previous career total in college and pro ball combined. It came with more swing and miss but club officials are hopeful that comes down as he continues to refine his swing.

THE FUTURE: McCarthy has the skill set to carve out a solid big league career—and he figures to come into spring training with a chance to win the center field job on Opening Day.

Year	Age	Club (Level)	Lge	AVG	G	AB	R	H	2B	3B	HR	RBI	BB	SO	SB	OBP	SLG
2021	23	Amarillo (AA)	Cent	.241	35	137	25	33	8	4	6	23	17	46	17	.333	.489
	23	Reno (AAA)	West	.262	50	191	38	50	6	7	9	31	20	49	12	.330	.508
	23	Arizona (MLB)	NL	.220	24	59	11	13	3	0	2	4	8	23	3	.333	.373
Major League Totals (1 year)				.220	24	59	11	13	3	0	2	4	8	23	3	.333	.373
Minor League Totals (4 years)				.270	196	742	126	200	44	18	20	106	77	188	68	.347	.458

16 DOMINIC CANZONE, OF

BA GRADE	
45	Risk: High

Born: Aug. 16, 1997. **B-T:** L-R. **HT:** 6-1. **WT:** 190. **Drafted:** Ohio State, 2019 (8th round). **Signed by:** Jeremy Kehrt.

TRACK RECORD: Canzone capped a solid career at Ohio State by putting together a big junior season in 2019, reaching base in a school-record 59 consecutive games and leading the Big Ten in a number of offensive categories. After missing the pandemic-canceled season in 2020, he started slowly in 2021 but eventually heated up in High-A, earning a promotion to Double-A and finishing with a strong showing in the Arizona Fall League.

SCOUTING REPORT: The lefthanded-hitting Canzone is a bat-first prospect with the potential to impact the game with his power and patience. Though he had below-average walk and chase rates in 2021, those numbers improved after an initial adjustment period at both High-A and Double-A. An adjustment to the finish on his swing helped him get more of his hard-hit balls in the air and toning down his leg kick helped him stay more under control. He likely profiles best in left field due to his below-average speed and arm strength. He was working out at first base in the fall in hopes of increasing his versatility.

THE FUTURE: Canzone is an advanced prospect with a bat that appears close to being major league-ready. The D-backs project to have a crowded outfield situation going forward, so he likely will need his bat to remain hot in order to push his way into the mix.

Year	Age	Club (Level)	Lge	AVG	G	AB	R	H	2B	3B	HR	RBI	BB	SO	SB	OBP	SLG
2021	23	Hillsboro (HiA)	West	.263	44	171	22	45	8	3	7	25	17	43	18	.337	.468
	23	Amarillo (AA)	Cent	.354	35	130	25	46	8	1	7	27	15	28	1	.425	.592
Minor League Totals (3 years)				.294	125	486	79	143	35	6	22	90	41	100	24	.354	.527

17 LUIS FRIAS, RHP

BA GRADE	
45	Risk: High

Born: May 23, 1998. **B-T:** R-R. **HT:** 6-3. **WT:** 245. **Signed:** Dominican Republic, 2015. **Signed by:** Jose Ortiz/Junior Noboa.

TRACK RECORD: Frias has worked his way steadily through the system since signing for $50,000 in 2015, adding size and improving the quality of his stuff along the way. He reached the majors in 2021, but did not exhibit the sort of command and control typically seen from a starter, leading many to assume his future role likely will be in relief.

SCOUTING REPORT: Frias averages about 95 mph with his fastball, occasionally touching 99 mph, holding his velocity deep into games. He throws a pair of breaking balls that can occasionally blend together. He also has a split-change that has yet to truly take hold. He threw strikes at High-A and Double-A last year, but struggled to limit walks during a five-start stint in Reno. He also walked five in 3.1 innings during a September callup.

THE FUTURE: Frias' lack of refinement has many thinking he might shift into a relief role, in which he could pare back his repertoire and focus mostly on his monster fastball and plus curveball. Still, starting isn't off the table. His path, at least in the short-term, could be determined based on how things shake out in spring training.

Year	Age	Club (Level)	Lge	W	L	ERA	G	GS	IP	H	HR	BB	SO	BB/9	SO/9	WHIP	AVG
2021	23	Hillsboro (HiA)	West	2	0	0.82	2	2	11	5	0	4	15	3.3	12.3	0.82	.139
	23	Amarillo (AA)	Cent	5	6	5.26	16	16	78	69	16	25	91	2.9	10.4	1.19	.228
	23	Reno (AAA)	West	2	1	5.82	5	5	21	21	1	16	20	6.7	8.3	1.71	.256
	23	Arizona (MLB)	NL	0	0	2.70	3	0	3	2	0	5	3	13.5	8.1	2.10	.200
Major League Totals (1 year)				0	0	2.70	3	0	3	2	0	5	3	13.50	8.10	2.10	.200
Minor League Totals (5 years)				19	18	3.80	66	63	294	236	19	128	332	3.9	10.2	1.24	.217

18 CORBIN MARTIN, RHP

BA GRADE
45 Risk: High

Born: Dec. 28, 1995. **B-T:** R-R. **HT:** 6-2. **WT:** 225. **Drafted:** Texas A&M, 2017 (2nd round). **Signed by:** Noel Gonzales-Luna (Astros).

TRACK RECORD: Martin rocketed through the Astros system, reaching the majors in 2019. Shortly after, he went down with Tommy John surgery and was subsequently dealt to the D-backs in the Zack Greinke trade. The D-backs thought they were getting a surefire rotation piece, but thus far Martin has yet to deliver on expectations, struggling to stay healthy in 2020 and then pitching poorly in the major leagues in 2021.

SCOUTING REPORT: There weren't many bright spots to Martin's 2021 season, in which he allowed 19 earned runs in 16 innings in the majors, but one was the fact that his pre-surgery stuff returned mostly intact. He sat in the 94 mph range with his fastball and exhibited the same movement profiles on his secondary pitches. Nothing he had seemed to fool big league hitters, however, and opinions vary on what went wrong. His command might have backed up and his confidence took a hit. He also was shut down again with more elbow problems, though he got back on the mound and was healthy before heading home for the offseason.

THE FUTURE: Rather than getting a chance to settle in after surgery, circumstances prompted the D-backs to bring Martin to the majors more quickly than they had hoped in 2021. They are hoping another year removed from the injury and a smoother path back will help him get back to being comfortable and confident on the mound.

Year	Age	Club (Level)	Lge	W	L	ERA	G	GS	IP	H	HR	BB	SO	BB/9	SO/9	WHIP	AVG
2021	25	Reno (AAA)	West	2	0	5.93	6	6	27	31	7	19	30	6.3	9.9	1.83	.279
	25	Arizona (MLB)	NL	0	3	10.69	5	3	16	23	5	14	13	7.9	7.3	2.31	.338
Major League Totals (2 years)				1	4	7.90	10	8	35	46	13	26	32	6.62	8.15	2.04	.311
Minor League Totals (5 years)				13	4	3.00	50	39	219	172	17	81	240	3.32	9.85	1.15	.214

19 ADRIAN DEL CASTILLO, C

BA GRADE
45 Risk: High

Born: Sept. 27, 1999. **B-T:** L-R. **HT:** 5-11. **WT:** 208. **Drafted:** Miami, 2021 (2nd round supplemental). **Signed by:** Eric Cruz.

TRACK RECORD: Del Castillo was considered one of the better college bats in his class entering the spring, but his production at the plate fell off, and with some clubs unsure about his defensive home, he fell to the 67th pick, where the D-backs snapped him up and paid him a $1 million bonus.

SCOUTING REPORT: Despite the down year, the D-backs were drawn to Del Castillo's bat. They see a quality lefthanded swing with an advanced approach and the ability to flat-out hit, evidenced by having more walks than strikeouts in his college career. They believe his pre-draft struggles were to due to changes he made to try to add power, and they hope that with his focus back on barreling balls up rather than lifting them, he'll eventually develop into a plus hitter with average power. The club seems to have fewer concerns about his defense than some others, seeing him as at least a decent receiver and blocker whose fringe-average arm can be offset by on-target accuracy and a quick release. Because of the pandemic, Del Castillo has had only one full season at catcher since high school, and the club hopes more experience will allow him to continue to develop behind the plate.

THE FUTURE: The D-backs hope Del Castillo eventually looks a little like Alex Avila in his best years. He figures to open this season in High-A.

Year	Age	Club (Level)	Lge	AVG	G	AB	R	H	2B	3B	HR	RBI	BB	SO	SB	OBP	SLG
2021	21	D-backs (R)	ACL	.600	2	5	1	3	0	0	0	0	2	1	0	.714	.600
	21	Visalia (LoA)	West	.244	22	78	12	19	6	2	1	14	9	28	0	.341	.410
Minor League Totals (1 year)				.265	24	83	13	22	6	2	1	14	11	29	0	.367	.422

20 TOMMY HENRY, LHP

Born: July 29, 1997. **B-T:** L-L. **HT:** 6-3. **WT:** 205. **Drafted:** Michigan, 2019 (2nd round supplemental). **Signed by:** Jeremy Kehrt.

BA GRADE	
45	Risk: High

TRACK RECORD: Henry was a big-game pitcher at Michigan and helped the Wolverines make a memorable run through the College World Series in 2019. Viewed as a relatively polished starter with a deep repertoire, Henry was pushed to Double-A to start his first full season and struggled with the aggressive assignment, logging a 5.21 ERA in 23 starts.

SCOUTING REPORT: Henry's fastball has ticked down to sit 91 mph and both his slider and curveball need improvement, with some sense he may be best served blending them into a slurvy offering. His changeup is solid-average and he learned in Double-A how much he needed to rely on it to keep hitters off his fastball. Henry struggled with below-average control throughout the year, but the D-backs' internal numbers showed his performance was more indicative of someone with a run and a half lower ERA.

THE FUTURE: Henry's upside remains limited by his lack of overpowering stuff, but the D-backs still view him as a potential back-end starter. He'll be tested at Triple-A Reno in 2022.

Year	Age	Club (Level)	Lge	W	L	ERA	G	GS	IP	H	HR	BB	SO	BB/9	SO/9	WHIP	AVG
2021	23	Amarillo (AA)	Cent	4	6	5.21	23	23	115	116	24	53	135	4.1	10.5	1.46	.268
Minor League Totals (3 years)				4	6	5.23	26	26	119	120	24	53	139	4.0	10.5	1.46	.268

21 SETH BEER, 1B/DH

Born: Sept. 18, 1996. **B-T:** L-R. **HT:** 6-3. **WT:** 225. **Drafted:** Clemson, 2018 (1st round). **Signed by:** Gavin Dickey (Astros).

BA GRADE	
40	Risk: Medium

TRACK RECORD: Beer became the fourth and final player from the Zack Greinke trade to reach the majors for the D-backs when he made his debut in September. He connected for a pinch-hit homer in his first big league at-bat, but suffered a season-ending shoulder injury in his first inning in the field diving for a ball.

SCOUTING REPORT: As always, Beer remains a bat-first, if not bat-only, prospect. He hits the ball to all fields, is good at working counts and makes a decent amount of contact even when expands the zone. Beer's power is closer to average than plus, but he gets to it enough to make a difference in games. Beer's defense at first base remains subpar, with evaluators differing only on whether it is playable. He is a slow mover with poor hands and is a liability in the field.

THE FUTURE: A universal DH would help Beer's cause, but many evaluators see him as a good hitter rather than a great one, projecting him more as a second-division slugger.

Year	Age	Club (Level)	Lge	AVG	G	AB	R	H	2B	3B	HR	RBI	BB	SO	SB	OBP	SLG
2021	24	Reno (AAA)	West	.287	100	362	73	104	33	0	16	59	39	76	0	.398	.511
	24	Arizona (MLB)	NL	.444	5	9	4	4	1	0	1	3	1	3	0	.500	.889
Major League Totals (1 year)				.444	5	9	4	4	1	0	1	3	1	3	0	.500	.889
Minor League Totals (4 years)				.292	289	1072	184	313	71	0	54	204	110	238	1	.392	.509

22 JOE ELBIS, RHP

Born: Sept. 24, 2002. **B-T:** R-R. **HT:** 6-1. **WT:** 170. **Signed:** Venezuela, 2019. **Signed by:** Cesar Geronimo/Francisco Cartaya/Tony Caballero.

BA GRADE	
50	Risk: Extreme

TRACK RECORD: Elbis was an athletic, projectable righthander who recently converted from the outfield to pitching when the D-backs signed him for $275,000 in 2019. He opened eyes in his debut in 2021, showing good command, a solid repertoire, pitching acumen and an impressive work ethic.

SCOUTING REPORT: Elbis does not overpower hitters with pure stuff, but he locates his 91-94 mph fastball well, commanding it to both sides of the plate and showing the ability to elevate. His changeup is his best secondary pitch, eliciting swings and misses and weak contact, and he showed an improved curveball after switching to a spike grip. He also has a slider that shows promise. He has a clean, sound delivery and a quick arm. During the Arizona Complex League season, Elbis took it upon himself to go to Chase Field to try to learn by watching big league pitching, which coaches saw as evidence of his drive to improve.

THE FUTURE: Just how much projection he has left is up for debate, but even without big gains in velocity or secondary stuff, he has the makings of a back-end big league starter.

Year	Age	Club (Level)	Lge	W	L	ERA	G	GS	IP	H	HR	BB	SO	BB/9	SO/9	WHIP	AVG
2021	18	D-backs (R)	ACL	3	2	3.40	9	7	39	39	4	4	46	0.9	10.4	1.08	.260
	18	Visalia (LoA)	West	0	1	3.86	3	3	14	13	0	3	13	1.9	8.4	1.14	.236
Minor League Totals (1 year)				3	3	3.52	12	10	54	52	4	7	59	1.2	9.9	1.10	.254

23 JUSTIN MARTINEZ, RHP

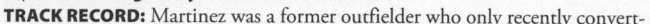

BA GRADE
50 Risk: Extreme

Born: July 30, 2001. **B-T:** R-R. **HT:** 6-3. **WT:** 195. **Signed:** Dominican Republic, 2018. **Signed by:** Cesar Geronimo/Jose Ortiz.

TRACK RECORD: Martinez was a former outfielder who only recently convert- ed to the mound when the D-backs took a $50,000 flier on his athleticism and arm strength by signing him in March 2018. He quickly made significant strides, improving his velocity into the upper 90s while showing some feel to spin a breaking ball, but he suffered a setback early in 2021 when he ultimately required Tommy John surgery in July.

SCOUTING REPORT: Martinez is known for a fastball that regularly sits in the upper 90s. He also has a slider that flashes plus but is inconsistent and a split-change that needs refinement. He struggled with his strike-throwing early last year but started to show improvement by picking up the tempo in his delivery to make things less rigid and more fluid. He still has work to do but continued to show enough to look like a starter. He has a strong frame and is a hard worker, someone coaches say is eager to soak up information.

THE FUTURE: Surgery will wipe out a good chunk of Martinez's 2022 season, but he is still young and will pitch most of 2023 at age 21. As such, he still has time to make good on his high-upside potential.

Year	Age	Club (Level)	Lge	W	L	ERA	G	GS	IP	H	HR	BB	SO	BB/9	SO/9	WHIP	AVG
2021	19	Visalia (LoA)	West	1	3	6.65	7	7	23	25	1	15	24	5.9	9.4	1.74	.284
Minor League Totals (4 years)				2	11	5.27	40	29	123	118	4	90	132	6.6	9.7	1.69	.248

24 CONOR GRAMMES, RHP

BA GRADE
50 Risk: Extreme

Born: July 13, 1997. **B-T:** R-R. **HT:** 6-2. **WT:** 205. **Drafted:** Xavier, 2019 (5th round). **Signed by:** Jeremy Kehrt.

TRACK RECORD: The D-backs bet on Grammes' athleticism when they drafted him out of Xavier despite the former two-way player's relative inexperience on the mound. He looked like a quick study during his time at instructional league in 2020, but he did not pitch well early in the 2021 season, then went down with an elbow injury that required Tommy John surgery.

SCOUTING REPORT: Before surgery, Grammes still had some of the best stuff in the system. His fastball averaged 96 mph to go with a slider, curveball and changeup, the latter two lagging behind the others. He is raw when it comes to his pitching acumen and had managed to get by on stuff and athleticism before last year. A former two-time state wrestling champion, he is an excellent competitor who keeps his emotions in check on the mound.

THE FUTURE: The injury pushes back Grammes' timeline and might point him more toward a future in the bullpen, but it will give him a chance to learn how hard he'll need to work in order to make it back. With a big fastball and usable secondary pitches, his stuff will play regardless of the role.

Year	Age	Club (Level)	Lge	W	L	ERA	G	GS	IP	H	HR	BB	SO	BB/9	SO/9	WHIP	AVG
2021	23	Hillsboro (HiA)	West	0	2	7.46	8	7	25	35	5	12	32	4.3	11.4	1.86	.327
Minor League Totals (3 years)				0	3	6.20	17	13	41	46	5	20	52	4.4	11.5	1.62	.284

25 ALVIN GUZMAN, OF

BA GRADE
50 Risk: Extreme

Born: Oct. 20, 2001. **B-T:** R-R. **HT:** 6-3. **WT:** 177. **Signed:** Dominican Republic, 2018. **Signed by:** Cesar Geronimo/Luis Baez.

TRACK RECORD: The D-backs gave Guzman $1.8 million, making him their top international signing in 2018, doing so on the strength of his athleticism, tools and feel to hit. Thus far, it hasn't come together for him in games on a consistent basis, but he did enjoy a stretch of production in the Arizona Complex League that gave a glimpse of what he is capable of doing.

SCOUTING REPORT: When Guzman is locked in at the plate, he can look like he has about as much ceil- ing as any player in the system. For those who believe in his potential, he is at least a four-tool player— maybe five if you expect the power to come along. He should stick in center field and has a strong and accurate arm. He has speed that can impact the game. Guzman can be inconsistent at the plate, getting too aggressive and giving away at-bats, and evaluators say he needs to shorten up his swing and make it more repeatable in addition to improving his approach.

THE FUTURE: Guzman has a lot he needs to clean up, but this would be a good time to do it since he is going into a protection year. He figures to get a shot at full-season ball in 2022.

Year	Age	Club (Level)	Lge	AVG	G	AB	R	H	2B	3B	HR	RBI	BB	SO	SB	OBP	SLG
2021	19	D-backs (R)	ACL	.208	42	125	28	26	6	1	3	13	18	50	15	.324	.344
Minor League Totals (2 years)				.220	99	364	67	80	17	4	4	37	34	114	29	.295	.321

26 TIM TAWA, 2B/OF

BA GRADE

40 Risk: High

Born: April 7, 1999. **B-T:** R-R. **HT:** 6-0. **WT:** 196. **Drafted:** Stanford, 2021 (11th round). **Signed by:** Andrew Allen.

TRACK RECORD: Tawa won Gatorade Player of the Year honors in football three times and baseball once during his prep career in Oregon and was seen as a legit baseball prospect after a big freshman year at Stanford. But injuries and poor performance hurt his stock, and after the D-backs selected him as a senior sign last year, he put together the most productive offensive season of any of the club's debut players.

SCOUTING REPORT: Tawa profiles as a versatile and athletic up-the-middle player. He has tools, namely his plus speed, and showed some ability to put together good at-bats and produce in Low-A, though he was old for the level. He has a simple, efficient swing with good bat speed and generated good batted-ball data in his debut. He played mostly second base and the outfield, logging the most innings in center, and is viewed as an above-average defender with an average arm at each of those positions.

THE FUTURE: Tawa suffered a left shoulder injury that might have affected his performance across two seasons at Stanford. Now healthy after surgery, the hope is that he is back to the type of prospect he appeared to be years ago. He profiles best as a super-utility player. He figures to open the year in High-A.

Year	Age	Club (Level)	Lge	AVG	G	AB	R	H	2B	3B	HR	RBI	BB	SO	SB	OBP	SLG
2021	22	D-backs (R)	ACL	.400	2	5	1	2	0	0	1	3	2	2	1	.571	1.000
2021	22	Visalia (LoA)	West	.264	36	140	27	37	9	2	5	19	22	36	13	.366	.464
Minor League Totals (1 year)				.269	38	145	28	39	9	2	6	22	24	38	14	.374	.483

27 JEFERSON ESPINAL, OF

BA GRADE

45 Risk: Extreme

Born: June 7, 2002. **B-T:** L-L. **HT:** 6-0. **WT:** 185. **Signed:** Dominican Republic, 2018. **Signed by:** Cesar Geronimo/Omar Rogers.

TRACK RECORD: Knowing he had an unrefined game, the D-backs gambled on Espinal's athleticism when they gave him a $200,000 bonus in 2018. In an up-and-down 2021 season, Espinal showed glimpses of the sort of impact profile he can provide while also looking like a player who still has a long developmental timeline ahead.

SCOUTING REPORT: Espinal has an array of tools along with a strong, athletic frame. He has blazing speed and the ability to stick in center field. Offensively, it's tough to figure out what he'll become. He performed poorly in Low-A to start the year and was sent back to Arizona, where he worked to retool his swing. With his upper and lower halves better synched up, he raked in the complex league, then returned to Low-A and performed there, as well, hitting a combined .330/.409/.482 over his final 31 games before a groin injury ended his season.

THE FUTURE: Espinal needs to improve his approach at the plate, and his reads and routes in the outfield need to get better, as well. He lacks good instincts, so reps and experience are of the utmost importance. But the tools are there, and his strong finish provides hope that he is making progress.

Year	Age	Club (Level)	Lge	AVG	G	AB	R	H	2B	3B	HR	RBI	BB	SO	SB	OBP	SLG
2021	19	D-backs (R)	ACL	.352	20	71	17	25	6	1	1	10	10	21	9	.446	.507
	19	Visalia (LoA)	West	.216	42	153	22	33	8	0	1	13	16	63	7	.288	.288
Minor League Totals (3 years)				.303	118	446	81	135	24	3	4	44	49	140	42	.376	.397

28 WILDERD PATIÑO, OF

BA GRADE

45 Risk: Extreme

Born: July 18, 2001. **B-T:** R-R. **HT:** 6-1. **WT:** 175. **Signed:** Venezuela, 2017. **Signed by:** Cesar Geronimo/Kristians Pereira.

TRACK RECORD: Patiño has been a well-regarded player within the organization for years, his strength, build and athleticism—not to mention his performance early in his career—giving evaluators reason to dream on a massive upside. As they did with almost all of their prospects last year, the D-backs pushed Patiño, starting him in Low-A. He might not have been ready for the challenge.

SCOUTING REPORT: Patiño fell flat in full-season ball, both expanding the zone and swinging and missing at well above-average rates. He probably deserves some slack due to a recurring groin issue. The injury bothered him at the start of the year and then cost him about 2 1/2 months in the middle. He might have pressed in hopes of making up for his subpar start and could not dig his way out. He also allowed his swing to get big, incorporating a leg kick that might have hurt his timing. At his best, Patiño is a physical, tooled-up player with the potential for an impact power/speed profile. He was seen as a possible center fielder but now is more likely to end up on a corner.

THE FUTURE: The club hopes Patiño returns to camp fully healthy, and that he is able to learn from his struggles last year. He figures to open the season back in Low-A.

Year	Age	Club (Level)	Lge	AVG	G	AB	R	H	2B	3B	HR	RBI	BB	SO	SB	OBP	SLG
2021	19	D-backs (R)	ACL	.250	8	28	2	7	1	1	0	1	0	9	0	.276	.357
	19	Visalia (LoA)	West	.210	30	119	18	25	2	1	2	8	5	49	6	.288	.294
Minor League Totals (4 years)				.266	112	399	58	106	14	7	3	43	34	128	26	.350	.358

29 JOSE FERNANDEZ, SS

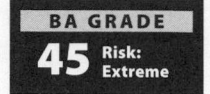

BA GRADE

45 Risk: Extreme

Born: Sept. 22, 2003. **B-T:** R-R. **HT:** 6-3. **WT:** 180. **Signed:** Venezuela, 2021. **Signed by:** Cesar Geronimo/Francisco Cartaya/Gregory Blanco.
TRACK RECORD: Fernandez signed for $275,000 in January 2021, far from the top bonus in the D-backs' international class. But he was pushed as aggressively as anyone, making his pro debut some six months later in the complex league. Given the age differential, he mostly held his own at the plate, showing some flashes of the ability that has many in the organization excited about his future.
SCOUTING REPORT: Fernandez has a loose, easy swing with a clean path and feel for the barrel. He has a lean frame with room to add significant strength, making it easier to envision at least above-average if not plus power. He swung and missed at an alarming 43 percent rate, though he was often playing against competition several years older. He has good hands and footwork and smooth actions at shortstop. For some, the only question about his future position is in how his body develops.
THE FUTURE: Those willing to dream see the frame and tools of modern-day, middle-of-the-lineup shortstop. His debut showed he has a ways to go, but he has the makeup and work ethic teams like to see when they project on developmental gains.

Year	Age	Club (Level)	Lge	AVG	G	AB	R	H	2B	3B	HR	RBI	BB	SO	SB	OBP	SLG
2021	17	D-backs (R)	ACL	.250	36	112	14	28	4	1	0	14	11	39	4	.320	.304
Minor League Totals (1 year)				.250	36	112	14	28	4	1	0	14	11	39	4	.320	.304

30 MANUEL PEÑA, 3B/2B

BA GRADE

45 Risk: Extreme

Born: Dec. 5, 2003. **B-T:** L-R. **HT:** 6-1. **WT:** 170. **Signed:** Dominican Republic, 2021. **Signed by:** Cesar Geronimo/Omar Rogers/Ronald Rivas.
TRACK RECORD: The D-backs liked Peña's sweet, lefthanded swing, his sound approach and his ability to stick on the infield dirt when they signed him for $1.2 million in January, giving him the largest bonus of any player in the club's 2020-21 international class. He debuted in the Dominican Summer League and held his own, impressing evaluators with the quality of his at-bats.
SCOUTING REPORT: Peña's supporters have little doubt about his ability to hit. He has a clean, loose swing and a good feel for putting the barrel on the ball. He gets good marks for his advanced approach at the plate. He also works deep counts and controls the zone well. Defensively, he has good hands and a solid, accurate throwing arm, but he lacks the kind of range necessary to stick at shortstop. Evaluators expect him to shift either to third or second. He impressed the organization with his mature work habits and his dedication and focus on improving.
THE FUTURE: After a solid debut, Peña likely makes his way stateside for the first time in 2022. Those who believe in him see a potential impact hitter in the mold of Eric Chavez or Rafael Devers, only with less power.

Year	Age	Club (Level)	Lge	AVG	G	AB	R	H	2B	3B	HR	RBI	BB	SO	SB	OBP	SLG
2021	17	D-backs1 (R)	DSL	.253	57	194	30	49	5	2	4	30	26	46	17	.342	.361
Minor League Totals (1 year)				.253	57	194	30	49	5	2	4	30	26	46	17	.342	.361

MORE PROSPECTS TO KNOW

31 COOPER HUMMEL, OF
Hummel has an elite approach and has tapped into more power in recent years, though he remains a below-average defender wherever he plays.

32 JORGE BARROSA, OF
Barrosa is a terrific defender in center field and can swing the bat from both sides of the plate. Questions about his level of impact are all that hold him back.

33 BUDDY KENNEDY, 3B
Kennedy enjoyed an impressive offensive season at two levels, but concerns about his defense hold him back—and probably are the only reason he hasn't been added to the 40-man roster.

34 JUAN CORNIEL, SS
Corniel, who signed for $325,000 in 2019, debuted in the complex league last year. He's a surefire shortstop with a chance to contribute at the plate.

35 DOMINIC FLETCHER, OF
Fletcher's aggressiveness at the plate got exposed a bit at Double-A last year, but he remains a terrific defender who profiles as an extra outfielder.

36 KENNY CASTILLO, C `SLEEPER`
Castillo has a knack for making hard contact, profiling as an offensive catcher with a strong arm who still has some growing to do behind the plate.

37 ALBERTO CIPRIAN, 3B
Part of the deal that sent Eduardo Escobar to the Brewers, Ciprian has a chance to hit for both average and power, though there are some questions about where he ends up defensively.

38 JUNIOR FRANCO, OF
Franco, listed at 5-foot-9, 165 pounds, draws comparisons to Kole Calhoun for his build and his bat. He put up big numbers in his pro debut in the complex league.

39 NEYFY CASTILLO, OF
Castillo has that always-coveted power-speed combo but needs to improve his low-average, high-strikeout tendencies.

40 JACOB STEINMETZ, RHP
Steinmetz, the first known practicing Orthodox Jewish player to be drafted, has the potential for a plus fastball and the makings of a wicked curve.

TOP PROSPECTS OF THE DECADE

Year	Player, Pos	2021 Org
2012	Trevor Bauer, RHP	Dodgers
2013	Tyler Skaggs, LHP	Deceased
2014	Archie Bradley, RHP	Phillies
2015	Archie Bradley, RHP	Phillies
2016	Dansby Swanson, SS	Braves
2017	Anthony Banda, LHP	Pirates
2018	Jon Duplantier, RHP	D-backs
2019	Jazz Chisholm, SS	Marlins
2020	Daulton Varsho, C/OF	D-backs
2021	Corbin Carroll, OF	D-backs

TOP DRAFT PICKS OF THE DECADE

Year	Player, Pos	2021 Org
2012	Stryker Trahan, C	Did not play
2013	Braden Shipley, RHP	Mexican League
2014	Touki Toussaint, RHP	Braves
2015	Dansby Swanson, SS	Braves
2016	Anfernee Grier, OF (1st rd supp)	American Assoc.
2017	Pavin Smith, 1B	D-backs
2018	*Matt McLain, SS	Reds
2019	Corbin Carroll, OF	D-backs
2020	Bryce Jarvis, RHP	D-backs
2021	Jordan Lawlar, SS	D-backs
	* Did not sign	

Atlanta Braves

BY CARLOS COLLAZO

The Braves reached the pinnacle of baseball during the 2021 season, beating the Astros in six games to claim the organization's fourth World Series championship and first since the 1995 season.

Atlanta did this despite losing its best player—outfielder Ronald Acuña Jr.—to a knee injury in the middle of the season and after only getting 48 games out of outfielder Marcell Ozuna, who dealt with injury and a domestic violence arrest that ended his season.

Even after winning the fourth straight division title, the Braves were an underdog in the postseason with the worst record of the entire field.

The team found success thanks to big games from lefthanders Max Fried and Charlie Morton (who suffered a broken leg in the World Series), excellent pitching out of the bullpen from Will Smith, Luke Jackson, AJ Minter and especially Tyler Matzek and offensive contributions from key trade deadline acquisitions Adam Duvall, Joc Pederson, Eddie Rosario and World Series MVP Jorge Soler.

In hindsight, Atlanta's 2021 trade deadline looks like one of the most successful in recent memory, as general manager Alex Anthopoulos continued to show a savvy ability to make in-season additions without giving up premium prospect packages in return. The Duvall/Pederson/Rosario/Soler outfield group helped get the Braves into the playoffs and then win it all, and it only cost the team righthander Kasey Kalich, catcher Alex Jackson, pinch hitter Pablo Sandoval and first baseman Bryce Ball.

Sandoval was a limited bench piece and each of Kalich, Jackson and Ball ranked in the back half of Atlanta's top 30 prospects a year ago.

Anthopoulos' unwillingness to deal from the team's premier prospect group leaves the organization with a solid farm system that should continue to help fill holes on the major league club in coming seasons. Graduations and offensive stagnation with top prospects Cristian Pache and Drew Waters limits the top-end upside of the system, but the team did see excellent seasons and big steps forward from up-the-middle prospects like Michael Harris II (the new No. 1 prospect) and catcher Shea Langeliers.

Pache and Waters are still young, and the same hitting development group that helped turn Austin Riley into an MVP candidate in 2021 is working with the two, but hitting depth falls off quickly beyond contact-oriented third baseman Vaughn Grissom and slugging outfielder Jesse Franklin.

Instead, the bulk of the organization's depth comes from righthanded pitching. The Braves

Austin Riley blossomed in 2021 as Atlanta flourished in the fall and won the World Series.

PROJECTED 2025 LINEUP

Catcher	Shea Langeliers	27
First Base	Austin Riley	28
Second Base	Ozzie Albies	28
Third Base	Vaughn Grissom	24
Shortstop	Dansby Swanson	31
Left Field	Michael Harris II	24
Center Field	Cristian Pache	26
Right Field	Ronald Acuña Jr.	27
Designated Hitter	Drew Waters	26
No. 1 Starter	Max Fried	31
No. 2 Starter	Mike Soroka	26
No. 3 Starter	Ian Anderson	27
No. 4 Starter	Kyle Muller	27
No. 5 Starter	Huascar Ynoa	27
Closer	Spencer Strider	26

have continued to show a savvy ability to draft and develop arms in the post-Brian Bridges scouting era under Dana Brown. Spencer Strider was a success story in 2021 after Atlanta took a shot on him in the fourth round in the 2020 draft, and Atlanta is looking to find similar results with power-armed, athletic 2021 drafted righthanders like Ryan Cusick, Spencer Schwellenbach and AJ Smith-Shawver.

The Braves will need to continue reinforcing the farm system while picking in the back half of the first round for the foreseeable future, but moving forward the team will be able to get more aggressive on the international market with signing sanctions now fully in the rearview mirror. ■

DEPTH CHART

ATLANTA BRAVES

TOP 2022 ROOKIES	RANK
Cristian Pache, OF	3
Kyle Muller, LHP	4
Bryce Elder, RHP	8

BREAKOUT PROSPECTS	RANK
Freddy Tarnok, RHP	11
AJ Smith-Shawver, RHP	18
Brandol Mezquita, OF	29

SOURCE OF TOP 30 TALENT

Homegrown	30	Acquired	0
College	13	Trade	0
Junior college	2	Rule 5 draft	0
High school	9	Independent league	0
Nondrafted free agent	0	Free agent/waivers	0
International	6		

LF
Jesse Franklin (10)
Stephen Paolini

CF
Michael Harris (1)
Cristian Pache (3)
Drew Waters (6)
Tyler Collins (28)
Justin Dean
Kadon Morton

RF
Brandol Mezquita (29)
Trey Harris

3B
Vaughn Grissom (12)
Ambiorvis Tavarez (30)
Justyn-Henry Malloy

SS
Braden Shewmake (7)
Beau Philip
Francisco Floyd

2B
Cal Conley (24)
Luke Waddell

1B
Greyson Jenista (26)
Drew Lugbauer

C
Shea Langeliers (2)
Logan Brown
Tyler Tolve
Javier Valdes

LHP

LHSP	LHRP
Kyle Muller (4)	Tucker Davidson (13)
Jared Shuster (15)	Jake Higginbotham
	Adam Shoemaker
	Gabriel Rodriguez
	Dylan Lee

RHP

RHSP	RHRP
Bryce Elder (8)	Spencer Strider (5)
Ryan Cusick (9)	Joey Estes (14)
Freddy Tarnok (11)	Daysbel Hernandez (19)
Darius Vines (16)	Brooks Wilson (20)
Spencer Schwellenbach (17)	Indigo Diaz (21)
AJ Smith-Shawver (18)	Jasseel de la Cruz (22)
Alan Rangel (27)	Victor Vodnik (23)
Nolan Kingham	William Woods (25)
Andrew Hoffman	Jared Johnson
	Rolddy Munoz
	Trey Riley
	Tyler Owens
	Roddery Munoz

1 MICHAEL HARRIS II, OF

Born: March 7, 2001. **B-T:** L-L. **HT:** 6-0. **WT:** 195.
Drafted: HS—Stockbridge, Ga., 2019 (3rd round).
Signed by: Kirk Fredriksson.

TRACK RECORD: Most of the scouting industry seemed to prefer Harris as a lefthanded pitcher out of Stockbridge (Ga.) in 2019. He touched 93 mph with his fastball and showed feel to spin a big curveball. Harris preferred hitting, though, and the Braves liked his upside enough as a position player to give him a chance with the bat. They drafted him in the third round as an outfielder and signed him for $547,500 to forgo a Texas Tech commitment. After flashing solid tools in his pro debut after signing, Harris impressed Braves officials in 2020 with quality at-bats against many of the team's top pitching prospects at the alternate training site. He carried that into 2021 with a breakout season at High-A Rome, finishing among the Braves organization leaders in hits (110), doubles (26), RBIs (67), stolen bases (27) and earning a selection to the Futures Game.

SCOUTING REPORT: Harris has developed rapidly into the consensus best pure hitter in the Braves' system. Officially listed by Major League Baseball as a switch-hitter, he took all his swings from the left side in 2021 and shows impressive feel to hit with loose wrists, easy hands and impressive plate coverage. Harris' plate coverage is so good that he gives away at-bats at times by being overly aggressive and chasing balls he can't drive, but he identifies pitches well. When he focused on eliminating his chases on the inner half during the second half of the season, his on-base percentage shot up to .400 over the final two months. Harris has plenty of strength in his filled-out frame and drops the bat head with force throughout the zone. He routinely produces exit velocities in the 110-114 mph range, and while he hit just seven home runs this year, he played his home games in one of the toughest offensive environments in minor league baseball. All of his seven home runs came on the road, and his home (.282/.361/.363) and road (.305/.363/.498) splits suggest above-average power potential his overall numbers might not indicate. Harris combines that power potential with plus speed and aggressive baserunning that make him a dangerous stolen base threat. In addition to his offensive prowess, Harris was voted the best defensive outfielder in High-A East by league managers. He draws praise for his instincts and ability in center field and

TOM PRIDDY/FOUR SEAM IMAGES

BA GRADE	SCOUTING GRADES
60 Risk: High	Hit: 60. Power: 55. Run: 55. Field: 60. Arm: 60.

Projected future grades on 20-80 scouting scale

BEST TOOLS

Best Hitter for Average	Michael Harris II
Best Power Hitter	Jesse Franklin
Best Strike-Zone Discipline	Vaughn Grissom
Fastest Baserunner	Cristian Pache
Best Athlete	Michael Harris
Best Fastball	Kyle Muller
Best Curveball	Freddy Tarnok
Best Slider	Bryce Elder
Best Changeup	Jared Shuster
Best Control	Darius Vines
Best Defensive Catcher	Shea Langeliers
Best Defensive Infielder	Braden Shewmake
Best Infield Arm	Beau Philip
Best Defensive Outfielder	Cristian Pache
Best Outfield Arm	Cristian Pache

could be an above-average or plus defender at the position if he maintains his plus speed. His thicker lower half and filled-out frame raise the possibility he will slow down in the future, but he should remain an above-average defender even if he has to eventually move to a corner outfield spot. His plus arm strength will play at any position.

THE FUTURE: With above-average or better tools across the board, Harris has a chance to be an impact, everyday big leaguer. He will move to Double-A Mississippi in 2022, where the Braves would like to see him continue to mature as a hitter. His defense gives him a shot to be a very well-rounded player. ■

Year	Age	Club (Level)	Lge	AVG	G	AB	R	H	2B	3B	HR	RBI	BB	SO	SB	OBP	SLG
2021	20	Rome (HiA)	East	.294	101	374	55	110	26	3	7	64	35	76	27	.362	.436
Minor League Totals (3 years)				.288	154	565	81	163	34	7	9	91	53	118	35	.356	.421

2 SHEA LANGELIERS, C

Born: Nov. 18, 1997. **B-T:** R-R. **HT:** 6-0. **WT:** 205. **Drafted:** Baylor, 2019 (1st round). **Signed by:** Darin Vaughan.

TRACK RECORD: Langeliers established himself as top defensive catcher in the 2019 draft class at Baylor and steadily raised his stock throughout his junior spring, leading the Braves to draft him ninth overall and sign him for an under-slot $3.9 million bonus. After making his brief pro debut at High-A Rome, Langeliers impressed at the alternate training site in 2020 and had a standout first full season at Double-A Mississippi in 2021. He finished third in Double-A South with 22 home runs and fourth with an .836 OPS while playing excellent defense behind the plate, earning a billing as the league's best prospect.

SCOUTING REPORT: Langeliers' defense is his primary asset, led by his plus-plus arm. He threw out 42% of attempted base stealers in 2021 and routinely records pop times to second base in the 1.90-second range with pristine accuracy. Pitchers love throwing to Langeliers and he has the makeup and baseball IQ to manage a staff, although he still needs to improve his pitch framing and mobility to become a true plus defender. Langeliers has continued to show above-average power as he's moved further away from a hamate injury in college, and his 22 home runs came while playing his home games in a difficult hitter's park. Langeliers will have to work to avoid creating holes in his swing—notably with high fastballs and sliders away—but he uses the entire field well and makes enough contact to be a fringe-average hitter. Braves officials have praised his ability to make adjustments.

THE FUTURE: Langeliers has a chance to make his big-league debut in 2022. If he reaches his offensive ceiling, he could be an above-average regular.

BA GRADE

55 Risk: High

SCOUTING GRADES:	Hitting: 45	Power: 55	Running: 40	Fielding: 60	Arm: 70

Year	Age	Club (Level)	Lge	AVG	G	AB	R	H	2B	3B	HR	RBI	BB	SO	SB	OBP	SLG
2021	23	Mississippi (AA)	South	.258	92	329	56	85	13	0	22	52	36	97	1	.338	.498
	23	Gwinnett (AAA)	East	.182	5	11	3	2	2	0	0	1	3	6	0	.357	.364
Minor League Totals (3 years)				.255	151	556	86	142	28	0	24	87	56	158	1	.327	.435

3 CRISTIAN PACHE, OF

Born: Nov. 19, 1998. **B-T:** R-R. **HT:** 6-2. **WT:** 215. **Signed:** Dominican Republic, 2015. **Signed by:** Matias Laureano.

TRACK RECORD: Pache signed with the Braves for $1.4 million as a 16-year-old out of the Dominican Republic and immediately stood out for his defensive prowess in center field. Pache filled out, added strength and became one of the most electric defensive prospects in baseball, but his offensive development has stalled. He began the 2021 season as the Braves' Opening Day center fielder, but he hit just .111 with 25 strikeouts in 68 plate appearances and was demoted to Triple-A for the rest of the season.

SCOUTING REPORT: Pache's 80-grade defense in center field is unimpeachable, but his bat remains a question mark. He has timing issues at the plate and often has to decide whether he's sitting on fastballs or breaking stuff, which creates inconsistencies. He has long had issues with a pull-heavy approach and posted the highest strikeout rate (27.5%) of his minor league career in 2021. Pache has gone back and forth with various handsets the Braves have tried to incorporate to get him in better position to hit, with varying levels of success. He has the strength to hit 20 home runs, but he projects to be no more than a below-average hitter. At the very least, Pache will save plenty of runs with his top-of-the-scale glovework, plus-plus speed and plus-plus arm strength in center field.

THE FUTURE: Pache's defense is valuable, but barring a step forward with his approach at the plate, he now seems more like a defensive specialist who hits at the bottom of the lineup rather than the potential All-Star of years past.

BA GRADE

55 Risk: High

SCOUTING GRADES:	Hitting: 40	Power: 50	Running: 70	Fielding: 80	Arm: 70

Year	Age	Club (Level)	Lge	AVG	G	AB	R	H	2B	3B	HR	RBI	BB	SO	SB	OBP	SLG
2021	22	Gwinnett (AAA)	East	.265	89	321	50	85	15	0	11	44	30	97	9	.330	.414
	22	Atlanta (MLB)	NL	.111	22	63	6	7	3	0	1	4	2	25	0	.152	.206
Major League Totals (2 years)				.119	24	67	6	8	3	0	1	4	2	27	0	.157	.209
Minor League Totals (5 years)				.280	517	1970	257	552	91	30	32	215	145	444	67	.330	.406

4 KYLE MULLER, LHP

BA GRADE
50 Risk: High

Born: Oct. 7, 1997. **B-T:** R-L. **HT:** 6-7. **WT:** 250. **Drafted:** HS—Dallas, 2016 (2nd round). **Signed by:** Nate Dion.

TRACK RECORD: Muller was one of the fast-risers of the prep ranks as a high school senior. He'd gone from sitting 87-89 mph to the low 90s when the Braves drafted him. His stuff has steadily progressed as he filled out his 6-foot-7 frame. After five years of strength gains, he flashed some of the best pure stuff in the Braves system in 2021 and received his first big league callup in June. Muller went 2-4, 4.17 in nine appearances (eight starts) with the Braves while striking out more than a batter per inning, but also showed he is still learning to harness his new power arsenal.

SCOUTING REPORT: Muller's fastball sits around 94 mph and routinely gets up into the upper 90s from the left side. Beyond the pure velocity, Muller's standout spin metrics and extension from his large frame allow his fastball to generate tons of swings and misses up in the zone. Muller's mid-80s slider earns plus grades at its best and his low-80s curveball is another above-average pitch, while his firm changeup is an average offering that gives him a complete four-pitch mix. What holds Muller back is below-average control. He stopped going over the top of his head in his windup to simplify his delivery and become more consistent. The changes cut his walk rate a bit, but it still remains below average.

THE FUTURE: The Braves have committed to developing Muller as a starter, but if his control doesn't improve, he has the stuff to be a closer. He has two options remaining, so there's still time.

SCOUTING GRADES:	Fastball: 70	Slider: 60	Curveball: 55	Changeup: 50	Control: 40

Year	Age	Club (Level)	Lge	W	L	ERA	G	GS	IP	H	HR	BB	SO	BB/9	SO/9	WHIP	AVG
2021	23	Atlanta (MLB)	NL	2	4	4.17	9	8	36	26	2	20	37	4.9	9.1	1.25	.202
	23	Gwinnett (AAA)	East	5	4	3.39	17	17	79	66	9	42	93	4.7	10.5	1.36	.223
Major League Totals (1 year)				2	4	4.17	9	8	37	26	2	20	37	4.91	9.08	1.25	.202
Minor League Totals (6 years)				25	14	3.10	85	84	406	330	27	186	429	4.12	9.50	1.27	.223

5 SPENCER STRIDER, RHP

BA GRADE
50 Risk: High

Born: Oct. 28, 1998. **B-T:** R-R. **HT:** 6-0. **WT:** 195. **Drafted:** Clemson, 2020 (4th round). **Signed by:** Billy Best.

TRACK RECORD: Strider was a high-profile pitching prospect in high school and pitched well when healthy at Clemson, but he missed all of 2019 after having Tommy John surgery and made only four starts in 2020 before the coronavirus pandemic canceled the season. The Braves were high on Strider's stuff and aptitude despite his limited innings and drafted him in the fourth round, signing him for $449,300. Strider rewarded that faith by vaulting four levels from Low-A Augusta to the majors.

SCOUTING REPORT: Strider uses an upper-90s fastball with riding life at the top of strike the zone to overwhelm his competition, and changes to his pitch mix helped set the stage for his meteoric rise. The Braves largely shelved his changeup and curveball and had him throw his plus-plus four-seam fastball up in the zone paired with a vertical slider down in the zone. Strider's slider improved with the focus on the pitch and has the potential to be an above-average offering if he improves its consistency. Strider began re-working the changeup into his arsenal in the second half of the season, but it's a fringy offering that remains a third pitch. He throws plenty of strikes with average control.

THE FUTURE: The Braves view Strider as a starter, although his two-pitch mix makes him a likely reliever in external evaluators' eyes. He will begin 2022 in Triple-A Gwinnett's rotation.

SCOUTING GRADES:	Fastball: 70	Slider: 55	Changeup: 45	Control: 50

Year	Age	Club (Level)	Lge	W	L	ERA	G	GS	IP	H	HR	BB	SO	BB/9	SO/9	WHIP	AVG
2021	22	Augusta (LoA)	East	0	0	0.59	4	4	15	6	0	5	32	2.9	18.8	0.72	.118
	22	Rome (HiA)	East	0	0	2.45	3	3	14	9	1	6	24	3.7	14.7	1.02	.170
	22	Mississippi (AA)	South	3	7	4.71	14	14	63	48	6	29	94	4.1	13.4	1.22	.211
	22	Gwinnett (AAA)	East	0	0	0.00	1	0	1	1	0	0	3	0.0	27.0	1.00	.250
	22	Atlanta (MLB)	NL	1	0	3.86	2	0	2	2	1	1	0	3.9	0.0	1.29	.250
Major League Totals (1 year)				1	0	3.86	2	0	2	2	1	1	0	3.86	0.00	1.29	.250
Minor League Totals (2 years)				3	7	3.64	22	21	94	64	7	40	153	3.83	14.65	1.11	.190

6 DREW WATERS, OF

Born: Dec. 30, 1998. **B-T:** B-R. **HT:** 6-2. **WT:** 185. **Drafted:** HS—Woodstock, Ga., 2017 (2nd round). **Signed by:** Dustin Evans.

TRACK RECORD: Waters was a local prospect from Woodstock, Ga. who the Braves drafted in the second round in 2017 and signed for $1.5 million. He progressed through the minors and won MVP of the Double-A Southern League in 2019, but the canceled 2020 minor league season hampered his development. Waters returned to play at Triple-A Gwinnett in 2021 and hit just .240 with an alarming 31% strikeout rate, leading the Braves to look for other, external options when they needed outfield help in the majors.

SCOUTING REPORT: A 6-foot-2 switch-hitter with long levers, Waters has long had a feel to hit but has struggled to find an approach. That was exploited by more advanced pitchers in 2021 and led to a disastrous season. The Braves want Waters to improve his mental approach at the plate and gain a better understanding of the pitches he can and cannot do damage with. Even with significant improvements, however, he projects to be no more than a fringe-average hitter. Waters' supplemental toolset is still quite loud. He has average power and is an asset in center field with his plus speed, plus arm strength and overall plus defensive ability.

THE FUTURE: Waters is still young and will enter his age-23 season in 2022. Whether he can make the necessary mental adjustments will determine whether he becomes a regular or never makes enough contact to crack the Braves' starting outfield.

BA GRADE
50 Risk: High

SCOUTING GRADES:	Hitting: 45	Power: 50	Running: 60	Fielding: 60	Arm: 60

Year	Age	Club (Level)	Lge	AVG	G	AB	R	H	2B	3B	HR	RBI	BB	SO	SB	OBP	SLG
2021	22	Gwinnett (AAA)	East	.240	103	404	70	97	22	1	11	37	47	142	28	.329	.381
Minor League Totals (5 years)				.283	401	1589	255	450	115	21	31	152	138	481	73	.347	.441

7 BRADEN SHEWMAKE, SS

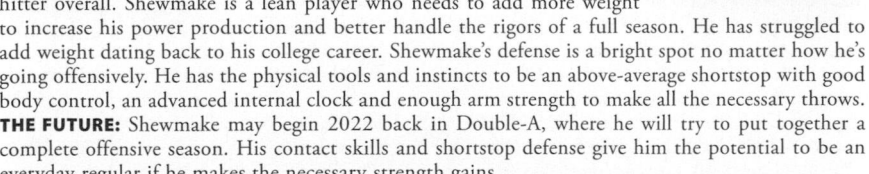

Born: Nov. 19, 1997. **B-T:** L-R. **HT:** 6-4. **WT:** 190. **Drafted:** Texas A&M, 2019 (1st round). **Signed by:** Darin Vaughan.

TRACK RECORD: The Braves used the second of their two-first round picks in 2019 to select Shewmake after he was a standout hitter in his college career at Texas A&M. He spent 2020 at the alternate training site and began his first full season at Double-A Mississippi in 2021. He got off to a .094/.144/.165 start that weighed down his overall numbers, but adjusted and hit .263/.300/.456 with 11 home runs the rest of the year.

SCOUTING REPORT: Despite the ugly numbers in his full-season debut, Shewmake hits velocity well, has natural bat-to-ball skills and shows a knack for shooting the ball the other way. The Braves were happy with the in-season adjustments he made and he has the traits to be an average hitter overall. Shewmake is a lean player who needs to add more weight to increase his power production and better handle the rigors of a full season. He has struggled to add weight dating back to his college career. Shewmake's defense is a bright spot no matter how he's going offensively. He has the physical tools and instincts to be an above-average shortstop with good body control, an advanced internal clock and enough arm strength to make all the necessary throws.

THE FUTURE: Shewmake may begin 2022 back in Double-A, where he will try to put together a complete offensive season. His contact skills and shortstop defense give him the potential to be an everyday regular if he makes the necessary strength gains.

BA GRADE
50 Risk: High

SCOUTING GRADES:	Hitting: 50	Power: 45	Running: 60	Fielding: 55	Arm: 50

Year	Age	Club (Level)	Lge	AVG	G	AB	R	H	2B	3B	HR	RBI	BB	SO	SB	OBP	SLG
2021	23	Mississippi (AA)	South	.228	83	324	40	74	14	3	12	40	17	75	4	.271	.401
Minor League Totals (3 years)				.259	148	571	84	148	32	5	15	80	42	115	17	.316	.412

8 BRYCE ELDER, RHP

Born: May 19, 1999. **B-T:** R-R. **HT:** 6-2. **WT:** 220. **Drafted:** Texas, 2020
(5th round). **Signed by:** Darin Vaughan.

TRACK RECORD: Elder emerged as Texas' ace as a sophomore and was off to a strong start as a junior in 2020 before the coronavirus pandemic canceled the college season. The Braves drafted him in the fifth round and signed him for an over-slot $847,500 bonus. Elder made his pro debut in 2021 and rocketed up the system, jumping from High-A and Triple-A to leading the minors with 137.2 innings pitched on his way to being named the Braves' minor league pitcher of the year.

SCOUTING REPORT: While the Braves have no shortage of pitchers with elite fastballs, Elder is a different type of pitcher with a five-pitch mix and arguably the best pitchability in the organization. He is a cerebral pitcher who has an advanced level of preparation, understands what he does well and knows how best to attack opposing hitters. Elder primarily uses a 90-94 mph sinker, a mid-80s slider with standout depth and an above-average changeup he is comfortable throwing in any situation. He also throws a four-seam fastball and an average curveball. Elder induces plenty of ground balls (56.9% ground ball rate) and has the secondary stuff to miss bats as well. He has the potential for above-average control but still adjusting his game to the professional strike zone, which doesn't allow him to work side-to-side as much as he did in college. Elder is very durable and has demonstrated his ability to work efficiently deep into games.

THE FUTURE: Elder is the safe bet to be a back-of-the-rotation starter with enough quality offspeed stuff to miss bats. He's in position to make his major league debut in 2022.

BA GRADE

45 Risk: Medium

SCOUTING GRADES:	Fastball: 50	Slider: 50	Curveball: 50	Changeup: 55	Control: 55

Year	Age	Club (Level)	Lge	W	L	ERA	G	GS	IP	H	HR	BB	SO	BB/9	SO/9	WHIP	AVG
2021	22	Rome (HiA)	East	2	1	2.60	9	9	45	38	2	20	55	4.0	11.0	1.29	.224
	22	Mississippi (AA)	South	7	1	3.21	9	9	56	39	7	17	60	2.7	9.6	1.00	.198
	22	Gwinnett (AAA)	East	2	3	2.21	7	7	36	18	1	20	40	4.9	9.8	1.04	.143
Minor League Totals (2 years)				11	5	2.75	25	25	138	95	10	57	155	3.73	10.13	1.10	.193

9 RYAN CUSICK, RHP

Born: Nov. 12, 1999. **B-T:** R-R. **HT:** 6-6. **WT:** 235. **Drafted:** Wake Forest, 2021
(1st round). **Signed by:** Billy Best.

TRACK RECORD: The Braves drafted Wake Forest lefthander Jared Shuster in 2020 and went back to the Demon Deacons pitching well in 2021. The Braves drafted Cusick with the 24th overall pick after he showed arguably the best fastball in the draft class as Wake's top starter and signed him for $2.7 million. Cusick reported to Low-A Augusta after signing and had a standout pro debut, posting a 2.76 ERA with 34 strikeouts against just four walks in 16.1 innings.

SCOUTING REPORT: A massive, 6-foot-6, 235-pound righthander, Cusick has thrown hard since his prep days in Connecticut. His fastball sits in the upper 90s and touches 102 mph with life, making it a dominant, plus-plus pitch that gets swings and misses in the strike zone. His fastball command has underwhelmed at times, but the pitch is overpowering enough to dominate hitters even without pinpoint accuracy. Cusick threw both a curveball and slider in college, but the Braves have emphasized throwing hard, vertical sliders with several of their pitching prospects. Cusick's slider flashes above-average and will be a focus early next year, with his average curveball and firm, below-average changeup options for another pitch down the road. Cusick showed below-average control throughout his college career, but a simplified approach in pro ball yielded average control in his debut.

THE FUTURE: Cusick is tentatively slated to begin 2022 at High-A Rome. He has mid-rotation potential with the fallback of a hard-throwing reliever.

BA GRADE

50 Risk: High

SCOUTING GRADES:	Fastball: 70	Slider: 55	Curveball: 50	Changeup: 40	Control: 50

Year	Age	Club (Level)	Lge	W	L	ERA	G	GS	IP	H	HR	BB	SO	BB/9	SO/9	WHIP	AVG
2021	21	Augusta (LoA)	East	0	1	2.76	6	6	16	15	1	4	34	2.2	18.7	1.16	.242
Minor League Totals (1 year)				0	1	2.76	6	6	16	15	1	4	34	2.20	18.73	1.16	.242

10 JESSE FRANKLIN, OF

Born: Dec. 1, 1998. **B-T:** L-L. **HT:** 6-1. **WT:** 215. **Drafted:** Michigan, 2020 (3rd round). **Signed by:** Jeremy Gordon.

TRACK RECORD: After two solid seasons at Michigan that included a 2019 trip to the College World Series finals, Franklin didn't get to play his junior season in 2020 after breaking his collarbone. The Braves still drafted him in the third round and signed him for $497,500. Franklin rewarded their faith in his pro debut at High-A Rome in 2021. He led the Braves system with 24 home runs and finished second with 188 total bases.

SCOUTING REPORT: Franklin has shown a contact-oriented, all-fields approach in the past, but the Braves wanted to let him cut loose and see how hard he could drive the ball in his pro debut. The change in approach revealed borderline plus-plus raw power in Franklin's bat, and he is now the best power prospect in their system. Franklin now projects to hit for plus power in games, but the tradeoff came in his hitting ability. His approach change resulted in more chase swings and an increased strikeout rate, dropping him to a potential fringe-average hitter. Franklin is an instinctive defensive outfielder. He can fill in as a center fielder with his impressive first step and clean routes, but his average speed and fringy arm strength make him a better fit for left field. He is an efficient basestealer despite his average pure speed.

THE FUTURE: The Braves want to see Franklin continue to show this sort of power while improving his contact and walk rates. His best-case scenario is an everyday left fielder, although he is more likely to end up a lefty-hitting, platoon power bat.

BA GRADE
45 Risk: Medium

SCOUTING GRADES:	Hitting: 45	Power: 60	Running: 50	Fielding: 55	Arm: 45

Year	Age	Club (Level)	Lge	AVG	G	AB	R	H	2B	3B	HR	RBI	BB	SO	SB	OBP	SLG
2021	22	Rome (HiA)	East	.244	101	360	55	88	24	2	24	61	34	115	19	.320	.522
Minor League Totals (2 years)				.244	101	360	55	88	24	2	24	61	34	115	19	.320	.522

11 FREDDY TARNOK, RHP

BA GRADE
45 Risk: High

Born: Nov. 24, 1998. **B-T:** R-R. **HT:** 6-3. **WT:** 185. **Drafted:** HS—Riverview, Fla., 2017 (3rd round). **Signed by:** Justin Clark.

TRACK RECORD: A two-way player out of high school in Florida, the Braves drafted Tarnok in the third round as a pitcher and signed him for $1.4 million. His development was slow going for his first four years, but in 2021 Tarnok took a step forward and reached Double-A Mississippi, where he dominated and posted a 2.60 ERA.

SCOUTING REPORT: Tarnok has come into his own physically and as a pitcher this year, and now gets his fastball up into the 95-98 mph range at times, with one of the best true curveballs in the system—a 12-to-6 downer that gets plus grades. Tarnok added strength, velocity and more comfort with his delivery during the 2020 covid season. He primarily pitched off that fastball/curveball combination in 2021, but as the year progressed, he worked in a slider and a changeup. Both pitches need more work to get consistent above-average grades, but Braves officials were happy with how comfortable he seemed with both by the end of the year. Previously, Tarnok's changeup was viewed as one of the best in the system, but it regressed this year while his curve improved. Among Braves minor leaguers with at least 10 starts, only Spencer Strider posted a better strikeout percentage than Tarnok (36.5%).

THE FUTURE: Tarnok is now close to or inside the top tier of Braves pitching prospects after showing the best bat-missing stuff of his pro career. He's got plenty of positive indicators between his size, deep pitch mix and command. Now he needs to do the same against more advanced hitters.

Year	Age	Club (Level)	Lge	W	L	ERA	G	GS	IP	H	HR	BB	SO	BB/9	SO/9	WHIP	AVG
2021	22	Rome (HiA)	East	3	2	4.76	7	5	28	21	6	13	48	4.1	15.3	1.20	.204
	22	Mississippi (AA)	South	3	2	2.60	9	9	45	35	2	15	61	3.0	12.2	1.11	.212
Minor League Totals (5 years)				14	20	4.06	73	55	271	245	20	109	293	3.62	9.74	1.31	.239

12 VAUGHN GRISSOM, SS/3B

BA GRADE
45 Risk: High

Born: Jan. 5, 2001. **B-T:** R-R. **HT:** 6-3. **WT:** 180. **Drafted:** HS—Oviedo, Fla., 2019 (11th round). **Signed by:** Jon Bunnell.

TRACK RECORD: The Braves liked Grissom's bat enough to sign him for $347,500 in the 11th round in 2019 and he just had one of the better offensive seasons in Atlanta's

system, posting a 143 wRC+ between Low-A and High-A.

SCOUTING REPORT: Grissom has showcased impressive contact ability since he joined pro ball, and that continued in 2021. He pairs that natural bat-to-ball ability with a solid understanding of the strike zone, and his walk-to-strikeout rate was one of the best marks in the system. While Grissom possesses solid foundational hitting skills, scouts have been wanting to see him drive the ball for more impact and home run production. He has raw power that shows up more in batting practice, and his top-end exit velocities stack up with some of the better sluggers in the system (113.2 max EV) but some evaluators believe he'll always hit for more average than power. His slugging numbers progressed as the year went on and he has room to add weight to his frame still, but some scouts note a lack of freedom in his swing that could limit his impact. He's stretched at shortstop due to limited range and athleticism. He has the arm strength for third and the hands to handle second.

THE FUTURE: Grissom should get his first test against upper-level minor league arms in 2022 where he'll look to hit for more impact. For now he profiles as a contact-oriented utility infielder.

Year	Age	Club (Level)	Lge	AVG	G	AB	R	H	2B	3B	HR	RBI	BB	SO	SB	OBP	SLG
2021	20	Augusta (LoA)	East	.311	75	280	52	87	15	4	5	33	34	49	13	.402	.446
	20	Rome (HiA)	East	.378	12	37	12	14	2	0	2	10	11	5	3	.519	.595
Minor League Totals (3 years)				.308	131	477	86	147	24	5	10	66	61	81	19	.399	.442

13 TUCKER DAVIDSON, LHP

BA GRADE

45 Risk: High

Born: March 25, 1996. **B-T:** L-L. **HT:** 6-2. **WT:** 215. **Drafted:** Midland (Texas) JC, 2016 (19th round). **Signed by:** Nate Dion.

TRACK RECORD: Davidson became the first Midland (Texas) JC draftee to make the majors when he debuted in 2020, and he threw 20 innings in 2021 before a forearm strain sidelined him for most of the season. Davidson did come back for the postseason and made a spot start in game five of the World Series, though he allowed four runs in two innings.

SCOUTING REPORT: While healthy, Davidson showed a better ability to attack the strike zone at the major league level this year. Establishing his 93 mph fastball allowed his secondary stuff to play up. It's a low-spin fastball, but Davidson pairs that with a firm slider in the upper 80s. The slider is now his go-to breaking ball, with above-average potential and his curveball features solid vertical depth that could give him a third average offering. He largely scrapped a mid-80s changeup (1% usage) in 2021 and the pitch is a distant fourth offering compared to his fastball and breaking pitches. Previously, Davidson's control has led opposing scouts to view him as a reliever, but the Braves have stuck with him as a starter and he looked to take a step forward in his control this year, albeit in a brief sample.

THE FUTURE: Davidson's playoff start suggests the Braves trust him, and he should be back in the mix for the team's pitching plans in 2022.

Year	Age	Club (Level)	Lge	W	L	ERA	G	GS	IP	H	HR	BB	SO	BB/9	SO/9	WHIP	AVG
2021	25	Gwinnett (AAA)	East	2	2	1.17	4	4	23	11	2	5	28	2.0	11.0	0.70	.141
	25	Atlanta (MLB)	NL	0	0	3.60	4	4	20	15	3	8	18	3.6	8.1	1.15	.205
Major League Totals (2 years)				0	1	4.15	5	5	22	18	4	12	20	4.98	8.31	1.38	.220
Minor League Totals (5 years)				22	26	2.76	95	66	404	367	17	151	394	3.36	8.77	1.28	.246

14 JOEY ESTES, RHP

BA GRADE

45 Risk: High

Born: Oct. 8, 2001. **B-T:** R-R. **HT:** 6-2. **WT:** 190. **Drafted:** HS—Lancaster, Calif., 2019 (16th round). **Signed by:** Kevin Martin.

TRACK RECORD: Estes ranked as the No. 239 prospect in the 2019 class, but the Braves managed to sign him in the 16th round with a $497,500 bonus. He's a competitive pitcher who was one of the better Low-A arms in the minors as a 19-year-old, finishing sixth with 99 innings and fourth with 127 strikeouts at the level.

SCOUTING REPORT: Estes works quickly on the mound and comes right at hitters with a solid, if unspectacular, three-pitch mix. His fastball gets up to 96-97 mph and typically sits in the 91-95 mph range, with standout riding life up in the zone and a flat approach angle. Estes also throws a low-80s slider with 8 o'clock tilt and an 83-86 mph changeup that he shows confidence in already. Both secondary offerings made progress this season, but neither flashes more than above-average at times, with most evaluators favoring the slider over the changeup for now. Estes' best skill is his feel for filling up the zone. He gets ahead in counts frequently, though as he climbs the minor league ladder he'll need to do a better job finishing off hitters with quality chase pitches. Despite his strike throwing and three-pitch mix, some scouts believe he profiles best as a reliever, with a bit of effort in his delivery.

THE FUTURE: Estes likely could have been promoted to Rome in 2021 given his performance. He should begin the 2022 season there, where he'll continue to be exceptionally young for the level.

Year	Age	Club (Level)	Lge	W	L	ERA	G	GS	IP	H	HR	BB	SO	BB/9	SO/9	WHIP	AVG
2021	19	Augusta (LoA)	East	3	6	2.91	20	20	99	66	7	29	127	2.6	11.6	0.96	.184
Minor League Totals (3 years)				3	7	3.39	25	25	109	76	7	36	135	2.97	11.15	1.03	.191

15 JARED SHUSTER, LHP

BA GRADE
45 Risk: High

Born: Aug. 3, 1998. **B-T:** L-L. **HT:** 6-3. **WT:** 210. **Drafted:** Wake Forest, 2020 (1st round). **Signed by:** Billy Best.

TRACK RECORD: The Braves made Shuster their first-round pick in 2020 after the southpaw saw a significant uptick in velocity during the shortened 2020 season, signing him for just under $2.2 million. That velocity didn't hold up in his first taste of pro ball this year, and while he pushed to Double-A, Shuster is still adjusting to the rigors of pro ball.

SCOUTING REPORT: Shuster stands out for his pitching ability and a devastating changeup that multiple Braves officials have said is better than righthander Ian Anderson's. The pitch is an easy plus offering that generates ugly swings and is thrown with confidence and 12 mph separation from his fastball. While that velocity gap is solid, Shuster sat with a fastball in the 88-92 mph range, touching 94. The shape of the pitch is solid, but so far it looks like his draft-year spike in velocity was more of a flash in the pan than a sign of a new normal. Shuster's slider is a low-80s breaking ball that generated whiffs at a decent clip this year, but scouts think it's more of an average offering at best. Shuster looked like he was still acclimating to the pro schedule, and he got hit around over three starts in Double-A (11.7 H/9), though he has continued to throw quality strikes.

THE FUTURE: Shuster's ceiling is somewhat limited given his velocity, though an out-pitch changeup and above-average control give him a chance to be a backend starter.

Year	Age	Club (Level)	Lge	W	L	ERA	G	GS	IP	H	HR	BB	SO	BB/9	SO/9	WHIP	AVG
2021	22	Rome (HiA)	East	2	0	3.70	15	14	58	47	10	15	73	2.3	11.3	1.06	.215
	22	Mississippi (AA)	South	0	0	7.36	3	3	14	19	5	5	17	3.1	10.4	1.64	.306
Minor League Totals (2 years)				2	0	4.44	18	17	73.0	66	15	20	90	2.47	11.10	1.18	.235

16 DARIUS VINES, RHP

BA GRADE
45 Risk: High

Born: April 30, 1998. **B-T:** R-R. **HT:** 6-1. **WT:** 190. **Drafted:** Cal State Bakersfield, 2019 (7th round). **Signed by:** Kevin Martin.

TRACK RECORD: Vines was drafted twice (by the Astros out of high school and Cubs out of junior college) before the Braves eventually signed him as a seventh rounder in 2019. After struggling in rookie ball, Vines took a step forward in 2021.

SCOUTING REPORT: Vines was older than his competition to start the year, and overwhelmed hitters with an ability to land his quality secondary offerings for strikes. His fastball averages 92 mph and has touched 95-96, but is average at best. He shines with secondary stuff and took a big step forward with a low-80s changeup that looks like an above-average offering. Vines has excellent feel to spin the ball and throws both a low-80s slider and a downer, mid-70s curveball with plenty of depth that was his calling card as an amateur. He has feel for both offerings, but went to the slider more frequently in 2021 and lands it in the zone consistently. Vines was a high school quarterback and is a good athlete who has shown strong ability to throw strikes with his entire arsenal.

THE FUTURE: How Vines' stuff plays against hitters in the upper minors will add more clarity to his future role, but for now he seems like a depth arm who could be a back-end starter or pitch in the pen.

Year	Age	Club (Level)	Lge	W	L	ERA	G	GS	IP	H	HR	BB	SO	BB/9	SO/9	WHIP	AVG
2021	23	Augusta (LoA)	East	2	0	2.25	8	8	36	24	3	10	48	2.5	12.0	0.94	.180
	23	Rome (HiA)	East	4	4	3.24	14	14	75	60	12	19	81	2.3	9.7	1.05	.214
Minor League Totals (3 years)				6	9	3.77	34	33	143	123	19	39	164	2.45	10.30	1.13	.226

17 SPENCER SCHWELLENBACH, RHP

BA GRADE
50 Risk: Extreme

Born: May 31, 2000. **B-T:** R-R. **HT:** 6-1. **WT:** 200. **Drafted:** Nebraska, 2021 (2nd round). **Signed by:** JD French.

TRACK RECORD: Schwellenbach was one of the best two-way prospects in the 2021 class. A shortstop and righthander, he strolled to the mound as a reliever for Nebraska—

with little to no pitching prep—and put 99 mph fastballs and solid secondaries over the plate. Atlanta's scouting staff drooled over his upside and signed him for $997,500.

SCOUTING REPORT: Schwellenbach is one of the better pure athletes in Atlanta's system, with incredible natural arm talent. However, he needed Tommy John surgery after the draft and has few innings under his belt. The 6-foot-1 righty has a chance to throw 100 mph in the future, and despite how little time he's spent honing his craft, showed impressive command of his fastball and a slider and changeup. Amateur scouts saw the secondary offerings as average or above-average pitches, while Braves officials think both pitches have a chance to be plus. The Braves are planning to stretch him out as a starter, where his athleticism and easy operation could serve him well.

THE FUTURE: Schwellenbach's surgery means he might not get into games until 2023 and there might not be a player in the system with higher variance. The Braves will try to continue adding to their reputation for developing arms and identifying two-way talents with the Nebraska product.

Year	Age	Club (Level)	Lge	W	L	ERA	G	GS	IP	H	HR	BB	SO	BB/9	SO/9	WHIP	AVG
2021	24	Augusta (LoA)	East	0	3	13.50	16	0	20	35	5	23	14	10.0	6.1	2.81	.389
Minor League Totals (4 years)				5	7	5.89	40	5	81	81	6	52	81	5.78	9.00	1.64	.259

18 AJ SMITH-SHAWVER, RHP

BA GRADE

50 Risk: Extreme

Born: Nov. 20, 2002. **B-T:** R-R. **HT:** 6-3. **WT:** 205.
Drafted: HS—Colleyville, Texas, 2021 (7th round). **Signed by:** Trey McNickle.

TRACK RECORD: A twitchy, multi-sport athlete out of high school, the Braves took a chance on Smith-Shawver's explosive arm speed, signing him to just under $1 million in the 7th round.

SCOUTING REPORT: Given Smith-Shawver's current stuff, athleticism and arm speed, there are officials in Braves camp who think the 6-foot-3 righthander could be one of the top prospects in the system in a few years. There's some refinement that needs to happen—particularly with his command—before that, and he did struggle in a brief pro debut but the toolset is tantalizing. Smith-Shawver touched 94-95 during the spring but with Atlanta he's been sitting in that range, getting up to 97 mph with solid vertical life. The spin on both his breaking balls is impressive as well. He threw a mid-80s gyro slider more frequently this summer than a 7 o'clock tilt, downer curve in the upper-70s—but both pitches have a chance to be above-average. On top of that, Smith-Shawver showed feel for a mid-80s changeup that was well beyond his years and experience level on the mound, forcing hitters well beyond his level to ground out on ugly swings in live at-bats.

THE FUTURE: Smith-Shawver was a prep quarterback and hasn't spent much time focusing on pitching, but Braves officials rave about his early progress and believe he is a potential breakout candidate.

Year	Age	Club (Level)	Lge	W	L	ERA	G	GS	IP	H	HR	BB	SO	BB/9	SO/9	WHIP	AVG
2021	18	Braves (R)	FCL	0	1	8.64	4	4	8	4	2	10	16	10.8	17.3	1.68	.143
Minor League Totals (1 year)				0	1	8.64	4	4	8	4	2	10	16	10.80	17.28	1.68	.143

19 DAYSBEL HERNANDEZ, RHP

BA GRADE

45 Risk: High

Born: Sept. 15, 1996. **B-T:** R-R. **HT:** 5-10. **WT:** 220. **Signed:** Cuba, 2017.
Signed by: Rolando Petit.

TRACK RECORD: After spending two years in Cuba's Serie Nacional, Hernandez signed for $190,000 in 2017 and took a big step forward in High-A in 2019. The Braves challenged Hernandez this year and assigned him to Triple-A, where he struggled initially before rebounding with Double-A Mississippi and finding more success in a return to Triple-A.

SCOUTING REPORT: Hernandez has never started a professional game and works with a hard two-pitch mix. His fastball sits with plus velocity for a reliever in the 96-99 mph range and he gets to 100 mph at peak. The pitch comes from a flat approach angle thanks in part to his 5-foot-10 frame and has impressive vertical life. He pairs the fastball with a hard slider that sits in the 87-89 mph range and will get into the low 90s, with sharp downward bite. The breaking ball is also a plus offering and he used both to rack up plenty of whiffs. What has held Hernandez back is his control. He's walked 11.3% of batters in the minors and that rate was worse in Double-A and Triple-A this season.

THE FUTURE: Hernandez has the two-pitch mix to be a middle-leverage reliever, but he'll need to sharpen his control to step into that role. If he's throwing strikes, he could debut in 2022.

Year	Age	Club (Level)	Lge	W	L	ERA	G	GS	IP	H	HR	BB	SO	BB/9	SO/9	WHIP	AVG
2021	24	Mississippi (AA)	South	3	1	2.76	26	0	32	23	3	16	46	4.4	12.7	1.19	.200
	24	Gwinnett (AAA)	East	0	1	7.45	10	0	9	8	1	7	12	6.5	11.2	1.55	.235
Minor League Totals (5 years)				10	6	3.18	92	0	133	93	8	69	164	4.67	11.10	1.22	.198

20 BROOKS WILSON, RHP

Born: March 15, 1996. **B-T:** L-R. **HT:** 6-2. **WT:** 205. **Drafted:** Stetson, 2018 (7th round). **Signed by:** Justin Clark.

BA GRADE
40 Risk: High

TRACK RECORD: Wilson was a two-way player at Stetson—where he was teammates with Mariners first rounder Logan Gilbert—and signed for just $80,000 as a seventh-round senior sign. His first two years in pro ball were sound, but he was outstanding in 2021, so much so that the Braves placed him on the 40-man roster after the season.

SCOUTING REPORT: Among Braves minor leaguers, only Indigo Diaz managed a better strikeout rate than Wilson's 41.4% mark in Double-A and Triple-A. Wilson throws from a high, three-quarter slot and has a 92-94 mph fastball that touches 96, a low-80s split-change and an upper-70s curveball he uses as a get-me-over pitch. The splitter is Wilson's bread-and-butter, a pitch that racked up tons of whiffs this year and falls out of the bottom of the zone. That pitch was the primary reason he was able to set career-bests in strikeout rates against upper-level minor league hitters. He struck out more than 40% of batters at both levels.

THE FUTURE: Braves officials have lauded Wilson's competitiveness, and given his performance, three-pitch mix and strike throwing, think he can be a multi-inning or low-leverage reliever.

Year	Age	Club (Level)	Lge	W	L	ERA	G	GS	IP	H	HR	BB	SO	BB/9	SO/9	WHIP	AVG
2021	25	Mississippi (AA)	South	3	1	2.45	33	0	44	32	3	17	73	3.5	14.9	1.11	.201
	25	Gwinnett (AAA)	East	0	0	1.50	6	0	6	2	0	2	11	3.0	16.5	0.67	.100
Minor League Totals (4 years)				10	6	2.24	80	11	165	134	8	53	182	2.89	9.93	1.13	.220

21 INDIGO DIAZ, RHP

Born: Oct. 14, 1998. **B-T:** R-R. **HT:** 6-5. **WT:** 250. **Drafted:** Michigan State, 2019 (27th round). **Signed by:** Freddy Perez.

BA GRADE
45 Risk: High

TRACK RECORD: A 27th-round pick in the 2019 draft, Diaz had a strong—albeit brief—pro debut in Rookie ball. In his first full season in 2021 he was one of the best pitchers in the Braves' system. His 47.4% strikeout rate led all minor league pitchers with at least 40 innings.

SCOUTING REPORT: A big, physical reliever, Diaz put in plenty of work over the offseason to get stronger and that resulted in louder pure stuff. The Braves always liked the carry on his fastball and now he's throwing the pitch in the 93-94 mph range and touching 97. That velocity doesn't stand out among relievers, but the traits of the pitch are solid and he does a nice job living in the top of the zone where he generates a ton of whiffs. His secondary offering is an 83-84 mph vertical slider that gets slurvy at times, but at its best plays off his fastball nicely at the bottom of the zone. He'll need to continue sharpening the breaking ball, because he isn't the sort of flamethrower one typically sees in big league bullpens and he tended to get fastball-reliant in 2021.

THE FUTURE: It'll be hard to replicate the season Diaz just had as he starts to face upper-level bats, but he has a chance to become a medium-leverage reliever with continued progress.

Year	Age	Club (Level)	Lge	W	L	ERA	G	GS	IP	H	HR	BB	SO	BB/9	SO/9	WHIP	AVG
2021	22	Rome (HiA)	East	4	1	1.00	18	0	27	11	0	7	54	2.3	18.0	0.67	.117
	22	Mississippi (AA)	South	2	1	1.50	14	0	18	10	1	9	29	4.5	14.5	1.06	.161
Minor League Totals (3 years)				7	2	1.63	38	0	55	30	1	18	98	2.93	15.94	0.87	.154

22 JASSEEL DE LA CRUZ, RHP

Born: June 26, 1997. **B-T:** R-R. **HT:** 6-1. **WT:** 195. **Signed:** Dominican Republic, 2015. **Signed by:** Matias Laureano.

BA GRADE
40 Risk: High

TRACK RECORD: De la Cruz was a low-profile signing who Atlanta signed to a $55,000 bonus out of the Dominican Republic, but as he progressed through the system his stuff took big steps forward. He showed an ability to start with effectiveness against Double-A pitching in 2019, but his control regressed significantly in 2021, where he struggled against Triple-A hitters.

SCOUTING REPORT: De la Cruz looked great in May when he threw strikes 65% of the time but fell off significantly after that and split time as a starter and reliever, with better results out of the bullpen. He has a firm fastball in the 94-96 mph range that gets to the upper 90s and has touched 100 mph in the past. The pitch has ordinary life, however, and missed a below-average number of bats. His slider is his go-to secondary, a mid-80s breaker that receives above-average and plus grades at times and has been up to 92 mph with big spin in the 2,700 rpm range. De la Cruz rarely uses a firm changeup that doesn't have much separation from his fastball and is predominantly a two-pitch righty. After improving his control in 2019, he walked a career-high 12.5% in 2021.

THE FUTURE: Without a consistent third offering and below-average control, De la Cruz profiles best out of the bullpen, where perhaps his fastball/slider combination can play better.

Year	Age	Club (Level)	Lge	W	L	ERA	G	GS	IP	H	HR	BB	SO	BB/9	SO/9	WHIP	AVG
2021	24	Gwinnett (AAA)	East	1	3	7.03	20	15	56	63	8	33	55	5.3	8.8	1.70	.278
Minor League Totals (6 years)				17	20	4.18	96	65	349	301	25	157	315	4.05	8.13	1.31	.232

23 VICTOR VODNIK, RHP

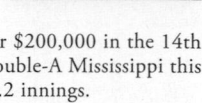

BA GRADE

45 Risk: Extreme

Born: Oct. 9, 1999. **B-T:** R-R. **HT:** 6-0. **WT:** 200. **Drafted:** HS—Rialto, Calif., 2018 (14th round). **Signed by:** Kevin Martin.

TRACK RECORD: The Braves took a shot on Vodnik's natural arm strength out of high school, despite plenty of rawness to his game, and signed him for $200,000 in the 14th round. He pitched well in his first full season in 2019, but struggled with Double-A Mississippi this year, and also dealt with a forearm strain and blisters that limited him to 33.2 innings.

SCOUTING REPORT: While Vodnik had some bright spots in the Arizona Fall League, his struggles largely carried over in his 23.2 innings there as well. Vodnik is a short righthander with a three-pitch mix led by an easy plus fastball that sat 95-96 and has been up to 100 mph. He also throws a firm changeup in the upper 80s and a slurvy slider in the low 80s. The former looked like his best secondary this season and features plenty of arm-side running action. The breaking ball has been crude going back to his prep days and is a question mark moving forward. After showing solid control during his first two years, Vodnik walked 14.7% of the batters he faced this year.

THE FUTURE: Vodnik will look to get back on track next year, where scouts will look to see if his regression in control was health-related or an accurate reflection of his skill in putting the ball over the plate. He projects as a reliever moving forward.

Year	Age	Club (Level)	Lge	W	L	ERA	G	GS	IP	H	HR	BB	SO	BB/9	SO/9	WHIP	AVG
2021	21	Mississippi (AA)	South	1	4	5.35	11	11	33	32	5	22	41	5.9	11.0	1.60	.252
Minor League Totals (4 years)				3	8	4.00	38	14	106	95	7	47	119	4.00	10.14	1.34	.240

24 CAL CONLEY, SS

BA GRADE

40 Risk: High

Born: July 17, 1999. **B-T:** B-R. **HT:** 5-10. **WT:** 185. **Drafted:** Texas Tech, 2021 (4th round). **Signed by:** Trey McNickle.

TRACK RECORD: Conley is the son of former professional player and coach Brian Conley and was the sparkplug of Texas Tech's lineup and the anchor of the team's defense this spring. The Braves signed him for $422,500 in the fourth round and assigned him to Low-A Augusta, where he struggled with the bat while playing shortstop and second.

SCOUTING REPORT: A tough, but smaller switch-hitting infielder, Conley stands out more for a collection of average-ish tools than any individual carrying tool. He's shown consistent contact ability and some pop from both sides in the past, though in his debut he swung and missed at an average rate and scouts don't believe his 15-home run power in college will translate to a wood bat. His top end exit velocity numbers this summer don't suggest average power production, though Conley should stick at a middle infield position where that's less of an issue. He's a solid runner with reliable hands and the Braves were happy with how he handled shortstop, though his arm strength and range fit better at second base. He has solid instincts and a good internal clock.

THE FUTURE: Conley will need to add more power to profile as anything more than a utility infield-type player who looks stretched as an everyday shortstop.

Year	Age	Club (Level)	Lge	AVG	G	AB	R	H	2B	3B	HR	RBI	BB	SO	SB	OBP	SLG
2021	21	Augusta (LoA)	East	.214	35	140	21	30	5	1	2	9	14	33	8	.304	.307
Minor League Totals (1 year)				.214	35	140	21	30	5	1	2	9	14	33	8	.304	.307

25 WILLIAM WOODS, RHP

BA GRADE

45 Risk: Extreme

Born: Dec. 29, 1998. **B-T:** R-R. **HT:** 6-3. **WT:** 190. **Drafted:** Dyersburg (Tenn.) JC, 2018 (23rd round). **Signed by:** JD French.

TRACK RECORD: Woods was one of the most anticipated lower-level prospects in Atlanta's system after improving his stuff in 2020. A forearm injury in 2021 sidelined him until mid-August and he threw 31.2 innings on the year.

SCOUTING REPORT: Woods has explosive pure stuff, headlined by a fastball that has consistently ticked up over the years and is now touching 99-100 mph and sitting in the mid-90s. In a bullpen role, Woods has the sort of arm strength to regularly throw in the 97-100 mph range in one-inning stints. He's gotten above-average grades on a mid-80s slider in the past, and that was his most frequently used secondary in his limited time in 2021. He also throws a firm changeup around 90 mph that could use more separation from his fastball but has looked like a promising third offering. Woods has shown scattered control at times, though he is athletic enough to improve in this area given more innings.

THE FUTURE: Woods is difficult to project given his injuries, lack of innings this year and with the lost 2020 season. Scouts haven't seen much of him at full strength and he's an entirely different pitcher today than he was in 2019. He has a chance to start, and the Braves continue to develop him in that role but might fit best as a power-armed reliever.

Year	Age	Club (Level)	Lge	W	L	ERA	G	GS	IP	H	HR	BB	SO	BB/9	SO/9	WHIP	AVG
2021	22	Rome (HiA)	East	0	1	4.66	4	4	9	10	3	4	7	3.7	6.5	1.45	.270
	22	Braves (R)	FCL	0	0	0.00	1	1	1	1	0	0	1	0.0	9.0	1.00	.250
Minor League Totals (4 years)				1	7	4.15	35	16	82	71	7	43	86	4.70	9.40	1.38	.231

26 GREYSON JENISTA, 1B/OF

Born: Dec. 7, 1996. **B-T:** L-R. **HT:** 6-4. **WT:** 210. **Drafted:** Wichita State, 2018 (2nd round). **Signed by:** Nate Dion.

TRACK RECORD: Jenista was a standout hitter at Wichita State and was named MVP in the Cape Cod League prior to being drafted for $1.2 million in the second round. Amateur scouts wondered if Jenista would ever tap into his impressive raw power in games. After struggling to do so in 2018 and 2019, he broke out with 19 home runs in Double-A in 2021.

SCOUTING REPORT: The physical, 6-foot-4 lefthanded slugger has standout raw power and posted some of the better top-end exit velocities in the organization. Jenista does plenty of damage on contact, but he whiffs at a high clip and is susceptible to big velocity. Fortunately, Jenista's swing decisions seem to be good ones and he used a career-best 15.5% walk rate to get on base at a .343 clip despite a .216 average. He struck out at a career-high rate as well, but those extra whiffs came with the best HR/FB ratio (26.8%) he's posted in full-season ball and a more pull-heavy approach. Jenista is a fine defender in a corner outfield spot with arm strength for right but with few first base prospects in the system, he played most of his innings in the infield this year.

THE FUTURE: Accessing his raw power more frequently was a step forward for Jenista. He now looks like a three-true-outcomes (57%) slugger who could be a power bench bat or platoon corner option.

Year	Age	Club (Level)	Lge	AVG	G	AB	R	H	2B	3B	HR	RBI	BB	SO	SB	OBP	SLG
2021	24	Mississippi (AA)	South	.216	89	273	45	59	7	2	19	42	51	118	7	.343	.465
Minor League Totals (3 years)				.236	280	920	120	217	34	8	32	131	128	304	14	.328	.395

27 ALAN RANGEL, RHP

Born: Aug. 21, 1997. **B-T:** R-R. **HT:** 6-2. **WT:** 170. **Signed:** Mexico, 2014. **Signed by:** Manuel Samaniego.

TRACK RECORD: Rangel signed with the Braves out of Mexico in 2014 and has largely been an unnoticed, under-the-radar arm who took his time progressing through the system. He repeated Low-A Rome three consecutive years from 2017-2019 but broke out in 2021 with more strikeouts and pushing to Double-A Mississippi in his age-23 season.

SCOUTING REPORT: Braves pitching coaches worked with Rangel to trust his stuff more, and that paid off with career high strikeout rates, topping 30% in both High-A and Double-A. He has a three-pitch mix featuring a fastball, changeup and curveball. His fastball ranges from 92-95 mph and touches 96, but the pitch has solid vertical life and some arm-side run. His best secondary is a low-80s changeup with good fastball separation. The pitch earned above-average grades and allowed him to dominate hitters and rack up whiffs. Rangel also throws a 12-to-6 curveball in the mid 70s that draws solid-average grades. Rangel has been an above-average strike thrower over his minor league career and his 6.1% walk rate in 2021 was one of the best marks in Atlanta's system.

THE FUTURE: Rangel's season was loud enough for the Braves to place him on the 40-man roster. He'll try to keep missing Triple-A bats in 2022, with a chance to be a big-league depth starter option.

Year	Age	Club (Level)	Lge	W	L	ERA	G	GS	IP	H	HR	BB	SO	BB/9	SO/9	WHIP	AVG
2021	23	Rome (HiA)	East	4	5	3.57	15	14	70	54	8	21	95	2.7	12.1	1.06	.205
	23	Mississippi (AA)	South	3	2	4.50	7	7	34	28	3	5	41	1.3	10.9	0.97	.220
Minor League Totals (7 years)				27	30	4.28	116	90	505	500	43	137	480	2.44	8.56	1.26	.256

28 TYLER COLLINS, OF

Born: March 6, 2003. **B-T:** L-R. **HT:** 5-11. **WT:** 180.
Drafted: HS—McKinney, Texas, 2021 (8th round). **Signed by:** Trey McNickle.
TRACK RECORD: A speedy, up-the-middle player out of McKinney Boyd
High in McKinney, Texas, Collins signed for $447,500 in the eighth round. He was assigned to the
Florida Complex League, where he was one of the more impressive 2021 draftee hitters.
SCOUTING REPORT: Speed is Collins' carrying tool at present. He's a double-plus runner who can
cover plenty of ground in the outfield and turn lightly hit balls into the gaps into extra base hits. His
production this summer was likely buoyed in part because of that standout running ability, and his
.500 BABIP is unsustainable moving forward. He's a contact hitter who can spray the ball around the
field, but at 5-foot-11, 180 pounds he lacks strength and power. His speed should allow him to play
center field with improvement in his reads, but he also played shortstop in high school and could
get some time at second base as a professional. His arm is a bit light. At either corner he would need
to add significantly more power to profile as an everyday bat.
THE FUTURE: Collins has a carrying tool with his running ability, but scouts will get a better idea of
his overall offensive profile in 2022 during full-season ball.

Year	Age	Club (Level)	Lge	AVG	G	AB	R	H	2B	3B	HR	RBI	BB	SO	SB	OBP	SLG
2021	18	Braves (R)	FCL	.347	23	75	16	26	4	2	0	7	7	23	12	.424	.453
Minor League Totals (1 year)				.347	23	75	16	26	4	2	0	7	7	23	12	.424	.453

29 BRANDOL MEZQUITA, OF

Born: July 14, 2001. **B-T:** R-R. **HT:** 6-0. **WT:** 170. **Signed:** Dominican
Republic, 2017. **Signed by:** Jonathan Cruz.
TRACK RECORD: Mezquita signed with the Braves in 2017, a year after the
class that had 13 players' contracts voided and resulted in former general manager John Coppolella
being banned for life. Mezquita has been one of the only bright spots on the international front for
the organization over the last few years.
SCOUTING REPORT: Mezquita impressed Atlanta hitting coaches with his power potential and gap-
to-gap hitting ability. He currently has an aggressive approach that features some swing-and-miss
(29% strikeouts) but he has posted impressive top-end exit velocity numbers which should continue
to improve and translate into more game power. A plus runner, Mezquita has played all three outfield
positions but has increasingly logged more time in left and right over the years. He has an above-average arm. Braves officials are impressed with his cultural adjustment and English skills, and believe
he has the mental acumen to make the necessary adjustments as he climbs the minor league ladder.
THE FUTURE: After spending a few years in rookie ball, Mezquita should begin the 2022 season in
Low-A Augusta. He is one of the organization's more intriguing, lower-level hitting prospects.

Year	Age	Club (Level)	Lge	AVG	G	AB	R	H	2B	3B	HR	RBI	BB	SO	SB	OBP	SLG
2021	19	Braves (R)	FCL	.308	43	146	18	45	8	2	3	25	19	50	15	.402	.452
Minor League Totals (4 years)				.253	129	419	55	106	15	2	8	63	60	142	27	.366	.356

30 AMBIORIS TAVAREZ, SS

Born: Nov. 12, 2003. **B-T:** R-R. **HT:** 6-0. **WT:** 168. **Signed:** Dominican
Republic, 2021. **Signed by:** Jonathan Cruz/Luis Santos.
TRACK RECORD: Tavarez is the first prominent international signing the
Braves have made since their international sanctions, and there will be pressure on him given his
$1.5 million price tag. Tavarez has yet to make his pro debut, but he did go to instructional league.
SCOUTING REPORT: Tavarez is one of the bigger question marks in the system given his lack of playing time, but international scouts were excited about his power potential from the right side. He has
lots of strength in his arms and wrists, with bat speed that should allow him to develop plus power
in the future as he fills out a projectable frame. Tavarez hasn't had much in-depth hitting instruction and will need to make improvements with his lower half and get a better understanding of the
foundation of his swing. However, his hands work well and the swing is loose and easy. Tavarez will
likely begin his career at shortstop, and he's got more than enough arm strength, but some evaluators
think his actions and limited range fit at third base.
THE FUTURE: Tavarez should make his pro debut in 202. He's a high-upside bat.

Year	Age	Club (Level)	Lge	AVG	G	AB	R	H	2B	3B	HR	RBI	BB	SO	SB	OBP	SLG
2021	17	Did not play															

MORE PROSPECTS TO KNOW

31 LUKE WADDELL, 2B/SS/3B

Waddell was one of the older players in the 2021 draft as a third-year eligible player and signed for $247,500 in the fifth round. He doesn't have standout tools, but is a contact-oriented lefthanded hitter who controls the zone well and can play all over the infield.

32 JUSTIN DEAN, OF

Dean is a double-plus runner in center field who plays with plenty of energy and is a good defender. He swung and missed at a high rate (30.3%) in Double-A and doesn't have much power but is an upper-level outfield depth option with defense, speed and some on-base ability.

33 TREY HARRIS, OF

Harris has solid raw power but struggled to access it consistently in his first full season at Double-A. He chases outside of the zone too frequently and will need to up his contact rate.

34 KADON MORTON, OF

Morton impressed Braves officials during instructs and has an interesting blend of power and speed. He'll need to dramatically cut down his whiff rate (35%) to make the most of his tool set.

35 LOGAN BROWN, C

Brown is a talented catch-and-throw backstop who has done an excellent job shutting down running games, but his bat prevents him from profiling as more than a defense-only backup.

36 JUSTYN-HENRY MALLOY, 3B

Malloy showed impressive on-base ability and zone recognition last spring and in his pro debut. He could provide value at a corner infield spot with athleticism, walks and some power.

37 JARED JOHNSON, RHP

Jonson has a fastball that can get to 99-100 mph at his best with a hard slider along with it, but he's still raw and needs to improve his strike-throwing. He could be a power-armed reliever if he improves his control but will likely move through the system slowly.

38 ADAM SHOEMAKER, LHP

Shoemaker is a tall and projectable 6-foot-6 lefthander who has steadily improved his velocity and has a chance to throw in the upper 90s in the future, with a hard slider as well. The Braves are working on refining his mechanics and getting him to a consistent, lower three-quarters arm slot.

39 DYLAN DODD, LHP

The Braves thought Dodd was one of the better true seniors in the 2021 class. He is an above-average strike-thrower with a fastball in the low 90s who has shown promise with a changeup and two breaking balls. He struggled in a brief pro debut this summer.

40 DREW LUGBAUER, 1B

Lugbauer has plus raw power and homered 18 times with Double-A Mississippi before terrorizing Arizona Fall League pitchers. He hit .346/.453/.692 in 16 AFL games. He swings and misses at a high rate and struck out 37% of the time in 2021.

TOP PROSPECTS OF THE DECADE

Year	Player, Pos.	2021 Org
2012	Julio Teheran, RHP	Tigers
2013	Julio Teheran, RHP	Tigers
2014	Lucas Sims, RHP	Reds
2015	Jose Peraza, 2B	Mets
2016	Sean Newcomb, LHP	Braves
2017	Dansby Swanson, SS	Braves
2018	Ronald Acuña Jr., OF	Braves
2019	Austin Riley, 3B	Braves
2020	Cristian Pache, OF	Braves
2021	Cristian Pache, OF	Braves

TOP DRAFT PICKS OF THE DECADE

Year	Player, Pos.	2021 Org
2012	Lucas Sims, RHP	Reds
2013	Jason Hursh, RHP	Did not play
2014	Braxton Davidson, OF	Frontier League
2015	Kolby Allard, LHP	Rangers
2016	Ian Anderson, RHP	Braves
2017	Kyle Wright, RHP	Braves
2018	*Carter Stewart, RHP	SoftBank (Japan)
2019	Shea Langeliers, C	Braves
2020	Jared Shuster, LHP	Braves
2021	Ryan Cusick, RHP	Braves
	*Did not sign	

Baltimore Orioles

BY JON MEOLI

The third season of a deliberate rebuild under executive vice president and general manager Mike Elias brought another year of losing in the big leagues. The Orioles lost an MLB-high 110 games and will draft No. 1 overall in 2022.

But Elias promised the club would work tirelessly to build an elite talent pipeline to Camden Yards, not provide a quick turnaround, and they're certainly on track for the former.

High draft picks and large bonus pools over the last few years have yielded some of Baltimore's top hitting prospects. Examples include 2019 No. 1 overall pick Adley Rutschman, plus Gunnar Henderson and Kyle Stowers. First-round pitchers they inherited in Grayson Rodriguez and DL Hall are some of the best mound prospects in the game. They have contributed to the Baltimore farm system being rated as one of the game's best.

The Orioles' reinvestment in Latin America led to the first ever seven-figure signings in that market in January 2020, and a coaching staff that preaches progressive development strategies and uses data to reinforce it has helped foster significant gains first on the mound in 2019 and at the plate in 2021. The Orioles' full-season minor league affiliates saw a 36-point jump in overall OPS and steep climbs in home run and walk rates.

That's where the strength of the organization is at present. Many of the hitters they drafted early in 2019 are thriving in the high minors, and even without 2020 top pick Heston Kjerstad playing a game due to complications from myocarditis, that class has several impressive pieces emerging as well.

The 2021 draft class was heavy on hitters again, with the Orioles focusing on those who make elite contact and control the strike zone and betting they can refine that to bring on more power.

Some of the Orioles' top hitting prospects could arrive at Camden Yards in 2022, joining a lineup that already features young regulars Cedric Mullins, Ryan Mountcastle, Austin Hays and Anthony Santander.

Baltimore's challenge, especially in the punishing American League East, is on the mound. Outside of lefthander John Means, whose May 2021 no-hitter was a season highlight, they have little to count on in the rotation. Five well-regarded prospects graduated and got extended rotation looks this year, and none had an ERA under five.

Those graduations mean that outside the special talents in Rodriguez and Hall, the system is unbalanced toward hitters. The Elias Orioles have shown a deliberate strategy of targeting arms in trades and late in the draft whose skill sets fit best with how

Outfielder Cedric Mullins' breakout season stuck out amid another dreadful year in Baltimore.

PROJECTED 2025 LINEUP

Catcher	Adley Rutschman	27
First Base	Ryan Mountcastle	28
Second Base	Jordan Westburg	26
Third Base	Coby Mayo	23
Shortstop	Gunnar Henderson	24
Left Field	Colton Cowser	25
Center Field	Cedric Mullins	30
Right Field	Kyle Stowers	27
Designated Hitter	Trey Mancini	33
No. 1 Starter	Grayson Rodriguez	25
No. 2 Starter	D.L. Hall	26
No. 3 Starter	John Means	32
No. 4 Starter	Kyle Bradish	28
No. 5 Starter	Bruce Zimmermann	30
Closer	Tyler Wells	30

they develop and improve pitchers. This requires a longer development track and leaves a talent gap behind their top few pitching prospects.

The ability to deliver pitching that can succeed in the crucible that is the AL East remains perhaps the singular challenge of this rebuild, even as the Orioles view their burgeoning success in developing hitters as a potential opportunity to make impact trades for pitchers when they're ready to win.

Rutschman's pending arrival in 2022 means the Orioles are closer to competing than they've been in years, but the expected lack of investment in the major league roster means they will perhaps be more interesting than good in the short term. ∎

BALTIMORE ORIOLES

TOP 2022 ROOKIES	RANK
Adley Rutschman, C	1
Grayson Rodriguez, RHP	2
Mike Baumann, RHP	11
BREAKOUT PROSPECTS	**RANK**
Connor Norby, 2B	12
Carter Baumler, RHP	18
Reed Trimble, OF	21

SOURCE OF TOP 30 TALENT

Homegrown	23	Acquired	7
College	12	Trade	7
Junior college	0	Rule 5 draft	0
High school	7	Independent league	0
Nondrafted free agent	0	Free agent/waivers	0
International	4		

LF
Mishael Deson
Robert Neustrom
Johnny Rizer

CF
Colton Cowser (5)
Reed Trimble (21)
Hudson Haskin (22)
Zach Watson
Donta' Williams

RF
Kyle Stowers (7)
Heston Kjerstad (8)
Yusniel Diaz (23)
John Rhodes (24)
Luis Gonzalez
Cristopher Cespedes

3B
Coby Mayo (10)
Anderson de los Santos (30)
Rylan Bannon
Pat Dorrian

SS
Gunnar Henderson (4)
Jordan Westburg (6)
Maikol Hernandez (13)
Joey Ortiz (16)
Darell Hernaiz

2B
Connor Norby (12)
Terrin Vavra (14)
Jahmai Jones (19)
Adam Hall (27)

1B
Tyler Nevin
J.D. Mundy

C
Adley Rutschman (1)
Samuel Basallo (15)

LHP

LHSP	LHRP
DL Hall (3)	Nick Vespi
Drew Rom (17)	
Kevin Smith (20)	
Alexander Wells (25)	
Zac Lowther (26)	
Cameron Bishop	

RHP

RHSP	RHRP
Grayson Rodriguez (2)	Brenan Hanifee
Kyle Bradish (9)	Felix Bautista
Mike Baumann (11)	Cody Sedlock
Carter Baumler (18)	Blaine Knight
Kyle Brnovich (28)	Isaac Mattson
Jean Pinto (29)	
Brandon Young	
Zach Peek	
Garrett Stallings	

1 ADLEY RUTSCHMAN, C

Born: Feb. 6, 1998. **B-T:** B-R. **HT:** 6-2. **WT:** 216.
Drafted: Oregon State, 2019 (1st round).
Signed by: Brandon Verley.

TRACK RECORD: The Orioles were made to wait longer than expected to see the 2019 No. 1 overall pick tear through the minors the way a generational amateur talent is expected. A College World Series champion and Most Outstanding Player for Oregon State in 2018 and the BA College Player of the Year in 2019, Rutschman got a late start to his 2019 pro debut due to illness, then spent the summer of 2020 at the Orioles' alternate training site refining his swing and beginning to build rapport with some of the top pitching prospects in the organization. His delayed first full season, however, could not have gone better. Beginning at Double-A Bowie, Rutschman was the top prospect in Double-A Northeast and appeared in the Futures Game before ending his season with Triple-A Norfolk. He hit .285/.397/.502 with 23 home runs and a 79-to-90 walk-to-strikeout ratio in 123 games. He led all minor league catchers with 543 plate appearances.

SCOUTING REPORT: Rutschman's calling card at the plate is his elite plate discipline, with his 14.5% walk rate the best in the organization and in the top 10% of all qualified hitters in the high minors. He paced the Orioles' internal swing decision metrics and rarely swings and misses, with a 6.7% whiff rate. His uncanny understanding of the strike zone means his already-modest strikeout numbers could fall as he advances to the majors and higher quality umpires. When pitchers do come into his zone, Rutschman can do damage. In the midst of his one rough stretch of the season, he and the Orioles identified an issue with his load and landed on a change that allows him to let the ball travel deeper. In doing so, he was able to drive the ball more consistently by staying on plane with the pitch, all without sacrificing power or contact to do so. His line drive rate was 17.2% at Bowie, but with the changes taking hold, that rate jumped to 26.6% the last two months at Triple-A. The adjustment helps Rutschman better tap into his potentially elite power while elevating his average when he's staying in the ballpark. Defensively, Rutschman made strides calling games and built on his strength of developing relationships with pitchers, who raved about working with him. He's already an advanced receiver and his strong arm helped him cut down 27% of basestealers. While his skill set is major league-ready, coaches and teammates appreciate how tirelessly Rutschman

BRIAN WESTERHOLT/FOUR SEAM IMAGES

BA GRADE	SCOUTING GRADES
75 Risk: Medium	Hit: 70. Power: 65. Run: 40. Field: 60. Arm: 70.

Projected future grades on 20-80 scouting scale

BEST TOOLS

Best Hitter for Average	Adley Rutschman
Best Power Hitter	Adley Rutschman
Best Strike-Zone Discipline	Adley Rutschman
Fastest Baserunner	Adam Hall
Best Athlete	Jordan Westburg
Best Fastball	DL Hall
Best Curveball	DL Hall
Best Slider	Grayson Rodriguez
Best Changeup	Grayson Rodriguez
Best Control	Grayson Rodriguez
Best Defensive Catcher	Adley Rutschman
Best Defensive Infielder	Jordan Westburg
Best Infield Arm	Coby Mayo
Best Defensive Outfielder	Zach Watson
Best Outfield Arm	Kyle Stowers

works to improve and shows genuine efforts for helping them do the same.

THE FUTURE: The composite of all of Rutschman's skills makes for a player who looks like he can be an above-average major leaguer in 2022. A forecast of multiple all-star appearances and consideration for MVP honors isn't far-fetched. Rutschman will be the cornerstone of the Orioles' planned turnaround, and his success in Triple-A means there's not much left for him to accomplish there. If he's not on the Opening Day roster, it won't be long before he's suiting up behind the plate at Camden Yards. ∎

Year	Age	Club (Level)	Lge	AVG	G	AB	R	H	2B	3B	HR	RBI	BB	SO	SB	OBP	SLG
2021	23	Bowie (AA)	NEast	.271	80	295	61	80	16	0	18	55	55	57	1	.392	.508
	23	Norfolk (AAA)	East	.312	43	157	25	49	9	2	5	20	24	33	2	.405	.490
Minor League Totals (3 years)				.278	160	582	105	162	33	3	27	101	99	117	4	.386	.485

2 GRAYSON RODRIGUEZ, RHP

Born: Nov. 16, 1999. **B-T:** L-R. **HT:** 6-5. **WT:** 220. **Drafted:** HS—Nacogdoches, Texas, 2018 (1st round). **Signed by:** Thom Dreier.

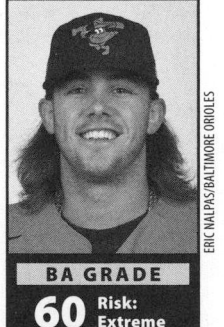

ERIC NALPAS/BALTIMORE ORIOLES

TRACK RECORD: Only one pitcher in the 30-plus years of the Orioles' Jim Palmer minor league pitcher of the year award had ever repeated before Rodriguez shared the honor in 2019 then took it on his own in 2021. Signed for $4.3 million as the 11th overall pick in 2018, Rodriguez spent the year leading up to his selection remaking his body and delivery. He has thrived in the Orioles' progressive new pitching system and become baseball's top pitching prospect. He led all minor league pitchers with 100 innings in strikeout rate: 14.1 per nine innings.

BA GRADE

70 Risk: High

SCOUTING REPORT: Rodriguez's dominance over his two full seasons took on different forms. He overpowered batters with his fastball in 2019, but used an advanced pitch mix to carve through Double-A Northeast lineups in 2021. Rodriguez's fastball averaged 97 mph for the season and frequently hit 100 early in the year before settling in the mid-to-high 90s late. It's an elite pitch with above-average spin and hop, and he locates it to all four quadrants of the strike zone. Rodriguez's slider, a plus pitch in the 79-85 mph range, has late bite and can be manipulated a variety of different ways. His screwball-like changeup is a swing-and-miss weapon against both righties and lefties. Rodriguez also has the potential for an above-average curveball, a pitch that he started to throw harder this year, and he occasionally mixes in a low-90s cutter. Physically, Rodriguez has a prototypical starter's frame with a durable and repeatable delivery that allows him to exhibit plus command.

THE FUTURE: Rodriguez's attributes give him the chance to be a mid-rotation starter at worst, with No. 2 starter potential at best. He'll start 2022 at Triple-A Norfolk, with the 22-year-old's major league debut not far off.

SCOUTING GRADES:	Fastball: 70	Slider: 70	Curveball: 55	Changeup: 65	Control: 60

Year	Age	Club (Level)	Lge	W	L	ERA	G	GS	IP	H	HR	BB	SO	BB/9	SO/9	WHIP	AVG
2021	21	Aberdeen (HiA)	East	3	0	1.54	5	5	23	11	2	5	40	1.9	15.4	0.69	.138
	21	Bowie (AA)	NEast	6	1	2.60	18	18	79	47	8	22	121	2.5	13.7	0.87	.165
Minor League Totals (4 years)				19	7	2.41	52	51	216	132	14	70	310	2.91	12.90	0.93	.172

3 DL HALL, LHP

Born: Sept. 19, 1998. **B-T:** L-L. **HT:** 6-0. **WT:** 180. **Drafted:** HS—Valdosta, Ga., 2017 (1st round). **Signed by:** Arthur McConnehead.

ERIC NALPAS/BALTIMORE ORIOLES

TRACK RECORD: The Orioles got a premium talent when Hall fell to them as the 21st pick in the 2017 draft and signed for $3 million. Hall has been impressive when healthy, and in each of his first two full seasons—the second featuring a trip to the Futures Game in 2019—he got better as the season went on. But after thriving at the team's alternate training site in 2020 and coming into 2021 with high expectations, Hall made just seven starts for Double-A Bowie, albeit dominant ones, before a stress reaction in his elbow ended his 2021 early.

BA GRADE

60 Risk: Extreme

SCOUTING REPORT: Hall honed his electric arsenal at the alternate site and hit 100 mph for the first time there. He carried that into 2021 in a significant way, with his fastball sitting in the high 90s and averaging 97 mph with above-average hop. The efforts of 2020 to distinguish his breaking balls paid off, with a plus slider in the mid 80s the best of his secondaries, followed by a slower curveball and a changeup. Hall's command, however, will be what determines his big league fate. It improved since his last game action in 2019, and while his walk rate of 4.6 per nine innings was still high, the Orioles believe he was more consistently around the strike zone without sacrificing the chase his dynamic arsenal creates.

THE FUTURE: Hall's stuff and control create the possibility of a high-leverage, late-inning reliever, but despite his injuries, he has a ceiling of a No. 3 starter. He'll be added to the 40-man roster this winter but could be back at Double-A Bowie in 2022.

SCOUTING GRADES:	Fastball: 70	Slider: 60	Curveball: 55	Changeup: 55	Control: 45

Year	Age	Club (Level)	Lge	W	L	ERA	G	GS	IP	H	HR	BB	SO	BB/9	SO/9	WHIP	AVG
2021	22	Bowie (AA)	NEast	2	0	3.13	7	7	31	16	4	16	56	4.6	15.9	1.01	.145
Minor League Totals (5 years)				8	12	2.99	53	49	217	147	14	122	284	5.06	11.78	1.24	.193

4 GUNNAR HENDERSON, SS/3B

Born: June 29, 2001. **B-T:** L-R. **HT:** 6-3. **WT:** 195. **Drafted:** HS—Selma, Ala., 2019 (2nd round). **Signed by:** David Jennings.

TRACK RECORD: Signed for an above-slot $2.3 million to keep him away from an Auburn commitment, Henderson has grown to be a darling of Orioles staff and scouts alike as a precociously talented hitter and relentless competitor. He quickly learned what it would take to face older pitchers at the alternate training site and used what he learned there to move quickly in 2021. Henderson was the Low-A East player of the month in May to begin 2021 and eventually was promoted twice, finishing at Double-A Bowie.

JOEY GARDNER

BA GRADE	
55	Risk: High

SCOUTING REPORT: Henderson has all the makings of a modern-day, bat-first shortstop and took strides toward that in 2021 as he embraced the challenges of playing above his level for most of the year. He's a potentially average hitter with plus power who has improved along with his competition, and while he struck out more often as he climbed the minors, his swing decisions and contact rates were better in High-A than Low-A. Henderson has a quiet setup but quick hands that allow him to get his barrel into the zone quickly and keep it there, and as he continues to connect his upper and lower body in his load, he'll tap into more pull power. While there's a risk he can outgrow shortstop for third base, Henderson is athletic for his size with a plus arm and above-average speed. His intelligent aggression on the bases shows how locked-in he is on a daily basis.

THE FUTURE: The Orioles haven't drafted and developed an all-star shortstop since Manny Machado, but Henderson has the talent to be the next one. He'll be back at Double-A Bowie to start 2022, with an MLB role in 2023 in play.

SCOUTING GRADES:	Hitting: 50	Power: 60	Running: 55	Fielding: 55	Arm: 60

Year	Age	Club (Level)	Lge	AVG	G	AB	R	H	2B	3B	HR	RBI	BB	SO	SB	OBP	SLG
2021	20	Delmarva (LoA)	East	.312	35	141	30	44	11	1	8	39	14	46	5	.369	.574
	20	Aberdeen (HiA)	East	.230	65	243	34	56	16	3	9	35	40	87	11	.343	.432
	20	Bowie (AA)	NEast	.200	5	15	4	3	1	0	0	0	2	10	0	.294	.267
Minor League Totals (3 years)				.258	134	507	89	131	33	6	18	85	67	171	18	.346	.454

5 COLTON COWSER, OF

Born: March 20, 2000. **B-T:** L-R. **HT:** 6-3. **WT:** 195. **Drafted:** Sam Houston State, 2021 (1st round). **Signed by:** Thom Dreier.

TRACK RECORD: Even selecting fifth overall in 2021, the Orioles feel they picked a premium college bat in Cowser, who signed for a below-slot $4.9 million. Cowser embodied the team's focus on hitters who make hard contact and don't strike out, which he demonstrated with USA Baseball's Collegiate National Team in 2019. He hit .374/.490/.680 with 16 homers and 17 steals in 55 games this spring to take Southland Conference player of the year honors in 2021. He spent a month at Low-A Delmarva to end his pro debut and walked more than he struck out.

JOEY GARDNER

BA GRADE	
55	Risk: High

SCOUTING REPORT: Cowser has always found the barrel, a skill that results in few whiffs and is aided by impressive swing decisions. He's the type to spray line drives to all fields, but his swing path is presently more geared toward contact versus power. The Orioles believe he's the rare college draftee who can add more strength and allow him to perhaps grow into 20-home run power to go along with his plus hit tool, and that any added power won't take away from his strengths of controlling the zone. Cowser is an above-average runner with good instincts in center field, giving him solid-average potential there with the arm to allow him to play either corner.

THE FUTURE: Part of the allure of selecting Cowser was how quickly he might climb to the majors, where his table-setting ability would fit right in. Developing more power could allow him to be more, but Cowser has the makings of a first-division regular at present. He could begin at High-A Aberdeen in 2022 and ride a fast track to Baltimore by 2023.

SCOUTING GRADES:	Hitting: 60	Power: 50	Running: 55	Fielding: 50	Arm: 55

Year	Age	Club (Level)	Lge	AVG	G	AB	R	H	2B	3B	HR	RBI	BB	SO	SB	OBP	SLG
2021	21	Orioles Orange (R)	FCL	.500	7	22	8	11	3	0	1	8	3	4	3	.560	.773
	21	Delmarva (LoA)	East	.347	25	98	22	34	5	0	1	26	22	19	4	.476	.429
Minor League Totals (1 year)				.375	32	120	30	45	8	0	2	34	25	23	7	.490	.492

6 JORDAN WESTBURG, SS/3B

Born: Feb. 18, 1999. **B-T:** R-R. **HT:** 6-3. **WT:** 200. **Drafted:** Mississippi State, 2020 (1st round supplemental). **Signed by:** David Jennings.

TRACK RECORD: In signing Westburg for $2.37 million as the 30th overall pick in 2020, the Orioles bet he was going to continue the improvements from his strong summer in 2019 in Cape Cod League and the first few weeks of the shortened college season. He did just that at instructional league in 2020. He began his pro career at Low-A Delmarva before beginning a three-level ascent to Double-A Bowie.

SCOUTING REPORT: While climbing the minors, Westburg showed an aptitude to adjust and rise to the competition level each time. An above-average hitter who made consistent contact with good swing decisions, Westburg abandoned a toe-tap late in the season and moved to a leg lift that caused his hard-contact rate to spike down the stretch at Bowie. As he moves forward with that and doesn't give up his ability to drive the ball late in counts, Westburg could have 20-home run power, especially if he pulls the ball more often. His strikeout concerns have been quieted by a year where his strikeout rates fell as he climbed levels, and he chased fewer than 20% of the time. He's a plus runner with the instincts and athleticism to play shortstop in the big leagues and the arm for third base, making him an asset anywhere on the infield.

THE FUTURE: Westburg's quiet competitiveness and confidence fit in well on an ascendant Orioles farm, and he projects to be an everyday big leaguer whose versatility may make him worth more than that in the major leagues. He should finish off Double-A Bowie to begin 2022 but has a chance to push for the majors by the end of the summer.

BA GRADE	
55	Risk: High

JOEY GARDNER

SCOUTING GRADES:	Hitting: 55	Power: 50	Running: 60	Fielding: 55	Arm: 60

Year	Age	Club (Level)	Lge	AVG	G	AB	R	H	2B	3B	HR	RBI	BB	SO	SB	OBP	SLG
2021	22	Delmarva (LoA)	East	.366	20	71	18	26	5	1	3	24	12	24	5	.484	.592
	22	Aberdeen (HiA)	East	.286	62	241	41	69	16	2	8	41	35	71	9	.389	.469
	22	Bowie (AA)	NEast	.232	30	112	15	26	6	2	4	14	14	32	3	.323	.429
Minor League Totals (2 years)				.285	112	424	74	121	27	5	15	79	61	127	17	.389	.479

7 KYLE STOWERS, OF

Born: Jan. 2, 1998. **B-T:** L-L. **HT:** 6-3. **WT:** 200. **Drafted:** Stanford, 2019 (2nd round supplemental). **Signed by:** Scott Walter.

TRACK RECORD: Signed for $884,200 thanks to his power potential and high average exit velocities at Stanford, Stowers was a short-season New York-Penn League all-star after debuting in 2019 but was left out of the team's alternate training site in 2020. He spent the year getting stronger and in 2021 led Orioles minor leaguers with 27 home runs over three levels. He shared the Brooks Robinson player of the year award with top prospect Adley Rutschman as he climbed from High-A Aberdeen to Triple-A Norfolk in his first full year.

SCOUTING REPORT: Stowers is a picture of controlled violence in his swing. He takes big hacks but rarely seems to over swing. He has natural loft in his swing, which allows him to display his plus-plus raw power on balls down. He's working on more consistently closing holes up in the zone, but has the ability to drive elevated pitches as well. Even with that development point, his 2021 season was defined by elite hard contact and barrel rates. Stowers has the typical swing-and-miss concerns of a big swinger, but it's less to do with chase than whiffing in the zone and missing mistakes. Correcting that would make him an even tougher out. Drafted as a center fielder, Stowers could still play there in a pinch, but his bat will play in right field, where he boasts a plus arm and above-average speed as well.

THE FUTURE: Even after a successful full-season debut, Stowers' assignment to the Arizona Fall League shows how quickly the Orioles want to get him to the majors. He has the potential to be a middle-of-the-order hitter and could be in the majors in 2022 after finishing his development at Triple-A Norfolk.

ERIC NALPAS/BALTIMORE ORIOLES

BA GRADE	
45	Risk: Medium

SCOUTING GRADES:	Hitting: 50	Power: 60	Running: 55	Fielding: 50	Arm: 60

Year	Age	Club (Level)	Lge	AVG	G	AB	R	H	2B	3B	HR	RBI	BB	SO	SB	OBP	SLG
2021	23	Aberdeen (HiA)	East	.275	36	131	25	36	6	1	7	32	27	55	3	.404	.496
	23	Bowie (AA)	NEast	.283	66	237	38	67	15	0	17	42	34	84	4	.377	.561
	23	Norfolk (AAA)	East	.272	22	81	10	22	2	0	3	11	12	32	1	.366	.407
Minor League Totals (3 years)				.259	179	653	92	169	36	2	33	108	93	224	13	.355	.472

8 HESTON KJERSTAD, OF

Born: Feb. 12, 1999. **B-T:** L-R. **HT:** 6-3. **WT:** 205. **Drafted:** Arkansas, 2020 (1st round). **Signed by:** Ken Guthrie.

TRACK RECORD: The Orioles feel Kjerstad would have been college baseball's best player had the 2020 season finished. Thus they believe they got a bargain when he signed for a below-slot $5.2 million as the No. 2 overall pick. They haven't gotten to see much of his promise on the field. Kjerstad has yet to appear in a game due to the effects of myocarditis—inflammation of the heart muscle—that was detected ahead of 2020 instructional league. He began working back to health in the spring, but was shut down again in June before resuming activities in August. He was swinging a bat again in September.

SCOUTING REPORT: Coming out of college, Kjerstad was touted as a potential middle-of-the-order bat with plus-plus raw power and the ability to utilize it in games. The moving parts of his swing introduced strikeout risk, but the Orioles saw the type of improvement over his college career to believe that could be managed. While Kjerstad has an above-average arm, his corner outfield profile puts pressure on his bat to produce at that level. The loss of muscle that can come from spending more than a year without physical activity raises concerns about whether he'll be able to hit for the power his position will require. The Orioles feel his swing is natural enough that he'll be able to regain it.

THE FUTURE: A positive outlook on Kjerstad's health at the end of 2021 has the Orioles hopeful he'll be able to begin his professional career in 2022, potentially at Low-A Delmarva. The uncertainty his health struggles created makes it unclear how easily Kjerstad will be able to reach his ceiling as an everyday bat-first outfielder.

BA GRADE
55 Risk: Extreme

SCOUTING GRADES:	Hitting: 50	Power: 70	Running: 40	Fielding: 50	Arm: 60

Year	Age	Club (Level)	Lge	AVG	G	AB	R	H	2B	3B	HR	RBI	BB	SO	SB	OBP	SLG
2021	22	Did not play—Injured															

9 KYLE BRADISH, RHP

Born: Sept. 12, 1996. **B-T:** R-R. **HT:** 6-3. **WT:** 175. **Drafted:** New Mexico State, 2018 (4th round). **Signed by:** Chad Hermansen (Angels).

TRACK RECORD: Bradish came to the Orioles as one of four pitchers acquired for Dylan Bundy in a December 2019 trade with the Angels. He quickly distinguished himself as the top piece in that deal. Bradish had struggled with the Angels, but he regained his mid-90s velocity upon reporting to his first spring with the Orioles. He impressed at the alternate training site in 2020, and needed just three scoreless outings at Double-A Bowie to end up at Triple-A Norfolk.

SCOUTING REPORT: A tall righthander with a unique, over-the-top delivery, Bradish comes at hitters from an uncomfortable angle with lively stuff. His fastball, a four-seamer with hop and cut, sits comfortably in the mid 90s and tops out at 97 mph. It can explode on hitters. A plus slider that averaged 86 mph is his top weapon against righthanded hitters, and a low-80s curveball is his go-to against lefthanders. Both the curveball and his firm changeup are under-utilized at times and aren't finished products. Bradish's walk rate jumped at Triple-A Norfolk, but he finished strong when he stopped trying to make perfect pitches and attacked with his best stuff in the strike zone. Further honing his delivery and getting to his best release point and timing more consistently, a challenge with his unique mechanics, will help that.

THE FUTURE: Bradish largely lived up to the internal buzz he generated during the 2020 shutdown. A No. 4 starter's role could be in play for Bradish should he grow more consistent and develop confidence in his entire arsenal. He could compete for a rotation spot in the majors in 2022.

DAN KUBUS/BALTIMORE ORIOLES

BA GRADE
50 Risk: High

SCOUTING GRADES:	Fastball: 60	Slider: 60	Curveball: 50	Changeup: 45	Control: 45

Year	Age	Club (Level)	Lge	W	L	ERA	G	GS	IP	H	HR	BB	SO	BB/9	SO/9	WHIP	AVG
2021	24	Bowie (AA)	NEast	1	0	0.00	3	3	13	7	0	5	26	3.3	17.1	0.88	.149
	24	Norfolk (AAA)	East	5	5	4.26	21	19	86	85	10	39	105	4.1	10.9	1.43	.254
Minor League Totals (4 years)				12	12	3.98	48	40	201	182	19	97	251	4.34	11.22	1.39	.238

10 COBY MAYO, 3B

Born: Dec. 10, 2001. **B-T:** R-R. **HT:** 6-5. **WT:** 215. **Drafted:** HS—Parkland, Fla., 2020 (4th round). **Signed by:** Brandon Verley.

TRACK RECORD: Prolific raw power as an amateur was the principal reason the Orioles signed Mayo for $1.75 million—more than $1 million above slot—in the five-round 2020 draft. Still, it would take work to translate that power into games, and Mayo ultimately did that after a spring training knee injury kept him back from a full-season affiliate. Once games began in the Florida Complex League, Mayo dominated and continued his rise with a month at Low-A Delmarva to end the year.

SCOUTING REPORT: Mayo used his time in extended spring training to improve his movement patterns and rotation to better allow him to get to his plus power in games and hit the ball in the air more consistently. His base is presently more stable than when he was an amateur. While tall, Mayo is athletic, allowing him to have a clean swing and catch the ball out front often. By combining the newfound loft in his swing with his natural strength, Mayo is hitting fewer ground balls and thus finding more hits when he stays in the park. He could be an average hitter as he continues to hone his approach, and his ability to control the strike zone and cut down on chase rate while still hitting for power in his debut season impressed the Orioles. Mayo could easily outgrow third base, but has a chance to be average there, with his plus arm an asset at the position.

THE FUTURE: Mayo doesn't have much pro experience, but has the makings of a middle-of-the-lineup, everyday third baseman after how he finished 2021. He could be back at Delmarva for 2022, and is a few years away from the majors, but he features some of the system's best offensive upside.

BA GRADE	
50	Risk: High

SCOUTING GRADES:	Hitting: 50	Power: 60	Running: 45	Fielding: 50	Arm: 60

Year	Age	Club (Level)	Lge	AVG	G	AB	R	H	2B	3B	HR	RBI	BB	SO	SB	OBP	SLG
2021	19	Orioles Black (R)	FCL	.324	23	71	17	23	6	0	3	13	11	13	6	.429	.535
	19	Orioles Orange (R)	FCL	.400	3	5	2	2	0	0	1	2	2	1	0	.571	1.000
	19	Delmarva (LoA)	East	.311	27	106	27	33	8	1	5	26	16	26	5	.416	.547
Minor League Totals (2 years)				.319	53	182	46	58	14	1	9	41	29	40	11	.426	.555

11 MIKE BAUMANN, RHP

BA GRADE	
50	Risk: High

Born: Sept. 10, 1995. **B-T:** R-R. **HT:** 6-4. **WT:** 225. **Drafted:** Jacksonville, 2017 (3rd round). **Signed by:** Arthur McConnehead.

TRACK RECORD: An imposing righthander signed for $500,000 in 2017, Baumann moved quickly and shared the Orioles' Jim Palmer minor league pitcher of the year award in a 2019 season where he struck out 10.3 batters per nine and pitched a nine-inning no-hitter. A flexor mass strain in his elbow at the alternate site in 2020, and a recurrence the following spring, meant Baumann wasn't himself for much of 2021, even as he made his major league debut.

SCOUTING REPORT: Baumann spent most of the year trying to sync up his delivery and establish that foundation for his season. Without it, he didn't consistently get into the upper 90s with his plus fastball, instead often pitching in the 93-94 mph range with it. His plus slider didn't always have the bite it did in 2019, and he didn't throw his curveball or changeup enough for anyone's liking. The fastball and slider give Baumann a high floor as a reliever, but the Orioles hope a healthy offseason will have Baumann comfortable with his delivery in spring training so they can keep developing him as a starter.

THE FUTURE: Should Baumann come into 2022 healthy, he has the stuff to be in the rotation mix for the Orioles in spring training. He can be a back-end starter if his whole arsenal is in play.

Year	Age	Club (Level)	Lge	W	L	ERA	G	GS	IP	H	HR	BB	SO	BB/9	SO/9	WHIP	AVG
2021	25	Delmarva (LoA)	East	0	0	0.00	2	2	5	0	0	3	6	5.4	10.8	0.60	.000
	25	Bowie (AA)	NEast	3	2	4.89	10	10	38	29	6	18	39	4.2	9.1	1.22	.204
	25	Norfolk (AAA)	East	1	1	2.00	6	6	27	18	0	13	26	4.3	8.7	1.15	.194
	25	Baltimore (MLB)	AL	1	1	9.90	4	0	10	13	2	6	5	5.4	4.5	1.90	.302
Major League Totals (1 year)				1	1	9.90	4	0	10	13	2	6	5	5.40	4.50	1.90	.302
Minor League Totals (5 years)				28	16	2.94	77	74	368	264	21	151	362	3.70	8.86	1.13	.201

12 CONNOR NORBY, 2B

BA GRADE
50 Risk: High

Born: June 8, 2000. **B-T:** R-R. **HT:** 5-10. **WT:** 190. **Drafted:** East Carolina, 2021 (2nd round). **Signed by:** Quincy Boyd.

TRACK RECORD: A near-consensus All-American who led the NCAA with 102 hits and was the American Athletic Conference player of the year in 2021, Norby particularly impressed the Orioles with his plate appearances against Vanderbilt aces Jack Leiter and Kumar Rocker in the NCAA super regional. Norby signed for slightly below slot at $1.7 million, and showed a patient, opposite-field approach in the final month of the season at Low-A Delmarva.

SCOUTING REPORT: Like many of the Orioles' 2021 draftees, Norby has a knack for making contact and barreling the ball in the strike zone. At this point, he can be an above-average hitter, albeit with an opposite-field approach at the moment that can limit his power. His ability to control the strike zone and recognize pitches mean he could grow to better recognize which pitches he can drive and increase his power potential. Norby has average speed and a fringe-average arm, but the Orioles believe he's more athletic than the second base-only tag might indicate.

THE FUTURE: Norby could be a solid-average regular who sets the table at the top of a lineup or helps turn it over at the bottom. It's possible he starts at High-A Aberdeen in 2022, putting him on track to potentially reach the majors in 2023 if he performs.

Year	Age	Club (Level)	Lge	AVG	G	AB	R	H	2B	3B	HR	RBI	BB	SO	SB	OBP	SLG
2021	21	Orioles Orange (R)	FCL	.182	7	22	3	4	2	0	0	2	1	7	1	.208	.273
	21	Delmarva (LoA)	East	.283	26	99	17	28	4	1	3	17	21	28	5	.413	.434
Minor League Totals (1 year)				.264	33	121	20	32	6	1	3	19	22	35	6	.380	.405

13 MAIKOL HERNANDEZ, SS

BA GRADE
50 Risk: Extreme

Born: Oct. 4, 2003. **B-T:** R-R. **HT:** 6-3. **WT:** 175. **Signed:** Venezuela, 2021. **Signed by:** Adel Granadillo/Geraldo Cabrera.

TRACK RECORD: The Orioles' return to the Latin American market in 2019 produced their largest ever signing class, then in January 2021 brought about their first two seven-figure signing bonuses. Hernandez's $1.2 million bonus was one of them. The projectable shortstop got better as his summer in the Dominican Republic went on, and came stateside for instructional camp in October.

SCOUTING REPORT: Hernandez came to the Orioles with a smooth athleticism that they believe will maintain as he grows into his tall frame, and he already boasts a clean swing with a good path through the zone. He has a good understanding of the strike zone, and improved as the summer went on at better getting to his high-end exit velocities and hitting line drives during games. He could grow into average power as an average hitter, in addition to being a plus runner with the potential to be an average shortstop and enough arm to move to third base if he outgrows his current position.

THE FUTURE: The Orioles haven't produced a homegrown, everyday major league infielder from Latin America since Jonathan Schoop, but Hernandez could be the next one. He should be in the Florida Complex League after extended spring training camp in 2022.

Year	Age	Club (Level)	Lge	AVG	G	AB	R	H	2B	3B	HR	RBI	BB	SO	SB	OBP	SLG
2021	17	Orioles1 (R)	DSL	.231	40	130	20	30	8	1	0	15	20	33	4	.340	.308
Minor League Totals (1 year)				.231	40	130	20	30	8	1	0	15	20	33	4	.340	.308

14 TERRIN VAVRA, 2B/OF

BA GRADE
45 Risk: High

Born: May 12, 1997. **B-T:** L-R. **HT:** 6-1. **WT:** 185. **Drafted:** Minnesota, 2018 (3rd round). **Signed by:** Brett Baldwin (Rockies).

TRACK RECORD: The latest in a talented baseball family to try and climb to the big leagues, Vavra began his career with the Rockies and was the 2019 South Atlantic League MVP for Asheville. He filled a high-minors infield void with the Orioles after being part of the 2020 trade for Mychal Givens, and was among their most productive minor league hitters before a back injury cost him nearly two months in 2021.

SCOUTING REPORT: On either side of his injury, Vavra showed an advanced eye at the plate and an ability to hit line drives with a smooth swing from the left side. He can have fringe-average power and be an above-average hitter thanks to his swing decisions and contact profile. Vavra's best fit is at second base, where he made just one error this season, and he projects long term as an average defender at the position. Additionally, he spent time in center field in 2021, a position that he has the athleticism for, even if his running is just average. His fringe-average arm will limit him to second base on the infield and could impact his ability to make an impact in the outfield.

THE FUTURE: Vavra's on-base ability and defensive versatility could make him an everyday fixture at the bottom of a lineup, or alternatively a table-setter up top. He could begin 2022 in Triple-A Norfolk.

Year	Age	Club (Level)	Lge	AVG	G	AB	R	H	2B	3B	HR	RBI	BB	SO	SB	OBP	SLG
2021	24	Orioles Orange (R)	FCL	.667	2	6	1	4	0	0	0	0	0	0	1	.667	.667
	24	Orioles Black (R)	FCL	.000	1	2	1	0	0	0	0	0	2	0	0	.500	.000
	24	Aberdeen (HiA)	East	.381	5	21	4	8	2	1	0	1	3	6	0	.458	.571
	24	Bowie (AA)	NEast	.248	40	149	28	37	10	1	5	20	29	42	6	.388	.430
Minor League Totals (4 years)				.304	194	721	135	219	52	7	19	99	122	150	34	.405	.474

15 SAMUEL BASALLO, C

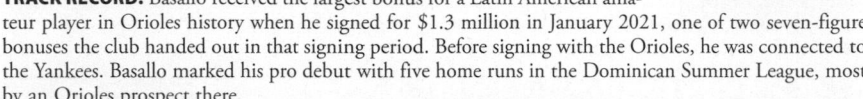

Born: Aug. 13, 2004. **B-T:** L-R. **HT:** 6-3. **WT:** 180. **Signed:** Dominican Republic, 2021. **Signed by:** Micheal Cruz/Geraldo Cabrera.

TRACK RECORD: Basallo received the largest bonus for a Latin American amateur player in Orioles history when he signed for $1.3 million in January 2021, one of two seven-figure bonuses the club handed out in that signing period. Before signing with the Orioles, he was connected to the Yankees. Basallo marked his pro debut with five home runs in the Dominican Summer League, most by an Orioles prospect there.

SCOUTING REPORT: Basallo's power is one of several promising tools, as it could be plus-plus power as he continues to grow into it and refine both his approach and his swing. As he learns how his body moves and reduces his chase rate, the Orioles see potential for him to improve on what was the best hard-hit rate in their Dominican group. While already big for his age, Basallo is athletic behind the plate with a plus arm that could keep him at the position as he continues to develop.

THE FUTURE: Basallo came stateside for the Orioles' fall instructional camp, indicating he could spend 2021 in the Florida Complex League. While he's a long way away, Basallo has the skills to grow into a bat-first, everyday catcher or possibly hit enough to play as a corner outfielder.

Year	Age	Club (Level)	Lge	AVG	G	AB	R	H	2B	3B	HR	RBI	BB	SO	SB	OBP	SLG
2021	16	Orioles1 (R)	DSL	.239	41	134	18	32	8	0	5	19	19	32	1	.338	.410
Minor League Totals (1 year)				.239	41	134	18	32	8	0	5	19	19	32	1	.338	.410

16 JOEY ORTIZ, SS/2B

Born: July 14, 1998. **B-T:** R-R. **HT:** 5-11. **WT:** 175. **Drafted:** New Mexico State, 2019 (4th round). **Signed by:** John Gillette

TRACK RECORD: Ortiz starred at New Mexico State at third base as a freshman and then for two years as a standout shortstop whose advanced glove was enough to get him drafted early on the second day in 2019. Ortiz added nearly 30 pounds of muscle and remade his swing during the 2020 shutdown to add a big league offensive profile to go with his glove. He was one of the Orioles' breakout prospects before requiring surgery to repair a torn left labrum.

SCOUTING REPORT: By adding loft to his swing and catching the ball out front to elevate it more consistently, Ortiz took what was a meek offensive skill set and created the potential to be an average hitter with fringe-average power. He cut his groundball rate by nearly 12% from 2019 to 2021. Despite bulking up and increasing his ability to impact the ball more consistently, Ortiz didn't lose much of his defensive promise. He primarily played shortstop, where he can at least be above-average, with the range for second and the arm for third when he played there.

THE FUTURE: There's always a major league role for a true shortstop, but Ortiz could be a big league regular because of his improved offensive profile. He didn't spend much time at Double-A Bowie before his injury, and should return there in 2022.

Year	Age	Club (Level)	Lge	AVG	G	AB	R	H	2B	3B	HR	RBI	BB	SO	SB	OBP	SLG
2021	22	Aberdeen (HiA)	East	.289	19	76	14	22	7	2	0	8	10	18	3	.382	.434
	22	Bowie (AA)	NEast	.233	16	60	11	14	2	0	4	9	6	14	1	.313	.467
Minor League Totals (3 years)				.251	91	331	48	83	11	2	5	34	46	69	6	.348	.341

17 DREW ROM, LHP

Born: Dec. 15, 1999. **B-T:** L-L. **HT:** 6-2. **WT:** 170. **Drafted:** HS—Fort Thomas, Ky., 2018 (4th round). **Signed by:** Adrian Dorsey.

TRACK RECORD: The last in a long line of projectable lefties the Orioles drafted last decade in hopes of them filling out and developing into big league starters, Rom has done that as he's climbed into the high minors.

SCOUTING REPORT: Rom hasn't yet developed a standout pitch, but a varied mix and precocious pitch-ability have helped him carve up hitters at every level. His fastball, which sat around 90 mph previously, was up to 94 mph at times late in the season and more consistently sat around 91-93. He experimented with dropping his arm slot against lefties to create different action on his two-seam fastball. His average slider is the best of his secondaries now, though there's work to be done on differentiating its movement from his fringe-average splitter, changeup and curveball. Rom knows how the pitches play off one another, and pitches backwards while taking advantage of his deception and angles.

THE FUTURE: Rom is aware of the challenges that face a finesse lefthander without premium velocity in the majors, but adding to his fastball and learning how to pitch backwards at an early stage keep a No. 5 starter profile in play. He should start back at Double-A Bowie in 2022, with a big league chance in play the following year.

Year	Age	Club (Level)	Lge	W	L	ERA	G	GS	IP	H	HR	BB	SO	BB/9	SO/9	WHIP	AVG
	21	Aberdeen (HiA)	East	8	0	2.79	14	13	67	60	6	17	73	2.3	9.7	1.14	.236
2021	21	Bowie (AA)	NEast	3	1	3.83	9	7	40	35	6	9	47	2.0	10.6	1.10	.230
Minor League Totals (4 years)				17	6	2.89	54	44	234	198	18	65	270	2.50	10.40	1.13	.225

18 CARTER BAUMLER, RHP

BA GRADE

50 Risk: Extreme

Born: Jan. 31, 2002. **B-T:** R-R. **HT:** 6-2. **WT:** 195. **Drafted:** HS—West Des Moines, Iowa, 2020 (5th round). **Signed by:** Scott Thomas.

TRACK RECORD: Baumler's $1.5 million, above-slot bonus remains the largest the Orioles have given to a pitcher under the Mike Elias regime, and what the athletic righthander showed in fall instructional camp in 2020 made them feel safe in that investment before an elbow injury required Tommy John surgery. Baumler spent 2021 recovering from that injury and finished his rehab progression at fall instructional camp to set the course for a normal offseason throwing program.

SCOUTING REPORT: Before his injury, Baumler worked with a fastball in the 88-92 mph range that topped out at 96 mph from a clean, repeatable delivery with a good arm path and plenty of physical projection to add to his heater. Baumler spent a month of his rehab honing his breaking ball and changeup, each of which had at least average potential before his year off. A classic high-ceiling, cold-weather arm, the Orioles believe Baulmer has plenty of capacity to improve.

THE FUTURE: Baumler is yet to throw a pitch in a professional game, but many believe he has No. 3 starter potential, even if he's years away from fulfilling that role. He should be a full-go come spring training and begin his affiliated career at Low-A Delmarva in 2022.

Year	Age	Club (Level)	Lge	W	L	ERA	G	GS	IP	H	HR	BB	SO	BB/9	SO/9	WHIP	AVG
2021	19	Did not play—Injured															

19 JAHMAI JONES, 2B

BA GRADE

40 Risk: Medium

Born: Aug. 4, 1997. **B-T:** R-R. **HT:** 6-0. **WT:** 204. **Drafted:** HS—Norcross, Ga., 2015 (2nd round). **Signed by:** Todd Hogan (Angels).

TRACK RECORD: With a father and brother who played in the NFL, Jones made his major league debut in 2020 to show his choice to play baseball was a sound one. After a slow development process as a high school draftee who signed for $1.1 million, Jones found his swing during the second half of 2019 at Double-A Mobile, after a tough first half. By the time he was traded to the Orioles for Alex Cobb in February 2021, his stock had plummeted significantly. He hit in spurts in the minors before struggling on his return to the big leagues late in the season.

SCOUTING REPORT: Jones had moments in 2021 where his average hit tool and fringe-average power showed up in games. Upon his arrival in the majors, he was attacked with inside fastballs and never made the proper adjustment, leading to plenty of strikeouts and weak contact. Jones' offensive profile complements a high-energy presence both on and off the field, as Jones' plus speed and athleticism have helped him transition from center field to second base. He could grow into an average defender at the position, but remains inexperienced there and is still smoothing out his actions.

THE FUTURE: Jones could grow into an everyday player for a second-division club and is still young, but has plenty to improve on based on his time in the majors in 2021.

Year	Age	Club (Level)	Lge	AVG	G	AB	R	H	2B	3B	HR	RBI	BB	SO	SB	OBP	SLG
2021	23	Aberdeen (HiA)	East	.500	3	8	2	4	0	0	1	2	0	1	0	.556	.875
	23	Norfolk (AAA)	East	.243	70	255	34	62	9	3	11	37	35	68	11	.337	.431
	23	Baltimore (MLB)	AL	.149	26	67	5	10	3	0	0	3	4	26	1	.208	.194
Major League Totals (2 years)				.176	29	74	7	13	3	0	0	4	4	28	1	.228	.216
Minor League Totals (6 years)				.258	557	2163	353	557	99	27	47	241	240	473	107	.338	.393

20 KEVIN SMITH, LHP

BA GRADE

40 Risk: Medium

Born: May 13, 1997. **B-T:** L-L. **HT:** 6-5. **WT:** 224. **Drafted:** Georgia, 2018 (7th round). **Signed by:** Tommy Jackson (Mets).

TRACK RECORD: Smith was the Mets' minor league pitcher of the year in 2019, his first full season, and was part of a trade that sent him to the Orioles for reliever Miguel Castro the following summer. He dominated in six appearances at Double-A Bowie to begin 2021 before Triple-A proved challenging. Smith struggled with walks and home runs at Norfolk.

SCOUTING REPORT: When he was at his best at Bowie early in the season, Smith used a four-seam and two-seam fastball in the 91-92 mph range, though they backed up to around 90 mph late in the year. His slider has plus potential, and his changeup can be average, and the whole arsenal plays up at times because of the deception his crossbody delivery provides. That deception relies on him controlling the ball and throwing strikes, something he struggled badly with in Triple-A, with fewer than half of his pitches in the zone.

THE FUTURE: Smith was Rule 5 eligible this winter and was added to the 40-man roster, putting a tighter timeline on him figuring out his command issues as he'll be needed in the major league mix come 2022. It's possible he could be a No. 5 starter or middle reliever as he has the pitches to attack hitters at both sides of the plate.

Year	Age	Club (Level)	Lge	W	L	ERA	G	GS	IP	H	HR	BB	SO	BB/9	SO/9	WHIP	AVG
2021	24	Bowie (AA)	NEast	0	1	1.04	6	5	26	18	1	10	37	3.5	12.8	1.08	.196
	24	Norfolk (AAA)	East	3	6	6.23	16	15	56	56	14	49	68	7.8	10.9	1.86	.257
Minor League Totals (4 years)				15	15	3.43	57	46	223	194	22	104	263	4.20	10.61	1.34	.237

21 REED TRIMBLE, OF

BA GRADE

45 Risk: High

Born: June 6, 2000. **B-T:** B-R. **HT:** 6-0. **WT:** 180. **Drafted:** Southern Mississippi, 2021 (2nd round supplemental). **Signed by:** David Jennings.

TRACK RECORD: As a second-year freshman who played just one full season because of Covid, Trimble made his year with the Golden Eagles count: he tied for the NCAA lead with 72 RBIs as their everyday right fielder. Trimble signed for a below-slot $800,000 deal after a standout performance in the NCAA regional, but didn't get to show his full potential in his pro debut as his playing time was limited.

SCOUTING REPORT: Trimble is on the raw side when it comes to Orioles draftees in 2021, but has all the markers of a player who can grow into a complete outfielder. He has polished swings and above-average bat speed from both sides of the plate with bat-to-ball skills and strike zone control that can make him at least an average hitter with potentially above-average power as he matures. His plus-plus speed is an asset on the bases and in center field, where it can make him an above-average defender. He boasts a solid-average arm as well.

THE FUTURE: Trimble could return to Low-A Delmarva for everyday center field duties in 2022 to begin his first full season and establish a path to a future as an everyday outfielder when the Orioles get competitive. Trimble's athleticism and switch-hitting give him an easy bench outfielder floor.

Year	Age	Club (Level)	Lge	AVG	G	AB	R	H	2B	3B	HR	RBI	BB	SO	SB	OBP	SLG
2021	21	Orioles Orange (R)	FCL	.333	6	15	3	5	1	0	0	2	3	4	2	.444	.400
	21	Delmarva (LoA)	East	.169	16	65	11	11	1	0	0	6	9	21	1	.276	.185
Minor League Totals (1 year)				.200	22	80	14	16	2	0	0	8	12	25	3	.309	.225

22 HUDSON HASKIN, OF

BA GRADE

45 Risk: High

Born: Dec. 31, 1998. **B-T:** R-R. **HT:** 6-2. **WT:** 200. **Drafted:** Tulane, 2020 (2nd round). **Signed by:** David Jennings.

TRACK RECORD: A draft-eligible sophomore who signed for $1.91 million after starring for two seasons with the Green Wave, Haskin spent most of his debut season at Low-A Delmarva and had a month at High-A Aberdeen before he fractured his thumb in late August.

SCOUTING REPORT: Every aspect of Haskin's game is influenced by his easy plus speed, most notably his ability to potentially play an above-average center field with an above-average arm at the highest level. His legs also are an asset on offense, with his 22 stolen bases among the best in the Orioles' system and his ability to beat out hits paramount to his attack. His swing is geared more to flat contact than loft and can get a little long, but there's still average potential for his hit tool, albeit with fringe-average power. As a quick-twitch athlete who is willing to put in the work, the Orioles hope he can increase his damage level as he continues to work his swing and develop physically.

THE FUTURE: Haskin didn't spend enough time at Aberdeen to warrant his starting above there in 2022, and will likely continue his efforts to be a second-division regular or platoon outfielder with the Ironbirds next spring. His speed and projection to stay in center field give Haskin a high floor at the major league level.

Year	Age	Club (Level)	Lge	AVG	G	AB	R	H	2B	3B	HR	RBI	BB	SO	SB	OBP	SLG
2021	22	Delmarva (LoA)	East	.276	57	217	44	60	13	1	5	33	22	60	17	.377	.415
	22	Aberdeen (HiA)	East	.275	26	91	15	25	6	2	0	9	10	18	5	.389	.385
Minor League Totals (2 years)				.276	83	308	59	85	19	3	5	42	32	78	22	.381	.406

23 YUSNIEL DIAZ, OF

Born: Oct. 7, 1996. **B-T:** R-R. **HT:** 6-1. **WT:** 195. **Signed:** Cuba, 2015.
Signed by: Ismael Cruz/Miguel Tosar/Roman Barinas (Dodgers).

TRACK RECORD: Signed for $15.5 million by the Dodgers and later used as the centerpiece in a trade that brought them Manny Machado in 2018, Diaz immediately became the Orioles' top prospect but has seen his career stall out through injury and poor performance. He missed time in 2021 at Triple-A Norfolk with a quadriceps strain and turf toe, but had a .498 OPS over two levels when he was healthy.

SCOUTING REPORT: Diaz's talent is still there in flashes, though the Orioles believe he needs a sustained period of health to best demonstrate it. Despite a good approach at the plate, his load remains an issue and keeps him from making consistent hard contact. He could be a fringe-average hitter with pull power if he cleans that up, which could put pressure on his bat as he's likely a corner outfielder despite some experience in center field. Diaz can be an average runner, but hasn't been aggressive on the bases since his 2018 trade, with his plus arm currently his best tool.

THE FUTURE: An inability to stay on the field has made Diaz a major question mark, but he still has the talent to be a second-division regular or bench outfielder if he regains consistency and health.

Year	Age	Club (Level)	Lge	AVG	G	AB	R	H	2B	3B	HR	RBI	BB	SO	SB	OBP	SLG
2021	24	Bowie (AA)	NEast	.179	11	39	3	7	3	0	1	6	4	13	1	.273	.333
	24	Norfolk (AAA)	East	.157	54	191	19	30	4	1	4	16	14	69	1	.225	.251
Minor League Totals (7 years)				.262	446	1670	232	438	75	20	47	231	187	400	30	.338	.416

24 JOHN RHODES, OF

Born: Aug. 15, 2000. **B-T:** R-R. **HT:** 6-0. **WT:** 200. **Drafted:** Kentucky, 2021 (3rd round). **Signed by:** Trent Friedrich.

TRACK RECORD: Rhodes became a draft-eligible sophomore when the draft was moved from June to July, and though he underperformed in 2021 compared to how he stood out before the shutdown in 2020, the Orioles signed him for an above-slot $1.38 million.

SCOUTING REPORT: Kentucky never found a defensive home for Rhodes, who played at the corners in the infield and outfield, but that was more down to his versatility and its desire to keep his bat in its lineup. Rhodes has good bat speed and showed increasingly powerful top-end exit velocities as well as an average hit tool. The challenge for Rhodes will be adding loft to his swing and getting his best swings off consistently without sacrificing his ability to put the ball in play or his impressive on-base numbers. The Orioles will keep him in the outfield, where he has work to do and can be average with experience.

THE FUTURE: Rhodes can be an average regular, perhaps on a second-division club, with the outside potential for more should he grow into the consistent game power a corner outfielder requires.

Year	Age	Club (Level)	Lge	AVG	G	AB	R	H	2B	3B	HR	RBI	BB	SO	SB	OBP	SLG
2021	20	Orioles Orange (R)	FCL	.154	5	13	3	2	0	0	0	3	3	3	0	.313	.154
	20	Orioles Black (R)	FCL	1.000	1	1	0	1	0	0	0	2	0	0	0	1.000	1.000
	20	Delmarva (LoA)	East	.266	23	94	20	25	4	0	2	18	9	16	6	.343	.372
Minor League Totals (1 year)				.259	29	108	23	28	4	0	2	23	12	19	6	.350	.352

25 ALEXANDER WELLS, LHP

Born: Feb. 27, 1997 **B-T:** L-L. **HT:** 6-1. **WT:** 190. **Signed:** Australia, 2015.
Signed by: Brett Ward/Mike Snyder.

TRACK RECORD: Wells was an all-star in each of his first four minor league seasons, including a 2017 season when he was the Orioles' minor league pitcher of the year. His 2021 got a late start due to an oblique strain in spring training, and he pitched well at Triple-A in between some big league outings that illustrated the challenges of being a soft-tossing, fly ball pitcher in the AL East.

SCOUTING REPORT: Pitching with a fastball that sits in the high 80s is difficult at any level, but Wells showed flashes of being able to locate the pitch well enough to get away with it in the majors. When he stays on the attack, it has pinpoint control in the strike zone where hitters can't get their best swings off, though his confidence in that attack can waver, leading to walks and bad misses. Wells developed a slider during the 2020 shutdown that gave him a harder breaking ball than his average curve, with the new slider effective in the majors. His changeup has above-average potential, and is necessary against righthanded hitters.

THE FUTURE: Without the ability to be a matchup reliever due to his velocity profile, Wells profiles best as a bulk pitcher or No. 5 starter in the majors. He'll be in the Orioles' rotation mix in 2022.

Year	Age	Club (Level)	Lge	W	L	ERA	G	GS	IP	H	HR	BB	SO	BB/9	SO/9	WHIP	AVG
2021	24	Norfolk (AAA)	East	6	3	3.29	13	10	54	49	6	7	48	1.2	7.9	1.02	.232
	24	Baltimore (MLB)	AL	2	3	6.75	11	8	42	53	10	16	26	3.4	5.5	1.62	.299
Major League Totals (1 year)				2	3	6.75	11	8	43	53	10	16	26	3.38	5.48	1.62	.299
Minor League Totals (6 years)				36	27	2.87	99	96	530	480	52	83	417	1.41	7.09	1.06	.239

26 ZAC LOWTHER, LHP

BA GRADE

40 Risk: Medium

Born: April 30, 1996. **B-T:** L-L. **HT:** 6-2. **WT:** 235. **Drafted:** Xavier, 2017 (2nd round supplemental). **Signed by:** Adrian Dorsey.

TRACK RECORD: After earning the Orioles' minor league pitcher of the year honors in 2018 and an all-star nod at Double-A Bowie in 2019, Lowther's career slowed significantly. He missed time with a shoulder strain in 2021 and was hit hard once he reached the big leagues. His time at Triple-A Norfolk wasn't much better, representing the first real struggles he's had as a pro.

SCOUTING REPORT: Lowther has never had premium velocity, with a four-seam fastball that averages 89-91 mph but plays up because of his ability to get down the mound and generate extension. It's not a hoppy fastball, though, which limits its effectiveness in the zone. He used his high-spin curveball effectively in the majors, as well as the slider he learned in the 2020 shutdown, but neither those nor his changeup project to be plus pitches. Lowther needs to be fine with his command and pitch backwards to succeed in the majors, and was able to pitch well in 2021 when he did that.

THE FUTURE: Lowther learned the margin for error that he'll have to live in to be a big league starter in 2021, and still has a chance to be a No. 5 starter or bulk pitcher with refinement.

Year	Age	Club (Level)	Lge	W	L	ERA	G	GS	IP	H	HR	BB	SO	BB/9	SO/9	WHIP	AVG
2021	25	Orioles Black (R)	FCL	0	0	0.00	1	0	2	1	0	0	3	0.0	11.6	0.43	.143
	25	Aberdeen (HiA)	East	0	1	6.75	1	1	2	4	0	1	5	3.4	16.9	1.88	.333
	25	Bowie (AA)	NEast	0	0	0.00	1	1	4	5	0	1	4	2.3	9.0	1.50	.278
	25	Norfolk (AAA)	East	0	5	6.53	8	8	30	33	4	16	33	4.8	9.8	1.62	.266
	25	Baltimore (MLB)	AL	1	3	6.67	10	6	29	36	6	13	30	3.9	9.1	1.65	.298
Major League Totals (1 year)				1	3	6.67	10	6	30	36	6	13	30	3.94	9.10	1.65	.298
Minor League Totals (5 years)				23	19	2.61	72	69	365	266	21	127	425	3.13	10.47	1.08	.203

27 ADAM HALL, 2B

BA GRADE

45 Risk: High

Born: May 22, 1999. **B-T:** R-R. **HT:** 6-0. **WT:** 170. **Drafted:** HS—London, Ont., 2017 (2nd round). **Signed by:** Chris Reitsma.

TRACK RECORD: Signed for an above-slot $1.3 million, Hall impressed in his full-season debut in 2019 at Low-A Delmarva. He wasn't at his best in 2021 with High-A Aberdeen and missed time late in the season with a quadriceps injury.

SCOUTING REPORT: Even in a down year, Hall's best tool remains his plus-plus speed, as evidenced by his 26 steals in 27 attempts to lead the organization. He also had one of the highest strikeout rates on the Orioles' farm (29.6%), and his swing-and-miss issues will keep him from being more than a fringe-average hitter. When he does connect, Hall's swing is level and results in singles and gap power, though he could grow into fringe-average power as he matures. While Hall is athletic enough to stay in the middle infield, he spent time in 2021 in center field, and could be average there while boosting a utility profile.

THE FUTURE: Hall's development stunted in the last two years, and he's been passed on the Orioles' depth chart by other highly-regarded infielders. Still, he offers enough speed and defensive versatility to envision a platoon or major league bench role with refinement. He was promoted to Double-A Bowie for the playoffs in 2021, and should return there next spring.

Year	Age	Club (Level)	Lge	AVG	G	AB	R	H	2B	3B	HR	RBI	BB	SO	SB	OBP	SLG
2021	22	Aberdeen (HiA)	East	.248	81	294	40	73	13	2	3	27	24	100	26	.335	.337
Minor League Totals (5 years)				.285	267	988	157	282	45	10	9	98	86	277	82	.368	.379

28 KYLE BRNOVICH, RHP

Born: Oct. 20, 1997. **B-T:** R-R. **HT:** 6-2. **WT:** 190. **Drafted:** Elon, 2019 (8th round). **Signed by:** Chris McAlpin (Angels).

BA GRADE	
45	**Risk:** High

TRACK RECORD: Brnovich was a three-year starter at Elon, earning Colonial Athletic Association rookie of the year honors as a freshman and pitching his way onto the Collegiate National Team after a standout sophomore season. He never appeared in a game after the Angels signed him for just below slot at $168,700, and was part of their December 2020 trade for Dylan Bundy.

SCOUTING REPORT: Brnovich impressed over two levels in his full-season debut thanks to an ability to pitch backwards and de-emphasize a fastball that has some hop but mostly sits in the 90 mph range. His curveball can be an above-average pitch with different movement profiles because of his knuckle grip. After not using his changeup much previously, Brnovich brought it along as the season progressed and it now looks like a future average pitch. He gets downhill with a slight hop in his delivery to create some deception and allow the stuff to play up, but he needs to pitch backwards to be at his most effective.

THE FUTURE: With further development of his secondary pitches Brnovich could take a No. 5 starter role. He may begin 2022 back at Double-A Bowie until a spot in Triple-A opens up.

Year	Age	Club (Level)	Lge	W	L	ERA	G	GS	IP	H	HR	BB	SO	BB/9	SO/9	WHIP	AVG
2021	23	Aberdeen (HiA)	East	4	1	2.36	8	8	34	18	4	11	48	2.9	12.6	0.84	.144
2021	23	Bowie (AA)	NEast	2	1	3.86	15	11	60	54	10	15	75	2.2	11.1	1.14	.232
Minor League Totals (3 years)				6	2	3.32	23	19	95	72	14	26	123	2.46	11.65	1.03	.201

29 JEAN PINTO, RHP

Born: Jan 9, 2001. **B-T:** R-R. **HT:** 5-11. **WT:** 175. **Signed:** Venezuela, 2019. **Signed by:** Marlon Urdaneta/Joel Chicarelli (Angels).

BA GRADE	
45	**Risk:** Very High

TRACK RECORD: One of two pitchers acquired when the Orioles traded Jose Iglesias to the Angels in December 2020, Pinto showed well with an impressive domestic debut. He made just five appearances in the FCL before a promotion to Low-A Delmarva.

SCOUTING REPORT: Pinto's fastball already sits in the low 90s while touching 95 mph, and his size means there's potentially room to grow into more. It's already an effective pitch, especially up in the strike zone, though he's working to be more consistent with the movement of the four-seamer. He missed bats with a changeup that could be above-average in the high 80s, while he uses a two-plane breaking ball in the 82-84 mph range for strikeouts as well. He's filled out physically since signing, especially in his lower half, but uses his whole body in his delivery and keeps a clean line to the plate.

THE FUTURE: Pinto has a ways to go before he can get near his ceiling as a back-end starter in the big leagues.

Year	Age	Club (Level)	Lge	W	L	ERA	G	GS	IP	H	HR	BB	SO	BB/9	SO/9	WHIP	AVG
2021	20	Orioles Black (R)	FCL	1	1	1.80	5	4	20	11	2	4	28	1.8	12.6	0.75	.155
	20	Delmarva (LoA)	East	1	1	2.51	9	7	46	29	1	13	56	2.5	10.8	0.90	.178
Minor League Totals (2 years)				2	3	2.29	17	14	79	52	3	20	103	2.29	11.78	0.92	.185

30 ANDERSON DE LOS SANTOS, 3B

Born: Jan. 11, 2004. **B-T:** R-R. **HT:** 5-11. **WT:** 185. **Signed:** Dominican Republic, 2021. **Signed by:** Geraldo Cabrera/Rafael Belen.

BA GRADE	
45	**Risk:** Extreme

TRACK RECORD: The Orioles handed out two seven-figure bonuses in the 2021 international signing class, but a $350,000 signee in de los Santos was one of the more impressive performers in their Latin American program.

SCOUTING REPORT: With a strong frame and good rotation in his swing, de los Santos generates excellent bat speed and thus produces plenty of hard contact and promising top-end exit velocities. His plate discipline is lagging, but that didn't manifest in many strikeouts. Swinging at better pitches and laying off ones he can't drive could make de los Santos a fringe-average hitter with at least above-average power. He signed as a shortstop but spent most of his time at third base in 2021, a position where he has more than enough arm strength.

THE FUTURE: By virtue of bringing de los Santos to their fall instructional camp, the Orioles are telegraphing a plan to have him play in the United States in 2022, likely in the Florida Complex League.

Year	Age	Club (Level)	Lge	AVG	G	AB	R	H	2B	3B	HR	RBI	BB	SO	SB	OBP	SLG
2021	17	Orioles1 (R)	DSL	.324	36	111	18	36	6	2	3	17	15	18	3	.409	.495
Minor League Totals (1 year)				.324	36	111	18	36	6	2	3	17	15	18	3	.409	.495

MORE PROSPECTS TO KNOW

31 BRENAN HANIFEE, RHP

The Orioles were prepared for Hanifee to break out after a productive year of remote work that had his plus sinker moving more consistently and his slider and changeup showing improvement. However, he had Tommy John surgery in May and missed the entire season.

32 BRANDON YOUNG, RHP

SLEEPER

Young, a 2020 nondrafted free agent, boasts a mid-90s fastball. If any of his secondary pitches takes a step forward, he has the physicality and makeup to be a big league starter.

33 ZACH WATSON, OF

A standout center fielder with deceptive power, Watson had the organization's first season with 20 home runs and 20 steals in the minors since DJ Stewart's in 2018 at Double-A Bowie.

34 MISHAEL DESON, OF

Acquired for reliever Mychal Givens in August 2020, Deson was the Florida Complex League's player of the month in August and ended his first U.S. season with an .822 OPS and 12 steals. Deson has plenty of room to physically mature and fulfill an offensive profile that's already promising due to his swing decisions and bat-to-ball skills.

35 LUIS GONZALEZ, OF

A power-hitting outfielder with plus raw power and natural elevation in his swing, Gonzalez signed for $450,000 in July 2019 out of the Dominican Republic. The Orioles still believe in those tools, even as he struggled badly in the Florida Complex League in his professional debut at age 18.

36 ZACH PEEK, RHP

A slight righthander with a low-90s fastball and a high-spin breaking ball, Peek's 12.2 strikeouts per nine innings was second in the organization to Grayson Rodriguez among pitchers with 90 innings. He was one of four pitchers the Orioles acquired from the Angels in the 2019 Dylan Bundy trade.

37 FELIX BAUTISTA, RHP

A 26-year-old reliever who is much more physical than his listed 6-foot-5, 190-pound size suggests, Bautista refined his control to keep his 100 mph fastball around the strike zone and struck out 77 in 46.2 innings to put himself on the major league radar for the Orioles in 2022.

38 ROBERT NEUSTROM, OF

Neustrom, a fifth-round pick in 2018, rebuilt his swing to gear it toward more power at Double-A Bowie and finished with 49 extra-base hits and a .790 OPS.

39 CODY SEDLOCK, RHP

The Orioles' 2016 first-round draft pick reached Triple-A Norfolk in 2021 and struck out over a batter per inning in a swingman role. His results took a step back because of an increase in home runs.

40 DONTA' WILLIAMS, OF

A senior sign out of Arizona, Williams is a true center fielder with above-average speed and impressive plate discipline.

TOP PROSPECTS OF THE DECADE

Year	Player, Pos	2021 Org
2012	Dylan Bundy, RHP	Angels
2013	Dylan Bundy, RHP	Angels
2014	Dylan Bundy, RHP	Angels
2015	Dylan Bundy, RHP	Angels
2016	Dylan Bundy, RHP	Angels
2017	Chance Sisco, C	Mets
2018	Austin Hays, OF	Orioles
2019	Yusniel Diaz, OF	Orioles
2020	Adley Rutschman, C	Orioles
2021	Adley Rutschman, C	Orioles

TOP DRAFT PICKS OF THE DECADE

Year	Player, Pos	2021 Org
2012	Kevin Gausman, RHP	Giants
2013	Hunter Harvey, RHP	Orioles
2014	Brian Gonzalez, LHP (3rd round)	Rockies
2015	D.J. Stewart, OF	Orioles
2016	Cody Sedlock, RHP	Orioles
2017	D.L. Hall, LHP	Orioles
2018	Grayson Rodriguez, RHP	Orioles
2019	Adley Rutschman, C	Orioles
2020	Heston Kjerstad, OF	Orioles
2021	Colton Cowser, OF	Orioles

Boston Red Sox

BY ALEX SPEIER

The Red Sox embarked on 2021 with an uncertain outlook but a clear mission.

In spring training, chief baseball officer Chaim Bloom—who in October 2019 had been entrusted with the task of reshaping and in many ways deconstructing the core that had won the 2018 World Series—suggested that regardless of the big league team's success in 2021, the organization's goal for the year was to identify the next wave of players who could serve as the foundation of multi-year contention.

The 2021 campaign brought the Red Sox—who had remade their roster with trades of Mookie Betts and Andrew Benintendi, among others—surprisingly close to an actual title, as the team made an unexpected run to the AL Championship Series. But as significant, the team continued to replenish a young talent base that had become thin.

Rookie righthanders Garrett Whitlock—an astute Rule 5 pick—and Tanner Houck both emerged as key contributors, while also showing arsenal improvements that pointed to a more successful pitching development infrastructure. Bobby Dalbec worked through struggles to become a formidable run producer down the stretch. Jarren Duran, after excelling in Triple-A, made his big league debut. It offered glimpses of greater promise moving forward.

The Red Sox experienced breakthrough seasons from existing talent and an influx of new young players. A pair of recent Red Sox first-rounders out of high school, Triston Casas and Nick Yorke, looked very much at home against older competition. With their highest draft pick in a half-century, the Red Sox took SoCal high school shortstop Marcelo Mayer with the No. 4 overall selection in the draft. He is viewed by some as a potential franchise player.

The Red Sox also added talent by—for them—non-traditional means. The selection of Whitlock—dominant as a multi-innings reliever, with a potential starter's pitch mix—in the Rule 5 draft represented a massive addition to the team's long-term pitching outlook. The trade of Benintendi just before spring training netted multiple prospects, including promising righthander Josh Winckowski. After the season, Boston landed prospects Alex Binelas and David Hamilton from the Brewers.

The idea of trading for prospects coming off a year in which the Red Sox were two wins from the World Series represented a marked contrast to anything the team had done in decades and offered evidence that Bloom's stated intention of further-

Rafael Devers delivered 38 home runs and 113 RBIs in his first all-star season at age 24.

PROJECTED 2025 LINEUP

Catcher	Christian Vazquez	34
First Base	Triston Casas	25
Second Base	Xander Bogaerts	32
Third Base	Rafael Devers	28
Shortstop	Marcelo Mayer	22
Left Field	Nick Yorke	23
Center Field	Jarren Duran	28
Right Field	Alex Verdugo	29
Designated Hitter	Bobby Dalbec	30
No. 1 Starter	Nate Eovaldi	35
No. 2 Starter	Chris Sale	36
No. 3 Starter	Garrett Whitlock	29
No. 4 Starter	Brayan Bello	26
No. 5 Starter	Tanner Houck	29
Closer	Bryan Mata	26

ing the team's short- and long-term goals was more than mere rhetoric. The result of his two-pronged efforts to add to the big league roster while also building out the farm system is an organization that has significantly upgraded the top end of its talent pool—Mayer, Casas, Yorke—while also creating depth both to reinforce the big league roster directly and to make trades.

It is premature to suggest whether Bloom's efforts will overcome what had been treated by the Red Sox as the inherent tension between the pursuit of short- and long-term success. But at the least, the totality of his moves over his first two-plus years suggests a very different modus operandi from that which preceded his arrival. ∎

BOSTON RED SOX

TOP 2022 ROOKIES	RANK
Jarren Duran, OF	4
Josh Winckowski, RHP	9
Kutter Crawford, RHP	15
BREAKOUT PROSPECTS	**RANK**
Brandon Walter, LHP	11
Wilkelman Gonzalez, RHP	13
Miguel Bleis, OF	20

SOURCE OF TOP 30 TALENT

Homegrown	22	Acquired	8
College	8	Trade	8
Junior college	0	Rule 5 draft	0
High school	6	Independent league	0
Nondrafted free agent	0	Free agent/waivers	0
International	8		

LF
Miguel Ugueto
Tyler Dearden

CF
Jarren Duran (4)
Tyler McDonough (16)
Miguel Bleis (20)
Ceddanne Rafaela (22)
Jhostynxon Garcia

RF
Gilberto Jimenez (23)
Juan Chacon
Nick Decker

3B
Blaze Jordan (7)
Brandon Howlett

SS
Marcelo Mayer (1)
Matthew Lugo (14)
Brainer Bonaci (18)
Christian Koss (26)

2B
Nick Yorke (3)
Jeter Downs (6)
David Hamilton (25)
Eddinson Paulino (28)

1B
Triston Casas (2)
Alex Binelas (17)

C
Nathan Hickey (24)
Ronaldo Hernandez (27)
Connor Wong (29)

LHP

LHSP	LHRP
Jay Groome (10)	Jeremy Wu-Yelland
Brandon Walter (11)	Brendan Cellucci
Chris Murphy (12)	

RHP

RHSP	RHRP
Brayan Bello (5)	Kutter Crawford (15)
Bryan Mata (8)	Connor Seabold (21)
Josh Winckowski (9)	Victor Santos
Wilkelman Gonzalez (13)	Durbin Feltman
Thaddeus Ward (19)	Eduard Bazardo
Noah Song (30)	Jacob Wallace
Chih-Jung Liu	Wyatt Olds
Nathanael Cruz	
Bradley Blalock	
Luis Perales	
Elmer Rodriguez	

1 MARCELO MAYER, SS

Born: Dec. 12, 2002. **B-T:** L-R. **HT:** 6-3. **WT:** 188.
Drafted: HS—Chula Vista, Calif., 2021 (1st round).
Signed by: J.J. Altobelli.

TRACK RECORD: Eastlake High featured an eventual first-rounder in 2019 in third baseman Keoni Cavaco—who was eventually drafted by the Twins in 2019—but whenever Red Sox area scout J.J. Altobelli went to see Cavaco, he invariably started raving about sophomore shortstop Marcelo Mayer. Based on his performance as an underclassman as well as a summer with Team USA's 18U National team in 2019, Mayer entered last spring as one of the top players in the draft class and never disappointed, batting .397/.555/.886 with 14 home runs, 31 walks, and eight strikeouts against top competition in San Diego County while showing ease and fluidity both in the batter's box and at shortstop. He was viewed as a candidate to go first overall in the 2021 draft, and the Red Sox felt the chance he'd get to them was remote. But when he remained available with the Sox in possession of the No. 4 pick, their highest in selection in more than 50 years, the team was elated and quickly selected him. Mayer signed for $6,664,000 to forgo a Southern California commitment and immediately stood out as the top prospect in the Florida Complex League in his pro debut, making the game look easy on both sides of the ball all summer long.

SCOUTING REPORT: Mayer is a natural, graceful player with an advanced feel for the strike zone and the ability to manipulate the barrel with a sweet, lefthanded swing. His swing is mechanically sound and allows him to take a versatile offensive approach, alternately drilling line drives and turning on pitches to get to power. He will swing and miss at times, but with his strong plate discipline and good swing decisions, he should draw enough walks to post high on-base percentages while hitting for power. Though Mayer has below-average speed, his excellent instincts, smooth actions, sure hands, and plus arm strength all suggest a potential defensive standout at shortstop. He may outgrow the position, although his size and lefthanded swing draw frequent comparisons to Corey Seager, who has remained a shortstop throughout his major league career. Mayer never lifted weights in high school, creating both the possibility of additional power as well as the risk that he gets too big as he adds strength to his lean frame and has to move off of shortstop. If he does, any additional power potential he gains would help him profile at third base, where he would project as a potentially elite defender, would maintain his status as a

TOM DiPACE

BA GRADE | **SCOUTING GRADES**

65 Risk: Very High

Hit: 65. Power: 55. Run: 40.
Field: 60. Arm: 60.

Projected future grades on 20-80 scouting scale

BEST TOOLS

Best Hitter for Average	Nick Yorke
Best Power Hitter	Blaze Jordan
Best Strike-Zone Discipline	Nick Yorke
Fastest Baserunner	Jarren Duran
Best Athlete	Gilberto Jimenez
Best Fastball	Brandon Walter
Best Curveball	Jay Groome
Best Slider	Bryan Mata
Best Changeup	Brayan Bello
Best Control	Connor Seabold
Best Defensive Catcher	Connor Wong
Best Defensive Infielder	Marcelo Mayer
Best Infield Arm	Marcelo Mayer
Best Defensive Outfielder	Ceddanne Rafaela
Best Outfield Arm	Gilberto Jimenez

standout player both in the batter's box and on the left side of the infield.

THE FUTURE: Mayer's defense at a premium position and sound swing and approach give him an easy projection of at least an above-average regular. His ultimate ceiling will be determined by whether he stays at shortstop or outgrows it, as well as how his power develops in pro ball. Still, few who scouted him as an amateur would be surprised if he emerges as an all-star and Red Sox franchise cornerstone. That ascent should start in earnest in 2022, when Mayer is likely to begin the season at Low-A Salem and could finish it at High-A Greenville. ■

Year	Age	Club (Level)	Lge	AVG	G	AB	R	H	2B	3B	HR	RBI	BB	SO	SB	OBP	SLG
2021	18	Red Sox (R)	FCL	.275	26	91	25	25	4	1	3	17	15	27	7	.377	.440
Minor League Totals (1 year)				.275	26	91	25	25	4	1	3	17	15	27	7	.377	.440

2 TRISTON CASAS, 1B

Born: Jan. 15, 2000. **B-T:** L-R. **HT:** 6-5. **WT:** 245. **Drafted:** HS—Plantation, Fla., 2018 (1st round). **Signed by:** Willie Romay.

TRACK RECORD: Casas has stood out for his immense raw power and mature, adaptable approach since his amateur days and was drafted 26th overall by the Red Sox in 2019. He held his own as one of the youngest players at every level of the minors and broke out with a banner year in 2021. Casas bounced between Double-A, Triple-A and playing for Team USA at the Tokyo Olympics and performed at every stop. He posted an .877 OPS at the highest levels of the minors during a disjointed year and led Team USA with three home runs and eight RBIs in Tokyo, earning raves from manager Mike Scioscia and other Team USA veterans.

SCOUTING REPORT: Casas is a massive presence in the batter's box at 6-foot-5, 245 pounds and possesses the plus-plus raw power expected from someone of his stature. While he occasionally sells out for power early in counts, he prides himself on being a well-rounded hitter who chokes up, spreads out his stance and uses the whole field with two strikes. While his hit-over-power approach has impressed, many evaluators believe he'll ultimately focus more on driving the ball in the air, with middle-of-the-order power numbers to follow. Casas should be able to make that shift given his professorial understanding of his swing, and still projects to be an above-average hitter. A former third baseman, Casas has a strong arm, soft hands and solid footwork at first base, where his size makes him an inviting target.

THE FUTURE: Casas will begin 2022 back in Triple-A and could reach the majors during the season. If his power develops as expected, he's a potential all-star first baseman who can anchor the lineup.

SCOUTING GRADES:	Hitting: 55	Power: 65	Running: 40	Fielding: 55	Arm: 50

Year	Age	Club (Level)	Lge	AVG	G	AB	R	H	2B	3B	HR	RBI	BB	SO	SB	OBP	SLG
2021	21	Portland (AA)	NEast	.284	77	275	57	78	12	2	13	52	49	63	6	.395	.484
	21	Worcester (AAA)	East	.242	9	33	6	8	3	1	1	7	8	8	1	.381	.485
Minor League Totals (4 years)				.265	208	741	129	196	41	8	34	140	116	191	10	.368	.479

3 NICK YORKE, 2B

Born: April 2, 2002. **B-T:** R-R. **HT:** 6-0. **WT:** 200. **Drafted:** HS—San Jose, Calif., 2020 (1st round). **Signed by:** Josh Labandeira.

TRACK RECORD: Most teams considered Yorke a potential second- or third-round pick in 2020, but the Red Sox went above industry consensus and made Yorke the surprise first-round pick of the draft when they took him 17th overall. Yorke entered his pro debut intent on proving doubters wrong and largely accomplished that mission. After a slow start, he caught fire during the summer to win the Low-A East batting title (.323) and OPS crown (.913) before receiving a late promotion to High-A Greenville.

SCOUTING REPORT: Yorke's quick, compact swing and excellent barrel control permits him the ability to hit the ball hard to all fields. He complements those physical gifts with excellent pitch recognition and plate discipline to earn consensus projections as a future plus to plus-plus hitter. While Yorke showed gap power early, he adjusted to create space with his body to drive the ball in the air to his pull side down the stretch, resulting in 11 homers in his final 35 games. While few doubt Yorke will hit, his defensive outlook is murkier. His fringe-average speed, which results in some difficulty making plays to his right, and long arm stroke create questions about his ability to stick at second base despite solid hands and average pure arm strength. If he can't stay at second, he's likely to land in left field.

THE FUTURE: Yorke's performance suggests a player who may be one of the best pure hitters in the minors. He profiles as a top-of-the-order hitter and will see the upper levels of the minors in 2022.

SCOUTING GRADES:	Hitting: 70	Power: 50	Running: 45	Fielding: 45	Arm: 50

Year	Age	Club (Level)	Lge	AVG	G	AB	R	H	2B	3B	HR	RBI	BB	SO	SB	OBP	SLG
2021	19	Salem (LoA)	East	.323	76	294	59	95	14	4	10	47	41	47	11	.413	.500
	19	Greenville (HiA)	East	.333	21	84	17	28	6	1	4	15	11	22	2	.406	.571
Minor League Totals (2 years)				.325	97	378	76	123	20	5	14	62	52	69	13	.412	.516

4 JARREN DURAN, OF

Born: Sept. 5, 1996. **B-T:** L-R. **HT:** 6-2. **WT:** 200. **Drafted:** Long Beach State, 2018 (7th round). **Signed by:** Justin Horowitz.

BA GRADE
55 Risk: High

TRACK RECORD: A line drive-hitting second baseman in college, Duran was drafted by the Red Sox in the seventh round in 2018 with the intention of moving him to the outfield. After a strong full-season debut that resulted in a Futures Game appearance, Duran remade his swing to generate more power at the alternate training site in 2020 and posted dazzling results that led to his first MLB callup last year. But after a solid start that included his first major league home run, his inability to handle fastballs at the top of the zone led to a 35.7% strikeout rate and resulted in a return to the minors.

SCOUTING REPORT: Duran's swing changes have transformed him from a slap hitter who used his double-plus speed to wreak havoc on the basepaths into a hitter who tries to launch balls for home runs. He incorporated a sizable leg lift and stride while lowering his hands to get in a better position to drive the ball in the air, which gave him increased power at Triple-A but made him vulnerable to elevated fastballs in the majors. He has tinkered extensively with his swing and is still trying to find the right balance between hitting for average and power, but he has a chance to be average at both. Duran is a blur at full speed, creating impact as a baserunner and allowing him to out-run indirect routes in center field. He is still learning the position but should emerge as a capable ball-tracker with a below-average arm.

THE FUTURE: Duran will likely open 2022 back in Triple-A. Despite his initial struggles, he has demonstrated the athleticism and aptitude to adjust and should re-emerge as the Red Sox's center fielder of the future.

SCOUTING GRADES:	Hitting: 50	Power: 50	Running: 70	Fielding: 50	Arm: 40

Year	Age	Club (Level)	Lge	AVG	G	AB	R	H	2B	3B	HR	RBI	BB	SO	SB	OBP	SLG
2021	24	Worcester (AAA)	East	.258	60	244	46	63	11	2	16	36	30	66	16	.357	.516
	24	Boston (MLB)	AL	.215	33	107	17	23	3	2	2	10	4	40	2	.241	.336
Major League Totals (1 year)				.215	33	107	17	23	3	2	2	10	4	40	2	.241	.336
Minor League Totals (4 years)				.307	259	1046	188	321	49	21	24	109	92	242	86	.372	.463

5 BRAYAN BELLO, RHP

Born: May 17, 1999. **B-T:** R-R. **HT:** 6-1. **WT:** 170. **Signed:** Dominican Republic, 2016. **Signed by:** Manny Nanita/Todd Claus/Rollie Pino.

BA GRADE
55 Risk: High

TRACK RECORD: Bello signed with the Red Sox for just $28,000 as a slender 17-year-old with a whippy arm during the 2016 international signing period. He progressively filled out as he matured and made his largest strength gains during the 2020 coronavirus shutdown, resulting in a significant uptick in velocity and stuff once minor league play resumed in 2021. Armed with new-found velocity, Bello's strikeout rate jumped more than 10% as he rose from High-A to Double-A and earned a selection to the Futures Game.

SCOUTING REPORT: Bello's athleticism produces a repeatable delivery that allows him to consistently attack the strike zone with his three-pitch mix. His fastball velocity improved from the low 90s before the shutdown to now sitting comfortably in the mid 90s and touching 98 mph. Bello's long arm path allows hitters to get a good read on his fastball, however, and its lack of movement means he has to command it to ensure its effectiveness. When he locates his fastball up in the zone, his changeup falls off of it as a plus offering, while his improving slider increasingly projects to be an above-average offering. He is in the process of developing a two-seamer to create a more complete pitch mix. Bello pounds the strike zone with above-average control and has limited his walks at every level.

THE FUTURE: Bello is likely to progress to Triple-A during the 2022 season and could emerge as a big league rotation option by the end of the year. He has mid-rotation potential as long as he maintains his velocity jump and improves his fastball command.

SCOUTING GRADES:	Fastball: 55	Slider: 55	Changeup: 60	Control: 50

Year	Age	Club (Level)	Lge	W	L	ERA	G	GS	IP	H	HR	BB	SO	BB/9	SO/9	WHIP	AVG
2021	22	Greenville (HiA)	East	5	0	2.27	6	6	31	25	3	7	45	2.0	12.8	1.01	.217
	22	Portland (AA)	NEast	2	3	4.66	15	15	63	66	5	24	87	3.4	12.3	1.41	.266
Minor League Totals (4 years)				19	15	3.98	60	59	280	265	17	79	325	2.54	10.43	1.23	.247

6 JETER DOWNS, 2B/SS

Born: July 27, 1998. **B-T:** R-R. **HT:** 5-11. **WT:** 180. **Drafted:** HS—Miami Gardens, Fla., 2017 (1st round supplemental). **Signed by:** Hector Otero (Reds).

TRACK RECORD: Originally drafted by the Reds in 2017, Downs was traded to the Dodgers in the deal for Yasiel Puig and Matt Kemp after the 2018 season and had a standout campaign in his lone year in the Dodgers' system, leading the Red Sox to acquire him in the trade that sent Mookie Betts to Los Angeles. Downs spent all of 2020 at the Red Sox's alternate training site and made his highly-anticipated organizational debut in 2021, but he was overmatched for much of the season in Triple-A. His low point came during a shocking 52-game stretch from July through mid September in which his approach unraveled completely and he hit .117/.207/.211.

BA GRADE

50 Risk: High

SCOUTING REPORT: At his best, Downs has an efficient, righthanded swing that allows him to let pitches travel deep. He drives balls hard from left-center to right-center with above-average power when he connects, but he is prone to stretches of poor pitch selection and giving away at-bats. He started pressing in 2021 and made poor swing decisions that led to both an alarming number of swings and misses and an inordinate amount of weak contact. While Downs flashes the traits of an average hitter, the lack of consistency in his approach has yielded a career .248 batting average in the minors. Defensively, Downs is an average defender at second base with decent hands and an average arm and can play shortstop in a pinch. He has just average speed but is a dangerous basestealer with his advanced reads and instincts.

THE FUTURE: Downs will get a do-over in Triple-A in 2022. He is young enough to re-establish himself as a potential everyday middle infielder.

SCOUTING GRADES:	Hitting: 45	Power: 55	Running: 50	Fielding: 50	Arm: 50

Year	Age	Club (Level)	Lge	AVG	G	AB	R	H	2B	3B	HR	RBI	BB	SO	SB	OBP	SLG
2021	22	Worcester (AAA)	East	.190	99	357	39	68	9	0	14	39	38	131	18	.272	.333
Minor League Totals (5 years)				.248	388	1444	225	358	70	9	57	201	177	373	87	.338	.427

7 BLAZE JORDAN, 1B

Born: Dec. 19, 2002. **B-T:** R-R. **HT:** 6-2. **WT:** 220. **Drafted:** HS—Southaven, Miss., 2020 (3rd round). **Signed by:** Danny Watkins.

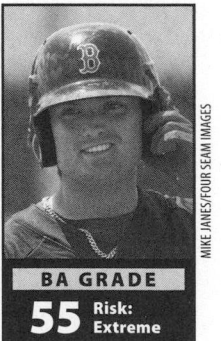

MIKE JANES/FOUR SEAM IMAGES

TRACK RECORD: Jordan's power made him a YouTube sensation as a 13-year-old, and the Red Sox were happy to draft him in the third round in 2020 and sign him away from Mississippi State for an over-slot $1.75 million bonus. Jordan delivered a positive early return on that investment in his pro debut, batting .362/.408/.667 with 12 extra-base hits in 19 games in the Florida Complex League to earn a quick promotion to Low-A Salem.

BA GRADE

55 Risk: Extreme

SCOUTING REPORT: Jordan's plus-plus power is a show-stopper. He hits towering home runs to all fields and gets to his power even with a disconnect in his upper and lower halves that should get smoothed out over time. Though he lacks any real semblance of an approach, he sees the ball well, allowing him to remain more controlled in the batter's box than might be expected. Jordan projects to be no more than a fringe-average hitter, but his pitch recognition gives him the foundation to get to his power enough to be an everyday player. Defensively, Jordan is a third baseman now but is likely to move to first base with his strong, physical frame at a young age. The Red Sox believe he can continue developing at third, which he does have the plus arm strength for.

THE FUTURE: Jordan is set to open 2022 in Low-A and is likely to move deliberately through the system. If everything clicks, he could emerge as a player with considerable power and run-production capabilities in the bottom half of the order.

SCOUTING GRADES:	Hitting: 45	Power: 70	Running: 40	Fielding: 45	Arm: 60

Year	Age	Club (Level)	Lge	AVG	G	AB	R	H	2B	3B	HR	RBI	BB	SO	SB	OBP	SLG
2021	18	Red Sox (R)	FCL	.362	19	69	12	25	7	1	4	19	6	13	1	.408	.667
	18	Salem (LoA)	East	.250	9	36	7	9	1	0	2	7	2	8	0	.289	.444
Minor League Totals (2 years)				.324	28	105	19	34	8	1	6	26	8	21	1	.368	.590

8 BRYAN MATA, RHP

Born: May 3, 1999. **B-T:** R-R. **HT:** 6-3. **WT:** 225. **Signed:** Venezuela, 2016.
Signed by: Alex Requena/Eddie Romero.

TRACK RECORD: Mata signed late in the 2015-16 international signing period for a $25,000 bonus but quickly shed his low profile when size and strength gains helped him develop the most powerful arsenal in the Red Sox's system. After a strong 2019 campaign, he showed an electric pitch mix at the alternate training site in 2020 to put himself in position to be a potential contributor in 2021. Instead, he suffered a forearm injury that required Tommy John surgery in April and wiped out his first year on the 40-man roster.

SCOUTING REPORT: Mata featured huge stuff prior to surgery, starting with a mid-to upper-90s two-seamer and a nasty, plus slider that darts out of the same tunnel. Both produced ground balls and swings and misses and largely kept batters in check on their own. Mata also has a four-seamer, an average changeup and a below-average but usable curveball at his disposal, allowing him to work to all quadrants of the strike zone. The movement he generates on his pitches can make it difficult for him to keep them in the strike zone, but he was making his delivery more compact to address his below-average control before he got hurt. While Mata has a sturdy starter's build and the pitch mix to stay in the rotation, he has yet to demonstrate he can stay healthy through a full season.

THE FUTURE: Mata will spend most of 2022 rehabbing and could return to an affiliate by mid-year. If his stuff comes back, he could emerge as a late-inning reliever or a carefully managed starter by 2023.

BRACE HEMMELGARN/MLB PHOTOS

BA GRADE
55 Risk: Extreme

SCOUTING GRADES:	Fastball: 70	Slider: 60	Curveball: 40	Changeup: 50	Control: 40

Year	Age	Club (Level)	Lge	W	L	ERA	G	GS	IP	H	HR	BB	SO	BB/9	SO/9	WHIP	AVG
2021	22	Did not play—injured															
Minor League Totals (5 years)				22	20	3.40	69	69	315	279	13	145	307	4.14	8.77	1.35	.242

9 JOSH WINCKOWSKI, RHP

Born: June 28, 1998. **B-T:** R-R. **HT:** 6-4. **WT:** 220. **Drafted:** HS—Estero, Fla., 2016 (15th round). **Signed by:** Matt O'Brien (Blue Jays).

TRACK RECORD: Winckowski was an unheralded 15th-round pick of the Blue Jays out of Estero (Fla.) High in 2016 and spent his first four pro seasons in the low minors throwing strikes with a low-90s fastball and slider. His velocity jumped into the mid 90s at 2020 instructional league and he showed improved action on his changeup, leading teams to target him in trades. Though Winckowski went unpicked in the Rule 5 draft, the Mets acquired him in the deal for Steven Matz prior to the 2021 season and the Red Sox acquired him two weeks later in the three-team trade that sent Andrew Benintendi to the Royals.

SCOUTING REPORT: Winckowski attacks the strike zone with a well-rounded repertoire. His above-average four-seam fastball sits 94-96 mph at times and gets swings and misses in the strike zone. He sometimes works below that velocity but is still effective when he does. He also uses a two-seam fastball in the low 90s to create different movement profiles and keep batters guessing. Winckowski's average slider and changeup both come in firm in the mid 80s and feature enough movement to spread the zone to both his arm and glove sides. He'll reshape the slider into a cutter to vary looks. Winckowski throws all his pitches for strikes with above-average control and is extremely efficient, allowing him to work deep into starts despite the lack of an overpowering, putaway pitch.

THE FUTURE: Winckowski was added to the 40-man roster in the offseason and is likely to make his big league debut in 2022. He may break in as a reliever but has the potential to be a solid No. 4 or 5 starter.

BA GRADE
45 Risk: Medium

SCOUTING GRADES:	Fastball: 55	Slider: 50	Changeup: 50	Control: 55

Year	Age	Club (Level)	Lge	W	L	ERA	G	GS	IP	H	HR	BB	SO	BB/9	SO/9	WHIP	AVG
2021	23	Portland (AA)	NEast	8	3	4.14	21	20	100	100	10	30	88	2.7	7.9	1.30	.253
	23	Worcester (AAA)	East	1	1	2.25	2	2	12	5	1	3	13	2.3	9.8	0.67	.122
Minor League Totals (6 years)				27	21	3.53	77	72	375	360	31	119	338	2.86	8.11	1.28	.248

10 JAY GROOME, LHP

Born: Aug. 23, 1998. **B-T:** L-L. **HT:** 6-6. **WT:** 250. **Drafted:** HS—Barnegat, N.J., 2016 (1st round). **Signed by:** Ray Fagnant.

TRACK RECORD: Groome was considered arguably the top high school pitcher in the country when the Red Sox drafted him 12th overall in 2016, but his career has been sidetracked by injuries. Groome missed all of 2018 and most of 2019 after having Tommy John surgery and saw his full-season return delayed when the coronavirus pandemic canceled the 2020 minor league season. He finally had a full, healthy season in 2021 and was inconsistent across outings but still rose to Double-A Portland.

SCOUTING REPORT: Groome's best stuff never fully came back following surgery, but his arsenal remains plenty potent. His fastball sits at 90-94 mph and touches 95-96 and he commands it to all quadrants of the strike zone.

BA GRADE
50 Risk: High

Though Groome's fastball lacks elite spin rates, hitters don't seem to pick it up, resulting in late swings and misses. His formerly elite curveball has not regained its bite since surgery but still works as an average offering. He's developed a slider that flashes above-average and an average changeup he can use below the zone. Groome has ballooned from 220 to 250 pounds, and his conditioning and stamina are issues. He often dominates early in outings only to fall apart after a few innings. He has reverse splits and dominates righthanded hitters while struggling against lefties.

THE FUTURE: The visions of Groome as a top-of-the-rotation starter have faded, but getting through a healthy 2021 represented a step forward. He could still emerge as either a back-of-the-rotation starter or a late-inning reliever if he remains healthy.

SCOUTING GRADES:	Fastball: 55	Slider: 50	Curveball: 50	Changeup: 50	Control: 55

Year	Age	Club (Level)	Lge	W	L	ERA	G	GS	IP	H	HR	BB	SO	BB/9	SO/9	WHIP	AVG
2021	22	Greenville (HiA)	East	3	8	5.29	18	18	81	76	12	32	108	3.5	11.9	1.32	.244
	22	Portland (AA)	NEast	2	0	2.30	3	3	15	12	0	4	26	2.3	14.9	1.02	.211
Minor League Totals (6 years)				8	17	4.96	41	41	163	145	18	71	222	3.91	12.23	1.32	.234

11 BRANDON WALTER, LHP

BA GRADE
50 Risk: High

Born: Sept. 8, 1996. **B-T:** L-L. **HT:** 6-2. **WT:** 200. **Drafted:** Delaware, 2019 (26th round). **Signed by:** Reed Gragnani.

TRACK RECORD: Walter had Tommy John surgery in his sophomore year at Delaware in 2017 and missed the entire 2018 season while rehabbing, but showed enough feel for pitching during his return as a redshirt junior to convince the Sox to take him as a day three selection. He was diligent in his work during the 2020 shutdown and returned as a different pitcher, with major gains in his entire arsenal that produced the most unexpected leap in the Sox system in 2021.

SCOUTING REPORT: Walter represents an unusual case: A pitcher whose age suggests reservations about his impressive numbers at two levels of Class A—particularly given that the Sox had him open the year out of the bullpen. But his stuff and pitch data suggest reason to believe in a big ceiling, making him a popular target in trade talks. The lefty throws from a low three-quarters arm slot and is a database-breaker for hitters, particularly now that his sinker sits at 93-95 mph with a sweeping slider and changeup that plays against both righties and lefties. His 5.4% walk rate is more indicative of Walter's ability to induce chases than control. He'll need to throw more strikes to stay in the rotation, but his raw stuff is elite.

THE FUTURE: Walter likely will be pushed to Double-A to open 2022, and the upper levels will give a greater indication of whether he's a late-blooming starter or if 2021 was a mirage. If his stuff holds and he harnesses his pitches in the zone, he may challenge the Sox to put him on an aggressive development track.

Year	Age	Club (Level)	Lge	W	L	ERA	G	GS	IP	H	HR	BB	SO	BB/9	SO/9	WHIP	AVG
2021	24	Salem (LoA)	East	1	1	1.45	13	2	31	21	0	6	46	1.7	13.4	0.87	.178
	24	Greenville (HiA)	East	4	3	3.70	12	12	58	46	6	14	86	2.2	13.3	1.03	.211
Minor League Totals (3 years)				9	5	2.86	38	14	123	93	8	28	171	2.05	12.55	0.99	.202

12 CHRIS MURPHY, LHP

BA GRADE
50 Risk: High

Born: June 5, 1998. **B-T:** L-L. **HT:** 6-1. **WT:** 175. **Drafted:** San Diego, 2019 (6th round). **Signed by:** J.J. Altobelli.

TRACK RECORD: The Sox took Murphy in the sixth round of the 2019 draft believing that he had swing-and-miss weapons and better command than his 12% walk rate at San Diego suggested. The lefthander has largely rewarded that view, emerging as a steady performer who at times dominated after his late-season promotion to Double-A in 2021. He went 8-5 with a 4.62 ERA between High-A Greenville and Double-A Portland in 2021, with a 30.2% strikeout rate on the year that included a 34.1% mark in Portland.

SCOUTING REPORT: Murphy leans hard on a 92-94 mph fastball—occasionally running it up to 96-97—that hitters struggle to pick up at the top of the zone, but sometimes the pitch loses ride and becomes vulnerable to hard contact, contributing to the 21 homers allowed in just over 100 innings. His best secondary offering is an above-average changeup that dives away from righties for swings and misses, while he features a curveball that shows average potential. His slider is currently a below-average offering, and may ultimately be reshaped into a cutter. Sox officials rave about his competitiveness, believing that his makeup will allow him to work past transitional bumps in the big leagues, and that his openness to pitch design work will help him find the arsenal he needs to be effective.

THE FUTURE: Murphy's dominance against lefties gives him a solid reliever floor, but so long as he throws enough strikes, Murphy's four-pitch mix gives him a chance to emerge by late 2022 or early 2023 as rotation depth with a No. 4 starter's ceiling.

Year	Age	Club (Level)	Lge	W	L	ERA	G	GS	IP	H	HR	BB	SO	BB/9	SO/9	WHIP	AVG
2021	23	Greenville (HiA)	East	5	3	4.21	14	14	68	62	17	23	81	3.0	10.7	1.24	.240
	23	Portland (AA)	NEast	3	2	5.45	7	6	33	30	4	13	47	3.6	12.8	1.30	.242
Minor League Totals (3 years)				8	6	3.74	31	30	135	115	22	43	162	2.87	10.83	1.17	.230

13 WILKELMAN GONZALEZ, RHP

BA GRADE

55 Risk: Extreme

Born: March 25, 2002. **B-T:** R-R. **HT:** 6-0. **WT:** 167. **Signed:** Venezuela, 2018. **Signed by:** Wilder Lobo/Rollie Pino.

TRACK RECORD: When the Sox scouted Gonzalez in Venezuela, they saw a slender pitcher with a mid-80s fastball, feel for a changeup, the ability to spin a curveball and plenty of projection as he filled out. After a respectable DSL debut in 2019, he used the shutdown to build strength and impressed in instructs in 2020 when he sat in the low 90s and topped out at 95. In 2021, he had a strong showing in the States, forging a 2.91 ERA with a 30.6% strikeout rate and 7.4% walk rate while logging 52.2 innings in the Florida Complex League and with Low-A Salem.

SCOUTING REPORT: Gonzalez features an easy, compact delivery that makes his fastball—which averages 93-94 mph and tops out at 97—appear to jump on hitters. He repeats his mechanics well and attacks the strike zone with his three-pitch mix. His changeup is currently his best secondary pitch and has plus potential, while his curveball remains inconsistent but flashes depth and sweep to give it above-average projection.

THE FUTURE: Gonzalez shows the potential for three above-average or better pitches, giving him mid-rotation potential if he can remain healthy and build upon his considerable development of the last two years.

Year	Age	Club (Level)	Lge	W	L	ERA	G	GS	IP	H	HR	BB	SO	BB/9	SO/9	WHIP	AVG
2021	19	Salem (LoA)	East	0	0	1.53	4	4	17	13	1	8	20	4.1	10.2	1.19	.206
	19	Red Sox (R)	FCL	4	2	3.60	8	7	35	29	1	8	46	2.1	11.8	1.06	.223
Minor League Totals (2 years)				4	5	3.09	26	25	99	76	5	40	110	3.64	10.00	1.17	.213

14 MATTHEW LUGO, SS

BA GRADE

50 Risk: High

Born: May 9, 2001. **B-T:** R-R. **HT:** 6-1. **WT:** 185. **Drafted:** HS—Florida, P.R., 2019 (2nd round). **Signed by:** Edgar Perez.

TRACK RECORD: The Red Sox drafted Lugo in 2019 and signed him for $1.1 million with the hope that he could develop as a solid defensive middle infielder—likely a second baseman—with above-average pop. Early in his pro career, his defense advanced ahead of expectations while his bat came around slowly. But after a rusty beginning to the 2021 season, Lugo closed his first full season of pro ball with a .303/.383/.429 line in his final 61 games in Low-A Salem.

SCOUTING REPORT: Lugo lets the ball travel and has a direct-to-the-ball swing that represents both a strength and limitation. On one hand, at a young age, he shows good pitch recognition that allows him to draw walks and limits his strikeouts. On the other hand, the approach results in a lot of ground balls and hinders his ability to take advantage of his considerable strength. Even so, his ability to hit for average and get on base down the stretch in 2021 suggested a player who is making gains, with the possibility that power (beyond the four homers and 28 extra-base hits he had in 105 games) will follow. Defensively, Lugo showed fluidity and good arm strength at shortstop that provides hope that he can remain an option at the position, though he has yet to develop the diversity of arm slots that characterizes most who excel at

the position. The nephew of Carlos Beltran, Lugo is considered very mature in his work ethic and habits.
THE FUTURE: Given the relatively limited game exposure Lugo received in Puerto Rico, he may follow a level-to-level progression, with an assignment to High-A Greenville for much or all of 2022 likely. If he develops 15-18 home run power, he's a potential everyday middle infielder.

Year	Age	Club (Level)	Lge	AVG	G	AB	R	H	2B	3B	HR	RBI	BB	SO	SB	OBP	SLG
2021	20	Salem (LoA)	East	.270	105	418	61	113	21	3	4	50	38	94	15	.338	.364
Minor League Totals (3 years)				.267	146	562	80	150	26	4	5	63	53	132	18	.338	.354

15 KUTTER CRAWFORD, RHP

BA GRADE
45 Risk: Medium

Born: April 1, 1996. **B-T:** R-R. **HT:** 6-1. **WT:** 210. **Drafted:** Florida Gulf Coast, 2017 (16th round). **Signed by:** Willie Romay.
TRACK RECORD: Crawford transferred to Florida Gulf Coast after two years at Indian Wells (Fla.) JC and delivered the best season (7-1, 1.71 ERA, 10.6 strikeouts per nine) in the program's history by anyone outside of Chris Sale. After the Red Sox took him as a 16th-round pick in 2017, Crawford delivered solid performances despite pitching through persistent discomfort as he moved up to Double-A, ultimately having Tommy John surgery at the end of 2019. He returned from the procedure in 2021 having improved his direction to the plate and with increased extension and velocity, allowing his arsenal to play up. He posted a 34.4% strikeout rate with a 5.2% walk rate across Double-A and Triple-A en route to his big league debut.
SCOUTING REPORT: Crawford holds his hands low while easing into the start of his delivery before seemingly jumping at the hitter, resulting in hitters mistiming and swinging through his 93-96 mph fastball at the top of the zone. He also has a cutter (which he sometimes reshapes into a slider) that can get swings and misses. He's working to develop an average third pitch, with some hope of doing so with a splitter.
THE FUTURE: Crawford represents near-term big league depth. At the least, he is capable of helping as a multi-inning reliever, but if he gets a reliable third pitch, he has a chance to emerge as a back-of-the-rotation starter.

Year	Age	Club (Level)	Lge	W	L	ERA	G	GS	IP	H	HR	BB	SO	BB/9	SO/9	WHIP	AVG
2021	25	Portland (AA)	NEast	3	2	3.30	10	10	46	33	7	5	64	1.0	12.4	0.82	.200
	25	Worcester (AAA)	East	3	4	5.21	10	9	48	49	5	15	67	2.8	12.5	1.32	.259
	25	Boston (MLB)	AL	0	1	22.50	1	1	2	5	1	2	2	9.0	9.0	3.50	.556
Major League Totals (1 year)				0	1	22.50	1	1	2	5	1	2	2	9.00	9.00	3.50	.556
Minor League Totals (5 years)				18	21	3.63	67	66	328	302	25	114	390	3.13	10.71	1.27	.245

16 TYLER MCDONOUGH, 2B/OF

BA GRADE
45 Risk: High

Born: April 2, 1999. **B-T:** B-R. **HT:** 5-10. **WT:** 180. **Drafted:** North Carolina State, 2021 (3rd round). **Signed by:** Kirk Fredriksson.
TRACK RECORD: McDonough returned to school after getting bypassed as a draft-eligible sophomore in 2020, a decision that proved wise when he emerged as one of the more reliable bats in the 2021 draft while hitting .339/.423/.631 with 15 homers in a season where he had a 53-game on-base streak. He hit the ground running in pro ball, hitting .296/.397/.491 while splitting time between second and center in 31 games in the Florida Complex League and Low-A Salem.
SCOUTING REPORT: McDonough showed a full array of skills both in college and pro ball, emerging as the sort of versatile, switch-hitting, multi-positional player now coveted in baseball. He shows solid bat-to-ball skills, strike zone recognition and modest pop from both sides of the plate. His average speed combined with strong instincts suggests a multi-dimensional player who can contribute in center or at second with low-teens power totals and double-digit steals—the sort of utility profile that once suggested a valuable reserve but that now fits a versatile everyday depiction.
THE FUTURE: McDonough could open 2022 in High-A, where he'll continue his development at both second and center while potentially incorporating more positions down the road. He is perhaps the most polished player drafted by the Red Sox in 2021, and his versatility could help him find a spot in the big leagues at some point in 2023.

Year	Age	Club (Level)	Lge	AVG	G	AB	R	H	2B	3B	HR	RBI	BB	SO	SB	OBP	SLG
2021	22	Red Sox (R)	FCL	.308	4	13	2	4	3	0	0	1	0	4	0	.308	.538
	22	Salem (LoA)	East	.296	27	108	23	32	4	4	3	14	17	24	3	.397	.491
Minor League Totals (1 year)				.298	31	121	25	36	7	4	3	15	17	28	3	.388	.496

17 ALEX BINELAS, 3B/1B

Born: May 26, 2000. **B-T:** L-R. **HT:** 6-3. **WT:** 225. **Drafted:** Louisville, 2021 (3rd round). **Signed by:** Jeff Simpson (Brewers)

BA GRADE
45 Risk: High

TRACK RECORD: Binelas was one of the top freshmen performers in the country in 2019, but required surgery to repair a broken hamate that ended his sophomore year prior to the pandemic. He struggled badly at the start of 2021, hurting his draft stock. But he rebounded to put up huge numbers—including 15 homers in his final 27 games—to convince his hometown Brewers to take him in the third round. He had a monster pro debut, hitting .309/.390/.583 with nine homers in 36 games (mostly in Low-A). The Brewers shipped Binelas and David Hamilton to the Red Sox along with Jackie Bradley Jr. for Hunter Renfroe in December.

SCOUTING REPORT: Binelas has what Red Sox chief baseball officer Chaim Bloom called "special power." Paired at Louisville with Henry Davis, Binelas produced similar exit velocities and launch angles to the No. 1 overall pick in the draft, driving the ball out to all fields and handling fastballs in the bottom half of the strike zone with a fluid swing. That said, the length in his stroke creates swings and misses on elevated pitches and creates questions about his future offensive profile. Defensively, he showed limited range at third but made routine plays. He's likely to spend most of his time at first but perhaps with cameos at third.

THE FUTURE: Binelas should open 2022 at High-A Greenville, with a chance to advance to Double-A by the end of the season if he can control his strikeout rate. He profiles as a bottom-half-of-the-order power hitter with enough thunder to remain valuable even if he's limited to first base.

Year	Age	Club (Level)	Lge	AVG	G	AB	R	H	2B	3B	HR	RBI	BB	SO	SB	OBP	SLG
2021	21	Brewers Gold (R)	ACL	.286	7	21	4	6	0	0	0	2	5	6	1	.444	.286
	21	Carolina (LoA)	East	.314	29	118	29	37	11	0	9	27	12	33	0	.379	.636
Minor League Totals (1 year)				.309	36	139	33	43	11	0	9	29	17	39	1	.390	.583

18 BRAINER BONACI, SS

Born: July 9, 2002. **B-T:** B-R. **HT:** 5-10. **WT:** 175. **Signed:** Venezuela, 2018. **Signed by:** Manny Padron/Junior Vizcaino/Eddie Romero.

BA GRADE
45 Risk: High

TRACK RECORD: The Red Sox believed that Bonaci had the potential for a well-rounded skill set when they signed him for $290,000, and that view remains intact after the switch-hitter posted a .245/.336/.383 line with 20 extra-base hits and 12 steals in as many attempts over 49 games between the Florida Complex League and Low-A Salem in 2021.

SCOUTING REPORT: Bonaci had good feel for both sides of the ball as an amateur, and then added muscle after signing in 2018. While he lost some of his physical gains during the pandemic (something he planned to address by working out in the offseason in Florida), as an 18-year-old, he showed feel to hit and unusual plate discipline given his age. While he moved from short to second to accommodate Marcelo Mayer, Bonaci adapted well to that position and appears capable of developing at both middle-infield positions, with a chance to develop into average or better power given his feel for the barrel and approach. He runs well and shows good instincts on the bases.

THE FUTURE: Bonaci seems likely to open 2022 back in Low-A Salem, but with a chance to move up at midseason and remain on a more aggressive development path than peers in his signing class. He has the potential to emerge as an everyday middle infielder with near-average or better tools across the board who, as a switch-hitter, may avoid platoon confinement.

Year	Age	Club (Level)	Lge	AVG	G	AB	R	H	2B	3B	HR	RBI	BB	SO	SB	OBP	SLG
2021	18	Red Sox (R)	FCL	.252	36	139	27	35	13	1	2	17	21	37	12	.358	.403
2021	18	Salem (LoA)	East	.224	13	49	5	11	3	1	0	8	3	8	0	.269	.327
Minor League Totals (2 years)				.264	110	417	66	110	30	4	5	62	47	85	30	.347	.391

19 THADDEUS WARD, RHP

Born: Jan. 16, 1997. **B-T:** R-R. **HT:** 6-3. **WT:** 192. **Drafted:** Central Florida, 2018 (5th round). **Signed by:** Stephen Hargett.

BA GRADE
50 Risk: Extreme

TRACK RECORD: The Red Sox saw untapped potential when scouting Ward as a sinker/slider swingman in college. Improved velocity and the development of a cutter in 2019—as well as work on a changeup and four-seamer—gave him a mix that contributed to one of the lowest ERAs (2.14) and highest strikeout rates (29.9%) of any pitcher to throw 100 innings. But after the shutdown of 2020, Ward made just two appearances in Double-A Portland in 2021 before blowing out his elbow in May and having Tommy John surgery in June.

SCOUTING REPORT: In 2019, Ward worked largely at 93-96 mph with his sinker while showing a slider with plus potential. Both the cutter and slider tunneled well off his sinker. The changeup was a point of emphasis for Ward during the 2020 shutdown. He is a good athlete with a repeatable delivery that created the expectation of control gains—but, of course, the return from Tommy John could set back that anticipated progression.

THE FUTURE: Ward seemed a candidate to fast-track after 2019, but the lost 2020 season followed by Tommy John surgery altered that trajectory completely and resulted in the Red Sox leaving him off the 40-man (and Rule 5 eligible) after the 2021 campaign. Pre-surgery, he had a No. 4 starter's ceiling with a middle-innings floor and a potential 2021 or 2022 big league debut. Now, it would represent success for him to return to the mound in games in 2022.

Year	Age	Club (Level)	Lge	W	L	ERA	G	GS	IP	H	HR	BB	SO	BB/9	SO/9	WHIP	AVG
2021	24	Portland (AA)	NEast	0	0	5.63	2	2	8	11	0	5	11	5.6	12.4	2.00	.324
Minor League Totals (4 years)				8	8	2.61	38	38	165	133	8	74	195	4.03	10.61	1.25	.220

20 MIGUEL BLEIS, OF

BA GRADE

50 Risk: Extreme

Born: March 1, 2004. **B-T:** R-R. **HT:** 6-3. **WT:** 170. **Signed:** Dominican Republic, $1.5 million. **Signed by:** Eddie Romero/Manny Nanita.

TRACK RECORD: The Red Sox signed Bleis to a $1.5 million bonus in January 2021 based on his size, athleticism and what assistant general manager Eddie Romero described as "extreme bat life." His solid performance in the DSL as a 17-year-old in 2021 (.252/.331/.420 with four homers and seven steals) did nothing to dispel that perception.

SCOUTING REPORT: Bleis has the hands and wrists to generate outstanding bat speed and loud contact with atypical frequency at a young age. He often features a fairly significant leg kick in his load, but has the athleticism and balance to make it work. He'll also adjust his swing and approach from that power-generating load, showing the ability to make mechanical adjustments to create a solid hit tool. In the outfield, he glides to the ball with speed and routes that seem suited to sticking in center.

THE FUTURE: Bleis is among the most exciting prospects in the system. He'll start progressing in the States in 2022. He's years away from the big leagues but has the potential to be an everyday player in center.

Year	Age	Club (Level)	Lge	AVG	G	AB	R	H	2B	3B	HR	RBI	BB	SO	SB	OBP	SLG
2021	17	Red Sox Red (R)	DSL	.252	36	119	17	30	6	1	4	17	12	25	7	.331	.420
Minor League Totals (1 year)				.252	36	119	17	30	6	1	4	17	12	25	7	.331	.420

21 CONNOR SEABOLD, RHP

BA GRADE

40 Risk: Medium

Born: Jan. 24, 1996. **B-T:** R-R. **HT:** 6-2. **WT:** 190. **Drafted:** Cal State Fullerton, 2017 (3rd round). **Signed by:** Demerius Pittman (Phillies).

TRACK RECORD: The Red Sox acquired Seabold and Nick Pivetta from the Phillies in August 2020 in exchange for relievers Brandon Workman and Heath Hembree, an imbalanced trade that could become more lopsided if Seabold emerges as a big league contributor. Though slowed by elbow inflammation to start the year, Seabold—true to the form he'd shown in the Phillies system—displayed a good feel for a four-pitch mix while going 4-3 with a 3.50 ERA, 22.9% strikeout rate and 8.4% walk rate in 54 Triple-A innings. He also made his big league debut (a three-inning start) in September.

SCOUTING REPORT: At his best, Seabold features a low-90s fastball that tops out in the mid 90s, but his velocity fluctuated (perhaps a reflection of his elbow issue), as he sometimes pitched closer to 88-91 mph. His changeup has swing-and-miss action though when his velocity is down, it becomes easier to spoil or put in play. Seabold also throws a slider and added a curveball to his mix in 2021. While the changeup shows potential as an above-average offering, his strongest attributes are his feel for sequencing and the ability to command his pitches in the zone. Durability and health are concerns for the slight righthander, who has thrown just over 150 professional innings since the start of 2019.

THE FUTURE: Seabold represents big league-ready, optionable depth for the Red Sox entering the 2022 season, with a chance to emerge at some point as a back-of-the-rotation option if healthy.

Year	Age	Club (Level)	Lge	W	L	ERA	G	GS	IP	H	HR	BB	SO	BB/9	SO/9	WHIP	AVG
2021	25	Red Sox (R)	FCL	0	0	3.18	2	2	5	3	0	3	12	4.8	19.1	1.06	.136
	25	Worcester (AAA)	East	4	3	3.50	11	11	54	43	6	19	52	3.2	8.7	1.15	.215
	25	Boston (MLB)	AL	0	0	6.00	1	1	3	3	1	2	0	6.0	0.0	1.67	.300
Major League Totals (1 year)				0	0	6.00	1	1	3	3	1	2	0	6.00	0.00	1.67	.300
Minor League Totals (5 years)				15	13	3.51	53	47	256	209	25	68	267	2.39	9.37	1.08	.218

22 CEDDANNE RAFAELA, OF/3B

BA GRADE

45 Risk: High

Born: Sept. 18, 2000. **B-T:** R-R. **HT:** 5-8. **WT:** 152. **Signed:** Curacao, 2017. **Signed by:** Dennis Neuman/Rollie Pino/Todd Claus.

TRACK RECORD: Rafaela has commanded attention since signing for $10,000 as someone whose tools vastly exceed his size. He's posted solid numbers throughout his career, including a .251/.305/.424 line with 10 homers and 23 steals in 102 games in Low-A Salem in 2021. Yet it was his defense that truly stood out. Rafaela, who'd moved around the infield in 2018-19, emerged as a dazzling outfielder in 2021, grading as easily the best in the system while opening a path as a super-utility player.

SCOUTING REPORT: Rafaela's unexpected bat speed is particularly apparent against lefties (.267/.304/.627 with four homers). His speed shows up on the bases and in the field, where Rafaela takes excellent routes and jumps on hard-to-reach contact to the outfield. His arm grades as above-average to plus in both the infield and outfield. His bat-to-ball skills are a double-edged sword, as he had a reasonable 18.3% strikeout rate but with a tendency to chase pitches on which he made weak contact. His 5.8% walk rate is concerning, and he'll need to hone his approach to have a chance to be more than a glove-first reserve.

THE FUTURE: With greater selectivity, Rafaela could become a super-utility player who is a plus defender at every position. If that doesn't happen, he looks like a valuable reserve who can fill in anywhere.

Year	Age	Club (Level)	Lge	AVG	G	AB	R	H	2B	3B	HR	RBI	BB	SO	SB	OBP	SLG
2021	20	Salem (LoA)	East	.251	102	394	73	99	20	9	10	53	25	79	23	.305	.424
Minor League Totals (4 years)				.255	200	761	134	194	30	15	19	99	53	149	51	.313	.409

23 GILBERTO JIMENEZ, OF

BA GRADE

50 Risk: Extreme

Born: July 8, 2000. **B-T:** B-R. **HT:** 5-11. **WT:** 212. **Signed:** Dominican Republic, 2017. **Signed by:** Eddie Romero/Manny Nanita.

TRACK RECORD: Since signing for $10,000, Jimenez has stood out as one of the best athletes in the system. The Red Sox hoped that his athleticism, hand-eye coordination and high contact rates would lead to five-tool impact. He hit for average at Low-A in 2021 but with little power.

SCOUTING REPORT: Jimenez, a natural righthanded hitter, took on switch-hitting upon entry into the Red Sox system and is still working to define his swing. He's a free-swinger who has produced a sky-high groundball rate. The Red Sox are trying to get him to be more upright in the box to gain leverage and tap into his considerable raw strength. Though he possesses double-plus speed once underway, it hasn't translated yet to stolen bases, creating concern about his reads. Speed and a powerful arm give him the chance to be an above-average outfielder in center or right.

THE FUTURE: Jimenez still has the tools to put the ball in play and use his speed to make an impact on the bases and defensively, but he'll need to start squaring up the ball to maintain that outlook.

Year	Age	Club (Level)	Lge	AVG	G	AB	R	H	2B	3B	HR	RBI	BB	SO	SB	OBP	SLG
2021	20	Salem (LoA)	East	.306	94	373	64	114	16	6	3	56	19	86	13	.346	.405
Minor League Totals (4 years)				.324	220	864	141	280	37	17	6	97	51	164	43	.370	.427

24 NATHAN HICKEY, C

BA GRADE

45 Risk: High

Born: Nov. 23, 1999. **B-T:** L-R. **HT:** 6-0. **WT:** 210. **Drafted:** Florida, 2021 (5th round). **Signed by:** Dante Ricciardi.

TRACK RECORD: Hickey posted a .316/.436/.539 line with nine homers in 60 games as a draft-eligible redshirt freshman in 2021. The Red Sox made a bet on his ability to continue catching, signing him to a $1 million bonus after taking him in the fifth round.

SCOUTING REPORT: Hickey features an unusual offensive profile for a catcher. He knows both the strike zone and his strengths within it, resulting in a 15.3% walk rate in college in 2021 compared to a strikeout rate of 14.2%. He makes plenty of hard contact, especially on pitches down in the zone, with the potential for an above-average hit tool and strength to suggest untapped power potential. He's far from a sure bet to stay behind the plate, where he lacks agility and technical polish when both receiving and blocking. While he has solid arm strength, he ended his 2021 college season at third base.

THE FUTURE: Hickey may move more deliberately than other college players with his offensive profile given the need to develop behind the plate, but he'll be given every chance to develop into a bat-first everyday catcher. If he can't stay at the position, he could fit in a corner.

Year	Age	Club (Level)	Lge	AVG	G	AB	R	H	2B	3B	HR	RBI	BB	SO	SB	OBP	SLG
2021	21	Red Sox (R)	FCL	.250	8	20	4	5	2	0	0	1	6	8	0	.429	.350
	21	Salem (LoA)	East	.125	3	8	1	1	0	0	0	1	3	2	0	.333	.125
Minor League Totals (1 year)				.214	11	28	5	6	2	0	0	2	9	10	0	.400	.286

25 DAVID HAMILTON, SS/2B

BA GRADE
45 Risk: High

Born: Sept. 29, 1997. **B-T:** L-R. **HT:** 5-10. **WT:** 175. **Drafted:** Texas, 2019 (8th round). **Signed by:** KJ Hendricks (Brewers).

TRACK RECORD: Hamilton's defense and on-base skills impressed as a sophomore at Texas, but a torn Achilles created concern that his exceptional speed might be diminished. The Brewers took him in the eighth round and signed him for $400,000. With the 2020 minor league season canceled, he played in an independent league, going 20-for-20 in steals. The Red Sox acquired him with Alex Binelas after the season in a trade sending Hunter Renfroe to Milwaukee.

SCOUTING REPORT: Hamilton has standout speed and timing, helping him both as a basestealer and giving him good lateral range in the middle infield. He has advanced pitch recognition and a good sense of the strike zone with strength in his swing, but he sometimes gets in trouble making hollow contact while trying to elevate the ball. He's at his best drilling firm liners to the gaps, something he did a lot against righties but not so much against southpaws. He has the lateral range for short but a fringy arm.

THE FUTURE: Hamilton's contact, speed and defense offer an old-school top-of-the-order skill set, while likely making him a valued part-timer against righties now.

Year	Age	Club (Level)	Lge	AVG	G	AB	R	H	2B	3B	HR	RBI	BB	SO	SB	OBP	SLG
2021	23	Wisconsin (HiA)	Cent	.263	68	270	50	71	14	7	5	31	35	58	41	.351	.422
	23	Biloxi (AA)	South	.248	33	133	16	33	5	4	3	12	15	32	11	.322	.414
Minor League Totals (2 years)				.258	101	403	66	104	19	11	8	43	50	90	52	.341	.419

26 CHRISTIAN KOSS, SS/2B

BA GRADE
40 Risk: High

Born: Jan. 27, 1998. **B-T:** R-R. **HT:** 6-1. **WT:** 182. **Drafted:** UC Irvine, 2019 (12th round). **Signed by:** Jon Lukens (Rockies).

TRACK RECORD: Koss had a strong Cape Cod League summer in 2018 but a junior year struggle dropped him to a 12th-round pick by the Rockies in 2019. He bounced back with a strong debut in the Pioneer League with impressive defense at short. The Red Sox acquired him after 2020 in exchange for lefthander Yoan Aybar, and Koss delivered a solid all-around season with High-A.

SCOUTING REPORT: Koss makes hard contact with a compact righthanded swing that is geared more for an up-the-middle approach with all-fields contact than power. That said, even while he grades as below-average in terms of power, he does have the strength to clear the fences from left to center. Koss spent all of 2021 at shortstop and showed the ability, body control and athleticism to make plus plays with a solid arm at the position. He's already seen time in pro ball at second and short, and some evaluators believe that he has the speed and reads to add outfield to his repertoire. He is an above-average runner.

THE FUTURE: Koss has the defensive ability and hit tool to project as a utilityman with at least the ability to get in the lineup against lefties and could make more contact against righties than a pure platoon player.

Year	Age	Club (Level)	Lge	AVG	G	AB	R	H	2B	3B	HR	RBI	BB	SO	SB	OBP	SLG
2021	23	Greenville (HiA)	East	.271	104	428	65	116	18	7	15	55	31	100	10	.325	.451
Minor League Totals (3 years)				.290	157	618	110	179	29	11	26	106	66	143	20	.366	.498

27 RONALDO HERNANDEZ, C

BA GRADE
40 Risk: High

Born: Nov. 11, 1997. **B-T:** R-R. **HT:** 6-1. **WT:** 230. **Signed:** Colombia, 2014. **Signed by:** Angel Contreras (Rays).

TRACK RECORD: The Red Sox acquired Hernandez from the Rays prior to the 2021 season. He hit .326/.369/.568 with 10 homers over his last 63 games at Double-A and Triple-A.

SCOUTING REPORT: Hernandez has significant raw power that shows up in games when he gets the barrel to the ball, something that can be challenging despite his solid contact rate due to a lack of plate discipline. Still, if he remains at catcher, his power would allow his offense to stand out at the position even if he grades as a 35 or 40 hitter. There's industry skepticism about his ability to stay behind the plate given technical shortcomings as a receiver and blocker, but the Red Sox were encouraged by progress he made in his receiving at the bottom of the zone and his blocking after going to one knee.

THE FUTURE: If Hernandez stays behind the plate, he could have a long career as a backup. The 2022 season is his last with an option.

Year	Age	Club (Level)	Lge	AVG	G	AB	R	H	2B	3B	HR	RBI	BB	SO	SB	OBP	SLG
2021	23	Portland (AA)	NEast	.280	92	336	44	94	26	1	16	53	11	70	0	.319	.506
	23	Worcester (AAA)	East	.333	7	27	1	9	3	0	0	5	1	7	0	.400	.444
Minor League Totals (7 years)				.291	432	1634	235	476	102	7	57	276	99	268	22	.340	.467

28 EDDINSON PAULINO, 3B/2B

BA GRADE

45 Risk: Extreme

Born: July 2, 2002. **B-T:** L-R. **HT:** 5-10. **WT:** 155. **Signed:** Dominican Republic, 2018. **Signed by:** Esau Medina/Eddie Romero

TRACK RECORD: Signed for just over $200,000 on the day he turned 16, Paulino has what one evaluator described as "special hand-eye coordination" that, in tandem with good swing decisions, has allowed him to excel in the DSL in 2019 and the Florida Complex League in 2021.
SCOUTING REPORT: Though Paulino looks like someone who might be knocked over by a fastball, he consistently finds the barrel against heaters in the strike zone, resulting in hard contact. He possesses a line drive stroke best geared for singles and doubles, projecting for below-average power despite his ability to square up pitches. His 11.3% walk rate and 15.8% strikeout rate highlight both his bat-to-ball skills and his plate discipline. He shows the agility to move around the infield with the potential to be average at multiple positions and his solid speed should result in some exposure in center field as he progresses.
THE FUTURE: After his standout performance in the FCL, Paulino should get his first taste of full-season ball in 2022. He joins the growing list of versatile, athletic, multi-positional Red Sox infielders.

Year	Age	Club (Level)	Lge	AVG	G	AB	R	H	2B	3B	HR	RBI	BB	SO	SB	OBP	SLG
2021	18	Red Sox (R)	FCL	.336	36	113	25	38	16	4	0	13	15	21	5	.436	.549
Minor League Totals (2 years)				.312	71	221	42	69	18	8	0	23	33	44	7	.415	.466

29 CONNOR WONG, C

BA GRADE

40 Risk: High

Born: May 19, 1996. **B-T:** R-R. **HT:** 6-1. **WT:** 181. **Drafted:** Houston, 2017 (3rd round). **Signed by:** Clint Bowers (Dodgers).

TRACK RECORD: The Red Sox acquired Wong from the Dodgers in the Mookie Betts trade, believing he had both growth potential behind the plate as well as the athleticism to move around the field in a reserve role. He stayed behind the plate all year and made his big league debut.
SCOUTING REPORT: Wong has wiry strength that helped contribute to solid power totals in the Dodgers system, but against Triple-A competition, pitchers exploited his pull-heavy approach by pitching away and getting weaker contact. He showed the ability to diversify his swing and line the ball to the opposite field in his big league cameo, giving hope that he could develop into a fringy hitter, though perhaps without much power. Wong is a terrific athlete who has emerged as a capable presence behind the plate. He's refined his receiving to the point of being at least average behind the plate, and while he has just average arm strength, his quick feet and transfer allow him to do a decent job of controlling the running game.
THE FUTURE: Wong's defense has developed to the point where he should have a future as a backup catcher—with the potential to add to his profile by moving around the infield.

Year	Age	Club (Level)	Lge	AVG	G	AB	R	H	2B	3B	HR	RBI	BB	SO	SB	OBP	SLG
2021	25	Worcester (AAA)	East	.256	50	199	22	51	13	0	8	26	9	58	7	.288	.442
2021	25	Boston (MLB)	AL	.308	6	13	3	4	1	1	0	1	1	7	0	.357	.538
Major League Totals (1 year)				.308	6	13	3	4	1	1	0	1	1	7	0	.357	.538
Minor League Totals (5 years)				.272	291	1103	161	300	63	9	56	186	86	366	25	.333	.498

30 NOAH SONG, RHP

BA GRADE

45 Risk: Extreme

Born: May 28, 1997. **B-T:** R-R. **HT:** 6-4. **WT:** 200. **Drafted:** Navy, 2019 (4th round). **Signed by:** Reed Gragnani.

TRACK RECORD: Song was one of the best college pitchers in the 2019 draft but slipped to the Red Sox in the fourth round based on the uncertainty created by his military commitment. He was given permission by the Navy to delay his report date to flight school, and dazzled in both the New York-Penn League and pitching for Team USA in the Premier12. But his petition to serve as a reservist while advancing in pro ball stalled amidst Department of Defense personnel and policy changes, leaving Song in limbo. He dropped the petition in mid 2020 and trained to be a pilot throughout 2021.
SCOUTING REPORT: No one has seen Song pitch since the Premier12 in November 2019, but when he was last on the mound, he showed mid-to-upper-90s four-seam velocity, a swing-and-miss slider, the potential for a solid to plus curveball and changeup and a repeatable, athletic delivery.
THE FUTURE: It's hard to know if Song will ever pitch professionally again, and if he does, whether he'll look anything like he did in 2019, when he showed mid-rotation potential.

Year	Age	Club (Level)	Lge	W	L	ERA	G	GS	IP	H	HR	BB	SO	BB/9	SO/9	WHIP	AVG
2021	24	Did not play															
Minor League Totals (2 years)				0	0	1.06	7	7	17.0	10	0	5	19	2.65	10.06	0.88	.167

MORE PROSPECTS TO KNOW

31 JEREMY WU-YELLAND, LHP
Wu-Yelland features the potential to dominate in the late innings thanks to a mid-90s fastball and hard slider from a low arm slot.

32 CHIH-JUNG LIU, RHP
Liu remains early in his pitching development, but features a broad array of up to a half-dozen pitches. If he can regain the mid-to-high-90s velocity he showed in Taiwan as an amateur, he could emerge as a mid-rotation starter.

33 JHOSTYNXON GARCIA, OF
Garcia had a head-turning debut in the DSL, showing a mature approach at the plate (.424 OBP) to go with a center fielder's instincts and athleticism and the potential for an average hit tool and power.

34 NATHANAEL CRUZ, RHP
SLEEPER
When healthy—which hasn't been often in his pro career—Cruz shows the potential for a four-pitch mix anchored by a mid-90s fastball.

35 MIGUEL UGUETO, OF
At 18, Ugueto put up a terrific .331/.370/.528 line as an 18-year-old in the FCL. He shows power potential but may be limited to left field.

36 BRADLEY BLALOCK, RHP
Blalock made a velocity bump from the high 80s to the low-to-mid 90s during the pandemic, and showed feel for three pitches during his first full pro season in 2021, when he struck out 21.8% of batters while posting a 4.27 ERA in 23 starts as a 21-year-old.

37 LUIS PERALES, RHP
Perales has an amazing arm, and was touching 98 mph in Dominican instructs after the 2021 season. But health issues (including a non-UCL arm injury) have limited him to two professional innings since he signed in 2019.

38 JUAN CHACON, OF
Chacon showed five-tool potential when the Red Sox signed him out of Venezuela for $900,000 in 2019, and his pandemic-delayed pro debut in the DSL in 2021 showed inconsistent flashes of that promise.

39 NICK DECKER, OF
At 21, Decker still displayed some of the lively tools in Low-A Salem that convinced the Red Sox to make him a second-rounder in 2018. His bat speed suggests potential impact, but he's struggled to stay healthy enough to prove it.

40 BRENDAN CELLUCCI, LHP
Though Cellucci struggled at times in High-A Greenville in 2021, he struck out 34% of batters while showing the fastball/breaking ball combination to move quickly if he ever harnesses his control.

TOP PROSPECTS OF THE DECADE

Year	Player, Pos	2021 Org
2012	Will Middlebrooks, 3B	Did not play
2013	Xander Bogaerts, SS	Red Sox
2014	Xander Bogaerts, SS/3B	Red Sox
2015	Blake Swihart, C	Nationals
2016	Yoan Moncada, 3B	White Sox
2017	Andrew Benintendi, OF	Royals
2018	Jay Groome, LHP	Red Sox
2019	Bobby Dalbec, 3B	Red Sox
2020	Triston Casas, 1B	Red Sox
2021	Triston Casas, 1B	Red Sox

TOP DRAFT PICKS OF THE DECADE

Year	Player, Pos	2021 Org
2012	Deven Marrero, SS	Marlins
2013	Trey Ball, LHP	Did not play
2014	Michael Chavis, SS	Pirates
2015	Andrew Benintendi, OF	Royals
2016	Jay Groome, LHP	Red Sox
2017	Tanner Houck, RHP	Red Sox
2018	Triston Casas, 3B	Red Sox
2019	Cameron Cannon, SS (2nd round)	Red Sox
2020	Nick Yorke, 2B	Red Sox
2021	Marcelo Mayer, SS	Red Sox

Chicago Cubs

BY KYLE GLASER

The Cubs best run of success in the past century ended in 2021. Now comes the challenge of once again trying to build a championship contender from the ground up.

The Cubs went 71-91 last season, their first losing record in seven years, and saw the departure of most of the remaining players who led the team to its first World Series championship since 1908.

The Cubs telegraphed a rebuild was near when they traded ace Yu Darvish to the Padres for Zach Davies and four teenaged prospects—three of whom had yet to play a professional game—before the season. After briefly flirting with contention early in the year, they lost 22 of 30 games going into the trade deadline and tore it all down. The Cubs traded cornerstones Anthony Rizzo, Kris Bryant and Javier Baez in addition to Craig Kimbrel, Joc Pederson, Ryan Tepera, Andrew Chafin, Jake Marisnick and Trevor Williams in a 15-day span in July In return, they received 10 prospects and young big leaguers Nick Madrigal and Codi Heuer.

The moves bolstered the Cubs farm system and pivoted the franchise's focus to the future. To that end, the Cubs hired former Cleveland executive Carter Hawkins to be the club's general manager after the season. Hawkins earned a strong reputation for player development during his 14 seasons in Cleveland's front office and will be tasked with overseeing Chicago's next wave of talent.

Still, while the Cubs prospect base is now stronger than it previously was, the team's return to contention will take time.

Only one of the Cubs' top 20 prospects has reached Triple-A. The players they acquired at the deadline were overwhelmingly in the Class A levels or below, with many yet to play above the complex leagues.

Additionally, the Cubs farm system was hit hard by injuries in 2021. Three of the Cubs top five prospects finished the season on the injured list including top pitching prospect Brailyn Marquez, who missed the entire season with a shoulder strain. Well-regarded pitching prospects Kohl Franklin (oblique) and Riley Thompson (shoulder) also missed the entire year, while talented righthanders Michael McAvene (elbow), Chris Clarke (hip) and Ben Leeper (elbow) missed significant time. The franchise's Double-A affiliate, the Tennessee Smokies, had a Covid-19 outbreak at the end of August that led to many of the club's top players finishing the year on the injured list.

On the positive side, outfielder Brennen Davis rocketed from High-A to Triple-A and won Futures Game MVP after hitting two home runs

Willson Contreras was the lone core position player left from the 2016 World Series champs.

PROJECTED 2025 LINEUP

Catcher	Miguel Amaya	26
First Base	Frank Schwindel	33
Second Base	Nick Madrigal	28
Third Base	Patrick Wisdom	33
Shortstop	Nico Hoerner	28
Left Field	Owen Caissie	22
Center Field	Pete Crow-Armstrong	23
Right Field	Brennen Davis	25
Designated Hitter	Ian Happ	30
No. 1 Starter	Brailyn Marquez	26
No. 2 Starter	Adbert Alzolay	30
No. 3 Starter	Jordan Wicks	25
No. 4 Starter	Caleb Kilian	28
No. 5 Starter	DJ Herz	24
Closer	Codi Heuer	28

at Coors Field. Shortstop Cristian Hernandez showed immense promise in his pro debut in the Dominican Summer League after the Cubs signed him for the largest bonus they've ever given to an international amateur. Lefthander D.J. Herz took a huge step forward at the Class A levels to give the Cubs a promising starting pitching prospect and the selection of Kansas State lefthander Jordan Wicks in the first round of the 2021 draft gave the organization another.

The Cubs' primary focus now is ensuring those prospects are developed to their fullest potential. How well they accomplish that goal will determine when, and if, the franchise return to championship contention. ∎

CHICAGO CUBS

TOP 2022 ROOKIES	RANK
Brennen Davis, OF	1
BREAKOUT PROSPECTS	**RANK**
James Triantos, 3B/2B	11
Drew Gray, LHP	28

SOURCE OF TOP 30 TALENT			
Homegrown	**21**	**Acquired**	**9**
College	6	Trade	8
Junior college	0	Rule 5 draft	0
High school	6	Independent league	1
Nondrafted free agent	0	Free agent/waivers	0
International	9		

LF
Yohendrick Pinango (10)
Jordan Nwogu (23)
Yonathan Perlaza

CF
Brennen Davis (1)
Pete Crow-Armstrong (4)
Kevin Alcantara (6)
Christopher Morel (29)
Ismael Mena
Christian Franklin

RF
Owen Caissie (8)
Nelson Velazquez (15)
Alexander Canario (20)
Greg Deichmann

3B
Reggie Preciado (14)
Luis Verdugo

SS
Cristian Hernandez (2)
Kevin Made (13)
Ed Howard (17)
Pedro Ramirez

2B
James Triantos (11)
Chase Strumpf (19)
Yeison Santana (24)

1B
Alfonso Rivas (26)
Jared Young
Nelson Maldonado

C
Miguel Amaya (12)
Moises Ballesteros (25)
Pablo Aliendo
Ethan Hearn

LHP

LHSP	LHRP
Brailyn Marquez (3)	Brendon Little
Jordan Wicks (5)	Bailey Horn
DJ Herz (9)	Burl Carraway
Drew Gray (28)	Jack Patterson

RHP

RHSP	RHRP
Caleb Kilian (7)	Manuel Rodriguez (27)
Ryan Jensen (16)	Ben Leeper (30)
Kohl Franklin (18)	Ethan Roberts
Riley Thompson (21)	Cayne Ueckert
Cory Abbott (22)	Scott Effross
Max Bain	Alexander Vizcaino
Chris Clarke	Eduarniel Nuñez
Daniel Palencia	Anderson Espinoza
Michael McAvene	Danis Correa
Matt Swarmer	
Cam Sanders	
Brad Depperman	

1 BRENNEN DAVIS, OF

Born: Nov. 2, 1999. **B-T:** R-R. **HT:** 6-4. **WT:** 210.
Drafted: HS—Chandler, Ariz., 2018 (2nd round).
Signed by: Steve McFarland.

TRACK RECORD: Davis is the son of former NBA point guard Reggie Theus, but his father is not a part of his life. He was raised by his mother Jakki, a former standout long jumper at Washington, on a ranch in Arizona, where he tended to goats, llamas, chickens, horses, cats, dogs and other animals as part of his childhood responsibilities growing up. Davis grew into a multi-sport standout and helped Basha (Chandler, Ariz.) High win the Arizona 6A state basketball championship as a junior while being named his region's defensive player of the year, but he stopped playing basketball as a senior to focus on baseball full-time. The decision paid off when the Cubs drafted him in the second round and signed him for an above-slot $1.1 million bonus to forgo a Miami commitment. After being limited by a broken finger in his first full season and spending 2020 at the alternate training site, Davis broke out in 2021. He missed the start of the season after he was hit by a pitch in the face during spring training and suffered a broken nose and a concussion, but he still rose from High-A to Triple-A and led all Cubs full-season minor leaguers in runs (66), doubles (25) and OPS (.869). He hit two home runs at the Futures Game in Denver and was named MVP.

SCOUTING REPORT: Davis is built like a basketball player with his long, lean 6-foot-4 frame. His long arms create excellent leverage in his swing and help him generate plus power to his pull side. He has progressively filled out as he's matured and still has room to get stronger and add more power. Davis' long levers previously made it difficult for him to be on time against fastballs, but he adjusted his swing to be shorter and quicker and now has no trouble catching up to velocity. He turns around both fastballs and breaking balls, covers the entire plate and drives the ball hard to all fields. Davis occasionally expands the strike zone, especially against secondary pitches down and away from lefthanded pitchers, but he generally forces pitchers to throw strikes. He projects to be an average hitter as long he maintains his patient approach and swing adjustments. Davis is a plus runner who uses his speed more effectively in the outfield than on the basepaths. He effortlessly runs down fly balls in all directions and projects to be an above-average defender in center field. He may slow down as he fills out and move to right field, where

BRIAN WESTERHOLT/FOUR SEAM IMAGES

BA GRADE	SCOUTING GRADES
60 Risk: Medium	Hit: 50. Power: 60. Run: 60. Field: 55. Arm: 60.

Projected future grades on 20-80 scouting scale

BEST TOOLS

Best Hitter for Average	Yohendrick Pinango
Best Power Hitter	Owen Caissie
Best Strike-Zone Discipline	Miguel Amaya
Fastest Baserunner	Ismael Mena
Best Athlete	Brennen Davis
Best Fastball	Ryan Jensen
Best Curveball	Riley Thompson
Best Slider	Manuel Rodriguez
Best Changeup	Jordan Wicks
Best Control	Caleb Kilian
Best Defensive Catcher	Pablo Aliendo
Best Defensive Infielder	Ed Howard
Best Infield Arm	Christopher Morel
Best Defensive Outfielder	Pete Crow-Armstrong
Best Outfield Arm	Nelson Velazquez

his plus arm strength will fit. Davis is a thoughtful, charitable individual who offered to pay off his mom's house with his signing bonus and donated 40 pairs of cleats to his high school. He continues to care for his pet llamas, Marco and Polo, in the offseason.

THE FUTURE: Davis has the talent to be an all-star and the personality to be a fan favorite in Chicago. He is likely to begin the 2022 season back at Triple-A, but with the Cubs firmly in a rebuilding period, his major league debut should come in 2022. ◼

Year	Age	Club (Level)	Lge	AVG	G	AB	R	H	2B	3B	HR	RBI	BB	SO	SB	OBP	SLG
2021	21	South Bend (HiA)	Cent	.321	8	28	6	9	2	0	2	5	3	6	2	.406	.607
	21	Tennessee (AA)	South	.252	76	266	50	67	20	0	13	36	36	97	6	.367	.474
	21	Iowa (AAA)	East	.268	15	56	10	15	3	0	4	12	11	15	0	.397	.536
Minor League Totals (4 years)				.277	167	584	108	162	36	3	27	86	78	168	18	.383	.488

2 CRISTIAN HERNANDEZ, SS

Born: Dec. 13, 2003. **B-T:** R-R. **HT:** 6-2. **WT:** 175. **Signed:** Dominican Republic, 2021. **Signed by:** Gian Guzmán/Louie Eljaua/Alex Suarez

TRACK RECORD: Hernandez showed elite swing mechanics from an early age in the Dominican Republic and established himself as arguably the top player in the 2020-21 international signing class. The Cubs signed him for $3 million, a franchise record for an international amateur, the first day the signing period opened. Hernandez began his pro career in the Dominican Summer League and delivered a promising early return on that investment. He posted an .822 OPS with 21 stolen bases and nearly as many walks (30) as strikeouts (39).

BA GRADE

60 Risk: Extreme

SCOUTING REPORT: Hernandez is the rare explosive athlete who is also a polished hitter for his age. He generates excellent bat speed, gets on plane early and keeps his barrel through the zone for a long time. He effortlessly drives the ball hard to all fields and projects to grow into plus power as he fills out his projectable, 6-foot-2 frame. Hernandez got off to a slow start in his pro debut, but he showed the ability to adjust and caught fire at the end of the season. He has a high baseball IQ and a preternatural ability to slow the game down. Hernandez is impressively coordinated for his age and has the hands, instincts and range to be an average defender at shortstop. He may outgrow the position as he fills out and has the plus arm strength for third base if he has to move.

THE FUTURE: Hernandez has the potential to be an impact hitter in the middle of the lineup, but he's a long way away. He is set to make his U.S. debut in 2022.

SCOUTING GRADES:	Hitting: 55	Power: 60	Running: 55	Fielding: 50	Arm: 60

Year	Age	Club (Level)	Lge	AVG	G	AB	R	H	2B	3B	HR	RBI	BB	SO	SB	OBP	SLG
2021	17	Cubs Blue (R)	DSL	.285	47	158	38	45	5	1	5	22	30	39	21	.398	.424
Minor League Totals (1 year)				.285	47	158	38	45	5	1	5	22	30	39	21	.398	.424

3 BRAILYN MARQUEZ, LHP

Born: Jan. 30, 1999. **B-T:** L-L. **HT:** 6-4. **WT:** 185. **Signed:** Dominican Republic, 2015. **Signed by:** Mario Encarnacion/Jose Serra/Alex Suarez/Louie Eljaua.

TRACK RECORD: Marquez signed with the Cubs for $600,000 when he was 16 and blossomed into one of the hardest-throwing lefthanded pitchers in the minors. He made his major league debut on the final day of the 2020 season and entered last year as the Cubs' No. 1 prospect, but he contracted Covid-19 before spring training and then suffered a shoulder strain trying to build up his arm strength. His shoulder injury lingered and caused him to abort multiple rehab attempts throughout the year, and he ended up missing the entire season.

BA GRADE

55 Risk: Extreme

SCOUTING REPORT: When healthy, Marquez overwhelms hitters with a fastball that sits at 96-98 mph and touches 102 with remarkably little effort. He pairs it with a mid-to-upper 80s slider with excellent depth and a 90-91 mph changeup he sells well with his arm speed. He also developed a low-80s curveball at the alternate training site in 2020 that he can land for strikes early in counts. Marquez's stuff is overpowering, but he's only a fair athlete and struggles to repeat his delivery and release point. His fastball sails high to his arm side when his delivery is not on time and he has yet to show he can throw his slider and changeup for strikes consistently. He has stretches where he pounds the strike zone, but he also has spurts of extreme wildness. He projects to have fringe-average control overall and will have to improve both his fitness and mechanics to reach average control.

THE FUTURE: Marquez is a wild card depending on the health of his shoulder. Provided his stuff returns intact, he has a chance to be a hard-throwing, mid-rotation starter if he improves his control. If not, he has the stuff to be a closer out of the bullpen.

SCOUTING GRADES:	Fastball: 80	Slider: 60	Curveball: 40	Changeup: 50	Control: 45

Year	Age	Club (Level)	Lge	W	L	ERA	G	GS	IP	H	HR	BB	SO	BB/9	SO/9	WHIP	AVG
2021	22	Did not play—injured															
Major League Totals (1 year)				0	0	67.50	1	0	1	2	0	3	1	40.50	13.50	7.50	.500
Minor League Totals (4 years)				16	12	3.19	57	55	257	232	14	101	287	3.54	10.05	1.30	.240

4 PETE CROW-ARMSTRONG, OF

Born: March 25, 2002. **B-T:** L-L. **HT:** 6-0. **WT:** 184. **Drafted:** HS—Los Angeles, 2020 (1st round). **Signed by:** Rusty McNamara (Mets).

TRACK RECORD: Crow-Armstrong starred at Harvard-Westlake High in Los Angeles, the same school that produced Lucas Giolito, Max Fried and Jack Flaherty, and was a two-time member of USA Baseball's 18U National Team in a decorated amateur career. The Cubs nearly drafted him with their first-round pick in 2020, but ultimately opted for local shortstop Ed Howard. The Mets drafted him three picks later and signed him for $3.359 million to forgo a Vanderbilt commitment. Crow-Armstrong's pro debut in 2021 was cut short after six games by a torn labrum in his right shoulder that required season-ending surgery. Despite the injury, the Cubs still acquired him at the trade deadline for Javier Baez and Trevor Williams.

BA GRADE

55 Risk: Extreme

SCOUTING REPORT: Crow-Armstrong is slightly built but has innate instincts that help him play bigger than his size. He has a sweet lefthanded swing geared for contact, has few holes in his swing path and controls the strike zone with a disciplined approach. He doesn't hit the ball particularly hard yet, but he projects to be at least an average hitter and should grow into 10-15 home run power as he adds strength to his lithe frame. Crow-Armstrong shines most brightly on defense. He's a confident, fluid defender in center field with plus speed, elite anticipation and graceful actions. His above-average arm keeps runners from taking extra bases and rounds out his plus-plus defensive ability.

THE FUTURE: Crow-Armstrong has the skills to be a Gold Glove-winning center fielder who hits at the top or bottom of a lineup. He should have no trouble dealing with the spotlight—his parents, Ashley Crow and Matthew Armstrong, are both accomplished actors in L.A.

SCOUTING GRADES:	Hitting: 50	Power: 40	Running: 60	Fielding: 70	Arm: 55

Year	Age	Club (Level)	Lge	AVG	G	AB	R	H	2B	3B	HR	RBI	BB	SO	SB	OBP	SLG
2021	19	St. Lucie (LoA)	SEast	.417	6	24	6	10	2	0	0	4	7	6	2	.563	.500
Minor League Totals (2 years)				.417	6	24	6	10	2	0	0	4	7	6	2	.563	.500

5 JORDAN WICKS, LHP

Born: Sept. 1, 1999. **B-T:** L-L. **HT:** 6-3. **WT:** 220. **Drafted:** Kansas State, 2021 (1st round). **Signed by:** Ty Nichols.

TRACK RECORD: Wicks led the Big 12 Conference in strikeouts last spring and set Kansas State's single-season (118) and career (230) strikeout records despite playing only two full seasons due to the coronavirus pandemic. The Cubs considered him a top 10 talent in the draft and were happily surprised he was available at No. 21, where they quickly selected him to make him the first Kansas State player ever picked in the first round. Wicks signed for $3,132,300 and made his brief pro debut with four abbreviated starts at Low-A Myrtle Beach.

BA GRADE

50 Risk: High

SCOUTING REPORT: Wicks is a polished lefthander who pounds the strike zone with five pitches. His four-seam and two-seam fastball both sit 92-93 mph and touch 95, and they each play up with late movement and deception out of his slightly crossfire delivery. His four-seamer gets excellent carry through the zone with cut and ride and his two-seamer features late run. Wicks expertly mixes his secondary pitches, headlined by a plus-plus changeup that was the best in the 2021 draft class. It's a tumbling pitch with late drop in the low 80s that he sells with his arm speed and gets early swings and misses. Wicks' mid-80s slider has improved to become an above-average pitch and his upper-70s curveball is a usable offering. Wicks works quickly and fills up the strike zone with plus control. He is an outstanding teammate who is eager to learn.

THE FUTURE: Wicks has weapons to get both righthanded and lefthanded hitters out and should move quickly up the minors. He projects to settle in as a No. 3 or 4 starter similar to Marco Gonzales.

SCOUTING GRADES:	Fastball: 55	Slider: 55	Curveball: 45	Changeup: 70	Control: 60

Year	Age	Club (Level)	Lge	W	L	ERA	G	GS	IP	H	HR	BB	SO	BB/9	SO/9	WHIP	AVG
2021	21	South Bend (HiA)	Cent	0	0	5.14	4	4	7	7	0	3	5	3.9	6.4	1.43	.250
Minor League Totals (1 year)				0	0	5.14	4	4	7	7	0	3	5	3.86	6.43	1.43	.250

6 KEVIN ALCANTARA, OF

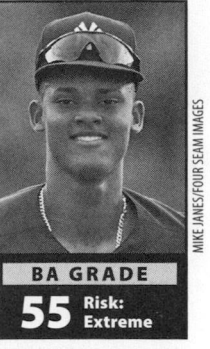

MIKE JANES/FOUR SEAM IMAGES

Born: July 12, 2002. **B-T:** R-R. **HT:** 6-6. **WT:** 188. **Signed:** Dominican Republic, 2018. **Signed by:** Edgar Mateo/Juan Piron (Yankees).

TRACK RECORD: Alcantara signed with the Yankees for $1 million during the 2018 international signing period and advanced out of the Dominican Summer League just nine games into his pro debut. He got off to a hot start during extended spring training and the beginning of the Florida Complex League season in 2021, leading the Cubs to acquire him with righthander Alexander Vizcaino for Anthony Rizzo at the trade deadline. Alcantara took off after joining the Cubs, posting a 1.024 OPS in the Arizona Complex League and becoming a scout favorite.

BA GRADE

55 Risk: Extreme

SCOUTING REPORT: Alcantara is physically gifted with his long, lean 6-foot-6 frame, growing strength and impressive athleticism. He has a balanced, powerful swing and generates plenty of leverage with his long arms. The ball jumps off his bat in the air to all fields with little effort, and he has a chance to grow into plus power as he gets stronger. Alcantara's swing gets long and will need to be shortened, but he's receptive to coaching and has already shown the ability to adjust. He recognizes spin well for his age, stays balanced through his swing and uses the whole field, giving him a chance to be an average hitter. Alcantara is a plus runner who covers lots of ground in center field with his long strides. He has a chance to stay in center but may outgrow the position as he fills out. He has average arm strength.

THE FUTURE: Alcantara's raw tools give him as much upside as anyone in the Cubs system. How his swing develops will determine whether he reaches his all-star potential.

SCOUTING GRADES:	Hitting: 50	Power: 60	Running: 55	Fielding: 55	Arm: 50

Year	Age	Club (Level)	Lge	AVG	G	AB	R	H	2B	3B	HR	RBI	BB	SO	SB	OBP	SLG
2021	18	Yankees (R)	FCL	.370	9	27	5	10	1	0	1	3	4	8	2	.452	.519
2021	18	Cubs (R)	ACL	.337	25	92	27	31	3	5	4	21	13	28	3	.415	.609
Minor League Totals (3 years)				.293	75	280	58	82	12	8	6	43	25	72	10	.357	.457

7 CALEB KILIAN, RHP

BARRY GOSSAGE/MLB PHOTOS VIA GETTY IMAGES

Born: June 2, 1997. **B-T:** R-R. **HT:** 6-4. **WT:** 180. **Drafted:** Texas Tech, 2019 (8th round). **Signed by:** Todd Thomas (Giants).

TRACK RECORD: Kilian led Texas Tech to back-to-back College World Series appearances as a member of the Red Raiders starting rotation and finished third in school history with 23 career wins. The Giants drafted him in the eighth round in 2019 and signed him for $397,500. Kilian impressed in his pro debut after signing and, after missing the 2020 season due to the coronavirus pandemic, rose to Double-A in a breakout 2021 campaign. The Cubs acquired him with outfielder Alexander Canario at the trade deadline for Kris Bryant, and Kilian continued his ascent with a star turn in the Arizona Fall League after the season.

BA GRADE

50 Risk: High

SCOUTING REPORT: Kilian previously succeeded with average stuff and plus control, but his stuff has ticked up to enhance his future outlook. His fastball now sits 91-94 mph and touches 97-98 mph. He has maintained his advanced feel for pitching through his velocity bump and manipulates his fastball to alternately give it cut, sink or ride depending on the hitter. Kilian primarily succeeds throwing different varieties of his fastball, but his curveball has improved to flash plus with good depth and he can mix in both an average cutter and changeup. Kilian locates his fastball on both edges of the plate and fills up the strike zone with all four of his pitches. He has a good feel for changing speeds and moving the ball around the strike zone.

THE FUTURE: Kilian's newfound velocity and advanced feel for pitching gives him a chance to be a mid-to-back of the rotation starter. He is in position to make his major league debut in 2022.

SCOUTING GRADES:	Fastball: 55	Curveball: 55	Cutter: 50	Changeup: 50	Control: 60

Year	Age	Club (Level)	Lge	W	L	ERA	G	GS	IP	H	HR	BB	SO	BB/9	SO/9	WHIP	AVG
2021	24	Eugene (HiA)	West	3	0	1.25	4	4	21	9	0	1	32	0.4	13.3	0.46	.122
	24	Richmond (AA)	NEast	3	2	2.43	11	11	63	51	2	8	64	1.1	9.1	0.94	.221
	24	Tennessee (AA)	South	1	2	4.02	4	4	15	15	3	4	16	2.3	9.2	1.21	.250
Minor League Totals (3 years)				7	4	2.09	26	25	116	82	5	15	129	1.16	9.98	0.83	.197

8 OWEN CAISSIE, OF

BILL MITCHELL

BA GRADE

55 Risk: **Extreme**

Born: July 8, 2002. **B-T:** L-R. **HT:** 6-4. **WT:** 190. **Drafted:** HS—Burlington, Ont., 2020 (2nd round). **Signed by:** Chris Kemlo (Padres).

TRACK RECORD: Caissie starred for the Canada's junior national team and rose to prominence as a high school senior when he hit a home run off Double-A pitcher Conner Overton that hit the batter's eye at the Blue Jays spring training stadium. The Padres drafted him 45th overall and signed him for $1.2 million, then traded him to the Cubs six months later as one of five players for Yu Darvish. Almost immediately, Caissie emerged as the best prospect in the Darvish trade. His power earned comparisons to Joey Gallo's during extended spring training and he rampaged through the Arizona Complex League with a 1.074 OPS. He finished the year with a promotion to Low-A Myrtle Beach.

SCOUTING REPORT: Caissie has the most power in the Cubs system and gets to it with remarkable ease. He has a compact, powerful lefthanded swing and keeps his barrel in the zone a long time. The ball jumps off his bat with his natural strength and leverage and frequently clears 400 feet to both his pull side and the opposite field. He puts together quality at-bats, keeps a good direction in his swing and controls the strike zone enough to project to be an average hitter with 35-plus home run power. Caissie is less refined defensively. He's a below-average right fielder who struggles with high fly balls and is short on game experience. He's a good athlete and hard worker and should improve in time. He has above-average arm strength.

THE FUTURE: Caissie checks all the boxes of a future middle-of-the-order run producer. His bat may allow him to rise quickly through the minors.

SCOUTING GRADES:	Hitting: 50	Power: 65	Running: 50	Fielding: 40	Arm: 55

Year	Age	Club (Level)	Lge	AVG	G	AB	R	H	2B	3B	HR	RBI	BB	SO	SB	OBP	SLG
2021	18	Cubs (R)	ACL	.349	32	109	20	38	7	1	6	20	26	39	1	.478	.596
	18	Myrtle Beach (LoA)	East	.233	22	73	15	17	4	0	1	9	16	28	0	.367	.329
Minor League Totals (2 years)				.302	54	182	35	55	11	1	7	29	42	67	1	.434	.489

9 D.J. HERZ, LHP

BA GRADE

50 Risk: **High**

Born: Jan. 4, 2001. **B-T:** L-R. **HT:** 6-2. **WT:** 175. **Drafted:** HS—Fayetteville, N.C., 2019 (8th round). **Signed by:** Billy Swoope.

TRACK RECORD: Herz played quarterback on the football team and guard on the basketball team in addition to being the ace lefthander at Sanford High in Fayetteville, N.C. The Cubs identified Herz early as a draft target and selected him in the eighth round in 2019, signing him for an above-slot $500,000 bonus. Herz looked primed for a breakout during 2020 spring training before the coronavirus pandemic canceled the minor league season, but he carried it over into 2021. Herz led the organization with 131 strikeouts while spending time at both Class A levels and averaged 14.4 strikeouts per nine innings, third-highest in the minors among pitchers who threw at least 80 innings.

SCOUTING REPORT: Herz is an athletic lefthander who continues to grow into more stuff every year. His fastball jumped from 88-91 to 92-95 mph and plays up with late carry and deception from his crossbody delivery. Hitters don't see his fastball and are consistently late on it. Herz's changeup has developed into a borderline plus-plus pitch with "insane" drop, in the words of one evaluator, and his tight, vertical curveball is at least an average pitch that ties up righthanded batters. Herz has three swing-and-miss pitches, but his long arm action and cross-body finish make it difficult for him to control his arsenal. He averaged nearly five walks per nine, hit eight batters and threw 14 wild pitches. His arm action also raises concerns about future injuries.

THE FUTURE: Herz has electric stuff but needs to improve his control to reach his mid-rotation potential. If he doesn't, he could still be a shutdown lefthanded reliever.

SCOUTING GRADES:	Fastball: 60	Curveball: 50	Changeup: 65	Control: 40

Year	Age	Club (Level)	Lge	W	L	ERA	G	GS	IP	H	HR	BB	SO	BB/9	SO/9	WHIP	AVG
2021	20	Myrtle Beach (LoA)	East	3	4	3.43	17	17	65	32	6	38	105	5.2	14.4	1.07	.152
	20	South Bend (HiA)	Cent	1	0	2.81	3	3	16	10	1	6	26	3.4	14.6	1.00	.175
Minor League Totals (3 years)				4	5	3.23	26	26	92	52	7	52	139	5.09	13.60	1.13	.168

10 YOHENDRICK PINANGO, OF

LARRY KAVE/MYRTLE BEACH PELICANS

Born: May 7, 2002. **B-T:** L-L. **HT:** 5-11. **WT:** 170. **Signed:** Venezuela, 2018. **Signed by:** Julio Figueroa/Hector Ortega/Louie Eljaua.

TRACK RECORD: Pinango stood out for his hitting ability as an amateur in Venezuela and signed with the Cubs for $400,000 in 2018. He lived up to the billing by leading the Dominican Summer League in hits in his pro debut and followed up by hitting .272 at offense-stifling Myrtle Beach in his first full season in 2021. He ended the year with a promotion to High-A South Bend.

SCOUTING REPORT: The best pure hitter in the Cubs system, Pinango has a quick, lefthanded swing and elite contact skills for his age. He rarely swings and misses, keeps his barrel in the zone for a long time and sprays balls from line to line. He complements those contact skills with a patient approach and is a consensus future plus hitter. Pinango swings down on the ball and mostly hits it on the ground, making it unlikely he'll ever elevate enough to be a home run threat, but he makes hard contact and posts above-average exit velocities for his age. Pinango is physically mature already and projects to be a left fielder with his average speed and arm strength. He has advanced instincts and plays under control on both sides of the ball.

THE FUTURE: Pinango's hitting ability gives him a chance to be a starting corner outfielder even with his lack of home run power. He may see Double-A as a 20-year-old in 2022.

BA GRADE

50 Risk: High

SCOUTING GRADES:	Hitting: 60	Power: 30	Running: 50	Fielding: 50	Arm: 50

Year	Age	Club (Level)	Lge	AVG	G	AB	R	H	2B	3B	HR	RBI	BB	SO	SB	OBP	SLG
2021	19	Myrtle Beach (LoA)	East	.272	84	324	50	88	16	2	4	27	24	57	8	.322	.370
	19	South Bend (HiA)	Cent	.289	24	97	9	28	4	1	1	9	7	12	0	.343	.381
Minor League Totals (2 years)				.306	170	661	102	202	40	3	5	72	58	89	35	.364	.398

11 JAMES TRIANTOS, 2B/SS

BA GRADE

55 Risk: Extreme

Born: Jan. 29, 2003. **B-T:** R-T. **HT:** 6-1. **WT:** 195. **Drafted:** HS—Vienna, Va. (2nd round). **Signed by:** Billy Swoope.

TRACK RECORD: Triantos was originally part of the 2022 draft class but reclassified for 2021. In the final game of his high school career, he took a perfect game into the seventh inning and hit the go-ahead home run to give Madison High the Virginia 6A state championship. Cubs scouting director Dan Kantrovitz was in attendance, and three weeks later the Cubs drafted Triantos in the second round. He signed for an above-slot $2.1 million.

SCOUTING REPORT: Triantos is a precocious hitter who possesses elite bat speed and an innate feel for the barrel. He consistently squares pitches up and drives them hard to all fields. He complements his physical abilities with a keen sense for making adjustments and solid plate discipline, helping him project to be a plus hitter with average power. A shortstop in high school, Triantos is now a second baseman and has a lot of work to do defensively. His hands and feet get disconnected and the game frequently speeds up on him, leading to sloppy errors. His above-average arm strength is negated by a poor arm action.

THE FUTURE: Triantos projects to hit enough to overshadow his defensive shortcomings. He'll make his full-season debut in 2022.

Year	Age	Club (Level)	Lge	AVG	G	AB	R	H	2B	3B	HR	RBI	BB	SO	SB	OBP	SLG
2021	18	Cubs (R)	ACL	.327	25	101	27	33	7	1	6	19	7	18	3	.376	.594
Minor League Totals (1 year)				.327	25	101	27	33	7	1	6	19	7	18	3	.376	.594

12 MIGUEL AMAYA, C

BA GRADE

50 Risk: High

Born: March 9, 1999. **B-T:** R-R. **HT:** 6-2. **WT:** 230. **Signed:** Panama, 2015. **Signed by:** Mario Encarnacion/Jose Serra/Alex Suarez/Louie Eljaua.

TRACK RECORD: Amaya starred for Panama at international tournaments throughout his youth and signed with the Cubs for $1 million in 2015. He received back-to-back Futures Game selections in 2018-19 and was invited to the alternate training site in 2020. Amaya opened 2021 at Double-A, but he played just 23 games before going on the injured list with forearm tightness in early June. He had a setback during his rehab and ultimately had Tommy John surgery in November.

SCOUTING REPORT: When healthy, Amaya is a well-rounded catcher who makes an impact on both sides of the ball. He is an extremely disciplined hitter who recognizes pitches and stays in the strike zone. He swings at the right pitches and has above-average power, but he frequently hits the ball on the ground and will have to learn to elevate more. Amaya is a big, physical presence behind the plate defensively.

His receiving and framing are average and he is a good blocker who keeps the ball in front of him. He shut down running games with a quick exchange and plus arm strength prior to surgery.

THE FUTURE: Amaya's surgery will keep him out all of the 2022 season. He is scheduled to return in 2023.

Year	Age	Club (Level)	Lge	AVG	G	AB	R	H	2B	3B	HR	RBI	BB	SO	SB	OBP	SLG
2021	22	Tennessee (AA)	South	.215	23	79	11	17	4	0	1	13	21	22	2	.406	.304
Minor League Totals (6 years)				.241	354	1270	165	306	75	3	28	170	157	258	15	.339	.371

13 KEVIN MADE, SS

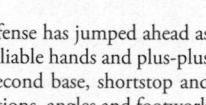

BA GRADE

50 Risk: Very High

Born: Sept. 10, 2002. **B-T:** R-R. **HT:** 5-10. **WT:** 160. **Signed:** Dominican Republic, 2019. **Signed by:** Louis Eljaua/Jose Serra/Gian Guzman.

TRACK RECORD: Made signed with the Cubs for $1.5 million as one of the top players in the 2019 international class. The Cubs pushed him aggressively in his professional debut, sending him straight to Low-A Myrtle Beach as an 18-year-old in 2021. Made impressively hit .272 facing older competition, but he also walked only six times in 58 games.

SCOUTING REPORT: Made's offense was his strength as an amateur, but his defense has jumped ahead as a pro. He is a borderline plus-plus defender at shortstop with quick reactions, reliable hands and plus-plus arm strength. Though he isn't the most electric or rangy defender, he plays second base, shortstop and third base "flawlessly" in the words of one evaluator and quickly picks up the actions, angles and footwork of each position. Made's swing is mechanically sound and he makes hard contact when he connects, but he's an extraordinarily aggressive hitter. He swings at almost any fastball and bails pitchers out by chasing fastballs well out of the strike zone. He does hit fastballs in the zone and recognizes breaking balls.

THE FUTURE: Made's defense will buy him time to improve his plate discipline. He'll move to High-A South Bend in 2022.

Year	Age	Club (Level)	Lge	AVG	G	AB	R	H	2B	3B	HR	RBI	BB	SO	SB	OBP	SLG
2021	18	Myrtle Beach (LoA)	East	.272	58	235	19	64	13	3	1	20	6	57	2	.296	.366
Minor League Totals (1 year)				.272	58	235	19	64	13	3	1	20	6	57	2	.296	.366

14 REGGIE PRECIADO, 3B

BA GRADE

50 Risk: Extreme

Born: May 16, 2003. **B-T:** B-R. **HT:** 6-5. **WT:** 185. **Signed:** Panama, 2019. **Signed by:** Chris Kemp/Richard Montenegro (Padres).

TRACK RECORD: Preciado starred for Panama in international tournaments throughout his youth and signed with the Padres for $1.3 million in 2019. He stood out during 2020 instructional league and was acquired by the Cubs as one of five players for Yu Darvish a few months later. Preciado skipped over the Dominican Summer League and made his debut in 2021 in the Arizona Complex League, where he hit .333 and finished tied for 10th in the league in hits.

SCOUTING REPORT: Preciado stands 6-foot-5 and has plenty of room to fill out his lanky frame. A switch-hitter, he has excellent hand-eye coordination, advanced barrel control and a natural feel for contact from both sides of the plate. Preciado's bat-to-ball skills and power potential give him plenty of offensive upside, but he'll need to tighten his plate discipline. He is extremely aggressive and prone to chasing pitches out of the strike zone. Preciado signed as a shortstop but has already outgrown the position. He's not particularly agile, but his reliable hands and above-average arm strength give him a chance to be an average defender at third base.

THE FUTURE: Preciado projects to be a power-hitting, everyday third baseman if he can fine-tune his approach. He'll still be 18 on Opening Day and has plenty of time.

Year	Age	Club (Level)	Lge	AVG	G	AB	R	H	2B	3B	HR	RBI	BB	SO	SB	OBP	SLG
2021	18	Cubs (R)	ACL	.333	34	141	28	47	10	3	3	25	11	35	7	.383	.511
Minor League Totals (1 year)				.333	34	141	28	47	10	3	3	25	11	35	7	.383	.511

15 NELSON VELAZQUEZ, OF

BA GRADE

45 Risk: High

Born: Dec. 26, 1998. **B-T:** R-R. **HT:** 6-0. **WT:** 190. **Drafted:** HS—Carolina, P.R., 2017 (5th round). **Signed by:** Edwards Guzman.

TRACK RECORD: Velazquez went to high school in Florida before moving back to Puerto Rico and becoming one of the island's top draft prospects in 2017. The Cubs drafted him in the fifth round and signed him for $400,000. Velazquez disappointed his first few seasons, but he began to show signs of life before the coronavirus pandemic hit. He broke out in 2021 and led the Cubs system in total bases (191) while advancing to Double-A Tennessee, then won MVP of the Arizona Fall League.

SCOUTING REPORT: Velazquez has long had loud tools and is finally turning them into production. He generates above-average power out of his compact, muscular build and has made swing adjustments to better access it. He previously struggled with fastballs and was too pull-oriented, but he flattened his swing to stay in the zone longer and now drives high-velocity fastballs to all fields. He remains prone to chasing breaking balls off the plate but makes enough contact overall to project to hit .240 with 20-plus home runs. Velazquez is a good athlete given his bulk and makes highlight-reel catches in both center and right field. He has average speed and plus arm strength.

THE FUTURE: Velazquez is on track to be at least a part-time outfielder in the majors. He was added to the 40-man roster last fall and may make his major league debut in 2022.

Year	Age	Club (Level)	Lge	AVG	G	AB	R	H	2B	3B	HR	RBI	BB	SO	SB	OBP	SLG
2021	22	South Bend (HiA)	Cent	.261	69	261	37	68	13	1	12	46	20	97	12	.321	.456
	22	Tennessee (AA)	South	.290	34	124	19	36	10	1	8	27	10	35	5	.358	.581
Minor League Totals (5 years)				.259	316	1151	160	298	64	10	45	169	98	377	42	.324	.449

16 RYAN JENSEN, RHP

BA GRADE
45 Risk: High

Born: Nov. 23, 1997. **B-T:** R-R. **HT:** 6-0. **WT:** 190. **Drafted:** Fresno State, 2019 (1st round). **Signed by:** Gape Zappin

TRACK RECORD: Jensen touched 98 mph and was the Mountain West Conference pitcher of the year as a junior at Fresno State, but the Cubs still went above industry consensus when they drafted him 27th overall in 2019. Concerns about Jensen's control appeared well-founded at the start of his full-season debut with High-A South Bend in 2021, but he locked in his delivery and release point midway through the year. He posted a 2.28 ERA in his final 11 starts and rose to Double-A.

SCOUTING REPORT: Jensen is undersized, but he is a power pitcher with a pair of plus-plus fastballs that overwhelm hitters. His four-seamer averages 96 mph and rides above barrels and his two-seamer averages 95 mph and breaks bats with its late run and bore. Jensen's mid-80s slider with lateral run is an above-average pitch and he introduced a vertical curveball last year that flashes average. His upper-80s changeup gets swings and misses in the strike zone but doesn't get chase swings. Jensen has an effortful delivery with a long arm action that leads to inconsistent mechanics and bouts of below-average control. He's a good athlete who took off when he found a consistent release point.

THE FUTURE: Jensen has the stuff to be a hard-throwing back-end starter if he maintains his delivery and release point. If not, his stuff should play in late relief.

Year	Age	Club (Level)	Lge	W	L	ERA	G	GS	IP	H	HR	BB	SO	BB/9	SO/9	WHIP	AVG
2021	23	South Bend (HiA)	Cent	2	7	4.50	16	16	62	42	8	24	75	3.5	10.9	1.06	.189
	23	Tennessee (AA)	South	1	0	3.00	4	4	18	14	2	7	15	3.5	7.5	1.17	.222
Minor League Totals (3 years)				3	7	3.91	26	26	92	63	10	45	109	4.40	10.66	1.17	.193

17 ED HOWARD, SS

BA GRADE
45 Risk: High

Born: Jan. 28, 2002. **B-T:** R-R. **HT:** 6-2. **WT:** 185. **Drafted:** HS—Chicago, 2020 (1st round). **Signed by:** John Pedrotty.

TRACK RECORD: Howard grew up on Chicago's South Side and led the city's Jackie Robinson West All-Star team to the Little League World Series in 2014. He followed with a standout career at Mount Carmel High, 15 miles south of Wrigley Field, and was drafted 16th overall by the Cubs in 2020. Howard jumped straight to Low-A Myrtle Beach for his pro debut in 2021 but struggled with the aggressive assignment. He hit just .225 with a 30% strikeout rate and missed nearly a month with a strained hamstring.

SCOUTING REPORT: Howard has long stood out for his athleticism and defense at shortstop. He is an electric, rangy defender who makes both the flashy and routine plays with his soft hands, plus arm strength and an excellent internal clock. He moves fluidly across the diamond, takes good angles to the ball and keeps his throws on target to project as a plus-plus defender. Howard's offense has further to go. He struggles to recognize or hit breaking balls and hits the ball on the ground too often. He has plenty of bat speed, shows solid hand-eye coordination and flashes average power, but his poor pitch recognition precludes him from being more than a below-average hitter.

THE FUTURE: Howard's defense will buy him time for his bat to develop. He'll start 2022 back in the Class A levels.

Year	Age	Club (Level)	Lge	AVG	G	AB	R	H	2B	3B	HR	RBI	BB	SO	SB	OBP	SLG
2021	19	Myrtle Beach (LoA)	East	.225	80	302	33	68	9	3	4	31	18	98	7	.277	.315
Minor League Totals (2 years)				.225	80	302	33	68	9	3	4	31	18	98	7	.277	.315

18 KOHL FRANKLIN, RHP

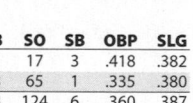

BA GRADE

50 Risk: Extreme

Born: Sept. 9, 1999. **B-T:** R-R. **HT:** 6-4. **WT:** 195. **Drafted:** HS—Broken Arrow, Okla., 2018 (6th round). **Signed by:** Ty Nichols.

TRACK RECORD: Franklin's projectable frame and athletic delivery enticed the Cubs to draft him in the sixth round in 2018 and give him an above-slot $540,000 signing bonus. He showed well during his pro debut at short-season Eugene, but injuries and the coronavirus pandemic have largely kept him off the mound in three of the last four seasons. He missed most of his senior year with a broken foot, lost 2020 due to the pandemic and missed all of last season with a strained oblique.

SCOUTING REPORT: The nephew of former closer Ryan Franklin, Kohl throws three pitches for strikes out of a loose, athletic delivery and has room to fill out his 6-foot-4 frame. His fastball sits 92-95 mph and projects to tick up as he gets stronger. He pairs his heater with a potentially plus changeup in the 80-84 mph range and an average spike curveball in the mid 70s that shows solid depth. Franklin pounds the strike zone and projects to have above-average control. His biggest question is his durability—he has thrown just 50.2 innings in four professional seasons.

THE FUTURE: Franklin began throwing bullpen sessions last fall and should be ready for 2022 spring training. He has mid-rotation potential but has to show he can stay on the mound.

Year	Age	Club (Level)	Lge	W	L	ERA	G	GS	IP	H	HR	BB	SO	BB/9	SO/9	WHIP	AVG
2021	21	Did not play—Injured															
Minor League Totals (3 years)				1	4	3.02	16	14	51	36	2	25	60	4.44	10.66	1.20	.194

19 CHASE STRUMPF, 3B/2B

BA GRADE

45 Risk: High

Born: March 8, 1998. **B-T:** R-R. **HT:** 6-1. **WT:** 191. **Drafted:** UCLA, 2019 (2nd round). **Signed by:** Tom Myers.

TRACK RECORD: Strumpf rose to prominence as the starting shortstop at national prep power JSerra High in SoCal and put together a solid three-year career at UCLA. The Cubs drafted him in the second round, No. 64 overall, and signed him for just over $1.05 million. Strumpf's full-season debut was delayed by the coronavirus pandemic, but he made up for lost time by racing to Double-A in 2021. He overcame a slow start to finish with a 1.028 OPS in his final month.

SCOUTING REPORT: Strumpf is the epitome of a "professional hitter" with a calm, patient approach, an easy swing and a natural feel for the barrel. He works counts until he gets a pitch to hit and smoothly drives balls from gap to gap. He fell into some bad habits trying to lift the ball at Double-A initially, but he eventually rediscovered his form to retain his status as a potential above-average hitter. Strumpf has sneaky power, particularly the other way to right-center, and should complement solid batting averages with double-digit homers. He is an average defender at second base and has started to play third base on occasion. He is more comfortable at second and his fringe-average arm fits best there.

THE FUTURE: Strumpf's hitting ability should make him at least a solid contributor. He'll see Triple-A in 2022.

Year	Age	Club (Level)	Lge	AVG	G	AB	R	H	2B	3B	HR	RBI	BB	SO	SB	OBP	SLG
2021	23	South Bend (HiA)	Cent	.309	16	55	15	17	4	0	0	7	7	17	3	.418	.382
	23	Tennessee (AA)	South	.211	62	213	25	45	15	0	7	29	38	65	1	.335	.380
Minor League Totals (3 years)				.236	117	403	65	95	31	0	10	53	68	124	6	.360	.387

20 ALEXANDER CANARIO, OF

BA GRADE

45 Risk: High

Born: May 7, 2000. **B-T:** R-R. **HT:** 6-1. **WT:** 165. **Signed:** Dominican Republic, 2016. **Signed by:** Ruddy Moreta (Giants).

TRACK RECORD: Canario signed with the Giants for $60,000 and quickly surpassed many players who signed for larger bonuses. He starred in both the Rookie-level Arizona League and short-season Northwest League before being invited to the Giants alternate training site in 2020, and he impressed against older competition. Canario scuffled in his full-season debut with Low-A San Jose in 2021, but the Cubs still acquired him with righthander Caleb Kilian at the trade deadline for Kris Bryant.

SCOUTING REPORT: Canario looks the part of a major leaguer with a physical, 6-foot-1 frame, good athleticism for his size and loads of strength. He has plus-plus bat speed and generates impressive torque when he rotates to produce plus-plus raw power to all fields. He hits the ball hard even when he's off-balance. Canario's power is prodigious, but he is prone to overswinging and chasing breaking balls in the dirt. His poor plate discipline limits him to a below-average hitter who may struggle to get to his power in games. Canario is an aggressive defender who plays hard in the outfield. He fits best in right field with his above-average speed and plus, accurate arm.

THE FUTURE: Canario's power gives him a carrying tool if he can get to it. He finished in High-A South Bend and may return there to start 2022.

Year	Age	Club (Level)	Lge	AVG	G	AB	R	H	2B	3B	HR	RBI	BB	SO	SB	OBP	SLG
2021	21	San Jose (LoA)	West	.235	65	238	43	56	14	3	9	29	33	79	15	.325	.433
	21	South Bend (HiA)	Cent	.224	42	170	19	38	6	1	9	28	10	46	6	.264	.429
Minor League Totals (5 years)				.267	277	1055	191	282	62	12	45	175	123	296	51	.348	.477

21 RILEY THOMPSON, RHP

BA GRADE
45 Risk: High

Born: July 9, 1996. **B-T:** L-R. **HT:** 6-4. **WT:** 210. **Drafted:** Louisville, 2018 (11th round). **Signed by:** Jacob Williams.

TRACK RECORD: Thompson had Tommy John surgery at Louisville and battled shoulder troubles after he returned, but the Cubs saw enough stuff to draft him in the 11th round and give him an above-slot $200,000 bonus. Thompson appeared to break through in 2019 at Low-A South Bend and pitched five no-hit innings with 10 strikeouts in the clinching game of the Midwest League championship series, but he hasn't pitched since. The coronavirus pandemic canceled the 2020 minor league season and he missed all of 2021 with shoulder discomfort.

SCOUTING REPORT: Thompson fits a starter's mold with a 6-foot-4, 210-pound frame and three pitches he can throw for strikes. His high-spin fastball ranges from 90-96 mph and touches higher in relief. His high-spin, mid-80s curveball is a plus pitch that puts hitters away and his average changeup with late sink gets swings and misses over the top. Thompson struggled to throw strikes in college, but he began throwing with more conviction and confidence in pro ball and now shows average control. His primary concern is durability. He has pitched more than 33 innings in a season only once in college or the minors.

THE FUTURE: Thompson started throwing bullpens in the fall and should be ready for 2022 spring training. He has starter stuff, but his health may limit him to relief.

Year	Age	Club (Level)	Lge	W	L	ERA	G	GS	IP	H	HR	BB	SO	BB/9	SO/9	WHIP	AVG
2021	24	Did not play—Injured															
Minor League Totals (3 years)				8	8	3.02	30	29	119	109	10	40	112	3.02	8.45	1.25	.242

22 CORY ABBOTT, RHP

BA GRADE
40 Risk: Medium

Born: Sept. 20, 1995. **B-T:** R-R. **HT:** 6-2. **WT:** 220. **Drafted:** Loyola Marymount, 2017 (2nd round). **Signed by:** Tom Myers.

TRACK RECORD: Abbott pitched the first perfect game in Loyola Marymount history and shot up draft boards to the second round in 2017, where the Cubs picked him 67th overall. He led the Double-A Southern League in strikeouts in 2019, but he took a step back during the coronavirus shutdown and struggled at both the alternate training site and instructional league. His struggles continued in 2021 with a 5.91 ERA at Triple-A and a 6.75 ERA in his major league debut.

SCOUTING REPORT: Abbott relies on precision more than stuff. His fastball is a fringy pitch that sits 92 mph and plays on the edges of the strike zone, but it gets crushed when he leaves it over the plate. His best pitch is a short, above-average 86-89 mph slider that gets swings and misses both in and out of the zone. His vertical mid-80s curveball is an average pitch with solid depth and he rounds out his arsenal with a rarely-used, below-average changeup. Despite his lack of big stuff, Abbott racks up strikeouts with his ability to locate to both sides of the plate. He has average control.

THE FUTURE: Abbott will likely settle in as a swingman but has an outside chance to be a back-of-the-rotation starter. He'll return to the majors in 2022.

Year	Age	Club (Level)	Lge	W	L	ERA	G	GS	IP	H	HR	BB	SO	BB/9	SO/9	WHIP	AVG
2021	25	Iowa (AAA)	East	5	6	5.91	19	19	96	97	20	53	130	5.0	12.2	1.56	.257
	25	Chicago (MLB)	NL	0	0	6.75	7	1	17	20	7	11	12	5.7	6.2	1.79	.286
Major League Totals (1 year)				0	0	6.75	7	1	17	20	7	11	12	5.71	6.23	1.79	.286
Minor League Totals (5 years)				21	20	3.63	72	72	372	317	44	147	445	3.56	10.78	1.25	.229

23 JORDAN NWOGU, OF

BA GRADE
45 Risk: High

Born: March 10, 1999. **B-T:** R-R. **HT:** 6-3. **WT:** 230. **Drafted:** Michigan, 2020 (3rd round). **Signed by:** John Pedrotty.

TRACK RECORD: Nwogu walked on at Michigan and became a three-year starter for the Wolverines. He led the team in most offensive categories during its run to the 2019 College World Series finals and got off to another hot start before the 2020 season shut down. The Cubs drafted him in the third round and signed him for $678,800. Nwogu made his pro debut at Low-A Myrtle Beach in 2021 and started slowly, but he improved as the year progressed and hit .296/.383/.415 over the final eight weeks.

SCOUTING REPORT: Nwogu is a physical specimen who received Division I football offers to play defensive end. He stands a muscular 6-foot-3, 230 pounds and gets to plus power and high-end exit velocities with ease. Nwogu's swing is stiff and a bit funky with its lack of extension, but he's short to the ball and makes loud contact when he connects. He is a smart, patient hitter with good strike-zone discipline. Nwogu is an above-average runner and uses his speed effectively to steal bases and cover ground in the outfield. He's not a particularly smooth defender, but he has the athleticism to become an average left fielder with more experience. He has a below-average arm.

THE FUTURE: Nwogu's power gives him a carrying tool. He has a chance to be a low-average, decent power slugger if he can clean up his swing.

Year	Age	Club (Level)	Lge	AVG	G	AB	R	H	2B	3B	HR	RBI	BB	SO	SB	OBP	SLG
2021	22	Myrtle Beach (LoA)	East	.248	94	323	48	80	12	2	10	40	42	105	16	.344	.390
Minor League Totals (2 years)				.248	94	323	48	80	12	2	10	40	42	105	16	.344	.390

24 YEISON SANTANA, SS

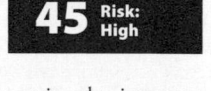

BA GRADE

45 Risk: High

Born: Dec. 7, 2000. **B-T:** R-R. **HT:** 5-11. **WT:** 170. **Signed:** Dominican Republic . **Signed by:** Felix Feliz/Chris Kemp (Padres).

TRACK RECORD: Santana signed with the Padres for $300,000 and finished fourth in batting average in the Rookie-level Arizona League in his pro debut. He continued to impress at instructional league in 2020 and was acquired by the Cubs as one of five players for Yu Darvish. Santana made his full-season debut at Low-A Myrtle Beach in 2021 but hit just .147 in 20 games. He was demoted to extended spring training in June and spent the rest of the season in the Arizona Complex League.

SCOUTING REPORT: Despite his poor season, Santana still holds promise as a young player with intriguing tools. He's an aggressive hitter who swings hard but has excellent hand-eye coordination and makes frequent contact. He primarily hits line drives, especially up the middle and the opposite way. Santana is a free swinger and will need to improve his pitch selection to only swing at pitches he can drive. His explosive hands and twitchy athleticism give him a chance to grow into double-digit home run power if he gets stronger. Santana is a high-energy defender at shortstop. He has decent range and above-average arm strength, but he often plays too fast and needs to learn to play more under control.

THE FUTURE: Santana is raw but has ability on both sides of the ball. He'll head back to Low-A in 2022.

Year	Age	Club (Level)	Lge	AVG	G	AB	R	H	2B	3B	HR	RBI	BB	SO	SB	OBP	SLG
2021	20	Cubs (R)	ACL	.292	32	89	19	26	3	1	1	15	11	24	6	.385	.382
	20	Myrtle Beach (LoA)	East	.147	20	75	8	11	2	0	0	1	9	28	3	.238	.173
Minor League Totals (4 years)				.277	129	458	88	127	11	11	4	71	76	120	18	.384	.376

25 MOISES BALLESTEROS, C

BA GRADE

50 Risk: Extreme

Born: November 8, 2003. **B-T:** L-R. **HT:** 5-10. **WT:** 195. **Signed:** Venezuela, 2021. **Signed by:** Louie Eljaua/Julio Figueroa/Hector Ortega.

TRACK RECORD: Ballesteros batted cleanup as the youngest player on Venezuela's team at the 2015 U-12 World Cup in Taiwan and remained one of the best hitters for his age throughout his amateur career. He signed with the Cubs for $1.5 million on the first day of the 2021 international period and made his professional debut in the Dominican Summer League. He hit .266 with 13 extra-base hits in 40 games and had more walks (31) than strikeouts (24).

SCOUTING REPORT: Ballesteros manages at-bats well for his age with a patient approach and good bat control from the left side. He has a strong upper body and makes hard contact when he connects, usually for doubles with the occasional home run. His contact skills and plate discipline give him a foundation to be an above-average hitter and his strength gives him a chance to grow into average power. Ballesteros has a stout, blocky body and will need to stay on top of his conditioning to remain a catcher. His blocking and receiving need work, but he does have plus arm strength and a quick release.

THE FUTURE: Ballesteros has a chance to be a bat-first, everyday catcher if he stays behind the plate. He may hit enough even if he has to move to another position.

Year	Age	Club (Level)	Lge	AVG	G	AB	R	H	2B	3B	HR	RBI	BB	SO	SB	OBP	SLG
2021	17	Cubs Red (R)	DSL	.266	48	154	22	41	10	0	3	25	31	24	6	.396	.390
Minor League Totals (1 year)				.266	48	154	22	41	10	0	3	25	31	24	6	.396	.390

26 ALFONSO RIVAS, 1B/OF

Born: Sept. 13, 1996. **B-T:** L-L. **HT:** 6-0. **WT:** 188. **Drafted:** Arizona, 2018 (4th round). **Signed by:** Scott Cousins (Athletics).

BA GRADE
40 Risk: Medium

TRACK RECORD: Rivas hit .326 during a decorated college career at Arizona and was drafted in the fourth round by the Athletics in 2018. He raced to Triple-A in his first full season and was acquired by the Cubs for Tony Kemp following a strong showing in the Arizona Fall League. Rivas wasn't invited to the alternate training site in 2020, but that didn't stop his progress. He hit his way out of Triple-A and made his major league debut with the Cubs in August, where he batted .318/.388/.409 in 18 games before suffering a season-ending finger injury.

SCOUTING REPORT: Rivas has a smooth, effortless lefthanded swing that makes a lot of contact. He has a balanced setup, stays in the strike zone and wears pitchers down until he gets a pitch to hit. He drives the ball on a line to all fields and racks up doubles. Rivas has below-average power, leading to questions about whether he can be an everyday player with such little power production. He is a plus defender at first base with good hands and above-average arm strength and can fill in at both left and right field, although he is a below-average defender at both spots.

THE FUTURE: Rivas' hitting ability gives him a chance to contribute at least off the bench. He's ready to fill that role in 2022.

Year	Age	Club (Level)	Lge	AVG	G	AB	R	H	2B	3B	HR	RBI	BB	SO	SB	OBP	SLG
2021	24	Iowa (AAA)	East	.284	58	197	22	56	13	0	4	32	35	49	0	.405	.411
	24	Chicago (MLB)	NL	.318	18	44	7	14	1	0	1	3	4	16	0	.388	.409
Major League Totals (1 year)				.318	18	44	7	14	1	0	1	3	4	16	0	.388	.409
Minor League Totals (4 years)				.288	241	874	117	252	55	5	14	120	139	213	9	.393	.411

27 MANUEL RODRIGUEZ, RHP

Born: Aug. 6, 1996. **B-T:** R-R. **HT:** 5-11. **WT:** 205. **Signed:** Mexico, 2016. **Signed by:** Sergio Hernandez/Louie Eljaua.

BA GRADE
40 Risk: Medium

TRACK RECORD: Rodriguez won the Mexican League's rookie of the year award as Yucatan's closer in 2015 and signed with the Cubs a year later for $400,000. He began to trend upward before the coronavirus pandemic hit and continued that rise when the minor leagues resumed in 2021. Rodriguez earned Futures Game selection and rose from Double-A to the majors, receiving his first big league callup in July. He made 20 relief appearances for the Cubs before finishing the year on the injured list with right shoulder inflammation.

SCOUTING REPORT: Rodriguez is a short, stout righthander with a big right arm. Both his four-seam and two-seam fastballs sit 97 mph and touch 99 with late life. His four-seamer cuts and rides above barrels and his heavy two-seamer drops below them. His fastball command can be scattered, which led to both of them getting hit in the majors. Rodriguez's vertical 87-90 mph slider is a swing-and-miss pitch when he gets it below the strike zone. His fastball-slider combination shuts down righthanded batters, but he doesn't have a changeup and struggles against lefties. He held righties to a .137 batting average and .430 OPS in the minors in 2021 compared to a .324 average and .960 OPS against lefties.

THE FUTURE: Rodriguez is ready to take over as a situational reliever who handles righties. He'll compete for an Opening Day roster spot.

Year	Age	Club (Level)	Lge	W	L	ERA	G	GS	IP	H	HR	BB	SO	BB/9	SO/9	WHIP	AVG
2021	24	Tennessee (AA)	South	1	1	2.03	13	0	13	8	1	10	19	6.8	12.8	1.35	.178
	24	Iowa (AAA)	East	0	0	0.00	7	0	7	6	0	2	8	2.5	9.8	1.09	.231
	24	Chicago (MLB)	NL	3	3	6.11	20	0	17	18	3	12	16	6.1	8.2	1.70	.257
Major League Totals (1 year)				3	3	6.11	20	0	18	18	3	12	16	6.11	8.15	1.70	.257
Minor League Totals (5 years)				11	10	3.94	175	0	205	190	9	113	256	4.95	11.22	1.48	.245

28 DREW GRAY, LHP

Born: May 10, 2003. **B-T:** L-L. **HT:** 6-3. **WT:** 190. **Signed:** HS—Bradenton, Fla., 2021 (3rd round). **Signed by:** Tom Clark.

BA GRADE
50 Risk: Extreme

TRACK RECORD: Gray grew up in Illinois and became the state's top player in his class before he transferred to IMG Academy in Florida. The move paid off when the Cubs drafted him in the third round, No. 93 overall, and signed him for an above-slot $900,000 to forgo an Arkansas commitment. Gray made his pro debut in the Arizona Complex League and struck out nine of the 16 batters he faced before continuing to impress in instructional league.

SCOUTING REPORT: Gray is an excellent athlete who starred as both an outfielder and pitcher in high school and was set to play both ways in college. His high-spin fastball ranges from 90-94 mph and gets swings and misses at the top of the zone when he locates it. He complements his heater with a high-spin, downer curveball in the mid 70s he buries for chase swings and a sweeping, low-80s slider that has a chance to be average. His below-average changeup is a fourth pitch he rarely uses. Gray struggles to keep his delivery in sync and repeat his release point at times, leading to bouts of below-average control. His body control and velocity should both improve as he fills out his projectable 6-foot-3 frame.

THE FUTURE: Gray requires projection but has promising ingredients. The Cubs view him as a potential breakout prospect in 2022.

Year	Age	Club (Level)	Lge	W	L	ERA	G	GS	IP	H	HR	BB	SO	BB/9	SO/9	WHIP	AVG
2021	18	Cubs (R)	ACL	0	1	0.00	2	2	4	3	0	1	9	2.3	20.3	1.00	.200
Minor League Totals (1 year)				0	1	0.00	2	2	4	3	0	1	9	2.25	20.25	1.00	.200

29 CHRISTOPHER MOREL, OF/3B

BA GRADE
45 Risk: Very High

Born: June 24, 1999. **B-T:** R-R. **HT:** 5-11. **WT:** 145. **Signed:** Dominican Republic, 2015. **Signed by:** Jose Estevez/Gian Guzman/Jose Serra.

TRACK RECORD: The Cubs signed Morel for $800,000 in 2015 as part of a strong international signing class that included Brailyn Marquez and Miguel Amaya. He moved slowly through the low minors but received a boost when the Cubs invited him to the alternate training site in 2020. Morel performed well enough to be added to the 40-man roster after the season and jumped to Double-A in 2021, where he struggled initially before finishing strong to earn a promotion to Triple-A.

SCOUTING REPORT: Morel is one of the most versatile athletes in the Cubs system. He's an explosive, plus runner who is an above-average defender at both shortstop and center field and can also play second base, third base, right field and left field. He has plus-plus arm strength, although his accuracy needs improvement. Morel has plenty of bat speed and borderline plus-plus raw power, but his swing gets long and he is extremely streaky with his pitch selection. He is particularly vulnerable against velocity high and inside. He hits the ball hard in the air when he connects, but he is prone to swinging and missing and needs to improve his consistency.

THE FUTURE: Morel projects to be a utilityman who provides occasional pop off the bench. He'll start 2022 back in Triple-A.

Year	Age	Club (Level)	Lge	AVG	G	AB	R	H	2B	3B	HR	RBI	BB	SO	SB	OBP	SLG
2021	22	Tennessee (AA)	South	.220	101	368	59	81	17	5	17	64	41	124	16	.300	.432
	22	Iowa (AAA)	East	.257	9	35	6	9	1	0	1	2	4	10	2	.333	.371
Minor League Totals (5 years)				.236	298	1087	172	256	47	14	34	157	102	288	51	.306	.398

30 BEN LEEPER, RHP

BA GRADE
45 Risk: Very High

Born: June 15, 1997. **B-T:** R-R. **HT:** 6-0. **WT:** 195. **Signed:** Oklahoma State, 2020 (NDFA). **Signed by:** Ty Nichols.

TRACK RECORD: Leeper had two Tommy John surgeries, an ulnar nerve transposition surgery, an emergency appendectomy and a sports hernia all by the time he was 18 and considered quitting baseball. Instead, he returned to Oklahoma State after his second Tommy John and became one of the top closers in the Big 12, leading the Cubs to sign him as a nondrafted free agent in 2020 for $20,000. Leeper raced to Triple-A in his first full season and posted a 1.29 ERA in 27 appearances, but elbow inflammation ended his season in early August.

SCOUTING REPORT: Leeper pounds the strike zone with premium stuff. His fastball sits 95-96 mph, touches 98 and gets swings and misses up in the zone. He complements his fastball with an 88-89 mph power slider with late tilt and drop that gets swings and misses as another plus pitch. He relies on his fastball-slider combination heavily and also has an average, upper-70s curveball and a firm, low-90s changeup he can mix in. He throws plenty of strikes with an aggressive, attacking mentality. Leeper's main concern is his health. He has never made more than 30 appearances in a season and often goes 3-5 days between outings.

THE FUTURE: Leeper has a chance to be a high-leverage reliever if he can stay healthy. His major league debut may come in 2022.

Year	Age	Club (Level)	Lge	W	L	ERA	G	GS	IP	H	HR	BB	SO	BB/9	SO/9	WHIP	AVG
2021	24	Tennessee (AA)	South	1	2	1.26	10	0	14	9	0	4	22	2.5	13.8	0.91	.167
	24	Iowa (AAA)	East	3	1	1.31	17	0	20	6	2	9	31	3.9	13.5	0.73	.091
Minor League Totals (1 year)				4	3	1.29	27	0	35	15	2	13	53	3.34	13.63	0.80	.125

MORE PROSPECTS TO KNOW

SLEEPER

31 PABLO ALIENDO, C

Aliendo is an athletic catcher with excellent catch-and-throw skills behind the plate. He has an easy, level swing that makes a lot of contact and has room to get stronger.

32 YONATHAN PERLAZA, OF

Perlaza signed for $1 million in 2015 and is starting to progress as a late bloomer. He is a capable hitter from both sides of the plate and has solid tools across the board, even if none are above average.

33 ETHAN ROBERTS, RHP

A fourth-round pick out of Tennessee Tech in 2018, Roberts struck out 72 batters in 54 innings across Double-A and Triple-A and was added to the 40-man roster. He generates extremely high spin rates on his 90-94 mph fastball, low-90s cutter and mid-80s slider to get swings and misses.

34 ALEXANDER VIZCAINO, RHP

One of two prospects acquired for Anthony Rizzo, Vizcaino has a fastball up to 98 mph and a deceptive, plus-plus changeup. He is also 24, has yet to pitch above High-A and battled a shoulder impingement last year.

35 GREG DEICHMANN, OF

One of two prospects acquired for Andrew Chafin, Deichmann is a solid defender who makes contact and draws walks from the left side. His previously plus-plus power has been sapped by injuries.

36 MAX BAIN, RHP

Bain weighed 300 pounds and sat in the mid 80s at Division II Northwood (Mich.), but he remade his body and added more than 10 mph after implementing Driveline's velocity training program. His 95-98 mph fastball and two above-average breaking balls will play if he improves his below-average control.

37 CHRIS CLARKE, RHP

The 6-foot-7 Clarke missed most of 2021 with a hip strain. He keeps the ball on the ground with a 92-95 mph sinker and plus, downer curveball with late bite that should profile well in relief.

38 ISMAEL MENA, OF

Mena is a speedy, lithe defender in center field with natural instincts for the position. He needs to get significantly stronger and requires a lot of projection as a hitter.

39 JARED YOUNG, 1B

Young bounced back from a poor 2019 to perform well at Triple-A Iowa last season. He has a sweet lefthanded swing and lines the ball all over the field, but he'll need to add power to profile as a corner-only defender.

40 CHRISTIAN FRANKLIN, OF

The Cubs' fourth-round pick in 2021 out of Arkansas, Franklin boasts power and patience at the plate and plays an impressive center field. He has to prove he can make contact against pro pitching.

TOP PROSPECTS OF THE DECADE

Year	Player, Pos.	2021 Org
2012	Brett Jackson, OF	Did not play
2013	Javier Baez, SS	Mets
2014	Javier Baez, SS	Mets
2015	Kris Bryant, 3B	Giants
2016	Gleyber Torres, SS	Yankees
2017	Eloy Jimenez, OF	White Sox
2018	Aramis Ademan, SS	Cubs
2019	Nico Hoerner, SS	Cubs
2020	Brailyn Marquez, LHP	Cubs
2021	Brailyn Marquez, LHP	Cubs

TOP DRAFT PICKS OF THE DECADE

Year	Player, Pos.	2021 Org
2012	Albert Almora, OF	Mets
2013	Kris Bryant, 3B	Giants
2014	Kyle Schwarber, C	Red Sox
2015	Ian Happ, OF	Cubs
2016	Thomas Hatch, RHP (3rd round)	Blue Jays
2017	Brendon Little, LHP	Cubs
2018	Nico Hoerner, SS	Cubs
2019	Ryan Jensen, RHP	Cubs
2020	Ed Howard, SS	Cubs
2021	Jordan Wicks, LHP	Cubs

Chicago White Sox

BY BILL MITCHELL

The 2021 season was certainly an interesting one for the White Sox, both in the big leagues and also with a thin farm system that struggled to win games at most levels.

Expectations remained high after the White Sox made the playoffs in 2020, the organization's first postseason appearance since 2008. Rick Renteria was replaced by Hall of Fame manager Tony La Russa, the latter's first managerial job in 10 years, in a controversial move. There was plenty of drama surrounding La Russa both before and during the season, with questions of how his "old school" managerial style would mesh with a newer generation of players. The White Sox also

had to deal with injuries to key performers Eloy Jimenez, Yasmani Grandal and Luis Robert. Andrew Vaughn, the team's first-round pick in 2019, started working out in left field the day after Jimenez suffered a pectoral injury in a spring training game, and instead of playing first base in Triple-A as expected, Vaughn broke camp with the big league team and wound up spending most of his rookie year handling left field.

Despite the setbacks, everything came together once the regular season started. The White Sox went 93-69 and won the American League Central division title to reach the postseason for the second straight year. Their season ended in the AL Division Series when they were defeated in four games by the eventual AL-champion Astros.

Just a handful of small trades were made to reinforce the MLB roster for the stretch run. With not a lot of depth to deal from in the farm system, the White Sox traded major leaguers Nick Madrigal and Codi Heuer to the Cubs for closer Craig Kimbrel. Minor league lefthander Konnor Pilkington was dealt to Cleveland for second baseman Cesar Hernandez, while fellow minor league lefty Bailey Horn was sent to the Cubs for reliever Ryan Tepera in a separate trade.

While the major league team met expectations, the performance of the minor league system was underwhelming. Double-A Birmingham was the only one of five domestic affiliates to post a winning record. Low-A Kannapolis was especially ineffective, losing its first 10 games en route to an abysmal 40-79 record, narrowly averting the worst record among all full-season affiliates. High-A Winston-Salem went 43-76 and Triple-A Charlotte went 45-75.

It was also not a good development year for the trio of young high school pitchers selected early in the 2019 and 2020 drafts. Righthanders Jared

Second-year outfielder Luis Robert shined when he was on the field but played in just 68 games.

PROJECTED 2025 LINEUP

Catcher	Zack Collins	30
First Base	Andrew Vaughn	27
Second Base	Colson Montgomery	23
Third Base	Yoan Moncada	30
Shortstop	Tim Anderson	32
Left Field	Eloy Jimenez	28
Center Field	Luis Robert	27
Right Field	Yoelqui Cespedes	27
Designated Hitter	Jose Abreu	38
No. 1 Starter	Lucas Giolito	30
No. 2 Starter	Dylan Cease	29
No. 3 Starter	Michael Kopech	29
No. 4 Starter	Norge Vera	25
No. 5 Starter	Reynaldo Lopez	31
Closer	Garrett Crochet	26

Kelley, Andrew Dalquist and Matthew Thompson struggled with inconsistency, injuries or both during their first full seasons. The depth of the system was bolstered by the early 2021 signings of a pair of Cuban players, both with baseball bloodlines. Outfielder Yoelqui Cespedes made it to Double-A in his pro debut while righthanded pitcher Norge Vera spent his first season in the Dominican Summer League.

Still, the White Sox will gladly take major league success if the cost is minor league struggles. After building up their farm system for years, the payoff has finally arrived with a team poised to control the AL Central for years to come and contend for a World Series. ■

CHICAGO WHITE SOX

TOP 2022 ROOKIES	RANK
Jake Burger, 3B	7
Jimmy Lambert, RHP	12
Jonathan Stiever, RHP	13
BREAKOUT PROSPECTS	**RANK**
Bryan Ramos, 3B	11
Jason Bilous, RHP	14

SOURCE OF TOP 30 TALENT			
Homegrown	29	Acquired	1
College	11	Trade	1
Junior college	0	Rule 5 draft	0
High school	6	Independent league	0
Nondrafted free agent	0	Free agent/waivers	0
International	12		

LF
Blake Rutherford (21)
Chase Krogman
Benyamin Bailey

CF
Yoelqui Cespedes (2)
Misael Gonzalez
James Beard
Cam Butler

RF
Micker Adolfo (18)
Luis Mieses (23)
Anderson Comas

3B
Wes Kath (4)
Jake Burger (7)
Bryan Ramos (11)
Wilfred Veras (29)
Luis Curbelo
Jayson Gonzalez
DJ Gladney

SS
Colson Montgomery (1)
Jose Rodriguez (5)
Romy Gonzalez (15)
Lenyn Sosa (17)
Wilber Sanchez (24)
Shawn Goosenberg

2B
Yolbert Sanchez (16)

1B
Harvin Mendoza

C
Adam Hackenberg (30)
Jefferson Mendoza
Victor Torres
Colby Smelley

LHP

LHSP	LHRP
Brooks Gosswein (27)	Bennett Sousa (26)
Ronaldo Guzman	Gil Luna (28)
Tommy Sommer	Fraser Ellard
	Hunter Schryver
	Anderson Severino
	Haylen Green

RHP

RHSP	RHRP
Norge Vera (3)	Caleb Freeman (22)
Andrew Dalquist (6)	Yoelvin Silven (25)
Jared Kelley (8)	Luke Shilling
Sean Burke (9)	Theo Denlinger
Matthew Thompson (10)	McKinley Moore
Jimmy Lambert (12)	Taylor Broadway
Jonathan Stiever (13)	Johnny Ray
Jason Bilous (14)	J.B. Olson
Tanner McDougal (19)	Noah Owen
Cristian Mena (20)	
Kade McClure	
Johan Dominguez	
Davis Martin	

1 COLSON MONTGOMERY, SS

Born: Feb. 27, 2002. **B-T:** L-R. **HT:** 6-4. **WT:** 205.
Drafted: HS—Huntingburg, Ind., 2021 (1st round).
Signed by: Justin Wechsler.

TRACK RECORD: Montgomery was a three-sport athlete in high school, excelling not just in baseball but also on the basketball court and football field as a star quarterback. He was especially notable for his basketball skills and finished as Southbridge (Ind.) High's leading career scorer. He drew interest from Division I basketball programs, including in-state powerhouse Indiana, but baseball was Montgomery's true love. He led his school to the Indiana Class 3A championship, earning second team All-America honors, and was committed to Indiana for baseball before the White Sox drafted him 22nd overall and signed him for $3.027 million. Montgomery was the first high schooler taken by the White Sox in the first round since Courtney Hawkins in 2012. Montgomery began his pro career in the Rookie-level Arizona Complex League and showed a solid set of tools across the board with a baseball savvy that allowed him to consistently play above his raw gifts.

SCOUTING REPORT: Montgomery has a smooth, lefthanded swing geared toward driving the ball to all fields. While he didn't hit a home run in his pro debut, balls regularly jump off his bat, and he has the natural strength to project above-average power as he matures. Montgomery's lanky, 6-foot-4 frame gives him long levers and some length to his swing, which could lead to higher strikeout totals. That was not an issue during ACL play, as Montgomery showed the ability to keep his hands in and stay short to the ball, making consistent contact. In addition to his above-average bat to ball skills, Montgomery showed a discerning eye at the plate, and the discipline to work deep into counts and take walks. While he didn't hit for a lot of power in games, his power metrics were strong with maximum exit velocities reaching upward of 106 mph. At present Montgomery's bat path is flat to downward at times, which led to lots of ground ball contact. As he optimizes his swing path for more power, adjusts to professional pitching and adds strength to his large frame, he should blossom into an above-average power hitter with a strong hit tool foundation. Defensively, Montgomery has a good chance to stay at shortstop despite his size. He is an average runner and moves well for his height with easy, smooth actions and good instincts. His above-average arm strength will be plenty for the left side of the infield, especially coupled with a good internal clock that keeps him from rushing his throws. He has all of the attri-

BILL MITCHELL

BA GRADE	SCOUTING GRADES
55 Risk: Extreme	**Hit:** 55. **Power:** 55. **Run:** 50. **Field:** 60. **Arm:** 55.

Projected future grades on 20-80 scouting scale

BEST TOOLS

Best Hitter for Average	Jose Rodriguez
Best Power Hitter	Romy Gonzalez
Best Strike-Zone Discipline	Colson Montgomery
Fastest Baserunner	James Beard
Best Athlete	Colson Montgomery
Best Fastball	Norge Vera
Best Curveball	Tanner McDougal
Best Slider	Jonathan Stiever
Best Changeup	Jason Bilous
Best Control	Norge Vera
Best Defensive Catcher	Adam Hackenberg
Best Defensive Infielder	Wilber Sanchez
Best Infield Arm	Wes Kath
Best Defensive Outfielder	James Beard
Best Outfield Arm	Micker Adolfo

butes needed to develop into an above-average defender, even if his size eventually slides him over to third base. He could excel at the position, where his smooth infield actions and above-average arm will play.

THE FUTURE: There's a lot to dream on with Montgomery, especially as he focuses strictly on baseball after playing multiple sports his whole life. An older prep player, he'll already be 20 next spring, putting him on target for an assignment to Low-A Kannapolis. He has what it takes to stay at shortstop even as he adds strength, but also should have the power to profile at third base if he needs to move. ∎

Year	Age	Club (Level)	Lge	AVG	G	AB	R	H	2B	3B	HR	RBI	BB	SO	SB	OBP	SLG
2021	19	White Sox (R)	ACL	.287	26	94	16	27	7	0	0	7	13	22	0	.396	.362
Minor League Totals (1 year)				.287	26	94	16	27	7	0	0	7	13	22	0	.396	.362

2 YOELQUI CESPEDES, OF

Born: Sept. 24, 1997. **B-T:** R-R. **HT:** 5-9. **WT:** 205. **Signed:** Cuba, 2021.
Signed by: Marco Paddy.

TRACK RECORD: Cespedes is a half-brother of longtime slugger Yoenis Cespedes and has been a known commodity in baseball circles since he played for Cuba's World Baseball Classic team in 2017. He defected from Cuba in 2019 but waited until the 2020-21 international signing period to sign with the White Sox for $2.05 million. After visa issues were resolved, Cespedes began his pro career in June at High-A Winston-Salem before moving up to Double-A Birmingham late in the season. He hit .285/.350/.463 in 72 games across both levels and ended his first professional year with an assignment to the Arizona Fall League.

BA GRADE
50 Risk: High

SCOUTING REPORT: Despite a two-year absence from competitive baseball, Cespedes put up good numbers at both levels. He has an aggressive swing that gets long at times, leading to questions about how much contact he will make long-term, but he's hit for high averages throughout his career and the White Sox have an excellent history of developing hitters from Cuba. Cespedes gets to his plus power in games and balls jump off his bat. He's an above-average runner who is slower out of the box but ticks up underway. A shoulder issue limited Cespedes to DH duties early in the season, but once he made his way to the outfield, he showed above-average defense with good reads, reactions and jumps. His above-average arm fits in right field.

THE FUTURE: Cespedes just needs to keep playing games to shake off the rust from his two years away from competition. He'll eventually fit in the White Sox outfield next to fellow Cuba native Luis Robert.

SCOUTING GRADES:	Hitting: 45	Power: 60	Running: 55	Fielding: 55	Arm: 55

Year	Age	Club (Level)	Lge	AVG	G	AB	R	H	2B	3B	HR	RBI	BB	SO	SB	OBP	SLG
2021	23	Winston-Salem (HiA)	East	.278	45	176	34	49	17	0	7	20	13	56	10	.355	.494
	23	Birmingham (AA)	South	.298	27	94	14	28	3	2	1	7	3	27	8	.340	.404
Minor League Totals (2 years)				.285	72	270	48	77	20	2	8	27	16	83	18	.350	.463

3 NORGE VERA, RHP

Born: June 1, 2000. **B-T:** R-R. **HT:** 6-4. **WT:** 185. **Signed:** Cuba, 2021.
Signed by: Marco Paddy/Ruddy Moreta/Doug Laumann.

TRACK RECORD: Vera was one of two top Cuban prospects signed by the White Sox in 2021, with his $1.5 million bonus just a bit less than that of outfielder Yoelqui Cespedes. The son of a former Cuban baseball star of the same name, Vera pitched in the Dominican Summer League after signing. He missed time with arm fatigue after not having pitched much in recent years, but he dominated when healthy. He didn't allow an earned run in 19.2 innings and had 34 strikeouts against five walks, albeit while facing much younger and less experienced hitters.

BA GRADE
55 Risk: Extreme

SCOUTING REPORT: Vera already possesses a plus fastball that sits 93-96 mph and touches 99-100. He has the frame to get bigger and stronger and add even more velocity as he matures, with the potential for it to become a plus-plus pitch. His slurvy breaking ball ranges from 78-82 mph with short, late movement, and will be a weapon working off his fastball with more use. Vera delivers a changeup with the same arm speed as the fastball, but it's still a bit too firm at 85-88 mph and a work in progress. He delivers his pitches with an easy, fluid, athletic delivery from a high three-quarters arm slot. Vera struggled to throw strikes his lone season in Cuba's major league, but his delivery and arm action portend above-average control.

THE FUTURE: Vera is ready to jump straight to a full-season affiliate in 2022. His innings will be closely monitored, but he has the stuff to be a mid-rotation starter if he can build up his durability.

SCOUTING GRADES:	Fastball: 70	Slider: 55	Changeup: 55	Control: 55

Year	Age	Club (Level)	Lge	W	L	ERA	G	GS	IP	H	HR	BB	SO	BB/9	SO/9	WHIP	AVG
2021	21	White Sox (R)	DSL	1	0	0.00	8	7	19	9	0	5	34	2.4	16.1	0.74	.141
Minor League Totals (1 year)				1	0	0.00	8	7	19	9	0	5	34	2.37	16.11	0.74	.141

4 WES KATH, 3B

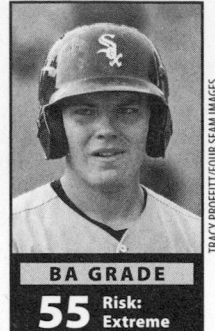

Born: Aug. 3, 2002. **B-T:** L-R. **HT:** 6-3. **WT:** 200. **Drafted:** HS—Scottsdale, Ariz., 2021 (2nd round). **Signed by:** John Kazanas.

TRACK RECORD: Kath was the top high school prospect in Arizona his senior year, leading Desert Mountain High to the state 5-A championship and capping his prep career with a long home run over the right field bullpen at Tempe Diablo Stadium. The White Sox selected him in the second round and signed him for an above-slot $1.8 million bonus to pass on his commitment to nearby Arizona State. Kath made his pro debut in the Arizona Complex League and flashed big power, but he also struck out 42 times in 115 plate appearances.

BA GRADE

55 Risk: Extreme

TRACY PROFFITT/FOUR SEAM IMAGES

SCOUTING REPORT: Kath's main draw is his plus power from the left side. He gets to his power with an easy stroke, and the planned offseason strength work will allow him to get even more power into the swing. Kath has the ability to make adjustments as a hitter and use the whole field, but he got caught trying to do too much at the plate in his pro debut and at times was clearly putting too much pressure on himself. He has the swing and underlying attributes to be an average hitter if he can adjust his approach and mindset. Kath is a below-average runner but has a good stride and picks up speed underway. He played shortstop as an amateur but has already moved to third base. Kath is a potentially average defender at the hot corner with good actions and plus arm strength.

THE FUTURE: Kath should be ready for full-season ball in 2022. He has a chance to be an everyday, power-hitting third baseman but is many years from that ceiling.

SCOUTING GRADES:	Hitting: 50	Power: 60	Running: 40	Fielding: 50	Arm: 60

Year	Age	Club (Level)	Lge	AVG	G	AB	R	H	2B	3B	HR	RBI	BB	SO	SB	OBP	SLG
2021	18	White Sox (R)	ACL	.212	28	104	15	22	0	2	3	15	8	42	1	.287	.337
Minor League Totals (1 year)				.212	28	104	15	22	0	2	3	15	8	42	1	.287	.337

5 JOSE RODRIGUEZ, SS

Born: May 13, 2001. **B-T:** R-R. **HT:** 5-11. **WT:** 175. **Signed:** Dominican Republic, 2018. **Signed by:** Ruddy Moreta.

TRACK RECORD: Rodriguez signed with the White Sox for $50,000 in 2018 and played his first two seasons exclusively in the Rookie levels. He entered the 2021 season relatively unknown but had the biggest breakout of any player in the White Sox system, vaulting up three levels to Double-A as a 20-year-old and finishing the season with a strong showing in the Arizona Fall League, where he became a favorite of rival scouts. He hit .301/.338/.469 overall and tied for eighth in the minors with 141 hits.

BA GRADE

50 Risk: High

BRIAN WESTERHOLT/FOUR SEAM IMAGES

SCOUTING REPORT: Rodriguez's tools are average across the board, but he has good instincts and an enthusiastic style of play that helps him play above them. He takes very big swings but has the discipline to make adjustments and shorten his swing with two strikes and put the ball in play. He mostly drives the ball for doubles but has the power to reach double-digit home runs. Rodriguez could become a plus defender at shortstop with more consistency. His good footwork allows him to make throws from various spots, but he sometimes plays out of control. He has a good internal clock and gets rid of the ball quickly. The best compliment about Rodriguez is that he's a ballplayer, and coaches love to have him on their team.

THE FUTURE: Rodriguez profiles best as a utility infielder, but improvement in his consistency and continued development as a hitter could make him a starter at either middle-infield position. He'll return to Double-A to start the 2022 season.

SCOUTING GRADES:	Hitting: 50	Power: 50	Running: 50	Fielding: 50	Arm: 50

Year	Age	Club (Level)	Lge	AVG	G	AB	R	H	2B	3B	HR	RBI	BB	SO	SB	OBP	SLG
2021	20	Kannapolis (LoA)	East	.283	78	336	58	95	22	4	9	32	21	57	20	.328	.452
	20	Winston-Salem (HiA)	East	.361	29	119	19	43	4	1	5	19	5	13	10	.381	.538
	20	Birmingham (AA)	South	.214	4	14	2	3	1	0	0	0	0	2	0	.214	.286
Minor League Totals (4 years)				.296	215	884	138	262	47	11	25	105	44	146	53	.331	.459

6 ANDREW DALQUIST, RHP

BRIAN WESTERHOLT/FOUR SEAM IMAGES

Born: Nov. 13, 2000. **B-T:** R-R. **HT:** 6-1. **WT:** 175. **Drafted:** HS—Redondo Beach, Calif., 2019 (3rd round). **Signed by:** Mike Baker.

TRACK RECORD: Dalquist emerged as one the top prep pitchers in the 2019 draft class with a breakout senior season at Redondo Union (Calif.) High. The White Sox drafted him in the third round and signed him for an above-slot $2 million to forgo an Arizona commitment. After making three brief appearances in his pro debut, Dalquist's only action in 2020 came at the White Sox's alternate training site and instructional league. He made his full-season debut at Low-A Kannapolis in 2021 and turned in mixed results with a 4.99 ERA in 23 starts, but also showed some encouraging signs.

SCOUTING REPORT: Dalquist has begun to grow into his projected velocity gains. After sitting 90-94 mph in high school, his fastball now ranges from 93-96 mph and still has room to increase. Dalquist complements his heater with a 81-83 mph slider with two-plane depth that flashes plus and a mid-70s, downer curveball with late bite that is potentially average, although he sometimes struggles to land it. Dalquist rounds out his arsenal with a mid-80s changeup he is beginning to use more and flashes above-average. Dalquist has plenty of stuff, but he walked 56 batters in 83 innings at Kannapolis. He struggles to keep his delivery in sync, often bouncing out of it and spraying his fastball to his arm side. He may repeat his delivery better as he gets stronger, but rival scouts question how much weight and strength he can add to his slender frame.

THE FUTURE: Dalquist's main task is to get his delivery under control. If he does, he could be a back-of-the-rotation starter.

BA GRADE
50 Risk: High

| SCOUTING GRADES: | Fastball: 55 | Slider: 60 | Curveball: 50 | Changeup: 55 | Control: 50 |

Year	Age	Club (Level)	Lge	W	L	ERA	G	GS	IP	H	HR	BB	SO	BB/9	SO/9	WHIP	AVG
2021	20	Kannapolis (LoA)	East	3	9	4.99	23	23	83	87	1	56	79	6.1	8.6	1.72	.269
Minor League Totals (3 years)				3	9	4.81	26	26	86	89	1	58	81	6.07	8.48	1.71	.266

7 JAKE BURGER, 3B

LAURA WOLFF/CHARLOTTE KNIGHTS

Born: April 10, 1996. **B-T:** R-R. **HT:** 6-2. **WT:** 230. **Drafted:** Missouri State, 2017 (1st round). **Signed by:** Clay Overcash.

TRACK RECORD: Burger's ascent to the majors in 2021 capped a remarkable comeback story. After being selected 11th overall in 2017, Burger missed all of 2018 and 2019 after twice rupturing his Achilles tendon and suffering a setback with a bruised heel. He briefly played in an independent league during the 2020 coronavirus shutdown before the White Sox added him to their alternate training site. Despite not having played an official game in nearly four years, Burger opened 2021 at Triple-A Charlotte and hit well enough to earn his first big league callup in early July, appearing in 15 games for the White Sox.

SCOUTING REPORT: Formerly a thick, burly masher, Burger has slimmed down since the early part of his career. He remains a dangerous hitter with a quick swing, plus raw power and the ability to drive balls from gap-to-gap with a solid approach. He struggled with strikeouts in his brief major league debut, but on the whole he keeps his strikeouts reasonable for a power hitter. Burger's improved fitness has primarily helped him in the field. His previously well below-average speed ticked up and he showed increased lateral agility at third base. He is able to make throws on the run from different angles and has an above-average arm.

THE FUTURE: Burger profiles best as a righthanded power hitter who bounces between third and first base. If he continues to stay healthy as he did in 2021, he may be able to hit his way into an everyday role.

BA GRADE
45 Risk: Medium

| SCOUTING GRADES: | Hitting: 55 | Power: 60 | Running: 40 | Fielding: 45 | Arm: 55 |

Year	Age	Club (Level)	Lge	AVG	G	AB	R	H	2B	3B	HR	RBI	BB	SO	SB	OBP	SLG
2021	25	Charlotte (AAA)	East	.274	82	310	46	85	16	2	18	54	24	91	0	.332	.513
	25	Chicago (MLB)	AL	.263	15	38	5	10	3	1	1	3	4	15	0	.333	.474
Major League Totals (1 year)				.263	15	38	5	10	3	1	1	3	4	15	0	.333	.474
Minor League Totals (4 years)				.270	133	504	71	136	26	4	23	83	38	121	0	.334	.474

8 JARED KELLEY, RHP

Born: Oct. 3, 2001. **B-T:** R-R. **HT:** 6-3. **WT:** 230. **Drafted:** HS—Refugio, Texas, 2020 (2nd round). **Signed by:** Tyler Wilt.

BILL MITCHELL

TRACK RECORD: Kelley was one of the top high school pitchers in the 2020 draft class, but the depth of pitching caused him to drop to the second round. The White Sox drafted him 47th overall and signed him for an above-slot $3 million bonus. Kelley pitched at the alternate training site and instructional league after signing and earned positive reviews, but he struggled in his pro debut at Low-A Kannapolis in 2021. Kelley battled shoulder fatigue and forearm tightness during the year and finished 0-7, 7.61 with 27 strikeouts and 26 walks in 23.2 innings.

SCOUTING REPORT: Kelley still flashes premium stuff with a fastball that touches 99 mph and a slider and changeup which each flash above-average.

BA GRADE

50 Risk: Extreme

He generates his fastball velocity with little effort and gets late run on the pitch. His 85-88 mph slider with late tilt has more cut to it at higher velocities and more sweep and depth when he slows it down. His changeup is a bit firm at 85-87 mph, but he has a feel for it and its armside life tunnels well off his fastball. Kelley's biggest hurdle is his conditioning, as he needs to get his big body leaner and more athletic. He generates power from his physical stature but needs to transfer that power more efficiently. Improvements to shoulder and core strength could pay dividends.

THE FUTURE: Kelley will spend much of his offseason in the weight room looking to add strength. External evaluators believe his ceiling is a hard-throwing reliever, but the White Sox internally still view him as a potential starter.

SCOUTING GRADES:	Fastball: 70	Slider: 55	Changeup: 55	Control: 45

Year	Age	Club (Level)	Lge	W	L	ERA	G	GS	IP	H	HR	BB	SO	BB/9	SO/9	WHIP	AVG
2021	19	White Sox (R)	ACL	0	2	13.50	2	2	2	3	2	4	2	13.5	6.8	2.63	.300
	19	Kannapolis (LoA)	East	0	5	6.86	10	10	21	21	1	22	25	9.4	10.7	2.05	.241
Minor League Totals (2 years)				0	7	7.61	12	12	23	24	3	26	27	9.89	10.27	2.11	.247

9 SEAN BURKE, RHP

Born: Dec. 18, 1999. **B-T:** R-R. **HT:** 6-6. **WT:** 230. **Drafted:** Maryland, 2021 (3rd round). **Signed by:** John Stott.

BILL MITCHELL

TRACK RECORD: Burke split his time playing baseball and basketball in high school and missed his freshman season at Maryland after having Tommy John surgery. He recovered to become the Terrapins' top starter as a redshirt sophomore in 2021 and ranked second in the Big Ten Conference with 107 strikeouts. The White Sox drafted him in the third round and signed him for $900,000. Burke moved quickly to Low-A Kannapolis after signing and posted a 2.65 ERA with 20 strikeouts and 10 walks in 17 innings for the Cannon Ballers.

SCOUTING REPORT: An athletic mover on the mound, Burke stands out for his pitchability and large, athletic frame. He has feel for all of his four pitches,

BA GRADE

45 Risk: High

coming from a low-effort, athletic delivery with clean arm action. The fastball was sitting 93-94 mph In his pro debut, touching 95-96. He generates good carry on the four-seam with easy velocity. Burke effectively pairs his two breaking balls. His above-average 12-to-6 curveball sits at 78-80 mph and allows him to effectively change a hitter's eye level. The curve sets up a slider at 83-84 mph with two-plane depth, tight spin, and power. He also mixes in a low-80s changeup that projects to be a average.

THE FUTURE: Burke doesn't possess any plus pitches, but he has well-rounded arsenal that will play up as he improves the control. He's got the chance to move quickly through the system, profiling best as a back-of-the-rotation innings-eater.

SCOUTING GRADES:	Fastball: 55	Slider: 55	Curveball: 55	Changeup: 50	Control: 50

Year	Age	Club (Level)	Lge	W	L	ERA	G	GS	IP	H	HR	BB	SO	BB/9	SO/9	WHIP	AVG
2021	21	White Sox (R)	ACL	0	0	0.00	2	2	3	1	0	1	5	3.0	15.0	0.67	.100
2021	21	Kannapolis (LoA)	East	0	1	3.21	5	5	14	9	0	10	20	6.4	12.9	1.36	.191
Minor League Totals (1 year)				0	1	2.65	7	7	17	10	0	11	25	5.82	13.24	1.24	.175

10 MATTHEW THOMPSON, RHP

Born: Aug. 11, 2000. **B-T:** R-R. **HT:** 6-3. **WT:** 195. **Drafted:** HS—Cypress, Texas, 2019 (2nd round). **Signed by:** Chris Walker.

TRACK RECORD: Thompson was a longtime standout on the showcase circuit as a high school underclassman and was drafted by the White Sox in the second round in 2019 even after a disappointing senior year. He signed for an above-slow $2.1 million to forgo a Texas A&M commitment. Thompson joined what was expected to be a dynamic rotation at Low-A Kannapolis with Jared Kelley and Andrew Dalquist in 2021 but, like his rotation-mates, Thompson struggled. He went 2-9, 5.99 in 20 starts between Kannapolis and the Arizona Complex League and was limited to 73.2 innings by a hip flexor strain.

BA GRADE

50 Risk: Extreme

SCOUTING REPORT: Thompson is regarded as the best athlete in the White Sox system, but that athleticism doesn't always translate to his on-field performance. His fastball velocity comes and goes, sometimes sitting 94-96 mph and running as high as 98, then at other times dipping into the 88-89 mph range. His fastball doesn't have a lot of deception, so batters pick it up easily. His curveball has depth but he struggles to land it for strikes, allowing hitters to sit on his fastball. Thompson also flashes an average changeup and is working to incorporate a slider into his repertoire to give him more of an east-west pitch. Despite his athleticism, Thompson has some stiffness in his delivery and he struggles to repeat it, leading to poor fastball command and fringy control. He is better pitching out of the stretch than the windup.

THE FUTURE: Thompson will head to High-A Winston-Salem in 2022 as a starter. His health, inconsistent velocity and command issues point to a future as a reliever.

SCOUTING GRADES:	Fastball: 60	Slider: 50	Curveball: 55	Changeup: 50	Control: 45

Year	Age	Club (Level)	Lge	W	L	ERA	G	GS	IP	H	HR	BB	SO	BB/9	SO/9	WHIP	AVG
2021	20	White Sox (R)	ACL	0	1	9.00	1	1	2	3	1	0	1	0.0	4.5	1.50	.333
2021	20	Kannapolis (LoA)	East	2	8	5.90	19	19	71	83	7	38	77	4.8	9.7	1.69	.296
Minor League Totals (3 years)				2	9	5.83	22	22	76	88	8	38	80	4.52	9.52	1.67	.296

11 BRYAN RAMOS, 3B

BA GRADE

50 Risk: Extreme

Born: March 12, 2002. **B-T:** R-R. **HT:** 6-2. **WT:** 190. **Signed:** Cuba, 2018. **Signed by:** Ruddy Moreta/Doug Laumann/Marco Paddy.

TRACK RECORD: After spending his 2019 pro debut season at 17 in the Rookie-level Arizona League and then missing 2020 due to the coronavirus pandemic, Ramos was the youngest player assigned to Low-A East in 2021. It was an aggressive assignment, but the native Cuban handled it well despite a lingering shoulder issue that limited him to a DH role for nearly half of his games played. His walk rate, contact rate and isolated slugging percentage all increased slightly from his last full season, and he was one of the few clear prospects on an otherwise barren Kannapolis team.

SCOUTING REPORT: Ramos is very athletic and his already broad-shouldered, strong body has gotten firmer and better balanced since his first season as a professional. He has a quick swing and quick hands, makes good zone decisions and hits to all fields with power. His bat path gets too steep at times, cutting him out of the zone, but he makes up for it with bat speed and strength. Primarily a third baseman, Ramos also saw time at second base and first base, but the hot corner is his best position. His feet and hands both work well there and his average arm may get stronger with more experience. Second base is not out of the question for Ramos long term.

THE FUTURE: Considering he won't turn 20 until midway through spring training, there's no reason to rush Ramos. He'll likely see an assignment to High-A to start 2022.

Year	Age	Club (Level)	Lge	AVG	G	AB	R	H	2B	3B	HR	RBI	BB	SO	SB	OBP	SLG
2021	19	Kannapolis (LoA)	East	.244	115	431	64	105	23	6	13	57	51	110	13	.345	.415
Minor League Totals (3 years)				.254	166	619	100	157	33	8	17	83	70	154	16	.348	.415

12 JIMMY LAMBERT, RHP

BA GRADE

40 Risk: Medium

Born: Nov. 18, 1994. **B-T:** R-R. **HT:** 6-2. **WT:** 190. **Drafted:** Fresno State, 2016 (5th round). **Signed by:** Adam Virchis.

TRACK RECORD: Lambert completed his first full season in 2021 since having Tommy John surgery, starting 19 games at Triple-A Charlotte and another four in the majors. The 2016 fifth-round pick had previously made his major league debut with two short outings in the 2020 season. **SCOUTING REPORT:** Lambert would get better grades on his four-pitch mix if he sharpened his command, but they all currently grade out as solid-average to a tick above-average offerings. His four-seam fastball sits 93-94 mph and gets good carry but is not an overpowering pitch. He generates swings and misses with a moderately sweeping slider, which tunnels off of his fastball as it moves away from right-handed batters as it approaches the plate. His mid-80s changeup has armside fade and tumble, and he gets heavy downward break on a mid-70s curveball. Lambert uses a simple, easy delivery that his athleticism allows him to repeat. His control and command still have a ways to go. **THE FUTURE:** The most optimistic projection for Lambert is as a fourth or fifth starter, although some observers believe he'll fit better in a swingman role.

Year	Age	Club (Level)	Lge	W	L	ERA	G	GS	IP	H	HR	BB	SO	BB/9	SO/9	WHIP	AVG
2021	26	Charlotte (AAA)	East	3	3	4.76	19	19	64	49	11	32	82	4.5	11.5	1.26	.210
	26	Chicago (MLB)	AL	1	1	6.23	4	3	13	16	3	6	10	4.2	6.9	1.69	.314
Major League Totals (2 years)				1	1	5.40	6	3	15	18	3	6	12	3.60	7.20	1.60	.305
Minor League Totals (5 years)				27	27	4.18	89	87	407	395	43	139	407	3.07	9.00	1.31	.257

13 JONATHAN STIEVER, RHP

BA GRADE

45 Risk: High

Born: May, 12, 1997. **B-T:** R-R. **HT:** 6-2. **WT:** 210. **Drafted:** Indiana, 2018 (5th round). **Signed by:** Adam Virchis.

TRACK RECORD: Stiever has gotten very brief cups of coffee with the White Sox in the last two seasons but spent most of 2021 with Triple-A Charlotte, struggling with inconsistent performance. He finished the Triple-A season with a 5.82 ERA and 13 home runs yielded in 74 innings but with an encouraging 10.7 strikeouts per nine innings. **SCOUTING REPORT:** Stiever's athleticism allows him to repeat his low-maintenance delivery as he explodes toward the plate, delivering the ball from an over-the-top slot. While his pitch mix consists of four pitches, Stiever relies heavily on his mid-90s fastball, touching 97-98, using it around 60% of the time in 2021. The pitch has easy velocity with run and average movement, and he attacks the zone and gets the heater to both sides of the plate. An improving 82-84 mph slider is his most-used secondary pitch. His 74 mph curveball has gone backward since 2019 and he needs to improve the consistency of its shape and the feel to land it. His infrequently-used changeup sits around 80-83 mph with heavy fade. **THE FUTURE:** Stiever will head to spring training looking to land a spot on the Opening Day roster. His ceiling is as a fourth starter, but his heavy fastball-slider mix would work well in a relief role.

Year	Age	Club (Level)	Lge	W	L	ERA	G	GS	IP	H	HR	BB	SO	BB/9	SO/9	WHIP	AVG
2021	24	Charlotte (AAA)	East	5	5	5.84	17	17	74	80	13	28	88	3.4	10.7	1.46	.265
	24	Chicago (MLB)	AL	0	0	—	1	0	0	4	0	0	0	—	—	—	1.000
Major League Totals (2 years)				0	1	14.21	3	2	6	11	4	4	3	5.68	4.26	2.37	.379
Minor League Totals (3 years)				15	16	4.26	56	56	247	247	33	64	281	2.33	10.24	1.26	.256

14 JASON BILOUS, RHP

BA GRADE

45 Risk: High

Born: Aug. 11, 1997. **B-T:** R-R. **HT:** 6-2. **WT:** 185. **Drafted:** Coastal Carolina, 2018 (13th round). **Signed by:** Kevin Burrell.

TRACK RECORD: Bilous jumped onto the White Sox's prospect radar this year. He dealt with lingering blister issues that may have impacted his performance. He also improved his once-poor control, and his strikeout rate jumped to nearly 12 batters per nine innings. **SCOUTING REPORT:** When he first joined the White Sox, Bilous was primarily using a fastball and slider, but he's since added to his mix and has gained confidence in his improved changeup and newer curveball. The key was getting his fastball velocity more consistent, and it now sits around 93 mph and touches 97 at its peak with late life and movement. His swing-and-miss pitch is a low-80s slider flashing plus and projecting as a future above-average pitch. His 12-to-6 curveball sits at 80-83 mph but it still tends to get slurvy. The improving changeup with fade projects as an above-average pitch, but it needs consistency. Bilous uses a high three-quarters delivery that gets rotational at times, and when he doesn't stay through his pitches his front side starts to fly open. **THE FUTURE:** As he continues to improve his control and get more consistency with his delivery, Bilous should reach his ceiling as a fourth starter. The White Sox added him to the 40-man roster.

Year	Age	Club (Level)	Lge	W	L	ERA	G	GS	IP	H	HR	BB	SO	BB/9	SO/9	WHIP	AVG
2021	23	Winston-Salem (HiA)	East	1	1	2.45	3	3	14	11	0	2	26	1.2	16.0	0.89	.208
	23	Birmingham (AA)	South	2	7	6.51	17	17	65	71	8	30	80	4.2	11.1	1.55	.278
Minor League Totals (4 years)				9	22	5.13	65	51	221	213	22	117	250	4.76	10.18	1.49	.254

15 ROMY GONZALEZ, SS/2B

BA GRADE
45 Risk: High

Born: Sept. 6, 1996. **B-T:** R-R. **HT:** 6-1. **WT:** 215. **Drafted:** Miami, 2018 (18th round). **Signed by:** Jose Ortega.

TRACK RECORD: Gonzalez has been in the White Sox organization since being drafted out of Miami in 2018, but this is his debut as a Top 30 prospect. He struggled at Low-A Kannapolis in 2019 but was able to use the 2020 downtime for a reset and to get healthy. After a strong season spent mostly with Double-A Birmingham, as well as brief stints in Triple-A and with the big league team, Gonzalez is now one of the organization's fastest-rising prospects. He adapted to shortstop after starting to play the position during the 2019 instructional league program.

SCOUTING REPORT: Considering his relative lack of experience at shortstop, Gonzalez already projects as an average defender, and it's where he's most confident on the field. His average speed and above-average arm will be enough for the position, and he demonstrates good game awareness and instincts. Above-average bat speed and good hands give him plenty of raw power, demonstrated by the 24 home runs he hit in just 93 minor league games in 2021. It's more than just the power for Gonzalez, as he shows good zone awareness and low chase numbers and consistently plays hard on the field.

THE FUTURE: Gonzalez will carve out some kind of role in the big leagues, most likely in a super-utility role considering his experience in the outfield and at all four infield positions.

Year	Age	Club (Level)	Lge	AVG	G	AB	R	H	2B	3B	HR	RBI	BB	SO	SB	OBP	SLG
2021	24	Birmingham (AA)	South	.267	78	303	52	81	11	0	20	47	38	97	21	.355	.502
	24	Charlotte (AAA)	East	.370	15	54	9	20	6	0	4	14	5	15	3	.417	.704
	24	Chicago (MLB)	AL	.250	10	32	4	8	3	0	0	2	1	11	0	.273	.344
Major League Totals (1 year)				.250	10	32	4	8	3	0	0	2	1	11	0	.273	.344
Minor League Totals (4 years)				.262	248	910	136	238	54	6	38	139	99	285	45	.341	.459

16 YOLBERT SANCHEZ, 2B/SS

BA GRADE
45 Risk: High

Born: March 3, 1997. **B-T:** R-R. **HT:** 5-11. **WT:** 176. **Signed:** Cuba, 2019. **Signed by:** Marco Paddy.

TRACK RECORD: The 2021 season was the first time that Sanchez faced age-appropriate competition since his 2017-18 season in the Cuban National Series. After signing with the White Sox in 2019 for $2.5 million, he played his first season in the Dominican Summer League, where, at 22, he was the oldest player on the circuit. He made up for lost time in 2021 with a promising season, followed by an assignment to the Arizona Fall League.

SCOUTING REPORT: Sanchez became more aggressive at the plate and was not just swinging to put balls in play, showing more pull-side power and a better contact rate in Double-A. He has a good bat path and bat-to-ball skills, with a balanced, handsy swing. While he's a hit-over-power type and more of a gap-to-gap hitter, Sanchez has average power that could improve with experience. While not a flashy defender, he shows good instincts at shortstop, projecting as an average defender with average range and an average arm. Sanchez spent more time at second base in 2021 while swapping middle infield positions with Lenyn Sosa for the majority of the season. He's a fringy runner but possesses baseball athleticism.

THE FUTURE: After not playing much over the preceding three years, it was beneficial for Sanchez to get a full season of minor league ball under his belt. The upcoming 2022 season will be his chance to really show his full potential.

Year	Age	Club (Level)	Lge	AVG	G	AB	R	H	2B	3B	HR	RBI	BB	SO	SB	OBP	SLG
2021	24	Winston-Salem (HiA)	East	.286	60	217	28	62	7	0	5	29	18	33	2	.340	.387
	24	Birmingham (AA)	South	.343	39	143	15	49	6	0	4	13	5	16	3	.369	.469
Minor League Totals (2 years)				.306	128	471	62	144	21	1	11	54	38	61	8	.360	.425

17 LENYN SOSA, SS

BA GRADE
45 Risk: High

Born: Jan. 25, 2000. **B-T:** R-R. **HT:** 6-0. **WT:** 180. **Signed:** Venezuela, 2016. **Signed by:** Amador Arias.

TRACK RECORD: Sosa has been young for each level since skipping over the Dominican Summer League and instead debuting in the Rookie-level Arizona League. He started to show his true potential at High-A Winston-Salem in 2021before being promoted to Double-A Birmingham.

SCOUTING REPORT: More of a line drive gap-to-gap hitter, Sosa has added strength to his lower half and showed more power at Winston-Salem, hitting 10 home runs while registering exit velos that were just above league average. However, Sosa needs to develop a more consistent approach, as he gets reactionary when he's not hitting well and tries to do too much. An aggressive hitter who walked in less than 4% of his plate appearances, Sosa needs to get himself in a better position to hit and make better swing decisions.

He split time between shortstop and second base. He's not rangy but has good hands and internal clock. **THE FUTURE:** Sosa struggled at the plate with Birmingham and likely will return there in 2022 for more seasoning. He profiles best as a utility infielder, able to handle all three infield positions.

Year	Age	Club (Level)	Lge	AVG	G	AB	R	H	2B	3B	HR	RBI	BB	SO	SB	OBP	SLG
2021	21	Winston-Salem (HiA)	East	.290	82	334	45	97	19	1	10	49	14	77	3	.321	.443
	21	Birmingham (AA)	South	.214	33	117	10	25	5	0	1	7	2	28	0	.240	.282
Minor League Totals (5 years)				.268	344	1387	190	372	76	8	24	165	64	267	14	.304	.386

18 MICKER ADOLFO, OF

BA GRADE
45 Risk: High

Born: Sept. 11, 1996. **B-T:** R-R. **HT:** 6-4. **WT:** 230. **Signed:** Dominican Republic, 2013. **Signed by:** Marco Paddy.

TRACK RECORD: Adolfo continues to show off his plus-plus raw power on the field when he is able to stay healthy. The native of the Dominican Republic signed with the White Sox for $1.6 million during the 2013 international period. His development has been slowed by injuries, the most recent being Tommy John surgery in 2018 and arthroscopic cleanup surgery in 2019. Finally healthy in 2021, Adolfo combined for 25 home runs between Double-A Birmingham and Triple-A Charlotte. That power comes with big strikeout totals. He fanned in 34% of his plate appearances.

SCOUTING REPORT: The time off the field has certainly slowed Adolfo's development as a hitter, but he'll continue to get opportunities not just because of the power but also his ability to play right field. He worked on his swing prior to the 2021 season, as his bat path gets steep at times and the bat is late getting into the zone. He needs to get behind the ball, control his center mass better and utilize his lower half. The White Sox staff believe his swing doesn't need a major overhaul, but rather small tweaks that will help the slugger find more consistency. Adolfo is a solid defender who tracks well and possesses a plus-plus arm.

THE FUTURE: Adolfo continued making up for lost time by playing in the Dominican Winter League this offseason. His power potential gives him a shot at an MLB role in 2022 or 2023 if he can stay healthy.

Year	Age	Club (Level)	Lge	AVG	G	AB	R	H	2B	3B	HR	RBI	BB	SO	SB	OBP	SLG
2021	24	Birmingham (AA)	South	.249	57	217	33	54	15	0	15	46	19	85	1	.318	.525
	24	Charlotte (AAA)	East	.240	44	150	23	36	9	1	10	23	12	53	3	.301	.513
Minor League Totals (8 years)				.248	465	1735	250	431	110	8	65	253	152	642	11	.321	.433

19 TANNER McDOUGAL, RHP

BA GRADE
50 Risk: Extreme

Born: April 3, 2003. **B-T:** R-R. **HT:** 6-5. **WT:** 185. **Drafted:** HS—Las Vegas, 2021 (5th round). **Signed by:** Mike Baker.

TRACK RECORD: The White Sox saved bonus pool money on many of their top ten draft picks, allotting much of the savings to sign McDougal, a fifth-round selection. A projectable righthanded high school pitcher from Las Vegas, the White Sox signed McDougal for a well above-slot bonus of $850,000. The former Oregon commit appeared in six games in the Arizona Complex League. He suffered an elbow injury and had Tommy John surgery in late October.

SCOUTING REPORT: With a tall, projectable frame and a loose arm, McDougal delivers a 92-94 mph fastball that touches 96. He lands his high-spin breaking ball that resembles a slurve at mid-80s slider speed, and has the makings of a plus pitch. He doesn't yet have a lot of feel for his 81-85 mph changeup, too often slowing down his arm during his delivery. Amateur scouts were concerned with his crossfire delivery that culminated in a violent head whack. Due to ample moving parts and violence in his delivery, many evaluators foresee an eventual move to the bullpen. Prior to the injury, White Sox staff worked with McDougal to get better direction toward the plate in hopes it would help the command and the shape of his fastball.

THE FUTURE: McDougal will spend the entire 2022 season rehabbing the elbow and will be 20 years old when he returns to the mound in 2023.

Year	Age	Club (Level)	Lge	W	L	ERA	G	GS	IP	H	HR	BB	SO	BB/9	SO/9	WHIP	AVG
2021	18	White Sox (R)	ACL	1	2	9.31	6	4	9	10	2	5	17	4.7	15.8	1.55	.278
Minor League Totals (1 year)				1	2	9.31	6	4	9	10	2	5	17	4.66	15.83	1.55	.278

20 CRISTIAN MENA, RHP

BA GRADE
50 Risk: Extreme

Born: Dec. 21, 2002. **B-T:** R-R. **HT:** 6-2. **WT:** 170. **Signed:** Dominican Republic, 2019. **Signed by:** Marino De Leon.

TRACK RECORD: Mena signed with the White Sox for $250,000 during the

2019 international signing period, finally making his pro debut in the 2021 Arizona Complex League. His projectable frame and mature demeanor marked him as one of more intriguing pitchers on the Rookie-level circuit.

SCOUTING REPORT: With a good feel for throwing strikes, Mena commands all three of his pitches, with his go-to offering a four-seam fastball sitting 91-93 mph, running it up to 95 mph at its peak. With plenty of room on his frame to add strength, his fastball velocity is expected to creep upward as he matures physically. His 78-81 mph curveball has 11-to-5 shape but will get slurvy at times. At its best, he adds more depth, getting closer to true 12-to-6 break. He mixes in a mid-80s changeup that performs inconsistently and is often shelved for long stretches. Mena uses an easy, athletic delivery, although he tends to get a little crossbody at times, affecting the shape of his pitches. Observers noted that the components of Mena's game were better than the results he had in Arizona.

THE FUTURE: Mena will be just 19 next season, so more time at the White Sox complex may be in order. But with the maturity he showed in his first season stateside, there's a good chance he gets to Low-A before the end of the summer.

Year	Age	Club (Level)	Lge	W	L	ERA	G	GS	IP	H	HR	BB	SO	BB/9	SO/9	WHIP	AVG
2021	18	White Sox (R)	ACL	1	4	7.82	13	12	48	69	8	21	62	3.9	11.5	1.86	.337
Minor League Totals (1 year)				1	4	7.82	13	12	48	69	8	21	62	3.91	11.54	1.86	.337

21 BLAKE RUTHERFORD, OF

BA GRADE
40 Risk: Medium

Born: May 2, 1997. **B-T:** L-R. **HT:** 6-3. **WT:** 205. **Drafted:** HS—West Hills, Calif., 2016 (1st round). **Signed by:** Bobby Dejardin (Yankees).

TRACK RECORD: Rutherford has spent quite a few years on prospect lists since being a first-round pick of the Yankees in 2016. He was the centerpiece of the package acquired in a 2017 mid-season trade that sent three big league players to New York. The anticipated power increase hasn't materialized, and he profiles as a left fielder defensively. Rutherford hit just 11 home runs during a full season with Triple-A Charlotte, a notorious hitters' haven.

SCOUTING REPORT: While expectations have been lowered, the White Sox believe Rutherford can be a contributor in the big leagues. His struggles at the plate come from having inconsistent at-bats and too often trying to do too much. Mechanical flaws in Rutherford's swing have contributed to his struggles, with holes that are easily recognizable versus lefthanders. Scouts note that there was an adjustment in his mentality at the plate over the course of 2021. He now goes to the plate looking for base hits and doesn't hunt for home runs. The last adjustment for Rutherford will be expanding on that mentality by marrying it with a swing path more conducive for hard flyball contact. Whether he can make those adjustments remains to be seen, as Rutherford has struggled to find his best approach at the plate throughout his professional career. He's mostly limited to left field, where he makes the routine plays but is hardly the center fielder or even above-average right fielder many envisioned.

THE FUTURE: Rutherford still occupies a spot on the White Sox 40-man roster. He'll likely return to Triple-A in 2022. He turns 25 in May, and time is running out on Rutherford's faded star.

Year	Age	Club (Level)	Lge	AVG	G	AB	R	H	2B	3B	HR	RBI	BB	SO	SB	OBP	SLG
2021	24	Charlotte (AAA)	East	.250	115	448	59	112	30	3	11	54	21	119	4	.286	.404
Minor League Totals (6 years)				.272	482	1843	244	502	105	21	30	228	143	433	38	.325	.401

22 CALEB FREEMAN, RHP

BA GRADE
45 Risk: High

Born: Feb. 23, 1998. **B-T:** R-R. **HT:** 6-1. **WT:** 195. **Drafted:** Texas Tech, 2019 (15th round). **Signed by:** Ryan Dorsey.

TRACK RECORD: Freeman's tantalizing stuff has often been coupled with inconsistency, even dating back to his final year at Texas Tech. He was expected to be the Red Raiders' closer in 2019 but was plagued by significant control and command woes. While there's still room for improvement, the results in his two pro seasons have been enough to justify their faith in his potential. Freeman reached Double-A Birmingham midway through 2021, posting a 2.70 ERA and an outstanding 22-to-5 strikeout-to-walk ratio across 16.2 innings.

SCOUTING REPORT: With three potential plus pitches, Freeman has a chance of developing into a high-leverage reliever. Due to his loud stuff, Freeman will continue to get plenty of opportunities to prove his mettle in that role over the coming years. His fastball ranges from 93-97 mph with excellent vertical break and late life, though it should be noted that he's had velocity dips dating back to his time at Texas Tech. Freeman's curveball, a true 12-to-6 downer in the high 70s, is another pitch with plus potential. Since joining the White Sox organization, he's added a mid-80s slider that he uses against righthanded batters almost exclusively. Freeman delivers his pitches with a balanced, high three-quarters delivery.

THE FUTURE: Freeman ended the 2021 season in the Arizona Fall League, having been sent there to prove himself against more advanced hitters. He responded with a solid fall season. He's on track to earn a spot in the White Sox bullpen before long if he continues to prove that he can command his impressive arsenal.

Year	Age	Club (Level)	Lge	W	L	ERA	G	GS	IP	H	HR	BB	SO	BB/9	SO/9	WHIP	AVG
2021	23	Winston-Salem (HiA)	East	2	2	3.62	25	0	27	22	5	14	33	4.6	10.9	1.32	.218
	23	Birmingham (AA)	South	0	1	2.70	14	0	16	15	2	5	22	2.7	11.9	1.20	.231
Minor League Totals (3 years)				6	5	2.88	56	0	69	52	9	28	93	3.67	12.19	1.17	.205

23 LUIS MIESES, OF

BA GRADE
40 Risk: High

Born: May 31, 2000. **B-T:** L-L. **HT:** 6-3. **WT:** 180. **Signed:** Dominican Republic, 2016. **Signed by:** Marino De Leon.

TRACK RECORD: It's been a slow climb for the tall, lanky Mieses since signing for $428,000 in 2016. He finally reached full-season ball in 2021.

SCOUTING REPORT: Mieses broke camp with the High-A squad, but his struggles there in May had him heading down the road from Winston-Salem to Kannapolis. Mieses righted the ship in Low-A and returned to Winston-Salem a much-improved hitter, best exemplified by the .930 OPS he compiled during the month of August. Like other hitters with similar physiques, Mieses has a long swing that's often prone to poor barrel control and bad misses. He needs to continue to stay balanced in the box yet swing with authority to best use his bat speed and raw power. Mieses has plenty of juice, posting a .227 isolated slugging in Winston-Salem, hitting 15 home runs in 2021, a new career high. He's a fringy defender taking shorter strides in the outfield, but his above-average arm will keep him in right field.

THE FUTURE: Mieses has a bat to dream on if he continues making adjustments and refining his swing to work with his long levers. The White Sox left him unprotected for the Rule 5 draft.

Year	Age	Club (Level)	Lge	AVG	G	AB	R	H	2B	3B	HR	RBI	BB	SO	SB	OBP	SLG
2021	21	Kannapolis (LoA)	East	.305	52	203	31	62	12	1	6	41	13	33	0	.347	.463
	21	Winston-Salem (HiA)	East	.236	58	220	30	52	19	2	9	33	11	48	0	.278	.464
Minor League Totals (5 years)				.254	276	1085	128	276	63	8	21	153	45	204	6	.287	.385

24 WILBER SANCHEZ, SS

BA GRADE
45 Risk: Extreme

Born: Feb. 21, 2002. **B-T:** R-R. **HT:** 5-10. **WT:** 160. **Signed:** Venezuela, 2019. **Signed by:** Amador Arias.

TRACK RECORD: Signed out of Venezuela in 2019, Sanchez made his pro debut the same year in the Dominican Summer League. He reached the states for the 2021 season, earning an assignment to the Arizona Complex League. Sanchez started getting attention from rival scouts this summer due his tools and scrappy play on the field. After 19 games in rookie ball, he made the jump to Low-A Kannapolis.

SCOUTING REPORT: Sanchez puts balls in play but with a limited amount of impact, battling pitchers with a repeatable stroke and strong bat-to-ball skills. He struggled in his first time away from the complex fields as he battled through slumps and noticeably put pressure on himself after bad at-bats. If his hit tool continues to improve, he has a chance to be a classic speedy top-of-the-order-type capable of putting pressure on the defense with his legs. Sanchez is an above-average defender at shortstop, charging balls hard and displaying easy infield actions, but some observers see him better at second base due to a lack of a true left-side-of-the-infield arm. His plus speed resulted in 17 stolen bases in 51 games, so his legs and baserunning acumen will be a big part of his game.

THE FUTURE: Sanchez should be more comfortable in a return to Kannapolis. He needs a lot more seasoning, especially at the plate, so expect him to be a one level per year-type of player for the time being.

Year	Age	Club (Level)	Lge	AVG	G	AB	R	H	2B	3B	HR	RBI	BB	SO	SB	OBP	SLG
2021	19	White Sox (R)	ACL	.269	19	78	10	21	3	0	2	8	5	23	6	.313	.385
	19	Kannapolis (LoA)	East	.200	34	115	12	23	2	1	4	13	7	55	11	.254	.339
Minor League Totals (2 years)				.257	105	370	54	95	18	4	6	46	40	111	30	.334	.376

25 YOELVIN SILVEN, RHP

BA GRADE
40 Risk: High

Born: June 26, 1999. **B-T:** R-R. **HT:** 6-1. **WT:** 176. **Signed:** Dominican Republic, 2018. **Signed by:** Guillermo Peralta/Ruddy Moreta.

TRACK RECORD: Signed by the White Sox during the 2018 international period, Silven debuted in the Dominican Summer League that same year. While nothing in Silven's profile

screamed prospect upon signing, he's shown enough potential in small samples to indicate that there may be something intriguing developing. He pitched at three levels in 2021, with the biggest improvement coming when he moved to the bullpen.

SCOUTING REPORT: Silven is a bulldog on the mound, although he can often struggle to control his emotions at times. His fastball ranges from 93-97 mph, but the pitch lacks bite or late life, making it fairly easy to barrel. The slider is a work in progress, as the organization is working to add velocity onto the pitch and was a key area of focus during instructional league. The pitch sat 80-82 mph during the regular season but was up to 86 mph during instructional league. Over the course of fall play, Silven and a pitching coach had an ongoing bet as to how hard he was going to throw the slider each day. It's a positive sign that he came out of the fall with a few extra bucks in his pocket.

THE FUTURE: Almost 19 when he signed with the White Sox, Silven will be 23 by midseason. After finishing the year with Double-A Birmingham, he's likely to return there to start 2022. Long-term, Silven projects to fill either a middle-inning relief role or that of a swingman, thriving primarily with his fastball-slider combo.

Year	Age	Club (Level)	Lge	W	L	ERA	G	GS	IP	H	HR	BB	SO	BB/9	SO/9	WHIP	AVG
2021	22	Kannapolis (LoA)	East	2	4	6.68	13	3	31	41	4	10	32	2.9	9.3	1.65	.304
	22	Winston-Salem (HiA)	East	0	0	2.77	7	2	13	9	3	2	11	1.4	7.6	0.85	.191
	22	Birmingham (AA)	South	0	0	7.71	4	0	4	8	0	2	3	3.9	5.8	2.14	.364
Minor League Totals (4 years)				3	14	4.34	57	17	164	181	18	37	176	2.03	9.68	1.33	.278

26 BENNETT SOUSA, LHP

BA GRADE **40** Risk: High

Born: April 6, 1995. **B-T:** L-L. **HT:** 6-3. **WT:** 220. **Drafted:** Virginia, 2018 (10th round). **Signed by:** Abe Fernandez.

TRACK RECORD: Sousa was a 10th-round pick by the White Sox in 2018 after a four-year career at Virginia. He was never a highly regarded prospect until a velocity jump in 2021 coupled with solid results put him on the radar. Sousa was added to the 40-man roster just before the deadline last November. His 13.5 strikeouts per nine innings was by far the best mark of his pro career.

SCOUTING REPORT: By the time he got to Triple-A, Sousa's fastball was sitting 93-97 mph with late life. Coming out of a high three-quarters delivery with deception, his fastball and slider combination play up. The slider is a reverse-split pitch. It's effective against righthanded batters, but less so left-on-left. Early in the season he was sitting 83-84 mph, but as his fastball velocity increased the slider also climbed, sitting 85-88 mph at season's end. With a strong one-two punch, Sousa looks like a potential bullpen option for the White Sox in 2022 with the ability to miss bats and provide some firepower in the later innings.

THE FUTURE: Sousa will head to big league camp looking to earn a spot in the White Sox bullpen, but more likely will be on the Charlotte-to-Chicago shuttle throughout the year.

Year	Age	Club (Level)	Lge	W	L	ERA	G	GS	IP	H	HR	BB	SO	BB/9	SO/9	WHIP	AVG
2021	26	Birmingham (AA)	South	0	1	3.28	20	0	24	14	4	15	38	5.5	13.9	1.18	.159
	26	Charlotte (AAA)	East	4	2	3.97	21	0	22	23	3	5	33	2.0	13.1	1.24	.258
Minor League Totals (4 years)				9	9	2.56	104	0	148	123	14	40	187	2.44	11.40	1.10	.224

27 BROOKS GOSSWEIN, LHP

BA GRADE **40** Risk: High

Born: Oct. 9, 1998. **B-T:** L-L. **HT:** 6-2. **WT:** 205. **Drafted:** Bradley, 2021 (4th round). **Signed by:** JJ Lally.

TRACK RECORD: Gosswein was picked by the White Sox after a four-year career at Bradley. He signed for a below-slot $200,000 bonus. While his college results were mixed, the White Sox see interesting tools to work with, most notably a five-pitch mix and solid command.

SCOUTING REPORT: With both a four-seam fastball and a two-seam sinker that range from 92-96 mph, Gosswein has an interesting arsenal that gives the White Sox staff something to work with as he develops. The two-seamer gets plenty of sink, but he needs to improve the differential between the two fastballs, as they'll often bleed together, creating suboptimal shape. Both of his breaking balls project as average pitches, with improvement coming once he gets more separation between the 79-81 mph curveball and 82-84 mph slider. Rounding out the diverse repertoire is a potentially above-average 83-85 mph changeup.

THE FUTURE: Gosswein is an arm-strength lefty who could fit as either a swingman or a versatile reliever. A solid showing in spring training could earn him an assignment to High-A Winston-Salem.

Year	Age	Club (Level)	Lge	W	L	ERA	G	GS	IP	H	HR	BB	SO	BB/9	SO/9	WHIP	AVG
2021	22	White Sox (R)	ACL	0	0	1.13	3	3	8	6	0	1	8	1.1	9.0	0.88	.214
	22	Kannapolis (LoA)	East	0	0	4.00	3	3	9	6	1	5	7	5.0	7.0	1.22	.200
Minor League Totals (1 year)				0	0	2.65	6	6	17	12	1	6	15	3.18	7.94	1.06	.207

28 GIL LUNA, LHP

BA GRADE

40 Risk: High

Born: July 29, 1999. **B-T:** L-L. **HT:** 5-10. **WT:** 173. **Drafted:** Arizona, 2021 (9th round). **Signed by:** John Kazanas.

TRACK RECORD: Luna wrapped up a four-year career at Arizona as one of the Wildcats' key bullpen pieces, finishing his senior year with a 1.69 ERA and 31 strikeouts in 21.1 innings. The White Sox drafted him in the ninth round, signing the diminutive lefthander for a money-saving $10,000.

SCOUTING REPORT: Luna delivers a 94-96 mph fastball coming out of a lower release point, giving the pitch deception. The slider flashes plus but for now is a below-average pitch projecting to be a future average offering that plays up because of the fastball velocity. The improvement of the breaking ball should ultimately give Luna a weapon to use against lefthanded batters. He needs to throw it harder, as right now it's in the 82-84 mph range and needs to be a few ticks harder to truly be effective. He shows confidence in his changeup, using it as a heavy focal point when attacking righthanded hitters.

THE FUTURE: Luna projects as a middle reliever, but with continued improvement to his slider he could be in the mix for a seventh or eighth inning role.

Year	Age	Club (Level)	Lge	W	L	ERA	G	GS	IP	H	HR	BB	SO	BB/9	SO/9	WHIP	AVG
2021	21	White Sox (R)	ACL	0	0	0.00	6	0	9	3	0	4	17	4.0	17.0	0.78	.103
	21	Kannapolis (LoA)	East	0	0	0.00	4	0	6	2	0	2	7	2.8	10.0	0.63	.111
Minor League Totals (1 year)				0	0	0.00	10	0	15	5	0	6	24	3.52	14.09	0.72	.106

29 WILFRED VERAS, 3B/1B

BA GRADE

45 Risk: Extreme

Born: Nov. 15, 2002. **B-T:** R-R. **HT:** 6-2. **WT:** 180. **Signed:** Dominican Republic, 2019. **Signed by:** Ruddy Moreta.

TRACK RECORD: Veras is part of a family that's become baseball royalty in the Dominican Republic. His father, Wilton, played two seasons with the Red Sox at the turn of the 21st century, but most notably, his mother is the sister of Fernando Tatis, Sr. Veras impressed opposing evaluators in the Arizona Complex League with his raw power and hitting skills.

SCOUTING REPORT: Veras has big raw power that he can get to with a strong, compact swing. A free swinger who makes minimal adjustments, he still has improvement ahead, but he's competitive in the box and grinds out at-bats. His long term defensive home is still in question. Veras split time at both corner infield positions, while also working out in the outfield. He's a below-average runner with an average arm.

THE FUTURE: Veras is still very much a work in progress, but the hit tool and raw power will give him plenty of opportunities to develop. He could break camp with the squad going to Low-A Kannapolis.

Year	Age	Club (Level)	Lge	AVG	G	AB	R	H	2B	3B	HR	RBI	BB	SO	SB	OBP	SLG
2021	18	White Sox (R)	ACL	.322	46	152	25	49	16	2	4	26	21	42	3	.416	.533
Minor League Totals (1 year)				.322	46	152	25	49	16	2	4	26	21	42	3	.416	.533

30 ADAM HACKENBERG, C

BA GRADE

40 Risk: High

Born: Sept. 8, 1999. **B-T:** R-R. **HT:** 6-1. **WT:** 225. **Drafted:** Clemson, 2021 (18th round). **Signed by:** Kevin Burrell.

TRACK RECORD: Hackenberg comes from an athletic family. His brother Christian was a quarterback drafted by the Jets. His other brother Brandon was a recent first-round pick in the 2021 Major League Soccer draft. Adam spent two years as Clemson's primary catcher.

SCOUTING REPORT: Already ranking as the top defensive catcher in the system, Hackenberg moves easily behind the plate and understands the game well, with a chance to be a plus defender. Blessed with a plus arm, Hackenberg threw out 44% of the basestealers during his stint with Kannapolis. He has more power in his bat than he showed in college, with good barrel-to-ball skills and ability to control the zone. He has average raw power but he shows the ability to get to it in games.

THE FUTURE: Hackenberg is advanced enough to start 2022 at High-A Winston-Salem, where the White Sox will get an indication whether his strong start is indicative of a step forward offensively.

Year	Age	Club (Level)	Lge	AVG	G	AB	R	H	2B	3B	HR	RBI	BB	SO	SB	OBP	SLG
2021	21	White Sox (R)	ACL	.211	6	19	3	4	3	0	0	2	4	0	0	.375	.368
	21	Kannapolis (LoA)	East	.346	21	81	8	28	4	1	1	11	4	16	0	.384	.457
Minor League Totals (1 year)				.320	27	100	11	32	7	1	1	13	8	16	0	.382	.440

MORE PROSPECTS TO KNOW

31. KADE McCLURE, RHP

The 2017 sixth-round pick has ranked higher in previous year's prospect lists. He made it to Triple-A after a strong half-season in Double-A, but his fastball has backed up.

32. LUKE SHILLING, RHP
SLEEPER

The 15th-round pick in 2018 out of Illinois showed promise when healthy, with a 93-98 mph fastball and two plus breaking balls, but has spent most of his career on the injured list and had Tommy John surgery in 2021. If healthy, he's got a chance to be a reliever prospect.

33. THEO DENLINGER, RHP

The second of two pitchers from Bradley taken in the top 10 rounds in 2021, Denlinger is already 25 but impressed in instructional league with his intimidating presence and 94-97 mph fastball. Off the field, he's an accomplished blacksmith.

34. JOHAN DOMINGUEZ, RHP

The former Brewers farmhand has picked up velocity, now touching 96-97 mph, and made it to the Arizona Fall League in 2021. He'll be 26 for all of the 2022 season, but he could prove to be a late bloomer.

35. McKINLEY MOORE, RHP

Moore has plenty of arm strength with a fastball up to 99 mph but is more of a thrower than a pitcher. His slider flashes plus as well.

36. FRASER ELLARD, LHP

The 2021 eighth-round pick from Liberty throws from a lower slot with a mid-90s fastball.

37. MISAEL GONZALEZ, OF

Gonzalez struggled with the bat in his first taste of full-season ball but won't turn 21 until May.

38. TAYLOR BROADWAY, RHP

The former Mississippi closer is fearless on the mound and gets good carry on his fastball. He'll move quickly and with his Southeastern Conference experience could get to Double-A in 2022.

39. JOHNNY RAY, RHP

The Texas Christian product struggled with getting batters out in college despite a plus fastball up to 98 mph. He showed progress in instructional league and could be a sleeper if he improves the life on his fastball and command of all four pitches.

40. DAVIS MARTIN, RHP

Martin commands all four pitches and had an increase in velocity in 2021, which saw him make it all the way to Double-A.

TOP PROSPECTS OF THE DECADE

Year	Player, Pos	2021 Org
2012	Addison Reed, RHP	Did not play
2013	Courtney Hawkins, OF	Atlantic League
2014	Jose Abreu, 1B	White Sox
2015	Carlos Rodon, LHP	White Sox
2016	Tim Anderson, SS	White Sox
2017	Yoan Moncada, 2B/3B	White Sox
2018	Eloy Jimenez, OF	White Sox
2019	Eloy Jimenez, OF	White Sox
2020	Luis Robert, OF	White Sox
2021	Andrew Vaughn, 1B	White Sox

TOP DRAFT PICKS OF THE DECADE

Year	Player, Pos	2021 Org
2012	Courtney Hawkins, OF	Atlantic League
2013	Tim Anderson, SS	White Sox
2014	Carlos Rodon, LHP	White Sox
2015	Carson Fulmer, RHP	Reds
2016	Zack Collins, C	White Sox
2017	Jake Burger, 3B	White Sox
2018	Nick Madrigal, SS	Cubs
2019	Andrew Vaughn, 1B	White Sox
2020	Garrett Crochet, LHP	White Sox
2021	Colson Montgomery, SS	White Sox

Cincinnati Reds

BY J.J. COOPER

It's easy to forget that a lot of things went well for Cincinnati in 2021.

The Reds got excellent production from National League Rookie of the Year Jonathan India, a season to remember out of outfielder Nick Castellanos and a resurgent bounceback year from first baseman Joey Votto.

The team also got solid work from a rotation fronted by Luis Castillo and Tyler Mahle. Wade Miley had his best season in years while rookie righthander Vladimir Gutierrez stepped in to claim the No. 5 starter's role.

But it wasn't enough.

Even with a solid lineup and rotation, the Reds  were undone by their bullpen, which was one of the worst in the majors, and finished seven games behind the Cardinals in the wild card race

No one reliever can fix a bullpen, but it was notable that Raisel Iglesias, the closer the Reds traded for virtually nothing in a salary dump in December 2020, was one of the best relievers in the American League in 2021. Iglesias' departure was a reminder that the Reds are going to have trouble getting out of the muddy middle of the NL while attempting to keep their payroll in the $125 million range.

There were more reminders at the beginning of the 2021-22 offseason of how difficult staying within those bounds can be. Catcher Tucker Barnhart was traded to the Tigers for a very modest return to clear his salary off the books. Miley was waived, even though he went 12-7, 3.32 in 163 innings.

In neither case could it be said the Reds were better off after those moves, but salary concerns forced them.

That leaves the Reds in a tricky spot. Their 83 wins in 2021 were the most the team has had since it won 90 in 2013 and the fourth-most games it's won in the 21st century.

The emergence of India, Gutierrez, Mahle and catcher Tyler Stephenson gives the club something to build around.

The club's top three prospects—shortstop Jose Barrero, righthander Hunter Greene and lefthander Nick Lodolo—should all settle into Cincinnati in 2022 as well. The bullpen also has a number of big league-ready prospects to choose from at some point in the near future.

Beyond those top three, there is depth in the Reds system, although much of it is at the lower levels of the minors. The Reds international scouting department has seen a recent resurgence. Shortstop Elly de la Cruz leads an impressive group of teenage prospects.

Rookie of the Year Jonathan India emerged as the Reds' second baseman and leadoff hitter.

PROJECTED 2025 LINEUP

Catcher	Tyler Stephenson	28
First Base	Rece Hinds	24
Second Base	Jonathan India	28
Third Base	Elly de la Cruz	23
Shortstop	Jose Barrero	27
Left Field	Nick Senzel	30
Center Field	Matt McLain	25
Right Field	Austin Hendrick	24
Designated Hitter	Jesse Winker	31
No. 1 Starter	Luis Castillo	32
No. 2 Starter	Nick Lodolo	27
No. 3 Starter	Hunter Greene	25
No. 4 Starter	Tyler Mahle	30
No. 5 Starter	Vladimir Gutierrez	29
Closer	Graham Ashcraft	27

At the same time, a lot of this team is old, expensive and in some cases almost immovable because of big contracts and poor production. Second baseman Mike Moustakas is set to make $34 million over the next two seasons, but doesn't have a clear spot in the lineup now that India has emerged. Third baseman Eugenio Suarez is delivering power, but he also hit .199/.293/.440 over the past two seasons. He's signed for the next three years at $11 million per year.

The question then becomes whether the Reds' young talent can help the team climb above .500, or whether the struggle to keep the payroll from climbing will force the team to sacrifice the depth it needs. ∎

DEPTH CHART

CINCINNATI REDS

TOP 2022 ROOKIES	RANK
Hunter Greene, RHP	2
Nick Lodolo, LHP	3
Dauri Moreta, RHP	15

BREAKOUT PROSPECTS	RANK
Ariel Almote, OF	21
Carlos Jorge, SS	25
Leonardo Balcazar, SS	27

SOURCE OF TOP 30 TALENT

Homegrown	29	Acquired	1
College	9	Trade	1
High School	1	Rule 5 draft	0
High School	8	Independent leagues	0
Nondrafted free agent	2	Free agents/waivers	0
International	9		

LF
Jay Allen (7)
Malvin Valdez

CF
TJ Friedl (20)
Mike Siani (30)
Justice Thompson
Jacob Hurtubise

R
Austin Hendrick (6)
Allan Cerda (14)
Ariel Almonte (21)
Yerlin Confidan (29)
Drew Mount

3B
Rece Hinds (8)

SS
Jose Barrero (1)
Elly de la Cruz (4)
Jose Torres (12)
Leonardo Balcazar (27)

2B
Tyler Callihan (17)
Ivan Johnson (18)
Alejo Lopez (24)
Carlos Jorge (25)
Francisco Urbanez

1B
Ruben Ibarra

C
Mat Nelson (11)
Daniel Vellojin (19)
Mark Kolozvary (26)
Jackson Miller

LHP

LHSP	LHRP
Nick Lodolo (3)	Evan Kravetz
Andrew Abbott (22)	
Reiver Sanmartin (28)	

RHP

RHSP	RHRP
Hunter Greene (2)	Bryce Bonnin (10)
Graham Ashcraft (9)	Dauri Moreta (15)
Carson Spiers (13)	Alexis Diaz (23)
Christian Roa (16)	Daniel Duarte
Lyon Richardson	Jared Solomon
James Marinan	Joe Boyle
Jose Franco	Steven Branche
Kevin Abel	Thomas Farr
Gabriel Aguilera	Rynardo Cruz
	Vincent Timpanelli
	Hunter Parks
	Braxton Roxby

1

JOSE BARRERO, SS

Born: April 5, 1998. **B-T:** R-R. **HT:** 6-2. **WT:** 175.
Signed: Cuba, 2017.
Signed by: Chris Buckley/Tony Arias/Miguel Machado/
Jim Stockel/Bob Engle/Hector Otero.

TRACK RECORD: For a team that rarely spends big on free agents, the Reds were always willing to spend on Cuban international free agents under the old format, where bonuses weren't strictly limited. The signings of Aroldis Chapman and Raisel Iglesias gave a big payoff. Vladimir Gutierrez and Barrero should give the Reds a couple more potentially valuable additions. Barrero signed for $5 million in 2017. A second baseman in Cuba, Barrero quickly took to shortstop in the U.S. A shoulder injury slowed his U.S. debut in 2018, but he had an excellent 2019 season at High-A. On the heels of that, the Reds aggressively promoted him to the majors late in 2020. Barrero showed he wasn't ready, but he responded by making improvements at the plate in the minors in 2021. He was called up to Cincinnati in September when Kyle Farmer went on the paternity list. When Farmer returned, Barrero got to branch out, playing some second base and center field. He hadn't played second base in a pro game since 2017 and his first game in center field was in the majors, but he showed his adaptability by picking up the new position quickly. Barrero changed his name (from Jose Garcia) to remember and honor his late mother Tania Barrero. She died in May 2021 because of a coronavirus-related illness.

SCOUTING REPORT: Barrero has developed into a solid offensive contributor with above-average power potential and average hitting ability. He is fully capable of crushing fastballs, but his success in the majors will be determined largely by his ability to either better hit or better lay off sliders out of the strike zone. He was regularly victimized by his tendency to chase in his first MLB stint in 2020. In 2021, he did a better job of laying off of sliders well out of the zone than he'd pulled off of in the past, but he's still vulnerable to good sliders just in or out of the strike zone low and away. Barrero is a plus runner who wisely picks out spots to steal. Defensively, Barrero is an above-average defender at shortstop thanks to a plus arm and solid body control. He is at his best coming in on choppers, which he can confidently barehand and fluidly throw to first. He's also excellent when he's fielding balls to his left, but he is less comfortable making plays deep in the hole to his right. He showed his

JOE ROBBINS/ICON SPORTSWIRE VIA GETTY IMAGES

BA GRADE	SCOUTING GRADES
55 Risk: Medium	Hit: 50. Power: 55. Run: 60. Field: 55. Arm: 60.

Projected future grades on 20-80 scouting scale

BEST TOOLS

Best Hitter for Average	Alejo Lopez
Best Power Hitter	Rece Hinds
Best Strike-Zone Discipline	Alejo Lopez
Fastest Baserunner	Elly de la Cruz
Best Athlete	Elly de la Cruz
Best Fastball	Bryce Bonnin
Best Curveball	Nick Lodolo
Best Slider	Graham Ashcraft
Best Changeup	Reiver Sanmartin
Best Control	Nick Lodolo
Best Defensive Catcher	Daniel Vellojin
Best Defensive Infielder	Jose Barrero
Best Infield Arm	Rece Hinds
Best Defensive Outfielder	Mike Siani
Best Outfield Arm	Yerlin Confidan

defensive versatility in Cincinnati last September.
THE FUTURE: Barrero has used only one of his three options, so there's still plenty of time for him to settle into his role with the Reds, even if it may not be on Opening Day in 2022. He has some defensive versatility, but the Reds have a long-term answer at second base and Barrero's bat fits better at shortstop than in center field. Kyle Farmer's surprising 2021 season means the Reds have another option, but Barrero should be a better defender with a better bat long term. ∎

Year	Age	Club (Level)	Lge	AVG	G	AB	R	H	2B	3B	HR	RBI	BB	SO	SB	OBP	SLG
2021	23	Chattanooga (AA)	South	.300	40	160	31	48	9	1	6	28	16	40	8	.367	.481
	23	Louisville (AAA)	East	.306	45	170	31	52	10	0	13	38	20	44	8	.392	.594
	23	Cincinnati (MLB)	NL	.200	21	50	4	10	4	1	0	3	3	17	1	.286	.320
Major League Totals (2 years)				.197	45	117	8	23	4	1	0	5	4	43	2	.242	.248
Minor League Totals (3 years)				.272	314	1216	181	331	78	6	33	174	80	279	44	.333	.428

2 HUNTER GREENE, RHP

Born: Aug. 6, 1999. **B-T:** R-R. **HT:** 6-5. **WT:** 230. **Drafted:** HS—Sherman Oaks, Calif., 2017 (1st round). **Signed by:** Rick Ingalls.

TRACK RECORD: After developing the hardest-throwing pitcher of the 21st century in Aroldis Chapman, the Reds now have the hardest-throwing starting pitcher in baseball. Fully recovered from his 2019 Tommy John surgery, Greene touched 105 mph during Reds spring training, 104 mph during the season and had three different starts where he had 30-plus pitches of 100 mph or harder. He earned a quick promotion to Triple-A Louisville but struggled at times against more experienced hitters. He missed one August start with an irritated AC joint in his right shoulder, but returned to make five more starts.

BA GRADE
55 Risk: High

SCOUTING REPORT: For as hard as Greene throws, his plus-plus fastball is hittable because it has relatively modest life and carry. If a hitter can time it, he can square it up. Nine of the 11 home runs Greene gave up after his promotion to Triple-A came against his fastball, usually when he pitched up in the zone. Greene's combination of a very smooth, fluid delivery and easy-to-pick-up release point means his fastball often doesn't play to its velocity. When Greene is throwing his plus slider for strikes, the combination of it and his fastball can be diabolical. Hitters have to be looking for his fastball, so even if they recognize his slider, all they can do is watch it go by. His improved slider is still inconsistent. Greene doesn't show much confidence in his high-80s changeup, but thanks to his fastball velocity it's an effective chase pitch against lefties. He has above-average control to go with his plus stuff.

THE FUTURE: There's every reason to develop Greene as a starter, although his fallback option is as the hardest-throwing closer in the game.

SCOUTING GRADES:	Fastball: 70	Slider: 60	Changeup: 45	Control: 55

Year	Age	Club (Level)	Lge	W	L	ERA	G	GS	IP	H	HR	BB	SO	BB/9	SO/9	WHIP	AVG
2021	21	Chattanooga (AA)	South	5	0	1.98	7	7	41	27	2	14	60	3.1	13.2	1.00	.186
	21	Louisville (AAA)	East	5	8	4.13	14	14	65	59	11	25	79	3.4	10.9	1.29	.240
Minor League Totals (4 years)				13	16	3.97	42	42	179	160	19	63	234	3.17	11.77	1.25	.237

3 NICK LODOLO, LHP

Born: Feb. 5, 1998. **B-T:** L-L. **HT:** 6-6. **WT:** 205. **Drafted:** Texas Christian, 2019 (1st round). **Signed by:** Paul Scott.

TRACK RECORD: One of the best high school arms in the 2016 draft class, Lodolo was picked 41st overall by the Pirates, but opted to head to Texas Christian. Lodolo's decision paid off when he became the top pitcher in the 2019 draft class. Picked seventh overall by the Reds, Lodolo worked on improving his changeup and adding a slider at the alternate site in 2020. Lodolo's innings were limited in 2021. He had a blister problem that cost him a month early in the season and was shut down with a minor shoulder strain late in the season.

BA GRADE
55 Risk: High

SCOUTING REPORT: While there's nothing spectacular about Lodolo's pitch assortment, he has the rare ability to locate everything he throws and confidence to throw offspeed pitches in fastball counts. His 86-88 mph slider is his lone plus pitch. It's effective against lefties and righties, as it has tight, late break. His average 93-96 mph fastball works because he can run it in and out—he mainly throws a sinker, but also mixes in a four-seamer, and he throws a cutter as well. His fringy, sweepy curveball became much less of a factor as he gained confidence in his slider. His average changeup has improved as a pro, and he's shown confidence to spot it against lefties and righties. Lodolo already has plus control with his repeatable delivery, and he projects to have future plus command.

THE FUTURE: Lodolo is unlikely to develop into an ace, but he is one of the safer bets in the minors to develop into a solid MLB starter. His confidence facing righthanded hitters and his command make everything play up, giving him a shot to be a reliable No. 3 or No. 4 starter.

SCOUTING GRADES:	Fastball: 50	Slider: 60	Cutter: 50	Curveball: 40	Changeup: 50	Control: 60

Year	Age	Club (Level)	Lge	W	L	ERA	G	GS	IP	H	HR	BB	SO	BB/9	SO/9	WHIP	AVG
2021	23	Chattanooga (AA)	South	2	1	1.84	10	10	44	31	1	9	68	1.8	13.9	0.91	.196
	23	Louisville (AAA)	East	0	1	5.40	3	3	6	7	2	2	10	2.7	13.5	1.35	.269
Minor League Totals (3 years)				2	3	2.35	21	21	69	56	4	11	108	1.43	14.09	0.97	.218

4 ELLY DE LA CRUZ, SS/3B

Born: Jan. 11, 2002. **B-T:** B-R. **HT:** 6-5. **WT:** 195. **Signed:** Dominican Republic, 2018. **Signed by:** Richard Jimenez.

TRACK RECORD: Few prospects have come as quickly out of nowhere into prominence as de la Cruz. Signed for just $65,000, de la Cruz made his Dominican Summer League debut in 2019 and then had to wait until 2021 to get into another game—he wasn't part of the Reds alternate site or instructional league in 2020. He played his way out of the Arizona Complex League by having 11 extra-base hits in just 11 games. Since signing he's grown three inches and added 35 pounds.

BA GRADE

60 Risk: Extreme

SCOUTING REPORT: No Reds prospect has a higher ceiling than de la Cruz. There are few players in the majors or minors with three 70s on their scouting report. De la Cruz is a plus-plus runner with a plus-plus arm and plus-plus raw power. His tool set and his frame draw comparisons to Pirates shortstop prospect Oneil Cruz. Coaches and scouts rave that de la Cruz's understanding of the game may be as impressive as his tools and he embraces working to get better. De la Cruz split his time between shortstop and third base. He has a legitimate shot to stick at short thanks to excellent hands and his railgun of an arm, but he would fit at third or in center field as well. The biggest concern with de la Cruz is his extremely aggressive at-bats. He approaches every at-bat as if he can hit everything. More advanced pitchers will force him to adjust, but he has the bat-to-ball skills to eventually do so.

THE FUTURE: De la Cruz looked like a future star in his U.S. debut. He has a lot of work ahead of him and his approach will have to improve, but he has a shot to hit in the middle of the lineup while also playing a premium defensive position. He should be ready for High-A Dayton.

SCOUTING GRADES:	Hitting: 50	Power: 60	Running: 70	Fielding: 55	Arm: 70

Year	Age	Club (Level)	Lge	AVG	G	AB	R	H	2B	3B	HR	RBI	BB	SO	SB	OBP	SLG
2021	19	Reds (R)	ACL	.400	11	50	13	20	6	2	3	13	4	15	2	.455	.780
2021	19	Daytona (LoA)	SEast	.269	50	197	22	53	12	7	5	29	10	65	8	.305	.477
Minor League Totals (2 years)				.291	104	412	59	120	29	10	9	68	28	125	13	.342	.476

5 MATT McLAIN, SS

Born: Aug. 6, 1999. **B-T:** R-R. **HT:** 5-11. **WT:** 180. **Drafted:** UCLA, 2021 (1st round). **Signed by:** Jimmy Moran.

TRACK RECORD: A two-time first-round pick, McLain spurned the D-backs as the 25th pick in the 2018 draft—he was the fast riser in a high school shortstop class that also included Brice Turang and Xavier Edwards. McLain's father was a college football player at UCLA, his mother was a college softball and volleyball player and his brothers Sean and Nick play baseball at Arizona State and UCLA, respectively.

SCOUTING REPORT: McLain's pro debut matched what he did at UCLA. He put together consistent at-bats and rarely swung and missed, but he didn't hit the ball particularly hard. He will have to rework his swing if he wants to hit for more power. His approach is contact-oriented, and his swing doesn't generate much of a load, but it does leave him able to control the barrel of the bat.

BA GRADE

55 Risk: High

He rarely fails to make contact, but he also posts modest exit velocities. Defensively, McLain makes all the plays at shortstop, he just doesn't always look like he does it easily. There's effort and a lack of fluidity to McLain's actions, but he has soft hands and an above-average arm that's enough to stay at the position. He also played center field as a freshman at UCLA and would fit there or at second base if needed.

THE FUTURE: Much like fellow Reds prospect Nick Lodolo, McLain is the kind of steady, solid contributor who is viewed as a relatively safe first-round pick. He's unlikely to be a regular all-star, but he should be a solid big leaguer. A return to High-A Dayton is possible to start the season, but he should spend much of 2022 at Double-A.

SCOUTING GRADES:	Hitting: 60	Power: 40	Running: 60	Fielding: 50	Arm: 55

Year	Age	Club (Level)	Lge	AVG	G	AB	R	H	2B	3B	HR	RBI	BB	SO	SB	OBP	SLG
2021	21	Reds (R)	ACL	.429	2	7	2	3	2	1	0	0	0	0	0	.429	1.000
	21	Dayton (HiA)	Cent	.273	29	99	15	27	6	0	3	19	17	24	10	.387	.424
Minor League Totals (1 year)				.283	31	106	17	30	8	1	3	19	17	24	10	.389	.462

6 AUSTIN HENDRICK, OF

Born: June 15, 2001. **B-T:** L-L. **HT:** 6-0. **WT:** 195. **Drafted:** HS—Imperial, Pa., 2020 (1st round). **Signed by:** Jeff Brookens.

TRACK RECORD: When the Reds picked Hendrick 12th overall in 2020, it was just the third time in draft history that Cincinnati had picked a prep outfielder in the top 15 picks of a draft. The previous two—Jay Bruce and Austin Kearns—both worked out. Hendrick's pro debut in 2021 didn't go as planned. A groin strain sidelined him for a month, and when he did play his power production was less than expected while his strikeout rate soared.

SCOUTING REPORT: Hendrick's first full pro season was a rather mixed bag. He struck out in 38% of his plate appearances and his exceptional bat speed did not lead to many home runs. He walked 19% of the time, however, and showed an advanced batting eye. Unlike many Class A hitters with strikeout issues, Hendrick doesn't really struggle with pitch recognition. His problem is he too often fouls off pitches he should drive. Hendrick's swing is quite steep. When he does connect it leads to plenty of long fly balls, but the loft in his swing means his barrel is not in the strike zone for very long. If he can fix that, Hendrick has the components to be a very productive hitter. His bat speed, batting eye and power give him the makings of at least an average hitter with plus power if he can fix his issues. His plus arm and fringe-average speed should work in right field, but as with most right fielders, it will depend on him being a very productive hitter.

THE FUTURE: Hendrick's 2021 season was disappointing, but the pieces are still there for him to be a potential middle-of-the-order hitter. He'll head to High-A Dayton with a healthy to-do list, but his top priority will be to make more quality contact.

BA GRADE

50 Risk: High

SCOUTING GRADES:	Hitting: 50	Power: 60	Running: 45	Fielding: 45	Arm: 60

Year	Age	Club (Level)	Lge	AVG	G	AB	R	H	2B	3B	HR	RBI	BB	SO	SB	OBP	SLG
2021	20	Daytona (LoA)	SEast	.211	63	209	30	44	16	0	7	29	51	100	4	.380	.388
Minor League Totals (2 years)				.211	63	209	30	44	16	0	7	29	51	100	4	.380	.388

7 JAY ALLEN, OF

Born: Nov. 22, 2002. **B-T:** R-R. **HT:** 6-3. **WT:** 190. **Drafted:** HS—Fort Pierce, Fla., 2021 (1st round). **Signed by:** Andrew Fabian.

TRACK RECORD: A Florida recruit in baseball, Allen also had college options in football and participated in the Elite 11 quarterback camp finals—a camp for prep quarterbacks considered among the best in the nation. Allen may have more development room ahead of him than most prep stars because he played three sports throughout high school—football bled into basketball season which bled into baseball season. He hasn't focused as much on baseball as many of his peers, but that hasn't slowed him down so far, and he homered in his first official pro at-bat.

SCOUTING REPORT: Allen showed both power and the ability to hit for average in his pro debut. He has a straightforward swing with a quick trigger. Last spring he showed a solid all-fields approach, although he was more pull-heavy in his pro debut. Allen turns in plus run times at his best, but those moments are rare, and his swing means he's often turning in average or slower times thanks to the time it takes for him to get underway. He accelerates quickly and has shown a solid understanding of how to read pitchers, which paid off with 14 stolen bases in 15 tries. The Reds had him play center field exclusively in his debut, but some scouts see him eventually ending up in left field. He should hit enough to fit at either spot.

THE FUTURE: Allen has a wide range of options ahead. In an ideal scenario, he'll be a center fielder with plus power and a plus hit tool. Even if he ends up in an outfield corner and doesn't develop as much power as expected, he still has a shot to be a future MLB regular.

BILL MITCHELL

BA GRADE

55 Risk: Extreme

SCOUTING GRADES:	Hitting: 50	Power: 50	Running: 55	Fielding: 55	Arm: 50

Year	Age	Club (Level)	Lge	AVG	G	AB	R	H	2B	3B	HR	RBI	BB	SO	SB	OBP	SLG
2021	18	Reds (R)	ACL	.328	19	61	20	20	3	1	3	11	8	12	14	.440	.557
Minor League Totals (1 year)				.328	19	61	20	20	3	1	3	11	8	12	14	.440	.557

8 RECE HINDS, 3B

Born: Sept. 5, 2000. **B-T:** R-R. **HT:** 6-4. **WT:** 215. **Drafted:** HS—Bradenton, Fla., 2019 (2nd round). **Signed by:** Sean Buckley.

TRACK RECORD: Hinds was viewed as one of the best power hitters in the 2019 draft class, but some teams shied away because of the strikeout issues that came with his power. A knee injury forced Hinds to miss two months from early June until early August. Upon his return to the Low-A Southeast league, he celebrated with four home runs and five consecutive two-hit games in his first five games back. Hinds' .515 slugging percentage was fourth best among Low-A Southeast hitters with 150 or more plate appearances and his .286 isolated power was the best among all Reds hitters with 100 or more plate appearances.

SCOUTING REPORT: Hinds has some of the best raw power and one of the stronger arms in the minors. Other than the Polo Grounds, there may not be a ballpark big enough to contain Hinds when he solidly connects. He has true all-fields power and drives the ball out to center field as often as he yanks it down the line. He has plenty of holes, but so far his hands and adjustability in his swing have proven better than expected, which has allowed him to make enough contact for his power to play. Hinds' range is limited at third base, but his plus-plus arm can turn anything he gets to into an out. He moves well enough to fit in right field if he doesn't stick at third base. He's an average runner now, but is likely to slow down as he matures.

THE FUTURE: Hinds' profile is somewhat reminiscent of J.D. Davis as a minor league third baseman with massive power and a big arm. He has made solid strides as far as making contact, but he'll have to steadily continue to improve to allow his power to play to its potential.

BA GRADE
55 Risk: Extreme

SCOUTING GRADES:	Hitting: 40	Power: 65	Running: 45	Fielding: 45	Arm: 70

Year	Age	Club (Level)	Lge	AVG	G	AB	R	H	2B	3B	HR	RBI	BB	SO	SB	OBP	SLG
2021	20	Reds (R)	ACL	.294	11	34	6	10	3	2	2	5	4	13	1	.390	.676
	20	Daytona (LoA)	SEast	.251	43	167	33	42	10	2	10	27	13	52	6	.319	.515
Minor League Totals (3 years)				.249	57	209	40	52	13	4	12	33	19	68	7	.326	.522

9 GRAHAM ASHCRAFT, RHP

Born: Feb. 11, 1998. **B-T:** L-R. **HT:** 6-2. **WT:** 220. **Drafted:** Alabama-Birmingham, 2019 (6th round). **Signed by:** Jonathan Reynolds.

TRACK RECORD: After a college career marred by injuries to both of his hips and a modest 2019 pro debut, Ashcraft was a revelation in 2021. He was the minors' hottest pitcher for much of the first half of the season and had a seven-start, 43-inning stretch when his only run was allowed via catcher's interference.

SCOUTING REPORT: Ashcraft's dominance and his struggles both stem from his all-power, all-the-time approach. At his best, Ashcraft can dominate a lineup with a 65-grade fastball, an above-average cutter and a plus slider. Everything is hard, but when he's throwing mid-90s fastballs with plenty of cut, knowing what's coming may not be enough for a hitter. But when Ashcraft is missing his spots, his simple approach allows hitters to simply look for a pitch to drive. Ashcraft is able to throw to the strike zone and let the movement of his fastball take care of the rest. He's unlikely to ever be a pitcher with the command to hit his spots, but he can throw strikes. His changeup is more a concept than a pitch right now, and he'll also flip over an early-count, well below-average curve.

BA GRADE
50 Risk: High

THE FUTURE: Ashcraft reached Double-A, but he has plenty of development of his secondaries left if he's going to be a starter. He'd have a quicker path as a reliever, where he could ride his pure power approach for one-inning stints. The dominance he demonstrates at his best is impressive, but he has to show he can sustain success. He also has to continue to demonstrate durability. It's been better as a pro, but it was an issue for him during his college career.

SCOUTING GRADES:	Fastball: 65	Slider: 60	Cutter: 55	Curveball: 30	Changeup: 30	Control: 45

Year	Age	Club (Level)	Lge	W	L	ERA	G	GS	IP	H	HR	BB	SO	BB/9	SO/9	WHIP	AVG
2021	23	Dayton (HiA)	Cent	4	1	2.33	8	8	38	28	0	13	55	3.0	12.8	1.06	.200
	23	Chattanooga (AA)	South	7	3	3.36	14	14	72	58	4	24	74	3.0	9.2	1.13	.218
Minor League Totals (3 years)				13	8	3.50	35	35	165	137	6	58	189	3.17	10.33	1.18	.222

10 BRYCE BONNIN, RHP

ALDRIN CAPULONG

Born: Oct. 11, 1998. **B-T:** R-R. **HT:** 6-2. **WT:** 190. **Drafted:** Texas Tech, 2020 (3rd round). **Signed by:** Paul Scott.

TRACK RECORD: A hitter who sporadically pitched for the first three years of his high school career, Bonnin established himself as one of the best prep arms in Texas in his senior season. He headed to Arkansas, but shoulder surgery meant he never pitched for the Razorbacks. He transferred to Texas Tech because the Red Raiders gave him the opportunity to start while Arkansas saw him as a future closer. In his second pro start, Bonnin struck out 11 of the 15 batters he faced in five perfect innings. His final three starts of the season after a promotion to High-A Dayton didn't go nearly as well.

BA GRADE

50 Risk: High

SCOUTING REPORT: Hunter Greene throws harder, but Bonnin's fastball is harder to hit than Greene's because of its combination of 94-99 mph velocity, a low release point which leads to a low vertical approach angle which hitters aren't used to seeing and the pitch's exceptional carry through the top of the zone. The Reds worked with Bonnin to get him to stop cutting his fastball and to help him finish a little less closed off in his delivery. The result was better vertical movement on his fastball as well as improved velocity. His slider is a plus pitch as well, but his cutter and changeup are still unrefined because he hasn't been able to use them much in games.

THE FUTURE: Bonnin carries plenty of reliever risk, but he also has some of the best stuff in the organization. His improved delivery buys him time to prove that he can start, and even if he can't his stuff is the type that can get saves.

SCOUTING GRADES:	Fastball: 70	Slider: 60	Cutter: 40	Changeup: 40	Control: 45

Year	Age	Club (Level)	Lge	W	L	ERA	G	GS	IP	H	HR	BB	SO	BB/9	SO/9	WHIP	AVG
2021	22	Reds (R)	ACL	0	0	2.25	1	1	4	2	0	1	7	2.3	15.8	0.75	.143
	22	Daytona (LoA)	SEast	4	0	1.41	7	7	32	18	0	8	44	2.3	12.4	0.81	.162
	22	Dayton (HiA)	Cent	0	2	7.36	3	3	11	7	4	8	20	6.6	16.4	1.36	.175
Minor League Totals (2 years)				4	2	2.87	11	11	47	27	4	17	71	3.26	13.60	0.94	.164

11 MAT NELSON, C

BA GRADE

50 Risk: High

Born: Jan. 14, 1999. **B-T:** R-R. **HT:** 5-11. **WT:** 190. **Drafted:** Florida State, 2021 (1st round supplemental). **Signed by:** Sean Buckley.

TRACK RECORD: Nelson was a star at Calvary Christian High in Clearwater, Fla., on a team that won 60 straight games and had Hall of Famer Roy Halladay on the coaching staff. He was an immediate starter as a freshman at Florida State. After going undrafted in 2020, he blossomed in 2021. His power improved, and his 23 home runs led all Division I hitters and vaulted him into the supplemental first round.

SCOUTING REPORT: Nelson took a pitch off his wrist in his 10th game as a Red and missed the rest of the season, although he returned to action at instructional league. He has a chance to be an extremely well-rounded catcher with an ability to get on base, hit for power and play solid defense behind the plate. He's good at blocking pitches in the dirt, and is an average receiver with a plus arm. Offensively, he uses the whole field, although he'll swing and miss enough to be a fringe-average hitter. He likes to get his arms extended. A pitcher who can work inside consistently can neutralize him, but he'll do enough damage on pitches on the middle or outer third of the plate to have above-average power.

THE FUTURE: Nelson was one of the older players in the 2021 draft class. That's mildly concerning, but otherwise he has the look of a valuable everyday catcher. With Tyler Stephenson just settling into the everyday job, Nelson has time to develop.

Year	Age	Club (Level)	Lge	AVG	G	AB	R	H	2B	3B	HR	RBI	BB	SO	SB	OBP	SLG
2021	22	Reds (R)	ACL	.000	2	4	1	0	0	0	0	0	2	2	0	.333	.000
	22	Dayton (HiA)	Cent	.208	8	24	3	5	2	1	0	3	4	15	0	.345	.375
Minor League Totals (1 year)				.179	10	28	4	5	2	1	0	3	6	17	0	.343	.321

12 JOSE TORRES, SS

BA GRADE

50 Risk: High

Born: Sept. 28, 1999. **B-T:** R-R. **HT:** 6-0. **WT:** 171. **Drafted:** North Carolina State, 2021 (3rd round). **Signed by:** Charlie Aliano.

TRACK RECORD: Torres was born in the Dominican Republic, but his family moved to the United States when he was a child. As a second-year freshman in 2021 thanks to the canceled 2020 season, he helped lead the Wolfpack to the College World Series.

SCOUTING REPORT: Torres was one of the best defensive shortstops in the 2021 draft class. He's only an average runner, but his hands, first step, body control and internal clock make him an extremely reliable, plus defender. He was bothered by an oblique injury early in 2021, but he has a plus arm when healthy. Offensively, he's steadily eliminated some of the concerns that have surrounded him. In 2020, he was an easy mark for any pitcher who could spin a breaking ball, but in 2021 both in college and pro ball he showed better pitch recognition against sliders and curves while continuing to punish fastballs. He has sneaky power, giving him a chance to get to 10-12 home runs a year.

THE FUTURE: Torres has been projected as a utiltyman whose glove will get him to the majors. He's showing signs that might be selling him short. He has a chance to be a regular if his bat continues to improve.

Year	Age	Club (Level)	Lge	AVG	G	AB	R	H	2B	3B	HR	RBI	BB	SO	SB	OBP	SLG
2021	21	Reds (R)	ACL	.300	3	10	3	3	0	1	1	2	2	2	1	.417	.800
	21	Daytona (LoA)	SEast	.337	25	95	15	32	4	3	4	17	8	17	6	.383	.568
Minor League Totals (1 year)				.333	28	105	18	35	4	4	5	19	10	19	7	.387	.590

13 CARSON SPIERS, RHP

BA GRADE

50 Risk: High

Born: Nov. 11, 1997. **B-T:** R-R. **HT:** 6-0. **WT:** 205. **Signed:** Clemson, 2020 (NDFA). **Signed by:** Charlie Aliano.

TRACK RECORD: When the 2020 draft was cut to five rounds, the Reds spent plenty of effort finding nondrafted pitchers who had the attributes to succeed in pro ball. Spiers looks like the best of an impressive bunch. The nephew of longtime MLB infielder Bill Spiers and the son of Clemson baseball star Michael Spiers, Carson was a reliable closer at Clemson, but he's become a useful starter in pro ball.

SCOUTING REPORT: Even though Spiers has moved from relieving in college to starting in pro ball, he's managed to add several ticks to his fastball, going from a 90-91 mph reliever to a starter who sits 92 mph and touches 96. He's also adjusted his pitch selection, switching from being a sinkerballer to a pitcher who thrives by throwing an average four-seam fastball with enough carry to stay above hitters' bats. His plus changeup is still his best pitch thanks to separation and deception, but he's also developed an average cutter and an average curve. All of Spiers' pitches work in part because he has plus control.

THE FUTURE: There's not much sexy about Spiers' assortment of pitches, but he's a durable, reliable starter who should pitch in the big leagues because of his multiple pitches and control. He should reach Double-A Chattanooga in 2022.

Year	Age	Club (Level)	Lge	W	L	ERA	G	GS	IP	H	HR	BB	SO	BB/9	SO/9	WHIP	AVG
2021	23	Daytona (LoA)	SEast	2	0	3.18	5	4	22	19	1	5	27	2.0	10.7	1.06	.241
	23	Dayton (HiA)	Cent	6	4	3.64	20	16	89	68	8	29	103	2.9	10.4	1.09	.215
Minor League Totals (1 year)				8	4	3.55	25	20	112	87	9	34	130	2.74	10.48	1.08	.220

14 ALLAN CERDA, OF

BA GRADE

55 Risk: Extreme

Born: Nov. 24, 1999. **B-T:** R-R. **HT:** 6-3. **WT:** 170. **Signed:** Dominican Republic, 2017. **Signed by:** Felix Romero.

TRACK RECORD: Cerda was part of a Reds 2017-18 international signing class that was limited to low-cost signings because of the team's spending spree in 2016. He's proven to be quite the find so far, and has posted a .360 or better on-base percentage at every stop. His 14 home runs were fifth best in the Low-A Southeast league.

SCOUTING REPORT: Cerda's hand-eye coordination and bat-to-ball skills are only adequate at best, but he makes up for that by having an excellent understanding of the strike zone. Hitting from a wide-open setup, Cerda will swing and miss at pitches in the zone, but he knows how to take a walk when pitchers nibble. He has above-average power to go with his average hit tool. When he was promoted to Dayton, Cerda largely transitioned to right field, which is his most likely eventual home because of his plus arm. Although he's still relatively skinny, he has slowed and is an above-average runner who is now average in center.

THE FUTURE: The Reds adding Cerda to their 40-man roster is a clear sign of how highly they value his well-rounded offensive game. He'll head back to High-A Dayton to start 2022.

Year	Age	Club (Level)	Lge	AVG	G	AB	R	H	2B	3B	HR	RBI	BB	SO	SB	OBP	SLG
2021	21	Daytona (LoA)	SEast	.242	66	227	42	55	14	4	14	42	31	85	1	.362	.524
	21	Dayton (HiA)	Cent	.273	21	77	15	21	8	1	3	13	10	20	1	.356	.519
Minor League Totals (4 years)				.250	177	609	114	152	39	5	32	116	86	206	7	.372	.488

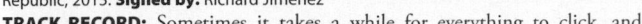

15 DAURI MORETA, RHP

BA GRADE

45 Risk: Medium

Born: April 15, 1996. **B-T:** R-R. **HT:** 6-2. **WT:** 186. **Signed:** Dominican Republic, 2015. **Signed by:** Richard Jimenez

TRACK RECORD: Sometimes it takes a while for everything to click, and Moreta didn't establish himself in full-season ball until his fifth season. After being left available and unpicked in the 2019 and 2020 Rule 5 drafts, Moreta took a massive step forward in 2021. He made it to Double-A for the first time, dominated there and in Triple-A and made it to Cincinnati at the end of the season.

SCOUTING REPORT: While it took a while for Moreta to get to Cincinnati, he should stay for quite a while. Moreta is the rare reliever with plus control. He fills the strike zone with his fastball, slider and a hard changeup. His mid-90s plus fastball can get above hitters' bats at the top of the strike zone thanks to its flat plane and above-average carry. He can reach back for 97-98 if he needs to as well. His mid-80s plus slider doesn't have a ton of movement but it pairs very well with his fastball. Those two pitches and his 87-89 mph, above-average changeup all can miss bats.

THE FUTURE: Moreta was better in almost every way in 2021 than he was pre-pandemic, but his step forward seems sustainable. Relievers with pinpoint control are rare, but Moreta has it to go with excellent stuff. The combination should make him a key part of the Reds bullpen for 2022 and beyond.

Year	Age	Club (Level)	Lge	W	L	ERA	G	GS	IP	H	HR	BB	SO	BB/9	SO/9	WHIP	AVG
2021	25	Chattanooga (AA)	South	4	0	1.35	18	0	26	17	3	5	37	1.7	12.5	0.83	.179
	25	Louisville (AAA)	East	2	0	0.68	24	0	26	14	2	4	21	1.4	7.2	0.68	.149
	25	Cincinnati (MLB)	NL	0	0	2.45	4	0	3	2	1	1	4	2.5	9.8	0.82	.154
Major League Totals (1 year)				0	0	2.45	4	0	4	2	1	1	4	2.45	9.82	0.82	.154
Minor League Totals (7 years)				16	10	3.18	172	0	252	196	19	86	332	3.07	11.86	1.12	.210

16 CHRISTIAN ROA, RHP

BA GRADE

50 Risk: High

Born: April 2, 1999. **B-T:** R-R. **HT:** 6-4. **WT:** 220. **Drafted:** Texas A&M, 2020 (2nd round). **Signed by:** Mike Partida.

TRACK RECORD: Ideally, Roa will be a big and durable starter, but so far he hasn't shown he can eat innings. He's yet to throw 60 innings in any official season stretching back to his high school career. His chance to do that at Texas A&M was torpedoed by the pandemic. He then missed instructional league in 2020 because of a sports hernia. In 2021, he missed time with an elbow flexor strain that limited him to 58.2 innings.

SCOUTING REPORT: Roa has the makings of four average or better pitches with average control. He's more of a sum-of-the-parts pitcher than one who depends on any one plus offering. His four-seam 91-94 mph fastball is a solid-average offering and he's shown he can bump it up to 96-97 when he reaches back. His low-80s changeup has developed into his best pitch, an above-average offering with solid deception and fade. It's his best two-strike pitch, as he can get swings and misses from hitters who chase it. His low-80s slider and high-70s curveball are both average as well. His ability to throw strikes with both breaking balls and his fastball keeps hitters guessing.

THE FUTURE: What Roa needs more than anything is a season when he can make 20-plus starts and get to 100 or more innings. He has the arsenal to be a No. 4 starter, but durability is a key component of filling that role.

Year	Age	Club (Level)	Lge	W	L	ERA	G	GS	IP	H	HR	BB	SO	BB/9	SO/9	WHIP	AVG
2021	22	Reds (R)	ACL	1	0	0.00	2	1	6	1	0	2	9	2.8	12.8	0.47	.045
	22	Daytona (LoA)	SEast	1	1	3.57	5	5	17	18	2	9	21	4.6	10.7	1.53	.261
	22	Dayton (HiA)	Cent	2	2	4.15	8	7	34	32	4	15	37	3.9	9.6	1.36	.244
Minor League Totals (2 years)				4	3	3.53	15	13	59	51	6	26	67	3.99	10.28	1.31	.230

17 TYLER CALLIHAN, 2B

BA GRADE

45 Risk: High

Born: June 22, 2000. **B-T:** L-R. **HT:** 6-0. **WT:** 205. **Drafted:** HS—Jacksonville, 2019 (3rd round). **Signed by:** Sean Buckley.

TRACK RECORD: Heading into the 2019 draft, Callihan was viewed as a very promising prep hitter with significant defensive questions. Three years later, he's still waiting to show what he can do. After losing the 2020 season like everyone else, he played just 29 games in 2021 before an elbow injury necessitated Tommy John surgery.

SCOUTING REPORT: Callihan showed up in better shape in 2021 and was reaping the benefits before his elbow injury. He has above-average bat speed and excellent hand-eye coordination. He was putting together plenty of quality at-bats before his injury, and his average speed made him a minor threat on the bases. Callihan should be an above-average hitter with average power, even if that power has yet to show up much in games. After playing second and third base in 2019, the Reds had Callihan focus on second base in 2021. He looked a little more agile and relatively sure-handed fielding balls he reached. The hope is he can be a fringe-average defender at second, which is playable thanks to his bat and good positioning. Callihan's arm was above-average before the surgery. Now, he'll have to show that it can bounce back.

THE FUTURE: Callihan should be back by the end of spring training. After getting less than 350 plate appearances in the past three seasons, he needs 120 games between Low-A and High-A in 2022. Optimistically, he could develop into a bat-first second baseman with a reliable enough glove.

Year	Age	Club (Level)	Lge	AVG	G	AB	R	H	2B	3B	HR	RBI	BB	SO	SB	OBP	SLG
2021	21	Daytona (LoA)	SEast	.299	23	87	14	26	6	0	2	10	8	13	5	.351	.437
Minor League Totals (3 years)				.273	80	311	44	85	16	6	8	43	18	63	16	.313	.441

18 IVAN JOHNSON, 2B

Born: Oct. 11, 1998. **B-T:** B-R. **HT:** 6-0. **WT:** 190. **Drafted:** Chipola (Fla.) JC, 2019 (4th round). **Signed by:** John Poloni.

BA GRADE
45 Risk: High

TRACK RECORD: After spending his freshman year at Georgia, Johnson transferred to Chipola (Fla.) JC for more playing time. He responded by hitting .389/.500/.606 and playing his way into the fourth round at a time when junior college hitters struggled to get drafted. After earning a promotion to High-A Dayton during the season, he finished the year by hitting six home runs in 17 games in the Arizona Fall League.

SCOUTING REPORT: Because of the lack of a clear alternative, the Reds have had Johnson play more at shortstop than second base early in his career. That's likely to change now that he's paired with Matt McLain and Elly de la Cruz. Johnson is better suited for second—or third, although he hasn't played there yet. His hands and consistency need some work, but his plus arm and body control give him a shot to be above-average at second, where he has a little more time to make the play. His righthanded swing can get a little bit big at times when it should be more contact-oriented, but both swings work and he has plus power when swinging lefty. He's a fringe-average runner.

THE FUTURE: Johnson is unlikely to stay at shortstop, but his hitting ability and athleticism should fit at second base. He's been productive so far, but there are evaluators who think Johnson has further upside.

Year	Age	Club (Level)	Lge	AVG	G	AB	R	H	2B	3B	HR	RBI	BB	SO	SB	OBP	SLG
2021	22	Daytona (LoA)	SEast	.263	52	186	27	49	14	2	6	23	27	61	8	.366	.457
	22	Dayton (HiA)	Cent	.265	27	98	17	26	5	0	4	18	14	39	3	.368	.439
Minor League Totals (3 years)				.261	125	472	71	123	29	3	16	63	59	146	22	.351	.436

19 DANIEL VELLOJIN, C

Born: March 15, 2000. **B-T:** B-R. **HT:** 5-11. **WT:** 160. **Signed:** Colombia, 2018. **Signed by:** Jose Valdelamar.

BA GRADE
45 Risk: High

TRACK RECORD: The decision to use an automated ball-strike system makes it tough to fully evaluate hitters and pitchers from the Low-A Southeast, as the league saw low batting averages but high on-base percentages due to plenty of walks. Vellojin was the epitome of the trend. His .401 on-base percentage led all minor league catchers in full-season ball, even though he hit only .247.

SCOUTING REPORT: Vellojin drew raves from scouts and coaches for his well-rounded combination of a discerning batting eye and a solid, well-rounded game behind the plate. He has a plus arm and is an above-average receiver. Vellojin shuts down the running game—he threw out 41% of basestealers in 2021. Vellojin does struggle significantly with his blocking. He led all full-season catchers with 102 wild pitches allowed (25 more than anyone else) and 11 passed balls. Offensively, Vellojin doesn't hit the ball very hard, but he makes extremely good swing decisions. It's very hard to get him to chase.

THE FUTURE: Vellojin has a lot of work ahead of him, but he has the foundational skills to be an everyday MLB catcher, although his on-base-heavy approach doesn't exactly fit the normal profile. When he heads to High-A Dayton next year, he needs to focus on improving his blocking.

Year	Age	Club (Level)	Lge	AVG	G	AB	R	H	2B	3B	HR	RBI	BB	SO	SB	OBP	SLG
2021	21	Daytona (LoA)	SEast	.247	88	283	56	70	21	1	7	34	72	73	5	.401	.403
Minor League Totals (3 years)				.256	177	589	116	151	34	6	12	97	129	127	16	.400	.396

20 T.J. FRIEDL, OF

BA GRADE

40 Risk: Medium

Born: Aug. 4, 1995. **B-T:** L-L. **HT:** 5-10. **WT:** 180. **Signed:** Nevada, 2016 (NDFA). **Signed by:** Rich Bordi/Sam Grossman.

TRACK RECORD: Friedl came to fame when he went undrafted as a draft-eligible sophomore in 2016. He then stood out for USA Baseball's Collegiate National Team, which helped him land a $735,000 bonus, which is the largest ever for a nondrafted free agent. Friedl's 2019 season was delayed because of a shoulder injury and ended in early July because of an ankle injury, which meant his return to action in 2021 marked the end of a 21-month layoff. He made the most of it and made his MLB debut in September.

SCOUTING REPORT: Friedl didn't get a chance to play a full game until his sixth MLB appearance. That sums up Friedl's likely role. He does a lot of things well, but probably not well enough to ever be a regular. He's a lefthanded hitter who works counts, knows how to draw a walk and has gotten stronger to the point where he has below-average power. He can play all three outfield spots, pinch-hit or serve as a defensive replacement. His above-average speed, average arm and above-average defense in the outfield are all useful.

THE FUTURE: Friedl went unpicked in two straight Rule 5 drafts before he made it to the majors. Even now, he'll be a player who lives on the edge of the MLB roster, as backup outfielders are luxuries when the bullpen or rotation needs help. He'll compete for a spot on Cincinnati's bench.

Year	Age	Club (Level)	Lge	AVG	G	AB	R	H	2B	3B	HR	RBI	BB	SO	SB	OBP	SLG
2021	25	Louisville (AAA)	East	.264	113	386	59	102	15	5	12	36	44	65	13	.357	.422
	25	Cincinnati (MLB)	NL	.290	14	31	9	9	1	0	1	2	4	2	0	.361	.419
Major League Totals (1 year)				.290	14	31	9	9	1	0	1	2	4	2	0	.361	.419
Minor League Totals (6 years)				.274	452	1651	270	453	83	26	32	170	191	325	79	.366	.414

21 ARIEL ALMONTE, OF

BA GRADE

50 Risk: Extreme

Born: Dec. 1, 2003. **B-T:** R-R. **HT:** 6-3. **WT:** 187. **Signed:** Dominican Republic, 2021.

TRACK RECORD: The biggest name in the Reds' 2020-2021 international signing class, Almonte impressed as an amateur by showing power and an advanced ability to recognize spin. His Dominican Summer League debut lived up to those expectations.

SCOUTING REPORT: Almonte showed a little bit of everything in his pro debut. He was second on the DSL Reds in home runs (five) and third in steals (25) while blistering line drive after line drive. He has already started to show plus power potential, with more likely to come as he fills out his still somewhat skinny frame. He shows excellent swing decisions for his age and squares up the ball consistently. In addition to hitting the ball hard, he shows the skills to post solid on-base percentages as well. He is a fringe-average runner who will likely slow down, but he should be fine in right field with a plus arm.

THE FUTURE: Almonte was one of the highest-priced outfielders in the 2021 international class. It looks to be money well spent. He has the foundational skills to be a fast-moving corner outfielder. He'll make his U.S. debut in 2022 while still a teenager.

Year	Age	Club (Level)	Lge	AVG	G	AB	R	H	2B	3B	HR	RBI	BB	SO	SB	OBP	SLG
2021	17	Reds (R)	DSL	.278	48	162	35	45	9	1	5	33	26	52	15	.398	.438
Minor League Totals (1 year)				.278	48	162	35	45	9	1	5	33	26	52	15	.398	.438

22 ANDREW ABBOTT, LHP

BA GRADE

45 Risk: High

Born: June 1, 1999. **B-T:** L-L. **HT:** 6-0. **WT:** 190. **Drafted:** Virginia, 2021 (2nd round). **Signed by:** Jeff Brookens.

TRACK RECORD: A little lefty, Abbott was coached in high school by an even smaller lefty in seven-time all-star Billy Wagner. Abbott doesn't throw nearly as hard as Wagner, but like Wagner, he was an excellent reliever. Abbott spent three years as a multi-inning, high-leverage reliever at Virginia. He was passed over in the shortened 2020 draft, which gave him a chance to start in 2021. After going 9-6, 2.87 for the Cavaliers, he vaulted into the second round.

SCOUTING REPORT: Abbott doesn't have a clear plus pitch, but three average to above-average offerings and plus control give him plenty of chances to compete. Working as a starter gave Abbott a chance to further refine and improve his average changeup, which pairs well with his above-average, high-70s, 12-to-6 curveball. Abbott's fastball has ticked up a little bit to sit 92-93 mph and he will touch 96-97 sporadically. His fastball has solid carry up in the strike zone. All three pitches work well together because he mixes them well. Coaches have long raved about Abbott's competitiveness and he has excellent durability.

THE FUTURE: Virginia has had 10 pitchers taken in the top 100 picks this century. Just two—Sean

Doolittle and Daniel Lynch—have put down significant roots in the big leagues. Abbott has a chance to be the third, although more likely as a No. 5 starter or multi-inning reliever.

Year	Age	Club (Level)	Lge	W	L	ERA	G	GS	IP	H	HR	BB	SO	BB/9	SO/9	WHIP	AVG
2021	22	Reds (R)	ACL	0	0	0.00	2	2	2	1	0	0	3	0.0	13.5	0.50	.143
	22	Daytona (LoA)	SEast	0	0	4.91	4	3	11	11	2	4	19	3.3	15.6	1.36	.250
Minor League Totals (1 year)				0	0	4.15	6	5	13	12	2	4	22	2.77	15.23	1.23	.235

23 ALEXIS DIAZ, RHP

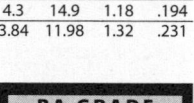

BA GRADE

45 Risk: High

Born: Sept. 24, 1996. **B-T:** R-R. **HT:** 6-2. **WT:** 224.
Drafted: HS—Naguabo, P.R., 2015 (12th round). **Signed by:** Will Harford.
TRACK RECORD: The younger brother of Mets closer Edwin Diaz, Alexis has proven to be a very useful developmental project. He sat 88-92 mph when the Reds drafted him in 2015. Now his slider can touch 88. He had Tommy John surgery in 2016 but has bounced back nicely. He earned a spot on the Reds' 40-man roster after an impressive season at Double-A Chattanooga.
SCOUTING REPORT: Because of his low three-quarters slot, Diaz has an exceptionally low release point. He has a very low approach angle on his 93-97 mph fastball. Diaz's above-average fastball has enough velocity to keep hitters looking for it, but really it's just the appetizer for his plus slider that he throws every bit as much as his fastball. It's thrown at 83-88 mph and looks like his fastball coming out of his hand. Diaz can throw it in the zone or out depending on the situation, flipping between a short, cutter-ish version as well as a bigger one that runs away from hitters' bats. His command is average, but he has below-average control thanks to his slider-heavy approach.
THE FUTURE: The best thing a pitcher can be is unusual. If you can throw hard and still be unlike anyone else hitters normally see, all the better. Diaz is a fireballer who has an unusual release point and a nice two-pitch mix. He could help Cincinnati at some point in 2022.

Year	Age	Club (Level)	Lge	W	L	ERA	G	GS	IP	H	HR	BB	SO	BB/9	SO/9	WHIP	AVG
2021	24	Chattanooga (AA)	South	3	1	3.83	35	0	42	30	2	20	70	4.3	14.9	1.18	.194
Minor League Totals (7 years)				15	12	4.03	95	18	199	177	15	85	265	3.84	11.98	1.32	.231

24 ALEJO LOPEZ, 2B/3B

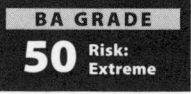

BA GRADE

40 Risk: Medium

Born: May 5, 1996. **B-T:** B-R. **HT:** 5-10. **WT:** 170. **Drafted:** HS—Phoenix, 2015 (27th round). **Signed by:** Dan Cholowsky.
TRACK RECORD: Of the 22 players who signed after being drafted in the 27th round in 2015, only Lopez has reached the majors. Six years after signing out of high school, he was called up to Cincinnati in late June. Lopez's grandfather and father played baseball in the Mexican League, and his father Alfonso is a vice president of the Mexican League's Puebla franchise.
SCOUTING REPORT: Lopez is a plus hitter who has hit wherever he's played. A career .303 hitter in the minors, Lopez has exceptional contact skills. He swings a lot, but he rarely swings and misses with a slap-heavy approach. Lopez has bottom-of-the-scale power. He is an extreme ground ball hitter who sprays the ball around the field. He's an average runner who isn't a basestealing threat. Defensively, Lopez is versatile, but his inability to really play shortstop limits him. He's best at second base, where his heady play, above-average arm and body control help him be average. He's fine in left field, but his bat is stretched there. The ball gets on him a little quickly at third.
THE FUTURE: Lopez is a big league-ready hitter but his lack of impact makes him better as a fill-in. He has survival skills, but he's most likely headed back to Triple-A Louisville to be ready whenever he is needed.

Year	Age	Club (Level)	Lge	AVG	G	AB	R	H	2B	3B	HR	RBI	BB	SO	SB	OBP	SLG
2021	25	Chattanooga (AA)	South	.362	25	105	18	38	9	0	0	13	12	11	3	.437	.448
	25	Louisville (AAA)	East	.303	67	251	54	76	18	0	6	31	33	21	6	.386	.446
	25	Cincinnati (MLB)	NL	.261	14	23	3	6	0	0	0	0	0	5	0	.261	.261
Major League Totals (1 year)				.261	14	23	3	6	0	0	0	0	0	5	0	.261	.261
Minor League Totals (7 years)				.303	417	1527	256	462	78	12	13	178	157	190	49	.375	.395

25 CARLOS JORGE, SS/2B

BA GRADE

50 Risk: Extreme

Born: Sept. 22, 2003. **B-T:** L-R. **HT:** 5-10. **WT:** 160. **Signed:** Dominican Republic, 2021. **Signed by:** Edgard Melo/Enmanuel Cartagena/Richard Jimenez.
TRACK RECORD: The DSL Reds were loaded with talent, but of all the intriguing prospects on the team, Jorge is the one who had the loudest debut. In a league with 46 teams, Jorge ranked in the top 10 in batting average (.346), OBP (.436), slugging (.579), stolen bases (27) and

total bases (92). He also led the league with 10 triples.

SCOUTING REPORT: Jorge impressed as an amateur, but he's proven to be even better than expected. He has a very simple, short swing that leads to tons of quality contact. While his frame doesn't portend a lot of strength gains, he made solid contact for a teenager in the DSL. He's short but not small. He's a plus-plus runner who is a real threat on the basepaths. Defensively, he has the skills to stay in the middle infield with an average arm and above-average range. His twitchy athleticism gives him an excellent first step.

THE FUTURE: It's hard not to think of Ozzie Albies or Vidal Brujan when watching Jorge. Like them, he is speedy, short but strong, and has plenty of offensive potential to go with defensive value.

Year	Age	Club (Level)	Lge	AVG	G	AB	R	H	2B	3B	HR	RBI	BB	SO	SB	OBP	SLG
2021	17	Reds (R)	DSL	.346	47	159	38	55	8	10	3	33	24	32	27	.436	.579
Minor League Totals (1 year)				.346	47	159	38	55	8	10	3	33	24	32	27	.436	.579

26 MARK KOLOZSVARY, C

BA GRADE
45 Risk: High

Born: Sept. 4, 1995. **B-T:** R-R. **HT:** 5-8. **WT:** 180. **Drafted:** Florida, 2017 (7th round). **Signed by:** Sean Buckley

TRACK RECORD: After barely playing in his first two years at Florida, Kolozsvary was supposed to be a backup as a junior. But Mike Rivera got hurt, Kolozsvary stepped in and impressed enough to get drafted by the Reds. Similarly, he emerged from obscurity—and a .188 batting average in 2019—to become Team USA's everyday catcher at the Olympics.

SCOUTING REPORT: After reworking his swing to try to hit for more power, Kolozsvary had an excellent start but struggled to sustain it. He hit .349 in May but .186 from June 1 until the end of the season. He's a solid defensive catcher who blocks and frames. Defensively, he's capable of serving as a solid backup, but his hitting will have to improve. Kolozsvary does have surprising above-average raw power, but his all-power approach led to significant contact issues. His swing-and-miss rate of 39% has to improve.

THE FUTURE: Added to the 40-man roster, Kolozsvary's defensive ability gives him a shot to become Tyler Stephenson's backup, but only if he gets much better at the plate. Without that improvement, he'll be stuck as a catcher on call at Triple-A in case of injuries.

Year	Age	Club (Level)	Lge	AVG	G	AB	R	H	2B	3B	HR	RBI	BB	SO	SB	OBP	SLG
2021	25	Chattanooga (AA)	South	.233	40	146	33	34	12	0	6	26	20	53	0	.341	.438
	25	Louisville (AAA)	East	.190	19	58	9	11	2	1	1	2	3	23	0	.299	.310
Minor League Totals (5 years)				.223	248	808	113	180	48	3	17	91	93	260	4	.330	.353

27 LEONARDO BALCAZAR, SS

BA GRADE
50 Risk: Extreme

Born: June 17, 2004. **B-T:** R-R. **HT:** 5-10. **WT:** 167. **Signed:** Venezuela, 2021. **Signed by:** Aguido Gonzalez/Ricardo Quintero/Richard Castro.

TRACK RECORD: Ariel Almonte and Malvin Valdez were considered the top players in the Reds' 2021 signing class and both are very good prospects. But shortstops Carlos Jorge and Balcazar have been at least as impressive if not more. Balcazar was the youngest player the Reds brought to their instructional league after the season.

SCOUTING REPORT: Balcazar has a chance to make an impact both at the plate and in the field. He showed advanced understanding of pitch selection and he has plus power potential as well. Unlike most teenagers, Balcazar showed he could clear the fence to all fields—he homered to center and right field in 2021. His athleticism is even more apparent in the field. He's a potentially above-average defender with a plus arm and shared the shortstop job with Jorge in the DSL. As is true with most 17-year-old shortstops, Balcazar will have to work on his consistency and reliability. Seven of his 11 errors were fielding errors.

THE FUTURE: Balcazar is an exciting blend of athleticism, potential and present skills. He's ready to come to the U.S. to play in the Arizona Complex League in 2022.

Year	Age	Club (Level)	Lge	AVG	G	AB	R	H	2B	3B	HR	RBI	BB	SO	SB	OBP	SLG
2021	17	Reds (R)	DSL	.259	29	112	26	29	5	4	6	15	13	29	8	.346	.536
Minor League Totals (1 year)				259	29	112	26	29	5	4	6	15	13	29	8	.346	.536

28 REIVER SANMARTIN, LHP

BA GRADE
40 Risk: Medium

Born: April 15, 1996. **B-T:** L-L. **HT:** 6-2. **WT:** 160. **Signed:** Colombia, 2015. **Signed by:** Hamilton Sarabia (Rangers).

TRACK RECORD: A $10,000 signing as a 19-year-old, Sanmartin was a regular participant on Colombia's international teams, including the team that played in the 2021 Olympics qualifier. Sanmartin was traded twice in two years. The first time he was swapped from the Rangers to the Yankees for righty Ronald Herrera. Two years later, he came to the Reds along with Sonny Gray in a deal that sent second baseman Shed Long to the Yankees. Sanmartin reached the majors in September and made two excellent starts for the Reds.

SCOUTING REPORT: Sanmartin is a testament to the value of plus-plus command and control. Sanmartin's plus changeup is not only his only plus pitch, it's really his only average pitch. His 87-91 mph two-seam and four-seam fastballs don't really scare hitters. They both feature below-average velocity and are relatively straight, but Sanmartin locates them precisely where he wants them. He is especially effective at dotting his two-seamer in on lefthanded hitters' hands. His 78-81 mph slider has decent tilt, but most of its effectiveness is because he rarely makes a mistake with its location.

THE FUTURE: Sanmartin has to have precise command because his mistakes will get punished. His low strikeout rate and also microscopic walk rate make him a useful No. 5 or No. 6 starter.

Year	Age	Club (Level)	Lge	W	L	ERA	G	GS	IP	H	HR	BB	SO	BB/9	SO/9	WHIP	AVG
2021	25	Chattanooga (AA)	South	2	0	0.50	4	3	18	8	0	5	23	2.5	11.5	0.72	.133
	25	Louisville (AAA)	East	8	2	3.94	21	14	82	80	6	23	89	2.5	9.7	1.25	.253
	25	Cincinnati (MLB)	NL	2	0	1.54	2	2	11	12	0	2	11	1.5	8.5	1.20	.267
Major League Totals (1 year)				2	0	1.54	2	2	12	12	0	2	11	1.54	8.49	1.20	.267
Minor League Totals (7 years)				33	25	3.22	95	75	428	429	24	87	403	1.83	8.48	1.21	.256

29 YERLIN CONFIDAN, OF

BA GRADE

50 Risk: Extreme

Born: Dec. 16, 2002. **B-T:** L-L. **HT:** 6-0. **WT:** 170. **Signed:** Dominican Republic, 2019. **Signed by:** Edgard Melo/Enmanuel Cartagena/Richard Jimenez.

TRACK RECORD: When Confidan signed with the Reds for $200,000 in 2019, his plus-plus arm was apparent, but there was a reasonable expectation that he would need time. Instead, he led the Arizona Complex League with 11 home runs and a .573 slugging percentage.

SCOUTING REPORT: Confidan has all the makings of a right fielder's tool set. He has big power and a big arm. When Confidan gets his long arms extended, he can hit tape-measure home runs. His peak exit velocity of 112 mph was among the best in the ACL and he consistently hits the ball hard. Scouts do worry that his batting average may plummet as he moves up the ladder if he doesn't become more selective. His aggressive approach leaves him vulnerable to chasing pitches out of the strike zone and his swing has some unavoidable length because of his long levers. Confidan is currently a below-average defender. He committed seven errors in just 43 games in the outfield, five of which were fielding errors.

THE FUTURE: Confidan's power, arm and defensive issues are reminiscent of the skill set of Juan Duran, a prominent international signee of the Reds 15 years ago. He had an excellent debut, but there are fears that Low-A Daytona may be a tougher test.

Year	Age	Club (Level)	Lge	AVG	G	AB	R	H	2B	3B	HR	RBI	BB	SO	SB	OBP	SLG
2021	18	Reds (R)	ACL	.315	50	178	33	56	9	2	11	34	12	48	7	.359	.573
Minor League Totals (1 year)				.315	50	178	33	56	9	2	11	34	12	48	7	.359	.573

30 MIKE SIANI, OF

BA GRADE

45 Risk: High

Born: July 16, 1999. **B-T:** L-L. **HT:** 6-1. **WT:** 188. **Drafted:** HS—Philadelphia, 2018 (4th round). **Signed by:** Jeff Brookens.

TRACK RECORD: Mike is the oldest of a trio of baseball-playing brothers. An elbow injury meant Mike couldn't play in the outfield until late May. He struggled to hit all season, but hit .300/.451/.450 with 10 steals in 14 games in the Arizona Fall League after the regular season.

SCOUTING REPORT: Siani is an exceptional center fielder defensively. He is fearless and has the mentality that any ball hit anywhere near center field should end up in his glove. His plus-plus defense would make him the Reds best defensive center fielder since Billy Hamilton was in his prime. He's also a plus runner and has a plus arm. But he hits for neither average nor power. Siani tries to drive the ball with a pull-heavy approach that relies on getting balls he can drive on the inner third of the plate. He doesn't really do much when he gets those pitches thanks to below-average power and the length to his swing. He was surprisingly bad against righthanders in 2021.

THE FUTURE: Siani's glove will buy him extra time to work through his offensive issues, but no center fielder gets to play if they don't hit at all. Siani has to make more and better contact in 2022.

Year	Age	Club (Level)	Lge	AVG	G	AB	R	H	2B	3B	HR	RBI	BB	SO	SB	OBP	SLG
2021	21	Dayton (HiA)	Cent	.216	97	352	60	76	13	4	6	26	50	103	30	.321	.327
Minor League Totals (4 years)				.247	264	1002	159	247	29	13	14	78	112	247	81	.332	.343

MORE PROSPECTS TO KNOW

31. LYON RICHARDSON, RHP

Richardson showed better velocity but struggled with consistency in 2021. A late-season elbow injury that required Tommy John surgery will sideline him until 2023.

32. DANIEL DUARTE, RHP

A very well-traveled pitcher who has bounced between the Mexican League and the U.S. and has already been a MiLB Rule 5 pick, Duarte got in better shape in 2021, which allowed his plus fastball and above-average slider to be more consistent. He was added to the 40-man roster in November.

33. JARED SOLOMON, RHP

SLEEPER

If not for Tommy John surgery late in 2020, Solomon would likely have pitched in Cincinnati in 2021. If his stuff bounces back to where it was pre-injury, he could make it to the big leagues in 2022. His fastball and slider give him a pair of potentially plus pitches.

34. MALVIN VALDEZ, OF

Valdez and Ariel Almonte were the big names in the Reds' 2021 international signing class. Valdez struggled a little in his Dominican Summer League debut, but he has the tools to be an MLB regular.

35. JAMES MARINAN, RHP

Marinan ranks among the Reds most-improved pitchers in 2021. He touched 98 mph at his best and went from starting the year in extended spring training to finishing it in the Arizona Fall League. He was added to the Reds' 40-man roster in November.

36. JOE BOYLE, RHP

When the Reds drafted Boyle, they knew they were getting a massive arm with massive control troubles. That's still true. Boyle walked more than a batter an inning in his four Low-A Southeast outings, but he also struck out 10 of the 17 batters he faced in his season finale.

37. JOSE FRANCO, RHP

Pushed a little beyond his level of readiness, Franco's statistics in 2021 at Low-A Daytona weren't pretty, but he has enough of a fastball and a pair of quality breaking balls to go with advanced understanding of the craft of pitching.

38. JACKSON MILLER, C

The Reds have a number of promising catchers, but Miller shouldn't get lost in the shuffle. He's battled illness and injuries, but when healthy he has the strength and swing to be a well-rounded catcher.

39. STEVEN BRANCHE, RHP

Yet another of the Reds' bevy of nondrafted free agent finds in 2020, the Rochester Institute of Tech (N.Y.) signee struck out 100 batters as a reliever in 2021. He can get to 98-99 mph regularly and has touched 100. His slider is effective as well.

40. THOMAS FARR, RHP

A fifth-round pick out of South Carolina, Farr has flashed excellent velocity at times (96-97 mph), although he hasn't been to those levels consistently as a starter. He has a solid feel for throwing his changeup and his slurvy slider is an average pitch as well.

TOP PROSPECTS OF THE DECADE

Year	Player, Pos	2021 Org
2012	Devin Mesoraco, C	Did not play
2013	Billy Hamilton, OF	White Sox
2014	Robert Stephenson, RHP	Rockies
2015	Robert Stephenson, RHP	Rockies
2016	Robert Stephenson, RHP	Rockies
2017	Nick Senzel, 3B/2B	Reds
2018	Nick Senzel, 3B/2B	Reds
2019	Nick Senzel, 3B/2B	Reds
2020	Hunter Greene, RHP	Reds
2021	Jose Barrero, SS	Reds

TOP DRAFT PICKS OF THE DECADE

Year	Player, Pos	2021 Org
2012	Nick Travieso, RHP	American Association
2013	Phillip Ervin, OF	Braves
2014	Nick Howard, RHP	Reds
2015	Tyler Stephenson, C	Reds
2016	Nick Senzel, 3B	Reds
2017	Hunter Greene, RHP	Reds
2018	Jonathan India, 3B	Reds
2019	Nick Lodolo, LHP	Reds
2020	Austin Hendrick, OF	Reds
2021	Matt McLain, SS	Reds

Cleveland Guardians

BY TEDDY CAHILL

For more than a century, the franchise was known as the Indians. But the 2021 club was the last to be known by that nickname.

In 2020, the organization announced it would change its nickname, but not until a new name was chosen. That happened on July 23, 2021, when Guardians was announced as the pick. The name was chosen in part in homage to the Guardians of Traffic statues that stand on the Hope Memorial Bridge just outside the entrance to Progressive Field.

While the name change was the most significant news for the organization, 2021 also marked  an important year for the direction of the club. In January, Cleveland traded Francisco Lindor and Carlos Carrasco to the Mets for Andres Gimenez, Isaiah Greene, Amed Rosario and Josh Wolf. Lindor was due to be a free agent after the 2021 season and his time with the organization had clearly been coming to an end, but that didn't make his departure any easier. Drafted eighth overall in 2011, he spent a decade with the organization and developed into a star.

On the field, Cleveland struggled to ever truly get going and it finished under .500 (80-82) for the first time since 2012. The pitching staff was beset by injuries, including to ace Shane Bieber, and its offense never really came together around Jose Ramirez. Cleveland became the first MLB team ever to be no-hit three times in one season.

Despite the disappointments, Cleveland did find some answers from younger players. Pitching injuries forced righthanders Aaron Civale, Triston McKenzie—the team's preseason No. 1 prospect—and Cal Quantrill into bigger roles and all three acquitted themselves well. Righthander Emmanuel Clase, another rookie, emerged as an answer at the back of the bullpen, compiling 24 saves. Rosario played well in his debut season in Cleveland and center fielder Myles Straw, acquired from the Astros in a trade deadline deal for Phil Maton, impressed down the stretch.

As Cleveland moves forward as the Guardians, it still has several key questions to answer. The AL Central is beginning to look much more competitive. The White Sox finished 13 games ahead of the second-place Cleveland and are in win-now mode under manager Tony La Russa. The Tigers are cycling up out of their rebuild, possibly as soon as 2022. The Royals would like to soon follow that same path, and the Twins are unlikely to again be as disappointing as they were in 2021.

The Guardians have help arriving from the

Emmanuel Clase notched 24 saves and finished fifth in AL Rookie of the Year voting.

PROJECTED 2025 LINEUP

Catcher	Bo Naylor	25
First Base	Nolan Jones	27
Second Base	Tyler Freeman	26
Third Base	Jose Ramirez	32
Shortstop	Brayan Rocchio	24
Left Field	Amed Rosario	29
Center Field	Myles Straw	30
Right Field	George Valera	24
Designated Hitter	Franmil Reyes	29
No. 1 Starter	Shane Bieber	30
No. 2 Starter	Triston McKenzie	27
No. 3 Starter	Cal Quantrill	30
No. 4 Starter	Daniel Espino	24
No. 5 Starter	Aaron Civale	30
Closer	Emmanuel Clase	27

farm system soon. They added 11 players to their 40-man roster in November to shield them from the Rule 5 draft. Their pitching pipeline shows no signs of slowing, and position players like Gabriel Arias, Tyler Freeman and Nolan Jones should soon be ready to help in Cleveland. It will be up to team president Chris Antonetti and general manager Mike Chernoff to integrate the coming youth wave successfully into the major league roster.

With Bieber and Ramirez still in place, there's no reason for Cleveland to take a big step back while the youth arrives. But the organization is entering the new year in a much different place than it was a year ago, which is reflected by more than just the new signage around Progressive Field. ∎

DEPTH CHART

CLEVELAND GUARDIANS

TOP 2022 ROOKIES	RANK
Gabriel Arias, SS	5
Logan Allen, LHP	9
Peyton Battenfield, RHP	14
BREAKOUT PROSPECTS	**RANK**
Carson Tucker, SS	17
Jhonkensy Noel, 3B/1B	20

SOURCE OF TOP 30 TALENT			
Homegrown	26	Acquired	4
College	10	Trade	4
Junior college	1	Rule 5 draft	0
High school	7	Independent league	0
Nondrafted free agent	0	Free agent/waivers	0
International	8		

LF
Richie Palacios (13)
Isaiah Greene

CF
Petey Halpin (22)
Steven Kwan (27)
Luis Durango Jr.
Will Brennan

RF
George Valera (4)
Alexfri Planez
Will Benson

3B
Nolan Jones (6)
Gabriel Rodriguez (18)
Jose Fermin

SS
Brayan Rocchio (3)
Gabriel Arias (5)
Angel Martinez (10)
Jose Tena (11)
Carson Tucker (17)
Jose Pastrano
Yordys Valdes
Jake Fox

2B
Tyler Freeman (1)
Ernie Clement (24)
Aaron Bracho (25)
Milan Tolentino

1B
Jhonkensy Noel (20)
Junior Sanquintin

C
Bo Naylor (7)
Bryan Lavastida (16)

LHP

LHSP	LHRP
Logan T. Allen (9)	Matt Turner
Doug Nikhazy (21)	Will Dion
Konnor Pilkington (30)	
Joey Cantillo	
Kirk McCarty	
Ryan Webb	
Adam Scott	

RHP

RHSP	RHRP
Daniel Espino (2)	Nick Mikolajchak
Gavin Williams (8)	Kevin Kelly
Tanner Burns (12)	Robert Broom
Peyton Battenfield (14)	Jerson Ramirez
Cody Morris (15)	
Ethan Hankins (19)	
Tobias Myers (23)	
Carlos Vargas (26)	
Xzavion Curry (28)	
Tommy Mace (29)	
Lenny Torres	

1 TYLER FREEMAN, SS/2B

Born: May 21, 1999. **B-T:** R-R. **HT:** 6-0. **WT:** 170.
Drafted: HS—Rancho Cucamonga, Calif., 2017 (2nd round supplemental).
Signed by: Mike Bradford.

TRACK RECORD: Since being drafted 71st overall in 2017 out of Etiwanda High, Freeman has been the most consistent hitter in Cleveland's system. He led the New York-Penn League in 2018 in a host of offensive categories, including batting average (.352) and slugging percentage (.511), as a 19-year-old. He followed that up with an impressive 2019, earning a promotion to High-A Lynchburg in his first year of full-season ball. Freeman spent the canceled 2020 minor league season at Cleveland's alternate training site and continued his previous ways when minor league play resumed in 2021. He was hitting .323 at Double-A in late June when he suffered a small tear in the labrum in his left shoulder. He briefly returned in July for five games but was unable to continue and ultimately had season-ending surgery in August. He has made good progress in his recovery and returned to baseball activities in December.

SCOUTING REPORT: Freeman stands out most for his hitting ability and excellent feel for the barrel. He has a very aggressive approach at the plate and rarely walks, but when he swings, he makes contact. He is a career .319/.378/.445 hitter with a miniscule 9.2% strikeout rate and projects to be at least a plus hitter. His pure hit tool stands out as one of the best not just in the system, but in the minors overall, and his contact-based approach fits the organization's philosophy well. Though on the smaller side, Freeman has always had some projectable power with his bat speed and ability to consistently square balls up. That power began to manifest in 2020, when he arrived at the alternate site noticeably stronger following the coronavirus shutdown. In 2021, a third of his hits went for extra bases, although he still hit just two home runs. While Freeman will likely never be a major home run threat, he posts solid exit velocities and does enough damage to keep pitchers honest. His ability to drive balls in the gaps combined with his average speed help him to produce plenty of doubles and he may grow into even more juice in time. Freeman was drafted as a shortstop and continues to develop there. He's improved his hands, infield actions and instincts, but he's still an average runner with average arm strength and limited range. Second base remains his most likely future position, but his ability to play shortstop has continually exceeded expectations as a professional. He also saw time at third base in 2021 to

BILL MITCHELL

BA GRADE	SCOUTING GRADES
55 Risk: High	Hit: 60. Power: 45. Run: 50. Field: 50. Arm: 50.

Projected future grades on 20-80 scouting scale

BEST TOOLS

Best Hitter for Average	Tyler Freeman
Best Power Hitter	Jhonkensy Noel
Best Strike-Zone Discipline	Richie Palacios
Fastest Baserunner	Quentin Holmes
Best Athlete	Will Benson
Best Fastball	Daniel Espino
Best Curveball	Gavin Williams
Best Slider	Daniel Espino
Best Changeup	Logan Allen
Best Control	Peyton Battenfield
Best Defensive Catcher	Bo Naylor
Best Defensive Infielder	Brayan Rocchio
Best Infield Arm	Gabriel Arias
Best Defensive Outfielder	Steven Kwan
Best Outfield Arm	Johnathan Rodriguez

enhance his versatility. He earns praise for his competitiveness and work ethic, traits that have helped him outperform expectations defensively, as well as expand his offensive skill set. Regardless of where Freeman ends up defensively, his bat will be his carrying tool and profiles just fine at second base.

THE FUTURE: Freeman should be back to full health at the start of the 2022 season. Cleveland added him to the 40-man roster in November to protect him from the Rule 5 draft and he could be in line for his major league debut sometime during the summer. He projects to be the Guardians' everyday second baseman of the future and one of the club's best pure hitters. ∎

Year	Age	Club (Level)	Lge	AVG	G	AB	R	H	2B	3B	HR	RBI	BB	SO	SB	OBP	SLG
2021	22	Akron (AA)	NEast	.323	41	164	26	53	14	2	2	19	8	21	4	.372	.470
Minor League Totals (5 years)				.319	272	1055	183	337	84	11	9	115	49	108	42	.378	.445

2 DANIEL ESPINO, RHP

Born: Jan. 5, 2001. **B-T:** R-R. **HT:** 6-1. **WT:** 205. **Drafted:** HS—Statesboro, Ga., 2019 (1st round). **Signed by:** Ethan Purser.

TRACK RECORD: Espino was born in Panama before moving with his family to the United States when he was 15. He enrolled at Georgia Premier Academy, where he was able to continue his education while also adopting a close to professional mindset on the diamond. He emerged as one of the top prep pitchers in the 2019 draft class and Cleveland selected him 24th overall, giving him a $2.5 million bonus to forgo a Louisiana State commitment. Espino's performance and mentality carried over to pro ball and he's been on a fast track since he was drafted. He reached High-A in 2021 as a 20-year-old and posted a 3.73 ERA over 20 total starts.

BA GRADE

55 Risk: High

SCOUTING REPORT: Espino is on the shorter side for a righthander, but his excellent athleticism and a rare combination of explosiveness and flexibility helps him access his lower half in a way most pitchers his size cannot. That helps him produce elite velocity with a fastball that sits at 96 mph and touches 99. He throws both a curveball and slider, with the slider earning better grades as a potential plus pitch. He also throws a firm changeup that needs refinement but has a chance to give him a fourth at least average offering. He has a long arm action but typically pitches with average control. Espino has swing-and-miss stuff—his 152 strikeouts ranked 15th in the minor leagues in just 91.2 innings—but he'll need to refine his command as he advances to face upper-level hitters who are less likely to chase out of the zone.

THE FUTURE: Espino is ready for the challenge of Double-A as a 21-year-old. He still needs to build innings and refine his command, but once he does, he has the potential to be a hard-throwing, mid-rotation starter.

SCOUTING GRADES:	Fastball: 70	Slider: 60	Curveball: 50	Changeup: 50	Control: 50

Year	Age	Club (Level)	Lge	W	L	ERA	G	GS	IP	H	HR	BB	SO	BB/9	SO/9	WHIP	AVG
2021	20	Lynchburg (LoA)	East	1	2	3.38	10	10	42	34	2	23	64	4.9	13.5	1.34	.217
	20	Lake County (HiA)	Cent	2	6	4.04	10	10	49	30	7	16	88	2.9	16.2	0.94	.170
Minor League Totals (3 years)				3	11	3.75	29	29	115	80	11	49	186	3.8	14.5	1.12	.191

3 BRAYAN ROCCHIO, SS

Born: Jan. 13, 2001. **B-T:** B-R. **HT:** 5-10. **WT:** 150. **Signed:** Venezuela, 2017. **Signed by:** Jhonathan Leyba.

TRACK RECORD: Cleveland made a big splash on the 2017 international market with the heralded signings of Aaron Bracho and George Valera, but their move to sign Rocchio flew more under the radar. Rocchio immediately jumped on an accelerated track and reached Double-A Akron as a 20-year-old in 2021, where he more than held his own on both sides of the ball. Ever the baseball rat, he returned home in the offseason to play in the Venezuelan Winter League and continued his strong performance at the plate.

BA GRADE

55 Risk: High

SCOUTING REPORT: Rocchio doesn't stand out physically but is nicknamed "The Professor" because of his high baseball IQ and game awareness. He has a smooth, consistent swing from both sides of the plate and excellent pitch recognition. He's an aggressive hitter who doesn't walk much, but consistently barrels up the ball and projects to be an above-average hitter. He is better at hitting righthanded than lefthanded. Rocchio began showing added power in 2021. His 15 home runs tripled his previous career high and his 46 extra-base hits were the second-most in Cleveland's organization. While he'll never be confused for a slugger, he now has enough pop to approach double-digit home runs. Rocchio faces zero questions about his ability to stick at shortstop. He's an above-average runner and has soft hands, average arm strength and excellent anticipation. His instincts and baseball IQ help his tools play up.

THE FUTURE: Rocchio has emerged as Cleveland's potential shortstop of the future. He'll see Triple-A in 2022 and should be in the majors for good by 2023.

SCOUTING GRADES:	Hitting: 55	Power: 40	Running: 55	Fielding: 60	Arm: 50

Year	Age	Club (Level)	Lge	AVG	G	AB	R	H	2B	3B	HR	RBI	BB	SO	SB	OBP	SLG
2021	20	Lake County (HiA)	Cent	.265	64	257	45	68	13	1	9	33	20	65	14	.337	.428
	20	Akron (AA)	NEast	.293	44	184	34	54	13	4	6	30	13	41	7	.360	.505
Minor League Totals (4 years)				.284	237	951	152	270	50	12	22	119	68	177	57	.347	.431

4 GEORGE VALERA, OF

Born: Nov. 13, 2000. **B-T:** L-L. **HT:** 5-10. **WT:** 160. **Signed:** Dominican Republic, 2017. **Signed by:** Jhonathan Leyba/Domingo Toribio.

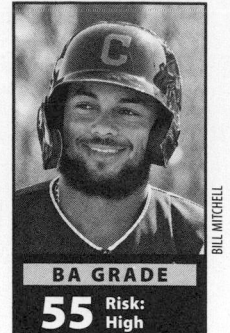

BILL MITCHELL

TRACK RECORD: Valera was born in New York and lived there until his family moved to the Dominican Republic when he was 13. Cleveland chose to make a splash on the international market in 2017 and Valera was its top signing for $1.3 million. Valera was limited by injuries early in his career but finally played his first full season in 2021. He spent most of the year at High-A Lake County before receiving a late-August promotion to Double-A Akron and posted a .260/.405/.505 slash line in 86 games between the two levels, although he did miss nearly a month with a right oblique strain.

SCOUTING REPORT: Valera is a potentially premium hitter and is beginning to blossom. He has a loose, compact lefthanded swing and keeps his bat in the zone for a long time. His advanced feel for the barrel, bat-to-ball skills, pitch recognition and plate discipline all help him make consistent, hard contact and give him the kind of above-average hitting ability the Guardians covet. He has above-average raw power and gets to it in games—his 19 home runs tied for second-most among the organization's minor leaguers. Valera profiles as a corner outfielder with average speed and arm strength. He has played all three outfield positions but is most experienced in right field. Valera's main challenge has been staying healthy. His 86 games in 2021 were a career high.

BA GRADE
55 Risk: High

THE FUTURE: Cleveland has been on the hunt for outfielders for several years and Valera could be one of the answers. He was added to the 40-man roster in November and has a chance to be in the majors for good by 2023.

SCOUTING GRADES:	Hitting: 55	Power: 55	Running: 50	Fielding: 50	Arm: 50

Year	Age	Club (Level)	Lge	AVG	G	AB	R	H	2B	3B	HR	RBI	BB	SO	SB	OBP	SLG
2021	20	Lake County (HiA)	Cent	.256	63	199	45	51	2	4	16	43	55	58	10	.430	.548
	20	Akron (AA)	NEast	.267	23	86	6	23	3	0	3	22	11	30	1	.340	.407
Minor League Totals (4 years)				.246	144	483	78	119	13	6	28	103	100	152	18	.381	.472

5 GABRIEL ARIAS, SS

Born: Feb. 27, 2000. **B-T:** R-R. **HT:** 6-1. **WT:** 201. **Signed:** Venezuela, 2016. **Signed by:** Luis Prieto/Yfrain Linares/Trevor Schumm (Padres).

TRACK RECORD: Arias was one of the top prospects in the 2016 international class and signed with the Padres for $1.9 million. He stood out for his defense from the outset and broke out offensively in the second half of the 2019 season after some early struggles. Cleveland acquired Arias at the 2020 trade deadline as a part of the deal for Mike Clevinger and Greg Allen. After facing some initial skepticism, Arias proved his offensive progress was sustainable in 2021. He jumped straight to Triple-A in his first year in Cleveland's organization and hit .284/.348/.454 as a 21-year-old while continuing to play his typically exceptional defense.

BA GRADE
55 Risk: High

SCOUTING REPORT: Arias is a good athlete with a lot of raw ability. The right-handed hitter has a smooth swing, and his bat speed and wiry strength give him surprising above-average power. Encouragingly, he has improved his strikeout rate in back-to-back seasons, dropping to a career-low 22.8% in 2021. His walk rate has also improved, although he still has a very aggressive approach at the plate. Arias is never going to be an on-base machine, but he's trending in the right direction and should be at least a fringe-average hitter who gets to his power enough. There have never been many doubts about Arias defensively. He has fluid actions, clean hands and plus-plus arm strength. Despite his below-average speed, he has plenty of range for shortstop with his anticipation and footwork and makes all the plays necessary.

THE FUTURE: Arias will get a chance in spring training to compete for Cleveland's starting shortstop job. Even if he doesn't break camp with the Guardians, his big league debut should come some time in 2022.

SCOUTING GRADES:	Hitting: 45	Power: 55	Running: 40	Fielding: 60	Arm: 70

Year	Age	Club (Level)	Lge	AVG	G	AB	R	H	2B	3B	HR	RBI	BB	SO	SB	OBP	SLG
2021	21	Columbus (AAA)	East	.284	115	436	64	124	29	3	13	55	39	110	5	.348	.454
Minor League Totals (5 years)				.274	412	1583	206	434	84	13	36	202	117	454	21	.327	.412

6 NOLAN JONES, 3B

Born: May 7, 1998. **B-T:** L-R. **HT:** 6-2. **WT:** 185. **Drafted:** HS—Bensalem, Pa., 2016 (2nd round). **Signed by:** Mike Kanen.

TRACK RECORD: Jones was expected to break through to the big leagues sooner than later, but it didn't quite come together for him in 2021. He started the season slowly with Triple-A Columbus before heating up in the summer. His season came to an early end when he suffered a high ankle sprain in late August that ultimately required surgery and cost him the final month of the season.

SCOUTING REPORT: Jones has an easy lefthanded swing and uses the whole field to hit. He is a patient hitter and led all Cleveland minor leaguers in walks in both 2018 and 2019, though his patience also means that he often works in deep counts and will always strike out fairly often as a result. In 2021, his walk rate decreased and his strikeout rate increased as he struggled with offspeed stuff, chasing more often than he has in the past. He has plus raw power and can drive the ball to all fields. Jones has dealt with questions about his ability to stay at third base throughout his career. He has plus arm strength and has worked hard to improve his glovework and infield actions, especially when ranging to his right. He also saw some action in the outfield as the Guardians work to increase his versatility and potentially open an additional route to Cleveland, where Jose Ramirez is still entrenched at third base.

THE FUTURE: Jones is coming off his worst offensive season as a professional, but he'll still be 23 on Opening Day and has the tools to develop into a big league corner bat. He'll likely make his MLB debut in 2022.

BA GRADE

50 Risk: Medium

SCOUTING GRADES:	Hitting: 45	Power: 60	Running: 50	Fielding: 50	Arm: 60

Year	Age	Club (Level)	Lge	AVG	G	AB	R	H	2B	3B	HR	RBI	BB	SO	SB	OBP	SLG
2021	23	Columbus (AAA)	East	.238	99	341	60	81	25	1	13	48	59	122	10	.356	.431
Minor League Totals (6 years)				.273	439	1525	261	416	91	9	51	219	310	510	23	.398	.445

7 BO NAYLOR, C

Born: Feb. 21, 2000. **B-T:** L-R. **HT:** 6-0. **WT:** 195. **Drafted:** HS—Mississauga, Ont., 2018 (1st round). **Signed by:** Mike Kanen.

TRACK RECORD: For perhaps the first time in his career, Naylor had an extended period of struggles in 2021. After a distinguished amateur career that led Cleveland to draft him 29th overall in 2019 and a fast start to his pro career, Naylor never got his bat going in Double-A. He hit just .188/.280/.332 in 87 games for the RubberDucks, although he was one of the youngest players at the level and was also dealing with the rigors of catching.

SCOUTING REPORT: Naylor's step back offensively was particularly surprising after his impressive performance in 2020 at the alternate training site. Initially, he was seen as being more of a contact hitter than a slugger, but his strikeout rate increased and his walk rate decreased as he struggled with more advanced pitching. He still has solid power and drives balls well to go with average speed. Naylor's athleticism plays well behind the plate as a blocker, and he earns high grades for his framing ability. He played a lot of third base as an amateur but has been exclusively a catcher the last three seasons and has proven he can handle the position.

THE FUTURE: Naylor will still be just 22 years old on Opening Day in 2022. He has a clear path to Cleveland, where he would join his older brother Josh, but he'll need to first work out his offensive issues.

BA GRADE

55 Risk: Very High

COURTESY OF AKRON RUBBERDUCKS

SCOUTING GRADES:	Hitting: 40	Power: 50	Running: 50	Fielding: 55	Arm: 60

Year	Age	Club (Level)	Lge	AVG	G	AB	R	H	2B	3B	HR	RBI	BB	SO	SB	OBP	SLG
2021	21	Akron (AA)	NEast	.188	87	313	41	59	13	1	10	44	37	112	10	.280	.332
Minor League Totals (4 years)				.227	227	829	118	188	34	14	23	126	101	244	22	.311	.385

8 GAVIN WILLIAMS, RHP

BILL MITCHELL

Born: July 26, 1999. **B-T:** L-R. **HT:** 6-6. **WT:** 238. **Drafted:** East Carolina, 2021 (1st round). **Signed by:** Pete Loizzo.

TRACK RECORD: Williams long had a big arm and lots of potential, but it took him a full four years at East Carolina to truly realize it. After primarily pitching out of the bullpen for his first three seasons, he took over a spot in the rotation in 2021 and produced an All-America season, going 10-1, 1.88 with 130 strikeouts in 81.1 innings. That turned him into a first-round pick, where Cleveland selected him 23rd overall and signed him for $2.25 million.

SCOUTING REPORT: Williams stands out for his size and arm strength. His fastball sits 95 mph, touches 101 and get swings and misses, especially up in the strike zone. He throws both a curveball and slider, with the 11-to-5 curve-ball being the better of the two pitches as a plus offering, although his short slider is an above-average pitch in its own right. He also has a firm changeup that is an average pitch at its best. Williams had control issues early in his college career but took a big step forward in 2021 and should pitch with average control. For a big, powerful pitcher, he has solid body control and has done a better job recently of repeating his delivery.

THE FUTURE: Williams did not pitch after signing and will likely make his professional debut at High-A in 2022. His loud stuff gives him mid-rotation upside as a starter.

BA GRADE

55 Risk: Very High

SCOUTING GRADES:	Fastball: 70	Slider: 55	Curveball: 60	Changeup: 50	Control: 50

Year	Age	Club (Level)	Lge	W	L	ERA	G	GS	IP	H	HR	BB	SO	BB/9	SO/9	WHIP	AVG
2021	21	Did not play															

9 LOGAN T. ALLEN, LHP

DAVID MONSEUR/ACCENT IMAGES PHOTOGRAPHY

Born: Sept. 5, 1998. **B-T:** R-L. **HT:** 6-0. **WT:** 180. **Drafted:** Florida International, 2020 (2nd round). **Signed by:** Jhonathan Leyba.

TRACK RECORD: Allen—who is not to be confused with lefthander Logan S. Allen, who arrived in the organization in 2019 in a trade with the Padres—was one of the organization's breakout prospects in 2021. After a decorated ama-teur career that led Cleveland to draft him in the second round in 2020, he rocketed to Double-A in his pro debut and went 9-0, 2.26 with 143 strikeouts against just 26 walks in 111.1 innings.

SCOUTING REPORT: Allen stands out for his feel and competitiveness on the mound, with the knocks on him long being his small size and lack of a big arm. His fastball has ticked up in the last couple years and now sits around 90 mph and can touch 95. The pitch plays up thanks to some deception in his delivery and his ability to locate it to all four quadrants of the strike zone.

BA GRADE

50 Risk: High

His best pitch is his changeup, which is a plus offering and a weapon he can use against both lefthanders and righthanders. His breaking ball has long lagged behind his other two pitches. He started exclusively throwing a slider in the fall of 2019, and it has the potential to be an average offering. His control was among the best in the draft class and that transferred to pro ball, where it showed plus. He was a two-way player in college and his athleticism plays well on the mound.

THE FUTURE: Allen put himself on the fast track to the big leagues and could well be in line for a 2022 debut. His ceiling is somewhat limited, but he can be a solid back-end starter.

SCOUTING GRADES:	Fastball: 50	Slider: 50	Changeup: 60	Control: 60

Year	Age	Club (Level)	Lge	W	L	ERA	G	GS	IP	H	HR	BB	SO	BB/9	SO/9	WHIP	AVG
2021	22	Lake County (HiA)	Cent	5	0	1.58	9	9	51	37	3	13	67	2.3	11.8	0.97	.200
	22	Akron (AA)	NEast	4	0	2.85	12	10	60	40	9	13	76	2.0	11.4	0.88	.186
Minor League Totals (2 years)				9	0	2.26	21	19	111	77	12	26	143	2.1	11.6	0.93	.193

10 ANGEL MARTINEZ, 2B/SS

Born: Jan. 27, 2002. **B-T:** B-R. **HT:** 6-0. **WT:** 165. **Signed:** Dominican Republic, 2018. **Signed by:** Jhonathan Leyba.

TRACK RECORD: Martinez is the son of former big league catcher Sandy Martinez, now the Nationals' Dominican Summer League manager. The younger Martinez signed with Cleveland for $500,000 in 2018 and was limited to the DSL and instructional league his first two seasons, but he made the biggest jump in the Guardians system of any position player prospect in 2021. He moved to Low-A Lynchburg and held his own as a 19-year-old, getting off to a fast start before slowing down in the second half.

SCOUTING REPORT: Martinez isn't the most tooled-up of the Guardians' lower-level infielders, but his baseball IQ and maturity make all his tools play up. The switch-hitter has a simple swing from both sides and can drive the ball to all fields with solid power potential, though it plays as doubles pop now. Martinez is an average runner, but still covers a lot of ground thanks to his instincts and makes sound decisions defensively. He also has a plus arm. He can play anywhere on the infield and split his time between second, third and shortstop.

THE FUTURE: Martinez's switch-hitting ability, power potential and defensive versatility make for a promising foundation, although he still has a long way to go. He'll head to High-A in 2022 and look to build on his previous gains.

BA GRADE 50 Risk: Very High

SCOUTING GRADES:	Hitting: 50	Power: 50	Running: 50	Fielding: 55	Arm: 60

Year	Age	Club (Level)	Lge	AVG	G	AB	R	H	2B	3B	HR	RBI	BB	SO	SB	OBP	SLG
2021	19	Lynchburg (LoA)	East	.241	97	377	62	91	20	6	7	46	43	88	13	.319	.382
Minor League Totals (2 years)				.265	153	599	99	159	30	13	8	73	72	117	24	.350	.399

11 JOSE TENA, SS/2B

BA GRADE 50 Risk: Very High

Born: March 20, 2001. **B-T:** L-R. **HT:** 5-10. **WT:** 160. **Signed:** Dominican Republic, 2017. **Signed by:** Anthony Roa/Jhonathan Leyba.

TRACK RECORD: Cleveland's 2017 international class has developed into a blockbuster. Outfielder George Valera and shortstop Brayan Rocchio have been the headliners of the group and Tena, a nephew of Juan Uribe, is fast closing in on them. After a strong season with High-A Lake County that saw him rank second in the league in hits (116), the 20-year-old finished the year by winning the Arizona Fall League batting title (.387).

SCOUTING REPORT: Tena has a smaller frame but that belies his ability. He has a loose, easy swing and good feel for the barrel, allowing him to consistently square up balls. He's an aggressive hitter who doesn't walk much and struck out in 26% of his plate appearances, a rate he'll have to manage while continuing to advance toward the major leagues. He's an above-average runner and as he's physically matured has developed solid power potential. Tena has an above-average arm, good hands and solid range thanks to his speed and athleticism. He mostly played shortstop at Lake County, while also seeing time at second and third base.

THE FUTURE: Tena elevated his profile with his performance in 2021. He'll look to build on his success in 2022 as he advances to Double-A Akron.

Year	Age	Club (Level)	Lge	AVG	G	AB	R	H	2B	3B	HR	RBI	BB	SO	SB	OBP	SLG
2021	20	Lake County (HiA)	Cent	.281	107	413	58	116	25	2	16	58	27	117	10	.331	.467
Minor League Totals (4 years)				.299	202	799	116	239	40	12	18	99	48	190	26	.345	.447

12 TANNER BURNS, RHP

BA GRADE 45 Risk: High

Born: Dec. 28, 1998. **B-T:** R-R. **HT:** 6-0. **WT:** 180. **Drafted:** Auburn, 2020 (1st round supplemental). **Signed by:** C.T. Bradford.

TRACK RECORD: A prominent player in high school and the highest-rated player from the class of 2017 to make it to college, Burns stepped right into the rotation at Auburn, where he learned alongside Casey Mize and under Tim Hudson. Cleveland in 2020 drafted him 36th overall, at the time the highest the organization had drafted a college pitcher since 2010. He made his professional debut in 2021 and though he was slowed by a two-week spell on the injured list due to elbow soreness, he acquitted himself well with High-A Lake County.

SCOUTING REPORT: Burns has solid all-around stuff and a good understanding of pitching. His fastball sits 93-94 mph and reaches 97. It's a plus pitch that plays up thanks to his ability to consistently locate it. He throws both a big, 12-to-6 curveball and a slider-cutter hybrid that sits around 90 mph. His curveball has long been the better of his breaking balls, but he worked over the offseason to reshape his slider and it became a solid offering itself. He also mixes in a changeup with good sinking action, but it's a clear fourth offering. He earns praise for his dedication to his craft, makeup and his desire to learn.

THE FUTURE: Burns is a bit undersized, and he doesn't have the biggest pure stuff, but between his aptitude, early success and Cleveland's track record of helping college pitchers improve, there's a lot to like. He'll advance to Double-A in 2022 and should continue to move quickly.

Year	Age	Club (Level)	Lge	W	L	ERA	G	GS	IP	H	HR	BB	SO	BB/9	SO/9	WHIP	AVG
2021	22	Lake County (HiA)	Cent	2	5	3.57	18	18	75	64	10	29	91	3.5	10.8	1.23	.229
Minor League Totals (2 years)				2	5	3.57	18	18	75	64	10	29	91	3.45	10.82	1.23	.229

13 RICHIE PALACIOS, 2B/OF

BA GRADE
45 Risk: High

Born: May 16, 1997. **B-T:** L-R. **HT:** 5-11. **WT:** 180. **Drafted:** Towson, 2018 (3rd round). **Signed by:** Aaron Etchison.

TRACK RECORD: Palacios had a decorated college career at Towson, where he became the fastest player in program history to reach 200 hits and set the program's single-season and career stolen base records. He got his pro career off to a strong start in 2018 but he tore the labrum in his right shoulder that offseason and had season-ending surgery in March. He worked out in Arizona in 2020 and hit the ground running in 2021, reaching Triple-A Columbus by the end of the season.

SCOUTING REPORT: Palacios has a good feel for the barrel and produces excellent bat speed. He has good plate discipline, knows how to work a walk and rarely strikes out. He has average power, which mostly has played as doubles pop to this point, but he's increasingly doing a better job of getting to it in games. He's a good athlete and has above-average speed. Where Palacios fits best defensively has long been a question and in 2021 he played second base and all three outfield positions. He's primarily been a second baseman and his hands work well enough on the infield, while his speed plays in the outfield.

THE FUTURE: The Guardians added Palacios to the 40-man roster in November, bringing him one step closer to joining his older brother Josh in the major leagues. Whether he ends up at second base or in the outfield, his bat will be the main attraction and he could be ready to help Cleveland sometime during 2022.

Year	Age	Club (Level)	Lge	AVG	G	AB	R	H	2B	3B	HR	RBI	BB	SO	SB	OBP	SLG
2021	24	Akron (AA)	NEast	.299	66	244	53	73	24	3	6	36	33	42	10	.389	.496
	24	Columbus (AAA)	East	.292	37	113	19	33	9	1	1	12	25	28	10	.434	.416
Minor League Totals (3 years)				.317	148	526	98	167	41	6	13	78	77	97	27	.409	.492

14 PEYTON BATTENFIELD, RHP

BA GRADE
45 Risk: High

Born: Aug. 10, 1997. **B-T:** R-R. **HT:** 6-4. **WT:** 224. **Drafted:** Oklahoma State, 2019 (9th round). **Signed by:** Jim Stevenson (Astros).

TRACK RECORD: Battenfield has been well traveled since the Astros drafted him in the ninth round in 2019. He was traded in January 2020 to the Rays in exchange for Austin Pruitt and at the 2021 trade deadline he was sent to Cleveland in exchange for DJ Johnson and Jordan Luplow. His trade to Cleveland came in the midst of a banner season that he finished with Double-A Akron.

SCOUTING REPORT: Battenfield was a reliever in college at Oklahoma State but found great success as a starter in 2021. His fastball sits in the low 90s, reaching 94-95 mph. The pitch plays up thanks to its incredible riding life. The pitch's movement combined with his ability to leverage his 6-foot-4 frame allows him to get swings and misses both up and down in the zone. He throws a big curveball, a cutter and a changeup, all of which are at least average offerings. His cutter has become his best secondary offering and all of his pitches play well off his fastball. Battenfield repeats his delivery well and fills up the strike zone, pitching with solid control.

THE FUTURE: Battenfield isn't overpowering but his ability to throw strikes with four pitches and his understanding of pitching fits well with Cleveland's philosophy. He'll start 2022 with Triple-A Columbus and could soon be in the mix at Progressive Field.

Year	Age	Club (Level)	Lge	W	L	ERA	G	GS	IP	H	HR	BB	SO	BB/9	SO/9	WHIP	AVG
2021	23	Bowling Green (HiA)	East	2	0	1.45	7	6	31	18	2	5	49	1.5	14.2	0.74	.162
	23	Montgomery (AA)	South	3	0	2.72	7	6	36	24	5	7	46	1.7	11.4	0.85	.179
	23	Akron (AA)	NEast	2	1	3.28	7	7	35	24	4	7	36	1.8	9.1	0.87	.183
Minor League Totals (3 years)				9	2	2.28	35	24	142	89	11	34	177	2.2	11.2	0.86	.173

15 CODY MORRIS, RHP

Born: Nov. 4, 1996. **B-T:** R-R. **HT:** 6-4. **WT:** 205. **Drafted:** South Carolina, 2018 (7th round). **Signed by:** Mike Bradford.

BA GRADE
50 Risk: Extreme

TRACK RECORD: Morris missed his freshman season at South Carolina due to Tommy John surgery before bouncing back for a solid college career. He's pitched well since Cleveland drafted him in 2018 and in 2021 overcame a delayed start to his season due to a strained lat muscle, delivering a breakout second-half performance after getting back to action in July. He finished the season with Triple-A Columbus.

SCOUTING REPORT: Listed at 6-foot-4 and 205 pounds, Morris has a strong build and a powerful arm. His fastball touched 99 mph in 2021 and averaged 96. He mixes in a changeup, a sharp curveball and this year also added a cutter that gets into the low 90s. His changeup is above-average and both his breaking balls are promising offerings. As important as his swing-and-miss power stuff ticking up this year was his improved command. He did a better job controlling his body and pitched with average control.

THE FUTURE: The gains Morris made in 2021 were very encouraging and the Guardians added him to the 40-man roster in November. Now he needs to show he can maintain his improvements over a full season. He'll start 2022 back in Columbus and could be in the mix to make his major league debut later in the season.

Year	Age	Club (Level)	Lge	W	L	ERA	G	GS	IP	H	HR	BB	SO	BB/9	SO/9	WHIP	AVG
2021	24	Guardians (R)	ACL	0	0	2.08	1	1	4	2	1	1	12	2.1	24.9	0.69	.133
	24	Akron (AA)	NEast	0	0	1.35	5	5	20	14	1	7	29	3.2	13.1	1.05	.197
	24	Columbus (AAA)	East	2	2	1.72	9	8	36	25	1	12	52	3.0	12.8	1.01	.191
Minor League Totals (3 years)				9	6	3.24	36	34	150	136	10	47	204	2.8	12.2	1.22	.239

16 BRYAN LAVASTIDA, C

Born: Nov. 27, 1998. **B-T:** R-R. **HT:** 6-0. **WT:** 200. **Drafted:** Hillsborough (Fla.) JC, 2018 (15th round). **Signed by:** Steffan Segui.

BA GRADE
45 Risk: High

TRACK RECORD: Lavastida was an infielder coming out of high school and began to convert to catching as a sophomore in junior college. Cleveland drafted him as a catcher in the 15th round in 2018 and continued to develop him behind the plate. While that project continues to progress, he's also impressed offensively and had a breakout 2021 season, reaching Triple-A Columbus.

SCOUTING REPORT: Lavastida has a balanced swing and a good approach at the plate, allowing him to control the strike zone well. He makes a lot of hard contact and has average raw power, though his line drive-oriented swing means his pop plays more as doubles power. Lavastida is a good athlete and moves well behind the plate and has average arm strength. He quickly picked up the mechanical aspects of catching and is continuing to progress with the finer points, like pitch-calling. While he hasn't appeared at any other position in the field as a professional, he has continued to work in the infield in practice settings.

THE FUTURE: Lavastida was added to the 40-man roster in November and after his breakout 2021 season it's possible he'll be ready to debut in Cleveland in 2022. His defense still needs some work to be a big league regular, but his bat gives him intriguing upside.

Year	Age	Club (Level)	Lge	AVG	G	AB	R	H	2B	3B	HR	RBI	BB	SO	SB	OBP	SLG
2021	22	Lake County (HiA)	Cent	.303	48	165	32	50	12	0	5	31	26	30	14	.399	.467
	22	Akron (AA)	NEast	.291	29	103	16	30	7	1	3	17	12	28	2	.373	.466
	22	Columbus (AAA)	East	.158	7	19	2	3	0	0	1	3	2	10	0	.238	.316
Minor League Totals (4 years)				.305	176	619	113	189	42	5	12	109	88	119	24	.397	.447

17 CARSON TUCKER, SS

Born: Jan. 24, 2002. **B-T:** R-R. **HT:** 6-2. **WT:** 180. **Drafted:** HS—Phoenix, 2020 (1st round). **Signed by:** Ryan Perry.

BA GRADE
50 Risk: Extreme

TRACK RECORD: Tucker got bigger and stronger going into his senior season and showed enough to convince Cleveland to draft him in the first round. He went 23rd overall, bettering his older brother Cole Tucker, who went 24th overall in 2014 to the Pirates. He made his pro debut in 2021 in the Arizona Complex League but was limited to just six games before a hand injury sidelined him.

SCOUTING REPORT: Tucker has solid all-around tools and stands out most for his feel for hitting and infield actions. He has a short, consistent swing and makes a lot of contact, a combination that should make him at least an average hitter. His swing is more geared to hitting line drives, but he can flash above-average power and his offseason strength gains should help him get to it. He's at least a plus runner. Tucker has worked hard at his defense and has a good natural feel for the position. His actions, above-average arm and speed give him the tools to be an above-average defender.

THE FUTURE: Tucker does a lot of things well on the diamond and may have better raw tools than his older brother at the same age. While the pandemic and his injury have greatly limited his time on the field early in his professional career, he'll play the 2022 season as a 20-year-old and can make up for lost time.

Year	Age	Club (Level)	Lge	AVG	G	AB	R	H	2B	3B	HR	RBI	BB	SO	SB	OBP	SLG
2021	19	Guardians (R)	ACL	.150	6	20	6	3	0	0	1	3	5	4	1	.320	.300
Minor League Totals (2 years)				.150	6	20	6	3	0	0	1	3	5	4	1	.320	.300

18 GABRIEL RODRIGUEZ, 3B/SS

BA GRADE
50 Risk: Extreme

Born: Feb. 22, 2002. **B-T:** R-R. **HT:** 6-2. **WT:** 174. **Signed:** Venezuela, 2018. **Signed by:** Hernan Albornoz.

TRACK RECORD: Rodriguez was the eighth-ranked player overall in the 2018 international class and headlined Cleveland's signing class that year. The Venezuelan got his professional career off to a good start in 2019, earning a midseason promotion to the Rookie-level Arizona League. He continued his precocious ways in 2021, as he was the second-youngest regular in Low-A East.

SCOUTING REPORT: Rodriguez stands out for his all-around skill set. He has a short, quick swing and can drive the ball to all fields. His power mostly plays as doubles pop now, but projects to eventually hit for solid power as he physically matures and learns how to employ the power-packed swing he can show during batting practice all the time. Rodriguez was praised for his advanced approach at the plate at the outset of his pro career but struck out in 27.3% of his plate appearances in 2021 and will need to make more consistent contact as he advances in the minor leagues. Signed as a shortstop, Rodriguez has started to fill out his 6-foot-2 frame and played more third base in 2021. His strong arm and instinctive infield actions play well on the hot corner and he's likely to settle in there.

THE FUTURE: Like most players who are young for their level, Rodriguez faced some challenges in 2021. He'll work in 2022 on making adjustments after his first full-season experience at High-A Lake County.

Year	Age	Club (Level)	Lge	AVG	G	AB	R	H	2B	3B	HR	RBI	BB	SO	SB	OBP	SLG
2021	19	Lynchburg (LoA)	East	.236	97	373	44	88	18	1	3	34	25	111	3	.288	.314
Minor League Totals (3 years)				.234	153	581	76	136	28	5	6	73	44	160	7	.300	.330

19 ETHAN HANKINS, RHP

BA GRADE
50 Risk: Extreme

Born: May 23, 2000. **B-T:** R-R. **HT:** 6-6. **WT:** 200. **Drafted:** HS—Gainesville, Ga., 2018 (1st round). **Signed by:** C.T. Bradford.

TRACK RECORD: Hankins was one of the stars of the showcase circuit in the summer of 2017 and was considered the best prep player in the draft class going into the spring. A minor shoulder injury caused him to slide on draft day and Cleveland was happy to select him with the final pick of the first round. After spending the 2020 season at the alternate site, he was sidelined in 2021 due to Tommy John surgery.

SCOUTING REPORT: Hankins has a long, lean frame and uncommon athleticism for a pitcher of his size. When he's healthy, he could run his fastball up to 97 mph and typically sat in the mid 90s with plus life. He has the makings of quality secondary pitches, but they'll need to become more consistent. His slider and changeup both have the ability to be above-average. He also throws a bigger curveball, though it lags behind his other pitches. Hankins controls his arsenal well, but it will be important for him to maintain his delivery as he grows into his large frame.

THE FUTURE: Between Cleveland's cautious approach with prep pitchers, the pandemic and, now, his injury, Hankins has thrown just 63 innings in pro ball. He turns 22 in May and should be able to get back to action soon after. He still has tremendous upside, but simply needs innings to help him realize it.

Year	Age	Club (Level)	Lge	W	L	ERA	G	GS	IP	H	HR	BB	SO	BB/9	SO/9	WHIP	AVG
2021	21	Did not play—Injured															
Minor League Totals (3 years)				0	3	2.71	16	15	63	47	4	30	77	4.3	11.0	1.22	.212

20 JHONKENSY NOEL, 3B/1B

BA GRADE
50 Risk: Extreme

Born: July 15, 2001. **B-T:** R-R. **HT:** 6-1. **WT:** 180. **Signed:** Dominican Republic, 2017. **Signed by:** Domingo Toribio/Jhonathan Leyba.

TRACK RECORD: Another member of Cleveland's banner 2017 international class, Noel signed on his 16th birthday and debuted the following year in the Dominican Summer League. Though he was hampered by hand and ankle injuries in 2021, he still delivered a breakout season and rose to High-A Lake County as a 20-year-old in his first full professional season.

SCOUTING REPORT: Noel has a big, strong frame and produces tremendous bat speed and raw power. He recorded a max exit velocity of 115 mph in 2021 and he doesn't have to sell out to get to his premium power. He controls the zone relatively well for a young power hitter, but there's no question he's an aggressive hitter looking to do damage at the plate. Noel spent most of his time at third base, but his below-average range may mean he eventually moves across the diamond to first base, where he's already playing some.

THE FUTURE: Noel's raw power is tantalizing, and he could be a middle-of-the-order hitter. But as a right-right corner infielder, there's a lot riding on his bat and he'll need to continue to develop as an overall hitter. Still, the Guardians thought enough of his potential to add him to the 40-man roster in November. He'll advance to Double-A Akron in 2022.

Year	Age	Club (Level)	Lge	AVG	G	AB	R	H	2B	3B	HR	RBI	BB	SO	SB	OBP	SLG
2021	19	Guardians (R)	ACL	.200	6	15	1	3	1	0	0	1	1	4	0	.294	.267
	19	Lynchburg (LoA)	East	.393	38	150	36	59	10	1	11	40	7	27	2	.426	.693
	19	Lake County (HiA)	Cent	.280	26	100	13	28	3	0	8	25	9	31	3	.351	.550
Minor League Totals (4 years)				.293	181	661	116	194	37	1	35	142	60	159	16	.367	.511

21 DOUG NIKHAZY, LHP

Born: Aug. 11, 1999. **B-T:** L-L. **HT:** 6-0. **WT:** 205. **Drafted:** Mississippi, 2021 (2nd round). **Signed by:** C.T. Bradford.

TRACK RECORD: Nikhazy was one of the most polished college pitchers in the 2021 draft class. He earned Freshman All-America honors in 2019, pitched for USA Baseball's Collegiate National Team and was named a first-team All-American in 2021. He didn't pitch in an official game after Cleveland drafted him, but he did participate in instructional league.

SCOUTING REPORT: Nikhazy has a slight frame and isn't overpowering but is an elite competitor and produced a stellar track record in college. His fastball gets up to 94-95 mph, but typically sits around 90. It plays up thanks to his over-the-top arm slot and the riding life on the pitch. He throws both a big, looping curveball and a slider that has late-biting action, both of which can be plus pitches. He also has a promising changeup but threw it only sparingly in college. He has above-average control.

THE FUTURE: Nikhazy's polish should enable him to move quickly in the minor leagues and he could begin his professional career at High-A. How much upside Nikhazy has will be determined by whether or not Cleveland can coax more velocity out of him.

Year	Age	Club (Level)	Lge	W	L	ERA	G	GS	IP	H	HR	BB	SO	BB/9	SO/9	WHIP	AVG
2021	21	Did not play															

22 PETEY HALPIN, OF

Born: May 26, 2002. **B-T:** L-R. **HT:** 6-0. **WT:** 185. **Drafted:** HS—Mountain View, Calif., 2020 (3rd round). **Signed by:** Carlos Muniz.

TRACK RECORD: Cleveland used top 100 draft picks in 2020 on Carson Tucker and Halpin, both of whom were committed to Texas. Halpin made his professional debut in 2021 with Low-A Lynchburg.

SCOUTING REPORT: Halpin has a top-of-the-order profile and a well-rounded skill set. He controls the strike zone well and makes adjustments quickly, helping him to make a lot of contact. His swing is geared toward hitting line drives and he's not a slugger, but he drives the ball into gaps often. The combination of that hard contact and his above-average speed makes for a lot of extra-base hits, and about a third of his hits this season went for extra bases. He's still learning to make the most of his speed on the bases and got thrown out 45% of the time as a basestealer. Halpin has good outfield actions and an average arm. If he can stay in center field—where he saw most of his action in 2021—he'd profile well. But if his range ends up being a better fit in left field, it would put more pressure on his bat.

THE FUTURE: Of the three prep hitters Cleveland drafted in 2020 (Tucker, Halpin and infielder Milan Tolentino), Halpin had the best professional debut. He showed off exciting offensive upside and will be ready for High-A in 2022.

Year	Age	Club (Level)	Lge	AVG	G	AB	R	H	2B	3B	HR	RBI	BB	SO	SB	OBP	SLG
2021	19	Lynchburg (LoA)	East	.294	54	221	34	65	14	6	1	18	21	50	11	.363	.425
Minor League Totals (2 years)				.294	54	221	34	65	14	6	1	18	21	50	11	.363	.425

23 TOBIAS MYERS, RHP

Born: Aug. 5, 1998. **B-T:** R-R. **HT:** 6-0. **WT:** 193. **Drafted:** HS—Winter Haven, Fla., 2016 (6th round). **Signed by:** Kelvin Colon (Orioles).

TRACK RECORD: Drafted in the sixth round in 2016 by the Orioles, Myers was traded at the deadline the following year to the Rays. He steadily climbed through the minor leagues to reach Triple-A Durham in 2021. Following the season, he was traded to the Guardians for Junior Caminero.

SCOUTING REPORT: Myers in 2021 saw his stuff tick up, as his fastball sat around 93-95 mph with some of the biggest vertical movement in the minor leagues. His best secondary offering is a mid-80s breaking ball that he calls a cutter. He also mixes in an above-average changeup and a big curveball. His stuff all plays up thanks to his plus control. Myers is a little undersized at 6 feet, 193 pounds, but his combination of stuff and control makes for an intriguing package. He has a starter profile, though his stuff would also play in relief.

THE FUTURE: The Guardians added Myers to the 40-man roster after acquiring him and he'll go to spring training in competition for a spot on staff, though he'll likely make his organizational debut with Triple-A Columbus.

Year	Age	Club (Level)	Lge	W	L	ERA	G	GS	IP	H	HR	BB	SO	BB/9	SO/9	WHIP	AVG
2021	22	Montgomery (AA)	South	5	3	3.32	13	10	59	49	8	10	81	1.5	12.2	0.99	.222
2021	22	Durham (AAA)	East	3	4	4.50	12	12	58	52	11	18	65	2.8	10.1	1.21	.234
Minor League Totals (6 years)				31	16	3.41	84	72	385	356	36	109	383	2.55	8.95	1.21	.244

24 ERNIE CLEMENT, 2B/3B

Born: March 22, 1996. **B-T:** R-R. **HT:** 6-0. **WT:** 170. **Drafted:** Virginia, 2017 (4th round). **Signed by:** Bob Mayer.

TRACK RECORD: Clement's reputation as a pure hitter dates back to his amateur days. That success translated to the professional ranks, as he continued to produce throughout the minor leagues. He made his major league debut in June, serving in a utility role for Cleveland. He spent most of September on the injured list but returned to action by the end of the season.

SCOUTING REPORT: Clement has an aggressive approach and an uncanny knack for putting the bat on the ball. He has below-average power and instead sprays the ball all over the field and takes advantage of his plus speed to get on base. Clement is a versatile defender and appeared at second base, third base, shortstop and left field in 2021. He has above-average instincts on the infield and good hands. His fringy arm strength means as an everyday player his best position is probably second base, but as a utility option he can handle the left side of the infield. His speed plays well in the outfield.

THE FUTURE: Clement's first taste of the big leagues was likely always going to come as a utility player. His challenge now is breaking into a crowded infield in Cleveland for a regular role. He'll likely ultimately settle in as a utility player, but his feel for hitting gives him a chance for more.

Year	Age	Club (Level)	Lge	AVG	G	AB	R	H	2B	3B	HR	RBI	BB	SO	SB	OBP	SLG
2021	25	Akron (AA)	NEast	.143	2	7	0	1	1	0	0	0	0	3	0	.143	.286
	25	Columbus (AAA)	East	.250	33	124	11	31	12	1	1	10	9	22	2	.294	.387
	25	Cleveland (MLB)	AL	.231	40	121	16	28	4	0	3	9	7	19	0	.285	.339
Major League Totals (1 year)				.231	40	121	16	28	4	0	3	9	7	19	0	.285	.339
Minor League Totals (5 years)				.275	283	1130	164	311	64	7	4	84	84	106	43	.331	.355

25 AARON BRACHO, 2B

Born: April 24, 2001. **B-T:** B-R. **HT:** 5-11. **WT:** 175. **Signed:** Venezuela, 2017. **Signed by:** Hernan Albornoz/Rafael Cariel.

TRACK RECORD: When Cleveland went big in the 2017 international market, Bracho and outfielder George Valera were the two most-hyped prospects in the group it signed. Bracho was banged up at the outset of his career and missed 2018 due to an arm injury, delaying his debut until 2019. After spending 2020 at the alternate site, he advanced to High-A Lake County in 2021, though he struggled at the plate and missed three weeks due to a thumb injury.

SCOUTING REPORT: A switch-hitter, Bracho produces good bat speed and has a quick, compact swing from both sides of the plate. He was lauded for his advanced approach early in his career but was more undisciplined in 2021 and struck out in more 31.9% of his plate appearances. His bat speed helps him drive balls better than his build might suggest and he has solid power potential. Bracho was signed as a shortstop, but he soon moved to second base. His hands and range are good enough to keep him there, but he's always going to be more of an offensive second baseman. He also saw time at both infield corners in 2021.

THE FUTURE: Bracho's 2021 struggles were a disappointment and led the Guardians not to add him to the 40-man roster, leaving him exposed to the Rule 5 draft. To get back on track, he'll need to get back to the disciplined plate approach he had early in his career. He'll likely begin 2022 back at Lake County.

Year	Age	Club (Level)	Lge	AVG	G	AB	R	H	2B	3B	HR	RBI	BB	SO	SB	OBP	SLG
2021	20	Lake County (HiA)	Cent	.174	70	241	27	42	9	0	7	27	32	89	1	.269	.299
Minor League Totals (4 years)				.213	108	376	57	80	20	2	15	60	60	118	5	.319	.396

26 CARLOS VARGAS, RHP

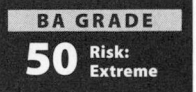

BA GRADE

50 Risk: Extreme

Born: Oct. 13, 1999. **B-T:** R-R. **HT:** 6-3. **WT:** 180. **Signed:** Dominican Republic, 2016. **Signed by:** Rafael Espinal.

TRACK RECORD: Cleveland's international department went through a transition in 2016 and its biggest signing in that class was Vargas, who signed for $275,000. Cleveland was excited enough about his ceiling that in November 2020 it added him to the 40-man roster to protect him from the Rule 5 draft, despite the fact he hadn't advanced past short-season ball. Vargas still hasn't pitched in a full-season league because he had Tommy John surgery in April, sidelining him for the 2021 season.

SCOUTING REPORT: When he signed as a 17-year-old in 2016, Vargas had an ultra-projectable frame and was already throwing 93 mph. His velocity has ticked up as expected, and before his injury his fastball touched 100 mph and sat in the upper 90s. His slider sits around 90 mph and is a plus pitch at its best. His changeup can be an average pitch and gives him a viable third offering. He improved his strike-throwing in 2019, cutting his walk rate considerably. He still needs to refine his command and learn how to get the most out of his electric stuff.

THE FUTURE: After missing so much game time the last two years, Vargas simply needs to get back into a regular routine. He'll be ready to return to action early in 2022 and will get his first taste of A ball.

Year	Age	Club (Level)	Lge	W	L	ERA	G	GS	IP	H	HR	BB	SO	BB/9	SO/9	WHIP	AVG
2021	21	Did not play—Injured															
Minor League Totals (3 years)				7	6	4.34	25	24	112	106	6	48	112	3.9	9.0	1.38	.252

27 STEVEN KWAN, OF

BA GRADE

45 Risk: High

Born: Sept. 5, 1997. **B-T:** L-L. **HT:** 5-9. **WT:** 175. **Drafted:** Oregon State, 2018 (5th round). **Signed by:** Conor Glassey.

TRACK RECORD: Kwan starred at Oregon State, helping to lead the Beavers to the 2018 national championship. While in college he built a strong track record for on-base skills and hitting, and that carried over to pro ball. He had a breakout 2021 season while splitting time between Double-A Akron and Triple-A Columbus.

SCOUTING REPORT: Kwan's size has always led to questions about his impact potential. What's never really been in doubt, however, is his ability to put the bat on the ball. He has excellent feel for the barrel and rarely strikes out—he whiffed in just 9% of his plate appearances in 2021. That fit with his profile as a slap-hitting leadoff hitter prior to 2021, but in 2021 he produced surprising power. While Akron and Columbus are both hitter-friendly ballparks, he did his best to answer questions about his ability to drive the ball. Kwan is an above-average runner and tracks balls well in center field.

THE FUTURE: Kwan's 2021 season led the Guardians to add him to their 40-man roster in November, setting him up to make his major league debut as soon as 2022. While he's likely to end up as a fourth outfielder in the long run, Kwan has exceeded expectations throughout his career and if his newfound power carries over to the big leagues he could do so again.

Year	Age	Club (Level)	Lge	AVG	G	AB	R	H	2B	3B	HR	RBI	BB	SO	SB	OBP	SLG
2021	23	Akron (AA)	NEast	.337	51	193	42	65	12	3	7	31	22	23	4	.411	.539
	23	Columbus (AAA)	East	.311	26	103	23	32	3	1	5	13	14	8	2	.398	.505
Minor League Totals (4 years)				.301	217	827	142	249	44	12	15	88	100	87	20	.380	.438

28 XZAVION CURRY, RHP

BA GRADE

45 Risk: High

Born: July 27, 1998. **B-T:** R-R. **HT:** 5-11. **WT:** 190. **Drafted:** Georgia Tech, 2019 (7th round). **Signed by:** Ethan Purser.

TRACK RECORD: Curry in 2017 became the first true freshman to be Georgia Tech's Opening Day starter since 1995. He was a stalwart in the Yellow Jackets' rotation for the next three years before being drafted by Cleveland. He didn't pitch in 2019 after signing due to shoulder inflammation and the 2020 season was canceled, delaying his professional debut until 2021. He made up for lost time, pitching at three levels to end the season with Double-A Akron.

SCOUTING REPORT: Curry is undersized for a righthander and isn't overpowering. His fastball sits in the low 90s, reaching 96 mph, but it plays up thanks to its shape and spin rate. He locates the pitch exceptionally well and can generate swings and misses with it. He relies heavily on his fastball, but also mixes in two breaking balls and a changeup. His slider has above-average potential and is his best secondary offering but it needs to be more consistent. Curry's whole arsenal plays up thanks to his plus control.

THE FUTURE: Curry's breakout season significantly elevated his profile. While he doesn't look like a traditional righthanded starter, he has a starter profile, and his style meshes well with the Guardians' approach. He'll start 2022 back in Akron.

Year	Age	Club (Level)	Lge	W	L	ERA	G	GS	IP	H	HR	BB	SO	BB/9	SO/9	WHIP	AVG
2021	22	Lynchburg (LoA)	East	3	0	1.07	5	5	25	12	1	4	38	1.4	13.5	0.63	.135
	22	Lake County (HiA)	Cent	5	1	2.66	13	13	67	53	10	12	80	1.6	10.6	0.96	.209
	22	Akron (AA)	NEast	0	0	3.86	1	1	4	6	2	0	5	0.0	9.6	1.29	.300
Minor League Totals (3 years)				8	1	2.30	19	19	98	71	13	16	123	1.5	11.3	0.89	.196

29 TOMMY MACE, RHP

BA GRADE

45 Risk: High

Born: Nov. 11, 1998. **B-T:** R-R. **HT:** 6-6. **WT:** 230. **Drafted:** Florida, 2021 (2nd supplemental round). **Signed by:** Andrew Krause.

TRACK RECORD: Mace was a key member of the Florida pitching staff for four years and spent the last three seasons in the Gators' rotation. Though he was highly regarded ahead of the 2020 draft, he opted to return to school for a fourth year and had a solid campaign. He did not pitch after the Guardians made him the 69th overall pick in 2021.

SCOUTING REPORT: Mace added some good weight in the last year and saw his velocity tick up. His fastball this spring averaged 93 mph and touched 97. He doesn't get a ton of life on the pitch but his ability to locate it to all quadrants of the strike zone helps it play up. He also throws a cutter, curveball and changeup, none of which project as a plus pitch. While Mace did post a career high strikeout rate this spring, he doesn't have the kind of stuff that stands out as swing and miss and instead relies on his above-average control to help it play up. He has a big 6-foot-6 frame and can create a tough angle for hitters.

THE FUTURE: Mace has the look of a back-of-the-rotation starter now, but the Guardians have had plenty of success in helping college pitchers take a step forward in pro ball. He'll look to start down that path in 2022 when makes his professional debut, likely with High-A Lake County.

Year	Age	Club (Level)	Lge	W	L	ERA	G	GS	IP	H	HR	BB	SO	BB/9	SO/9	WHIP	AVG
2021	22	Did not play															

30 KONNOR PILKINGTON, LHP

BA GRADE

45 Risk: High

Born: Sept. 12, 1997. **B-T:** L-L. **HT:** 6-3. **WT:** 240. **Drafted:** Mississippi State, 2018 (3rd round). **Signed by:** Warren Hughes (White Sox).

TRACK RECORD: Pilkington was a reliable starter throughout his college career at Mississippi State. He carried that success into pro ball after the White Sox drafted him in the third round in 2018. In 2021 he was traded to Cleveland in exchange for Cesar Hernandez and impressed with Double-A Akron after the deal.

SCOUTING REPORT: Pilkington's stuff has ticked up in pro ball and his fastball now works in the low 90s. His changeup is his best secondary offering, and he throws it against both righthanded and lefthanded hitters. He throws both a curveball and a slider and both pitches are average offerings. While his stuff isn't overpowering, he pounds the strike zone and has a good feel for pitching, helping him to get swings and misses. He pitches with above-average control.

THE FUTURE: After Pilkington's strong finish to the season, the Guardians added him to their 40-man roster in November. He'll open the 2022 season in the rotation for Triple-A Columbus and could soon push his way into the mix in Cleveland. His profile fits the kind of pitcher the Guardians develop well and could end up as an innings-eating starter.

Year	Age	Club (Level)	Lge	W	L	ERA	G	GS	IP	H	HR	BB	SO	BB/9	SO/9	WHIP	AVG
2021	23	Birmingham (AA)	South	4	4	3.48	14	14	62	36	9	21	71	3.1	10.3	0.92	.173
	23	Akron (AA)	NEast	3	2	2.33	8	7	38	25	2	18	49	4.2	11.4	1.11	.187
Minor League Totals (4 years)				12	16	3.84	55	53	244	196	21	94	269	3.5	9.9	1.19	.222

MORE PROSPECTS TO KNOW

31 LENNY TORRES, RHP
Torres was the 41st overall pick of the 2018 draft and his big arm got his career off to a fast start, but he missed 2019 due to Tommy John surgery and struggled in 2021. His fastball-slider combination has plus potential.

32 ISAIAH GREENE, OF
Greene was traded to Cleveland in the Francisco Lindor deal in January 2021. He made his professional debut in the Arizona Complex League and stands out for his disciplined approach at the plate.

33 MILAN TOLENTINO, 2B/SS
Tolentino built a long track record of success as a prep player, including playing shortstop for USA Baseball's 18U National Team at the 2019 World Cup. He has an excellent baseball IQ and does a lot of things well on the diamond, but there are some questions about his impact potential offensively.

34 JOEY CANTILLO, LHP
Cantillo was a part of the package Cleveland received from San Diego in exchange for Mike Clevinger at the 2020 trade deadline. He was sidelined most of the 2021 season due to an oblique injury. He isn't overpowering but throws a lot of strikes with his three-pitch arsenal.

35 JOSE PASTRANO, 2B/SS
Pastrano was the organization's top signing in the 2019 international signing class. He's a switch-hitter with a good feel for the strike zone to go with above-average speed and athleticism.

36 HUNTER GADDIS, RHP   SLEEPER
Gaddis has a big, long build at 6-foot-6 and has a good fastball-slider combination. His fastball sits in the low 90s and reaches 94-95 mph. He can get swings and misses with both offerings.

37 LUIS DURANGO JR., OF
Durango was one of the top players in Panama in 2019 and was Cleveland's second-biggest signing in the international class, behind only Jose Pastrano. He has an advanced hitting approach and well-above-average speed. He has a chance to fit a traditional top-of-the-order, center field profile.

38 YORDYS VALDES, SS
Born in Cuba, Valdes came to America when he was 12 and was drafted in the second round in 2019. He shines defensively thanks to his range, infield actions and arm strength. His bat is not as advanced, however.

39 WILL BRENNAN, OF
A two-way player at Kansas State, Brennan has been a full-time outfielder since he was drafted in 2019. His control of the strike zone is one of his best tools and his above-average speed plays well in center field.

40 JAKE FOX, SS
Cleveland drafted 21 players in 2021 and Fox was one of just two position players in the class. He has an unorthodox lefthanded swing but has a good feel for putting the bat on the ball and makes good use of his above-average speed.

TOP PROSPECTS OF THE DECADE

Year	Player, Pos	2021 Org
2012	Francisco Lindor, SS	Mets
2013	Francisco Lindor, SS	Mets
2014	Francisco Lindor, SS	Mets
2015	Francisco Lindor, SS	Mets
2016	Bradley Zimmer, OF	Guardians
2017	Francisco Mejia, C	Rays
2018	Francisco Mejia, C	Rays
2019	Triston McKenzie, RHP	Guardians
2020	Nolan Jones, 3B	Guardians
2021	Triston McKenzie, RHP	Guardians

TOP DRAFT PICKS OF THE DECADE

Year	Player, Pos	2021 Org
2012	Tyler Naquin, OF	Reds
2013	Clint Frazier, OF	Yankees
2014	Bradley Zimmer, OF	Guardians
2015	Brady Aiken, LHP	Guardians
2016	Will Benson, OF	Guardians
2017	Quentin Holmes, OF (2nd round)	Guardians
2018	Bo Naylor, C	Guardians
2019	Daniel Espino, RHP	Guardians
2020	Carson Tucker, SS	Guardians
2021	Gavin Williams, RHP	Guardians

Colorado Rockies

BY KYLE NEWMAN

After making consecutive playoff appearances for the first time in franchise history in 2017 and 2018, the Rockies went into a free fall.

The result has been three straight fourth-place finishes in the National League West, including a turbulent 2021 that began with the trade of star Nolan Arenado to the Cardinals in a one-sided offseason deal. The rocky year continued with general manager Jeff Bridich resigning in April, followed by the departure of farm director Zach Wilson in July.

Now, a new but familiar face has taken over at GM and is determined to rediscover the Rockies' identity using their draft-and-build philosophy. Bill Schmidt, the club's longtime scouting director, was named the team's fourth GM on Oct. 2 after filling in for Bridich on an interim basis.

The Rockies have the front end of their rotation in place with German Marquez, Kyle Freeland and Antonio Senzatela all under contract. But for the time being, pressing issues remain at the back end of the rotation, in the bullpen and in the lineup.

Who will step up as the Rockies' shortstop of the future following Trevor Story's possible departure in free agency? Who will be the team's closer? And who can pick up the slack in a lineup short on power?

The good and bad news for the Rockies is they may have these answers in their farm system, but the majority of those answers are still far away. Plus, for the Rockies to make up the ground between themselves and the Dodgers, Giants and Padres in the division standings, they need their latest wave of recently graduated prospects to start living up to their billing.

That list includes middle infielders Brendan Rodgers and Garrett Hampson, outfielder Sam Hilliard, righthander Peter Lambert and lefthanders Ryan Rolison and Ben Bowden, as well as newcomers Colton Welker and Ryan Vilade, both of whom debuted in September. All have reached the majors but have yet to establish themselves, though Rodgers has shown the most promise when he's managed to stay healthy.

The Rockies' system had much more talent in the years leading up to their back-to-back playoff appearances in 2017-18 with the likes of Story, Marquez and Ryan McMahon. When all that talent graduated, the Rockies' farm was naturally left depleted, and it has taken a few years to recover.

Such a recovery was best seen in the Rockies' low-level affiliates in 2021. The Arizona Complex League club finished in first place, while Low-A

German Marquez was one of the few remaining Rockies stars left from the 2018 playoff team.

PROJECTED 2025 LINEUP

Catcher	Drew Romo	23
First Base	Michael Toglia	26
Second Base	Brendan Rodgers	28
Third Base	Ryan McMahon	30
Shortstop	Ezequiel Tovar	23
Left Field	Zac Veen	23
Center Field	Benny Montgomery	22
Right Field	Brenton Doyle	27
Designated Hitter	Ryan Vilade	26
No. 1 Starter	German Marquez	30
No. 2 Starter	Kyle Freeland	30
No. 3 Starter	Antonio Senzatela	32
No. 4 Starter	Austin Gomber	31
No. 5 Starter	Ryan Rolison	27
Closer	Robert Stephenson	32

Fresno and High-A Spokane both made it to their league championships. All three teams boasted an array of top prospects, though fans won't see them at Coors Field for another couple of years at the earliest. Plus, a dearth of projectable top-end starting pitchers remains an organization-wide problem.

That all means 2022 sets up to be another rebuilding year for the Rockies. As Schmidt and Co. wait for the club's re-formed nucleus to adjust to the big leagues, new farm director Chris Forbes has his hands full making sure the Rockies' premium talent continues to progress on schedule. If that happens, the club could contend in its ultra-competitive division in a few years. ∎

COLORADO ROCKIES

TOP 2022 ROOKIES	RANK
Ryan Rolison, LHP	4
Elehuris Montero, 3B	8
Colton Welker, 3B/1B	14
BREAKOUT PROSPECTS	**RANK**
Jaden Hill, RHP	11
Warming Bernabel, 3B	16
Noah Davis, RHP	21

SOURCE OF TOP 30 TALENT

Homegrown	26	Acquired	4
College	11	Trade	4
Junior college	1	Rule 5 draft	0
High school	6	Independent league	0
Nondrafted free agent	0	Free agent/waivers	0
International	8		

LF
Zac Veen (1)
Ryan Vilade (6)
Isaac Collins
Willie Abreu
Yorvis Torrealba

CF
Benny Montgomery (5)
Bladimir Restituyo (24)
Jameson Hannah (26)

RF
Brenton Doyle (7)
Yanquiel Fernandez (18)
Niko Decolati
Casey Golden

3B
Elehuris Montero (8)
Aaron Schunk (12)
Colton Welker (14)
Warming Bernabel (16)
Julio Carreras
Mateo Gil

SS
Ezequiel Tovar (9)
Adael Amador (10)
Taylor Snyder

2B
Adrian Pinto (19)
Jack Blomgren
Eddy Diaz
Alan Trejo
Bret Boswell
Hunter Stovall

1B
Michael Toglia (2)
Grant Lavigne (25)
Colin Simpson
Cole Zabowski

C
Drew Romo (3)
Willie MacIver
Hunter Goodman
Brian Serven
Max George
Bryant Quijada

LHP

LHSP	LHRP
Ryan Rolison (4)	Helcris Olivarez (15)
Sam Weatherly (17)	Yoan Aybar (27)
Joe Rock (22)	Reagan Todd (28)
Nick Bush	PJ Poulin
Colten Schmidt	Ever Moya
	Felix Ramires

RHP

RHSP	RHRP
Jaden Hill (11)	Julian Fernandez (20)
Chris McMahon (13)	Justin Lawrence (29)
Noah Davis (21)	Gavin Hollowell (30)
Karl Kauffmann (23)	Tommy Doyle
Bryan Perez	Antonio Santos
Jordy Vargas	Chad Smith
Ryan Feltner	Shelby Lackey
Mitchell Kilkenny	Jake Bird
Case Williams	Logan Cozart
Will Ethridge	Juan Mejia
Will Gaddis	Blake Goldsberry
McCade Brown	

1 ZAC VEEN, OF

Born: Dec. 12, 2001. **B-T:** L-R. **HT:** 6-4. **WT:** 190.
Drafted: HS—Port Orange, Fla., 2020 (1st round).
Signed by: John Cedarburg.

TRACK RECORD: A talented high school player considered on the fringe of first-round consideration entering his senior year, Veen became the biggest riser during the shortened 2020 season after getting stronger and showing improved power at Spruce Creek (Fla.) High. The Rockies drafted him ninth overall and gave him a $5 million signing bonus to pass up a scholarship offer from Florida. Veen impressed in instructional league after signing and followed up with a sensational pro debut at Low-A Fresno in 2021. Despite a slow start that saw him go his first 120 at-bats without a homer, Veen batted .301 with 15 home runs, 75 RBIs, 36 stolen bases and a .900 OPS for the Grizzlies, becoming one of only four players in the minors to have at least 15 home runs and 35 stolen bases. He did that while impressing defensively both in left and right field and notching eight outfield assists in just 95 games.

SCOUTING REPORT: Veen is a true five-tool player and has the potential to be a longtime anchor in the Rockies outfield. He presently has an all-pull approach and can be a bit aggressive, but he consistently drives balls hard on a line, handles all types of pitches and rakes equally against both righties and lefties in a way that is rare for a young, lefthanded hitter. Veen still has some tinkering to do to shorten his swing and could stand to use the whole field better, but he's already shown he can make adjustments and has a chance to be a plus hitter with the amount of hard contact he makes. Veen has plus raw power and is increasingly learning to add leverage to his swing to access it. He is a potential 30-home run threat once he fills out his athletic, projectable frame and has the hand-eye coordination and barrel awareness to add that power without sacrificing his ability to hit for average. In addition to his immense hitting potential, Veen is a dynamic, aggressive baserunner with long strides that create sneaky speed and make him a stolen base threat. Though he has just average pure foot speed, his aggressiveness makes him an above-average runner who covers a lot of ground in a short time with his long strides and long arms that allow him to reach for the bag on slides and get in just ahead of throws. Veen's long strides also enable him to make rangy plays to both his right and left in the outfield. He gets good reads off the bat, takes clean routes and charges in on balls well to project as a potential plus defender in the corners. His arm is his weakest tool, but it's still average and makes him playable in both right and left field. In addition to his physical skills, Veen plays extremely hard and has an above-average internal clock for his age.

THE FUTURE: Veen will likely get an invitation to major league spring training and should start the 2022 season at High-A Spokane. On the low end, Veen projects to be an everyday big leaguer who reliably puts up 15 home runs and 10 steals per year while hitting for a high average. On the high end, if he makes the necessary adjustments to his approach, he could be a 30-home run threat who hits for average, steals bases and is a perennial all-star. ∎

LARRY GOREN/FOUR SEAM IMAGES

BA GRADE	SCOUTING GRADES
60 Risk: High	Hit: 60. **Power:** 60. **Run:** 50. Field: 60. **Arm:** 50.

Projected future grades on 20-80 scouting scale

BEST TOOLS

Best Hitter for Average	Drew Romo
Best Power Hitter	Michael Toglia
Best Strike-Zone Discipline	Drew Romo
Fastest Baserunner	Eddy Diaz
Best Athlete	Brenton Doyle
Best Fastball	Julian Fernandez
Best Curveball	Case Williams
Best Slider	Yoan Aybar
Best Changeup	Ryan Rolison
Best Control	Mitchell Kilkenny
Best Defensive Catcher	Drew Romo
Best Defensive Infielder	Ezequiel Tovar
Best Infield Arm	Ezequiel Tovar
Best Defensive Outfielder	Brenton Doyle
Best Outfield Arm	Brenton Doyle

Year	Age	Club (Level)	Lge	AVG	G	AB	R	H	2B	3B	HR	RBI	BB	SO	SB	OBP	SLG
2021	19	Fresno (LoA)	West	.301	106	399	83	120	27	4	15	75	64	126	36	.399	.501
Minor League Totals (2 years)				.301	106	399	83	120	27	4	15	75	64	126	36	.399	.501

2 MICHAEL TOGLIA, 1B

Born: Aug. 16, 1998. **B-T:** B-L. **HT:** 6-5. **WT:** 226. **Drafted:** UCLA, 2019 (1st round). **Signed by:** Matt Hattabaugh.

TRACK RECORD: The Rockies drafted Toglia in the 37th round out of high school in 2016 and drafted him again with the 23rd overall pick in 2019 after his strong career at UCLA. Toglia spent 2020 at the alternate training site before making his full-season debut in 2021. Despite a slow start, Toglia hit his way from High-A to Double-A and had his signature moment in July when he hit a home run at Coors Field in the Futures Game.

SCOUTING REPORT: A big, physical switch-hitter, Toglia hit 22 home runs in his first full season and is only just starting to tap into his power potential. He is an extremely patient hitter who sometimes lets hittable pitches go by, depressing both his batting average and power production. Once he learns to be more aggressive, he has the strength and feel for the barrel to be an average hitter with plus power. He is much more potent from the left side and will need to adjust his pull-heavy approach against better pitching. Toglia is remarkably nimble for his size. He's a plus defender with premium scooping ability at first base and is playable in the corner outfield with his fringy but respectable speed. His arm strength is just fringy, but it's enough to turn the 3-6-3 double play.

THE FUTURE: Toglia is the Rockies' long-awaited heir apparent at first base and is on track to reach Triple-A during the 2022 season. The Rockies re-signed C.J. Cron for the next two years to help bridge the gap, but once Cron leaves, first base will be Toglia's for the foreseeable future.

BA GRADE
50 Risk: High

SCOUTING GRADES:	Hitting: 50	Power: 60	Running: 45	Fielding: 65	Arm: 45

Year	Age	Club (Level)	Lge	AVG	G	AB	R	H	2B	3B	HR	RBI	BB	SO	SB	OBP	SLG
2021	22	Spokane (HiA)	West	.234	74	282	50	66	10	2	17	66	42	91	7	.333	.465
	22	Hartford (AA)	NEast	.217	41	143	16	31	10	1	5	18	23	51	3	.331	.406
Minor League Totals (3 years)				.233	156	570	91	133	27	3	31	110	93	187	11	.342	.454

3 DREW ROMO, C

Born: Aug. 29, 2001. **B-T:** B-R. **HT:** 6-1. **WT:** 205. **Drafted:** HS—The Woodlands, Texas, 2020 (1st round supplemental). **Signed by:** Jeff Edwards.

TRACK RECORD: Romo earned raves as the best defensive high school catcher since Austin Hedges and was drafted 35th overall in 2020 by the Rockies, who signed him for $2,095,800 to forgo a commitment to Louisiana State. Romo entered the year known as a defense-first catcher with a questionable bat, but he silenced concerns about his offense with an excellent pro debut at Low-A Fresno. He finished fourth in Low-A West with a .314 average and backed up the hype about his defense to lead the Grizzlies to the league's best record.

SCOUTING REPORT: Romo's defense behind the plate is borderline elite for his age. He has sound footwork and receiving skills, consistently posts pop times in the 1.9-second range with his above-average, accurate arm and quick release and has an advanced baseball IQ for his age. There's still room for development in his game-calling, and he also has the talent to take his blocking to an even higher level. Romo is a switch-hitter but is vastly better lefthanded. He hit .351 as a lefty compared to .218 as a righty and may be best served dropping switch-hitting. He has above-average bat speed, stays balanced in his swing and has strong strike zone discipline, allowing him to project as an above-average hitter from the left side. Romo has plenty of bat speed and raw strength, but his contact-first approach will likely limit him to fringe-average power production.

THE FUTURE: Romo's on track to become a Gold Glove-caliber defender and fill the Rockies' gaping hole at catcher. The club expects him to be their starting catcher in three years.

LARRY GOREN/FOUR SEAM IMAGES

BA GRADE
50 Risk: High

SCOUTING GRADES:	Hitting: 50	Power: 45	Running: 50	Fielding: 70	Arm: 60

Year	Age	Club (Level)	Lge	AVG	G	AB	R	H	2B	3B	HR	RBI	BB	SO	SB	OBP	SLG
2021	19	Fresno (LoA)	West	.314	79	312	48	98	17	2	6	47	19	50	23	.345	.439
Minor League Totals (2 years)				.314	79	312	48	98	17	2	6	47	19	50	23	.345	.439

4 RYAN ROLISON, LHP

Born: July 11, 1997. **B-T:** R-L. **HT:** 6-2. **WT:** 213. **Drafted:** Mississippi, 2018 (1st round). **Signed by:** Zack Zulli.

TRACK RECORD: Rolison's strong sophomore season at Ole Miss propelled him into the first round, where the Rockies drafted him 22nd overall and signed him for $2,912,300. Rolison pitched extremely well in two difficult environments at Rookie-level Grand Junction and High-A Lancaster to start his career and was invited to the Rockies alternate training site in 2020. Expected to rise quickly in 2021, Rolison was instead derailed by poor health. He had surgery to remove his appendix in June and broke a bone in his throwing hand while fielding a grounder in August. He made up for lost time by pitching in the Dominican Winter League after the season and was added to the 40-man roster in November.

SCOUTING REPORT: Rolison is a classic pitchability lefty who relies on commanding a varied arsenal to succeed. His fastball sits in the low 90s and mostly serves to set up his breaking stuff. His 12-to-6 curveball in the upper 70s is a plus pitch he can manipulate the power and depth of, and his slider is a slightly tighter version of his curveball that also flashes plus. He is still mastering his changeup, which flashes average at its best. Rolison fills up the strike zone with plus control and has an advanced feel for setting hitters up and reading swings. He has worked to improve the armside command of his fastball, which he'll need to open up the entire plate.

THE FUTURE: Rolison has the potential to be a steady, reliable starter at the back of the rotation. He may start 2022 back at Triple-A but should make his major league debut during the year.

BA GRADE
45 Risk: Medium

SCOUTING GRADES:	Fastball: 40	Slider: 55	Curveball: 60	Changeup: 50	Control: 60

Year	Age	Club (Level)	Lge	W	L	ERA	G	GS	IP	H	HR	BB	SO	BB/9	SO/9	WHIP	AVG
2021	23	Rockies (R)	ACL	0	0	7.11	2	2	6	10	0	2	9	2.8	12.8	1.89	.370
	23	Spokane (HiA)	West	0	0	3.60	1	1	5	4	1	2	3	3.6	5.4	1.20	.250
	23	Hartford (AA)	NEast	2	1	3.07	3	3	14	11	1	2	20	1.2	12.3	0.89	.204
	23	Albuquerque (AAA)	West	2	2	5.91	10	10	45	51	7	16	45	3.2	8.9	1.47	.280
Minor League Totals (4 years)				12	12	4.35	50	50	232	228	33	70	243	2.72	9.44	1.29	.255

5 BENNY MONTGOMERY, OF

Born: Sept. 9, 2002. **B-T:** R-R. **HT:** 6-4. **WT:** 200. **Drafted:** HS—Lewisberry, Pa., 2021 (1st round). **Signed by:** Ed Santa.

TRACK RECORD: Montgomery emerged as arguably the best player in a historically strong Northeast high school draft class in 2021, with his freakish athleticism drawing large crowds of scouts to every game. The Rockies drafted him eighth overall and signed him for $5 million, the most ever for a player from Pennsylvania, to forgo a Virginia commitment. Montgomery reported to the Arizona Complex League after signing and had a solid pro debut, albeit in only 14 games, and finished the year in instructional league.

SCOUTING REPORT: Montgomery's raw tools are immense. He has plus-plus speed, plus arm strength and the athleticism to develop into a plus defender in center field, although he needs to improve his jumps and routes going into the gaps. He also has plus raw power he'll show off in batting practice. The question is how much Montgomery will hit. He has a large hitch in his swing, which currently is more rigid and less fluid than it needs to be, and his timing and balance have a long way to go for him to be even a fringe-average hitter. He has plenty of bat speed and decent hand-eye coordination, but he'll need to prove he can make adjustments against higher-level pitching. His swing is consistently compared to Hunter Pence's, which can be both a good and bad thing with how funky and awkward it gets.

THE FUTURE: Montgomery has a wide range of outcomes depending on how his swing develops. If it clicks, he could be an above-average, everyday center fielder. If it doesn't, he'll struggle to get out of the low minors like previous athletic prep outfielders.

BILL MITCHELL

BA GRADE
55 Risk: Extreme

SCOUTING GRADES:	Hitting: 45	Power: 55	Running: 70	Fielding: 60	Arm: 60

Year	Age	Club (Level)	Lge	AVG	G	AB	R	H	2B	3B	HR	RBI	BB	SO	SB	OBP	SLG
2021	18	Rockies (R)	ACL	.340	14	47	7	16	0	1	0	6	5	9	5	.404	.383
Minor League Totals (1 year)				.340	14	47	7	16	0	1	0	6	5	9	5	.404	.383

6 RYAN VILADE, OF

Born: Feb. 18, 1999. **B-T:** R-R. **HT:** 6-2. **WT:** 226. **Drafted:** HS—Stillwater, Okla., 2017 (2nd round). **Signed by:** Jesse Retzlaf.

TRACK RECORD: The Rockies forfeited their first-round pick in 2017 after signing Ian Desmond and made Vilade their first selection when they took him in the second round, No. 48 overall. Vilade cruised through the lower levels of the minors and spent 2020 at the alternate training site before opening 2021 at Triple-A Albuquerque. He put up just middling numbers in the hitter-friendly environment of Albuquerque, but he still earned an invitation to the Futures Game at Coors Field in July and received his first big league callup in September.

SCOUTING REPORT: Vilade was drafted for his bat and hasn't disappointed in that aspect. His smooth, line-drive approach and natural feel for contact has produced a career .289 batting average in the minors. Vilade makes hard contact and has raw power, but he's hit more than 10 home runs only once in three full seasons. He'll need to put the ball into the air more in order to become an everyday, big league lineup pillar. Vilade began his career as a shortstop, moved to third base and is now strictly a corner outfielder. He is a below-average defender anywhere on the field, and his reads and routes in the outfield must improve. His average arm projects better in left field rather than right. A solid athlete, Vilade also began playing first base over the past year in an attempt to add to his versatility.

THE FUTURE: Vilade's hitting ability will buy him time to improve his defense. He'll need to access more power to be an everyday player.

BA GRADE
45 Risk: Medium

ROB TRINGALI/GETTY IMAGES

SCOUTING GRADES:	Hitting: 55	Power: 40	Running: 45	Fielding: 40	Arm: 50

Year	Age	Club (Level)	Lge	AVG	G	AB	R	H	2B	3B	HR	RBI	BB	SO	SB	OBP	SLG
2021	22	Albuquerque (AAA)	West	.284	117	468	82	133	28	5	7	44	38	92	12	.339	.410
	22	Colorado (MLB)	NL	.000	3	6	0	0	0	0	0	0	1	1	0	.143	.000
Major League Totals (1 year)				.000	3	6	0	0	0	0	0	0	1	1	0	.143	.000
Minor League Totals (5 years)				.289	402	1551	274	448	78	21	29	180	170	314	58	.360	.422

7 BRENTON DOYLE, OF

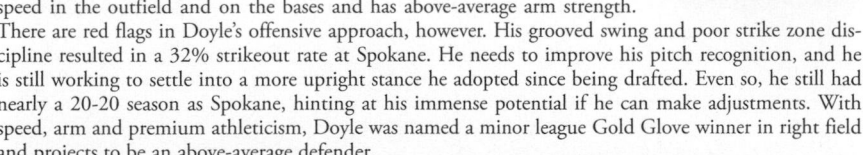

Born: May 14, 1998. **B-T:** R-R. **HT:** 6-3. **WT:** 200. **Drafted:** Shepard (W.Va.), 2019 (4th round). **Signed by:** Ed Santa.

TRACK RECORD: Doyle was set to attend Virginia Military Institute before he rerouted to Division II Shepherd in West Virginia, where he performed like a Division I-caliber player facing D-II competition. The Rockies drafted him in the fourth round in 2019 and he promptly won the Pioneer League batting title in his pro debut before impressing at instructional league in 2020. Doyle made his full-season debut in 2021 at High-A Spokane and didn't quite live up to enormous expectations, but he still put together a well-rounded season and led the Indians to the High-A West championship series.

SCOUTING REPORT: Doyle stands out foremost for his impactful raw tools. He's physically strong with borderline plus-plus raw power, has above-average speed in the outfield and on the bases and has above-average arm strength. There are red flags in Doyle's offensive approach, however. His grooved swing and poor strike zone discipline resulted in a 32% strikeout rate at Spokane. He needs to improve his pitch recognition, and he is still working to settle into a more upright stance he adopted since being drafted. Even so, he still had nearly a 20-20 season as Spokane, hinting at his immense potential if he can make adjustments. With speed, arm and premium athleticism, Doyle was named a minor league Gold Glove winner in right field and projects to be an above-average defender.

THE FUTURE: Doyle must start putting the ball in play more in order to fulfill his everyday potential. If he can, he'll succeed Charlie Blackmon as the Rockies' starting right fielder.

BA GRADE
50 Risk: High

SCOUTING GRADES:	Hitting: 45	Power: 55	Running: 55	Fielding: 55	Arm: 60

Year	Age	Club (Level)	Lge	AVG	G	AB	R	H	2B	3B	HR	RBI	BB	SO	SB	OBP	SLG
2021	23	Spokane (HiA)	West	.279	97	390	70	109	16	2	16	47	30	134	21	.336	.454
Minor League Totals (3 years)				.312	148	570	112	178	27	5	24	80	61	181	38	.383	.504

8 ELEHURIS MONTERO, 3B

Born: Aug. 17, 1998. **B-T:** R-R. **HT:** 6-3. **WT:** 235. **Signed:** Dominican Republic, 2014. **Signed by:** Angel Ovalles (Cardinals).

TRACK RECORD: Signed at 16 by the Cardinals, Montero won Most Valuable Player of the Low-A Midwest League in 2018 but missed a large chunk of 2019 with hand and wrist injuries. He spent 2020 at the Cardinals' alternate training site and was traded to the Rockies before the 2021 season as the top prospect in the deal that sent Nolan Arenado to St. Louis. Montero delivered a strong organizational debut in his first year in the Rockies system, leading the organization with 228 total bases and finishing second with 28 home runs and 86 RBIs as he rose from Double-A to Triple-A.

BA GRADE

50 Risk: High

SCOUTING REPORT: A big, physical masher at 6-foot-3, 235 pounds, Montero is an aggressive hitter who makes consistent hard contact that results in power to all fields. His above-average bat speed, a powerful frame and compact swing yields above-average power he gets to in games. Montero's approach still needs to be refined. He's an early-count swinger who needs to become more disciplined to get the most from his offensive skill set. Montero has plus arm strength at third base, but his big frame limits his mobility. His below-average speed and footwork make him a below-average defender and he spent an increasing amount of time at first base this year. Unless he slims down and gets quicker, first base is likely his long-term home.

THE FUTURE: Montero has the offensive tools to be an impact hitter in the middle of the Rockies lineup if he can tweak his approach. Where he fits on the field is still to be determined, with a strong chance he ends up at DH.

SCOUTING GRADES:	Hitting: 50	Power: 55	Running: 40	Fielding: 45	Arm: 60

Year	Age	Club (Level)	Lge	AVG	G	AB	R	H	2B	3B	HR	RBI	BB	SO	SB	OBP	SLG
2021	22	Hartford (AA)	NEast	.279	92	323	46	90	11	1	22	69	43	90	0	.361	.523
	22	Albuquerque (AAA)	West	.278	28	108	23	30	9	1	6	17	10	20	0	.355	.546
Minor League Totals (7 years)				.271	480	1778	276	482	104	9	60	278	182	429	5	.344	.441

9 EZEQUIEL TOVAR, SS

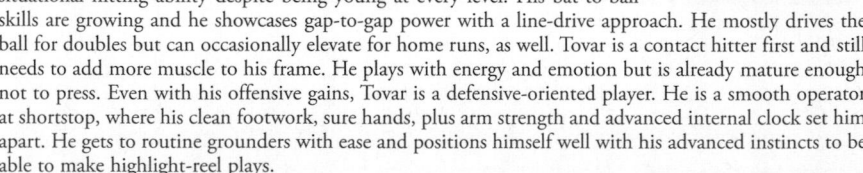

Born: Aug. 1, 2001. **B-T:** R-R. **HT:** 6-0. **WT:** 162. **Signed:** Venezuela, 2017. **Signed by:** Rolando Fernandez/Orlando Medina.

TRACK RECORD: Tovar was Colorado's top international signing in 2017, signing for $800,000 on his 16th birthday. He turned heads during his progression through the low minors and, after making two key changes, broke out in his full-season debut in 2021. Originally a switch-hitter, Tovar began batting righthanded only in 2021. He also made significant strength gains during the coronavirus shutdown. With those two changes, he hit .287 with 30 doubles, 15 home runs, 72 RBIs and 24 stolen bases across Low-A and High-A while earning raves as one of the best defensive shortstops in the minor leagues.

BA GRADE

50 Risk: High

SCOUTING REPORT: Tovar has long displayed above-average bat control and situational hitting ability despite being young at every level. His bat-to-ball skills are growing and he showcases gap-to-gap power with a line-drive approach. He mostly drives the ball for doubles but can occasionally elevate for home runs, as well. Tovar is a contact hitter first and still needs to add more muscle to his frame. He plays with energy and emotion but is already mature enough not to press. Even with his offensive gains, Tovar is a defensive-oriented player. He is a smooth operator at shortstop, where his clean footwork, sure hands, plus arm strength and advanced internal clock set him apart. He gets to routine grounders with ease and positions himself well with his advanced instincts to be able to make highlight-reel plays.

THE FUTURE: Tovar still has several years of growth ahead of him, but he's talented enough defensively to eventually be the Rockies' starting shortstop. His offensive gains will be tested at Double-A in 2022.

SCOUTING GRADES:	Hitting: 50	Power: 45	Running: 50	Fielding: 65	Arm: 60

Year	Age	Club (Level)	Lge	AVG	G	AB	R	H	2B	3B	HR	RBI	BB	SO	SB	OBP	SLG
2021	19	Fresno (LoA)	West	.309	72	298	60	92	21	3	11	54	14	38	21	.346	.510
	19	Spokane (HiA)	West	.239	32	134	19	32	9	0	4	18	3	19	3	.266	.396
Minor League Totals (4 years)				.271	212	851	142	231	40	11	17	99	65	159	57	.328	.404

10 ADAEL AMADOR, SS/2B

Born: April 11, 2003. **B-T:** B-R. **HT:** 6-0. **WT:** 160. **Signed:** Dominican Republic, 2019. **Signed by:** Rolando Fernandez/Martin Cabrera.

TRACK RECORD: Amador made his name on the Dominican Republic's 15U national team and signed with the Rockies for $1.5 million as one of the top players in the 2019 international class. His pro debut was delayed by the coronavirus pandemic, but he made up for lost time in 2021. He finished in the top 10 in the Arizona Complex League leaders in hits, runs, walks and stolen bases and led the ACL Rockies to the league's best record.

SCOUTING REPORT: Amador is a polished hitter for his age and has a history of excelling against older competition. He has quick hands and a short swing with a solid bat path that results in hard drives from gap to gap. He will need to continue to add strength to his relatively small frame, although he already has a thicker lower half that is already helping him tap into growing power. He commands the strike zone and has a good approach at the plate for a player who has seen very little pro action, helping him project to be an above-average hitter who should reach double-digit home runs. Defensively, Amador has only an average arm and average speed at shortstop and too often relies on his natural ability rather than sound footwork and fundamentals. He projects better at second base long-term.

THE FUTURE: While Amador is advanced compared to other international signings of his age, he still has a long way to go. He'll be tested at Low-A in 2022, and will need to prove that his small frame isn't a negative on either side of the ball.

BILL MITCHELL

BA GRADE
55 Risk: Extreme

SCOUTING GRADES:	Hitting: 55	Power: 45	Running: 45	Fielding: 50	Arm: 50

Year	Age	Club (Level)	Lge	AVG	G	AB	R	H	2B	3B	HR	RBI	BB	SO	SB	OBP	SLG
2021	18	Rockies (R)	ACL	.299	47	164	41	49	10	1	4	24	27	29	10	.394	.445
Minor League Totals (1 year)				.299	47	164	41	49	10	1	4	24	27	29	10	.394	.445

11 JADEN HILL, RHP

BA GRADE
55 Risk: Extreme

Born: Dec. 22, 1999. **B-T:** R-R. **HT:** 6-4. **WT:** 235. **Drafted:** Louisiana State, 2021 (2nd round). **Signed by:** Zack Zulli.

TRACK RECORD: Hill has been a prized pitching prospect since his prep days in Arkansas, but injuries have since marred his development. He was limited to six games across 2019 and 2020 at Louisiana State because of elbow problems and the pandemic and then lasted only 29.2 innings in 2021 before tearing his ulnar collateral ligament. The injury required Tommy John surgery and sent the projected first-round pick tumbling down the draft board. The Rockies gambled on him in the second round and signed him for the full slot value of $1,689,500.

SCOUTING REPORT: When healthy, Hill has three plus pitches in a mid-90s fastball, a mid-80s changeup and a wipeout slider. But his velocity, command and offspeed were all inconsistent in the seven starts he made prior to getting hurt in 2021, resulting in a 6.67 ERA. Hill's injury history goes beyond just his time at LSU. He broke his collarbone playing football and broke his wrist playing basketball in high school and has little extended track record of success, largely because of his frequent injuries. He is an excellent athlete with a powerful 6-foot-4, 234-pound frame, but he has yet to demonstrate the ability to consistently command his pitches to both sides of the plate.

THE FUTURE: Hill's offseason throwing program has him on track to make his pro debut in 2022. His athleticism and stuff give him enormous upside, but he needs to accumulate innings and prove he can stay healthy.

Year	Age	Club (Level)	Lge	W	L	ERA	G	GS	IP	H	HR	BB	SO	BB/9	SO/9	WHIP	AVG
2021	21	Did not play—Injured															

12 AARON SCHUNK, 3B

BA GRADE
50 Risk: High

Born: July 24, 1997. **B-T:** R-R. **HT:** 6-2. **WT:** 205. **Drafted:** Georgia, 2019 (2nd round). **Signed by:** Sean Gamble.

TRACK RECORD: A two-way star in college at Georgia, Schunk made third base his primary focus as a pro and turned in a solid debut season at short-season Boise in 2019 after the Rockies drafted him in the second round. He spent 2020 at the alternate training site and instructional league and made his full-season debut in 2021 at High-A Spokane, where he split time between third base (44 starts) and second base (35) and struggled at the plate.

SCOUTING REPORT: Schunk has just fringe power and doesn't fit the profile of a typical slugging third baseman. At his best, he takes competitive at-bats with a contact-driven approach and drives doubles from gap to gap. Schunk swung and missed way too frequently at Spokane, however, ringing up a 31% strikeout rate. Optimistic evaluators still see the potential for him to be an average hitter with his approach and natural bat-to-ball skills. Schunk is a slightly above-average runner and a good athlete who is a potential plus defender at third base. He is also developing at second base and saw a couple starts at first, too, where he is raw. Schunk has solid instincts on the bases and in the field that help his tools play up.

THE FUTURE: Schunk should start 2022 in Double-A and has the ability and work ethic to be a future everyday player for the Rockies. How his bat and power grow remain to be seen.

Year	Age	Club (Level)	Lge	AVG	G	AB	R	H	2B	3B	HR	RBI	BB	SO	SB	OBP	SLG
2021	23	Spokane (HiA)	West	.223	89	358	57	80	12	4	8	45	25	111	13	.286	.346
Minor League Totals (3 years)				.250	135	531	88	133	24	6	14	68	39	136	17	.313	.397

13 CHRIS MCMAHON, RHP

BA GRADE 50 Risk: High

Born: Feb. 4, 1999. **B-T:** R-R. **HT:** 6-2. **WT:** 217. **Drafted:** Miami, 2020 (2nd round). **Signed by:** Rafael Reyes.

TRACK RECORD: Knee and back injuries limited McMahon's time on the mound in college, but he was dominant when healthy. He posted a 2.25 ERA with 123 strikeouts in 112.1 career innings for Miami, then signed with the Rockies for $1,637,400 after Colorado drafted him No. 46 overall. He proceeded to impress in instructional league, then put up a 4.17 ERA in 22 games (20 starts) in his professional debut for High-A Spokane in 2021.

SCOUTING REPORT: McMahon's fastball sits in the low 90s and can run up to 95 mph with some late action that can induce weak contact. He has above-grade command and also features a hybrid breaking pitch that moves like a slurve, as well as an average changeup that's still a work in progress. He battles on the mound, attacks hitters, has good instincts and is athletic, but will probably need to shorten his arm action as he faces better hitting. His slider and curve also need more consistency.

THE FUTURE: McMahon's ceiling is as a mid- to back-end starter if he can continue to hone his control and develop his changeup to keep hitters off a non-dominant fastball. He'll likely start 2022 in Double-A..

Year	Age	Club (Level)	Lge	W	L	ERA	G	GS	IP	H	HR	BB	SO	BB/9	SO/9	WHIP	AVG
2021	22	Spokane (HiA)	West	10	3	4.17	22	20	114	119	13	32	119	2.5	9.4	1.32	.268
Minor League Totals (2 years)				10	3	4.17	22	20	114	119	13	32	119	2.5	9.4	1.32	.268

14 COLTON WELKER, 3B/1B

BA GRADE 45 Risk: Medium

Born: Oct. 9, 1997. **B-T:** R-R. **HT:** 6-1. **WT:** 235. **Drafted:** HS—Parkland, Fla., 2016 (4th round). **Signed by:** Rafael Reyes.

TRACK RECORD: Welker dominated his first three seasons after the Rockies selected him in the fourth round in 2016. He hit .329 for Rookie-level Grand Junction in his pro debut, .350 for Low-A Asheville in 2017 and .333 to win the California League batting title for High-A Lancaster in 2018. Welker hasn't been able to build on that success since. A shoulder injury limited him to 98 games in 2019 and, after spending 2020 at the alternate site and getting added to the 40-man roster, he was suspended 80 games for using the performance-enhancing substance DHCMT. He debuted for the Rockies on Sept. 8 and hit .189 in 37 at-bats.

SCOUTING REPORT: Welker has possibly the best pure bat-to-ball skills in the organization, but his recent offensive struggles have seeded doubts. At his best, he has a line-drive, on-base approach with a flat swing conducive to contact. He's a cerebral hitter, but he needs to work on staying within his approach and not trying to do too much. He is prone to selling out for power and losing his swing mechanics. Welker has good hands and a strong arm, but he is a slow runner with limited mobility in the field who fits better at first base than third base. He still needs to get better at scooping low throws out of the dirt.

THE FUTURE: Welker will be a part of the Rockies' plans in 2022. He has time to grow as a backup at third base behind Ryan McMahon and first base behind C.J. Cron.

Year	Age	Club (Level)	Lge	AVG	G	AB	R	H	2B	3B	HR	RBI	BB	SO	SB	OBP	SLG
2021	23	Rockies (R)	ACL	.200	2	5	0	1	1	0	0	1	1	1	0	.333	.400
	23	Spokane (HiA)	West	.194	8	31	5	6	1	0	3	7	2	10	0	.257	.516
	23	Albuquerque (AAA)	West	.286	23	84	13	24	5	1	3	18	12	20	0	.378	.476
	23	Colorado (MLB)	NL	.189	19	37	7	7	1	0	0	2	3	11	0	.250	.216
Major League Totals (1 year)				.189	19	37	7	7	1	0	0	2	3	11	0	.250	.216
Minor League Totals (6 years)				.308	363	1391	199	429	95	5	40	230	120	272	18	.363	.470

15 HELCRIS OLIVAREZ, LHP

BA GRADE

50 Risk: Extreme

Born: Aug. 8, 2000. **B-T:** L-L. **HT:** 6-3. **WT:** 200. **Signed:** Dominican Republic, 2016. **Signed by:** Rolando Fernandez/Arnaldo Gomez/Orlando Medina/Frank Roa.

TRACK RECORD: Signed for a mere $77,000 in 2016, Olivarez spent his first two seasons in the Dominican Summer League before making his stateside debut for Rookie-level Grand Junction in 2019. He turned in a raw but promising summer in the Pioneer League and had a big 2020 with solid showings at the alternate training site and in instructional league. Olivarez was added to the 40-man roster after the season and entered 2021 with big expectations, but he posted a 6.05 ERA for High-A Spokane.

SCOUTING REPORT: Olivarez's raw stuff is electric. He has easy fastball velocity up to 100 mph and usually sits in the high 90s. But his command is questionable and his offspeed pitches need honing, with an average changeup and a curveball that can be flat. Cleaning up and simplifying his delivery will help him achieve the release-point consistency needed to become a bonafide starter. He already creates uncomfortable at-bats from either side, but to complement his plus heat, Olivarez needs to keep a better lid on his emotions on the mound.

THE FUTURE: Olivarez's can be a hard-throwing back-end starter if he can learn to command his fastball. If the command doesn't come soon, he profiles as a late-inning bullpen arm.

Year	Age	Club (Level)	Lge	W	L	ERA	G	GS	IP	H	HR	BB	SO	BB/9	SO/9	WHIP	AVG
2021	20	Spokane (HiA)	West	4	9	6.05	22	21	99	89	10	68	112	6.1	10.1	1.58	.248
Minor League Totals (5 years)				14	15	4.35	67	49	248	203	20	142	289	5.15	10.5	1.39	.227

16 WARMING BERNABEL, 3B

BA GRADE

50 Risk: Extreme

Born: Aug. 6, 2002. **B-T:** R-R. **HT:** 6-0. **WT:** 180. **Signed:** Dominican Republic, 2018. **Signed by:** Rolando Fernandez/Martin Cabrera.

TRACK RECORD: The Rockies signed Bernabel for $900,000 out of the Dominican Republic in 2018 and quickly converted him from shortstop to third base. He had a sluggish start in the Dominican Summer League but tore it up in 2021 by hitting .312/.367/.516 in 43 games split between the Arizona Complex League and Low-A Fresno.

SCOUTING REPORT: Bernabel is a free-swinger with raw power who rarely misses mistake pitches. That power should continue to grow, as it has throughout his short minor league career thus far. A bat-first prospect, Bernabel knows how to battle and make contact when behind in the count. Strikeouts aren't really an issue despite his free-swinging ways. His line drive, pull-side approach is underscored by good balance and bat speed. Bernabel has a strong arm at third base but still has room to improve his footwork, lateral quickness, fluidity and internal clock. He is an average runner.

THE FUTURE: Bernabel has some gaps in his game to shore up, especially defensively, but his bat has him on a path toward Coors Field. He should be tested by Double-A pitching at some point in 2022.

Year	Age	Club (Level)	Lge	AVG	G	AB	R	H	2B	3B	HR	RBI	BB	SO	SB	OBP	SLG
2021	19	Rockies (R)	ACL	.432	22	74	18	32	5	0	6	31	5	12	5	.453	.743
	19	Fresno (LoA)	West	.205	21	83	9	17	6	0	1	7	7	14	4	.287	.313
Minor League Totals (2 years)				.276	98	369	64	102	24	2	11	69	28	55	12	.340	.442

17 SAM WEATHERLY, LHP

BA GRADE

45 Risk: High

Born: May 28, 1999. **B-T:** L-L. **HT:** 6-4. **WT:** 205. **Drafted:** Clemson, 2020 (3rd round). **Signed by:** Jordan Czarniecki.

TRACK RECORD: After starting his college career as a reliever, Weatherly switched to a starting role in 2020 and impressed. He went 2-0 with a 0.79 ERA in four starts as the Friday starter at Clemson and the Rockies drafted him No. 81 overall, signing him for $755,300. Weatherly impressed in instructional league and then got plenty of seasoning with Low-A Fresno in 2021, posting a 4.83 ERA with 96 strikeouts in 15 starts. A shoulder injury limited him down the stretch.

SCOUTING REPORT: Weatherly features a mid-90s fastball that can touch 97 mph with power finish. He has an effective changeup that induces swings and misses and his slider has the potential to be a plus pitch. While Weatherly has loud stuff, he needs to reign in his below-average control and work ahead of hitters more. He especially needs to improve his command of his slider. There are days when Weatherly is dominant and days when he's not filling up the zone. He is a good athlete and has a high pitching IQ.

THE FUTURE: Weatherly has the raw stuff to become a mid-rotation starter. If his strike-throwing doesn't improve, he profiles as a lefthanded setup man.

Year	Age	Club (Level)	Lge	W	L	ERA	G	GS	IP	H	HR	BB	SO	BB/9	SO/9	WHIP	AVG
2021	22	Fresno (LoA)	West	4	6	4.83	15	15	69	59	7	32	96	4.2	12.5	1.32	.233
Minor League Totals (2 years)				4	6	4.83	15	15	69	59	7	32	96	4.2	12.5	1.32	.233

18 YANQUIEL FERNANDEZ, OF

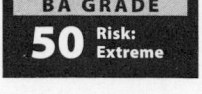

BA GRADE
50 Risk: Extreme

Born: Jan. 1, 2003. **B-T:** L-L. **HT:** 6-2. **WT:** 207. **Signed:** Cuba, 2019.
Signed by: Rolando Fernandez/Marc Russo/Raul Gomez.

TRACK RECORD: Fernandez signed with the Rockies out of Cuba for $295,000 in 2019, and it quickly became apparent he had the talent to match some of the top players in that year's international class. He made his pro debut as an 18-year-old in the Dominican Summer League in 2021 and ranked sixth in the league with a .937 OPS.

SCOUTING REPORT: Fernandez is a physical lefthanded hitter with a power stroke. It's a loose swing with good bat speed, leverage and strength behind it, posting top-end exit velocities that approach 110 mph. It should be at least plus raw power once he fills out, with a chance to be a 30 home run hitter in his prime. He recognizes pitches well for his age and generally stays within the strike zone. Fernandez has big offensive upside and is a smart player, but his lack of mobility restricts him defensively. He has a strong arm, but he's a well below-average runner who might slow down more, with some risk he could go to first base.

THE FUTURE: Fernandez will have to mash given his defensive limits, but he has the offensive upside to hit in the middle of a lineup.

Year	Age	Club (Level)	Lge	AVG	G	AB	R	H	2B	3B	HR	RBI	BB	SO	SB	OBP	SLG
2021	18	Rockies (R)	DSL	.333	54	177	29	59	17	0	6	34	22	26	0	.406	.531
Minor League Totals (1 year)				.333	54	177	29	59	17	0	6	34	22	26	0	.406	.531

19 ADRIAN PINTO, SS/2B

BA GRADE
50 Risk: Extreme

Born: Sept. 22, 2002. **B-T:** R-R. **HT:** 5-6. **WT:** 156. **Signed:** Venezuela, 2019. **Signed by:** Orlando Medina/Rolando Fernandez.

TRACK RECORD: At 5-foot-6, Pinto is typically the smallest player on the field. That didn't deter the Rockies, who signed him for $120,000 out of Venezuela, and he was outstanding in his pro debut in 2021. Pinto had more than twice as many walks (38) as strikeouts (18) in the Dominican Summer League, ranking second in the league in both batting average (.360) and on-base percentage (.486) and fourth in slugging percentage (.543).

SCOUTING REPORT: Pinto has a small but strong, compact build. He has outstanding hand-eye coordination and a short, quick stroke, rarely swinging and missing. His ability to recognize pitches and swing at good pitches are already advanced for his age, with a short strike zone that he doesn't often expand. Pinto is more of an on-base threat than a power threat, but he has some sneaky pop for his size and isn't just a slap hitter. Pinto's tools jump out as well. He's a plus-plus runner who led the DSL with 41 stolen bases. He has a plus arm too. He he spent most of his time last year at second base, his most likely defensive home.

THE FUTURE: Pinto has yet to make his U.S. debut, but he's a breakout candidate and one of the organization's most exciting players below the full-season level.

Year	Age	Club (Level)	Lge	AVG	G	AB	R	H	2B	3B	HR	RBI	BB	SO	SB	OBP	SLG
2021	18	Colorado (R)	DSL	.360	54	175	64	63	15	4	3	27	38	18	41	.486	.543
Minor League Totals (1 year)				.360	54	175	64	63	15	4	3	27	38	18	41	.486	.543

20 JULIAN FERNANDEZ, RHP

BA GRADE
45 Risk: High

Born: Dec. 5, 1995. **B-T:** R-R. **HT:** 6-6. **WT:** 235. **Signed:** Dominican Republic, 2012. **Signed by:** Rolando Fernandez.

TRACK RECORD: Fernandez took a long, circuitous route to his major league debut in 2021. He originally signed with the Rockies in 2012 and was selected by the Giants in the 2017 Rule 5 draft. He missed the 2018 season after having Tommy John surgery and was claimed off waivers after the season by the Marlins. He never pitched for them due to injury and re-signed with Rockies following the 2019 season. Fernandez finally got on the mound for the first time in four years in 2021. He began at Double-A and worked his way up to Triple-A, where he posted a 0.64 ERA in 14 appearances to earn a September callup.

SCOUTING REPORT: Fernandez touched 105 mph before surgery and is back bringing the heat. In his MLB debut Sept. 5, he threw the fastest Rockies pitch in the Statcast era at 102.4 mph. When Fernandez commands his fastball, he is nearly unhittable. But that command hasn't been nearly as consistent as he needs. He's been a bit over-reliant on his power fastball to get him through the minors, meaning his slider and changeup aren't as sharp as they need to be. His slider needs more depth and his changeup needs to be thrown with more consistency and confidence, especially early in the count.

THE FUTURE: Fernandez will be a part of the Rockies' bullpen plans in 2022. It will likely be another growth year as he continues to hone his offspeed pitches and overall command.

Year	Age	Club (Level)	Lge	W	L	ERA	G	GS	IP	H	HR	BB	SO	BB/9	SO/9	WHIP	AVG
2021	25	Hartford (AA)	NEast	2	2	3.45	30	0	28	25	4	12	24	3.8	7.5	1.29	.229
	25	Albuquerque (AAA)	West	1	0	0.64	14	0	14	10	0	4	18	2.6	11.6	1.00	.204
	25	Colorado (MLB)	NL	0	0	10.80	6	0	7	9	2	4	4	5.4	5.4	1.95	.310
Major League Totals (1 year)				0	0	10.80	6	0	7	9	2	4	4	5.40	5.40	1.95	.310
Minor League Totals (8 years)				10	9	3.40	172	0	191	154	7	98	175	4.63	8.26	1.32	.220

21 NOAH DAVIS, RHP

BA GRADE
45 Risk: High

Born: April 22, 1997. **B-T:** R-R. **HT:** 6-2. **WT:** 195. **Drafted:** UC Santa Barbara, 2018 (11th round). **Signed by:** Rick Ingalls (Reds).

TRACK RECORD: Davis had Tommy John surgery his junior year at UC Santa Barbara, but the Reds liked his stuf and gave him an above-slot $127,500 bonus to sign as an 11th-round pick. Davis returned to make his pro debut a year later and, after waiting out the coronavirus pandemic, was off to a strong start at High-A Dayton in 2021 when the Rockies acquired him as one of two prospects for Mychal Givens at the trade deadline. Davis showed well at High-A Spokane after the trade and was added to the 40-man roster after the season.

SCOUTING REPORT: Davis has a well-rounded four-pitch mix headlined by a 93-94 mph fastball that can get up to 96 mph with slight sink. He complements his fastball with a mid-to-high-80s slider, a high-70s curveball and a developing changeup. His potentially plus curveball is his best secondary, and he is confident throwing it in any count. Davis' control is inconsistent and has been below-average at its worst. The Rockies primarily want him to throw more fastballs and continue to develop his fastball command. Davis' biggest concern is his health. In addition to his Tommy John surgery, he has also battled shoulder soreness and blister issues at various points.

THE FUTURE: Davis has the stuff to be a back-end starter if he can hone his control and stay healthy. He'll move to Double-A in 2022.

Year	Age	Club (Level)	Lge	W	L	ERA	G	GS	IP	H	HR	BB	SO	BB/9	SO/9	WHIP	AVG
2021	24	Dayton (HiA)	Cent	3	6	3.60	13	13	65	44	3	35	77	4.9	10.7	1.22	.193
	24	Spokane (HiA)	West	3	1	3.60	6	6	35	32	3	8	29	2.1	7.5	1.14	.250
Minor League Totals (4 years)				7	10	3.48	32	32	142	116	14	56	141	3.5	8.9	1.21	.224

22 JOE ROCK, LHP

BA GRADE
45 Risk: High

Born: July 29, 2000. **B-T:** L-L. **HT:** 6-6. **WT:** 200. **Drafted:** Ohio, 2021 (2nd round supplemental). **Signed by:** Ed Santa.

TRACK RECORD: The Rockies selected Rock at No. 68 overall and signed him for $953,100 after he led Ohio in ERA (2.33), wins (eight), complete games (four) and strikeouts (117) as a junior. He made his brief pro debut with eight innings in the Arizona Complex League and struck out 11 of the 29 batters he faced.

SCOUTING REPORT: Rock's fastball sits in the mid-90s with cut, and he can pump it up to 96 mph. He is fairly skinny in his 6-foot-6 frame and still has room to get stronger and add more velocity. Rock also has a mid-80s power curveball and a developing changeup that he's building confidence in A somewhat deceptive delivery and a lower arm slot make his pitches difficult for hitters to pick up, but also hampers his control. Rock has struggled with walks at various points throughout his career and needs to learn to be around the strike zone more with his deceptive mechanics.

THE FUTURE: Rock has the body and raw stuff to be a back-end starter if he continues to fill out, improves his changeup and hones his control. He'll begin 2022 at one of the Class-A levels.

Year	Age	Club (Level)	Lge	W	L	ERA	G	GS	IP	H	HR	BB	SO	BB/9	SO/9	WHIP	AVG
2021	20	Rockies (R)	ACL	1	0	1.13	4	2	8	5	0	1	11	1.1	12.4	0.75	.179
Minor League Totals (1 year)				1	0	1.13	4	2	8	5	0	1	11	1.1	12.4	0.75	.179

23 KARL KAUFFMANN, RHP

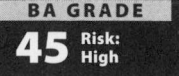

BA GRADE

45 Risk: High

Born: Aug. 15, 1997. **B-T:** R-R. **HT:** 6-2. **WT:** 200. **Drafted:** Michigan, 2019 (2nd round supplemental). **Signed by:** Ed Santa.

TRACK RECORD: After leading Michigan to a runner-up finish in the 2019 College World Series, the Rockies drafted Kauffmann No. 77 overall and elected to rest him that summer because of his high workload in college. A shoulder injury limited his development at the alternate site in 2020. The righthander made his pro debut in 2021 with High-A Spokane and the Rockies elevated him to Double-A after just two impressive starts, where he pitched to a 7.35 ERA in 19 games (18 starts).

SCOUTING REPORT: Kauffmann relies on command and grittiness to elevate an ordinary pitch mix. He's comfortable throwing his low-90s sinker to both sides of the plate, but hitters weren't fooled by it (.398 wOBA against) and he needs to throw it in the strike zone more frequently. Kauffmann also deploys a low-90s four-seamer and an average changeup that needs more development, but neither miss many bats. His best secondary offering is his mid-80s slider which looks extremely similar to his fastball out of his hand and projects as an above-average pitch.

THE FUTURE: Kauffmann's ceiling is an innings eater at the back of a rotation, though he could profile as a reliever as well. The Rockies challenged Kauffmann in 2021, unworried by the growing pains at Double-A, and the same will likely be true in Triple-A in 2022.

Year	Age	Club (Level)	Lge	W	L	ERA	G	GS	IP	H	HR	BB	SO	BB/9	SO/9	WHIP	AVG
2021	23	Spokane (HiA)	West	1	1	2.89	2	2	9	5	0	2	6	1.9	5.8	0.75	.167
	23	Hartford (AA)	NEast	2	11	7.35	19	18	82	123	18	41	65	4.5	7.1	2.00	.343
Minor League Totals (3 years)				3	12	6.90	21	20	91	128	18	43	71	4.2	7.0	1.87	.329

24 BLADIMIR RESTITUYO, OF

BA GRADE

40 Risk: High

Born: July 2, 2001. **B-T:** R-R. **HT:** 5-10. **WT:** 155. **Signed:** Dominican Republic, 2017. **Signed by:** Rolando Fernandez/Frank Roa.

TRACK RECORD: After signing with the Rockies for $200,000 on his 16th birthday, Restituyo spent 2018 in the Dominican Summer League, then hit .259 in 55 games in a strong first impression stateside in the Northwest League in 2019. He stood out during the 2020 instructional league, and spent all of 2021 with Low-A Fresno, slashing .259/.288/.334 as the Grizzlies' everyday center fielder.

SCOUTING REPORT: With growing gap-to-gap doubles power and sneaky pop, Restituyo has plenty of potential offensively. But he'll have to clean up certain glaring deficiencies, such as his tendency to be over-anxious in the box and his swing-and-miss rate on breaking balls. He struck out at a 25.2% clip in 2021 and needs to work on his strike zone discipline overall. A middle infielder converted to the outfield, Restituyo has above-average range to his left and right but needs to work on his footwork and reads on flies over his head. Strong arm. He's a fast, aggressive baserunner (69 steals in his career) who can put pressure on the opposing defense.

THE FUTURE: Restituyo projects as a reserve outfielder at the big league level, although his defensive versatility and speed could help him carve out a larger role. He'll be tested in High-A in 2022.

Year	Age	Club (Level)	Lge	AVG	G	AB	R	H	2B	3B	HR	RBI	BB	SO	SB	OBP	SLG
2021	19	Fresno (LoA)	West	.259	84	290	37	75	7	3	3	24	12	73	31	.288	.334
Minor League Totals (4 years)				.275	219	839	121	231	35	12	13	96	25	193	69	.300	.392

25 GRANT LAVIGNE, 1B

BA GRADE

40 Risk: High

Born: Aug. 27, 1999. **B-T:** L-R. **HT:** 6-4. **WT:** 220. **Drafted:** HS—Bedford, N.H., 2018 (1st round supplemental). **Signed by:** Mike Garlatti.

TRACK RECORD: New Hampshire isn't known for its baseball, but by getting drafted at No. 42 overall, Lavigne has a chance to become the first hitter drafted out of high school in the state to make it to the majors. He tore up the Pioneer League in 2018, slashing .350/.477/.519 with a .996 OPS, but came back down to earth in Low-A Asheville in 2019 (.236 average with 29.3 strikeout percentage). He played in instructional league in 2020 then was tested in Fresno and Spokane in 2021.

SCOUTING REPORT: Plate discipline is Lavigne's strength, as he's a patient (and sometimes too patient) hitter. He has a major-league frame, but lacks consistent power to all fields. With a smooth bat path and above-average bat speed, he has gap-to-gap potential, but tends to be too pull-happy. When he's struggling, he's not letting his natural strength and bat speed work for him. His speed is slightly above average for his size. He has an unimpressive arm and a long way to go overall on defense; improving his footwork has been a continued emphasis.

THE FUTURE: Lavigne's ceiling is as an average everyday first baseman, but he needs to flash more power and the glove must improve drastically if he's to be more than a reserve. Double-A will be a big test in 2022..

Year	Age	Club (Level)	Lge	AVG	G	AB	R	H	2B	3B	HR	RBI	BB	SO	SB	OBP	SLG
2021	21	Fresno (LoA)	West	.281	72	260	49	73	13	4	7	40	39	73	7	.388	.442
	21	Spokane (HiA)	West	.225	32	111	17	25	5	1	2	18	22	39	2	.362	.342
Minor League Totals (4 years)				.269	289	1017	163	274	50	7	22	160	174	281	29	.386	.397

26 JAMESON HANNAH, OF

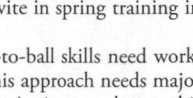

Born: Aug. 10, 1997. **B-T:** L-L. **HT:** 5-9. **WT:** 185. **Drafted:** Dallas Baptist, 2018 (2nd round). **Signed by:** Chris Reilly (Athletics).

TRACK RECORD: It's been a winding road since Oakland drafted Hannah No. 50 overall in 2018. The A's traded him to the Reds at the 2019 deadline, then Cincinnati flipped him to Colorado after the 2020 season in a deal that sent Hannah and Robert Stephenson to the Rockies in exchange for Jeff Hoffman and Case Williams. He impressed as a non-roster invite in spring training in 2021 before slashing .255/.324/.351 in 71 games in Double-A.

SCOUTING REPORT: There's not a lot of power in Hannah's swing and his bat-to-ball skills need work. He struck out at a 32.8% clip in 2021 after a 23.5% strikeout rate in 2019, so his approach needs major refinement. He's much better at making consistent hard contact against righties. Against southpaws, his power is negligible and he hit a paltry .178 from that side in 2021. He has plus speed but it's not showing up on the basepaths yet. He has wide range in center field but his arm is average for the position and would be a better fit for left, where he's also seen time.

THE FUTURE: Hannah profiles as a fourth outfielder who can add speed and occasional sparks to a lineup, but he doesn't have the hit tools to project as a starter. He'll be tested in Triple-A in 2022.

Year	Age	Club (Level)	Lge	AVG	G	AB	R	H	2B	3B	HR	RBI	BB	SO	SB	OBP	SLG
2021	23	Hartford (AA)	NEast	.255	79	302	41	77	16	2	3	17	29	99	11	.324	.351
Minor League Totals (4 years)				.267	212	830	109	222	48	7	6	64	76	227	25	.334	.364

27 YOAN AYBAR, LHP

Born: July 3, 1997. **B-T:** L-L. **HT:** 6-2. **WT:** 210. **Signed:** Dominican Republic, 2013. **Signed by:** Jonathan Cruz/Eddie Romero (Red Sox).

TRACK RECORD: After four seasons in Boston's system as an outfielder, Aybar converted to pitcher ahead of the 2018 season. The move paid off, as Aybar posted a 4.58 ERA across 44 appearances at Low-A and High-A in 2019. He was traded to Colorado after the 2020 season in exchange for shortstop prospect Christian Koss, and the Rockies placed Aybar on their 40-man roster. The southpaw had a bumpy 2021 in Double-A with a 6.22 ERA in 49 appearances.

SCOUTING REPORT: Aybar has a mid-90s fastball that tops out at 99 mph with cut. When he commands that pitch to both sides, he's nearly unhittable. And even when the heater isn't totally sharp, it's still electric enough to get him out of trouble. His offspeed pitches need sharpening, as his high-80s slider doesn't have consistent cut and he's still growing confidence in his low-80s changeup. He's still raw in his pitchability and his overall command needs refinement. His arsenal limits homers and there's more strikeout potential in his arm than his 23.7% K rate in 2021.

THE FUTURE: Everything comes down to command for Aybar. If he can pinpoint his blazing fastball and his offspeed pitches progress, he could be a focal point of the Rockies' bullpen in a couple years. He'll likely start 2022 in Triple-A and could pitch himself into a second-half call-up.

Year	Age	Club (Level)	Lge	W	L	ERA	G	GS	IP	H	HR	BB	SO	BB/9	SO/9	WHIP	AVG
2021	23	Hartford (AA)	NEast	2	6	6.22	49	0	46	50	8	33	53	6.4	10.3	1.79	.266
Minor League Totals (4 years)				5	10	5.06	110	0	132	111	9	88	150	6.0	10.2	1.51	.222

28 REAGAN TODD, LHP

Born: Aug. 30, 1995. **B-T:** L-L. **HT:** 6-3. **WT:** 218. **Drafted:** Colorado Mesa, 2018 (32nd round). **Signed by:** Marc Gustafson.

TRACK RECORD: A local product who starred at Regis Jesuit High School, Todd played two seasons at Arizona State before transferring to Colorado Mesa. The Rockies took him in the 32nd round, and he signed for just $1,000. Todd has grinded through the minors in the three years since. After a rough debut in 2018, he had a flashy 1.86 ERA across 26 games at the Class-A levels in 2019. The 2021 season brought growing pains in the high minors, but Todd capped the year with an all-star appearance in the Arizona Fall League.

SCOUTING REPORT: Todd's low-90s fastball tops out at 95 mph with run, and he pairs it with a low-80s slider that has two-plane break. That breaking ball improved over the past couple years, along with his fastball and developing changeup. Earlier in his minor league career he had a tendency to overthrow, but that's been corrected. He knows how to attack hitters and pitch to their weaknesses, battles through tough innings, and can finish hitters off deep in the count (31.4% K rate in 2021). Todd has solid command with room for improvement.

THE FUTURE: If Todd continues to rise as quickly as he has, he could debut in the Rockies' bullpen in 2022. He'll likely begin the season in Triple-A.

Year	Age	Club (Level)	Lge	W	L	ERA	G	GS	IP	H	HR	BB	SO	BB/9	SO/9	WHIP	AVG
2021	25	Hartford (AA)	NEast	4	2	4.36	39	0	43	39	7	15	59	3.1	12.3	1.25	.245
	25	Albuquerque (AAA)	West	1	0	5.40	10	0	8	11	1	8	10	8.6	10.8	2.28	.333
Minor League Totals (4 years)				10	5	4.32	92	3	110	117	15	42	140	3.4	11.4	1.44	.275

29 JUSTIN LAWRENCE, RHP

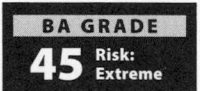

BA GRADE

45 Risk: Extreme

Born: Nov. 25, 1994. **B-T:** R-R. **HT:** 6-3. **WT:** 213. **Drafted:** Daytona (Fla.) JC, 2015 (12th round). **Signed by:** John Cedarburg.

TRACK RECORD: The Rockies drafted Lawrence in the 12th round in 2015 and he evolved into one of the club's most intriguing bullpen prospects. After a couple unimpressive seasons to start his career, Lawrence burst onto the radar with dominant seasons in the South Atlantic League in 2017 and the California League in 2018. He rode a wave of momentum into 2019 spring training as a non-roster invitee, but then sputtered to a 8.76 ERA across 38 games in the high minors. Then, Lawrence was suspended 80 games for the performance-enhancing substance DHCMT. He rebounded in 2021 with his Rockies debut, but struggled against big-league hitters with a 8.64 ERA in 19 games.

SCOUTING REPORT: Lawrence has a high-90s fastball with sink and he can routinely touch triple digits. His funky arm angle – which is somewhere between three-quarters and sidearm – creates deception throughout an at-bat. He has an aggressive demeanor on the mound and attacks hitters with his heater. The sharpness of his low-80s slider is improving. His command needs to get better, too, as evidenced by his 22% walk rate in the bigs in 2021.

THE FUTURE: Command and the consistency of his secondary pitches are what's keeping Lawrence from sticking in the Rockies' bullpen, where he will have plenty of chances again in 2022.

Year	Age	Club (Level)	Lge	W	L	ERA	G	GS	IP	H	HR	BB	SO	BB/9	SO/9	WHIP	AVG
2021	26	Albuquerque (AAA)	West	6	5	4.73	31	0	32	32	3	12	30	3.3	8.4	1.36	.256
	26	Colorado (MLB)	NL	1	0	8.64	19	0	16	21	0	19	17	10.3	9.2	2.40	.333
Major League Totals (1 year)				1	0	8.64	19	0	17	21	0	19	17	10.3	9.2	2.40	.333
Minor League Totals (7 years)				11	23	5.13	211	0	230	231	18	108	225	4.2	8.8	1.48	.262

30 GAVIN HOLLOWELL, RHP

BA GRADE

40 Risk: High

Born: Nov. 4, 1997. **B-T:** R-R. **HT:** 6-7. **WT:** 215. **Drafted:** St. John's, 2019 (6th round). **Signed by:** Mike Garlatti.

TRACK RECORD: After dominating his first two years for St. John's, Hollowell took a step back his junior year, but the Rockies selected him at No. 189 anyway. He immediately impressed in Grand Junction in 2019, posting a 2.89 ERA in 17 games with seven saves as the team's closer. He worked to fine-tune his delivery during instructional league in 2020. Then he recovered from injury to put up another strong (albeit short) year in Low-A Fresno with a 2.45 ERA in 22 games in 2021, with four saves. Hollowell is 12-of-13 in save opportunities as a pro.

SCOUTING REPORT: His fastball sits around 95 mph and is combined with his mid-80s power slurve, which is his out pitch and a big reason why he's tallied a 36.4% strikeout rate so far. He has solid command with both pitches and walks very few batters, while also showing the ability to keep the ball in the yard (three homers allowed across 42.2 innings). He morphed a crouched-style delivery into an upright one, allowing him to use his height and frame to generate more movement on both pitches.

THE FUTURE: Hollowell is a projectable back-end bullpen arm, especially if his strikeout rate stays steady. He'll be tested in the high minors in 2022.

Year	Age	Club (Level)	Lge	W	L	ERA	G	GS	IP	H	HR	BB	SO	BB/9	SO/9	WHIP	AVG
2021	23	Rockies (R)	ACL	1	0	0.00	2	0	2	2	0	2	2	9.0	9.0	2.00	.286
	23	Fresno (LoA)	West	2	0	2.45	22	0	22	15	1	5	31	2.1	12.7	0.91	.185
Minor League Totals (3 years)				6	0	2.53	41	0	43	31	3	12	63	2.5	13.3	1.01	.196

MORE PROSPECTS TO KNOW

31. BRYAN PEREZ, RHP

A nephew of Edinson Volquez, Perez looked sharp as a 17-year-old in the Dominican Summer League, where he showed a smooth delivery and good feel for pitching. He works off a fastball that sits at 93-96 mph, touches 98 and complements it with a potential plus curveball.

32. JORDY VARGAS, RHP

The son of former big league reliever Yorkis Perez, Vargas posted a 1.30 ERA and struck out 46 in 34.2 innings as a 17-year-old in the Dominican Summer League. He's 6-foot-3 with a starter profile, touching 97 mph with his fastball, a plus curveball with tight rotation and good feel for a changeup.

33. NIKO DECLOLATI, OF

The 24-year-old fourth outfielder hopeful is a strong defender with some discipline and some speed but limited impact potential.

34. WILLIE MacIVER, C

MacIver played a lot of third base in college but has committed to catching in pro ball. His bat broke out at High-A Spokane to earn a Futures Game bid, but his production dried up at Double-A..

35. EDDY DIAZ, SS/2B

The speedy middle infielder led the Rockies' organization with 48 steals in 2021. He's the first Cuban player ever signed by Colorado. He needs to show he can hit after batting .192 at High-A Spokane.

36. RYAN FELTNER, RHP

One of the organization's fastest rising arms a year ago, Feltner debuted Sept. 5 and got roughed up in two big league starts. He throws a mid-90s fastball, a slider and a changeup.

37. TOMMY DOYLE, RHP

After cruising through his first three seasons of pro ball as a closer with a power fastball and wipeout slider, Doyle struggled to a 9.64 ERA in Double-A in 2021. He suffered a labrum tear but the Rockies are hopeful he returns to the mound in 2022.

38. HUNTER STOVALL, 3B/2B/OF

The super utilityman is coming off a strong season with Spokane in which he slashed .316/.393/.438. He has a line-drive, gap-to-gap approach in the box.

39. CASEY GOLDEN, OF

Oblique and ankle injuries limited him to 47 games in 2021, when the 27-year old was about two years older than the average Double-A player, but there's undeniable power in his bat, as he has 86 career homers and won the 2019 California League home run derby.

40. HUNTER GOODMAN, C

The Rockies took Goodman in the fourth round in 2021, and he's an aggressive power hitter capable of blasting long home runs. A utility player at Memphis, the Rockies used the 2021 season and instructional league to work on his raw catching skills.

TOP PROSPECTS OF THE DECADE

Year	Player, Pos	2021 Org
2012	Drew Pomeranz, LHP	Padres
2013	Nolan Arenado, 3B	Cardinals
2014	Jon Gray, RHP	Rockies
2015	David Dahl, OF	Brewers
2016	Jon Gray, RHP	Rockies
2017	Brendan Rodgers, SS	Rockies
2018	Brendan Rodgers, SS	Rockies
2019	Brendan Rodgers, SS/2B	Rockies
2020	Brendan Rodgers, SS/2B	Rockies
2021	Brendan Rodgers, SS/2B	Rockies

TOP DRAFT PICKS OF THE DECADE

Year	Player, Pos	2021 Org
2012	David Dahl, OF	Brewers
2013	Jon Gray, RHP	Rockies
2014	Kyle Freeland, LHP	Rockies
2015	Brendan Rodgers, SS	Rockies
2016	Riley Pint, RHP	Rockies
2017	Ryan Vilade, 3B (2nd round)	Rockies
2018	Ryan Rolison, LHP	Rockies
2019	Michael Toglia, 1B	Rockies
2020	Zac Veen, OF	Rockies
2021	Benny Montgomery, OF	Rockies

Detroit Tigers

BY EMILY WALDON

The Tigers entered 2021 faced with the challenge of reversing their trajectory in the standings after two consecutive last-place finishes in the American League Central.

There were a lot of changes in 2021, almost all of them positive for the rebuilding Tigers.

Detroit's decision to hire former Astros manager A.J. Hinch was arguably their strongest offseason move entering 2021 as the organization works toward a return to contention. MLB had suspended Hinch for the 2020 season following his involvement in the Astros' sign-stealing scandal.

Along with Hinch, the Tigers signed former University of Michigan pitching coach Chris Fetter, who had a history with Hinch from their days in the Padres organization.

Fetter's experience with developing young arms through the Wolverines' program made him well-suited for the role of bringing along righthander Casey Mize and lefthander Tarik Skubal. Mize and Skubal, the preseason Nos. 2 and 3 prospects, stayed in the rotation all year and improved Tigers starters' ERA from last in the AL in 2020 to seventh in 2021.

As was the case in 2020, the Tigers' challenge of juggling Covid protocols and injuries expedited the callups of several new faces, including Jason Foley, Jacob Robson and Matt Manning. While none produced a truly noteworthy season, the development exposure was a move the Tigers hope to continue building on in 2022.

An improvement, albeit a small one landed the Tigers in a third-place finish of 77-85, their first 70-plus win season since 2016.

The Tigers pulled a Rule 5 draft coup by selecting center fielder Akil Baddoo from the Twins. The 23-year-old rookie hit .259/.330/.436 with 13 home runs and 18 stolen bases in 124 games, while essentially jumping from a partial season at High-A in 2019. Not only does Baddoo represent a free find, he appears to be a lineup fixture for a club that needs to add offensive production.

The return of minor leagues brought with it a chance for Tigers prospects to prove themselves. Riley Greene, the fifth overall pick in 2019, started at Double-A Erie and finished at Triple-A Toledo, earning Minor League All-Star Team honors for a .301/.387/.534 season that included 24 home runs in 124 games.

The Tigers shifted some player development pieces in the front office as well. David Littlefield, the long-time vice president of player development, was moved to a special assignment scout's role and replaced by Ryan Garko.

Former Dodgers pitching coordinator Gabe

Casey Mize, the No. 1 overall pick in 2018, emerged as the Tigers' top starting pitcher.

PROJECTED 2025 LINEUP

Catcher	Dillon Dingler	26
First Base	Spencer Torkelson	25
Second Base	Ryan Kreidler	27
Third Base	Gage Workman	25
Shortstop	Javier Baez	32
Left Field	Roberto Campos	22
Center Field	Akil Baddoo	26
Right Field	Riley Greene	24
Designated Hitter	Jeimer Candelario	31
No. 1 Starter	Casey Mize	28
No. 2 Starter	Tarik Skubal	28
No. 3 Starter	Jackson Jobe	22
No. 4 Starter	Eduardo Rodriguez	32
No. 5 Starter	Matt Manning	27
Closer	Gregory Soto	30

Ribas was named the Tigers' new director of pitching, replacing Dan Hubbs, who was hired by Detroit in 2019.

Detroit also had the No. 3 overall selection in the draft and used it to select righthander and High School Player of the Year Jackson Jobe. The Tigers returned to previous draft form, selecting five pitchers among their first six picks, including Texas righthander Ty Madden at No. 32 overall.

With Greene and 2020 top overall pick Spencer Torkelson poised to reach Detroit fairly quickly in 2022, the Tigers, in turn, should be able to bolster an aging lineup and continue to cultivate the development of the young arms that they have been working to acquire. ∎

DETROIT TIGERS

TOP 2022 ROOKIES	RANK
Riley Greene, OF	1
Spencer Torkelson, 1B	2
BREAKOUT PROSPECTS	**RANK**
Cristian Santana, SS	11
Colt Keith, 3B	13
Reese Olson, RHP	15

SOURCE OF TOP 30 TALENT			
Homegrown	27	Acquired	3
College	13	Trade	3
Junior college	0	Rule 5 draft	0
High school	5	Independent league	0
Nondrafted free agent	2	Free agent/waivers	0
International	7		

LF
Bryant Packard (28)
Jacob Robson
Austin Murr
Danny Woodrow
Kerry Carpenter

CF
Riley Greene (1)
Parker Meadows (26)
Jose de la Cruz (23)
Eric de la Rosa

RF
Roberto Campos (8)
Daniel Cabrera (16)
Kingston Liniak
Ulrich Bojarski

3B
Gage Workman (5)
Ryan Kreidler (7)
Colt Keith (13)

SS
Izaac Pacheco (10)
Cristian Santana (11)
Manuel Sequera (12)
Adinso Reyes (24)
Abel Bastidas (27)
Trei Cruz
Jose King
Wenceel Perez

2B
Kody Clemens (17)
Andre Lipcius (30)
John Valente

1B
Spencer Torkelson (2)
Reynaldo Rivera
Jimmy Kerr

C
Dillon Dingler (4)
Eliezer Alfonzo (25)
Danuerys De La Cruz
Cooper Johnson
Sam McMillan
Brady Policelli

LHP

LHSP	LHRP
Joey Wentz (9)	Jack O'Loughlin
Carlos Pena	Adam Wolf
	Max Green
	Jared Tobey
	Andrew Magno

RHP

RHSP	RHRP
Jackson Jobe (3)	Jason Foley (21)
Ty Madden (6)	Paul Richan (29)
Dylan Smith (14)	Wladimir Pinto
Reese Olson (15)	Gerson Moreno
Beau Brieske (18)	Zack Hess
Tyler Mattison (19)	Nolan Blackwood
Alex Faedo (20)	Hugh Smith
Wilmer Flores (22)	Logan Shore
Garrett Hill	Brad Bass
Tanner Kohlhepp	Ethan DeCaster
Elvin Rodriguez	Rony Garcia
Wilkel Hernandez	Angel De Jesus
Carlos Guzman	
Franklin Perez	

1 RILEY GREENE, OF

Born: Sept. 28, 2000. **B-T:** L-L. **HT:** 6-3. **WT:** 200.
Drafted: HS—Oviedo, Fla., 2019 (1st round).
Signed by: RJ Burgess.

MIKE JANES/FOUR SEAM IMAGES

BA GRADE	SCOUTING GRADES
65 Risk: Medium	Hit: 60. Power: 60. Run: 55. Field: 60. Arm: 55.

Projected future grades on 20-80 scouting scale

TRACK RECORD: Greene has yet to lose any momentum since being selected fifth overall in 2019. He signed for $6.18 million and hit the ground running in 2019, cascading three levels and hitting a combined .271/.347/.403 as he rose to Low-A West Michigan. Following the canceled 2020 minor league season, the Tigers challenged Greene once again in 2021 with an assignment to Double-A Erie. Once again, Greene excelled, hitting .298/.381/.525 and joining Spencer Torkelson as the Tigers' representatives at the Futures Game in Denver. The Tigers tested Greene again in August with a promotion to Triple-A Toledo, where Greene exceeded expectations both offensively and defensively. Over 40 games with the Mud Hens, Greene slashed .308/.400/.553 with a .954 OPS and eight home runs to bring his single-season total to 29 homers. Although Greene was among the Tigers' selections for the Arizona Fall League, a head injury suffered at the end of his Triple-A season continued to produce concussion-like symptoms, forcing the Tigers to retract Greene's participation. He cleared concussion protocol shortly after and began his offseason routine in preparation for the 2022 season.
SCOUTING REPORT: Greene has drawn plaudits for his elite feel and instincts as a hitter since he was a high school underclassman. Mixing exceptional talent with a mature approach and a high IQ, Greene possesses elite bat speed with a fluid, balanced stroke and does damage with plus raw power. As a power hitter, Greene made major strides in 2021 as he blossomed into a true longball threat. Despite aggressive assignments, Greene hit 24 home runs and produced strong slugging metrics across the board. This showed up in the analytical data as well, with Greene's max exit velocity reaching 113.9 mph. Hitting the ball hard will not be a problem for Greene, but his ability to balance potential plus power with easy plus contact and hitting ability is what sets him apart from other prospects. He has continued to display advanced plate discipline and barrel control at every level, and he shows the ability to make adjustments from at-bat to at-bat when fooled. His physical gifts and advanced feel at the plate make him a potential plus-plus hitter who contends for batting titles and he has a chance to grow into 20-plus home run power. Defensively, the Tigers' have played Greene plenty in center field, but he projects to be a cor-

BEST TOOLS

Best Hitter for Average	Riley Greene
Best Power Hitter	Spencer Torkelson
Best Strike-Zone Discipline	Andre Lipcius
Fastest Baserunner	Parker Meadows
Best Athlete	Dillon Dingler
Best Fastball	Erick Pinales
Best Curveball	Wilmer Flores
Best Slider	Zack Hess
Best Changeup	Beau Brieske
Best Control	Beau Brieske
Best Defensive Catcher	Dillon Dingler
Best Defensive Infielder	Ryan Kreidler
Best Infield Arm	Gage Workman
Best Defensive Outfielder	Riley Greene
Best Outfield Arm	Jose de la Cruz

ner outfielder down the road. No matter where Greene plays, his decisions are made with enough confidence to make difficult plays look easy thanks to fluid actions. His above-average speed and arm strength give him a future in right field.
THE FUTURE: Greene only seems to thrive with every challenge, leading to the belief that he could make a case for a major league promotion before the all-star break, if not sooner. His consistent contact and fluid defense should allow him to seize a starting role quickly and begin his ascent to a perennial all-star who hits for average and power. ■

Year	Age	Club (Level)	Lge	AVG	G	AB	R	H	2B	3B	HR	RBI	BB	SO	SB	OBP	SLG
2021	20	Erie (AA)	NEast	.298	84	326	59	97	16	5	16	54	41	102	12	.381	.525
	20	Toledo (AAA)	East	.308	40	159	36	49	9	3	8	30	22	51	4	.400	.553
Minor League Totals (3 years)				.292	181	706	129	206	33	11	29	112	85	216	21	.375	.493

2 SPENCER TORKELSON, 1B/3B

Born: Aug. 26, 1999. **B-T:** R-R. **HT:** 6-1. **WT:** 220. **Drafted:** Arizona State, 2020 (1st round). **Signed by:** Joey Lothrop.

TRACK RECORD: Torkelson broke Barry Bonds' freshman home run record at Arizona State and established himself early as the top prospect in the 2020 draft class. The Tigers drafted him first overall and signed him for $8.146 million, the largest signing bonus for any player since MLB implemented the draft pool system in 2012. Torkelson reported to the Tigers' alternate training site after he signed and made his pro debut in 2021. He hit 30 home runs as he jumped three levels from High-A to Triple-A and was selected for the Futures Game in Denver. The Tigers sent Torkelson to the Arizona Fall League after the season, but his campaign was cut short by a sprained ankle.

BA GRADE

65 Risk: Medium

SCOUTING REPORT: With strength in both physical appearance and performance, Torkelson punishes baseballs to all fields with 80-grade raw power and hits jaw-dropping home runs that demoralize opposing pitchers. More than just an all-or-nothing slugger, Torkelson complements his power with a polished eye for the strike zone, excellent hand-eye coordination and a mature approach that make him a plus hitter. Torkelson played his entire college career at first base and, even though the Tigers announced him as a third baseman on draft day, first base is his present and future home. Torkelson is only a fringe-average runner, but his natural athleticism, average arm strength and steady footwork have him positioned as to be at least an average defender.

THE FUTURE: After steamrolling his way through three affiliates, Torkelson has a chance to make the Tigers' roster out of spring training. If he doesn't, his debut should come shortly after.

SCOUTING GRADES:	Hitting: 60	Power: 70	Running: 45	Fielding: 50	Arm: 50

Year	Age	Club (Level)	Lge	AVG	G	AB	R	H	2B	3B	HR	RBI	BB	SO	SB	OBP	SLG
2021	21	West Michigan (HiA)	Cent	.312	31	109	21	34	11	1	5	28	24	28	3	.440	.569
	21	Erie (AA)	NEast	.263	50	175	33	46	10	0	14	36	30	50	1	.373	.560
	21	Toledo (AAA)	East	.238	40	147	35	35	8	1	11	27	23	36	1	.350	.531
Minor League Totals (2 years)				.267	121	431	89	115	29	2	30	91	77	114	5	.383	.552

3 JACKSON JOBE, RHP

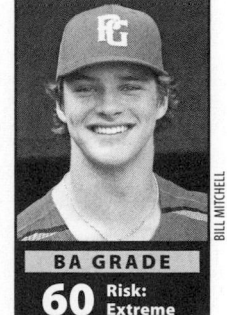

Born: July 30, 2002. **B-T:** R-R. **HT:** 6-2. **WT:** 190. **Drafted:** HS—Oklahoma City, 2021 (1st round). **Signed by:** Steve Taylor.

TRACK RECORD: The son of professional golfer Brandt Jobe, Jackson carried Heritage Hall (Oklahoma City) High to the Oklahoma 4A state championship as its star shortstop and top pitcher and won BA's 2021 High School Player of the Year award. Though he had pro potential as a position player, he was the best high school pitcher in the class, leading the Tigers to select him third overall as a pitcher and sign him for $6.9 million to forgo his commitment to Mississippi. Jobe did not pitch after signing and did not take part in instructional league.

BA GRADE

60 Risk: Extreme

SCOUTING REPORT: Jobe stands at a projectable 6-foot-2, 190 pounds and has plenty of room to add strength and fill out his frame. His fastball sits 92-94 mph and touches 96 with solid movement. His primary weapon is a plus-plus, high-spin slider with depth and bite that he expertly locates to both sides of the plate. His low-80s changeup with late dive is steadily improving and shows plus potential, and his above-average spike curveball with 11-to-5 break and depth could improve the more he works it into his arsenal. Jobe repeats his low-effort delivery and clean arm action for above-average control and is an excellent athlete with an advanced feel for pitching on the mound.

THE FUTURE: Jobe's arsenal and mature understanding of his craft could help him rise faster than most high school pitchers. He has at least mid-rotation potential and will begin his pro career in 2022.

SCOUTING GRADES:	Fastball: 60	Slider: 70	Curveball: 55	Changeup: 60	Control: 55

Year	Age	Club (Level)	Lge	W	L	ERA	G	GS	IP	H	HR	BB	SO	BB/9	SO/9	WHIP	AVG
2021	18	Did not play															

4 DILLON DINGLER, C

Born: Sept. 17, 1998. **B-T:** R-R. **HT:** 6-3. **WT:** 210. **Drafted:** Ohio State, 2020 (2nd round). **Signed by:** Austin Cousino.

TRACK RECORD: Dingler played both catcher and center field his freshman year at Ohio State before moving behind the plate full-time as a sophomore. His athleticism helped make him arguably the best defensive catcher in the 2020 draft class, and the Tigers drafted him 38th overall and signed him for $1,952,300. Dingler reported to the Tigers alternate training site after signing and made his pro debut in 2021. He quickly hit his way up to Double-A Erie, but he suffered a fractured finger tip on his left hand in early August when he got crossed up on a sign and finished the year slowly.

SCOUTING REPORT: Dingler has a physical, well-proportioned frame and is a good athlete on both sides of the ball. He is a plus runner, rare for a catcher, and has cat-like reflexes behind the plate. He is relatively new to the position and is still learning it, but he has consistently improved both his framing and receiving with experience and projects to be an above-average defender. His best asset is his near plus-plus arm that shuts down the running game. While Dingler's defense outshines his offense, he has increasingly learned to tap into his above-average raw power and does damage when he connects. He swings and misses too much to be more than an average hitter, but he projects to hit enough for a catcher.

THE FUTURE: Dingler is fully recovered from his finger injury and will be ready for spring training. He is the Tigers' catcher of the future and will be an asset behind the plate for their talented young pitchers.

BA GRADE
50 Risk: High

SCOUTING GRADES:	Hitting: 50	Power: 50	Running: 60	Fielding: 55	Arm: 65

Year	Age	Club (Level)	Lge	AVG	G	AB	R	H	2B	3B	HR	RBI	BB	SO	SB	OBP	SLG
2021	22	Lakeland (LoA)	SEast	.333	3	12	1	4	1	0	0	2	0	3	0	.333	.417
	22	West Michigan (HiA)	Cent	.287	32	122	25	35	6	1	8	24	13	36	0	.376	.549
	22	Erie (AA)	NEast	.202	50	188	24	38	3	3	4	20	9	62	1	.264	.314
Minor League Totals (2 years)				.239	85	322	50	77	10	4	12	46	22	101	1	.310	.407

5 GAGE WORKMAN, SS

Born: Oct. 24, 1999. **B-T:** B-R. **HT:** 6-3. **WT:** 202. **Drafted:** Arizona State (4th round). **Signed by:** Joey Lothrop.

TRACK RECORD: A teammate of Spencer Torkelson's at Arizona State, Workman quietly shined in Torkelson's shadow and was selected in the fourth round by the Tigers in 2020, the same year they picked Torkelson first overall. After primarily playing third base in college, Workman spent most of his pro debut at shortstop and climbed from Low-A to High-A while showing an intriguing power-speed combination with 55 extra-base hits and 31 stolen bases.

SCOUTING REPORT: Labeled "insanely athletic" by multiple observers, Workman is a defensive stalwart whose offense remains a work in progress. He's a switch-hitter who is significantly better from the left side, but he does flash above-average power from both sides of the plate. He swings and misses too often to be more than an average hitter and will rely on his power to make an impact. Workman is extremely fluid defensively with clean hands, average range and an above-average arm strength. He's an average defender at both shortstop and third base and can play whichever his team needs. Though he's just an average runner, his instincts on the basepaths make him a stolen-base threat.

THE FUTURE: Workman's power and defense give him a path to an everyday job on the left side of the infield. He'll move to Double-A in 2022.

MIKE JANES/FOUR SEAM IMAGES

BA GRADE
50 Risk: High

SCOUTING GRADES:	Hitting: 50	Power: 55	Running: 50	Fielding: 50	Arm: 55

Year	Age	Club (Level)	Lge	AVG	G	AB	R	H	2B	3B	HR	RBI	BB	SO	SB	OBP	SLG
2021	21	Lakeland (LoA)	SEast	.256	51	195	26	50	16	4	3	19	30	60	22	.357	.426
	21	West Michigan (HiA)	Cent	.237	67	257	42	61	21	2	9	39	23	97	9	.302	.440
Minor League Totals (2 years)				.246	118	452	68	111	37	6	12	58	53	157	31	.326	.434

6 TY MADDEN, RHP

Born: Feb. 21, 2000. **B-T:** R-R. **HT:** 6-3. **WT:** 215. **Drafted:** Texas, 2021 (1st round supplemental). **Signed by:** George Schaefer.

TRACK RECORD: A 34th-round pick of the Royals out of high school, Madden spent three years in Texas' starting rotation and won Big 12 Conference pitcher of the year in 2021. Expected to be one of the top pitchers selected in the draft, he instead slid to the supplemental first round, where the Tigers excitedly scooped him up with the 32nd overall pick and signed him for an above-slot $2.5 million bonus. The Tigers opted not to send him to an affiliate after he pitched 113.2 innings for the Longhorns in the spring.

SCOUTING REPORT: Madden combines top-end velocity with above-average control and is more consistent than most pitchers his age. His fastball sits 94-96 mph and touches 99 mph and is extremely effective when he pitches down in the zone with it. He complements his heater with a plus slider in the mid-80s that draws swings and misses and rounds out his arsenal with a developing curveball with solid depth and changeup with late fade, both of which project to be average pitches. Madden gets hit when he pitches up in the zone, so keeping the ball down is paramount to his success. He throws plenty of strikes and is a confident, poised presence on the mound.

THE FUTURE: Madden's struggles pitching up in the zone raise questions, but his arsenal and demeanor are more than enough for him to be a solid back-end starter. He is set to make his pro debut in 2022 and could rise up the system quickly.

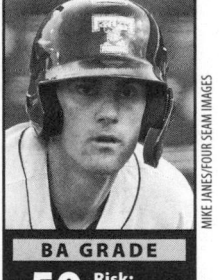

EDDIE KELLY/PROLOOK PHOTOS

BA GRADE

50 Risk: High

SCOUTING GRADES:	Fastball: 60	Slider: 60	Curveball: 50	Changeup: 50	Control: 55

Year	Age	Club (Level)	Lge	W	L	ERA	G	GS	IP	H	HR	BB	SO	BB/9	SO/9	WHIP	AVG
2021	21	Did not play															

7 RYAN KREIDLER, SS

Born: Nov. 12, 1997. **B-T:** R-R. **HT:** 6-4. **WT:** 208. **Drafted:** UCLA, 2019 (4th round). **Signed by:** Tim McWilliam.

TRACK RECORD: The son of sports writer and author Mark Kreidler, Ryan long drew raves for his defense but didn't hit until his junior year at UCLA. The Tigers drafted him in the fourth round in 2019 and signed him for $517,400. Kreidler spent 2020 at the Tigers alternate training site and emerged as a vastly improved hitter in 2021. He hit .270 with 22 home runs, 58 RBIs and 15 stolen bases between Double-A Erie and Triple-A Toledo and became the fastest-rising prospect in the Tigers system.

SCOUTING REPORT: Kreidler is a strong, physical presence at 6-foot-4, 208 pounds and is impressively athletic for his size. He has a quick first step, moves extremely well with light feet and is a cerebral defender with excellent instincts and a knack for reading swings. His soft hands and plus arm strength make him a plus defender anywhere on the infield, and he often sets the defense with his natural leadership qualities. Kreidler generates plus raw power with ease and has improved his ability to get to it, but he swings and misses too often against better pitching and projects to be a below-average hitter. His average speed and solid instincts make him a base-stealing threat.

THE FUTURE: Kreidler's infield defense and power make him a strong utility candidate, and he could be a starter if he keeps improving offensively. He is in position to make his debut in 2022.

MIKE JANES/FOUR SEAM IMAGES

BA GRADE

50 Risk: High

SCOUTING GRADES:	Hitting: 40	Power: 55	Running: 50	Fielding: 60	Arm: 60

Year	Age	Club (Level)	Lge	AVG	G	AB	R	H	2B	3B	HR	RBI	BB	SO	SB	OBP	SLG
2021	23	Erie (AA)	NEast	.256	88	347	67	89	15	0	15	36	32	119	10	.325	.429
	23	Toledo (AAA)	East	.304	41	135	28	41	8	0	7	22	24	39	5	.407	.519
Minor League Totals (3 years)				.258	189	710	123	183	36	4	24	78	76	219	24	.336	.421

8 ROBERTO CAMPOS, OF

Born: June 14, 2003. **B-T:** R-R. **HT:** 6-3. **WT:** 200. **Signed:** Cuba, 2019. **Signed by:** Aldo Perez/Oliver Arias.

TRACK RECORD: Campos was one of the top amateur players in Cuba before he left the country at age 16 to train in the Dominican Republic and showcase himself for MLB teams. The Tigers signed him for $2.85 million in 2019, the largest international signing bonus they awarded that year. Campos' pro debut was delayed by the coronavirus pandemic, but he finally got his career underway in 2021 in the Florida Complex League. He hit just .221 but also showed his power with eight home runs and a .441 slugging percentage in the FCL.

SCOUTING REPORT: Campos has a frame physically developed beyond his years. He already stands 6-foot-3, 200 pounds and still has room to get even bigger and stronger. Campos is a power hitter first and foremost. He has the bat speed and strength to drive the ball out to any part of the field and boasts plus raw power that could still tick up as he matures. Campos shows flashes of advanced instincts in the batter's box but still has some edges that need polishing. He doesn't strike out often but is still learning what pitches he can drive. Campos is an average runner who may slow down as he gets bigger. He plays center field now but projects to move to right, where his above-average arm strength will fit.

THE FUTURE: Campos is set to make his full-season debut with Low-A Lakeland in 2022. His ascent will be more of a slow and steady progression than a quick rise, but he has a chance to be an everyday corner outfielder if everything clicks.

MIKE JANES/FOUR SEAM IMAGES

BA GRADE

55 Risk: Extreme

SCOUTING GRADES:	Hitting: 50	Power: 55	Running: 45	Fielding: 50	Arm: 55

Year	Age	Club (Level)	Lge	AVG	G	AB	R	H	2B	3B	HR	RBI	BB	SO	SB	OBP	SLG
2021	18	Tigers West (R)	FCL	.228	39	136	20	31	5	0	8	19	17	41	3	.316	.441
Minor League Totals (1 year)				.228	39	136	20	31	5	0	8	19	17	41	3	.316	.441

9 JOEY WENTZ, LHP

Born: Oct. 6, 1997. **B-T:** L-L. **HT:** 6-5. **WT:** 220. **Drafted:** HS—Prairie Village, Kan., 2016 (1st round supplemental). **Signed by:** Nate Dion (Braves).

TRACK RECORD: The Tigers acquired Wentz in the 2019 trade that sent Shane Greene to the Braves, but the lefthander suffered an elbow injury shortly after that required Tommy John surgery. He returned to the mound in 2021 and went an unsightly 0-7, 4.50 in 18 starts between High-A and Double-A, but he struck out 10.3 batters per nine innings and got better as the year went on.

SCOUTING REPORT: Wentz is a big, physical presence at 6-foot-5, 220 pounds and has feel to manipulate his three-pitch mix and keep opposing batters on the defensive. His low-90s fastball plays up with late life and pairs well with his above-average, mid-80s changeup. He mixes in an average curveball with late break and mixes his pitches to keep batters guessing. Wentz's control has long been fringe-average and he is erratic in general. He will often cruise for three or four innings before unraveling.

THE FUTURE: Wentz is still young and could see his stuff tick up as he moves farther away from surgery. He projects as a back-end starter who caps at five innings or a long reliever.

BA GRADE

50 Risk: High

SCOUTING GRADES:	Fastball: 55	Curveball: 50	Changeup: 55	Control: 45

Year	Age	Club (Level)	Lge	W	L	ERA	G	GS	IP	H	HR	BB	SO	BB/9	SO/9	WHIP	AVG
2021	23	Lakeland (LoA)	SEast	0	3	6.75	5	5	18	23	5	8	24	3.9	11.6	1.66	.311
	23	Erie (AA)	NEast	0	4	3.71	13	13	53	41	7	33	58	5.6	9.8	1.39	.209
Minor League Totals (6 years)				19	26	3.43	97	97	443	356	35	185	477	3.76	9.68	1.22	.222

10 IZAAC PACHECO, SS

Born: Nov. 18, 2002. **B-T:** L-R. **HT:** 6-4. **WT:** 225.
Drafted: HS—Friendswood, Texas, 2021 (2nd round). **Signed by:** George Schaefer.
TRACK RECORD: Pacheco showed some of the biggest power in the high school class but also swung and missed more than ideal. The Tigers took the optimistic view and drafted Pacheco in the second round, No. 39 overall, and signed him for an above-slot $2.75 million to forgo a Texas A&M commitment. Pacheco made his pro debut in the Florida Complex League after signing and showed impressive physicality and raw power, but he hit just .226 with one home run and a 34% strikeout rate.
SCOUTING REPORT: Pacheco is every bit of 6-foot-4, 225 pounds and has a powerful lefthanded swing. He looks for pitches on the inner half of the plate and turns on them with giant hacks, sometimes rotating and landing on one knee a la Adrian Beltre. He has plus-plus raw power, solid bat speed and natural loft in his swing. How much Pacheco will get to his power is in question. He recognizes pitches, but struggles with anything on the outer half and swings and misses an inordinate amount. He projects to be no more than a below-average hitter and has substantial gains to make to get there. Pacheco plays a solid shortstop for his large frame with clean hands and plus arm strength, but his future home is third base, where he could be an above-average defender.
THE FUTURE: Pacheco's biggest challenge will be proving he can make enough contact to get to his power. If he can, he has to be a dangerous lefthanded power threat in the Tigers' lineup.

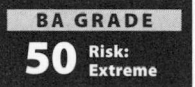

MIKE JANES/FOUR SEAM IMAGES

BA GRADE
55 Risk: **Extreme**

SCOUTING GRADES:	Hitting: 40	Power: 55	Running: 45	Fielding: 55	Arm: 60

Year	Age	Club (Level)	Lge	AVG	G	AB	R	H	2B	3B	HR	RBI	BB	SO	SB	OBP	SLG
2021	18	Tigers West (R)	FCL	.226	30	106	16	24	4	2	1	7	18	43	1	.339	.330
Minor League Totals (1 year)				.226	30	106	16	24	4	2	1	7	18	43	1	.339	.330

11 CRISTIAN SANTANA, SS

BA GRADE
50 Risk: **Extreme**

Born: Nov. 25, 2003. **B-T:** R-R **HT:** 6-0. **WT:** 165. **Signed:** Dominican Republic, 2021. **Signed by:** Aldo Perez/Carlos Santana
TRACK RECORD: The Tigers persistently tracked Santana's progress as an amateur in the Dominican Republic and signed him to a team-record $2.95 million bonus when the 2021 international signing period opened. He rewarded the club's renewed focus on the international market by performing well in his Dominican Summer League debut, hitting .269/.421/.520 in 54 games.
SCOUTING REPORT: Santana is already showing signs of developing into a future impact bat. He has an advanced approach at the plate, mature pitch recognition and a fluid swing that leads to loads of hard contact. He posted exit velocities up to 106 mph in the DSL, an impressive number for an 18-year-old, and his swing is geared toward lifting the ball in the air. He'll need to continue to grow into his frame to tap into more power, but the foundation is there. He projects as a future average infielder defensively with advanced footwork and instincts beyond his years. Santana's arm is average, but his quickness and natural feel allow him to navigate the infield with ease.
THE FUTURE: Santana's development path is going to take a long time and the Tigers don't plan to expedite it, but he shows exciting hitting qualities.

Year	Age	Club (Level)	Lge	AVG	G	AB	R	H	2B	3B	HR	RBI	BB	SO	SB	OBP	SLG
2021	17	Tigers (R)	DSL	.269	54	171	40	46	12	2	9	27	30	46	12	.421	.520
Minor League Totals (1 year)				.269	54	171	40	46	12	2	9	27	30	46	12	.421	.520

12 MANUEL SEQUERA, SS

BA GRADE
50 Risk: **Extreme**

Born: Sept. 28, 2002. **B-T:** R-R. **HT:** 6-1. **WT:** 170. **Signed:** Venezuela, 2019. **Signed by:** Jesus Mendoza
TRACK RECORD: Considered by many to be one Detroit's top signings during the 2019 international signing period. Sequera added strength over the shutdown and re-emerged a power hitting shortstop likely to move off of the position. He spent the summer in the Florida Complex League with the Tigers East squad, winning the circuit's home run title and ranking No. 8 on the FCL Top 10 Prospects list.
SCOUTING REPORT: A physical player with a broad shouldered power hitter's build. The added muscle and physicality manifested itself in big power numbers for Sequera, as he showed a knack for the barrel,

deploying a simple, fluid righthanded swing with natural loft, and few moving parts outside a pronounced leg kick. The simplicity of Sequera's load allows him to adjust to pitch height and sit back on breaking balls. His bat-to-ball skills are above-average, and enough to overcome aggressive, and at times immature swing decisions. As this area of Sequera's game adds refinement his strikeout numbers should decrease. In the field Sequera is limited by a lack of range. He made 39 starts at shortstop this summer, but looks likely to move off of the position long term. He projects to move to third base where his strong throwing arm should suffice. A below-average runner, Sequera's game is predicated on hard contact and bat-to-ball skills. **THE FUTURE:** With a strong debut season under his belt, Sequera should see assignment to Low-A Lakeland out of camp, where he's likely to see time at a variety of spots in the infield. His combination of feel to hit, above-average power, and a strong throwing arm give him the look of a potential power-hitting corner infielder.

Year	Age	Club (Level)	Lge	AVG	G	AB	R	H	2B	3B	HR	RBI	BB	SO	SB	OBP	SLG
2021	18	Tigers East (R)	FCL	.246	46	171	31	42	12	0	11	40	15	57	1	.314	.509
Minor League Totals (1 year)				.246	46	171	31	42	12	0	11	40	15	57	1	.314	.509

13 COLT KEITH, 3B

BA GRADE
50 Risk: Extreme

Born: Aug. 14, 2001. **B-T:** L-R. **HT:** 6-3. **WT:** 211. **Drafted:** HS—Biloxi, Miss., 2020 (5th round). **Signed by:** Mike Smith.

TRACK RECORD: The Tigers nabbed Keith, the 2019 Mississippi High School Player of the Year, for $500,000 in the fifth round of the 2020 draft. The pandemic delayed his pro debut to 2021, when Keith slashed .286/.396/.393 at three levels, reaching High-A West Michigan by the end of the season.

SCOUTING REPORT: Keith was a legitimate two-way prospect in high school at both shortstop and pitcher. He hasn't pitched so far as a professional—Detroit likes his profile at third base long-term—but it's easy to see his natural athleticism. He shows a plus arm at third base while continuing to develop feel for the position. He also flashes plus run times, although he's likely to settle in as an average runner. Offensively, Keith showed impressive bat-to-ball skills amid a challenging assignment. He hit just two homers, but scouts still believe there's plus raw power in his lefthanded swing. Much of Keith's development hinges on continued maturation of his approach while also tapping into his power more consistently as his frame fills out.

THE FUTURE: Detroit's crowded pool of infield prospects may ultimately push Keith to an outfield spot, but he has the upside of an everyday big leaguer.

Year	Age	Club (Level)	Lge	AVG	G	AB	R	H	2B	3B	HR	RBI	BB	SO	SB	OBP	SLG
2021	19	Tigers East (R)	FCL	.714	2	7	2	5	1	0	0	4	3	0	0	.800	.857
	19	Tigers West (R)	FCL	.500	1	2	0	1	0	1	0	1	0	0	0	.333	1.500
	19	Lakeland (LoA)	SEast	.320	44	147	32	47	6	3	1	21	30	39	4	.436	.422
	19	West Michigan (HiA)	Cent	.162	18	68	7	11	1	1	1	6	8	27	0	.250	.250
Minor League Totals (2 years)				.286	65	224	41	64	8	5	2	32	41	66	4	.396	.393

14 DYLAN SMITH, RHP

BA GRADE
45 Risk: High

Born: May 28, 2000. **B-T:** R-R. **HT:** 6-2. **WT:** 180. **Drafted:** Alabama, 2021 (3rd round). **Signed by:** Mike Smith.

TRACK RECORD: Smith emerged as Alabama's ace during his junior spring and the Tigers made him their third-round selection in the 2021 draft and signed him to an above-slot bonus of $1.12 million. Smith, who was initially drafted by the Padres in 2018 out of high school, steadily added muscle to his projectable frame and watched his fastball velocity tick up throughout college.

SCOUTING REPORT: Smith reportedly added 30 pounds of good weight in college and his fastball now touches 95 mph while sitting comfortably in the 92-93 mph range. He shows hitters a four-pitch mix, but scouts believe his slider is his strongest secondary offering. It's a mid-to-upper 80s pitch with slurvy shape that Smith uses as a putaway pitch. Scouts see his work-in-progress changeup developing into a fringe-average pitch, and his low-80s curveball has shown good depth, working in tandem with his four-seam to keep hitters off balance. Smith was a reliever his first two years at Alabama before moving to the starting rotation following an improvement in command of his arsenal entering the 2021 spring.

THE FUTURE: Set to make his pro debut in 2022, Smith needs to prove to scouts those command gains can hold in the pro ranks. If he does, he'll remain on a starter's track.

Year	Age	Club (Level)	Lge	W	L	ERA	G	GS	IP	H	HR	BB	SO	BB/9	SO/9	WHIP	AVG
2021	21	Did not play															

15 REESE OLSON, RHP

BA GRADE **45** Risk: High

Born: July 31, 1999. **B-T:** R-R. **HT:** 6-1. **WT:** 160.
Drafted: HS—Gainesville, Ga., 2018 (13th round). **Signed by:** Steve Smith (Brewers).
TRACK RECORD: Olson was drafted by the Brewers in 2018 and then dealt to the Tigers at the 2021 trade deadline in exchange for lefthander Daniel Norris. Prior to the deal, Olson posted a 4.30 ERA at Milwaukee's High-A Wisconsin affiliate, the same club he pitched for in 2019 when it was previously a Low-A affiliate. Detroit promoted him to Double-A Erie shortly after the trade, where he made five starts.
SCOUTING REPORT: Olson's four-pitch mix grabs the attention of scouts, but so does his violent delivery and inconsistent command. He attacks hitters with a mid-90s fastball and scouts believe there's still room for a touch more velocity. However, despite above-average velocity, the pitch lacks movement, and deception at release. He mixes a trio of strong secondaries that all generated whiffs at a rate of 40% or higher in 2021. The best of that group is an above-average changeup with heavy fade and tumble, generating both ground balls and whiffs at a high rate. His pair of breaking balls show distinctive shape and sharp break. His low-80s sweeper slider sees higher usage than the curveball in large part due to its dominance against righthanded hitters. His curveball is a mid-to-high-70s downer, with two-plane break, and is used primarily versus lefthanders as an alternative to his changeup. Olson needs to demonstrate more consistent command of his arsenal to project long term in a starting role, as he walked nearly 12% of hitters with High-A Wisconsin in 2021.
THE FUTURE: There's considerable reliever risk, but due to Olson's fastball velocity and deep quality mix of secondaries he could become an effective multi-inning relief option down the road.

Year	Age	Club (Level)	Lge	W	L	ERA	G	GS	IP	H	HR	BB	SO	BB/9	SO/9	WHIP	AVG
2021	21	Wisconsin (HiA)	Cent	5	4	4.30	14	14	69	58	5	35	79	4.6	10.3	1.35	.228
	21	West Michigan (HiA)	Cent	1	0	0.00	2	2	11	6	0	2	14	1.6	11.5	0.73	.154
	21	Erie (AA)	NEast	2	1	4.74	5	5	24	18	1	14	21	5.1	7.7	1.30	.202
Minor League Totals (4 years)				12	14	4.34	52	37	210	197	14	102	204	4.38	8.76	1.43	.249

16 DANIEL CABRERA, OF

BA GRADE **45** Risk: High

Born: Sept. 5, 1998. **B-T:** L-L. **HT:** 6-3. **WT:** 200. **Drafted:** Louisiana State, 2020 (2nd round supplemental). **Signed by:** Mike Smith.
TRACK RECORD: Cabrera was a consistent three-year performer in college at Louisiana State, and the Tigers knew him well when they made him their second-round selection in 2020 thanks to general manager Al Avila's connection to the program. Cabrera posted a .910 OPS and hit 22 homers as an amateur in the SEC, but his professional debut wasn't particularly powerful. He hit .242/.300/.395 in 99 games with High-A West Michigan and struggled mightily after being promoted to Double-A Erie, hitting .174 in 17 games.
SCOUTING REPORT: Cabrera lacks a true carrying tool, but he's always impressed scouts with a fluid lefthanded swing, solid hand-eye coordination and bat speed. His approach was tested at times in 2021, especially against upper-level pitching, and he's susceptible to effective breaking balls when his swing mechanics fall out of sync. His swing is heavily hands driven which can lead to a variety of timing issues, and professional pitchers exploited this. Defensively, Cabrera worked hard to improve his athleticism to the point where he's a viable option in right field in addition to left field. Despite his average speed, Cabrera boasts above-average arm strength and advanced instincts which boost his overall fielding grade.
THE FUTURE: Set to turn 24 years old in September, Cabrera was considered a potential quick-mover as an amateur, but he'll need to refine his eye to jump back on a fast track.

Year	Age	Club (Level)	Lge	AVG	G	AB	R	H	2B	3B	HR	RBI	BB	SO	SB	OBP	SLG
2021	22	West Michigan (HiA)	Cent	.242	99	380	54	92	19	6	9	64	34	95	7	.300	.395
	22	Erie (AA)	NEast	.174	17	69	8	12	2	0	4	9	1	18	1	.197	.377
Minor League Totals (2 years)				.232	116	449	62	104	21	6	13	73	35	113	8	.285	.392

17 KODY CLEMENS, 2B

BA GRADE **40** Risk: High

Born: May 15, 1996. **B-T:** L-R. **HT:** 6-1. **WT:** 170. **Drafted:** Texas, 2018 (3rd round). **Signed by:** Mike Lea.
TRACK RECORD: The son of seven-time Cy Young Award winner Roger Clemens, Kody was the 2018 Big 12 Conference player of the year at Texas. Detroit drafted the younger Clemens in the third round of the 2018 draft and signed him to a $600,000 bonus. His development has been slow, but he reached Triple-A Toledo in 2021 and was added to the 40-man roster after the season.

SCOUTING REPORT: Clemens is touted for his raw power and aggressive infield defense. He logged the bulk of his defensive action at second base, where he showed a quick first step and above-average instincts. Clemens' arm isn't flashy, but his accuracy and quick release balance that out. He also spent time in right field for the first time as a professional. It took Clemens some time to rediscover his natural raw power, but he ultimately hit a career-best 18 homers with Toledo, showing improved ability to hit to all fields with a fluid line-drive stroke. It's above-average raw power, but his flatter bat path leads to a high rate of ground balls. Further adjustments to add more loft to his barrel at contact could reap the rewards a high average exit velocity of 90.4 mph usually produces.

THE FUTURE: Clemens will need to show his bat can continue to adjust to upper-level pitching in 2022.

Year	Age	Club (Level)	Lge	AVG	G	AB	R	H	2B	3B	HR	RBI	BB	SO	SB	OBP	SLG
2021	25	Lakeland (LoA)	SEast	.182	3	11	0	2	0	0	0	2	0	4	0	.182	.182
2021	25	Toledo (AAA)	East	.247	97	369	66	91	15	6	18	59	36	94	4	.312	.466
Minor League Totals (3 years)				.247	280	1029	138	254	53	15	35	144	110	256	19	.320	.430

18 BEAU BRIESKE, RHP

BA GRADE
40 Risk: High

Born: April 5, 1998. **B-T:** R-R. **HT:** 6-3. **WT:** 200. **Drafted:** Colorado State-Pueblo, 2019 (27th round). **Signed by:** Joey Lothrop

TRACK RECORD: Following a pedestrian high school career, mostly as an outfielder, Brieske grew three inches during his freshman year at Glendale Community College and converted to full-time pitching. He transferred to Division II Colorado State-Pueblo his junior season and struck out 116 batters across 79.2 innings. The Tigers selected Brieske in the 27th round of the 2019 draft.

SCOUTING REPORT: Brieske made the most of the time allotted by the shutdown of 2020, connecting with his junior college pitching coach and following a rigorous regiment. Assigned to High-A West Michigan out of minor league camp, evaluators saw not only improved stuff, but pitchability and feel for the game. Mixing a four-pitch arsenal led by a fastball sitting 92-95 mph with above-average spin and ride, Brieske works the top of the zone with his heater before attacking low gloveside with a tight slider in the mid 80s and low armside with a changeup in the low 80s. The changeup is an above-average offering with hard armside run and an average of over 10 mph of separation from his fastball. Early in counts he'll show a 12-6 curveball in the mid-to-high 70s, but it's a fringe pitch used to change hitters' eye levels.

THE FUTURE: A combination of three average or better pitches, above-average command, and a brilliant understanding of sequencing, Brieske has quickly developed into a legitimate starting pitching prospect as he enters 2022. Brieske should return to Double-A Erie to begin the season after making eight strong starts there in 2021.

Year	Age	Club (Level)	Lge	W	L	ERA	G	GS	IP	H	HR	BB	SO	BB/9	SO/9	WHIP	AVG
2021	23	West Michigan (HiA)	Cent	6	3	3.45	13	13	62	49	5	15	76	2.2	10.9	1.02	.213
2021	23	Erie (AA)	NEast	3	1	2.66	8	8	44	36	2	8	40	1.6	8.2	1.00	.225
Minor League Totals (3 years)				12	5	3.12	32	21	127	98	9	33	147	2.34	10.42	1.03	.214

19 TYLER MATTISON, RHP

BA GRADE
40 Risk: High

Born: September 5, 1999. **B-T:** R-R. **HT:** 6-4. **WT:** 235. **Drafted:** Bryant, 2021 (4th round). **Signed by:** Jim Bretz

TRACK RECORD: The Tigers were sold on Mattison's increased velocity and power pitcher's build, selecting the Northeast Conference's Pitcher of the Year in the fourth round of the 2021 draft out of Bryant for an under-slot $400,000 bonus. Mattison is the highest draft pick in Bryant history. He did not make his professional debut in 2021.

SCOUTING REPORT: Scouts highlighted the uptick in velocity early in 2021, noting Mattison seemed more confident attacking the strike zone. His fastball sits in the 92-95 mph range and touches 97 mph with natural downhill plane, and Mattison held his velocity deep into starts. Scouts view Mattison's changeup as his strongest secondary, and it pairs well with his curveball. Both have solid-average potential. He also added a cutter/slider hybrid into his arsenal, but threw it less frequently and scouts think he needs to gain more confidence in the offering. Mattison repeats his delivery well, throwing all his pitches from a high arm slot.

SCOUTING REPORT: Mattison is already one of the more advanced college pitchers in the Tigers' pipeline and will likely open the 2022 season at High-A West Michigan. Considering his age and evolving arsenal, Mattison could move quickly through Detroit's system.

Year	Age	Club (Level)	Lge	W	L	ERA	G	GS	IP	H	HR	BB	SO	BB/9	SO/9	WHIP	AVG
2021	21	Did not play															

 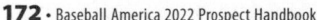

20 ALEX FAEDO, RHP

BA GRADE

40 Risk: High

Born: Nov. 12, 1995. **B-T:** R-R. **HT:** 6-5. **WT:** 225. **Drafted:** Florida, 2017 (1st round). **Signed by:** RJ Burgess.

TRACK RECORD: Faedo was named the Most Outstanding Player in the 2017 College World Series in his final season at Florida, and it was no surprise when the Tigers locked him in as their first-round selection in 2017 for $3.5 million. Injuries, including Tommy John surgery as well as a positive test for Covid-19, and ineffectiveness have plagued Faedo's career to this point. He hasn't pitched since 2019, when he struck out 134 hitters with Double-A Erie. The figure ranked third among all Tigers prospects that season, behind only Tarik Skubal and Matt Manning.

SCOUTING REPORT: Since his days at Florida, Faedo's slider has always been his signature pitch. There was concern early in his professional career about a drop in his fastball velocity, but the pitch slowly worked back to its previous form. With those two pitches Faedo also blends a changeup that was below-average at the close of the 2019 season. There were also questions about how much his unorthodox delivery would hinder the progression of his command and control.

THE FUTURE: Faedo's rehab work will dictate his future with the Tigers, and there's a growing likelihood he transitions to a relief role once he returns.

Year	Age	Club (Level)	Lge	W	L	ERA	G	GS	IP	H	HR	BB	SO	BB/9	SO/9	WHIP	AVG
2021	25	Did not play—Injured															
Minor League Totals (3 years)				11	17	3.96	46	46	236.1	207	35	60	244	2.28	9.29	1.13	.232

21 JASON FOLEY, RHP

BA GRADE

40 Risk: High

Born: Nov. 1, 1995. **B-T:** R-R. **HT:** 6-4. **WT:** 215. **Signed:** Sacred Heart, 2016 (NDFA). **Signed by:** Jim Bretz

TRACK RECORD: The Tigers signed Foley, who was college teammates at Sacred Heart with Tigers infielder Zack Short, as a nondrafted free agent. Scouts were impressed by a velocity spike that led to regular triple-digit readings. Foley broke out with Class-A West Michigan in 2017, but Tommy John surgery cost him his 2018 season. The pandemic wiped out 2020, but Foley made his big league debut in June 2021.

SCOUTING REPORT: Foley's signature is unquestionably his plus fastball, which has regained its upper-90s velocity since surgery. Despite premium velocity, hitters timed Foley's four-seam fastball fairly well in the minors, and he worked with the Tigers to add a two-seamer to his repertoire. The pitch features heavy arm-side run and sink, but he's still learning to command the pitch's heavy movement. The two fastball variations played off of each other, allowing his four-seam to play up as a swing-and-miss pitch when elevated. He has gained more confidence in his tight mid-80s slider, which missed bats at a high rate in 2021. He works primarily with a sinker-slider mix, looking to drive weak ground ball contact at a high rate. He'll mix in a split-changeup that misses bats even as he's gaining feel for the pitch.

THE FUTURE: For Foley, the biggest question will be his health. If he's able to maintain longevity, the Tigers should have a dependable relief option for years to come.

Year	Age	Club (Level)	Lge	W	L	ERA	G	GS	IP	H	HR	BB	SO	BB/9	SO/9	WHIP	AVG
2021	25	Toledo (AAA)	East	1	1	4.41	32	0	34	34	5	19	36	4.9	9.4	1.53	.264
2021	25	Detroit (MLB)	AL	0	0	2.61	11	0	10	8	1	5	6	4.4	5.2	1.26	.216
Major League Totals (1 year)				0	0	2.61	11	0	10	8	1	5	6	4.35	5.23	1.26	.216
Minor League Totals (6 years)				7	7	3.60	98	0	122	115	9	50	127	3.68	9.34	1.35	.245

22 WILMER FLORES, RHP

BA GRADE

45 Risk: Very High

Born: Feb. 20, 2001. **B-T:** R-R. **HT:** 6-4. **WT:** 225. **Signed:** Arizona Western, 2020 (NDFA). **Signed by:** Joey Lothrop

TRACK RECORD: The younger brother of major leaguer Wilmer Flores, the righthander signed as a nondrafted free agent in 2020 out of Arizona Western JC. He began his professional career with four appearances in the Florida Complex League before seeing promotion to Low-A Lakeland in mid-July.

SCOUTING REPORT: Flores deploys a four-pitch arsenal that leans heavily on a fastball and curveball combination. The fastball is a higher spin four-seam with natural cut sitting 93-95 mph touching 98 mph at peak. He commands the fastball fairly well showing a healthy preference to his armside. His low-80s curveball features 11-5 movement with heavy two-plane break and moderate depth. His command of the pitch comes and goes, but at it's best he can land it on the bottom of the zone to steal strikes, or bury it glove side for chases and whiffs. He throws a high-80s cutter and a mid-80s changeup as well, but each pitch was hit hard in 2021 and grades out as below-average. Evaluators like the power of Flores fastball and curveball combination and can envision the righthander settling into a middle relief role.

THE FUTURE: The Detroit scouting department did a good job identifying Flores' upside and signed him as an NDFA. He rewarded the organization with a strong performance across a pair of levels. With high octane stuff and the ability to miss bats and throw strikes, Flores has the look of a feature middle relief arm used in single inning appearances.

Year	Age	Club (Level)	Lge	W	L	ERA	G	GS	IP	H	HR	BB	SO	BB/9	SO/9	WHIP	AVG
2021	20	Tigers West (R)	FCL	2	1	4.85	3	2	13	15	0	2	18	1.4	12.5	1.31	.288
	20	Lakeland (LoA)	SEast	4	3	3.40	11	11	53	47	1	22	72	3.7	12.2	1.30	.239
Minor League Totals (1 year)				6	4	3.68	14	13	66.0	62	1	24	90	3.27	12.27	1.30	.249

23 JOSE DE LA CRUZ, OF

BA GRADE

45 Risk: Extreme

Born: Jan. 3, 2002. **B-T:** R-R. **HT:** 6-0. **WT:** 216. **Signed:** Dominican Republic, 2018. **Signed by:** Aldo Perez/Carlos Santana.

TRACK RECORD: De la Cruz's $1.8 million bonus was the largest of any Tigers 2018 international signing. He dazzled in his Dominican Summer League debut the next summer, slashing .307/.375/.556 with 11 home runs. He impressed again in the Rookie-level Florida Complex League in 2021, earning a promotion to Low-A Lakeland, where he hit .127 in 39 games.

SCOUTING REPORT: De la Cruz has drawn praise for his all-out style of play and intriguing mix of tools. He has the ability to produce hard contact thanks to his plus bat speed, but it comes with plenty of swing-and-miss. De la Cruz's strikeout rates hovered around 30% in rookie ball and ballooned to 46.8% in his first taste of Low-A. Still, De la Cruz was just 19 years old and some scouts are optimistic he'll cut that number down with more reps. Defensively, De la Cruz boasts plus speed and a plus arm, which profiles well across the outfield. Some scouts seem to believe right field could be the best fit for him as he fills out.

THE FUTURE: After getting his feet wet with Lakeland in 2021, De la Cruz's chances of advancing depend strongly on cutting his strikeout rate.

Year	Age	Club (Level)	Lge	AVG	G	AB	R	H	2B	3B	HR	RBI	BB	SO	SB	OBP	SLG
2021	19	Tigers East (R)	FCL	.270	44	159	20	43	9	1	4	15	17	58	7	.361	.415
	19	Lakeland (LoA)	SEast	.127	39	142	15	18	3	1	1	10	10	74	6	.209	.183
Minor League Totals (2 years)				.247	139	526	90	130	25	7	16	64	45	207	29	.327	.413

24 ADINSO REYES, SS

BA GRADE

45 Risk: Extreme

Born: Oct. 22, 2001. **B-T:** R-R. **HT:** 6-1. **WT:** 195. **Signed:** Dominican Republic, 2018. **Signed by:** Aldo Perez.

TRACK RECORD: The Tigers signed Reyes to a $1.45 million bonus in 2018, coveting his natural strength and projectable frame. He debuted the following year in the Dominican Summer League and hit .331/.379/.508. The missed year of development in 2020 didn't help the 20-year-old, who struggled in 2021, hitting a combined .184/.272/.356 during his time in the Rookie-level Florida Complex League.

SCOUTING REPORT: There's plenty to dream on with Reyes. In addition to his pure strength, Reyes has a knack for hard contact and flashes the ability to drive the ball to all fields. He's still a work in progress at the plate with several elements of his swing and approach needing refinement. Reyes' overly aggressive approach and downward bat path are both potential areas of improvement, and he chased pitches outside the zone at an alarming rate of 47.4%. His naturally long swing led to a high rate of in-zone swing and miss and his habit of chopping downward led to a near 50% ground ball rate. He struggled mightily versus breaking balls, but did show the ability to handle velocity. Defensively, evaluators are optimistic he can handle shortstop because of his arm strength and smooth footwork, but note he has the athleticism to handle third base if his size pushes him in that direction.

THE FUTURE: Reyes has upside, but he'll have to make significant adjustments to his swing and approach. He's expected to move through the system slowly.

Year	Age	Club (Level)	Lge	AVG	G	AB	R	H	2B	3B	HR	RBI	BB	SO	SB	OBP	SLG
2021	19	Tigers East (R)	FCL	.244	12	41	5	10	2	0	2	6	4	13	0	.326	.439
	19	Tigers West (R)	FCL	.164	36	122	16	20	5	0	5	12	8	60	1	.254	.328
Minor League Totals (2 years)				.272	110	405	65	110	27	1	14	66	26	124	4	.336	.447

25 ELIEZER ALFONZO, C

BA GRADE
40 Risk: High

Born: Sept. 23, 1999. **B-T:** B-R. **HT:** 5-10. **WT:** 155. **Signed:** Venezuela, 2016. **Signed by:** Alejandro Rodriguez/Raul Leiva.

TRACK RECORD: Alfonzo has quietly drawn praise for his developmental progress since signing with Detroit out of Venezuela in 2016, especially after breaking out in the Dominican Summer League in 2018 by hitting .391/.485/.500 in 33 games. He split his time between Low-A Lakeland and High-A West Michigan in 2021, hitting .287 with eight homers between the two levels.

SCOUTING REPORT: Alfonzo moves more quickly than his solid frame might suggest and can add more defensive polish if he continues to keep his weight in check. In 59 games behind the plate, Alfonzo allowed just one passed ball. At the plate, he has solid bat-to-ball skills and a compact swing geared to contact. He doesn't walk much, and needs to shore up his approach against more advanced pitching, especially against breaking stuff. Coaches who have worked with Alfonzo point out his natural leadership ability.

THE FUTURE: After posting respectable production at High-A West Michigan in 2021, Alfonzo is expected to return to the level to start 2022.

Year	Age	Club (Level)	Lge	AVG	G	AB	R	H	2B	3B	HR	RBI	BB	SO	SB	OBP	SLG
2021	21	Lakeland (LoA)	SEast	.308	39	156	25	48	7	1	7	29	12	11	2	.363	.500
	21	West Michigan (HiA)	Cent	.272	59	213	21	58	11	0	1	26	16	24	1	.319	.338
Minor League Totals (5 years)				.304	253	878	115	267	40	3	10	126	91	87	16	.370	.391

26 PARKER MEADOWS, OF

BA GRADE
40 Risk: High

Born: Nov. 2, 1999. **B-T:** L-R. **HT:** 6-5. **WT:** 205. **Drafted:** HS—Loganville, Ga., 2018 (2nd round). **Signed by:** Bryson Barber.

TRACK RECORD: Meadows is the younger brother of current Rays outfielder Austin Meadows. Parker, who was drafted in the second round in 2018, has yet to put it all together offensively and spent nearly all of 2021 with High-A West Michigan, hitting .208/.290/.330 over 94 games.

SCOUTING REPORT: The Tigers may be waiting for the bat to come around, but there's no denying the defensive potential. Few outfielders have the ability to move as well as Meadows. He produces some of the fastest sprint speeds in the system, and his advanced routes and instincts allow him to handle center field without issue. He also has a plus arm. Offensively, Meadows has struggled to shorten his naturally long swing. While Meadows has plenty of raw power, he has yet to tap into it on a regular basis.

THE FUTURE: Meadows is one of the best defensive outfielders in the system, but he needs to start hitting consistently.

Year	Age	Club (Level)	Lge	AVG	G	AB	R	H	2B	3B	HR	RBI	BB	SO	SB	OBP	SLG
2021	21	Lakeland (LoA)	SEast	.273	3	11	2	3	1	0	0	1	0	3	0	.333	.364
	21	West Michigan (HiA)	Cent	.208	94	355	50	74	15	2	8	44	37	99	9	.290	.330
Minor League Totals (4 years)				.224	251	902	124	202	34	5	19	95	94	246	26	.303	.336

27 ABEL BASTIDAS, SS

BA GRADE
45 Risk: Extreme

Born: No. 24, 2003. **B-T:** S-R. **HT:** 6-2. **WT:** 165. **Signed:** Venezuela, 2021. **Signed by:** Jesus Mendoza

TRACK RECORD: The Tigers thought highly enough of Bastidas to sign him to a $1.175 million bonus, the second-largest deal in their 2021 international signing class. He appeared in 54 games with Detroit's Dominican Summer League team, slashing .188/.324/.276.

SCOUTING REPORT: Bastidas is still in the early stages of his development, but it's clear his bat is going to be the focal point as his body fills out. He produces a fluid swing from both sides of the plate and showed good hand-eye coordination as an amateur. He doesn't impact the ball with much authority now, but there's plenty of physical projection left on his long and lanky frame, and scouts project potential for future average power. As an amateur, Bastidas trained with Cesar and Maicer Izturis and received praise for his polished defensive profile. Bastidas' slick glove remains intact. He manages the infield with light footwork, an above-average arm, good throwing accuracy and instincts well beyond his years.

THE FUTURE: Detroit is working to bolster its international presence and Bastidas, along with Cristian Santana, represents a strong step forward. Now, Tigers player development must work with Bastidas on his offensive development while his body matures.

Year	Age	Club (Level)	Lge	AVG	G	AB	R	H	2B	3B	HR	RBI	BB	SO	SB	OBP	SLG
2021	17	Tigers (R)	DSL	.188	54	181	24	34	4	3	2	27	35	46	12	.324	.276
Minor League Totals (1 year)				.188	54	181	24	34	4	3	2	27	35	46	12	.324	.276

28 BRYANT PACKARD, OF

Born: Oct. 6, 1997. **B-T:** L-R. **HT:** 6-3. **WT:** 200. **Drafted:** East Carolina, 2019 (5th round). **Signed by:** Taylor Black.

TRACK RECORD: Packard was the American Athletic Conference player of the year as a sophomore at East Carolina, and the Tigers made him their fifth-round pick the next year in 2019. His offensive prowess showed up in his pro debut, when he posted a 162 wRC+ with Low-A West Michigan and advanced to High-A. He returned to High-A in 2021, but hit just .222/.310/.369.

SCOUTING REPORT: Packard has been viewed as a bat-first prospect since his college days. He possesses an advanced, fluid lefthanded stroke and has enough strength in his frame to produce easy raw power. Packard has a polished eye and trimmed his strikeout rate by 2.5% in 2021 compared to 2019. Packard's limited athleticism and lack of speed make him best suited to left field. If that's the case, he'll need to do damage at the plate with consistency. While Packard has earned praise regarding his work ethic, his limited athleticism and lack of speed make his profile best suited for left field. His offense will continue to be his selling tool as long as it stands up against advanced pitching.

THE FUTURE: The Tigers still believe in Packard's bat and are likely to test him in 2022 against upper-level pitching.

Year	Age	Club (Level)	Lge	AVG	G	AB	R	H	2B	3B	HR	RBI	BB	SO	SB	OBP	SLG
2021	23	West Michigan (HiA)	Cent	.222	54	198	30	44	11	0	6	22	17	53	5	.310	.369
Minor League Totals (3 years)				.252	93	333	51	84	19	0	9	38	38	91	7	.344	.390

29 PAUL RICHAN, RHP

Born: March 26, 1997. **B-T:** R-R. **HT:** 6-2. **WT:** 200. **Drafted:** San Diego, 2018 (2nd round supplemental). **Signed by:** Alex Lontayo (Cubs).

TRACK RECORD: The Cubs made Richan their second-round pick in 2018 out of San Diego. He was one of two pitchers dealt to the Tigers in the 2019 Nick Castellanos deal, along with righty Alex Lange. Richan opened 2021 with Double-A Erie, but threw just 29 innings before being placed on the injured list in late June, ending his season.

SCOUTING REPORT: None of Richan's pitches grades as better than average, but his whole arsenal gets a boost thanks to impressive command and a smooth delivery. Richan's fastball sits between 88-92 mph, touching as high as 94 mph. It doesn't generate many whiffs, but Richan locates it well. His primary offspeed is a low-80s slider that gets swings and misses at an above-average rate. Richan also mixes in a curveball and a changeup that are dependable pieces, but lack the impact of his fastball or slider.

THE FUTURE: Richan doesn't have much margin for error, but he has enough control and deception to profile as a potential low-leverage big league relief option.

Year	Age	Club (Level)	Lge	W	L	ERA	G	GS	IP	H	HR	BB	SO	BB/9	SO/9	WHIP	AVG
2021	24	Erie (AA)	NEast	0	0	3.72	8	8	29	25	7	9	26	2.8	8.1	1.17	.234
Minor League Totals (4 years)				12	9	3.65	40	39	182	179	21	34	172	1.68	8.49	1.17	.257

30 ANDRE LIPCIUS, 3B

Born: May 22, 1998. **B-T:** R-R. **HT:** 6-1. **WT:** 190. **Drafted:** Tennessee, 2019 (3rd round). **Signed by:** Harold Zonder.

TRACK RECORD: Lipcius hit 16 homers as a junior at Tennessee in 2019, enticing the Tigers to select the nuclear engineering major in the third round of that year's draft and add him to their strong infield pipeline. That power hasn't translated to pro ball. He's hit just 14 home runs in 677 minor league at-bats and his only slugging percentage better than .400 came in a 22-game sample at High-A this past season.

SCOUTING REPORT: Advanced hand-eye coordination helps Lipcius post consistent contact rates. While scouts see no major flaws in his swing from the right side, there's some question as to whether he'll ever hit for much power. Versatility has been his calling card dating back to his college days at Tennessee, and Lipcius split his time defensively between third base and second base in 2021. He leans on his advanced instincts at both positions and is a fluid defender despite speed that is just average.

THE FUTURE: Lipcius' future depends entirely on his offensive progression, and he faces a crowded infield depth chart at the upper levels of Detroit's system.

Year	Age	Club (Level)	Lge	AVG	G	AB	R	H	2B	3B	HR	RBI	BB	SO	SB	OBP	SLG
2021	23	West Michigan (HiA)	Cent	.277	22	83	14	23	4	2	3	13	12	16	3	.357	.482
	23	Erie (AA)	NEast	.235	94	341	51	80	18	2	9	46	39	82	4	.312	.378
Minor League Totals (3 years)				.254	183	677	97	172	38	4	14	88	78	155	10	.329	.384

MORE PROSPECTS TO KNOW

31. TREI CRUZ, SS

The switch-hitter has shown plus raw power in the past but has yet to turn it into meaningful in-game thump. While he was drafted as a solid defender at shortstop, Cruz's lack of speed leads some scouts to believe he profiles better at second base.

32. DANUERYS DE LA CRUZ, C

SLEEPER

A standout at the plate and behind it in the Florida Complex League, de la Cruz displayed strong catch-and-throw skills, and plus raw power at the plate.

33. TANNER KOHLHEPP, RHP

The Tigers can't seem to say no to big righthanded arms. The 6-foot-4 Kohlhepp was a relief ace at Notre Dame thanks to a sinking fastball that touches the upper 90s and plays up thanks to his arm action. He could move quickly in either a starter or relief role.

34. COOPER JOHNSON, C

Still viewed as one of the top defensive catchers in the farm system with a cannon from behind the plate, all eyes are on Johnson's ability to tap into consistent offense to add more value.

35. ELVIN RODRIGUEZ, RHP

Rodriguez's progression has been slow, but the Tigers saw enough to add him to the 40-man roster to prevent him from becoming a minor league free agent. Rodriguez shows arm strength and a steady mound demeanor, but he may be better suited for a relief role.

36. JACOB ROBSON, OF

The 27-year-old Robson reached the big leagues in 2021 after spending multiple years in the upper levels, and has the speed and athleticism to handle all three outfield positions. He has battled a concerning swing-and-miss rate, though, and the Tigers outrighted Robson off the 40-man roster in November.

37. WILKEL HERNANDEZ, RHP

Hernandez impressed at the alternate site in 2020, but had Tommy John surgery that October and missed all of 2021. Scouts still like his potential, assuming he isn't rushed back too quickly.

38. GARRETT HILL, RHP

Hill stood out at the 2021 Arizona Fall League and is adept at sequencing his four-pitch mix, including a 90-93 mph fastball that plays up because of his deceptive release point. But control and command are still a work in progress for the 25-year-old, who was left unprotected ahead of the Rule 5 draft.

39. AUSTIN MURR, OF

Murr's profile in college was unusual as a contact-oriented first baseman with limited power but impressive on-base skills at North Carolina State. The Tigers played him mostly in the corner outfield in his 2021 debut and he fared well, hitting .319/.440/.393, with one homer, while reaching High-A.

40. ZACK HESS, RHP

The Louisiana State product's development has been slower than expected, but he reached Double-A Erie in 2021. Hess generates plenty of whiffs as a relief option, but also walked 34 batters in 49.2 innings at High-A West Michigan in 2021.

TOP PROSPECTS OF THE DECADE

Year	Player, Pos	2021 Org
2012	Jacob Turner, RHP	Did not play
2013	Nick Castellanos ,3B/OF	Reds
2014	Nick Castellanos, 3B/OF	Reds
2015	Steven Moya, OF	Orix (Japan)
2016	Michael Fulmer, RHP	Tigers
2017	Matt Manning, RHP	Tigers
2018	Franklin Perez, RHP	Tigers
2019	Casey Mize, RHP	Tigers
2020	Casey Mize, RHP	Tigers
2021	Spencer Torkelson, 1B	Tigers

TOP DRAFT PICKS OF THE DECADE

Year	Player, Pos	2021 Org
2012	Jake Thompson, RHP (2nd rd)	Mexican League
2013	Jonathon Crawford, RHP	Atlantic League
2014	Derek Hill, OF	Tigers
2015	Beau Burrows, RHP	Twins
2016	Matt Manning, RHP	Tigers
2017	Alex Faedo, RHP	Tigers
2018	Casey Mize, RHP	Tigers
2019	Riley Greene, OF	Tigers
2020	Spencer Torkelson, 3B	Tigers
2021	Jackson Jobe, RHP	Tigers

Houston Astros

BY CHANDLER ROME

Reception across the league and in opposing ballparks may signal otherwise, but the Astros are slowly starting to emerge from their scandal-stained past. A redemptive season of sorts ended with an American League pennant and two wins shy of a World Series championship.

More important for its longterm sustainability, Houston has a first- and second-round draft pick in 2022 for the first time in two years, finally finishing one of the punishments levied by Major League Baseball for electronic sign-stealing. The two picks alone won't salvage a farm system still in decline, but it could afford general manager James Click a chance to bolster its foundation.

Click entered the 2022 off-season expected to expand his baseball operations and scouting staff. He hired Sara Goodrum from the Brewers as farm director, making her one of the highest-ranking women in a baseball front office. Assistant GM Pete Putila held the title prior to his promotion in 2020.

Under Putila's watch, Houston turned itself into a pitching development destination. Their American League Championship Series win against the Red Sox was, in part, a testament to the Astros' prestigious pitching development. Luis Garcia carried a no-hitter into the sixth inning of a pennant-clinching win. Two days earlier, Framber Valdez threw eight innings of one-run ball inside Fenway Park.

Each signed for less than $25,000, prolonging Houston's propensity to discover and develop Latin American pitching prospects other teams pass over. Garcia finished second in AL Rookie of the Year voting. Cristian Javier, who signed for $10,000, finished third for the same award in 2020. He should shift back into the 2022 rotation alongside Valdez and Garcia.

Pitching still dominates the pipeline. Hunter Brown has replaced Forrest Whitley as the team's most promising pitching prospect, but for the system to take a step forward, Whitley must materialize into something resembling the reputation that preceded him. The former top prospect had Tommy John surgery in March and has appeared in just 23 games of affiliated ball since 2018.

The Astros have been able to compensate for Whitley's collapse by finding small-school gems late in drafts.

Both Shawn Dubin and Jonathan Bermudez came from NAIA schools in the 13th round or later and were added to Houston's 40-man roster after the season. Both could make a major league impact in 2022, along with Brown.

Position player development is another mat-

Kyle Tucker's breakout season helped lead the Astros to the brink of another World Series title.

PROJECTED 2025 LINEUP

Position	Player	Age
Catcher	Korey Lee	26
First Base	Joe Perez	25
Second Base	Jose Altuve	34
Third Base	Alex Bregman	31
Shortstop	Jeremy Peña	27
Left Field	Chas McCormick	30
Center Field	Jake Meyers	29
Right Field	Kyle Tucker	28
Designated Hitter	Yordan Alvarez	28
No. 1 Starter	Lance McCullers Jr.	31
No. 2 Starter	Framber Valdez	31
No. 3 Starter	Luis Garcia	27
No. 4 Starter	Cristian Javier	28
No. 5 Starter	Jose Urquidy	30
Closer	Hunter Brown	26

ter entirely. Chas McCormick and Jake Meyers graduated to the majors and held down center field during the 2021 season to become success stories, but little top-flight talent exists behind them. Top prospect Korey Lee could make his major league debut in 2022. Shortstop Jeremy Peña is almost guaranteed to do the same after Carlos Correa departed as a free agent.

Beyond them, though, the Astros have little on which to rely for lineup replacements. The nature of their position player core does not necessarily demand it—six of nine everyday players from the 2021 team are under contract through at least 2023—but Click preaches sustainability. Building the farm back up is a crucial step toward that. ∎

DEPTH CHART

HOUSTON ASTROS

TOP 2022 ROOKIES	RANK
Korey Lee, C	1
Jeremy Peña, SS	2

BREAKOUT PROSPECTS	RANK
Cristian Gonzalez, SS	15
Yainer Diaz, C	16
Chayce McDermott, RHP	18

SOURCE OF TOP 30 TALENT			
Homegrown	28	Acquired	2
College	15	Trade	1
Junior College	1	Rule 5 draft	1
High School	5	Independent leagues	0
Nondrafted free agent	1	Free agents/waivers	0
International	6		

LF
Matthew Barefoot (14)
Logan Cerny

CF
Pedro León (4)
Colin Barber (19)
Jordan Brewer (20)
Zach Daniels (22)

RF
Tyler Whitaker (9)
Alex McKenna (17)
Justin Dirden

3B
Joe Perez (5)
Grae Kessinger (12)
Corey Julks

SS
Jeremy Peña (2)
Cristian Gonzalez (15)
Dauri Lorenzo (21)

2B
Shay Whitcomb (26)
Luis Santana
J.C. Correa

1B
JJ Matijevic

C
Korey Lee (1)
Yanier Diaz (16)
Michael Papierski
Juan Santander
Scott Manea

LHP

LHSP	LHRP
Jonathan Bermudez (27)	Brayan De Paula
Parker Mushinski	Kit Scheetz

RHP

RHSP	RHRP
Hunter Brown (3)	Shawn Dubin (11)
Alex Santos (6)	Jojanse Torres (24)
Tyler Ivey (7)	Seth Martinez (28)
Jaime Melendez (8)	Jonathan Sprinkle
Peter Solomon (10)	Blair Henley
Forrest Whitley (13)	Austin Hansen
Chayce McDermott (18)	Jose Alberto Rivera
Jimmy Endersby (23)	Joe Record
Brett Conine (25)	Misael Tamarez
Jairo Solis (29)	Alimber Santa
Tyler Brown (30)	

1 KOREY LEE, C

Born: July 25, 1998. **B-T:** R-R. **HT:** 6-2. **WT:** 210.
Drafted: California, 2019 (first round).
Signed by: Tom Costic.

TONY FARLOW/FOUR SEAM IMAGES

TRACK RECORD: Fourteen years after the Astros drafted and developed Stanford product Jason Castro as their catcher of the future, another California-based backstop is following a similar path. The Astros surprised the industry by selecting Lee in the first round of the 2019 draft at No. 32 overall. Many teams thought Lee would be available in later rounds, but the Astros pounced due to their confidence in a bat that showed promise in his final collegiate season at California hitting behind Andrew Vaughn. The team hoped Lee's athleticism would pay dividends behind the plate. He signed for $1.75 million and delivered a solid, if unspectacular, debut season in Rookie ball in 2019. The upside and potential Houston saw finally manifested in Lee's first full minor league season in 2021. Lee hit .277/.340/.438 with 11 home runs in 88 games and reached Triple-A Sugar Land during a revealing campaign that included noticeable adjustments to both his batting and catching stances. He continued to make contact and control the strike zone across three minor league levels while distinguishing himself as a defensive standout. The Astros exposed Lee to both first base and third base in 2021, but his short-term future is behind the plate, where his athleticism is obvious and an opportunity for imminent major league playing time looms.
SCOUTING REPORT: Making so many adjustments left Lee somewhat inconsistent throughout the 2021 season, but his upside is apparent. He now catches in a one-knee stance to generate quicker releases with a plus-plus throwing arm. He produces pop times as low as 1.8 seconds in the one-knee stance. He shortened his arm slot to help the throws, too, but it has led to some accuracy issues. The two major changes sometimes leave Lee looking ragged behind the plate but his consistency and work ethic outweigh the occasional off days. He's developed into a better receiver but still needs work. Concerns still surround Lee's bat, but scouts believe he can hit enough to become an everyday catcher. He hit far too many ground balls to his pull side during his first minor league season, necessitating a few stance alterations. Lee came into pro ball with a busy batting stance—complete with a long stride and too much pre-pitch movement. Lee is far more stable and quiet now, which allows him to use his whole body, drive the ball

BA GRADE	SCOUTING GRADES
55 Risk: High	Hit: 50. Power: 50. Run: 40. Field: 55. Arm: 70.

Projected future grades on 20-80 scouting scale

BEST TOOLS

Best Hitter for Average	Yainer Diaz
Best Power Hitter	Scott Schreiber
Best Strike-Zone Discipline	Grae Kessinger
Fastest Baserunner	Michael Sandle
Best Athlete	Zach Daniels
Best Fastball	Hunter Brown
Best Curveball	Hunter Brown
Best Slider	Shawn Dubin
Best Changeup	Jaime Melendez
Best Control	Brett Conine
Best Defensive Catcher	Korey Lee
Best Defensive Infielder	Jeremy Peña
Best Infield Arm	Jeremy Peña
Best Defensive Outfielder	Jordan Brewer
Best Outfield Arm	Pedro Leon

more frequently and hit line drives. Lee can still tap into more of his above-average power, and the strides he made in 2021 portend well for the future.
THE FUTURE: Lee is the Astros' catcher of the future and is nearly ready for the major leagues. Both Castro and starter Martin Maldonado are signed only through 2022 and the team traded longtime third catcher Garrett Stubbs to clear a space on the 40-man roster and at Triple-A Sugar Land, where Lee should spend most of 2022. His MLB debut could come during the season. ∎

Year	Age	Club (Level)	Lge	AVG	G	AB	R	H	2B	3B	HR	RBI	BB	SO	SB	OBP	SLG
2021	22	Asheville (HiA)	East	.330	29	109	24	36	5	0	3	14	12	24	1	.397	.459
	22	Corpus Christi (AA)	Cent	.254	50	185	25	47	9	1	8	27	17	35	3	.320	.443
	22	Sugar Land (AAA)	West	.229	9	35	2	8	4	0	0	4	2	9	0	.263	.343
Minor League Totals (3 years)				.273	152	553	82	151	24	5	14	73	59	117	12	.348	.410

2 JEREMY PEÑA, SS

Born: Sept. 22, 1997. **B-T:** R-R. **HT:** 6-0. **WT:** 202. **Drafted:** Maine, 2018 (3rd round). **Signed by:** Bobby St. Pierre.

TRACK RECORD: Even after fracturing his left wrist while diving for a ball in April, Peña cemented himself as the Astros' heir apparent to Carlos Correa at shortstop during the 2021 season. He returned from a four-month absence to abuse pitching at Triple-A Sugar Land, collecting 16 extra-base hits in a 30-game cameo with the Skeeters. The Astros included Peña on their playoff taxi squad before he departed for a winter ball assignment in the Dominican Republic. Peña drew rave reviews from major league coaches and players for his presence and makeup during his time on the taxi squad and was added to the 40-man roster in November.

BA GRADE
55 Risk: High

SCOUTING REPORT: Known as an above-average defender since his third-round selection in the 2018 draft, Peña is making the offensive strides and showing a power surge that will make him an everyday major league option. He came back from a four-month injury absence with more muscle and tapped into the power some waited long to see. Peña's power may come at the expense of strike-zone control and an ability to hit for average, but his transformation from a handsy college hitter to one who can unearth more power is evident. Peña's body and build have generated praise from across the sport, but he has not sacrificed plus defense at shortstop, where he shows one of the organization's best infield arms. His major league bloodlines—his father, Geronimo, played seven major league seasons—influence a makeup about which many rave.

THE FUTURE: Peña's offensive adjustments make him a potential everyday regular at shortstop. He should start the 2022 season at Triple-A Sugar Land and, provided he produces similar offensive numbers, will be in position to make his major league debut during the season.

SCOUTING GRADES:	Hitting: 50	Power: 45	Running: 55	Fielding: 60	Arm: 60

Year	Age	Club (Level)	Lge	AVG	G	AB	R	H	2B	3B	HR	RBI	BB	SO	SB	OBP	SLG
2021	23	Astros (R)	FCL	.348	7	23	3	8	1	1	0	2	2	6	1	.444	.478
2021	23	Sugar Land (AAA)	West	.287	30	122	22	35	4	2	10	19	6	35	5	.346	.598
Minor League Totals (4 years)				.291	182	690	119	201	31	10	18	85	73	150	29	.371	.443

3 HUNTER BROWN, RHP

Born: Aug. 29, 1998. **B-T:** R-R. **HT:** 6-2. **WT:** 212. **Drafted:** Wayne State (Mich.), 2019 (5th round). **Signed by:** Scott Oberhelman.

TRACK RECORD: Brown burst onto the draft scene in 2019, striking out 114 batters in 85.1 innings as a junior at Division II Wayne State. The Astros took him in the fifth round that June and signed him for $325,000. Brown's first full minor league season in 2021 featured much of the same traits that attracted the Astros. He struck out 131 batters in 101.1 innings with a 4.04 ERA between Double-A Corpus Christi and Triple-A Sugar Land. The performance put Brown, a Detroit native who grew up idolizing Justin Verlander, in the thick of conversations to join him in the Astros' rotation.

BA GRADE
55 Risk: High

SCOUTING REPORT: Brown relies on a power four-seam fastball that sits in the mid-to-upper 90s and can reach 99 mph. He can elevate the pitch when needed and misses bats due to the late riding life it generates. Brown possesses two breaking pitches, a spike curveball in the low 80s and a sweeping slider that generates swings and misses. Both his four-seamer and curveball are major league-caliber, but a lack of consistency prevents Brown from being a bona fide, big-league starting pitching prospect. He is frequently unable to repeat his delivery and has the occasional propensity to lose his release point. His fastball command issues are apparent and must be solved for him to stick as a starter, although he could still be dominant in the bullpen.

THE FUTURE: Brown should begin 2022 at Triple-A Sugar Land, where perhaps a year of seasoning will yield the breakout season many within the organization envision.

SCOUTING GRADES:	Fastball: 70	Slider: 50	Curveball: 60	Changeup: 50	Control: 40

Year	Age	Club (Level)	Lge	W	L	ERA	G	GS	IP	H	HR	BB	SO	BB/9	SO/9	WHIP	AVG
2021	22	Corpus Christi (AA)	Cent	1	4	4.20	13	11	49	45	6	29	76	5.3	13.9	1.50	.245
	22	Sugar Land (AAA)	West	5	1	3.88	11	8	51	47	6	21	55	3.7	9.7	1.33	.246
Minor League Totals (3 years)				8	7	4.14	36	25	124	105	12	68	164	4.94	11.90	1.40	.229

4 PEDRO LEON, OF/SS

Born: May 28, 1998. **B-T:** R-R. **HT:** 5-10. **WT:** 170. **Signed:** Cuba, 2020.
Signed by: Charlie Gonzalez.

TRACK RECORD: The Astros invested $4 million in Leon as the crown jewel of their 2020 international signing class, stating their belief the Cuban center fielder could be a "rapid mover" to the majors. He had a 1.098 OPS in two seasons in Serie Nacional, including an all-star appearance as a 20-year-old. The pandemic prevented Leon from playing in 2020 and a visa issue delayed his arrival to spring training in 2021, but he still jumped straight to Double-A to begin his professional career. The Astros informed Leon he would see loads of time at shortstop upon signing him and, despite not playing the position since childhood, Leon made 48 of his first 71 minor league starts at shortstop.

BA GRADE
45 Risk: High

SCOUTING REPORT: Leon has enough athleticism and defensive aptitude to handle both center field and shortstop. He flashes plus-plus speed and has plus arm strength, as evidenced by a throw clocked at 98 mph from center field in spring training. However, many of the plus tools promised before Leon's arrival never materialized during his first minor league season. He has a long swing and struggled first with velocity at Double-A and then with breaking pitches in the Arizona Fall League. Though strong in his frame, his small stature and contact concerns preclude him from having more than fringe-average power. Leon's learning curve is steep, but his makeup and initial adaptation are encouraging. After striking out 33 times in his first 85 plate appearances, he posted a .766 OPS the rest of the season while earning a promotion to Triple-A.

THE FUTURE: Leon's best path to the big leagues is in center field, but he must continue to adjust offensively to be an everyday player. He is widely viewed as a future utilityman.

SCOUTING GRADES:	Hitting: 45	Power: 45	Running: 60	Fielding: 50	Arm: 60

Year	Age	Club (Level)	Lge	AVG	G	AB	R	H	2B	3B	HR	RBI	BB	SO	SB	OBP	SLG
2021	23	Astros (R)	FCL	.222	3	9	0	2	0	0	0	1	0	2	1	.222	.222
	23	Corpus Christi (AA)	Cent	.249	52	185	29	46	7	1	9	33	25	67	13	.359	.443
	23	Sugar Land (AAA)	West	.131	17	61	11	8	2	0	0	2	14	23	4	.293	.164
Minor League Totals (1 year)				.220	72	255	40	56	9	1	9	36	39	92	18	.339	.369

5 JOE PEREZ, 3B

Born: Aug. 12, 1999. **B-T:** R-R. **HT:** 6-2. **WT:** 198. **Drafted:** HS—Southwest Ranches, Fla., 2017 (2nd round). **Signed by:** Charlie Gonzalez.

TRACK RECORD: The Astros drafted Perez in the second round and signed him for $1.6 million in 2017 knowing he'd need Tommy John surgery. He had it one day after his selection, starting a circuitous career that finally seems on track. His Tommy John recovery, a shoulder surgery in 2018 and the coronavirus pandemic limited Perez to just 209 professional plate appearances prior to the 2021 season. He lost around 15 pounds during the pandemic to become more durable and reached Double-A Corpus Christi during his first full minor league season. Perez posted an .849 OPS and showed serviceable enough defense at third base to earn a spot on Houston's 40-man roster.

BA GRADE
45 Risk: High

SCOUTING REPORT: Perez isn't an excitable player but boasts an offensive skill set many feel will give him a chance to make the major leagues. He is still a power-over-hit offensive prospect, but he demonstrated a better ability to use the opposite field in 2021 while making far more contact and staging competitive at-bats. Perez's swing can still get too long, but he has enough strength to produce above-average power. The Astros will keep pushing him at third base—where a plus arm can compensate for a lack of range—but could expose him to left field to increase his value.

THE FUTURE: Perez reshaped his body and refined his focus to put himself back on the map in 2021. Having another season similar in 2022 at Triple-A Sugar Land would make him an intriguing bench option in the major leagues.

SCOUTING GRADES:	Hitting: 50	Power: 50	Running: 40	Fielding: 45	Arm: 60

Year	Age	Club (Level)	Lge	AVG	G	AB	R	H	2B	3B	HR	RBI	BB	SO	SB	OBP	SLG
2021	21	Fayetteville (LoA)	East	.300	12	50	7	15	4	0	2	8	9	13	0	.407	.500
	21	Asheville (HiA)	East	.354	25	99	24	35	11	0	8	26	10	21	1	.413	.707
	21	Corpus Christi (AA)	Cent	.267	69	281	34	75	19	0	8	27	24	80	2	.322	.420
Minor League Totals (5 years)				.262	160	622	89	163	41	2	25	88	57	169	7	.326	.455

6 ALEX SANTOS, RHP

Born: Feb. 10, 2002. **B-T:** R-R. **HT:** 6-4. **WT:** 194. **Drafted:** HS—Bronx, N.Y., 2020 (2nd round supplemental). **Signed by:** Bobby St. Pierre.

TRACK RECORD: The Astros selected Santos No. 72 overall in the 2020 draft despite him missing his entire senior high school season due to the pandemic. Rapsodo data from Santos' bullpen sessions during the shutdown, coupled with his continued presence on the showcase circuit, gave Houston confidence in its selection. Santos did not appear in a professional game until 2021, when he threw 41.2 innings for Low-A Fayetteville and demonstrated some of the potential that tantalized the Astros.

SCOUTING REPORT: Santos sits in the low-to-mid 90s with a high-spin four-seam fastball that can sneak up on hitters and always seems to miss bats. His fastball is usually 91-93 mph, but can touch 95 in spurts. Santos' ability to spin both the four-seamer and a plus curveball align well with the Astros' pitching philosophies. His confidence is growing in a fading changeup that he barely threw in high school, and it now has average potential. Continued progression of the changeup and a slider will serve Santos well if he hopes to start in the major leagues. Santos' arm action and failure to repeat his delivery consistently leave some wondering whether he's better suited as a reliever, but his strike-throwing ability stood out throughout the draft circuit.

THE FUTURE: Perhaps no young pitcher in Houston's system has more upside as a potential starter than Santos. He'll need to refine his repeatability and curtail some of his bouts of bad command, but hope is high given his age and relative inexperience.

BA GRADE
50 Risk: Extreme

SCOUTING GRADES:	Fastball: 55	Curveball: 60	Changeup: 50	Control: 50

Year	Age	Club (Level)	Lge	W	L	ERA	G	GS	IP	H	HR	BB	SO	BB/9	SO/9	WHIP	AVG
2021	19	Fayetteville (LoA)	East	2	2	3.46	12	7	42	31	2	30	48	6.5	10.4	1.46	.205
Minor League Totals (2 years)				2	2	3.46	12	7	42	31	2	30	48	6.48	10.37	1.46	.205

7 TYLER IVEY, RHP

Born: May 12, 1996. **B-T:** R-R. **HT:** 6-4. **WT:** 195. **Drafted:** Grayson (Texas) JC, 2017 (3rd round). **Signed by:** Jim Stevenson.

TRACK RECORD: Ivey is a Rowlett, Texas, native who made his major league debut during a spot start at the Rangers' Globe Life Park in May 2021. The emotions of a hometown debut, coupled with a family tragedy and an elbow injury he hid from the organization, caused the lanky righthander to take four months off from baseball. Ivey was diagnosed with thoracic outlet syndrome, but he did not require surgery and made one minor league rehab appearance in the Florida Complex League in late September. Coupled with persistent elbow pain in spring training and in May at Triple-A Sugar Land, Ivey threw just 17.2 innings all season.

BA GRADE
50 Risk: Extreme

SCOUTING REPORT: Ivey has a herky-jerky delivery and a high leg kick that generates most of the attention. The Astros have made some minor adjustments so he can better control the running game, but by and large allow Ivey to continue his unorthodox ways given his good command. He averaged just 90 mph with his four-seam fastball during his major league debut due to his injured elbow. When healthy, Ivey is in the low-to-mid 90s with the pitch and can touch 96. His delivery affords some deception on the fastball, which Ivey elevates well, and a high-spin curveball that pairs effectively with it. Ivey's changeup is still evolving to go along with a slider that can have cutter-like tendencies. Ivey has demonstrated the command and control some scouts doubted he'd discover due to his delivery and now has fringe-average control overall.

THE FUTURE: Ivey is a potential middle-to-back-of-the-rotation starter candidate if he can stay healthy. With two elbow injuries in three seasons, that's a big if.

SCOUTING GRADES:	Fastball: 50	Slider: 50	Curveball: 60	Changeup: 45	Control: 55

Year	Age	Club (Level)	Lge	W	L	ERA	G	GS	IP	H	HR	BB	SO	BB/9	SO/9	WHIP	AVG
2021	25	Astros (R)	FCL	0	0	0.00	1	1	2	1	0	1	3	4.5	13.5	1.00	.167
	25	Sugar Land (AAA)	West	0	1	4.91	4	3	11	14	2	8	13	6.6	10.6	2.00	.304
	25	Houston (MLB)	AL	0	0	7.71	1	1	5	6	1	1	3	1.9	5.8	1.50	.316
Major League Totals (1 year)				0	0	7.71	1	1	5	6	1	1	3	1.93	5.79	1.50	.316
Minor League Totals (5 years)				8	10	3.13	55	41	215	171	14	72	263	3.01	10.99	1.13	.213

8 JAIME MELENDEZ, RHP

Born: Sept. 26, 2001. **B-T:** L-R. **HT:** 5-8. **WT:** 190. **Signed:** Mexico, 2019.
Signed by: Miguel Pintor.

TRACK RECORD: Melendez signed for $195,000 out of Mexico in May 2019 as a slender prospect known more for his craftiness and pitchability than over-powering stuff. He appeared in 11 complex league games upon his arrival and did not pitch in 2020 due to the coronavirus pandemic. Melendez added more than 20 pounds to his frame and upped his velocity to ascend three levels of the minors during a breakout 2021. He reached Double-A Corpus Christi for his final three appearances of the season.

SCOUTING REPORT: Melendez draws comparisons to a fellow Mexican Astros pitcher: Jose Urquidy. Melendez throws from a high slot and is armed with a sneaky fastball that has substantial carry. After sitting 87-91 mph when he signed, Melendez now sits at 91-93 mph with his fastball and touches 95 on occasion. He generates swings and misses up in the strike zone, aligning perfectly with the Astros' organization-wide pitching philosophy. His changeup has developed into one of the organization's best. It has a similar spin rate to his fastball and some two-seam action. He throws a short slider with late break that has plus potential along with a curveball seen as average. His deception, ability to mix all four of his pitches and average control make him an intriguing starting candidate.

THE FUTURE: Melendez has four average pitches that he mixes and commands well, but durability remains a concern. He has the upside to be a starter but some evaluators feel he's destined for middle relief. A full season at Double-A in 2022 may help clear up his future.

BA GRADE
45 Risk: High

SCOUTING GRADES:	Fastball: 55	Slider: 50	Curveball: 45	Changeup: 55	Control: 50

Year	Age	Club (Level)	Lge	W	L	ERA	G	GS	IP	H	HR	BB	SO	BB/9	SO/9	WHIP	AVG
2021	19	Fayetteville (LoA)	East	2	2	0.49	6	3	18	7	1	5	38	2.5	18.7	0.65	.111
	19	Asheville (HiA)	East	2	3	4.78	11	7	32	34	2	24	41	6.8	11.5	1.81	.268
	19	Corpus Christi (AA)	Cent	0	1	5.87	3	1	7	8	0	4	11	4.7	12.9	1.57	.235
Minor League Totals (2 years)				5	9	3.34	31	16	86	69	3	49	129	5.11	13.45	1.37	.214

9 TYLER WHITAKER, OF

TOM DIPACE

Born: Aug. 2, 2002. **B-T:** R-R. **HT:** 6-4. **WT:** 190. **Drafted:** HS—Las Vegas, 2021 (third round). **Signed by:** Ryan Leake.

TRACK RECORD: In their final draft without a first- or second-round pick as punishment for their electronic sign-stealing scandal, the Astros took Whitaker 87th overall and praised him as a potential first-rounder who fell into their lap. Houston paid Whitaker $1.5 million—more than $800,000 over slot value—to break his commitment to Arizona. Whitaker played pri-marily right field during his senior season due to a team need, but the Astros view him as a center fielder long term. He started in center field in 19 of his 29 games in the Florida Complex League in his pro debut.

SCOUTING REPORT: Whitaker is toolsy and raw, but exudes enough energy and athleticism to portend well for his future. He has room to add more size and muscle to his lanky 6-foot-4 frame, and his athleticism is apparent. He has plus-plus speed and plus raw power, but his grooved swing produces too many swings and misses. He struck out 40 times in 114 plate appearances in the FCL and projects to be a below-average hiter. Whitaker has enough tools to play all three outfield positions. His plus arm profiles in right field ,but his enticing speed will keep him in center field for now.

THE FUTURE: Whitaker needs more seasoning and playing time, but he stands out as a bright spot in a system light on young position player talent. His first full season in 2022 should start in Low-A Fayetteville.

BA GRADE
50 Risk: Extreme

SCOUTING GRADES:	Hitting: 40	Power: 55	Running: 60	Fielding: 45	Arm: 55

Year	Age	Club (Level)	Lge	AVG	G	AB	R	H	2B	3B	HR	RBI	BB	SO	SB	OBP	SLG
2021	18	Astros (R)	FCL	.202	29	104	16	21	2	1	3	6	9	40	8	.263	.327
Minor League Totals (1 year)				.202	29	104	16	21	2	1	3	6	9	40	8	.263	.327

10 PETER SOLOMON, RHP

Born: Aug. 16, 1996. **B-T:** R-R. **HT:** 6-4. **WT:** 211. **Drafted:** Notre Dame, 2017 (fourth round). **Signed by:** Nick Venuto.

TRACK RECORD: Solomon and Astros teammate Brandon Bielak played together at Notre Dame, where Solomon struggled as a starter and was relegated to the bullpen. The Astros turned him back into a starter after selecting him in the fourth round of the 2017 draft. He thrived before Tommy John surgery sidelined him for most of 2019 and the pandemic prevented him from pitching in 2020. Solomon put it all together in 2021, making his major league debut as a fill-in long reliever while demonstrating his potential future as a back-end starter with an impressive season at Triple-A Sugar Land.

BA GRADE

45 Risk: High

SCOUTING REPORT: Solomon's four-seam fastball only averages 92 mph and is too straight at times, but it generates late ride that helps him miss bats at its best. He can run his four-seamer up to 96 mph in short spurts out of the bullpen. Solomon pairs his fastball with a new cutter he developed prior to Tommy John surgery that hovers around the mid 80s and proved effective in a short major league cameo. His slider is fringe-average and takes a back seat to a downer curveball and changeup that both continue to creep toward above-average **THE FUTURE:** Solomon showed enough command and durability in 2021 to project as a back-end starter. He should begin the 2022 season in Sugar Land as a depth option for the Astros rotation.

SCOUTING GRADES:	Fastball: 50	Cutter: 45	Curveball: 55	Changeup: 55	Control: 50

Year	Age	Club (Level)	Lge	W	L	ERA	G	GS	IP	H	HR	BB	SO	BB/9	SO/9	WHIP	AVG
2021	24	Sugar Land (AAA)	West	8	1	4.70	21	18	97	89	16	42	112	3.9	10.3	1.34	.235
	24	Houston (MLB)	AL	1	0	1.29	6	0	14	10	0	8	10	5.1	6.4	1.29	.217
Major League Totals (1 year)				1	0	1.29	6	0	14	10	0	8	10	5.14	6.43	1.29	.217
Minor League Totals (5 years)				17	2	3.43	48	34	207	174	19	78	240	3.39	10.43	1.22	.224

11 SHAWN DUBIN, RHP

BA GRADE

45 Risk: High

Born: Sept. 6, 1995. **B-T:** R-R. **HT:** 6-1. **WT:** 171. **Drafted:** Georgetown (Ky.), 2018 (13th round). **Signed by:** Travis Coleman.

TRACK RECORD: Dubin signed for $1,000 after a circuitous college career during which he almost gave up playing baseball. He finished at NAIA Georgetown (Ky.) after Buffalo shuttered its program. Dubin has added 30 pounds and substantial fastball velocity since reaching pro ball. He struck out 12.5 per nine innings at Triple-A Sugar Land in 2021 and was added to the Astros' 40-man roster after the season despite throwing just 49.2 innings due to elbow inflammation.

SCOUTING REPORT: After hovering around 90 mph in college, Dubin's fastball now sits anywhere from 93-96 mph with explosive life and reaches 99 mph. His plus slider, which he didn't throw until college, sweeps enough to generate swings and misses from both righties and lefties and is a legitimate out pitch. Both his slider and curveball are high spin and aided by a deceptive delivery. He can incorporate a cutter he learned at Houston's alternate site along with a developing changeup. Dubin's delivery is now far more efficient and he uses his lower half more instead of the whippy, long stride he showed in college. **THE FUTURE:** Dubin's plus slider and a fastball that plays up in short spurts make him an obvious reliever candidate, but the Astros are still giving him a chance to start with a five-pitch mix.

Year	Age	Club (Level)	Lge	W	L	ERA	G	GS	IP	H	HR	BB	SO	BB/9	SO/9	WHIP	AVG
2021	25	Sugar Land (AAA)	West	4	3	3.44	16	8	49	35	4	19	69	3.4	12.5	1.09	.201
Minor League Totals (4 years)				13	9	3.70	55	32	190	136	11	76	251	3.61	11.91	1.12	.199

12 GRAE KESSINGER, SS/3B

BA GRADE

45 Risk: High

Born: Aug. 25, 1997. **B-T:** R-R. **HT:** 6-2. **WT:** 204. **Drafted:** Mississippi, 2019 (2nd round). **Signed by:** Travis Coleman.

TRACK RECORD: No Astros prospect has richer bloodlines than Kessinger, whose father, uncle and, most notably, his grandfather, Don, all played professionally. Houston selected Grae in the second round of the 2019 draft out of Ole Miss and paid him $750,000. He spent his first full minor league season at Double-A Corpus Christi and ended it with a stint in the Arizona Fall League.

SCOUTING REPORT: Kessinger does a lot of things well but nothing spectacular. His baseball instincts and makeup mask some shortcomings. Kessinger's exit velocities jumped after he added some pre-pitch hand movement and widened the base of his stance to produce more line drive contact. He displays some of the organization's best strike zone control and pitch recognition but has below-average raw power. Kessinger is an average defender with an average arm at shortstop and could easily shift to second or third base if asked. He played first base in the Arizona Fall League, but only due to team roster construction.

THE FUTURE: The Astros view Kessinger as a major league average defender at shortstop but will continue to move him around the infield. He projects to be a utilityman, but if he can tap into some power, he could ascend to greater heights.

Year	Age	Club (Level)	Lge	AVG	G	AB	R	H	2B	3B	HR	RBI	BB	SO	SB	OBP	SLG
2021	23	Corpus Christi (AA)	Cent	.209	86	297	46	62	9	0	9	26	27	81	12	.287	.330
Minor League Totals (3 years)				.219	148	508	76	111	19	0	11	46	56	117	21	.307	.321

13 FORREST WHITLEY, RHP

BA GRADE 50 Risk: Extreme

Born: Sept. 15, 1997. **B-T:** R-R. **HT:** 6-7. **WT:** 238.
Drafted: HS—San Antonio, Texas, 2016 (1st round). **Signed by:** Noel Gonzales-Luna.

TRACK RECORD: Whitley's fall from baseball's top pitching prospect continued in 2021 when he had Tommy John surgery after a few spring training bullpen sessions. He's thrown just 59.2 innings in affiliated ball since 2018—and had a 7.99 ERA. He finished the 2019 season at Triple-A with a 12.21 ERA but Houston still put him on its 40-man roster. Whitley flashed promise at the team's alternate training site in 2020 and in some summer camp simulated games at Minute Maid Park

SCOUTING REPORT: Whitley hasn't pitched to his potential since 2017. A series of changes always seem to follow him, be it with his delivery, training regimen or weight, and none have stuck. His arsenal remains one of the organization's best: a plus four-seam fastball at 92-97 mph complemented by two high-spin breaking balls and a plus changeup. His collection of five pitches that are all above average or plus remains unmatched, but commanding that arsenal is another issue entirely. His fastball tends to sail over the top of the strike zone and his cutter was often a ball out of his hand before surgery. He also struggled to keep his composure when things weren't going well.

THE FUTURE: Whitley still possesses front-of-the-rotation type stuff. He could return to game action in summer 2022 and will try to actualize his tantalizing promise.

Year	Age	Club (Level)	Lge	W	L	ERA	G	GS	IP	H	HR	BB	SO	BB/9	SO/9	WHIP	AVG
2021	23	Did not play—Injured															
Minor League Totals (5 years)				9	15	4.71	57	47	197	171	18	95	289	4.34	13.20	1.35	.232

14 MATTHEW BAREFOOT, OF

BA GRADE 45 Risk: High

Born: Sept. 20, 1997. **B-T:** R-L. **HT:** 6-0. **WT:** 205. **Drafted:** Campbell, 2019 (6th round). **Signed by:** Gavin Dickey.

TRACK RECORD: Barefoot signed for $150,000 as a sixth-round pick in 2019 after destroying mid-major college pitching for three seasons at Campbell and earning the Cape Cod League MVP award in 2018. He purchased a pitching machine, indoor batting cage and Rapsodo machine during the coronavirus pandemic to produce a breakout 2021 season. Barefoot hit .301 with 36 extra-base hits between Low-A and High-A before hitting a wall with a .525 OPS and .299 slugging percentage in 36 games at Double-A Corpus Christi.

SCOUTING REPORT: Barefoot is a "backwards" player who throws lefthanded and hits righthanded. He has simplified his swing since college and is able to make easy, elevated line-drive contact with elite hand-eye coordination. He's shown prodigious home run power at the lower minor leagues, but it profiles as doubles power against better pitching. Still, his approach is sound and he projects to at least hit for average. Barefoot has plus speed and uses it efficiently to steal bases. He struggles with reads and routes in center field, making him a better corner option. He has an average arm that fits better in left than right.

THE FUTURE: Barefoot profiles as a platoon player or fourth outfielder unless he taps into more power. He must conquer higher-level pitching better than he did in his brief Double-A cameo in 2021.

Year	Age	Club (Level)	Lge	AVG	G	AB	R	H	2B	3B	HR	RBI	BB	SO	SB	OBP	SLG
2021	23	Fayetteville (LoA)	East	.344	16	64	14	22	4	1	4	17	7	21	10	.392	.625
	23	Asheville (HiA)	East	.287	49	195	26	56	14	1	12	35	12	64	7	.341	.554
	23	Corpus Christi (AA)	Cent	.175	36	137	13	24	5	0	4	16	7	50	4	.226	.299
Minor League Totals (3 years)				.242	124	467	58	113	24	2	20	70	34	152	22	.300	.430

15 CRISTIAN GONZALEZ, SS

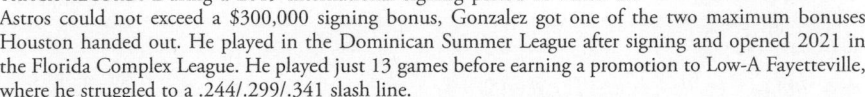

BA GRADE

50 Risk: Extreme

Born: Oct. 22, 2001. **B-T:** R-R. **HT:** 6-3. **WT:** 180. **Signed:** Dominican Republic, 2019. **Signed by:** Roman Ocumarez/Alfredo Ulloa/Jose Lima.

TRACK RECORD: During a 2019 international signing period in which the Astros could not exceed a $300,000 signing bonus, Gonzalez got one of the two maximum bonuses Houston handed out. He played in the Dominican Summer League after signing and opened 2021 in the Florida Complex League. He played just 13 games before earning a promotion to Low-A Fayetteville, where he struggled to a .244/.299/.341 slash line.

SCOUTING REPORT: Gonzalez has a projectable body that is still filling out. He is nimble but long-limbed, leading to questions about where his true defensive position is. The Astros play Gonzalez primarily at shortstop, where he shows a plus arm that could translate to the outfield if needed. Gonzalez has enough athleticism to stick at shortstop and the Astros intend to try it. He has above-average power and makes harder contact than some of his stats may suggest, but a stiff swing and poor strike zone discipline limit his production. As Gonzalez adds more weight and adjusts his swing, more of this power should manifest.

THE FUTURE: Gonzalez has physical upside, but needs to figure out his swing, approach and defensive home. He will likely open 2022 back in Fayetteville.

Year	Age	Club (Level)	Lge	AVG	G	AB	R	H	2B	3B	HR	RBI	BB	SO	SB	OBP	SLG
2021	19	Astros (R)	FCL	.310	13	42	8	13	2	0	2	13	5	10	3	.383	.500
	19	Fayetteville (LoA)	East	.244	30	123	19	30	4	1	2	14	9	41	1	.299	.341
Minor League Totals (2 years)				.235	106	371	59	87	12	4	5	48	33	107	15	.303	.329

16 YAINER DIAZ, C

BA GRADE

45 Risk: High

Born: Sept. 21, 1998. **B-T:** R-R. **HT:** 6-0. **WT:** 195. **Signed:** Dominican Republic, 2016. **Signed by:** Rigo de Los Santos/Jhonathan Leyba/Koby Perez (Cleveland).

TRACK RECORD: Cleveland signed Diaz for $25,000 during the 2016 international signing period. Five years later, the Astros acquired him and Phil Maton in exchange for Myles Straw at the trade deadline. Diaz played just 12 games at Low-A Fayetteville before earning a promotion to High-A Asheville. He hit .396/.438/.781 in 105 plate appearances there to finish his season batting .324.

SCOUTING REPORT: Diaz is an above-average hitter and a well-sequenced swing that easily produces contact. His hit-over-power profile does not fit a typical catcher, but the Astros are intrigued by the possibility. His exit velocities are near major league average and he hits hard line drives to all fields, but needs to tap into more power within his thick frame. His pitch selection needs to improve, and that may help in unlocking some power. Diaz has an above-average arm, but needs to refine his receiving and defense if he will stick behind the plate. He plays first base, too.

THE FUTURE: Diaz has hit at every level and passed every test. Facing more advanced pitching at Double-A in 2022 could dictate his immediate trajectory.

Year	Age	Club (Level)	Lge	AVG	G	AB	R	H	2B	3B	HR	RBI	BB	SO	SB	OBP	SLG
2021	22	Lynchburg (LoA)	East	.314	61	239	30	75	19	1	5	50	15	42	1	.357	.464
	22	Fayetteville (LoA)	East	.229	12	48	3	11	2	0	1	7	0	4	1	.224	.333
	22	Asheville (HiA)	East	.396	25	96	28	38	4	0	11	33	8	17	2	.438	.781
Minor League Totals (5 years)				.328	235	908	128	298	54	8	27	179	41	129	5	.360	.494

17 ALEX McKENNA, OF

BA GRADE

45 Risk: High

Born: Sept. 6, 1997. **B-T:** R-R. **HT:** 6-2. **WT:** 204. **Drafted:** Cal Poly, 2018 (4th round). **Signed by:** Tim Costic.

TRACK RECORD: McKenna won Big West Conference player of the year honors in 2018 at Cal Poly and received a $432,500 signing bonus after the Astros selected him in the fourth round. He played just 65 games after dislocating his finger and straining a hamstring during his first minor league season in 2019. He reshaped his body during the coronavirus shutdown and got off to a torrid start at High-A Asheville in 2021, hitting .305/.389/.616, but he encountered more injury issues during an unproductive stint in Double-A Corpus Christi to end his season.

SCOUTING REPORT: McKenna shows above-average raw power, but it comes with a propensity for swings and misses. He is a feast or famine hitter with huge exit velocities and a bevy of strikeouts. His ability to handle advanced pitching is suspect after a subpar end to his 2021 season at Double-A, and he is likely a below-average hitter, at best. McKenna's above-average speed and instincts translate well in the outfield, but his range is suspect in center field. He has an average arm. .

THE FUTURE: McKenna profiles best as a fourth outfielder who doesn't hit enough to play everyday in a corner. He'll return to Double-A in 2022.

Year	Age	Club (Level)	Lge	AVG	G	AB	R	H	2B	3B	HR	RBI	BB	SO	SB	OBP	SLG
2021	23	Asheville (HiA)	East	.305	41	164	41	50	8	2	13	31	21	62	7	.389	.616
	23	Corpus Christi (AA)	Cent	.206	38	131	12	27	5	1	2	15	17	55	1	.314	.305
Minor League Totals (3 years)				.270	188	697	94	188	28	6	23	94	72	234	21	.355	.426

18 CHAYCE McDERMOTT, RHP

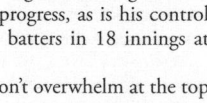

BA GRADE

45 Risk: High

Born: Aug. 22, 1998. **B-T:** L-R. **HT:** 6-3. **WT:** 197. **Drafted:** Ball State, 2021 (4th round). **Signed by:** Scott Oberhelman.

TRACK RECORD: McDermott redshirted in 2018 at Ball State while recovering from Tommy John surgery, suffered another injury in 2019 and threw just three times before the coronavirus pandemic stopped college baseball in 2020. He ended his only full collegiate season in 2021 with 13.6 strikeouts per nine innings, and the Astros took him in the fourth round and signed him for $372,500. McDermott continued piling up punchouts at Low-A Fayetteville, striking out 33 in 18.1 innings during his professional debut.

SCOUTING REPORT: McDermott has a solid set of four pitches. He misses bats with an above-average fastball that sits 92-96 mph and can get up to 98 on occasion. He pairs his heater with two potentially above-average breaking pitches in his 12-to-6 curveball in the mid 70s and a tilting slider that gets chase swings out of the strike zone. McDermott's changeup is still a major work in progress, as is his control of both breaking pitches. Even during his excellent pro debut, he walked 10 batters in 18 innings at Fayetteville.

THE FUTURE: McDermott's pitch mix gives him the potential to start, but he won't overwhelm at the top of a rotation. He should have a full season at a Class A affiliate in 2022.

Year	Age	Club (Level)	Lge	W	L	ERA	G	GS	IP	H	HR	BB	SO	BB/9	SO/9	WHIP	AVG
2021	22	Fayetteville (LoA)	East	0	0	3.44	6	4	18	11	3	10	33	4.9	16.2	1.15	.172
	22	Astros (R)	FCL	0	0	0.00	1	0	3	1	0	1	7	3.0	21.0	0.67	.100
Minor League Totals (1 year)				0	0	2.95	7	4	21	12	3	11	40	4.64	16.88	1.08	.162

19 COLIN BARBER, OF

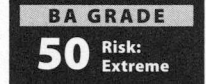

BA GRADE

50 Risk: Extreme

Born: Dec. 4, 2000. **B-T:** L-L. **HT:** 6-0. **WT:** 194. **Drafted:** HS—Chico, Calif., 2019 (4th round). **Signed by:** Tim Costic.

TRACK RECORD: Barber received a $1 million signing bonus after the Astros took him in the fourth round of the 2019 draft. He played 20 games of independent ball during the coronavirus pandemic and joined the Astros' alternate training site in September for developmental purposes. He was touted as a potential breakout candidate when minor league play resumed in 2021, but he played just 16 games at High-A Asheville before injuring his shoulder and having season-ending surgery.

SCOUTING REPORT: Barber has retooled his stance and swing to eliminate some of the rollover ground balls to the right side that previously plagued him. He digs his heel into the ground before starting his hands and finishes with his top hand up, allowing him to loft the ball and capitalize on his above-average raw power from the left side. Barber's patient approach disappeared during his brief 2021 season in favor of an aggressive, strikeout-filled stint that caused some worry. He has above-average speed and an average arm that could stick in center field or profile well in right. Within the organization, Barber's elite work ethic and determined demeanor have drawn comparisons to Alex Bregman.

THE FUTURE: Barber has perhaps more upside than any of the Astros' crew of young, recently drafted outfielders, but he has to show he's healthy. He should start 2022 back at Asheville.

Year	Age	Club (Level)	Lge	AVG	G	AB	R	H	2B	3B	HR	RBI	BB	SO	SB	OBP	SLG
2021	20	Asheville (HiA)	East	.214	16	42	10	9	1	0	3	7	9	22	1	.365	.452
Minor League Totals (2 years)				.248	44	141	29	35	6	1	5	13	28	51	3	.380	.411

20 JORDAN BREWER, OF

BA GRADE

45 Risk: Extreme

Born: Aug. 1, 1997. **B-T:** R-L. **HT:** 6-1. **WT:** 195. **Drafted:** Michigan, 2019 (3rd round). **Signed by:** Scott Oberhelman.

TRACK RECORD: Brewer played football and baseball in high school before blossoming into the Big Ten Conference player of the year at Michigan during its run to the 2019 College World Series finals. The Astros drafted him in the third round that July and gave him a $500,000 signing bonus. A nagging toe injury limited Brewer to 16 games in 2019 and left knee surgery sidelined him for most of 2020. He spent his first full minor league season at Low-A Fayetteville, stealing 21 bases and hitting .275/.375/.410 in 297 plate appearances.

SCOUTING REPORT: Brewer has a bevy of tantalizing tools that haven't yet come together. He is one of the fastest and most athletic players in the Astros organization and showcases plus speed. He has above-average raw power, but a grooved swing prevents him from displaying it much in games. Brewer swings and misses inside the strike zone too often and needs to improve his overall approach. He is an average defender in center field with an average arm but played in the more corners during his Michigan tenure despite his running ability.

THE FUTURE: Brewer held his own at Low-A despite some offensive flaws. He'll move up in 2022, where better pitching may be the best test for his toolsy profile.

Year	Age	Club (Level)	Lge	AVG	G	AB	R	H	2B	3B	HR	RBI	BB	SO	SB	OBP	SLG
2021	23	Fayetteville (LoA)	East	.275	65	251	49	69	12	2	6	41	34	80	21	.375	.410
Minor League Totals (3 years)				.249	81	305	54	76	12	2	7	44	36	86	23	.341	.370

21 DAURI LORENZO, SS

BA GRADE

45 Risk: Extreme

Born: Oct. 29, 2002. **B-T:** B-R. **HT:** 6-0. **WT:** 195. **Drafted:** Dominican Republic, Year 2019. **Signed by:** Roman Ocumarez/Francisco Ulloa/Leocadio Guevara.

TRACK RECORD: The Astros signed Lorenzo as the crown jewel of their 2019 international class, giving him a $1.8 million bonus. He did not play in 2020 due to the coronavirus pandemic but flashed spurts of promise at instructional league. Lorenzo got a late start in 2021 and played 41 games in the Florida Complex League in his pro debut, hitting .248/.316/.312 in 157 plate appearances.

SCOUTING REPORT: Only 19 years old, Lorenzo appeals to the Astros because of his mature approach. He is a switch hitter who is better from the right side, but he has a swing that stays through the strike zone and allows him to make easy contact from both sides. He is still filling out and has yet to show much power. Though heralded as a shortstop when he signed, the Astros played Lorenzo primarily at second base in his debut. He has an average arm and speed, but a lack of quickness at shortstop makes him more suited for the keystone.

THE FUTURE: Lorenzo is the latest in a long line of promising, young Latin infielders in the Astros system. He should get to Low-A in 2022, where his mature approach and contact-centric swing will be tested.

Year	Age	Club (Level)	Lge	AVG	G	AB	R	H	2B	3B	HR	RBI	BB	SO	SB	OBP	SLG
2021	18	Astros (R)	FCL	.248	41	141	15	35	6	0	1	12	14	35	5	.316	.312
Minor League Totals (1 year)				.248	41	141	15	35	6	0	1	12	14	35	5	.316	.312

22 ZACH DANIELS, OF

BA GRADE

45 Risk: Extreme

Born: Jan. 23, 1999. **B-T:** R-R. **HT:** 6-1. **WT:** 211. **Drafted:** Tennessee, 2020 (4th round). **Signed by:** Landon Townsley.

TRACK RECORD: The Astros drafted Daniels in the fourth round in 2020 after a loud 17-game showing prior to college baseball's shutdown. He had struggled the previous summer in the Cape Cod League and during his first two seasons at Tennessee, when he hit .176 and struck out 69 times in 64 games. The Astros saw enough in that small sample to give Daniels $400,000, but his first professional season matched the results of his early college days. He hit .224/.342/.358 with 129 strikeouts in 85 games across both Class A levels.

SCOUTING REPORT: Daniels has some of the loudest and most tantalizing tools in the Astros farm system. He is a plus-plus runner with plus raw power and enough quick twitch ability to put on an amazing batting practice show. But games demonstrate his lack of feel for hitting and a grooved swing that generates too many swings and misses inside the strike zone, preventing him from making much offensive impact. He has an average arm and speed that profiles well in center field. Daniels is the most athletic player in the Astros' system, which affords him a better chance to make adjustments.

THE FUTURE: Daniels must continue to make adjustments in games to realize the potential the Astros have for him. He will likely open 2022 back in High-A.

Year	Age	Club (Level)	Lge	AVG	G	AB	R	H	2B	3B	HR	RBI	BB	SO	SB	OBP	SLG
2021	22	Fayetteville (LoA)	East	.228	45	167	29	38	5	1	6	30	26	65	14	.345	.377
	22	Asheville (HiA)	East	.219	40	146	24	32	8	0	3	18	23	64	8	.339	.336
Minor League Totals (2 years)				.224	85	313	53	70	13	1	9	48	49	129	22	.342	.358

23 JIMMY ENDERSBY, RHP

Born: Jan. 16, 1998. **B-T:** R-R. **HT:** 6-1. **WT:** 194. **Signed:** NDFA—
Concordia-Irvine (Calif.), 2020. **Signed by:** Ryan Leake.

TRACK RECORD: Endersby threw just 45.1 collegiate innings in a circuitous
career. He came to Cal State Fullerton as an infielder and made occasional relief appearances, but
transitioned to a full-time pitcher once he transferred to Division II Concordia-Irvine (Calif.) in 2020.
Endersby made just five starts there before the pandemic shutdown, but the Astros still signed him as
an undrafted free agent for $20,000 following the five-round draft. Endersby reached Double-A Corpus
Christi with a 3.90 ERA and struck out 10.2 batters per nine innings in his first professional season.

SCOUTING REPORT: Endersby has an excellent arsenal for someone with so little in-game pitching experience. He throws a 92-95 mph four-seam fastball that reaches as high as 2,600 rpms with the elevation and
ride Houston desires. He throws a big breaking curveball and slider he's still developing to go along with a
below-average changeup. Endersby's command and control suffer at times from a lack of experience, but
the Astros are helping him adjust quickly.

THE FUTURE: Endersby should start 2022 back in Double-A. As he gains more innings and experience,
he could cement himself as valuable rotation depth.

Year	Age	Club (Level)	Lge	W	L	ERA	G	GS	IP	H	HR	BB	SO	BB/9	SO/9	WHIP	AVG
2021	23	Asheville (HiA)	East	2	1	4.85	8	4	29	29	3	13	43	3.9	13.0	1.42	.252
	23	Corpus Christi (AA)	Cent	5	6	3.48	16	13	67	56	5	40	67	5.4	9.0	1.43	.231
Minor League Totals (1 year)				7	7	3.90	24	17	97	85	8	53	110	4.92	10.21	1.42	.238

24 JOJANSE TORRES, RHP

Born: Aug. 4, 1995. **B-T:** R-R. **HT:** 6-2. **WT:** 188. **Signed:** Dominican
Republic, 2018. **Signed by:** Roman Ocumarez/Oz Ocampo.

TRACK RECORD: The Astros signed Torres for $150,000 as a 22-year-old dur-
ing the 2018 international signing period. He dominated the Class A levels in 2019 and was invited to
summer camp in 2020. Torres threw a few times in exhibitions at Minute Maid Park, but was shut down
with elbow soreness shortly after. He appeared in eight games for Triple-A Sugar Land in 2021 before he
having season-ending arthroscopic surgery to remove a bone chip from his right elbow.

SCOUTING REPORT: Torres has a tremendous four-seam fastball that sits in the high 90s and touches 100
mph. He is unafraid to challenge hitters with it and has had success in the minors doing so. His changeup
could be his best secondary pitch, especially with the velocity difference off his fastball. He also throws a
hard, mid-80s slider that gets chase swings along with a curveball, but he does not have enough consistency with either pitch. His control and command are suspect and will be tested against better competition.

THE FUTURE: Torres' age and injury history invite questions whether he has time to develop the command and breaking pitches to be a starter. His overpowering fastball and changeup combination profile
best out of the bullpen.

Year	Age	Club (Level)	Lge	W	L	ERA	G	GS	IP	H	HR	BB	SO	BB/9	SO/9	WHIP	AVG
2021	25	Sugar Land (AAA)	West	0	3	7.32	8	5	19	19	4	19	23	8.7	10.5	1.93	.257
Minor League Totals (4 years)				13	5	2.55	45	23	155	114	8	73	178	4.23	10.31	1.20	.201

25 BRETT CONINE, RHP

Born: Oct. 16, 1996. **B-T:** R-R. **HT:** 6-3. **WT:** 218. **Drafted:** Cal State
Fullerton, 2018 (11th round). **Signed by:** Ryan Leake.

TRACK RECORD: Conine closed throughout his three-year career at Cal State
Fullerton, but the Astros drafted him in 2018 with the intention to develop him as a starter. He had a
2.20 ERA and reached Double-A Corpus Christi during his first minor league season before continuing
his impressive ascent at the alternate training site in 2020. His performance suggested Conine could be a
major league depth option in 2021, but his command and performance regressed at Triple-A Sugar Land,
where he finished with a 5.66 ERA and 1.500 WHIP.

SCOUTING REPORT: Conine is a finesse righthander who mixes his four-pitch arsenal well, relying on
changing eye levels and deception more than bat-missing ability. His four-seam fastball sits 89-92 mph,
but he's shown the ability to hit 94-95. A big, overhand curveball is his out pitch. He's shown good feel
for an above-average changeup and needs to refine his slider, which he uses primarily early in counts but
only started throwing in 2019.

THE FUTURE: Conine took a step back in 2021. He should start 2022 back in Triple-A, where he could
reestablish himself as a depth starter on the big league doorstep.

Year	Age	Club (Level)	Lge	W	L	ERA	G	GS	IP	H	HR	BB	SO	BB/9	SO/9	WHIP	AVG
2021	24	Sugar Land (AAA)	West	8	4	5.66	25	18	98	105	20	43	83	3.9	7.6	1.50	.267
Minor League Totals (4 years)				17	9	3.57	61	36	244.2	219	27	83	254	3.05	9.34	1.23	.235

26 SHAY WHITCOMB, SS

Born: Sept. 28, 1998. **B-T:** R-R. **HT:** 6-3. **WT:** 202. **Drafted:** UC San Diego, 2020 (5th round). **Signed by:** Ryan Leake.

BA GRADE: 40 Risk: High

TRACK RECORD: Whitcomb signed for $56,000 after Houston took him with its final pick during the five-round draft in 2020. He flew under the radar at Division II UC San Diego, but popped onto the Astros' radar with a strong showing in the Cape Cod League after his sophomore year. Whitcomb affirmed the Astros' faith in him with a strong debut season in 2021 that ended at High-A Asheville. He and and Yankees top prospect Anthony Volpe were the only two minor league players that finished 2021 with at least 20 homers, 25 doubles and 30 stolen bases.

SCOUTING REPORT: Whitcomb has above-average raw power and some of the organization's highest exit velocities. He gets pull-happy and is strikeout-prone, creating worry that his swing-and-miss issues will be exploited by advanced pitching. Offense will be Whitcomb's ticket to advancement. He is a fringe-average runner and a below-average defender at shortstop. With limited range, bad footwork and a below-average throwing arm, some scouts think he is destined for second base while others contend he may slug his way onto a corner.

THE FUTURE: Whitcomb quieted some doubts with his excellent 2021, but will face stiffer competition in 2022, when he could reach Double-A.

Year	Age	Club (Level)	Lge	AVG	G	AB	R	H	2B	3B	HR	RBI	BB	SO	SB	OBP	SLG
2021	22	Fayetteville (LoA)	East	.282	41	163	32	46	3	0	7	22	20	53	14	.369	.429
	22	Asheville (HiA)	East	.300	58	233	49	70	22	0	16	56	19	81	16	.358	.601
Minor League Totals (2 years)				.293	99	396	81	116	25	0	23	78	39	134	30	.363	.530

27 JONATHAN BERMUDEZ, LHP

Born: Oct. 16, 1995. **B-T:** L-L. **HT:** 6-2. **WT:** 237. **Drafted:** Southeastern (Fla.), 2018 (23rd round). **Signed by:** Evan Brannon.

BA GRADE: 40 Risk: High

TRACK RECORD: Bermudez had a 1.95 ERA and earned NAIA pitcher of the year honors at Southeastern (Fla.) in 2018, after which Houston selected him in the 23rd round and gave him a $75,000 signing bonus. He reached Double-A Corpus Christi during the 2019 season, but the Astros did not include him in their 60-man player pool during the 2020 season. Bermudez came back with a breakout 2021 season, garnering Astros minor league pitcher of the year honors and a spot on the club's 40-man roster after a strong showing at Triple-A Sugar Land.

SCOUTING REPORT: Bermudez is a pitchability lefty with enough deception to project as a back-end starter. His four-seam fastball sits 91-93 mph with enough rise and run to miss some bats. Both his changeup and splitter have huge tailing action and sit in the low to mid 80s. He throws two variations of a slider: one short with cut in the low 80s and a sweeper in the high 70s. Bermudez hides the ball well in his delivery and has some funk to keep hitters off balance. Astros officials think he has more velocity in his big frame, too. He throws plenty of strikes with average control.

THE FUTURE: Bermudez broke out in 2021 and is on the major league doorstep because of it. He should start 2022 in Triple-A and could be in line for his major league debut.

Year	Age	Club (Level)	Lge	W	L	ERA	G	GS	IP	H	HR	BB	SO	BB/9	SO/9	WHIP	AVG
2021	25	Corpus Christi (AA)	Cent	3	5	3.32	18	15	78	72	7	21	106	2.4	12.1	1.18	.238
	25	Sugar Land (AAA)	West	2	1	3.06	7	5	32	21	3	13	40	3.6	11.1	1.05	.181
Minor League Totals (4 years)				12	9	3.43	58	30	202	173	15	70	249	3.11	11.08	1.20	.230

28 SETH MARTINEZ, RHP

Born: Aug. 29, 1994. **B-T:** R-R. **HT:** 6-2. **WT:** 200. **Drafted:** Arizona State, 2016 (17th round). **Signed by:** Scott Cousins (Athletics).

BA GRADE: 40 Risk: High

TRACK RECORD: The A's gave Martinez a $70,000 signing bonus after selecting him in the 17th round of the 2016 draft out of Arizona State. He peaked at Double-A in the A's organization before the Astros selected him in the minor league phase of the 2020 Rule 5 draft. Martinez had a 2.81 ERA in 36 relief appearances at Triple-A Sugar Land before the Astros summoned him for his major league debut in September. He appeared in three games and survived the offseason 40-man churn.

SCOUTING REPORT: Martinez has morphed into a long reliever after beginning his career as a starter. He throws five pitches, but his most recent success came after the Astros' player development staff overhauled his slider. Martinez now throws a horizontal, sweeping slider as opposed to the two-plane offering he had with Oakland. Martinez's four-seam fastball sits in the low 90s and he mixes in a cutter, sinker and a changeup to remain unpredictable. His control is above average and hitters struggle to square him up.

THE FUTURE: Martinez is already 27, but he has a spot on the 40-man roster and will figure into the Astros bullpen. He should bounce between Triple-A Sugar Land and the majors during the 2022 season.

Year	Age	Club (Level)	Lge	W	L	ERA	G	GS	IP	H	HR	BB	SO	BB/9	SO/9	WHIP	AVG
2021	26	Sugar Land (AAA)	West	5	3	2.81	36	0	57	35	5	20	78	3.1	12.2	0.95	.171
	26	Houston (MLB)	AL	0	0	15.00	3	0	3	5	0	3	3	9.0	9.0	2.67	.385
Major League Totals (1 year)				0	0	15.00	3	0	3	5	0	3	3	9.00	9.00	2.67	.385
Minor League Totals (6 years)				20	23	3.06	144	11	303	253	22	77	288	2.28	8.55	1.09	.227

29 JAIRO SOLIS, RHP

Born: Dec. 22, 1999. **B-T:** R-R. **HT:** 6-2. **WT:** 205. **Signed:** Venezuela, 2016. **Signed by:** Oz Ocampo/Tom Shafer/Roman Ocumarez/Enrique Brito.

BA GRADE
45 Risk: Extreme

TRACK RECORD: Solis signed for $450,000 as a 16-year-old during the 2016 international signing period, but has thrown just 112 innings in the four subsequent seasons. He hasn't appeared in a game since 2018, after which he had Tommy John surgery and missed the 2019 season. The Astros added Solis to their 40-man roster after a look at his stuff during the 2020 instructional league. He reported to spring training in 2021, but elbow problems persisted. An initial surgery to remove loose bodies did not solve it, and Solis had his second Tommy John surgery in June.

SCOUTING REPORT: When healthy, Solis has some of the best upside of any starting pitching prospect in the Astros system. He's shown above-average control at times with a four-pitch mix. He threw 93-94 mph in spring training and has shown the ability to touch 98. Solis' above-average changeup is his best secondary pitch and he shows feel for both a slider and curveball, though they both get slurvy. Some scouts say he's too thin and needs to add muscle, but his constant injuries make it difficult.

THE FUTURE: The timing of Solis' second Tommy John won't allow him to pitch until late 2022. He's still young enough to be excited about, but his injuries provide obvious concern.

Year	Age	Club (Level)	Lge	W	L	ERA	G	GS	IP	H	HR	BB	SO	BB/9	SO/9	WHIP	AVG
2021	21	Did not play—Injured															
Minor League Totals (3 years)				5	7	3.05	28	21	112	100	4	53	120	4.26	9.64	1.37	.240

30 TYLER BROWN, RHP

Born: Oct. 2, 1998. **B-T:** R-R. **HT:** 6-4. **WT:** 242. **Drafted:** Vanderbilt, 2020 (3rd round). **Signed by:** Landon Townsley.

BA GRADE
40 Risk: High

TRACK RECORD: Brown closed for a Vanderbilt team that won the 2019 College World Series and set the school's single-season saves record with 17. He left in second place on the school's all-time saves list. Houston signed him for $577,000 after taking him in the third round of the 2020 draft. The Astros believe Brown is a starter, but his debut season did not go well. He finished with a 6.95 ERA and a 1.68 WHIP between High-A Asheville and Double-A Corpus Christi.

SCOUTING REPORT: Brown has solid strike-throwing ability and a starter's repertoire, but many evaluators wonder whether he's better suited to go back to the bullpen because of his high-effort delivery. He sits 90-92 mph with his four-seam fastball as a starter and primarily complements it with an above-average slider that hovers around 78-81 mph. He has both an average changeup and a below-average curveball.

THE FUTURE: Brown's professional debut left a lot to be desired, but the fact the Astros moved him to Double-A despite his struggles signaled confidence in him putting it together. He should start 2022 back in Double-A.

Year	Age	Club (Level)	Lge	W	L	ERA	G	GS	IP	H	HR	BB	SO	BB/9	SO/9	WHIP	AVG
2021	22	Asheville (HiA)	East	3	5	7.25	15	11	63	71	14	32	68	4.6	9.7	1.63	.278
	22	Corpus Christi (AA)	Cent	1	3	6.26	8	4	27	26	4	24	40	7.9	13.2	1.83	.252
Minor League Totals (2 years)				4	8	6.95	23	15	91	97	18	56	108	5.56	10.72	1.69	.271

MORE PROSPECTS TO KNOW

31 LOGAN CERNY, OF
Cerny fits the Astros' recent profile for amateur outfielders: raw and extremely toolsy. He has plus-plus speed, above-average raw power and enough athleticism to believe he could be a plus-defender in the outfield, but questions surround his offensive approach and ability to make contactl.

32 JOSE ALBERTO RIVERA, RHP
The Angels selected Rivera in the 2021 Rule 5 Draft but returned him to the Astros before the season. Rivera's fastball has been clocked at 102 mph, but he threw just 11.1 innings in 2021.

33 JOE RECORD, RHP
Record had a nice debut season for the Astros and made the Fall Stars Game in the Arizona Fall League after being selected from the Twins in the minor league Rule 5 Draft. He's a reliever with a four-seam fastball in the mid to high 90s.

34 JONATHAN SPRINKLE, RHP
Sprinkle signed as an undrafted free agent in 2020 and reached Double-A in 2021. He's a relief prospect who relies on a mid 90s cutter along with a slider and changeup. He struck out 79 in 44 innings in 2021.

35 MISAEL TAMAREZ, RHP
Tamarez flashed a velocity increase in 2021, sitting mid to high 90s with his fastball to go along with an above-average slider. His control and command need improvement.

36 JUSTIN DIRDEN, OF
Dirden signed out of Southeast Missouri State as an undrafted free agent in 2020 and finished his first professional season with a .934 OPS in 350 plate appearances. He has average power from the left side and is a plus defender in right field.

37 COREY JULKS, 3B
SLEEPER

Julks had his most consistent season in 2021, slugging .491 with an .841 OPS at Double-A. He sequenced his swing better and started using his pull side more, eschewing the inside-out approach he had earlier in his career.

38 ALIMBER SANTA, RHP
An 18-year-old Dominican signed for $70,000 in 2021, Santa had a velocity spike at instructional league, sitting 98 mph with a big breaking curveball. He is still working on his slider.

39 JJ MATIJEVIC, 1B
A drug suspension in 2019 stalled Matijevic's ascent. He boasts above-average power and slugged 25 home runs in 2021 but needs to shore up defense at first base.

40 SCOTT MANEA, C
Since arriving from the Mets in the J.D. Davis trade, Manea has shown above-average power and is improving his receiving skills behind the plate.

TOP PROSPECTS OF THE DECADE

Year	Player, Pos	2021 Org
2012	Jon Singleton, 1B/OF	Mexican League
2013	Carlos Correa, SS	Astros
2014	Carlos Correa, SS	Astros
2015	Carlos Correa, SS	Astros
2016	A.J. Reed, 1B	Did not play
2017	Francis Martes, RHP	Astros
2018	Forrest Whitley, RHP	Astros
2019	Forrest Whitley, RHP	Astros
2020	Forrest Whitley, RHP	Astros
2021	Forrest Whitley, RHP	Astros

TOP DRAFT PICKS OF THE DECADE

Year	Player, Pos	2021 Org
2012	Carlos Correa, SS	Astros
2013	Mark Appel, RHP	Phillies
2014	*Brady Aiken, LHP	Guardians
2015	Alex Bregman, SS	Astros
2016	Forrest Whitley, RHP	Astros
2017	J.B. Bukauskas, RHP	D-backs
2018	Seth Beer, OF	D-backs
2019	Korey Lee, C	Astros
2020	Alex Santos, RHP (2nd round supp)	Astros
2021	Tyler Whitaker, OF (3rd round)	Astros
	* Did not sign	

Kansas City Royals

BY BILL MITCHELL

The Royals compiled their fifth straight losing season in 2021, finishing fourth in the American League Central with a 74-88 record, but advances in the minor leagues provide a more optimistic view for the future. Three of the Royals' four full-season affiliates finished with winning records. Even better, Double-A Northwest Arkansas and High-A Quad Cities both captured their respective league championships.

Several key Royals hitters made significant strides in 2021, representing a notable step forward for Kansas City's hitting development program under the direction of Alec Zumwalt.

First baseman Nick Pratto and catcher MJ Melendez made drastic improvements after subpar 2019 seasons, highlighted by Melendez leading the minors with 41 home runs and Pratto finishing tied for second with 36. Shortstop Bobby Witt Jr. continued his meteoric rise, reaching Triple-A in his first full season and winning Minor League Player of the Year. All three were first-team minor league all-stars for BA.

Other hitters who took big strides forward include first baseman Vinnie Pasquantino and second baseman Michael Massey. Outfielder Kyle Isbel made his MLB debut with two separate stints in Kansas City.

Not to be overlooked, Kansas City's pitching development program also experienced success, with 2018 draft picks Daniel Lynch and Kris Bubic becoming key parts of the Royals' rotation and fireballing righthander Carlos Hernandez pitching well in 24 games in his first real taste of the big leagues. Jackson Kowar and Jon Heasley, two other members of the 2018 draft class, also made their MLB debuts in 2021.

The Royals dipped into the high school ranks early in the 2021 draft to add to that talent base, taking pitchers Frank Mozzicato, Ben Kudrna and Shane Panzini in the first, second and fourth rounds, while also adding catcher Carter Jensen in the third round. Jensen made his debut in the Arizona Complex League, while the three pitchers did not appear in games until instructional league. The Royals signed all 21 of their draft choices before the signing deadline.

Following the major league struggles but minor league successes, the Royals revamped their front office in September. General manager Dayton Moore was promoted to president of baseball operations. Replacing Moore in the GM seat is longtime lieutenant J.J. Picollo. Gene Watson returned to the Royals after one year in an advisory role with the Angels and will be vice president/assistant GM

Shortstop Nicky Lopez hit .330 in the second half of 2021 to emerge as an everyday player.

PROJECTED 2025 LINEUP

Catcher	MJ Melendez	26
First Base	Nick Pratto	26
Second Base	Nick Loftin	26
Third Base	Bobby Witt Jr.	25
Shortstop	Nicky Lopez	30
Left Field	Andrew Benintendi	30
Center Field	Michael A. Taylor	34
Right Field	Kyle Isbel	28
Designated Hitter	Salvador Perez	35
No. 1 Starter	Daniel Lynch	28
No. 2 Starter	Asa Lacy	26
No. 3 Starter	Brady Singer	28
No. 4 Starter	Kris Bubic	27
No. 5 Starter	Jackson Kowar	28
Closer	Carlos Hernandez	28

of major league scouting. Scouting director Lonnie Goldberg, in his 14th year with the Royals, became vice president/player personnel. Danny Ontiveros moved into the role of scouting director.

The revamped front office will be tasked with turning all of the Royals' minor league success into major league success. The ascension of Lynch, Kowar and the rest of the young pitchers was a promising first step, and there is existing talent in the majors led by Salvador Perez, who hit 48 home runs in 2021 to set a new single-season record for a catcher.

With Witt, Pratto and Melendez on the doorstep, the Royals' return to a winning record appears near. ∎

DEPTH CHART

KANSAS CITY ROYALS

TOP 2022 ROOKIES	RANK
Bobby Witt Jr., SS	1
Nick Pratto, 1B	4
Kyle Isbel, OF	6
BREAKOUT PROSPECTS	**RANK**
Alec Marsh, RHP	11
Jon Heasley, RHP	13
Anthony Veneziano, LHP	21

SOURCE OF TOP 30 TALENT

Homegrown	29	Acquired	1
College	15	Trade	1
Junior college	0	Rule 5 draft	0
High school	10	Independent league	0
Nondrafted free agent	0	Free agent/waivers	0
International	4		

LF
Darryl Collins
Brewer Hicklen

CF
Kyle Isbel (6)
John Rave
Diego Hernandez
Tucker Bradley

RF
Erick Pena (17)
Seuly Matias
Tyler Gentry
Eric Cole

3B
Emmanuel Rivera (30)
Nathan Eaton

SS
Bobby Witt Jr. (1)
Nick Loftin (12)
Daniel Vazquez (25)
Maikel Garcia (28)
Brennon McNair

2B
Michael Massey (15)
Clay Dungan
Peyton Wilson

1B
Nick Pratto (4)
Vinnie Pasquantino (10)

C
MJ Melendez (3)
Carter Jensen (16)
Omar Hernandez

LHP

LHSP
Asa Lacy (2)
Frank Mozzicato (7)
Angel Zerpa (20)
Anthony Veneziano (21)
Austin Cox (22)
AJ Block
Drew Parrish

LHRP
Josh Dye
Emilio Marquez
Caden Monke

RHP

RHSP
Jackson Kowar (5)
Ben Kudrna (8)
Jonathan Bowlan (9)
Alec Marsh (11)
Jon Heasley (13)
Ben Hernandez (14)
Noah Murdock (23)
Shane Panzini (24)
Zack Haake (27)
Samuel Valerio
Harrison Beethe
Anderson Paulino

RHRP
Will Klein (18)
Dylan Coleman (19)
Nathan Webb (26)
Collin Snider (29)
Christian Cosby
Isaiah Henry
Jose Cuas
Kasey Kalich

1 BOBBY WITT JR., SS

Born: June 14, 2000. **B-T:** R-R. **HT:** 6-1. **WT:** 185.
Drafted: HS—Colleyville, Texas, 2019 (1st round).
Signed by: Chad Lee.

TRACK RECORD: Expectations have long been high for the son of former pitcher and 18-year major league veteran Bobby Witt. The younger Witt has been successful at every level, going back to youth baseball and continuing through his high school career at Colleyville (Texas) Heritage High, where he was named BA High School Player of the Year in 2019. The second overall pick in that year's draft has met every challenge thrown his way since signing for a full-slot bonus of $7,789,000 and debuting that summer in the Rookie-level Arizona League. He handled the advanced pitching at the alternate training site in 2020 and was challenged in 2021 with an assignment to Double-A for his first full season. To say that Witt exceeded expectations would be an understatement, as his 2021 season split between Double-A and Triple-A was one for the ages. After a slow start when he made the necessary adjustments, Witt obliterated Double-A pitching and moved up to Triple-A at midseason. He finished in the top five in the minor leagues in hits (144), runs (99), home runs (33) and RBIs (97) and finished just shy of a 30-30 season with 29 stolen bases, all in his age-21 season at the highest levels of the minors. In recognition of his outstanding season, Witt was named BA Minor League Player of the Year.

SCOUTING REPORT: Witt checks all of the boxes for a true five tool player, with all of his tools grading plus or better. What really makes him special is his cognitive ability and unique baseball instincts that allow him to simplify the game. He started the 2021 season relatively slowly but stuck to his game, improving his pitch selection and driving balls in the zone, and it wasn't long before he began performing at a higher level. Whenever he faces more advanced pitching, Witt and the Royals staff don't make mechanical adjustments to his short, compact swing or to his approach. Instead, they let his athleticism and instincts take over. The strength that he's added with maturity has given more power to his swing and allows him to hit balls hard to all fields. He controls the barrel very well and has become more aggressive with his swing while also cutting down on his swings and misses. Witt's speed that he showed while stealing 29 bases in 2021 was a surprise to many, and he could swipe more bags as he gains experience. He also showed he could leg out infield hits and regularly take an extra base. In addition to his well-rounded offen-

EDDIE KELLY/PROLOOK PHOTOS

BA GRADE	SCOUTING GRADES
75 Risk: Medium	Hit: 60. Power: 70. Run: 70. Field: 60. Arm: 60.

Projected future grades on 20-80 scouting scale

BEST TOOLS

Best Hitter for Average	Vinnie Pasquantino
Best Power Hitter	MJ Melendez
Best Strike-Zone Discipline	Nick Loftin
Fastest Baserunner	Tyler Tolbert
Best Athlete	Bobby Witt Jr.
Best Fastball	Will Klein
Best Curveball	Frank Mozzicato
Best Slider	Asa Lacy
Best Changeup	Jackson Kowar
Best Control	Angel Zerpa
Best Defensive Catcher	Sebastian Rivero
Best Defensive Infielder	Nick Pratto
Best Infield Arm	Maikel Garcia
Best Defensive Outfielder	Kyle Isbel
Best Outfield Arm	Seuly Matias

sive game, Witt is the complete package on defense at shortstop with steady hands and a strong, accurate arm. What also separates Witt is how hard he works behind the scenes, a factor contributing to how simple the game appears for him. His makeup is outstanding and he's a good teammate, helping others with their individual games.

THE FUTURE: Witt will soon take his place in the Royals' lineup. He projects to be a franchise cornerstone who impacts games at the plate, on the bases and in the field. His major league debut will come in 2022 barring injury, and may be as soon as Opening Day. ∎

Year	Age	Club (Level)	Lge	AVG	G	AB	R	H	2B	3B	HR	RBI	BB	SO	SB	OBP	SLG
2021	21	NW Arkansas (AA)	Cent	.295	61	244	44	72	11	4	16	51	25	67	14	.369	.570
	21	Omaha (AAA)	East	.285	62	253	55	72	24	0	17	46	26	64	15	.352	.581
Minor League Totals (3 years)				.283	160	661	129	187	37	9	34	124	64	166	38	.350	.520

2 ASA LACY, LHP

Born: June 2, 1999. **B-T:** L-L. **HT:** 6-4. **WT:** 215. **Drafted:** Texas A&M, 2020 (1st round). **Signed by:** Josh Hallgren.

TRACK RECORD: Lacy finally made his pro debut one year after the Royals drafted the hard-throwing southpaw fourth overall out of Texas A&M. After signing with the Royals for a $6,670,000 bonus, Lacy spent 2020 at the alternate training site and opened 2021 at High-A Quad Cities. Expected to move quickly, Lacy instead struggled to a 5.19 ERA and walked more than seven batters per nine innings in an underwhelming season, albeit while flashing exhilarating pure stuff.

BA GRADE
60 Risk: High

SCOUTING REPORT: The centerpiece of Lacy's arsenal is a plus-plus fastball that regularly touches 97-98 mph with sharp downward tilt. His three off-speed pitches all flash plus and get swings and misses in the strike zone. His high-80s slider, which sometimes looks more like a cutter, is a wipeout strikeout pitch against both righthanded and lefthanded batters. His changeup has late life and projects as a plus offering when he commands it, and his curveball has good bite. To improve his below-average control, Lacy needs to keep his feet and head in sync during his delivery in order to maintain a more fluid direction to the plate. But rival scouts are not yet concerned with his struggles to consistently throw strikes because of the quality of his pitches.

THE FUTURE: After four starts in the Arizona Fall League, where he showed loud stuff with very high strikeout and high walk rates, Lacy will be ready to move up to Double-A in 2022.

SCOUTING GRADES:	Fastball: 70	Slider: 60	Curveball: 55	Changeup: 60	Control: 40

Year	Age	Club (Level)	Lge	W	L	ERA	G	GS	IP	H	HR	BB	SO	BB/9	SO/9	WHIP	AVG
2021	22	Quad Cities (HiA)	Cent	2	5	5.19	14	14	52	41	5	41	79	7.1	13.7	1.58	.222
Minor League Totals (2 years)				2	5	5.19	14	14	52	41	5	41	79	7.1	13.7	1.58	.222

3 MJ MELENDEZ, C

Born: Nov. 28, 1998. **B-T:** L-R. **HT:** 6-1. **WT:** 185. **Drafted:** HS—Miami, 2017 (2nd round). **Signed by:** Alex Mesa.

TRACK RECORD: Melendez was one of several hitters at High-A Wilmington in 2019 to have a very difficult season at the plate. The improvement of the hitters from that season to 2021 was remarkable and a testament to the Royals' improved hitting development program. Melendez made perhaps the most drastic turnaround of all, culminating in him leading the minor leagues with 41 home runs and finishing fifth with a 1.011 OPS as he climbed from Double-A to Triple-A. Even more significant was how he cut his strikeout rate from nearly 40% in 2019 to 21.7% in 2021.

BA GRADE
55 Risk: Medium

SCOUTING REPORT: Melendez went to work on his swing and approach right after the 2019 season, resulting in a shorter swing, a toned-down leg kick, a better stance and a more relaxed approach. As a result, he is now able to pick up spin earlier, which leads to fewer chase swings out of the strike zone. Moving away from being a dead-pull hitter allowed Melendez to open up the opposite side of the field. He took well to the challenge of Triple-A, getting on base at a higher rate than in Double-A while maintaining his over-the-fence power. Melendez still has work to do with his receiving and blocking behind the plate, but he's athletic and flexible enough to keep improving. Blessed with a plus-plus arm, he continues to throw out runners at a high rate. In 2021, he threw out potential base stealers at a 31% rate.

THE FUTURE: Melendez will benefit from a full season at Triple-A, especially with Salvador Perez firmly entrenched at catcher in Kansas City. He played a few games at third base after his promotion to Omaha and will continue to get experience at other positions.

SCOUTING GRADES:	Hitting: 45	Power: 60	Running: 45	Fielding: 60	Arm: 70

Year	Age	Club (Level)	Lge	AVG	G	AB	R	H	2B	3B	HR	RBI	BB	SO	SB	OBP	SLG
2021	22	NW Arkansas (AA)	Cent	.285	79	298	58	85	18	0	28	65	43	76	2	.372	.628
	22	Omaha (AAA)	East	.293	44	150	37	44	4	3	13	38	32	39	1	.413	.620
Minor League Totals (5 years)				.241	391	1398	206	337	79	17	73	260	188	483	18	.333	.479

4 NICK PRATTO, 1B

Born: Oct. 6, 1998. **B-T:** L-L. **HT:** 6-1. **WT:** 195. **Drafted:** HS—Huntington Beach, Calif., 2017 (1st round). **Signed by:** Rich Amaral.

TRACK RECORD: Like teammate MJ Melendez, Pratto suffered through a miserable 2019 season at High-A Wilmington and went to work improving his swing and approach at the plate. The work paid off in 2021 as Pratto hit 36 home runs while rising from Double-A to Triple-A, tied for the second most home runs in the minor leagues, and finished the season with a .988 OPS.

SCOUTING REPORT: The key changes that Pratto made revolved around developing a new approach and mindset at the plate and adapting a more efficient bat path to allow his barrel to get into the zone sooner. This was helped further by the innate bat speed and quickness in his hands. Pratto now hits the ball in the air with more authority and will continue to add strength to his frame. Pratto sees the ball well and has shown that he can pick up spin, and a key factor in his improvement was better pitch selection. He doesn't miss his pitch to hit, especially those at higher velocities. Pratto also handles lefthanded pitchers well. While not a burner, Pratto continues to reach double-digit stolen bases every year, with sneaky instincts allowing his speed to play up on the bases. He's at least a plus defender at first base, with some plus-plus grades given to his glove and projections that he will win Gold Glove awards.

BA GRADE
55 Risk: Medium

THE FUTURE: First base has been a position of need for the Royals since Eric Hosmer departed as a free agent. Pratto will head to spring training vying to earn playing time in the big leagues, although additional Triple-A seasoning would provide long-term benefit for his career.

SCOUTING GRADES:	Hitting: 55	Power: 60	Running: 45	Fielding: 60	Arm: 55

Year	Age	Club (Level)	Lge	AVG	G	AB	R	H	2B	3B	HR	RBI	BB	SO	SB	OBP	SLG
2021	22	NW Arkansas (AA)	Cent	.271	61	221	44	60	13	4	15	43	46	80	7	.404	.570
	22	Omaha (AAA)	East	.259	63	224	54	58	15	3	21	55	37	77	5	.367	.634
Minor League Totals (5 years)				.248	427	1547	250	383	97	13	63	240	201	529	61	.337	.449

5 JACKSON KOWAR, RHP

Born: Oct. 4, 1996. **B-T:** R-R. **HT:** 6-5. **WT:** 180. **Drafted:** Florida, 2018 (1st round). **Signed by:** Jim Buckley.

TRACK RECORD: Of the five college pitchers the Royals took in the first two rounds of the 2018 draft, Kowar was the fourth to make it to the big leagues, with his debut coming on June 7, 2021. The former Florida righthander struggled to command his fastball in the majors and logged an ugly 11.27 ERA in nine appearances (eight starts), but he was solid throughout the rest of the season in Triple-A.

SCOUTING REPORT: Kowar's plus-plus changeup continues to be the gem of his arsenal. He throws his changeup with confidence and its trapdoor action makes it a tough pitch to barrel. Kowar complements his changeup with a fastball that sits 94-95 mph but plays down from its velocity at times. When his fastball gets up in the zone, it flattens out and there's not a lot of deception.

BA GRADE
50 Risk: Medium

When he's on top of the pitch it has two-seam running life in on righthanded batters and late sinking action. Kowar's curveball was a below-average pitch he used infrequently in college, but he worked on it extensively at the alternate training site in 2020. It has improved to the point that it's now an above-average pitch with the potential to be a plus offering. It has 11-to-5 shape with good spin, and will be more effective when he lands it for strikes with greater frequency. Kowar uses a three-quarters delivery with a full stroke and the ball comes out clean, giving him average control.

THE FUTURE: Kowar will be ready for another chance at the majors in 2022. He has the velocity and stuff to be a mid-rotation starter and will head to spring training looking for a spot in the Royals' rotation.

SCOUTING GRADES:	Fastball: 60	Curveball: 55	Changeup: 70	Control: 50

Year	Age	Club (Level)	Lge	W	L	ERA	G	GS	IP	H	HR	BB	SO	BB/9	SO/9	WHIP	AVG
2021	24	Omaha (AAA)	East	9	4	3.46	17	16	80	66	7	34	115	3.8	12.8	1.24	.220
	24	Kansas City (MLB)	AL	0	6	11.27	9	8	30	43	7	20	29	5.9	8.6	2.08	.336
Major League Totals (1 year)				0	6	11.27	9	8	30	43	7	20	29	5.9	8.6	2.08	.336
Minor League Totals (4 years)				16	15	3.49	52	51	255	226	21	89	281	3.1	9.9	1.23	.236

6 KYLE ISBEL, OF

Born: March 3, 1997. **B-T:** L-R. **HT:** 5-11. **WT:** 183. **Drafted:** Nevada-Las Vegas, 2018 (3rd round). **Signed by:** Kenny Muñoz.

TRACK RECORD: Isbel broke camp with the big league team in 2021 in what was really just his second full season since being drafted in the third round in 2018. The UNLV product struggled at the plate in his first Royals stint but hit much better after his late-season return from Triple-A Omaha.

SCOUTING REPORT: Isbel showed much more confidence when he returned to the Royals' lineup in September, posting a .286/.362/.452 batting line in his final 11 games, as he was more focused at the plate, his swing path improved, and he wasn't as pull-conscious. The expected power started to emerge in Triple-A, where he hit more line drives and fly balls than in the past, with his 15 home runs with Omaha being a career high. Isbel continues to improve his outfield defense, impressive considering he started his college career as an infielder. He played all three outfield positions with Omaha, spending more time in center field and emerging as a plus defender with the plus speed to cover the ground. He's able to close on balls in the gap and gets good initial reads and angles, and his outfield instincts have improved. His arm grade jumped to above-average thanks in part to the accuracy of his throws. Isbel stole 22 bases during his time with Omaha, giving another positive note to his game.

THE FUTURE: With his strong Triple-A season and the improvement he showed upon his return to Kansas City, Isbel has a very good chance of earning a spot on the Opening Day roster, either a starting job or as a fourth outfielder.

BA GRADE

45 Risk: Low

SCOUTING GRADES:	Hitting: 55	Power: 45	Running: 60	Fielding: 60	Arm: 55

Year	Age	Club (Level)	Lge	AVG	G	AB	R	H	2B	3B	HR	RBI	BB	SO	SB	OBP	SLG
2021	24	Omaha (AAA)	East	.269	105	394	62	106	18	3	15	55	45	91	22	.357	.444
	24	Kansas City (MLB)	AL	.276	28	76	16	21	5	2	1	7	7	23	2	.337	.434
Major League Totals (1 year)				.276	28	76	16	21	5	2	1	7	7	23	2	.337	.434
Minor League Totals (4 years)				.277	228	877	154	243	49	8	29	117	88	200	57	.352	.450

7 FRANK MOZZICATO, LHP

Born: June 10, 2003. **B-T:** L-L. **HT:** 6-3. **WT:** 175. **Drafted:** HS—Manchester, Conn., 2021 (1st round). **Signed by:** Casey Fahy.

TRACK RECORD: Mozzicato was an under-the-radar draft prospect until his stock soared in his senior season, when he pitched four straight no-hitters and showed one of the best curveballs in the country. The Royals pulled a surprise when they selected Mozzicato seventh overall in the draft and signed him for a $3,547,500 bonus, about $3 million under slot. Mozzicato reported to the Royals training facility in Surprise, Ariz., after signing but did not pitch in games during the regular season. He made his unofficial debut during instructional league.

SCOUTING REPORT: Mozzicato's curveball is his money offering. It's at least a plus pitch with some observers believing it could eventually be plus-plus because of its high spin rate, sharp bite and good depth. It has 1-to-7 shape, and he showed in instructs that he can fold it into the zone for a strike and expand the zone with it when ahead in the count. His fastball sits 90-93 mph with good vertical movement, and with his size and athleticism he should be able to add velocity with more experience and physical maturity. Like most prep pitchers, Mozzicato didn't have to use a changeup much during his high school career, but it's a potential plus pitch that is hard for hitters to see because he sells it with arm speed and it looks like his fastball coming out of his hand. He repeats his delivery and has good feel to pitch.

THE FUTURE: After getting his feet wet in the pro game, Mozzicato will be ready for a full-season assignment in 2022, with a likely limit on his total innings throughout the season.

BILL MITCHELL

BA GRADE

55 Risk: Extreme

SCOUTING GRADES:	Fastball: 55	Curveball: 60	Changeup: 55	Control: 50

Year	Age	Club (Level)	Lge	W	L	ERA	G	GS	IP	H	HR	BB	SO	BB/9	SO/9	WHIP	AVG
2021	18	Did not play															

8 BEN KUDRNA, RHP

Born: Jan. 30, 2003. **B-T:** R-R. **HT:** 6-3. **WT:** 203. **Drafted:** HS—Overland Park, Kan., 2021 (2nd round). **Signed by:** Matt Price.

TRACK RECORD: Kudrna started building his reputation at the 2020 Area Code Games and continued with a strong senior season at Blue Valley Southwest High in Overland Park, Kan., about 30 miles south of Kansas City. The Royals selected the local product in the second round, 43rd overall, and signed him for an above-slot $3 million bonus. Like Royals first-round pick Frank Mozzicato, Kudrna was held out of games during the regular season and didn't pitch until instructional league in the fall.

SCOUTING REPORT: Kudrna presents an imposing presence on the mound and backs it up by attacking hitters with a 96-98 mph fastball. He generates easy velocity from his loose, quick arm and makes hitters uncomfortable with his downhill angle and late hop on his pitches. He may have more velocity in the tank as he adds strength to his solid, high-waisted frame with broad shoulders. Kudrna is still developing his slider and shows the potential to turn it into an above-average pitch with depth and tilt. He began incorporating his changeup, a hard pitch that he throws with arm speed and deception, more during instructs. Kudrna is very competitive on the mound, with Royals coaches noting he bears down and gets better with men on base.

THE FUTURE: Kudrna will likely make his professional debut with Low-A Columbia in 2022. He has a chance to be a hard-throwing, mid-rotation starter.

BILL MITCHELL

BA GRADE
55 Risk: Extreme

SCOUTING GRADES:	Fastball: 60	Slider: 55	Changeup: 50	Control: 50

Year	Age	Club (Level)	Lge	W	L	ERA	G	GS	IP	H	HR	BB	SO	BB/9	SO/9	WHIP	AVG
2021	18	Did not play															

9 JONATHAN BOWLAN, RHP

Born: Dec. 1, 1996. **B-T:** R-R. **HT:** 6-6. **WT:** 248. **Drafted:** Memphis, 2018 (2nd round). **Signed by:** Travis Ezi.

TRACK RECORD: Heeding the advice of Royals officials to get his body in better shape, Bowlan arrived at spring training in 2021 with a significantly improved physique. It appeared to pay off when he began the 2021 season with three outstanding starts at Double-A Northwest Arkansas, but after being pulled early in his fourth start, it was determined he needed Tommy John surgery. The injury robbed Bowlan of what was looking like his breakthrough season and the chance to represent his country as a member of the United States Olympic qualifying team.

SCOUTING REPORT: Bowlan uses a four-pitch mix highlighted by a 93-97 mph fastball. His fastball jumps on hitters because of the extension he gets in his delivery out of his big, 6-foot-6 frame and plays as a plus pitch with late

BA GRADE
50 Risk: High

explosion in the strike zone. Bowlan's biggest change in 2021 was the addition of a curveball to complement his low-80s slider and give him a second breaking ball. His nascent 80-82 mph curve with downward break gives hitters a different look from his slider and plays well off his other pitches. Bowlan's slider has late bite and he has a good feel for his changeup, which he throws to both righthanded and lefthanded batters. His pitches play up because of how well he controls and commands them. Bowlan repeats his clean delivery and pounds the strike zone effectively, and the above-average life and deception on all of his pitches allow him to go right after hitters.

THE FUTURE: Bowlan's work ethic and dedication to conditioning will help him during the injury rehab process. The Royals hope he may return late in the 2022 season, but it may be 2023 before he gets back on the mound.

SCOUTING GRADES:	Fastball: 60	Slider: 55	Curveball: 55	Changeup: 50	Control: 60

Year	Age	Club (Level)	Lge	W	L	ERA	G	GS	IP	H	HR	BB	SO	BB/9	SO/9	WHIP	AVG
2021	24	NW Arkansas (AA)	Cent	2	0	1.59	4	4	17	13	0	3	25	1.6	13.2	0.94	.206
Minor League Totals (4 years)				14	9	3.68	39	36	198	185	15	35	198	1.6	9.0	1.11	.246

10 VINNIE PASQUANTINO, 1B

Born: Oct. 10, 1997. **B-T:** L-L. **HT:** 6-4. **WT:** 245. **Drafted:** Old Dominion, 2019 (11th round). **Signed by:** Jim Farr.

TRACK RECORD: Pasquantino was an unheralded 11th-round pick out of Old Dominion in 2019. He stood an ungainly 6-foot-4, 245 pounds, but his bat held promise and earned quiet praise from evaluators. He returned from the coronavirus shutdown an improved hitter and defender and broke out in 2021. He hit .300/.394/.563 with 24 home runs and 84 RBIs as he rose from High-A to Double-A and had as many walks as strikeouts (64).

BA GRADE

50 Risk: High

SCOUTING REPORT: Pasquantino is a determined hitter with a high level of focus at the plate. He regularly takes professional at-bats and his strikeout-to-walk rate is rare for a power hitter in the modern era. Instead of making a lot of mechanical changes to his swing, Pasquantino instead has focused on seeing the ball well, keeping his eyes behind the ball, letting pitches travel deep and taking pitches in the right situations. He works hard on improving his defense and is now at least an average defender at first base, with the work ethic to continue improving. He provides a big target for infielders throwing to first and is athletic enough for the position. While he'll always be a well below-average runner, he makes up for the lack of speed with good baserunning instincts and reads on the bases. What makes Pasquantino even more special is his gregarious personality, outstanding makeup and passion for the game.

THE FUTURE: Pasquantino didn't miss a beat after his midseason promotion. He has a chance to be a power-hitting first baseman or DH.

SCOUTING GRADES:	Hitting: 60	Power: 60	Running: 30	Fielding: 50	Arm: 45

Year	Age	Club (Level)	Lge	AVG	G	AB	R	H	2B	3B	HR	RBI	BB	SO	SB	OBP	SLG
2021	23	Quad Cities (HiA)	Cent	.291	61	237	44	69	20	3	13	42	33	38	4	.384	.565
	23	NW Arkansas (AA)	Cent	.310	55	200	35	62	17	0	11	42	31	26	2	.405	.560
Minor League Totals (3 years)				.298	173	648	122	193	54	5	38	137	91	104	6	.386	.573

11 ALEC MARSH, RHP

BA GRADE

50 Risk: High

Born: May 14, 1998. **B-T:** R-R. **HT:** 6-2. **WT:** 220. **Drafted:** Arizona State, 2019 (2nd round supplemental). **Signed by:** Kenny Munoz.

TRACK RECORD: Marsh entered 2021 as one of several picks to click in the Royals system after gaining strength during the 2020 shutdown, giving his fastball a significant velocity bump while also developing more separation between his breaking balls. But Marsh made just six regular-season starts at Double-A before being shut down because of biceps soreness and arm fatigue. He returned to make one start in the Arizona Fall League.

SCOUTING REPORT: Despite limited looks in 2021, Marsh showed enough to remain one of the better pitching prospects in the Royals system. He attacks the zone with a fastball that sits at 96 mph and tickles triple-digits. He aggressively goes right at hitters, throwing four pitches, all potential plus offerings, for strikes. Marsh's two breaking balls tended to blend together earlier in his career, but he now gets enough separation to make them distinct pitches. His mid-80s slider is a hard, tight pitch that sometimes resembles a cutter, and his curveball that ranges from the high 70s to low 80s has solid depth. His changeup has natural depth and he throws it with good arm speed. His delivery is clean and repeatable.

THE FUTURE: Marsh has all the attributes of a starting pitcher, but he could also thrive as a power arm at the back of the bullpen. He could be a contributor to the big league team in 2022 if he stays healthy.

Year	Age	Club (Level)	Lge	W	L	ERA	G	GS	IP	H	HR	BB	SO	BB/9	SO/9	WHIP	AVG
2021	23	NW Arkansas (AA)	Cent	1	3	4.97	6	6	25	20	4	13	42	4.6	14.9	1.30	.217
Minor League Totals (2 years)				1	4	4.45	19	19	59	50	9	17	80	2.6	12.3	1.14	.229

12 NICK LOFTIN, SS

BA GRADE

50 Risk: High

Born: Sept. 25, 1998. **B-T:** R-R. **HT:** 6-1. **WT:** 185. **Drafted:** Baylor, 2020 (1st round supplemental). **Signed by:** Josh Hallgren.

TRACK RECORD: Loftin was generally regarded as a solid all-around performer when the Royals made him the 32nd overall pick in the 2020 draft. So far, the Baylor product has come as advertised. He made his professional debut at High-A Quad Cities in 2021, helping them win a championship. He was one of three players to tie for the league lead in batting average (.289), including teammate Michael Massey.

SCOUTING REPORT: Loftin is a gap-to-gap contact hitter favoring his pull side with sneaky pop that should increase as he gets stronger. A minor wrist injury slowed his start to the season, but he finished strong down the stretch, posting a 1.014 OPS over the final two months of the season. He shows good strike zone awareness and walks nearly as often as he strikes out. Loftin is solid at shortstop with a good first step, a quick release, and good hands and range. He also saw time at second and third base, and with his athleticism he'd thrive in a utility role if that's his future. Loftin is an average runner, but his instincts allow his speed to play up both in the field and on the bases. He draws raves for his leadership quality, and his work ethic and off-the-charts instincts allow his tools to play up.

THE FUTURE: Loftin's development path has often been compared to Royals star Whit Merrifield. If he can live up to that, he'll be around the game for a long time.

Year	Age	Club (Level)	Lge	AVG	G	AB	R	H	2B	3B	HR	RBI	BB	SO	SB	OBP	SLG
2021	22	Quad Cities (HiA)	Cent	.289	90	356	67	103	22	5	10	57	42	60	11	.373	.463
Minor League Totals (2 years)				**.289**	**90**	**356**	**67**	**103**	**22**	**5**	**10**	**57**	**42**	**60**	**11**	**.373**	**.463**

13 JON HEASLEY, RHP

BA GRADE

45 Risk: Medium

Born: Jan. 27, 1997. **B-T:** R-R. **HT:** 6-3. **WT:** 215. **Drafted:** Oklahoma State, 2018 (13th round). **Signed by:** Chad Lee.

TRACK RECORD: Heasley was Kansas City's 18th-round pick in 2018 out of Oklahoma State and has since surpassed other more high-profile pitching prospects in the organization. He reached the majors in 2021 and made three starts for the Royals. He spent the bulk of the season at Double-A Northwest Arkansas, where he went 7-3, 3.33 and struck out 10.3 batters per nine innings.

SCOUTING REPORT: Heasley stands out for his bulldog mentality and extreme competitiveness on the mound, allowing his stuff to play up. His fastball sits 93-95 mph with sink and touches 97. His solid-average 12-to-6 curveball in the low 80s is thrown with depth and spin, and he has good feel for a mid-80s changeup that projects to be above-average. Heasley repeats his delivery well and pounds the strike zone with above-average control of all three of his pitches.

THE FUTURE: With a strong body, pitchability and resilience, Heasley is capable of filling multiple roles on a pitching staff. His ceiling is a back-of-the-rotation starter, but he can also provide value in a swingman role or as a multi-inning reliever.

Year	Age	Club (Level)	Lge	W	L	ERA	G	GS	IP	H	HR	BB	SO	BB/9	SO/9	WHIP	AVG
2021	24	NW Arkansas (AA)	Cent	7	3	3.33	22	21	105	95	18	34	120	2.9	10.3	1.22	.244
2021	24	Kansas City (MLB)	AL	1	1	4.91	3	3	15	15	3	3	6	1.8	3.7	1.23	.278
Major League Totals (1 year)				**1**	**1**	**4.91**	**3**	**3**	**15**	**15**	**3**	**3**	**6**	**1.84**	**3.68**	**1.23**	**.278**
Minor League Totals (4 years)				**16**	**11**	**3.58**	**59**	**52**	**269**	**243**	**33**	**84**	**275**	**2.8**	**9.2**	**1.22**	**.239**

14 BEN HERNANDEZ, RHP

BA GRADE

50 Risk: Extreme

Born: July 1, 2001. **B-T:** R-R. **HT:** 6-2. **WT:** 210. **Drafted:** HS—Chicago, 2020 (2nd round). **Signed by:** Scott Melvin.

TRACK RECORD: Hernandez broke camp with Low-A Columbia at the start of the 2021 season, his first full pro season after the Royals drafted him in the second round of the 2020 draft. Arm fatigue limited the Chicago high school product to nine starts before he was shut down, although he returned for three late-season starts in the Arizona Complex League and also pitched in Kansas City's fall instructional league.

SCOUTING REPORT: The gem of Hernandez's arsenal is a plus changeup that he throws with fade and deception, and it's been his bread-and-butter offering dating back to high school, where it was routinely recognized as the top changeup in the 2020 high school class. Hernandez pitches off a 94-96 mph fastball that jumps out of his hand with armside run and sink, inducing plenty of ground balls. Hernandez's curveball has always been a distant third pitch, but it showed improvement during the season. The Royals' staff worked with him to throw it more aggressively, particularly in the lower quadrants. With the added bite, the breaking ball provides Hernandez with another weapon to pair with his fastball/changeup combination. He throws all three offerings from an easy, deceptive delivery.

THE FUTURE: Reports from instructional league were very favorable, so Hernandez should be ready to go back to full-season ball in 2022. Concerns that he would be better suited for a bullpen role have been allayed by the improvement in the curveball, along with his pitchability and athleticism.

Year	Age	Club (Level)	Lge	W	L	ERA	G	GS	IP	H	HR	BB	SO	BB/9	SO/9	WHIP	AVG
2021	19	Royals Gold (R)	ACL	0	0	4.50	3	3	4	5	0	0	2	0.0	4.5	1.25	.313
	19	Columbia (LoA)	East	1	2	4.31	9	9	31	32	2	17	31	4.9	8.9	1.56	.271
Minor League Totals (2 years)				**1**	**2**	**4.33**	**12**	**12**	**35**	**37**	**2**	**17**	**33**	**4.3**	**8.4**	**1.53**	**.276**

15 MICHAEL MASSEY, 2B

Born: March 22, 1998. **B-T:** L-R. **HT:** 6-0. **WT:** 190. **Drafted:** Illinois, 2019 (4th round). **Signed by:** Scott Melvin.

TRACK RECORD: Healthy for the first time since his sophomore season at Illinois, Massey broke out in 2021. He hit a career-best 21 homers for High-A Quad Cities and tied for the High-A Central batting title (.289) with teammate Nick Loftin.

SCOUTING REPORT: Massey has plus raw power, but his lack of experience and poor health prevented him from showing it consistently. That changed in 2021. His 21 homers were more than his entire three-year college career combined (17). Massey has a solid approach at the plate, with good strike zone awareness and bat speed, and stays short to the ball. Defensively, Massey has played only second base but he could likely handle third base or a utility role. He is a solid-average defender with an average arm. Despite just average speed, his reads and baserunning instincts allow his speed to play up. Massey draws positive reviews for his character and makeup.

THE FUTURE: Massey shares many of the same attributes as Loftin. Both players will move to Double-A Northwest Arkansas and form a promising double-play tandem in 2022.

Year	Age	Club (Level)	Lge	AVG	G	AB	R	H	2B	3B	HR	RBI	BB	SO	SB	OBP	SLG
2021	23	Quad Cities (HiA)	Cent	.289	99	388	76	112	27	2	21	87	33	68	12	.351	.531
Minor League Totals (3 years)				.283	141	561	108	159	34	2	26	112	46	96	16	.347	.490

16 CARTER JENSEN, C

Born: July 3, 2003. **B-T:** L-R. **HT:** 6-1. **WT:** 210. **Drafted:** HS—Kansas City, 2021 (3rd round). **Signed by:** Matt Price.

TRACK RECORD: The Royals twice dipped into the greater Kansas City area high school ranks in the 2021 draft, taking righthander Ben Kudrna in the second round and Jensen in the third round. After signing for an over-slot $1,097,500, Jensen appeared in 19 games in the Rookie-level Arizona Complex League and impressed with his performance during instructional league.

SCOUTING REPORT: Jensen has a strong, mature build and an advanced lefthanded bat with plus raw power. He stands out for his feel to hit, all-fields approach, and an ability to slow the game down. He'll need to learn to make adjustments against lefthanded pitchers, especially against good breaking balls. Like most catchers coming into pro ball from the prep ranks, Jensen has a lot of work ahead of him defensively. He has the athleticism, flexibility, strong hands and tools to stay behind the plate, with an above-average arm that shows average or better pop times consistently.

THE FUTURE: Lefthanded-hitting catchers with power are valuable, so Jensen will be given time to develop. He needs defensive instruction and plenty of reps, but has youth on his side.

Year	Age	Club (Level)	Lge	AVG	G	AB	R	H	2B	3B	HR	RBI	BB	SO	SB	OBP	SLG
2021	17	Royals Blue (R)	ACL	.500	1	2	1	1	1	0	0	0	0	1	0	.500	1.000
	17	Royals Gold (R)	ACL	.273	18	55	8	15	1	1	1	7	10	19	4	.385	.382
Minor League Totals (1 year)				.281	19	57	9	16	2	1	1	7	10	20	4	.388	.404

17 ERICK PEÑA, OF

Born: Feb. 20, 2003. **B-T:** L-R. **HT:** 6-3. **WT:** 199. **Signed:** Dominican Republic, 2019 **Signed by:** Edis Perez.

TRACK RECORD: Peña was Kansas City's top international signing in 2019, inking a $3.9 million bonus. He made his long-awaited debut in 2021 and struggled badly in the Arizona Complex League, batting .161 with 57 strikeouts in 40 games.

SCOUTING REPORT: Peña has a promising set of tools, including projected above-average power, but he has a hitch in his swing that needs to be fixed. The Royals worked with him on creating more separation with his hands, which he'll need to live up to his previous projections as an average hitter. Peña has grown more muscular since he signed and is limited to a corner outfield spot defensively. He has the outfield instincts and average arm strength to handle either corner position.

THE FUTURE: The Royals believe Peña's work ethic and aptitude will help him make the necessary adjustments. He'll be just 19 years old in 2022 and could reach Low-A Columbia.

Year	Age	Club (Level)	Lge	AVG	G	AB	R	H	2B	3B	HR	RBI	BB	SO	SB	OBP	SLG
2021	18	Royals Blue (R)	ACL	.161	40	137	14	22	10	1	3	15	15	57	4	.256	.314
Minor League Totals (1 year)				.161	40	137	14	22	10	1	3	15	15	57	4	.256	.314

18 WILL KLEIN, RHP

Born: Nov. 28, 1999. **B-T:** R-R. **HT:** 6-5. **WT:** 230. **Drafted:** Eastern Illinois, 2020 (5th round). **Signed by:** Scott Melvin.

BA GRADE
45 Risk: High

TRACK RECORD: Klein was Kansas City's final pick in the shortened five-round 2020 draft, and it's already looking like the Royals have found excellent value. A converted catcher, Klein pitched his first two college seasons in Eastern Illinois' bullpen before moving into the starting rotation prior to the abbreviated 2020 season. The Royals used him exclusively in a reliever role during his pro debut, and Klein struck out nearly 41% of hitters he faced with High-A Quad Cities.

SCOUTING REPORT: Klein attacks hitters with a plus four-seam fastball that sits at 96-97 mph with good vertical break and touches 100 mph. Batters struggled to catch up to his fastball, with 43% of balls hit to the opposite field against Klein in 2021. He pitched in two-inning stints with Quad Cities and held his velocity. Klein arrived in Kansas City's organization with two distinct breaking balls, but has since shelved his slider/cutter in favor of refining his curveball. It's a hard breaker, sitting at 83-85 mph, and batters struggled with it as Klein messed with their eye levels, whiffing nearly 45% of the time. He's also working on a split-grip changeup, but it's not a regular part of his repertoire. Batters hit just .173 against Klein, but he struggled with control issues, walking 5.63 batters per nine innings.

THE FUTURE: Developing command and control will dictate Klein's future, and even subtle improvements will enhance his potent two-pitch mix. He's a candidate for a high-leverage bullpen role if he throws more strikes.

Year	Age	Club (Level)	Lge	W	L	ERA	G	GS	IP	H	HR	BB	SO	BB/9	SO/9	WHIP	AVG
2021	21	Quad Cities (HiA)	Cent	7	1	3.20	36	0	70	43	4	44	121	5.6	15.5	1.24	.173
Minor League Totals (2 years)				7	1	3.20	36	0	70	43	4	44	121	5.63	15.48	1.24	.173

19 DYLAN COLEMAN, RHP

Born: Sept. 16, 1996. **B-T:** R-R. **HT:** 6-5. **WT:** 230. **Drafted:** Missouri State, 2018 (4th round). **Signed by:** Troy Hoerner (Padres).

BA GRADE
40 Risk: Medium

TRACK RECORD: Coleman was a member of Missouri State's starting rotation when the Padres drafted him in the fourth round of the 2018 draft, but he struggled to hold velocity deep into starts in college. Those issues continued as a professional even after San Diego shifted him to the bullpen. But Coleman returned from the pandemic layoff in a new organization—Kansas City acquired him in 2020 as the player to be named later in the a deal for Trevor Rosenthal—and with renewed velocity. The harder fastball helped spark Coleman's ascension through the upper levels, culminating in his big league debut.

SCOUTING REPORT: Coleman began to rediscover his velocity and the bite on his slider while pitching in a semi-pro league in Missouri before joining the Royals. His fastball, which had dropped to the upper 80s by the end of his Padres tenure, sat at 98 mph in his brief big league showing and touched as high as 101 mph in 2021. The Royals staff worked with Coleman to throw his slider harder, getting it into the 84-88 mph range with nasty late break and enough separation from the fastball to mess with hitters' timing. His repertoire creates a powerful one-two punch out of the bullpen and the ability to generate swings and misses in bunches.

THE FUTURE: After a breakout 2021 season, Coleman looks like a potential bullpen option for Kansas City in 2022 and could work his way into high-leverage opportunities.

Year	Age	Club (Level)	Lge	W	L	ERA	G	GS	IP	H	HR	BB	SO	BB/9	SO/9	WHIP	AVG
2021	24	NW Arkansas (AA)	Cent	1	1	2.92	18	0	24	19	2	5	37	1.8	13.5	0.97	.211
	24	Omaha (AAA)	East	4	0	3.55	27	0	33	19	2	17	56	4.6	15.3	1.09	.167
	24	Kansas City (MLB)	AL	0	0	1.42	5	0	6	5	0	1	7	1.4	10.0	0.95	.208
Major League Totals (1 year)				0	0	1.42	5	0	6	5	0	1	7	1.42	9.95	0.95	.208
Minor League Totals (4 years)				10	6	3.23	90	2	114	90	6	50	161	3.9	12.7	1.22	.215

20 ANGEL ZERPA, LHP

Born: Sept. 27, 1999. **B-T:** L-L. **HT:** 6-0. **WT:** 211. **Signed:** Venezuela, 2016. **Signed by:** Richard Castro/Joelvis Gonzalez/Orlando Estevez.

BA GRADE
40 Risk: Medium

TRACK RECORD: Zerpa was a surprise addition to the 40-man roster just before the 2020 deadline despite never having pitched above the Rookie levels. However, the native Venezuelan proved that the Royals made a wise decision, as he moved across three levels of the minors. He finished 2021 with a single late-season start in Kansas City, pitching five innings and yielding just two unearned runs in his big league debut.

SCOUTING REPORT: More of a pitchability-over-stuff type, Zerpa has plenty of weapons at his disposal.

A lower arm slot adds an element of deception to his arsenal and helps his pedestrian raw stuff play up. The fastball ticked up in 2021, ranging from 91-96 mph, with a four-seamer that he commands to his glove side and a two-seamer with good movement that he uses when he falls behind in the count. Zerpa's slurvy slider is a hard pitch at 85-88 mph with late bite and sweep. His changeup sits 86-87 mph, a firm pitch that's best when it is inducing grounders. Zerpa is a competitor and has no fear, as scouts noted that his velocity would tick up as he faced better competition.

THE FUTURE: Zerpa could fill any number of roles on a big league staff. He has the look of a high-floor, back-end of the rotation or swingman type, but he's going to have a career in the major leagues.

Year	Age	Club (Level)	Lge	W	L	ERA	G	GS	IP	H	HR	BB	SO	BB/9	SO/9	WHIP	AVG
2021	21	Quad Cities (HiA)	Cent	4	0	2.59	8	8	41	32	2	8	53	1.7	11.5	0.96	.205
	21	NW Arkansas (AA)	Cent	0	3	5.96	13	13	45	51	7	19	54	3.8	10.7	1.54	.287
	21	Omaha (AAA)	East	0	1	20.25	1	1	1	2	1	1	1	6.8	6.8	2.25	.333
	21	Kansas City (MLB)	AL	0	1	0.00	1	1	5	3	0	1	4	1.8	7.2	0.80	.176
Major League Totals (1 year)				0	1	0.00	1	1	5	3	0	1	4	1.80	7.20	0.80	.176
Minor League Totals (5 years)				16	17	3.51	60	53	256	230	21	65	236	2.3	8.3	1.15	.240

21 ANTHONY VENEZIANO, LHP

BA GRADE

45 Risk: High

Born: Sept. 1, 1997. **B-T:** L-L. **HT:** 6-5. **WT:** 205. **Drafted:** Coastal Carolina, 2019 (10th round). **Signed by:** Joe Barbera.

TRACK RECORD: Kansas City's 10th-round pick in 2019, Veneziano wasn't on many radars until a heavily scouted appearance late in 2021 minor league spring training, where he flashed a fastball up to 97 mph. The Coastal Carolina product built on his solid spring, enjoying a very good season with High-A Quad Cities, where he struck out 127 batters in 93.2 innings. He was especially tough down the stretch for the eventual High-A Central champions.

SCOUTING REPORT: Veneziano attacks hitters with a heavy, bat-missing arsenal out of an easy three-quarters arm slot and repeatable motion. His sinking fastball sits 94-97 mph and plays above his velocity due to his whippy arm motion and good extension. Veneziano needs to become more confident in his secondary offerings to take another step forward. His breaking ball is a slurvy slider that he commands inconsistently. He also throws an average changeup with tumble and fade.

THE FUTURE: Veneziano is nowhere near a finished product, but he has the upside of a mid-rotation starter. He should move to Double-A in 2022.

Year	Age	Club (Level)	Lge	W	L	ERA	G	GS	IP	H	HR	BB	SO	BB/9	SO/9	WHIP	AVG
2021	23	Quad Cities (HiA)	Cent	6	4	3.75	22	22	93	76	11	37	127	3.6	12.2	1.21	.222
Minor League Totals (3 years)				9	8	4.36	35	33	140	141	17	50	171	3.2	11.0	1.36	.260

22 AUSTIN COX, LHP

BA GRADE

45 Risk: High

Born: March 28, 1997. **B-T:** L-L. **HT:** 6-4. **WT:** 185. **Drafted:** Mercer, 2018 (5th round). **Signed by:** Jim Buckley.

TRACK RECORD: Cox consistently ranked between No. 9 and No. 16 in Kansas City's Top 30 Prospects since the Royals made him their 2018 fifth-round selection out of Mercer, but his 2021 season represented a bit of a step back. Cox spent almost all season with Double-A Northwest Arkansas and was not added to the 40-man roster after the season.

SCOUTING REPORT: Cox has always pitched off the strength of his plus fastball, but his velocity was down a few ticks in 2021, mostly sitting 90-92 mph. He also shelved his inconsistent slider, instead choosing to focus on his curveball and changeup. The curveball made strides and is now considered an above-average pitch, delivered in the upper 70s with good depth and downward movement. His upper-80s changeup is too firm and hasn't developed into a reliable pitch. In the past, Cox's arsenal played up because of his command, but he labored to keep his delivery under control in 2021 and walked 3.57 batters per nine innings at Double-A. This heightened concerns about a potential shift to the bullpen.

THE FUTURE: Cox will head to spring training looking to regain velocity and smooth his delivery. He's shown the ability to get results previously, so a few adjustments may get him back on track.

Year	Age	Club (Level)	Lge	W	L	ERA	G	GS	IP	H	HR	BB	SO	BB/9	SO/9	WHIP	AVG
2021	24	NW Arkansas (AA)	Cent	4	1	3.00	15	15	63	54	8	25	56	3.6	8.0	1.25	.232
	24	Omaha (AAA)	East	0	0	18.00	2	1	5	9	3	5	4	9.0	7.2	2.80	.375
Minor League Totals (4 years)				13	8	3.30	50	48	232	204	23	83	240	3.2	9.3	1.24	.233

23 NOAH MURDOCK, RHP

BA GRADE
45 Risk: High

Born: Aug. 20, 1998. **B-T:** R-R. **HT:** 6-8. **WT:** 190. **Drafted:** Virginia, 2019 (7th round). **Signed by:** Jim Farr.

TRACK RECORD: Murdock's velocity has slowly returned since he had Tommy John surgery his sophomore year at Virginia, but a rash of injuries limited the 6-foot-8 righty to just seven games with High-A Quad Cities in 2021. Minor soreness wiped out his spring training and he then injured his hamstring while pitching in extended spring training. Once healthy, Murdock settled into the rotation at High-A Quad Cities and posted a 3.18 ERA in 22.2 innings.

SCOUTING REPORT: Murdock creates deception from the excellent extension driven by his long levers. His two-seam fastball has plus velocity, sitting 93-97 mph, and ample horizontal movement. His curveball mirrors the movement of his fastball, keeping hitters off-balance, and is thrown with high spin efficiency. He'll flash feel for an average changeup, but his fastball and curveball combination is his main point of attack. With unique movement and a deceptive operation, Murdock makes for an uncomfortable at-bat, although it also limits him to below-average control.

THE FUTURE: Murdock could be effective in a relief role where his fastball would play up. He should see Double-A in 2022.

Year	Age	Club (Level)	Lge	W	L	ERA	G	GS	IP	H	HR	BB	SO	BB/9	SO/9	WHIP	AVG
2021	22	Quad Cities (HiA)	Cent	2	1	3.18	7	6	22	15	0	11	19	4.4	7.5	1.15	.181
Minor League Totals (3 years)				5	2	2.55	18	12	60	50	2	22	62	3.3	9.3	1.20	.222

24 SHANE PANZINI, RHP

BA GRADE
50 Risk: Extreme

Born: Oct. 30, 2001. **B-T:** R-R. **HT:** 6-3. **WT:** 220. **Drafted:** HS—Red Bank, N.J., 2021 (4th round). **Signed by:** Casey Fahy.

TRACK RECORD: Panzini was the third of a trio of high school pitchers selected by the Royals early in the 2021 draft, signing an above-slot $997,500 bonus as a fourth-rounder. The New Jersey native was held out of games before seeing action during instructional league.

SCOUTING REPORT: Panzini aggressively attacks hitters with a heavy fastball that sits 89-92 mph with life and a high spin rate. His velocity, generated by his strong lower half, has touched higher and has room to increase. Panzini presently lacks a true swing-and-miss secondary. His slider is a future average pitch with sweep and horizontal movement. He infrequently throws a changeup, and he'll need to show it more as he gets his feet wet in pro ball. Panzini shows a repeatable delivery that should portend average control.

THE FUTURE: Panzini projects as a reliever, but the Royals will start him for now. He is set to open the 2022 season at Low-A Columbia.

Year	Age	Club (Level)	Lge	W	L	ERA	G	GS	IP	H	HR	BB	SO	BB/9	SO/9	WHIP	AVG
2021	19	Did not play															

25 DANIEL VAZQUEZ, SS

BA GRADE
50 Risk: Extreme

Born: Dec. 15, 2003. **B-T:** R-R. **HT:** 6-2. **WT:** 170. **Signed:** Dominican Republic, 2021. **Signed by:** Edis Perez.

TRACK RECORD: Vazquez signed with the Royals for $1.5 million during the January 2021 international signing period and appeared in 32 games with the Royals' Dominican Summer League team. He then participated in both Kansas City's Dominican and Arizona instructional leagues, and scouts who saw him stateside were impressed with the young shortstop.

SCOUTING REPORT: Vazquez certainly looks the part, with a wiry, athletic frame and long levers. He impressed with his actions at shortstop, soft hands, and whippy action from a plus throwing arm. He's agile on the field with good lateral movement. Defensively, Vazquez profiles as a starting shortstop, although he needs plenty of reps and to add more strength to his frame. Little has come into focus so far at the plate for Vazquez. He showed nice rhythm and timing and a propensity to battle deep into counts. Vazquez utilizes a high leg lift timing mechanism, and his swing produces a line drive stroke now, although he could one day hit 10-15 homers a year as he grows into his body.

THE FUTURE: It will be several years before the Royals really know what they have in Vazquez. He's expected to spend the 2022 season in the Arizona Complex League.

Year	Age	Club (Level)	Lge	AVG	G	AB	R	H	2B	3B	HR	RBI	BB	SO	SB	OBP	SLG
2021	17	Royals Blue (R)	DSL	.186	32	102	17	19	3	1	1	10	14	31	4	.280	.265
Minor League Totals (1 year)				.186	32	102	17	19	3	1	1	10	14	31	4	.280	.265

26 NATHAN WEBB, RHP

BA GRADE
45 Risk: High

Born: Aug. 20, 1997. **B-T:** R-R. **HT:** 6-2. **WT:** 215. **Drafted:** HS—Lee's Summit, Mo., 2016 (34th round). **Signed by:** Matt Price.

TRACK RECORD: For those outside the Royals organization, Webb was a surprise addition to the 40-man roster in November. The Kansas City native, who worked on the Kauffman Stadium grounds crew as a teenager, boosted his stock in his first full season in 2021, when he split the year between Low-A Columbia and High-A Quad Cities. He struck out 13.5 batters per nine innings between the two levels with a walk rate of 3.2 per nine innings. Webb was on the mound to get the final out when Quad Cities won the High-A Central championship.

SCOUTING REPORT: A big bump in velocity during his first full season put Webb on the radar, with his fastball now sitting 97-98 mph, and touching 100 mph. Webb focused on staying behind his four-seam fastball to create more vertical break coming into 2021, and the results followed. It's now a true swing-and-miss pitch that dominates the upper quadrants of the strike zone. His east-to-west slider improved during the season, a nice complement to the fastball. While his changeup will flash tumble and fade, it's a work in progress and clearly a distant third offering. His high three-quarters delivery, which was slow and methodical before, now gets more efficient movement to the plate, contributing to the increase in fastball velocity.

THE FUTURE: Webb will head to big league spring training. His most likely starting point for 2022 is Double-A Northwest Arkansas, but continued refinement may lead to a major league opportunity at some point.

Year	Age	Club (Level)	Lge	W	L	ERA	G	GS	IP	H	HR	BB	SO	BB/9	SO/9	WHIP	AVG
2021	23	Columbia (LoA)	East	0	2	3.38	18	0	26	14	3	12	43	4.1	14.5	0.98	.154
	23	Quad Cities (HiA)	Cent	4	1	4.41	17	0	32	26	2	9	46	2.5	12.7	1.07	.215
Minor League Totals (6 years)				13	14	5.56	83	25	235	241	26	111	262	4.26	10.05	1.50	.265

27 ZACH HAAKE, RHP

BA GRADE
45 Risk: High

Born: Oct. 8, 1996. **B-T:** R-R. **HT:** 6-5. **WT:** 186. **Drafted:** Kentucky, 2018 (6th round). **Signed by:** Mike Farrell.

TRACK RECORD: Durability concerns continue to be part of the equation for Haake, who missed six weeks with an oblique injury in 2021 and also missed two months in 2019 with shoulder soreness. He pitched well with High-A Quad Cities when healthy, posting a 3.74 ERA in 45.2 innings. Kansas City then sent Haake to the Arizona Fall League, where he struggled at times.

SCOUTING REPORT: Injuries and inconsistency have made Haake difficult to project dating back to his underwhelming college career, but his long frame and pitch mix have continued to earn him chances to start when healthy. His fastball sits 93-96 mph with armside run, and he also has feel for a potentially plus changeup, his most consistent secondary. Continued development of Haake's mid-80s slider will be key for him. Sometimes it tends to flatten out, resembling more of a cutter, but it was a potent swing-and-miss offering against High-A Central hitters this year, generating a 49% whiff rate. Haake walked 4.34 batters per nine innings and will need to tighten his strike-throwing.

THE FUTURE: Some evaluators feel Haake has regressed over the last two years and Kansas City did not add him to its 40-man roster, leaving him unprotected ahead of the Rule 5 Draft. It's becoming increasingly likely he winds up in a relief role before long.

Year	Age	Club (Level)	Lge	W	L	ERA	G	GS	IP	H	HR	BB	SO	BB/9	SO/9	WHIP	AVG
2021	24	Royals Blue (R)	ACL	0	0	2.25	2	2	4	4	0	0	5	0.0	11.3	1.00	.286
	24	Royals Gold (R)	ACL	0	0	0.00	2	2	4	1	0	1	6	2.3	13.5	0.50	.077
	24	Quad Cities (HiA)	Cent	4	1	3.74	11	10	45	35	9	22	47	4.3	9.3	1.25	.208
Minor League Totals (4 years)				8	7	2.84	41	39	149	111	12	66	166	4.0	10.0	1.19	.208

28 MAIKEL GARCIA, SS

BA GRADE
40 Risk: High

Born: March 3, 2000. **B-T:** R-R. **HT:** 6-0. **WT:** 161. **Signed:** Venezuela, 2016. **Signed by:** Richard Castro.

TRACK RECORD: Garcia signed as an international free agent out of Venezuela in 2016 and debuted the following year. He spent three consecutive seasons in rookie ball, making limited impact offensively, then missed all of 2020 because of the pandemic. Garcia made his full-season debut this year with Low-A Columbia and showed much better feel for contact, hitting .303 in 51 games, and kept on hitting after his promotion to High-A Quad Cities. Kansas City added Garcia to its 40-man roster in November.

SCOUTING REPORT: Long considered a glove-first shortstop, Garcia added strength and improved his barrel accuracy at the plate, posting a contact rate close to 85% in 2021. His approach and strike zone control improved, too. But Garcia has very little power in his thin, wiry frame and a bail move in the box at times, instead relying on spraying line drives to all fields. Garcia still has plenty of value defensively. He's at least an above-average shortstop—some evaluators believe he's a plus defender—and his hands and feet work together well, giving him good range. While not a burner, Garcia has good instincts on the bases, resulting in 35 stolen bases in 41 attempts in 2021.

THE FUTURE: Garcia needs to get stronger to make an impact at the upper levels, but his defense and speed give him a high floor.

Year	Age	Club (Level)	Lge	AVG	G	AB	R	H	2B	3B	HR	RBI	BB	SO	SB	OBP	SLG
2021	21	Columbia (LoA)	East	.303	51	195	40	59	13	3	1	26	38	33	24	.409	.415
	21	Quad Cities (HiA)	Cent	.281	53	217	38	61	8	4	3	24	24	40	11	.351	.396
Minor League Totals (5 years)				.266	261	983	157	261	35	13	5	103	122	171	83	.344	.343

29 COLLIN SNIDER, RHP

BA GRADE

40 Risk: High

Born: Oct. 10, 1995. **B-T:** R-R. **HT:** 6-4. **WT:** 195. **Drafted:** Vanderbilt, 2017 (12th round). **Signed by:** Nick Hamilton.

TRACK RECORD: Snider could be the next success story for the Royals' pitching development program. Drafted in the 12th round out of Vanderbilt in 2017, Snider primarily pitched out of the bullpen in college. He never struck out more than six batters per nine innings as a professional until 2021, when he broke out in the upper levels and reached Triple-A. Snider was especially effective with Double-A Northwest Arkansas, posting a 2.97 ERA while striking out more than a batter an inning.

SCOUTING REPORT: Snider's fastball now sits at 97 mph and touches 99—the primary reason for his surge in 2021. His high-spin two-seamer has run and sink and plays well with his other pitches. The other key was improving his 86-88 mph slider, which added movement and plays well off his fastball. The improvement in the slider gives Snider a swing-and-miss pitch that he didn't have before, but he needs to keep improving the consistency and command of it. His changeup, which he uses infrequently, is very much a work in progress, struggling for shape and strikes. Snider delivers his pitches from a three-quarters arm slot with a longer arm stroke.

THE FUTURE: Snider was added to the 40-man roster at the deadline and will head to spring training with the big league club looking for a spot in the Royals' bullpen. He's an intriguing sinker/slider power arm.

Year	Age	Club (Level)	Lge	W	L	ERA	G	GS	IP	H	HR	BB	SO	BB/9	SO/9	WHIP	AVG
2021	25	NW Arkansas (AA)	Cent	2	1	2.97	27	0	36	32	1	14	41	3.5	10.2	1.27	.241
	25	Omaha (AAA)	East	3	2	6.30	21	0	30	39	7	12	23	3.6	6.9	1.70	.312
Minor League Totals (5 years)				18	13	4.11	125	10	232	269	27	59	170	2.29	6.59	1.41	.287

30 EMMANUEL RIVERA, 3B

BA GRADE

40 Risk: High

Born: June 29, 1996. **B-T:** R-R. **HT:** 6-2. **WT:** 225. **Drafted:** HS—San Juan, P.R., 2015 (19th round). **Signed by:** Johnny Ramos.

TRACK RECORD: Rivera last ranked among Kansas City's top 30 prospects entering the 2019 season. A power surge, plus a trip to the big leagues, has the Puerto Rico native back on the radar. Despite a hamate injury that cost him a month, Rivera smacked 19 homers in just 255 at-bats with Triple-A Omaha in 2021, and also hit .256 in 29 games with Kansas City. He then played winter ball for Mayaguez in the Puerto Rican League.

SCOUTING REPORT: Always known as a steady hitter and defender at third base, Rivera long lacked the desired power for the position. He tapped into his more consistently in 2021, though, showing simple mechanics at the plate. Rivera creates a long path through the strike zone and drives the ball to all fields while showing movement patterns that are simple and repeatable. Rivera is an average defender at third base with good range and solid hands. He has a plus throwing arm with solid zip and carry. While he's a below-average runner, Rivera is a smart baserunner and can take an extra base in the right situation.

THE FUTURE: Rivera will report to spring training looking to build on his breakout season and grab a spot on the major league roster.

Year	Age	Club (Level)	Lge	AVG	G	AB	R	H	2B	3B	HR	RBI	BB	SO	SB	OBP	SLG
2021	25	NW Arkansas (AA)	Cent	.267	4	15	1	4	0	0	0	1	2	4	0	.333	.267
	25	Omaha (AAA)	East	.286	63	255	48	73	17	2	19	57	22	58	3	.348	.592
	25	Kansas City (MLB)	AL	.256	29	90	13	23	4	0	1	5	8	21	2	.316	.333
Major League Totals (1 year)				.256	29	90	13	23	4	0	1	5	8	21	2	.316	.333
Minor League Totals (6 years)				.272	522	1963	255	533	105	20	46	291	154	367	36	.329	.416

MORE PROSPECTS TO KNOW

31 SEULY MATIAS, OF

Matias still has two plus-plus tools in his power and arm, but has made only incremental progress so far in improving his hit tool. Multiple hand injuries have also been an issue.

32 CLAY DUNGAN, SS

SLEEPER

Dungan plays above his tools as a grinder who can flat-out hit. He profiles best as a utility infielder who could hit his way into an occasional starting role.

33 DARRYL COLLINS, OF

A solid natural hitter from the Netherlands, Collins is just starting to show more power but still has a long way to go. A below-average arm limits him to left field.

34 PEYTON WILSON, 2B

The 2021 second-rounder out of Alabama combines plus running ability and twitchy athleticism with a plus arm, leading to the possibility he could assume a super-utility role with Kansas City.

35 NATHAN EATON, 3B/OF

Eaton is a prototypical, grinder ballplayer who plays above his tools. He's capable of filling in at multiple positions.

36 SAMUEL VALERIO, RHP

Valerio pitched in just four games in Rookie ball in 2021 due to a shoulder injury, but when healthy he's got an electric fastball that touches triple-digits.

37 AJ BLOCK, LHP

Block was a nondrafted free agent in 2020 from Washington State. He's a polished lefthander who enjoyed a solid first pro season, mostly at High-A Quad Cities, where he struck out 98 batters in 85 innings. He features a sinker/slider combo with plus command and control.

37 DREW PARRISH, LHP

The undersized lefthander with a low-90s fastball pitched well in Double-A, fanning 95 batters in 83 innings. Scouts see a bullpen future for the Florida State product.

38 OMAR HERNANDEZ, C

A 20-year-old of Cuban descent who lives in Spain, Hernandez struggled at the plate in his full-season debut. He's got catch-and-throw skills, and his bat showed improvement at instructional league.

39 TYLER GENTRY, OF

The 2020 third-round pick missed much of his debut pro season to injury but has enough in-game power to potentially move up the list next year.

40 BREWER HICKLEN, OF

A 25-year-old ex-college football player, Hicklen got off to a slow start at Double-A before putting it together over the last two months of the season. Hicklen is noted for his off-the-charts makeup and leadership skills.

TOP PROSPECTS OF THE DECADE

Year	Player, Pos	2021 Org
2012	Mike Montgomery, LHP	Samsung (Korea)
2013	Kyle Zimmer, RHP	Royals
2014	Kyle Zimmer, RHP	Royals
2015	Adalberto Mondesi, SS	Royals
2016	Adalberto Mondesi, SS	Royals
2017	Josh Staumont, RHP	Royals
2018	Nick Pratto, 1B	Royals
2019	Brady Singer, RHP	Royals
2020	Bobby Witt Jr., SS	Royals
2021	Bobby Witt Jr., SS	Royals

TOP DRAFT PICKS OF THE DECADE

Year	Player, Pos	2021 Org
2012	Kyle Zimmer, RHP	Royals
2013	Hunter Dozier, SS	Royals
2014	Brandon Finnegan, LHP	Reds
2015	Ashe Russell, RHP	Royals
2016	A.J. Puckett, RHP (2nd round)	Braves
2017	Nick Pratto, 1B	Royals
2018	Brady Singer, RHP	Royals
2019	Bobby Witt Jr., SS	Royals
2020	Asa Lacy, LHP	Royals
2021	Frank Mozzicato, LHP	Royals

Los Angeles Angels

BY MIKE DiGIOVANNA

Shohei Ohtani turned in the finest two-way season in MLB history—but it wasn't enough.

The Ruthian exploits of two-way sensation Shohei Ohtani, a unanimous choice for American League MVP in 2021, couldn't keep the Angels from a sixth straight losing season and seventh without a playoff berth.

Major injuries to center fielder Mike Trout and third baseman Anthony Rendon, combined with the usual lack of starting pitching and bullpen depth, torpedoed the club, leading to another winter of upheaval. But this time, the changes were felt more in player development than on the big league staff.

Scouting director Matt Swanson was reassigned and replaced by Tim McIlvaine.

Pro scouting director Nate Horowitz left the organization, and minor league field coordinator Chad Tracy was not retained. Former Cardinals ace Chris Carpenter, a three-time all-star and 2005 National League Cy Young Award winner, was hired as a minor league pitching consultant.

Among the objectives under second-year general manager Perry Minasian is to implement a more aggressive mound mindset from the big league club down through the minor leagues. That bulldog mentality was reflected in the signing of former Mets righthander Noah Syndergaard to a one-year, $21 million deal in November and the selection of hard-throwing righthander Sam Bachman with the ninth pick in the 2021 draft.

The Angels want more pitchers who can miss bats. Syndergaard and Ohtani fit the bill. So do Bachman, who combines a triple-digit fastball and tight-spinning slider, and second-round pick Ky Bush, a lefthander with a mid-90s fastball and plus slider.

Bachman and Bush topped a 2021 Angels draft class in which all 20 picks were pitchers—all but one from the college ranks—in a clear attempt to address a longstanding shortage of pitching.

The Angels need to hit on at least a few of those arms to push themselves into playoff contention and ease the stress on a top-heavy payroll that will surpass $171 million for the 11th straight year.

An infusion of young pitchers should also boost a system that has graduated several promising youngsters—outfielders Jo Adell and Brandon Marsh, first baseman Jared Walsh, second baseman David Fletcher and pitchers Griffin Canning and Jose Suarez—to the big leagues in recent years but is still thin in potential high-impact players, especially power hitters.

There is no shortage of athletic middle infielders, with Jeremiah Jackson, Kyren Paris, Arol Vera, Denzer Guzman and Werner Blakely heading the

PROJECTED 2025 LINEUP

Catcher	Max Stassi	34
First Base	Jared Walsh	31
Second Base	Kyren Paris	23
Third Base	Anthony Rendon	35
Shortstop	David Fletcher	31
Left Field	Mike Trout	33
Center Field	Brandon Marsh	27
Right Field	Jo Adell	26
Designated Hitter	Shohei Ohtani	30
No. 1 Starter	Shohei Ohtani	30
No. 2 Starter	Reid Detmers	25
No. 3 Starter	Patrick Sandoval	28
No. 4 Starter	Griffin Canning	29
No. 5 Starter	Jose Suarez	27
Closer	Sam Bachman	25

group, but none is close to the big leagues.

A dozen pitching prospects—Chris Rodriguez, Reid Detmers, Austin Warren, Andrew Wantz, Packy Naughton, Janson Junk, Kyle Tyler, Oliver Ortega, Jose Marte, Elvis Peguero, Cooper Criswell and Jhonathan Diaz—made their MLB debuts.

But Detmers, the team's top prospect, and Rodriguez are the only potential high-impact arms from that group, and Rodriguez will miss most, if not all, of 2022 because of shoulder surgery.

The return of a healthy Trout and Rendon and a rotation headed by Ohtani and Syndergaard provide hope for 2022, but it may be another year or two before the big league club gets a significant bump from the farm system. ∎

LOS ANGELES ANGELS

TOP 2022 ROOKIES	RANK
Reid Detmers, LHP	1
Austin Warren, RHP	11
Orlando Martinez, OF	19
BREAKOUT PROSPECTS	**RANK**
D'Shawn Knowles, OF	14
Adrian Placencia, 2B/SS	17
Luke Murphy, RHP	20

SOURCE OF TOP 30 TALENT			
Homegrown	27	Acquired	3
College	9	Trade	3
Junior college	0	Rule 5 draft	0
High school	8	Independent league	0
Nondrafted free agent	1	Free agent/waivers	0
International	9		

LF
Orlando Martinez (19)
Erik Rivera
Jose Reyes
Trent Deveaux
Brennon Lund

CF
Jordyn Adams (4)
D'Shawn Knowles (14)
Natanael Santana (30)

RF
Alexander Ramirez (10)

3B
Brendon Davis

SS
Jeremiah Jackson (5)
Arol Vera (7)
Denzer Guzman (8)
Livan Soto
Jose Guzman

2B
Kyren Paris (3)
Adrian Placencia (17)
Michael Stefanic (22)
Werner Blakely (23)

1B
David MacKinnon
Jose Bonilla

C
Edgar Quero (27)
Anthony Mulrine
Michael Cruz

LHP

LHSP	LHRP
Reid Detmers (1)	Ryan Smith
Ky Bush (6)	Jose Salvador
Mason Albright (29)	Connor Higgins
Jhonathan Diaz	
Packy Naughton	
Adam Seminaris	
Brent Killam	

RHP

RHSP	RHRP
Sam Bachman (2)	Austin Warren (11)
Landon Marceaux (9)	Chase Silseth (12)
Jack Kochanowicz (25)	Davis Daniel (13)
Coleman Crow (28)	Jose Marte (15)
Alejandro Hidalgo	Chris Rodriguez (16)
Kyle Tyler	Janson Junk (18)
Zach Linginfelter	Luke Murphy (20)
Aaron Hernandez	Oliver Ortega (21)
John Swanda	Mason Erla (24)
	Elvis Peguero (26)
	Andrew Wantz
	Cooper Criswell
	Robinson Pina
	Nathan Burns
	Ivan Armstrong

1 REID DETMERS, LHP

Born: July 8, 1999. **B-T:** L-L. **HT:** 6-2. **WT:** 210.
Drafted: Louisville, 2020 (1st round).
Signed by: John Burden.

TRACK RECORD: Detmers was picked out of high school by the Braves in the 32nd round of the 2017 draft but opted to attend college instead. At Louisville, Detmers was part of a stacked roster that also included future first-round picks Bobby Miller (Dodgers) and Henry Davis (Pirates). The Angels thought enough of Detmers' mix of stuff and polish to make him the 10th overall pick in 2020 and sign him for a bonus of $4.67 million. Detmers rocketed from the Angels alternate training site in 2020 to Anaheim in 2021. He jumped straight to Double-A to start his pro career and dominated in 12 starts for the Trash Pandas before being promoted to Triple-A Salt Lake, where he made only two starts before being called up to the majors to make his big league debut on Aug. 1. In the majors less than 14 months after being drafted and after only 62 innings in the minors, Detmers got roughed up for a 7.40 ERA in five big league starts, although he showed promise with a six-inning, one-run effort in an Aug. 15 start against the Astros to earn his first big league win. Detmers was placed on the Covid-19 injured list on Aug. 25 and pitched only one more game, the regular-season finale.

SCOUTING REPORT: Detmers came out of college with excellent command of a low-90s fastball and a big-breaking, a mid-70s curveball, but his arsenal changed in pro ball to enhance his already-bright outlook. His fastball velocity ticked up to 93-97 mph and a new upper-80s slider emerged as a weapon to handle righthanded batters, giving him a complete, four-pitch mix. Detmers works his high-spin fastball with late riding action at the top of the zone and gets swings and misses when he locates it. It pairs exceptionally well with his plus-plus curveball, which averages more than six feet of drop and freezes batters at the knees. His new slider is a hard breaker in the mid-80s that barrels down and in on righthanders and gives him a second potentially plus breaking pitch, and his improving 79-83 mph changeup 79-83 mph is most effective when he drops it to the front foot of righthanded hitters. Detmers has a compact, easily repeatable delivery that should ward off most mechanical issues and good feel for and command of his four-pitch mix. He moves the ball around the strike zone with above-average

STEPH CHAMBERS/GETTY IMAGES

BA GRADE	SCOUTING GRADES
55 Risk: Medium	Fastball: 55. CB: 70. SL: 60. CHG: 50. Control: 50.

Projected future grades on 20-80 scouting scale

BEST TOOLS

Best Hitter for Average	Michael Stefanic
Best Power Hitter	Alexander Ramirez
Best Strike-Zone Discipline	Kyren Paris
Fastest Baserunner	Jordyn Adams
Best Athlete	Jordyn Adams
Best Fastball	Sam Bachman
Best Curveball	Reid Detmers
Best Slider	Coleman Crow
Best Changeup	Alejandro Hidalgo
Best Control	Landon Marceaux
Best Defensive Catcher	Edgar Quero
Best Defensive Infielder	Livan Soto
Best Infield Arm	Kevin Maitan
Best Defensive Outfielder	Jordyn Adams
Best Outfield Arm	Natanael Santana

control and mixes and matches his pitches to keep hitters guessing.

THE FUTURE: Detmers was just beginning to understand how his pitches work and how best to set hitters up before his 2021 season was derailed by Covid-19. He could eventually pitch his way into a frontline role, especially if he gains more strength and adds velocity, but because he lacks an overpowering fastball, most project him as a No. 3 or 4 starter. Detmers should contend for a rotation spot in 2022. ∎

Year	Age	Club (Level)	Lge	W	L	ERA	G	GS	IP	H	HR	BB	SO	BB/9	SO/9	WHIP	AVG
2021	21	Rocket City (AA)	South	2	4	3.50	12	12	54	45	10	18	97	3.0	16.2	1.17	.223
	21	Salt Lake (AAA)	West	1	0	1.13	2	2	8	7	0	1	11	1.1	12.4	1.00	.233
	21	Los Angeles (MLB)	AL	1	3	7.40	5	5	20	26	5	11	19	4.8	8.3	1.79	.295
Major League Totals (1 year)				1	3	7.40	5	5	21	26	5	11	19	4.79	8.27	1.79	.295
Minor League Totals (2 years)				3	4	3.19	14	14	62	52	10	19	108	2.76	15.68	1.15	.224

2 SAM BACHMAN, RHP

Born: Sept. 30, 1999. **B-T:** R-R. **HT:** 6-1. **WT:** 235. **Drafted:** Miami (Ohio), 2021 (1st round). **Signed by:** John Burden.

TRACK RECORD: Bachman showed some of the best pure stuff in college baseball at Miami (Ohio) and steadily raised his draft stock throughout his junior year. Angels general manager Perry Minasian attended Bachman's final start of the year, when the righthander pitched 6.1 dominant innings against Ball State, and six weeks later, the Angels drafted Bachman with the ninth overall pick. Bachman signed for a well below-slot $3,847,500 and made his professional debut with five starts for High-A Tri-City, where he went 0-2, 3.77 with 15 strikeouts and four walks in 14.1 innings.

BA GRADE
55 Risk: High

SCOUTING REPORT: The burly Bachman is a pure power pitcher with two potentially dominant pitches in his fastball and slider. His fastball sits 94-97 with hard run and sink out of his low-three quarters arm slot and touches 101 mph. He pairs his plus-plus fastball with a tight, vertical slider in the upper 80s that dives late to draw swings both in and out of the zone. It's another plus-plus pitch that batters have a tough time squaring up and mostly induces ground balls when they do make contact. Bachman has an improving, mid-80s changeup that flashes average and will be critical for him to develop if he is to remain in the starting rotation. His delivery isn't particularly fluid and he averaged less than five innings per start in 2021.

THE FUTURE: Bachman's two-pitch mix, delivery and durability questions point to a future as a setup man or closer, but the Angels believe his combination of velocity, movement and physicality will fit in the rotation. He is set to make his full-season debut in 2022.

SCOUTING GRADES:	Fastball: 70	Slider: 70	Changeup: 50	Control: 50

Year	Age	Club (Level)	Lge	W	L	ERA	G	GS	IP	H	HR	BB	SO	BB/9	SO/9	WHIP	AVG
2021	21	Tri-City (HiA)	West	0	2	3.77	5	5	14	13	1	4	15	2.5	9.4	1.19	.245
Minor League Totals (1 year)				0	2	3.77	5	5	14	13	1	4	15	2.5	9.4	1.19	.245

3 KYREN PARIS, SS/2B

Born: Nov. 11, 2001. **B-T:** R-R. **HT:** 6-0. **WT:** 180. **Drafted:** HS—Oakley, Calif., 2019 (2nd round). **Signed by:** Brian Tripp.

TRACK RECORD: Paris signed with the Angels for an over-slot $1.4 million as the 55th overall pick in the 2019 draft, but he's played just 50 games in three years. He was limited to three games by a broken hamate bone in 2019, missed the 2020 season due to the coronavirus pandemic and played only 47 games in 2021 after suffering a non-displaced fracture in his fibula. Even in that limited time, he stood out as a hitter at Low-A Inland Empire and earned a late promotion to High-A Tri-City as a 19-year-old.

BA GRADE
50 Risk: High

SCOUTING REPORT: Paris' bat is well ahead of the glove. He has quick hands, good timing and a natural feel to hit, and his strength belies his small stature. He was more of an opposite-field, line-drive hitter when the Angels drafted him, an approach that pairs well with his plus speed, but he began to hit the ball harder to the gap and down the line in left field last season. He projects to be an above-average hitter and has enough power to project 12-16 home runs. Paris committed 12 errors in only 29 games in the field last season, mostly throwing. He has occasional lapses in footwork and a tendency to peek at runners, causing errant throws. He lacks the arm strength, range or quick release to be a shortstop, but he could be an average second baseman if he improves his reliability. In addition to his tools, Paris earns high praise for his makeup and work ethic.

THE FUTURE: Paris has the components of a big league hitter and projects to be an offensive second baseman. He may see Double-A as a 20-year-old in 2022.

SCOUTING GRADES:	Hitting: 55	Power: 40	Running: 60	Fielding: 40	Arm: 45

Year	Age	Club (Level)	Lge	AVG	G	AB	R	H	2B	3B	HR	RBI	BB	SO	SB	OBP	SLG
2021	19	Angels (R)	ACL	.357	5	14	3	5	0	0	1	1	1	3	2	.400	.571
	19	Inland Empire (LoA)	West	.274	29	106	29	29	5	6	2	18	27	41	16	.434	.491
	19	Tri-City (HiA)	West	.231	13	52	6	12	2	1	1	6	2	20	4	.273	.365
Minor League Totals (3 years)				.269	50	182	42	49	8	7	4	27	33	68	22	.393	.456

4 JORDYN ADAMS, OF

Born: Oct. 18, 1999. **B-T:** R-R. **HT:** 6-2. **WT:** 195. **Drafted:** HS—Cary, N.C., 2018 (1st round). **Signed by:** Chris McAlpin.

TRACK RECORD: Adams was committed to North Carolina to play both baseball and football before the Angels drafted him 16th overall in 2018 and signed him for an over-slot $3.475 million bonus. After spending 2020 at the alternate training site, he opened the 2021 season at High-A Tri-City but suffered a hamstring strain in the third game of the season that sidelined him for five weeks. Adams struggled to find a consistent swing after he returned and finished the year batting .217 with five home runs and 38% strikeout rate.

BA GRADE

50 Risk: Very High

SCOUTING REPORT: Adams is an elite athlete and an 80-grade runner with excellent bat speed and wiry strength. But after making progress translating those tools into production at the alternate training site, he seemed to plateau in 2021. Like many young players, Adams gets in trouble when his swing gets long, which prevents him from catching up to fastballs and often leads to strikeouts and weak contact. When he finds a more efficient swing, he will be able to tap into the above-average raw power that makes him such an enticing prospect. Adams tracks pitches well and knows the strike zone, but his swing issues and overall lack of feel for the barrel prevent him from projecting as more than a below-average hitter. Adams might be big league ready on defense, where his speed and athleticism play well in center field. He has refined his jumps and has run cleaner routes in the past two seasons, he has a strong, accurate arm and has already shown an ability to rob homers with leaping catches at the wall.

THE FUTURE: Adams has upside, but his future will depend on his swing development.

SCOUTING GRADES:	Hitting: 40	Power: 45	Running: 80	Fielding: 60	Arm: 55

Year	Age	Club (Level)	Lge	AVG	G	AB	R	H	2B	3B	HR	RBI	BB	SO	SB	OBP	SLG
2021	21	Tri-City (HiA)	West	.217	71	277	37	60	7	2	5	27	28	116	18	.290	.310
Minor League Totals (4 years)				.244	209	802	113	196	30	8	13	76	98	257	39	.332	.350

5 JEREMIAH JACKSON, SS/2B

Born: March 26, 2000. **B-T:** R-R. **HT:** 6-0. **WT:** 180. **Drafted:** HS—Mobile, Ala., 2018 (2nd round). **Signed by:** J.T. Zink.

TRACK RECORD: Jackson has moved slowly since the Angels drafted him with the 57th overall pick in 2018. He spent his first two seasons in the Rookie levels, including hitting a Pioneer-League record 23 homers for Orem in 2019, and briefly appeared at the alternate training site in 2020 before making his full-season debut with Low-A Inland Empire in 2021. Jackson got off to a miserable start but began to catch fire before he suffered a significant quad strain in mid June that limited him to just 51 games. He went to the Arizona Fall League after the season and hit .161 with a 38% strikeout rate.

BA GRADE

50 Risk: Very High

SCOUTING REPORT: Jackson has long had a boom-or-bust approach that results in jaw-dropping home runs and gobs of strikeouts. He made some progress in 2021 seeing the ball better, recognizing secondary pitches and not expanding the zone as much, but he still posted a 33% strikeout rate. Jackson has a loose, explosive swing and he has refined his setup and timing mechanism to get his hands and body going earlier. He destroys pitches to his pull side and has improved at driving pitches on the outer half the other way, but still projects as a below-average hitter. Jackson is rangy on defense with a quick first step and above-average speed. He has the agility and arm strength to stick at shortstop and is an adequate second baseman, but there's also a chance he could move to center field.

THE FUTURE: Jackson has 30-homer potential but will have to tone down his swing and develop a more effective two-strike approach. He is on track to see Double-A in 2022.

SCOUTING GRADES:	Hitting: 40	Power: 60	Running: 55	Fielding: 45	Arm: 55

Year	Age	Club (Level)	Lge	AVG	G	AB	R	H	2B	3B	HR	RBI	BB	SO	SB	OBP	SLG
2021	21	Angels (R)	ACL	.381	6	21	5	8	1	0	2	4	1	7	2	.409	.714
	21	Inland Empire (LoA)	West	.263	45	167	29	44	14	3	8	46	24	65	11	.352	.527
Minor League Totals (4 years)				.266	159	617	107	164	39	10	40	133	64	227	28	.336	.556

6 KY BUSH, LHP

Born: Nov. 12, 1999. **B-T:** L-L. **HT:** 6-6. **WT:** 240. **Drafted:** St. Mary's, 2021 (2nd round). **Signed by:** Scott Richardson.

TRACK RECORD: Bush took a circuitous route to professional baseball. The Utah native headed for Washington State after high school, but after a rough freshman season and some turnover in the coaching staff, he transferred to Central Arizona JC, where his 2020 season was wiped out by the coronavirus pandemic. Bush then transferred to St. Mary's for the 2021 season and emerged as one of the best college pitchers on the West Coast. He posted a 2.99 ERA with 112 strikeouts and just 19 walks in 78.1 innings for the Gaels, leading the Angels to draft him in the second round and sign him for an over-slot $1.75 million.

BA GRADE
45 Risk: High

SCOUTING REPORT: Bush is a large-bodied lefthander at 6-foot-6, 240 pounds. He has a four-pitch mix out of his over-the-top delivery, headlined by a fastball that sits at 94 mph and touches 96 mph with late riding action. Bush struggled with his fastball command his first two years of college but gained a better feel of it at St. Mary's, in part because he lost weight and gained better control of his delivery. Bush's best secondary pitch is an above-average slider with more vertical drop than horizontal movement. His slow curveball and changeup are fringy pitches that are works in progress. Despite his large frame, Bush was athletic enough to play basketball in high school and has a good blend of stuff, feel and average control.

THE FUTURE: The Angels believe Bush is just scratching the surface of his potential. With an improved curveball and changeup, he could be a mid-to-back-of the rotation starter.

SCOUTING GRADES:	Fastball: 60	Slider: 55	Curveball: 55	Changeup: 45	Control: 50

Year	Age	Club (Level)	Lge	W	L	ERA	G	GS	IP	H	HR	BB	SO	BB/9	SO/9	WHIP	AVG
2021	21	Tri-City (HiA)	West	0	2	4.50	5	5	12	14	0	5	20	3.8	15.0	1.58	.292
Minor League Totals (1 year)				0	2	4.50	5	5	12	14	0	5	20	3.75	15.00	1.58	.292

7 AROL VERA, SS

Born: Sept. 12, 2002. **B-T:** B-R. **HT:** 6-2. **WT:** 200. **Signed:** Venezuela, 2019. **Signed by:** Marion Urdaneta/Andres Garcia/Joel Chicharelli.

TRACK RECORD: Vera signed with the Angels for $2 million as one of the top prospects in the 2019 international class, but he was confined to an Arizona apartment during the coronavirus shutdown and gained more than 20 pounds, setting off alarm bells in the Angels player development department. Vera returned slimmer and more athletic in 2021 and had an explosive pro debut in the Rookie-level Arizona Complex League, leading to a promotion to Low-A Inland Empire at the end of the season.

BA GRADE
50 Risk: Extreme

SCOUTING REPORT: Vera is a physical, projectable switch-hitter who hits balls hard from both sides of the plate. He shows an advanced, all-fields approach from the left side in particular and generates all of his power from that side. Vera has a tendency to chase pitches out of the strike zone, but the Angels are confident that will improve with experience and maturity. He is more of a gap-to-gap doubles hitter, but with added strength and better pitch selection, he could develop the power to hit 15-20 homers. Vera is an average runner and earns high marks for poise, makeup and character. He has emerged as one of the smoothest, most fundamentally sound defenders in the system, with sure hands and an above-average arm. Though he lost a considerable amount of weight last year, Vera is still a little thick in his lower half, which could portend an eventual move to third base.

THE FUTURE: Vera's hitting ability and poise on defense give him some of the highest upside of any position player in the Angels system. He'll return to Low-A to begin the 2022 season.

SCOUTING GRADES:	Hitting: 55	Power: 50	Running: 45	Fielding: 55	Arm: 55

Year	Age	Club (Level)	Lge	AVG	G	AB	R	H	2B	3B	HR	RBI	BB	SO	SB	OBP	SLG
2021	18	Angels (R)	ACL	.317	38	145	24	46	16	3	0	17	12	39	2	.384	.469
	18	Inland Empire (LoA)	West	.280	19	82	10	23	0	0	0	5	6	20	9	.344	.280
Minor League Totals (1 year)				.304	57	227	34	69	16	3	0	22	18	59	11	.370	.401

8 DENZER GUZMAN, SS

Born: Feb. 8, 2004. **B-T:** R-R. **HT:** 6-1. **WT:** 180. **Signed:** Dominican Republic, 2021. **Signed by:** Domingo Garcia.

TRACK RECORD: Once the pandemic-delayed international signing period opened in Jan. 2021, the Angels snapped up Guzman, one of the best pure hitters in his class, for a $2 million bonus. The 17-year-old had a solid pro debut in the Dominican Summer League, showing good power, plate discipline and speed, with 14 extra-base hits, 20 walks and 24 strikeouts in 164 plate appearances and 11 stolen bases in 18 attempts.

SCOUTING REPORT: Guzman has a knack for barreling balls with a loose, effortless swing that he starts with a small leg kick to create a good rhythm. He has an advanced approach and knowledge of the strike zone for his age and makes hard, consistent contact on pitches in all parts of the zone. Guzman has plenty of raw power to his pull side and, because of his big-time bat speed, should tap into even more as he matures and adds more loft to his swing. He's an average runner who probably will be less of a base-stealing threat as his body fills out physically. Guzman is a solid defender with good footwork and hands and the potential to have a plus arm that will fit on the left side of the infield. He has a chance to stick at shortstop, but his below-average speed could force the organization to move him to third base. Guzman is mature for his age and earns high marks for makeup and aptitude.

THE FUTURE: Guzman is set to make his stateside debut in the Arizona Complex League in 2022. He is many years away but has the potential to be an everyday infielder with a potent bat if everything clicks.

BA GRADE
50 Risk: Extreme

SCOUTING GRADES:	Hitting: 55	Power: 50	Running: 45	Fielding: 50	Arm: 55

Year	Age	Club (Level)	Lge	AVG	G	AB	R	H	2B	3B	HR	RBI	BB	SO	SB	OBP	SLG
2021	17	Angels (R)	DSL	.213	44	141	21	30	10	1	3	27	20	24	11	.311	.362
Minor League Totals (1 year)				.213	44	141	21	30	10	1	3	27	20	24	11	.311	.362

9 LANDON MARCEAUX, RHP

Born: Oct. 8, 1999. **B-T:** R-R. **HT:** 6-0. **WT:** 179. **Drafted:** Louisiana State, 2021 (3rd round). **Signed by:** Brandon McArthur.

TRACK RECORD: Marceaux was a two-time member of USA Baseball's 18U national team and was drafted by the Yankees in the 37th round out of high school. He instead made his way to Louisiana State and spent three years in the Tigers rotation, capped by going 7-7, 2.54 with 116 strikeouts and 26 walks in 102.2 innings in 2021. The Angels drafted him in the third round and signed him for $765,300. Marceaux made only two brief starts in the Arizona Complex League in his pro debut, a decision by the Angels to play it safe given his college workload.

SCOUTING REPORT: Marceaux's stuff won't wow anybody, but few pitching prospects have a better command of their repertoires. His fastball sits at 90-93 mph with some run and a little bit of sink, his low-80s slider is an average pitch, his low-80s changeup is above-average and his upper-70s curveball is fringy but improving. Marceaux succeeds by spotting his pitches on the edges of the strike zone and avoiding hitters' hot zones with surgical precision. He has a repeatable, low-effort delivery that gives him plus control and a high-three-quarters arm slot that creates some downhill plane on his pitches.

THE FUTURE: Marceaux's stuff leaves him little margin for error, but his ability to command the ball and keep hitters off-balance gives him a chance to rise as a back-of-the-rotation starter. He'll likely open the 2022 season at High-A Tri-City but could be advanced enough to jump straight to Double-A.

BILL MITCHELL

BA GRADE
45 Risk: High

SCOUTING GRADES:	Fastball: 45	Slider: 50	Curveball: 45	Changeup: 55	Control: 60

Year	Age	Club (Level)	Lge	W	L	ERA	G	GS	IP	H	HR	BB	SO	BB/9	SO/9	WHIP	AVG
2021	21	Angels (R)	ACL	0	1	14.73	2	2	4	7	0	0	6	0.0	14.7	1.91	.389
Minor League Totals (1 year)				0	1	14.73	2	2	4	7	0	0	6	0.00	14.73	1.91	.389

10 ALEXANDER RAMIREZ, OF

Born: Aug. 29, 2002. **B-T:** R-R. **HT:** 6-2. **WT:** 180. **Signed:** Dominican Republic, 2018. **Signed by:** Frank Tejada.

TRACK RECORD: The Angels signed Ramirez for $1 million when he was 16 on the belief he had the potential to grow into a middle-of-the-order slugger. Ramirez showed that pop with 17 extra-base hits in 39 games in the Dominican Summer League in 2019 and, after he was quarantined in Arizona during the coronavirus pandemic in 2020, regained his power stroke in his stateside debut in 2021. He hit .276 with a .908 OPS and 16 extra-base hits in 35 games in the Arizona Complex League and earned a promotion to Low-A Inland Empire at the end of the year.

BA GRADE
50 Risk: Extreme

SCOUTING REPORT: Ramirez is big, strong and muscular with an athletic frame, and he's shown an ability to barrel the ball to all fields. There is some length to his swing, which, combined with an aggressive approach, has led to a 34.7% strikeout rate, but he showed a better feel to hit last summer and produced some of the organization's top exit velocities with his electric bat speed. Ramirez still has to prove he can handle spin and progress with his pitch recognition, but he has the physical potential to be a fringe-average hitter with plus power. Ramirez is an average runner with solid defensive instincts and an above-average arm, although he is still growing into his body and has occasional coordination issues. Though he has the athleticism and instincts to play center field, he projects more as a power-hitting corner outfielder long-term.

THE FUTURE: Ramirez has the potential to hit 30 homers a season if everything comes together. He'll return to Inland Empire to open the 2022 season.

SCOUTING GRADES:	Hitting: 45	Power: 60	Running: 50	Fielding: 45	Arm: 50

Year	Age	Club (Level)	Lge	AVG	G	AB	R	H	2B	3B	HR	RBI	BB	SO	SB	OBP	SLG
2021	18	Angels (R)	ACL	.276	35	127	30	35	7	4	5	27	22	50	3	.396	.512
	18	Inland Empire (LoA)	West	.083	19	72	4	6	0	1	0	4	7	34	1	.185	.111
Minor League Totals (2 years)				.218	93	353	71	77	15	10	9	50	45	143	10	.325	.394

11 AUSTIN WARREN, RHP

BA GRADE
40 Risk: Medium

Born: Feb. 5, 1996. **B-T:** R-R. **HT:** 6-0. **WT:** 170. **Drafted:** UNC Wilmington, 2018 (6th round). **Signed by:** Chris McAlpin.

TRACK RECORD: A former shortstop, Warren didn't begin pitching until his sophomore year of college at UNC Wilmington. He was hardly a top prospect, signing for only $7,500 as a senior sign in the sixth round, but he rose quickly through the Angels system and made his major league debut in July. Warren immediately impressed the Angels' coaching staff with his repertoire and poise and was pitching in high-leverage situations by mid-August.

SCOUTING REPORT: Warren generates velocity that belies his smallish frame. His four-seam fastball sits 93-94 mph and touched 96 mph in the big leagues last season. He held opponents to a .130 average in at-bats ending with his heater and produced a 25.6% whiff-rate with the pitch. His best pitch is a wipeout slider that sits 86-88 mph with nearly three feet of drop. It's a plus pitch and his go-to swing-and-miss offering. His firm, upper 80s changeup is more of a show-me pitch. Warren pounds the zone, frequently getting ahead of pitchers with first-pitch strikes, and keeps the ball on the ground.

THE FUTURE: Warren has a combination of confidence and fearlessness that was immediately evident in his major league debut. He has positioned himself for a middle-relief role with the Angels..

Year	Age	Club (Level)	Lge	W	L	ERA	G	GS	IP	H	HR	BB	SO	BB/9	SO/9	WHIP	AVG
2021	25	Salt Lake (AAA)	West	2	3	6.19	22	1	36	42	5	18	45	4.5	11.2	1.65	.292
	25	Los Angeles (MLB)	AL	3	0	1.77	16	0	20	16	0	5	20	2.2	8.9	1.03	.205
Major League Totals (1 year)				3	0	1.77	16	0	20	16	0	5	20	2.21	8.85	1.03	.205
Minor League Totals (4 years)				5	14	4.23	77	1	121	121	14	57	160	4.23	11.87	1.47	.259

12 CHASE SILSETH, RHP

BA GRADE
45 Risk: High

Born: May 18, 2000. **B-T:** R-R. **HT:** 6-0. **WT:** 217. **Drafted:** Arizona, 2021 (11th round). **Signed by:** Jayson Durocher.

TRACK RECORD: Silseth began his college career as a reliever at Tennessee before transferring to JC Southern Nevada, where he made six starts before the 2020 season shut down due to the coronavirus pandemic. He transferred to Arizona and was the Wildcats' Friday night starter in 2021, with his top moment coming when he went toe-to-toe with All-American Kumar Rocker in the College World Series, The Angels drafted Silseth in the 11th round and signed him for an over-slot $485,000 bonus.

SCOUTING REPORT: Silseth has a lively fastball that averages 96 mph and touches 98 mph. He has a good feel for a slurvy curveball with 12-to-6 break in the 78-82 mph range and a tight mid-80s slider. Both have a chance to be plus pitches, although he gets more swings and misses with his curveball. Silseth also keeps hitters off-balance with a low-80s splitter with good depth that is often mistaken for a changeup. He generally throws strikes early in his outings, but his command suffers as games wear on and he gets tired.

THE FUTURE: Silseth's four-pitch arsenal may allow him to remain in the rotation. His command and durability are indicators that he might have more success as a power arm out of the bullpen.

Year	Age	Club (Level)	Lge	W	L	ERA	G	GS	IP	H	HR	BB	SO	BB/9	SO/9	WHIP	AVG
2021	21	Angels (R)	ACL	0	0	4.50	1	0	2	1	0	1	4	4.5	18.0	1.00	.143
	21	Rocket City (AA)	South	0	2	13.50	2	2	3	6	1	0	3	0.0	8.1	1.80	.353
Minor League Totals (1 year)				0	2	10.13	3	2	5	7	1	1	7	1.69	11.81	1.50	.292

13 DAVIS DANIEL, RHP

Born: June 11, 1997. **B-T:** R-R. **HT:** 6-1. **WT:** 190. **Drafted:** Auburn, 2019 (7th round). **Signed by:** Todd Hogan.

BA GRADE
40 Risk: Medium

TRACK RECORD: Daniel had Tommy John surgery after throwing just two innings for Auburn as a junior in 2019, but the Angels still drafted him in the seventh round and signed him for $172,500. Daniel began generating buzz when he returned during instructional league in 2020 and carried that momentum into his pro debut in 2021. He rose three levels from High-A to Triple-A and led the Angels system with 154 strikeouts.

SCOUTING REPORT: Daniel has a full four-pitch arsenal, but he mostly goes after hitters with his fastball. His high-spin four-seamer sits 91-92 mph and touches 95 mph with above-average ride and cut to generate swings and misses at the top of the strike zone. He complements his fastball with a mid-70s, 12-to-6 curveball, an improving, low-80s changeup and a low-80s slider. None of them project to be more than average, but Daniel is a smart pitcher who knows when to throw them for maximum effectiveness. He throws plenty of strikes with above-average control and creates some deception with an old-school delivery in which he tilts his glove angle to hide the ball.

THE FUTURE: Daniel has a chance to be a back-of-the-rotation starter if his secondaries continue to progress. He also has experience as a reliever, so where he pitches in the big leagues will be based on need.

Year	Age	Club (Level)	Lge	W	L	ERA	G	GS	IP	H	HR	BB	SO	BB/9	SO/9	WHIP	AVG
2021	24	Tri-City (HiA)	West	3	2	2.31	9	9	46	26	4	20	64	3.9	12.3	0.99	.163
	24	Rocket City (AA)	South	1	3	2.68	9	9	47	39	4	8	66	1.5	12.6	1.00	.222
	24	Salt Lake (AAA)	West	0	2	10.29	5	4	21	37	7	6	24	2.6	10.3	2.05	.381
Minor League Totals (3 years)				4	7	3.92	23	22	115	102	15	34	154	2.67	12.09	1.19	.236

14 D'SHAWN KNOWLES, OF

Born: Jan. 16, 2001. **B-T:** B-R. **HT:** 5-11. **WT:** 180. **Signed:** Bahamas, 2017. **Signed by:** Carlos Gomez.

BA GRADE
45 Risk: High

TRACK RECORD: The switch-hitting Knowles signed with the Angels for $850,000 out of the Bahamas when he was 16 and slowly made his way through the low minors. He made his full-season debut in 2021 at Low-A Inland Empire and showed elite speed and defensive versatility while starting games at all three outfield positions and shortstop. But he also hit just .227/.280/.355 and showed he has a long way to go offensively.

SCOUTING REPORT: Knowles shows flashes of ability but has yet to find consistency. At his best, he drives the ball to both gaps with a clean, compact swing from both sides of the plate and average raw power. He has developed into a great base-stealer, is learning to bunt and is working on a better two-strike approach. Knowles also has stretches when he swings and misses at the top of the strike zone in bunches and takes zig-zag routes in center field. He goes to the gaps well and is even better at charging balls with his above-average arm strength and quick release, but he struggles to find the wall going back. Regardless of whether he's going good or bad, Knowles earns raves for his work ethic, enthusiasm and love of the game.

THE FUTURE: Knowles projects more as a speedy utility man than a regular. He'll move to High-A in 2022.

Year	Age	Club (Level)	Lge	AVG	G	AB	R	H	2B	3B	HR	RBI	BB	SO	SB	OBP	SLG
2021	20	Inland Empire (LoA)	West	.227	84	361	61	82	21	5	5	48	25	114	31	.280	.355
Minor League Totals (4 years)				.254	206	836	145	212	45	12	16	105	79	255	45	.320	.394

15 JOSE MARTE, RHP

BA GRADE
40 Risk: Medium

Born: June 14, 1996. **B-T:** R-R. **HT:** 6-3. **WT:** 180. **Signed:** Dominican Republic, 2015. **Signed by:** Ruddy Moreta (Giants).

TRACK RECORD: Marte did not rise above the Class A levels in his first four pro seasons with the Giants, but after idling in 2020, he moved from the rotation to the bullpen in 2021 and excelled at Double-A. The Angels acquired Marte as one of three prospects for Tony Watson at the trade deadline, and he made his major league debut for them in August.

SCOUTING REPORT: The power-armed Marte throws a heavy two-seam fastball that sits 96-97 mph with big sink and run. The sinker consistently plays as a plus pitch when he keeps it down in the zone and is difficult for batters to elevate, part of the reason he rarely allows home runs. Marte complements his sinker with a sluvy, mid-80s slider with more drop than break. He replaced the changeup he threw earlier in his career with an upper-80s cutter as his third pitch. Marte has long struggled with his fastball command and overall control. He needs to improve the consistency of his secondary pitches and be more effective at finishing batters off once he gets them in two-strike counts.

THE FUTURE: Marte has a lot of things to work on, but his stuff gives him a chance to be a middle reliever in the majors. He'll try to win a bullpen spot in spring training.

Year	Age	Club (Level)	Lge	W	L	ERA	G	GS	IP	H	HR	BB	SO	BB/9	SO/9	WHIP	AVG
2021	25	Eugene (HiA)	West	0	0	0.00	5	0	6	3	0	0	14	0.0	19.9	0.47	.130
	25	Richmond (AA)	NEast	2	0	3.57	19	0	22	21	0	15	36	6.0	14.3	1.59	.247
	25	Rocket City (AA)	South	0	0	0.00	3	0	3	1	0	2	5	6.0	15.0	1.00	.100
	25	Salt Lake (AAA)	West	1	2	8.59	7	0	7	10	0	5	7	6.1	8.6	2.05	.323
	25	Los Angeles (MLB)	AL	0	1	9.00	4	0	4	4	1	3	5	6.8	11.3	1.75	.267
Major League Totals (1 year)				0	1	9.00	4	0	4	4	1	3	5	6.75	11.25	1.75	.267
Minor League Totals (6 years)				16	24	4.71	97	61	306	305	19	160	316	4.71	9.29	1.52	.260

16 CHRIS RODRIGUEZ, RHP

BA GRADE
50 Risk: Extreme

Born: July 20, 1998. **B-T:** R-R. **HT:** 6-2. **WT:** 185. **Drafted:** HS—Miami, 2016 (4th round). **Signed by:** Ralph Reyes.

TRACK RECORD: After missing most of 2018 and 2019 because of back injuries and 2020 because of the coronavirus pandemic, Rodriguez broke camp with the Angels in 2021 and worked his way into high-leverage relief by going 2-0 with a 2.30 ERA in his first eight appearances. But shoulder injuries derailed his season, and he underwent capsule repair surgery in October that will sideline him for most, if not all, of 2022.

SCOUTING REPORT: Rodriguez would do well to smooth out a delivery that is a little high-effort at times, but he showed last season that he has the stuff to pitch in the big leagues. His four-pitch mix features a sinking fastball that sits 94-96 mph with and late tailing action, a wipeout, 89-90 mph slider that induces plenty of swings and misses, a big overhand curveball in the mid 80s with more than four feet of vertical drop and a 88-90 mph changeup with screwball-like action. Rodriguez throws plenty of strikes with his premium arsenal, but he hasn't been able to stay on the mound. He has thrown more than 30 innings only once in four seasons, and that was in 2017.

THE FUTURE: Rodriguez has the stuff to succeed as a starter or reliever in the majors, but another major injury has clouded his future. He'll spend the year rehabbing and try to make it back healthy in 2023.

Year	Age	Club (Level)	Lge	W	L	ERA	G	GS	IP	H	HR	BB	SO	BB/9	SO/9	WHIP	AVG
2021	22	Rocket City (AA)	South	0	0	4.26	5	5	12	15	1	5	17	3.6	12.1	1.58	.283
	22	Salt Lake (AAA)	West	0	1	5.87	3	2	7	7	1	6	5	7.0	5.9	1.70	.250
	22	Los Angeles (MLB)	AL	2	1	3.64	15	2	29	28	0	15	29	4.6	8.8	1.45	.243
Major League Totals (1 year)				2	1	3.64	15	2	29	28	0	15	29	4.55	8.80	1.45	.243
Minor League Totals (6 years)				5	4	4.78	32	29	98	101	4	32	108	2.94	9.92	1.36	.264

17 ADRIAN PLACENCIA, 2B/SS

BA GRADE
50 Risk: Extreme

Born: June 2, 2003. **B-T:** B-R. **HT:** 5-11. **WT:** 170. **Signed:** Dominican Republic, 2019. **Signed by:** Jochy Cabrera/Rusbell Cabrera.

TRACK RECORD: The switch-hitting Placencia signed with the Angels for $1.1 million as one of the youngest players in the 2019-2020 international class. After spending 2020 in instructional league, he made his professional debut in the Rookie-level Arizona Complex League in 2021. Placencia cleaned up some of his footwork and throwing mechanics on defense and showed glimpses of offensive potential, but he hit just .175/.326/.343 in 43 games.

SCOUTING REPORT: Placencia has an advanced feel for contact from both sides of the plate. He has quick hands and the barrel of his bat moves quickly through the zone. He limits his chase swings and doesn't

 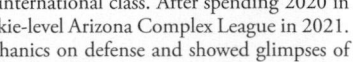

strike out often. Despite that strong foundation, Placencia struggled to hit in his pro debut in part because he doesn't consistently hit the ball hard. He flashes surprising power for his small frame and has some natural lift in his swing, but on a pitch-to-pitch basis, he struggles to do damage. Defensively, Placencia has smooth actions, soft hands and an average arm with a quick exchange. He is a below-average runner and is better at second base than shortstop.

THE FUTURE: Placencia profiles better as a utilityman than an everyday player, but he's still young and has time to add strength to his frame. He may see Low-A Inland Empire in 2022.

Year	Age	Club (Level)	Lge	AVG	G	AB	R	H	2B	3B	HR	RBI	BB	SO	SB	OBP	SLG
2021	18	Angels (R)	ACL	.175	43	143	29	25	3	3	5	19	28	49	4	.326	.343
Minor League Totals (1 year)				.175	43	143	29	25	3	3	5	19	28	49	4	.326	.343

18 JANSON JUNK, RHP

BA GRADE

40 Risk: Medium

Born: Jan. 15, 1996. **B-T:** R-R. **HT:** 6-1. **WT:** 177. **Drafted:** Seattle, 2017 (22nd round). **Signed by:** Mike Thurman (Yankees).

TRACK RECORD: Junk was a largely anonymous 22nd-round pick in the Yankees system his first three pro seasons, but he broke out in 2021 at Double-A Somerset and was acquired by the Angels for Andrew Heaney at the trade deadline. He continued his ascent in his new organization and received his first MLB callup in September, posting a 3.86 ERA in four abbreviated starts.

SCOUTING REPORT: Junk used the coronavirus shutdown in 2020 to adjust his attitude and take a more aggressive, attacking mindset to the mound. With that new mindset, his fastball has become his best pitch at 93-97 mph with a high spin rate and good carry at the top of the strike zone. He also used the shutdown to alter the shape of his slider, which was too slurvy and similar to his curveball. His low-80s slider is now a sweeper pitch with late horizontal break and drop that gets plenty of swings and misses. Junk rounds out his arsenal with a fringy 79-80 mph curveball and a fringy changeup he mostly throws to lefthanded hitters. He throws plenty of strikes with average control but is on the small side for a starter, leading to some durability concerns.

THE FUTURE: Junk's size and fastball-slider combination might be better suited for a middle-relief role. He'll look to break camp with the Angels in 2022.

Year	Age	Club (Level)	Lge	W	L	ERA	G	GS	IP	H	HR	BB	SO	BB/9	SO/9	WHIP	AVG
2021	25	Somerset (AA)	NEast	4	1	1.78	14	12	65	43	6	20	68	2.7	9.3	0.96	.185
	25	Rocket City (AA)	South	2	2	5.27	5	5	27	32	5	7	29	2.3	9.6	1.43	.281
	25	Los Angeles (MLB)	AL	0	1	3.86	4	4	16	20	5	2	10	1.1	5.5	1.35	.294
Major League Totals (1 year)				0	1	3.86	4	4	16	20	5	2	10	1.10	5.51	1.35	.294
Minor League Totals (5 years)				18	17	3.87	69	46	282	276	30	106	259	3.39	8.28	1.36	.252

19 ORLANDO MARTINEZ, OF

BA GRADE

45 Risk: High

Born: Feb. 17, 1998. **B-T:** L-L. **HT:** 6-0. **WT:** 195. **Signed:** Cuba, 2017. **Signed by:** Frankie Thon Jr.

TRACK RECORD: Martinez signed with the Angels for $250,000 out of Cuba in 2017 and has steadily risen up their system. After impressing at the Class A levels his first two seasons, Martinez returned from the coronavirus shutdown and set new career highs in doubles (23), home runs (16) and total bases (178) with Double-A Rocket City, all despite the league being pitcher friendly.

SCOUTING REPORT: Martinez has a smooth, lefthanded swing and a natural feel to hit, but he sacrificed some contact to access more power last season. Though he has more of a hit-over-power profile, Martinez could add power as he continues to learn what pitches he can drive with authority and what pitches he should lay off of. He has decent speed but is not a base-stealing threat. Though he is not Gold Glove-caliber on defense, he has shown the ability to play all three outfield positions with good jumps, clean, direct routes and a strong, accurate arm.

THE FUTURE: Martinez does not have the eye-popping tools of a potential all-star, but he is the type of prospect whose whole is greater than the sum of his parts. He could be a versatile extra outfielder or platoon player and will open 2022 in Triple-A..

Year	Age	Club (Level)	Lge	AVG	G	AB	R	H	2B	3B	HR	RBI	BB	SO	SB	OBP	SLG
2021	23	Rocket City (AA)	South	.258	102	400	58	103	23	2	16	54	30	119	5	.313	.445
Minor League Totals (4 years)				.272	255	1046	151	284	61	7	33	138	87	263	19	.328	.438

20 LUKE MURPHY, RHP

BA GRADE

45 Risk: High

Born: Nov. 5, 1999. **B-T:** R-R. **HT:** 6-5. **WT:** 190. **Drafted:** Vanderbilt, 2021 (4th round). **Signed by:** Joel Murrie.

TRACK RECORD: The end of Murphy's college career was much better than the beginning. After sitting out the 2019 season recovering from Tommy John surgery and pitching only four times in pandemic-shortened 2020 season, Murphy spent 2021 as Vanderbilt's closer and went 4-1, 2.40 with nine saves. The Angels drafted him in the fourth round and signed him for $747,500.

SCOUTING REPORT: The lanky Murphy relies heavily on a fastball that sits at 94-95 mph and touches 98-99. He has good command of the four-seamer and locates it in all four quadrants of the strike zone. His best secondary offering is a sweeping slider with movement that has the potential to be a wipeout pitch. He is developing a curveball and changeup but didn't throw either pitch much in college. Murphy didn't start at Vanderbilt, but he worked multiple innings regularly and can be stretched out.

THE FUTURE: Murphy's fastball-slider combination is suited to a high-leverage relief role. He could move quickly and reach the upper levels of the minors in 2022.

Year	Age	Club (Level)	Lge	W	L	ERA	G	GS	IP	H	HR	BB	SO	BB/9	SO/9	WHIP	AVG
2021	21	Tri-City (HiA)	West	0	1	3.00	7	0	9	7	0	1	15	1.0	15.0	0.89	.206
Minor League Totals (1 year)				0	1	3.00	7	0	9	7	0	1	15	1.00	15.00	0.89	.206

21 OLIVER ORTEGA, RHP

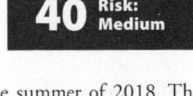

BA GRADE

40 Risk: Medium

Born: Oct. 2, 1996. **B-T:** R-R. **HT:** 6-0. **WT:** 200. **Signed:** Dominican Republic, 2014. **Signed by:** Domingo Garcia/Alfredo Ulloa.

TRACK RECORD: Ortega signed with the Angels for $10,000 as a late-blooming 18-year-old and spent his first five seasons as a starter before moving to the bullpen in 2021. He struggled early at Double-A Rocket City but found his bearing after a promotion to Triple-A Salt Lake and received his first big league callup in September. After making eight relief appearances for the Angels, he went to the Dominican Winter League and posted a 0.69 ERA in 13 appearances.

SCOUTING REPORT: Ortega has plenty of stuff to pitch in relief and is getting comfortable with the role. His four-seam fastball sits 96-97 mph and touches 99 mph with cutting action out of the bullpen. His funky, 12-to-6 knuckle curveball sits in the low 80s with nearly four feet of drop and sometimes spins like a lefthanded breaking ball. His rarely thrown changeup is firm at 89 mph and has a lot more run than his fastball. Ortega's stuff is loud, but his control is below-average. He will look dominant at times and then walk two or three batters in a row.

THE FUTURE: Ortega could provide solid middle relief for the Angels as soon as 2022. He'll look to win an Opening Day bullpen spot in spring training.

Year	Age	Club (Level)	Lge	W	L	ERA	G	GS	IP	H	HR	BB	SO	BB/9	SO/9	WHIP	AVG
2021	24	Rocket City (AA)	South	2	3	6.16	25	0	30	33	3	13	46	3.8	13.5	1.50	.266
	24	Salt Lake (AAA)	West	0	0	3.75	9	0	12	11	2	5	15	3.8	11.3	1.33	.229
	24	Los Angeles (MLB)	AL	1	0	4.82	8	0	9	12	1	2	4	1.9	3.9	1.50	.333
Major League Totals (1 year)				1	0	4.82	8	0	9	12	1	2	4	1.93	3.86	1.50	.333
Minor League Totals (7 years)				13	22	4.06	106	46	308	256	20	144	346	4.21	10.11	1.30	.224

22 MICHAEL STEFANIC, 2B

BA GRADE

40 Risk: Medium

Born: Feb. 24, 1996. **B-T:** R-R. **HT:** 5-10. **WT:** 180. **Signed:** Westmont (Calif.), 2018 (NDFA). **Signed by:** Ben Diggins.

TRACK RECORD: After going undrafted despite starring at NAIA Westmont, Stefanic sent his resume and a homemade prospect video to all 30 clubs in the summer of 2018. The Angels needed a low-level infielder and signed him with the thought he'd be an organizational player. Stefanic instead hit at every level leading up to a breakout 2021 season. He finished second in the minor leagues with 165 hits and tied for fifth with a .336 batting average as he rose from Double-A to Triple-A.

SCOUTING REPORT: Stefanic is an extreme contact hitter who rarely swings and misses, doesn't chase and has the bat control to put almost any pitch in play. He grew stronger and started showing his power—to the pull side as well as right-center—in 2021. There is little doubt he can be an average hitter with double-digit home runs in the majors, but that might not be enough to overcome his defense. Stefanic isn't very athletic defensively and has to substantially improve his lateral mobility. He has limited range at second base and his below-average arm doesn't play well at third base. He has bottom-of-the-scale speed and lacks first-step quickness.

THE FUTURE: Stefanic's bat is legitimate, but he will have to improve defensively to be a utilityman. If he can play third base and add corner outfield to his resume, he could earn a spot on a big league bench.

Year	Age	Club (Level)	Lge	AVG	G	AB	R	H	2B	3B	HR	RBI	BB	SO	SB	OBP	SLG
2021	25	Rocket City (AA)	South	.345	21	87	11	30	5	0	1	9	7	15	0	.406	.437
	25	Salt Lake (AAA)	West	.334	104	404	67	135	21	0	16	54	45	62	6	.408	.505
Minor League Totals (4 years)				.314	241	904	130	284	44	3	20	115	86	129	15	.388	.436

23 WERNER BLAKELY, SS/2B

BA GRADE 45 Risk: Extreme

Born: Feb. 21, 2002. **B-T:** L-R. **HT:** 6-3. **WT:** 185. **Drafted:** HS—Detroit, 2020 (4th round). **Signed by:** Drew Dominguez.

TRACK RECORD: Blakely grew up in Detroit and emerged as Michigan's top high school player in the 2020 draft class. He did not get a chance to play his senior season due to the coronavirus pandemic, but the Angels still drafted him in the fifth round and gave him an above-slot $900,000 bonus to pass up an Auburn commitment. Blakely made his pro debut in the Arizona Complex League in 2021 and showed some ability to draw walks, but he hit just .182 with a 37% strikeout rate.

SCOUTING REPORT: Blakely has a lot to dream on with his long, lean, projectable frame and immense athleticism. He has a good eye and patient approach at the plate, but he swings and misses a lot in the strike zone with an uppercut swing. The Angels tinkered with his swing throughout his first season, and it began to look better at the end of the year. Blakely should add power as he packs more muscle onto his frame and is athletic enough to remain an above-average runner even as he gets bigger. A shortstop now, Blakely has the actions and arm strength to play all three infield positions, but most think he'd be best in center field.

THE FUTURE: Blakely is a prototypical high-risk, high-reward prospect with plenty of projection. His swing development will determine what kind of career he has.

Year	Age	Club (Level)	Lge	AVG	G	AB	R	H	2B	3B	HR	RBI	BB	SO	SB	OBP	SLG
2021	19	Angels (R)	ACL	.182	44	148	22	27	6	0	3	19	33	69	15	.339	.284
Minor League Totals (2 years)				.182	44	148	22	27	6	0	3	19	33	69	15	.339	.284

24 MASON ERLA, RHP

BA GRADE 40 Risk: High

Born: Aug. 19, 1997. **B-T:** R-R. **HT:** 6-4. **WT:** 200. **Drafted:** Michigan State, 2021 (17th round). **Signed by:** Drew Dominguez.

TRACK RECORD: Erla was passed over in the five-round 2020 draft, so he returned to Michigan State for a fifth season and went 5-6, 3.50 with 80 strikeouts and only three home runs allowed in 79.2 innings. The Angels drafted him in the 17th round and he immediately showed promise in his pro debut with 11 strikeouts and no walks in 7.1 innings across two levels.

SCOUTING REPORT: The big-bodied Erla has good command of a fastball that averages 95-96 mph and touches 98 mph in short bursts. He added a low-90s cutter that has more slider-like action after being drafted to give him a potentially average secondary pitch, He has shown a good feel for a mid-80s changeup and iis still developing a mid-80s slider that is more of a slurve. He throws all of his pitches for strikes with average control.

THE FUTURE: Erla is already 24, but his velocity and strike-throwing capabilities make him a sleeper candidate. He will remain a starter for now and can slide into relief if needed.

Year	Age	Club (Level)	Lge	W	L	ERA	G	GS	IP	H	HR	BB	SO	BB/9	SO/9	WHIP	AVG
2021	23	Angels (R)	ACL	1	0	0.00	2	1	5	2	0	0	9	0.0	16.2	0.40	.125
	23	Tri-City (HiA)	West	0	1	3.86	1	1	2	2	0	0	2	0.0	7.7	0.86	.200
Minor League Totals (1 year)				1	1	1.23	3	2	7	4	0	0	11	0.00	13.50	0.55	.154

25 JACK KOCHANOWICZ, RHP

BA GRADE 45 Risk: Extreme

Born: Dec. 22, 2000. **B-T:** L-R. **HT:** 6-6. **WT:** 220. **Drafted:** HS—Philadelphia, 2019 (3rd round). **Signed by:** Kennard Jones.

TRACK RECORD: Kochanowicz signed for an over-slot $1.25 million bonus as a third-round pick in 2019 and had to wait almost two years to make his professional debut. The layoff showed at Low-A Inland Empire in 2021, where Kochanowicz surrendered 102 hits in 83.1 innings and got tagged for an 6.91 ERA while averaging barely four innings per outing.

SCOUTING REPORT: Kochanowicz is a big-bodied righthander with an athletic and relatively fluid delivery that produces lively fastballs in the 93-97 mph range. His high-spin, big-breaking, mid-70s curveball with big drop and late horizontal movement gives him a second potential plus pitch if he can command it, and his changeup shows average potential. Kochanowicz struggled to throw his offspeed pitches for strikes in 2021, forcing him to throw his fastball over the middle, where it was crushed. He should improve as he gains better command of the heater and learns to attack different parts of the zone with it. The Angels love his work ethic and inquisitive nature and believe he will grow from the adversity.

THE FUTURE: Kochanowicz's focus in 2022 will be on fastball command and getting ahead in counts. He needs to do that and start throwing his secondaries for strikes to live up to his starter potential.

Year	Age	Club (Level)	Lge	W	L	ERA	G	GS	IP	H	HR	BB	SO	BB/9	SO/9	WHIP	AVG
2021	20	Inland Empire (LoA)	West	4	2	6.91	20	18	83	102	12	35	73	3.8	7.9	1.64	.297
Minor League Totals (3 years)				4	2	6.91	20	18	83	102	12	35	73	3.78	7.88	1.64	.297

26 ELVIS PEGUERO, RHP

BA GRADE
40 Risk: High

Born: March 20, 1997. **B-T:** R-R. **HT:** 6-5. **WT:** 208. **Signed:** Dominican Republic, 2015. **Signed by:** Arturo Peña (Yankees).

TRACK RECORD: Peguero is a native of Cotui, the rural Dominican Republic town that produced former Angels pitcher Ramon Ortiz. He signed with the Yankees for $50,000 in 2015 and was acquired in a trade-deadline deal for Andrew Heaney last summer. Peguero spent his first three professional seasons as a starter but was moved to the bullpen in 2019, a better fit for his power two-pitch mix. He jumped three levels in 2021 and made his big league debut in late August, getting roughed up in three appearances.

SCOUTING REPORT: Peguero features a heavy sinking fastball that averages 96 mph with late tailing action. It is a difficult pitch to lift when it's down in the zone. His vertical upper-80s slider has plenty of drop but lacks sharpness and he struggles to land it. Peguero uses his lanky frame well to throw downhill and puts the ball over the plate, but he has trouble hitting his spots and too often leaves the ball in hittable zones

THE FUTURE: Peguero has the pure stuff to pitch in the back of a bullpen, but his lack of command makes him more likely to be a middle reliever.

Year	Age	Club (Level)	Lge	W	L	ERA	G	GS	IP	H	HR	BB	SO	BB/9	SO/9	WHIP	AVG
2021	24	Hudson Valley (HiA)	East	3	1	2.51	15	0	32	22	2	11	40	3.1	11.1	1.02	.186
	24	Somerset (AA)	NEast	1	0	1.50	6	0	12	6	1	5	17	3.8	12.8	0.92	.140
	24	Rocket City (AA)	South	1	1	8.44	4	0	5	7	2	1	8	1.7	13.5	1.50	.304
	24	Salt Lake (AAA)	West	0	0	6.75	6	0	8	9	0	2	7	2.3	7.9	1.38	.281
	24	Los Angeles (MLB)	AL	0	1	27.00	3	0	2	7	0	3	0	11.6	0.0	4.29	.538
Major League Totals (1 year)				0	1	27.00	3	0	2	7	0	3	0	11.57	0.00	4.29	.538
Minor League Totals (6 years)				10	18	4.80	79	22	214	217	20	89	188	3.75	7.92	1.43	.258

27 EDGAR QUERO, C

BA GRADE
45 Risk: Extreme

Born: April 6, 2003. **B-T:** B-R. **HT:** 5-11. **WT:** 170. **Signed:** Cuba, 2021. **Signed by:** Brian Parker.

TRACK RECORD: The switch-hitting Quero jumped onto the radar of talent evaluators when he hit .400 in the 15U World Cup in Panama in 2018. He signed for $200,000 last winter, one of 11 six-figure bonuses the Angels handed out during the 2020-2021 international signing period. Quero hit so well in 29 Arizona rookie-league games (.253, .945 OPS, four homers, 24 RBIs) that he earned a promotion to Low-A Inland Empire in late August.

SCOUTING REPORT: Quero has an advanced approach at the plate for his age and a knack for barreling the ball, with most of his pull power coming from the left side. He should develop more power as he matures physically and gains strength. Though there is some swing-and-miss in his game, he rarely chases pitches out of the zone and had almost as many walks (23) as strikeouts (28) in the ACL. Defensively, Quero is athletic with good receiving skills and an average arm, and he's already impressing coaches with his ability to call a game and work with pitchers.

THE FUTURE: It has been more than a decade since the Angels developed a decent homegrown catcher. Quero has the potential to end that streak, although he's a few years away.

Year	Age	Club (Level)	Lge	AVG	G	AB	R	H	2B	3B	HR	RBI	BB	SO	SB	OBP	SLG
2021	18	Angels (R)	ACL	.253	29	87	21	22	8	1	4	24	23	28	1	.440	.506
	18	Inland Empire (LoA)	West	.206	10	34	2	7	2	0	1	6	5	16	1	.310	.353
Minor League Totals (1 year)				.240	39	121	23	29	10	1	5	30	28	44	2	.405	.463

28 COLEMAN CROW, RHP

BA GRADE

40 Risk: High

Born: Dec. 30, 2000. **B-T:** R-R. **HT:** 6-0. **WT:** 175. **Drafted:** HS—Zebulon, Ga., 2019 (28th round). **Signed by:** Todd Hogan.

TRACK RECORD: The Angels drafted Crow in the 28th round out of high school in 2019 but gave him a $317,500 signing bonus— fifth-round money—to buy him out of his Kennesaw State commitment. Crow did not pitch after being drafted and lost the 2020 season to the coronavirus pandemic, but he finally made his pro debut in 2021 and excelled at Low-A Inland Empire. He went to the Arizona Fall League after the season and posted a 1.38 ERA in five games as one of the league's youngest players and earned a selection to the AFL Fall Stars Game.

SCOUTING REPORT: Though small in stature, Crow has a feisty mound demeanor and a penchant for battling through tough situations. His fastball sits 91-92 mph and touches 95 and he spins his slurvy, low-80s slider extremely well, generating 3,000 rpms on the pitch. He complements his two primary offerings with a low-80s changeup with split action and late run and is mixing in a two-seam fastball with tailing and sinking action. Crow has just fringy control, but he throws enough strikes in short bursts.

THE FUTURE: Crow could be a solid depth piece if he gains more fastball velocity and better commands his secondary pitches. A move to the bullpen could help his stuff tick up.

Year	Age	Club (Level)	Lge	W	L	ERA	G	GS	IP	H	HR	BB	SO	BB/9	SO/9	WHIP	AVG
2021	20	Inland Empire (LoA)	West	4	3	4.19	13	10	62	68	7	29	62	4.2	9.0	1.56	.273
Minor League Totals (3 years)				4	3	4.19	13	10	62	68	7	29	62	4.19	8.95	1.56	.273

29 MASON ALBRIGHT, LHP

BA GRADE

45 Risk: Extreme

Born: Nov. 26, 2002. **B-T:** L-L. **HT:** 6-0. **WT:** 190.
Drafted: HS—Bradenton, Fla., 2021 (12th round). **Signed by:** Brandon McArthur.

TRACK RECORD: Albright moved from Maryland to Florida to attend IMG Academy as a senior in 2021. He appeared headed for Virginia Tech after he wasn't picked during the first two days of the draft, but the Angels took him in the 12th round and bought him out of that commitment with a $1,247,500 signing bonus, the largest ever given to a player taken outside of the first 10 rounds.

SCOUTING REPORT: Albright has an advanced feel for and command of his three-pitch mix, which is headlined by a fastball that sits between 90-92 mph and touches 94 mph. He throws a big, sweeping mid-70s breaking ball from a slightly lower arm slot that is more slurve than slider and has and decent feel for a low-80s changeup. His fastball command, namely when to throw the pitch for a strike and when to move it off the plate, was a focus at instructional league. He is only 19 and has plenty of room for physical growth.

THE FUTURE: With some added velocity and command of his secondary pitches, Albright could work his way into the back of a big league rotation. He'll likely see Low-A Inland Empire in 2022.

Year	Age	Club (Level)	Lge	W	L	ERA	G	GS	IP	H	HR	BB	SO	BB/9	SO/9	WHIP	AVG
2021	18	Angels (R)	ACL	1	0	0.00	3	2	8	3	0	2	8	2.3	9.0	0.63	.107
Minor League Totals (1 year)				1	0	0.00	3	2	8	3	0	2	8	2.25	9.00	0.63	.107

30 NATANAEL SANTANA, OF

BA GRADE

45 Risk: Extreme

Born: July 27, 2001. **B-T:** R-R. **HT:** 6-3. **WT:** 190. **Signed:** Dominican Republic, 2019. **Signed by:** Giovanni Hernandez/Aneudi Mercado/Joel Chicarelli.

TRACK RECORD: Santana signed with the Angels as a 17-year-old and spent his first pro season in the Dominican Summer League, where he hit .258 with a .778 OPS. After losing the 2020 season to the coronavirus pandemic, Santana put up decent numbers in the Rookie-level Arizona Complex League but also struck out 70 times in 182 plate appearances for a 38.5% strikeout rate.

SCOUTING REPORT: Santana is a late-bloomer who didn't play baseball as a youngster, so his all-around game is not as refined or advanced as that of most top international prospects. But he has the kind of raw tools, athleticism and physicality to dream on. He has plus raw power, plus speed and above-average arm strength. His plate discipline and pitch recognition, as well as his reads and routes in the outfield, have improved. The question is whether Santana will be able to hit.

THE FUTURE: Santana has looked comfortable and competent in center field, but his body will probably push him to a corner outfield spot. He may reach Low-A Inland Empire in 2022.

Year	Age	Club (Level)	Lge	AVG	G	AB	R	H	2B	3B	HR	RBI	BB	SO	SB	OBP	SLG
2021	19	Angels (R)	ACL	.239	48	163	30	39	8	2	2	14	11	70	13	.313	.350
Minor League Totals (2 years)				.249	102	345	64	86	13	3	7	41	45	136	25	.361	.365

MORE PROSPECTS TO KNOW

31. LIVAN SOTO, SS/2B
The 21-year-old Venezuelan is one of the best defenders in the system, with good instincts and fast-twitch actions, a good first step, quick hands and an arm strong enough to stick at shortstop. He showed a little more pop in 2021, but his strikeout rate jumped from 13% in his first three seasons to 24%.

32. JHONATHAN DIAZ, LHP
Signed as a minor league free agent, Diaz averages 90 mph with his two-seam fastball. He spins the ball extremely well with a 79 mph slider that features 44.6 inches of drop and 15.7 inches of break and a looping 74 mph curve that drops 64 inches. He also has good feel of an 86 mph changeup.

33. BRENDON DAVIS, 3B `SLEEPER`
A fifth-round pick of the Dodgers in 2015, Davis was picked in the 2020 minor league Rule 5 draft. The versatile 24-year-old from Lakewood, Calif., jumped from High-A to Double-A to Triple-A in 2021.

34. ALEJANDRO HIDALGO, RHP
The 18-year-old from Venezuela, who signed during the 2019-20 international period, sat 92-94 mph with his fastball and showed advanced feel to spin a curveball last summer in the Arizona Complex League, where he went 3-2, 4.67 in seven games.

35. DAVID MACKINNON, 1B
A 32nd-round pick out of Hartford in 2017, MacKinnon is among the best in the system at strike-zone management, he's beginning to hit mistakes and he's a solid defender.

36. RYAN SMITH, LHP
The 24-year-old gets a ton of run with a four-seam fastball that sits 92-93 mph and touches 96 mph and good horizontal movement with an upper-70s slider. He jumped four levels in 2021, combining to go 7-7, 4.24 ERA in 24 games.

37. PACKY NAUGHTON, LHP
The crafty 25-year-old, acquired from the Reds in 2020, works from a slightly funky, low-three-quarters arm slot that adds deception to his three-pitch mix, a low-90s fastball, a low-80s changeup with good armside run and an 83 mph slider. He reached the big leagues for the first time in 2021.

38. ANDREW WANTZ, RHP
The 26-year-old from UNC Greensboro, a seventh-round pick in 2018, increased his fastball velocity from 88-92 mph to 91-95 mph and added a cutter to his arsenal last season.

39. KYLE TYLER, RHP
A 20th-round pick out of Oklahoma in 2018, Tyler led Double-A Rocket City's rotation, which included top prospect Reid Detmers, for much of 2021. He pounds the strike zone with above-average command of a fastball that sits 91-93 mph with a natural cut. His 12-to-6 breaking ball is improving.

40. ZACH LINGINFELTER, RHP
The 6-foot-5, 240-pound righty's four-seam fastball sits at 94-95 mph and touches 98 mph, and an upper-80s slider pairs well with a firm two-seam sinking fastball that he began throwing last season, when he went 2-7, 4.11 in 27 games. His short, late-breaking curveball in the mid 80s looks promising.

TOP PROSPECTS OF THE DECADE

Year	Player, Pos.	2021 Org
2012	Mike Trout, OF	Angels
2013	Kaleb Cowart, 3B	Yankees
2014	Taylor Lindsey, 2B	Did not play
2015	Andrew Heaney, LHP	Yankees
2016	Taylor Ward, C	Angels
2017	Jahmai Jones, OF	Orioles
2018	Shohei Ohtani, RHP/DH	Angels
2019	Jo Adell, OF	Angels
2020	Jo Adell, OF	Angels
2021	Jo Adell, OF	Angels

TOP DRAFT PICKS OF THE DECADE

Year	Player, Pos.	2021 Org
2012	R.J. Alvarez, RHP (3rd round)	Brewers
2013	Hunter Green, LHP (2nd round)	Did not play
2014	Sean Newcomb, LHP	Braves
2015	Taylor Ward, C	Angels
2016	Matt Thaiss, C	Angels
2017	Jo Adell, OF	Angels
2018	Jordyn Adams, OF	Angels
2019	Will Wilson, SS	Giants
2020	Reid Detmers, LHP	Angels
2021	Sam Bachman, RHP	Angels

Los Angeles Dodgers

BY KYLE GLASER

The Dodgers have been a beacon of stability in the major leagues for nearly a decade. Entering the 2022 season, that status is somewhat tenuous.

The Dodgers won 106 games last season and reached the National League Championship Series, where they fell to the eventual-champion Braves in six games. It was the Dodgers' third time winning at least 100 games in the last four full seasons, and they have either won the World Series or lost to the eventual champion each of the last five years.

Now, the Dodgers face the daunting challenge of continuing that success without some of the cornerstones who made it possible. Franchise shortstop Corey Seager left in free agency after the season to sign a 10-year, $325 million contract with the Rangers. Clayton Kershaw and Kenley Jansen, the two longest-tenured Dodgers and franchise fixtures, became free agents and remained unsigned when the lockout began in December.

The possibility of losing Seager, Kershaw and Jansen would be enough to throw off any team, but the Dodgers face more uncertainty even beyond that. Max Scherzer, who went 7-1, 1.98 in 11 starts for the Dodgers after they acquired him at the trade deadline, left in free agency to sign a three-year, $130 million contract with the Mets. Cody Bellinger hit .165 in a miserable season that was the latest chapter in his stunning decline from his 2019 NL MVP campaign. Dustin May will be out most of the 2022 season after having Tommy John surgery. Trevor Bauer remains in limbo as both the Pasadena police department and MLB investigate sexual assault claims made against the pitcher last summer.

With so many stars either gone or their ability to contribute in question, the Dodgers' seemingly perpetual ability to replenish what was lost will face its stiffest challenge.

The good news is the Dodgers have plenty of capable candidates.

Former BA Minor League Player of the Year Gavin Lux began to show signs of life at the end of last season and is slated to step into an everyday role in 2022, likely as the Dodgers' starting second baseman. Righthander Tony Gonsolin struggled with his command in 2021 but still owns a career 2.85 ERA and will move into a larger role in the rotation.

And, as always, the Dodgers have talent in the upper minors ready to come up and help. Third baseman Miguel Vargas and second baseman Michael Busch are polished, talented hitters who will open the year in Triple-A, while righthander Ryan Pepiot finished last season in Triple-A and

Young Dodgers ace Walker Buehler finished fourth in NL Cy Young Award voting.

PROJECTED 2025 LINEUP

Catcher	Will Smith	30
First Base	Michael Busch	27
Second Base	Gavin Lux	27
Third Base	Miguel Vargas	25
Shortstop	Trea Turner	32
Left Field	Andy Pages	24
Center Field	Cody Bellinger	29
Right Field	Mookie Betts	32
Designated Hitter	Max Muncy	34
No. 1 Starter	Walker Buehler	30
No. 2 Starter	Julio Urias	28
No. 3 Starter	Dustin May	27
No. 4 Starter	Bobby Miller	26
No. 5 Starter	Tony Gonsolin	31
Closer	Brusdar Graterol	26

has the stuff to impact the major league club during the year. Fellow righthanders Bobby Miller, Landon Knack and Clayton Beeter all finished last season at Double-A and could conceivably make their debuts during the season, as well.

The Dodgers don't need their young big leaguers or rising prospects to be instant stars. The club still has as much star power as any team in the majors with Walker Buehler and Julio Urias leading the pitching staff, and Mookie Betts, Trea Turner, Max Muncy, Justin Turner and Will Smith pacing the lineup. Rather, it will be incumbent on their young players to step into supporting roles and ensure a lack of depth doesn't derail the club's championship hopes. ∎

LOS ANGELES DODGERS

TOP 2022 ROOKIES	RANK
Miguel Vargas, 3B	3
Michael Busch, 2B	4
Ryan Pepiot, RHP	5
BREAKOUT PROSPECTS	**RANK**
Yeiner Fernandez, C	18
Peter Heubeck, RHP	20
Rayne Doncon, SS	21

SOURCE OF TOP 30 TALENT

Homegrown	29	Acquired	1
College	13	Trade	1
Junior college	0	Rule 5 draft	0
High school	3	Independent league	0
Nondrafted free agent	1	Free agent/waivers	0
International	12		

LF
Devin Mann (27)
Ryan Ward
Carlos Rincon

CF
James Outman (15)
Drew Avans
Jonny DeLuca

RF
Andy Pages (6)
Jose Ramos (13)
Luis Rodriguez

3B
Miguel Vargas (3)
Kody Hoese (19)
Brandon Lewis

SS
Wilman Diaz (10)
Jacob Amaya (14)
Rayne Doncon (21)
Alex De Jesus (25)
Leonel Valera

2B
Michael Busch (4)
Eddys Leonard (8)
Jorbit Vivas (23)

1B
Justin Yurchak (26)
Ryan Noda

C
Diego Cartaya (1)
Yeiner Fernandez (18)
Carson Taylor (28)
Hunter Feduccia

LHP

LHSP	LHRP
Maddux Bruns (11)	Justin Bruihl (22)
Robinson Ortiz	Austin Drury

RHP

RHSP	RHRP
Bobby Miller (2)	Andre Jackson (9)
Ryan Pepiot (5)	Clayton Beeter (12)
Landon Knack (7)	Michael Grove (24)
Nick Nastrini (16)	Carlos Duran (29)
Gavin Stone (17)	Nick Robertson
Peter Heubeck (20)	Edgardo Henriquez
Hyun-il Choi (30)	Emmet Sheehan
Kendall Williams	Cameron Gibbens
Maximo Martinez	Alec Gamboa
Jesus Vargas	Justin Hagenman
	Kyle Hurt

1 DIEGO CARTAYA, C

Born:: Sept. 7, 2001. **B-T:** R-R. **HT:** 6-3. **WT:** 219.
Signed: Venezuela, 2018.
Signed by: Luis Marquez/Roman Barinas/Cliff Nuiter/ Jean Castro.

TRACK RECORD: Cartaya represented Venezuela at international tournaments from the time he was 10 years old and emerged early as the country's top player in his class. He maintained that status through his teenage years and signed with the Dodgers for $2.5 million on the first day of the 2018-19 international signing period. Cartaya immediately impressed in the Rookie-level Arizona League in his pro debut and was the youngest player the Dodgers invited to their alternate training site in 2020, where he understandably struggled against older competition. A back muscle flareup delayed his full-season debut in 2021, but he reported to Low-A Rancho Cucamonga in late May and became an instant star. He hit 10 home runs in 31 games while showing uncommon poise and maturity defensively behind the plate before his season was cut short by injuries. He went on the injured list with a strained hamstring in July and re-injured his back in August while he was rehabbing. The Dodgers shut him down for the year.

SCOUTING REPORT: Though only 20 years old, Cartaya is a big, physical masher who is a force at the plate. He is an extraordinarily mature hitter who expertly manages the strike zone, recognizes pitches out of the hand and makes ear-ringing contact with controlled, powerful swings. His efficient swing and natural strength create booming, all-fields power with remarkable ease, and he stays through the big part of the field in his approach to hit towering drives from left-center to right-center. Cartaya turns around premium velocity, stays on breaking balls, covers the entire plate and rarely chases out of the strike zone, giving pitchers little recourse to avoid damage. He struggles at times with changeups and pitches fading down and away from him, but he still projects to be an above-average hitter with plus power, if not more. Cartaya is a good athlete who is impressively limber for his size behind the plate. He presents a good target for his pitchers, frames well at the bottom of the strike zone and controls the run game with his plus-plus arm strength. He still needs to improve his framing at the top of the strike zone and his game-calling, but he has all the tools to be a plus defender. He will have to watch his size to maintain his athleticism and mobility in blocking as he gets older. Unable to return home to Venezuela during the coronavirus pandemic, Cartaya lived with Dodgers Triple-A manager Travis Barbary in South Carolina

JASON REED/RANCHO CUCAMONGA QUAKES

BA GRADE	SCOUTING GRADES
65 Risk: V. High	Hit: 55. Power: 60. Run: 30. Field: 60. Arm: 70.

Projected future grades on 20-80 scouting scale

BEST TOOLS

Best Hitter for Average	Miguel Vargas
Best Power Hitter	Andy Pages
Best Strike-Zone Discipline	Jacob Amaya
Fastest Baserunner	Jeren Kendall
Best Athlete	James Outman
Best Fastball	Bobby Miller
Best Curveball	Clayton Beeter
Best Slider	Carlos Duran
Best Changeup	Ryan Pepiot
Best Control	Landon Knack
Best Defensive Catcher	Diego Cartaya
Best Defensive Infielder	Jacob Amaya
Best Infield Arm	Leonel Valera
Best Defensive Outfielder	Jeren Kendall
Best Outfield Arm	Jose Ramos

during the 2020 shutdown and rapidly learned English. He is an exceptionally hard worker who expertly retains scouting report information and invests deeply in his relationships with pitchers. He is a natural-born leader who remains poised in adverse situations and is comfortable communicating in both English and Spanish.

THE FUTURE: Cartaya's repeated back injuries are concerning, but if he can stay healthy, he has the talent to be a franchise catcher who hits in the middle of a lineup and contends for Gold Glove awards. He is expected to be ready for the start of spring training and will likely spend most of the 2022 season at High-A Great Lakes. ■

Year	Age	Club (Level)	Lge	AVG	G	AB	R	H	2B	3B	HR	RBI	BB	SO	SB	OBP	SLG
2021	19	R. Cucamonga (LoA)	West	.298	31	114	31	34	6	0	10	31	18	37	0	.409	.614
Minor League Totals (3 years)				.288	80	299	67	86	18	2	14	53	34	79	1	.369	.502

2 BOBBY MILLER, RHP

Born: April 5, 1999. **B-T:** R-R. **HT:** 6-5. **WT:** 220. **Drafted:** Louisville, 2020 (1st round). **Signed by:** Marty Lamb.

TRACK RECORD: Miller spent his first two seasons at Louisville moving between the starting rotation and the bullpen and didn't become a full-time starter until 2020. He made only four starts before the coronavirus pandemic canceled the season, but the Dodgers saw enough to draft him 29th overall. Miller immediately impressed at the alternate training site and instructional league after being drafted and made his highly anticipated pro debut in 2021. He continued to show premium stuff and advanced to Double-A, but strict pitch limits and a right oblique strain limited him to just 56.1 innings.

BA GRADE
60 Risk: High

SCOUTING REPORT: Miller is an intimidating presence at 6-foot-5, 220 pounds and aggressively goes after hitters with a high-powered arsenal. He attacks the strike zone with a riding 95-98 mph four-seam fastball that touches 100 and a 94-97 mph two-seam fastball with hard tail and sink. His fastballs have similar horizontal movement and run together at times, but his four-seamer should be a plus-plus offering once he learns to separate it. Miller's main secondary pitch is a high-spin, 84-87 mph slider with late, two-plane break that draws swings and misses. His firm, 86-89 mph changeup with fade and sink is another potentially plus pitch that misses bats. He also has a tight-spinning, 78-81 mph curveball he can land for strikes. Miller has tightened his delivery to throw strikes more consistently and now has average control. He still has to prove he can maintain his stuff over longer outings—he completed five innings only once in 17 appearances in 2021.

THE FUTURE: Miller has the stuff to be a No. 2 or 3 starter but still has to prove his durability. He'll open 2022 back at Double-A.

SCOUTING GRADES:	Fastball: 70	Slider: 50	Curveball: 60	Changeup: 60	Control: 50

Year	Age	Club (Level)	Lge	W	L	ERA	G	GS	IP	H	HR	BB	SO	BB/9	SO/9	WHIP	AVG
2021	22	Great Lakes (HiA)	Cent	2	2	1.91	14	11	47	30	1	11	56	2.1	10.7	0.87	.178
	22	Tulsa (AA)	Cent	0	0	4.82	3	3	9	10	1	2	14	1.9	13.5	1.29	.256
Minor League Totals (2 years)				2	2	2.40	17	14	56	40	2	13	70	2.08	11.18	0.94	.192

3 MIGUEL VARGAS, 3B

Born: Nov. 17, 1999. **B-T:** R-R. **HT:** 6-3. **WT:** 205. **Signed:** Cuba, 2017. **Signed by:** Roman Barinas/Mike Tosar.

TRACK RECORD: Vargas is the son of Cuban baseball legend Lazaro Vargas, a former Serie Nacional MVP who led two Cuba to two Olympic gold medals in the 1990s. The younger Vargas emerged as one of Cuba's top hitters as an amateur and left the country with his father in 2015, signing with the Dodgers for $300,000 two years later. After signing, Vargas immediately established himself as one of the best hitters in the Dodgers system. He hit .330 in his pro debut, .308 the following year and had his best season yet in 2021. He hit .319 with a career-high 23 home runs while advancing to Double-A and finished third in the minors in hits.

BA GRADE
60 Risk: High

SCOUTING REPORT: Vargas is a natural-born hitter with an uncanny feel for the barrel. His flat swing keeps his bat in the zone for a long time and covers the entire plate, allowing him to drive balls no matter where they're pitched. His inside-out swing naturally drives balls the other way into the right-center gap, but he began turning on pitches in 2021 and surprised even Dodgers officials with his above-average pull-side power. He rarely strikes out and is a consensus plus hitter. Vargas faces more questions defensively. He catches balls hit at him and has solid hands, but his slow feet limit his range and mobility at third base. He is a fringy defender with a slightly better than average arm and may have to move to first.

THE FUTURE: Vargas draws comparisons to fellow countryman Yuli Gurriel as a hitter and has similar impact potential. He'll open 2022 at Triple-A and could make his major league debut during the year.

SCOUTING GRADES:	Hitting: 65	Power: 55	Running: 45	Fielding: 45	Arm: 50

Year	Age	Club (Level)	Lge	AVG	G	AB	R	H	2B	3B	HR	RBI	BB	SO	SB	OBP	SLG
2021	21	Great Lakes (HiA)	Cent	.314	37	156	31	49	11	1	7	16	9	32	4	.366	.532
	21	Tulsa (AA)	Cent	.321	83	327	67	105	16	1	16	60	36	57	7	.386	.523
Minor League Totals (7 years)				.316	297	1174	209	371	80	8	32	183	123	208	31	.384	.480

4 MICHAEL BUSCH, 2B

Born: Nov. 9, 1997. **B-T:** L-R. **HT:** 6-1. **WT:** 210. **Drafted:** North Carolina, 2019 (1st round). **Signed by:** Jonah Rosenthal.

BA GRADE

55 Risk: High

TRACK RECORD: Busch starred as one of college baseball's top hitters at North Carolina and was drafted 31st overall by the Dodgers in 2019. He was limited to 10 games in his pro debut after he was hit by a pitch that broke his right hand and lost the 2020 season to the coronavirus pandemic. Busch finally got to play his first full season in 2021 and jumped straight to Double-A Tulsa, where he finished among the organization leaders in every offensive category despite being hit by a pitch on his right hand again and playing at less than full strength for a month.

SCOUTING REPORT: Busch has some of the best hitting traits in the Dodgers system. He stays balanced in the box, is disciplined with his pitch selection and makes a lot of hard contact with a short, efficient swing. He drives the ball up through the middle of the field and has grown into above-average power with the ability to leave the park from left-center to right-center. Busch handles all types of pitches, but he's too passive at times and falls behind in counts. After Dodgers manager Dave Roberts challenged him to hit .300 during an August phone call, Busch got more aggressive and hit .346 the final month of the season. A first baseman in college, Busch has transitioned to second base and become an adequate defender who makes the routine plays. His range is limited and his below-average arm creates issues turning double plays, but he's playable with shifts.

THE FUTURE: Busch resembles Max Muncy as both a hitter and defender and projects to be a similar player. He'll begin 2022 at Triple-A.

SCOUTING GRADES:	Hitting: 55	Power: 55	Running: 45	Fielding: 45	Arm: 40

Year	Age	Club (Level)	Lge	AVG	G	AB	R	H	2B	3B	HR	RBI	BB	SO	SB	OBP	SLG
2021	23	Tulsa (AA)	Cent	.267	107	409	84	109	27	1	20	67	70	129	2	.386	.484
Minor League Totals (3 years)				.259	117	433	89	112	27	1	20	69	77	134	2	.385	.464

5 RYAN PEPIOT, RHP

Born: Aug. 21, 1997. **B-T:** R-R. **HT:** 6-3. **WT:** 215. **Drafted:** Butler, 2019 (3rd round). **Signed by:** Stephen Head.

BA GRADE

55 Risk: High

TRACK RECORD: Pepiot set Butler's single-season (126) and career (306) strikeout records and became the highest Bulldogs player ever drafted when the Dodgers selected him in the third round in 2019. His star rose when he struck out Cody Bellinger, Gavin Lux and Matt Beaty during a summer camp outing at Dodger Stadium in 2020 and followed with a standout performance at the alternate training site. Pepiot jumped straight to Double-A for his full-season debut in 2021 and finished second in the Dodgers system in strikeouts (127), but he also had the second-most walks (47) and struggled after a promotion to Triple-A.

SCOUTING REPORT: Pepiot's stuff is as good as anyone's in the Dodgers system. His fastball sits 94-98 mph with hard armside run and his changeup is a devastating, 80-grade offering with late drop that gets wild swings and misses. He commands his changeup remarkably well and will throw it in any count against any hitter. Pepiot complements his primary offerings with a short, tight slider in the upper 80s that flashes average but is inconsistent, and he also has a fringy 12-to-6 curveball in the upper 70s. Pepiot has plenty of stuff, but he has long battled below-average control. He is prone to rushing through his delivery and drifting out of his balance point, leading to poor fastball command and short outings when he gets either too much of the plate or not enough of it.

THE FUTURE: Pepiot has the stuff to be a mid-rotation starter if he can corral his delivery. If not, his fastball and changeup will play in late relief. He is in position to make his major league debut in 2022.

SCOUTING GRADES:	Fastball: 70	Slider: 50	Curveball: 45	Changeup: 80	Control: 40

Year	Age	Club (Level)	Lge	W	L	ERA	G	GS	IP	H	HR	BB	SO	BB/9	SO/9	WHIP	AVG
2021	23	Tulsa (AA)	Cent	3	4	2.87	15	13	59	30	7	26	81	3.9	12.2	0.94	.149
	23	Oklahoma City (AAA)	West	2	5	7.13	11	9	41	54	12	21	46	4.5	9.9	1.80	.305
Minor League Totals (3 years)				5	9	4.11	39	32	125	99	19	60	158	4.33	11.41	1.28	.214

6 ANDY PAGES, OF

Born: Dec. 8, 2000. **B-T:** R-R. **HT:** 6-1. **WT:** 212. **Signed:** Cuba, 2018.
Signed by: Luis Marquez/Roman Barinas/Manelik Pimentel

TRACK RECORD: Pages starred in Cuba's junior leagues as an amateur and signed with the Dodgers for $300,000 in 2018. He broke out in the Rookie-level Pioneer League the following year and was set to be traded to the Angels in a Feb. 2020 deal before Angels owner Arte Moreno canceled the trade. It turned out to be a fortuitous development for the Dodgers. Pages made his full-season debut with High-A Great Lakes in 2021 and hit a franchise-record 31 home runs, most in High-A Central. He also led the league runs (96), slugging percentage (.539) and OPS (.933) and was named MVP.

BA GRADE

55 Risk: Very High

SCOUTING REPORT: Few prospects hit the ball in the air as hard and as far as Pages. His bat speed, strength and uphill swing path combine to produce towering home runs that clear scoreboards and leave all parts of the stadium. Pages destroys pitches below the waist, but his swing path makes him vulnerable to elevated fastballs. He is a cerebral hitter who has shown the ability to adjust, providing optimism he'll make enough contact to be a fringe-average hitter. He keeps his strikeouts reasonable for a power hitter and walks plenty to maintain high on-base percentages. Pages is a below-average runner who struggles with his weight at times. He runs into outs with poor decision-making on the basepaths and is an inconsistent defender in right field who is easily distracted. When focused, he's an average defender with a plus-plus, albeit inaccurate, arm.

THE FUTURE: Pages has the potential to be an everyday, power-hitting corner outfielder, but he has lots of areas to improve. He'll see Double-A in 2022.

SCOUTING GRADES:	Hitting: 45	Power: 60	Running: 40	Fielding: 50	Arm: 70

Year	Age	Club (Level)	Lge	AVG	G	AB	R	H	2B	3B	HR	RBI	BB	SO	SB	OBP	SLG
2021	20	Great Lakes (HiA)	Cent	.265	120	438	96	116	25	1	31	88	77	132	6	.394	.539
Minor League Totals (4 years)				.267	235	839	192	224	56	3	60	179	132	246	23	.395	.555

7 LANDON KNACK, RHP

Born: July 15, 1997. **B-T:** R-R. **HT:** 6-2. **WT:** 220. **Drafted:** East Tennessee State, 2020 (2nd round). **Signed by:** Marty Lamb.

TRACK RECORD: Knack spent two seasons at Walters State (Tenn.) JC before transferring to East Tennessee State, where he had continued success with average stuff and plus control. Knack's velocity jumped as a senior to vault him up draft boards to the second round, where the Dodgers selected him 60th overall. Knack missed the first month of the 2021 season with a strained hamstring and missed another three weeks later in the year after he re-injured it, but he still rose from High-A to Double-A and posted 82 strikeouts against just eight walks in 62.1 innings.

BA GRADE

50 Risk: High

SCOUTING REPORT: Knack sat in the low 90s most of his college career, but his stuff has progressively ticked up. His fastball jumped to 92-95 mph as a senior and now sits 93-96 mph and touches 98 with cut and ride to make it a plus pitch. The added separation from his fastball has also turned his fading, 80-84 mph changeup into a plus pitch he sells with his arm speed to get swings and misses over the top. Knack's fastball-changeup combination makes him a reverse-splits pitcher who is better against lefties than righties. His low-80s, high-spin slider flashes above-average but needs more power and break, and his average, 77-79 mph curveball is the fourth pitch in his arsenal. Knack is able to stay out of hitters' hot zones with his plus-plus control. He is a natural strike-thrower who locates in all parts of the strike zone and consistently delivers quick, efficient outings.

THE FUTURE: Knack projects to be a steady, reliable No. 4 starter who pitches above that in his best years. He'll head to Triple-A in 2022.

SCOUTING GRADES:	Fastball: 60	Slider: 55	Curveball: 50	Changeup: 60	Control: 70

Year	Age	Club (Level)	Lge	W	L	ERA	G	GS	IP	H	HR	BB	SO	BB/9	SO/9	WHIP	AVG
2021	23	Great Lakes (HiA)	Cent	5	0	2.50	10	5	39	31	2	5	55	1.1	12.5	0.91	.215
	23	Tulsa (AA)	Cent	2	1	4.37	6	6	22	19	6	3	27	1.2	10.7	0.97	.221
Minor League Totals (2 years)				7	1	3.18	16	11	62	50	8	8	82	1.16	11.84	0.93	.217

8 EDDYS LEONARD, 2B/SS/OF

Born: Nov. 10, 2000. **B-T:** R-R. **HT:** 6-0. **WT:** 180. **Signed:** Dominican Republic, 2017. **Signed by:** Roman Barinas/Luis Marquez/Maneleik Pimentel.

TRACK RECORD: The Dodgers signed Leonard for $200,000 when he was 17, taking a shot on his raw athleticism and fast bat speed. Leonard moved slowly through the Rookie levels and missed the 2020 season due to the coronavirus pandemic, but he finally played his first full season in 2021 and had the biggest breakout of any player in the Dodgers system. He hit .296 with 22 home runs and 81 RBIs as he moved from Low-A to High-A and finished second in OPS (.929) among all prospects in the organization.

SCOUTING REPORT: Few hitters in the Dodgers system can match Leonard's bat speed. He has electric hands that get his barrel to the zone remarkably quickly, and the ball comes off fast and loud when he connects. Leonard has long crushed fastballs and began staying on righthanded sliders in 2021, which fueled his breakout. Leonard's bat speed gives him above-average raw power, and he began elevating to his pull-side this year to access it in games. He stays balanced through his swing and has few pitch types or locations that cause him to struggle. Leonard is still searching for a home defensively. He's an erratic infielder who is better at second base than shortstop and may have to move to center field. He's a fringy to below-average defender at every spot with average speed and arm strength.

THE FUTURE: Leonard's bat gives him a chance to be a multi-positional, everyday player. He'll see Double-A in 2022.

BA GRADE	
50	Risk: High

SCOUTING GRADES:	Hitting: 55	Power: 50	Running: 50	Fielding: 40	Arm: 50

Year	Age	Club (Level)	Lge	AVG	G	AB	R	H	2B	3B	HR	RBI	BB	SO	SB	OBP	SLG
2021	20	R. Cucamonga (LoA)	West	.295	66	261	59	77	19	2	14	57	34	74	6	.399	.544
	20	Great Lakes (HiA)	Cent	.299	41	164	30	49	10	2	8	24	17	42	3	.375	.530
Minor League Totals (4 years)				.284	207	767	155	218	46	8	30	118	107	209	24	.386	.482

9 ANDRE JACKSON, RHP

Born: May 1, 1996. **B-T:** R-R. **HT:** 6-3. **WT:** 210. **Drafted:** Utah, 2017 (12th round). **Signed by:** Brian Compton.

TRACK RECORD: Jackson primarily played the outfield at Utah but also showed intriguing arm strength during 12 relief appearances. Though he posted a 6.53 ERA and missed all of 2017 after having Tommy John surgery, the Dodgers drafted him as a pitcher in the 12th round and signed him for an over-slot $247,500 bonus. Jackson made the decision look prescient when he tied for second in the organization in strikeouts in his first full season as a pitcher in 2019. He spent 2020 at the alternate training site and made his major league debut in 2021 with a 2.31 ERA in 11.2 innings.

SCOUTING REPORT: Jackson is slowly learning to harness his immense athleticism and arm strength. His fastball ranges widely from 90-98 mph, but at

BA GRADE	
45	Risk: Medium

his best he sits 93-96 mph and gets swings and misses up in the zone. After initially struggling to find a consistent secondary pitch, Jackson has developed impressive feel and command for a plus, 83-85 mph changeup that gets swings and misses from both righties and lefties. He sells the pitch well with his arm speed and gets batters waving over it with its late drop. Jackson experimented with a curveball, cutter and slider before settling on a short slider in the mid 80s. It has a chance to be an average pitch as he becomes more consistent throwing it for strikes. Jackson's control has improved with experience but remains fringy. He throws more strikes at the lower end of his velocity range.

THE FUTURE: Jackson's stuff and control fit best in the bullpen, but he's still improving and could start if they tick up. He'll return to the majors in 2022.

SCOUTING GRADES:	Fastball: 55	Slider: 45	Changeup: 60	Control: 45

Year	Age	Club (Level)	Lge	W	L	ERA	G	GS	IP	H	HR	BB	SO	BB/9	SO/9	WHIP	AVG
2021	25	R. Cucamonga (LoA)	West	0	0	1.59	1	1	5	4	1	1	5	1.6	7.9	0.88	.182
	25	Tulsa (AA)	Cent	3	2	3.27	15	13	63	46	12	20	75	2.8	10.7	1.04	.201
	25	Oklahoma City (AAA)	West	2	3	5.13	6	5	26	26	6	9	23	3.1	7.9	1.33	.250
	25	Los Angeles (MLB)	NL	0	1	2.31	3	0	12	10	1	6	10	4.6	7.7	1.37	.238
Major League Totals (1 year)				0	1	2.31	3	0	12	10	1	6	10	4.63	7.71	1.37	.238
Minor League Totals (5 years)				15	12	3.53	65	61	278	232	28	132	320	4.27	10.36	1.31	.226

10 WILMAN DIAZ, SS

Born: Nov. 15, 2003. **B-T:** R-R. **HT:** 6-2. **WT:** 182. **Signed:** Venezuela,
2021. **Signed by:** Roman Barinas/Jean Castro/Jose Briceño.

BILL MITCHELL

BA GRADE	
55	Risk: **Extreme**

TRACK RECORD: Diaz established himself as the top player in Venezuela for his age and signed with the Dodgers for $2,697,500 on the first day of the 2020-21 international signing period. He had trouble getting out of Venezuela due to coronavirus restrictions and arrived late to the Dodgers' Dominican complex, forcing him to play catch-up throughout the DSL season. Diaz had no such issues when he arrived in Arizona for instructional league, where his athleticism and offensive potential stood out.

SCOUTING REPORT: Diaz has all the ingredients to hit with advanced plate discipline, short actions and a loose, easy swing. He does a good job staying behind the ball and has plenty of room to add strength. Diaz projects to be an above-average hitter with at least average power, but he still has some swing work ahead. The Dodgers plan to work with him on staying in his legs more and keeping his hands closer to his body to create a more linear bat path. Diaz is more polished on defense. He's a borderline plus runner with plenty of range, sure hands and plus arm strength from shortstop. He's a good athlete who projects to stay at the position even as he adds weight and strength.

THE FUTURE: Diaz's swing development will determine if he reaches his above-average, everyday potential. He is set to make his U.S. debut in the Arizona Complex League in 2022.

SCOUTING GRADES:	Hitting: 55	Power: 50	Running: 60	Fielding: 55	Arm: 60

Year	Age	Club (Level)	Lge	AVG	G	AB	R	H	2B	3B	HR	RBI	BB	SO	SB	OBP	SLG
2021	17	Dodgers Shoemaker (R)	DSL	.235	24	85	13	20	5	1	1	9	9	26	8	.309	.353
Minor League Totals (1 year)				.235	24	85	13	20	5	1	1	9	9	26	8	.309	.353

11 MADDUX BRUNS, LHP

BA GRADE	
55	Risk: **Extreme**

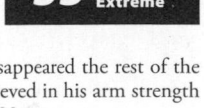

Born: June 20, 2002. **B-T:** L-L. **HT:** 6-2. **WT:** 205. **Drafted:** HS—Mobile, Ala., 2021 (1st round). **Signed by:** Benny Latino.

TRACK RECORD: Bruns touched 97 mph at Perfect Game National to establish himself as one of the top pitchers in the 2021 draft class, but his control disappeared the rest of the summer and was hit-or-miss throughout his senior spring. The Dodgers still believed in his arm strength and drafted him in the first round, No. 29 overall, and signed him for $2,197,500.

SCOUTING REPORT: Bruns has a strong, 6-foot-2 frame and attacks hitters with a potent four-pitch mix. His fastball sits 93-95 mph, touches 97 and is a plus pitch with the deception he generates out of his crossfire delivery. His 82-84 mph slider is another plus pitch with tough angle and late bite, and his high-arching, 74-76 mph curveball also shows plus at its best. He also has advanced touch and feel for a fading changeup that projects to be average. While Bruns' stuff is unquestioned, he has well below-average control and struggles to stay around the strike zone. The Dodgers believe his control can become average with adjustments to his timing, delivery and mindset, but he's not a natural strike-thrower.

THE FUTURE: Bruns has to prove he can throw enough strikes to reach his mid-rotation potential. He'll try to show he can at Low-A Rancho Cucamonga in 2022.

Year	Age	Club (Level)	Lge	W	L	ERA	G	GS	IP	H	HR	BB	SO	BB/9	SO/9	WHIP	AVG
2021	19	Dodgers (R)	ACL	0	2	16.20	4	4	5	8	2	7	5	12.6	9.0	3.00	.364
Minor League Totals (1 year)				0	2	16.20	4	4	5	8	2	7	5	12.60	9.00	3.00	.364

12 CLAYTON BEETER, RHP

BA GRADE	
50	Risk: **Very High**

Born: Oct. 9, 1998. **B-T:** R-R. **HT:** 6-2. **WT:** 220. **Drafted:** Texas Tech, 2020 (2nd round supplemental). **Signed by:** Clint Bowers.

TRACK RECORD: Beeter had Tommy John surgery in high school but recovered to become a standout closer at Texas Tech before taking over as the Friday night starter. The Dodgers drafted him 66th overall in 2020 and signed him for $1,196,500. Beeter made his pro debut in 2021 and posted a 3.44 ERA between High-A Great Lakes and Double-A Tulsa, but he mostly worked as an "opener" and never threw more than 3.1 innings in an outing.

SCOUTING REPORT: Beeter is a strong, physical righthander who pitches almost exclusively with his fastball and curveball. His plus fastball sits 93-95 and touches 98 with ride through the top of the strike zone and his is curveball is a high-spin, top-to-bottom offering in the mid 80s that drops below the zone for swings and misses. Beeter rarely throws his below-average, low-80s changeup and gets hit hard by lefties as a result. His long arm action leads to a lack of deception and fringe-average control

THE FUTURE: Beeter is universally seen as a future reliever. His fastball-curveball combination is good enough for him to potentially be a setup man.

Year	Age	Club (Level)	Lge	W	L	ERA	G	GS	IP	H	HR	BB	SO	BB/9	SO/9	WHIP	AVG
2021	22	Great Lakes (HiA)	Cent	0	4	3.13	23	22	37	28	3	15	55	3.6	13.3	1.15	.212
	22	Tulsa (AA)	Cent	0	2	4.20	5	5	15	10	2	7	23	4.2	13.8	1.13	.189
Minor League Totals (2 years)				0	6	3.44	28	27	52	38	5	22	78	3.78	13.41	1.15	.205

13 JOSE RAMOS, OF

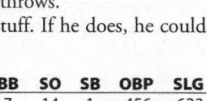

BA GRADE
50 Risk: Very High

Born: Jan. 1, 2001. **B-T:** R-R. **HT:** 6-1. **WT:** 200. **Signed:** Panama, 2018.
Signed by: Luis Marquez/Cliff Nuiter.
TRACK RECORD: Ramos signed with the Dodgers for $30,000 out of Panama when he was 17 and immediately emerged as a potential sleeper in the system. He delivered on that promise in his U.S. debut in 2021. Ramos torched the Arizona Complex League to earn a promotion after only 15 games to Low-A Rancho Cucamonga, where he hit .313/.377/.559 over the final two months.
SCOUTING REPORT: Ramos is a strong, aggressive hitter who feasts on fastballs. He has a smooth, rhythmic swing with plenty of bat speed and strength. He turns fastballs around 400-plus feet with his plus raw power and posts some of the highest exit velocities of any Dodgers prospect. Ramos struggles to recognize breaking balls, but he's adept at working himself into fastball counts and playing to his strengths. Ramos is a playable defender in center field and above-average in right field with his average speed and clean routes and reads. His best tool is his plus-plus, accurate arm that makes jaw-dropping throws.
THE FUTURE: Ramos will have to better learn to recognize or lay off breaking stuff. If he does, he could be an everyday, power-hitting right fielder.

Year	Age	Club (Level)	Lge	AVG	G	AB	R	H	2B	3B	HR	RBI	BB	SO	SB	OBP	SLG
2021	20	Dodgers (R)	ACL	.383	15	60	13	23	6	0	3	15	7	14	1	.456	.633
	20	R. Cucamonga (LoA)	West	.313	47	195	30	61	18	3	8	44	16	57	1	.377	.559
Minor League Totals (2 years)				.305	119	462	77	141	39	3	13	86	43	117	11	.380	.487

14 JACOB AMAYA, SS

BA GRADE
45 Risk: High

Born: Sept. 3, 1998. **B-T:** R-R. **HT:** 6-0. **WT:** 180. **Drafted:** HS—West Covina, Calif., 2017 (11th round). **Signed by:** Bobby Darwin.
TRACK RECORD: Amaya grew up in suburban Los Angeles and is the grandson of former Brooklyn Dodgers prospect Frank Amaya. The Dodgers kept the connection going when they drafted the younger Amaya in the 11th round in 2017 and signed him for an above-slot $247,500. Amaya quickly established himself as the best defensive shortstop in the Dodgers system, but longstanding questions about his bat only increased after he hit .216/.303/.343 at Double-A Tulsa in 2021.
SCOUTING REPORT: Amaya is a gifted defensive shortstop with elite instincts for the position. He is always in the right place, secures every ball with his soft, reliable hands and makes every throw with his plus, accurate arm. He's not the rangiest or flashiest defender, but he makes every play and is elite at nuances such as tags and relays. Amaya's bat is further behind. He previously demonstrated elite-strike zone discipline but tried to hit for power in 2021 and started chasing and overswinging. He's an undersized hitter who is best when he drives singles the other way with his short, direct stroke.
THE FUTURE: Amaya's defense gives him a chance to stick as a utilityman. He'll try to make the necessary offensive adjustments in 2022.

Year	Age	Club (Level)	Lge	AVG	G	AB	R	H	2B	3B	HR	RBI	BB	SO	SB	OBP	SLG
2021	22	Tulsa (AA)	Cent	.216	113	417	60	90	15	1	12	47	52	103	5	.303	.343
Minor League Totals (5 years)				.254	330	1226	213	311	57	11	25	161	199	273	28	.359	.379

15 JAMES OUTMAN, OF

BA GRADE
45 Risk: High

Born: May 14, 1997. **B-T:** L-R. **HT:** 6-3. **WT:** 215. **Drafted:** Sacramento State, 2018 (7th round). **Signed by:** Tom Kunis.
TRACK RECORD: Outman was a standout middle linebacker in high school, but he chose to pursue baseball and became a three-year starting outfielder at Sacramento State. He led the Western Athletic Conference with 11 home runs as a junior in 2018 and was drafted by the Dodgers in the seventh round. Outman immediately starred on defense and progressively improved as a hitter leading

up to a breakout 2021. He posted a career-high .869 OPS while advancing to Double-A and finished the year with a star turn in the Arizona Fall League.

SCOUTING REPORT: Outman is a physical, athletic specimen more usually seen playing football. He is a plus runner at 6-foot-3, 215 pounds with quick initial burst and elite acceleration in center field. He ticks up to nearly plus-plus speed underway and runs down long flies to both gaps and at the wall. The Dodgers refined Outman's lefthanded swing to get his upper and lower halves more in sync. He still has a hand hitch and has to cheat to get to velocity, but he sees pitches well and crushes fastballs when he connects.

THE FUTURE: Outman is a nearly-ready fourth outfielder with his defense and power at the plate. He'll head to Triple-A in 2022.

Year	Age	Club (Level)	Lge	AVG	G	AB	R	H	2B	3B	HR	RBI	BB	SO	SB	OBP	SLG
2021	24	Great Lakes (HiA)	Cent	.250	65	248	50	62	12	8	9	30	45	88	21	.385	.472
	24	Tulsa (AA)	Cent	.289	39	166	40	48	9	1	9	24	18	51	2	.369	.518
Minor League Totals (4 years)				.249	278	1064	199	265	44	16	48	143	143	323	55	.350	.456

16 NICK NASTRINI, RHP

BA GRADE

50 Risk: Extreme

Born: Feb. 18, 2000. **B-T:** R-R. **HT:** 6-3. **WT:** 215. **Drafted:** UCLA, 2021 (4th round). **Signed by:** Dennis Moeller.

TRACK RECORD: Nastrini entered his junior year at UCLA considered a potential first-round pick, but he suffered the yips and walked 38 batters in 31.1 innings. The Dodgers still took a shot on his potent stuff and drafted him in the fourth round, signing him for an above-slot $497,500. Nastrini rediscovered his control as a pro and dominated in six starts at Low-A Rancho Cucamonga, then became the talk of instructional league with a sensational showing.

SCOUTING REPORT: Nastrini is a sturdy, physical righthander who flashes three plus or better pitches. His fastball sits 92-96 mph as a starter with high spin rates at the top of the strike zone. His short, tight 84-88 mph slider is a plus pitch that tunnels well off his fastball and his 78-82 mph, high-spin curveball with depth and sweep is another plus offering. His firm, 87-88 mph changeup with split action is developing. Nastrini's control is the wild card. He is a good athlete with a polished delivery and threw strikes in the past, but he presently has well below-average control and has some mental hurdles to overcome.

THE FUTURE: The Dodgers are optimistic Nastini will find his way back and become a mid-rotation starter. His first big test will come at High-A Great Lakes in 2022.

Year	Age	Club (Level)	Lge	W	L	ERA	G	GS	IP	H	HR	BB	SO	BB/9	SO/9	WHIP	AVG
2021	21	Dodgers (R)	ACL	0	0	0.00	1	1	1	1	0	0	2	0.0	18.0	1.00	.333
	21	R. Cucamonga (LoA)	West	0	0	2.08	6	6	13	6	2	7	30	4.9	20.8	1.00	.130
Minor League Totals (1 year)				0	0	1.93	7	7	14	7	2	7	32	4.50	20.57	1.00	.143

17 GAVIN STONE, RHP

BA GRADE

45 Risk: High

Born: Oct. 15, 1998. **B-T:** R-R. **HT:** 6-1. **WT:** 175. **Drafted:** Central Arkansas, 2020 (5th round). **Signed by:** Brian Kraft.

TRACK RECORD: After spending most of his first two seasons in the bullpen, Stone moved into Central Arkansas' starting rotation in 2020 and threw a no-hitter in his final start before the coronavirus pandemic shut down the season. The Dodgers drafted him in the fifth round and signed him for a below-slot $97,500. Stone made his pro debut in 2021 and was one of the surprises of the season. He led the Dodgers organization with 138 strikeouts as he rose from Low-A to High-A.

SCOUTING REPORT: Stone's fastball sat 90-92 mph in college but ticked up to 93-97 in his pro debut. His fastball plays up with run and ride from his low release point to make it an above-average pitch that gets swings and misses in the strike zone. Stone uses his fastball heavily, but his slider and changeup are also viable weapons. His mid-80s slider flashes average and he began incorporating a firm, 86-89 mph changeup as last year progressed and flashed a plus offering with split action and late dive. Stone is undersized and has some effort to his delivery, but he has above-average control and holds his velocity through his starts.

THE FUTURE: Stone largely projects to be a multi-inning reliever. He still has some physical projection left and could potentially blossom into a back-end starter.

Year	Age	Club (Level)	Lge	W	L	ERA	G	GS	IP	H	HR	BB	SO	BB/9	SO/9	WHIP	AVG
2021	22	R. Cucamonga (LoA)	West	1	2	3.73	18	17	70	69	5	20	101	2.6	13.0	1.27	.253
	22	Great Lakes (HiA)	Cent	1	0	3.86	5	5	21	18	2	5	37	2.1	15.9	1.10	.234
Minor League Totals (2 years)				2	2	3.76	23	22	91	87	7	25	138	2.47	13.65	1.23	.249

18 YEINER FERNANDEZ, C

BA GRADE
50 Risk: Extreme

Born: Sept. 19, 2002. **B-T:** R-R. **HT:** 5-9. **WT:** 170. **Signed:** Venezuela, 2019. **Signed by:** Roman Barinas/Jean Castro/Cristian Guzman.

TRACK RECORD: Fernandez played for Venezuela in the 2015 Little League World Series and built a long track record of hitting to become one of the top catchers in his class. The Dodgers signed him for $717,500 and sent him to the Arizona Complex League for his pro debut in 2021, where he hit .319/.382/.454 and received a late promotion to Low-A Rancho Cucamonga.

SCOUTING REPORT: Fernandez hardly cuts an imposing figure with his short, stocky build, but has elite hand-eye coordination and barrel control and sprays line drives all over the field. He handles upper-90s velocity and has sneaky power that could become average once he starts to pull the ball. He is aggressive and doesn't walk much, but he recognizes pitches and rarely swings and misses. Fernandez was a second baseman who converted to catching and is still learning to play the position. He's a good athlete with soft hands and is making progress with his blocking, throwing and game-calling. He has a chance to be an average defender with a plus, accurate arm, but that requires a lot of projection.

THE FUTURE: Fernandez's bat will buy him time to develop his defense. He is playable enough at second base to be a catcher/infielder utilityman.

Year	Age	Club (Level)	Lge	AVG	G	AB	R	H	2B	3B	HR	RBI	BB	SO	SB	OBP	SLG
2021	18	Dodgers (R)	ACL	.319	35	141	24	45	11	1	2	15	10	27	1	.382	.454
	18	R. Cucamonga (LoA)	West	.516	7	31	4	16	1	0	1	10	2	3	0	.559	.645
Minor League Totals (1 year)				.355	42	172	28	61	12	1	3	25	12	30	1	.414	.488

19 KODY HOESE, 3B

BA GRADE
45 Risk: High

Born: July 13, 1997. **B-T:** R-R. **HT:** 6-4. **WT:** 200. **Drafted:** Tulane, 2019 (1st round). **Signed by:** Benny Latino.

TRACK RECORD: Hoese finished tied for fifth in the nation with 23 home runs his junior season at Tulane and was drafted 26th overall by the Dodgers in 2019. He posted an .863 OPS in his pro debut and was the Dodgers' best hitter at the alternate training site in 2020, but he struggled badly in his first full season in 2021. He hit just .188 with two home runs in 59 games at Double-A Tulsa and missed two months with an intercostal strain. He finished the year by hitting .200/.250/.327 in an underwhelming showing in the Arizona Fall League.

SCOUTING REPORT: Hoese is a divisive player who draws widely disparate opinions depending on when scouts saw him. At his best, he is a balanced hitter with a short, compact swing and drives balls to all fields with his natural strength and leverage. Other times he jumps out of his legs, gets around the ball with a long swing and his bat speed disappears. Hoese shows above-average hitting ability and power when his swing is right, but the latter swing shows up too frequently. Hoese is a below-average runner who gets what's hit to him at third base but lacks range. His arm strength fluctuates from below-average to above-average due to his inconsistent arm slot.

THE FUTURE: Hoese has a lot to prove in 2022, including that he can consistently maintain his best swing against upper-level pitching. He may open the season back at Double-A.

Year	Age	Club (Level)	Lge	AVG	G	AB	R	H	2B	3B	HR	RBI	BB	SO	SB	OBP	SLG
2021	23	Dodgers (R)	ACL	.258	10	31	2	8	1	0	0	3	2	4	0	.294	.290
	23	Tulsa (AA)	Cent	.188	59	229	26	43	7	0	2	17	15	55	2	.241	.245
Minor League Totals (3 years)				.233	110	407	57	95	16	2	7	49	35	84	3	.297	.334

20 PETER HEUBECK, RHP

BA GRADE
50 Risk: Extreme

Born: July 22, 2002. **B-T:** R-R. **HT:** 6-3. **WT:** 170. **Drafted:** HS—Baltimore, 2021 (3rd round). **Signed by:** Paul Murphy.

TRACK RECORD: Heubeck emerged as one of the top prep pitchers in the Northeast and led Gilman High to the Maryland Class A state title in the spring, highlighted by a 15-strikeout performance in the semifinals. The Dodgers drafted him in the third round and signed him for a $1,269,500 bonus. Heubeck impressed with nine strikeouts in only four innings in the Arizona Complex League after signing, and then became a favorite of Dodgers officials during instructional league.

SCOUTING REPORT: Heubeck is a thin, projectable 6-foot-3 righthander who keeps trending up. His fastball sits 90-91 mph with elite riding life at the top of the strike zone and should tick up as he fills out physically. Heubeck complements his fastball with a plus, 12-to-6 curveball in the low 80s with impressive depth and power. He effectively throws his fastball up and curveball down to give him the north-south profile teams covet. Heubeck mostly relies on those two pitches but has flashed an average changeup. He

has an easy delivery and a clean arm action that give him average control.
THE FUTURE: Heubeck has a promising foundation but needs to get stronger. He'll head to Low-A Rancho Cucamonga in 2022.

Year	Age	Club (Level)	Lge	W	L	ERA	G	GS	IP	H	HR	BB	SO	BB/9	SO/9	WHIP	AVG
2021	18	Dodgers (R)	ACL	0	0	0.00	2	1	4	1	0	2	9	4.5	20.3	0.75	.077
Minor League Totals (1 year)				0	0	0.00	2	1	4	1	0	2	9	4.50	20.25	0.75	.077

21 RAYNE DONCON, SS

BA GRADE

50 Risk: Extreme

Born: Sept. 22, 2003. **B-T:** R-R. **HT:** 6-2. **WT:** 176. **Signed:** Dominican Republic, 2021. **Signed by:** Domingo Toribio/Laiky Uribe/Roman Barinas.
TRACK RECORD: Doncon used the 2020 coronavirus shutdown to get stronger and enhanced his stock on the international market. The Dodgers signed him for $497,500 out of the Dominican Republic on the first day the 2021 signing period opened. Doncon continued to blossom physically after he signed and outperformed many of his more touted classmates in the DSL in his pro debut. He hit .283/.387/.455 while showing an intriguing power-speed combination and made a loud first impression on Dodgers officials at instructional league after the season.
SCOUTING REPORT: Doncon is a long, lean 6-foot-2 with a high waist and lots of physical projection to dream on. He has fast bat speed, excellent natural timing in the batter's box and consistently barrels fastballs. He has a flat swing plane that results in a lot of low line drives, but he has a chance to grow into average or better power as he gets stronger and fills out physically. Doncon remains lean and is a capable shortstop with good actions and a plus arm. He is a tick below average runner who projects to slow down as he continues to fill out, so he may eventually have to move to third base.
THE FUTURE: Doncon's offensive potential has the Dodgers excited. He will make his stateside debut in the Arizona Complex League in 2022.

Year	Age	Club (Level)	Lge	AVG	G	AB	R	H	2B	3B	HR	RBI	BB	SO	SB	OBP	SLG
2021	17	Dodgers Bautista (R)	DSL	.283	31	99	20	28	4	2	3	15	16	28	7	.387	.455
Minor League Totals (1 year)				.283	31	99	20	28	4	2	3	15	16	28	7	.387	.455

22 JUSTIN BRUIHL, LHP

BA GRADE

40 Risk: Medium

Born: June 26, 1997. **B-T:** L-L. **HT:** 6-2. **WT:** 215. **Signed:** Santa Rosa (Calif.) JC, 2017 (NDFA). **Signed by:** Tom Kunis.
TRACK RECORD: Bruihl had Tommy John surgery in high school and pitched one season at Cal Poly before he transferred to Santa Rosa (Calif.) JC. He pitched well enough to earn a scholarship to Cal, but he instead chose to sign with the Dodgers as a nondrafted free agent. Bruihl slowly rose through the lower minors before breaking out in 2021. He vaulted from Double-A to the majors and made 21 appearances out of the Dodgers bullpen, where he posted a 2.89 ERA.
SCOUTING REPORT: Bruihl's low arm slot and slightly crossfire delivery make it difficult to pick the ball up, especially for lefties. His hard, 88-89 mph cutter darts across the plate with late gloveside bite and his sweeping, 77-80 mph curveball gets lunging, off-balance swings Bruihl has average control but is prone to walks because he has to stay on the edges of the plate. His deception and pitch movement helped him hold lefties to a .150 batting average and .359 OPS in his debut, but righties hit .292 with an .830 OPS.
THE FUTURE: The Dodgers found situations to use Bruihl successfully even with the three-batter minimum. His ability to neutralize lefties should keep him in the bullpen moving forward.

Year	Age	Club (Level)	Lge	W	L	ERA	G	GS	IP	H	HR	BB	SO	BB/9	SO/9	WHIP	AVG
2021	24	Tulsa (AA)	Cent	1	0	1.20	8	0	15	7	1	3	20	1.8	12.0	0.67	.140
	24	Oklahoma City (AAA)	West	3	0	3.57	18	1	22	22	2	7	30	2.8	11.9	1.28	.259
	24	Los Angeles (MLB)	NL	0	1	2.89	21	2	19	13	1	7	11	3.4	5.3	1.07	.203
Major League Totals (1 year)				0	1	2.89	21	2	19	13	1	7	11	3.38	5.30	1.07	.203
Minor League Totals (4 years)				14	2	3.73	72	1	111	90	4	43	145	3.49	11.76	1.20	.214

23 JORBIT VIVAS, 2B/3B

BA GRADE

45 Risk: High

Born: March 9, 2001. **B-T:** L-R. **HT:** 5-10. **WT:** 171. **Signed:** Venezuela, 2017. **Signed by:** Luis Marquez/Roman Barinas/Andres Simancas.
TRACK RECORD: Vivas was an undersized shortstop with a track record of hitting when the Dodgers signed him for $300,000 out of Venezuela in 2017. He never really grew and he moved off of shortstop, but he's continued to hit. Vivas made his full-season debut in 2021 and hit .321 with 14 home runs, 87 RBIs and an .893 OPS as he rose from Low-A to High-A. The Dodgers added

him to their 40-man roster after the season to protect him from the Rule 5 draft.

SCOUTING REPORT: Vivas hardly stands out with his small, unimposing frame, but he's a talented hitter who frequently outperforms his more physically gifted peers. He consistently puts the bat on the ball with his excellent hand-eye coordination and natural ability to manipulate the barrel. He has a sharp eye at the plate and rarely chases, forcing pitchers to throw strikes and not missing when they do. Vivas posts below-average exit velocities, but he picks out pitches to drive and has gotten strong enough to sneak them over the fence. Vivas is a below-average runner with a fringy arm and is limited to second base defensively. He makes routine plays but is challenged on the move.

THE FUTURE: Vivas' size and lack of athleticism lead to skepticism he'll succeed at higher levels. He'll try to silence those doubts at Double-A in 2022.

Year	Age	Club (Level)	Lge	AVG	G	AB	R	H	2B	3B	HR	RBI	BB	SO	SB	OBP	SLG
2021	20	R. Cucamonga (LoA)	West	.311	83	328	73	102	20	4	13	73	27	42	5	.389	.515
	20	Great Lakes (HiA)	Cent	.318	23	85	12	27	6	0	1	14	13	13	3	.422	.424
Minor League Totals (4 years)				.296	211	788	149	233	54	8	16	130	85	121	34	.389	.445

24 MICHAEL GROVE, RHP

Born: Dec. 18, 1996. **B-T:** R-R. **HT:** 6-3. **WT:** 200. **Drafted:** West Virginia, 2018 (2nd round). **Signed by:** Jonah Rosenthal

TRACK RECORD: Grove looked like a future first-round pick as an underclassman at West Virginia, but he had Tommy John surgery during his sophomore year and missed his entire junior season as well. The Dodgers still drafted him in the second round and gave him an above-slot $1,229,500 bonus. Grove's stuff took three years to return, but it finally happened at Double-A Tulsa in 2021. Even though he showed poor control and posted a 7.86 ERA, the Dodgers still added him to their 40-man roster after the season.

SCOUTING REPORT: Grove rebuilt himself into a power pitcher and now possesses the most imposing stuff of his career. He generates 94-97 mph fastballs that touch 99 as a starter with little effort out of his strong, athletic delivery. He complements his heater with a hard slider at 86-89 mph and a power curveball at 78-81 mph that both have downer action and get swings and misses. While everything looks good on paper, Grove's fastball is straight and he tends to leave it over the plate, where it gets crushed, and he lacks a soft offering to keep batters from gearing up. His uptick in stuff has also come with a downgrade in his control, which is now below-average and prevents him from lasting long in his starts.

THE FUTURE: The Dodgers hope Grove's stuff will play in relief moving forward. His transition to the bullpen may come in 2022.

Year	Age	Club (Level)	Lge	W	L	ERA	G	GS	IP	H	HR	BB	SO	BB/9	SO/9	WHIP	AVG
2021	24	Tulsa (AA)	Cent	1	4	7.86	21	19	71	85	19	42	88	5.3	11.2	1.79	.290
Minor League Totals (3 years)				1	9	7.12	42	40	123	146	26	61	161	4.48	11.81	1.69	.291

25 ALEX DE JESUS, SS

Born: March 22, 2002. **B-T:** R-R. **HT:** 6-2. **WT:** 170. **Signed:** Dominican Republic, 2018. **Signed by:** Luis Marquez/Laiky Uribe/Manelik Pimentel.

TRACK RECORD: De Jesus signed with the Dodgers for $500,000 out of the Dominican Republic in 2018 and quickly emerged as one of their most promising low-level prospects. He got into bad swing habits during the coronavirus shutdown and hit .210 with a 38% strikeout rate the first two months of the 2021 season at Low-A Rancho Cucamonga, but after he made adjustments to get back to his former swing, he hit .314/.440/.490 the rest of the year.

SCOUTING REPORT: When De Jesus is right, he has a fast, direct swing with natural loft and drives balls hard in the air from gap to gap. He got too aggressive in his approach and struggled against righthanded spin during the early part of 2021, but as he eased back and fixed his load, trigger and bat path, he began to resemble the potential average hitter with above-average power previously seen. De Jesus is a below-average runner with a big, strong body and projects to move off of shortstop. His reliable hands, quick first step and plus arm strength should help him be an average third baseman. De Jesus is a smart, mature player who takes coaching well and puts in the work to improve.

THE FUTURE: De Jesus' midseason improvement provides hope he can still be a power-hitting, everyday infielder. He'll head to High-A Great Lakes in 2022.

Year	Age	Club (Level)	Lge	AVG	G	AB	R	H	2B	3B	HR	RBI	BB	SO	SB	OBP	SLG
2021	19	R. Cucamonga (LoA)	West	.268	97	351	67	94	25	1	12	73	69	128	1	.386	.447
Minor League Totals (3 years)				.273	154	568	88	155	38	2	15	107	89	200	6	.370	.426

26 JUSTIN YURCHAK, 1B

BA GRADE
40 Risk: High

Born: Sept. 17, 1996. **B-T:** L-R. **HT:** 6-1. **WT:** 204. **Drafted:** Binghamton, 2017 (12th round). **Signed by:** Joel Grampietro (White Sox).

TRACK RECORD: Yurchak played on the same high school team as Braves pitcher Ian Anderson and became one of college baseball's best pure hitters, first at Wake Forest and then Binghamton. The White Sox drafted Yurchak in the 12th round in 2017 and traded him a year later to the Dodgers for lefthanded reliever Manny Banuelos. Yurchak continued to hit at every stop and finally gained some notoriety in 2021 when he hit .365 across High-A and Double-A, the highest batting average in the minors.

SCOUTING REPORT: Yurchak can make contact on par with almost anyone in the minors. He has an efficient lefthanded swing that can make contact with almost any pitch in any location and he stays in the strike zone with a sharp eye and advanced, patient approach. He rarely swings and misses, puts together elite quality at-bats and has a knack for getting hits in clutch situations. Yurchak doesn't hit the ball very hard, however, and his well below-average power makes it tough to find him somewhere to play. He is a below-average runner with fringy arm strength and is limited to first base defensively.

THE FUTURE: Yurchak's pure contact skills from the left side give him a shot to reach the majors. He'll have to develop more power or defensive versatility to carve out a stable bench role.

Year	Age	Club (Level)	Lge	AVG	G	AB	R	H	2B	3B	HR	RBI	BB	SO	SB	OBP	SLG
2021	24	Great Lakes (HiA)	Cent	.356	62	225	42	80	10	1	5	31	38	47	2	.446	.476
	24	Tulsa (AA)	Cent	.383	30	115	21	44	8	0	2	27	13	22	0	.436	.504
Minor League Totals (5 years)				.321	311	1116	212	358	67	4	29	167	179	214	3	.412	.466

27 DEVIN MANN, 1B/2B/OF

BA GRADE
40 Risk: High

Born: Feb. 11, 1997. **B-T:** R-R. **HT:** 6-3. **WT:** 180. **Drafted:** Louisville, 2018 (5th round). **Signed by:** Marty Lamb.

TRACK RECORD: A contact hitter in college at Louisville, Mann got stronger and made swing changes after the Dodgers drafted him in the fifth round in 2018. The changes helped him become one of the top power hitters in the High-A California League in his first full season, but he lost those strength gains and his swing regressed during the coronavirus shutdown. Mann struggled at Double-A Tulsa when minor league play resumed in 2021, but he eventually rounded into form and hit .279 with an .852 OPS over the season's final three months.

SCOUTING REPORT: Mann is a tall, lanky righthanded hitter with strong strike-zone discipline, good pitch recognition and above-average contact ability even when he isn't going well. He's adept at working counts and drives balls from gap to gap when he's right. Mann's slow start depressed his overall numbers in 2021, but he showed his ability to adjust and still projects to be an average hitter with double-digit home run power with the way he finished. Mann has long been a stiff, below-average second baseman, but he began playing first base and the outfield in Tulsa. He gets excellent reads in the corner outfield and covers enough ground with his long gait.

THE FUTURE: Mann's hitting ability and newfound defensive versatility give him a chance to be a bench option. He'll head to Triple-A in 2022.

Year	Age	Club (Level)	Lge	AVG	G	AB	R	H	2B	3B	HR	RBI	BB	SO	SB	OBP	SLG
2021	24	Tulsa (AA)	Cent	.244	110	369	51	90	27	1	14	62	49	100	6	.350	.436
Minor League Totals (4 years)				.259	278	979	142	254	61	4	35	156	131	247	18	.356	.437

28 CARSON TAYLOR, C

BA GRADE
40 Risk: High

Born: June 2, 1999. **B-T:** B-R. **HT:** 6-2. **WT:** 205. **Drafted:** Virginia Tech, 2020 (4th round). **Signed by:** Paul Murphy.

TRACK RECORD: Taylor split his time between catcher, first base and DH at Virginia Tech and got off to a blistering start in 2020 before the coronavirus pandemic canceled the season. The Dodgers drafted him in the fourth round and signed him for $397,500. Taylor jumped to High-A Great Lakes for his pro debut and shook off a slow start to hit .294 with an .842 OPS from June through the end of the season. Most importantly, he made needed defensive strides and capably handled a high-octane Loons pitching staff.

SCOUTING REPORT: The switch-hitting Taylor is firmly a bat-first catcher. He's a patient hitter who controls the strike zone and consistently conducts high-level at-bats from both sides of the plate. He's a better hitter from the right side, but he made adjustments to improve his lefthanded swing and projects to be an average hitter overall. Taylor has below-average power, so most of his offensive production will come from making contact and getting on-base. Taylor's defense is improving and has an outside chance to get to average. His receiving and framing are solid, but his blocking, throwing and game-calling all have a ways to go. He's physically large and has below-average mobility and athleticism, which often leads to inconsistent timing and footwork on his throws.

THE FUTURE: Taylor will have to keep improving defensively to be a backup catcher. He'll move to Double-A Tulsa in 2022.

Year	Age	Club (Level)	Lge	AVG	G	AB	R	H	2B	3B	HR	RBI	BB	SO	SB	OBP	SLG
2021	22	Great Lakes (HiA)	Cent	.278	79	291	52	81	16	1	9	54	45	63	1	.371	.433
Minor League Totals (2 years)				.278	79	291	52	81	16	1	9	54	45	63	1	.371	.433

29 CARLOS DURAN, RHP

BA GRADE
40 Risk: High

Born: July 30, 2001. **B-T:** R-R. **HT:** 6-7. **WT:** 230. **Signed:** Dominican Republic, 2018. **Signed by:** Luis Marquez/Maneleik Pimentel.

TRACK RECORD: Duran stood 6-foot-7 by the time he was 17 years old and signed with the Dodgers for $300,000 in 2018 out of the Dominican Republic. He made his full-season debut in 2021 and posted an unsightly 5.56 ERA across both Class A levels, but he finished tied for fourth in the organization with 115 strikeouts and flashed one of the best sliders in the minor leagues.

SCOUTING REPORT: Duran previously threw a four-seam fastball that stayed straight and got crushed up in the zone, so he switched to a 92-95 mph two-seamer that gets plus sink and run and still has room to improve. In any form, his fastball is merely a setup pitch for his plus-plus, mid-80s slider. Duran hides the ball well behind his big frame and the pitch turns hard with late sweep and dive, repeatedly getting righties to chase it down and away. Duran's sinker-slider combination dominates righthanded batters, but his well below-average changeup leaves him vulnerable to lefties. He has good body control for his size and throws enough strikes to project fringe-average control.

THE FUTURE: Duran's ability to dominate with his slider bodes well for a situational relief role in the majors. He'll remain a starter for now to work on his entire arsenal.

Year	Age	Club (Level)	Lge	W	L	ERA	G	GS	IP	H	HR	BB	SO	BB/9	SO/9	WHIP	AVG
2021	19	R. Cucamonga (LoA)	West	2	4	5.25	20	18	73	81	9	24	109	2.9	13.3	1.43	.266
	19	Great Lakes (HiA)	Cent	0	1	8.59	2	2	7	10	0	6	6	7.4	7.4	2.18	.323
Minor League Totals (4 years)				3	11	4.19	47	45	163	166	13	53	184	2.92	10.14	1.34	.257

30 HYUN-IL CHOI, RHP

BA GRADE
40 Risk: High

Born: May 27, 2000. **B-T:** R-R. **HT:** 6-2. **WT:** 200. **Signed:** South Korea, 2018. **Signed by:** Jon Deeble/Allen Lin/Simon Kim.

TRACK RECORD: Choi had a chance to be a top pick in the Korea Baseball Organization draft out of high school but instead signed with the Dodgers for $300,000. He led the Rookie-level Arizona League in strikeouts in his pro debut in 2019 and, after spending the coronavirus shutdown in South Korea, posted a 3.55 ERA in 106.1 innings as he moved from Low-A to High-A in his full-season debut in 2021. He finished among the organization's leaders in innings, ERA, wins (8), strikeouts (106) and WHIP (0.969) and was named the Dodgers' minor league pitcher of the year.

SCOUTING REPORT: Choi is extremely polished for his age and has advanced command of a four-pitch arsenal. His fastball ranges from 90-94 mph with late armside run and plays up with his ability to locate it precisely on both sides of the plate. His best secondary pitch is an average, 80-84 mph split-changeup that plays well off his fastball in part because of how well he locates the pitch. Choi's 80-84 mph slider flashes average but is inconsistent and he rarely uses his slow, 72-74 mph curveball, but he can locate both with plus control. Choi works quickly and efficiently and holds his stuff and command for the better part of five innings before slowing down.

THE FUTURE: Choi's command and pitchability give him a chance to rise as a swingman. He may see Double-A in 2022.

Year	Age	Club (Level)	Lge	W	L	ERA	G	GS	IP	H	HR	BB	SO	BB/9	SO/9	WHIP	AVG
2021	21	R. Cucamonga (LoA)	West	8	3	3.17	15	2	65	47	8	7	75	1.0	10.3	0.83	.197
	21	Great Lakes (HiA)	Cent	0	3	4.17	9	9	41	38	4	11	31	2.4	6.8	1.20	.248
Minor League Totals (3 years)				13	7	3.20	38	22	171	142	18	29	177	1.52	9.30	1.00	.224

MORE PROSPECTS TO KNOW

31 RYAN WARD, OF
Ward can hit for average and power from the left side and now needs to find a defensive home.

32 KENDALL WILLIAMS, RHP
Williams is a tough competitor with a projectable body. The next step is getting stronger to help his average stuff tick up.

33 LEONEL VALERA, SS
Valera is a slick defensive shortstop with plus raw power, but he has to improve his plate discipline and pitch recognition to make more contact.

34 NICK ROBERTSON, RHP
Robertson floods the strike zone with his mid-90s fastball, power slider and firm changeup and could join the Dodgers bullpen in 2022.

35 BRANDON LEWIS, 3B
Lewis hit 30 home runs last season and has massive raw power, but whether he'll make enough contact against upper-level pitching is a question.

36 LUIS RODRIGUEZ, OF
Rodriguez's athleticism and hitting ability have gone backward since he signed with the Dodgers for $2,667,500. Fixing his undisciplined approach is priority No. 1.

37 EMMET SHEEHAN, RHP
SLEEPER

The sixth-round pick out of Boston College stood out in his pro debut with his low-slot, running 95-99 mph fastball that generated elite swing-and-miss rates.

38 RYAN NODA, 1B
Noda hit 29 home runs at Double-A and packs big power from the left side, but his ability to make consistent contact is a question.

39 EDGARDO HENRIQUEZ, RHP
The 19-year-old righthander already sits 97-98 mph on his fastball and has the potential to be a high-leverage reliever.

40 DREW AVANS, OF
Avans is undersized but plays hard and is a capable outfielder and basestealer, making him a potential callup option.

TOP PROSPECTS OF THE DECADE

Year	Player, Pos	2021 Org
2012	Zach Lee, RHP	Reds
2013	Hyun-Jin Ryu, LHP	Blue Jays
2014	Joc Pederson, OF	Braves
2015	Corey Seager, SS	Dodgers
2016	Corey Seager, SS	Dodgers
2017	Cody Bellinger, 1B	Dodgers
2018	Walker Buehler, RHP	Dodgers
2019	Keibert Ruiz, C	Nationals
2020	Gavin Lux, SS/2B	Dodgers
2021	Keibert Ruiz, C	Nationals

TOP DRAFT PICKS OF THE DECADE

Year	Player, Pos	2021 Org
2012	Corey Seager, 3B	Dodgers
2013	Chris Anderson, RHP	Did not play
2014	Grant Holmes, RHP	Athletics
2015	Walker Buehler, RHP	Dodgers
2016	Gavin Lux, SS	Dodgers
2017	Jeren Kendall, OF	Dodgers
2018	*J.T. Ginn, RHP	Mets
2019	Kody Hoese, 3B	Dodgers
2020	Bobby Miller, RHP	Dodgers
2021	Maddux Bruns, LHP	Dodgers
	*Did not sign	

Miami Marlins

BY JOSH NORRIS

Slowly but surely, the Marlins are laying the groundwork to return to playoff contention. They finished fourth in the National League East, just two games in front of the withered husk of the Nationals.

By season's end, though, there were hints of what was to come. Although breakout righthander Sixto Sanchez missed all season with a shoulder injury that eventually required surgery, Edward Cabrera was right there to flash his potential in the upper minors. Cabrera, too, dealt with injuries, but he recovered in time to run roughshod over the upper minors en route to his MLB debut.

Behind him, 2020 draft picks Max Meyer (first round) and Jake Eder (fourth) put together two of the better pitching seasons in the minors. Their years were made all the more impressive because of their aggressive career-opening assignments to Double-A. Meyer made it to Triple-A, but Eder's season ended with Tommy John surgery in August.

The biggest breakout in the system, though, belonged to a 6-foot-8 righthander who hopes to follow Sandy Alcantara's path to the front of the rotation. The year belonged to Eury Perez, an 18-year-old righthander who cut through the competition at two Class A stops and ascended all the way to the top spot among a pitching-rich system.

More than his pure stuff, Perez impressed evaluators for his strike-throwing ability and innate control of his long limbs. Most pitchers of Perez's size struggle to sync up their bodies throughout their career, but Perez, who will begin 2022 still 18 years old, showed no signs of those struggles.

One day soon, the Marlins hope Sanchez, Cabrera, Meyer, Eder and Perez will give them an array of choices to combine with Alcantara, Trevor Rogers, Elieser Hernandez and Pablo Lopez.

The Marlins' system isn't just pitching, though. The organization was delighted to see Kahlil Watson, a high school shortstop from Raleigh, N.C., whom BA ranked as the No. 6 overall prospect in the class, fall to them with the 16th overall selection. His combination of offensive upside and chance to stick at shortstop helped him nearly vault to the No. 1 spot in the organization.

The Marlins also saw flashes of brilliance from young shortstop Jazz Chisholm, as well as other upside-filled moments from first baseman Lewin Diaz and outfielder Jesus Sanchez. That is a credit to Marlins pro scouting. All three of Chisholm, Diaz and Sanchez were acquired through deadline deals in recent years.

After the year, the Marlins moved to secure one of their prized pieces by locking Sandy Alcantara

Lefty Trevor Rogers followed up a smashing 2020 debut with a strong rookie season.

PROJECTED 2025 LINEUP

Catcher	Joe Mack	22
First Base	Lewin Diaz	28
Second Base	Kahlil Watson	21
Third Base	Brian Anderson	31
Shortstop	Jazz Chisholm	27
Left Field	Peyton Burdick	28
Center Field	Bryan de la Cruz	28
Right Field	Jesus Sanchez	27
Designated Hitter	Avisail Garcia	34
No. 1 Starter	Sandy Alcantara	29
No. 2 Starter	Trevor Rogers	27
No. 3 Starter	Pablo Lopez	29
No. 4 Starter	Eury Perez	21
No. 5 Starter	Sixto Sanchez	26
Closer	Edward Cabrera	26

into a long-term deal, then added outfielder Avisail Garcia via free agency. Of course any system flush with pitching needs a rock-solid catcher to guide the youngsters, so Miami dealt with Pittsburgh to add Gold Glove backstop Jacob Stallings.

The Braves won the 2021 World Series even without all-world outfielder Ronald Acuña Jr. The Phillies have reigning MVP Bryce Harper and ace righty Zack Wheeler in tow for years. The Mets opened free agency by securing Max Scherzer's services for the next three seasons.

All this is to say that the road ahead won't be easy for the Marlins, but their young talent in the majors and on the farm could be just the cobblestones they need to build a bridge to October. ■

MIAMI MARLINS

TOP 2022 ROOKIES	RANK
Sixto Sanchez, RHP	3
Edward Cabrera, RHP	4
BREAKOUT PROSPECTS	**RANK**
Dax Fulton, LHP	11
Cody Morissette, 2B	17

SOURCE OF TOP 30 TALENT

Homegrown	25	Acquired	5
College	7	Trade	5
Junior College	0	Rule 5 Draft	0
High School	8	Independent League	0
Nondrafted Free Agent	0	Free Agent/Waivers	0
International	10		

LF
Griffin Conine (27)
Brady Allen
Tanner Allen

CF
Peyton Burdick (7)
Victor Mesa Jr. (25)
Kevin Guerrero (29)

RF
JJ Bleday (10)
Jerar Encarnacion (24)

3B
Jose Salas (8)
Cristhian Rodriguez (30)
Joe Dunand

SS
Kahlil Watson (2)
Jose Devers (13)
Nasim Nuñez (15)
Yiddi Cappe (18)

2B
Ian Lewis (9)
Cody Morissette (17)
Jordan McCants (19)

1B
Troy Johnston
Lazaro Alonso

C
Joe Mack (12)
Nick Fortes (21)
Payton Henry (23)
Ronald Hernandez (28)

LHP

LHSP	LHRP
Jake Eder (6)	Jefry Yan
Dax Fulton (11)	Antonio Velez
Braxton Garrett (14)	Andrew Nardi
Will Stewart	Jake Fishman
Patrick Monteverde	Josh Simpson
Zach King	

RHP

RHSP	RHRP
Eury Perez (1)	Jordan Holloway (20)
Sixto Sanchez (3)	Nick Neidert (22)
Edward Cabrera (4)	Josh Roberson
Max Meyer (5)	Dylan Bice
Zach McCambley (16)	Raul Brito
Chris Mokma (26)	Colton Hock
Evan Fitterer	
George Soriano	
Hunter Perdue	

1 EURY PEREZ, RHP

Born: April 15, 2003. **B-T:** R-R. **HT:** 6-8. **WT:** 200.
Signed: Dominican Republic, 2019.
Signed by: Fernando Seguignol.

TOM DIPACE

BA GRADE	SCOUTING GRADES
60 Risk: Extreme	**FB:** 70. **CHG:** 60. **CB:** 50. **CTL:** 60

Projected future grades on 20-80 scouting scale

TRACK RECORD: As an amateur, Perez was already 6-foot-5 and a lanky 155 pounds when he signed with the Marlins for $200,000. He's gained both height and weight since then, reaching 6-8, 200 pounds, but has maintained his surprising body control and coordination. Perez's first shot at a professional debut was scuttled by the coronavirus pandemic, though he did attend Miami's instructional league. He proved advanced enough to skip over both extended spring training and the Florida Complex League and opened the 2021 season in the rotation at Low-A Jupiter, where he dominated despite being the youngest player in the spot on Opening Day. His finest moment came on Aug. 7, when he struck out a season-high 11 hitters in 4.2 no-hit innings against Tampa. Perez proved advanced enough to move to High-A Beloit for four starts at season's end. He was excellent after the promotion as well, with his only real clunker coming in his last start of the season against Cleveland phenom Daniel Espino.

SCOUTING REPORT: Perez's success can be credited to the three C's: coordination, control and command. All of these would be solid for any 18-year-old pitcher getting his first shot at pro ball, but given the circumstances surrounding the canceled 2020 season and his massive frame, they were exceptional. Perez works with a three-pitch mix of a four-seam fastball, changeup and curveball, the first two of which already show the makings of plus or better offerings. His fastball ranges between 93-96 mph and has touched a few ticks higher while settling in at an average of roughly 95 mph with excellent riding life up in the zone. The Marlins were pleased with the pitch's analytical characteristics and the way it played against more experienced hitters. Perez's changeup, which averaged 83 mph, shows solid fading action when he properly executes it. Other times it plays too firm and he'll at times slow his arm down when he throws it. Nevertheless, this changeup projects to eventually be a plus offering, and he is willing to throw it in any count and against both righties and lefties. Perez's curveball parks in the 77-80 mph range and needs the most work of his secondary pitches. He spins the ball well and uses his curveball as an early-count offering to steal strikes, but he needs to add more consistency and power to the offering to help it realize its average to above-average potential. Despite his already massive frame,

BEST TOOLS

Best Hitter for Average	Kahlil Watson
Best Power Hitter	Peyton Burdick
Best Strike-Zone Discipline	Nasim Nuñez
Fastest Baserunner	Nasim Nuñez
Best Athlete	Kahlil Watson
Best Fastball	Eury Perez
Best Curveball	Dax Fulton
Best Slider	Max Meyer
Best Changeup	Antonio Velez
Best Control	Antonio Velez
Best Defensive Catcher	Nick Fortes
Best Defensive Infielder	Nasim Nuñez
Best Infield Arm	Nasim Nuñez
Best Defensive Outfielder	Monte Harrison
Best Outfield Arm	Jerar Encarnacion

Perez still has plenty of projection remaining. The Marlins have tasked him with gaining roughly 20 more pounds of good weight so he can add more power behind his already dynamic arsenal and take on an even bigger workload.

THE FUTURE: After a successful stint at High-A to end his season, Perez is likely to return to the level to begin 2022, when he'll be among the youngest players in the league. He has the upside of a front-end starter. He's part of a group of young, talented Marlins pitchers that also includes fellow prospects Sixto Sanchez, Edward Cabrera, Max Meyer and Jake Eder. ∎

Year	Age	Club (Level)	Lge	W	L	ERA	G	GS	IP	H	HR	BB	SO	BB/9	SO/9	WHIP	AVG
2021	18	Jupiter (LoA)	SEast	2	3	1.61	15	15	56	32	2	21	82	3.4	13.2	0.95	.163
	18	Beloit (HiA)	Cent	1	2	2.86	5	5	22	11	5	5	26	2.1	10.6	0.73	.145
Minor League Totals (1 year)				3	5	1.96	20	20	78	43	7	26	108	3.00	12.46	0.88	.158

2 KAHLIL WATSON, SS

Born: April 16, 2003. **B-T:** L-R. **HT:** 5-9. **WT:** 178. **Drafted:** HS—Wake Forest, N.C., 2021 (1st round).

TRACK RECORD: Watson used the summer showcase circuit to cement his status as one of the top prospects in the country but took a curious tumble on draft night. The Marlins stopped his slide at No. 16 and signed him away from his North Carolina State commitment for $4,540,790. Watson had a successful but short debut in the Florida Complex League before his season was cut short by a hamstring strain. He got back on the field at the team's development camp in October.

SCOUTING REPORT: Watson's prodigious bat speed is his biggest asset. He uses an extremely strong lower half to whip his bat through the zone and produce all-fields power without a lot of wasted movement. He does so while maintaining the barrel malleability to hit for plenty of average as well. Watson shows well against mid-90s fastballs and displays the strike zone discipline to confidently take borderline pitches. There are a few minor kinks to be worked out, such as a small hitch in his load that affects his timing and balance, but he's so strong and has such barrel awareness that he can still be a plus hitter with above-average power. Watson has the speed and the athleticism to stick at shortstop, but he needs to improve his footwork. He is a plus runner and makes plenty of highlight-reel plays with his range and above-average arm strength, but he also commits clunkers on routine plays and needs to improve his focus on defense.

THE FUTURE: Watson will get his first full-season test in 2022 at Low-A Jupiter. If he shores his defense, he can be a true five-tool talent.

BA GRADE
60 Risk: Extreme

SCOUTING GRADES:	Hitting: 60	Power: 55	Running: 60	Fielding: 55	Arm: 55

Year	Age	Club (Level)	Lge	AVG	G	AB	R	H	2B	3B	HR	RBI	BB	SO	SB	OBP	SLG
2021	18	Marlins (R)	FCL	.394	9	33	13	13	3	2	0	5	8	7	4	.524	.606
Minor League Totals (1 year)				.394	9	33	13	13	3	2	0	5	8	7	4	.524	.606

3 SIXTO SANCHEZ, RHP

Born: July 29, 1998. **B-T:** R-R. **HT:** 6-0. **WT:** 234. **Signed:** Dominican Republic, 2015. **Signed by:** Carlos Salas (Phillies).

TRACK RECORD: After making seven dominant starts for the Marlins during the shortened 2020 season, Sanchez was expected to take his place atop the Marlins' rotation and vault into stardom in 2021. Instead, he didn't throw a single pitch. Injuries and setbacks plagued Sanchez all season long, eventually culminating in surgery in July to repair a capsular tear in his right shoulder.

SCOUTING REPORT: When healthy, Sanchez mixes an elite fastball that averages 99 mph with a devastating, plus-plus changeup that plays well against both righthanded and lefthanded hitters. Both of his breaking balls play average or better as well, with his slider a potentially plus pitch and his curveball just a tick behind. Sanchez is one of the rare power pitchers with plus control of his stuff, giving him a rare package of precision and power few pitchers in the majors or minors can match. Sanchez has long had concerns about his health and durability and he tailed off in the postseason during his dominant 2020 showing. His success masked the fact that he had gotten quite heavy, which adds to the list of things that will need to be watched as he develops.

THE FUTURE: Sanchez is tentatively expected to be ready for 2022 spring training. If Sanchez's stuff returns intact after he completed his rehab, he should resume his place near the top of the Marlins' rotation.

BA GRADE
60 Risk: Extreme

SCOUTING GRADES:	Fastball: 70	Slider: 55	Curveball: 55	Changeup: 70	Control: 60

Year	Age	Club (Level)	Lge	W	L	ERA	G	GS	IP	H	HR	BB	SO	BB/9	SO/9	WHIP	AVG
2021	22	Did not play—Injured															
Major League Totals (1 year)				3	2	3.46	7	7	39	36	3	11	33	2.54	7.62	1.21	.250
Minor League Totals (5 years)				23	18	2.58	68	59	335	278	9	64	294	1.72	7.89	1.02	.223

4 EDWARD CABRERA, RHP

Born: April 13, 1998. **B-T:** R-R. **HT:** 6-5. **WT:** 217. **Signed:** Dominican Republic, 2015. **Signed by:** Albert Gonzalez/Sandy Nin/Domingo Ortega.

TRACK RECORD: Cabrera signed with the Marlins for $100,000 in 2015 and broke out with a big year in 2019. Injuries to his back and biceps limited him each of the past two seasons, but he still earned his first callup to the majors in 2021 and made seven starts down the stretch. He struggled to a 5.81 ERA with 19 walks in 26.1 innings in his debut, but his pure stuff was encouraging nonetheless.

SCOUTING REPORT: Cabrera's biggest weapon is his fastball, which sits in the upper 90s, and can be even more effective with improved command. If he can throw more quality strikes with his heater, his upside will become more attainable. Already armed with a three-pitch mix of a fastball, curveball and changeup, Cabrera began working on a slider this year in Triple-A. The aver-

BA GRADE

55 Risk: High

age pitch features short, sweeping break in the upper 80s and served as a fine complement to his plus, low-80s, downer curveball. Both breaking pitches take a backseat to his hard changeup, which averages 93 mph. At its best, the changeup shows late fade life away from lefties and is deceptive because of the conviction with which he throws it. Cabrera relied heavily on his offspeeds in Triple-A, where he threw his fastball just 26% of the time.

THE FUTURE: Cabrera has mid-rotation potential, but he needs to sharpen his command and fringe-average control to reach that ceiling. He'll likely begin the 2022 season back in Triple-A for more seasoning

SCOUTING GRADES:	Fastball: 70	Slider: 50	Curveball: 60	Changeup: 50	Control: 45

Year	Age	Club (Level)	Lge	W	L	ERA	G	GS	IP	H	HR	BB	SO	BB/9	SO/9	WHIP	AVG
2021	23	Jupiter (LoA)	SEast	0	0	0.00	2	2	6	4	0	0	11	0.0	16.5	0.67	.182
	23	Pensacola (AA)	South	2	1	2.77	5	5	26	19	3	6	33	2.1	11.4	0.96	.211
	23	Jacksonville (AAA)	East	1	3	3.68	6	6	29	22	4	19	48	5.8	14.7	1.40	.206
	23	Miami (MLB)	NL	0	3	5.81	7	7	26	24	6	19	28	6.5	9.6	1.63	.247
Major League Totals (1 year)				0	3	5.81	7	7	26	24	6	19	28	6.49	9.57	1.63	.247
Minor League Totals (6 years)				19	25	3.54	78	67	341	311	27	116	361	3.06	9.53	1.25	.242

5 MAX MEYER, RHP

Born: March 12, 1999. **B-T:** L-R. **HT:** 6-0. **WT:** 196. **Drafted:** Minnesota, 2020 (1st round). **Signed by:** Shaeffer Hall.

TRACK RECORD: After two dominant years in Minnesota's bullpen, Meyer entered the 2020 season as part of the Golden Gophers' rotation. He made only four starts before the coronavirus pandemic shut down the season, but the Marlins were confident enough in what they saw to draft him third overall. Meyer jumped straight to Double-A to start his pro career and, though his stuff was inconsistent, his numbers were superb. His 2.27 ERA ranked fourth in the minors among pitchers who threw at least 100 innings and his 130 strikeouts were the second-most in the Marlins system.

SCOUTING REPORT: Meyer's bread and butter is his fastball and slider com-

BA GRADE

55 Risk: High

bination. His plus fastball typically sits in the low 90s and gets up to 96-97 when he needs a few extra notches. His plus slider was the clear leader in his arsenal as an amateur, a true downer weapon that generated swings and misses. The pitch was much less consistent in his pro debut, though it showed flashes of its formerly monstrous self. Meyer had a slightly lower arm slot in 2021 than he had as an amateur, a possible reason for inconsistency. Meyer's fringy changeup is still a work in progress and shows little movement, instead relying on the separation from his fastball to disrupt batters' timing. Though undersized, Meyer is an exceptional athlete and throws all his pitches for strikes with above-average control.

THE FUTURE: Meyer ended the season at Triple-A and should return to the level in 2022. If he can find consistency, improve his changeup and sharpen his command, he could pitch in the middle of a rotation.

SCOUTING GRADES:	Fastball: 60	Slider: 60	Changeup: 45	Control: 55

Year	Age	Club (Level)	Lge	W	L	ERA	G	GS	IP	H	HR	BB	SO	BB/9	SO/9	WHIP	AVG
2021	22	Pensacola (AA)	South	6	3	2.41	20	20	101	84	7	40	113	3.6	10.1	1.23	.226
	22	Jacksonville (AAA)	East	0	1	0.90	2	2	10	6	1	2	17	1.8	15.3	0.80	.167
Minor League Totals (2 years)				6	4	2.27	22	22	111	90	8	42	130	3.41	10.54	1.19	.221

6 JAKE EDER, LHP

Born: Oct. 9, 1998. **B-T:** L-L. **HT:** 6-4. **WT:** 215. **Drafted:** Vanderbilt, 2020 (4th round). **Signed by:** JT Zink.

TRACK RECORD: Eder was poised to use the 2020 season as a coming-out party after moving from Vanderbilt's bullpen to the rotation, but the coronavirus pandemic cut that chance short. Marlins area scout JT Zink was still convinced by what he saw to push the Marlins to draft Eder in the fourth round, and Eder quickly rewarded that faith by jumping straight to Double-A in his pro debut. Eder dominated early and was one of the best pitchers in the minors, but his debut was cut short in August when he suffered a torn left elbow ligament and had Tommy John surgery.

BA GRADE

55 Risk: Extreme

SCOUTING REPORT: Before his injury, Eder's stuff placed him among the game's best pitching prospects. His fastball parks in the low 90s and can bump a few ticks higher with excellent riding life up in the zone. His breaking ball can sometimes look like a slider and other times look like a curveball depending on his intent. If he wants to get swings and misses, he'll add more sweep. If he wants to get early-count strikes, he'll take something off and drop it into the zone. Eder's changeup is at its best when thrown in the low 80s, where it shows solid fading life, but it straightens when it gets too firm. A small mechanical adjustment with the way Eder took the ball from his glove at the beginning of his delivery paid immediate dividends in terms of command and control. Eder now shows potentially plus command of his arsenal and his heady, competitive makeup helps him gut through times when he's not at his best.

THE FUTURE: Eder will miss the 2022 season rehabbing from his surgery. If he can make a full recovery, he has a chance to pitch toward the middle of a rotation.

SCOUTING GRADES:	Fastball: 60	Slider: 60	Changeup: 50	Control: 60

Year	Age	Club (Level)	Lge	W	L	ERA	G	GS	IP	H	HR	BB	SO	BB/9	SO/9	WHIP	AVG
2021	22	Pensacola (AA)	South	3	5	1.77	15	15	71	43	3	27	99	3.4	12.5	0.98	.169
Minor League Totals (2 years)				3	5	1.77	15	15	71	43	3	27	99	3.41	12.49	0.98	.169

7 PEYTON BURDICK, OF

Born: Feb. 26, 1997. **B-T:** R-R. **HT:** 6-0. **WT:** 205. **Drafted:** Wright State, 2019 (3rd round). **Signed by:** Nate Adcock.

TRACK RECORD: Burdick was the Horizon League player of the year in 2019 and parlayed the award into becoming a third-round pick of the Marlins that season. He showed well in his first year as a pro but had to wait until 2021 for his full-season debut because of the coronavirus pandemic. He jumped straight to Double-A for his full-season debut and hit 23 home runs to tie for the league lead in the Double-A South before receiving a promotion to Triple-A.

BA GRADE

50 Risk: High

SCOUTING REPORT: Burdick uses his smaller frame to generate surprising strength, which results in raw power that easily grades as plus. He tends to favor that side of his game over hitting for average, which sometimes leads to his swing getting too big and his approach becoming overly pull-heavy. The Marlins also worked with Burdick during the season to close a hole at the top of the strike zone which was caused by a stride that had a tendency to get too long. When that happened, it forced his bat path to work under the strike zone, leaving him vulnerable to anything elevated. Burdick is most likely a corner outfielder, but he's playable in center field if needed. His power profiles in a corner and his above-average arm would serve him well in right field. Evaluators inside the Marlins organization love his makeup and dedication to the game.

THE FUTURE: Burdick ended the season in Triple-A and will return to the level in 2022, when he'll try to add a little more balance to his game without sacrificing his enviable power potential. He profiles as a right fielder who can move to center every so often.

SCOUTING GRADES:	Hitting: 40	Power: 60	Running: 50	Fielding: 50	Arm: 55

Year	Age	Club (Level)	Lge	AVG	G	AB	R	H	2B	3B	HR	RBI	BB	SO	SB	OBP	SLG
2021	24	Pensacola (AA)	South	.231	106	373	71	86	17	2	23	52	76	135	9	.376	.472
	24	Jacksonville (AAA)	East	.143	8	28	5	4	3	0	0	1	3	11	0	.226	.250
Minor League Totals (3 years)				.257	183	661	136	170	40	6	34	117	113	218	16	.382	.490

8 JOSE SALAS, SS

Born: April 26, 2003. **B-T:** B-R. **HT:** 6-2. **WT:** 191. **Signed:** Venezuela, 2019.
Signed by: Angel Izquierdo.

TRACK RECORD: After growing up in Orlando, Salas moved to Venezuela as a teen and signed with the Marlins as an international free agent in 2019 for $2.8 million. His pro debut was delayed a year by the coronavirus pandemic, but he got onto the field during 2020 instructional league and made his official pro debut in 2021. He hit .370/.458/.511 during an exceptional 28-game stint in the Florida Complex League and received a promotion to Low-A Jupiter to end the season.

SCOUTING REPORT: Salas is a balanced switch-hitter who shows hints of being an above-average hitter with above-average power. His power is presently gap to gap and goes more often for doubles than homers, but he flashed his potential with a long home run in Jupiter. Salas is a better hitter from the left side simply because he faces more righties, but overall he shows a quick, leveraged swing from both sides of the plate. He has strong, fast hands that allow him to manipulate the barrel to different parts of the zone. While Salas makes plenty of contact, he has a tendency to swing at pitches he can't drive and needs to refine his approach and pitch selection. Defensively, Salas has solid actions, an above-average arm and plenty of range with his plus speed to develop into a reliable everyday shortstop. He needs to focus on staying more engaged on every play and remembering where he needs to be on the field.

THE FUTURE: Salas will likely return to Low-A in 2022, where he, Ian Lewis and Kahlil Watson will form an enviable trio of middle-of-the-diamond talents.

BA GRADE
50 Risk: Extreme

SCOUTING GRADES:	Hitting: 55	Power: 55	Running: 60	Fielding: 50	Arm: 55

Year	Age	Club (Level)	Lge	AVG	G	AB	R	H	2B	3B	HR	RBI	BB	SO	SB	OBP	SLG
2021	18	Marlins (R)	FCL	.370	28	92	14	34	10	0	1	11	11	23	8	.458	.511
	18	Jupiter (LoA)	SEast	.250	27	108	12	27	4	0	1	8	11	28	6	.333	.315
Minor League Totals (1 year)				.305	55	200	26	61	14	0	2	19	22	51	14	.391	.405

9 IAN LEWIS, 2B

Born: Feb. 4, 2003. **B-T:** B-R. **HT:** 5-10. **WT:** 177. **Signed:** Bahamas, 2019.
Signed by: Carlos Herazo.

TRACK RECORD: Lewis was part of a strong Marlins 2019 international signing class that included righthander Eury Perez and shortstop Jose Salas. He signed for $950,000, the top bonus for any Bahamian player in the class, and drew acclaim for his blend of tools, athleticism and projectability in his pro debut. Lewis hit .302/.354/.497 in the Florida Complex League and drew universal praise as one of the league's top prospects.

SCOUTING REPORT: Lewis is an aggressive hitter who hunts fastballs he can drive. That approach helped him produce exit velocities up to 110 mph and drive 40% of his hits for extra bases. The switch-hitting Lewis combines that aggression with excellent bat-to-ball skills from both sides of the plate with a whippy swing and strong hands. He has excellent barrel accuracy for his age, and also shows the ability to foul off tough pitches in order to get something he can drive. The Marlins worked with Lewis to maintain a more consistent posture throughout his swing. When he gets out of whack, his stride gets too long and his shoulders dip, which causes his bat path to divert from its ideal course. Defensively, Lewis is likely to move to either second or third base. He has quick feet and a strong arm as well as excellent body control while turning double plays. He accelerates well into his above-average speed and has the potential to move around the diamond.

THE FUTURE: After a successful turn in the FCL, Lewis will likely head to Low-A Jupiter, where he'll be part of a high-upside trio of players with Salas and 2021 first-rounder Kahlil Watson.

BA GRADE
50 Risk: Extreme

SCOUTING GRADES:	Hitting: 50	Power: 55	Running: 55	Fielding: 50	Arm: 50

Year	Age	Club (Level)	Lge	AVG	G	AB	R	H	2B	3B	HR	RBI	BB	SO	SB	OBP	SLG
2021	18	Marlins (R)	FCL	.302	43	149	24	45	10	5	3	27	11	24	9	.354	.497
Minor League Totals (1 year)				.302	43	149	24	45	10	5	3	27	11	24	9	.354	.497

10 JJ BLEDAY, OF

Born: Nov. 10, 1997. **B-T:** L-L. **HT:** 6-2. **WT:** 197. **Drafted:** Vanderbilt, 2019 (1st round). **Signed by:** Christian Castorri.

NINO MENDEZ

TRACK RECORD: Bleday led the nation in home runs for Vanderbilt in 2019 and played a starring role as the Commodores won the College World Series. The Marlins drafted him fourth overall and signed him for $6.67 million. Bleday moved to Double-A Pensacola and scuffled badly to a .212/.323/.373 slash line, but he made a swing adjustment after the year and redeemed himself with a star showing in the Arizona Fall League that included the Top Star award in the league's annual Fall Stars Game and a key role on the league-champion Mesa Solar Sox.

BA GRADE
45 Risk: High

SCOUTING REPORT: Bleday's 2021 was rough, but he still maintained a strong knowledge of the strike zone and used the whole field. After he lowered his hands in his stance in the AFL, his barrel became more adjustable and he started driving balls in the middle of the strike zone he'd been missing all season long. The Marlins also worked with Bleday to stand taller at address in order to keep him from getting stuck on his backside and making weak contact on pitches he should hit hard. The adjustments give Bleday a chance to be a fringe-average hitter, although he needs to prove he can maintain them over a full season. Bleday's power also became amplified with the changes and he began to show average power potential for the first time. Bleday is a potentially plus defender in right field with the average speed and plus arm strength to stick at the position. With his offensive changes, he now has a chance to profile at the position.

THE FUTURE: Bleday still has a ways to go to look like the hitter the Marlins thought they were drafting, but he's at least on the right track. He'll head to Triple-A in 2022, where he'll hope to build on the outstanding showing he had in the AFL.

SCOUTING GRADES:	Hitting: 45	Power: 50	Running: 50	Fielding: 60	Arm: 60

Year	Age	Club (Level)	Lge	AVG	G	AB	R	H	2B	3B	HR	RBI	BB	SO	SB	OBP	SLG
2021	23	Pensacola (AA)	South	.212	110	397	52	84	22	3	12	54	64	101	5	.323	.373
Minor League Totals (3 years)				.223	148	537	65	120	30	3	15	73	75	130	5	.320	.374

11 DAX FULTON, LHP

BA GRADE
45 Risk: High

Born: Oct. 16, 2001. **B-T:** L-L. **HT:** 6-7. **WT:** 225. **Drafted:** HS—Mustang, Okla., 2020 (2nd round). **Signed by:** James Vilade.

TRACK RECORD: Fulton was the second of six pitchers Miami picked in the five-round 2020 draft. The selection was made with an eye toward upside considering Fulton was recovering from the Tommy John surgery he'd had during his senior season of high school. With no minor league season because of the pandemic, Fulton got on the mound at instructional league, then made his official debut in 2021 at Low-A Jupiter.

SCOUTING REPORT: Fulton works primarily with a three-pitch mix of a four-seam fastball, curveball and changeup. The first two offerings were his mainstays as an amateur, while the changeup was a work in progress all year long. The fastball averaged around 93 mph and touched as high as 96 and was thrown with good angle. His curveball showed 1-to-7 break in the mid 70s and flashed solid-average depth and bite down in the zone. The changeup will be the key to whether Fulton remains a starter. Fulton used Rapsodo and Edgertronic cameras to help find a grip that got him an ideal combination of movement and velocity separation from his fastball. Fulton is also massive in stature, and scouts were concerned about the lack of athleticism they saw in his movements and wondered if they would lower his ultimate ceiling as a result.

THE FUTURE: Fulton and Eury Perez moved in tandem from Low-A to High-A in 2021, and both are likely to return to the level to begin 2022. Fulton has a ceiling of a back-end starter and a floor of a bullpen arm.

Year	Age	Club (Level)	Lge	W	L	ERA	G	GS	IP	H	HR	BB	SO	BB/9	SO/9	WHIP	AVG
2021	19	Jupiter (LoA)	SEast	2	4	4.30	15	14	58	50	3	30	66	4.6	10.1	1.36	.229
	19	Beloit (HiA)	Cent	0	1	5.49	5	5	19	21	3	8	18	3.7	8.2	1.47	.276
Minor League Totals (2 years)				2	5	4.60	20	19	78	71	6	38	84	4.37	9.65	1.39	.241

12 JOE MACK, C

Born: Dec. 27, 2002. **B-T:** L-R. **HT:** 6-1. **WT:** 210.
Drafted: HS—East Amherst, N.Y., 2021 (1st round supplemental).

BA GRADE

50 Risk: Extreme

TRACK RECORD: The Marlins' early picks in the 2021 draft represented something of a coup. First, they had shortstop Kahlil Watson, whom BA ranked as the No. 6 prospect in the class, fall into their laps with the 16th pick. Then, in the supplemental round, with pick 31, they landed Mack, the No. 22 player in the class based on his blend of skills on both sides of the ball. He signed for $2.5 million to keep him away from a commitment to Clemson.
SCOUTING REPORT: Mack burnished his stock on the summer showcase circuit, which was all the more impressive after his high school season was wiped out by the pandemic. The Marlins loved Mack's hittability and think it could be unlocked further by becoming more aggressive on pitches he can drive. He has plenty of raw power, too, which was on display at the team's instructional league program in Miami, where Mack drove a ball into the third deck of the big league stadium. Behind the plate, Mack shows the athleticism that helped him play both basketball and volleyball as a high schooler. He's got a strong throwing arm as well, which scouts project to be plus as he moves through the system. He's a below-average runner, which is to be expected for a catcher.
THE FUTURE: Mack got his feet wet as a pro in the Florida Complex League, where he walked nearly as often as he struck out. He'll likely make the jump to full-season ball in 2022 at Low-A Jupiter.

Year	Age	Club (Level)	Lge	AVG	G	AB	R	H	2B	3B	HR	RBI	BB	SO	SB	OBP	SLG
2021	18	Marlins (R)	FCL	.132	19	53	9	7	1	0	1	2	20	22	0	.373	.208
Minor League Totals (1 year)				.132	19	53	9	7	1	0	1	2	20	22	0	.373	.208

13 JOSE DEVERS, SS

Born: Dec. 7, 1999. **B-T:** L-R. **HT:** 6-0. **WT:** 174. **Signed:** Dominican Republic, 2016. **Signed by:** Juan Rosario (Yankees).

BA GRADE

45 Risk: High

TRACK RECORD: The cousin of Red Sox star third baseman Rafael Devers, Jose was dealt from the Yankees to the Marlins as part of the package that brought Giancarlo Stanton to New York. He's shown plenty of potential in his time with his new club, but hasn't been able to stay on the field consistently. Devers made his big league debut on April 24, but a shoulder injury limited him to just 80 at-bats all season between the majors and minors, and he's played just 80 games combined between the 2019 and 2021 seasons.
SCOUTING REPORT: Devers has the skill set of a player who can hit at the top or bottom of the order while causing havoc on the basepaths. He makes plenty of contact—his career strikeout rate is just 14.1%—and is working to improve his swing decisions. As those improve, he'll learn to unleash his swing on pitches he can slash into the alleyways before letting his plus speed take over. He also needs to continue to add strength in order to better withstand the rigors of a long season. He's a surefire shortstop going forward, with potentially plus defense that will help make up for a throwing arm that is just average.
THE FUTURE: Devers missed most of the season with an impingement in his right shoulder but should be ready for spring training. If he can return to health, he has table setter skills and the chops to stick up the middle.

Year	Age	Club (Level)	Lge	AVG	G	AB	R	H	2B	3B	HR	RBI	BB	SO	SB	OBP	SLG
2021	21	Jacksonville (AAA)	East	.231	12	39	4	9	1	1	0	3	1	5	0	.250	.308
	21	Miami (MLB)	NL	.244	21	41	7	10	3	0	0	5	3	11	0	.304	.317
Major League Totals (1 year)				.244	21	41	7	10	3	0	0	5	3	11	0	.304	.317
Minor League Totals (5 years)				.275	199	745	97	205	30	10	1	52	49	117	37	.335	.346

14 BRAXTON GARRETT, LHP

Born: Aug. 5, 1997. **B-T:** R-L. **HT:** 6-2. **WT:** 202. **Drafted:** HS—Florence, Ala., 2016 (1st round). **Signed by:** Mark Willoughby.

BA GRADE

40 Risk: Medium

TRACK RECORD: Garrett was the Marlins' first-round pick in 2016, then had Tommy John surgery midway through his 2017 season. He missed all of 2018 rehabbing before finally getting a full season's worth of innings in 2019 between High-A and Double-A. He was at the Marlins' alternate training site in 2020 and made his big league debut that September. In 2021, Garrett bounced back and forth between Triple-A and Miami.
SCOUTING REPORT: Garrett's stuff has diminished somewhat over the years. He still works with a four-pitch repertoire fronted by a low-90s fastball and buttressed primarily with a pair of breaking balls. His curveball sits in the mid 70s while his slider, which is the more frequently thrown of the two pitches, has

an average velocity around 84 mph. The slider also shows above-average spin rate as well as other analytical characteristics that make it the superior breaking ball. Garrett's changeup sits in the mid 80s and might be more effective with a touch more separation from his fastball.

THE FUTURE: If Garrett is to stick in the big leagues, he'll have to improve his control and command. He walked 5.3 hitters per nine innings in his time with the Marlins, and scouts think he might be better suited as a left-on-left reliever who relies heavily on his breaking pitches.

Year	Age	Club (Level)	Lge	W	L	ERA	G	GS	IP	H	HR	BB	SO	BB/9	SO/9	WHIP	AVG
2021	23	Jacksonville (AAA)	East	5	4	3.89	18	18	85	73	10	32	86	3.4	9.0	1.23	.231
	23	Miami (MLB)	NL	1	2	5.03	8	7	34	42	3	20	32	5.3	8.5	1.82	.318
Major League Totals (2 years)				2	3	5.18	10	9	42	50	6	25	40	5.40	8.64	1.80	.311
Minor League Totals (4 years)				12	11	3.64	43	43	208	182	26	78	221	3.38	9.58	1.25	.232

15 NASIM NUÑEZ, SS

BA GRADE

45 Risk: High

Born: Aug. 18, 2000. **B-T:** B-R. **HT:** 5-9. **WT:** 158. **Drafted:** HS—Suwanee, Ga., 2019 (2nd round). **Signed by:** Christian Castorri.

TRACK RECORD: Nuñez was one of the best infield defenders available in the 2019 draft class, and the Marlins were intrigued enough by his upside to spend $2.2 million to buy him out of his Clemson commitment. His first season as a pro was mostly spent in the Rookie-level Gulf Coast League, and he was invited to Miami's alternate training site in 2020. Injuries limited Nuñez to just 52 games in 2021.

SCOUTING REPORT: Nuñez is one of the best defensive shortstops in the minor leagues, with true 80-grade potential. His instincts are so sharp, scouts say, that it appears he is moving toward the ball before it is hit. He has the range to track down balls to his right and left and will go all-out to get fly balls even if it means sacrificing his body. His arm is strong enough to make accurate throws from different angles at any spot on the diamond. Nuñez's bat lags well behind his glove. His average exit velocity in 2021 was roughly 84 mph and he has just nine extra-base hits—and zero home runs—in 454 plate appearances. His saving graces on offense are a keen knowledge of the strike zone and the kind of blazing speed to have swiped 61 bases in 103 games over his career.

THE FUTURE: With middle infielders Kahlil Watson, Ian Lewis and Jose Salas coming behind him, Nuñez will likely move to High-A Beloit in 2022. He has the upside of a rock-solid defensive shortstop who hits toward the bottom of a lineup.

Year	Age	Club (Level)	Lge	AVG	G	AB	R	H	2B	3B	HR	RBI	BB	SO	SB	OBP	SLG
2021	20	Jupiter (LoA)	SEast	.243	52	189	33	46	2	1	0	10	35	46	33	.366	.265
Minor League Totals (3 years)				.222	103	374	71	83	7	2	0	22	70	94	61	.347	.251

16 ZACH McCAMBLEY, RHP

BA GRADE

45 Risk: High

Born: May 4, 1999. **B-T:** L-R. **HT:** 6-2. **WT:** 220. **Drafted:** Coastal Carolina, 2020 (3rd round). **Signed by:** Blake Newsome.

TRACK RECORD: After a knee injury kept him from being drafted out of high school, McCambley put together three strong collegiate seasons to earn the Marlins' third-round selection in 2020. He was part of a group of six pitchers the Marlins assembled in the shortened 2020 draft.

SCOUTING REPORT: McCambley attacks hitters with a three-pitch mix of four-seam fastball, curveball and changeup. The fastball sits in the low 90s, touches up to 96 mph and is accentuated by a near-elite spin rate of roughly 2,700 revolutions per minute and glove-side life. His curveball is an 11-to-5 breaker in the low 80s with excellent spin and horizontal break. The pitch can get a bit out of whack when he throws it too hard. McCambley's changeup sits in the mid 80s and shows flashes of action but oftentimes comes in too firm. McCambley's arsenal plays down somewhat by a lack of command—but not control; he put together a strikeout-to-walk rate of better than 4.5 to 1. The issue stems from an inability to repeat his delivery, which is up tempo and can lack rhythm, particularly when he's forced to pitch from the stretch.

THE FUTURE: McCambley reached Double-A Pensacola by the end of the season and should return there to begin 2022. If he can remedy his command problems, he has a chance to fit toward the back of a rotation. If not, he fits in middle relief.

Year	Age	Club (Level)	Lge	W	L	ERA	G	GS	IP	H	HR	BB	SO	BB/9	SO/9	WHIP	AVG
2021	22	Beloit (HiA)	Cent	2	4	3.79	11	11	57	52	10	6	73	1.0	11.5	1.02	.234
	22	Pensacola (AA)	South	1	6	5.18	9	9	40	41	11	20	47	4.5	10.6	1.53	.270
Minor League Totals (2 years)				3	10	4.36	20	20	97	93	21	26	120	2.41	11.13	1.23	.249

17 CODY MORISSETTE, 2B

Born: Jan. 16, 2000. **B-T:** L-R. **HT:** 6-0. **WT:** 175. **Drafted:** Boston College, 2021 (2nd round).

BA GRADE
45 Risk: High

TRACK RECORD: Morissette was snapped up by Miami in the second round and signed for $1,403,200. Morissette dealt with a hand injury at multiple points, which made his .895 OPS for Boston College more impressive. He made it to Low-A Jupiter in his pro debut.

SCOUTING REPORT: Morissette's bat will be his calling card as a pro. He did not perform well in his first foray at the next level, and he and the team's player development staff went to work at instructional league to make Morissette's swing more connected and compact while making him less vulnerable to pitches at the top of the strike zone. The early results helped him show more power to the pull side while shooting line drives the other way as well. Defensively, the Marlins are going to move Morissette around the diamond in an effort to find the most comfortable spot. He has a strong arm but needs to correct a funky, arrhythmic stroke. He's an average runner with the instincts to push for extra bases.

THE FUTURE: The Marlins hope the work Morissette did at instructional league will lead to better results in 2022, when he'll likely advance to High-A Beloit. He projects as a hit-over-power utility infielder.

Year	Age	Club (Level)	Lge	AVG	G	AB	R	H	2B	3B	HR	RBI	BB	SO	SB	OBP	SLG
2021	21	Jupiter (LoA)	SEast	.204	34	137	22	28	8	1	1	10	20	38	0	.308	.299
Minor League Totals (1 year)				.204	34	137	22	28	8	1	1	10	20	38	0	.308	.299

18 YIDDI CAPPE, SS

Born: Sept. 17, 2002. **B-T:** R-R. **HT:** 6-3. **WT:** 175. **Signed:** Cuba, 2021. **Signed by:** Marlins International Scouting Department.

BA GRADE
50 Risk: Extreme

TRACK RECORD: Though he was eligible to sign in 2019, Cappe chose to wait until teams' bonus pools reset in order to maximize his value. Ultimately, Cappe inked with Miami for roughly $3 million and spent his first pro season in the Dominican Summer League.

SCOUTING REPORT: As an amateur, Cappe drew raves for his projectable body, quick feet and light actions at shortstop. He has a quick transfer and a plus throwing arm as well. Those factors will likely lead to him sticking at shortstop in the long term. His long levers might lead to holes in his swing, but he showed strong strike zone knowledge in his first pro test (a strikeout rate of just 16.2%), and internal evaluators praised his barrel accuracy. He's gained good weight over the past year but still has a long way to go to fully grow into his body. His average exit velocity in his first pro season was just shy of 82 mph, so adding strength will be a focal point of his early-career development. Cappe is an above-average runner now but could lose a step or two as he matures and adds the needed muscle.

THE FUTURE: Cappe is part of a glut of talented middle-infield prospects that includes Top 10 talents Kahlil Watson, Jose Salas and Ian Lewis. Cappe will likely move to Low-A Jupiter in 2022.

Year	Age	Club (Level)	Lge	AVG	G	AB	R	H	2B	3B	HR	RBI	BB	SO	SB	OBP	SLG
2021	18	Marlins (R)	DSL	.270	54	189	31	51	17	1	2	27	19	35	9	.329	.402
Minor League Totals (1 year)				.270	54	189	31	51	17	1	2	27	19	35	9	.329	.402

19 JORDAN McCANTS, SS

Born: May 21, 2002. **B-T:** L-R. **HT:** 6-1. **WT:** 165. **Drafted:** HS— Pensacola, Fla., 2021 (3rd round).

BA GRADE
50 Risk: Extreme

TRACK RECORD: McCants was Miami's fourth pick in 2021 and ranked as the No. 88 prospect in the class. He signed for $800,000 and started in the Florida Complex League.

SCOUTING REPORT: McCants is blessed with skills of a table-setter, including potentially 70-grade speed. The Marlins acknowledge that McCants is unlikely to stick at shortstop because of fringe-average arm strength, but he should wind up at either second base or center field for the long term. In the batter's box, the Marlins see plenty of potential because of McCants' ability to get the barrel to the ball. There's a long way to go in terms of McCants learning how his body works and getting himself in the best positions to make the most of his abilities, but Miami is willing to invest the time.

THE FUTURE: There was a bit of concern with McCants' age, given that he was already 19 on draft day, but he's shown already that he's not done growing and has added 15 pounds of good weight to his frame. He'll join a cavalcade of young middle-diamond prospects clustered in Miami's lower levels next season.

Year	Age	Club (Level)	Lge	AVG	G	AB	R	H	2B	3B	HR	RBI	BB	SO	SB	OBP	SLG
2021	19	Marlins (R)	FCL	.224	23	76	10	17	1	0	0	4	6	22	1	.286	.237
Minor League Totals (1 year)				.224	23	76	10	17	1	0	0	4	6	22	1	.286	.237

20 JORDAN HOLLOWAY, RHP

BA GRADE

40 Risk: Medium

Born: June 13, 1996. **B-T:** R-R. **HT:** 6-6. **WT:** 236. **Drafted:** HS—Arvada, Colo., 2014 (20th round). **Signed by:** Scott Stanley.

TRACK RECORD: The road to the big leagues hasn't been easy for Holloway, who had Tommy John surgery in 2017 and didn't make it past High-A until his major league debut, which came on July 26, 2020, as the Marlins churned through arms during the tumultuous pandemic season. He dealt with a groin injury in 2021, which he split mostly between Triple-A and the big leagues.

SCOUTING REPORT: Although he is primarily a relief prospect at this point, Holloway works with a five-pitch mix fronted by four- and two-seam fastballs which each sat at roughly 95 mph. He backs the fastballs chiefly with a hard, high-80s slider which got swings and misses at a rate of nearly 38%, as well as a low-80s curveball which plays up due to its excellent depth. Holloway rounds out his repertoire with a low-90s changeup which lags behind both of his breaking balls.

THE FUTURE: Holloway started four games this season, but his injury history makes it unlikely he re-emerges from the bullpen on a full-time basis. More likely his role is as a power arm in the middle innings.

Year	Age	Club (Level)	Lge	W	L	ERA	G	GS	IP	H	HR	BB	SO	BB/9	SO/9	WHIP	AVG
2021	25	Jupiter (LoA)	SEast	0	0	13.50	2	2	2	7	0	1	2	4.5	9.0	4.00	.538
	25	Jacksonville (AAA)	East	0	5	4.88	8	6	31	29	5	14	29	4.0	8.3	1.37	.248
	25	Miami (MLB)	NL	2	3	4.00	13	4	36	23	3	26	36	6.5	9.0	1.36	.177
Major League Totals (2 years)				2	3	3.96	14	4	36	25	3	27	36	6.69	8.92	1.43	.188
Minor League Totals (7 years)				13	35	4.72	86	80	338	316	29	181	276	4.82	7.36	1.47	.246

21 NICK FORTES, C

BA GRADE

40 Risk: Medium

Born: Nov. 11, 1996. **B-T:** R-R. **HT:** 5-11. **WT:** 198. **Drafted:** Mississippi, 2018 (4th round). **Signed by:** Mark Willoughby.

TRACK RECORD: Fortes was the Marlins' fourth-round pick in 2018 and had largely gone unsung in the system until 2021, when he showed enough on both sides of the ball to earn his first big league callup.

SCOUTING REPORT: Fortes has raised his profile in an organization largely bereft of catching talent at the upper levels. His bat speed is on par with some of the system's higher-profile prospects, and he's long had the bat-to-ball skills to keep his strikeout totals low. He'd also had a reputation as a player who could marry that bat speed, discipline and barrel malleability, and in 2021 those skills came together for a peek at his potential. Fortes drew raves for the way he worked with the system's high-end pitching prospects. He also showed improvements in the way he received and blocked, and threw out 27% of potential base-stealers during his time in the minor leagues. He's a surprising athlete for a catcher and an average runner.

THE FUTURE: The catcher position is muddled in Miami behind Jacob Stallings, so Fortes should get plenty of chances to build on his outburst toward the end of the 2021 season. He has the ceiling of a backup catcher who develops strong rapports with his pitching staffs.

Year	Age	Club (Level)	Lge	AVG	G	AB	R	H	2B	3B	HR	RBI	BB	SO	SB	OBP	SLG
2021	24	Pensacola (AA)	South	.251	57	195	21	49	10	1	3	23	22	36	5	.338	.359
	24	Jacksonville (AAA)	East	.237	38	135	16	32	7	0	4	21	10	18	0	.322	.378
	24	Miami (MLB)	NL	.290	14	31	6	9	0	0	4	7	3	8	1	.353	.677
Major League Totals (1 year)				.290	14	31	6	9	0	0	4	7	3	8	1	.353	.677
Minor League Totals (4 years)				.232	190	655	71	152	30	3	10	84	68	108	6	.318	.333

22 NICK NEIDERT, RHP

BA GRADE

40 Risk: Medium

Born: Nov. 20, 1996. **B-T:** R-R. **HT:** 6-1. **WT:** 202. **Drafted:** HS—Suwanee, Ga., 2015 (2nd round). **Signed by:** Dustin Evans (Mariners).

TRACK RECORD: A second-round pick of the Mariners in 2015, Neidert was traded to Miami in the deal that sent Dee Strange-Gordon to Seattle. He missed most of the 2019 season after having surgery to repair a torn meniscus, then made his big league debut in the truncated 2020 season. He spent 2021 shuttling back and forth between Triple-A and the big leagues.

SCOUTING REPORT: Neidert has a full four-pitch complement but works most frequently with a four-seam fastball that averaged 93 mph in the minor leagues but touched as high as 97 and a mid-80s slider with sharp downward break at its best. His changeup sat around 84 mph in the minor leagues and showed a solid separation from his fastball of roughly nine mph. Neidert also has a seldom-used curveball, thrown in the low 80s. The solid control he showed in the minor leagues evaporated in the big leagues, where he walked 23 hitters in 35.2 innings. Neidert's delivery is stiff and rigid, with a stabbing action in the back which does not typically lend itself to precision around the strike zone.

THE FUTURE: Neidert's likely role is the one he played in 2021: a starter who fits at the back of a rotation for a second-division club. If he improves his command and control, he could have a touch more ceiling.

Year	Age	Club (Level)	Lge	W	L	ERA	G	GS	IP	H	HR	BB	SO	BB/9	SO/9	WHIP	AVG
2021	24	Jacksonville (AAA)	East	6	4	3.67	14	13	68	71	8	21	52	2.8	6.8	1.34	.264
	24	Miami (MLB)	NL	1	2	4.54	8	7	35	31	4	23	21	5.8	5.3	1.51	.246
Major League Totals (2 years)				1	2	4.70	12	7	44	41	5	25	25	5.11	5.11	1.50	.259
Minor League Totals (6 years)				39	27	3.26	108	107	529	498	49	123	466	2.09	7.92	1.17	.249

23 PAYTON HENRY, C

BA GRADE
40 Risk: Medium

Born: June 24, 1997. **B-T:** R-R. **HT:** 6-2. **WT:** 215. **Drafted:** HS—Pleasant Grove, Utah, 2016 (6th round). **Signed by:** Jeff Scholzen (Brewers).

TRACK RECORD: Henry was the Brewers' sixth-round pick in 2016 and reached High-A in 2019. He was dealt from Milwaukee to Miami in the summer of 2021 for John Curtiss. He made his big league debut on Sept. 17.

SCOUTING REPORT: For one scintillating turn in big league spring training, Henry looked like the Brewers' catcher of the future. He's largely failed to hit since then, and is now viewed as more of a glove-first backup. He still hit the ball fairly hard in the minor leagues and doesn't strike out an exorbitant amount, but he doesn't get the ball in the air enough to turn his positive traits into assets. He had four passed balls in 511 innings in the minor leagues and caught runners at a 36% clip as well, seemingly giving him the chops needed to stick in the big leagues.

THE FUTURE: Scouts are not bullish on Henry's bat, but his defensive prowess gives him a chance to be the kind of glove-first catcher who carves out a career as a backup and hits toward the bottom of a lineup.

Year	Age	Club (Level)	Lge	AVG	G	AB	R	H	2B	3B	HR	RBI	BB	SO	SB	OBP	SLG
2021	24	Biloxi (AA)	South	.315	30	111	11	35	5	1	1	10	12	32	0	.392	.405
	24	Nashville (AAA)	East	.262	19	61	7	16	3	0	1	9	4	17	0	.338	.361
	24	Jacksonville (AAA)	East	.188	22	69	7	13	2	0	4	8	10	26	0	.300	.391
	24	Miami (MLB)	NL	.267	5	15	0	4	1	0	0	0	1	5	0	.313	.333
Major League Totals (1 year)				.267	5	15	0	4	1	0	0	0	1	5	0	.313	.333
Minor League Totals (6 years)				.245	369	1297	171	318	71	5	37	193	126	429	3	.331	.393

24 JERAR ENCARNACION, OF

BA GRADE
40 Risk: High

Born: Oct. 27, 1997. **B-T:** R-R. **HT:** 6-5. **WT:** 239. **Signed:** Dominican Republic, 2015. **Signed by:** Albert Gonzalez/Sandy Nin.

TRACK RECORD: Encarnacion vaulted up prospect boards in 2019 with a big year, then was cost a shot at an encore by the pandemic. The 2021 season, too, didn't go as planned. Hand and leg injuries limited Encarnacion to just 65 games, spent mostly at Double-A Pensacola.

SCOUTING REPORT: Extremely tall players are always likely to have plenty of holes pitchers can exploit, and Encarnacion is no different. When he was on the field, he had trouble getting to his massive raw power because of extreme swing-and-miss issues that led to a 38.3% strikeout rate. As a player with big power at the expense of hittability, his skill set is not unlike that of fellow Marlins prospects Griffin Conine and Peyton Burdick. Encarnacion plays surprisingly good defense for a player his size, and his throwing arm is the best in the organization. He's an average runner who would fit just fine in right field, but the Marlins also exposed him to first base a bit this season.

THE FUTURE: Encarnacion is likely headed back to Double-A Pensacola to begin next season, when he'll work on unlocking the raw power he's shown in the past. He fits best as a powerful backup outfielder.

Year	Age	Club (Level)	Lge	AVG	G	AB	R	H	2B	3B	HR	RBI	BB	SO	SB	OBP	SLG
2021	23	Jupiter (LoA)	SEast	.200	2	5	1	1	0	0	0	1	1	3	0	.333	.200
	23	Pensacola (AA)	South	.222	63	230	24	51	12	1	9	28	24	99	5	.308	.400
Minor League Totals (6 years)				.253	315	1189	150	301	61	8	35	159	85	384	15	.309	.406

25 VICTOR MESA JR., OF

BA GRADE
40 Risk: High

Born: Sept. 8, 2001. **B-T:** L-L. **HT:** 6-0. **WT:** 195. **Signed:** Cuba, 2018. **Signed by:** Fernando Seguignol.

TRACK RECORD: When Mesa Jr. and his brother, Victor Victor Mesa, signed with the Marlins in 2019, Victor Victor was viewed as the prize. As their careers have played out, Mesa Jr., who got a $1 million bonus, has performed better. Being the younger of the brothers, Mesa Jr. spent his official first full year as a pro exclusively at Low-A Jupiter.

SCOUTING REPORT: Mesa Jr. showed hints of his potential in 2021, but the Marlins believe there's plenty more to come if he can tighten up his swing mechanics. Outside scouts noticed a significant bat tip, and internal evaluators worked with Mesa Jr. to correct the way he stepped in the bucket and alter the way he loads his hands. Before the changes, Mesa Jr.'s mechanics cost him balance and minimized the barrel accuracy he's displayed in games. His average exit velocity of roughly 89 mph was among the best in the organization. On defense, scouts see a player who can still fit in center field despite speed that has diminished slightly as he's gotten older and stronger. He got exposure to both outfield corners in 2021 as well, and his above-average arm strength would fit well in right field.

THE FUTURE: Mesa Jr. will move up to High-A Beloit in 2022, when he'll try to build on the improvements he's made since joining the Marlins. He has a ceiling of a second-division regular.

Year	Age	Club (Level)	Lge	AVG	G	AB	R	H	2B	3B	HR	RBI	BB	SO	SB	OBP	SLG
2021	19	Jupiter (LoA)	SEast	.266	111	428	66	114	21	11	5	71	33	102	12	.316	.402
Minor League Totals (3 years)				.272	158	604	105	164	30	15	6	95	57	131	19	.331	.401

26 CHRIS MOKMA, RHP

BA GRADE
40 Risk: High

Born: Feb. 11, 2001. **B-T:** R-R. **HT:** 6-4. **WT:** 210. **Drafted:** HS—Holland, Mich., 2019 (12th round). **Signed by:** Nate Adcock.

TRACK RECORD: Mokma was set to go to Michigan State before the Marlins signed him for $557,000. He got his feet wet in the Gulf Coast League in 2019 before spending all of 2021 with Low-A Jupiter.

SCOUTING REPORT: Mokma was a projectable arm coming out of the draft, and there's still a considerable amount of rawness to his game. He works with a full four-pitch mix fronted by a low-90s fastball that peaked at 94 this past season. Scouts who saw Mokma believe that he should add more velocity as he continues to get stronger, and also noted that his heater plays well when thrown up in the zone. His best offspeed pitch in scouts' eyes is his changeup, which is also the least frequently thrown of his secondary pitches. The changeup is a mid-80s offering which got swings and misses roughly a quarter of the time it was thrown. Scouts preferred his mid-70s curveball to his low-80s slider, seeing the former as potentially average and the latter as more of a fringy offering.

THE FUTURE: Given his Michigan roots, Mokma will likely be just fine in the early-season climate he could face in 2022 at High-A Beloit. He has a ceiling in the back of a rotation.

Year	Age	Club (Level)	Lge	W	L	ERA	G	GS	IP	H	HR	BB	SO	BB/9	SO/9	WHIP	AVG
2021	20	Jupiter (LoA)	SEast	2	7	6.60	20	20	92	122	17	28	78	2.7	7.6	1.62	.314
Minor League Totals (3 years)				2	8	6.09	25	25	105	134	17	30	90	2.57	7.71	1.56	.307

27 GRIFFIN CONINE, OF

BA GRADE
40 Risk: High

Born: July 11, 1997. **B-T:** L-R. **HT:** 6-1. **WT:** 213. **Drafted:** Duke, 2018 (2nd round). **Signed by:** Jason Beverlin (Blue Jays).

TRACK RECORD: Conine was drafted by Toronto in 2018, then traded to Miami in 2020. Conine is best known for his power, and he spent all summer battling with Royals prospect M.J. Melendez for the minor league home run lead.

SCOUTING REPORT: Obviously, Conine has a ton of power. His raw juice grades as nearly double-plus, and his maximum exit velocity of 116 mph was the second-highest in the organization. The next step will be to add some hittability to that immense power. Marlins player development staff acknowledge that Conine has holes he needs to close at the top of the strike zone and against offspeed pitches away so he can be more than a player who pulverizes fastballs. Defensively, he needs to improve his routes, jumps and angles to the ball and also needs to do better when it comes to setting his feet before throwing to bases. He's a below-average runner.

THE FUTURE: Conine is likely to return to Double-A Pensacola to continue working on becoming a more complete hitter while also sharpening his outfield defense. His power is alluring, but there's a long way to go before it will play at the highest level.

Year	Age	Club (Level)	Lge	AVG	G	AB	R	H	2B	3B	HR	RBI	BB	SO	SB	OBP	SLG
2021	23	Beloit (HiA)	Cent	.247	66	235	45	58	7	2	23	59	46	103	3	.382	.587
	23	Pensacola (AA)	South	.176	42	159	18	28	4	0	13	25	12	82	0	.243	.447
Minor League Totals (4 years)				.246	245	912	147	224	45	6	65	181	116	375	10	.340	.522

28 RONALD HERNANDEZ, C

Born: Oct. 23, 2003. **B-T:** B-R. **HT:** 6-1. **WT:** 155. **Signed:** Venezuela, 2021. **Signed by:** Fernando Seguignol.

BA GRADE
45 Risk: Extreme

TRACK RECORD: Venezuela has been the go-to destination for catching prospects in recent years, and the Marlins snapped up one of the best available in the most recent crop when they signed Hernandez once the pandemic-delayed international period opened on Jan. 15, 2021. Hernandez spent his debut season in the DSL, where he showed impressive command of the strike zone. **SCOUTING REPORT:** As an amateur, Hernandez showed off quick feet, plus arm strength that produced sub-2.0 second pop times and the quick footwork that should help keep him behind the plate in the long run. In the DSL and again at the Marlins' postseason instructional camp at their big league stadium, Hernandez showed a strong sense of plate discipline. During the regular season, that skill allowed him to have nearly as many walks (31) as strikeouts (32). As an amateur he showed doubles power that was expected to amplify as he matured, as well as the strong hand-eye coordination to translate into bat-to-ball skills. Hernandez is also bilingual and has already shown a strong baseball aptitude for a player his age. **THE FUTURE:** After debuting in the DSL, Hernandez should move stateside in 2022, when he'll begin to show exactly what kind of ceiling he has going forth.

Year	Age	Club (Level)	Lge	AVG	G	AB	R	H	2B	3B	HR	RBI	BB	SO	SB	OBP	SLG
2021	17	Marlins (R)	DSL	.209	43	134	30	28	5	3	3	26	31	32	3	.365	.358
Minor League Totals (1 year)				.209	43	134	30	28	5	3	3	26	31	32	3	.365	.358

29 KEVIN GUERRERO, OF

Born: April 17, 2004. **B-T:** R-R. **HT:** 6-3. **WT:** 165. **Drafted:** Dominican Republic, 2021. **Signed by:** Fernando Seguignol.

BA GRADE
45 Risk: Extreme

TRACK RECORD: Guerrero was part of the class the Marlins inked as soon as the most recent international period opened on Jan. 15, 2021. Guerrero opened his career in the DSL, where he hit for average and got on base but showed almost no power. **SCOUTING REPORT:** Given his 6-foot-3, 165-pound frame, it's no surprise that Guerrero's future will be based around the way his body develops. His goal in the coming years will be to pack on as much muscle as possible, and internally the Marlins expect him to be the type of prospect who takes a little while to bloom. Beyond simply getting stronger, Guerrero needs to tighten up his swing mechanics to help his limbs work more in sync with one another throughout the course of his swing. He's an average runner with the skills to stick in center field, but could move to right field if he slows down a tick. **THE FUTURE:** After getting his feet wet in 2021, Guerrero will move stateside in 2022, when he'll likely play in extended spring training and the Florida Complex League. Guerrero's development will take time, but he should be worth the wait.

Year	Age	Club (Level)	Lge	AVG	G	AB	R	H	2B	3B	HR	RBI	BB	SO	SB	OBP	SLG
2021	17	Marlins (R)	DSL	.260	39	131	24	34	3	1	0	11	23	33	13	.373	.298
Minor League Totals (1 year)				.260	39	131	24	34	3	1	0	11	23	33	13	.373	.298

30 CRISTHIAN RODRIGUEZ, SS

Born: Dec. 23, 2001. **B-T:** L-R. **HT:** 6-1. **WT:** 160. **Signed:** Dominican Republic, 2018. **Signed by:** Fernando Seguignol.

BA GRADE
45 Risk: Extreme

TRACK RECORD: Rodriguez was added to the fold on the strength of a projectable frame and strong defensive actions at shortstop. Rodriguez spent his first two seasons as a pro (with the pandemic in the middle) playing in the DSL and Florida Complex League. **SCOUTING REPORT:** Judging Rodriguez on his stats alone doesn't tell the full story. Scouts who saw him this year in the FCL saw a player with bat speed and power waiting to be tapped. His swing mechanics are complex, leading him to be late on hittable pitches as a result. The Marlins worked extensively with Rodriguez to increase the mobility in Rodriguez's hips to help him pull the ball with more authority. On defense, Rodriguez has split his time between shortstop and third base, and he's shown smooth hands and footwork and a strong arm at both spots. He needs to add more strength to his frame. **THE FUTURE:** After time at both of the Marlins' complexes, Rodriguez should move to full-season ball in 2022, when he'll be part of a large glut of young, talented infielders clustered at Low-A Jupiter.

Year	Age	Club (Level)	Lge	AVG	G	AB	R	H	2B	3B	HR	RBI	BB	SO	SB	OBP	SLG
2021	19	Marlins (R)	FCL	.218	46	156	20	34	12	2	0	18	15	59	3	.295	.321
Minor League Totals (3 years)				.229	110	410	68	94	24	6	4	43	52	137	7	.321	.346

MORE PROSPECTS TO KNOW

31 EVAN FITTERER, RHP

Fitterer was the Marlins' fifth-round pick in 2019 out of high school in California. He has a solid, projectable arsenal but was limited by injuries to just 30.1 innings in the regular season.

32 GEORGE SORIANO, RHP

Signed out of the Dominican Republic in 2015, Soriano whiffed 114 in 89.1 innings between two Class A stops. He works primarily with a low-90s fastball and a solid slider in the low 80s.

33 ANDREW NARDI, LHP

Nardi was Miami's 16th-rounder in 2019, out of Arizona, and has the look of a big league reliever. He pairs a low-90s fastball with glove-side life with an outstanding sweeper slider.

34 ANTONIO VELEZ, LHP

An NDFA in 2020 out of Florida State, Velez excelled in his first test in pro ball and earned marks for having the best control and changeup in the system. His low-90s fastball is amplified by vertical break that borders on double-plus, as well as a low-80s changeup.

35 JOSH ROBERSON, RHP

SLEEPER

A 17th-rounder out of UNC Wilmington in 2017, Roberson showed a mid-to-upper-90s fastball this season as he zoomed to Double-A. The fastball also showed excellent spin, induced vertical break and was accentuated by a deceptive approach angle. He pairs the fastball with a hard, high-spin slider. Roberson needs to improve his control and command to reach his ceiling.

36 BRADY ALLEN, OF

The Marlins' fifth-rounder in the 2021 draft showed bat-to-ball skills and above-average raw power in college, but an elbow injury shortly after signing caused him to not make his pro debut.

37 MONTE HARRISON, OF

Harrison has long been intriguing because of his tool set, but he's never hit enough to stick in the big leagues when he's gotten chances. He struck out at a 37% clip this year at Triple-A. If he is to capitalize on his elite defense in center field, he'll have to make contact more often.

38 BRYSON BRIGMAN, 2B/SS

Brigman showed solid bat-to-ball skills in Triple-A in 2021, albeit with little power. He's a tough out and has the chops to play up the middle, likely at second base, and should get a taste of the big leagues.

39 BENNETT HOSTETLER, C

Hostetler was the Marlins' 18th-round pick in 2021 out of North Dakota State. He acquitted himself well at two Class A stops and Marlins amateur scouts were sold on him as one of the sneakier bats in the class. Now, the organization will attempt to convert him into a catcher.

40 DYLAN BICE, RHP

A minor league Rule 5 pick of Miami's from 2020, Bice is a relief-only prospect who marries a mid-90s fastball with excellent vertical break primarily with a low-80s slider. He also throws a curveball and a changeup.

TOP PROSPECTS OF THE DECADE

Year	Player, Pos	2021 Org
2012	Christian Yelich, OF	Brewers
2013	Jose Fernandez, RHP	Deceased
2014	Andrew Heaney, LHP	Yankees
2015	Tyler Kolek, RHP	Marlins
2016	Tyler Kolek, RHP	Marlins
2017	Braxton Garrett, LHP	Marlins
2018	Sandy Alcantara, RHP	Marlins
2019	Victor Victor Mesa, OF	Marlins
2020	Sixto Sanchez, RHP	Marlins
2021	Sixto Sanchez, RHP	Marlins

TOP DRAFT PICKS OF THE DECADE

Year	Player, Pos	2021 Org
2012	Andrew Heaney, LHP	Yankees
2013	Colin Moran, 3B	Pirates
2014	Tyler Kolek, RHP	Marlins
2015	Josh Naylor, 1B	Guardians
2016	Braxton Garrett, LHP	Marlins
2017	Trevor Rogers, LHP	Marlins
2018	Connor Scott, OF	Marlins
2019	JJ Bleday, OF	Marlins
2020	Max Meyer, RHP	Marlins
2021	Kahlil Watson, SS	Marlins

Milwaukee Brewers

BY BEN BADLER

While the Brewers' farm system leans heavily on position players, the organization has created one of the better pitching development pipelines in the game.

That was evident in 2021, as the Brewers ranked third in MLB in fewest runs allowed and did it behind the strength of their homegrown arms. Corbin Burnes, a fourth-round pick in 2016, won the National League Cy Young award, while Brandon Woodruff (11th round in 2014) finished fifth. Freddy Peralta—a Mariners international signing who the Brewers traded for when he was a teenager in Rookie ball—posted a 2.81 ERA with 195 strikeouts in 144.1 innings. Devin Williams, a second-rounder in 2013, built upon his 2020 NL Rookie of the Year campaign as one of the game's most dominant relievers.

The Brewers got a glimpse of the next potential impact arm on the way when lefthander Aaron Ashby came up in August. Ashby was throwing 90-94 mph when the Brewers drafted him in the fourth round in 2018, but his velocity cranked up to 94-99 mph in 2021. Backing it up with a slider that's a wipeout pitch at times along with a quality changeup, Ashby is now the No. 1 prospect in the organization.

Ashby pitched out of the bullpen down the stretch and made a pair of relief appearances against the Braves in the NL Division Series, though the Brewers view him as a long-term starter and could have him follow the path of Burnes and Woodruff by using him as a reliever before stretching him back out into a starting role.

Milwaukee's pitching staff led the club to an NL Central title and their fourth consecutive playoff appearance, though they exited swiftly in the NLDS against the Braves.

The Brewers' offense ranked 16th in the big leagues in on-base percentage and 23rd in slugging, and while its farm system leans heavily toward position players, the reality is that there aren't many young hitters poised to make a major league impact in 2022.

Shortstop Brice Turang is the top position player prospect in the system. He should be up at some point in 2022, and while he has shown good strike-zone discipline and improved defense at shortstop, he slugged just .362 between Double-A and Triple-A last year. Center fielder Garrett Mitchell has more raw power, explosiveness and higher-end tools, though his unconventional swing makes him a more polarizing prospect. Center fielder Sal Frelick and second baseman Tyler Black—Milwaukee's top two draft picks in 2021—are polished college players who could move

Righthander Corbin Burnes led the Brewers' staff and took home the NL Cy Young Award.

PROJECTED 2025 LINEUP

Catcher	Jeferson Quero	22
First Base	Rowdy Tellez	30
Second Base	Brice Turang	25
Third Base	Luis Urias	28
Shortstop	Willy Adames	29
Left Field	Christian Yelich	33
Center Field	Sal Frelick	25
Right Field	Garrett Mitchell	26
Designated Hitter	Keston Hiura	28
No. 1 Starter	Corbin Burnes	30
No. 2 Starter	Brandon Woodruff	32
No. 3 Starter	Aaron Ashby	27
No. 4 Starter	Freddy Peralta	29
No. 5 Starter	Ethan Small	28
Closer	Devin Williams	30

quickly but probably won't arrive before 2023.

Venezuela has also become a strong pipeline of talent for the Brewers over the last few years under Mike Groopman, who led their international scouting before leaving after the 2021 season to become an assistant general manager with the Red Sox. Assistant international director Luis Perez and Latin America crosschecker Fernando Veracierto—both integral to the team's Venezuelan scouting—remain with the Brewers. Outfielder Hedbert Perez, catcher Jeferson Quero and outfielder Jackson Chourio all are top 10 prospects in the organization who signed out of Venezuela, with Chourio the only one who signed for at least $1 million. ■

DEPTH CHART

MILWAUKEE BREWERS

TOP 2022 ROOKIES	RANK
Aaron Ashby, LHP	1
Brice Turang, SS	2
BREAKOUT PROSPECTS	**RANK**
Hendry Mendez, OF	11
Russell Smith, LHP	14
Logan Henderson, RHP	19

SOURCE OF TOP 30 TALENT

Homegrown	29	Acquired	1
College	11	Trade	1
Junior college	4	Rule 5 draft	0
High school	3	Independent league	0
Nondrafted free agent	0	Free agent/waivers	0
International	11		

LF
Carlos Rodriguez (23)
Luis Medina

CF
Sal Frelick (3)
Garrett Mitchell (4)
Jackson Chourio (10)
Joe Gray (12)
Korry Howell (29)

RF
Hedbert Perez (6)
Joey Wiemer (8)
Hendry Mendez (11)
Tristen Lutz

3B
Zavier Warren (17)
Jesus Parra
Alexander Perez

SS
Brice Turang (2)
Eduardo Garcia (15)
Freddy Zamora (16)
Gregory Barrios (26)
Daniel Guilarte (27)
Ethan Murray (30)

2B
Tyler Black (5)
Felix Valerio (21)
Jheremy Vargas (22)
Hayden Cantrelle

1B
Thomas Dillard
Ernesto Martinez

C
Jeferson Quero (7)
Mario Feliciano (18)
Nick Kahle

LHP

LHSP	LHRP
Aaron Ashby (1)	Clayton Andrews
Ethan Small (9)	
Antoine Kelly (13)	
Russell Smith (14)	

RHP

RHSP	RHRP
Logan Henderson (19)	Abner Uribe (20)
Alec Bettinger (24)	Victor Castaneda (25)
Dylan File (28)	Taylor Floyd
Justin Jarvis	J.T. Hintzen
Max Lazar	Alexis Ramirez
Justin Bullock	Leo Crawford
Carlos Luna	Lucas Erceg
Miguel Segura	Zack Brown

1 AARON ASHBY, LHP

Born: May 24, 1998. **B-T:** R-L. **HT:** 6-2. **WT:** 181.
Drafted: Crowder (Mo.) JC, 2018 (4th round).
Signed by: Drew Anderson.

DANIEL SHIREY/MLB PHOTOS VIA GETTY IMAGES

TRACK RECORD: A nephew of former all-star righthander Andy Ashby, Aaron showed up at Crowder (Mo.) JC throwing in the mid 80s with a solid breaking ball, but he walked 56 batters in 66 innings split between starting and relieving as a freshman in 2017. Ashby's stuff ticked up the next year. He went from 88-91 mph early in the season to 90-94 mph later on. He struck out 156 batters in 74.2 innings and signed with the Brewers for $520,000 as their fourth-round pick. Ashby won the organization's minor league pitcher of the year award in his full-season debut in 2019 and was the Brewers' best pitcher at instructional league in 2020, where his stuff played up in short bursts to 94-97 mph. Ashby's stuff continued its upward trajectory in 2021. He piled up strikeouts but still had command issues while splitting time between the rotation and the bullpen in Triple-A Nashville. Triple-A East managers chose Ashby as having the best breaking pitch in the league, which he used to strike out 14.2 batters per nine innings, tops in Triple-A among pitchers with at least 60 innings. However, in his major league debut on June 30, Ashby didn't get out of the first inning, allowing seven runs (four earned) with three walks and no strikeouts. He had a 3.48 ERA the rest of the season, then pitched in a pair of playoff games against the Braves in the National League Division Series.
SCOUTING REPORT: Ashby has developed into a power pitcher from the left side whose fastball sits in the mid 90s as a starter and touches 99 mph. It has solid sink and run to it, but his below-average fastball command has led to harder contact against it and worse outcomes than his raw stuff would suggest. Ashby has a true putaway pitch in his slider, a plus pitch that flashes plus-plus at times. It's a sharp, biting slider with two-plane break, good depth and late tilt, making it effective against both lefties and righties. Ashby does a good job executing the pitch to make it look like a strike before it darts out of the zone and underneath barrels. Ashby's changeup has made significant strides to the point it's at least an average pitch and flashes plus against righties. It's a firm changeup at 87-91 mph, and at its best it has late diving action down in the zone. Ashby also throws a 77-81 mph curveball, though he rarely uses it and primarily goes to his slider when throwing a breaking ball. Ashby has the pure stuff to miss plenty of bats, but he also

BA GRADE	SCOUTING GRADES
60 Risk: High	**FB:** 60. **SL:** 65. **CHG:** 55. **CB:** 50. **CTL:** 45.

Projected future grades on 20-80 scouting scale

BEST TOOLS

Best Hitter for Average	Sal Frelick
Best Power Hitter	Joey Weimer
Best Strike-Zone Discipline	Brice Turang
Fastest Baserunner	Garrett Mitchell
Best Athlete	Sal Frelick
Best Fastball	Abner Uribe
Best Curveball	Cam Robinson
Best Slider	Aaron Ashby
Best Changeup	Ethan Small
Best Control	Alec Bettinger
Best Defensive Catcher	Jeferson Quero
Best Defensive Infielder	Brice Turang
Best Infield Arm	Eduardo Garcia
Best Defensive Outfielder	Garrett Mitchell
Best Outfield Arm	Joey Weimer

adds deception by varying the leg lifts and tempo in his delivery to try to disrupt the hitter's timing. **THE FUTURE:** Ashby has the stuff to develop into a No. 2 or 3 starter, but improving his fastball command will be critical to do so. The Brewers' plan is to develop Ashby as a starter long term, though depending on their 2022 rotation, they could deploy him as a reliever before transitioning him to a starting role as they did with their top three starters, Corbin Burnes, Brandon Woodruff and Freddy Peralta. ■

Year	Age	Club (Level)	Lge	W	L	ERA	G	GS	IP	H	HR	BB	SO	BB/9	SO/9	WHIP	AVG
2021	23	Nashville (AAA)	East	5	4	4.41	21	12	63	55	4	32	100	4.6	14.2	1.37	.227
2021	23	Milwaukee (MLB)	NL	3	2	4.55	13	4	32	25	4	12	39	3.4	11.1	1.17	.210
Major League Totals (1 year)				3	2	4.55	13	4	32	25	4	12	39	3.41	11.08	1.17	.210
Minor League Totals (4 years)				12	17	3.75	58	45	247	214	13	109	301	3.97	10.97	1.31	.233

2 BRICE TURANG, SS

Born: Nov. 21, 1999. **B-T:** L-R. **HT:** 6-0. **WT:** 175. **Drafted:** HS—Corona, Calif., 2018 (1st round). **Signed by:** Wynn Pelzer.

TRACK RECORD: Turang had buzz as the potential top overall pick in the 2018 draft entering his senior year, but a middling season dropped him to the Brewers at No. 21 overall. Turang has rebounded to move quickly and reached Triple-A in 2021 as a 21-year-old, though he has yet to dominate at any level. **SCOUTING REPORT:** Turang stands out for his athleticism, plus speed and ability to control the strike zone. He tracks and recognizes pitches well, doesn't chase much and makes frequent contact with a flat swing path from the left side geared to hit line drives to all fields. While Turang has gotten stronger, he still has a slender frame and below-average power. Turang whips the barrel through the zone well with good bat speed, but he will need to drive the ball with more impact moving forward. Some believe Turang can develop into a 15-20 home run hitter as he gets into his physical prime and learns which pitches he can pull, but others are skeptical he will get there. Turang's most noticeable strides have come on defense, where he has proven himself a reliable defender at shortstop. He has good anticipation, moves his hands and feet well and has good body control. While some previously thought Turang might end up at second base, he has quieted those concerns by showing improved range to his left and at least average arm strength. **THE FUTURE:** Turang has the talent to be an above-average regular if he adds power. If he doesn't, he may be more of a utilityman or a low-end regular. He will open 2022 back at Triple-A and could make his major league debut during the season.

BA GRADE
50 Risk: Medium

SCOUTING GRADES:	Hitting: 55	Power: 40	Running: 60	Fielding: 50	Arm: 50

Year	Age	Club (Level)	Lge	AVG	G	AB	R	H	2B	3B	HR	RBI	BB	SO	SB	OBP	SLG
2021	21	Biloxi (AA)	South	.264	73	288	40	76	14	3	5	39	28	48	11	.329	.385
	21	Nashville (AAA)	East	.245	44	143	19	35	7	0	1	14	32	35	9	.381	.315
Minor League Totals (4 years)				.261	288	1063	178	277	46	10	10	108	174	218	64	.364	.351

3 SAL FRELICK, OF

Born: April 19, 2000. **B-T:** L-R. **HT:** 5-9. **WT:** 175. **Drafted:** Boston College, 2021 (1st round). **Signed by:** Ty Blankmeyer.

TRACK RECORD: Undrafted out of high school, Frelick developed into one of the most exciting players in college baseball at Boston College in 2021. The Brewers drafted him with the 15th overall pick and signed him for $4 million. Frelick got off to a quick start in his pro debut, hitting .329/.414/.466 in 35 games across three levels. **SCOUTING REPORT:** Frelick packs quick-twitch, explosive athleticism into a smaller, 5-foot-9 frame with plus-plus speed and high-end contact skills. He does a good job of hitting the ball where it is pitched, using his quick hands to pull fastballs up and in while shooting pitches on the outer third to the opposite field. Frelick has a small strike zone and doesn't expand much, with the bat-to-ball skills to make contact even when he does chase. He doesn't get off his best swings on pitches down, instead slapping the ball into the ground and relying on his wheels. Frelick has sneaky pop for his size and can pull a ball out when he gets a pitch up in the zone, but he doesn't project to be a power threat and will likely be a 10-15 home run hitter. An infielder in high school, Frelick primarily played right field his first two years at BC before moving to center field in 2021 and became the Atlantic Coast Conference defensive player of the year. He has good instincts and range in center field with fringe-average arm strength. **THE FUTURE:** Frelick has a chance to hit at the top of a lineup and play good defense at a premium position. He will likely start at High-A Wisconsin in 2022 and has a chance to reach Milwaukee by 2023.

BA GRADE
55 Risk: Very High

SCOUTING GRADES:	Hitting: 60	Power: 40	Running: 70	Fielding: 55	Arm: 45

Year	Age	Club (Level)	Lge	AVG	G	AB	R	H	2B	3B	HR	RBI	BB	SO	SB	OBP	SLG
2021	21	Brewers Gold (R)	ACL	.467	4	15	4	7	1	1	0	4	2	2	3	.529	.667
	21	Carolina (LoA)	East	.437	16	71	17	31	6	1	1	12	9	10	6	.494	.592
	21	Wisconsin (HiA)	Cent	.167	15	60	7	10	1	1	1	5	10	13	3	.296	.267
Minor League Totals (1 year)				.329	35	146	28	48	8	3	2	21	21	25	12	.414	.466

4 GARRETT MITCHELL, OF

Born: Sept. 4, 1998. **B-T:** L-R. **HT:** 6-3. **WT:** 215. **Drafted:** UCLA, 2020 (1st round). **Signed by:** Daniel Cho/Corey Rodriguez.

TRACK RECORD: Mitchell hit .349/.418/.566 as a sophomore at UCLA and got off to a strong start as a junior in 2020 before the coronavirus pandemic shut down the season. The Brewers drafted Mitchell with the 20th overall pick and signed him for $3,242,900. Mitchell made his pro debut in 2021. He dominated at High-A Wisconsin despite missing three weeks with a leg injury, but his performance hit a wall after a promotion to Double-A Biloxi.

SCOUTING REPORT: Mitchell immediately jumps out for his physicality and athleticism and has raw tools that grade out among the best in the minors. He's an 80 runner underway, is a plus defender in center field with good range and has a plus arm. Mitchell shows plus raw power in batting practice, but neither his swing nor approach allow his power to manifest in games. Mitchell has some choppiness to his stroke and struck out 27% of the time in 2021. Instead of an approach geared to drive the ball in the air, he often slaps the ball on the ground. Mitchell is a patient hitter—he walked in 17% of his plate appearances—but he will likely need a significant swing adjustment to be a more consistent offensive performer against upper-level pitching and better tap into his power.

THE FUTURE: Mitchell's defense at a premium position and offensive upside give him a chance to be an above-average, everyday player if he can modify his swing and approach, but the risk of whether that will materialize makes him a divisive player. He will likely head back to Double-A Biloxi to start 2022.

BA GRADE
55 Risk: **Very High**

SCOUTING GRADES:	Hitting: 50	Power: 50	Running: 80	Fielding: 60	Arm: 60

Year	Age	Club (Level)	Lge	AVG	G	AB	R	H	2B	3B	HR	RBI	BB	SO	SB	OBP	SLG
2021	22	Wisconsin (HiA)	Cent	.359	29	92	33	33	5	2	5	20	28	30	12	.508	.620
	22	Biloxi (AA)	South	.186	35	129	16	24	1	0	3	10	18	41	5	.291	.264
Minor League Totals (2 years)				.258	64	221	49	57	6	2	8	30	46	71	17	.388	.412

5 TYLER BLACK, 2B

Born: July 26, 2000. **B-T:** L-R. **HT:** 6-2. **WT:** 190. **Drafted:** Wright State, 2021 (1st round supplemental). **Signed by:** Pete Vuckovich Jr.

TRACK RECORD: Black was the Horizon League freshman of the year in 2019 and, after the 2020 season shut down due to the coronavirus pandemic, returned in 2021 to hit .383/.496/.683 with more walks (39) than strikeouts (25) for Wright State. Many scouts considered him one of the best hitters in the 2021 draft, and the Brewers selected him 33rd overall and signed him for $2.2 million. Black reported to Low-A Carolina after he signed and showed a patient approach, but he looked fatigued and out of rhythm at the end of a long year.

SCOUTING REPORT: Black manages his at-bats well with a keen eye for the strike zone. He doesn't chase much and makes consistent, quality contact when he does swing. Black starts his swing with a big leg kick, then whips his hands through the zone quickly. He stays inside the ball well, enabling him to handle good pitches on the inner third and use the whole field. He has a particular knack for driving pitches down in the strike zone. Black's strengths lie mostly in his on-base skills, but he has a chance to develop average power. Black is athletic—he also played football and hockey in high school—but he is a rough defender with clunky footwork and below-average range at second base. He's an average runner with a below-average arm after he had right shoulder surgery to repair a torn labrum in 2020.

THE FUTURE: Black has the hitting potential to be an offensive-minded, everyday second baseman if he can be just an adequate defender. He will begin his first full season at one of the Class A affiliates in 2022.

BA GRADE
50 Risk: **High**

SCOUTING GRADES:	Hitting: 55	Power: 50	Running: 50	Fielding: 45	Arm: 40

Year	Age	Club (Level)	Lge	AVG	G	AB	R	H	2B	3B	HR	RBI	BB	SO	SB	OBP	SLG
2021	20	Brewers Blue (R)	ACL	.500	3	6	4	3	0	0	1	2	6	2	2	.750	1.000
	20	Carolina (LoA)	East	.222	23	81	11	18	4	0	0	6	20	29	3	.388	.272
Minor League Totals (1 year)				.241	26	87	15	21	4	0	1	8	26	31	5	.426	.322

6 HEDBERT PEREZ, OF

Born: April 4, 2003. **B-T:** L-L. **HT:** 5-11. **WT:** 180. **Signed:** Venezuela, 2019.
Signed by: Reinaldo Hidalgo.

TRACK RECORD: The son of former major league outfielder Robert Perez, Hedbert trained in his father's program in Venezuela before signing with the Brewers for $700,000 when he was 16. He was so advanced that the Brewers brought him to their alternate training site as a 17-year-old in 2020 before he made his pro debut in the Rookie-level Arizona Complex League in 2021. Perez hit well in the ACL before a late promotion to Low-A Carolina as an 18-year-old, where he struggled as he slid into a free-swinging mentality.

SCOUTING REPORT: Perez's strength is in the batter's box. He has fast bat speed from a fluid, compact lefthanded swing and a good path through the hitting zone. Perez has added significant weight and strength over the last couple of years, driving the ball with easy, above-average power he taps into in games. He has a fairly sound idea of the strike zone for his age, but he gets himself into trouble trying to swing for the fences at times. Perez's speed and arm strength have regressed as he's added bulk, decreasing his chances of sticking in center field. He's now a solid-average runner with fringe-average arm strength. The Brewers will continue to develop him in center, it's more likely he heads to a corner long term.

THE FUTURE: The most optimistic projections see Perez as an offensive difference-maker with good defense on a corner spot, but he's many years from that ceiling. He is set to return to Low-A Carolina to begin 2022.

BA GRADE
55 Risk: Extreme

SCOUTING GRADES:	Hitting: 55	Power: 60	Running: 50	Fielding: 50	Arm: 45

Year	Age	Club (Level)	Lge	AVG	G	AB	R	H	2B	3B	HR	RBI	BB	SO	SB	OBP	SLG
2021	18	Brewers Gold (R)	ACL	.333	32	120	19	40	11	0	6	21	8	34	2	.394	.575
	18	Carolina (LoA)	East	.169	16	65	5	11	2	0	1	7	1	25	0	.206	.246
Minor League Totals (1 year)				.276	48	185	24	51	13	0	7	28	9	59	2	.330	.459

7 JEFERSON QUERO, C

BILL MITCHELL

Born: Oct 8, 2002. **B-T:** R-R. **HT:** 5-10. **WT:** 165. **Signed:** Venezuela, 2019.
Signed by: Reinaldo Hidalgo

TRACK RECORD: Quero signed for $200,000 out of Venezuela in 2019 and quickly emerged as one of the Brewers' best players in their class as well as one of the best catchers in Latin America for his year. Quero impressed mightily in his pro debut in the Arizona Complex League in 2021. He demonstrated advanced ability behind the plate, in the batter's box and an overall maturity beyond his years, but the year ended on a sour note when he had surgery to repair a separated left shoulder after the season.

SCOUTING REPORT: Quero earns high marks for his defensive skills. He's an athletic catcher who is quick and agile, blocks balls well with the soft hands and has the advanced receiving skills to comfortably handle high-octane stuff and steal strikes. He has a plus arm, too, that often records pop times into the low 1.9-second range in games. Quero is a smart player and has a vocal, high-energy style that endears him to managers. He has the attributes to become a plus defender, but he's not just a glove-only catcher. Quero has a solid grasp of the strike zone, good bat control and advanced contact skills with the ability to use the whole field. His average bat speed is a question mark, but he flashes average raw power when he connects.

THE FUTURE: Quero has similarities to Nationals catcher Keibert Ruiz at the same age. Teenage catchers carry plenty of risk, but Quero could be on the verge of a breakout at Low-A Carolina in 2022.

BA GRADE
55 Risk: Extreme

SCOUTING GRADES:	Hitting: 55	Power: 50	Running: 40	Fielding: 60'	Arm: 60

Year	Age	Club (Level)	Lge	AVG	G	AB	R	H	2B	3B	HR	RBI	BB	SO	SB	OBP	SLG
2021	18	Brewers Blue (R)	ACL	.309	23	68	15	21	5	1	2	8	12	10	4	.434	.500
Minor League Totals (1 year)				.309	23	68	15	21	5	1	2	8	12	10	4	.434	.500

8 JOEY WEIMER, OF

Born: Feb. 11, 1999. **B-T:** R-R. **HT:** 6-5. **WT:** 215. **Drafted:** Cincinnati, 2020 (4th round). **Signed by:** Jeff Bianchi.

BA GRADE
50 Risk: Very High

TRACK RECORD: Wiemer showed a promising mix of size, athleticism and tools in college at Cincinnati, albeit with an unorthodox swing and a middling .264/.379/.408 career slash line. The Brewers bet on his athleticism and drafted him in the fourth round in 2020, signing him for $150,000. After a slow start in his pro debut in 2021, Wiemer took off after a midseason swing adjustment and hit .295/.403/.556 with 27 home runs and 30 stolen bases in 109 games across both Class A levels. He continued mashing in the Arizona Fall League before a bruised left thumb ended his year.

SCOUTING REPORT: Wiemer's tools are among the best in the Brewers' system. He has plus-plus raw power and was able to tap into more frequently as a pro than he did in college. Wiemer's swing had a ton of moving parts as an amateur, and while there is still a lot of noise with his hands getting his swing started, he quieted a big leg kick and replaced it with a toe tap, which helped him be more consistent with his timing. Wiemer's swing-and-miss rates may increase as he faces better pitching, but he kept his strikeout rate to a manageable 22% in his pro debut and showed patience with a 13% walk rate. Wiemer has surprising speed for a 6-foot-5, 215-pound outfielder. He's a plus runner underway and can play center field, although right field is his likely long-term home. He has the attributes to be a plus defender in right, including an 80-grade arm.

THE FUTURE: Wiemer has the tools to be an impact player, but his swing still leaves some unanswered questions. If Wiemer keeps producing at Double-A in 2022, his stock could take a leap.

SCOUTING GRADES:	Hitting: 45	Power: 70	Running: 60	Fielding: 55	Arm: 80

Year	Age	Club (Level)	Lge	AVG	G	AB	R	H	2B	3B	HR	RBI	BB	SO	SB	OBP	SLG
2021	22	Carolina (LoA)	East	.276	75	268	53	74	11	2	13	44	45	69	22	.391	.478
	22	Wisconsin (HiA)	Cent	.336	34	128	33	43	7	0	14	33	18	36	8	.428	.719
Minor League Totals (2 years)				.295	109	396	86	117	18	2	27	77	63	105	30	.403	.556

9 ETHAN SMALL, LHP

Born: Feb. 14, 1997. **B-T:** L-L. **HT:** 6-3. **WT:** 215. **Drafted:** Mississippi State, 2019 (1st round). **Signed by:** Scott Nichols.

BA GRADE
45 Risk: High

TRACK RECORD: Small had Tommy John surgery at Mississippi State but returned to rank second in the Southeastern Conference in ERA and first in strikeouts in 2019 as a redshirt junior. The Brewers drafted him 28th overall and signed him for $1.8 million. Small made his full-season debut in 2021 and raced to Triple-A while posting a 1.98 ERA across 18 starts. He missed most of July and August with a strained tendon in his left middle finger, but made up the lost innings in winter ball pitching for Escogido in the Dominican League.

SCOUTING REPORT: Small won't overpower anyone, but he keeps hitters off balance. His high-spin fastball sits at 89-93 and his best pitch is his plus changeup, which he disguises to look like a fastball out of his hand before it parachutes underneath bats. Small is a competitive pitcher who leans heavily on his changeup and doesn't use his breaking stuff much, with a curveball and slider that are both fringe-average at times. Small will vary his leg lifts and the tempo of his delivery to try to disrupt the hitter's timing. Small was known for his polish and strike-throwing at Mississippi State, but his control regressed in 2021 with an overly-high 13% walk rate.

THE FUTURE: Small has a chance to develop into a solid back-end starter if he can find a breaking ball and rediscover his previous control. He should make his major league debut in 2021, possibly as a reliever given the Brewers' current rotation.

SCOUTING GRADES:	Fastball: 50	Slider: 45	Curveball: 45	Changeup: 60	Control: 50

Year	Age	Club (Level)	Lge	W	L	ERA	G	GS	IP	H	HR	BB	SO	BB/9	SO/9	WHIP	AVG
2021	24	Brewers Gold (R)	ACL	0	0	0.00	1	1	2	0	0	1		0.0	9.0	2.00	.400
	24	Biloxi (AA)	South	2	2	1.96	8	8	41	26	1	21	67	4.6	14.6	1.14	.184
	24	Nashville (AAA)	East	2	0	2.06	9	9	35	27	3	21	24	5.4	6.2	1.37	.216
Minor League Totals (3 years)				4	4	1.74	25	25	98	66	4	46	128	4.21	11.72	1.14	.192

10 JACKSON CHOURIO, OF

Born: March 11, 2004. **B-T:** R-R. **HT:** 6-1. **WT:** 165. **Signed:** Venezuela, 2021. **Signed by:** Fernando Veracierto/Luis Perez.

TRACK RECORD: Chourio was the top prospect the Brewers signed in their 2020-21 international class when the signing period opened. He got off to a slow start in his pro debut in the Dominican Summer League as a 17-year-old, but he finished on a tear and put together quality at-bats even when his numbers were down early in the year.

SCOUTING REPORT: Chourio is an explosive, quick-burst athlete. That explosiveness is evident in his fast, whippy bat speed, which helps the ball jump off his bat more than expected for a hitter with such a wiry frame. His five home runs were the most among either of Milwaukee's two DSL clubs, and he has physical projection remaining to grow into plus power. More than just a slugger, Chourio stands out for his ability to recognize pitches, manage at-bats and make frequent contact for his age. He has a chance to be an average hitter as he continues to mature and develop. Chourio signed as a shortstop, but his fringy arm strength doesn't fit at the position and he is more comfortable in center field, where he played nearly all of his games in his pro debut. He's a plus runner who glides around well in the outfield and has the attributes to develop into an above-average defender.

THE FUTURE: Chourio is still several years away, but he has a chance to be a power-speed threat in the middle of the field. He will make his United States debut in the Rookie-level Arizona Complex League in 2022.

BA GRADE
50 Risk: Extreme

SCOUTING GRADES:	Hitting: 50	Power: 55	Running: 60	Fielding: 55	Arm: 45

Year	Age	Club (Level)	Lge	AVG	G	AB	R	H	2B	3B	HR	RBI	BB	SO	SB	OBP	SLG
2021	17	Brewers2 (R)	DSL	.296	45	159	31	47	7	1	5	25	23	28	8	.386	.447
Minor League Totals (1 year)				.296	45	159	31	47	7	1	5	25	23	28	8	.386	.447

11 HENDRY MENDEZ, OF

BA GRADE
50 Risk: Extreme

Born: Nov. 7, 2003. **B-T:** L-L. **HT:** 6-3. **WT:** 180. **Signed:** Dominican Republic, 2021. **Signed by:** Gary Peralta.

TRACK RECORD: During the tryout process in the Dominican Republic, Mendez was a 5-foot-11 lefty with uneven hitting performance who projected as a corner outfielder. By the time the Brewers signed him for $800,000 on Jan. 15, 2021, his stock had climbed significantly, as he had grown to 6-foot-3, 180 pounds and showed impressive contact skills. That carried over into his pro debut, as Mendez hit well in both the Dominican Summer League and the Rookie-level Arizona Complex League as a 17-year-old in 2021, striking out in just 9% of his plate appearances.

SCOUTING REPORT: Mendez is a student of the game with a mature plan at the plate for his age, staying disciplined within the strike zone to draw more walks than strikeouts. Mendez has some unconventional components to his swing, which results in a lot of balls on the ground. Driving the ball in the air more will be important as he moves up, but he already hits the ball hard now with the bat speed and physical projection to grow into plus raw power. Mendez's offensive game will carry him, as he spent time in center field and right field in 2021 but projects as a corner outfielder long term. He's an average runner who likely slows down and has an average arm.

THE FUTURE: Mendez is polished enough to see Low-A Carolina as an 18-year-old at some point in 2022.

Year	Age	Club (Level)	Lge	AVG	G	AB	R	H	2B	3B	HR	RBI	BB	SO	SB	OBP	SLG
2021	17	Brewers1 (R)	DSL	.296	21	54	10	16	5	1	1	9	7	2	0	.391	.481
	17	Brewers Blue (R)	ACL	.333	19	63	6	21	4	2	0	10	10	10	3	.425	.460
Minor League Totals (1 year)				.316	40	117	16	37	9	3	1	19	17	12	3	.409	.470

12 JOE GRAY JR., OF

BA GRADE
45 Risk: Very High

Born: March 12, 2000. **B-T:** R-R. **HT:** 6-1. **WT:** 195.

Drafted: HS—Hattiesburg, Miss., 2017 (2nd round). **Signed by:** Scott Nichols.

TRACK RECORD: One of the most tooled-up, dynamic athletes in the 2018 draft, Gray also carried significant risk as a high school outfielder with a lot of rawness to his offensive game. Signed for $1,113,500 as a second-round pick, Gray struggled to stay on the field and performed poorly when he did play his first two years in Rookie ball. The 2021 season marked a turnaround for

Gray, who was excellent in his full-season debut with Low-A Carolina before slowing down upon an early July promotion to High-A Wisconsin.

SCOUTING REPORT: Gray's free-swinging habits got him into trouble early in his career, but he did a better job of managing his at-bats in Low-A, allowing his above-average raw power to play in games. His chase tendencies and swing holes became more of an issue after his promotion and after the season in the Arizona Fall League. Gray's defense never went into a slump. His speed and arm strength are both plus tools, with his instincts in center field giving him a chance to be a plus defender.

THE FUTURE: Gray's swing and miss might ultimately end up holding him back, but he's a much improved player from a year ago with power and defensive skills at a premium position that still make him intriguing. He likely returns to High-A Wisconsin to start the 2022 season.

Year	Age	Club (Level)	Lge	AVG	G	AB	R	H	2B	3B	HR	RBI	BB	SO	SB	OBP	SLG
2021	21	Carolina (LoA)	East	.289	51	190	40	55	15	7	12	53	33	61	12	.407	.632
	21	Wisconsin (HiA)	Cent	.219	59	215	32	47	7	2	8	37	20	70	11	.306	.381
Minor League Totals (4 years)				.226	165	592	105	134	31	10	25	108	84	192	32	.340	.439

13 ANTOINE KELLY, LHP

BA GRADE **50** Risk: Extreme

Born: Dec. 5, 1999. **B-T:** L-L. **HT:** 6-6. **WT:** 205. **Drafted:** Wabash Valley (Ill.) JC, 2019 (2nd round). **Signed by:** Harvey Kuenn Jr.

TRACK RECORD: The arrows were pointing in the right direction in 2020 for Kelly, who was one of the most electric players at Milwaukee's alternate training site. Then in November that year, Kelly had surgery for thoracic outlet syndrome. The rehab kept him out of action until July 13 and he pitched just 19.1 innings, showing promising stuff but struggling badly with his control.

SCOUTING REPORT: When he was healthy in 2020, Kelly showed a plus fastball that sat at 93-97 mph and touched 98 mph, a plus slider and a changeup that flashed average. By the end of 2021, Kelly was still showing a power fastball and at times a quality slider, but he had little ability to corral it in the strike zone. Much of that wildness was expected coming back from his operation, and evaluators noted that the physical struggles seemed to add a mental hurdle for him as well.

THE FUTURE: While Kelly's command needed tightening before the surgery, he had previously shown the potential to develop into a mid-rotation or better starter. He's much more of a wild card at this point, with more risk he ends up in the bullpen long term.

Year	Age	Club (Level)	Lge	W	L	ERA	G	GS	IP	H	HR	BB	SO	BB/9	SO/9	WHIP	AVG
2021	21	Brewers Blue (R)	ACL	0	0	0.00	1	0	1	0	0	0	0	0.0	0.0	0.00	.000
2021	21	Carolina (LoA)	East	0	1	6.88	7	7	17	13	0	16	24	8.5	12.7	1.71	.213
	21	Wisconsin (HiA)	Cent	0	1	54.00	1	1	1	3	0	3	3	20.3	20.3	4.50	.500
Minor League Totals (3 years)				0	3	5.47	19	18	51	42	2	28	72	4.94	12.71	1.37	.230

14 RUSSELL SMITH, LHP

BA GRADE **45** Risk: High

Born: Sept. 10, 1998. **B-T:** L-L. **HT:** 6-9. **WT:** 235. **Drafted:** Texas Christian, 2021 (2nd round). **Signed by:** K.J. Hendricks.

TRACK RECORD: Smith was a 38th-round pick of the Cubs coming out of high school as a projectable 6-foot-9 pitcher with issues syncing up his delivery. His time at Texas Christian cleared those problems up. Smith stepped right into Texas Christian's rotation as a freshman, missed the 2019 season because of Tommy John surgery, but once again impressed in the rotation in 2020 and 2021, going 7-3, 3.83 as a redshirt junior.

SCOUTING REPORT: It's hard to think of much better fits than giving the Brewers a crafty, unconventional pitcher with plus command of his fastball and changeup. Smith's plus changeup is something he's able to consistently keep down and away from righthanded hitters. He also does a good job spotting his average 90-94 mph fastball. If the Brewers can help him improve his fringe-average slider and/or help him find a little more arm speed (which could improve his slider on its own), he could go from being a useful multi-inning reliever/back-of-the rotation starter to a fast-moving mid-rotation starter.

THE FUTURE: The Brewers were very cautious about not overtaxing college pitchers who threw full seasons. Smith has yet to make his pro debut, but he could jump straight to High-A Wisconsin in 2022.

Year	Age	Club (Level)	Lge	W	L	ERA	G	GS	IP	H	HR	BB	SO	BB/9	SO/9	WHIP	AVG
2021	22	Did not play															

15 EDUARDO GARCIA, SS

BA GRADE
45 Risk: High

Born: July 10, 2002. **B-T:** R-R. **HT:** 6-2. **WT:** 188. **Signed:** Venezuela, 2018. **Signed by:** Reinaldo Hidalgo.

TRACK RECORD: Garcia signed with the Brewers for $1.1 million on his 16th birthday in 2018. A broken ankle limited him to just 10 games in 2019, then the coronavirus pandemic wiped out the 2020 season, so Garcia had yet to play much heading into the 2021 season. He spent most of 2021 in the Rookie-level Arizona Complex League before a September bump to Low-A Carolina.

SCOUTING REPORT: Garcia stands out most on the defensive side. He moves around well at shortstop, where he has soft hands, good footwork and a plus arm. He's a fringe-average runner with good instincts and body control, giving him a chance to be an above-average defender. Garcia shows the power potential to be a 15-20 home run hitter and did make some strides with his early-count swing decisions in 2021, but he still struck out in 29% of his plate appearances and has to do a better job managing his at-bats.

THE FUTURE: Garcia's first full season in 2022—likely starting in Wisconsin—should offer a more revealing look at his future and whether he can do enough at the plate to develop into an everyday regular.

Year	Age	Club (Level)	Lge	AVG	G	AB	R	H	2B	3B	HR	RBI	BB	SO	SB	OBP	SLG
2021	18	Brewers Blue (R)	ACL	.385	3	13	3	5	2	0	1	3	1	2	0	.429	.769
	18	Brewers Gold (R)	ACL	.238	33	122	24	29	10	3	3	24	9	40	2	.316	.443
	18	Carolina (LoA)	East	.333	10	33	8	11	4	0	0	7	6	13	1	.452	.455
Minor League Totals (2 years)				.275	56	200	41	55	18	3	5	37	22	64	4	.371	.470

16 FREDDY ZAMORA, SS

BA GRADE
45 Risk: High

Born: Nov. 1, 1998. **B-T:** R-R. **HT:** 6-1. **WT:** 190. **Drafted:** Miami, 2020 (2nd round). **Signed by:** Lazaro Llanes.

TRACK RECORD: Zamora didn't play his junior year at Miami in 2020 after tearing an anterior cruciate ligament in his knee during a preseason practice, but the Brewers still drafted him in the second round. Zamora's pro debut in 2021 got off to a slow start. He batted .245/.360/.283 in 28 games by the end of June, but from then on he hit .324/.424/.481 in his final 64 games.

SCOUTING REPORT: Zamora has the tools to stick at shortstop. He's an above-average runner with quick footwork who moves well laterally and has soft hands, along with a solid-average arm. He was error-prone in college and showed that at times on routine plays in pro ball, though some of that could have been getting back to game speed from his lost 2020 season. At the plate, Zamora controls the strike zone and makes frequent contact, albeit without much impact.

THE FUTURE: There's a path for Zamora to develop into a steady shortstop who hits toward the bottom of a lineup if he can produce more damage on contact. He likely opens 2022 with High-A Wisconsin.

Year	Age	Club (Level)	Lge	AVG	G	AB	R	H	2B	3B	HR	RBI	BB	SO	SB	OBP	SLG
2021	22	Carolina (LoA)	East	.287	70	268	58	77	13	1	5	40	45	57	9	.396	.399
	22	Wisconsin (HiA)	Cent	.342	22	79	12	27	9	0	1	9	12	19	1	.435	.494
Minor League Totals (2 years)				.300	92	347	70	104	22	1	6	49	57	76	10	.404	.421

17 ZAVIER WARREN, 3B/C

BA GRADE
45 Risk: High

Born: Jan. 8, 1999. **B-T:** B-R. **HT:** 6-0. **WT:** 190. **Drafted:** Central Michigan, 2020 (3rd round). **Signed by:** Pete Vuckovich Jr.

TRACK RECORD: Warren was primarily a shortstop at Central Michigan, though he spent some time behind the plate in college. Warren started to transition to catching after signing and played 20 games there in his pro debut in 2021, though he spent most of his time at third base.

SCOUTING REPORT: Wherever Warren ends up, his bat stands out the most. He has good rhythm and balance, solid bat-to-ball skills and good strike-zone discipline. Warren's on-base skills stick out more than his power, though he does make hard contact and could unlock more power as he learns which pitches he can drive. Warren's defense at catcher is understandably still a long way from being major league ready. He might continue catching in 2022, but it's unlikely he sticks there long term. An average runner with an average arm, Warren looked much better at third base, where he has quick reactions off the bat.

THE FUTURE: Catching can take a toll on a player's offensive game, so a move off that position could help Warren take off, even if it raises the bar for what he will need to produce at the plate.

Year	Age	Club (Level)	Lge	AVG	G	AB	R	H	2B	3B	HR	RBI	BB	SO	SB	OBP	SLG
2021	22	Carolina (LoA)	East	.251	53	191	34	48	8	2	10	30	33	49	1	.374	.471
	22	Wisconsin (HiA)	Cent	.267	36	135	21	36	7	1	3	18	18	32	5	.357	.400
Minor League Totals (1 year)				.258	89	326	55	84	15	3	13	48	51	81	6	.367	.442

18 MARIO FELICIANO, C

Born: Nov. 20, 1998. **B-T:** R-R. **HT:** 6-1. **WT:** 195. **Drafted:** HS—Florida, P.R., 2016 (2nd round supplemental). **Signed by:** Charlie Sullivan.

BA GRADE
45 Risk: High

TRACK RECORD: Feliciano made his major league debut in 2021, drawing an 11th-inning walk and coming around to score the winning run in a May 1 victory over the Dodgers. That was Feliciano's only big league plate appearance and little else went right for him during the year. A right shoulder impingement limited his playing time, and when he did get on the field at Triple-A Nashville, he struggled.

SCOUTING REPORT: While his numbers dropped in 2021, Feliciano has generally been an offensive-minded catcher when healthy. He has above-average raw power that he generates from a loose swing with some length to it, but his proclivity to expand the strike zone eats away at his productivity and leads to too many empty swings. Behind the plate, Felciiano is agile and athletic and shows a solid-average arm when healthy. That often wasn't the case in 2021, though, and his slower transfer led him to throw out just 19% of basestealers.

THE FUTURE: It's possible that injuries simply masked Feliciano's true ability last year, but the 2022 season will be critical for Feliciano to rebound on both sides of the ball. He should start 2022 back in Triple-A.

Year	Age	Club (Level)	Lge	AVG	G	AB	R	H	2B	3B	HR	RBI	BB	SO	SB	OBP	SLG
2021	22	Brewers Gold (R)	ACL	.360	7	25	7	9	3	1	0	4	1	6	0	.448	.560
	22	Nashville (AAA)	East	.210	32	105	12	22	2	0	3	19	4	26	1	.246	.314
	22	Milwaukee (MLB)	NL	.000	1	0	1	0	0	0	0	0	1	0	0	1.000	.000
Major League Totals (1 year)				.000	1	0	1	0	0	0	0	0	1	0	0	1.000	.000
Minor League Totals (6 years)				.253	337	1261	166	319	59	12	29	170	90	328	17	.312	.388

19 LOGAN HENDERSON, RHP

Born: March 2, 2002. **B-T:** R-R. **HT:** 5-11. **WT:** 194. **Drafted:** McLennan (Texas) JC, 2021 (4th round). **Signed by:** K.J. Hendrick.

BA GRADE
50 Risk: Extreme

TRACK RECORD: There was little debate over who the best pitcher in junior college baseball was in 2021. After a modest start, Henderson dominated all comers over the final two months of the season to earn pitcher of the year honors. He threw a seven-inning perfect game and led NJCAA Division I with 166 strikeouts. In the Junior College World Series, he made two starts, allowing one run while striking out 31 in just 16 innings.

SCOUTING REPORT: Henderson is a shorter righthander with a high-spin low-90s fastball that plays above average thanks to its hop and the lower approach angles that help get on top of hitters' bats at the top of the zone. His changeup is an above-average pitch with solid deception. His slider is not as developed yet, but it will flash average. Henderson has above-average control of all three pitches. It's that advanced control for his age and his remaining projectability that give him a shot to develop into a reliable mid-rotation starter.

THE FUTURE: Henderson will play the entire 2022 season as a 20-year-old, so he's significantly younger than most college draftees. He should head to Low-A Carolina to begin his pro career. There's reason to believe the best is yet to come as he should get stronger and throw harder as he matures.

Year	Age	Club (Level)	Lge	W	L	ERA	G	GS	IP	H	HR	BB	SO	BB/9	SO/9	WHIP	AVG
2021	19	Did not play															

20 ABNER URIBE, RHP

Born: June 20, 2000. **B-T:** R-R. **HT:** 6-2. **WT:** 200. **Signed:** Dominican Republic, 2018. **Signed by:** Elvis Cruz.

BA GRADE
45 Risk: Very High

TRACK RECORD: The Brewers signed Uribe out of the Dominican Republic for $85,000 in 2018, when he was an 18-year-old with a low-90s fastball. The next year, Uribe's fastball reached the mid 90s, and by the time he got to instructional league in 2020, he touched 101 mph. Uribe made his full-season debut in 2021 as a 21-year-old in Low-A Wisconsin, where he lit up radar guns with erratic control. That continued after the season in the Arizona Fall League, where he walked 17 in nine innings.

SCOUTING REPORT: Uribe is one of the hardest throwers on the planet. He tops out at 103 mph, sitting in the mid-to-upper 90s and regularly cracking triple digits. Some scouts thought his fastball was more hittable than the pure velocity would suggest, but Uribe has shown feel for a slider that could be an average pitch and he posted a 35% strikeout rate in Carolina. He has a changeup but rarely throws it. Uribe profiles best as a reliever, and to stick around in that role he will need to make massive improvements with his control. His feel for pitching is still raw and he has trouble syncing up his delivery, leading him to throw 14 wild pitches and issue 6.7 walks per nine innings in 2021.

THE FUTURE: Uribe's arm strength gives him a chance to develop into a power reliever, but he will have to tame his wildness to realize that potential.

Year	Age	Club (Level)	Lge	W	L	ERA	G	GS	IP	H	HR	BB	SO	BB/9	SO/9	WHIP	AVG
2021	21	Carolina (LoA)	East	1	0	4.01	17	4	33	24	2	25	52	6.7	13.9	1.46	.195
Minor League Totals (4 years)				6	2	4.79	36	6	62	49	3	46	80	6.68	11.61	1.53	.224

21 FELIX VALERIO, 2B/SS

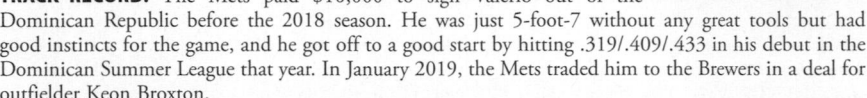

BA GRADE
45 Risk: Very High

Born: Dec. 26, 2000. **B-T:** R-R. **HT:** 5-7. **WT:** 165. **Signed:** Dominican Republic, 2018. **Signed by:** Anderson Taveras/Gerardo Cabrera (Mets).

TRACK RECORD: The Mets paid $10,000 to sign Valerio out of the Dominican Republic before the 2018 season. He was just 5-foot-7 without any great tools but had good instincts for the game, and he got off to a good start by hitting .319/.409/.433 in his debut in the Dominican Summer League that year. In January 2019, the Mets traded him to the Brewers in a deal for outfielder Keon Broxton.

SCOUTING REPORT: Valerio's best asset is plate discipline. His stature gives him a smaller strike zone that he has to cover, and he does a good job of not chasing much off the plate. He drew nearly as many walks (69) as strikeouts (71) in 2021, making frequent contact when he does swing with a 14% strikeout rate. Valerio was mostly a spray hitter early in his career, and while his power is still below-average, he added a little more loft to his swing and surprised with 11 home runs. An average runner, Valerio has played all around the infield, but he is a below-average defender with a below-average arm that fits best at second.

THE FUTURE: Valerio doesn't quite project as an everyday player yet, but his contact skills and plate discipline could offer sneaky value if he continues to hit at the upper levels.

Year	Age	Club (Level)	Lge	AVG	G	AB	R	H	2B	3B	HR	RBI	BB	SO	SB	OBP	SLG
2021	20	Carolina (LoA)	East	.314	85	309	71	97	24	3	6	63	54	49	27	.430	.469
	20	Wisconsin (HiA)	Cent	.229	29	118	19	27	13	0	5	16	15	22	4	.321	.466
Minor League Totals (4 years)				.302	222	047	160	256	67	5	14	119	120	113	63	.399	.443

22 JHEREMY VARGAS, SS/3B/2B

BA GRADE
45 Risk: Very High

Born: May 10, 2003. **B-T:** R-R. **HT:** 5-10. **WT:** 160. **Signed:** Venezuela, 2019. **Signed by:** Jose Rodriguez.

TRACK RECORD: Vargas signed with the Brewers for $650,000 when the 2019-20 international signing period opened on July 2, 2019. Vargas stood out more for his game savvy than his tools, and he continued to show that in his pro debut in 2021 in the Arizona Complex League.

SCOUTING REPORT: Vargas doesn't have a plus tool and he won't immediately stick out for his size or explosiveness. What he does have are instincts and feel for the game that are advanced for an 18-year-old. Vargas is a smart player who has a knack for slowing the game down and playing under control on both sides of the ball. There are some unconventional parts to his swing, but he manages his at-bats well, draws walks and sprays line drives, albeit with well-below-average power. An average runner with a solid-average arm, Vargas doesn't make the acrobatic plays other shortstops make, but he's a reliable, sure-handed defender with good instincts who committed just two errors in 2021, spending time at shortstop, third base and second base.

THE FUTURE: If Vargas can get stronger to be able to do more damage as he faces more advanced pitchers, he could develop into a utility infielder. He should spend 2022 with Low-A Carolina.

Year	Age	Club (Level)	Lge	AVG	G	AB	R	H	2B	3B	HR	RBI	BB	SO	SB	OBP	SLG
2021	18	Brewers Blue (R)	ACL	.230	44	135	22	31	2	3	2	20	29	42	8	.374	.333
Minor League Totals (1 year)				.230	44	135	22	31	2	3	2	20	29	42	8	.374	.333

23 CARLOS RODRIGUEZ, OF

BA GRADE
40 Risk: High

Born: Dec. 7, 2000. **B-T:** L-L. **HT:** 5-10. **WT:** 165. **Signed:** Venezuela, 2017. **Signed by:** Jose Rodriguez.

TRACK RECORD: Rodriguez was a prominent 2017 international signing out of Venezuela, landing a $1.355 million bonus. He has shown good bat control and moved quickly, reaching High-A Carolina as a 20-year-old in 2021.

SCOUTING REPORT: Rodriguez has a knack for finding the barrel with his short lefthanded stroke. He has good hand-eye coordination that leads to impressive plate coverage and a lot of contact. While Rodriguez has gotten stronger, he still has minimal power—he hit just one home run in 2021—creating questions about how he profiles at the big league level. That's especially true now that it looks like his future is in an outfield corner. Rodriguez played some center field last year but mostly played the corners. He has a chance to be a good defender on a wing, with average speed and good instincts.

THE FUTURE: Stretched thin in center field, Rodriguez will need to develop more thump to become a big league corner outfielder. His contact skills and instincts give him a chance though, and he will be one of the youngest players in Double-A next year at 21.

Year	Age	Club (Level)	Lge	AVG	G	AB	R	H	2B	3B	HR	RBI	BB	SO	SB	OBP	SLG
2021	20	Wisconsin (HiA)	Cent	.267	94	345	43	92	17	4	1	38	35	75	15	.336	.348
Minor League Totals (4 years)				.299	198	755	110	226	34	6	6	84	48	117	34	.346	.384

24 ALEC BETTINGER, RHP

Born: July 13, 1995. **B-T:** R-R. **WT:** 6-2. **WT:** 210. **Drafted:** Virginia, 2017 (10th round). **Signed by:** James Fisher.

TRACK RECORD: When the Brewers drafted Bettinger as a senior sign in 2017, his $10,000 bonus helped the team go over slot to sign Tristen Lutz, Brendan Murphy and Nick Egnatuk. Bettinger has proven more than just a money saver. He made an auspicious debut in early May. Called up to give a breather to a spent pitching staff, Bettinger gave up two grand slams and 11 earned runs in four innings, tying the record for the most earned runs allowed in an MLB debut.

SCOUTING REPORT: Bettinger was much better in his other three MLB appearances, but his awful MLB debut is a reminder of how he doesn't have much margin for error. He's the type of crafty, funky and deceptive righthander who relies on plus command to succeed. When he nibbles, it's intentional, as he has to stay on the edges of the strike zone. His 89-92 mph fringe-average fastball has good carry, but the lack of velocity limits its effectiveness. He relies on a cross-fire delivery to add deception. Bettinger's average mid-70s curve is effective if he locates it down in the zone, but hitters tee off if he leaves it up. He also spots his average 86-88 mph cutter, which helps keep hitters off his fastball. He has shown little confidence in a below-average changeup.

THE FUTURE: Bettinger is unlikely to ever be a regular member of the Brewers' rotation, but he can provide spot starts as well as serve as a low-leverage multi-inning reliever thanks to his durability and control.

Year	Age	Club (Level)	Lge	W	L	ERA	G	GS	IP	H	HR	BB	SO	BB/9	SO/9	WHIP	AVG
2021	25	Nashville (AAA)	East	3	7	4.75	21	18	96	104	15	26	98	2.4	9.1	1.34	.272
	25	Milwaukee (MLB)	NL	0	1	13.50	4	1	10	18	3	3	5	2.7	4.5	2.10	.391
Major League Totals (1 year)				0	1	13.50	4	1	10	18	3	3	5	2.70	4.50	2.10	.391
Minor League Totals (5 years)				17	27	4.45	87	76	411	406	45	118	400	2.58	8.76	1.27	.258

25 VICTOR CASTANEDA, RHP

Born: Aug. 27, 1998. **B-T:** R-R. **HT:** 6-1. **WT:** 185. **Signed:** Mexico, 2017. **Signed by:** Taylor Green

TRACK RECORD: The Mexican native was signed by the Brewers during the summer of 2017 as a precocious 18-year-old coming off nine appearances for Toros de Tijuana of the Mexican League. Castaneda skipped complex ball and was assigned directly to the Brewers Rookie-level affiliate Helena, where the righty made 14 appearances. He spent 2019 alternating between a starting role and the bullpen, working as Wisconsin's closer for a stretch of the season. Fast forward to 2021, and Castaneda is now focused on developing as a starting pitcher. Between High-A and Triple-A, Castaneda made 22 starts to middling results, and ultimately was left off of the 40-man roster this winter.

SCOUTING REPORT: Castaneda has a unique four-pitch mix, led by the unusual combination of both a changeup and a splitter. He throws each in any count to any handedness, selling them with good arm speed. His four-seam fastball sits 90-93 mph with moderate hop and arm-side run. It's an effective pitch in right-on-right matchups, but it's easily identified by lefthanders and subsequently hit. He works from a semi-windup, with a long arm stroke that dips back before delivering from a high three-quarters slot. This plays up the deception on his fastball versus righthanders, and allows him to sell his changeup and splitter off of his four-seam. He features a sweepy high-70s slider versus righthanders, but runs into too many barrels versus lefties for it to be an effective pitch in off-handed matchups. Castaneda's changeup and splitter are major league pitches now, but the right-on-right split-heavy nature of his four-seam and slider pairing leaves him stuck between a true identity as a starter or reliever. He's most likely destined for a multi-inning relief role with the ability to challenge lefthanded hitters with a variety of offspeed options.

THE FUTURE: A shorter righthander with some history as a reliever early in his professional career, Castaneda has work to do to shake the future reliever label. He'll likely head to Double-A to begin 2022, where he should continue to develop as a starter.

Year	Age	Club (Level)	Lge	W	L	ERA	G	GS	IP	H	HR	BB	SO	BB/9	SO/9	WHIP	AVG
2021	22	Wisconsin (HiA)	Cent	5	7	5.20	20	20	97	90	18	37	114	3.4	10.6	1.31	.243
	22	Nashville (AAA)	East	1	1	2.25	3	2	12	9	0	8	17	6.0	12.8	1.42	.205
Minor League Totals (4 years)				15	17	4.65	78	35	224	226	32	82	241	3.29	9.67	1.37	.259

26 GREGORY BARRIOS, SS

BA GRADE

45 Risk: Extreme

Born: April 8, 2004. **B-T:** B-R. **HT:** 6-0. **WT:** 180. **Signed:** Venezuela, 2021.
Signed by: Jose Rodriguez/Fernando Veracierto.

TRACK RECORD: Barrios was one of the top Venezuelan shortstops in the 2020-21 signing class when the Brewers landed him for $1 million in Jan. 2021. He made his pro debut in 2021 in the Dominican Summer League.

SCOUTING REPORT: Barrios was one of the top defensive shortstops from Latin America in his class. While not as explosive as fellow 2021 Venezuelan signing Jackson Chourio, Barrios is a smooth, instinctive fielder with a good internal clock. An average runner with solid-average arm strength, Barrios is light on his feet with good body control and soft hands. Barrios is a switch-hitter, though he's much better from the right side and might end up hitting exclusively righthanded. Most of his at-bats came as a lefty, dragging down his offensive production, though he also took some at-bats from the right side against righthanders. Barrios does have a keen eye for the strike zone and makes frequent contact with a line-drive approach. There's some physical projection for Barrios to grow into more power, but right now he's mostly a singles hitter with limited pop.

THE FUTURE: Barrios shows promise as a true shortstop who will need to develop his offensive game, but with contact skills and strike-zone judgment intact to build from. He should head to the Rookie-level Arizona Complex League for the 2022 season.

Year	Age	Club (Level)	Lge	AVG	G	AB	R	H	2B	3B	HR	RBI	BB	SO	SB	OBP	SLG
2021	17	Brewers1 (R)	DSL	.208	30	101	19	21	4	0	0	6	14	14	9	.302	.248
Minor League Totals (1 year)				.208	30	101	19	21	4	0	0	6	14	14	9	.302	.248

27 DANIEL GUILARTE, SS

BA GRADE

45 Risk: Extreme

Born: Oct. 29, 2003. **B-T:** R-R. **HT:** 6-1. **WT:** 165. **Signed:** Venezuela, 2021. **Signed by:** Trino Aguilar.

TRACK RECORD: Between Jackson Chourio, Gregory Barrios and Guilarte, the Brewers signed three Venezuelan prospects for seven-figure deals after the 2020-21 international signing period opened on Jan. 15, 2021. Guilarte signed for $1 million, though he didn't play in 2021 due to a left shoulder injury.

SCOUTING REPORT: Guilarte is built like Eduardo Garcia was when they signed him out of Venezuela, a wiry shortstop but with better tools at the same stage. He got faster leading up to his signing date, to where he's now a plus runner with a plus arm, with the defensive actions that give him a good chance to stick at shortstop. The lost 2021 season creates more uncertainty with projecting Guilarte's offensive game, though as an amateur he showed a solid idea of the strike zone and contact skills. Guilarte has good bat speed and the strength projection to grow into more pop, but his power is mostly to the alleys right now and his swing is geared more for low line drives rather than loft.

THE FUTURE: Losing the 2021 season hampers Guilarte's development, but he's with the tools and ability to play a premium position still intact.

Year	Age	Club (Level)	Lge	AVG	G	AB	R	H	2B	3B	HR	RBI	BB	SO	SB	OBP	SLG
2021	17	Did not play—Injured															

28 DYLAN FILE, RHP

BA GRADE

40 Risk: High

Born: June 4, 1996. **B-T:** R-R. **HT:** 6-1. **WT:** 205. **Drafted:** Dixie State (Utah), 2017 (21st round). **Signed by:** Jeff Scholzen.

TRACK RECORD: A standout at Dixie State, File lowered his arm slot to low three-quarters as a pro. That, along with his impressive control, has helped him exceed expectations. Milwaukee added him to the 40-man roster after the 2020 season, but File's 2021 season was somewhat of a struggle. He missed the first half of the season recovering from a stress fracture in his right elbow. When he returned, he was a little homer-prone at Triple-A Nashville.

SCOUTING REPORT: File is the epitome of a crafty back-of-the-rotation starter. He sits 88-92 mph with his fastball and can brush 94 at his best. That offering does not scare hitters, but he does hit his spots. File's average low-80s slider was his best pitch in 2021 and his slower, loopier mid-70s curve will flash average, but nothing he throws is above average. His fringe-average 82-85 mph changeup could use a little more separation from his fastball. File repeats his delivery well, and at his best, his lower arm slot is a tough look for righthanded hitters. File relies on his plus control and ability to mix four pitches to be effective. **THE FUTURE:** File's fringy stuff means his margin of error will generally be quite narrow. Triple-A batters hit .314 against him in 2021. He will likely need to rely even more on his two breaking balls going forward. He profiles as a useful Triple-A starter who can be called on as a fill-in when needed.

Year	Age	Club (Level)	Lge	W	L	ERA	G	GS	IP	H	HR	BB	SO	BB/9	SO/9	WHIP	AVG
2021	25	Brewers Blue (R)	ACL	0	0	3.38	2	2	2	5	0	0	3	0.0	10.1	1.88	.385
	25	Wisconsin (HiA)	Cent	0	1	7.20	2	2	5	7	1	4	6	7.2	10.8	2.20	.333
	25	Nashville (AAA)	East	2	4	5.27	9	9	42	53	7	12	36	2.5	7.6	1.52	.314
Minor League Totals (5 years)				26	23	3.88	76	71	381	413	39	79	332	1.87	7.85	1.29	.278

29 KORRY HOWELL, OF

Born: Sept. 1, 1998. **B-T:** R-R. **HT:** 6-3. **WT:** 180. **Drafted:** Kirkwood (Iowa) CC, 2018 (12th round). **Signed by:** Drew Anderson.

TRACK RECORD: Howell was not heavily recruited as a high school senior, so he spent two seasons at Kirkwood (Iowa) CC. Milwaukee selected Howell in the 12th round in 2018 and signed him for a well above-slot bonus of $210,000. After meager production over his first two years as a pro, Howell made the most of the 2020 shutdown, adding muscle to his frame and improving his plate approach. The efforts were repaid with a breakout season across High-A and Double-A in 2021.
SCOUTING REPORT: A converted infielder, Howell spent a majority of his last two professional seasons patrolling center field. He was moved to the outfield in 2019 and has taken to the position, while still logging time at his natural position of shortstop. In fact, versatility became a major part of his profile in 2021, as he started five or more games at five different positions during the season. He's a high-end athlete, with twitch and plus or better foot speed that translates to aggressive baserunning and range in the field. At the plate, Howell is still a work in progress, but he has an enticing combination of bat speed-driven power to his pull side, a discerning eye at the plate and above-average on-base ability. Howell's bat-to-ball skills are still below-average, leading to a high amount of swing and miss. Howell is an excellent fastball hitter, but struggled versus breaking balls and changeups in 2021. Many evaluators noted he'll need to improve his ability to hit spin and cut down on the whiffs in order to develop into an everyday regular.
THE FUTURE: A tooled-up and versatile slugger with the ability to fill in at a variety of premium positions, Howell was left off of Milwaukee's 40-man roster, indicative of the need for further refinement in his game. He'll likely return to Double-A Biloxi to begin the 2022 campaign.

Year	Age	Club (Level)	Lge	AVG	G	AB	R	H	2B	3B	HR	RBI	BB	SO	SB	OBP	SLG
2021	22	Wisconsin (HiA)	Cent	.248	69	258	65	64	12	4	12	36	34	88	20	.361	.465
	22	Biloxi (AA)	South	.235	28	98	18	23	5	1	4	15	12	44	4	.318	.429
Minor League Totals (3 years)				.250	216	752	133	188	33	8	18	79	97	250	55	.348	.387

30 ETHAN MURRAY, SS

Born: May 13, 2000. **B-T:** R-R. **HT:** 6-0. **WT:** 200. **Drafted:** Duke, 2021 (5th round). **Signed by:** Taylor Frederick.

TRACK RECORD: Murray was a Freshman All-American at Duke in 2019, when he started all 58 games at shortstop and hit .305/.391/.445. He posted similar numbers in 2021, when the Brewers drafted him in the fifth round and signed him for $272,500.
SCOUTING REPORT: Murray is a reliable defender at shortstop, where he plays under control with solid hands and an above-average arm. He's a below-average runner whose range and actions lead some scouts to think he might move off the position, possibly rotating around the infield as a utility type. Murray performed well at Duke because has a good grasp of the strike zone and got on base at a strong clip. He has a big, aggressive swing but has below-average power, so some scouts are skeptical on how his offensive game will translate to the higher levels.
THE FUTURE: Murray lacks a big ceiling, but he could develop into a solid utility player. He got a taste of Low-A Carolina after signing and could return there for 2022.

Year	Age	Club (Level)	Lge	AVG	G	AB	R	H	2B	3B	HR	RBI	BB	SO	SB	OBP	SLG
2021	21	Brewers Blue (R)	ACL	.227	8	22	1	5	1	0	0	3	3	2	0	.320	.273
	21	Carolina (LoA)	East	.232	28	112	19	26	3	2	3	14	17	29	3	.341	.375
Minor League Totals (1 year)				.231	36	134	20	31	4	2	3	17	20	31	3	.338	.358

MORE PROSPECTS TO KNOW

31 JUSTIN JARVIS, RHP

Jarvis can run his fastball into the mid 90s and flash a big curveball at times. He posted a 5.40 ERA and 5.0 walks per nine innings at High-A Wisconsin, but the Brewers saw enough to send him to the Arizona Fall League as a 21-year-old.

32 TAYLOR FLOYD, RHP

SLEEPER

A 10th-round pick from Texas Tech in 2019, Floyd is a low-slot reliever with a low-90s sinker and a slider that sweeps across the zone. It's an unusual look for hitters, which helps Floyd's stuff play up to post an 84-24 strikeout-to-walk mark in 56 innings in 2021, finishing the year in Double-A.

33 THOMAS DILLARD, 1B/C

The Brewers have tried Dillard behind the plate, but he spends most of his time at first base. It's a high offensive bar to clear at the position, but Dillard did show signs of life with the bat in 2021, hitting .247/.365/.444 in 108 games between High-A and Double-A as a 23-year-old.

34 TRISTEN LUTZ, OF

Signed for $2,352,000 as a supplemental first-rounder out of high school in 2017, Lutz has strength and raw power, but he has scuffled in games, hitting .217/.291/.362 in 64 games in Double-A in 2021.

35 MAX LAZAR, RHP

Lazar missed the 2021 season due to Tommy John surgery but should be back by midseason 2022. His upper-80s fastball has below-average velocity, but he had a sparkling 119-15 strikeout-to-walk ratio in 85 innings in 2019 because of his deception and ability to change speeds.

36 LUIS MEDINA, OF

A big-ticket international signing out of Venezuela in 2019, Medina is a corner outfielder with big raw power, but he struggled as an 18-year-old in the Rookie-level Arizona Complex League with an overaggressive approach and holes in his swing.

37 HAYDEN CANTRELLE, 2B

Cantrelle led Brewers minor leaguers in walks with 82 in 90 games between High-A and Double-A in 2021. He will need to show more than just a patient approach, as he hit a combined .171/.368/.307.

38 CLAYTON ANDREWS, LHP/OF

Andrews is primarily a reliever with a plus changeup that he sells well off a fastball that sits 89-93 mph and touches 95. But he also serves as an occasional two-way player with solid defense in center field, adding an extra wrinkle of versatility to his game.

39 JESUS PARRA, 3B/1B

Parra struggled as an 18-year-old in the Arizona Complex League in his stateside debut. He's a physical third baseman with a chance to hit for power, but he will have to cut down on his empty swings.

40 ERNESTO MARTINEZ, 1B

Martinez is a 6-foot-6 lefty whose raw power grades out among the best in the organization. He performed well in Low-A last year as a 22-year-old, but he has a long swing with holes that could get exposed against better pitching.

TOP PROSPECTS OF THE DECADE

Year	Player, Pos	2021 Org
2012	Wily Peralta, RHP	Tigers
2013	Wily Peralta, RHP	Tigers
2014	Jimmy Nelson, RHP	Dodgers
2015	Tyrone Taylor, OF	Brewers
2016	Orlando Arcia, SS	Braves
2017	Lewis Brinson, OF	Marlins
2018	Lewis Brinson, OF	Marlins
2019	Keston Hiura, 2B	Brewers
2020	Brice Turang, SS	Brewers
2021	Brice Turang, SS	Brewers

TOP DRAFT PICKS OF THE DECADE

Year	Player, Pos	2021 Org
2012	Clint Coulter, C	Cardinals
2013	Devin Williams, RHP (2nd round)	Brewers
2014	Kodi Medeiros, LHP	White Sox
2015	Trent Grisham, OF	Padres
2016	Corey Ray, OF	Brewers
2017	Keston Hiura, 2B	Brewers
2018	Brice Turang, SS	Brewers
2019	Ethan Small, LHP	Brewers
2020	Garrett Mitchell, OF	Brewers
2021	Sal Frelick, OF	Brewers

Minnesota Twins

BY CARLOS COLLAZO

After finishing first or second in the American League Central for four straight seasons, the Twins took a huge step backwards in 2021, finishing with a 73-89 record and landing in the bottom of the division for the first time since 2016.

The Twins were around league average as an offensive club but ranked No. 26 in baseball with a 4.83 team ERA. Pitching will be a question mark for the team moving forward, especially after trading righthander Jose Berrios to the Blue Jays at the trade deadline. Berrios was one of the most successful homegrown starters the Twins have developed in years, though he did bring back Austin Martin, the organization's new top prospect, as well as righthander Simeon Woods Richardson, who ranks No. 8.

Minnesota added two additional Top 30 Prospects in a July trade that sent Nelson Cruz to the Rays for righthanders Joe Ryan (No. 4) and Drew Strotman (17).

While the trades of Berrios and Cruz were certainly retooling efforts, the Twins managed to extend outfielder Byron Buxton to an incentive-laden, seven-year contract worth at least $100 million. That keeps the homegrown star in Minnesota through his age-34 season, and he was playing like an MVP contender in 2021 before injuries cut his season short.

To field a competitive team around Buxton and third baseman Josh Donaldson, the Twins will need plenty of reinforcement from a farm system that lacks impact talent at the top but is one of the deepest in baseball.

Martin and former No. 1 overall pick Royce Lewis are a solid 1-2 at the top of the system, but both have significant questions with impact and pure hitting ability, respectively. Beyond that, Minnesota is overflowing with righthanded starters and relievers who could impact the major league team sooner rather than later.

Jordan Balazovic (No. 3), Ryan, Josh Winder (6) and Jhoan Duran (10) are Top 10 Prospects who should impact the club in the short term, while 2021 first-rounder Chase Petty (No. 7), Woods Richardson and Matt Canterino (9) are a strong foundation beyond that.

The Twins also have several intriguing corner profile types, led by third baseman Jose Miranda, who hit .344/.401/.572 with 30 home runs and dramatically improved his prospect status by showing more power and a refined offensive approach.

Hitting on first-rounders and top international signings will be key for Minnesota moving forward to add more impact to a system strong on lower-upside depth pieces. Graduations of top prospects

Second baseman Jorge Polanco blasted a career-high 33 home runs in a rebound season.

PROJECTED 2025 LINEUP

Catcher	Ryan Jeffers	28
First Base	Alex Kirilloff	27
Second Base	Luis Arraez	28
Third Base	Jose Miranda	27
Shortstop	Royce Lewis	26
Left Field	Austin Martin	26
Center Field	Byron Buxton	31
Right Field	Trevor Larnach	28
Designated Hitter	Miguel Sano	32
No. 1 Starter	Jordan Balazovic	26
No. 2 Starter	Joe Ryan	29
No. 3 Starter	Josh Winder	28
No. 4 Starter	Chase Petty	22
No. 5 Starter	Simeon Woods Richardson	24
Closer	Jhoan Duran	27

like Alex Kirilloff, Trevor Larnach and Ryan Jeffers have impacted the system, as have struggles by recent first-rounders Aaron Sabato, a college first baseman taken in 2020, and high school shortstop Keoni Cavaco, taken the year before.

The Twins will be picking among the top 10 picks again in the 2022 draft, which should help, but development of high-upside, but risky young position players like Emmanuel Rodriguez, Noah Miller, Danny De Andrade, Kala'i Rosario and Misael Urbina as well as righthander Marco Raya will be important.

The Twins also have several players beyond the top 30 who could become big league contributors as soon as 2022. ■

DEPTH CHART

MINNESOTA TWINS

TOP 2022 ROOKIES	RANK
Jordan Balazovic, RHP	3
Joe Ryan, RHP	4
Jose Miranda, 3B/2B	5
BREAKOUT PROSPECTS	**RANK**
Steven Hajjar, LHP	13
Danny De Andrade, SS/3B	21
Marco Raya, RHP	30

SOURCE OF TOP 30 TALENT

Homegrown	22	Acquired	8
College	9	Trade	7
Junior College	0	Rule 5 draft	0
High School	10	Independent leagues	0
Nondrafted free agent	0	Free agents/waivers	1
International	3		

LF
Edouard Julien (26)
Misael Urbina (28)
Alerick Soularie

CF
Austin Martin (1)
Gilberto Celestino (20)
Jimmy Kerrigan

RF
Emmanuel Rodriguez (11)
Matt Wallner (25)
Kala'i Rosario (27)
Mark Contreras

3B
Jose Miranda (5)
Danny De Andrade (21)
Keoni Cavaco (22)
Seth Gray

SS
Royce Lewis (2)
Noah Miller (14)
Jermaine Palacios (29)

2B
Spencer Steer (15)
Yunior Severino
Anthony Prato

1B
Aaron Sabato (19)
Christian Encarnacion-Strand
Andrew Bechtold

C
Ben Rortvedt
Charles Mack
Noah Cardenas
Patrick Winkel

LHP

LHSP	LHRP
Steven Hajjar (13)	Jovani Moran (23)
Cade Povich	Zach Featherstone

RHP

RHSP	RHRP
Jordan Balazovic (3)	Jhoan Duran (10)
Joe Ryan (4)	Cole Sands (16)
Josh Winder (6)	Drew Strotman (17)
Chase Petty (7)	Chris Vallimont (24)
Simeon Woods Richardson (8)	Sean Mooney
Matt Canterino (9)	Yennier Cano
Louie Varland (12)	Casey Legumina
Blayne Enlow (18)	Tyler Beck
Marco Raya (30)	Ben Gross
Sawyer Gipson-Long	

1 AUSTIN MARTIN, OF/SS

Born: March 23, 1999. **B-T:** R-R. **HT:** 6-0. **WT:** 185.
Drafted: Vanderbilt, 2020 (1st round).
Signed by: Nate Murrie (Blue Jays).

TRACK RECORD: A standout collegian and All-American at Vanderbilt, Martin was in the conversation to be the No. 1 overall pick in the 2020 draft, as teams liked his bat even if they debated where he'd end up playing defensively. The Blue Jays were excited to see him fall to No. 5 overall, where they signed him for $7,000,825—the second-biggest bonus of the class. The Blue Jays traded Martin and righthander Simeon Woods Richardson to the Twins in his first pro season to acquire righthander Jose Berrios in July 2021. Martin was assigned to Double-A, where he showed excellent on-base ability, though scouts wondered about his overall impact and future defensive home.

SCOUTING REPORT: Martin developed a reputation as one of the best pure hitters in his draft class, and that hitting ability and on-base skills create a strong foundation for his value as a player. Scouts noted that Martin's bat path got longer and his hand load got more complicated, which created some timing issues this season compared to a simple and quick-firing path in college. He continued to show above-average bat speed, but scouts internally and externally wonder what sort of power Martin will grow into. His exit velocities were below-average and he totaled just 25 extra-base hits in 418 plate appearances. Gaining more strength and hitting the ball with authority more frequently will determine whether Martin becomes an impact regular or more of an average, everyday type player. His best offensive attribute might be his plate discipline and batting eye. Martin's .414 on-base percentage was the 10th-best mark among upper-level hitters with 300 plate appearances in 2021. Of the top 25 hitters in that category, the 22-year-old Martin was the youngest. He rarely expands the zone and chases bad pitches. Martin is a strong athlete with above-average running ability who can put pressure on opposing teams on the bases, but his future defensive home is still in question. He split time equally between shortstop and center field this season but is a much more instinctive and natural defender in the outfield, where his throwing struggles are less of an issue. His arm strength is fine, and Martin has received solid feedback on his glove work and range at shortstop, but he struggles to set himself up well on throws and his accuracy has been problematic dating back to college. Because of that, many scouts think Martin

EDDIE KELLY/PROLOOK PHOTOS

BA GRADE	SCOUTING GRADES
60 Risk: High	Hit: 65. Power: 50. Run: 55. Field: 50. Arm: 50.

Projected future grades on 20-80 scouting scale

BEST TOOLS

Best Hitter for Average	Austin Martin
Best Power Hitter	Jose Miranda
Best Strike-Zone Discipline	Austin Martin
Fastest Baserunner	Royce Lewis
Best Athlete	Royce Lewis
Best Fastball	Chase Petty
Best Curveball	Jordan Balazovic
Best Slider	Josh Winder
Best Changeup	Simeon Woods Richardson
Best Control	Joe Ryan
Best Defensive Catcher	Ben Rortvedt
Best Defensive Infielder	Jermaine Palacios
Best Infield Arm	Jermaine Palacios
Best Defensive Outfielder	Austin Martin
Best Outfield Arm	Emmanuel Rodriguez

will wind up in the outfield, where he'll be more good than great in center and where his power output could make him a tougher offensive profile if he has to move to left field.

THE FUTURE: Martin's bat-to-ball skills and batting eye give him impressive carrying traits that will make a big league role in some capacity extremely likely. The biggest question moving forward is how much impact he can make at the plate. The development of his currently below-average power will be crucial to determining if Martin is just a fine regular or an impact, 60 grade-caliber hitter. ■

Year	Age	Club (Level)	Lge	AVG	G	AB	R	H	2B	3B	HR	RBI	BB	SO	SB	OBP	SLG
2021	22	New Hampshire (AA)	NEast	.281	56	196	43	55	10	2	2	16	37	53	9	.424	.383
	22	Wichita (AA)	Cent	.254	37	134	24	34	8	0	3	19	23	30	5	.399	.381
Minor League Totals (2 years)				.270	93	330	67	89	18	2	5	35	60	83	14	.414	.382

2 ROYCE LEWIS, SS

Born: June 5, 1999. **B-T:** R-R. **HT:** 6-2. **WT:** 200. **Drafted:** HS—San Juan Capistrano, Calif., 2017 (1st round). **Signed by:** John Leavitt.

TRACK RECORD: Lewis has had a bit of an up-and-down minor league career since going No. 1 overall in the 2017 draft. He hit well and showed developing power in the lower levels of the minors in 2017-18 before struggling with consistency at the plate in 2019 when he made his way to Double-A. After the season in 2019, Lewis took off in the Arizona Fall League, where he was named MVP. He missed the 2021 season with a torn right anterior cruciate ligament.

SCOUTING REPORT: If you're just looking at overall upside, it would be hard to take any player in Minnesota's system over Lewis. He has plenty of bat speed, plus raw power, elite range and quickness with 70-grade running ability when healthy. He was also showing progress defensively at shortstop the last time scouts saw him regularly playing—with above-average potential at the game's most valued non-catching position. However, Lewis also comes with plenty of question marks, and missing the last two seasons due to the Covid-19 pandemic and a knee injury have only made him tougher to figure out. Lewis has plenty of moving parts in his swing that have led to inconsistencies, and he's also gotten pull-happy and had trouble covering the outer half of the plate. He's a versatile defender who has also played third, second and center—with plus defensive potential in the outfield.

THE FUTURE: Perhaps no player in Minnesota's system could have used a full 2021 season more than Lewis, but he'll get back to action in 2022, where he'll look to have his first full season in the upper minors and continue refining his approach at the plate.

SCOUTING GRADES:	Hitting: 45	Power: 55	Running: 70	Fielding: 55	Arm: 55

Year	Age	Club (Level)	Lge	AVG	G	AB	R	H	2B	3B	HR	RBI	BB	SO	SB	OBP	SLG
2021	22	Did not play—injured															
Minor League Totals (4 years)				.266	302	1204	210	320	63	10	30	150	106	240	68	.331	.409

BA GRADE
60 Risk: Extreme

3 JORDAN BALAZOVIC, RHP

Born: Sept. 17, 1998. **B-T:** R-R. **HT:** 6-5. **WT:** 215. **Drafted:** HS—Mississauga, Ont., 2016 (5th round). **Signed by:** Walt Burrows.

TRACK RECORD: The Twins liked Balazovic's physical upside and developing fastball out of high school, and they signed the top-ranked Canadian prospect in the 2016 class to a $515,000 bonus in the fifth round. The big righthander made the Futures Game in 2019, and after being sidelined early in 2021 due to a back injury, pitched well in a shortened season in his first try at Double-A.

SCOUTING REPORT: Balazovic has a solid blend of three pitches and a north-south approach that could play up thanks to a funky delivery that features a high front side and some length in the back of his arm action. While some scouts might be bothered by his forearm flying out, he does a good job getting on time at foot strike and has generally been an above-average strike-thrower, though in 2021 his walk rate jumped to 8.9%. Balazovic's fastball has continued to tick up and sat in the 95-96 mph range. He establishes the zone well with the pitch and uses a low-80s, 12-to-6 curveball and upper-80s split-changeup down in the zone off of it. Scouts thought he added more depth to the breaking ball this year and it could be a 55-grade offering, while the changeup needs more refinement to become above-average but is a fine third offering for now.

THE FUTURE: Balazovic looks like a solid No. 3 starter who will find success more by spotting his fastball up in the zone and successfully pairing his secondaries down. There's no one wipeout offering here yet, but his pitch mix works well in tandem. He could make his big league debut in 2022 if he stays healthy.

BA GRADE
55 Risk: High

SCOUTING GRADES:	Fastball: 55	Curveball: 55	Changeup: 50	Control: 55

Year	Age	Club (Level)	Lge	W	L	ERA	G	GS	IP	H	HR	BB	SO	BB/9	SO/9	WHIP	AVG
2021	22	Wichita (AA)	Cent	5	4	3.62	20	20	97	98	9	38	102	3.5	9.5	1.40	.255
Minor League Totals (6 years)				23	16	3.41	69	58	325	292	23	106	354	2.94	9.81	1.23	.235

4 JOE RYAN, RHP

Born: June 5, 1996. **B-T:** R-R. **HT:** 6-2. **WT:** 205. **Drafted:** Cal State Stanislaus, 2018 (7th round). **Signed by:** Alan Hull (Rays).

TRACK RECORD: The Twins acquired Ryan and righthander Drew Strotman from the Rays when they sent Nelson Cruz and minor league righthander Calvin Faucher to Tampa Bay in July. After the trade, Ryan made just two starts for Triple-A St. Paul in August before he was called up to the majors in September, where he pitched well in five starts.

SCOUTING REPORT: Ryan has always been a fastball-dominant pitcher. He used that pitch to power through the minors. While evaluators wanted to see him take strides with his secondaries, he continued to pitch overwhelmingly off his fastball (65.8%) with the Twins and continued to find success with it. The pitch has below-average velocity (91.2 mph) and spin, but a low slot and impressive carry up in the zone has allowed it to perplex and stymie hitters, nonetheless. Scouts did like the improvement of Ryan's slider, which he used 16% of the time in his brief MLB debut. The pitch comes in around 80 mph, and he generated whiffs with it 35.3% of the time. After that, Ryan also occasionally threw an 83 mph changeup and slow curveball. Ryan has an easy delivery with deception and has always been an above-average strike thrower who aggressively attacks hitters and challenges them in the zone.

THE FUTURE: Evaluators would still like to see Ryan improve his secondaries so he is better equipped to turn over a lineup, but his fastball has proven to be effective against big league hitters. Ryan profiles as a solid back-of-the-rotation starter with No. 3 upside with further secondary improvement. It's tough to be a one-pitch starter for long in the majors.

BA GRADE
50 Risk: Medium

SCOUTING GRADES:	Fastball: 65	Slider: 50	Curveball: 40	Changeup: 50	Control: 55

Year	Age	Club (Level)	Lge	W	L	ERA	G	GS	IP	H	HR	BB	SO	BB/9	SO/9	WHIP	AVG
2021	25	Durham (AAA)	East	4	3	3.63	12	11	57	35	8	10	75	1.6	11.8	0.79	.175
	25	St. Paul (AAA)	East	0	0	2.00	2	2	9	5	1	2	17	2.0	17.0	0.78	.161
	25	Minnesota (MLB)	AL	2	1	4.05	5	5	26	16	4	5	30	1.7	10.1	0.79	.168
Major League Totals (1 year)				2	1	4.05	5	5	26	16	4	5	30	1.69	10.13	0.79	.168
Minor League Totals (4 years)				15	8	2.67	50	42	226	143	19	53	326	2.11	12.98	0.87	.178

5 JOSE MIRANDA, 3B/2B

Born: June 29, 1998. **B-T:** R-R. **HT:** 6-2. **WT:** 210. **Drafted:** HS—Guaynabo, P.R., 2016 (2nd round). **Signed by:** Freddie Thon.

TRACK RECORD: Miranda showed a solid approach and feel for hitting out of high school in 2016, when he was part of a deep Puerto Rican infield class. The Twins signed him for $775,000 in the second round and he flashed offensive potential at times in the minors before having a breakout 2021 campaign. He led the minors in hits and was one of just two players with 30 or more home runs and doubles, along with Royals shortstop Bobby Witt Jr.

SCOUTING REPORT: Miranda's success in 2021 stems in large part from a more mature, selective approach at the plate. He did a better job narrowing the strike zone and being more selective for pitches he could drive early in counts, while still showing impressive bat-to-ball ability to stay alive on pitcher's pitches when behind, and showed solid production against breaking balls. Miranda has plus raw power and averaged 90.2 mph exit velocity this year, while topping out around 113 mph. Scouts seem split on whether he'll be a hit-over-power bat or vice versa, but he has the strength and contact ability for either depending on his approach. Miranda is a bat-first prospect who is limited defensively. He's a below-average athlete who might be a 30-grade runner, which means third base or first base might be a better fit than second. He does have plus arm strength and solid hands, so he'll convert what comes to him, but overall it's a below-average defensive profile.

THE FUTURE: The Twins have a number of multi-position, corner-type bats and now Miranda is solidly in that group and should make his major league debut in 2022.

BA GRADE
50 Risk: Medium

MIKE JANES/FOUR SEAM IMAGES

SCOUTING GRADES:	Hitting: 55	Power: 55	Running: 30	Fielding: 40	Arm: 55

Year	Age	Club (Level)	Lge	AVG	G	AB	R	H	2B	3B	HR	RBI	BB	SO	SB	OBP	SLG
2021	23	Wichita (AA)	Cent	.345	47	194	36	67	8	0	13	38	17	25	4	.408	.588
	23	St. Paul (AAA)	East	.343	80	341	61	117	24	0	17	56	25	49	0	.397	.563
Minor League Totals (6 years)				.282	486	1891	264	534	100	5	66	294	132	250	10	.340	.445

6 JOSH WINDER, RHP

Born: Oct. 11, 1996. **B-T:** R-R. **HT:** 6-5. **WT:** 210. **Drafted:** Virginia Military Institute, 2018 (7th round). **Signed by:** Matt Williams.

TRACK RECORD: Winder was one of the Twins' most improved arms during the shutdown 2020 season, improving his physicality and showing much better velocity during instructs. He pitched well in his first stints in Double-A and Triple-A in 2021, though he missed the second half of the season with shoulder fatigue.

SCOUTING REPORT: Winder is a big and athletic righthander who has always thrown strikes, and now his improved stuff across the board is yielding more strikeouts, with a career-best 10.0 K/9 this season. His fastball sits around 95 mph and touches 98. He pairs that fastball with three solid or better secondaries. The Twins love Winder's mid-80s slider, which has cutter shape and was his most-used secondary this year, but he also throws a firm upper-80s changeup that generates tons of whiffs and gets plus grades from scouts. He also throws a 12-to-6 curve in the low 80s but uses the pitch more frequently against lefthanded hitters. With his improved stuff, Winder has continued to throw strikes and showcase impressive feel for pitching, and he walked just 1.6 batters per nine across both levels in 2021.

THE FUTURE: If Winder were healthy, his combination of size, stuff and command would make for a compelling case as the organization's top pitching prospect. He's still solidly in the mix for that label even with his shoulder fatigue, and it does sound like the Twins are happy with his progress, but it adds a bit more risk. Winder has No. 3 starter potential.

BA GRADE
55 Risk: High

SCOUTING GRADES:	Fastball: 55	Slider: 60	Curveball: 50	Changeup: 60	Control: 55

Year	Age	Club (Level)	Lge	W	L	ERA	G	GS	IP	H	HR	BB	SO	BB/9	SO/9	WHIP	AVG
2021	24	Wichita (AA)	Cent	3	0	1.98	10	10	54	41	5	10	65	1.7	10.7	0.93	.208
	24	St. Paul (AAA)	East	1	0	4.67	4	4	17	14	4	3	15	1.6	7.8	0.98	.219
Minor League Totals (4 years)				14	3	2.82	44	44	236	185	20	49	240	1.87	9.14	0.99	.214

7 CHASE PETTY, RHP

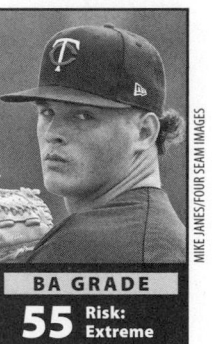

MIKE JANES/FOUR SEAM IMAGES

Born: April 4, 2003. **B-T:** R-R. **HT:** 6-1. **WT:** 190. **Drafted:** HS—Linwood, N.J., 2021 (1st round). **Signed by:** John Wilson.

TRACK RECORD: Petty was the hardest-throwing high school arm in the 2021 class, and after touching 102 mph he joined an exclusive group of prep flamethrowers you can count on one hand. With that velocity comes plenty of risk, as many hard-throwing high school righthanders have struggled to reach their lofty expectations, but the Twins were excited enough with Petty to make him their first prep righthander in the first round since Kohl Stewart (2013).

SCOUTING REPORT: With Petty's fastball and slider, he has a pair of pitches that have legitimate 70-grade potential. The fastball velocity speaks for itself, but scouts also loved the immense life on the pitch. Petty gets tremendous arm-side run and sink on his fastball which should make it tough for opposing hitters to barrel up, even if it's not the four-seam riding life that's currently popular in front offices. Petty didn't use his changeup much in high school, so it's a heavy projection pitch that he'll need to develop more feel with, but some scouts with Minnesota think it can become a plus offering as well. Petty is short but strong, and he's a plus athlete with impressive arm speed, although he gets erratic at times and there's plenty of effort in his delivery. The Twins have been working to keep Petty's arm slot up in the three-quarter range, where he's able to get bowling ball life on his fastball and two-plane, snapdragon bite on the slider. When his slot drops, his fastball runs too much and his slider gets sweepy.

THE FUTURE: Petty's upside is significant, but his specific player demographic is inherently risky and he'll need plenty of time to develop.

BA GRADE
55 Risk: Extreme

SCOUTING GRADES:	Fastball: 70	Slider: 70	Changeup: 55	Control: 50

Year	Age	Club (Level)	Lge	W	L	ERA	G	GS	IP	H	HR	BB	SO	BB/9	SO/9	WHIP	AVG
2021	18	Twins (R)	FCL	0	0	5.40	2	1	5	6	0	1	6	1.8	10.8	1.40	.300
Minor League Totals (1 year)				0	0	5.40	2	1	5	6	0	1	6	1.80	10.80	1.40	.300

8 SIMEON WOODS RICHARDSON, RHP

Born: Sept. 27. 2000. **B-T:** R-R. **HT:** 6-3. **WT:** 210. **Drafted:** HS—Sugar Land, Texas, 2018 (2nd round). **Signed by:** Ray Corbett (Mets).

TRACK RECORD: One of the youngest players in the 2018 draft class, Woods Richardson signed for $1.85 million as the No. 48 overall pick. He has already been traded twice in his career. The Mets sent him to the Blue Jays in a package for Marcus Stroman and the Blue Jays then traded him to the Twins in 2021, along with Austin Martin, for righthander Jose Berrios.

SCOUTING REPORT: A Top 100 prospect entering the 2021 season, Woods Richardson struggled in his first stint in the upper minors, posting a 5.91 ERA between Double-A New Hampshire and Wichita. He throws from a high arm slot that offers some deception, but his delivery has been described as mechanical and stiff at times, and his arm can be late at foot strike. Woods Richardson has been an impressive strike thrower despite that in the past,

BA GRADE

50 Risk: High

though his walk rate ballooned this year to a career-worst 5.7 BB/9 mark. His fastball sits in the low 90s and will touch 95 mph at peak, but it's not an overpowering pitch. It has cut action that allows it to tunnel nicely with an arm side fading changeup around 80 mph that earns plenty of plus grades and is one of the best in the Minnesota system. He also throws a steep, downer, mid-70s curveball and a slider (mostly to righties) a few ticks harder. Woods Richardson shows feel to land his breaking stuff and both have solid movement, but hitters have managed to track them well.

THE FUTURE: Woods Richardson profiles as a back-end starter at best who succeeds with precision and deception—as well as an out-pitch changeup—though some scouts think he'd be best served in a multi-inning relief role.

SCOUTING GRADES:	Fastball: 50	Slider: 55	Curveball: 50	Changeup: 60	Control: 60

Year	Age	Club (Level)	Lge	W	L	ERA	G	GS	IP	H	HR	BB	SO	BB/9	SO/9	WHIP	AVG
2021	20	New Hampshire (AA)	NEast	2	4	5.76	11	11	45	42	5	26	67	5.2	13.3	1.50	.246
	20	Wichita (AA)	Cent	1	1	6.75	4	3	8	6	0	8	10	9.0	11.3	1.75	.207
Minor League Totals (4 years)				10	15	4.21	48	44	177	159	12	62	229	3.15	11.62	1.25	.237

9 MATT CANTERINO, RHP

Born: Dec. 14, 1997. **B-T:** R-R. **HT:** 6-2. **WT:** 222. **Drafted:** Rice, 2019 (2nd round). **Signed by:** Greg Runser.

TRACK RECORD: Canterino ranked as the No. 34 prospect in the 2019 draft class as a productive starter with plenty of funk. The Twins signed him for $1.1 million in the second round and he's been highly effective on the mound in his pro career (1.13 ERA), but was limited to just 23 innings in 2021 after dealing with multiple elbow strains.

SCOUTING REPORT: Fans will love watching Canterino pitch thanks to his high-energy approach on the mound. He has an intense and effortful delivery, but he's always shown impressive touch and feel, and in pro ball his spin rates and extension have been exceptional. This year, Canterino pitched in the 94-95 mph range with his fastball and touched 97, but the induced vertical break of the pitch is what truly sets it apart and allows it to play up. Canterino

BA GRADE

55 Risk: Extreme

throws a hard vertical slider and a curveball with more depth in the low 80s. Both breaking balls have a chance to be solid-average or above-average. His best secondary might be a changeup that he improved dramatically after entering pro ball, a low-80s offering that has solid arm-side movement and depth. He has shown impressive command of his entire pitch mix and in his six starts before going down struck out 45 batters to just four walks.

THE FUTURE: Canterino's fastball quality, four-pitch mix and command give him middle-of-the-rotation upside, but his elbow injuries this year and the fact that he still hasn't pitched above High-A add plenty of risk to the profile. He has yet to pitch more than 25 innings in a season since being drafted.

SCOUTING GRADES:	Fastball: 65	Slider: 55	Curveball: 50	Changeup: 55	Control: 55

Year	Age	Club (Level)	Lge	W	L	ERA	G	GS	IP	H	HR	BB	SO	BB/9	SO/9	WHIP	AVG
2021	23	Cedar Rapids (HiA)	Cent	1	0	0.86	5	5	21	10	1	4	43	1.7	18.4	0.67	.135
	23	Fort Myers (LoA)	SEast	0	0	0.00	1	1	2	0	0	0	2	0.0	9.0	0.00	.000
Minor League Totals (3 years)				2	1	1.13	13	13	48	18	1	12	76	2.25	14.25	0.63	.110

10 JHOAN DURAN, RHP

Born: Jan. 8, 1998. **B-T:** R-R. **HT:** 6-5. **WT:** 230. **Signed:** Dominican Republic, 2015. **Signed by:** Jose Ortiz/Junior Noboa (D-backs).

TRACK RECORD: The Twins acquired Duran in a 2018 deal that sent Eduardo Escobar to the D-backs—who originally signed the massive righthander for just $65,000 in 2014. Duran trended up after joining the Twins organization, reaching Double-A in his first full season, but hit a roadblock in 2021 when an elbow strain limited him to just 16 innings at Triple-A St. Paul.

SCOUTING REPORT: Duran has a pair of offerings that have gotten 70-grade reviews in the past. His four-seam fastball touches 100 mph and sat 97-98 this year, while his sinker-splitter hybrid—which he has dubbed the 'splinker'— has a unique velocity and movement profile that combines the traits of both offerings and has racked up plenty of whiffs in the past. He also throws a power curve in the low 80s with big spin rates. The pitch looks like a real swing-and-miss offering at times, though he struggles to land it for strikes. Duran also throws a changeup in the mid 80s, but the pitch remains a significant work in progress. Duran has faced starter/reliever questions thanks to a delivery that regularly gets out of sync in addition to the fact that he lacks a softer secondary that could keep hitters off his fastball/splinker combo.

THE FUTURE: Duran likely would have been in the mix for Minnesota's pitching staff in the second half of the 2021 season if he were healthy. He reportedly threw well in the fall and will look to get back on track in 2022, where he'll try to refine his pitching at Triple-A and potentially make his big league debut.

BA GRADE
50 Risk: High

SCOUTING GRADES:	Fastball: 70	Splitter: 60	Curveball: 50	Changeup: 30	Control: 45

Year	Age	Club (Level)	Lge	W	L	ERA	G	GS	IP	H	HR	BB	SO	BB/9	SO/9	WHIP	AVG
2021	23	St. Paul (AAA)	East	0	3	5.06	5	4	16	16	1	13	22	7.3	12.4	1.81	.258
Minor League Totals (7 years)				23	29	3.99	82	80	390	364	24	144	388	3.3	9.0	1.30	.246

11 EMMANUEL RODRIGUEZ, OF

BA GRADE
50 Risk: Extreme

Born: Feb. 28, 2003. **B-T:** L-L. **HT:** 5-10. **WT:** 165. **Signed:** Dominican Republic, 2019. **Signed by:** Manuel Luciano.

TRACK RECORD: The Twins' top international target in the 2019 class, Rodriguez signed for $2.5 million but his pro debut was delayed by the canceled 2020 season. Instead, he debuted in 2021 in the Florida Complex League, where he posted a 124 wRC+ with 10 home runs.

SCOUTING REPORT: Rodriguez packs plenty of power into his lefthanded swing, and his top-end exit velocities were among the best in the system despite his age and modest frame. That power translated into games immediately, though it comes with a strikeout rate (36.6%) and a swing that borders on being too steep. Despite the swing-and-miss, Rodriguez does have a good idea of the strike zone, and despite a .214 average he got on base at a solid clip (.346) thanks to a 15% walk rate. Rodriguez is a solid runner now and is playing center field at an adequate level, but his plus arm strength could allow him to move to right field in the future if his speed backs up. He certainly has the power potential to profile there. Rodriguez has dealt with a few injuries over the past few years, including a hand injury and some back issues.

THE FUTURE: Rodriguez will try to cut down his whiff rate and could be ready for Low-A Fort Myers.

Year	Age	Club (Level)	Lge	AVG	G	AB	R	H	2B	3B	HR	RBI	BB	SO	SB	OBP	SLG
2021	18	Twins (R)	FCL	.214	37	126	31	27	5	2	10	23	23	56	9	.346	.524
Minor League Totals (1 year)				.214	37	126	31	27	5	2	10	23	23	56	9	.346	.524

12 LOUIE VARLAND, RHP

BA GRADE
45 Risk: High

Born: Dec. 9, 1997. **B-T:** L-R. **HT:** 6-1. **WT:** 205. **Drafted:** Concordia (Minn.), 2019 (15th round). **Signed by:** Joe Bisenius.

TRACK RECORD: A relatively unheralded draft prospect, Varland is a local product—he grew up in St. Paul and went to college there as well—who signed in the 15th round for $115,000. He turned in an exceptional first full pro season, winning the Twins minor league pitcher of the year award after posting a 2.10 ERA between Low-A Fort Myers and High-A Cedar Rapids.

SCOUTING REPORT: Varland's success has come with increased fastball velocity. After pitching in the 90-92 mph range as an amateur, Varland's fastball sat in the 94-95 mph range this season, peaking at 98-99 mph. It's a flat approach angle fastball that he throws for strikes well and earns plus grades. Varland's most-used secondary is a hard slider in the mid 80s that gets average grades. He also throws an average changeup in the upper-80s that has good sink and could improve in the future, plus an occasional, show-me curveball in the upper 80s with solid raw spin rates, but below-average scouting grades. Varland's been an average strike-thrower in the past, but this season he walked just 2.6 batters per nine.

THE FUTURE: Varland has the repertoire and control to be a back-end starter with his newfound fastball velocity and has a fallback option as a hard-throwing reliever otherwise.

Year	Age	Club (Level)	Lge	W	L	ERA	G	GS	IP	H	HR	BB	SO	BB/9	SO/9	WHIP	AVG
2021	23	Fort Myers (LoA)	SEast	4	2	2.09	10	8	47	41	2	16	76	3.0	14.5	1.20	.228
	23	Cedar Rapids (HiA)	Cent	6	2	2.10	10	10	55	41	4	14	66	2.3	10.7	0.99	.202
Minor League Totals (3 years)				10	5	2.10	23	19	112	91	7	34	152	2.74	12.25	1.12	.218

13 STEVEN HAJJAR, LHP

BA GRADE
45 Risk: High

Born: Aug. 7, 2000. **B-T:** R-L. **HT:** 6-5. **WT:** 215. **Drafted:** Michigan, 2021 (2nd round). **Signed by:** Jeff Pohl.

TRACK RECORD: Hajjar was a talented draft prospect dating back to his prep days, and a bump in fastball velocity during the summer prior to his draft year at Michigan helped raise his draft stock significantly. That stuff didn't hold during the spring, but Hajjar still showed a solid pitch mix and control—enough for the Twins to sign him for $1,129,700 in the second round.

SCOUTING REPORT: Where Hajjar's velocity settles into is probably one of the bigger questions for the big lefthander now. He pitched in the low 90s for the most part with Michigan, and while he didn't get into an official pro game this summer, he reportedly touched 97 and was sitting comfortably above 93 mph in bullpens with the Twins. Hajjar threw a curveball, slider and changeup in college, though he will likely use the slider and changeup the most at the pro level. His slider has been up to 87 and flashes hard, biting action at its best, while he's made tremendous progress over the last three years with a low-80s changeup that has impressive tumble. There's a bit of funk in Hajjar's delivery that could add some deception to his overall operation, and for the most part he's done a good job throwing strikes.

THE FUTURE: Hajjar has starter traits and back-end stuff now, though the quality of his fastball could tick his ceiling up.

Year	Age	Club (Level)	Lge	W	L	ERA	G	GS	IP	H	HR	BB	SO	BB/9	SO/9	WHIP	AVG
2021	20	Did not play															

14 NOAH MILLER, SS

BA GRADE
50 Risk: Extreme

Born: Nov. 12, 2002. **B-T:** B-R. **HT:** 6-0. **WT:** 185. **Drafted:** HS—Fredonia, Wis., 2021 (1st round supplemental). **Signed by:** Joe Bisenius.

TRACK RECORD: The younger brother of Guardians shortstop Owen Miller, Noah is a savvy defensive shortstop with an impressive baseball IQ. One of the better defenders in the 2021 prep class, the Twins signed him for $1.7 million to buy out his Alabama commitment and he impressed in his pro debut in the Florida Complex League.

SCOUTING REPORT: Slick defending is the calling card with Miller for the time being. He has all the intangibles to stay at shortstop in the long run, outside of foot speed. He has good instincts, a quick first step and an internal clock that's advanced beyond his age. He can make throws from multiple angles and arm slots and generally has a good understanding of when to let loose and when he can hold back on his throws. A switch-hitter, Miller is a hit-over-power bat currently who will need to add strength as he develops. Some amateur scouts thought he could grow into average power, but he's not there yet. His righthanded swing is freer and easier than his left side, so refining that left side will be key for his offensive development. Miller is an average runner.

THE FUTURE: The recent track record of Wisconsin hitters is quite good, and Miller will look to follow players like Gavin Lux, Jarred Kelenic and Daulton Varsho.

Year	Age	Club (Level)	Lge	AVG	G	AB	R	H	2B	3B	HR	RBI	BB	SO	SB	OBP	SLG
2021	18	Twins (R)	FCL	.238	22	84	11	20	3	1	2	14	9	26	1	.316	.369
Minor League Totals (1 year)				.238	22	84	11	20	3	1	2	14	9	26	1	.316	.369

15 SPENCER STEER, 2B/3B

BA GRADE
45 Risk: High

Born: Dec. 7, 1997. **B-T:** R-R. **HT:** 5-11. **WT:** 185. **Drafted:** Oregon, 2019 (3rd round). **Signed by:** Kyle Blackwell.

TRACK RECORD: Steer was a standout performer throughout his collegiate career with Oregon and also stood out on the Cape Cod League. After an impressive 2019 pro debut,

Steer began tapping into more power in 2021, advancing to Double-A Wichita and drawing positive reviews from scouts both inside and outside the org for his all-around game.

SCOUTING REPORT: While Steer doesn't have massive top-end exit velocity numbers, he makes hard contact consistently and hit 24 home runs and 18 doubles between High-A and Double-A in 2021. That's a great sign for a contact-oriented bat like Steer, who only struck out at a combined 21.5% rate this season. He's a versatile defender who can handle several positions—including shortstop in a pinch—with good hands, adequate arm strength and enough arm for whatever position he's at. His best defensive position is second, but he should be able to move around the defensive spectrum depending on team need. Steer is an average runner, but he's opportunistic and savvy on the base paths and generally draws positive reviews for his baseball instincts in general, and for his competitiveness and intensity on the field.

THE FUTURE: Steer needs more at-bats against upper-level minor league pitching, but his power increase makes him one of the risers of the system and his defensive versatility gives him multiple avenues to a big league role.

Year	Age	Club (Level)	Lge	AVG	G	AB	R	H	2B	3B	HR	RBI	BB	SO	SB	OBP	SLG
2021	23	Cedar Rapids (HiA)	Cent	.274	45	168	37	46	7	1	10	24	35	32	4	.409	.506
	23	Wichita (AA)	Cent	.241	65	249	45	60	11	2	14	42	20	73	4	.304	.470
Minor League Totals (3 years)				.264	174	667	122	176	36	6	28	99	89	138	13	.362	.462

16 COLE SANDS, RHP

BA GRADE
45 Risk: High

Born: July 17, 1997. **B-T:** R-R. **HT:** 6-3. **WT:** 215. **Drafted:** Florida State, 2018 (5th round). **Signed by:** Brett Dowdy.

TRACK RECORD: Sands turned in career bests in strikeout and walk rates during his draft year with Florida State in 2018, turning that into a $600,000 fifth-round bonus. He pitched well at the lower levels in 2019 and in 2021 had another strong season with Double-A Wichita, though his control regressed (1.8 BB/9 in 2019 to 3.9 BB/9).

SCOUTING REPORT: In a time where north-south pitching profiles and vertical fastballs sit at the popular table, Sands is a lower three-quarters slot righty with an east-west three-pitch mix. He sits in the 93-94 mph range with his fastball and touches 96, but the pitch has more arm-side running life than carry up in the zone. His secondaries match that movement profile as well. His 78-82 mph curveball has huge raw spin rates (around 2,900 rpm) but is more of a sweeping pitch with lateral movement that he showed good feel to land for strikes. His low-80s changeup also has lateral, fading life that could play off his fastball nicely with about 10 mph of separation, and it's flashed plus in the past. After showing glimpses of improved command, Sands looks more like a fringe-average strike-thrower which gives him some reliever risk.

THE FUTURE: Sands has No. 4 or No. 5 starter upside with improved command, but probably profiles best as a unique look out of the pen.

Year	Age	Club (Level)	Lge	W	L	ERA	G	GS	IP	H	HR	BB	SO	BB/9	SO/9	WHIP	AVG
2021	23	Wichita (AA)	Cent	4	2	2.46	19	18	80	59	6	35	96	3.9	10.8	1.17	.203
Minor League Totals (4 years)				11	5	2.58	37	36	178	140	10	54	204	2.74	10.33	1.09	.217

17 DREW STROTMAN, RHP

BA GRADE
45 Risk: High

Born: Sept. 3, 1996. **B-T:** R-R. **HT:** 6-3. **WT:** 195. **Drafted:** St. Mary's, 2017 (4th round). **Signed by:** Allan Hull (Rays).

TRACK RECORD: Mostly a reliever in college, the Rays developed Strotman as a starter and dealt him to the Twins in the Nelson Cruz trade that also landed Minnesota righthander Joe Ryan. Strotman pitched exclusively at Triple-A in 2021 with solid stuff, but control that got him into trouble at times.

SCOUTING REPORT: Strotman has a four-pitch mix headlined by a fastball that sat in the 94-95 mph range and has been up to 99-100 mph. The pitch is ordinary in terms of movement and spin, and he needs to do a better job spotting the pitch on the edges of the zone moving forward. His best secondary is a hard cutter/slider that sits in the upper 80s and is currently his best in-zone swing-and-miss offering. Strotman also has a mid-to-upper-80s changeup that gets whiffs more as a chase offering versus lefthanded hitters. A curveball around 80 mph is his fourth offering and doesn't project as anything more than a change of pace pitch.

THE FUTURE: Strotman has the stuff to pitch in a No. 4 or No. 5 role if he can get his control back to pre-Tommy John surgery levels, but if that doesn't happen his fastball could play up in a bullpen role. Strotman is on the 40-man roster with a chance to make his big league debut in 2022.

Year	Age	Club (Level)	Lge	W	L	ERA	G	GS	IP	H	HR	BB	SO	BB/9	SO/9	WHIP	AVG
2021	24	Durham (AAA)	East	7	2	3.39	13	12	58	50	3	33	62	5.1	9.6	1.42	.235
	24	St. Paul (AAA)	East	3	3	7.33	12	12	54	65	9	30	42	5.0	7.0	1.76	.298
Minor League Totals (5 years)				15	11	4.09	54	49	233	213	15	102	213	3.94	8.23	1.35	.246

18 BLAYNE ENLOW, RHP

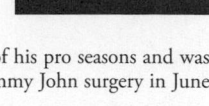

BA GRADE

50 Risk: Extreme

Born: March 21, 1999. **B-T:** R-R. **HT:** 6-3. **WT:** 170.
Drafted: HS—St. Amant, La., 2017 (3rd round). **Signed by:** Greg Runser.
TRACK RECORD: The Twins signed Enlow for $2 million out of high school to pry him from a Louisiana State commitment. He has pitched well in all four of his pro seasons and was off to a strong start in 2021 with High-A Cedar Rapids before undergoing Tommy John surgery in June after just three starts and 14.2 innings.
SCOUTING REPORT: Enlow has a solid mix of four offerings and was trending in the right direction this year with a bit more fastball velocity, more movement on his breaking ball and impressive feel for a hard cutter that he can land to both sides of the plate. Enlow has been up to 97 mph with his fastball, but the development of his breaking stuff is probably the most encouraging sign for his profile. He has impressive touch on a low-80s curveball that he can land for strikes or bury below the zone for whiffs. His upper-80s cutter is now a pitch he can use for swings and misses in the zone or to keep hitters off the barrel. On top of his fastball and breaking stuff, Enlow has a firm changeup in the upper 80s that improved significantly in 2020 and gives him a fourth reliable offering.
THE FUTURE: Enlow profiles as a back-end starter if healthy, but he'll miss all or most of the 2022 season recovering from surgery.

Year	Age	Club (Level)	Lge	W	L	ERA	G	GS	IP	H	HR	BB	SO	BB/9	SO/9	WHIP	AVG
2021	22	Cedar Rapids (HiA)	Cent	1	1	1.84	3	3	14	13	1	6	23	3.7	14.1	1.30	.250
Minor League Totals (5 years)				15	13	3.27	50	41	240	220	14	83	208	3.12	7.81	1.26	.243

19 AARON SABATO, 1B

BA GRADE

45 Risk: High

Born: June 4, 1999. **B-T:** R-R. **HT:** 6-2. **WT:** 230. **Drafted:** North Carolina, 2020 (1st round). **Signed by:** Ty Dawson.
TRACK RECORD: Sabato set North Carolina's freshman home run record (18) in 2019 and showed some of the best raw power in the 2020 class as a draft-eligible sophomore. The Twins signed him for $2.75 million with the 27th overall pick and watched him look overmatched early and quite good late in his debut pro season this year.
SCOUTING REPORT: As a right-right, first base-only defensive profile, almost all Sabato's value is riding on his bat and massive raw power. Early this season with Low-A Fort Myers, Sabato was extremely passive and looked overmatched by fastballs north of 93 mph. He struggled to get to pitches on the inner half and in general seemed out of sync and off time. He was promoted to High-A Cedar Rapids in late August and the fresh start seemed good for him, as he managed a 1.015 OPS with eight home runs and a heavier pull approach. Sabato has a keen eye at the plate—his 92 walks ranked second in the minors only to org mate Edouard Julien—rarely expands the zone and does plenty of damage on contact, but will need to find a way to lower his 32% strikeout rate. He's a bottom-of-the-scale runner limited to first base defensively.
THE FUTURE: Sabato should get a chance at Double-A in 2022, where he'll put his power and patient approach to the test against better arms.

Year	Age	Club (Level)	Lge	AVG	G	AB	R	H	2B	3B	HR	RBI	BB	SO	SB	OBP	SLG
2021	22	Fort Myers (LoA)	SEast	.189	85	286	48	54	15	0	11	42	73	117	1	.365	.357
	22	Cedar Rapids (HiA)	Cent	.253	22	75	21	19	3	0	8	15	19	32	0	.402	.613
Minor League Totals (2 years)				.202	107	361	69	73	18	0	19	57	92	149	1	.373	.410

20 GILBERTO CELESTINO, OF

BA GRADE

40 Risk: Medium

Born: Feb. 13, 1999. **B-T:** R-L. **HT:** 6-0. **WT:** 170. **Signed:** Dominican Republic, 2015. **Signed by:** Oz Ocampo/Roman Ocumarez (Astros).
TRACK RECORD: Celestino was a top prospect in the 2015 international class who signed with the Astros for $2.5 million. The Twins acquired him in a trade that sent Ryan Pressly to Houston, and injuries on the big league roster led to Celestino making his big league debut in 2021, where he looked overmatched at the plate.
SCOUTING REPORT: Celestino has shown the ability to hit for average and get on base in the upper minors and was off to a strong start with Triple-A St. Paul (125 wRC+) but scouts believe he wasn't quite

ready for big league arms. He hits the ball hard when he gets a pitch in his hitting zone, but he also doesn't elevate the ball frequently and struggles with velocity on the inner half. Celestino controls the zone well and makes solid swing decisions, but scouts believe he'll be a below-average power hitter. Celestino can handle center field, and he played all three outfield positions both in Triple-A and for the Twins. Despite an 80th percentile sprint speed according to Baseball Savant, some scouts believe he's a fringe runner who is better in a corner—though he's always been praised for his route running and reads off the bat.

THE FUTURE: Celestino profiles as an extra outfielder off the bench who will need to tap into more power to raise his ceiling.

Year	Age	Club (Level)	Lge	AVG	G	AB	R	H	2B	3B	HR	RBI	BB	SO	SB	OBP	SLG
2021	22	Wichita (AA)	Cent	.250	21	84	10	21	5	0	2	7	11	24	0	.344	.381
	22	St. Paul (AAA)	East	.290	49	183	27	53	13	0	5	24	24	43	4	.384	.443
	22	Minnesota (MLB)	AL	.136	23	59	7	8	3	0	2	3	3	14	0	.177	.288
Major League Totals (1 year)				.136	23	59	7	8	3	0	2	3	3	14	0	.177	.288
Minor League Totals (6 years)				.275	374	1417	193	389	80	10	28	162	156	296	65	.351	.404

21 DANNY DE ANDRADE, SS/3B

BA GRADE

50 Risk: Extreme

Born: April 10, 2004. **B-T:** R-R. **HT:** 5-11. **WT:** 173. **Signed:** Venezuela, 2021. **Signed by:** Fred Guerrero/Luis Lajara.

TRACK RECORD: De Andrade is a Venezuelan shortstop and third baseman who trained in the Dominican Republic as an amateur and was an early standout in the 2020-21 international class. He signed with the Twins for $2.2 million on Jan. 15 and made his Dominican Summer League debut, where he showed contact ability and impressive defensive tools as a 17-year-old.

SCOUTING REPORT: De Andrade is more polished on the defensive side of the ball now. He has impressive hands, quick actions, good body control and a sound internal clock that give him a chance to stick at shortstop despite fringe-average or solid speed at best. His arm strength is certainly strong enough for him to stick on the left side of the infield, but some scouts think he might be a better fit for third base as he adds strength and physicality to his frame. Offensively, De Andrade has a short, quick swing and contact-driven, aggressive approach. He swings frequently and will chase outside of the zone, so in the future he'll likely need to become more selective to do more damage. He's a gap-to-gap doubles hitter now, but scouts think he has a chance to get to above-average power potential in the future.

THE FUTURE: De Andrade is one of the focal points of Minnesota's next wave of international prospects and should make his domestic debut in 2022.

Year	Age	Club (Level)	Lge	AVG	G	AB	R	H	2B	3B	HR	RBI	BB	SO	SB	OBP	SLG
2021	17	Twins (R)	DSL	.264	50	178	16	47	13	1	0	16	15	27	6	.340	.348
Minor League Totals (1 year)				.264	50	178	16	47	13	1	0	16	15	27	6	.340	.348

22 KEONI CAVACO, SS

BA GRADE

50 Risk: Extreme

Born: June 2, 2001. **B-T:** R-R. **HT:** 6-2. **WT:** 195. **Drafted:** HS—Chula Vista, Calif., 2019 (1st round). **Signed by:** John Leavitt.

TRACK RECORD: Cavaco blew up late in the draft process during his senior spring season in high school, when he showed some of the most exciting raw tools in the class. The Twins signed him for $4.05 million as the 13th overall pick, but he has struggled mightily in his brief two years in the lower minors.

SCOUTING REPORT: The one silver lining for Cavaco at this point is his 2021 season showed flashes of the promise he showed in high school. In June and July, he hit .292/.376/.427 between the FCL and Low-A Fort Myers. Consistency in his approach and consistency in being on the field has been more of a challenge. He missed time with a concussion and hamstring issues this year, and he is behind the curve from an approach and mechanical standpoint. Cavaco has plus raw power, but he can't access it regularly thanks to poor direction in his lower half and bat path, as well as a chase rate that has been described as "unsustainable." He drew mixed reviews for his defensive ability, with some scouts saying he looked better than expected at shortstop and others believing the game still speeds up on him.

THE FUTURE: There are still significant holes in Cavaco's game, but there's no denying his toolset is among the most intriguing in the system.

Year	Age	Club (Level)	Lge	AVG	G	AB	R	H	2B	3B	HR	RBI	BB	SO	SB	OBP	SLG
2021	20	Twins (R)	FCL	.222	3	9	2	2	1	0	0	2	1	3	1	.300	.333
	20	Fort Myers (LoA)	SEast	.233	60	236	27	55	6	2	2	24	18	89	5	.296	.301
Minor League Totals (3 years)				.217	88	332	38	72	11	2	3	32	23	127	7	.276	.289

23 JOVANI MORAN, LHP

BA GRADE

40 Risk: Medium

Born: April 24, 1997. **B-T:** L-L. **HT:** 6-1. **WT:** 167. **Drafted:** HS—Florida, P.R., 2015 (7th round). **Signed by:** Freddie Thon.

TRACK RECORD: Moran signed for $275,000 as one of the top pitching prospects in Puerto Rico in 2015 and quickly transitioned to a full-time reliever role after joining the organization. After a strong 2019 season, Moran excelled at Double-A Wichita and Triple-A St. Paul in 2021, posting the best overall full-season strikeout rate of his career and earning a big league debut.

SCOUTING REPORT: Moran relies mostly on a two-pitch mix led by a 92-93 mph fastball that gets up to the 97-98 mph range at peak and an out pitch changeup in the 80-81 mph range. His fastball is ordinary—especially by reliever standards—and got hit hard in his brief big league sample. The pitch was also his least effective offering in the minors. His changeup is a real weapon. It has received double-plus grades and generated a 51% whiff rate in the majors. He also throws a low-80s, high-spin slider but largely scrapped the pitch in his major league stint. Control has always been a question mark and weak link for Moran, and that was still the case in 2021, with a walk rate of 4.3 per nine innings in the minors.

THE FUTURE: Moran has a chance to provide low-leverage innings out of the bullpen again in 2022, but his upside could be capped without improving his fastball velocity, shape or command.

Year	Age	Club (Level)	Lge	W	L	ERA	G	GS	IP	H	HR	BB	SO	BB/9	SO/9	WHIP	AVG
2021	24	Wichita (AA)	Cent	2	1	1.91	20	0	37	14	3	14	64	3.4	15.3	0.74	.112
	24	St. Paul (AAA)	East	2	1	3.03	15	0	29	14	3	18	45	5.5	13.7	1.08	.140
	24	Minnesota (MLB)	AL	0	0	7.88	5	0	8	9	0	7	10	7.9	11.3	2.00	.290
Major League Totals (1 year)				0	0	7.88	5	0	8	9	0	7	10	7.88	11.25	2.00	.290
Minor League Totals (7 years)				18	10	2.64	112	7	225	130	12	107	333	4.27	13.30	1.05	.168

24 CHRIS VALLIMONT, RHP

BA GRADE

45 Risk: High

Born: March 18, 1997. **B-T:** R-R. **HT:** 6-5. **WT:** 220. **Drafted:** Mercyhurst (Pa.), 2018 (5th round). **Signed by:** Alex Smith (Marlins).

TRACK RECORD: Vallimont signed for $300,000 in the fifth round with the Marlins in 2018 after a stellar three-year career at Division II Mercyhurst (Pa.). The Twins acquired him and Sergio Romo in 2019 in exchange for Lewin Diaz. After pitching well in 2019, Vallimont struggled against Double-A bats in 2021, but the Twins still added him to the 40-man roster in November.

SCOUTING REPORT: Vallimont gave up plenty of hits (1.638 WHIP) and walks (5.8 BB/9) this season, but still has an intriguing four-pitch mix. His fastball sits in the 92-93 mph range and has been up to 95-96, and analysts love the metrics beyond the velocity, especially the extreme carry and vertical break of the offering. His go-to secondary and most effective pitch this year was a mid-80s slider with spin in the 2,500 rpm range and solid sweeping action. The 6-foot-5 righty also throws an upper-70s curveball and a low-80s changeup. All his offerings have average or a tick better potential, but he needs to take a big step forward with the consistency of his command against upper-level bats.

THE FUTURE: The Twins have developed Vallimont as a starter, and he has a deep arsenal and the physical frame, but his control might make him a better fit for the pen, where perhaps his velocity could tick up.

Year	Age	Club (Level)	Lge	W	L	ERA	G	GS	IP	H	HR	BB	SO	BB/9	SO/9	WHIP	AVG
2021	24	Fort Myers (LoA)	SEast	0	0	0.00	1	1	3	2	0	0	6	0.0	18.0	0.67	.182
	24	Wichita (AA)	Cent	5	7	6.03	21	21	91	91	15	61	130	6.0	12.9	1.67	.258
Minor League Totals (4 years)				13	18	4.56	57	56	251	210	25	125	306	4.49	10.99	1.34	.226

25 MATT WALLNER, OF

BA GRADE

45 Risk: Very High

Born: Dec. 12, 1997. **B-T:** L-R. **HT:** 6-5. **WT:** 220. **Drafted:** Southern Mississippi, 2019 (1st round supplemental). **Signed by:** Derrick Dunbar.

TRACK RECORD: Wallner set Southern Mississippi's career home runs record (58) and parlayed that power potential into a $1.8 million bonus as the Twins' 39th overall pick in the 2019 draft. After homering eight times in his pro debut in 2019, Wallner clubbed 15 at High-A Cedar Rapids in 2021 and performed well in an 18-game stint in the Arizona Fall League (1.011 OPS).

SCOUTING REPORT: Power is Wallner's calling card and the physical 6-foot-5 outfielder posts some of the best top-end exit velocity numbers in the system, along with first baseman Aaron Sabato. He has 70 or 80-grade raw power, but his plate discipline, the length of his swing and his swing-and-miss rate will severely limit his overall offensive upside and deflate his average. Wallner struck out at a 33.3% clip with Cedar Rapids—while old for the level—and chases outside the zone at an above-average rate. He's pull-happy, which suits his power, but will also leave him susceptible to secondary offerings and more advanced pitching. A former pitcher, Wallner has plus arm strength that fits well in right field, where he is a fringy, but adequate defender and runner.

THE FUTURE: Wallner will never compete for a batting title, but his power production could make him a big league contributor. He should get his first test against upper-level minor league pitching in 2022.

Year	Age	Club (Level)	Lge	AVG	G	AB	R	H	2B	3B	HR	RBI	BB	SO	SB	OBP	SLG
2021	23	Twins (R)	FCL	.333	2	6	2	2	0	0	0	0	0	2	0	.333	.333
	23	Cedar Rapids (HiA)	Cent	.264	66	258	39	68	14	2	15	47	28	98	0	.350	.508
Minor League Totals (3 years)				.262	133	516	83	135	35	4	23	81	52	180	1	.354	.479

26 EDOUARD JULIEN, 2B/3B/OF

BA GRADE 45 Risk: Extreme

Born: April 30, 1999. **B-T:** L-R. **HT:** 6-2. **WT:** 195. **Drafted:** Auburn, 2019 (18th round). **Signed by:** Jack Powell.

TRACK RECORD: Julien was a prominent amateur player dating back to his prep days when he impressed scouts with his lefthanded swing with the Canadian Junior National Team. The Twins signed Julien for $493,500 in the 18th round of the 2019 draft as an eligible sophomore. He led all minor league hitters with 110 walks in his first pro season in 2021.

SCOUTING REPORT: Julien has one of the keenest eyes in minor league baseball. He rarely expands the zone, and his chase rate is reportedly among the best in the minors. He walked at a 24.5% clip in Low-A Fort Myers and after being promoted to High-A Cedar Rapids still walked at a 19.4% rate. Some scouts have put plus raw power grades on him as well, and Julien smacked 18 home runs and 28 doubles between both levels. Just seven minor league hitters managed 15+ homers, 25+ doubles and a .400+ on-base percentage in 2021 (including Jose Miranda) and of that group, only Yankees shortstop Anthony Volpe was younger than Julien. Julien played first, second, third and left field, but he profiles best at a corner and is likely a better fit in the outfield than in the dirt with below-average speed and fringy defensive ability.

THE FUTURE: The Twins have plenty of corner profiles in front of Julien, but he excels at getting on base and has some power to go with it. How his approach fairs against upper-level pitching is the next question.

Year	Age	Club (Level)	Lge	AVG	G	AB	R	H	2B	3B	HR	RBI	BB	SO	SB	OBP	SLG
2021	22	Fort Myers (LoA)	SEast	.299	47	147	41	44	12	1	3	24	50	54	21	.490	.456
	22	Cedar Rapids (HiA)	Cent	.247	65	247	52	61	16	0	15	48	60	90	13	.397	.494
Minor League Totals (3 years)				.266	112	394	93	105	28	1	18	72	110	144	34	.434	.480

27 KALA'I ROSARIO, OF

BA GRADE 45 Risk: Extreme

Born: July 2, 2002. **B-T:** R-R. **HT:** 6-1. **WT:** 205. **Drafted:** HS—Waiakea, Hawaii, 2020 (5th round). **Signed by:** John Leavitt.

TRACK RECORD: Rosario was the top draft prospect out of Hawaii in 2020, separating himself by posting massive exit velocities at showcases like the Area Code Games and showing a good ability to use the entire field. The Twins signed Rosario for $270,000 in the fifth round and he was solid in his pro debut in the Florida Complex League (109 wRC+).

SCOUTING REPORT: Rosario is an impressive, physical athlete with a strong frame and raw power that gets both 70 and 80 future grades. His exit velocities stack up with the better sluggers in the system, though that translated into just five home runs in 51 games this summer. He has the power to tally many more as he learns to drive the ball more consistently in games and cut down a below-average swing-and-miss rate. Rosario struck out at a 31.7% rate, though his swing decisions themselves are solid and he doesn't chase out of the zone at an exorbitant rate. Rosario spent time in left field (78 innings) and right field (229 innings) this summer and is definitely a corner outfielder whose arm strength fits best for left field.

THE FUTURE: Rosario has huge power upside and should get a chance at full-season ball for the first time in 2022 during his age-20 season. He's praised for a strong work ethic.

Year	Age	Club (Level)	Lge	AVG	G	AB	R	H	2B	3B	HR	RBI	BB	SO	SB	OBP	SLG
2021	18	Twins (R)	FCL	.277	51	188	32	52	10	4	5	40	19	66	4	.341	.452
Minor League Totals (2 years)				.277	51	188	32	52	10	4	5	40	19	66	4	.341	.452

28 MISAEL URBINA, OF

BA GRADE 45 Risk: Extreme

Born: April 26, 2002. **B-T:** R-R. **HT:** 6-0. **WT:** 175. **Signed:** Venezuela, 2018. **Signed by:** Fred Guerrero.

TRACK RECORD: One of the top prospects in the 2018 international class, Urbina signed for $2.75 million. After impressing in the Dominican Summer League in 2019, Urbina made his stateside debut in 2021, where he struggled with the bat with Low-A Fort Myers.

SCOUTING REPORT: Urbina impressed with his bat-to-ball skills in the DSL, and he still made an above-average amount of contact in his first test in full season ball. But the quality of his contact was poor and opposing scouts turned in lower complimentary tools grades for Urbina almost across the board compared to a year ago. The Twins tried to quiet Urbina's hands in his load, while also narrowing his stance to unlock more power, but he finished the year with just a .286 slugging percentage and .095 ISO. He does have solid zone recognition. A year ago, Urbina was cited as a plus runner with a chance to stick in center field, but his run tool grades this year have regressed and some scouts think he's a better fit for left field moving forward with below-average arm strength. Urbina is an aggressive runner on the base paths, who stole 16 bags in 22 tries.

THE FUTURE: Urbina will be looking to bounce back in 2022, his age-20 campaign. It sounds like the Twins are still excited about his potential, but he needs to develop more power.

Year	Age	Club (Level)	Lge	AVG	G	AB	R	H	2B	3B	HR	RBI	BB	SO	SB	OBP	SLG
2021	19	Fort Myers (LoA)	SEast	.191	101	367	50	70	12	4	5	52	54	82	16	.299	.286
Minor League Totals (2 years)				.220	151	550	84	121	26	9	7	78	77	96	35	.327	.338

29 JERMAINE PALACIOS, SS

BA GRADE

40 Risk: High

Born: July 19, 1996. **B-T:** R-R. **HT:** 6-0. **WT:** 145. **Signed:** Venezuela, 2013. **Signed by:** Jose Leon.

TRACK RECORD: Palacios signed with the Twins for $70,000 in 2013 and was traded to the Rays in 2018 for righthander Jake Odorizzi. Minnesota reacquired him as a minor league free agent prior to the 2021 season and watched him hit 19 home runs and 17 doubles while playing strong defense at shortstop with Double-A Wichita.

SCOUTING REPORT: Palacios has a case as the best defensive shortstop in the system. He has soft hands and impressive actions in the field, with a strong arm from multiple angles and arm slots. His instincts are sound, and he is confident at all infield positions—he logged innings at each—earning plus defensive grades overall. The offensive profile is a bigger question. He hit well in his third stint against Double-A pitching, but skeptics will point to the fact that he was old for the level and a long history of generally underwhelming as a hitter. He posted near league-average exit velocities in 2021 and he does solid damage on contact, though he tends to expand the zone and swing and miss at below-average rates. Some scouts have noted he struggles against secondary offerings.

THE FUTURE: Despite his age and questions on the bat, Palacios' power output and defensive ability make him an intriguing sleeper to keep an eye on.

Year	Age	Club (Level)	Lge	AVG	G	AB	R	H	2B	3B	HR	RBI	BB	SO	SB	OBP	SLG
2021	24	Wichita (AA)	Cent	.259	110	410	69	106	17	0	19	54	46	109	18	.340	.439
Minor League Totals (8 years)				.264	603	2208	334	582	105	29	40	295	180	454	80	.324	.392

30 MARCO RAYA, RHP

BA GRADE

45 Risk: Extreme

Born: Aug. 7, 2002. **B-T:** R-R. **HT:** 6-0. **WT:** 165. **Drafted:** HS—Laredo, Texas, 2020 (4th round). **Signed by:** Trevor Brown.

TRACK RECORD: Raya was an arrow-up player during his senior season in high school prior to the 2020 season being shut down, but the Twins still liked his upside and feel for spin enough to sign him for $410,000 in the fourth round. There's a lot of unknown with Raya, as he missed the 2021 season with shoulder fatigue and has yet to make an official pro start.

SCOUTING REPORT: Despite Raya's lack of professional track record, Minnesota is still high on the 6-foot righthander's upside and stuff. While he didn't pitch an official game in the 2021 season, he joined the team in instructs and reportedly had his fastball sitting at 97 mph consistently in a short outing, with a good slider and curveball. His fastball sat in the 92-93 mph range as an amateur, but it's still up in the air what sort of fastball quality he will have over the course of a professional season. His breaking balls have both shown promise at times and he seems to have an innate feel for spinning the ball, while his changeup quality is to be determined. While Raya isn't physically imposing, he's worked hard over the last few years to add strength to his frame.

THE FUTURE: Raya is one of the bigger question marks in the system and should finally make his pro debut in 2022, when he'll still be in his age-19 season.

Year	Age	Club (Level)	Lge	W	L	ERA	G	GS	IP	H	HR	BB	SO	BB/9	SO/9	WHIP	AVG
2021	18	Did not play—Injured															

MORE PROSPECTS TO KNOW

31 CADE POVICH, LHP

SLEEPER

Povich signed for $500,000 in the third round and had a strong 10-inning pro debut. He added velocity quickly after joining the Twins—he touched 95 mph at instructs—and could move quickly.

32 ALERICK SOULARIE, 2B/OF

Soularie missed time in 2021 with a broken left foot and struggled against quality pitching when he was healthy, though he does have solid bat speed, zone control and some feel for the barrel. Scouts believe he's more likely to wind up in left field than stick in the infield.

33 YUNIOR SEVERINO, 2B/3B

Severino has big power potential with an impressive average exit velocity around 90 mph and he hammers fastballs. He needs to improve his approach against secondary offerings of all types, however.

34 BEN RORTVEDT, C

Rortvedt is on the 40-man roster and got into 39 games with the Twins in 2021 during his debut season at the level. He has a grooved swing and is very limited offensively, but is a plus pitch framer and could be a solid defensive-oriented backup or emergency catcher.

35 SEAN MOONEY, RHP

Mooney is a short, lower slot righthander who has a flat vertical approach angle fastball that gets more whiffs than 91-92 mph velocity would suggest. He racked up 71 strikeouts in just 42 innings in 2021 but needs to improve his control.

36 SAWYER GIPSON-LONG, RHP

Gipson-Long has a three-pitch mix and attacks the zone effectively, with poise on the mound and game-prep that is lauded by scouts. His fastball-changeup-curveball combination is ordinary, but he gets plenty of extension that could help it play up.

37 YENNIER CANO, RHP

Cano is a 27-year-old righthander, but he has an explosive fastball regularly in the upper 90s with lots of sinking action and a hard slider he commands well that gets plus grades. He could impact the Twins bullpen as soon as 2022.

38 CASEY LEGUMINA, RHP

Legumina split time as a starter and reliever in 2021, but could have a future 70-grade fastball out of the bullpen, as well as a plus slider and average changeup. His fastball is currently in the 93-94 mph range with impressive carry from a flat approach angle.

39 MARK CONTRERAS, OF

Contreras came out of nowhere to hit 20 home runs and 30 doubles with Double-A Wichita and Triple-A St. Paul. He's a solid corner outfielder and posts some of the system's best exit velocities.

40 TYLER BECK, RHP

Beck has a solid four-pitch mix with a fastball in the low 90s, but a curveball and slider with high spin rates and solid results in High-A Cedar Rapids and Double-A Wichita this season. His fastball isn't the firmest, but it has solid vertical life.

TOP PROSPECTS OF THE DECADE

Year	Player, Pos.	2021 Org
2012	Miguel Sano, 3B/SS	Twins
2013	Miguel Sano, 3B	Twins
2014	Byron Buxton, OF	Twins
2015	Byron Buxton, OF	Twins
2016	Byron Buxton, OF	Twins
2017	Nick Gordon, SS	Twins
2018	Royce Lewis, SS	Twins
2019	Royce Lewis, SS	Twins
2020	Royce Lewis, SS/3B	Twins
2021	Alex Kirilloff, OF/1B	Twins

TOP DRAFT PICKS OF THE DECADE

Year	Player, Pos.	2021 Org
2012	Byron Buxton, OF	Twins
2013	Kohl Stewart, RHP	Cubs
2014	Nick Gordon, SS	Twins
2015	Tyler Jay, LHP	Did not play
2016	Alex Kirilloff, OF	Twins
2017	Royce Lewis, SS	Twins
2018	Trevor Larnach, OF	Twins
2019	Keoni Cavaco, SS	Twins
2020	Aaron Sabato, 1B	Twins
2021	Chase Petty, RHP	Twins

New York Mets

BY MATT EDDY

Year one of Steve Cohen's ownership produced high highs and low lows.

The Mets entered 2021 with World Series aspirations but ultimately finished 11.5 games off the pace in the National League East, where the Braves' 88 wins were enough to win the division. New York entered the all-star break in first place but went 29-45 in the second half.

Cohen, a billionaire hedge fund manager who assumed the reins late in 2020, installed Sandy Alderson as president. Their first two general manager hires were dismissed before the season ended.

First, they brought on D-backs assistant GM Jared Porter but promptly fired him in January 2021 after it came to light that he  sent explicit, unsolicited texts to a female reporter in 2016 while working for the Cubs. Porter's assistant Zack Scott stepped in as acting GM and helped negotiate the trade that brought Francisco Lindor and Carlos Carrasco from Cleveland for Amed Rosario, Andres Gimenez and two lower-level prospects. Lindor signed a 10-year, $341 million extension.

Scott shepherded the Mets through most of the season before he was arrested and charged with driving while intoxicated in late August. New York fired Scott on Nov. 1 and hired Billy Eppler as its new GM a few weeks later. Eppler served as Angels GM from 2015 to 2020, before that serving as pro scouting director and AGM for the Yankees.

Cohen, Alderson and Eppler got right to work. They signed free agents Max Scherzer, Starling Marte, Mark Canha and Eduardo Escobar for a total outlay of nearly $255 million.

The signings help offset the free agent departures of Marcus Stroman, Javier Baez, Michael Conforto and Noah Syndergaard. Just as significantly the imports should add competitive fire on the field and team leadership in the clubhouse.

Syndergaard signing with the Angels yielded a compensatory draft pick after the second round in 2022. The Mets will add another pick when Conforto signs. The Mets will choose 11th and 14th overall in 2022, the former a compensatory pick for failing to sign Vanderbilt righthander Kumar Rocker as the 10th overall pick in 2021.

In total, the Mets will have a bonus pool for the 2022 draft that ranks at or near the top of the heap. That will be key for replenishing the top of a farm system that has been thinned by the trades of prospects, particularly first-round high school outfielders Jarred Kelenic and Pete Crow-Armstrong.

A number of young position prospects took steps forward in 2021, led by catcher Francisco Alvarez and third baseman Brett Baty. That duo plus shortstop Ronny Mauricio and third base-

Pete Alonso continued to hit bombs while also improving his feel to hit and first base defense.

PROJECTED 2025 LINEUP

Catcher	Francisco Alvarez	23
First Base	Pete Alonso	30
Second Base	Ronny Mauricio	24
Third Base	Mark Vientos	25
Shortstop	Francisco Lindor	31
Left Field	Brett Baty	25
Center Field	Starling Marte	36
Right Field	Brandon Nimmo	32
Designated Hitter	Dominic Smith	30
No. 1 Starter	Jacob deGrom	37
No. 2 Starter	Matt Allan	24
No. 3 Starter	J.T. Ginn	26
No. 4 Starter	Tylor Megill	29
No. 5 Starter	David Peterson	29
Closer	Edwin Diaz	31

man Mark Vientos could all be MLB ready by the second half of 2023, which could go a long way toward restocking what was the fourth-oldest offense in the NL in 2021.

The Mets hired Astros minor league hitting coordinator Jeremy Barnes before the 2021 season, and he rose to the title of farm director, where his lead initiative will be to enhance bat speed, add strength and improve the exit velocities of the organization's young hitters.

Barnes can point to success stories—including Chas McCormick, Jake Meyers and Jeremy Peña—in which Houston turned college performers into pro prospects and even major leaguers. ■

DEPTH CHART

NEW YORK METS

TOP 2022 ROOKIES	RANK
Brett Baty, 3B/OF	2
Mark Vientos, 3B	4
Adam Oller, RHP	20
BREAKOUT PROSPECTS	**RANK**
Dominic Hamel, RHP	12
Luis Rodriguez, LHP	17
Vincent Perozo, C	25

SOURCE OF TOP 30 TALENT

Homegrown	27	Acquired	3
College	9	Trade	1
Junior college	0	Rule 5 draft	1
High school	5	Independent league	0
Nondrafted free agent	0	Free agent/waivers	1
International	13		

LF
Nick Plummer (13)
Carlos Cortes (16)

CF
Jaylen Palmer (15)
Jake Mangum (28)
Stanley Consuegra

RF
Alex Ramirez (7)
Khalil Lee (8)

3B
Brett Baty (2)
Mark Vientos (4)
Jose Peroza (21)
Justin Guerrera

SS
Ronny Mauricio (3)
Wilmer Reyes
William Lugo

2B
Kevin Kendall (27)
Luke Ritter (29)
Travis Blankenhorn
Wyatt Young

1B
JT Schwartz (26)
Warren Saunders

C
Francisco Alvarez (1)
Hayden Senger (23)
Vincent Perozo (25)
Patrick Mazeika

LHP

LHSP	LHRP
Luis Rodriguez (17)	Keyshawn Askew
Javier Atencio (24)	Thomas Szapucki
Josh Walker	

RHP

RHSP	RHRP
Matt Allan (5)	Robert Dominguez (22)
J.T. Ginn (6)	Eric Ozre
Joel Diaz (9)	Daison Acosta
Calvin Ziegler (10)	Colin Holderman
Jose Butto (11)	Michel Otañez
Dominic Hamel (12)	Brian Metoyer
Mike Vasil (14)	Yenssy Diaz
Junior Santos (18)	Jake Reed
Jordany Ventura (19)	Antonio Santos
Adam Oller (20)	Ryley Gilliam
Joander Suarez (30)	Bryce Montes de Oca
Carson Seymour	Dedniel Nuñez
Tony Dibrell	Josh Cornielly
Jorge De Leon	Levi David

1 FRANCISCO ALVAREZ, C

Born: Nov. 19, 2001. **B-T:** R-R. **HT:** 5-10. **WT:** 233.
Signed: Venezuela, 2018.
Signed by: Andres Nuñez/Ismael Perez.

TRACK RECORD: When the Mets signed Alvarez for a franchise international amateur record $2.7 million in 2018, they knew they were acquiring a player with a high upside. They just might not have expected him to realize so much of his upside so soon. Alvarez moved quickly to the Rookie-advanced Appalachian League in his 2019 pro debut and put up a .916 OPS as a 17-year-old catcher. His batting dominance manifested at the same age and in the same league as similar break-throughs by Vladimir Guerrero Jr. in 2016 and Wander Franco in 2018. Alvarez made the most of his time at the Mets' alternate training site in 2020 during the coronavirus shutdown, wowing scouts and emerging from it as the organization's clear-cut No. 1 prospect. He retains that standing following a powerful full-season debut in 2021. In a year spent primarily at High-A Brooklyn, he hit .272/.388/.554 with 24 home runs in 99 games and led all qualified 19-year-olds in full-season ball with a .941 OPS. His peer group included standout 2020 first-round picks Jordan Walker, Nick Yorke, Zac Veen and Robert Hassell III. Alvarez shined at the Mets' fall hitting camp after the season, where he helped mentor fellow young players, and participated in Dominican instructional league in November.

SCOUTING REPORT: Alvarez combines rare hitting attributes at the plate with the tools, personality and motivation to develop into a championship catcher. At the plate, Alvarez has incredible awareness and shows no fear. He has plus offensive upside, both in terms of hitting for average and power. Alvarez makes adjustments within at-bats and has the sort of natural timing and ability to pick up spin to hit breaking pitches. His power is the product of good weight transfer and a short, fast bat path to crush baseballs, especially to right-center field. Alvarez is a motivated defensive catcher who should get to average overall. One reason the Mets promoted him out of Low-A St. Lucie after 15 games was that they wanted him to hone his framing with a human umpire, rather than the automated balls and strikes at Low-A Southeast. He receives the ball well but needs to fine-tune his presentation to buy strikes for his pitchers. His raw arm strength is plus but plays down to average because of inefficient throwing mechanics. He threw out 23% of basestealers in 2021. Alvarez dramatically improved his rate of passed balls but

MIKE JANES/FOUR SEAM IMAGES

BA GRADE	SCOUTING GRADES
65 Risk: High	Hit: 60. **Power:** 60. **Run:** 30. Field: 50. **Arm:** 55.

Projected future grades on 20-80 scouting scale

BEST TOOLS

Best Hitter for Average	Francisco Alvarez
Best Power Hitter	Mark Vientos
Best Strike-Zone Discipline	Francisco Alvarez
Fastest Baserunner	Jaylen Palmer
Best Athlete	Ronny Mauricio
Best Fastball	Michel Otañez
Best Curveball	Brian Metoyer
Best Slider	J.T. Ginn
Best Changeup	Jose Butto
Best Control	J.T. Ginn
Best Defensive Catcher	Nick Meyer
Best Defensive Infielder	Brett Baty
Best Infield Arm	Ronny Mauricio
Best Defensive Outfielder	Jake Mangum
Best Outfield Arm	Stanley Consuegra

still has a tendency to use his hands more than his body when blocking pitches in the dirt. The Mets expect him to improve his defensive consistency because of his drive and passion to improve.

THE FUTURE: Alvarez planned to spend the offseason in Miami to continue developing his game. He should spend the bulk of 2022 at Double-A as a 20-year-old, with an MLB debut possible in 2023 after some Triple-A seasoning. It's rare for catchers as young as Alvarez to play regularly in the majors, but few young catchers have his precociousness. He has a chance to be a middle-of-the-order hitter and team leader behind the plate. ∎

Year	Age	Club (Level)	Lge	AVG	G	AB	R	H	2B	3B	HR	RBI	BB	SO	SB	OBP	SLG
2021	19	St. Lucie (LoA)	SEast	.417	15	48	12	20	5	0	2	12	15	7	2	.567	.646
	19	Brooklyn (HiA)	East	.247	84	279	55	69	13	1	22	58	40	82	6	.351	.538
Minor League Totals (3 years)				.285	141	484	99	138	28	1	31	96	76	126	9	.393	.539

2 BRETT BATY, 3B/OF

BA GRADE

60 Risk: High

Born: Nov. 13, 1999. **B-T:** L-R. **HT:** 6-3. **WT:** 210. **Drafted:** HS—Austin, Texas, 2019 (1st round). **Signed by:** Harry Shelton.

TRACK RECORD: Baty was one of the best high school hitters in a loaded 2019 draft, but his age—he turned 20 in November of his draft year—pushed him down the board to the Mets at 12th overall. He showed impressive raw power in his pro debut but struck out enough to introduce skepticism. Baty got into better shape for 2020 and impressed the Mets at the alternate training site. A loud full-season debut in 2021, which included a .292/.382/.473 batting line with 12 home runs in 91 games as he reached Double-A, validated his hard work. He also put on a show during batting practice at the Futures Game.

SCOUTING REPORT: Baty is a disciplined hitter with feel for the barrel, incredible raw power and greater athletic ability than his physical 6-foot-3 frame suggests. While he will show double-plus raw power in batting practice, Baty focuses on making hard contact to all fields in games. He is unafraid to work deep counts and has a chance to hit for a high average with plus on-base ability. Scouts are optimistic that Baty can get to above-average and possibly plus power, despite a batting profile that was heavy on ground balls in 2021. That's because he hits the ball hard consistently, and his doubles should turn into home runs as his batting approach continues to mature against advanced pitchers. Baty's conditioning work paid off on defense, where he showed greater quickness at third base, a strong, accurate arm and an ability to throw from different angles. He tried his hand at left field and showed the potential to be playable there.

THE FUTURE: Baty made a ton of progress in 2021 and looks like a future regular, potentially an impact one. His rise to Double-A and trial in left field indicate he is in the Mets' plans for 2022, with an MLB debut possible in the summer.

SCOUTING GRADES	Hitting: 60	Power: 55	Speed: 50	Fielding: 50	Arm: 60

Year	Age	Club (Level)	Lge	AVG	G	AB	R	H	2B	3B	HR	RBI	BB	SO	SB	OBP	SLG
2021	20	Brooklyn (HiA)	East	.242	100	392	55	95	14	5	19	63	24	101	9	.290	.449
	20	Binghamton (AA)	NEast	.323	8	31	3	10	1	0	1	1	2	11	2	.364	.452
Minor League Totals (4 years)				.262	281	1120	152	293	51	13	27	136	62	251	19	.302	.403

3 RONNY MAURICIO, SS

BA GRADE

55 Risk: High

Born: April 4, 2001. **B-T:** B-R. **HT:** 6-3. **WT:** 166. **Signed:** Dominican Republic, 2017. **Signed by:** Marciano Alvarez/Gerardo Cabrera.

TRACK RECORD: The headliner of the Mets' international signing class of 2017, Mauricio has wowed scouts with his bat speed and incredible raw power from day one. But that power hasn't always played in games. Mauricio's time in Low-A in 2019 and at the alternate training site in 2020 could best be described as uneven. His power manifested in 2021 in the form of 20 home runs, including 19 at High-A Brooklyn, a park notoriously stingy for home runs to right field.

SCOUTING REPORT: Mauricio has tantalizing power and an improving feel for the strike zone, but after hitting .248 in 2021 with a sub-.300 on-base percentage has clear areas for refinement. He's a tall, long-levered hitter who doesn't walk often, so that limits his OBP upside. Like most switch-hitters, Mauricio is stronger from the left side of the plate and makes more authoritative contact and chases less out of the zone from that side. Mauricio hit a wall in June, but the Mets challenged him to make better contact in the zone. His chase rate shrank from 52% in May to 33% in August, while his 90th percentile exit velocity climbed to 109.5 mph in August and 111.1 in September. Mauricio reads the ball well off the bat, has soft hands and a strong arm at shortstop. He doesn't run well. Moving to third base or right field are possible outcomes if he outgrows shortstop.

THE FUTURE: Mauricio's questionable on-base ability will move him down the lineup, but his glove and power will keep him in play. He should enter the MLB picture in 2023.

SCOUTING GRADES	Hitting: 40	Power: 60	Speed: 40	Fielding: 55	Arm: 60

Year	Age	Club (Level)	Lge	AVG	G	AB	R	H	2B	3B	HR	RBI	BB	SO	SB	OBP	SLG
2021	20	Brooklyn (HiA)	East	.242	100	392	55	95	14	5	19	63	24	101	9	.290	.449
	20	Binghamton (AA)	NEast	.323	8	31	3	10	1	0	1	1	2	11	2	.364	.452
Minor League Totals (4 years)				.262	281	1120	152	293	51	13	27	136	62	251	19	.302	.403

4 MARK VIENTOS, 3B/OF

Born: Dec. 11, 1999. **B-T:** R-R. **HT:** 6-4. **WT:** 185. **Drafted:** HS—Plantation, Fla., 2017 (2nd round). **Signed by:** Cesar Aranguren.

TRACK RECORD: Vientos spent two years in short-season ball after being the youngest player drafted in 2017. He flashed power indicators at pitcher-friendly Low-A Columbia in 2019, but not until 2021 did he reach his extra-base upside. That's when Vientos slugged 25 home runs in 83 games, most of them at Double-A Binghamton, and his .300 isolated slugging ranked second only to the Yankees' Anthony Volpe among 21-or-younger players who batted at least 300 times.

SCOUTING REPORT: Vientos has massive raw power and can reach the deepest recesses of left field. His swing is geared to do damage in the air and he can take the ball out to all fields. The majority of his 2021 home runs were hit to right field. Vientos has improved his pitch recognition, especially against breaking stuff from righthanders, and after catching up to the speed of Double-A he compiled a 1.043 OPS in his final 60 games. He doesn't flinch at velocity and could become a near-average hitter with plus power. Drafted as a shortstop, Vientos shifted to third base as a pro. He is playable there and has a plus arm. Some scouts believe his thick lower half could force him to first base, but Vientos has shown a renewed focus on conditioning this offseason. He tried his hand at left field, but rival scouts are not convinced because he is a well below-average runner.

THE FUTURE: Vientos is a competitive player who carries a chip on his shoulder for not being widely viewed in the same tier as the Mets' other top position prospects. He has a chance to change perceptions, because his MLB debut is on deck for 2022 if he hits at Triple-A. He could become a fixture on an infield corner.

BA GRADE
55 Risk: High

SCOUTING GRADES	Hitting: 45	Power: 60	Speed: 30	Fielding: 45	Arm: 60

Year	Age	Club (Level)	Lge	AVG	G	AB	R	H	2B	3B	HR	RBI	BB	SO	SB	OBP	SLG
2021	21	Binghamton (AA)	NEast	.281	72	274	43	77	16	0	22	59	26	87	0	.346	.580
	21	Syracuse (AAA)	East	.278	11	36	9	10	2	0	3	4	7	13	0	.395	.583
Minor League Totals (5 years)				.269	305	1140	155	307	71	1	52	203	107	299	2	.335	.470

5 MATT ALLAN, RHP

Born: April 17, 2001. **B-T:** R-R. **HT:** 6-3. **WT:** 225. **Drafted:** HS—Sanford, Fla., 2019 (3rd round). **Signed by:** Jon Updike.

TRACK RECORD: The top high school pitcher in the 2019 draft, Allan slid to the Mets in the third round and signed for $2.5 million, the equivalent of late first-round money. Allan made a handful of brief appearances in short-season leagues his pro debut before truly shining at the Mets' alternate training site in 2020. He carried that progress into 2021 spring training but had Tommy John surgery in May, right before the minor league season began. He missed the entire season and will be out for at least half of 2022.

SCOUTING REPORT: While Allan's timeline has been adjusted by elbow surgery, he has the repertoire, physicality and determination to pitch in a big league rotation one day. Prior to surgery, he sat in the mid 90s and touched higher with a four-seam fastball with riding life. Allan's curveball was the best among preps in the 2019 draft. It's a high-70s breaking pitch with tight spin and at least plus potential. He commands his curve but was frustrated that he lost feel for the pitch at spring training when he tried to get a tighter break. Allan improved his changeup at the alternate site in 2020 by mastering his hand and wrist position at release. That addition gave him three pitches with plus potential.

THE FUTURE: Allan took his Tommy John rehab slowly in 2021 and probably will not be ready before July 2022. With just 10 official pro innings under his belt, he's going to need a long runway to build endurance and work toward his MLB debut. No Mets pitching prospect has a higher upside than Allan, who could fit the mold of No. 3 starter.

BA GRADE
60 Risk: Extreme

SCOUTING GRADES:	Fastball: 60	Curveball: 60	Changeup: 50	Control: 50

Year	Age	Club (Level)	Lge	W	L	ERA	G	GS	IP	H	HR	BB	SO	BB/9	SO/9	WHIP	AVG
2021	20	Did not play—Injured															
Minor League Totals (2 years)				1	0	2.61	6	5	10	10	0	5	14	4.35	12.19	1.45	.250

6 J.T. GINN, RHP

Born: May 20, 1999. **B-T:** R-R. **HT:** 6-2. **WT:** 200. **Drafted:** Mississippi State, 2020 (2nd round). **Signed by:** Jet Butler.

TRACK RECORD: Ginn made it to campus at Mississippi State despite being the 30th overall pick out of high school by the Dodgers in 2018. He won Southeastern Conference freshman of the year honors in 2019 but didn't get a chance for an encore after having Tommy John surgery early in 2020, before the pandemic canceled the college season. The Mets drafted Ginn in the second round in 2020 as an eligible sophomore and signed him for $2.9 million, which was late first-round money. After rehabbing elbow surgery, Ginn made his first pro start for Low-A St. Lucie on June 3.

BA GRADE

55 Risk: High

SCOUTING REPORT: As Ginn regained feel and shape on his pitches, his upside came into sharper focus. He works fast, throws strikes and keeps the ball on the ground. He allowed just three home runs and 22 walks in 18 starts, while his 62% groundball rate ranked second in the minors for pitchers with at least 90 innings. Ginn pitched in the low 90s with plus sink and boring action to break bats. He reaches back for 95 mph when motivated. Ginn is able to work inside against hitters on both sides of the plate from his extreme first base setup. He is a strong athlete with good feel for a low-80s slider he can land for strikes or expand off the plate for chases. The pitch has heavy vertical movement and can be used to back-foot lefthanded batters. Ginn needs to develop more conviction in his changeup, because when he executes it he gets swings and misses.

THE FUTURE: Ginn's average velocity trended up in his final starts of 2021 as he moved farther away from surgery. Armed with three pitches and plus control, he projects as a No. 3 or 4 starter, and one who could be MLB ready late in 2022 or early 2023.

SCOUTING GRADES:	Fastball: 55	Slider: 60	Changeup: 50	Control: 60

Year	Age	Club (Level)	Lge	W	L	ERA	G	GS	IP	H	HR	BB	SO	BB/9	SO/9	WHIP	AVG
2021	22	St. Lucie (LoA)	SEast	2	1	2.56	8	8	38	26	3	10	35	2.3	8.2	0.93	.195
	22	Brooklyn (HiA)	East	3	4	3.38	10	10	53	49	0	12	46	2.0	7.8	1.14	.240
Minor League Totals (2 years)				5	5	3.03	18	18	92	75	3	22	81	2.15	7.92	1.05	.223

7 ALEX RAMIREZ, OF

Born: Jan. 13, 2003. **B-T:** R-R. **HT:** 6-3. **WT:** 170. **Signed:** Dominican Republic, 2019. **Signed by:** Gerardo Cabrera/Fernando Encarnacion.

TRACK RECORD: The Mets made Ramirez their top international target in 2019 and signed the Dominican center fielder for $2.05 million. Like all players in his signing class, he had his pro debut pushed back a season by the pandemic. Ramirez played so well at extended spring training in 2021 that the Mets challenged him with an assignment to Low-A St. Lucie on June 1. As a result, he gained more game experience than more famous prospects from his signing class, including the Yankees' Jasson Dominguez.

BA GRADE

55 Risk: Extreme

SCOUTING REPORT: Ramirez combines dynamic tools, quick wrists, solid pitch recognition and an overall easiness to his game to project as a future regular—but only if he can clean up his hit tool. He has a loose whippy swing, but his moves to the ball are too exaggerated. Top prospect Francisco Alvarez, showcasing his leadership ability, worked with Ramirez at the Mets' October hitting camp to be more direct to the ball. The Mets are heartened that Ramirez makes contact in the zone and hits the ball hard. He also narrows his zone with two strikes, but like many young players, he simply chases too much. He has the upside to reach near-average as a hitter with above-average power. Tall and twitchy, Ramirez has added lots of good weight since signing. He is an average runner who might be able to hold down center field but faces a possible move to right, where his plus arm would play.

THE FUTURE: Ramirez was one of three players age 18 or younger to bat at least 300 times in 2021, when both his upside potential and extreme youth were evident. Like Ronny Mauricio, he has longer levers to contend with while hitting. If everything clicks, Ramirez could be the Mets' right fielder of the future.

SCOUTING GRADES	Hitting: 40	Power: 55	Speed: 50	Fielding: 55	Arm: 60

Year	Age	Club (Level)	Lge	AVG	G	AB	R	H	2B	3B	HR	RBI	BB	SO	SB	OBP	SLG
2021	18	St. Lucie (LoA)	SEast	.258	76	302	41	78	15	4	5	35	23	104	16	.326	.384
Minor League Totals (1 year)				.258	76	302	41	78	15	4	5	35	23	104	16	.326	.384

8 KHALIL LEE, OF

Born: June 26, 1998. **B-T:** L-L. **HT:** 5-10. **WT:** 170. **Drafted:** HS—Oakton, Va., 2016 (3rd round). **Signed by:** Jim Farr (Royals).

TRACK RECORD: Drafted by the Royals out of high school in 2016, Lee had reached Double-A by the time the pandemic struck. The Royals traded him to the Mets following the lost 2020 minor league season, acquiring Andrew Benintendi from the Red Sox as part of a three-team deal. Lee advanced to Triple-A Syracuse in 2021 and led all qualified players at that level with a .451 on-base percentage and 18.3% walk rate. His .951 OPS ranked eighth.

SCOUTING REPORT: Injuries pressed Lee into emergency big league duty in May. He wasn't ready and went just 1-for-18 with 13 strikeouts. The Mets were encouraged by how he recovered at Triple-A and by how his aggressiveness ticked up late in the season. In his final 30 games he hit .311/482/.600 with 13 extra-base hits. Lee has bat speed and above-average raw power to his pull side but faces questions about his overall feel for hitting. He tended toward passivity at Triple-A and swung at just 37% of pitches, placing him in the 1st percentile in terms of aggressiveness for the level. Lee runs well but is not the burner his past stolen base totals suggest. He is capable in center field but better in right, where his plus arm is an asset.

THE FUTURE: Lee offers more floor than ceiling and could serve as an extra outfielder as soon as 2022. His window to playing time opens wider if he can prove himself in center field or get to more power by attacking pitches he can damage.

BA GRADE
45 Risk: Medium

SCOUTING GRADES	Hitting: 45	Power: 45	Speed: 55	Fielding: 55	Arm: 60

Year	Age	Club (Level)	Lge	AVG	G	AB	R	H	2B	3B	HR	RBI	BB	SO	SB	OBP	SLG
2021	23	Syracuse (AAA)	East	.274	102	292	67	80	20	2	14	37	71	115	8	.451	.500
	23	New York (MLB)	NL	.056	11	18	2	1	1	0	0	1	0	13	0	.056	.111
Major League Totals (1 year)				.056	11	18	2	1	1	0	0	1	0	13	0	.056	.111
Minor League Totals (6 years)				.259	501	1741	312	451	92	21	51	229	293	600	105	.382	.424

9 JOEL DIAZ, RHP

Born: Feb. 26, 2004. **B-T:** R-R. **HT:** 6-2. **WT:** 200. **Signed:** Dominican Republic, 2021. **Signed by:** Moises de Mota/Oliver Dominguez.

TRACK RECORD: The Mets emphasized volume during the 2020-21 international signing period, preferring to spread their bonus pool money around rather than focusing large sums on few players. They might have unearthed a gem in Diaz, a 6-foot-2 Dominican righthander whose fastball velocity jumped in the period leading up to his signing in January 2021. He made a loud pro debut in the Dominican Summer League, allowing three earned runs in 50.1 innings and not allowing any in his first 10 starts. Diaz's 0.54 ERA was the fourth lowest by a qualified pitcher in the DSL since at least 2006 and the lowest by a 17-year-old in that time.

SCOUTING REPORT: Diaz is a strike thrower with three pitches, good velocity and the projectable, athletic frame to add even more. His fastball ranges from 92-96 mph after sitting more in the high 80s when other teams were scouting him as an amateur. Diaz was reaching his peak velocity more often later in the season. Life on the pitch was evident from the 11.3 strikeouts per nine innings, .163 opponent average and zero home runs he allowed in 15 starts. Diaz is a strong, fluid pitcher who has uncommon feel for his secondary pitches for such a young pitcher. His changeup with late fade played as above-average to plus in his debut, and he threw it 20% of the time. He tended to introduce his high-70s curveball the second time through the order, but if he struggled to control it or get chases he would ditch it in favor of his change.

THE FUTURE: Diaz's starts were appointment viewing for Mets player development staff, who would make a point to tune in to the internal livestream of DSL games to watch him pitch. They should be able to watch him in person in 2022, when an assignment to Low-A St. Lucie is possible. With so much distance to cover, Diaz is a boom or bust pitching prospect with a wide range of possible outcomes.

BA GRADE
50 Risk: Extreme

SCOUTING GRADES:	Fastball: 60	Curveball: 50	Changeup: 55	Control: 50

Year	Age	Club (Level)	Lge	W	L	ERA	G	GS	IP	H	HR	BB	SO	BB/9	SO/9	WHIP	AVG
2021	17	DSL Mets (R)	DSL	0	2	0.54	15	15	50	29	0	9	63	1.6	11.3	0.75	.164
Minor League Totals (1 year)				0	2	0.54	15	15	50	29	0	9	63	1.61	11.26	0.75	.164

10 CALVIN ZIEGLER, RHP

Born: Oct. 3, 2002. **B-T:** R-R. **HT:** 6-0. **WT:** 205. **Drafted:** HS—Ocoee, Fla., 2021 (2nd round). **Signed by:** Jon Updike/John Kosciak.

TRACK RECORD: Ziegler is an Ontario prep who took unusual measures to be seen by scouts after not being drafted in 2020. With Canada on tighter Covid restrictions in 2021, Ziegler traveled south to pitch in tournaments for TNXL Academy, a Florida charter school, and later the Ohio Warhawks travel team. He hit his stride late in the spring and appealed to the Mets in the second round, both for his upside and asking price. He signed for $910,000, and the Mets planned to channel the $710,000 in bonus pool savings to first-rounder Kumar Rocker, the Vanderbilt righthander who ultimately did not sign.

SCOUTING REPORT: The top Canadian pitcher drafted in 2021, Ziegler delivers quality stuff from a powerful, athletic delivery. In his best outings before the draft, he pitched at 93-95 mph and topped out at 97 with a fastball featuring armside run. His curveball has plus potential at 78-84 mph with tight break and top-to-bottom shape. He threw more strikes with his curve as the spring unfolded. Ziegler will need to develop his firm mid-80s changeup that shows tail and sink when executed. Improved control, location and mound presence helped Ziegler put everything together in 2021.

THE FUTURE: Ziegler did not pitch for a Mets affiliate after signing because he had to clear up visa issues, but he threw a few bullpen sessions when he got to the complex in Port St. Lucie, Fla. The Mets will have a better idea of what they have in Ziegler in 2022 when he gains his first pro experience.

TOM DIPACE

BA GRADE
50 Risk: Extreme

SCOUTING GRADES:	Fastball: 60	Curveball: 55	Changeup: 45	Control: 45

Year	Age	Club (Level)	Lge	W	L	ERA	G	GS	IP	H	HR	BB	SO	BB/9	SO/9	WHIP	AVG
2021	18	Did not play															

11 JOSE BUTTO, RHP

BA GRADE
45 Risk: High

Born: March 19, 1998. **B-T:** R-R. **HT:** 6-1. **WT:** 205. **Signed:** Venezuela, 2017. **Signed by:** Hector Rincones.

TRACK RECORD: Nothing about Butto's development has been conventional. He signed out of Venezuela at age 19 in 2017 and didn't reach a full-season league until he was 21. Butto took his greatest developmental strides at instructional league in 2020, following the canceled minor league season, when he threw a ton of strikes and limited hard contact. He pitched his way to Double-A in late July, positioning him for an MLB role in 2022.

SCOUTING REPORT: Butto is an athletic strike-thrower with the best changeup in the organization. His low-80s circle-change sinks and fades slightly as it nears the plate and at peak features 12 mph or more of separation from his fastball. Butto sells his changeup because it comes from the same tunnel as his fastball, a four-seamer that ranges from 92-96 mph and sits near 93 with good vertical finish. His fastball and change helped him generate a 16.1% swinging-strike rate that ranked 16th in the minors among pitchers with at least 90 innings. Developing his curveball would give him a glove-side weapon to attack righthanded hitters and solidify Butto as a rotation prospect. His curve is a fringe pitch in the low 80s with 12-to-6 break and average depth that he tends to cast early. He has upped its usage to 16% versus righthanded hitters. He is a flyball pitcher who can be homer-prone when he loses feel for his changeup.

THE FUTURE: As a three-pitch starter who has had some success at Double-A, Butto is lined up for MLB innings at some point in 2022. He projects as a No. 5 starter or quality reliever.

Year	Age	Club (Level)	Lge	W	L	ERA	G	GS	IP	H	HR	BB	SO	BB/9	SO/9	WHIP	AVG
2021	23	Brooklyn (HiA)	East	1	4	4.32	12	12	58	51	11	15	60	2.3	9.3	1.13	.232
	23	Binghamton (AA)	NEast	3	2	3.12	8	8	40	33	6	9	50	2.0	11.2	1.04	.219
Minor League Totals (5 years)				13	19	3.39	74	64	321.1	290	34	86	315	2.41	8.82	1.17	.239

12 DOMINIC HAMEL, RHP

BA GRADE
45 Risk: High

Born: March 2, 1999. **B-T:** R-R. **HT:** 6-2. **WT:** 206. **Drafted:** Dallas Baptist, 2021 (3rd round). **Signed by:** Gary Brown.

TRACK RECORD: Hamel spent two years at Yavapai (Ariz.) JC before transferring to Dallas Baptist in 2020—just in time for the pandemic to interfere with his draft year. He made just four starts and went unselected in the five-round 2020 draft. After ranking ninth in Division I with 136 strikeouts in 2021 he went inside the top 100 picks. Hamel looked sharp in brief pro debut.

SCOUTING REPORT: The Mets like Hamel's pitch attributes and believe he has the potential to advance quickly, especially if he can round out his repertoire. His fastball had some of the best characteristics in the 2021 draft. Hamel ranges from 91-94 mph and bumps 95 with extreme spin and vertical break. The pitch bores to his arm side. Hamel's slider shows above-average to plus potential and is thrown in the low 80s with high spin. He also throws a fringe curveball in the mid 70s and has a below-average changeup. Both could be improved to keep lefthanded hitters off his fastball. Hamel throws plenty of strikes and stays over the mound well with a repeatable delivery.

THE FUTURE: The next step for Hamel is either adding a few ticks to his fastball or bringing up the quality of his secondary pitches. Even without those improvements, he profiles as a future major league pitcher because his fastball and pitchability are assets.

Year	Age	Club (Level)	Lge	W	L	ERA	G	GS	IP	H	HR	BB	SO	BB/9	SO/9	WHIP	AVG
2021	22	FCL Mets (R)	FCL	0	0	0.00	2	2	3	0	0	0	7	0.0	21.0	0.00	.000
Minor League Totals (1 year)				0	0	0.00	2	2	3	0	0	0	7	0.00	21.00	0.00	.000

13 NICK PLUMMER, OF

Born: July 31, 1996. **B-T:** L-L. **HT:** 5-10. **WT:** 200. **Drafted:** HS—Bloomfield Hills, Mich., 2015 (1st round). **Signed by:** Jason Bryans (Cardinals).

TRACK RECORD: When the Cardinals drafted Plummer 23rd overall in 2015, he was the first Michigan high schooler to go in the first round since 1997 and the first position prep since Derek Jeter in 1992. Plummer's time with St. Louis was marked with disappointment. A wrist injury wiped out what would have been his full-season debut in 2016, and he had not advanced past Class A before the pandemic wiped out 2020.

SCOUTING REPORT: Plummer began to realize his upside potential in 2021 by hitting .280/.415/.479 with 15 home runs at Double-A and Triple-A. His on-base percentage ranked inside the top 20 in the minor leagues, but it wasn't enough for the Cardinals to retain him, so he headed for minor league free agency at age 25. The Mets signed him to a one-year major league deal. Plummer is a 5-foot-10, lefthanded hitter with enticing bat speed and athletic ability. Plummer spread out his batting stance in 2021 after previously using a leg kick, and the results were palpable. He hit the ball where it was pitched, took his walks and set personal bests for offensive production across the board. His best position is left field, but he is capable at all three spots and has a below-average arm. He runs well but isn't a big basestealing threat.

THE FUTURE: While Plummer's tools may be short to profile for everyday play, he has the components to succeed as an extra outfielder. He and Khalil Lee will vie for MLB outfield at-bats in 2022.

Year	Age	Club (Level)	Lge	AVG	G	AB	R	H	2B	3B	HR	RBI	BB	SO	SB	OBP	SLG
2021	24	Springfield (AA)	Cent	.283	90	311	52	88	17	4	13	46	53	108	9	.404	.489
	24	Memphis (AAA)	East	.267	27	75	19	20	3	2	2	8	20	18	4	.455	.440
Minor League Totals (7 years)				.221	460	1469	239	324	69	17	33	152	279	541	42	.363	.358

14 MIKE VASIL, RHP

Born: March 19, 2000. **B-T:** L-R. **HT:** 6-5. **WT:** 225. **Drafted:** Virginia, 2021 (8th round). **Signed by:** Daniel Coles.

TRACK RECORD: Vasil lined up as one of the top prep pitchers in the 2018 draft before an arm injury shut him down early that spring. The Boston prep subsequently withdrew his name from the draft. Vasil never quite launched at Virginia and had a 4.52 ERA over 81.2 innings in his draft year of 2021. Still, the Mets had good reports and drafted him in the eighth round.

SCOUTING REPORT: The Mets were thrilled with what they saw from Vasil in his first pro summer and regard him as their best late-round pick from the 2021 draft. In seven innings in the Florida Complex League, he struck out 10, walked none and allowed three hits in seven innings. Vasil topped out at 97 mph in his pro debut but sits more in the low 90s with some occasional run on his four-seam fastball. His mid-80s slider is thrown with power in the high 80s and flashes plus at times. Vasil shows a well-rounded starter's arsenal with an upper-70s curveball and mid-80s changeup with average potential. Those pitches help keep opposing hitters off-balance, especially lefthanded ones. He has good tempo and throws enough strikes to stay in the rotation.

THE FUTURE: Vasil has a chance to develop four average or better pitches to go with an average command and control profile. Ultimately, he could fit at the back of a rotation or in a bulk reliever-type role.

Year	Age	Club (Level)	Lge	W	L	ERA	G	GS	IP	H	HR	BB	SO	BB/9	SO/9	WHIP	AVG
2021	21	FCL Mets (R)	FCL	0	0	1.29	3	3	7	3	0	0	10	0.0	12.9	0.43	.125
Minor League Totals (1 year)				0	0	1.29	3	3	7	3	0	0	10	0.00	12.86	0.43	.125

15 JAYLEN PALMER, 3B/OF

BA GRADE

45 Risk: High

Born: July 31, 2000. **B-T:** R-R. **HT:** 6-4. **WT:** 208. **Drafted:** HS—Flushing, N.Y., 2018 (22nd round). **Signed by:** John Kosciak.

TRACK RECORD: Palmer went to high school in the shadow of Citi Field in Flushing, N.Y., and was a 22nd-round find by area scout John Kosciak. Palmer was moving in the right direction in Rookie ball in 2019 and kept his momentum at the alternate training site in 2020. He looked sharp at Low-A St. Lucie in the first half of 2021 but got exposed at High-A Brooklyn with a .189 average and strikeout rate bordering on 39%.

SCOUTING REPORT: Palmer is a favorite of Mets coaches for his energetic style of play, athleticism and positive demeanor. He is one of the fastest players in the organization and one of the top defensive center fielders, thanks to the vacuum created by the trade of Pete Crow-Armstrong. How Palmer's bat develops will determine his MLB future. He knows the strike zone, isn't afraid to work deep counts and take his walks; he just needs to refine his swing decisions to offer at a higher rate of balls he can damage. Palmer shows solid-average power in batting practice and hits the ball hard consistently. His average exit velocity of 90 mph in Low-A Southeast is squarely above-average. The Mets hope that as his decisions improve that his offensive outlook will improve to near average. Drafted as a shortstop, Palmer has embraced versatility in pro ball by playing third base, second base and the outfield. His best position may be center field with his above-average range solid arm.

THE FUTURE: Palmer does many things well and is driven. If he hits, there will be an MLB role for him, most likely as a multi-positional player.

Year	Age	Club (Level)	Lge	AVG	G	AB	R	H	2B	3B	HR	RBI	BB	SO	SB	OBP	SLG
2021	20	St. Lucie (LoA)	SEast	.276	66	246	51	68	13	4	2	24	39	81	23	.378	.386
	20	Brooklyn (HiA)	East	.189	39	143	28	27	5	2	4	15	25	65	7	.314	.336
Minor League Totals (4 years)				.258	192	718	133	185	34	9	14	78	103	281	36	.356	.389

16 CARLOS CORTES, OF

BA GRADE

45 Risk: High

Born: June 30, 1997. **B-T:** L-L. **HT:** 5-7. **WT:** 197. **Drafted:** South Carolina, 2018 (3rd round). **Signed by:** Daniel Cortes.

TRACK RECORD: Cortes' offensive production had been muted by the pitcher-friendly New York-Penn and Florida State leagues in past seasons. That wasn't the case in 2021, when he popped a career-high 14 home runs at Double-A Binghamton and ranked third in the Mets system with a .230 isolated slugging, trailing only young boppers Francisco Alvarez and Mark Vientos. Cortes was out of action most of September after a Covid outbreak at Binghamton forced the cancelation of 11 games down the stretch. He got back into action in the Arizona Fall League.

SCOUTING REPORT: Cortes has a good eye at the plate and a strong lefthanded swing geared to hit the ball in the air. Few minor league hitters had a higher flyball rate than Cortes, who hit two-thirds of his batted balls in the air in 2021. If he turns more doubles into homers as he matures, his power could get to big league average, to go along with a near-average feel to hit. He slugged .583 against Double-A righthanders in 2021 and could have strong-side platoon utility for an MLB club. Finding a defensive home for the ambidextrous Cortes is more challenging. Drafted as second baseman, he lacked the arm strength throwing righthanded to stick at the keystone. He throws better from his natural left side and is playable in left field. Cortes actually is most at home at first base, but his 5-foot-7 stature is a profile mismatch there.

THE FUTURE: The Mets declined to add Cortes to the 40-man roster, making him eligible for the Rule 5 draft. He has the bat to be a 26th man on an MLB roster, if not the defensive versatility.

Year	Age	Club (Level)	Lge	AVG	G	AB	R	H	2B	3B	HR	RBI	BB	SO	SB	OBP	SLG
2021	24	Binghamton (AA)	NEast	.257	79	304	50	78	26	1	14	57	35	85	1	.332	.487
Minor League Totals (4 years)				.257	253	940	140	242	57	6	29	149	104	196	8	.335	.423

17 LUIS RODRIGUEZ, LHP

BA GRADE

50 Risk: Extreme

Born: Dec. 3, 2002. **B-T:** L-L. **HT:** 6-3. **WT:** 190. **Signed:** Dominican Republic, 2019. **Signed by:** Kelvin Dominguez.

TRACK RECORD: The Mets have two pitchers named Luis Rodriguez from the Dominican Republic in the low levels of their system. Luis Raul Rodriguez is a 6-foot-3 lefthander who has developed into the system's top southpaw. He signed with little fanfare at age 16 in 2019 and had his debut season wiped out by the pandemic in 2020. Rodriguez came out of nowhere to pitch his way onto the Florida Complex League roster in 2021 and earned a seven-inning look at Low-A St. Lucie late in the season as an 18-year-old.

SCOUTING REPORT: Rodriguez has exciting stuff, athleticism and physicality from the left side, giving him one of the higher upsides among pitchers in the organization. As he has physically matured, he has found more velocity from his low three-quarters arm slot. In 2021, he topped out at 97 mph and pitched consistently in the mid 90s. Rodriguez's low-80s slider sweeps hard to his glove side and has wipeout potential, especially when he gets it into the 85-86 mph range. Rodriguez is mostly a two-pitch pitcher who has toyed around with a changeup on the side. The Mets believe he has enough arm speed to make it work, but it is still on his developmental to-do list.

THE FUTURE: The Mets challenged Rodriguez at a young age in 2021, believing that struggling is an important part of players' development. He should get a chance to find his footing in 2022 at a Class A affiliate. Those highest on Rodriguez's upside see midrotation upside.

Year	Age	Club (Level)	Lge	W	L	ERA	G	GS	IP	H	HR	BB	SO	BB/9	SO/9	WHIP	AVG
2021	18	FCL Mets (R)	FCL	0	1	1.69	4	2	5	2	0	3	11	5.1	18.6	0.94	.111
	18	St. Lucie (LoA)	SEast	0	1	7.71	3	2	7	10	1	2	5	2.6	6.4	1.71	.345
Minor League Totals (1 year)				0	2	5.11	7	4	12	12	1	5	16	3.65	11.68	1.38	.255

18 JUNIOR SANTOS, RHP

BA GRADE

50 Risk: Extreme

Born: Aug. 16, 2001. **B-T:** R-R. **HT:** 6-7. **WT:** 244. **Signed:** Dominican Republic, 2018. **Signed by:** Anderson Taveras/Gerardo Cabrera.

TRACK RECORD: Santos signed at age 16 in 2017, then spent 2018 and 2019 in short-season leagues. He broke his foot in 2020, which prohibited him from working off a mound even at the alternate training site when the season was canceled. Santos showed durability in 2021, when he tossed 96 innings at Low-A St. Lucie in his most extended pro look.

SCOUTING REPORT: Santos has a distinguishing 6-foot-7, near 250-pound frame, but he has not separated from the pack with his overall stuff or command. Santos pitches at 93 mph with good two-seam run and tops at 97 in some starts. He had little trouble throwing his fastball for strikes even with the automated balls and strikes in use in Low-A Southeast. Putting batters away was more of a challenge. Santos gets caught in between on his breaking pitch, a low-80s slider with downer action. He had tried a curveball in the past, but it didn't fit with his lower three-quarters arm slot. Santos throws a firm changeup in the mid 80s that lacks action and hasn't been successful at keeping lefthanded hitters at bay. Despite his size, Santos is quick to the plate and good at holding baserunners.

THE FUTURE: Some scouts think Santos could one day start at the back of a rotation. Others see more of a swingman role as a possibility. A lot depends on how well he sharpens his breaking pitch.

Year	Age	Club (Level)	Lge	W	L	ERA	G	GS	IP	H	HR	BB	SO	BB/9	SO/9	WHIP	AVG
2021	19	St. Lucie (LoA)	SEast	6	6	4.59	21	16	96	108	8	38	79	3.6	7.4	1.52	.287
Minor League Totals (4 years)				7	12	4.15	49	40	187	193	13	69	154	3.33	7.43	1.40	.268

19 JORDANY VENTURA, RHP

BA GRADE

50 Risk: Extreme

Born: July 6, 2000. **B-T:** R-R. **HT:** 6-0. **WT:** 162. **Signed:** Dominican Republic, 2018. **Signed by:** Andres Nuñez.

TRACK RECORD: The Mets signed Ventura as a 17-year-old out of the Dominican Republic in 2018, and he began to catch scouts' attention in 2019 as he climbed from the Dominican Summer League to Rookie-advanced Kingsport, striking out 34 in 33 innings. Ventura looked good at the Mets' alternate training site in 2020 and carried the momentum into spring training in 2021, but he had Tommy John surgery just before the season started.

SCOUTING REPORT: Ventura was a breath of fresh air in a Mets system that was short on upside arms prior to focusing on pitchers in the 2021 draft and experiencing breakthrough seasons from young Dominican pitchers such as righthander Joel Diaz and lefty Luis Rodriguez. Ventura is an athletic righthander with a three-pitch profile, a quick arm and the room to improve his entire repertoire. In 2020 he pitched at 91-92 mph and bumped 94, but the Mets think he can sit a few ticks higher based on his ease of operation and projected physical gains. Ventura was fastball-focused in his last game action but has flashed a curveball with late snap and a changeup that he sells convincingly.

THE FUTURE: Ventura lost game reps in 2020 and 2021 but should be ready to get into Class A games by the second half of 2022. His rehab from Tommy John was going extremely well, and the Mets are excited about his breakout potential.

Year	Age	Club (Level)	Lge	W	L	ERA	G	GS	IP	H	HR	BB	SO	BB/9	SO/9	WHIP	AVG
2021	20	Did not play—Injured															
Minor League Totals (3 years)				2	3	3.36	18	14	59	45	3	26	57	3.97	8.69	1.20	.215

20 ADAM OLLER, RHP

BA GRADE

45 Risk: High

Born: Oct. 17, 1994. **B-T:** R-R. **HT:** 6-4. **WT:** 225. **Drafted:** Northwestern State, 2016 (20th round). **Signed by:** Phil Huttmann (Pirates).

TRACK RECORD: Drafted in the 20th round by the Pirates out of college in 2016, Oller was released after three seasons. He considered retiring but latched on in the independent Frontier League, where a 45-to-2 strikeout-to-walk ratio got him signed by the Giants. He pitched well as a 24-year-old at Low-A in 2019 before the Mets took him in the minor league Rule 5 draft that offseason.

SCOUTING REPORT: Oller came from out of nowhere to lead all Mets minor league pitchers with 120 innings and 138 strikeouts in 2021. For that, Oller was named the organization's minor league pitcher of the year. He impressed the Mets with his bulldog demeanor, increased velocity and improved changeup to earn a 40-man roster spot in the offseason. Oller pitches at 93 mph and touches 96, and that velocity boost allows him to compete in the zone and set up his quality secondaries. His swing-and-miss slider is an above-average pitch with low spin but outstanding velocity at 86 mph and a peak of 89. That speed makes it tough to time for batters sitting fastball. Oller's mid-80s changeup is firm but effective because it drops and runs to his arm side. He lands it for strikes and has at least average control overall.

THE FUTURE: Oller has a role on a big league pitching staff, potentially at the back of a rotation or in a bulk or middle relief role. He is 27 years old and will probably make his MLB debut in 2022.

Year	Age	Club (Level)	Lge	W	L	ERA	G	GS	IP	H	HR	BB	SO	BB/9	SO/9	WHIP	AVG
2021	26	Binghamton (AA)	NEast	5	3	4.03	15	15	76	66	8	29	95	3.4	11.3	1.25	.230
	26	Syracuse (AAA)	East	4	1	2.45	8	8	44	27	1	18	43	3.7	8.8	1.02	.179
Minor League Totals (6 years)				24	20	4.05	99	56	380	360	37	115	395	2.72	9.35	1.25	.250

21 JOSE PEROZA, 3B/2B

BA GRADE

45 Risk: High

Born: June 15, 2000. **B-T:** R-R. **HT:** 6-1. **WT:** 221. **Signed:** Venezuela, 2016. **Signed by:** Ismael Perez/Hector Rincones.

TRACK RECORD: Strength comes natural to Peroza, who grew up on a farm in Venezuela before training at Carlos Guillen's academy. He signed with the Mets for $280,000 in 2016. After three seasons spent in short-season leagues, plus a fourth lost to the pandemic, Peroza emerged as one of the organization's better offensive performers in a 2021 season spent at two Class A levels.

SCOUTING REPORT: Peroza is a big-bodied infielder who plays capable defense at three positions, and the breakout the organization expected in 2020 manifested a year later. He does a lot of things at the plate that the Mets value: he hits the ball hard in the air with angle and takes his walks. Peroza ranked fourth in the organization with 54 walks and a .365 on-base percentage. He focused on improving his load to prevent his head from moving so much in 2021 and he saw the ball better and got the most out of his above-average raw power. Peroza saw most of his time at third base, where he compensates for below-average range with a borderline plus arm. He's playable at second base and first base.

THE FUTURE: Peroza could hit his way to a big league role with a near-average hit tool and average power if he continues to develop. He probably fits best as a bat-first multi-position player.

Year	Age	Club (Level)	Lge	AVG	G	AB	R	H	2B	3B	HR	RBI	BB	SO	SB	OBP	SLG
2021	21	St. Lucie (LoA)	SEast	.274	64	226	46	62	15	1	7	47	41	67	5	.404	.442
	21	Brooklyn (HiA)	East	.218	38	133	20	29	7	0	5	17	13	44	1	.293	.383
Minor League Totals (5 years)				.259	237	851	128	220	56	5	24	142	91	252	16	.341	.421

22 ROBERT DOMINGUEZ, RHP

BA GRADE

50 Risk: Extreme

Born: Nov. 30, 2001. **B-T:** R-R. **HT:** 6-5. **WT:** 195. **Signed:** Venezuela, 2019. **Signed by:** Ismael Perez/Andres Nuñez.

TRACK RECORD: Teams passed over Dominguez when he was first eligible to sign at age 16 in 2018. He moved from Venezuela to the Dominican Republic to train in 2019, and after a series of mechanical adjustments his velocity spiked to 97 mph. The Mets signed him that November right before his 18th birthday. Dominguez made his pro debut in the Florida Complex League in 2021, and while he struck out 10 batters in 12 innings, poor control and command resulted in a 2.00 WHIP.

SCOUTING REPORT: Scouts who see Dominguez at his best are attracted to his fastball velocity, promise of a slider and athletic 6-foot-5 frame. From the Mets' perspective, getting him on the mound and in the strike zone have been challenges. Dominguez dealt with shoulder trouble in 2020 and other off-field maladies in 2021 that put him behind schedule. As a result he made just 12 appearances—none facing more than eight batters—in Rookie ball rather than getting development time in the rotation. Dominguez topped out near 99 mph and averaged 95 with decent ride through the zone. He has some feel for spin

and the potential for an average slider, but it's a low-80s pitch now that he tends to telegraph by cutting off his delivery and not getting the same extension as his fastball delivery. He has not shown much aptitude for a changeup. As a result, lefthanded batters are comfortable in the box because they can sit fastball. Dominguez has put on weight since signing and needs to make conditioning more of a priority.
THE FUTURE: The Mets would like to develop Dominguez as a starter so that he benefits from a consistent routine and has the ability to sharpen his secondary pitches in side sessions. Ultimately his best big league role is probably power reliever—if his slider progresses and he develops just fringe command.

Year	Age	Club (Level)	Lge	W	L	ERA	G	GS	IP	H	HR	BB	SO	BB/9	SO/9	WHIP	AVG
2021	19	FCL Mets (R)	FCL	1	1	8.25	10	1	12	15	1	9	10	6.8	7.5	2.00	.300
Minor League Totals (1 year)				1	1	8.25	10	1	12	15	1	9	10	6.75	7.50	2.00	.300

23 HAYDEN SENGER, C

BA GRADE
45 Risk: High

Born: April 3, 1997. **B-T:** R-R. **HT:** 6-1. **WT:** 210. **Drafted:** Miami (Ohio), 2018 (24th round). **Signed by:** Chris Hervey.
TRACK RECORD: Senger and Nick Meyer were college catchers drafted by the Mets in 2018. The two played for different Class A affiliates in 2019 but spent the 2021 season as teammates at Double-A Binghamton. Meyer has the best defensive reputation in the organization, while Senger offers more offensive production with a solid catching foundation.
SCOUTING REPORT: Senger has the attributes of a future backup catcher with a near-average bat for the position and an above-average arm. His swing is clean and geared toward taking the ball where it's pitched. Senger's exit velocities are above-average and he manipulates the barrel well, but his power output is minimal. The Mets want to see him become more direct to the ball and not fly open when he gets pull-happy. Senger blocks well behind the plate and throws well. He worked to improve his transfer on throws in the Arizona Fall League and is learning the finer points of game-calling that come with experience.
THE FUTURE: The Mets left Senger off the 40-man roster and thus exposed to selection in the Rule 5 draft. He is ready for Triple-A in 2022 and could be on call in the event of an MLB catching emergency.

Year	Age	Club (Level)	Lge	AVG	G	AB	R	H	2B	3B	HR	RBI	BB	SO	SB	OBP	SLG
2021	24	Brooklyn (HiA)	East	.302	11	43	10	13	5	1	2	4	3	16	0	.362	.605
	24	Binghamton (AA)	NEast	.254	50	181	23	46	13	1	3	10	16	62	0	.337	.387
Minor League Totals (4 years)				.254	183	631	81	160	46	4	10	68	57	173	0	.345	.387

24 JAVIER ATENCIO, LHP

BA GRADE
50 Risk: Extreme

Born: Nov. 26, 2001. **B-T:** L-L. **HT:** 6-0. **WT:** 160. **Signed:** Venezuela, 2018. **Signed by:** Andres Nuñez.
TRACK RECORD: The Mets signed Atencio as a 16-year-old in 2018, and while he hasn't yet advanced beyond the Dominican Summer League, he showed promise in 2021. The 19-year-old lefty ranked second in the DSL with 76 strikeouts and seventh with a 1.58 ERA. Had it not been so difficult to transfer players in the time of Covid, the Mets probably would have brought Atencio to the U.S.
SCOUTING REPORT: Atencio tops out at 96 mph and throws a power curveball, while his north-south approach proved to be too much for DSL hitters to handle. They hit just .171. Atencio pitches at 92 mph with plus ride characteristics up in the zone. He complements that with a breaking pitch that pairs slider velocity—nearly 80 mph—with more of a curveball shape. He commands the pitch well and generated one of the higher whiff rates in the minor leagues by burying it effectively. He doesn't really throw a changeup at this stage, preferring to change speeds with his curve that ranges from the mid 70s to low 80s.
THE FUTURE: The emergence of Atencio and Luis Rodriguez in 2021 gave the Mets some much-needed lefthanded presence. Atencio will probably get a shot in full-season ball in 2022 and has rotation upside.

Year	Age	Club (Level)	Lge	W	L	ERA	G	GS	IP	H	HR	BB	SO	BB/9	SO/9	WHIP	AVG
2021	19	DSL Mets1 (R)	DSL	1	3	2.44	15	14	48	28	1	19	76	3.6	14.3	0.98	.171
Minor League Totals (2 years)				1	4	3.43	27	22	84	70	3	35	101	3.75	10.82	1.25	.227

25 VINCENT PEROZO, C

BA GRADE
50 Risk: Extreme

Born: March 6, 2003. **B-T:** L-R. **HT:** 6-0. **WT:** 170. **Signed:** Venezuela, 2019. **Signed by:** Robert Espejo.
TRACK RECORD: The Mets signed Perozo out of Venezuela in 2019, and two years later he made his pro debut in the Florida Complex League as an 18-year-old. While his 2021 season appeared to be a dud on the surface, in reality he was playing through a shoulder injury and probably

would have been one of the top prospects in the Dominican Summer League had he been held back. As a sign of his esteem in the industry, Perozo was a popular ask from other clubs in trade talks.

SCOUTING REPORT: Perozo is a lefthanded-hitting catcher with a pro body and swing geared to do damage. He was limited to mostly first base and DH in the FCL because of a left shoulder injury that shut him down in mid August. He attempted to rehab it but ultimately had surgery in mid September. Perozo has good timing and rhythm in his swing and the type of power upside to one day get to 20 homers. He has a good knowledge of the strike zone, as evidenced by his 10 walks and 21 strikeouts in 18 games. Behind the plate, Perozo receives well and has a strong understanding of calling games and helping his pitchers get strikes. His average arm is hindered by a slower transfer, though his overall footwork is good. He projects to be at least an average catch-and-throw receiver.

THE FUTURE: Scouts who have seen Perozo at his best see the potential for a future regular catcher who hits enough to stay in the lineup. He has a long trek ahead of him but could be worth the wait.

Year	Age	Club (Level)	Lge	AVG	G	AB	R	H	2B	3B	HR	RBI	BB	SO	SB	OBP	SLG
2021	18	FCL Mets (R)	FCL	.173	18	52	7	9	2	0	1	6	10	21	0	.348	.269
Minor League Totals (1 year)				.173	18	52	7	9	2	0	1	6	10	21	0	.348	.269

26 JT SCHWARTZ, 1B

Born: Dec. 17, 1999. **B-T:** L-R. **HT:** 6-4. **WT:** 215. **Drafted:** UCLA, 2021 (4th round). **Signed by:** Rusty McNamara.

BA GRADE
45 Risk: Very High

TRACK RECORD: Schwartz was a draft prospect as a SoCal high school shortstop before enrolling at UCLA as a top recruit in 2018. He shifted to first base in college and thrived when he was on the field. Schwartz redshirted as a freshman and missed his sophomore year to the pandemic before breaking out in 2021, when he led the Pacific-12 Conference with a .396 average while drawing 37 walks to 28 strikeouts. The Mets drafted him in the fourth round.

SCOUTING REPORT: Schwartz has demonstrated an ability to discern balls from strikes and get his bat on fastballs, but his power production has to improve. He hit .195 with little power in a 25-game debut at Low-A St. Lucie. The Mets are working with Schwartz to clean up his movement patterns and add muscle to his lanky 6-foot-4 frame. If he can sync up his upper and lower halves and add bat speed, then enhanced exit velocities could follow. But for now his EVs are well below-average for a first baseman. He shows occasional power in batting practice. Schwartz has below-average speed and fringe range at first base. He missed time with a shoulder injury in 2021 and previously had hip surgery and knee problems.

THE FUTURE: Adopting more of a power-over-hit mentality and embracing the idea of taking more chances will help Schwartz move away from his college approach. He will be a key player to watch in 2022.

Year	Age	Club (Level)	Lge	AVG	G	AB	R	H	2B	3B	HR	RBI	BB	SO	SB	OBP	SLG
2021	21	St. Lucie (LoA)	SEast	.195	25	82	9	16	5	0	0	8	13	12	2	.320	.256
Minor League Totals (1 year)				.195	25	82	9	16	5	0	0	8	13	12	2	.320	.256

27 KEVIN KENDALL, SS/2B

Born: June 25, 1999. **B-T:** L-R. **HT:** 5-10. **WT:** 175. **Drafted:** UCLA, 2021 (7th round). **Signed by:** Rusty McNamara.

BA GRADE
45 Risk: Very High

TRACK RECORD: Kendall stood out at UCLA in 2021 for his athleticism, versatility and performance. He had underwhelmed in college to that point—and he missed 2020 with a wrist injury—but a big junior year got him drafted by the Mets in the seventh round. Kendall shined in his pro debut for Low-A St. Lucie, hitting for average while showing strong plate discipline and speed.

SCOUTING REPORT: The Mets' scouting department views the lefthanded-hitting Kendall as a similar athlete to Adam Frazier, a player whose ability to hit and play multiple positions have created MLB value. That will be Kendall's ticket to advancement in pro ball, too. His strongest offensive assets are his swing decisions, high contact rate on pitches in the zone and plus speed that borders on double-plus. The Mets worked with all their hitters invited to instructional league in 2021 to improve their strength and learn to impact the ball with greater frequency. Kendall is a plus defender at shortstop and second base with an average arm. He even proved to be above-average in center field, where he played at UCLA in deference to Reds first-rounder Matt McLain.

THE FUTURE: Kendall's encouraging pro debut and strong showing at instructs sets him up for a productive 2022 season. His upside may fall short of MLB regular but should be enough for utility consideration.

Year	Age	Club (Level)	Lge	AVG	G	AB	R	H	2B	3B	HR	RBI	BB	SO	SB	OBP	SLG
2021	22	St. Lucie (LoA)	SEast	.327	31	113	22	37	7	2	1	11	15	24	8	.421	.451
Minor League Totals (1 year)				.327	31	113	22	37	7	2	1	11	15	24	8	.421	.451

28 JAKE MANGUM, OF

BA GRADE 40 Risk: High

Born: March 8, 1996. **B-T:** B-L. **HT:** 6-1. **WT:** 179. **Drafted:** Mississippi State, 2019 (4th round). **Signed by:** Jet Butler.

TRACK RECORD: Mangum's father and grandfather played in the NFL, and Jake has that competitive drive in common with them. He stayed an extra year at Mississippi State to set the Southeastern Conference's all-time hits record and then signed with the Mets as a 2019 fourth-rounder. Mangum's pro debut was uninspiring, but changes made at the alternate training site in 2020 helped set the stage for a productive 2021 spent mostly at Double-A Binghamton.

SCOUTING REPORT: Mangum altered his hand position to improve his attack angle to the ball. The results became obvious later in the season as he learned he could accomplish more by swinging less. Mangum hit .340/.395/.526 in his final 53 games, at one point reaching base in 29 straight games. He doesn't take a ton of walks but doesn't strike out often, either. Mangum is the best defensive outfielder in the system and an above-average runner with an above-average arm and range in center field.

THE FUTURE: Mangum is driven to reach the major leagues. If his gains from the second half of 2021 hold, then he will do just that, most likely as an extra outfielder.

Year	Age	Club (Level)	Lge	AVG	G	AB	R	H	2B	3B	HR	RBI	BB	SO	SB	OBP	SLG
2021	25	Brooklyn (HiA)	East	.206	9	34	7	7	1	0	2	6	3	15	0	.289	.412
	25	Binghamton (AA)	NEast	.294	75	303	56	89	21	4	7	41	16	58	14	.342	.459
Minor League Totals (3 years)				.272	137	519	92	141	27	6	9	65	34	99	31	.337	.399

29 LUKE RITTER, 2B/1B

BA GRADE 40 Risk: High

Born: Feb. 15, 1997. **B-T:** R-R. **HT:** 5-11. **WT:** 187. **Drafted:** Wichita State, 2019 (7th round). **Signed by:** Nathan Beuster.

TRACK RECORD: The Mets' 2019 draft strategy centered around pooling surplus bonus dollars after the third round in order to go over slot to sign prep pitchers Josh Wolf and Matt Allan. That resulted in the Mets focusing on college seniors in rounds four through 10. Fourth-rounder Jake Mangum and Ritter have developed into notable prospects after signing for a combined $30,000.

SCOUTING REPORT: Ritter led Wichita State with a 1.003 OPS as a senior and earned high grades for his makeup and versatility. He jumped to High-A in 2021, and while at age 24 he was old for the level, he showed the same bat intrigue and leadership ability. Ritter puts the bat on the ball frequently and gets it in the air. He has average power potential that was masked by his pitcher-friendly home park in Brooklyn. He hit 12 of his 14 homers on the road. He broke the hamate bone in his left hand in July, missed four weeks and then hit just three homers the rest of the way. Ritter is playable at second base and first base with near-average fielding and throwing ability, and he's athletic enough to learn to play corner outfield.

THE FUTURE: Ritter has the competitive drive to will himself into the big league conversation as a multi-positional option with power. Next up is the proving ground of Double-A.

Year	Age	Club (Level)	Lge	AVG	G	AB	R	H	2B	3B	HR	RBI	BB	SO	SB	OBP	SLG
2021	24	Brooklyn (HiA)	East	.232	73	250	31	58	9	0	14	44	25	94	3	.311	.436
Minor League Totals (3 years)				.238	141	479	70	114	24	1	18	80	58	144	8	.330	.405

30 JOANDER SUAREZ, RHP

BA GRADE 40 Risk: Very High

Born: Feb. 27, 2000. **B-T:** R-R. **HT:** 6-3. **WT:** 223. **Signed:** Venezuela, 2018. **Signed by:** Carlos Perez.

TRACK RECORD: Suarez signed at age 18 and spent two seasons in Rookie ball, then he had his full-season debut pushed back a year by the pandemic. He made six starts for Low-A St. Lucie in 2021 before having Tommy John surgery in mid June.

SCOUTING REPORT: Suarez missed bats in Low-A Southeast but otherwise proved to be more wild and more hittable than he had shown previously. His 93 mph fastball gets good vertical ride and tops out at 95. His mid-70s curveball has true 12-to-6 life. Suarez also throws a firm, high-80s changeup with run to his arm side. His curve and change get swings and misses, but his fastball is the only pitch he can regularly land for strikes.

THE FUTURE: Suarez probably will miss the 2022 season as he recovers from Tommy John surgery. His most likely future role is lower-leverage reliever.

Year	Age	Club (Level)	Lge	W	L	ERA	G	GS	IP	H	HR	BB	SO	BB/9	SO/9	WHIP	AVG
2021	21	St. Lucie (LoA)	SEast	0	3	7.66	6	6	24	28	3	16	26	5.8	9.5	1.78	.280
Minor League Totals (4 years)				1	4	4.10	25	18	86	71	4	37	92	3.89	9.67	1.26	.223

MORE PROSPECTS TO KNOW

31 ERIC ORZE, RHP
The 24-year-old reliever pitched at three levels up to Triple-A in 2021, striking out 12.1 per nine innings to go with a 3.08 ERA in 49.2 innings. He pitches at 92-94 mph with an average low-80s splitter with swing-and-miss potential and a fringy slider.

32 DAISON ACOSTA, RHP
SLEEPER

The 23-year-old Dominican righthander missed the season rehabbing from Tommy John surgery but resumed throwing after the season. The Mets remain high on Acosta, who has an interesting fastball/slider mix and unique angles created by his long limbs.

33 STANLEY CONSUEGRA, OF
Consuegra is a 21-year-old outfielder who has interesting tools but a spotty track record for health, with his lone uninterrupted season coming in 2018. An appendectomy cost him two months in 2021, but when healthy he showed some power, some speed and a terrific outfield arm in the FCL.

34 WILMER REYES, SS/2B
The breakout star of the Mets' 2020 instructional league, Reyes contended with a knee injury that kept him out most of 2021 before he returned to play in the Arizona Fall League. He has some feel to hit and the versatility to play all over the infield.

35 MICHEL OTAÑEZ, RHP
The 24-year-old moved to the bullpen in 2021 and found a few extra ticks. He averages 98 mph and bumps 101. He walked 41 in 40.1 innings at High-A and lacks feel for his slider and changeup.

36 COLIN HOLDERMAN, RHP
The 6-foot-7 reliever has velocity up to 99 mph but needs to learn to trust his slider to keep hitters off his straight fastball. He's 26 and coming off his most dominant pro season. He reached Double-A.

37 KEYSHAWN ASKEW, LHP
Drafted in the 10th round in 2021 out of Clemson, Askew is a 6-foot-4 lefthander with a sidearm slot and low-90s heat up to 95 mph with late run. He gets good depth on a low-70s curveball that plays up with his uptempo motion and delivery that is all arms and legs.

38 CARSON SEYMOUR, RHP
Drafted in the sixth round in 2021 out of Kansas State, Seymour hit 98 mph in his pro debut with a power slider at 87-90. A move to the bullpen could expedite his development.

39 BRIAN METOYER, RHP
The 25-year-old reliever, a 40th-round pick in 2018, climbed to Double-A and missed bats with a 96 mph fastball and the best curveball in the system. His breaking ball has crazy spin and a high whiff rate. He just needs to land it for strikes more often.

40 CARLOS DOMINGUEZ, OF
The Dominican outfielder finished one off the FCL pace with 10 home runs. He signed late and already is 22, but he has big power and some speed to go with swing-and-miss concerns.

TOP PROSPECTS OF THE DECADE

Year	Player, Pos.	2021 Org
2012	Zack Wheeler, RHP	Phillies
2013	Zack Wheeler, RHP	Phillies
2014	Noah Syndergaard, RHP	Mets
2015	Noah Syndergaard, RHP	Mets
2016	Steven Matz, LHP	Blue Jays
2017	Amed Rosario, SS	Guardians
2018	Andres Gimenez, SS	Guardians
2019	Andres Gimenez, SS	Guardians
2020	Ronny Mauricio, SS	Mets
2021	Francisco Alvarez, C	Mets

TOP DRAFT PICKS OF THE DECADE

Year	Player, Pos	2021 Org
2012	Gavin Cecchini, SS	Angels
2013	Dominic Smith, 1B	Mets
2014	Michael Conforto, OF	Mets
2015	Desmond Lindsay, OF (2nd round)	Mets
2016	Justin Dunn, RHP	Mariners
2017	David Peterson, LHP	Mets
2018	Jarred Kelenic, OF	Mariners
2019	Brett Baty, 3B	Mets
2020	Pete Crow-Armstrong, OF	Cubs
2021	*Kumar Rocker, RHP	None

*Did not sign

New York Yankees

BY JOSH NORRIS

I n 2020, the Yankees stood pat at the trade deadline and lost to the Rays in the Division Series.

A year later, the team went wild at the end of July, acquiring Joey Gallo and Joely Rodriguez from the Rangers, Anthony Rizzo from the Cubs and Andrew Heaney from the Angels in an attempt to balance their lineup and boost their chances in the postseason. The team also spun a pair of infield prospects to Pittsburgh for reliever Clay Holmes.

The deadline moves followed an offseason in which New York refurbished its rotation by acquiring righthander Jameson Taillon from the Pirates and signing two-time Cy Young Award winner Corey Kluber. True to their history, both pitchers spent time on the injured list, though Kluber threw a no-hitter in May.

Instead, all their action bought them was one additional game, a bludgeoning at the hands of the Red Sox in the AL Wild Card Game in Fenway Park. To make the wound's sting all the more acute, Boston used righthander Garrett Whitlock, whom it had plucked from the Yankees in the preceding Rule 5 draft, to end its rival's season.

All those transactions sapped the Yankees' system of plenty of its prospect power—chief among the losses was righthander Roansy Contreras, who went to Pittsburgh in the Taillon deal and blossomed into one of the year's biggest breakout pitchers. The Gallo deal also cost the system intriguing infield prospect Ezequiel Duran, and the Rizzo trade cost upside prospects Alexander Vizcaino and Kevin Alcantara.

Among the players who remained in the system, the biggest gains came from a pair of shortstops. Anthony Volpe, the team's first-round pick in 2019, dominated both Class A levels and had one of the best all-around seasons in the minors. He vaulted to the No. 1 spot in the system and was untouchable in trade talks. The same is true for Oswald Peraza, who continued hitting the ball hard while getting it in the air more often, resulting in a much louder offensive profile to pair with excellent defense.

A host of Yankees arms had breakthrough seasons as well, including righthander Hayden Wesneski and lefty Ken Waldichuk. Both pitchers ended the 2019 season at Rookie-level Pulaski but finished 2021 in the upper levels.

Some of the system's former high-value prospects spun their wheels and kept themselves from factoring into the big club's season. Righthander Deivi Garcia struggled mightily with control and command all season long, and

MVP contender Aaron Judge is the centerpiece of the Yankees' lineup for years to come.

PROJECTED 2025 LINEUP

Catcher	Austin Wells	25
First Base	DJ Lemahieu	36
Second Base	Gleyber Torres	28
Third Base	Anthony Volpe	24
Shortstop	Oswald Peraza	25
Left Field	Joey Gallo	31
Center Field	Jasson Dominguez	22
Right Field	Aaron Judge	33
Designated Hitter	Giancarlo Stanton	35
No. 1 Starter	Gerrit Cole	34
No. 2 Starter	Luis Severino	31
No. 3 Starter	Jordan Montgomery	32
No. 4 Starter	Luis Gil	27
No. 5 Starter	Hayden Wesneski	27
Closer	Jonathan Loaisiga	30

outfielder Estevan Florial continued to deal with swing-and-miss issues, particularly at pitches in the zone. Righthander Clarke Schmidt was injured in the very early days of spring training and missed a large chunk of the year recovering.

Following the season, the Yankees fired hitting coaches P.J. Pilittere and Marcus Thames, as well as third base coach Phil Nevin. The moves were an attempt to get the team's lineup, which is stocked with star-quality players, to more consistently perform at its peak.

If that goal is achieved, perhaps the Yankees can end their current World Series drought, which stands as the longest in franchise history. ■

DEPTH CHART

NEW YORK YANKEES

TOP 2022 ROOKIES	RANK
Clarke Schmidt, RHP	13
Deivi Garcia, RHP	14
BREAKOUT PROSPECTS	**RANK**
Randy Vasquez, RHP	12
Antonio Gomez, C	22

SOURCE OF TOP 30 TALENT

Homegrown	27	Acquired	3
College	9	Trade	2
Junior college	2	Rule 5 draft	0
High school	2	Independent league	0
Nondrafted free agent	1	Free agent/waivers	1
International	13		

LF
Everson Pereira (11)
Elijah Dunham (18)
Aldenis Sanchez

CF
Jasson Dominguez (3)
Estevan Florial (15)
Brandon Lockridge (23)
Raimfer Salinas

RF
Jake Sanford
Madison Santos

3B
Marcos Cabrera
James Nelson

SS
Anthony Volpe (1)
Oswald Peraza (2)
Trey Sweeney (7)
Alexander Vargas (28)
Hans Montero (29)

2B
Oswaldo Cabrera (8)
Cooper Bowman
Benjamin Cowles

1B
Anthony Garcia (27)
Tyler Hardman
Andres Chaparro

C
Austin Wells (5)
Josh Breaux (20)
Antonio Gomez (22)
Anthony Seigler

LHP

LHSP	LHRP
Ken Waldichuk (10)	J.P. Sears (26)
Brock Selvidge (17)	Matt Krook
Robert Ahlstrom	

RHP

RHSP	RHRP
Luis Gil (4)	Ron Marinaccio (21)
Hayden Wesneski (6)	Stephen Ridings (24)
Luis Medina (9)	Greg Weissert (30)
Randy Vasquez (12)	Albert Abreu
Clarke Schmidt (13)	Jhony Brito
Deivi Garcia (14)	Mitch Spence
Brendan Beck (16)	Zach Greene
Yoendrys Gomez (19)	Barrett Loseke
Beck Way (25)	Braden Bristo
Juan Carela	Nick Ernst
Josue Panacual	Jack Neely
Will Warren	Zach Messinger
Tyrone Yulie	
Yarison Ruiz	

1 ANTHONY VOLPE, SS

Born: April 28, 2001. **B-T:** R-R. **HT:** 5-11. **WT:** 180.
Drafted: HS—Morristown, N.J., 2019 (1st round).
Signed by: Matt Hyde.

MIKE JANES/FOUR SEAM IMAGES

TRACK RECORD: Entering the 2021 season, Volpe's career could be best described as incomplete. Drafted in the first round in 2019, his first test in pro ball at Rookie-level Pulaski was marred by a case of mononucleosis. The 2020 season was canceled because of the coronavirus pandemic, and the Yankees did not hold a domestic instructional league, which left Volpe to do as much development as he could through independent training and via remote work with the organization's coaches. He emerged from the shutdown with renewed health and added strength, which he used to produce one of the finest seasons in the minor leagues. In a season split evenly between Low-A Tampa and High-A Hudson Valley he hit .294/.423/.604 with 27 home runs and 33 stolen bases in 109 games. What Volpe did in 2021 not only positioned him as a clear piece of the organization's long term plans, it exceeded even the Yankees' wildest expectations.

SCOUTING REPORT: Volpe entered what appeared to be a standard minor league offseason in 2020 with the goal of increasing his peak exit velocity. He had much longer than expected to achieve that goal, but quickly showed off his more powerful swing by producing average and maximum exit velocities of 91.5 and 108.3 mph before a move from Low-A to High-A. He's gone all-in on the Yankees' internal motto of "Hit Strikes Hard" and produces some of the highest quality at-bats in the organization. He controls at-bats from the moment he gets in the box and does not relent no matter the count. He shows no fear with two strikes and is content to foul off pitches until he gets something he can do damage on. Whether he's facing premium velocity, high spin or extreme changes of speed, Volpe stays balanced and on time, often resulting in a ball hit with authority. The combination of increased strength and a mature approach have produced a player who earns future plus grades for both his hitting and power. In the field, Volpe shows quick actions and instincts as well as solid hands and footwork, all of which make up for fringe-average range and a near-average arm boosted by strong accuracy and a solid internal clock. Scouts are split on whether he can remain a shortstop, mostly because of his fringy arm, but even his doubters acknowledge his outstanding work ethic could help him work to increase his arm strength. Volpe is an above-average runner as

BA GRADE	SCOUTING GRADES
65 Risk: High	Hit: 60. Power: 60. Run: 55. Field: 50. Arm: 45.

Projected future grades on 20-80 scouting scale

BEST TOOLS

Best Hitter for Average	Anthony Volpe
Best Power Hitter	Anthony Garcia
Best Strike-Zone Discipline	Anthony Volpe
Fastest Baserunner	Oswald Peraza
Best Athlete	Estevan Florial
Best Fastball	Stephen Ridings
Best Curveball	Clarke Schmidt
Best Slider	Greg Weissert
Best Changeup	Ron Marinaccio
Best Control	Jhony Brito
Best Defensive Catcher	Antonio Gomez
Best Defensive Infielder	Oswald Peraza
Best Infield Arm	Oswald Peraza
Best Defensive Outfielder	Estevan Florial
Best Outfield Arm	Estevan Florial

well—his stolen base totals were somewhat inflated in Low-A due to the rules designed to promote increased activity on the bases—and he has enough speed and aptitude to steal double-digit bases. From the first day of minor league spring training, scouts buzzed about Volpe's combination of skills, instincts and makeup.

THE FUTURE: After conquering both Class A levels, Volpe's next test will be Double-A Somerset. The biggest question he'll have to answer is whether he faces a move to second base, either in deference to fellow prospect Oswald Peraza or a free agent import. ∎

Year	Age	Club (Level)	Lge	AVG	G	AB	R	H	2B	3B	HR	RBI	BB	SO	SB	OBP	SLG
2021	20	Tampa (LoA)	SEast	.302	54	199	56	60	18	5	12	49	51	43	21	.455	.623
	20	Hudson Valley (HiA)	East	.286	55	213	57	61	17	1	15	37	27	58	12	.391	.587
Minor League Totals (3 years)				.276	143	533	132	147	42	8	29	97	101	139	39	.406	.548

2 OSWALD PERAZA, SS

Born: June 15, 2000. **B-T:** R-R. **HT:** 5-11. **WT:** 186. **Signed:** Venezuela, 2016. **Signed by:** Roney Calderon/Jose Gavidia.

BA GRADE
55 Risk: High

TRACK RECORD: Peraza signed with the Yankees in 2016 and quickly opened evaluators' eyes with a burgeoning hit tool and the chops to stick up the middle. He held his own as a 19-year-old in his first taste of full-season ball toward the end of 2019 at Low-A Charleston. Added to the 40-man roster after the 2020 season, Peraza produced a breakout in 2021, when he eclipsed his career totals for doubles (26) and home runs (18) while climbing from High-A to Triple-A.

SCOUTING REPORT: After the 2020 season, the Yankees' hitting department suggested that Peraza could get more out of his game simply by changing his approach. He hit the ball plenty hard but needed to get the ball in the air more often. The changes worked. In 2019, Peraza carried one of the highest groundball rates in the minors. He moved to the middle of the pack in 2021. In other words, he's getting the most out of his quality contact. His next hurdle will be hitting against breaking balls. Multiple scouts noted he was vulnerable to spin, though he showed improvement and adjustability as the season wore on. Peraza is likely to stick at shortstop, though he's not the twitchiest athlete. Instead, he relies on above-average speed, strong instincts and reaction times to make plays.

THE FUTURE: Peraza has taken the leap and upped his prospect status in the process. The next step will be to add polish to his game and prepare for his big league debut, which should come sometime in 2022.

SCOUTING GRADES:	Hitting: 60	Power: 50	Running: 55	Fielding: 55	Arm: 55

Year	Age	Club (Level)	Lge	AVG	G	AB	R	H	2B	3B	HR	RBI	BB	SO	SB	OBP	SLG
2021	21	Hudson Valley (HiA)	East	.306	28	111	20	34	10	0	5	16	12	24	16	.386	.532
	21	Somerset (AA)	NEast	.294	79	326	51	96	16	2	12	40	23	82	20	.348	.466
	21	Scranton/W-B (AAA)	East	.286	8	28	5	8	0	0	1	2	2	5	2	.323	.393
Minor League Totals (5 years)				.280	274	1087	183	304	48	8	23	123	95	227	82	.353	.402

3 JASSON DOMINGUEZ, OF

Born: Feb. 7, 2003. **B-T:** B-R. **HT:** 5-10. **WT:** 210. **Signed:** Dominican Republic, 2019. **Signed by:** Juan Rosario/Lorenzo Piron/Edgar Mateo.

BA GRADE
60 Risk: Extreme

TRACK RECORD: Some scouts labeled Dominguez as one of the best international prospects they had seen when he signed out of the Dominican Republic for $5.1 million in 2019. The lost season in 2020 pushed his debut back further but only increased the anticipation. He started the year in the Florida Complex League before moving to Low-A Tampa, where he held his own as one of a handful of 18-year-olds in full-season ball. Despite his inexperience, Dominguez participated in the 2021 Futures Game.

SCOUTING REPORT: Dominguez has thickened up considerably into a much stockier player, which leads to questions about whether he can stick in center field. He's already slowed down and now earns grades closer to average than the plus-plus times scouts once saw. If Dominguez moves to a corner, his average arm, which has also backed up, will play in right field. At the plate, Dominguez went through the expected growing pains of dealing with pitchers who were more experienced and knew how to attack him with spin. The quality of his at-bats and swing decisions got better as the season went on, culminating in a .777 OPS in September. Outside evaluators noted plenty of excellent impact on contact, and he produced average and maximum exit velocities of 86 and 111 mph during his time in Low-A.

THE FUTURE: Though he did not show the star-level performance that would be expected of a player with his hype, Dominguez certainly held his own, especially considering the long layoff after signing. There's quite a bit of polish still to apply, but Dominguez could reach a ceiling of an impact MLB regular.

SCOUTING GRADES:	Hitting: 55	Power: 60	Running: 50	Fielding: 50	Arm: 50

Year	Age	Club (Level)	Lge	AVG	G	AB	R	H	2B	3B	HR	RBI	BB	SO	SB	OBP	SLG
2021	18	Yankees (R)	FCL	.200	7	20	5	4	0	0	0	1	6	6	2	.407	.200
	18	Tampa (LoA)	SEast	.258	49	186	26	48	9	1	5	18	21	67	7	.346	.398
Minor League Totals (1 year)				.252	56	206	31	52	9	1	5	19	27	73	9	.353	.379

4 LUIS GIL, RHP

Born: June 3, 1998. **B-T:** R-R. **HT:** 6-2. **WT:** 185. **Signed:** Dominican Republic, 2014. **Signed by:** Luis Lajara (Twins).

TRACK RECORD: Four years after signing with the Twins, Gil was dealt to the Yankees for outfielder Jake Cave in 2018. He entered 2019 as part of a pack of talented righthanders that also included Luis Medina, Roansy Contreras and Alexander Vizcaino. Contreras and Vizcaino have since been traded, while Medina continues to show flashes of dominance. Gil put together a strong season thanks to further development of his changeup and was rewarded with his first big league callup, where he posted a 3.07 ERA in six starts.

SCOUTING REPORT: Gil is a hard-throwing starter with a classic pitcher's frame built to withstand the rigors of a high workload. His hallmark is a lively fastball that averages 96 mph and his mid-80s slider continues to be his best secondary weapon and a potential plus pitch. One of the keys to his future will be the development of his low-90s changeup, which needs to show more movement and separation from his fastball to be an effective third pitch. His fringy control caught up with him at Triple-A, where he walked 15% of hitters, and remains a limiting factor.

THE FUTURE: After a taste of the big leagues in 2021, Gil should battle for a spot on the Opening Day roster. If his changeup and control improve, he can be part of the starting rotation. If not, he could be an effective late-inning reliever.

BA GRADE
55 Risk: High

SCOUTING GRADES:	Fastball: 60	Slider: 60	Changeup: 50	Control: 45

Year	Age	Club (Level)	Lge	W	L	ERA	G	GS	IP	H	HR	BB	SO	BB/9	SO/9	WHIP	AVG
2021	23	Somerset (AA)	NEast	1	1	2.64	7	7	30	24	2	13	50	3.8	14.7	1.21	.207
	23	Scranton/W-B (AAA)	East	4	0	4.81	13	10	48	35	7	32	67	5.9	12.4	1.38	.202
	23	New York (MLB)	AL	1	1	3.07	6	6	29	20	4	19	38	5.8	11.7	1.33	.183
Major League Totals (1 year)				1	1	3.07	6	6	29	20	4	19	38	5.83	11.66	1.33	.183
Minor League Totals (7 years)				13	13	3.08	82	63	286	208	16	169	381	5.31	11.98	1.32	.201

5 AUSTIN WELLS, C

Born: July 12, 1999. **B-T:** L-R. **HT:** 6-1. **WT:** 200. **Drafted:** Arizona, 2020 (1st round). **Signed by:** Troy Afenir.

TRACK RECORD: The Yankees drafted Wells out of high school in 2018 and again in the first round in 2020 when he was a draft-eligible sophomore at Arizona. The coronavirus pandemic cost Wells most of his final collegiate season and limited him to remote training during the regular season. In his pro debut in 2021, he showed hitting ability, power and patience and produced one of the best overall years in the system as he moved from Low-A to High-A.

SCOUTING REPORT: Wells shows a smooth, loose, repeatable swing capable of producing loud contact to all sectors. He expertly manages the strike zone, which shows up in his strikeout and walk totals, although those numbers were somewhat buttressed by spending the first part of the season in Low-A Southeast, which used automated balls and strikes. The Yankees did

BA GRADE
50 Risk: High

tweak Wells' approach to make him more aggressive in two-strike counts. With his swing, strength and approach, he projects to be a plus hitter with average power. Few outside the organization believe Wells can stick behind the plate as a catcher. His lack of twitchiness, struggles blocking pitches and well below-average arm strength make him a below-average defender. Even if he moves off catcher, he has the bat to profile at either first base or left field.

THE FUTURE: Wells will head to Double-A in 2022. Regardless of what position he ends up at, he has a chance to be the impact lefthanded hitter the Yankees have lacked in recent years.

SCOUTING GRADES:	Hitting: 60	Power: 50	Running: 50	Fielding: 40	Arm: 40

Year	Age	Club (Level)	Lge	AVG	G	AB	R	H	2B	3B	HR	RBI	BB	SO	SB	OBP	SLG
2021	21	Tampa (LoA)	SEast	.258	65	236	61	61	17	4	9	54	51	62	11	.398	.479
2021	21	Hudson Valley (HiA)	East	.274	38	146	21	40	6	1	7	22	20	55	5	.376	.473
Minor League Totals (2 years)				.264	103	382	82	101	23	5	16	76	71	117	16	.390	.476

6 HAYDEN WESNESKI, RHP

Born: Dec. 5, 1997. **B-T:** R-R. **HT:** 6-3. **WT:** 210. **Drafted:** Sam Houston State, 2019 (6th round). **Signed by:** Brian Rhees.

TRACK RECORD: A 33rd-round pick by the Rays out of high school, Wesneski instead went to Sam Houston State, improved his fitness and saw a corresponding jump in stuff. That led the Yankees to take him in the sixth round in 2019. Wesneski got his feet wet in Rookie ball in his pro debut, then made great strides via remote training during the canceled 2020 season and rocketed from High-A to Triple-A in 2021.

SCOUTING REPORT: Wesneski works with an arsenal of four- and two-seam fastballs, a slider, a changeup, a curveball and a newly added cutter. The four-seamer parks in the mid 90s and has peaked at 99 mph with heavy sinking life. His average slider has short, sweepy break, while his curveball is potentially plus and acts more like a powerful slurve with horizontal and vertical break. His changeup is a potentially average pitch and is thrown in the low 80s. Wesneski's delivery features a deep shoulder load, a three-quarters slot and a wider release point that leads to fringy control. He'll have to improve his direction to the plate in order to help his stuff maintain its consistency.

THE FUTURE: After reaching Triple-A for his last two starts of 2021, Wesneski is likely to return to the level. There, he'll work on continuing to develop his cutter, learning how to better sequence his wide arsenal and honing his control and command to reach his ceiling as a No. 4 or 5 starter.

BA GRADE
50 Risk: High

SCOUTING GRADES:	Fastball: 70	Slider: 50	Curveball: 60	Changeup: 50	Control: 45

Year	Age	Club (Level)	Lge	W	L	ERA	G	GS	IP	H	HR	BB	SO	BB/9	SO/9	WHIP	AVG
2021	23	Hudson Valley (HiA)	East	1	1	1.49	7	7	36	24	2	9	47	2.2	11.6	0.91	.194
	23	Somerset (AA)	NEast	8	4	4.01	15	15	83	76	11	22	92	2.4	10.0	1.18	.241
	23	Scranton/W-B (AAA)	East	2	1	3.27	3	2	11	10	0	5	12	4.1	9.8	1.36	.244
Minor League Totals (3 years)				12	7	3.52	43	24	159	142	14	42	181	2.38	10.27	1.16	.237

7 TREY SWEENEY, SS

Born: April 24, 2000. **B-T:** L-R. **HT:** 6-4. **WT:** 200. **Drafted:** Eastern Illinois, 2021 (1st round). **Signed by:** Steve Lemke.

TRACK RECORD: Undrafted out of high school, Sweeney showed enough improvement during his time at Eastern Illinois for the Yankees to draft him 20th overall in 2021. He signed for $3 million and reached Low-A Tampa in his pro debut, where he showed the same hitting ability and plate discipline that were his hallmarks in college.

SCOUTING REPORT: Sweeney earns praise for his polished offensive skill set and ability to command the strike zone and get pitches to drive. He blasted three home runs during the regular season with Tampa, then added one more during the playoffs. The Yankees have identified areas for improvement, including smoothing out his bat path and working to make his exit velocities more consistent. If he makes those adjustments, he could be a plus hitter with average power. Sweeney has fringe-average pure foot speed, but his advanced instincts make him a plus baserunner. Defensively, Sweeney's athleticism, above-average arm strength and solid baseball IQ could allow him to stick up the middle even if he has to move off of shortstop.

BA GRADE
50 Risk: High

THE FUTURE: Sweeney will likely begin 2022 at High-A Hudson Valley. He's behind Anthony Volpe and Oswald Peraza on the organization depth chart, but has a chance to surface as an everyday infielder in the Bronx.

SCOUTING GRADES:	Hitting: 60	Power: 50	Running: 45	Fielding: 50	Arm: 55

Year	Age	Club (Level)	Lge	AVG	G	AB	R	H	2B	3B	HR	RBI	BB	SO	SB	OBP	SLG
2021	21	Yankees (R)	FCL	.600	3	5	4	3	0	0	1	1	4	2	1	.778	1.200
	21	Tampa (LoA)	SEast	.245	29	110	26	27	4	4	6	13	18	29	3	.357	.518
Minor League Totals (1 year)				.261	32	115	30	30	4	4	7	14	22	31	4	.384	.548

8 OSWALDO CABRERA, 2B/3B

Born: March 1, 1999. **B-T:** B-R. **HT:** 6-0. **WT:** 200. **Signed:** Venezuela, 2015.
Signed by: Borman Landaeta.

TRACK RECORD: Cabrera signed with the Yankees in 2015 and slowly wound his way through the system. He always made plenty of contact but failed to produce much power. That changed in 2021. He relocated to Tampa during the coronavirus shutdown and added strength and power to his game. His hard work paid off with 29 home runs in 2021 between Double-A and Triple-A and a .272/.330/.553 overall slash line.

SCOUTING REPORT: Cabrera has gained 55 pounds since signing and has become visibly stronger and more filled out. He has increased his average exit velocity by 5 mph jump over the past two seasons and also begun putting the ball in the air more. He's accomplished that while maintaining his excellent bat-to-ball skills, giving him a chance to hit for both average power. Cabrera has slowed down as he's filled out and is now a below-average runner. He can play shortstop in a pinch but is better suited for a utility role in which he sees time at second and third base. He has the potential to be an above-average or plus defender at either of the latter two positions with his solid hands and actions and above-average arm strength.

THE FUTURE: He will likely start the 2022 season back at Triple-A. If he can maintain his improvements, he could make his major league debut during the season.

MIKE JANES/FOUR SEAM IMAGES

BA GRADE

50 Risk: High

SCOUTING GRADES:	Hitting: 40	Power: 50	Running: 40	Fielding: 60	Arm: 55

Year	Age	Club (Level)	Lge	AVG	G	AB	R	H	2B	3B	HR	RBI	BB	SO	SB	OBP	SLG
2021	22	Somerset (AA)	NEast	.256	109	437	61	112	29	1	24	78	36	118	20	.311	.492
	22	Scranton/W-B (AAA)	East	.500	9	30	11	15	2	1	5	11	5	9	1	.583	1.133
Minor League Totals (6 years)				.262	528	2007	257	526	113	8	51	271	146	376	50	.314	.403

9 LUIS MEDINA, RHP

Born: May 3, 1999. **B-T:** R-R. **HT:** 6-3. **WT:** 195. **Signed:** Dominican Republic, 2015. **Signed by:** Juan Rosario.

TRACK RECORD: Medina's path through the minors has been bumpy, to say the least. He signed with the Yankees in 2015 and was celebrated for his triple-digit fastball, but he didn't make it past the Class A levels until 2021, largely due to ghastly command and control. After physical and mental tweaks to help him find the strike zone more, Medina went 6-4, 3.39 in 22 appearances (21 starts) between High-A and Double-A with a high strikeout rate (11.3 K/9) but also a high walk rate (5.1 BB/9).

SCOUTING REPORT: Medina's pure stuff is tremendous. His fastball lives in the upper 90s and peaks at 103 mph, and he pairs it with a hard, downer curveball and an improving changeup. When it's on, his curveball is a true wipeout pitch that can generate plenty of swings and misses. Medina's average changeup doesn't have big-time movement but can upset hitters' timing because of the conviction with which he throws it as well as the velocity separation. As ever, improving his below-average control is going to be the key to his success. If he can find the zone more often, he could keep his future as a starter alive. To do so, he'll have to find more consistency with his delivery and work to keep his arm more on time and in sync.

BA GRADE

50 Risk: High

THE FUTURE: Medina is already on the 40-man roster, so his big league debut could come as soon as next season. He still has to conquer Triple-A, where he'll face much more seasoned hitters who will give his control its biggest test yet.

SCOUTING GRADES:	Fastball: 70	Curveball: 60	Changeup: 50	Control: 40

Year	Age	Club (Level)	Lge	W	L	ERA	G	GS	IP	H	HR	BB	SO	BB/9	SO/9	WHIP	AVG
2021	22	Hudson Valley (HiA)	East	2	1	2.76	7	7	32	18	4	19	50	5.2	13.8	1.13	.162
	22	Somerset (AA)	NEast	4	3	3.67	15	14	73	65	7	41	83	5.0	10.1	1.44	.239
Minor League Totals (6 years)				10	17	4.73	69	67	289	241	24	204	350	6.35	10.89	1.54	.227

10 KEN WALDICHUK, LHP

Born: Jan. 8, 1998. **B-T:** L-L. **HT:** 6-4. **WT:** 220. **Drafted:** St. Mary's, 2019 (5th round). **Signed by:** Tyler Robertson.

TRACK RECORD: Waldichuk went undrafted out of high school but improved dramatically during his three years at St. Mary's. The Yankees drafted him in the fifth round in 2019, then let him get his feet wet at Rookie-level Pulaski. Waldichuk developed remotely during the lost 2020 season, then came out of the gate on fire in 2021, when he went the first 34 innings before allowing a run. He finished the year with 163 strikeouts, tied for fourth in the minors, as he climbed from High-A to Double-A.

BA GRADE
50 Risk: High

SCOUTING REPORT: Waldichuk is the Yankees' preeminent king of funk. He stymies hitters not only with his stuff, but a slinger-type delivery that confuses hitters with arms, legs and angles. All of that movement allows his stuff to play up. His arsenal starts with a four-seam fastball that sits 92-93 mph with tail and carry at the top of the zone. Waldichuk backs up his fastball with an array of average offspeed pitches. His slider flashes excellent depth at the bottom of the zone and he also has a slurvier curveball that has similar shape but less velocity than his slider. His changeup flashes above-average to plus and may end up his best secondary. Waldichuk's control will be the true key to his success. His delivery is difficult to repeat and yields fringy control which, combined with his lack of a true out pitch, was part of the reason he was less successful after moving to Double-A.

THE FUTURE: Waldichuk should move to Triple-A to begin 2022. He'll need to improve his command and control and find a separator offspeed pitch in order to remain a starter.

SCOUTING GRADES:	Fastball: 60	Slider: 50	Curveball: 45	Changeup: 55	Control: 45

Year	Age	Club (Level)	Lge	W	L	ERA	G	GS	IP	H	HR	BB	SO	BB/9	SO/9	WHIP	AVG
2021	23	Hudson Valley (HiA)	East	2	0	0.00	7	7	30	12	0	13	55	3.8	16.1	0.82	.120
	23	Somerset (AA)	NEast	4	3	4.20	16	14	79	64	13	38	108	4.3	12.3	1.29	.218
Minor League Totals (3 years)				6	5	3.17	33	31	139	95	15	58	212	3.75	13.69	1.10	.190

11 EVERSON PEREIRA, OF

BA GRADE
50 Risk: High

Born: April 10, 2001. **B-T:** R-R. **HT:** 5-10. **WT:** 191. **Signed:** Venezuela, 2017. **Signed by:** Roney Calderon.

TRACK RECORD: Pereira's career has been stalled greatly by both injuries and the pandemic. His 2019 season was limited to just 18 games because of a severely sprained ankle, and then nearly all his 2020 work was done remotely because of the pandemic until instructional league convened in the Dominican Republic. He entered the year still needing to deliver upon the potential promised by his enviable tool set, then did so in emphatic fashion.

SCOUTING REPORT: Pereira's best tools lie on the offensive side of the ball, where he shows high-end bat speed and exit velocities, as well as a bat path that keeps the barrel in the zone a long time. In combination, those traits helped him produce incredible power numbers, especially once he reached High-A. He finished third on High-A Hudson Valley with 14 home runs despite playing just 27 games with the team. The biggest thing to clean up right now is swinging and missing at pitches in the strike zone, which he did at a rate of 41% all season. On defense he has a chance to stick in center field but will likely move to a corner, where his average speed and strong throwing arm should serve him well.

THE FUTURE: The Yankees added Pereira to the 40-man roster to keep him from being selected in the Rule 5 Draft. He should reach Double-A at some point next season.

Year	Age	Club (Level)	Lge	AVG	G	AB	R	H	2B	3B	HR	RBI	BB	SO	SB	OBP	SLG
2021	20	Yankees (R)	FCL	.375	3	8	3	3	2	0	1	3	3	2	0	.545	1.000
	20	Tampa (LoA)	SEast	.361	19	72	17	26	5	1	5	22	10	21	4	.446	.667
	20	Hudson Valley (HiA)	East	.259	27	108	27	28	3	0	14	32	15	38	5	.354	.676
Minor League Totals (4 years)				.266	108	425	77	113	21	3	24	85	47	147	15	.341	.499

12 RANDY VASQUEZ, RHP

BA GRADE
50 Risk: High

Born: Nov. 3, 1998. **B-T:** R-R. **HT:** 6-0. **WT:** 165. **Signed:** Dominican Republic, 2018. **Signed by:** Arturo Pena.

TRACK RECORD: The Yankees added Vasquez as part of their 2017-18 class, which also included Everson Pereira and the since-traded Ezequiel Duran. He was solid over his first two seasons, during which time he advanced to Rookie-level Pulaski. He came back from the lost 2020 season and was set to be traded to the Rangers in an early version of the trade that brought Joey Gallo to New York. That version was scuttled by an injury to Texas lefty John King, so Vasquez stayed with the Yankees and shot all the way to Double-A.

SCOUTING REPORT: Vasquez used a couple of key changes to fuel his big year. First, he added a two-seam fastball to go with his four-seamer. To make that pitch more effective, he lowered his arm slot. The aim was to give Vasquez a pitch profile that was more horizontal, and it worked. His four-seamer sat in the mid 90s and touched as high as 98, while his two-seamer came in a tick lower and played as a potentially average pitch. He showed huge spin—an average of more than 3,000 rpms—on both his low-80s curveball and high-80s slider as well. His changeup came along, but at an average of 88 mph still could use a bit more separation from his fastball.

THE FUTURE: Because he signed late, Vasquez did not need to be added to the 40-man roster. He'll likely return to Double-A, and has a future as a potential back-end rotation piece.

Year	Age	Club (Level)	Lge	W	L	ERA	G	GS	IP	H	HR	BB	SO	BB/9	SO/9	WHIP	AVG
2021	22	Tampa (LoA)	SEast	3	3	2.34	13	11	50	35	2	23	58	4.1	10.4	1.16	.189
2021	22	Hudson Valley (HiA)	East	3	0	1.75	6	6	36	33	0	8	53	2.0	13.3	1.14	.241
	22	Somerset (AA)	NEast	2	1	4.22	4	4	21	23	2	7	19	3.0	8.0	1.41	.258
Minor League Totals (4 years)				13	6	2.62	43	39	192	143	11	78	211	3.65	9.87	1.15	.203

13 CLARKE SCHMIDT, RHP

BA GRADE

45 Risk: Medium

Born: Feb. 20, 1996. **B-T:** R-R. **HT:** 6-1. **WT:** 209. **Drafted:** South Carolina, 2017 (1st round). **Signed by:** Billy Godwin.

TRACK RECORD: The Yankees took Schmidt in 2017 knowing he'd need Tommy John surgery. He had the surgery, then made his pro debut late in the 2018 season. In 2019, he showed the potential the Yankees sought when they drafted him, and developed enough in 2020 at the alternate training site to make his big league debut in 2020. Schmidt strained his pitching elbow in the early days of spring training, which kept him out until a rehab appearance on July 26 and limited him to just 6.1 big league innings in 2021.

SCOUTING REPORT: At his best, Schmidt mixes an excellent two-seam fastball with a hard, low-80s curveball which rates as the best in the system. He also added a slider this season to give him more options and a more natural pairing with his sinker. The slider checks in at around 86 mph on average and is understandably behind his curveball. Schmidt also has a four-seam fastball in roughly the same velo range as his sinker, as well as a changeup in the high 80s, but his two-seamer and curveball are his clear money pitches. The next step will be for his command and control to improve.

THE FUTURE: Because his workload was so small in 2021—just 44.1 innings between the minors and majors—it is hard to envision Schmidt as a viable rotation candidate in 2022. It is more likely he'll either head to Triple-A or be utilized as a multi-inning option out of the bullpen.

Year	Age	Club (Level)	Lge	W	L	ERA	G	GS	IP	H	HR	BB	SO	BB/9	SO/9	WHIP	AVG
2021	25	Yankees (R)	FCL	0	0	0.00	1	1	3	1	0	0	5	0.0	15.0	0.33	.111
	25	Tampa (LoA)	SEast	0	0	3.00	1	1	3	1	0	2	4	6.0	12.0	1.00	.111
	25	Somerset (AA)	NEast	0	1	4.26	2	2	6	5	2	2	5	2.8	7.1	1.11	.208
	25	Scranton/W-B (AAA)	East	0	6	2.10	6	5	25	25	4	8	32	2.8	11.2	1.29	.245
	25	New York (MLB)	AL	0	0	5.68	2	1	6	11	1	5	6	7.1	8.5	2.53	.355
Major League Totals (2 years)				0	1	6.39	5	2	13	18	1	10	13	7.11	9.24	2.21	.316
Minor League Totals (4 years)				6	10	3.14	37	34	152	127	11	46	178	2.72	10.54	1.14	.225

14 DEIVI GARCIA, RHP

BA GRADE

45 Risk: Medium

Born: May 19, 1999. **B-T:** R-R. **HT:** 5-10. **WT:** 167. **Signed:** Dominican Republic, 2015. **Signed by:** Miguel Benitez.

TRACK RECORD: After signing in 2015, Garcia and his signature curveball rose through the system on the way to a spot as its top pitching prospect. He made his big league debut on Aug. 30, 2020, and opened a game in the Yankees' playoff series against the Rays that year. This season, the wheels came off. His command and control vanished, and his 68 walks were the most by any pitcher in the organization.

SCOUTING REPORT: A great deal of Garcia's issues with control and command stem from the introduction of a slider and a delivery that has gotten out of whack as a result. Specifically, he started to fly open with his stride and his arm slot wandered, leading to a lot of pitches sprayed all over the zone but particularly high and to his armside. The drop in his arm slot was particularly noticeable on his curveball, which lacked any semblance of its former dominance and was his least-thrown offspeed pitch. A lot of analytical components point to Garcia's rebound potential, but he must first fix his mechanical issues and rebuild his confidence after a season that was 180 degrees from what was expected.

THE FUTURE: After a rough 2021 season, Garcia will head back to Triple-A to try to start fresh and re-establish some of his dented prospect stock. He's an extraordinarily driven, competitive pitcher, and he has age still firmly on his side, but there's a lot of work to be done.

Year	Age	Club (Level)	Lge	W	L	ERA	G	GS	IP	H	HR	BB	SO	BB/9	SO/9	WHIP	AVG
2021	22	Scranton/W-B (AAA)	East	3	7	6.85	24	22	90	102	21	68	97	6.8	9.6	1.88	.285
	22	New York (MLB)	AL	0	2	6.48	2	2	8	8	1	4	7	4.3	7.6	1.44	.250
Major League Totals (2 years)				3	4	5.27	8	8	43	43	7	10	40	2.11	8.44	1.24	.253
Minor League Totals (5 years)				20	27	4.19	89	79	384	313	44	193	513	4.52	12.01	1.32	.223

15 ESTEVAN FLORIAL, OF

Born: Nov. 25, 1997. **B-T:** L-L. **HT:** 6-1. **WT:** 195. **Signed:** Haiti, 2015.
Signed by: Esteban Castillo.

TRACK RECORD: After a 2017 season in which he was the system's most bal-lyhooed prospect, Florial's progress came to a screeching halt thanks to a series of injuries to his hands and wrists in the next two seasons. He was limited to 149 non-rehab games over those seasons, then spent 2020 at the team's alternate training site. He got off to a hot start in 2021 at Double-A, then looked completely overmatched after a promotion to Triple-A.

SCOUTING REPORT: As ever, Florial has plenty of strong tools. Internal evaluators rate his defense and throwing arm as the best among the system's outfielders, and his athleticism also grades out as the organization's best. He still is capable of hitting the ball plenty hard—his exit velocities in the minors maxed out at 111 mph—but he still swings and misses far too often, particularly at pitches in the strike zone, and he struck out at a nearly 31% clip in Triple-A. To that end, the Yankees have been working with Florial to find a bat path that keeps his barrel in the zone for a longer amount of time. They've seen some month-over-month results, but he still needs plenty of seasoning. His speed and athleticism will give him plenty of chances to stick in center field, but his bat will determine how often his name is written into the lineup.

THE FUTURE: Florial made a few cameos in New York and hit his first big league home run, but overall still showed he had plenty of holes to close if he is to ever live up to his potential.

Year	Age	Club (Level)	Lge	AVG	G	AB	R	H	2B	3B	HR	RBI	BB	SO	SB	OBP	SLG
2021	23	Somerset (AA)	NEast	.229	9	35	5	8	2	0	4	6	4	9	0	.308	.629
	23	Scranton/W-B (AAA)	East	.218	78	312	65	68	17	1	13	41	42	112	13	.315	.404
	23	New York (MLB)	AL	.300	11	20	3	6	2	0	1	2	5	6	1	.440	.550
Major League Totals (2 years)				.304	12	23	3	7	2	0	1	2	5	8	1	.429	.522
Minor League Totals (6 years)				.263	479	1854	331	488	92	25	59	260	228	605	86	.345	.435

16 BRENDAN BECK, RHP

Born: Oct. 6, 1998. **B-T:** R-R. **HT:** 6-2. **WT:** 205. **Drafted:** Stanford, 2021 (2nd round). **Signed by:** Tyler Robertson.

TRACK RECORD: Beck is the younger brother of Tristan Beck, who also pitched at Stanford and was the Braves' fourth-round pick in 2018. The younger Beck shined for the Cardinal in 2021, helping lead the team to a national seed and a berth in the College World Series. The Yankees liked his pitch mix, polish and competitiveness, and signed him for $1,050,000 in the second round.

SCOUTING REPORT: Perhaps the most important development affecting Beck's draft stock was his spike in velocity. His fastball moved from an 88-92 mph offering to a 91-96 mph pitch in his final year in college. The Yankees like Beck's slider the best out of all his offspeed pitches, but project his low-80s changeup and high-70s curveball to each be at least above-average. As an amateur, scouts preferred his changeup as the best of that trio, followed by his slider and curve. He also should have above-average control once he reaches his peak. The entirety of Beck's repertoire should be accentuated by his feel to pitch and intense competitive streak.

THE FUTURE: Beck did not pitch after signing, but his pedigree and age will likely allow him to leap immediately to High-A Hudson Valley once the 2022 season begins. He has the potential to pitch in the back of a rotation thanks to his arsenal, pitching acumen and a body built to eat innings.

Year	Age	Club (Level)	Lge	W	L	ERA	G	GS	IP	H	HR	BB	SO	BB/9	SO/9	WHIP	AVG
2021	22	Did not play															

17 BROCK SELVIDGE, LHP

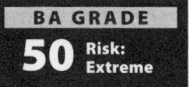

BA GRADE

50 Risk: Extreme

Born: Aug. 28, 2002. **B-T:** R-L. **HT:** 6-3. **WT:** 205. **Drafted:** HS—Chandler, Ariz., 2021 (3rd round). **Signed by:** Troy Afenir.

TRACK RECORD: Entering the season, Selvidge was on a track that could have seen him become the first Arizona prep lefty to go in the first round since Matthew Liberatore in 2018. Instead, his year didn't quite go as planned, and he fell somewhat. He regained his stock a bit thanks to MLB's new draft combine, and the Yankees felt confident enough to take him in the third round.

SCOUTING REPORT: As an amateur, Selvidge's bread and butter was a fastball that peaked at 95 mph and a pair of breaking pitches which each projected as at least average. His low-80s slider was a potentially average pitch, while the Yankees believe his curveball—which he'd scrapped earlier in the season—could get to plus as it develops. His changeup, thrown in the low 80s, showed tumble and was thrown with good arm speed and conviction, but is less developed and consistent than his other three pitches. Selvidge's command and control wavered during his senior season, but the Yankees believe it could get to average as he rebounds. He also earned raves for his makeup and competitive streak as an amateur.

THE FUTURE: After getting his feet wet in the Rookie-level Florida Complex League, Selvidge should slide into the rotation at Low-A Tampa in 2022. He's got the ceiling of a No. 4 starter.

Year	Age	Club (Level)	Lge	W	L	ERA	G	GS	IP	H	HR	BB	SO	BB/9	SO/9	WHIP	AVG
2021	18	Yankees (R)	FCL	0	0	2.45	3	2	3	2	0	1	4	2.5	9.8	0.82	.154
Minor League Totals (1 year)				0	0	2.45	3	2	3	2	0	1	4	2.45	9.82	0.82	.154

18 ELIJAH DUNHAM, OF

BA GRADE

45 Risk: High

Born: May 29, 1998. **B-T:** L-L. **HT:** 6-0. **WT:** 213. **Signed:** Indiana, 2020 (NDFA). **Signed by:** Mike Gibbons/Mitch Colahan.

TRACK RECORD: In a normal world, Dunham would have heard his name called at some point in the 2020 draft. With the draft shortened to just five rounds because of the pandemic, however, Dunham went unpicked and instead signed with the Yankees as a free agent a week later.

SCOUTING REPORT: In his first test as a pro, Dunham showed an intriguing combination of power and speed and finished the year as one of just seven minor leaguers with 13 or more home runs, 28 or more stolen bases and fewer than 100 strikeouts. He hit the ball plenty hard, with an average exit velocity of 89.2 mph and a maximum of 111 mph. The next step is getting Dunham to hit the ball in the air more often to make the most of his bat-to-ball skills and hard contact. Defensively, he likely fits as a left fielder who can use his plus speed to cover plenty of ground.

THE FUTURE: Dunham will likely move to Double-A Somerset, where he'll give his strong contact and on-base skills their first test against more advanced pitching.

Year	Age	Club (Level)	Lge	AVG	G	AB	R	H	2B	3B	HR	RBI	BB	SO	SB	OBP	SLG
2021	23	Tampa (LoA)	SEast	.276	29	98	32	27	6	2	4	25	25	23	11	.441	.500
2021	23	Hudson Valley (HiA)	East	.257	64	241	40	62	19	0	9	32	22	62	17	.325	.448
Minor League Totals (1 year)				.263	93	339	72	89	25	2	13	57	47	85	28	.362	.463

19 YOENDRYS GOMEZ, RHP

BA GRADE

50 Risk: Extreme

Born: Oct. 15, 1999. **B-T:** R-R. **HT:** 6-3. **WT:** 175. **Signed:** Venezuela, 2016. **Signed by:** Alan Atacho.

TRACK RECORD: The lost 2020 season limited Gomez to remote training, while a shoulder injury kept him from debuting until a month into the 2021 season. His year lasted 23.2 innings before he contracted Covid-19 and had to go on the injured list. Beyond that, Gomez had elbow surgery, which will cost him an undetermined amount of time.

SCOUTING REPORT: When he was on the mound in 2021, Gomez showed the same live arm as always. His four-seam fastball averaged 95 mph and topped at 99 while showing excellent shape, particularly in regard to its vertical break. He backed the fastball primarily with a slider—a newer pitch in his repertoire—in the mid 80s with an excellent amount of the horizontal sweeping action that has become en vogue of late. He still boasts a third pitch changeup in the high 80s. The pitch could become more effective if it gains more separation from his fastball.

THE FUTURE: The Yankees added Gomez to their 40-man roster after the 2020 season, but they will have to wait until his elbow is healed to reap those benefits.

Year	Age	Club (Level)	Lge	W	L	ERA	G	GS	IP	H	HR	BB	SO	BB/9	SO/9	WHIP	AVG
2021	21	Tampa (LoA)	SEast	0	0	3.42	9	9	23	14	3	9	29	3.4	11.0	0.97	.163
Minor League Totals (5 years)				8	9	3.65	44	41	163	138	9	68	165	3.76	9.13	1.27	.231

20 JOSH BREAUX, C

Born: Oct. 7, 1997. **B-T:** R-R. **HT:** 6-1. **WT:** 220. **Drafted:** McLennan (Texas) JC, 2018 (2nd round). **Signed by:** Mike Leuzinger.

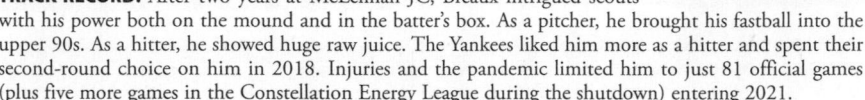

BA GRADE
45 Risk: High

TRACK RECORD: After two years at McLennan JC, Breaux intrigued scouts with his power both on the mound and in the batter's box. As a pitcher, he brought his fastball into the upper 90s. As a hitter, he showed huge raw juice. The Yankees liked him more as a hitter and spent their second-round choice on him in 2018. Injuries and the pandemic limited him to just 81 official games (plus five more games in the Constellation Energy League during the shutdown) entering 2021.
SCOUTING REPORT: Early in the season, it looked as if the book on Breaux would be the same as ever: Big power, lots of swing and miss and little chance to stick behind the plate. As the year went on, he made some changes and saw big results. First, he stood taller in the box and narrowed his stance. He also worked with Yankees coaches to eliminate some of the bigger moving parts in his swing while also improving his swing decisions. The changes worked, and from June 1 through the end of his tenure with High-A, Breaux hit .290/.340/.590. He regressed upon reaching Double-A, but overall the year included some of the most positive markers of his career. He has a plus arm behind the plate, but he needs to get to it more quickly in order to throw out more runners. He also needs to improve his blocking and receiving.
THE FUTURE: If Breaux can continue to build upon the strides he made at the beginning of the season, he could have a future as an offense-oriented backup. He's likely to return to Double-A in 2022.

Year	Age	Club (Level)	Lge	AVG	G	AB	R	H	2B	3B	HR	RBI	BB	SO	SB	OBP	SLG
2021	23	Hudson Valley (HiA)	East	.252	64	250	34	63	12	0	17	46	22	73	0	.308	.504
	23	Somerset (AA)	NEast	.240	26	100	14	24	8	0	6	17	4	26	1	.274	.500
Minor League Totals (3 years)				.259	171	657	82	170	39	0	36	125	45	179	1	.305	.482

21 RON MARINACCIO, RHP

Born: July 1, 1995. **B-T:** R-R. **HT:** 6-2. **WT:** 205. **Drafted:** Delaware, 2017 (19th round). **Signed by:** Stewart Smothers.

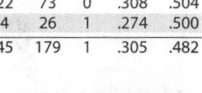

BA GRADE
40 Risk: Medium

TRACK RECORD: Of the 17 pitchers the Yankees drafted and signed in 2017, five have already made their big league debuts—each with a different organization. Marinaccio could become the sixth at some point in 2022. New York's player development staff pointed to Marinaccio before the season as a player to watch, and he delivered with 105 strikeouts, the most by any pitcher in the minors who threw fewer than 70 innings.
SCOUTING REPORT: A major piece of Marinaccio's breakout centered around a velocity spike. His four-seam fastball jumped roughly five mph from 2019 until 2021 and now averages around 95 mph with a peak of 98. He pairs the fastball primarily with a dastardly changeup that averaged around 84 mph and got swings and misses at a near-elite rate, as well as an average separation of more than 10 mph from his fastball. Marinaccio also has a slider in the low 80s with excellent sweeper break that got plenty of swings and misses as well. Working in concert, the three pitches give Marinaccio weapons to neutralize hitters from both sides of the plate.
THE FUTURE: Marinaccio was added to the Yankees' 40-man roster to protect him from the Rule 5 Draft. He'll likely make his big league debut in 2022 as a reliever who can work multiple innings per outing.

Year	Age	Club (Level)	Lge	W	L	ERA	G	GS	IP	H	HR	BB	SO	BB/9	SO/9	WHIP	AVG
2021	25	Somerset (AA)	NEast	1	1	1.82	22	0	39	17	2	19	64	4.3	14.5	0.91	.129
	25	Scranton/W-B (AAA)	East	1	0	2.36	18	0	26	18	2	8	41	2.7	13.8	0.98	.186
Minor League Totals (5 years)				5	3	3.16	88	0	148	106	5	57	214	3.46	12.98	1.10	.198

22 ANTONIO GOMEZ, C

Born: Nov. 13, 2001. **B-T:** R-R. **HT:** 6-2. **WT:** 212. **Signed:** Venezuela, 2018. **Signed by:** Edgar Mateo/Raul Gonzalez.

BA GRADE
50 Risk: Extreme

TRACK RECORD: The Yankees inked Gomez, who ranked as the No. 14 player available in his signing class, in 2018. He opened his career by ranking No. 5 on the 2019 Gulf Coast League Top 20, then placed No. 10 on the 2021 list.
SCOUTING REPORT: Injuries and the pandemic limited Gomez to just 15 professional games entering 2021, when he more than tripled that total by playing in 46 games between the FCL and Low-A. For now, Gomez's loudest tool is his throwing arm, a true plus-plus weapon which helps him regularly produce pop times below 2.0 seconds. He needs lots more polish when it comes to receiving and blocking, both of which scouts have pegged as inconsistent at best. At the plate, he needs to improve his plate discipline. He believes he can hit anything, which leads him to swing at anything. He has power to his pull side,

but scouts also noted that he needs to close a hole on the outer half before he can tap into his raw juice regularly. As would be expected from a catcher, Gomez is a well below-average runner.

THE FUTURE: Gomez made his full-season debut in 2021 and is likely to return to Low-A. Right now, he has the ceiling of a defensive-minded backup with the skills to hit toward the bottom of an order.

Year	Age	Club (Level)	Lge	AVG	G	AB	R	H	2B	3B	HR	RBI	BB	SO	SB	OBP	SLG
2021	19	Yankees (R)	FCL	.305	29	95	18	29	8	1	2	16	16	31	4	.416	.474
	19	Tampa (LoA)	SEast	.197	17	61	10	12	2	0	2	7	10	18	1	.310	.328
Minor League Totals (3 years)				.269	61	208	39	56	15	1	5	31	30	58	5	.369	.423

23 BRANDON LOCKRIDGE, OF

BA GRADE
45 Risk: High

Born: March 14, 1997. **B-T:** R-R. **HT:** 6-0. **WT:** 192. **Drafted:** Troy, 2018 (5th round). **Signed by:** Mike Wagner

TRACK RECORD: Lockridge was a second baseman for the first part of his college career before converting to the outfield, where his high-end speed would be more of an asset. He showed a burner's skill set and an improved eye in his draft year, leading the Yankees to take him in the fifth round. In 2021, he was one of just three players in the minor leagues to hit 16 or more doubles, 13 or more home runs and steal 18 or more bases while playing in 75 or fewer games.

SCOUTING REPORT: Above all, Lockridge has the speed and power traits which teams covet. Thirty-eight percent of his career hits have gone for extra bases, and his stolen base efficiency increased greatly in 2021, when he was successful on 18 of 20 tries. In Hudson Valley, Lockridge suffered a 70-point dropoff in batting average when hitting against righthanders. Upon moving to Double-A, that hole seemed to close. Though his numbers against lefties were still much better, he produced an .870 OPS against righties. If that improvement can be maintained, Lockridge's path to the big leagues became much clearer.

THE FUTURE: Lockridge was left exposed by the Yankees in the Rule 5 draft, which was delayed until the end of the lockout. Lockridge at his peak could provide speed, power and solid defense in center field.

Year	Age	Club (Level)	Lge	AVG	G	AB	R	H	2B	3B	HR	RBI	BB	SO	SB	OBP	SLG
2021	24	Hudson Valley (HiA)	East	.256	32	125	18	32	6	2	3	22	9	27	5	.309	.408
	24	Somerset (AA)	NEast	.328	43	174	33	57	10	0	10	24	13	58	13	.382	.557
Minor League Totals (4 years)				.269	222	878	134	236	54	10	26	110	79	246	43	.336	.442

24 STEPHEN RIDINGS, RHP

BA GRADE
40 Risk: Medium

Born: Aug. 14, 1995. **B-T:** R-R. **HT:** 6-8. **WT:** 220. **Drafted:** Haverford (Pa.), 2016 (8th round). **Signed by:** Matt Sherman (Cubs).

TRACK RECORD: Ridings lasted three seasons with the Cubs before being dealt to the Royals in 2019. He stayed two seasons with Kansas City before signing with the Yankees as a minor league free agent. Ridings carved at the upper levels in 2021 before earning his first big league callup.

SCOUTING REPORT: Ridings' calling card is his high-velocity fastball. In the minors, the pitch touched 100 mph and averaged roughly 97. But velocity is only part of the reason the Yankees have tabbed Ridings' heater as the best in the system. The pitch also shows well analytically, with plus or better marks in terms of spin rate as well as horizontal and vertical break. Put simply, the pitch is hard, lively and very difficult to hit. The key to Ridings' ascent, however, lies with the improvement of his breaking ball. The pitch, a tight, high-80s slider, got swings and misses more than half the time in the minor leagues. Ridings' work with Yankees strength guru Eric Cressey has also helped create a more fluid delivery.

THE FUTURE: Ridings is a powerful reliever with a massive frame and two excellent weapons to dominate hitters. The Yankees added him to their 40-man roster to protect him from the Rule 5 Draft.

Year	Age	Club (Level)	Lge	W	L	ERA	G	GS	IP	H	HR	BB	SO	BB/9	SO/9	WHIP	AVG
2021	25	Somerset (AA)	NEast	4	0	0.47	14	0	19	8	0	2	30	1.0	14.2	0.53	.123
	25	Scranton/W-B (AAA)	East	1	0	2.70	8	0	10	8	2	2	12	1.8	10.8	1.00	.211
	25	New York (MLB)	AL	0	0	1.80	5	0	5	4	0	2	7	3.6	12.6	1.20	.235
Major League Totals (1 year)				0	0	1.80	5	0	5.0	4	0	2	7	3.60	12.60	1.20	.235
Minor League Totals (6 years)				12	8	4.25	69	19	142.0	110	13	68	200	4.31	12.68	1.25	.212

25 BECK WAY, RHP

BA GRADE
40 Risk: High

Born: Aug. 6, 1999. **B-T:** R-R. **HT:** 6-4. **WT:** 200. **Drafted:** Northwest Florida State JC, 2020 (4th round). **Signed by:** Chuck Bartlett.

TRACK RECORD: Way started his career at Division II Belmont-Abbey (N.C.) before moving to Northwest Florida State JC in his draft year, which was limited to 40 innings because of

the pandemic. He spent his first official season as a pro between both Class A levels.

SCOUTING REPORT: Way relies mainly on a mix of four- and two-seam fastballs, as well as a slider and changeup. He also added a cutter during the remote-training sessions during the 2020 shutdown. His slider is by far his most commonly used pitch, thrown nearly as often as all three of his fastballs combined. The slider is a sweepy pitch, with a nearly elite 14 inches of horizontal break and a swing-and-miss rate of 50%. Way's sinker and four-seamer each averaged between roughly 94-95 mph, and the four-seamer showed exceptional horizontal break at the top of the zone. Way's changeup is still a bit of a work in progress and needs to show more separation from his fastballs to be more effective. His extremely loose arm and slinger action led to command and control issues, and he got crushed in a small sample at High-A.

THE FUTURE: Way will likely return to High-A to begin 2022, and has the stuff to carve out a role as a reliever. To do so, he'll need to greatly improve his ability to throw quality strikes.

Year	Age	Club (Level)	Lge	W	L	ERA	G	GS	IP	H	HR	BB	SO	BB/9	SO/9	WHIP	AVG
2021	21	Tampa (LoA)	SEast	3	1	2.68	15	14	47	23	2	29	54	5.6	10.3	1.11	.144
	21	Hudson Valley (HiA)	East	1	2	7.71	4	4	16	18	3	9	29	5.0	16.0	1.65	.281
Minor League Totals (2 years)				4	3	3.98	19	18	63	41	5	38	83	5.40	11.79	1.25	.183

26 J.P. SEARS, LHP

BA GRADE
40 Risk: High

Born: Feb. 19, 1996. **B-T:** R-L. **HT:** 5-11. **WT:** 180. **Drafted:** The Citadel, 2017 (11th round). **Signed by:** Ben Sanderson (Mariners).

TRACK RECORD: The Mariners popped Sears in the 11th round in 2017, then shipped him to New York with righty Juan Then in exchange for reliever Nick Rumbelow. Sears broke out in 2021 and finished No. 3 in strikeouts (136) and strikeout percentage (32.8) in the system.

SCOUTING REPORT: Sears works with a three-pitch arsenal of a low-90s fastball, mid-80s changeup and a low-80s slider. His fastball shows well in plenty of analytical characteristics, including horizontal break and vertical approach angle—and was the most effective pitches in his mix despite average velocity and spin rates. Sears' slider—which has been recently introduced into his mix—is the more effective of the two offspeed pitches, garnering a swing-and-miss rate of nearly 46%. His changeup is a clear third pitch, and scouts believe it could have a ceiling as an average offering. He showed excellent control in 2021, with just 2.7 walks per nine innings and a strikeout-to-walk rate of roughly 4.7 over 106 innings.

THE FUTURE: Like fellow breakout reliever Ron Marinaccio, Sears was added to the 40-man roster in November to keep him out of the Rule 5 Draft. He has a future as a multi-inning reliever.

Year	Age	Club (Level)	Lge	W	L	ERA	G	GS	IP	H	HR	BB	SO	BB/9	SO/9	WHIP	AVG
2021	25	Somerset (AA)	NEast	3	2	4.09	15	8	50	45	6	18	71	3.2	12.6	1.24	.242
	25	Scranton/W-B (AAA)	East	7	0	2.87	10	10	53	41	5	11	65	1.9	11.0	0.98	.215
Minor League Totals (5 years)				16	13	3.07	66	34	234	178	21	68	286	2.61	10.98	1.05	.210

27 ANTHONY GARCIA, 1B/OF

BA GRADE
45 Risk: Extreme

Born: Sept. 5, 2000. **B-T:** B-R. **HT:** 6-5. **WT:** 204. **Signed:** Dominican Republic, 2017. **Signed by:** Jose Sabino.

TRACK RECORD: The Yankees inked Garcia for $500,000 in 2017 on the strength of a tool kit fronted by positively preposterous power from both sides of the plate. He led the Gulf Coast League with 10 home runs in 2018, then dealt with injuries and was limited to just six games in 2019. He was the only minor leaguer in 2021 with 14 or more home runs in fewer than 130 at-bats.

SCOUTING REPORT: Garcia hits balls hard, often. Scouts graded his raw power as easily double-plus from both sides of the plate, and his average exit velocity of 91.4 mph ranked among the system's very best. His maximum exit velocity of 116 mph was the highest in the organization. Garcia has improved the quality of his at-bats by leaps and bounds, and his chase rate is surprisingly low for a player who still struck out in nearly 33% of his plate appearances. He played mostly first base and didn't look great doing it, so he's likely a DH in the big leagues. His 20-grade speed makes that outcome even more probable.

THE FUTURE: After a smashing turn in Low-A, Garcia could return there for more seasoning in 2022. His likely future is as a player who keeps getting chances thanks to true light-tower power.

Year	Age	Club (Level)	Lge	AVG	G	AB	R	H	2B	3B	HR	RBI	BB	SO	SB	OBP	SLG
2021	20	Yankees (R)	FCL	.318	23	66	19	21	1	0	8	21	18	25	10	.459	.697
	20	Tampa (LoA)	SEast	.291	16	55	16	16	2	0	6	16	13	25	5	.426	.655
Minor League Totals (4 years)				.254	98	331	64	84	13	5	25	69	59	147	18	.363	.550

28 ALEXANDER VARGAS, SS

Born: Oct. 29, 2001. **B-T:** B-R. **HT:** 5-11. **WT:** 162. **Signed:** Cuba, 2018.
Signed by: Edgar Mateo/Esteban Castillo/Rudy Gomez.

BA GRADE
45 Risk: Extreme

TRACK RECORD: As an amateur, Vargas was expected to sign with Cincinnati. Instead, the Yankees added him to a haul that also included future trade pieces Kevin Alcantara and Maikol Escotto. He showed promise in his first season as a pro—split between the two complex-league affiliates—before repeating the Rookie-level Florida Complex League in 2021.
SCOUTING REPORT: Vargas has continued to add strength to his frame and now checks in at a much more formidable 162 pounds, but he still has a long way to go. His average exit velocity in 2021 was roughly 83 mph, among the lowest in the entire system. As he continues to gain strength, the Yankees believe his raw tools will be better amplified. Outside evaluators would like to see more consistency in his game. They note the potential for plus defense and plus speed, but also that he gets lackadaisical and takes plays off. Sometimes he'll make the highlight-reel play, other times he'll boot routine grounders. They also note a tendency to get out of his approach and become too much of a free-swinger.
THE FUTURE: After two years in the lowest levels of the minor leagues sandwiched around a pandemic, Vargas will need to move up at least to Low-A Tampa.

Year	Age	Club (Level)	Lge	AVG	G	AB	R	H	2B	3B	HR	RBI	BB	SO	SB	OBP	SLG
2021	19	Yankees (R)	FCL	.273	42	150	37	41	7	1	3	26	20	40	17	.362	.393
Minor League Totals (3 years)				.251	90	343	66	86	17	8	4	44	38	68	32	.335	.382

29 HANS MONTERO, SS

Born: Dec. 25, 2003. **B-T:** R-R. **HT:** 5-11. **WT:** 160. **Signed:** Dominican Republic, 2021. **Signed by:** Juan Piron/Juan Rosario/Victor Mata.

BA GRADE
45 Risk: Extreme

TRACK RECORD: Under normal conditions, the Yankees would have added Montero to their system on July 2, 2020. Instead, the pandemic scuttled the traditional signing day and the two sides made it official when the period opened on Jan. 21, 2021. He made his pro debut in the Dominican Summer League, which began play in July.
SCOUTING REPORT: Montero ranked as the No. 23 prospect available in the class once the period opened. He was lauded as an amateur for a well-rounded skill set that included 55-grade speed, a strong arm and soft hands, all of which should help him stick at shortstop in the long run. Offensively, he has a short, compact swing from the right side that's geared more for line drives than home runs. Understandably, he still needs to add strength to his frame to get the most out of his bat. His 83 mph average exit velocity was among the lowest in the system.
THE FUTURE: Montero's likely next stop is domestic extended spring training followed by the Florida Complex League. He projects as a glove-first shortstop who hits toward the bottom of an order.

Year	Age	Club (Level)	Lge	AVG	G	AB	R	H	2B	3B	HR	RBI	BB	SO	SB	OBP	SLG
2021	17	Yankees1 (R)	DSL	.200	51	190	31	38	5	1	1	22	33	74	15	.339	.253
Minor League Totals (1 year)				.200	51	190	31	38	5	1	1	22	33	74	15	.339	.253

30 GREG WEISSERT, RHP

Born: Feb. 4, 1995. **B-T:** R-R. **HT:** 6-2. **WT:** 215. **Drafted:** Fordham, 2016 (18th round). **Signed by:** Scott Lovekamp/Cesar Presbott.

BA GRADE
40 Risk: High

TRACK RECORD: Weissert has slowly wound his way through the system. He's been exclusively a reliever from the moment he entered pro ball and excelled in his time in both 2019 and 2021 at the upper levels of the system. Internal evaluators grade Weissert's slider as the system's best.
SCOUTING REPORT: Weissert's slider, thrown nearly 46% of the time, is a low-80s pitch that shows outstanding spin at nearly 2,800 rpms on average as well as an elite 19 inches of horizontal break. To make the slider even more effective, Weissert will need to throw it for strikes more often. Weissert primarily pairs the slider with a two-seam fastball which averages around 93 mph and has improved its shape and sink after work with the Yankees' pitching development team. Weissert also has a four-seam fastball and a changeup, but he works primarily as a sinker-slider pitcher. Improving his strike-throwing ability would make all of Weissert's stuff play up.
THE FUTURE: Weissert is likely to return to Triple-A to begin 2022. His ceiling is as a low-leverage reliever.

Year	Age	Club (Level)	Lge	W	L	ERA	G	GS	IP	H	HR	BB	SO	BB/9	SO/9	WHIP	AVG
2021	26	Somerset (AA)	NEast	1	2	0.71	12	0	12	9	0	5	20	3.6	14.2	1.11	.191
	26	Scranton/W-B (AAA)	East	3	1	1.96	28	0	36	20	2	22	40	5.4	9.8	1.15	.156
Minor League Totals (6 years)				13	14	3.16	151	0	222	162	11	110	282	4.45	11.42	1.22	.200

MORE PROSPECTS TO KNOW

31 ALBERT ABREU, RHP

Abreu qualifies for this list by the skin of his teeth, needing just one out in 2022 to graduate from the realm of prospects. He showed flashes of his potential out of the big league bullpen but will need to significantly tighten his control and command to reach his ceiling.

32 RAIMFER SALINAS, OF

Salinas has intriguing tools, but he has not turned them into skills. Scouts in 2021 saw a player who squared balls frequently but ran bad routes in the outfield and had become a below-average runner.

33 COOPER BOWMAN, 2B

Bowman was the Yankees' fourth-round selection in 2021, was among the most athletic players in their draft class and possesses blazing speed on the basepaths.

34 ANDRES CHAPARRO, 3B/1B

Chaparro was one of the standouts in the organization in terms of pure production and he continued to hit for power in the Arizona Fall League. His thick frame makes it extremely probable he'll have to move to first base.

35 JUAN CARELA, RHP

SLEEPER

Carela is part of the Yankees' next wave of young, hard-throwing righthanded starters. He already brings his fastball into the mid 90s and shows flashes of a plus slider and analytical characteristics which amplify his entire repertoire.

36 MATT KROOK, LHP

As ever, Krook possesses wicked stuff that would get him to the big leagues with improved control and command. His sinker-slider package gets tons of grounders, and he struck out more than 11 hitters per nine innings as well.

37 JHONY BRITO, RHP

Tabbed as having the best control in the system, Brito's average arsenal plays a bit better than would be expected thanks to how well he commands it, as well as some intriguing analytical characteristics.

38 ZACH GREENE, RHP

The eighth-rounder from 2019 out of South Alabama used a low-90s fastball with excellent induced vertical break and vertical approach angle to whiff 38.2% of hitters he faced in 2021. He backs the fastball most frequently with a high-80s slider, but also has a curveball and changeup in his mix.

39 MADISON SANTOS, OF

Santos, signed out of the Dominican Republic in 2018, didn't produce big-time numbers this season after moving to L0w-A, but he did hit the ball harder than most players in the organization.

40 ANTHONY SEIGLER, C

Quite simply, Seigler has not produced since the Yankees made him their first-round pick in 2018. He has not been healthy, either, and has played just 95 games overall. If he can stay on the field, perhaps he can tap into the promise he showed as an amateur.

TOP PROSPECTS OF THE DECADE

Year	Player, Pos	2021 Org
2012	Jesus Montero, C	Did not play
2013	Mason Williams, OF	Mets
2014	Gary Sanchez, C	Yankees
2015	Luis Severino, RHP	Yankees
2016	Jorge Mateo, SS	Orioles
2017	Gleyber Torres, SS	Yankees
2018	Gleyber Torres, SS	Yankees
2019	Estevan Florial, OF	Yankees
2020	Jasson Dominguez, OF	Yankees
2021	Jasson Dominguez, OF	Yankees

TOP DRAFT PICKS OF THE DECADE

Year	Player, Pos	2021 Org
2012	Ty Hensley, RHP	Frontier League
2013	Eric Jagielo, 3B	Did not play
2014	Jacob Lindgren, LHP (2nd round)	White Sox
2015	James Kaprielian, RHP	Athletics
2016	Blake Rutherford, OF	White Sox
2017	Clarke Schmidt, RHP	Yankees
2018	Anthony Seigler, C	Yankees
2019	Anthony Volpe, SS	Yankees
2020	Austin Wells, C	Yankees
2021	Trey Sweeney, SS	Yankees

Oakland Athletics

BY MARK CHIARELLI

The Athletics appear headed toward another transitory phase.

Oakland stumbled down the stretch in 2021, falling out of the American League playoff race in late August to finish 86-76 and third in the AL West. The late-season slide came despite a series of win-now moves at the deadline, including acquiring all-star outfielder Starling Marte on an expiring contract from the Marlins in a deal for former top prospect lefthander Jesus Luzardo.

They're now approaching a confluence of events familiar to longtime A's employees and fans alike. Key members of a core that helped Oakland play to a 97-win pace from 2018-20 are getting older—and more expensive. The window is closing at a time when Oakland faces payroll limitations under owner John Fisher without knowing what ballpark it will call home in several years.

Those realities seemed to manifest early in the offseason. Oakland allowed the Padres to hire longtime manager Bob Melvin, who was still under contract, without receiving compensation. Melvin had been in his post with the A's for more than 10 years. Free agency looms for first baseman Matt Olson, third baseman Matt Chapman and righthander Frankie Montas after the 2023 season, and rotation stalwarts Chris Bassitt and Sean Manaea are entering the final year of their deals in 2022.

Baseball's lockout and subsequent transaction freeze may delay the inevitable by several weeks, but it seems unlikely all of those players remain in Oakland to start the 2022 season.

The good news for A's fans? Oakland has rarely shown much of an appetite for a full-scale teardown under Billy Beane's leadership, winning at least 70 games in all but two seasons since the turn of the century. The front office is going to have to get creative yet again.

Oakland's farm system is in need of reinforcements and ranked 27th in Baseball America's midseason organization talent rankings. The system has thinned in recent years as the A's supplemented their MLB roster with talent and haven't seen much, if any, results from a number of high-profile draft picks, including lefthander A.J Puk and outfielders Austin Beck and Kyler Murray.

But Oakland's last two drafts appear quite promising. Catcher Tyler Soderstrom, the 2020 first-rounder, was one of the most impressive hitters in the lower minors in 2021. The A's went back to the high school ranks again in 2021, taking another California native, shortstop Max Muncy, in the first round. The emergence of some of their

Matt Olson earned his first all-star nod in 2021 but has just two seasons left before free agency.

PROJECTED 2025 LINEUP

Catcher	Sean Murphy	30
First Base	Matt Olson	31
Second Base	Max Muncy	22
Third Base	Matt Chapman	32
Shortstop	Nick Allen	26
Left Field	Zack Gelof	25
Center Field	Ramon Laureano	30
Right Field	Tyler Soderstrom	23
Designated Hitter	Lawrence Butler	24
No. 1 Starter	Frankie Montas	32
No. 2 Starter	Sean Manaea	33
No. 3 Starter	James Kaprielian	31
No. 4 Starter	Cole Irvin	31
No. 5 Starter	A.J. Puk	30
Closer	Lou Trivino	33

college picks, including third baseman Zack Gelof, who briefly reached Triple-A, and righthander Mason Miller, who touched 100 mph at instructs, has Oakland officials excited.

Oakland also saw several breakout performances. Lawrence Butler emerged as an intriguing power-speed threat, hitting 19 homers and stealing 29 bases. Righthander Colin Peluse's workhorse effort in 2021 vaulted him up the system list.

Depending on Oakland's payroll outlook and upcoming trade decisions, an influx of new names could soon join the system, too. It will take a series of shrewd moves to return the A's to the top of a crowded AL West, but Oakland's front office group has done it before. ∎

DEPTH CHART

OAKLAND ATHLETICS

TOP 2022 ROOKIES	RANK
Nick Allen, SS	3
A.J. Puk, LHP	6
Daulton Jefferies, RHP	7
BREAKOUT PROSPECTS	**RANK**
Denzel Clarke, OF	13
Mason Miller, RHP	16
Angel Arevalo, SS/CF	29

SOURCE OF TOP 30 TALENT

Homegrown	27	Acquired	3
College	16	Trade	3
Junior college	0	Rule 5 draft	0
High school	4	Independent league	0
Nondrafted free agent	0	Free agent/waivers	0
International	7		

LF
Denzel Clarke (13)
Cody Thomas (20)
Junior Perez (28)

CF
Pedro Pineda (5)
Michael Guldberg (21)
Mickey McDonald (26)
Austin Beck
Buddy Reed

RF
Brayan Buelvas (8)
Luis Barrera (18)

3B
Zack Gelof (2)
Logan Davidson (15)
Jonah Bride (22)
Brett Harris (30)

SS
Nick Allen (3)
Max Muncy (4)
Robert Puason (17)
Angel Arevalo (29)
Drew Swift

2B
Max Schuemann (27)
Jhoan Paulino

1B
Lawrence Butler (9)
Jordan Diaz (14)
Dermis Garcia

C
Tyler Soderstrom (1)
Carlos Amaya
Kyle McCann
C.J. Rodriguez
Shane McGuire

LHP

LHSP	LHRP
A.J. Puk (6)	Jose Dicochea
Hogan Harris (24)	
Brady Basso (25)	

RHP

RHSP	RHRP
Daulton Jefferies (7)	Jack Weisenburger
Colin Peluse (10)	Aiden McIntyre
Jeff Criswell (11)	Garrett Acton
Brent Honeywell (12)	Brian Howard
Mason Miller (16)	Wandisson Charles
Jorge Juan (19)	Bryce Conley
Brady Feigl (23)	Ryan Castellani
Jack Cushing	Pedro Santos
Parker Dunshee	
Tyler Baum	
Grant Holman	

1 TYLER SODERSTROM, C/1B

Born: Nov. 24, 2001. **B-T:** L-R. **HT:** 6-2. **WT:** 200.
Drafted: HS—Turlock, Calif., 2020 (1st round).
Signed by: Kevin Mello.

TRACK RECORD: The Athletics closed the 2010s with multiple misfires at the top of the draft, but going over slot to draft Soderstrom No. 26 overall in 2020 looks like quite a reversal of fortune. Oakland had plenty of familiarity with Soderstrom, the son of 1993 Giants first-rounder Steve Soderstrom. He grew up less than two hours from Oakland in Turlock, Calif., and played for the Athletics' Area Code team. It didn't take Soderstrom long to impress A's brass once he turned pro, either. Soderstrom was one of the most impressive hitters at Oakland's alternate training site in 2020 despite being just 18 years old. He carried that momentum into 2021, impressing in spring training and crushing Low-A West pitching. His 145 wRC+ with Stockton was tied for fifth-best among all hitters with 200 or more plate appearances. An oblique injury prematurely ended Soderstrom's season in late July, and a flareup of the same injury kept Soderstrom from participating in the Arizona Fall League after the season.

SCOUTING REPORT: The chorus of praise surrounding Soderstrom only grew louder in 2021. The 19-year-old posted some of the best average exit velocities of any hitter in Oakland's system, consistently beating Low-A pitching with a swing and approach some scouts believe could handle big league pitching right now. Soderstrom's picturesque lefty swing stays in the strike zone for a long time and he's adept at backspinning the baseball, showing plus raw power to all fields. Soderstrom doesn't fear long at-bats and shows advanced strike-zone recognition, especially with breaking balls, for his age. There's the occasional overaggressive swing decisions that come with youth, but scouts feel comfortable projecting all those ingredients will add up to a middle-of-the-order big league bat. Which position Soderstrom ultimately plays when he arrives in the majors remains an open question. Soderstrom never caught full-time as a high schooler and was understandably quite raw in his initial professional foray into catching. While he's far from a finished product, opposing evaluators were encouraged by the gains Soderstrom made in just a year. He shows a surprising amount of lateral agility despite his bigger, strength-based frame, and his arm flashes above-average at times. Many believe Soderstrom's blocking and receiving will continue to develop with more in-game reps and he's shown the necessary willingness to work at it. Soderstrom has shown enough athletic ability

LARRY GOREN/FOUR SEAM IMAGES

BA GRADE	SCOUTING GRADES
60 Risk: High	Hit: 60. **Power:** 60. **Run:** 40. Field: 40. **Arm:** 55.

Projected future grades on 20-80 scouting scale

BEST TOOLS

Best Hitter for Average	Tyler Soderstrom
Best Power Hitter	Lawrence Butler
Best Strike-Zone Discipline	Jonah Bride
Fastest Baserunner	Denzel Clarke
Best Athlete	Denzel Clarke
Best Fastball	Wandisson Charles
Best Curveball	Pedro Santos
Best Slider	Jack Weisenburger
Best Changeup	Jeff Criswell
Best Control	Jack Cushing
Best Defensive Catcher	CJ Rodriguez
Best Defensive Infielder	Nick Allen
Best Infield Arm	Jeremy Eierman
Best Defensive Outfielder	Buddy Reed
Best Outfield Arm	Buddy Reed

to suggest he could handle a corner if Oakland eventually moves him off catcher, potentially in either left field or at first base.

THE FUTURE: Soderstrom's bat is special. He projects to be a potential .300 hitter with 25 or more homers at his peak, and could compete against upper-level pitching in 2022. That will lead to an interesting debate for the A's. His bat will most likely be ready for the majors long before his glove if he sticks at catcher. The A's will have to decide if they have the appetite to wait on his defense to develop behind the plate or move him to another position where he could reach the majors more quickly. ∎

Year	Age	Club (Level)	Lge	AVG	G	AB	R	H	2B	3B	HR	RBI	BB	SO	SB	OBP	SLG
2021	19	Stockton (LoA)	West	.306	57	222	39	68	20	1	12	49	27	61	2	.390	.568
Minor League Totals (2 years)				.306	57	222	39	68	20	1	12	49	27	61	2	.390	.568

2 ZACK GELOF, 3B

Born: Oct. 19, 1999. **B-T:** R-R. **HT:** 6-3. **WT:** 205. **Drafted:** Virginia, 2021 (2nd round). **Signed by:** Tripp Faulk.

TRACK RECORD: No 2021 Athletics draft pick made a stronger first impression than Gelof, who reached Triple-A Las Vegas by the end of 2021 when the A's needed infield depth. Gelof was a solid performer in college, serving as the leadoff hitter on a Virginia team that reached the 2021 College World Series. He spent most of his pro debut at Low-A Stockton, posting a .941 OPS.

SCOUTING REPORT: Gelof is physically strong and flashed plus raw power, mostly to his pull side, in college. The A's believed he could maintain his all-fields approach but unlock that power more regularly as a professional. So far, that's proving prescient. Gelof did significant damage in his short time in Stockton, approaching average exit velocities of 90 mph, and hit seven homers in just 32 games. Gelof hunted fastballs in college and struggled at times with breaking balls, an area he'll have to shore up against more advanced pitching. He'll also have to prove he can stay at third base. Gelof dealt with an elbow injury while at Virginia that affected his throwing mechanics, although the A's are confident he can stick at the position. He showed an average arm when making throws on the run, but struggled setting his feet and making throws over the top. He's an above-average runner and athletic enough to handle a corner outfield position if Oakland opts for a change.

THE FUTURE: The A's believe Gelof has the bat, approach and makeup to jump on the fast track, potentially arriving in Oakland as early as 2023.

BA GRADE
50 Risk: High

SCOUTING GRADES:	Hitting: 50	Power: 55	Running: 50	Fielding: 50	Arm: 50

Year	Age	Club (Level)	Lge	AVG	G	AB	R	H	2B	3B	HR	RBI	BB	SO	SB	OBP	SLG
2021	21	Athletics (R)	ACL	1.000	1	2	1	2	0	0	0	2	0	0	2	1.000	1.000
	21	Stockton (LoA)	West	.298	32	124	26	37	8	1	7	22	19	36	11	.393	.548
	21	Las Vegas (AAA)	West	.583	3	12	3	7	1	0	0	6	1	2	0	.615	.667
Minor League Totals (1 year)				.333	36	138	30	46	9	1	7	30	20	38	13	.422	.565

3 NICK ALLEN, SS

Born: Oct. 8, 1998. **B-T:** R-R. **HT:** 5-8. **WT:** 170. **Drafted:** HS—San Diego, 2017 (3rd round). **Signed by:** Anthony Aliotti.

TRACK RECORD: It didn't take Allen long to become one of the minors' best defensive shortstops after the A's made him their third-round selection in 2017, giving him a $2 million bonus that was nearly three times his slot value. His bat is now catching up. Allen opened 2021 at Double-A Midland, then started at shortstop for Team USA in the Tokyo Olympics. Oakland promoted Allen to Triple-A Las Vegas when he returned, and Allen hit .313 in September after taking some time to adjust.

SCOUTING REPORT: Allen's glove is major league ready now, and he could compete for Gold Gloves one day. His deft hands, instincts and footwork at shortstop allow him to make exceptional defensive plays look easy, and he made the routine plays more consistently in 2021 as well. Whether the 5-foot-8 shortstop reaches his everyday ceiling hinges on the incremental development of his bat, which took another step forward in 2021. The A's worked diligently with Allen to avoid chasing power and instead employ a flighted, gap-to-gap approach more suited to his inside-out bat stroke. Allen has average bat speed and opposing evaluators are concerned he'll struggle against premium big league velocity. He displays a solid understanding of the strike zone, and the A's believe he made progress laying off high fastballs.

THE FUTURE: Allen profiles as a second-division regular at shortstop who could easily handle a Nick Punto-esque super-utility role if needed. He should compete for Oakland's starting shortstop job in 2022.

BA GRADE
45 Risk: Medium

SCOUTING GRADES:	Hitting: 50	Power: 30	Running: 50	Fielding: 80	Arm: 55

Year	Age	Club (Level)	Lge	AVG	G	AB	R	H	2B	3B	HR	RBI	BB	SO	SB	OBP	SLG
2021	22	Midland (AA)	Cent	.319	50	204	31	65	9	2	6	31	18	46	8	.374	.471
	22	Las Vegas (AAA)	West	.243	39	136	17	33	8	0	0	10	11	30	4	.302	.301
Minor League Totals (5 years)				.267	317	1226	170	327	59	15	10	114	104	241	56	.330	.364

4 MAX MUNCY, SS

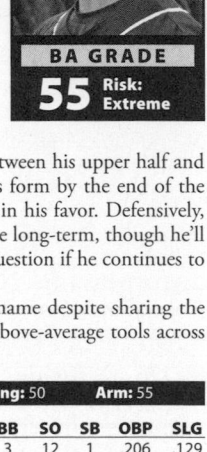

BILL MITCHELL

BA GRADE

55 Risk: Extreme

Born: Aug. 25, 2002. **B-T:** R-R. **HT:** 6-1. **WT:** 180. **Drafted:** HS—Thousand Oaks, Calif., 2021 (1st round). **Signed by:** Dillon Tung.

TRACK RECORD: Muncy's path to Oakland was representative of the unusual nature of scouting during a pandemic. With their travel limited to essentially as far as they could drive, the Athletics saw plenty of the California native in the spring leading up to the 2021 draft, including during the state's high school playoffs in June with the draft pushed back to July. They went slightly over slot to sign Muncy to a $2.85 million deal after selecting him No. 25 overall. He made his pro debut in the Arizona Complex League in early August.

SCOUTING REPORT: Muncy stands out for his athleticism and high-energy style of play. He showed above-average hitting ability as an amateur and the A's were impressed by the rotational acceleration in his swing. Muncy tinkered with his setup and swing early in his high school season, losing connectivity between his upper half and lower half that led to an uptick in strikeouts. He reverted back to his previous form by the end of the season, shortening his swing and allowing his strong hands and wrists to work in his favor. Defensively, Muncy is a solid-average defender at shortstop and the A's believe he'll stick there long-term, though he'll need to continue to clean up his actions. A move to third base isn't out of the question if he continues to grow into his wiry frame.

THE FUTURE: Muncy, who is not related to the Dodgers slugger of the same name despite sharing the same Aug. 25 birth date, is commended for his makeup and has a chance for above-average tools across the board, though he has a long way to go to get there.

SCOUTING GRADES:	Hitting: 55	Power: 55	Running: 55	Fielding: 50	Arm: 55

Year	Age	Club (Level)	Lge	AVG	G	AB	R	H	2B	3B	HR	RBI	BB	SO	SB	OBP	SLG
2021	18	Athletics (R)	ACL	.129	11	31	3	4	0	0	0	4	3	12	1	.206	.129
Minor League Totals (1 year)				.129	11	31	3	4	0	0	0	4	3	12	1	.206	.129

5 PEDRO PIÑEDA, OF

BA GRADE

55 Risk: Extreme

Born: Sept. 6, 2003. **B-T:** R-R. **HT:** 6-1. **WT:** 180. **Signed:** Dominican Republic, 2020. **Signed by:** Juan Carlos de la Cruz.

TRACK RECORD: The Athletics first became enamored with Piñeda as a 14-year-old in the Dominican Republic. He made his professional debut this year in the Dominican Summer League, displaying the same enticing mix of raw tools that made him one of the top international prospects in his class. Oakland moved Piñeda up to the Arizona Complex League in late July and he ranked as the league's No. 5 prospect.

SCOUTING REPORT: Piñeda is a dynamic athlete growing into his 180-pound frame, and there's more projection left. That strength helps him already generate aggressive, violent bat speed that leads to easy plus raw power, including at least one memorable opposite field homer in extended spring training as a 17-year-old. There's some lift to Piñeda's swing that leads to swings and misses in the strike zone, but he has worked to cut down the length of his swing. He shows advanced pitch recognition for his age and impressed scouts in Arizona by his selectivity. Piñeda is a plus runner with an above-average arm right now, making it easy to dream on his potential as a center fielder, but he will need to refine his routes and instincts. A shift to a corner outfield spot isn't out of the question if he slows down as he packs more strength onto his frame.

THE FUTURE: Still quite raw, Piñeda has one of the highest ceilings in Oakland's system but his path to the big leagues will be a slow burn. He's expected to return to the ACL to begin 2022.

SCOUTING GRADES:	Hitting: 50	Power: 60	Running: 50	Fielding: 50	Arm: 60

Year	Age	Club (Level)	Lge	AVG	G	AB	R	H	2B	3B	HR	RBI	BB	SO	SB	OBP	SLG
2021	17	Athletics (R)	DSL	.200	10	35	4	7	1	1	0	1	5	13	3	.300	.286
	17	Athletics (R)	ACL	.258	23	62	15	16	2	2	1	8	13	28	3	.403	.403
Minor League Totals (1 year)				.237	33	97	19	23	3	3	1	9	18	41	6	.368	.361

6 A.J. PUK, LHP

Born: April 25, 1995. **B-T:** L-L. **HT:** 6-7. **WT:** 248. **Drafted:** Florida, 2016 (1st round). **Signed by:** Trevor Schaffer.

TRACK RECORD: Puk ranked as the top prospect in the 2016 draft and was the first college pitcher drafted when Oakland selected him sixth overall. He still hasn't thrown 300 career innings because of a slew of injuries that include both Tommy John surgery and a shoulder surgery. That trend continued in 2021. Puk missed a month early in the season with a left biceps strain and pitched almost primarily in relief upon returning, splitting time between Triple-A Las Vegas and Oakland.

SCOUTING REPORT: Puk's velocity dipped to 92-94 mph and the A's deployed him cautiously early in the season, avoiding throwing him in back-to-back games out of the bullpen. Puk lowered his arm slot in early June and his fastball velocity crept back up into his accustomed 96-97 mph range. He pitched better from that point onward, and the A's called up Puk to Oakland to aid their bullpen in mid August. When healthy, Puk's arsenal still looks potent. The A's like the extension Puk gets on his fastball and his plus upper-80s slider generated a 46.4% whiff rate in the big leagues. He flashes a plus changeup at 89-91 mph, but struggled to find the feel for it at times out of the bullpen. Oakland believes Puk made subtle improvements to the lower half of his delivery in the second half of 2021.

THE FUTURE: Puk will be 27 years old in April and has yet to make a big league start. There are evaluators, both internally and externally, who believe a future as a mid-rotation starter is possible while also acknowledging a high-leverage relief role is a more likely outcome considering his injury history.

BA GRADE

50 Risk: High

| SCOUTING GRADES: | Fastball: 70 | Slider: 60 | Changeup: 55 | Control: 50 |

Year	Age	Club (Level)	Lge	W	L	ERA	G	GS	IP	H	HR	BB	SO	BB/9	SO/9	WHIP	AVG
2021	26	Las Vegas (AAA)	West	2	5	6.10	29	4	48	61	12	19	58	3.5	10.7	1.64	.303
	26	Oakland (MLB)	AL	0	3	6.08	12	0	13	18	1	6	16	4.1	10.8	1.80	.310
Major League Totals (2 years)				2	3	4.74	22	0	25	28	2	11	29	4.01	10.58	1.58	.280
Minor League Totals (6 years)				12	20	4.43	84	42	232	213	22	89	320	3.46	12.43	1.30	.239

7 DAULTON JEFFERIES, RHP

Born: Aug. 2, 1995. **B-T:** L-R. **HT:** 6-0. **WT:** 185. **Drafted:** California, 2016 (1st round supplemental). **Signed by:** Jermaine Clark.

TRACK RECORD: Shoulder injuries beset Jefferies' final year of college at California in 2016 and Tommy John surgery wiped out nearly all of the ensuing two years of his professional career. He reached Double-A upon returning in 2019 and walked just nine batters in 79 total innings. He impressed the A's at their alternate training site in 2020 and was in contention for their final starting rotation spot out of spring training in 2021, but ultimately spent most of the season with Triple-A Las Vegas. He dealt with both right biceps tendinitis and a right flexor strain in his elbow during the season.

SCOUTING REPORT: Jefferies relies on his advanced command and throws a variety of fastballs. Both his four and two-seam heater sit in the 92-94 mph range and he's comfortable throwing his cutter, which is a tick slower, to both righties and lefties. Jefferies can move his fastballs around the strike zone but doesn't miss many bats with them. His best swing-and-miss offering is an upper-80s changeup with considerable horizontal break that tumbles away from lefthanders. He's shown the ability to manipulate the changeup, sometimes getting it to behave more like a splitter. He has yet to land on a consistent breaking ball. He featured a slurvy low-80s pitch that generated an average amount of whiffs but he threw less than 15% of the time.

THE FUTURE: If Jefferies can stay healthy, he profiles as a back-of-the-rotation starter who can compete for innings in Oakland in 2022.

BA GRADE

45 Risk: Medium

| SCOUTING GRADES: | Fastball: 50 | Cutter: 55 | Curveball: 50 | Changeup: 60 | Control: 65 |

Year	Age	Club (Level)	Lge	W	L	ERA	G	GS	IP	H	HR	BB	SO	BB/9	SO/9	WHIP	AVG
2021	25	Las Vegas (AAA)	West	5	1	4.91	15	15	77	90	13	11	68	1.3	8.0	1.31	.288
	25	Oakland (MLB)	AL	1	0	3.60	5	1	15	11	1	4	8	2.4	4.8	1.00	.208
Major League Totals (2 years)				1	1	5.82	6	2	17	16	3	6	9	3.18	4.76	1.29	.250
Minor League Totals (5 years)				7	3	3.93	49	37	176	182	21	23	189	1.17	9.65	1.16	.263

8 BRAYAN BUELVAS, OF

Born: June 8, 2002. **B-T:** R-R. **HT:** 5-11. **WT:** 155. **Signed:** Colombia, 2018. **Signed by:** Tito Quintero.

TRACK RECORD: Buelvas signed for less than $100,000 out of Colombia in 2018, but he turned heads in his Arizona League debut the following year in 2019, hitting .300/.392/.506 as a 17-year-old. Buelvas was one of three teenagers invited to Oakland's alternate training site in 2020, joining Tyler Soderstrom and Robert Puason, and spent all of 2021 at Low-A Stockton, where he was again one of the youngest players at 19 years old.

SCOUTING REPORT: Buelvas' barrel accuracy, strike-zone awareness and sneaky power bely his understated frame. He hit 16 home runs for Stockton, albeit while hitting for less average than some expected. Buelvas is still trying to find the right balance of contact and power, at times lengthening his swing and expanding his approach as he chases power Opposing evaluators mostly envision Buelvas settling into an above-average hitter with more of a gap-to-gap approach once he finds that balance. Buelvas is an instinctive defender who impresses the longer you watch him. Solid throwing accuracy allows his average arm to play up and he's capable of playing all three outfield positions, but his average foot speed may ultimately be better suited in a corner as he continues to fill out physically.

THE FUTURE: Buelvas lacks an obvious carrying tool, but those most bullish on him see a hit-over-power everyday corner outfielder.

BA GRADE

50 Risk: High

SCOUTING GRADES:	Hitting: 55	Power: 50	Running: 50	Fielding: 55	Arm: 55

Year	Age	Club (Level)	Lge	AVG	G	AB	R	H	2B	3B	HR	RBI	BB	SO	SB	OBP	SLG
2021	19	Stockton (LoA)	West	.219	88	347	54	76	11	4	16	50	37	95	17	.306	.412
Minor League Totals (3 years)				.244	155	585	84	143	26	12	19	91	67	155	33	.333	.427

9 LAWRENCE BUTLER, 1B/OF

Born: July 10, 2000. **B-T:** L-R. **HT:** 6-2. **WT:** 215. **Drafted:** HS—Atlanta, 2018 (6th round). **Signed by:** Jemel Spearman.

TRACK RECORD: Butler elevated his stock as much as any prospect in Oakland's system in 2021. The A's tabbed Butler as a developmental project out of high school and he struggled mightily with strikeouts in his first two professional seasons. That changed in 2021, when he broke out in his first taste of full-season ball, posting the second-best isolated power (.236) of any qualified hitter in Low-A West with Stockton. He ended the year hitting .340 in 14 games with High-A Lansing.

BA GRADE

45 Risk: High

SCOUTING REPORT: Butler's combination of power and speed is mesmerizing. His powerful, lofted swing produces 70-grade raw power with exit velocities maxing out north of 110 mph, putting him among the most powerful hitters in Oakland's system. Like many long-levered young power hitters, Butler fights a tendency to lengthen his swing, leaving him susceptible to swings and misses. There are concerns about his 33% strikeout rate, but that represented an improvement compared to his pro debut. Butler isn't a hacker—if anything, he can be overly deferential and his swing rates were among the lowest in Oakland's system. He's an instinctive, plus runner who stole nearly 30 bases in 2021 and spent time at all three outfield positions in addition to first base. Butler may be better suited for first base in the long run as he matures, but his athleticism gives him a shot to handle a corner outfield position. He also receives raves for his competitiveness and makeup.

THE FUTURE: A return to High-A Lansing is likely for Butler as he continues to prove he can make enough contact to allow his head-turning power to play.

SCOUTING GRADES:	Hitting: 45	Power: 70	Running: 55	Fielding: 50	Arm: 45

Year	Age	Club (Level)	Lge	AVG	G	AB	R	H	2B	3B	HR	RBI	BB	SO	SB	OBP	SLG
2021	20	Stockton (LoA)	West	.263	88	335	62	88	20	4	17	67	55	131	26	.364	.499
	20	Lansing (HiA)	Cent	.340	14	50	14	17	4	0	2	8	4	15	3	.389	.540
Minor League Totals (4 years)				.239	203	683	116	163	33	8	24	112	103	279	33	.337	.416

10 COLIN PELUSE, RHP

Born: June 11, 1998. **B-T:** R-R. **HT:** 6-3. **WT:** 230. **Drafted:** Wake Forest, 2019 (9th round). **Signed by:** Neil Avent.

TRACK RECORD: A dismal 5.52 ERA hurt Peluse's draft stock as a junior at Wake Forest in 2019 and he entered the A's system as an unheralded ninth-round selection. Peluse added considerable strength to his lower half during the 2020 shutdown and surprised the A's by touching 98 mph in short bursts at instructional league that fall. He carried that momentum through 2021, posting a 3.66 ERA in 86 innings at High-A Lansing before being promoted to Double-A Midland to end the season.

SCOUTING REPORT: Peluse's fastball settles into the 94-95 mph range with decent shape in a starting role. He deploys it aggressively, throwing it for strikes roughly 70% of the time, and hunts the first-pitch advantage in a manner more like a reliever than a starter. Peluse's secondaries are less refined. He worked with the A's analytics department, including staff astrophysicist Samantha Schultz, to reshape his slider, seeking a pitch with more late life that could miss more bats, and also tinkered with the pitch's grip. Peluse's third offering is a changeup with decent arm-side run that he doesn't always trust. He shows average command and a feel to pitch.

THE FUTURE: Some evaluators see Peluse as a multi-inning battering ram out of the bullpen, while others believe he has the upside of a No. 4 starter if he improves his secondaries.

BA GRADE

45 Risk: High

SCOUTING GRADES:		Fastball: 55		Slider: 55		Changeup: 50		Control: 50	

Year	Age	Club (Level)	Lge	W	L	ERA	G	GS	IP	H	HR	BB	SO	BB/9	SO/9	WHIP	AVG
2021	23	Lansing (HiA)	Cent	7	3	3.66	18	15	86	82	10	22	92	2.3	9.6	1.21	.251
	23	Midland (AA)	Cent	2	0	1.80	3	3	15	9	1	4	17	2.4	10.2	0.87	.176
Minor League Totals (3 years)				11	4	3.17	29	23	125	112	12	32	135	2.30	9.72	1.15	.238

11 JEFF CRISWELL, RHP

BA GRADE

45 Risk: High

Born: March 10, 1999. **B-T:** R-R. **HT:** 6-4. **WT:** 225. **Drafted:** Michigan, 2020 (2nd round). **Signed by:** Rich Sparks.

TRACK RECORD: Criswell was an All-Big Ten first-team selection at Michigan in 2019, logging 106 innings primarily as a starter until the College World Series, where he starred in a relief role. He was expected to anchor Michigan's rotation in 2020, but the pandemic ended his season after 24 innings. He has pitched sparingly since. Criswell missed nearly all of 2021 dealing with arm trouble, throwing just 12 innings for High-A Lansing, but pitched in the Arizona Fall League.

SCOUTING REPORT: Criswell teases the potential for four potential above-average offerings, but he needs to prove he can sustain them in a starting role. His fastball touched 98 mph in shorter instructional league outings in 2020 and sat 93-95 mph in the AFL in 2021. He pairs his fastball with a vertically-breaking mid-80s slider that he commands well and a low-80s changeup that dives off the plate. Both pitches flash plus and generate swings and misses, although he struggled to command them in his limited AFL time. Criswell occasionally features a solid-average curveball as a fourth offering, too. He has ample arm strength, but his effortful delivery and inconsistent foot strike concern evaluators who watch him.

THE FUTURE: Criswell's professional debut hasn't allayed fears of reliever risk, but those highest on him still see a potential mid-to-back of the rotation arm.

Year	Age	Club (Level)	Lge	W	L	ERA	G	GS	IP	H	HR	BB	SO	BB/9	SO/9	WHIP	AVG
2021	22	Lansing (HiA)	Cent	0	0	4.50	5	5	12	9	1	4	12	3.0	9.0	1.08	.200
Minor League Totals (2 years)				0	0	4.50	5	5	12	9	1	4	12	3.00	9.00	1.08	.200

12 BRENT HONEYWELL JR., RHP

BA GRADE

45 Risk: High

Born: March 31, 1995. **B-T:** R-R. **HT:** 6-2. **WT:** 195. **Drafted:** Walters State (Tenn.) JC, 2014 (2nd round supplemental). **Signed by:** Brian Hickman (Rays).

TRACK RECORD: Honeywell ranked in the Rays top 30 seven consecutive seasons, reaching Tampa Bay's No. 1 spot in 2018, but missed three consecutive seasons returning from a trio of elbow surgeries. Honeywell returned in 2021 and finally made his big league debut for the Rays, but pitched mostly in a bulk-innings role for Triple-A Durham. Squeezed for 40-man roster spots, the Rays traded Honeywell to the Athletics in November.

SCOUTING REPORT: There is hope that another year removed from injury will allow Honeywell's stuff to further regain its crispness. Honeywell always relied on a deep arsenal and he turned to all of his pitches in 2021. His fastball velocity is nearly back, sitting 93-96 mph, and he occasionally uses a low-90s cutter as well. Honeywell still throws two distinct breaking balls, a mid-80s slider and a slower curveball, although he trusted the slider more in 2021. Honeywell continues to flash a plus changeup and sprinkles in his putaway screwball as a fifth offering. All of his secondaries miss an average amount of bats, but his command isn't always consistent.

THE FUTURE: The Athletics saw oft-injured righthander James Kaprielian settle into their rotation in 2021. A similar redemption story for Honeywell represents a best-case scenario.

Year	Age	Club (Level)	Lge	W	L	ERA	G	GS	IP	H	HR	BB	SO	BB/9	SO/9	WHIP	AVG
2021	26	Durham (AAA)	East	5	4	3.97	31	13	81	74	13	24	67	2.6	7.4	1.20	.241
	26	Tampa Bay (MLB)	AL	0	0	8.31	3	2	4	5	2	3	4	6.23	8.31	1.85	.278
Major League Totals (1 year)				0	0	8.31	3	2	4	5	2	3	4	6.23	8.31	1.85	.278
Minor League Totals (7 years)				36	23	3.06	110	91	498	431	40	117	525	2.12	9.49	1.10	.232

13 DENZEL CLARKE, OF

Born: May 1, 2000. **B-T:** R-R. **HT:** 6-5. **WT:** 220. **Drafted:** Cal State Northridge, 2021 (4th round). **Signed by:** Dillon Tung.

TRACK RECORD: Clarke surged up draft boards following a strong second half at Cal State Northridge, and the A's made him their fourth-round selection in 2021, coveting his power-speed potential and makeup they ascertained during pre-draft conversations. He debuted in the Arizona Complex League, appearing in seven games. Clarke's mother, Donna, was an Olympian heptathlete for Canada in 1984 and he is cousins with the Guardians' Naylor brothers, Josh and Bo.

SCOUTING REPORT: Clarke boasts enormous tools, headlined by easy plus raw power that allows for home run potential even on fly balls he doesn't barrel. He rebuilt his swing mechanics following his freshman year in college, working with several instructors, including hitting coach Craig Wallenbrock, to find a solution that allowed him to access his power more consistently. He reduced his leg kick and adopted more of a simplified, balanced approach. He still has swing-and-miss concerns, and at times he struggles to sync his upper and lower half when he gets overly aggressive, but he now shows fringe-average hitting potential. Clarke is a plus runner who shows good defensive instincts, although his fringe-average arm may push him to left field. Clarke's impressive frame still has room to add more strength, too.

THE FUTURE: It's a risk-reward profile, but Clarke is one of Oakland's most intriguing prospects as he enters full-season ball in 2022.

Year	Age	Club (Level)	Lge	AVG	G	AB	R	H	2B	3B	HR	RBI	BB	SO	SB	OBP	SLG
2021	21	Athletics (R)	ACL	.316	7	19	2	6	2	0	1	1	3	6	1	.409	.579
Minor League Totals (1 year)				.316	7	19	2	6	2	0	1	1	3	6	1	.409	.579

14 JORDAN DIAZ, 1B/3B

Born: Aug. 13, 2000. **B-T:** R-R. **HT:** 5-9. **WT:** 190. **Signed:** Colombia, 2016. **Signed by:** Jose Quintero.

TRACK RECORD: Diaz has consistently demonstrated advanced hitting ability since he signed with the A's out of Colombia for $275,000 in 2016. That continued in 2021 with High-A Lansing. Diaz finished fourth in batting average (.288) and tied for 10th in wRC+ (121) among qualified High-A Central hitters despite being one of the league's youngest hitters at 20 years old. He also appeared on Colombia's Olympic qualifying roster. The A's added Diaz to their 40-man roster in November.

SCOUTING REPORT: An innate feel for the barrel and a solid swing path allows Diaz to consistently hit for average, and his power is slowly catching up. Diaz likes to deploy his hitting ability and swings the bat freely. He owned one of the highest swing percentages in the A's system and also posted one of its lowest walk rates (6.8%), but his contact skills so far have allowed him to maintain a manageable strikeout rate. Diaz's future defensive home has yet to crystallize. Diaz's stocky frame has raised concerns in the past, although he looked a bit more spry in 2021. He flashes the ability to handle third base, but still needs to clean up his footwork. The A's shifted Diaz to first base more in 2021, but he's undersized for the position, and also briefly tried him in left field, where his foot speed was tested.

THE FUTURE: Opposing teams have coveted Diaz in trade talks in the past. His pure hitting ability may be good enough to make up for the defensive ambiguity.

Year	Age	Club (Level)	Lge	AVG	G	AB	R	H	2B	3B	HR	RBI	BB	SO	SB	OBP	SLG
2021	20	Lansing (HiA)	Cent	.288	90	333	46	96	24	1	13	56	25	58	2	.337	.483
Minor League Totals (5 years)				.271	258	933	116	253	59	4	23	148	68	152	7	.324	.417

15 LOGAN DAVIDSON, SS/3B

Born: Dec. 26, 1997. **B-T:** B-R. **HT:** 6-3. **WT:** 210. **Drafted:** Clemson, 2019 (1st round). **Signed by:** Neil Avent.

BA GRADE
45 Risk: High

TRACK RECORD: Davidson's blend of all-around performance, power potential and defense made him the 29th overall pick out of Clemson in 2019. Those tools haven't translated to production so far in pro ball, and he posted a .620 OPS with Double-A Midland in 2021.

SCOUTING REPORT: Even as an amateur, Davidson's lack of wood bat success raised questions about his pure hitting ability. Those concerns followed him into pro ball. He struck out 30% of the time in 2021, although it's worth noting he bypassed the Class A levels completely because of the canceled 2020 minor league season. The A's have worked with the switch-hitting Davidson to shorten his swing and tighten his approach, helping him learn which pitches he can hunt in the strike zone. Davidson still shows above-average power potential and averaged a nearly 90 mph exit velocity in 2021. He is much more impactful from the left side and hit all seven of his home runs lefthanded while posting just a .359 OPS righthanded during the season. Defensively, Davidson has the footwork, actions and instincts to play an average shortstop. He makes most of the routine plays and he has an accurate throwing arm. Most evaluators agree he could handle third base or a multi-positional infield role.

THE FUTURE: The A's are still waiting for Davidson's bat to come around, but his defensive chops should allow him to reach the big leagues as a versatile infield defender with power off the bench.

Year	Age	Club (Level)	Lge	AVG	G	AB	R	H	2B	3B	HR	RBI	BB	SO	SB	OBP	SLG
2021	23	Midland (AA)	Cent	.212	119	448	53	95	22	1	7	48	62	155	4	.307	.313
Minor League Totals (3 years)				.221	173	653	95	144	29	1	11	60	93	210	9	.319	.319

16 MASON MILLER, RHP

Born: Aug. 24, 1998. **B-T:** R-R. **HT:** 6-5. **WT:** 200. **Drafted:** Gardner-Webb, 2021 (3rd round). **Signed by:** Neil Avent.

BA GRADE
50 Risk: Extreme

TRACK RECORD: Miller weighed just 155 pounds and his fastball sat in the mid-to-upper 80s at Division III Waynesburg (Pa.) when doctors discovered he had Type 1 diabetes, explaining confounding weight loss early in his college career. His velocity returned—and then some—as he incrementally gained weight, and he dominated his final two seasons. Miller transferred to Division I Gardner-Webb in 2021 and led all Big South Conference pitchers with 121 strikeouts. The A's made him their third-round selection, and he briefly debuted in the Arizona Complex League.

SCOUTING REPORT: Miller's fastball touched triple digits at instructional league and settles in at 94-96 mph as a starter. The pitch isn't shaped like the bat-missing, vertically-oriented fastballs currently en vogue. Instead, Miller relies more on its horizontal break and his solid command of the pitch. His low-80s slider plays off his fastball and generates more whiffs thanks to its two-plane break as it dives out of the zone. He also features a mid-80s changeup that showed signs of improvement upon getting to pro ball. A starter throughout college, Miller repeats his delivery well and has prototypical size, although he fought his control at times early in his career at Waynesburg.

THE FUTURE: Miller turns 24 in August and has the look of a potential fast-riser. He could arrive in the majors as a power reliever before settling into a mid-rotation starting role.

Year	Age	Club (Level)	Lge	W	L	ERA	G	GS	IP	H	HR	BB	SO	BB/9	SO/9	WHIP	AVG
2021	22	Athletics (R)	ACL	0	1	1.50	3	2	6	4	0	3	9	4.5	13.5	1.17	.190
Minor League Totals (1 year)				0	1	1.50	3	2	6	4	0	3	9	4.50	13.50	1.17	.190

17 ROBERT PUASON, SS

Born: Sept. 11, 2002. **B-T:** B-R. **HT:** 6-3. **WT:** 187. **Signed:** Dominican Republic, 2019. **Signed by:** Amauris Reyes.

BA GRADE
50 Risk: Extreme

TRACK RECORD: The A's signed Puason to a $5.1 million bonus in 2019, tied with Yankees outfielder Jasson Dominguez for the largest bonus in that year's international class. Oakland sent Puason to their alternate training site in 2020 with the pandemic delaying his official pro debut until 2021. The A's opted for Puason to bypass rookie ball and sent him to Low-A Stockton, where he was the league's youngest qualified hitter at 18 years old. He was mostly overmatched, striking out more than 40% of the time.

SCOUTING REPORT: Puason is a toolsy, gifted athlete capable of the occasional jaw-dropping feat, but most observers felt he wasn't ready for full-season ball after seeing pitchers expose both his swing and approach. His steep, uphill swing doesn't stay in the strike zone very long, leading to a significant amount of swings and misses and a nearly 60% groundball rate when he does make contact. He also lacks a consistent approach, chasing pitches at one of the highest clips in the A's system. Defensively, Puason shows glimpses of excellence, displaying a plus throwing arm and impressive range at shortstop. But the game speeds up on him at times and he struggles to consistently make the routine play (29 errors in 2021). Puason is a plus runner but he's still developing the necessary instincts to translate his speed on the basepaths.

THE FUTURE: Puason will likely repeat Low-A after an erratic start to his pro career. His physical skills are impressive, but his development arc will be a long, slow burn.

Year	Age	Club (Level)	Lge	AVG	G	AB	R	H	2B	3B	HR	RBI	BB	SO	SB	OBP	SLG
2021	18	Stockton (LoA)	West	.215	91	302	43	65	12	1	3	27	24	139	3	.282	.291
Minor League Totals (1 year)				.215	91	302	43	65	12	1	3	27	24	139	3	.282	.291

18 LUIS BARRERA, OF

Born: Nov. 15, 1995. **B-T:** L-L. **HT:** 6-0. **WT:** 195. **Signed:** Dominican Republic, 2012. **Signed by:** Raymond Abreu.

BA GRADE
40 Risk: Medium

TRACK RECORD: The A's hoped Barrera's strong performance at their alternate training site in 2020 portended another step forward in 2021, nearly a decade after they signed him. The A's briefly summoned Barrera for his big league debut, a four-game stint in late May, but he spent the majority of 2021 with Triple-A Las Vegas, where he didn't hit for much impact and finished with a .741 OPS.

SCOUTING REPORT: Barrera fits the classic hit-over-power slasher profile. His flat bat path is geared toward contact, which allows his plus speed to play on the basepaths, but his swing doesn't produce much in-game power. Most aspects of Barrera's game are aggressive, especially his approach. He swung at nearly 48% of all pitches he saw in 2021. He makes it work thanks to his pure hitting ability, but he would benefit from a bit more selectivity. Barrera is a solid thrower who plays all three defensive positions, although he's a bit stretched in center field.

THE FUTURE: Barrera's speed, defense and contact ability should allow him to compete for a part-time role in the A's outfield in 2022, but the clock is ticking.

Year	Age	Club (Level)	Lge	AVG	G	AB	R	H	2B	3B	HR	RBI	BB	SO	SB	OBP	SLG
2021	25	Las Vegas (AAA)	West	.276	96	341	53	94	16	6	4	37	39	67	10	.348	.393
	25	Oakland (MLB)	AL	.250	6	8	1	2	0	0	0	0	0	2	0	.250	.250
Major League Totals (1 year)				.250	6	8	1	2	0	0	0	0	0	2	0	.250	.250
Minor League Totals (9 years)				.279	534	1917	287	535	88	43	25	220	171	388	72	.339	.409

19 JORGE JUAN, RHP

Born: March 6, 1999. **B-T:** R-R. **HT:** 6-8. **WT:** 200. **Signed:** Dominican Republic, 2017. **Signed by:** Juan Carlos de la Cruz.

BA GRADE
50 Risk: Extreme

TRACK RECORD: Juan was a virtual unknown outside of the A's organization until his breakout 2021 season. He struck out 31 batters in 21 innings with Low-A Stockton and earned a quick promotion to High-A Lansing. An arm injury ended his season in mid-August, but the A's still added him to their 40-man roster in November.

SCOUTING REPORT: Juan is built like a throwback NBA power forward. He is listed at 6-foot-8, 200 pounds and likely weighs closer to 250 pounds. His fastball velocity has gradually increased as he's added strength to his hulking frame. His heater now sits in the mid 90s and touches 99 mph with unique angle. Juan snaps off a mid-80s power breaking ball with considerable vertical break that flashes plus. He generates plenty of whiffs when he buries it as chase pitch, but needs to locate it in the strike zone more consistently. Juan's third pitch is a 90 mph changeup with lateral run that he uses infrequently. Throwing strikes is an ongoing battle for Juan, but he surprises evaluators with his ability to repeat his delivery despite his height, giving him a chance to start. He'll need to show he can locate his changeup consistently to engender more confidence that he can remain in the rotation.

THE FUTURE: The A's decision to protect Juan suggests he could move quickly if shifted to a relief role. His injury clouds his 2022 outlook, but he has become a power arm to watch in the system.

Year	Age	Club (Level)	Lge	W	L	ERA	G	GS	IP	H	HR	BB	SO	BB/9	SO/9	WHIP	AVG
2021	22	Stockton (LoA)	West	1	1	3.86	6	4	21	15	2	7	31	3.0	13.3	1.05	.203
	22	Lansing (HiA)	Cent	0	2	11.12	2	2	5	7	2	6	9	9.5	14.3	2.29	.280
Minor League Totals (4 years)				2	13	4.88	36	18	103	86	5	68	124	5.92	10.80	1.49	.226

20 CODY THOMAS, OF

BA GRADE

45 Risk: High

Born: Oct. 8, 1994. **B-T:** L-R. **HT:** 6-4. **WT:** 211. **Drafted:** Oklahoma, 2016 (13th round). **Signed by:** Josh Herzenberg (Dodgers).

TRACK RECORD: Thomas was a two-sport athlete at Oklahoma and competing with Baker Mayfield for quarterback reps before turning to baseball full-time in 2016, his only full season of college baseball. The A's acquired Thomas and reliever Adam Kolarek from the Dodgers in a Feb. 2021 trade that sent Sheldon Neuse to Los Angeles. Thomas spent all season with Triple-A Las Vegas and hit 18 homers in its hitting-friendly environment until an Achilles injury ended his season in late July.

SCOUTING REPORT: Evaluators marvel at Thomas' raw power, but question how consistently he'll access it. His 90 mph average exit velocity with Las Vegas ranked among the highest marks in Oakland's system, although he played in just 59 games. As with several of their most prolific power hitters, the A's asked Thomas to work on shortening the length of his swing. His heavy pull-side approach and swing-and-miss concerns (36% whiff rate) limit his pure hitting potential to fringe-average. Defensively, Thomas is a capable corner outfielder, although his arm is just average despite his quarterback background.

THE FUTURE: The A's added Thomas to their 40-man roster in November. He draws some comparisons to A's outfielder Seth Brown because of his age and offensive profile.

Year	Age	Club (Level)	Lge	AVG	G	AB	R	H	2B	3B	HR	RBI	BB	SO	SB	OBP	SLG
2021	26	Las Vegas (AAA)	West	.289	59	218	46	63	20	4	18	52	25	78	0	.363	.665
Minor League Totals (6 years)				.259	496	1883	315	488	100	25	99	330	183	622	26	.333	.497

21 MICHAEL GULDBERG, OF

BA GRADE

45 Risk: High

Born: June 22, 1999. **B-T:** R-R. **HT:** 6-0. **WT:** 175. **Drafted:** Georgia Tech, 2020 (3rd round). **Signed by:** Jemel Spearman.

TRACK RECORD: Guldberg's college career was shortened by a shoulder injury as a freshman and the canceled 2020 season, but he hit .374 when in the lineup for Georgia Tech. He impressed the A's immediately in instructional league after they drafted him in the third round in 2020 and began the 2021 season with High-A Lansing. Hamstring and shoulder injuries limited Guldberg to just 49 games.

SCOUTING REPORT: A lean, wiry athlete, Guldberg's speed and solid instincts allows him to play a plus defensive center field and cover plenty of ground. He played almost exclusively in center for Lansing and his average arm should allow him to stick there, but past experience at left field and second base allows for the A's to envision a potential super-utility role if his bat can take another step. Guldberg makes plenty of contact and shows decent bat speed, but his swing isn't geared toward in-game power. The A's believe there's the potential for fringe-average power as he adds strength to his frame.

THE FUTURE: The A's are encouraged by the glimpses they've seen from Guldberg, but he needs to stay healthy. His defense, speed and versatility allows for at least a potential part-time big league role.

Year	Age	Club (Level)	Lge	AVG	G	AB	R	H	2B	3B	HR	RBI	BB	SO	SB	OBP	SLG
2021	22	Lansing (HiA)	Cent	.259	48	174	29	45	9	2	5	18	17	36	11	.347	.420
Minor League Totals (2 years)				.259	48	174	29	45	9	2	5	18	17	36	11	.347	.420

22 JONAH BRIDE, 1B/3B/C

BA GRADE

40 Risk: Medium

Born: Dec. 27, 1995. **B-T:** R-R. **HT:** 5-10. **WT:** 200. **Drafted:** South Carolina, 2018 (3rd round). **Signed by:** Neil Avent.

TRACK RECORD: Bride was an unheralded senior sign in 2018 after starting every game for South Carolina in each of his final two seasons. He climbed to Double-A Midland in 2021 and was one of the league's most consistent performers. Bride walked as frequently as he struck out, his 17.1% walk rate was best among Double-A Central qualified hitters. The A's sent him to the Arizona Fall League after the season and added him to their 40-man roster in November.

SCOUTING REPORT: If there's a defensive position open, chances are Bride is willing to try it. He spent time at first, third and second base this year with Midland, then went to the AFL to learn how to play catcher. Offensively, Bride's swing is a bit unorthodox, beginning with a slightly open stance before closing his stride and stepping almost toward first base, but was impactful at Double-A. He rarely swings and misses, especially on fastballs in the strike zone, and he has excellent strike-zone discipline—his 17% chase rate was among the best of all A's minor leaguers. Bride doesn't have a loud carrying tool, and he's the type of player who tends to impress evaluators over longer periods of time instead of short looks.

THE FUTURE: Bride is a classic skills-over-tools versatile performer in the mold of Austin Nola or Kyle Farmer. He could reach the majors in 2022.

Year	Age	Club (Level)	Lge	AVG	G	AB	R	H	2B	3B	HR	RBI	BB	SO	SB	OBP	SLG
2021	25	Midland (AA)	Cent	.265	78	264	45	70	11	2	9	49	57	57	2	.407	.424
Minor League Totals (4 years)				.274	251	875	130	240	46	6	22	141	125	191	7	.381	.416

23 BRADY FEIGL, RHP

BA GRADE **40** Risk: Medium

Born: Nov. 27, 1995. **B-T:** R-R. **HT:** 6-4. **WT:** 235. **Drafted:** Mississippi, 2018 (5th round). **Signed by:** Kelcey Mucker.

TRACK RECORD: The A's selected Feigl in the fifth round of the 2018 draft, signing him to a $300,000 bonus after he performed well as Mississippi's Saturday starter. He's been a reliable year-over-year option since. Feigl spent most of 2021 with Double-A Midland, posting the league's fourth-best expected fielding independent ERA (3.85) of any pitcher with 70 or more innings. Still, the A's did not protect Feigl ahead of the Rule 5 draft.

SCOUTING REPORT: Feigl's pitch mix isn't overpowering, but his deceptive delivery, command and pitchability allows him to minimize damage. His fastball averages nearly 93 mph with natural cut and sink, enhancing his groundball-oriented approach. Feigl throws the pitch with deceptive angle and can command it to any quadrant of the strike zone, but it generates a below-average amount of swings and misses. He also displays feel for spin, throwing an above-average mid-80s slider with late life and a curveball that's a beat slower. Feigl's two breaking balls tend to blend together, and the A's want to see more distinction between the two pitches. He also mixes in a fringe-average changeup. A's player development staffers believe the pitch could improve even more with better sequencing.

THE FUTURE: Feigl largely projects as a back-of-the-rotation starter, but his arsenal may play up in a relief role like long-time A's stalwart Yusmeiro Petit.

Year	Age	Club (Level)	Lge	W	L	ERA	G	GS	IP	H	HR	BB	SO	BB/9	SO/9	WHIP	AVG
2021	25	Midland (AA)	Cent	7	7	3.96	20	20	102	94	13	34	106	3.0	9.3	1.25	.242
	25	Las Vegas (AAA)	West	1	2	8.55	5	5	20	23	5	12	17	5.4	7.7	1.75	.295
Minor League Totals (4 years)				14	22	4.30	63	58	283	276	31	89	276	2.83	8.79	1.29	.255

24 HOGAN HARRIS, LHP

BA GRADE **45** Risk: High

Born: Dec. 26, 1996. **B-T:** R-L. **HT:** 6-3. **WT:** 230. **Drafted:** Louisiana-Lafayette, 2018 (3rd round). **Signed by:** Kelcey Mucker.

TRACK RECORD: Harris missed all of 2021 recovering from Tommy John surgery before returning to pitch in the Arizona Fall League. The lefthander has logged just 54.2 career innings, all coming in 2019. Oblique injuries at Louisiana Lafayette hampered his 2018 draft stock and he didn't make his pro debut that season because of an elbow strain.

SCOUTING REPORT: Harris is still working his way back and threw mostly fastballs and changeups in his return in the AFL. His fastball sits in the low 90s with late sink and has touched 95 at its best. His above-average changeup sits in the mid 70s and can miss bats at the bottom of the strike zone. Harris throws a slow, arcing low-70s curveball sparingly, and has shown an ability to manipulate a slider in the past. Harris' strike-throwing looked tentative in his return—he walked 14 batters in 10 innings—and command has been an issue in the past, but some of that should be expected as he eases back to health. Harris used his rehab time to clean up his body, and he's also made a series of changes in pro ball to alleviate timing issues in his delivery that leads to bouts of erraticism.

THE FUTURE: Harris has the ceiling of a back-end starter if he can remain healthy. His primary goal is just to make it through a full season in 2022.

Year	Age	Club (Level)	Lge	W	L	ERA	G	GS	IP	H	HR	BB	SO	BB/9	SO/9	WHIP	AVG
2021	24	Did not play—Injured															

25 BRADY BASSO, LHP

BA GRADE **45** Risk: High

Born: Oct. 8, 1997. **B-T:** R-L. **HT:** 6-2. **WT:** 210. **Drafted:** Oklahoma State, 2019 (16th round). **Signed by:** Chris Reilly.

TRACK RECORD: Basso flashed premium stuff but erratic control at Oklahoma State, walking 6.5 batters per nine innings in his draft year. The A's gave him $75,000 in the 16th round and he pitched well out of the bullpen in a limited rookie ball debut. The A's moved Basso to a starting role in 2021 and were encouraged with the results until an elbow injury that required Tommy John surgery ended his season in mid June.

SCOUTING REPORT: Basso worked with Oakland's pitching development staff to smooth out his delivery, unlocking more consistent velocity. His fastball sat 94-95 mph and touched 97 mph with good spin and shape from the left side before he got hurt. He threw a hard slider in college that has morphed into a low-90s cutter as a professional. The gem of his arsenal might end up being his hammer of an upper-70s curveball, which High-A hitters whiffed on nearly 80% of the time in a small sample. Basso also features a work-in-progress changeup. There's some length in the back of Basso's arm stroke and he needed to prove he could maintain the changes to his delivery over time, even before elbow surgery.

THE FUTURE: The A's believed they had unlocked a potential gem in Basso, but his injury clouds his future. Basso has yet to pitch above High-A and turns 25 in October.

Year	Age	Club (Level)	Lge	W	L	ERA	G	GS	IP	H	HR	BB	SO	BB/9	SO/9	WHIP	AVG
2021	23	Lansing (HiA)	Cent	2	2	4.71	7	4	21	21	2	7	26	3.0	11.1	1.33	.247
Minor League Totals (3 years)				2	2	3.09	22	5	47	41	2	15	64	2.89	12.34	1.20	.228

26 MICKEY McDONALD, OF

BA GRADE 40 Risk: Medium

Born: June 2, 1995. **B-T:** L-R. **HT:** 6-2. **WT:** 175. **Drafted:** Illinois-Chicago, 2017 (18th round). **Signed by:** Kevin Mello.

TRACK RECORD: McDonald posted a .607 OPS across three levels in 2019 when teams last saw him in his age-24 season, but he re-emerged an improved player in 2021 and reached Triple-A Las Vegas. He he hit .333 at the minors' highest level and showed intriguing defensive versatility.

SCOUTING REPORT: McDonald fits the A's mold as an older, under-the-radar performer without an obvious carrying tool. He ditched switch-hitting in 2021, choosing instead to hit solely from the left side, and his success surprised opposing evaluators. He showed a compact swing and a contact-oriented approach, putting the ball in play enough to allow his above-average speed (18 steals) to play on the bases. McDonald's gets on base, but he doesn't have much power potential. He is a solid defender who can handle all three outfield positions, and McDonald also played some third base.

THE FUTURE: McDonald played his way into the A's logjam of outfielders vying for a part-time role in the majors. His lack of power puts pressure on his hitting ability, but McDonald's speed and defense help his chances.

Year	Age	Club (Level)	Lge	AVG	G	AB	R	H	2B	3B	HR	RBI	BB	SO	SB	OBP	SLG
2021	26	Midland (AA)	Cent	.273	50	172	25	47	6	1	1	16	25	47	8	.378	.337
	26	Las Vegas (AAA)	West	.333	56	192	44	64	11	3	1	22	26	42	10	.423	.438
Minor League Totals (5 years)				.269	362	1251	192	336	45	13	6	109	145	308	65	.350	.340

27 MAX SCHUEMANN, 2B/SS

BA GRADE 40 Risk: Medium

Born: June 11, 1997. **B-T:** R-R. **HT:** 6-1. **WT:** 190. **Drafted:** Eastern Michigan, 2018 (20th round). **Signed by:** Richard Sparks.

TRACK RECORD: Schuemann starred at both Portage (Mich.) Northern High and Eastern Michigan, so it's only fitting his breakout season began at High-A Lansing in 2021. He vaulted three levels up to Triple-A and tied for fifth among all minor leaguers with 52 steals, tormenting opposing pitchers and catchers in the first year of MLB's experimental pickoff rules in High-A.

SCOUTING REPORT: Schuemann is a plus runner, but his base-stealing ability benefits from strong baseball instincts that show up across several facets of his game. He's stretched a bit thin at shortstop, his natural defensive position, but he's added versatility, playing second base and all three outfield positions with Double-A Midland. Schuemann showed impressive bat-to-ball skills but modest impact at the plate. His below-average power potential puts more strain on his hit tool, and he'll need to continue to hone in his approach against veteran pitching.

THE FUTURE: After adding more versatility to complement his running ability, Schuemann has the ceiling of a versatile up-and-down utility player.

Year	Age	Club (Level)	Lge	AVG	G	AB	R	H	2B	3B	HR	RBI	BB	SO	SB	OBP	SLG
2021	24	Lansing (HiA)	Cent	.224	54	201	43	45	11	1	5	20	25	50	34	.347	.363
	24	Midland (AA)	Cent	.320	57	219	38	70	13	1	2	21	23	46	17	.398	.416
	24	Las Vegas (AAA)	West	.231	8	26	2	6	1	1	0	1	5	7	1	.355	.346
Minor League Totals (4 years)				.255	258	909	159	232	55	4	10	83	96	209	88	.352	.358

28 JUNIOR PEREZ, OF

Born: July 4, 2001. **B-T:** R-R. **HT:** 6-1. **WT:** 200. **Signed:** Dominican Republic, 2017. **Signed by:** Felix Perez/Trevor Schumm (Padres).

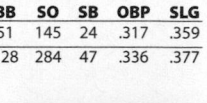

BA GRADE

45 Risk: Very High

TRACK RECORD: The A's acquired Perez from the Padres in 2019 as the player to be named later for Jorge Mateo on the strength of Perez's strong debut showing in the Rookie-level Arizona League. Perez failed to replicate that success in his first taste of full-season ball, striking out 37.6% of the time with Low-A Stockton in 2021 en route to a .207/.317/359 slash line.

SCOUTING REPORT: Perez's plus power remains his calling card, although he now faces heightened concerns about his ability to make enough quality contact for it to show up. He struggles to time pitches and his rotational, lofted swing doesn't stay on plane for very long, leading to lots of swings and misses in the strike zone. When Perez does make contact, it's loud. His exit velocities max out north of 110 mph. Perez was more of a power-speed threat as an amateur, but he's already started to slow down as he's grown stronger. He now projects to be a future fringe-average runner and is likely destined for a corner.

THE FUTURE: Perez showed some ability late in the season to make adjustments and cut down on his swings and misses. He'll have to do so again in 2022 after a difficult Low-A debut.

Year	Age	Club (Level)	Lge	AVG	G	AB	R	H	2B	3B	HR	RBI	BB	SO	SB	OBP	SLG
2021	19	Stockton (LoA)	West	.207	95	329	54	68	16	5	8	34	51	145	24	.317	.359
Minor League Totals (4 years)				.216	207	742	124	160	36	9	22	99	128	284	47	.336	.377

29 ANGEL AREVALO, SS/OF

Born: Oct. 2, 2003. **B-T:** R-R. **HT:** 5-11. **WT:** 160. **Signed:** Venezuela, 2020. **Signed by:** Oswaldo Troconis.

BA GRADE

45 Risk: Extreme

TRACK RECORD: Arevalo was the A's most impactful Venezuelan signee in their 2020 international class. He initially signed as a long-term physical projection candidate and has incrementally added strength. He made his pro debut in the Dominican Summer League in 2021 and hit a promising .297/.438/.473 with nearly as many walks (18) as strikeouts (19).

SCOUTING REPORT: The A's were encouraged by Arevalo's diligent work during the 2020 coronavirus shutdown, and his strength gains showed this summer. Arevalo begins his swing with a wide stance at the plate and employs a modest leg kick and occasional toe tap as a timing mechanism. His swing isn't necessarily geared for in-game power right now, but he has average power potential because of his strength. Initially signed as an outfielder, Arevalo played mostly shortstop in his debut. He is an above-average runner and thrower, and the A's hope he can stay up the middle at either position.

THE FUTURE: Arevalo is promising but a long way away. He should make his U.S. debut in the Arizona Complex League in 2022.

Year	Age	Club (Level)	Lge	AVG	G	AB	R	H	2B	3B	HR	RBI	BB	SO	SB	OBP	SLG
2021	17	Athletics (R)	DSL	.297	27	74	16	22	5	4	0	15	18	19	1	.438	.473
Minor League Totals (1 year)				.297	27	74	16	22	5	4	0	15	18	19	1	.438	.473

30 BRETT HARRIS, 3B

Born: June 24, 1998. **B-T:** R-R. **HT:** 6-3. **WT:** 208. **Drafted:** Gonzaga, 2021 (7th round). **Signed by:** Jim Coffman.

BA GRADE

40 Risk: High

TRACK RECORD: Harris's season in 2021 at Gonzaga made him a favorite of Northwest area scouts. He hit .350 for the Zags, leading them to a No. 2 seed in the NCAA Tournament, and was named the West Coast Conference's defensive player of the year at third base. The A's drafted him in the seventh round and signed him for a below-slot $120,000.

SCOUTING REPORT: Harris will turn 24 in June, but he's the type of player Oakland's player development program tends to maximize. He's a plus defender at third base with impressive hands and instincts, and has the versatility to handle either shortstop or second base in a pinch. Harris showed quality pitch recognition in college and the A's were enthused by his all-fields approach and low-maintenance swing that give average hitting potential. Harris' power potential remains in question. He posted a .148 isolated power in a limited debut at High-ALansing, but amateur scouts predicted below-average power out of the draft.

THE FUTURE: Harris' glove and hitting ability make him an intriguing potential utility infielder. He'll make his full-season debut back at Lansing in 2022.

Year	Age	Club (Level)	Lge	AVG	G	AB	R	H	2B	3B	HR	RBI	BB	SO	SB	OBP	SLG
2021	23	Athletics (R)	ACL	.667	2	3	2	2	0	0	0	3	2	0	0	.800	.667
	23	Lansing (HiA)	Cent	.222	25	81	14	18	3	0	3	11	8	20	3	.323	.370
Minor League Totals (1 year)				.238	27	84	16	20	3	0	3	14	10	20	3	.347	.381

MORE PROSPECTS TO KNOW

31 JACK WEISENBURGER, RHP

Weisenburger's plus slider veers away from righthanded batters and it generated a 40% whiff rate. He pairs it with a well-shaped mid-90s fastball. Weisenburger's breaking ball moves so much that he struggles to control it, but has the makings of a single-inning MLB reliever.

32 AIDEN McINTYRE, RHP

A starter-turned-reliever, McIyntre's 92-94 mph fastball has the spin characteristics and shape that generates plenty of swing and misses at the top of the zone. Continued changeup improvement could lead to a role in Oakland's bullpen sooner rather than later.

33 CARLOS AMAYA, C

Amaya was an under-the-radar signing out of Venezuela in 2019 and hit his way out of the Dominican Summer League in 2021. The A's are impressed with his advanced strike-zone command.

34 DERMIS GARCIA, 1B

The Yankees signed Garcia to a $3 million bonus in 2014 on the strength of his double-plus raw power. It's still his loudest tool, but he also fights massive swing-and-miss. He made subtle improvements in the second half of 2021, and the A's signed him as a minor league free agent in November.

35 WANDISSON CHARLES, RHP

The A's hoped the flame-throwing Charles would emerge as a potential bullpen piece at some point in 2021. Instead, he missed all season with injury, although he returned to pitch in winter ball. Charles can touch triple-digits when healthy, albeit with shaky control.

36 GARRETT ACTON, RHP

Acton signed as a nondrafted free agent in 2020 after serving as Illinois' closer. His invisball mid-90s fastball generated nearly a 40% whiff rate in his first taste of pro ball. His slider gave hitters fits, too, and he could be another quick-moving relief option.

37 BRIAN HOWARD, RHP

Howard creates unique angle via his 6-foot-9 frame and pitched better than his 5.81 ERA indicated for Triple-A Las Vegas in 2021, showing a slight uptick in fastball velocity. He could make for an intriguing multi-inning reliever.

38 JACK CUSHING, RHP

Cushing is a pitchability righty who commands his modest arsenal with pinpoint accuracy. Improved changeup consistency would help his fastball-slider combination succeed even more.

39 JHOAN PAULINO, 3B/2B

Plus raw power is Paulino's calling card, although swing-and-miss issues and a lack of game reps are a bit concerning. He's a breakout candidate with Low-A Stockton in 2022.

40 AUSTIN BECK, OF

Pro ball has been mostly unkind to Oakland's 2017 first-round pick. Beck struck out 34% of the time while repeating High-A. Beck still has plenty of tools—speed, power, defense—but his wickedly fast bat doesn't stay in the zone long, and he struggles mightily with breaking balls.

TOP PROSPECTS OF THE DECADE

Year	Player, Pos	2021 Org
2012	Jarrod Parker, RHP	Did not play
2013	Addison Russell, SS	Mexican League
2014	Addison Russell, SS	Mexican League
2015	Daniel Robertson, SS	Brewers
2016	Franklin Barreto, SS	Angels
2017	Franklin Barreto, SS	Angels
2018	A.J. Puk, LHP	Athletics
2019	Jesus Luzardo, LHP	Marlins
2020	Jesus Luzardo, LHP	Marlins
2021	Tyler Soderstrom, C	Athletics

TOP DRAFT PICKS OF THE DECADE

Year	Player, Pos	2021 Org
2012	Addison Russell, SS	Mexican League
2013	Billy McKinney, OF	Dodgers
2014	Matt Chapman, 3B	Athletics
2015	Richie Martin, SS	Orioles
2016	A.J. Puk, LHP	Athletics
2017	Austin Beck, OF	Athletics
2018	Kyler Murray, OF	NFL
2019	Logan Davidson, SS	Athletics
2020	Tyler Soderstrom, C	Athletics
2021	Max Muncy, SS	Athletics

Philadelphia Phillies

BY CHRIS HILBURN-TRENKLE

The 2021 Phillies finished over .500, at 82-80, for the first time since 2011, but it wasn't enough to take the National League East crown.

Philadelphia finished 6.5 games back of the eventual World Series champion Braves, and were officially eliminated from postseason contention on the final day of September after being swept by Atlanta in a three-game set.

Outfielder Bryce Harper continued to live up to his lofty contract, leading the majors in OPS+ en route to his second NL MVP award, and righthander Zack Wheeler narrowly missed out on winning his first Cy Young Award while leading an inconsistent rotation.

The Phillies simply did not have enough quality bats and arms, and they weren't helped by the decline of third baseman Alec Bohm, who finished second in NL Rookie of the Year voting in 2020. Bohm was jettisoned back and forth between the majors and Triple-A Lehigh Valley, while former top prospect Spencer Howard failed to improve upon his pedestrian 2020 season. Howard was traded in July to the Rangers for righthanders Kyle Gibson and Ian Kennedy and prospect Hans Crouse, who ranks as the Phillies' No. 7 prospect.

Meanwhile down on the farm, big improvements from Bryson Stott, Johan Rojas and Logan O'Hoppe helped bolster one of the weaker farm systems in baseball. Stott was named the organization's minor league player of the year and looks to be on the verge of making his MLB debut.

Righthander Mick Abel, the team's 2020 first-round pick, impressed evaluators inside and outside the organization thanks to his impressive four-pitch mix and advanced approach for his age. The Phillies doubled down in the 2021 draft, selecting talented prep righthander Andrew Painter in the first round to give them two exciting young arms at the top of the system.

The organization rebuilt its farm system through the draft, selecting 14 pitchers in the 20-round draft, including intriguing collegiate righthanders Griff McGarry and Christian McGowan and prep projection righthander Micah Ottenbreit.

The Phillies added two more quality bats, Jordan Viars and Ethan Wilson, giving them six new Top 30 Prospects.

But with just one Top 100 Prospect in the organization—Abel—there is plenty of work to be done to strengthen the farm system.

President of baseball operations Dave Dombrowski in August dismissed assistant general managers Bryan Minniti and Scott Proefrock, as well as farm director Josh Bonifay.

Ranger Suarez's 1.36 ERA was the fifth-lowest by a pitcher with at least 10 starts since 1920.

PROJECTED 2025 LINEUP

Catcher	J.T. Realmuto	34
First Base	Matt Vierling	28
Second Base	Jean Segura	35
Third Base	Alec Bohm	28
Shortstop	Bryson Stott	27
Left Field	Ethan Wilson	25
Center Field	Johan Rojas	24
Right Field	Bryce Harper	32
Designated Hitter	Rhys Hoskins	32
No. 1 Starter	Zack Wheeler	35
No. 2 Starter	Aaron Nola	32
No. 3 Starter	Mick Abel	23
No. 4 Starter	Zach Eflin	31
No. 5 Starter	Ranger Suarez	29
Closer	Connor Brogdon	30

Dombrowski stated that he wanted everyone in the organization to be on the same page, which led him to hire Preston Mattingly, son of Don Mattingly, to take over as farm director.

Mattingly, who previously worked in the Padres organization as manager of scouting and coordinator of major league advance scouting and game planning, plans to combine an "old school" and "new school" approach to the farm system, and he noted he wants there to be one "consistent message," as he told NBC Sports Philadelphia's Jim Salisbury.

The organization took the step of understanding it needs to revamp its entire farm system. But now comes the hard part of executing a plan. ■

DEPTH CHART

PHILADELPHIA PHILLIES

TOP 2022 ROOKIES	RANK
Bryson Stott, SS	3
Hans Crouse, RHP	7
Bailey Falter, LHP	24
BREAKOUT PROSPECTS	**RANK**
Erik Miller, LHP	11
Cristian Hernandez, RHP	16
Alexeis Azuaje, 2B	20

SOURCE OF TOP 30 TALENT

Homegrown	**27**	**Acquired**	**3**
College	6	Trades	2
Junior college	2	Rule 5 draft	0
High school	8	Independent leagues	0
Nondrafted free agents	0	Free agents/waivers	1
International	11		

LF
Ethan Wilson (5)
Jordan Viars (13)

CF
Johan Rojas (4)
Simon Muzziotti (10)
Mickey Moniak (21)
Yhoswar Garcia (24)

RF
Matt Vierling (8)
Jhailyn Ortiz (14)

3B
Kendall Simmons

SS
Bryson Stott (3)
Luis Garcia (15)
Nick Maton (20)
Casey Martin (30)
Jamari Baylor

2B
Luke Williams (17)
Alexeis Azuaje (23)
Hao Yu Lee (27)
Daniel Brito
Nicolas Torres

1B
Darick Hall

C
Logan O'Hoppe (6)
Rafael Marchan (9)
Rickardo Perez (25)
Donny Sands
Andrick Nava

LHP

LHSP	LHRP
Erik Miller (11)	Cristopher Sanchez (26)
Bailey Falter (22)	Erubiel Armenta
Scott Moss (29)	Kyle Dohy
Ethan Lindow	JoJo Romero
Jordi Martinez	Rafael Marcano
Matt Osterberg	Damon Jones

RHP

RHSP	RHRP
Mick Abel (1)	Andrew Baker
Andrew Painter (2)	Andrew Schultz
Hans Crouse (7)	Ben Brown
Griff McGarry (12)	Eduar Segovia
Cristian Hernandez (16)	Starlyn Castillo
Christian McGowan (18)	Billy Sullivan
Micah Ottenbreit (19)	Blake Brown
Francisco Morales (28)	
Jose Pena Jr.	
Victor Vargas	
Noah Skirrow	

1 MICK ABEL, RHP

Born: Aug. 18, 2001. **B-T:** R-R. **HT:** 6-5. **WT:** 190.
Drafted: HS—Portland, Ore., 2020 (1st round).
Signed By: Zach Friedman.

MIKE JANES/FOUR SEAM IMAGES

BA GRADE	SCOUTING GRADES
60 Risk: High	**FB:** 65. **SL:** 60. **CHG:** 60. **CB:** 50. **CTL:** 55.

Projected future grades on 20-80 scouting scale

TRACK RECORD: Abel first emerged on the scene after striking out Riley Greene as a junior in 2019 and continued to gain steam over the next year. He ranked as the top high school pitcher in the 2020 draft class thanks to an impressive four-pitch arsenal, pitchability and the best command in the class. The Phillies were ecstatic to draft him at No. 15 overall, making him the first high school pitcher selected in the first round out of Oregon since Matt Smith in 1994. He signed with the team for $4.1 million, then joined the organization at instructional league in the fall, where he lived up to his lofty draft status. The 20-year-old righthander had an encouraging full-season debut in 2021, ranking as the top pitcher in the Low-A Southeast by league managers and pitching to a 4.43 ERA in 14 starts, while showing off an arsenal of four pitches that flashed plus. Abel missed the last two months of the season with a shoulder injury, but it wasn't considered serious and he rejoined the team at instructional league.

SCOUTING REPORT: Abel's high school team didn't take the field in 2020 due to the coronavirus pandemic, but he showed no rust in his pro debut. He has an athletic build at 6-foot-5, 190 pounds with projection remaining and a clean delivery. His fastball is his best pitch, sitting from 94-97 mph and topping out at 99. It's a swing-and-miss offering with huge vertical break and averages 2,500 rpm, giving hitters headaches. Abel's slider was voted the best breaking pitch in the 2020 prep class by scouting directors and it lived up to its reputation in 2021. It's a firm, hard pitch that sits in the mid-to-high 80s and blends well with his fastball, diving late on hitters. He's made significant progress improving his changeup. It's a plus high-80s offering with tumble and fading life, giving him a third swing-and-miss weapon. Abel's curveball is a clear fourth pitch, but it has good spin metrics and flashes plus at times. His control faltered at points, but he's an aggressive strike-thrower, as evidenced by his 13.3 strikeouts per nine innings, and he tunnels his pitches off of each other with ease. Abel ran into trouble with his delivery in the middle of the season, which caused his command to worsen. He was spending his time at instructional league getting the consistency back with his delivery to allow his command to catch up to his stuff. The Phillies aren't concerned and rave about his makeup and work ethic, and the

organization firmly believes it has a future top-of-the-rotation starter.

THE FUTURE: It wasn't a perfect debut for Abel, but he still stood out as one of the top pitching prospects in baseball, with three plus pitches, a fourth average offering and room to keep improving. He should start the 2022 season at High-A, where he will continue to hone his changeup, curveball and delivery. He has all the ingredients to pitch in the middle to front of a big league rotation. If everything goes as planned, Abel should make his major league debut during the 2023 season. ∎

BEST TOOLS

Best Hitter for Average	Bryson Stott
Best Power Hitter	Jhailyn Ortiz
Best Strike-Zone Discipline	Rafael Marchan
Fastest Baserunner	Yhoswar Garcia
Best Athlete	Yhoswar Garcia
Best Fastball	Mick Abel
Best Curveball	James McArthur
Best Slider	Francisco Morales
Best Changeup	Griff McGarry
Best Control	Josh Hendrickson
Best Defensive Catcher	Rafael Marchan
Best Defensive Infielder	Jonathan Guzman
Best Infield Arm	Jonathan Guzman
Best Defensive Outfielder	Johan Rojas
Best Outfield Arm	Jhailyn Ortiz

Year	Age	Club (Level)	Lge	W	L	ERA	G	GS	IP	H	HR	BB	SO	BB/9	SO/9	WHIP	AVG
2021	19	Clearwater (LoA)	SEast	1	3	4.43	14	14	44	27	5	27	66	5.4	13.3	1.21	.174
Minor League Totals (2 years)				1	3	4.43	14	14	44	27	5	27	66	5.44	13.30	1.21	.174

2 ANDREW PAINTER, RHP

Born: April 10, 2003. **B-T:** R-R. **HT:** 6-7. **WT:** 215. **Drafted:** HS—Fort Lauderdale, Fla., 2021 (1st round). **Signed by:** Victor Gomez.

TRACK RECORD: The No. 2 prep pitcher in the 2021 draft class, Painter became the highest drafted player ever out of the power program Calvary Christian High in Fort Lauderdale. He signed with the Phillies for $3.9 million after being taken 13th overall. Painter impressed in a brief pro debut, striking out 12, walking none and allowing four hits in six scoreless innings in the Florida Complex League.

SCOUTING REPORT: Painter has an advanced approach for a prep arm to go along with an impressive four-pitch arsenal, led by a fastball that ticked up from the low 90s in 2020 to sitting in the mid 90s and touching 98 mph at instructional league. The pitch has shown encouraging metrics and is a plus offering. Painter shows confidence in his changeup, throwing the pitch in any count and to both lefthanded and righthanded hitters while adding a different spin axis to it this summer. He throws an above-average mid-80s slider with good spin, and he rounds out his mix with a curveball that flashes plus at times. Painter has plus control, an easy arm action and a repeatable delivery out of an imposing 6-foot-7 frame, giving him the upside to develop into a future No. 2 or 3 starter.

THE FUTURE: Painter spent his time at instructional league honing his offspeed offerings, including getting his curveball to a more consistent point and keeping the same spin axis on his changeup that he showed this summer. He'll make his full-season debut in 2022.

MIKE JANES/FOUR SEAM IMAGES

BA GRADE
60 Risk: Extreme

SCOUTING GRADES:	Fastball: 60	Slider: 60	Curveball: 50	Changeup: 50	Control: 60

Year	Age	Club (Level)	Lge	W	L	ERA	G	GS	IP	H	HR	BB	SO	BB/9	SO/9	WHIP	AVG
2021	18	Phillies (R)	FCL	0	0	0.00	4	4	6	4	0	0	12	0.0	18.0	0.67	.190
Minor League Totals (1 year)				0	0	0.00	4	4	6	4	0	0	12	0.00	18.00	0.67	.190

3 BRYSON STOTT, SS/2B

Born: Oct. 6, 1997. **B-T:** L-R. **HT:** 6-3. **WT:** 200. **Drafted:** Nevada-Las Vegas, 2019 (1st round). **Signed by:** Mike Garcia.

TRACK RECORD: The Phillies' pick as 2021 minor league player of the year had a breakthrough season, making his first Futures Game appearance, conquering High-A and Double-A and showing increased power with 16 home runs, one more than he hit in 171 collegiate games. He rounded out the year with 10 games in Triple-A and a stint in the Arizona Fall League.

SCOUTING REPORT: Stott spent the 2020 summer at the alternate training site, where he added strength to his frame and worked on hitting the ball to all fields. He also incorporated bat speed training and improved his plate discipline against advanced pitchers. Those improvements carried over to 2021 as Stott showed better recognition of finding the right pitch to hit and raised his walk rate. Stott's power gains give him a fifth average or better tool, and the added juice didn't lead to more swing-and-miss or cause him to be too pull-happy. Stott is an above-average runner and has good actions at shortstop. He has an above-average arm and grades out as an above-average defender with the ability to move to second base if needed.

THE FUTURE: Stott's 2021 season reinforced the organization's belief that he will be an everyday big leaguer, and he'll make his MLB debut some time next season.

BA GRADE
55 Risk: High

SCOUTING GRADES:	Hitting: 55	Power: 50	Running: 55	Fielding: 55	Arm: 55

Year	Age	Club (Level)	Lge	AVG	G	AB	R	H	2B	3B	HR	RBI	BB	SO	SB	OBP	SLG
2021	23	Jersey Shore (HiA)	East	.288	22	73	18	21	4	0	5	10	22	22	3	.453	.548
	23	Reading (AA)	NEast	.301	80	312	49	94	22	2	10	36	35	78	6	.368	.481
	23	Lehigh Valley (AAA)	East	.303	10	33	4	10	0	0	1	3	8	8	1	.439	.394
Minor League Totals (3 years)				.298	160	584	101	174	35	5	22	76	89	147	15	.390	.488

4 JOHAN ROJAS, OF

Born: Aug. 14, 2000. **B-T:** R-R. **HT:** 6-0. **WT:** 175. **Signed:** Dominican Republic, 2018. **Signed by:** Carlos Salas.

TRACK RECORD: Few players in the organization improved as much during the season as Rojas, who put an exclamation mark on the 2021 campaign with a red-hot September in his first month at High-A, hitting .344/.419/.563 with nearly as many walks (seven) as strikeouts (eight) while showing an exciting power/speed combination. Rojas spent the fall at instructional league.

SCOUTING REPORT: Rojas has tools scouts can dream on, with plus-plus speed, plus defense, an above-average arm and plus raw power that led to a career-high 11 homers. But he's had trouble accessing those tools in games. He took a big step forward in 2021, improving his approach at the plate and swing decisions, getting a better launch angle on the ball to lower his ground-ball rate and cutting down on his swing-and-miss while showing higher exit velocities. He showed better recognition against spin and offspeed pitches, doing more damage than he had before while continuing to show impressive bat speed and bat-to-ball skills and doing more harm to pitches over the middle of the plate. Rojas spent his time at instructional league continuing to work on his approach, launch angle and offspeed recognition as well as pulling the ball. The organization believes it has an everyday center fielder who has the upside of an all-star if everything clicks.

THE FUTURE: Rojas will likely get more reps in at winter ball before starting the 2022 season back at High-A Jersey Shore.

BA GRADE
55 Risk: Extreme

SCOUTING GRADES: Hitting: 50 | Power: 60 | Running: 70 | Fielding: 60 | Arm: 55

Year	Age	Club (Level)	Lge	AVG	G	AB	R	H	2B	3B	HR	RBI	BB	SO	SB	OBP	SLG
2021	20	Phillies (R)	FCL	.750	1	4	2	3	0	0	1	3	0	0	1	.750	1.500
	20	Jersey Shore (HiA)	East	.344	17	64	16	22	3	1	3	11	7	8	8	.419	.563
	20	Clearwater (LoA)	SEast	.240	78	313	51	75	15	3	7	38	26	69	25	.305	.374
Minor League Totals (4 years)				.280	224	878	141	246	41	19	15	98	65	155	67	.339	.421

5 ETHAN WILSON, OF

Born: Nov. 7, 1999. **B-T:** L-L. **HT:** 6-1. **WT:** 210. **Drafted:** South Alabama, 2021 (2nd round). **Signed By:** Mike Stauffer.

TRACK RECORD: An under-the-radar prospect coming out of the Alabama prep ranks, Wilson had an excellent three-year career at South Alabama, earning freshman All-America honors in 2019 and fighting through a slow start in 2021 to finish with a .318/.419/.528 slash line with 25 extra-base hits. The Phillies were drawn to Wilson's hitting ability and power, snatching him up in the second round.

SCOUTING REPORT: Wilson skipped Rookie ball and started his pro career at Low-A, where he struggled to a .215/.282/.374 mark. The Phillies were still pleased with what they saw from the corner outfielder. Wilson drew praise in his pro debut for the quality of his at-bats, impressive bat speed, ability to impact the ball and solid defense all over the outfield. The lefthanded hitter has plus power with an all-fields approach out of a 6-foot-1, 210-pound frame to make him the top hitter in the organization with the potential for 25-30 homers and a .270 average in the big leagues. Wilson showed an uncharacteristically high swing-and-miss rate after entering pro ball, and he spent his time at instructional league working to make more contact, control the strike zone and clean up his swing path. Wilson is a below-average runner and a solid-average defender without much arm strength, meaning he'll likely end up in left field.

THE FUTURE: The organization believes Wilson's combination of hitting ability and power will allow him to move through the system quickly. He'll likely start the 2022 season at a Class A level, but if he hits he won't be there for long.

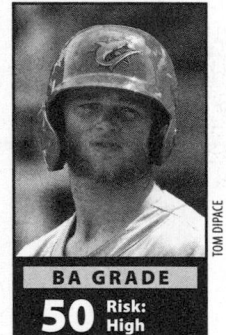
TOM DIPACE

BA GRADE
50 Risk: High

SCOUTING GRADES: Hitting: 55 | Power: 60 | Running: 40 | Fielding: 45 | Arm: 45

Year	Age	Club (Level)	Lge	AVG	G	AB	R	H	2B	3B	HR	RBI	BB	SO	SB	OBP	SLG
2021	21	Clearwater (LoA)	SEast	.215	30	107	15	23	4	2	3	17	10	25	2	.282	.374
Minor League Totals (1 year)				.215	30	107	15	23	4	2	3	17	10	25	2	.282	.374

6 LOGAN O'HOPPE, C

Born: Feb. 9, 2000. **B-T:** R-R. **HT:** 6-2. **WT:** 185. **Drafted:** HS—West Islip, N.Y., 2018 (23rd round). **Signed by:** Alex Agostino.

TRACK RECORD: O'Hoppe is one of the most popular players in the organization, drawing rave reviews for his makeup, work ethic and dedication to his craft. He turned in an impressive full-season debut, climbing from High-A all the way to Triple-A at 21 years old. Along the way, O'Hoppe hit .270/.331/.458 with 17 home runs in 104 games. He wrapped up his impressive season in the Arizona Fall League.

SCOUTING REPORT: O'Hoppe spent time at the alternate training site in 2020 working on his bat-to-ball skills and after the season went to Driveline Baseball in Seattle. There he worked on flattening out his bat path to lower his swing and miss. His work paid off in 2021, with improved bat-to-ball skills and impact to go with a good approach and the lowest strikeout rate of his pro career. He's got plus raw power, with the chance to hit 20-25 home runs in the big leagues, but it's his defensive profile that leads the way. He has a good release on throws, blocks balls in the dirt well, has a strong arm and shows a polished and advanced approach behind the plate. He has all the tools to be a plus defensive catcher.

THE FUTURE: After O'Hoppe's encouraging season, the Phillies want him to continue improving his pitch recognition and swing path. He'll start the 2022 season in the upper minors and could make his MLB debut during the season.

BA GRADE
50 Risk: High

SCOUTING GRADES:	Hitting: 50	Power: 55	Running: 30	Fielding: 60	Arm: 60

Year	Age	Club (Level)	Lge	AVG	G	AB	R	H	2B	3B	HR	RBI	BB	SO	SB	OBP	SLG
2021	21	Jersey Shore (HiA)	East	.270	85	318	43	86	17	2	13	48	30	63	6	.335	.459
	21	Reading (AA)	NEast	.296	13	54	6	16	1	0	3	7	1	9	0	.333	.481
	21	Lehigh Valley (AAA)	East	.190	6	21	2	4	1	0	1	3	2	4	0	.261	.381
Minor League Totals (3 years)				.273	183	664	90	181	41	5	24	105	55	153	11	.329	.458

7 HANS CROUSE, RHP

Born: Sept. 15, 1998. **B-T:** R-R. **HT:** 6-5. **WT:** 208. **Drafted:** HS—Dana Point, Calif., 2017 (2nd round). **Signed by:** Steve Flores (Rangers).

TRACK RECORD: Coming into this season, Crouse had just 42 career appearances to his name since being drafted by the Rangers in the second round in 2017. He impressed in 2018 between short-season ball and Low-A, but missed time in 2019 due to bone spurs in his elbow that led to surgery in the offseason. Crouse didn't appear at the alternate training site or instructional league in 2020 due to personal reasons. The Phillies acquired him along with Kyle Gibson and Ian Kennedy in the 2021 deadline deal that sent former top prospect Spencer Howard to Texas. Crouse made his MLB debut in September.

SCOUTING REPORT: Crouse was the Rangers No. 1 prospect coming into the 2019 season due to his explosive arsenal, but he showed decreased fastball velocity with the Phillies, sitting 93-94 mph after previously reaching 97. He pairs his sinking fastball with a plus hard slider that has late diving life, and his changeup, which he developed while dealing with bone spurs in his elbow during the 2019 season, gives him a third above-average or better offering. Crouse has worked to tone down his violent delivery, and he has good feel for locating his pitches and throwing strikes with average control. The fact that Crouse stayed healthy in 2021 is an encouraging sign, but the Phillies want to see him get his fastball velocity back up to the upper 90s at its best. He has the stuff of a mid-rotation starter but needs to stay healthy and continue throwing strikes.

THE FUTURE: The Phillies were pleased with Crouse's arsenal and motor in 2021. He'll likely begin the 2022 season at Triple-A but could find himself back in the big leagues before long.

BA GRADE
50 Risk: High

SCOUTING GRADES:	Fastball: 60	Slider: 60	Changeup: 55	Control: 50

Year	Age	Club (Level)	Lge	W	L	ERA	G	GS	IP	H	HR	BB	SO	BB/9	SO/9	WHIP	AVG
2021	22	Frisco (AA)	Cent	3	2	3.35	13	13	51	27	5	19	54	3.4	9.5	0.90	.157
	22	Reading (AA)	NEast	2	2	2.73	6	6	29	24	3	12	38	3.6	11.5	1.21	.222
	22	Lehigh Valley (AAA)	East	0	0	6.23	1	1	4	5	1	3	6	6.2	12.5	1.85	.294
	22	Philadelphia (MLB)	NL	0	2	5.14	2	2	7	4	2	7	2	9.0	2.6	1.57	.16
Major League Totals (1 year)				0	2	5.14	2	2	7	4	2	7	2	9.00	2.57	1.57	.167
Minor League Totals (5 years)				16	8	3.27	62	58	247	192	25	79	266	2.87	9.68	1.10	.213

8 MATT VIERLING, OF/1B

Born: Sept. 16, 1996. **B-T:** R-R. **HT:** 6-3. **WT:** 205. **Drafted:** Notre Dame, 2018 (5th round). **Signed by:** Justin Morgenstern.

TRACK RECORD: The 2018 fifth-rounder from Notre Dame had an impressive debut season before struggling to a .232 mark at High-A in 2019. He was on the Phillies' 2020 instructional league roster, where he stood out for significant strength gains and improved bat speed. His gains carried over to the 2021 season, where he excelled at Double-A and posted a 126 OPS+ in 71 big league at-bats, including starting in multiple games down the stretch as the Phillies chased a wild card.

SCOUTING REPORT: Vierling showed some of the best exit velocities in the organization during spring training, turning in 115-116 mph speeds off the bat thanks to the strength gains he made during the 2020 shutdown. The Phillies believe his power now grades out at plus, and his bat-to-ball skills have improved as well, though he needs to cut down on swing-and-miss. Vierling is an impressive athlete who can play both corner infield spots and anywhere in the outfield, with plus speed and above-average defense in center field to go with a plus arm. The Phillies believe Vierling's bat and ability to play multiple positions will make him a super-utility player who could carve out a long big league career.

THE FUTURE: After ending the season in the big leagues, Vierling should be back in the mix for a spot on the MLB roster for 2022 Opening Day.

BA GRADE

45 Risk: Medium

SCOUTING GRADES:	Hitting: 45	Power: 55	Running: 60	Fielding: 55	Arm: 60

Year	Age	Club (Level)	Lge	AVG	G	AB	R	H	2B	3B	HR	RBI	BB	SO	SB	OBP	SLG
2021	24	Reading (AA)	NEast	.345	24	87	16	30	6	1	6	16	12	18	5	.422	.644
	24	Lehigh Valley (AAA)	East	.248	55	206	25	51	6	1	5	31	24	46	5	.331	.359
	24	Philadelphia (MLB)	NL	.324	34	71	11	23	3	1	2	6	4	20	2	.364	.479
Major League Totals (1 year)				.324	34	71	11	23	3	1	2	6	4	20	2	.364	.479
Minor League Totals (4 years)				.267	259	958	114	256	53	5	23	119	83	198	39	.332	.405

9 RAFAEL MARCHAN, C

Born: Feb. 25, 1999. **B-T:** B-R. **HT:** 5-9. **WT:** 196. **Signed:** Venezuela, 2015. **Signed by:** Jesus Mendez.

TRACK RECORD: Marchan's excellent defense in 2020 spring training impressed Joe Girardi, and after spending time at the alternate training site he made his big league debut in September, collecting four hits in eight at-bats. Marchan spent the 2021 season getting juggled back and forth between Triple-A and the majors, struggling mightily with the bat and posting a .203 average in 67 games at Triple-A and a .231 average in 20 games with the Phillies.

SCOUTING REPORT: Marchan makes his money behind the dish, where he's a plus-plus defender thanks to above-average blocking skills, a strong throwing arm and the ability to handle pitchers. Marchan has a patient approach at the plate, with some of the lowest whiff and chase rates in the organization and does a good job of putting the ball in play. He needs to improve his bat speed, however, to get more impact on the ball. Marchan is working on reducing his groundball rate and needs to develop more physicality, with well below-average power currently. His plus-plus defense gives him the floor of a big league backup catcher, but if he improves his bat speed and power he could turn into an everyday player.

THE FUTURE: With J.T. Realmuto entrenched at catcher in Philadelphia, the best role Marchan can aspire to is backup. He might fill a share of that role in 2022 if the Phillies don't sign a veteran backstop this offseason.

BA GRADE

45 Risk: Medium

SCOUTING GRADES:	Hitting: 45	Power: 30	Running: 40	Fielding: 70	Arm: 60

Year	Age	Club (Level)	Lge	AVG	G	AB	R	H	2B	3B	HR	RBI	BB	SO	SB	OBP	SLG
2021	22	Reading (AA)	NEast	.200	1	5	1	1	1	0	0	0	0	1	0	.200	.400
	22	Lehigh Valley (AAA)	East	.203	67	237	28	48	7	0	0	19	23	45	1	.283	.232
	22	Philadelphia (MLB)	NL	.231	20	52	7	12	1	1	1	4	4	10	0	.286	.346
Major League Totals (2 years)				.267	23	60	10	16	1	1	2	7	5	12	0	.323	.417
Minor League Totals (5 years)				.265	278	1007	117	267	48	3	0	98	84	125	19	.327	.319

10 SIMON MUZZIOTTI, OF

Born: Dec. 27, 1998. **B-T:** L-L. **HT:** 6-1. **WT:** 198. **Signed:** Venezuela, 2016. **Signed by:** Claudio Scerrato.

TRACK RECORD: Muzziotti followed up an impressive 2019 season in what was then the pitcher-friendly High-A Florida State League with an encouraging showing in 2020 spring training, standing out for his ability to drive the ball. After the coronavirus pandemic shuttered the 2020 minor league season, he returned to the field for instructional league, where he was one of the team's best hitters. Muzziotti missed the majority of the 2021 campaign due to visa issues that kept him in Venezuela, but was solid once he arrived, hitting .296 in 71 at-bats, the majority of which came at Triple-A Lehigh Valley.

BA GRADE
55 Risk: Extreme

SCOUTING REPORT: Muzziotti stood out for his improved bat speed and bat-to-ball skills in 2021, grading out as one of the top two hitters in the system along with Bryson Stott, and he added strength to his frame as he looks to tap into more power. He's also added loft to his swing to reduce his groundball rate, which was the highest in the system in 2019. Muzziotti can be a free swinger at times and is working to make improvements in his approach at the plate to focus on not expanding early in counts. Muzziotti stands out in center field, where his plus speed, instincts, routes and average arm make him a plus defender. Muzziotti might never hit for more than 10-15 home runs, but he rounds out his tool set with three above-average or better tools.

THE FUTURE: After missing two seasons due to the pandemic and visa issues, Muzziotti needs to get back into game form. He participated in the Arizona Fall League before going home to play winter ball. He'll start the 2022 season back in the upper minors.

SCOUTING GRADES:	Hitting: 55	Power: 40	Running: 55	Fielding: 60	Arm: 50

Year	Age	Club (Level)	Lge	AVG	G	AB	R	H	2B	3B	HR	RBI	BB	SO	SB	OBP	SLG
2021	22	Phillies (R)	FCL	.333	1	3	1	1	1	0	0	0	0	1	0	.333	.667
	22	Clearwater (LoA)	SEast	.300	3	10	1	3	0	1	0	1	1	2	0	.364	.500
	22	Jersey Shore (HiA)	East	.412	4	17	4	7	1	0	0	3	2	2	0	.474	.471
	22	Reading (AA)	NEast	.313	4	16	1	5	2	0	0	6	1	2	0	.353	.438
	22	Lehigh Valley (AAA)	East	.200	8	25	2	5	0	0	0	2	5	4	2	.333	.200
Minor League Totals (6 years)				.270	293	1140	139	308	47	14	4	98	79	138	59	.318	.346

11 ERIK MILLER, LHP

BA GRADE
50 Risk: High

Born: Feb. 13, 1998. **B-T:** L-L. **HT:** 6-5. **WT:** 240. **Drafted:** Stanford, 2019 (4th round). **Signed by:** Joey Davis.

TRACK RECORD: A 2019 fourth-rounder from Stanford who signed for an under-slot $428,300 deal, Miller rose to Low-A Lakewood in his abbreviated debut, then impressed at instructional league following the canceled 2020 minor league season. Miller missed most of the 2021 season due to injury, but was sharp in his return in the Arizona Fall League, striking out 12 in 10 innings of three-run (two earned) ball.

SCOUTING REPORT: Miller has an imposing build from the left side at 6-foot-5, 240 pounds with a big fastball with running life and carry up in the zone. The pitch previously topped out at 96 mph, but Miller sat 96-99 mph in short stints during his time in Arizona, giving it the look of a potential plus offering. Miller was aggressive in attacking hitters in the AFL, showing the ability to beat hitters in the zone. He complements his fastball with a hard, low-80s slider with three-quarter tilt and crossbreaking action that flashes plus. He rounds out his arsenal with a mid-80s changeup. Miller has struggled to throw strikes during his brief pro career, and needs to focus on repeating his delivery to allow him to more easily access his impressive stuff.

THE FUTURE: Miller needs to show he can stay on the field for a full season, but he could be a fast riser if he does so while throwing more strikes. He'll likely start the 2022 season at High-A Jersey Shore.

Year	Age	Club (Level)	Lge	W	L	ERA	G	GS	IP	H	HR	BB	SO	BB/9	SO/9	WHIP	AVG
2021	23	Phillies (R)	FCL	0	0	0.00	2	2	3	1	0	3	2	7.4	4.9	1.09	.083
	23	Clearwater (LoA)	SEast	0	0	3.18	2	2	5	4	0	5	10	7.9	15.9	1.59	.190
	23	Jersey Shore (HiA)	East	0	0	0.00	1	1	3	3	0	3	4	8.1	10.8	1.80	.231
Minor League Totals (3 years)				1	0	1.48	16	12	49	33	0	26	68	4.81	12.58	1.21	.184

12 GRIFF McGARRY, RHP

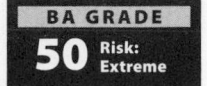

BA GRADE

50 Risk: Extreme

Born: June 8, 1999. **B-T:** R-R. **HT:** 6-2. **WT:** 190. **Drafted:** Virginia, 2021 (5th round). **Signed by:** Kellan McKeon.

TRACK RECORD: McGarry struggled to throw strikes throughout his collegiate career at Virginia, walking 8.8 batters per nine innings. He compensated for it with three swing-and-miss weapons, posting 12.5 strikeouts per nine. The Phillies were willing to take a gamble on his pure stuff in the fifth round, and he rewarded them with an encouraging pro debut between the Class A levels. He rounded out the year in instructional league.

SCOUTING REPORT: McGarry might have the best pure stuff of any pitcher in the system, with a 70-grade fastball and a pair of plus offspeeds in his slider and changeup. McGarry's fastball was sitting 96-99 mph this summer, and his mid-80s slider is a dangerous swing-and-miss weapon with two-plane break. But McGarry will only go as far as his bottom-of-the-scale control takes him. This season he changed his delivery to make him more directional toward home plate, and the Phillies felt that change helped his control. The organization was impressed with his ability to throw strikes at instructs, and he also threw his changeup more during games this fall. The Phillies feel like McGarry could help them in the majors as soon as next year, but his control will need to improve for him to get to that point.

THE FUTURE: McGarry should start the 2022 season back at High-A, but the Phillies will be aggressive in pushing him through the system. He has the stuff to be a mid-rotation starter, but will have to throw more strikes to get there.

Year	Age	Club (Level)	Lge	W	L	ERA	G	GS	IP	H	HR	BB	SO	BB/9	SO/9	WHIP	AVG
2021	22	Clearwater (LoA)	SEast	0	0	3.27	5	1	11	6	0	7	22	5.7	18.0	1.18	.154
	22	Jersey Shore (HiA)	East	1	0	2.70	3	3	13	7	0	7	21	4.7	14.2	1.05	.152
Minor League Totals (1 year)				1	0	2.96	8	4	24	13	0	14	43	5.18	15.90	1.11	.153

13 JORDAN VIARS, OF

BA GRADE

50 Risk: Extreme

Born: July 18, 2003. **B-T:** L-L. **HT:** 6-4. **WT:** 215. **Drafted:** HS—Frisco, Texas, 2021 (3rd round). **Signed by:** Tommy Field.

TRACK RECORD: Viars was an under-the-radar talent coming out of Reed High in Frisco, Texas, who the Phillies were happy to nab in the third round in 2021 and convince him to forgo a commitment to Arkansas. He started his pro career in the Florida Complex League, where he posted a .255/.406/.468 slash line in 47 at-bats before ending the year in instructs.

SCOUTING REPORT: Viars has a huge frame with impact power potential from the left side. Viars gets to his power with leverage out of a crouched stance, with plus raw juice currently that could grow into more. He has quick bat speed and impressed the organization with the quality of his at-bats in his debut, showing strike zone discipline and patience at the plate. He has the athleticism to fit in the corner outfield, but he's expected to slow down as he matures and could move to the corner infield. He worked on adjusting to velocity and spin at instructional league. He has a good feel for the barrel, and averaged 90 mph exit velocities at instructs, topping out at 112 mph.

THE FUTURE: Viars should start the 2022 season at Low-A Clearwater. If everything clicks, Viars projects to be an everyday big leaguer who hits 25-30 homers, but he's years away from reaching that point.

Year	Age	Club (Level)	Lge	AVG	G	AB	R	H	2B	3B	HR	RBI	BB	SO	SB	OBP	SLG
2021	17	Phillies (R)	FCL	.255	22	47	13	12	1	0	3	18	11	12	2	.406	.468
Minor League Totals (1 year)				.255	22	47	13	12	1	0	3	18	11	12	2	.406	.468

14 JHAILYN ORTIZ, OF

BA GRADE

45 Risk: High

Born: Nov. 18, 1998. **B-T:** R-R. **HT:** 6-3. **WT:** 264. **Signed:** Dominican Republic, 2015. **Signed by:** Sal Agostinelli.

TRACK RECORD: Signed for $4 million out of the Dominican Republic in 2015, Ortiz had yet to live up to that contract going into last season, with a .227 average over 1,167 at-bats across his first four seasons. He broke out in a big way in 2021 at High-A Jersey Shore, crushing 19 home runs and slashing .262/.358/.521 to earn a promotion to Double-A.

SCOUTING REPORT: Ortiz came into the season in the best shape of his life, with a more healthy diet and a focused, diligent approach that stood out to coaches. He cut down on the length in his swing, which helped him catch up to mid-90s fastballs, and showed an improved ability to see pitches and perform against spin. Ortiz's bat speed and improved pitch selection allowed him to more easily tap into his light-tower power, which led to a career-high 23 homers between High-A and Double-A. Ortiz is athletic for his size, with the ability to play center field currently, although he fits best in a corner, with the plus arm strength to fit in right field. Ortiz needs to continue cutting down on his swing and miss, keep his swing shorter, improve his bat-to-ball skills and stay on top of his weight, but this season was a big step in the right direction.

THE FUTURE: Ortiz would have been Rule 5 draft eligible this winter, but the Phillies put him on the 40-man roster. He stayed in shape by playing in the winter Dominican League and should start the 2022 season at Double-A.

Year	Age	Club (Level)	Lge	AVG	G	AB	R	H	2B	3B	HR	RBI	BB	SO	SB	OBP	SLG
2021	22	Jersey Shore (HiA)	East	.262	74	263	52	69	11	0	19	48	29	86	4	.358	.521
	22	Reading (AA)	NEast	.208	21	77	7	16	1	0	4	6	9	27	0	.307	.377
Minor League Totals (6 years)				.232	414	1507	223	350	69	7	71	223	144	510	21	.316	.429

15 LUIS GARCIA, SS

Born: Oct. 1, 2000. **B-T:** B-R. **HT:** 5-11. **WT:** 195. **Signed:** Dominican Republic, 2017. **Signed by:** Carlos Salas.

BA GRADE 45 Risk: High

TRACK RECORD: One of the top players in the 2017 international class who signed with the Phillies for $2.5 million, Garcia won the Rookie-level Gulf Coast League batting title in 2018, struggled mightily at Low-A in 2019 and spent the 2020 season at the alternate training site, where he added muscle to his frame. He was slow out of the gate in 2021, but an encouraging August led to a September promotion to High-A.

SCOUTING REPORT: Garcia's strength gains helped him tap into more power this season, hitting a career-high 13 home runs and posting the highest exit velocities of his professional career. Those power gains led to higher exit velocities at instructional league, where he topped out at 108 mph. Garcia has a tendency to get heavy on his front leg at the plate, and he made mechanical changes to get behind the ball better and stay on the ball. Garcia raised his walk rate significantly from the 2019 season and showed improved bat speed, an area of emphasis coming into the season. He'll need to continue showing improvement with his bat speed, pitch recognition skills and staying on the right bat path to reduce his groundball rate. Garcia is a plus defender at shortstop with easy actions, solid range and an above-average arm who can also play second base. He spent his time at instructional league working at different positions around the infield, and the Phillies added him to the 40-man roster this winter.

THE FUTURE: Garcia could be a useful defensive option off the bench in the majors, but he'll need significant improvement from his bat to get him to that point.

Year	Age	Club (Level)	Lge	AVG	G	AB	R	H	2B	3B	HR	RBI	BB	SO	SB	OBP	SLG
2021	20	Clearwater (LoA)	SEast	.246	87	333	57	82	16	5	11	42	54	93	11	.356	.423
	20	Jersey Shore (HiA)	East	.224	16	58	6	13	2	0	2	8	10	19	4	.333	.362
Minor League Totals (4 years)				.238	273	1026	132	244	43	11	18	118	123	265	36	.325	.354

16 CRISTIAN HERNANDEZ, RHP

Born: Sept. 23, 2000. **B-T:** R-R. **HT:** 6-3. **WT:** 180. **Signed:** Venezuela, 2017. **Signed by:** Ebert Velasquez.

BA GRADE 50 Risk: Extreme

TRACK RECORD: Hernandez was given one of the smaller bonuses in the Phillies' 2017 international class that included shortstop Luis Garcia, but quickly impressed in the Dominican Summer League in 2018 before missing the 2019 season due to injury and the 2020 season due to the coronavirus pandemic. He took a step forward in his full-season debut in 2021, pitching to a 3.69 ERA with 11 strikeouts per nine innings at Low-A Clearwater.

SCOUTING REPORT: Hernandez stood out to opposing scouts in his first full season, with an imposing 6-foot-3 build from the right side with some projectability remaining, and a fastball that sat 93-94 mph and topped out at 96. He shows feel for the pitch, as well as a curveball with good spin that has the potential to be a plus pitch. He rounds out his arsenal with a pair of average offerings in his changeup and slider. Hernandez's velocity backed up slightly during instructional league, a sign of fatigue after his first full season in professional baseball. Hernandez has solid-average control and projects for average command.

THE FUTURE: Hernandez was one of the breakout players in the organization in 2021 and should start the 2022 season at High-A Jersey Shore. He has the stuff to project as a No. 5 starter, but needs to show he can maintain his fastball velocity deep into the season.

Year	Age	Club (Level)	Lge	W	L	ERA	G	GS	IP	H	HR	BB	SO	BB/9	SO/9	WHIP	AVG
2021	20	Phillies (R)	FCL	0	0	1.80	2	2	5	2	1	0	8	0.0	14.4	0.40	.118
	20	Clearwater (LoA)	SEast	2	7	3.69	18	15	70	62	11	29	86	3.7	11.0	1.29	.235
Minor League Totals (2 years)				4	10	3.12	33	30	139	126	14	39	143	2.53	9.28	1.19	.238

17 LUKE WILLIAMS, 2B/3B/OF

BA GRADE
40 Risk: Medium

Born: Aug. 9, 1996. **B-T:** R-R. **HT:** 6-1. **WT:** 186. **Drafted:** HS—Dana Point, Calif., 2015 (3rd round). **Signed by:** Demerius Pittman.

TRACK RECORD: Williams had a storybook 2021 season, going from a non-prospect to helping Team USA qualify for the Summer Olympics, posting eight hits in 18 at-bats. After returning from representing Team USA, Williams quickly earned a promotion to the major leagues and hit a walk-off home run in his first big league start. He stayed in the big leagues for the majority of the season, hitting .245 in 98 at-bats.

SCOUTING REPORT: Williams isn't going to wow anyone with his tools, but he stands out thanks to his defensive versatility, having played every position but catcher during his time in the big leagues. Williams improved his hit tool coming into the season and showed a high barrel frequency, albeit with little power. He's a line-drive hitter with a patient approach, but his lack of power likely prevents him from being more than a quality reserve. Williams is a plus runner and a good defender with a solid arm, making just two errors in 209.2 innings spread across seven positions.

THE FUTURE: Williams' positional flexibility should help him earn a spot in the big leagues again in 2022.

Year	Age	Club (Level)	Lge	AVG	G	AB	R	H	2B	3B	HR	RBI	BB	SO	SB	OBP	SLG
2021	24	Lehigh Valley (AAA)	East	.270	32	126	21	34	5	2	0	15	12	29	7	.329	.341
	24	Philadelphia (MLB)	NL	.245	58	98	8	24	4	0	1	6	10	23	2	.315	.316
Major League Totals (1 year)				.245	58	98	8	24	4	0	1	6	10	23	2	.315	.316
Minor League Totals (7 years)				.238	472	1661	215	396	78	6	23	166	165	376	100	.312	.334

18 CHRISTIAN McGOWAN, RHP

BA GRADE
50 Risk: Extreme

Born: March 7, 2000. **B-T:** R-R. **HT:** 6-3. **WT:** 205. **Drafted:** Eastern Oklahoma State JC, 2021 (7th round). **Signed by:** Tommy Field.

TRACK RECORD: McGowan worked primarily as a reliever in his freshman season at Eastern Oklahoma State JC before transitioning to the rotation in 2020 and breaking out in 2021, with a 2.55 ERA and 13.3 strikeouts per nine innings. The Phillies scooped up McGowan in the seventh round, and he made four appearances between the Florida Complex League and Low-A Clearwater before finishing the season in instructional league.

SCOUTING REPORT: McGowan has an impressive four-pitch arsenal from the right side, led by his two-seam and four-seam fastballs that sat 94-97 mph at instructs. The two-seamer has hard sinking action, and the pitches play well off each other. He attacks lefties with a high-80s changeup that has good deception and arm speed, making it an above-average offering. He also throws a hard, mid-80s slider with diving action that has earned above-average to plus grades. McGowan is a good athlete with a repeatable delivery, but needs to throw more strikes after walking 30 batters in 74 innings in 2021.

THE FUTURE: After not throwing many innings in junior college, the Phillies could opt to start McGowan at Low-A Clearwater in 2022, with a promotion to High-A not far off.

Year	Age	Club (Level)	Lge	W	L	ERA	G	GS	IP	H	HR	BB	SO	BB/9	SO/9	WHIP	AVG
2021	21	Phillies (R)	FCL	0	0	0.00	1	1	1	0	0	0	3	0.0	27.0	0.00	.000
	21	Clearwater (LoA)	SEast	0	0	0.00	3	0	4	2	0	1	5	2.3	11.3	0.75	.154
Minor League Totals (1 year)				0	0	0.00	4	1	5	2	0	1	8	1.80	14.40	0.60	.118

19 MICAH OTTENBREIT, RHP

BA GRADE
50 Risk: Extreme

Born: May 7, 2003. **B-T:** R-R. **HT:** 6-4. **WT:** 190. **Drafted:** HS—Trenton, Mich., 2021 (4th round). **Signed by:** Derrick Ross.

TRACK RECORD: One of the top prep pitchers in the state of Michigan, Ottenbreit ranked No. 280 on the BA 500. The Phillies were excited to nab Ottenbreit in the fourth round, signing him for an above-slot deal of $775,000. He made his debut in the Florida Complex League, appearing in five games.

SCOUTING REPORT: Ottenbreit is a classic projection arm at 6-foot-4, 190 pounds from the right side who just turned 18 years old in May. He has a good feel to pitch, with a three-pitch mix led by a fastball that sits in the low 90s and topped out at 95 mph at instructional league and has the potential for more velocity as he adds strength and matures. His curveball is his best secondary, a mid-70s offering with good depth that had excellent spin rates topping out above 3,000 rpm at instructs. The pitch needs more power, but has the potential to be a plus or better offering in the future. Ottenbreit has also shown good feel to throw his low-80s changeup. He needs to improve his command and pitch selection, but the organization was pleased with the progress he made.

THE FUTURE: Ottenbreit should make his full-season debut in 2022 in the Clearwater rotation and could be a candidate to make a jump in the next few years as he matures and grows into his body.

Year	Age	Club (Level)	Lge	W	L	ERA	G	GS	IP	H	HR	BB	SO	BB/9	SO/9	WHIP	AVG
2021	18	Phillies (R)	FCL	1	0	4.50	5	0	6	6	0	3	4	4.5	6.0	1.50	.273
Minor League Totals (1 year)				1	0	4.50	5	0	6	6	0	3	4	4.50	6.00	1.50	.273

20 NICK MATON, SS/2B

BA GRADE
40 Risk: Medium

Born: Feb. 18, 1997. **B-T:** L-R. **HT:** 6-2. **WT:** 178. **Drafted:** Lincoln Land (Ill.) JC, 2017 (7th round). **Signed by:** Justin Morgenstern.

TRACK RECORD: A 2017 seventh-rounder out of Lincoln Land (Ill.) Community College, Maton signed for $353,400, quickly made his Double-A debut two years later and impressed at the alternate training site in 2020. Maton struggled mightily at Triple-A this season, hitting .199 in 206 at-bats, but held his own in the big leagues with a .256 average in 117 at-bats.

SCOUTING REPORT: Maton's development took a step forward in 2020 at the alternate site, as he stood out for his improved pitch recognition and made harder contact against advanced arms. His development backed up this year, as he struggled mightily against offspeeds, with a high chase rate. Maton has no trouble handling high velocity, but major league pitchers were able to neutralize him with spin. Maton makes solid contact and projects to be a fringe-average hitter, with line-to-line power that shouldn't lead to more than 10-15 home runs in the big leagues. He's improved his range at shortstop, and has the ability to play there, second base and third base, with an above-average arm. He's an average runner. Maton likely won't hit enough to be more than a reserve infielder, but his defensive ability gives him value.

THE FUTURE: Maton will likely start the 2022 season at Triple-A, where he'll look to improve upon his 2021 stint.

Year	Age	Club (Level)	Lge	AVG	G	AB	R	H	2B	3B	HR	RBI	BB	SO	SB	OBP	SLG
2021	24	Lehigh Valley (AAA)	East	.199	63	206	29	41	11	2	5	27	38	60	3	.332	.345
	24	Philadelphia (MLB)	NL	.256	52	117	16	30	7	1	2	14	10	39	2	.323	.385
Major League Totals (1 year)				.256	52	117	16	30	7	1	2	14	10	39	2	.323	.385
Minor League Totals (5 years)				.249	349	1221	156	304	63	11	22	142	161	295	30	.340	.373

21 MICKEY MONIAK, OF

BA GRADE
40 Risk: Medium

Born: May 13, 1998. **B-T:** L-R. **HT:** 6-2. **WT:** 195. **Drafted:** HS—Carlsbad, Calif., 2016 (1st round). **Signed by:** Mike Garcia.

TRACK RECORD: Moniak, the 2016 No. 1 overall pick, spent the 2020 summer at the alternate training site before making his major league debut in mid September. He added muscle to his frame during the following offseason and stood out to manager Joe Girardi in 2021 spring training, but struggled between the majors and Triple-A, hitting .238 with 15 home runs in 99 games at Lehigh Valley. He was scheduled to appear in the Arizona Fall League, but pulled out due to an injury.

SCOUTING REPORT: Moniak added 10 pounds of muscle to his frame during the offseason and it resulted in the most consistent hard contact of his career, with exit velocities topping out between 110 and 113 mph as he showed average power to all fields. Moniak worked during 2020 to cut down on his free-swinging approach, but posted the highest strikeout rate (24.7%) of his career at Triple-A in 2021. He improved his bat speed and showed solid bat-to-ball skills, but doesn't reach base enough to be anything more than an extra outfielder. Moniak is a good athlete, a solid defender at all three outfield positions, an average runner and has an average arm.

THE FUTURE: Moniak's lack of an above-average tool prevents him from being an MLB regular. He'll likely spend the 2022 season between the majors and Triple-A.

Year	Age	Club (Level)	Lge	AVG	G	AB	R	H	2B	3B	HR	RBI	BB	SO	SB	OBP	SLG
2021	23	Lehigh Valley (AAA)	East	.238	99	365	42	87	15	8	15	65	31	101	5	.299	.447
	23	Philadelphia (MLB)	NL	.091	21	33	3	3	0	0	1	3	3	16	0	.167	.182
Major League Totals (2 years)				.128	29	47	6	6	0	0	1	3	7	22	0	.241	.191
Minor League Totals (5 years)				.252	501	1905	235	481	104	34	37	259	125	456	47	.301	.401

22 BAILEY FALTER, LHP

BA GRADE
40 Risk: Medium

Born: April 24, 1997. **B-T:** R-L. **HT:** 6-4. **WT:** 175. **Drafted:** HS—Chino Hills, Calif., 2015 (5th round). **Signed by:** Demerius Pittman.

TRACK RECORD: After faring well in his upper minors debut at Double-A Reading in 2019, Falter made the Phillies 2020 instructional league roster, impressed in five May starts at Triple-A Lehigh Valley in 2021 and quickly appeared in his first major league game in June. Falter was set to join the Phillies starting rotation in July before being placed on the Covid injured list, which caused him to miss a month of games. He made his first big league start on the final day of the regular season.

SCOUTING REPORT: Falter emerged on the radar this year thanks to improvement in his fastball, with the pitch ranging from 91-94 mph from the left side. He gets good extension and riding life on the pitch, making it difficult to hit up in the zone. Falter throws a pair of breaking balls in a mid-70s curveball and mid-80s slider, which has sweeping life. Falter threw the slider 23.4% of the time at the big league level and had a 30.3% whiff rate on the pitch. It projects as an average offering. He rounds out his operation with a mid-80s changeup with tumbling life that flashes average, although he rarely threw the pitch in the big leagues. Falter was a consistent strike-thrower in the minors and was even better in the big leagues, with 1.6 walks per nine innings compared to 9.1 strikeouts.

THE FUTURE: The Phillies believe Falter can be a back-of-the-rotation starter, but he'll need to improve his changeup to give him a better weapon against righthanded hitters or be destined for a bullpen role.

Year	Age	Club (Level)	Lge	W	L	ERA	G	GS	IP	H	HR	BB	SO	BB/9	SO/9	WHIP	AVG
2021	24	Lehigh Valley (AAA)	East	2	0	1.76	8	6	30	23	3	8	44	2.4	12.9	1.01	.205
	24	Philadelphia (MLB)	NL	2	1	5.61	22	1	33	34	5	6	34	1.6	9.1	1.19	.262
Major League Totals (1 year)				2	1	5.61	22	1	34	34	5	6	34	1.60	9.09	1.19	.262
Minor League Totals (7 years)				26	25	3.06	83	80	412	407	31	81	391	1.77	8.53	1.18	.258

23 ALEXEIS AZUAJE, 2B

Born: April 24, 2002. **B-T:** R-R. **HT:** 5-10. **WT:** 155. **Signed:** Venezuela, 2018. **Signed by:** Rafael Alvarez and Ebert Velasquez.

BA GRADE
40 Risk: High

TRACK RECORD: Signed by the Phillies out of Venezuela in 2018, Azuaje spent the 2019 season in the Dominican Summer League before the coronavirus pandemic shuttered the 2020 minor league season. He made his U.S. debut in 2021 with an encouraging stint in the Florida Complex League. He continued to impress with the bat in instructional league.

SCOUTING REPORT: Azuaje stands out for his ability as a hitter, with a flat swing that leads to line-to-line contact with improved bat speed, and he has good recognition of spin. He is an aggressive hitter who makes plenty of contact, but that aggressiveness leads to a high chase rate and few walks. Azuaje could develop into a plus hitter if he's able to show a more selective approach. He has deceptive power and hit five home runs with six doubles in the FCL. Azuaje is an excellent athlete with plus-plus running ability and ran a 6.41-second 60-yard dash in 2018. Azuaje has a bat-first profile, and is a fringe-average defender at second base with a fringe-average arm, but his speed allows his range to play up.

THE FUTURE: After an impressive 2021 season, Azuaje should make his full-season debut at Low-A Clearwater in 2022.

Year	Age	Club (Level)	Lge	AVG	G	AB	R	H	2B	3B	HR	RBI	BB	SO	SB	OBP	SLG
2021	19	Phillies (R)	FCL	.400	19	45	17	18	6	0	5	16	4	5	4	.509	.867
Minor League Totals (2 years)				.304	68	230	58	70	20	3	10	35	8	46	17	.356	.548

24 YHOSWAR GARCIA, OF

Born: Sept. 13, 2001. **B-T:** R-R. **HT:** 6-1. **WT:** 155. **Signed:** Venezuela, 2020. **Signed by:** Ebert Velasquez.

BA GRADE
45 Risk: Extreme

TRACK RECORD: One of the top prospects in the 2019-2020 international class, Garcia's signing with the Phillies was delayed a year due to a discrepancy with his age, with Garcia presenting himself as a year younger than he was. Garcia spent the 2020 season at home in Venezuela working on his conditioning, then made his pro debut in 2021 with Low-A Clearwater, but missed the majority of the season after fouling a ball off his leg.

SCOUTING REPORT: Garcia has some of the loudest tools in the organization. The player nicknamed "The Drone" is an excellent athlete, with plus-plus speed, a plus arm and plus defensive ability in center field, with good range and instincts that should allow him to stick there. Garcia makes solid contact at the plate, but shows some chase tendencies and needs to improve the level of his at-bats. Opposing scouts are skeptical of his future impact due to his lack of power out of a 6-foot-1, 155-pound frame. Garcia has worked to put on muscle, but it'll be a continued focus moving forward. He's a line-drive, gap-to-gap hitter and does damage on the basepaths due to his speed and instincts.

THE FUTURE: Garcia is still a raw talent who's likely years away from reaching his potential, but his tool package gives the organization reason for excitement. He'll start the 2022 season back at Low-A.

Year	Age	Club (Level)	Lge	AVG	G	AB	R	H	2B	3B	HR	RBI	BB	SO	SB	OBP	SLG
2021	19	Clearwater (LoA)	SEast	.229	18	70	7	16	1	1	0	8	6	23	11	.299	.271
Minor League Totals (1 year)				.229	18	70	7	16	1	1	0	8	6	23	11	.299	.271

25 RICKARDO PEREZ, C

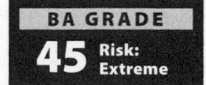

BA GRADE
45 Risk: Extreme

Born: Dec. 4, 2003. **B-T:** L-R. **HT:** 6-1. **WT:** 172. **Signed:** Venezuela, 2021.
Signed by: Ebert Velasquez.

TRACK RECORD: Perez was the headliner of the Phillies 2020-2021 international signing class, agreeing to a $1.2 million deal. Perez made his professional debut in 2021, appearing in 43 games in the Dominican Summer League. He put up solid numbers as a 17-year-old, hitting .256/.370/.281. Perez finished the year at instructs, and continued to hit well.
SCOUTING REPORT: Perez shot up to 6-foot-1 and his prospect status rose with his height. He stands out for a smooth stroke from the left side as well as the ability to barrel balls in games. He has an adjustable, quick swing and projects for average power in the future thanks to his bat control and loft in his swing. He has solid catch-and-throw skills and improved his arm strength, with his arm projecting as average. Perez is a well below-average runner and needs to watch his conditioning, as his body has not aged well.
THE FUTURE: Perez is still a bat-first catcher, but his improvement defensively gives him an avenue to stick at the position moving forward. He should make his stateside debut in 2021.

Year	Age	Club (Level)	Lge	AVG	G	AB	R	H	2B	3B	HR	RBI	BB	SO	SB	OBP	SLG
2021	17	Phillies Red (R)	DSL	.256	43	121	15	31	3	0	0	9	22	15	3	.370	.281
Minor League Totals (1 year)				.256	43	121	15	31	3	0	0	9	22	15	3	.370	.281

26 CRISTOPHER SANCHEZ, LHP

BA GRADE
40 Risk: High

Born: Dec. 12, 1996. **B-T:** L-L. **HT:** 6-1. **WT:** 165. **Signed:** Dominican Republic, 2013. **Signed by:** Daniel Santana (Rays).

TRACK RECORD: Sanchez, acquired from the Rays in the 2019 offseason for third baseman Curtis Mead, spent the majority of the 2021 season at Triple-A Lehigh Valley, where he showed swing-and-miss stuff, but issued far too many walks (5.9 per nine innings). He made his big league debut in June and appeared in seven games, allowing 16 hits and striking out 13 in 12.2 innings.
SCOUTING REPORT: Sanchez relies on a mid-90s fastball with sinking life that comes in on hitters looking like a changeup due to his crossfire three-quarters delivery. His delivery hurts his fastball command, and the pitch was hit hard at the big league level. His mid-80s slider is his best offspeed offering, a pitch he uses to attack righthanded hitters down and in. It flashes above-average to plus. His changeup is a below-average offering with little movement and deception. Sanchez's lack of a third pitch and below-average control make it likely he'll end up in a bullpen role long term.
THE FUTURE: After finishing the season in Philadelphia, Sanchez should compete for a spot on the 2022 Opening Day roster.

Year	Age	Club (Level)	Lge	W	L	ERA	G	GS	IP	H	HR	BB	SO	BB/9	SO/9	WHIP	AVG
2021	24	Lehigh Valley (AAA)	East	5	6	4.68	19	17	73	58	4	48	89	5.9	11.0	1.45	.211
	24	Philadelphia (MLB)	NL	1	0	4.97	7	1	12	16	1	7	13	5.0	9.2	1.82	.320
Major League Totals (1 year)				1	0	4.97	7	1	13	16	1	7	13	4.97	9.24	1.82	.320
Minor League Totals (8 years)				22	22	4.56	109	57	343	345	18	161	308	4.22	8.07	1.47	.260

27 HAO YU LEE, 2B

BA GRADE
40 Risk: High

Born: Feb. 3, 2003. **B-T:** R-R. **HT:** 5-10. **WT:** 190. **Signed:** Taiwan, 2021.
Signed by: Youngster Wang.

TRACK RECORD: Lee signed for $500,000 out of Taiwan in June 2021, and it didn't take long for him to make his U.S. debut. He appeared in nine games in the Florida Complex League, collecting eight hits in 22 at-bats (.364), with five extra-base hits. Lee then impressed members of the organization with his play at instructional league.
SCOUTING REPORT: Lee is a bat-first second baseman who showed off his knack for hitting in three weeks at instructs. He has impressive bat-to-ball skills, above-average barrel awareness, plus bat speed and a good approach, projecting to be an above-average hitter in the future. He hits the ball hard for his size, and should be able to add more power as he matures, with the ability to top out around 15 home runs. He's a good athlete and a solid-average defender at second base with a fringe-average arm, but it'll be his bat that leads the way.
THE FUTURE: After making his stateside debut quickly after signing, Lee is in line to make his full-season debut at Low-A Clearwater in 2022 as a 19-year-old.

Year	Age	Club (Level)	Lge	AVG	G	AB	R	H	2B	3B	HR	RBI	BB	SO	SB	OBP	SLG
2021	18	Phillies (R)	FCL	.364	9	22	9	8	2	2	1	5	3	5	0	.440	.773
Minor League Totals (1 year)				.364	9	22	9	8	2	2	1	5	3	5	0	.440	.773

28 FRANCISCO MORALES, RHP

BA GRADE

40 Risk: High

Born: Oct. 27, 1999. **B-T:** R-R. **HT:** 6-5. **WT:** 260. **Signed:** Venezuela, 2016. **Signed by:** Jesus Mendez.

TRACK RECORD: Morales struggled mightily in his upper minors debut after spending the 2020 shutdown in Orlando working on his conditioning and the development of his changeup. Morales posted a 6.94 ERA and walked 6.5 batters per nine innings at Double-A Reading before closing out the year with two scoreless starts at Triple-A Lehigh Valley.

SCOUTING REPORT: Morales has long stood out for two impressive weapons in his mid-90s fastball and sharp, high-80s slider, but he had trouble throwing the pitches for strikes this season due to a lack of repeatability with his high-effort delivery. Morales will need to work on spotting his fastball, as he threw it over the middle of the plate far too often this season and it often plays below its velocity due to a lack of movement and command. His changeup lacks deception, making it a below-average offering.

THE FUTURE: The 2022 season is a make-or-break year for Morales. If he can improve his fastball command and changeup development he can remain a starter. If not, his plus slider gives him a future in a bullpen role.

Year	Age	Club (Level)	Lge	W	L	ERA	G	GS	IP	H	HR	BB	SO	BB/9	SO/9	WHIP	AVG
2021	21	Reading (AA)	NEast	4	13	6.94	22	20	83	76	11	60	110	6.5	11.9	1.64	.240
2021	21	Lehigh Valley (AAA)	East	0	1	0.00	2	2	8	6	0	7	7	7.3	7.3	1.50	.188
Minor League Totals (5 years)				12	29	4.78	74	59	286	252	26	166	358	5.22	11.27	1.46	.232

29 SCOTT MOSS, LHP

BA GRADE

40 Risk: High

Born: Oct. 6, 1994. **B-T:** L-L. **HT:** 6-6. **WT:** 225. **Drafted:** Florida, 2016 (4th round). **Signed by:** Greg Zunino (Reds).

TRACK RECORD: The 2016 fourth-rounder from Florida was traded to the Guardians in July 2019 as part of a three-team deal that sent righthander Trevor Bauer to the Reds. Moss spent the 2020 season at the alternate training site. He had the worst year of his pro career in 2021 while dealing with neck, back and shoulder injuries. The Guardians designated him for assignment after the season, and the Phillies claimed him on waivers in November.

SCOUTING REPORT: Moss was expected to compete for a spot in the big leagues in 2021, but was sidetracked by various injuries and a walk rate that rose to 6.6 per nine innings. Moss relies on a three-pitch mix led by a low-90s fastball that tops out at 94 mph. He gets good riding life at the top of the zone and solid extension on the pitch. He improved his slider over the last two seasons, and it flashes plus. He rounds out his arsenal with a changeup. Moss has average command, but his control has backed up from average to below-average.

THE FUTURE: If Moss can throw more consistent strikes he could help the Phillies at the back of the rotation. He'll compete for a roster spot in 2022.

Year	Age	Club (Level)	Lge	W	L	ERA	G	GS	IP	H	HR	BB	SO	BB/9	SO/9	WHIP	AVG
2021	26	Columbus (AAA)	East	1	5	7.08	9	7	20	20	2	15	29	6.6	12.8	1.72	.247
Minor League Totals (6 years)				42	22	3.45	96	94	457.0	403	36	188	485	3.70	9.55	1.29	.234

30 CASEY MARTIN, SS

BA GRADE

40 Risk: Extreme

Born: April 7, 1999. **B-T:** R-R. **HT:** 5-11. **WT:** 175. **Drafted:** Arkansas, 2020 (3rd round). **Signed by:** Tommy Field.

TRACK RECORD: Martin's excellent freshman season helped propel Arkansas to the 2018 College World Series finals, but he regressed over the next two seasons and questions about his hit tool led him to fall to the third round in the 2020 draft. Martin continued to struggle in his first pro season. He had ankle surgery in October, but should be ready for spring training.

SCOUTING REPORT: Martin has a pull-heavy approach, a high chase rate and struggles to hit offspeed pitches away. Martin needs to improve his bat speed, as well as do a better job of barreling the ball. He has plus raw power, but tends to sell out for home runs and frequently expands the zone. He's an impressive athlete, a plus runner and has a plus arm, but needs to improve his consistency defensively at shortstop. He can play second base in a pinch, and his speed and arm would profile well in center field as well.

THE FUTURE: Time is running out for Martin to prove he can hit enough to progress up the minor league ladder. He'll return to Jersey Shore in 2022, where he'll look to have a breakthrough year.

Year	Age	Club (Level)	Lge	AVG	G	AB	R	H	2B	3B	HR	RBI	BB	SO	SB	OBP	SLG
2021	22	Clearwater (LoA)	SEast	.223	69	264	33	59	17	0	6	35	28	68	15	.316	.356
	22	Jersey Shore (HiA)	East	.136	29	110	15	15	4	0	1	7	13	52	2	.232	.200
Minor League Totals (2 years)				.198	98	374	48	74	21	0	7	42	41	120	17	.291	.310

MORE PROSPECTS TO KNOW

31 ERUBIEL ARMENTA, LHP   SLEEPER

Armenta turned in an impressive minor league debut, rising from Low-A Clearwater to Double-A Reading and striking out 49 batters in 23 innings in 16 appearances. He throws up to 95 mph from the left side with a changeup that flashes plus, but needs to cut down on his walk rate.

32 DANIEL BRITO, 2B

A breakthrough 2021 season was stopped short when Brito collapsed on the field during a July 31 game. Brito had two surgeries and was taken to a rehab facility in September, with no update on whether he will play in 2022.

33 ANDREW BAKER, RHP

The 2021 11th-rounder has excellent metrics on his pitches, with a high-spin mid-90s fastball and a high-spin low-80s curveball, but he struggled to throw strikes in his minor league debut.

34 NICOLAS TORRES, 2B/OF

Torres has good bat-to-ball skills, a solid approach at the plate, a good baseball IQ and provides defensive versatility, with the ability to play all three outfield spots, shortstop, second and third base.

35 ETHAN LINDOW, LHP

The 23-year-old lefthander didn't have trouble with High-A hitters, but struggled after a promotion to Double-A Reading. Lindow has two potentially above-average offerings in his curveball and changeup, but his lack of fastball velocity (89-90 mph) makes it unlikely he'll settle into a big league rotation.

36 EDUAR SEGOVIA, RHP

Segovia struggled to throw strikes in his full-season debut at Low-A Clearwater, but he has a pair of potential swing-and-miss weapons in his mid-90s fastball and hard slider, both of which have intriguing metrics.

37 JAMARI BAYLOR, SS

The injury bug has bit Baylor hard since he was drafted in the third round in 2019. Now healthy, he stands out for his bat-to-ball skills and solid pop, but there are questions regarding whether he can fit in the infield defensively.

38 DONNY SANDS, C

Acquired in November from the Yankees, Sands made his upper minors debut in 2021 and showed significantly more power, with a career-high 18 home runs in 94 games.

39 BEN BROWN, RHP

In his first year back since having Tommy John surgery in 2019, Brown made seven appearances between the Class A levels. His fastball topped out at 98 mph and he showed feel for a curveball.

40 JORDI MARTINEZ, LHP

Martinez stood out in a small sample in his full-season debut, holding hitters to a .212 average at Low-A Clearwater. He has an average slider and a fastball that sits 90-95 mph, but it should play up in a relief role.

TOP PROSPECTS OF THE DECADE

Year	Player, Pos	2021 Org
2012	Trevor May, RHP	Mets
2013	Jesse Biddle, LHP	Braves
2014	Maikel Franco, 3B	Braves
2015	J.P. Crawford, SS	Mariners
2016	J.P. Crawford, SS	Mariners
2017	J.P. Crawford, SS	Mariners
2018	J.P. Crawford, SS	Mariners
2019	Sixto Sanchez, RHP	Marlins
2020	Spencer Howard, RHP	Rangers
2021	Spencer Howard, RHP	Rangers

TOP DRAFT PICKS OF THE DECADE

Year	Player, Pos	2021 Org
2012	Shane Watson, RHP (1st round supp)	Did not play
2013	J.P. Crawford, SS	Mariners
2014	Aaron Nola, RHP	Phillies
2015	Cornelius Randolph, SS	Phillies
2016	Mickey Moniak, OF	Phillies
2017	Adam Haseley, OF	Phillies
2018	Alec Bohm, 3B	Phillies
2019	Bryson Stott, SS	Phillies
2020	Mick Abel, RHP	Phillies
2021	Andrew Painter, RHP	Phillies

Pittsburgh Pirates

BY MARK CHIARELLI

Yes, even for a 100-loss team, the final week of the regular season can provide optimism. For the Pirates, it was a fleeting glimpse at what the future—and the fruits of yet another arduous rebuild—might one day hold.

Pittsburgh quietly called up a pair of baseball's Top 100 Prospects. Fireballing righthander Roansy Contreras came first, striking out four batters over three scoreless innings against the Cubs on Sept. 29. Shortstop Oneil Cruz, debuting in Pittsburgh's second-to-last game of the season, then homering a day later in Game 162.

To be clear: It will take far more than two prospects to turn the Pirates around. They lost 101 games and finished 34 games out of first place in the National League Central. They were on pace to lose 110 games in the shortened 2020 season, and they've finished last three years in a row.

The 2022 season figures to be more of the same, but there's something bubbling under the surface.

Pittsburgh has built one of baseball's deepest farm systems under general manager Ben Cherington, who has systematically augmented all levels of the system. He has acquired 15 of the team's 30 best prospects via a series of trades.

He also made a splash in the 2021 draft.

The Pirates selected Louisville catcher Henry Davis No. 1 overall and signed him to a $6.5 million bonus, nearly $2 million below slot. The added financial flexibility provided a path to landing a trio of talented high schoolers in righthander/shortstop Bubba Chandler, lefthander Anthony Solometo and outfielder Lonnie White Jr. over the first three rounds of the draft. All four players ranked among the 32 best prospects in the draft.

Pittsburgh also added nine prospects in a trade deadline fire sale headlined by sending all-star second baseman Adam Frazier to the Padres.

There were in-house successes, too.

Catcher Endy Rodriguez, acquired via the Mets in the three-team Joe Musgrove after the 2020 season, impressed team officials with his blend of versatility and aptitude at the plate for Low-A Bradenton. Outfielder Matt Fraizer, who wasn't invited to the team's alternate site in 2020, emerged from the shutdown with a revamped approach and crushed High-A pitching, earning a promotion to Double-A Altoona.

By the end of the season, the Pirates had five of the Top 100 Prospects in baseball, with Contreras nearly making it six.

It wasn't perfect. Pittsburgh dealt with a rash of injuries to some of its top prospects. Cruz, Contreras and second baseman Nick Gonzales all

Bryan Reynolds rebounded from an abysmal 2020 to make the National League all-star team.

PROJECTED 2025 LINEUP

Catcher	Henry Davis	25
First Base	Endy Rodriguez	25
Second Base	Nick Gonzales	26
Third Base	Ke'Bryan Hayes	28
Shortstop	Liover Peguero	24
Left Field	Bryan Reynolds	30
Center Field	Travis Swaggerty	27
Right Field	Oneil Cruz	26
Designated Hitter	Matt Fraizer	27
No. 1 Starter	Roansy Contreras	25
No. 2 Starter	Quinn Priester	24
No. 3 Starter	Michael Burrows	25
No. 4 Starter	Carmen Mlodzinski	26
No. 5 Starter	Mitch Keller	29
Closer	Jared Jones	23

missed multiple weeks. But it was progress.

Since Cherington's arrival, the Pirates have worked diligently to overhaul player development, hoping to shed the reputation of an organization that often failed to get the most out of talented players. They've taken a more holistic approach to player development under new farm director John Baker, and the returns this year were promising. Both High-A Greensboro and Low-A Bradenton made the postseason, featuring a slew of players who will one day form a core in Pittsburgh.

Patience may still be required for Pirates fans in 2022. But the sheer volume of talent making its way through the farm system suggests more exciting days are eventually coming. ∎

PITTSBURGH PIRATES

TOP 2022 ROOKIES	RANK
Oneil Cruz, SS	1
Roansy Contreras, RHP	5
Travis Swaggerty, OF	15
BREAKOUT PROSPECTS	**RANK**
Anthony Solometo, LHP	11
Maikol Escotto, SS	19
Rodolfo Nolasco, OF	21

SOURCE OF TOP 30 TALENT			
Homegrown	**15**	**Acquired**	**15**
College	5	Trade	15
Junior college	0	Rule 5 draft	0
High school	7	Independent league	0
Nondrafted free agent	0	Free agent/waivers	0
International	3		

LF
Jack Suwinski (24)
Canaan Smith-Njigba (28)
Cal Mitchell

CF
Lonnie White Jr. (14)
Travis Swaggerty (15)
Ji-Hwan Bae (25)
Connor Scott (26)
Jared Oliva
Lolo Sanchez
Sammy Siani

RF
Matt Fraizer (12)
Rodolfo Nolasco (21)
Hudson Head (23)

3B
Rodolfo Castro (20)
Jared Triolo

SS
Oneil Cruz (1)
Liover Peguero (5)
Maikol Escotto (19)

2B
Nick Gonzales (3)
Diego Castillo (16)
Tucupita Marcano (27)

1B
Mason Martin
Alexander Mojica

C
Henry Davis (2)
Endy Rodriguez (7)
Abrahan Gutierrez (22)
Carter Bins

LHP

LHSP	**LHRP**
Anthony Solometo (11)	Trey McGough
Omar Cruz	

RHP

RHSP	**RHRP**
Roansy Contreras (4)	Tahnaj Thomas (18)
Quinn Priester (6)	Kyle Nicolas (29)
Michael Burrows (8)	Oliver Mateo
Jared Jones (9)	Santiago Florez
Carmen Mlodzinski (10)	Eddy Yean
Bubba Chandler (13)	Blake Cederlind
Miguel Yajure (17)	Austin Roberts
Cody Bolton (30)	JC Flowers
Luis Ortiz	Luis Oviedo
Braxton Ashcraft	Will Kobos
Max Kranick	Enmanuel Mejia
Brennan Malone	Colin Selby
Nick Garcia	
Logan Hofmann	
Owen Kellington	
Ricky DeVito	
Adrian Florencio	

1 ONEIL CRUZ, SS

Born: Oct. 4, 1998. **B-T:** L-R. **HT:** 6-7. **WT:** 210.
Signed: Dominican Republic, 2015.
Signed by: Patrick Guerrero/Franklin Taveras/
Bob Engle (Dodgers).

TRACK RECORD: Cruz tests the imagination of evaluators and scouts alike. He first worked out for clubs as a 15-year-old amateur standing at 6-foot-1 in 2015 and signed with the Dodgers for $950,000, but he grew nearly six inches before making his pro debut the following year. The Dodgers traded him to the Pirates for Tony Watson at the 2017 trade deadline. Cruz has been something of a baseball unicorn since as a 6-foot-7 shortstop, inviting annual skepticism that, at some point, a position change is necessary. Yet the immensely talented Cruz continues to stave off such a decision. He spent most of 2021 manning shortstop at Double-A Altoona, where his .530 slugging percentage ranked ninth among all Double-A Northeast hitters with at least 200 plate appearances. Cruz missed nearly seven weeks with a forearm injury, but he made a brief stop in Triple-A after returning and was summoned to Pittsburgh in October. He dazzled in a two-game cameo, homering in his second game while also becoming the tallest starting shortstop in MLB history.

SCOUTING REPORT: Cruz boasts plus power, speed and throwing ability and has a legitimate chance to stick in the infield. He possesses otherworldly raw power, generating elite exit velocities with the leverage created by his long levers. Cruz already owns the Pirates' record for exit velocity in the Statcast era—a 118.2 mph single in his debut—and is capable of producing 30-homer seasons at his peak. He'll always battle strikeouts, and his swings and misses are sometimes exacerbated by his aggressive approach. He walked just 7.2% of the time with Altoona, and pitchers can exploit both the inherent length of his swing and his eagerness. There are times pitchers can catch Cruz guessing while hunting specific pitches, but he showed an ability to make adjustments in his approach within an at-bat. Cruz easily has a plus arm, but there is less consensus on where he should deploy it. The Pirates believe Cruz has the ingredients to stick at shortstop, citing his smooth hands and surprisingly deft infield actions. He will always face concerns about his range and ability to handle the demands of the position over a full season, but increased shifting could mitigate some of those worries. Some of his 16 errors came from rushing

MIKE JANES/FOUR SEAM IMAGES

BA GRADE	SCOUTING GRADES
65 Risk: Medium	Hit: 50. Power: 70. Run: 60. Field: 50. Arm: 60.

Projected future grades on 20-80 scouting scale

BEST TOOLS

Best Hitter for Average	Nick Gonzales
Best Power Hitter	Oneil Cruz
Best Strike-Zone Discipline	Tucupita Marcano
Fastest Baserunner	Jasiah Dixon
Best Athlete	Bubba Chandler
Best Fastball	Roansy Contreras
Best Curveball	Michael Burrows
Best Slider	Oliver Mateo
Best Changeup	Omar Cruz
Best Control	Trey McGough
Best Defensive Catcher	Carter Bins
Best Defensive Infielder	Jared Triolo
Best Infield Arm	Oneil Cruz
Best Defensive Outfielder	Travis Swaggerty
Best Outfield Arm	Travis Swaggerty

his throwing mechanics. Cruz is also a plus runner, leading to speculation about a long-term home in either center or right field, but he has yet to appear in the outfield outside of practice settings.

THE FUTURE: The Pirates will give Cruz a chance to win the starting shortstop job out of spring training. While he needs refinement, and the development of other players may ultimately dictate his position, Cruz has the highest impact potential of any player in the system and has one of baseball's most dynamic skill sets. ■

Year	Age	Club (Level)	Lge	AVG	G	AB	R	H	2B	3B	HR	RBI	BB	SO	SB	OBP	SLG
2021	22	Altoona (AA)	NEast	.292	62	250	51	73	15	5	12	40	20	64	18	.346	.536
	22	Indianapolis (AAA)	East	.524	6	21	11	11	1	0	5	7	8	5	1	.655	1.286
	22	Pittsburgh (MLB)	NL	.333	2	9	2	3	0	0	1	3	0	4	0	.333	.667
Major League Totals (1 year)				.333	2	9	2	3	0	0	1	3	0	4	0	.333	.667
Minor League Totals (6 years)				.281	404	1522	250	427	85	23	49	207	144	419	60	.342	.463

2 HENRY DAVIS, C

Born: Sept. 21, 1999. **B-T:** R-R. **HT:** 6-2. **WT:** 210. **Drafted:** Louisville, 2021 (1st round). **Signed by:** Adam Bourassa.

TRACK RECORD: Davis played his way up draft boards as Louisville's starting catcher in 2021 and emerged as the clear-cut top collegiate hitter in a class bereft of a true top prospect. The Pirates coveted his profile and drafted him No. 1 overall, signing him for a below-slot $6.5 million. The Pirates sent Davis to High-A Greensboro after a brief tune-up in the Florida Complex League, and he hit a pair of homers in six games before an oblique injury ended his season in late August.

SCOUTING REPORT: The Pirates believe Davis' swing is tailored to combat modern pitching, even if it looks a bit unorthodox. He greets pitchers with an open, crouched stance, cocks his hands back during his load, then attacks with an ample leg kick and a stride that looks like he's closing back up as he steps toward the pitcher. Davis worked diligently at Louisville to flatten his bat path, and the Pirates were drawn to his ability to handle both fastballs and breaking balls from various arm angles. Davis is built like a fullback and punishes mistakes with his natural strength and mature strike-zone recognition. Scouts have adored Davis' plus-plus arm dating back to high school, but he has faced longstanding concerns about his blocking and receiving. He's athletic enough to handle catching, and some of his defensive concerns could be allayed by the introduction of an automatic ball-strike system.

THE FUTURE: Davis' advanced offensive ability and the Pirates' logjam of catchers at the lower levels could lead to an aggressive assignment in 2022. He projects to be the organization's catcher of the future and has all-star potential on account of his bat.

BA GRADE

60 Risk: High

SCOUTING GRADES:	Hitting: 60	Power: 55	Running: 45	Fielding: 45	Arm: 70

Year	Age	Club (Level)	Lge	AVG	G	AB	R	H	2B	3B	HR	RBI	BB	SO	SB	OBP	SLG
2021	21	Pirates Black (R)	FCL	.429	2	7	1	3	2	0	1	4	0	2	0	.429	1.143
	21	Greensboro (HiA)	East	.263	6	19	6	5	0	1	2	3	4	8	1	.375	.684
Minor League Totals (1 year)				.308	8	26	7	8	2	1	3	7	4	10	1	.387	.808

3 NICK GONZALES, 2B

Born: May 27, 1999. **B-T:** R-R. **HT:** 5-10. **WT:** 190. **Drafted:** New Mexico State, 2020 (1st round). **Signed by:** Derrick Van Dusen.

TRACK RECORD: Gonzales arrived at New Mexico State as a walk-on and transformed into one of college baseball's best hitters. The Pirates drafted him seventh overall in 2020, making him the first pick of general manager Ben Cherington's tenure. Gonzales' pro debut in 2021 was interrupted by a broken finger in late May that cost him more than a month, and he started slowly when he returned. But Gonzales turned in a much more productive finish, hitting .322/.424/.661 with 13 homers from Aug. 1 through the end of the season and .380/.483/.539 in the Arizona Fall League.

SCOUTING REPORT: At his best, Gonzales is a hitting machine who sprays line drives to all fields with a simple, inside-out swing optimized for hard contact. He has a sound, mature approach and rarely chases, forcing pitchers to beat him in the zone. Gonzales swung and missed in the strike zone more than expected in his pro debut and posted a surprisingly high 27% strikeout rate, but he still hit over .300 to retain his status as a borderline plus-plus hitter. Gonzales hit 13 of his 18 home runs at his hitter-friendly home park in Greensboro, leading to skepticism about his power. Even so, he's strong in his frame and projects to reach double-digit home runs. Gonzales plays functional defense at second base and his average arm can make every throw, but his promise is largely tied to his bat.

THE FUTURE: Gonzales is ready for the upper levels and will see Double-A in 2022. He has the ceiling of an offensive-minded second baseman who makes an occasional all-star team.

BA GRADE

55 Risk: Medium

SCOUTING GRADES:	Hitting: 65	Power: 50	Running: 55	Fielding: 50	Arm: 50

Year	Age	Club (Level)	Lge	AVG	G	AB	R	H	2B	3B	HR	RBI	BB	SO	SB	OBP	SLG
2021	22	Greensboro (HiA)	East	.302	80	324	53	98	23	4	18	54	40	101	7	.385	.565
Minor League Totals (2 years)				.302	80	324	53	98	23	4	18	54	40	101	7	.385	.565

4 ROANSY CONTRERAS, RHP

Born: Nov. 7, 1999. **B-T:** R-R. **HT:** 6-0. **WT:** 197. **Signed:** Dominican Republic, 2016. **Signed by:** Juan Rosario (Yankees).

TRACK RECORD: Contreras raised his stock as much as any pitching prospect in 2021, gains initially set in motion while he was still in the Yankees' system. His improvement continued when the Pirates acquired him after the 2020 season in the trade that sent Jameson Taillon to New York. Contreras struck out 36% of batters as he rifled through Double-A and Triple-A, though he missed two months with a forearm strain. Contreras returned in September and continued to impress, culminating in his MLB debut with the Pirates at the end of the season.

BA GRADE
55 Risk: High

SCOUTING REPORT: Contreras has worked diligently to add strength and refine his pitch mix, and the result is an attack rooted in brute force. His fastball now tops out at 98 mph after operating primarily in the low 90s with the Yankees, and it explodes out of his hand at an angle that confuses hitters. He added a slider late in his tenure with the Yankees, giving him two distinct breaking balls, and both flash plus albeit with inconsistent command. Even his changeup, which he uses less frequently, has above-average potential. The Pirates worked with Contreras to better sync the release point of his breaking pitches with his fastball, unlocking more deception and improved spin rates on his curveball, which now tickles 2,900 rpm with better depth. Contreras' command wavers when he gets over-aggressive with his delivery, but his athleticism allows him to make adjustments on the fly. The larger concern is whether the 6-foot Contreras can sustain hold up under a starter's workload for a full season.

THE FUTURE: Contreras will enter spring training with a chance to win a spot in the Pirates' rotation. He has the ceiling of a mid-rotation starter.

SCOUTING GRADES:	Fastball: 60	Slider: 55	Curveball: 55	Changeup: 50	Control: 50

Year	Age	Club (Level)	Lge	W	L	ERA	G	GS	IP	H	HR	BB	SO	BB/9	SO/9	WHIP	AVG
2021	21	Altoona (AA)	NEast	3	2	2.65	12	12	54	37	5	12	76	2.0	12.6	0.90	.185
	21	Indianapolis (AAA)	East	0	0	2.45	1	1	3	4	0	1	6	2.5	14.7	1.36	.267
	21	Pittsburgh (MLB)	NL	0	0	0.00	1	1	3	3	0	1	4	3.0	12.0	1.33	.273
Major League Totals (1 year)				0	0	0.00	1	1	3	3	0	1	4	3.00	12.00	1.33	.273
Minor League Totals (5 years)				19	13	3.13	63	60	307	250	24	87	289	2.55	8.46	1.10	.219

5 LIOVER PEGUERO, SS

Born: Dec. 31, 2000. **B-T:** R-R. **HT:** 6-1. **WT:** 200. **Signed:** Dominican Republic, 2017. **Signed by:** Cesar Geronimo (D-backs).

TRACK RECORD: The D-backs signed Peguero out of the Dominican Republic for $475,000 in 2017, and arrow-up indicators followed shortly thereafter. The Pirates took notice and acquired Peguero with righthander Brennan Malone for Starling Marte before the 2020 season, the first significant trade of the Ben Cherington era. The Pirates sent Peguero to the alternate training site in 2020 to soak up the atmosphere among older competition. Peguero made his full-season debut in 2021 and posted a .776 OPS in 95 games with High-A Greensboro as one of the league's youngest regulars at 20 years old.

BA GRADE
55 Risk: High

SCOUTING REPORT: Peguero's blend of dynamic ability and enthusiasm is intriguing, though considerable refinement is needed. His strong hands and wrists generate wicked bat speed and exit velocities, and he continues to steadily add strength to what was once a wiry, high-waisted frame. Peguero is aggressive in all facets of the game. Sometimes that works against him at the plate, evident in his 25% strikeout rate. Continued improvement, especially at recognizing spin, should allow him to unlock an above-average bat and average power. Peguero has all the tools to play shortstop and turns in plenty of highlight-reel plays, but he lacks consistency. He also flashes explosive speed and will likely settle into above-average running ability as he matures, which also leaves the door open for a potential shift to the outfield if his defense plateaus.

TRACK RECORD: Peguero is still quite young and appears ready for the upper levels. He has the ceiling of a first-division regular at shortstop, but a ways to go to get there.

SCOUTING GRADES:	Hitting: 55	Power: 50	Running: 55	Fielding: 50	Arm: 55

Year	Age	Club (Level)	Lge	AVG	G	AB	R	H	2B	3B	HR	RBI	BB	SO	SB	OBP	SLG
2021	20	Greensboro (HiA)	East	.270	90	374	67	101	19	2	14	45	33	105	28	.332	.444
Minor League Totals (4 years)				.285	191	748	136	213	33	10	20	104	64	185	46	.343	.436

6 QUINN PRIESTER, RHP

Born: Sept. 15, 2000. **B-T:** R-R. **HT:** 6-3. **WT:** 210. **Drafted:** HS—Cary, Ill., 2019 (1st round). **Signed by:** Anthony Wycklendt.

TRACK RECORD: The Pirates drafted Priester No. 18 overall in 2019 and signed him for $3.4 million out of high school. He became a darling of scouts the following year at instructional league, where he touched 98 mph and showed improved stuff in short stints following the canceled minor league season. Priester was a popular breakout candidate entering 2021 and posted a 3.04 ERA in 97.2 innings for High-A Greensboro, where he was one of the youngest starting pitchers at the level.

BA GRADE

55 Risk: High

SCOUTING REPORT: Priester didn't quite hold his previous velocity gains and settled into the 94-95 mph range before tailing off at the end of the season. Still, he looks the part of the prototype starting pitcher with a strong frame. He throws two fastballs—a four-seamer and a sinker—and pairs them with a plus curveball, average slider and fringy changeup. Priester added his slider during the coronavirus shutdown while seeking a pitch he could throw to his glove side. It's a harder offering that sits 89-91 mph and is sometimes confused for a cutter, but is plenty effective. He could stand to throw his fringe-average changeup with more conviction. All of Priester's pitches play well off the same plane, and he fills up the strike zone with above-average control. He does have some rigidity in his throwing stroke and his delivery can become methodical at times. Priester didn't miss an overwhelming amount of bats in his debut, but his near 55% groundball rate ranked second among Pirates minor league starters with 90 innings.

THE FUTURE: Priester will still be just 21 years old on Opening Day. He will likely open in Double-A and has the ceiling of a mid-rotation starter.

SCOUTING GRADES:	Fastball: 60	Slider: 50	Curveball: 60	Changeup: 45	Control: 55

Year	Age	Club (Level)	Lge	W	L	ERA	G	GS	IP	H	HR	BB	SO	BB/9	SO/9	WHIP	AVG
2021	20	Greensboro (HiA)	East	7	4	3.04	20	20	97	82	8	39	98	3.6	9.0	1.24	.225
Minor League Totals (3 years)				8	5	3.08	29	28	134	114	9	53	139	3.55	9.31	1.24	.228

7 ENDY RODRIGUEZ, C/1B

Born: May 26, 2000. **B-T:** B-R. **HT:** 6-0. **WT:** 170. **Signed:** Dominican Republic, 2018. **Signed by:** Anderson Taveras (Mets).

TRACK RECORD: Rodriguez was an "older" $10,000 signee at 18 by the Mets and was trending upward when the Pirates acquired him in the three-team deal that sent Joe Musgrove to the Padres after the 2020 season. Rodriguez continued that momentum in his full-season debut in 2021, winning the Low-A Southeast batting title (.294) and posting the league's lowest strikeout rate (17.7%).

BA GRADE

50 Risk: High

SCOUTING REPORT: Rodriguez receives a steady drumbeat of praise as an ultra-athletic, switch-hitting catcher. He has a clean, direct swing from both sides of the plate and his lefthanded swing is geared for power. Rodriguez projects as a plus hitter thanks to his combination of impressive strike-zone recognition, bat speed and feel for the barrel. He posted the lowest swinging-strike rate (8.3%) of any hitter in his league. Rodriguez has a wiry frame, but he has a chance to sustain average power if he can add more strength. Defensively, Rodriguez is an agile mover behind the plate who adeptly handles velocity. He's still raw—he never caught full time until turning pro—but he's a quick learner who has made strides with his blocking and receiving. The Pirates internally rave about his energy and leadership behind the plate. Rodriguez didn't look out of place in looks at first base and left field, and he may be athletic enough to handle second base.

THE FUTURE: Rodriguez is one of several recent acquisitions who has transformed the Pirates' catching depth, along with Henry Davis, Abrahan Gutierrez and Carter Bins. Divvying up those reps will be a challenge, but Rodriguez is ready for High-A Greensboro in 2022.

SCOUTING GRADES:	Hitting: 60	Power: 50	Running: 45	Fielding: 50	Arm: 55

Year	Age	Club (Level)	Lge	AVG	G	AB	R	H	2B	3B	HR	RBI	BB	SO	SB	OBP	SLG
2021	21	Bradenton (LoA)	SEast	.294	98	377	73	111	25	6	15	73	50	77	2	.380	.512
Minor League Totals (4 years)				.288	164	594	114	171	45	9	19	110	85	121	8	.383	.490

8 MICHAEL BURROWS, RHP

Born: Nov. 8, 1999. **B-T:** R-R. **HT:** 6-1. **WT:** 192. **Drafted:** HS—Waterford, Conn., 2018 (11th round). **Signed by:** Eddie Charles.

TRACK RECORD: The Pirates bought Burrows out of a Connecticut commitment in 2018 with a $500,000 bonus, hoping to unlock a cold-weather prep pitcher with intriguing spin rates. Burrows showed flashes as a 19-year-old in the short-season New York-Penn League in 2019, then added strength to his frame during the Covid-19 shutdown. He joined High-A Greensboro's rotation in 2021 and dominated when healthy, striking out 66 hitters in 49 innings, but he missed nearly two months with an oblique injury. The Pirates sent Burrows to the Arizona Fall League to recoup some of those lost innings after the season.

BA GRADE
50 Risk: High

SCOUTING REPORT: Burrows primarily torments hitters with two plus offerings. His fastball, previously in the low 90s at the start of his pro career, now sits 94-97 mph thanks to his strength gains. The pitch has plenty of ride to miss barrels at the top of the strike zone. His high-spin, upper-70s curveball plays off his fastball with hard vertical break, and he's comfortable throwing it in any count. The Pirates believe his third pitch, a mid-80s changeup, has potential, but Burrows rarely throws it in games, and few external evaluators have seen it. One of Burrows' Arizona Fall League objectives was to use his changeup more and become comfortable using it behind in counts. Burrows' command can waver at times, leading to efficiency issues, and he has yet to throw more than 50 innings in a season.

THE FUTURE: Burrows has No. 4 starter potential if his changeup develops. Even if it doesn't, he could settle into a high-leverage role either as a closer or multi-inning battering ram equipped with two devastating pitches.

SCOUTING GRADES:	Fastball: 60	Curveball: 60	Changeup: 45	Control: 45

Year	Age	Club (Level)	Lge	W	L	ERA	G	GS	IP	H	HR	BB	SO	BB/9	SO/9	WHIP	AVG
2021	21	Greensboro (HiA)	East	2	2	2.20	13	13	49	24	3	20	66	3.7	12.1	0.90	.143
Minor League Totals (4 years)				4	5	2.78	28	27	107	74	5	44	118	3.71	9.96	1.11	.194

9 JARED JONES, RHP

Born: Aug. 6, 2001. **B-T:** L-R. **HT:** 6-0. **WT:** 180. **Drafted:** HS—La Mirada, Calif., 2020 (2nd round). **Signed by:** Brian Tracy.

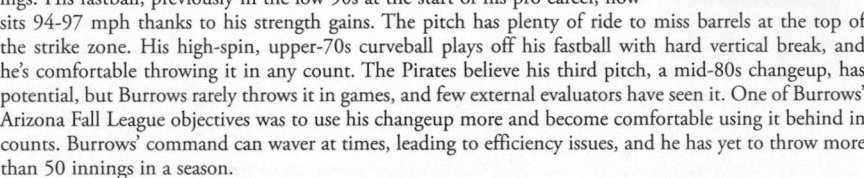

TRACK RECORD: Jones was a famous two-way prospect in high school and was selected for USA Baseball's Junior National Teams three times as an amateur. The Pirates drafted him in the second round in 2020 and gave him an above-slot $2.2 million to be a full-time pitcher. Jones made his pro debut in 2021 with Low-A Bradenton and missed plenty of bats with 103 strikeouts in 66 innings, but he also struggled with walks and posted a 4.64 ERA in a pitcher-friendly league.

BA GRADE
55 Risk: Very High

SCOUTING REPORT: Jones is a metrics darling with a live arm. His fastball sits 94-96 mph and can touch as high as 99. He throws two distinct, high-spin breaking balls that mirror his fastball and flash plus, though he struggles to consistently locate both at the same time. Jones leans on his mid-to-upper-80s slider more because he commands it better, and he also throws a low-80s curveball with more vertical break. He also mixes in an upper-80s changeup that has average potential. He throws it with good arm speed, but it needs more separation from his fastball. Jones has plenty of stuff but needs to hone his command to showcase it more consistently. His 6-foot frame and effortful delivery may portend a future shift to the bullpen, but he is immensely athletic and the Pirates believe he'll continue to improve as a starter. He draws raves for his competitiveness on the mound.

THE FUTURE: Jones can be downright electric on the right night and shows the ceiling of a mid-rotation starter, but he has a lot of work to do to get there.

SCOUTING GRADES:	Fastball: 60	Slider: 60	Curveball: 55	Changeup: 50	Control: 45

Year	Age	Club (Level)	Lge	W	L	ERA	G	GS	IP	H	HR	BB	SO	BB/9	SO/9	WHIP	AVG
2021	19	Bradenton (LoA)	SEast	3	6	4.64	18	15	66	63	6	34	103	4.6	14.1	1.47	.245
Minor League Totals (2 years)				3	6	4.64	18	15	66	63	6	34	103	4.64	14.05	1.47	.245

10 CARMEN MLODZINSKI, RHP

Born: Feb. 19, 1999. **B-T:** R-R. **HT:** 6-2. **WT:** 231. **Drafted:** South Carolina, 2020 (1st round supplemental). **Signed by:** Cam Murphy.

BA GRADE
50 Risk: High

TRACK RECORD: Mlodzinski had a limited track record at South Carolina because of a foot injury in 2019 and the pandemic-shortened 2020 season, but the Pirates saw enough in limited time to draft him 31st overall and sign him for $2.05 million. Mlodzinski got his pro career off to a hot start with 51 strikeouts in 37.1 innings at High-A Greensboro before he suffered right shoulder stiffness that sidelined him for more than a month. He was limited to shorter outings upon returning in August, but he still made it to Triple-A for one relief appearance. He finished the year in the Arizona Fall League.
SCOUTING REPORT: Mlodzinski has long had a deep arsenal, if not a true swing-and-miss pitch. He set out to change that in 2021 by relying more on a traditional four-seam fastball with carry through the zone as opposed to his typical sinker-heavy approach. Mlodzinski's four-seamer sits 93-95 mph and touches 98 and has the potential to play up from his low arm slot, aided even more by his effortful-yet-deceptive delivery. Mlodzinski also throws an average cutter with late life and his assortment of secondaries includes an above-average slider, an above-average, mid-80s changeup he throws with impressive arm speed and the occasional fringy curveball. Sequencing and efficiency can be an issue for Mlodzinski, and he sometimes struggled to finish at-bats. His velocity also tends to fluctuate
THE FUTURE: The health of Mlodzinski's shoulder and his lack of a true out pitch are concerns. He still has the upside of a back-end starter and could arrive in Pittsburgh sooner rather than later.

SCOUTING GRADES: Fastball: 55 Slider: 55 Cutter: 50 Curveball: 45 Changeup: 55 Control: 50

Year	Age	Club (Level)	Lge	W	L	ERA	G	GS	IP	H	HR	BB	SO	BB/9	SO/9	WHIP	AVG
2021	22	Greensboro (HiA)	East	2	3	3.93	14	14	50	45	7	20	64	3.6	11.4	1.29	.237
	22	Indianapolis (AAA)	East	0	1	4.50	1	0	2	3	0	2	2	9.0	9.0	2.50	.333
Minor League Totals (2 years)				2	4	3.96	15	14	52	48	7	22	66	3.78	11.35	1.34	.241

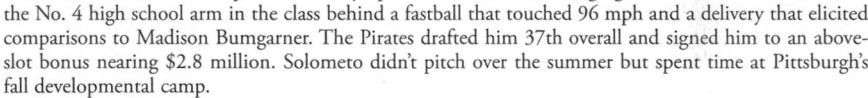

11 ANTHONY SOLOMETO, LHP

BA GRADE
55 Risk: Extreme

Born: Dec. 2, 2002. **B-T:** L-L. **HT:** 6-5. **WT:** 220. **Drafted:** HS— Pennsauken, N.J., 2021 (2nd round). **Signed by:** Dan Radcliff.
TRACK RECORD: Solometo pitched his way up 2021 draft boards, emerging as the No. 4 high school arm in the class behind a fastball that touched 96 mph and a delivery that elicited comparisons to Madison Bumgarner. The Pirates drafted him 37th overall and signed him to an above-slot bonus nearing $2.8 million. Solometo didn't pitch over the summer but spent time at Pittsburgh's fall developmental camp.
SCOUTING REPORT: Solometo's entire operation is memorable. The tall, gangly lefty begins his windup with a big step toward third base, then swings his right leg up into an exaggerated leg kick, holding the ball in his hands above his head. From there, he brings the ball down into a deep, long arm action before exploding down the mound, releasing it from a low arm slot. All the moving parts create considerable deception, only aiding what the Pirates believe is a plus fastball thanks to its low-to-mid-90s velocity, command and ability to throw it in any count. He pairs it with a slider that dives at the foot of right-handed batters and flashes plus. His changeup is more developmental but flashes solid-average potential. Naturally, such an intricate delivery invites skepticism and requires some maintenance, but Solometo's athleticism allows him to repeat it surprisingly well.
THE FUTURE: Solometo is more advanced than the average prep pitcher, and the Pirates were impressed with his competitiveness and makeup. He has mid-rotation upside.

Year	Age	Club (Level)	Lge	W	L	ERA	G	GS	IP	H	HR	BB	SO	BB/9	SO/9	WHIP	AVG
2021	18	Did not play															

12 MATT FRAIZER, OF

BA GRADE
50 Risk: High

Born: Jan. 12, 1998. **B-T:** L-R. **HT:** 6-3. **WT:** 205. **Drafted:** Arizona, 2019 (3rd round). **Signed by:** Derrick Van Dusen.
TRACK RECORD: Fraizer was the Pirates system's breakout star in 2021. He underwhelmed in his 2019 pro debut, posting a .553 OPS in 43 games for short-season West Virginia. The pandemic wiped out Fraizer's 2020 season like many others, but he broke out with High-A Greensboro in 2021, hitting .314/.401/.578 to lead High-A West in all three triple-slash categories. He was one of the

few Pirates prospects to earn a midseason promotion. He joined Double-A Altoona in August.

SCOUTING REPORT: Fraizer's revelatory season was rooted in a series of changes to simplify his swing and approach, allowing him to access his raw tools more consistently. He quieted his hands to eliminate counter-movement during his load, better incorporated his lower half and sought more extension to drive the ball in the air. Fraizer hit plenty of ground balls to start the season, but he began showing power to all fields by June as he grew more comfortable with his new swing. Fraizer has impressive overall bat speed and made plenty of hard contact against pitchers of both hands, though his swing can get big at times. He's a plus runner who has a shot to stick in center field, but his fringe-average arm may play better in left.

THE FUTURE: Fraizer tapped into his power more consistently than at any point in his career, and the outfield-needy Pirates took notice. Now, he'll have to prove his swing changes against upper-level pitchers.

Year	Age	Club (Level)	Lge	AVG	G	AB	R	H	2B	3B	HR	RBI	BB	SO	SB	OBP	SLG
2021	23	Greensboro (HiA)	East	.314	75	303	64	95	14	3	20	50	43	74	14	.401	.578
	23	Altoona (AA)	NEast	.288	37	132	20	38	12	3	3	18	13	34	1	.356	.492
Minor League Totals (3 years)				.284	155	589	104	167	31	7	23	83	70	146	20	.362	.477

13 BUBBA CHANDLER, RHP/SS

BA GRADE
55 Risk: Extreme

Born: Sept. 14, 2002. **B-T:** B-T. **HT:** 6-3. **WT:** 200. **Drafted:** HS—Bogart, Ga., 2021 (3rd round). **Signed by:** Cam Murphy.

TRACK RECORD: Chandler expected to play both baseball and football at Clemson until the Pirates offered him $3 million—late first-round money—to turn pro as a 2021 third-round pick. They landed one of the draft's most compelling prospects. A four-star quarterback recruit, Chandler surged up baseball draft boards after touching 97 mph last spring while showing promise as a legit two-way player. Chandler made his pro debut by appearing in 11 games as a shortstop and DH in the Florida Complex League.

SCOUTING REPORT: Chandler is an elite athlete capable of throwing a football 50 yards lefthanded and easily dunking a basketball. He's a switch-hitter with real raw power. But the Pirates view him first as a pitcher, where most evaluators feel he has immense upside. Chandler has a fast, strong arm and already runs his fastball into the low-to-mid 90s from a high arm slot. His secondaries were inconsistent as an amateur, but his breaking ball showed above-average spin and he throws a work-in-progress changeup. He's also experimented with both a slider and a cutter. Chandler's mechanics are quite raw. He has never focused on baseball full time. At the plate, Chandler is a switch-hitter with solid raw power, albeit with swing-and-miss concerns. He has the range and arm strength to handle shortstop.

THE FUTURE: There are few comparisons for Chandler, and the Pirates plan to allow him to pursue both pitching and hitting. It may be a slow burn, but his athleticism and raw skills create immense upside.

Year	Age	Club (Level)	Lge	AVG	G	AB	R	H	2B	3B	HR	RBI	BB	SO	SB	OBP	SLG
2021	18	Pirates Black (R)	FCL	.167	11	30	3	5	1	0	1	2	5	16	0	.324	.300
Minor League Totals (1 year)				.167	11	30	3	5	1	0	1	2	5	16	0	.324	.300

14 LONNIE WHITE JR., OF

BA GRADE
55 Risk: Extreme

Born: Dec. 31, 2002. **B-T:** R-R. **HT:** 6-3. **WT:** 212. **Drafted:** HS—Malvern, Pa., 2021 (2nd round supplemental). **Signed by:** Dan Radcliff.

TRACK RECORD: White ranked as the No. 32 prospect in the 2021 draft, but a two-sport commitment to Penn State to play both baseball and football created signability questions. Pittsburgh went nearly $500,000 over slot to sign White, taking him No. 64 overall. He debuted in the Florida Complex League, hitting .258 with a pair of homers in nine games.

SCOUTING REPORT: White was a four-star wide receiver recruit and his explosiveness shows up frequently on the diamond. He's a powerful athlete with ample strength and bat speed. His plus raw power from the right side already puts him among some of the most powerful bats in Pittsburgh's system, and he showed a track record of in-game, impactful hitting ability as an amateur. There are swing-and-miss concerns—he struck out 42% of the time in his nine-game FCL debut—but the Pirates noted he already showed impressive adjustability in approach and think he'll improve in that area now that he's focusing on baseball for the first time. White is a plus runner who covers a ton of ground in center field and also shows impressive instincts.

THE FUTURE: White's blend of power, speed and performance create high upside. The Pirates are eager to see how he progresses with a full year to focus solely on baseball.

Year	Age	Club (Level)	Lge	AVG	G	AB	R	H	2B	3B	HR	RBI	BB	SO	SB	OBP	SLG
2021	18	Pirates Black (R)	FCL	.258	9	31	6	8	2	0	2	5	2	14	0	.303	.516
Minor League Totals (1 year)				.258	9	31	6	8	2	0	2	5	2	14	0	.303	.516

15 TRAVIS SWAGGERTY, OF

BA GRADE

50 Risk: High

Born: Aug. 19, 1997. **B-T:** L-L. **HT:** 5-11. **WT:** 200. **Drafted:** South Alabama, 2018 (1st round). **Signed by:** Darren Mazeroski

TRACK RECORD: Swaggerty represented a relatively safe profile ahead of the 2018 draft as a lefthanded outfielder with extensive college track record at South Alabama, where he hit 28 homers and walked more than he struck out. Pittsburgh selected Swaggerty 10th overall, intrigued by the power-speed potential. But the consistency Swaggerty showed in college hasn't materialized as a professional. He slugged just .381 in 2019 at High-A Bradenton, then spent all of 2020 at Pittsburgh's alternate site. His 2021 season ended after 12 games with Triple-A Indianapolis when he dislocated his non-throwing shoulder diving back to first base, requiring season-ending surgery.

SCOUTING REPORT: Swaggerty always showed advanced understanding of the strike zone, but too often he chased power at the expense of contact. The Pirates believed Swaggerty was heading toward a breakout season, noting that his improved swing decisions led to more frequent hard contact, and he appeared more upright in his setup at the plate compared to two years ago. Evaluators may need more convincing when it comes to Swaggerty's bat, but few question his defensive chops. He's a plus defender with an above-average arm. Swaggerty likely would have been regarded as one of the best defensive center fielders in the upper levels had he stayed healthy.

THE FUTURE: Pittsburgh rued the timing of Swaggerty's injury as it cycled through center field options in the big leagues in 2021. He has the ceiling of a second-division starter if he can demonstrate more consistent hitting ability.

Year	Age	Club (Level)	Lge	AVG	G	AB	R	H	2B	3B	HR	RBI	BB	SO	SB	OBP	SLG
2021	23	Indianapolis (AAA)	East	.220	12	41	6	9	0	0	3	7	6	8	3	.333	.439
Minor League Totals (4 years)				.255	185	699	113	178	30	5	17	67	85	182	35	.339	.385

16 DIEGO CASTILLO, 2B/3B

BA GRADE

45 Risk: High

Born: Oct. 28, 1997. **B-T:** R-R. **HT:** 6-0. **WT:** 185. **Signed:** Venezuela, 2014. **Signed by:** Roney Calderon (Yankees).

TRACK RECORD: Castillo was a skilled, instinctual infielder when the Yankees signed him as part of their historic 2014 international signing class that shattered their bonus pool at the time. But Castillo moved slowly through New York's system until his breakout season in 2021, when he hit 19 homers across two levels. The Yankees dealt Castillo and shortstop Hoy Park to Pittsburgh at the deadline for reliever Clay Holmes, and the Pirates added Castillo to their 40-man roster after the season.

SCOUTING REPORT: Castillo always possessed strong barrel awareness and feel for contact, but without power production. He used baseball's shutdown in 2020 to add strength to his frame and work diligently with the Yankees' hitting instructors to tamp down his overaggressive approach, learning which pitches to seek and destroy. The changes resulted in higher exit velocities and noticeably more damage, suggesting average power potential. Castillo also turned in a 10% walk rate, the best of his career. He's a below-average runner, and evaluators don't envision Castillo sticking at shortstop, but he's fundamentally sound and has an average arm at both second and third base.

THE FUTURE: Some evaluators now see Castillo as a future big league hitter without a true defensive home. He's one of several utility types with a shot at winning the Pirates' second base job in 2022.

Year	Age	Club (Level)	Lge	AVG	G	AB	R	H	2B	3B	HR	RBI	BB	SO	SB	OBP	SLG
2021	23	Somerset (AA)	NEast	.277	58	224	44	62	18	0	11	32	21	34	8	.345	.504
	23	Altoona (AA)	NEast	.282	28	110	11	31	3	0	5	16	10	9	1	.342	.445
	23	Indianapolis (AAA)	East	.278	18	54	18	15	3	0	3	7	13	13	0	.414	.500
Minor League Totals (7 years)				.270	556	2140	306	578	95	15	27	229	168	253	52	.326	.366

17 MIGUEL YAJURE, RHP

BA GRADE

40 Risk: Medium

Born: May 1, 1998. **B-T:** R-R. **HT:** 6-1. **WT:** 220. **Signed:** Venezuela, 2015. **Signed by:** Cesar Suarez/Ricardo Finol (Yankees).

TRACK RECORD: A right forearm injury limited Pittsburgh's opportunity to evaluate Yajure his first year in the organization after being dealt from the Yankees in the Jameson Taillon trade. Yajure signed with New York for just $30,000 in 2015, then missed all of 2017 after having Tommy John surgery. New York summoned him for his MLB debut in the shortened 2020 season, but 2021 represented Yajure's first opportunity at sustaining a role in the big leagues.

SCOUTING REPORT: Yajure relies on pitchability more than pure stuff. As such, his margin for error is thinner than others, but he combats hitters with a deep arsenal that runs six pitches deep. He throws a low-90s fastball with decent shape to it, but big league hitters hit .429 against it in a small sample. Yajure added a low-90s cutter in 2019, and his most effective secondary is a 12-6 curveball he throws in the upper 70s and tunnels with his four-seamer. Yajure also throws a solid-average changeup and mixes in a slider as well. His minor league track record suggests he can throw his entire arsenal for strikes, though his command has wavered as a big leaguer.

THE FUTURE: Pittsburgh needs Yajure to stay healthy and add more strength. If he can, he'll have an opportunity to compete for innings in Pittsburgh and settle in as a back-of-the-rotation starter.

Year	Age	Club (Level)	Lge	W	L	ERA	G	GS	IP	H	HR	BB	SO	BB/9	SO/9	WHIP	AVG
2021	23	Pittsburgh (MLB)	NL	0	2	8.40	4	3	15	17	6	7	11	4.2	6.6	1.60	.283
	23	Indianapolis (AAA)	East	2	3	3.09	9	9	43	33	6	13	40	2.7	8.2	1.05	.209
	23	Bradenton (LoA)	SEast	0	1	6.75	2	2	4	6	1	1	5	2.3	11.3	1.75	.333
Major League Totals (2 years)				0	2	6.14	7	3	22	20	7	12	19	4.91	7.77	1.45	.241
Minor League Totals (6 years)				16	17	2.60	72	65	339	300	17	84	291	2.23	7.72	1.13	.238

18 TAHNAJ THOMAS, RHP

Born: June 16, 1999. **B-T:** R-R. **HT:** 6-4. **WT:** 190. **Signed:** Bahamas, 2016. **Signed by:** Koby Perez (Indians).

TRACK RECORD: Thomas was a shortstop in the Bahamas as an amateur and first tried pitching in 2016 only out of necessity—his travel team ran out of arms at a tournament. But he quickly took to it and converted full time shortly after, signing with Cleveland that year. He was traded to the Pirates two years later, and he showed immense upside as a developmental arm. Thomas was one of several high-profile arms in High-A Greensboro's rotation in 2021 and struggled, walking more than five batters per nine innings.

SCOUTING REPORT: Thomas is highly athletic and can touch triple digits thanks to his considerable arm strength. He sits in the upper 90s when he stays on top of his fastball out of a high arm slot. It shows impressive ride and late life in the zone. But Thomas struggles to sync his delivery, causing the quality of his fastball to suffer, and scouts noted he sometimes throttles down in velocity to throw strikes. Breaking pitch development is key to Thomas' trajectory. So far, he's shown a streaky ability to land his slurvy slider for strikes but doesn't consistently spin it. He also throws an average changeup, though multiple evaluators speculated he may benefit from swapping it for more of a splitter to pair with the power fastball.

THE FUTURE: Thomas was always going to move slowly because of his lack of pitching experience. The Pirates still believe he can start, citing his competitiveness, athleticism and development window. He'll need to find a consistent breaking ball, and his strike-throwing needs to take a leap forward, but he has the fallback option of a high-leverage reliever.

Year	Age	Club (Level)	Lge	W	L	ERA	G	GS	IP	H	HR	BB	SO	BB/9	SO/9	WHIP	AVG
2021	22	Greensboro (HiA)	East	3	3	5.19	16	16	60	61	13	35	62	5.2	9.2	1.58	.256
Minor League Totals (5 years)				5	11	4.63	52	47	167	152	24	92	182	4.96	9.81	1.46	.240

19 MAIKOL ESCOTTO, SS

Born: June 4, 2002. **B-T:** R-R. **HT:** 5-11. **WT:** 180. **Signed:** Dominican Republic, 2018. **Signed by:** Esteban Castillo/Victor Mata/Juan Rosario.

TRACK RECORD: The Yankees signed Escotto for $350,000 out of the Dominican Republic in 2018, and he was an arrow-up name after posting a .981 OPS in his pro debut in the Dominican Summer League. He was one of four players traded to the Pirates in the Jameson Taillon trade in January 2021 and spent all season with Low-A Bradenton.

SCOUTING REPORT: Escotto has considerable upside and ran the gamut of experiences in his first year of full-season ball. The 19-year-old posted an .801 OPS and hit all seven of his regular season homers through July—but his OPS afterward was just .593. Escotto has a simple, efficient swing with the chance for above-average power potential, generating exit velocities up to 109 mph with Bradenton. The Pirates were impressed with how his swing played against sliders early in the year. But Escotto's high strikeout (30.4%) and grouball (53.8%) rates were concerns. He'll need to continue to add strength to impact the ball more effectively throughout a full season. Escotto's actions checked out defensively at shortstop, where he displays the requisite range and arm to stick at the position, though he could eventually move across the keystone as an offensive-minded second baseman depending on how his body matures.

THE FUTURE: Plenty of refinement at the lower levels is needed for Escotto, but the raw ingredients of a high-upside middle infield prospect remain.

Year	Age	Club (Level)	Lge	AVG	G	AB	R	H	2B	3B	HR	RBI	BB	SO	SB	OBP	SLG
2021	19	Bradenton (LoA)	SEast	.234	89	320	61	75	13	1	7	38	54	116	22	.354	.347
Minor League Totals (2 years)				.263	134	501	108	132	24	5	15	64	86	173	35	.381	.421

20 RODOLFO CASTRO, 2B/3B

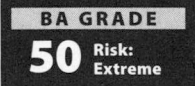

BA GRADE

45 Risk: High

Born: May 21, 1999. **B-T:** B-R. **HT:** 6-0. **WT:** 210. **Signed:** Dominican Republic, 2015. **Signed by:** Rene Gayo/Juan Mercaso/Jose Ortiz.

TRACK RECORD: Castro became a sensation in 2021, six years after he signed for $150,000 as an international free agent from the Dominican Republic. Despite never appearing above High-A, he impressed at Pittsburgh's alternate training site during the shutdown. He opened 2021 at Double-A Altoona, but the Pirates summoned him for a one-game MLB debut in April. He returned in July and his first five big league hits were homers—a modern era record.

SCOUTING REPORT: Castro is an energetic free-swinger with considerable raw power from both sides of the plate. Such a profile comes with stark highs and lows. Castro posted just a .458 OPS over his final 22 games following his homer-happy start, striking out 31% of the time. Castro's swing is geared for damage—his max exit velocity in Pittsburgh was 112.5 mph—but he struggles with breaking balls and doesn't walk much. He's a solid-average runner and is a serviceable defender at shortstop, second and third base.

THE FUTURE: Castro could compete for Pittsburgh's starting second base job in 2021 and has a future as utility infielder with thump.

Year	Age	Club (Level)	Lge	AVG	G	AB	R	H	2B	3B	HR	RBI	BB	SO	SB	OBP	SLG
2021	22	Altoona (AA)	NEast	.242	72	285	43	69	14	1	12	47	19	72	7	.295	.425
	22	Indianapolis (AAA)	East	.286	8	35	7	10	4	0	3	8	3	11	0	.342	.657
	22	Pittsburgh (MLB)	NL	.198	31	86	9	17	2	0	5	8	6	27	0	.258	.395
Major League Totals (1 year)				.198	31	86	9	17	2	0	5	8	6	27	0	.258	.395
Minor League Totals (6 years)				.248	412	1502	210	373	90	15	54	239	122	400	26	.308	.436

21 RODOLFO NOLASCO, OF

BA GRADE

50 Risk: Extreme

Born: Sept. 23, 2001. **B-T:** R-R. **HT:** 6-1. **WT:** 175. **Signed:** Dominican Republic, 2018. **Signed by:** Victor Santana.

TRACK RECORD: Pittsburgh signed Nolasco for $235,000 in 2018 after he stood out for his raw power, and he performed well in his first taste of Rookie ball in 2019. A spring training injury delayed Nolasco's season in 2021, and the Pirates opted to keep him in the Florida Complex League. Nolasco showed power, homering eight times and leading the FCL in slugging (.552).

SCOUTING REPORT: Nolasco's raw power rivals any hitter in Pittsburgh's system. He's physically strong and continues to add strength to his frame, resulting in ample bat speed. He crushes fastballs when he's on time. Nolasco also shows breaking ball recognition, but his swing mechanics suggest he will always have to manage swing-and-miss. He struck out 26% of the time in the FCL. Nolasco will likely be a below-average runner as he matures, limiting him to a corner outfield spot. He split time between right field and DH in 2021.

THE FUTURE: Nolasco is a long way away, but few 20-year-olds can match his raw power. He's ready for Low-A Bradenton in 2022.

Year	Age	Club (Level)	Lge	AVG	G	AB	R	H	2B	3B	HR	RBI	BB	SO	SB	OBP	SLG
2021	19	Pirates Gold (R)	FCL	.284	42	134	27	38	8	2	8	32	26	43	0	.409	.552
Minor League Totals (2 years)				.294	96	333	70	98	21	5	13	66	42	69	3	.388	.505

22 ABRAHAN GUTIERREZ, C

BA GRADE

45 Risk: High

Born: Oct. 31, 1999. **B-T:** R-R. **HT:** 6-0. **WT:** 215. **Signed:** Venezuela, 2017. **Signed by:** Carlos Salas (Phillies).

TRACK RECORD: Gutierrez was set to sign with the Braves for $3.53 million in 2017, a record at the time for an international amateur catcher, but MLB voided the deal because of the Braves' international infractions. He eventually signed with the Phillies for $550,000 and showed encouraging bat-to-ball skills but inconsistent conditioning. The Pirates acquired Gutierrez at the 2021 deadline in a deal for reliever Braeden Ogle, and he exceeded their expectations at Low-A Bradenton.

SCOUTING REPORT: The Pirates were impressed with Gutierrez's mature approach. He was one of Pittsburgh's most selective hitters, walking more than he struck out, while also posting one of the lower chase rates in the system. He doesn't post overwhelming exit velocities and there's some length to his swing, leading to fringe-average power potential. Gutierrez will have to work diligently to maintain his body, and the Phillies said he did a better job of it in 2021. He also earned positive reviews for improvements with pitch-calling and receiving. Gutierrez's fringy arm is susceptible to basestealers.

THE FUTURE: Pittsburgh suddenly has a glut of catching prospects, but Gutierrez distinguished himself after the trade deadline. He has the hitting ability and defensive chops to project as a part-time MLB catcher.

Year	Age	Club (Level)	Lge	AVG	G	AB	R	H	2B	3B	HR	RBI	BB	SO	SB	OBP	SLG
2021	21	Clearwater (LoA)	SEast	.288	50	177	30	51	10	0	5	32	37	31	0	.420	.429
2021	21	Bradenton (LoA)	SEast	.294	22	68	16	20	8	2	0	4	16	13	0	.448	.471
Minor League Totals (5 years)				.275	231	825	108	227	46	3	11	105	101	143	5	.360	.378

23 HUDSON HEAD, OF

BA GRADE

45 Risk: High

Born: April 8, 2001. **B-T:** L-L. **HT:** 6-1. **WT:** 180. **Drafted:** HS—San Antonio, Texas, 2019 (3rd round). **Signed by:** Kevin Ham (Padres).

TRACK RECORD: Teams didn't have much history with Head, who was a high school quarterback in Texas, prior to his emergence as a popup prospect for the 2019 draft. That didn't stop the Padres from signing him for $3 million in the third round. He flashed explosive tools in limited instructional league looks with San Diego, and was sent to Pittsburgh in the Joe Musgrove trade after the 2020 season. Head showed power but struck out 31.6% of the time with Low-A Bradenton in 2021.

SCOUTING REPORT: Scouts struggled to evaluate Head in 2021. He showed above-average power potential at times, hitting 15 homers, with bat speed to produce above-average exit velocities from his wiry frame. But multiple evaluators expected a bit more physicality based on what he had shown previously in 2019. Head also struggled with premium velocity at times, especially at the top of the zone, leading to concerns his swing is a bit grooved. He also struggled mightily against lefthanders. The Pirates worked with Head to shorten his swing throughout the season. Defensively, Head is a solid defender with the arm to handle any outfield position, but his speed and arm may ultimately play better in a corner.

THE FUTURE: Those bullish on Head will give him a mulligan for 2021, citing his age and uneven development timeline. He has the floor of a fourth outfielder with more upside if he can make more contact.

Year	Age	Club (Level)	Lge	AVG	G	AB	R	H	2B	3B	HR	RBI	BB	SO	SB	OBP	SLG
2021	20	Bradenton (LoA)	SEast	.213	101	348	67	74	16	1	15	50	68	137	3	.362	.394
Minor League Totals (3 years)				.231	133	468	86	108	23	4	16	62	83	166	6	.367	.400

24 JACK SUWINSKI, OF

BA GRADE

45 Risk: High

Born: July 29, 1998. **B-T:** L-L. **HT:** 6-2. **WT:** 206. **Drafted:** HS—Chicago, 2016 (15th round). **Signed by:** Troy Hoerner (Padres).

TRACK RECORD: The Padres popped Suwinski, a cold-weather high school product, in the 15th round of the 2016 draft, signing him for $550,000. He spent six years in San Diego's system, rising to Double-A San Antonio, where he hit a career-high 15 homers in just 66 games in 2021. The Pirates acquired him in a trade deadline deal for all-star second baseman Adam Frazier.

SCOUTING REPORT: Suwinski hits the ball hard. His 90 mph average exit velocity ranked among the best in Pittsburgh's system upon his arrival. He also hit the ball in the air more frequently than any point in his career previously, tapping into his pull-side power. That equation yielded his best season as a pro and led to Pittsburgh adding Suwinski to the 40-man roster after the season. His 28% strikeout rate and issues against same-side pitchers are concerns for evaluators, who note there's some stiffness in his swing. But he also walks plenty, is unafraid of deep counts and minimizes chase thanks to an advanced understanding of the strike zone. Suwinski isn't a dynamic athlete defensively, but he's an average runner with a solid-average arm who played almost exclusively at both corner outfield positions in 2021.

THE FUTURE: His struggles against lefties may limit Suwinski to a platoon role, but his power and plate discipline should allow him to reach the big leagues in relatively short order.

Year	Age	Club (Level)	Lge	AVG	G	AB	R	H	2B	3B	HR	RBI	BB	SO	SB	OBP	SLG
2021	22	San Antonio (AA)	Cent	.269	66	216	47	58	8	4	15	37	45	74	7	.398	.551
	22	Altoona (AA)	NEast	.252	45	151	21	38	9	0	4	21	25	51	4	.359	.391
Minor League Totals (6 years)				.237	493	1737	257	412	75	18	50	217	230	513	29	.331	.387

25 JI-HWAN BAE, 2B/OF

BA GRADE

45 Risk: High

Born: July 26, 1999. **B-T:** L-R. **HT:** 6-1. **WT:** 185. **Signed:** South Korea, 2018. **Signed by:** Fu-Chun Chiang/Tony Harris.

TRACK RECORD: Bae planned to sign with the Braves in 2017 until his contract was disapproved after MLB disciplined Atlanta for violating international signing rules. He signed with the Pirates in 2018 for $1.25 million. A year later, he served a 30-game suspension after he was convicted of assaulting his ex-girlfriend in South Korea. After including Bae at their alternate site in 2020, Pittsburgh sent him to Double-A Altoona in 2021.

SCOUTING REPORT: Speed and contact skills define Bae's game, although added strength allowed him to impact the ball a bit more in 2021. He hit the first eight homers of his pro career in the U.S. With that came more swing-and-miss concerns from evaluators. Most agree Bae still projects as a table-setter type who should use his barrel control skills and legit 70-grade speed, with the caveat that his baserunning instincts still need work. His defensive position remains in question. Pittsburgh moved him to second base in 2021, and scouts weren't overly impressed with his actions. Bae also played nine games in center field, where his speed may end up being more of an asset.

THE FUTURE: Without a defined defensive home, Bae may settle into a speedy super-utility role, putting even more stress on his contact skills.

Year	Age	Club (Level)	Lge	AVG	G	AB	R	H	2B	3B	HR	RBI	BB	SO	SB	OBP	SLG
2021	21	Altoona (AA)	NEast	.278	83	320	63	89	12	5	7	31	38	83	20	.359	.413
	21	Pirates Gold (R)	FCL	.333	1	3	1	1	0	0	1	1	0	0	0	.333	1.333
	21	Pirates Black (R)	FCL	.500	1	4	2	2	0	0	0	1	0	0	0	.500	.500
Minor League Totals (4 years)				.297	206	784	159	233	43	12	8	84	96	176	61	.378	.413

26 CONNOR SCOTT, OF

BA GRADE
45 Risk: High

Born: Oct 8, 1999. **B-T:** L-L. **HT:** 6-3. **WT:** 187. **Drafted:** HS—Tampa, 2018 (1st round). **Signed by:** Donovan O'Dowd (Marlins).

TRACK RECORD: Scott was the 13th overall pick in 2018, out of Tampa's Plant High, which also produced Astros outfielder Kyle Tucker and Mets first baseman Pete Alonso. The Marlins signed Scott for $4,038,200 to keep him from following Alonso's path to playing at Florida. He scuffled in his first two seasons before the pandemic, but produced much better in terms of batting average in 2021 at High-A Beloit. Pittsburgh acquired Scott and righthander Kyle Nicolas from Miami in a November 2021 trade for Gold Glove catcher Jacob Stallings.

SCOUTING REPORT: The development for Scott was always going to take a while and was contingent on him getting stronger, which has happened slowly but surely. The result this year was a solid season that flew a bit under the radar. Scott was one of five players in the minor leagues who—in fewer than 100 games—accumulated 25 doubles, 10 home runs and 14 stolen bases while striking out fewer than 100 times. Further, he was one of just two players to accomplish those feats at age 21 or younger. The Marlins worked with Scott at instructional league to hone his swing decisions, which they believe will help him access more pull-side power as he continues to get stronger. Defensively, scouts see Scott as a potentially average center fielder with a plus arm and above-average speed.

THE FUTURE: Scott's first test at the upper levels should come in 2022, when he'll advance to Double-A. He has the ceiling of a regular center fielder on a second-division club or a backup on a championship contender.

Year	Age	Club (Level)	Lge	AVG	G	AB	R	H	2B	3B	HR	RBI	BB	SO	SB	OBP	SLG
2021	21	Beloit (HiA)	Cent	.276	96	395	80	109	25	6	10	46	31	92	14	.333	.446
Minor League Totals (4 years)				.253	268	1050	167	266	56	15	16	100	97	265	46	.319	.381

27 TUCUPITA MARCANO, 2B/OF

BA GRADE
40 Risk: Medium

Born: Sep 16, 1999. **B-T:** L-R. **HT:** 6-0. **WT:** 170. **Signed:** Venezuela, 2016. **Signed by:** Antonio Alejos, Chris Kemp, Yfrain Linares (Padres).

TRACK RECORD: The Padres signed Marcano out of Venezuela for $320,000 in 2016. He built a reputation as a hitting machine against older pitchers and made San Diego's Opening Day roster in 2021 despite never playing in the upper levels. Marcano was the key prospect included in the Padres' deadline deal with Pittsburgh for second baseman Adam Frazier. He spent the rest of the season with Triple-A Indianapolis.

SCOUTING REPORT: Without much power, Marcano's profile heavily relies on his exceptional barrel awareness and strike-zone control. He makes it work, using his direct, compact lefthanded swing and deft pitch recognition allows him to spray line drives to all fields at will. Marcano rarely generates much impact, though, because he lacks sufficient strength in his thin frame. Scouts believe Marcano looks most comfortable at second base, but is likely ticketed for a utility role in the big leagues because of his versatility. He appeared at second base, shortstop, third base and both corner outfield positions in 2021.

THE FUTURE: It's easy to forget Marcano will be just 22 years old on Opening Day. He's yet another potential option in the Pirates' wide-open second base competition entering 2022.

Year	Age	Club (Level)	Lge	AVG	G	AB	R	H	2B	3B	HR	RBI	BB	SO	SB	OBP	SLG
2021	21	El Paso (AAA)	West	.273	45	172	31	47	7	2	6	27	27	26	4	.366	.442
	21	Indianapolis (AAA)	East	.230	48	183	29	42	4	1	1	12	26	33	8	.325	.279
	21	San Diego (MLB)	NL	.182	25	44	7	8	1	0	0	3	6	9	0	.280	.205
Major League Totals (1 year)				.182	25	44	7	8	1	0	0	3	6	9	0	.280	.205
Minor League Totals (5 years)				.271	305	1179	177	319	39	11	10	125	152	135	52	.354	.348

28 CANAAN SMITH-NJIGBA, OF

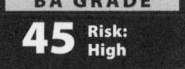

BA GRADE
45 Risk: High

Born: April 30, 1999. **B-T:** L-R. **HT:** 6-0. **WT:** 240. **Drafted:** HS—Rockwall, Texas, 2017 (4th round). **Signed by:** Mike Leuzinger (Yankees).

TRACK RECORD: The Pirates acquired Smith-Njigba via the Yankees in the January 2021 Jameson Taillon trade. He missed six weeks with a thigh injury in 2021, but got on base at a nearly 40% clip when healthy for Double-A Altoona and earned a promotion to Triple-A Indianapolis at the end of the season. Pittsburgh added Smith-Njigba to the 40-man roster after the season.

SCOUTING REPORT: Smith-Njigba packs a lot of strength onto his sturdy 240-pound frame, leading to impressive exit velocities. His discerning eye allows him to wait for pitches he can punish. He needs to hit the ball in the air more to maximize his bat speed. His groundball rate spiked to 66% in 2021. Smith-Njigba's body is mature for his age, but he was a star high school quarterback, while his younger brother Jaxon is a star wide receiver at Ohio State. He's an average runner underway and shows impressive basestealing instincts. Defensively, he's likely limited to left field as a fringe-average defender and thrower.

THE FUTURE: Smith-Njigba's combination of hitting ability and power potential could be enough to carve out a corner outfield role in the big leagues.

Year	Age	Club (Level)	Lge	AVG	G	AB	R	H	2B	3B	HR	RBI	BB	SO	SB	OBP	SLG
2021	22	Altoona (AA)	NEast	.274	66	219	11	60	11	0	6	40	45	66	13	.398	.406
	22	Indianapolis (AAA)	East	.095	7	21	1	2	0	0	0	2	2	9	0	.174	.095
Minor League Totals (5 years)				.275	299	1028	145	283	61	4	25	160	186	279	34	.387	.415

29 KYLE NICOLAS, RHP

BA GRADE
45 Risk: High

Born: Feb. 22, 1999. **B-T:** R-R. **HT:** 6-4. **WT:** 223. **Drafted:** Ball State, 2020 (2nd round supplemental). **Signed by:** Joe Dunigan (Marlins).

TRACK RECORD: Nicolas' strikeout and walk rates improved at Ball State in the brief 2020 season, leading to the Marlins to draft him with the 61st overall pick. He spent his first year as a pro between High-A Beloit and Double-A Pensacola. The Pirates acquired him with Connor Scott in a deal for catcher Jacob Stallings in November.

SCOUTING REPORT: Nicolas' pure stuff is excellent. His mix is fronted by a four-seam fastball that averages 94 mph and has touched as high as 98. The pitch gets swings and misses thanks to its spin rate, horizontal break and vertical approach angle. Nicolas backs his fastball with a trio of a low-80s curveball, a mid-80s slider and a mid-80s changeup, with the curveball being thrown the most frequently. None of his offspeed pitches jumps off the page for anything but velocity, though both breaking balls get swings and misses at above-average or better rates. The changeup needs the most work, and its development was a focal point throughout the year.

THE FUTURE: Nicolas has the body and arm of a power pitcher, but in his first test as a pro did not show the control or command required to start. If that doesn't improve, he's likely bound for a bullpen role.

Year	Age	Club (Level)	Lge	W	L	ERA	G	GS	IP	H	HR	BB	SO	BB/9	SO/9	WHIP	AVG
2021	22	Beloit (HiA)	Cent	3	2	5.28	13	12	59	57	13	24	86	3.6	13.0	1.36	.246
	22	Pensacola (AA)	South	3	2	2.52	8	8	39	23	3	25	50	5.7	11.4	1.22	.167
Minor League Totals (2 years)				6	4	4.18	21	20	99	80	16	49	136	4.45	12.36	1.30	.216

30 CODY BOLTON, RHP

BA GRADE
45 Risk: High

Born: June 19, 1998. **B-T:** R-R. **HT:** 6-3. **WT:** 185. **Drafted:** HS—Tracy, Calif., 2017 (6th round). **Signed by:** Mike Sansoe.

TRACK RECORD: A velocity bump helped Bolton rise to Double-A Altoona in 2019 and emerge as one of Pittsburgh's top prospects. He hasn't pitched in an official game since. Bolton missed all of 2021 after having knee surgery in May. Injuries have frequently stalled his development: He missed time with a forearm injury in 2018 and a groin strain in 2019.

SCOUTING REPORT: Bolton's pitch mix is aggressive. His fastball touches 97 mph and regularly sits 93-96. His two-seam fastball is a touch slower, but generates plenty of ground balls, and he added a cutterish slider in 2019 that flashed above-average. His lengthy arm path concerned evaluators in the past, but he was a solid strike-thrower at the lower levels. Bolton spent much of 2021 rehabbing at the Pirates' complex in Florida, and the team is encouraged with the improvements he has made with his conditioning.

THE FUTURE: Bolton needs to stay healthy to achieve his ceiling of a No. 4 starter, though the lost development and concerns with his delivery could ultimately push him to the bullpen.

Year	Age	Club (Level)	Lge	W	L	ERA	G	GS	IP	H	HR	BB	SO	BB/9	SO/9	WHIP	AVG
2021	23	Did not play—Injured															
Minor League Totals (4 years)				11	11	3.36	39	39	172	142	14	45	169	2.36	8.86	1.09	.222

MORE PROSPECTS TO KNOW

31 MASON MARTIN, 1B
Martin's mammoth lefthanded power rivals anyone in the minors, but swing-and-miss concerns render him to a risky three-outcome type profile.

32 CAL MITCHELL, OF
Mitchell's smooth, lofted lefthanded swing invites comparisons to Michael Brantley and he shows a superb feel to hit. But he also swings frequently, fights a tendency to expand the zone and has, so far, shown just modest power, creating a bit of a challenging profile in left field.

33 LUIS ORTIZ, RHP   SLEEPER
A $25,000 signing out of the Dominican Republic in 2018, Ortiz has steadily added strength and velocity. He sat in the mid 90s and touched 99 mph late in 2021. He pairs his fastball with a swing-and-miss, mid-80s slider and a burgeoning changeup. He has some reliever risk but also breakout potential.

34 BRAXTON ASHCRAFT, RHP
Ashcraft gradually added strength to his starter's frame and was up to 97 mph in 2021, missing more bats than ever before. He had Tommy John Surgery in August and is a name to keep an eye on.

35 CARTER BINS, C
The Pirates acquired Bins at the trade deadline. He's an above-average defensive catcher who handles premium velocity well and gets on base, though there's plenty of strikeouts as well.

36 NICK GARCIA, RHP
Garcia ranked as the No. 56 prospect in the 2020 draft as a converted pitcher after beginning his college career as a third baseman at Division III Chapman. Garcia's sinker-heavy approach generated some intriguing underlying data, but he needs to throw his secondaries for strikes more frequently.

37 OLIVER MATEO, RHP
Mateo is purely a reliever who has two legitimate 70-grade pitches: a triple-digit fastball and a wipe-out slider that elicited a nearly 70% whiff rate when he threw it in the zone. The problem? He walked nearly 10 batters per nine innings, though Pittsburgh believes it may have unlocked better command with a midseason mechanical alteration.

38 JARED TRIOLO, 3B
A plus defender at third base with an unorthodox swing, Triolo began to tap into his power more by narrowing his approach and managing the length to his swing.

39 SANTIAGO FLOREZ, RHP
Scouts love Florez's two-plane breaking ball almost as much as Florez loves throwing it. He uses it more often than his fastball and can land his entire arsenal for strikes.

40 LOLO SANCHEZ, OF
It feels like ages ago when the Pirates made Sanchez their big international signing of 2015. His plate discipline took a step forward in 2021 and his athleticism remains intact, giving him a shot to play all three outfield positions.

TOP PROSPECTS OF THE DECADE

Year	Player, Pos	2021 Org
2012	Gerrit Cole, RHP	Yankees
2013	Gerrit Cole, RHP	Yankees
2014	Gregory Polanco, OF	Pirates
2015	Tyler Glasnow, RHP	Rays
2016	Tyler Glasnow, RHP	Rays
2017	Austin Meadows, OF	Rays
2018	Mitch Keller, RHP	Pirates
2019	Mitch Keller, RHP	Pirates
2020	Mitch Keller, RHP	Pirates
2021	Ke'Bryan Hayes, 3B	Pirates

TOP DRAFT PICKS OF THE DECADE

Year	Player, Pos	2021 Org
2012	*Mark Appel, RHP	Phillies
2013	Austin Meadows, OF	Rays
2014	Cole Tucker, SS	Pirates
2015	Kevin Newman, SS	Pirates
2016	Will Craig, 3B	Kiwoom (Korea)
2017	Shane Baz, RHP	Rays
2018	Travis Swaggerty, OF	Pirates
2019	Quinn Priester, RHP	Pirates
2020	Nick Gonzales, SS	Pirates
2021	Henry Davis, C	Pirates
	*Did not sign	

St. Louis Cardinals

BY CHRIS HILBURN-TRENKLE

A season that looked to be spinning out of control after the Cardinals were swept by the Braves to fall to 53-55 in early August was brought back on course when the Cardinals won eight out of their next nine games. They finished August four games over .500, then won a franchise-record 17 games in a row in September to nab the second wild card spot and advance to the playoffs for the third straight season.

Outfielder Dylan Carlson, the team's No. 1 prospect in 2020 and 2021, solidified his starting spot by appearing in 149 games and finishing third in National League Rookie of the Year voting. Fellow outfielder Tyler O'Neill, the team's No. 2 prospect in 2019, finished top 10  in MVP voting and announced himself as a star, while young arms Genesis Cabrera and Kodi Whitley provided value out of the bullpen.

But the results weren't as encouraging down on the farm, where the Cardinals' domestic affiliates finished with the worst winning percentage in baseball at .394. That winning percentage ranks 1,552nd out of 1,556 organization overall records since 1963, according to Baseball-Reference. That sample encompasses the modern history of the minor leagues.

The Cardinals' system was weakened by trades for all-stars Nolan Arenado and Paul Goldschmidt, but it was not helped by subpar drafting in recent years.

Shortstop Delvin Perez, the 23rd overall pick in 2016, was not added to the 40-man roster in the offseason after several underwhelming seasons. Neither was 2015 first-round outfielder Nick Plummer, who qualified for minor league free agency and signed an MLB deal with the Mets.

In 2017, the Cardinals lost their first-round pick after signing outfielder Dexter Fowler, and then lost their second-round pick and supplemental second-round pick due to a hacking scandal, which left them severely hamstrung in that year's draft.

There is reason for optimism, however. The Cardinals hit on their 2018 first-round pick Nolan Gorman, a powerful slugger on the verge of making his big league debut, and 2020 first-rounder Jordan Walker, who ranks as the team's No. 1 prospect after an impressive debut season that saw him conquer the Class A levels.

In the 2021 draft, the Cardinals accumulated 11 collegiate arms, four of whom rank among the organization's top 30 prospects. First-rounder Michael McGreevy was one of the most polished arms in the draft class and could be a quick riser through the system thanks to his plus-plus control and impressive arsenal of pitches.

And the system saw some players take big leaps

Outfielder Tyler O'Neill won a Gold Glove and finished top 10 in National League MVP voting.

PROJECTED 2025 LINEUP

Catcher	Ivan Herrera	25
First Base	Jordan Walker	23
Second Base	Nolan Gorman	25
Third Base	Nolan Arenado	34
Shortstop	Paul DeJong	31
Left Field	Tyler O'Neill	30
Center Field	Harrison Bader	31
Right Field	Dylan Carlson	26
Designated Hitter	Paul Goldschmidt	37
No. 1 Starter	Jack Flaherty	29
No. 2 Starter	Dakota Hudson	30
No. 3 Starter	Matthew Liberatore	25
No. 4 Starter	Steven Matz	34
No. 5 Starter	Michael McGreevy	25
Closer	Alex Reyes	30

forward, including third baseman Juan Yepez, who put up stellar numbers between Double-A and Triple-A.

Outfielder Lars Nootbaar jumped to the No. 6 spot among the team's top 30 prospects thanks to his plus hit tool and steady defense, which led him to spend the second half of the season on the big league roster.

But the system, which ranked No. 20 at the midseason organization talent rankings, still has plenty of room for improvement.

It appears that the Cardinals nailed the 2020 draft, and the 2021 haul is promising as well. But there remains work to be done down on the farm. ∎

ST. LOUIS CARDINALS

TOP 2022 ROOKIES	RANK
Nolan Gorman, 3B/2B	2
Matthew Liberatore, LHP	3
Juan Yepez, 1B/3B/OF	9
BREAKOUT PROSPECTS	**RANK**
Andre Pallante, RHP	16
Dionys Rodriguez, RHP	21
Inohan Paniagua, RHP	31

SOURCE OF TOP 30 TALENT			
Homegrown	**27**	**Acquired**	**3**
College	12	Trade	3
Junior college	0	Rule 5 draft	0
High school	8	Independent league	0
Nondrafted free agent	0	Free agent/waivers	0
International	7		

LF
Alec Burleson (10)
L.J. Jones

CF

Joshua Baez (7)
Tre Fletcher (22)
Carlos Carmona
Mike Antico

RF
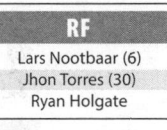
Lars Nootbaar (6)
Jhon Torres (30)
Ryan Holgate

3B
Jordan Walker (1)
Nolan Gorman (2)
Malcom Nunez (17)
Osvaldo Tovalin

SS

Masyn Winn (8)
Delvin Perez (25)
Jeremy Rivas
Kramer Robertson

2B
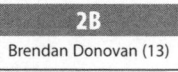
Brendan Donovan (13)

1B
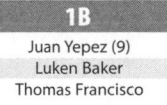
Juan Yepez (9)
Luken Baker
Thomas Francisco

C
Ivan Herrera (5)
Julio Rodriguez (27)

LHP

LHSP	LHRP
Matthew Liberatore (3)	Alfredo Ruiz
Zack Thompson (12)	Evan Sisk
Connor Thomas (28)	Garrett Williams
Levi Prater	

RHP

RHSP	RHRP
Michael McGreevy (4)	Edwin Nunez (18)
Masyn Winn (8)	Kodi Whitley (19)
Tink Hence (11)	Dionys Rodriguez (21)
Austin Love (14)	Jake Walsh (24)
Gordon Graceffo (15)	Jose Davila (29)
Andre Pallante (16)	Freddy Pacheco
Angel Rondon (20)	Tommy Parsons
Alec Willis (23)	Ian Bedell
Zane Mills (26)	Alvaro Seijas
Inohan Paniagua	Griffin Roberts

1 JORDAN WALKER, 3B

Born: May 22, 2002. **B-T:** R-R. **HT:** 6-5. **WT:** 220.
Drafted: HS—Decatur, Ga., 2020 (1st round).
Signed by: Charles Peterson.

TRACK RECORD: Walker used an impressive start to the 2020 spring before the coronavirus pandemic shut down the season to vault himself forward on draft boards, resulting with a selection by the Cardinals with the 21st pick in the draft. He signed for a below-slot deal of $2.9 million to forego a commitment to Duke. He then had one of the best pro debuts of any 2020 draftee, hitting his way out of Low-A Palm Beach in 2021 after 27 games and ranking as the No. 2 prospect in Low-A Southeast. He continued to hit well at High-A Peoria, where he ranked as the No. 3 prospect in High-A Central. He stood out for his combination of power and feel for hitting, thus solidifying himself as the top prospect in the organization. Walker finished the season hitting .317/.388/.548 between the Class A levels with 14 home runs, 25 doubles and 14 stolen bases in 82 games, earning the organization's minor league player of the year honors while shooting onto the Top 100 Prospects ranking.

SCOUTING REPORT: Walker has an imposing 6-foot-5, 220-pound frame and rare strength for a teenager, crushing a ball at 116 mph off the bat in his first month as a professional. He's got a good feel for hitting and an advanced approach for the game, impressing the organization with the way he made adjustments on the fly. The length to Walker's swing produces some swing-and-miss issues, but he does a good job of catching up to velocity and has good knowledge of the strike zone. Walker hits the ball to all fields and should project for at least an average hit tool in the future to go along with plus-plus power as he matures. He posted a 15% walk rate and 17% strikeout rate at Low-A, but struggled to a 6% walk rate and 27% strikeout rate against more advanced pitchers at High-A, which is common for a young hitter facing more advanced arms. Some scouts believe he'll continue to have trouble with spin due to his aggressiveness as a hitter. However, Walker does a good job of making adjustments on the fly and rarely makes the same mistake twice. Walker is a good athlete, runs well for his size and worked hard to improve at third base. He has good footwork and above-average arm strength, but he will need to improve his instincts and reactions to stick at the hot corner. Opposing scouts are split on whether he will fit at third base, with some believing he'll end up at first base or right field,

TOM DiPACE

BA GRADE	SCOUTING GRADES
60 Risk: High	Hit: 50. Power: 70. Run: 45. Field: 45. Arm: 55.

Projected future grades on 20-80 scouting scale

BEST TOOLS

Best Hitter for Average	Juan Yepez
Best Power Hitter	Jordan Walker
Best Strike-Zone Discipline	Lars Nootbaar
Fastest Baserunner	Masyn Winn
Best Athlete	Masyn Winn
Best Fastball	Edwin Nunez
Best Curveball	Michael McGreevy
Best Slider	Seth Elledge
Best Changeup	Matthew Liberatore
Best Control	Michael McGreevy
Best Defensive Catcher	Julio Rodriguez
Best Defensive Infielder	Delvin Perez
Best Infield Arm	Masyn Winn
Best Defensive Outfielder	Tre Fletcher
Best Outfield Arm	Joshua Baez

where his arm and offensive ability will profile well. Walker has an excellent work ethic, which should help give him a chance to stick at third base moving forward.

THE FUTURE: Walker's combination of tools and performance fit the profile of a future middle-of-the-order masher who could one day hit 35 home runs in a season. After the way he performed at the Class A levels in 2021, he looks ready for an assignment to Double-A, and it's not out of the question that he could make it to Triple-A by the end of the 2022 season, setting himself up for a 2023 major league debut. ∎

Year	Age	Club (Level)	Lge	AVG	G	AB	R	H	2B	3B	HR	RBI	BB	SO	SB	OBP	SLG
2021	19	Palm Beach (LoA)	SEast	.374	27	99	24	37	11	1	6	21	18	21	1	.475	.687
	19	Peoria (HiA)	Cent	.292	55	226	39	66	14	3	8	27	15	66	13	.344	.487
Minor League Totals (2 years)				.317	82	325	63	103	25	4	14	48	33	87	14	.388	.548

2 NOLAN GORMAN, 3B/2B

Born: May 10, 2000. **B-T:** L-R. **HT:** 6-1. **WT:** 210. **Drafted:** HS—Phoenix, 2018 (1st round). **Signed by:** Mauricio Rubio.

TRACK RECORD: The top prep power hitter in the 2018 draft class, Gorman spent the 2019 season at the Class A levels before impressing at 2020 spring training and spending the summer at the alternate training site, where he continued to stand out offensively. He made his upper minors debut in 2021 and put together his best year as a pro. Gorman led the Cardinals organization with 231 total bases and finished third with 25 home runs as he climbed from Double-A Springfield to Triple-A Memphis, and did it while lowering his strikeout rate the higher he climbed.

BA GRADE

60 Risk: High

SCOUTING REPORT: Gorman transitioned from third base to second base after the Cardinals acquired Nolan Arenado from the Rockies before the season. He impressed the organization with his range and actions while continuing to work on improving his footwork turning double plays. He has plus arm strength and projects to be a fringe-average, but playable, defender at the keystone. Regardless of position, it'll be Gorman's bat that makes him an above-average everyday player. He has plus-plus raw power and can hit a home run out of any park. He destroys pitches down in the zone and consistently posts high exit velocities. Gorman is an aggressive hitter who doesn't walk much and is prone to chasing, but he makes enough contact to regularly access his power.

THE FUTURE: Gorman is on track to be a middle-of-the order slugger who hits 30-35 home runs per year. He is in position to make his major league debut sometime during the 2022 season.

SCOUTING GRADES:	Hitting: 45	Power: 70	Running: 40	Fielding: 45	Arm: 60

Year	Age	Club (Level)	Lge	AVG	G	AB	R	H	2B	3B	HR	RBI	BB	SO	SB	OBP	SLG
2021	21	Memphis (AAA)	East	.274	76	303	45	83	14	1	14	48	20	63	3	.320	.465
	21	Springfield (AA)	Cent	.288	43	177	26	51	6	0	11	27	18	52	4	.354	.508
Minor League Totals (4 years)				.269	307	1173	185	316	63	8	57	181	117	343	10	.340	.483

3 MATTHEW LIBERATORE, LHP

Born: Nov. 6, 1999. **B-T:** L-L. **HT:** 6-5. **WT:** 200. **Drafted:** HS—Glendale, Ariz., 2018 (1st round). **Signed by:** David Hamlett (Rays).

TRACK RECORD: The top prep pitcher in the 2018 draft class, Liberatore surprisingly fell in the draft before the Rays scooped him up with the 16th overall pick. He impressed in his full-season debut at Low-A in 2019 before being traded to the Cardinals in the deal that sent Randy Arozarena to Tampa Bay. The Cardinals aggressively pushed Liberatore to Triple-A to start the 2021 season despite the fact he was 21 years old and had never pitched above Low-A. He understandably struggled at the start of the season but improved as the year progressed and logged a 2.67 ERA in his final 10 starts.

BA GRADE

55 Risk: Medium

SCOUTING REPORT: Liberatore has a well-rounded four-pitch arsenal and is polished beyond his years. His fastball velocity ranges from 89-93 mph on some days to 92-96 mph on others, but it gets carry at the top of the zone with good running life at any velocity to remain an effective pitch. Liberatore throws a trio of impressive secondaries, led by an above-average, upper-70s curveball that has hard, late snap and downer action. His curveball was his clear out pitch in previous years, but it's arguably been surpassed by his above-average, low-80s slider with late, three-quarters tilt. His changeup gives him a fourth above-average offering as a low-80s pitch he sets up well and uses to finish off batters. Liberatore is a cerebral pitcher with a good feel for mixing his pitches and reading swings. His repeatable delivery and clean arm action from the left side portend at least above-average control.

THE FUTURE: Liberatore has the pitchability and well-rounded arsenal to be a solid No. 3 starter. It shouldn't be long before he makes his big league debut in 2022.

SCOUTING GRADES:	Fastball: 55	Slider: 55	Curveball: 55	Changeup: 55	Control: 55

Year	Age	Club (Level)	Lge	W	L	ERA	G	GS	IP	H	HR	BB	SO	BB/9	SO/9	WHIP	AVG
2021	21	Memphis (AAA)	East	9	9	4.04	22	18	124	123	19	33	123	2.4	8.9	1.25	.257
Minor League Totals (4 years)				17	13	3.36	47	42	236	214	21	77	236	2.94	9.01	1.23	.242

4 MICHAEL McGREEVY, RHP

Born: July 8, 2000. **B-T:** R-R. **HT:** 6-4. **WT:** 215. **Drafted:** UC Santa Barbara, 2021 (1st round). **Signed by:** Michael Garciaparra.

TRACK RECORD: McGreevy made an immediate impact at UC Santa Barbara by earning freshman All-America honors as a reliever in 2019 and posting a 0.99 ERA in four starts in 2020 before the coronavirus pandemic shut down the season. He built on that success and solidified himself as the best pitcher on the West Coast during his junior season, posting a 2.92 ERA with 115 strikeouts and only 11 walks in 101.2 innings. The Cardinals drafted him 18th overall and signed him for $2.75 million. McGreevy made seven starts split between the Florida Complex League and Low-A Palm Beach after he signed, throwing no more than two innings in any outing.

BA GRADE
55 Risk: High

SCOUTING REPORT: McGreevy is a control artist who also happens to have four above-average or better pitches. His fastball sits in the low 90s and tops out at 96 mph. The pitch plays up with armside sink and finish, and he is able to effectively locate it to both sides of the plate. McGreevy's curveball is his most effective secondary offering as a top-to-bottom hammer that flashes plus. He rounds out his four-pitch mix with a mid-80s slider and a changeup that flash above-average as well. McGreevy ties everything together with plus-plus control. He floods the strike zone with all of his pitches and his few misses are very small. McGreevy is an excellent athlete with a strong, durable build at 6-foot-4, 200 pounds and still has some projection remaining.

THE FUTURE: McGreevy has all the ingredients to be a mid-rotation starter. He should start the season at High-A and could move quickly.

SCOUTING GRADES:	Fastball: 55	Slider: 50	Curveball: 60	Changeup: 50	Control: 70

Year	Age	Club (Level)	Lge	W	L	ERA	G	GS	IP	H	HR	BB	SO	BB/9	SO/9	WHIP	AVG
2021	20	Cardinals (R)	FCL	0	2	10.80	2	2	1	4	0	1	3	5.4	16.2	3.00	.444
	20	Palm Beach (LoA)	SEast	0	0	9.00	5	5	6	10	1	1	4	1.5	6.0	1.83	.357
Minor League Totals (1 year)				0	2	9.39	7	7	8	14	1	2	7	2.35	8.22	2.09	.378

5 IVAN HERRERA, C

Born: June 1, 2000. **B-T:** R-R. **HT:** 5-11. **WT:** 220. **Signed:** Panama, 2016. **Signed by:** Damaso Espino.

TRACK RECORD: Herrera signed with the Cardinals for $200,000 when he was 16 and immediately became one of the most productive hitters in their system. He spent 2020 spring training learning under Yadier Molina's tutelage and was invited to the Cardinals alternate training site in the summer. Herrera jumped to Double-A in 2021 and experienced his first offensive struggles with a career-worst .229/.342/.403 slash line, but he still hit 17 home runs and earned a promotion to Triple-A Memphis for his last game of the season.

SCOUTING REPORT: Known for his above-average hitting ability, Herrera has a compact swing and makes solid contact. He has a good approach at the plate and does a good job of controlling the strike zone with low chase rates. Herrera posts low exit velocities and doesn't hit the ball very hard with

BA GRADE
50 Risk: High

fringe-average power, but he makes so much contact he is still able to pick up extra-base hits. Herrera's defense behind the plate is further behind. His receiving regressed during the coronavirus shutdown and he struggled with drops throughout the 2021 season. At his best, Herrera flashes good hands, moves well and has average arm strength, but he has long demonstrated a lack of focus and intensity that prevents him from performing up to his capabilities of being an above-average defender.

THE FUTURE: Herrera will have to improve his defense to be Yadier Molina's successor as the Cardinals catcher. He will still be only 21 when he begins next season at Triple-A and has plenty of time to rebound both offensively and defensively from a difficult 2021.

SCOUTING GRADES:	Hitting: 55	Power: 45	Running: 30	Fielding: 55	Arm: 50

Year	Age	Club (Level)	Lge	AVG	G	AB	R	H	2B	3B	HR	RBI	BB	SO	SB	OBP	SLG
2021	21	Springfield (AA)	Cent	.231	98	363	50	84	13	0	17	63	60	96	2	.346	.408
	21	Memphis (AAA)	East	.000	1	4	0	0	0	0	0	0	0	0	0	.000	.000
Minor League Totals (5 years)				.278	265	959	142	267	44	4	28	162	129	226	6	.375	.420

6 LARS NOOTBAAR, OF

Born: Sept. 8, 1997. **B-T:** L-R. **HT:** 6-3. **WT:** 210. **Drafted:** Southern California, 2018 (8th round). **Signed by:** Michael Garciaparra.

TRACK RECORD: Drafted in the eighth round in 2018 out of Southern California, Nootbaar advanced from Low-A all the way to Double-A in his first full season in 2019. He spent the summer of 2020 working as a mechanic during the coronavirus shutdown, but the time away from the field didn't hurt him. Nootbaar broke out offensively at Triple-A Memphis in 2021 and earned his first callup to the majors in late June. He returned to the majors for good in late July and appeared in 58 games overall for the Cardinals, mostly as a pinch-hitter and defensive replacement.

BA GRADE

45 Risk: Medium

SCOUTING REPORT: Nootbaar's intelligence and work ethic stand out in the organization. He's shown an ability to catch up quickly to each new assignment and has progressed rapidly in limited time as a professional. Nootbaar has the tools to be an above-average hitter with his advanced, patient approach at the plate. He rarely swings at bad pitches and has had nearly as many walks as strikeouts throughout every level of his career. Nootbaar possesses good bat speed and his strong, 6-foot-3, 210-pound frame should allow him to access more power in the future. His power is currently fringy, however. Nootbaar is a good athlete with average arm strength who should be able to stick in either corner outfield spot. He has below-average speed but covers enough ground with his long strides and solid route-running.

THE FUTURE: Nootbaar's improvements have turned him from an up-and-down player to a potential everyday outfielder. He'll likely be on the Cardinals' Opening Day roster in 2022.

SCOUTING GRADES:	Hitting: 55	Power: 45	Running: 40	Fielding: 50	Arm: 50

Year	Age	Club (Level)	Lge	AVG	G	AB	R	H	2B	3B	HR	RBI	BB	SO	SB	OBP	SLG
2021	23	Memphis (AAA)	East	.308	35	117	21	36	2	1	6	19	17	25	1	.404	.496
	23	St. Louis (MLB)	NL	.239	58	109	15	26	3	1	5	15	13	28	2	.317	.422
Major League Totals (1 year)				.239	58	109	15	26	3	1	5	15	13	28	2	.317	.422
Minor League Totals (4 years)				.261	192	656	74	171	16	3	15	83	84	123	7	.347	.363

7 JOSHUA BAEZ, OF

Born: June 28, 2003. **B-T:** R-R. **HT:** 6-4. **WT:** 220. **Drafted:** HS—Brookline, Mass., 2021 (2nd round). **Signed by:** Jim Negrych.

TRACK RECORD: Baez impressed on the high school summer showcase circuit with an impressive array of tools and a physical, 6-foot-3, 220-pound frame. He struggled with strikeouts during his high school senior season, but the Cardinals still drafted him with the 54th overall pick and gave him an over-slot $2.25 million signing bonus to forgo a Vanderbilt commitment. Baez reported to the Florida Complex League after signing and showed off his big tools, but he also hit .158 with 28 strikeouts in 95 plate appearances.

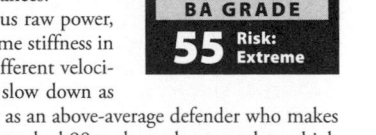

TOM DIPACE

BA GRADE

55 Risk: Extreme

SCOUTING REPORT: Baez has impressive bat speed and plus-plus raw power, but there are questions surrounding his ability to hit. He has some stiffness in his swings and a hand drop that hurts his ability to adapt to different velocities. Baez played center field in high school, but he's likely to slow down as he matures and will need to move to a corner, where he profiles as an above-average defender who makes good reads and takes good routes. He has a plus-plus arm and touched 98 mph on the mound as a high school senior. The Cardinals believe he will improve as a hitter as he gets more at-bats under his belt. Baez was one of the youngest players in the draft and didn't turn 18 until the end of June.

THE FUTURE: Baez is a high-risk, high-reward player. He has the strength and physicality to dream about him hitting 30-plus home runs in the major leagues, but he'll need to make significantly more contact to get to that point. He'll likely start the 2022 season at Low-A.

SCOUTING GRADES:	Hitting: 40	Power: 70	Running: 40	Fielding: 55	Arm: 70

Year	Age	Club (Level)	Lge	AVG	G	AB	R	H	2B	3B	HR	RBI	BB	SO	SB	OBP	SLG
2021	18	Cardinals (R)	FCL	.158	23	76	18	12	3	1	2	8	14	28	5	.305	.303
Minor League Totals (1 year)				.158	23	76	18	12	3	1	2	8	14	28	5	.305	.303

8 MASYN WINN, SS/RHP

TOM DIPACE

Born: March 21, 2002. **B-T:** R-R. **HT:** 5-11. **WT:** 180. **Drafted:** HS—Kingwood, Texas, 2020 (2nd round). **Signed by:** Jabari Barnett.

TRACK RECORD: Winn excelled at both shortstop and on the mound for Kingwood (Texas) High and stood out with an impressive two-way performance at the World Wood Bat Association Championships in the fall of 2019. He lost most of his senior year due to the coronavirus pandemic, but the Cardinals still drafted him 54th overall and gave him an above-slot $2.1 million signing bonus to forgo an Arkansas commitment. Winn made his pro debut in 2021 and played shortstop nearly exclusively in 97 games across both Class A levels, but he did make one appearance as a pitcher.

SCOUTING REPORT: Winn has arguably the strongest arm of any shortstop in the majors and minors. By the middle of July he already had 15 throws across the diamond at 92 mph or harder, more than twice as many as all major league infielders combined. The Cardinals were pleased with Winn's development as a hitter at Low-A, but opposing scouts are split on whether he will hit enough to remain a position player moving forward. He does a good job staying in the middle of the field and adjusting his swing, but he struggles mightily with spin and is overly prone to chasing out of the strike zone. He'll need to work on his approach and strike-zone discipline to become even a below-average hitter, and he has below-average power. The Cardinals would like to give Winn more opportunities on the mound in 2022. His fastball sits in the mid 90s and touches 98 to go with a hard slider that flashes plus and a developing changeup.

THE FUTURE: Winn will start the 2022 season back at High-A. He will get more opportunities to prove himself as a two-way prospect, but he is trending toward ending up a pitcher long-term.

BA GRADE
50 Risk: Very High

SCOUTING GRADES:	Hitting: 40	Power: 40	Running: 70	Fielding: 60	Arm: 80
SCOUTING GRADES:	Fastball: 70	Slider: 55	Changeup: 50	Control: 40	

Year	Age	Club (Level)	Lge	AVG	G	AB	R	H	2B	3B	HR	RBI	BB	SO	SB	OBP	SLG
2021	19	Palm Beach (LoA)	SEast	.262	61	237	50	62	15	3	3	34	40	60	16	.370	.388
	19	Peoria (HiA)	Cent	.209	36	148	26	31	4	2	2	10	6	40	16	.240	.304
Minor League Totals (2 years)				.242	97	385	76	93	19	5	5	44	46	100	32	.324	.356

9 JUAN YEPEZ, 1B

Born: Feb. 19, 1998. **B-T:** R-R. **HT:** 6-1. **WT:** 200. **Signed:** Venezuela, 2014. **Signed by:** Rolando Petit (Braves).

TRACK RECORD: Yepez signed with the Braves out of Venezuela in 2014 and was traded to the Cardinals in 2017 in exchange for Matt Adams. Yepez didn't look like much of a prospect his first three years in the organization but broke out in a big way in 2021. He hit .286 with 27 home runs, 77 RBIs and a .969 OPS as he rose to Triple-A Memphis and was added to the Cardinals roster for the National League Wild Card Game. Yepez went to the Arizona Fall League after the season and continued to swing the bat well with seven home runs and a 1.028 OPS in 23 games.

SCOUTING REPORT: Yepez gained about 20 pounds of muscle coming into the 2021 season, which led to more hard contact and the best season of his career. Now that he's gotten stronger, Yepez checks a lot of boxes as a hitter. He consistently barrels the ball, shows a patient approach and rarely chases pitches out of the strike zone. He has struggled at times with spin, but he destroys fastballs at any velocity. He has improved facing lefthanded pitching to reduce his platoon split and altogether projects to be an average hitter with above-average power. Yepez previously was versatile enough to play first base, third base and left field, but the added bulk and muscle has reduced his mobility. He is a well below-average runner and below-average defender who is limited strictly to first base and may have to be a DH.

THE FUTURE: Yepez is blocked by Paul Goldschmidt in St. Louis, but the permanent addition of the DH in the National League would open up a spot for him. He should make his major league debut in 2022.

BA GRADE
45 Risk: Medium

SCOUTING GRADES:	Hitting: 50	Power: 55	Running: 30	Fielding: 40	Arm: 50

Year	Age	Club (Level)	Lge	AVG	G	AB	R	H	2B	3B	HR	RBI	BB	SO	SB	OBP	SLG
2021	23	Springfield (AA)	Cent	.270	19	63	11	17	4	0	5	14	9	13	0	.387	.571
	23	Memphis (AAA)	East	.289	92	304	56	88	25	0	22	63	42	69	1	.382	.589
Minor League Totals (7 years)				.274	475	1678	237	460	114	5	53	263	155	392	23	.340	.443

10 ALEC BURLESON, OF/1B

Born: Nov. 25, 1998. **B-T:** L-L. **HT:** 6-2. **WT:** 212. **Drafted:** East Carolina, 2020 (2nd round supplemental). **Signed by:** T.C. Calhoun.

TRACK RECORD: Burleson excelled as a two-way player throughout his college career at East Carolina, including earning a selection to the USA Baseball Collegiate National team, and was drafted by the Cardinals in the supplemental second round in 2020. He made his pro debut in 2021 and rose three levels from High-A to Triple-A, hitting a combined .270/.329/.454 with 22 home runs in 119 games.

SCOUTING REPORT: Previously known as a contact-oriented hitter who rarely struck out, Burleson began taking bigger swings and increased his power production in his pro debut. He shows a propensity for barreling the ball and making hard contact in games, although the added power has come with more strikeouts as he's started expanding the zone. Burleson's bat path is still relatively flat, but he has a chance to add more loft to his swing and hit for even more power in the future. He should even out as an average hitter with average power. Burleson at times plays average defense in left and right field, but his arm is fringy despite his two-way background and he needs to be more consistent. He can also play first base, where he shows good footwork and actions.

THE FUTURE: Burleson should start the 2022 season back at Triple-A. His major league debut won't be far off if he continues to swing the bat well.

BA GRADE
45 Risk: Medium

SCOUTING GRADES:	Hitting: 50	Power: 50	Running: 40	Fielding: 45	Arm: 45

Year	Age	Club (Level)	Lge	AVG	G	AB	R	H	2B	3B	HR	RBI	BB	SO	SB	OBP	SLG
2021	22	Peoria (HiA)	Cent	.286	11	42	8	12	1	0	4	10	6	15	1	.367	.595
	22	Springfield (AA)	Cent	.288	63	260	34	75	10	0	14	44	19	59	2	.333	.488
	22	Memphis (AAA)	East	.234	45	154	19	36	7	0	4	22	17	27	0	.310	.357
Minor League Totals (2 years)				.270	119	456	61	123	18	0	22	76	42	101	3	.329	.454

11 TINK HENCE, RHP

BA GRADE
55 Risk: Extreme

Born: Aug. 6, 2002. **B-T:** R-R. **HT:** 6-1. **WT:** 175. **Drafted:** HS—Pine Bluff, Ark., 2020 (2nd round supplemental). **Signed by:** Dirk Kinney.

TRACK RECORD: The Cardinals drafted Hence in the supplemental second round in 2020 and signed him to an over-slot $1.15 million deal to lure him away from Arkansas. He was brought along slowly in 2021, appearing in just eight games in the Florida Complex League.

SCOUTING REPORT: Hence saw his prospect status shoot up during his senior year after an impressive summer showcase circuit. He has a projectable body with room to fill out, and is already throwing a fastball that sits 90-93 mph and tops out at 95-96 mph from the right side. His breaking balls are his best weapons, a slider and curveball that he shows feel to spin. Both flash plus potential, and he rounds out his arsenal with a changeup that flashes average at times. The Cardinals intentionally brought Hence along slowly, wanting him to have a full season of preparation under his belt before making his full-season debut in 2022. They were encouraged by his mound presence and feel for pitching that he showed in the FCL.

THE FUTURE: Hence has the arsenal to one day start in the major leagues, but he's years away from reaching that point. He'll make his full-season debut in 2022.

Year	Age	Club (Level)	Lge	W	L	ERA	G	GS	IP	H	HR	BB	SO	BB/9	SO/9	WHIP	AVG
2021	18	Cardinals (R)	FCL	0	1	9.00	8	1	8	11	1	3	14	3.4	15.8	1.75	.306
Minor League Totals (2 years)				0	1	9.00	8	1	8	11	1	3	14	3.38	15.75	1.75	.306

12 ZACK THOMPSON, LHP

BA GRADE
45 Risk: High

Born: Oct. 28, 1997. **B-T:** L-L. **HT:** 6-2. **WT:** 225. **Drafted:** Kentucky, 2019 (1st round). **Signed by:** Jason Bryans.

TRACK RECORD: After a dominant junior season at Kentucky the Cardinals drafted Thompson in the first round in 2019, and he made 11 appearances out of the bullpen at High-A Palm Beach after signing. He stood out in 2020 at spring training, then spent the summer at the alternate training site. Thompson made his upper minors debut at Triple-A Memphis in 2021, where he struggled mightily, proving to be far too hittable and posting 5.5 walks per nine innings and a 7.06 ERA.

SCOUTING REPORT: Thompson previously stood out for his loud arsenal, including a fastball that sat 91-94 mph and topped out at 97, but opposing scouts watched as his velocity backed up significantly early in the 2021 season. He sat 87-88 mph with big running life and pitched with restriction in his shoulder. Thompson's velocity began to pick up as the season progressed, and he was back to sitting 91-94 mph in the Arizona Fall League, where he struck out 22 batters over 17.1 innings of work. His slider sat in the low 80s in the AFL with a low spin rate and flat break, and his plus curveball had high spin rates exceeding 3,000 rpm. However, the curve has very little power, sitting 69-72 mph. Thompson rounds out his arsenal with a changeup that flashes average. Thompson has struggled with his below-average control at times, and it's imperative that he throws more consistent strikes, especially if his velocity continues to fluctuate. **THE FUTURE:** Thompson once looked like a mid-rotation arm, but the 2021 season was a step in the wrong direction. He'll head back to Triple-A Memphis in 2022, where he'll look to regain his velocity and improve his strike-throwing ability.

Year	Age	Club (Level)	Lge	W	L	ERA	G	GS	IP	H	HR	BB	SO	BB/9	SO/9	WHIP	AVG
2021	23	Memphis (AAA)	East	2	10	7.06	22	19	93	114	18	57	82	5.5	7.9	1.84	.302
Minor League Totals (3 years)				2	10	6.56	35	21	108	133	18	61	105	5.07	8.72	1.79	.302

13 BRENDAN DONOVAN, 2B/OF

BA GRADE
45 Risk: High

Born: Jan. 16, 1997. **B-T:** L-R. **HT:** 6-1. **WT:** 195. **Drafted:** South Alabama, 2018 (7th round). **Signed by:** Clint Brown

TRACK RECORD: The 2018 seventh-rounder from South Alabama played in just four games in the New York-Penn League after signing before making his full-season debut at Low-A in 2019, where he put up solid numbers. Donovan wasn't at the Cardinals alternate training site in 2020 but started the 2021 season on a tear, quickly advancing out of High-A after 25 games. He spent 50 games at Double-A Springfield before finishing the season at Triple-A Memphis. He hit .308 with two homers in the Arizona Fall League to wrap up the season.

SCOUTING REPORT: Donovan wasn't much of a prospect coming into the year but his performance helped shoot him onto the prospect scene. He's a line-to-line hitter who gets on base, has a patient approach and doesn't have much swing and miss. He projects to be a plus hitter, with a high contact rate and the ability to hit mid-90s velocity, but the rest of his tools are below-average to fringe-average. Donovan has slightly below-average power and is a fringe-average defender at second base and third base. Some opposing scouts think he'll need to move permanently to left field. The Cardinals were pleased with his development this year and added him to the 40-man roster after the season.

THE FUTURE: Donovan provides good value as a lefthanded bat off the bench on a Cardinals team stocked with righthanded hitters. He should make his big league debut in 2022.

Year	Age	Club (Level)	Lge	AVG	G	AB	R	H	2B	3B	HR	RBI	BB	SO	SB	OBP	SLG
2021	24	Peoria (HiA)	Cent	.295	25	95	15	28	6	0	2	13	10	15	7	.385	.421
	24	Springfield (AA)	Cent	.319	50	185	35	59	10	1	4	28	25	39	8	.411	.449
	24	Memphis (AAA)	East	.288	33	111	23	32	5	0	6	25	15	23	4	.389	.495
Minor League Totals (4 years)				.284	226	810	145	230	49	5	20	121	115	175	23	.386	.431

14 AUSTIN LOVE, RHP

BA GRADE
45 Risk: High

Born: Jan. 26, 1999. **B-T:** R-R. **HT:** 6-3. **WT:** 232. **Drafted:** North Carolina, 2021 (3rd round). **Signed by:** T.C. Calhoun

TRACK RECORD: Love worked as a full-time reliever in his first two seasons at North Carolina in 2019 and 2020, but transitioned to the starting rotation for the 2021 season. He put up impressive numbers in 2021 while his draft stock shot up significantly. The Cardinals scooped him up in the third round of the July draft, and Love made seven appearances between the Florida Complex League and Low-A Palm Beach after signing. He allowed one earned run in eight innings.

SCOUTING REPORT: Love uses a fastball that sat 91-94 mph as a starter and topped out at 97-98 mph. He has a pair of offspeed offerings that flash above-average, with a mid-80s slider with vertical break and a mid-80s changeup with fade and tumble. Love stood out to Cardinals officials after signing for the way he competed and his ability to command his three-pitch mix. Some opposing scouts feel Love profiles better in the bullpen, where his fastball would play up, but the Cardinals plan to use him as a starter.

THE FUTURE: Love has the pitch mix and control to profile as a back-end starter, but he could also become a high-leverage reliever.

Year	Age	Club (Level)	Lge	W	L	ERA	G	GS	IP	H	HR	BB	SO	BB/9	SO/9	WHIP	AVG
2021	22	Cardinals (R)	FCL	0	0	1.80	5	5	5	2	1	0	9	0.0	16.2	0.40	.118
	22	Palm Beach (LoA)	SEast	0	0	0.00	2	0	3	1	0	1	4	3.0	12.0	0.67	.111
Minor League Totals (1 year)				0	0	1.13	7	5	8	3	1	1	13	1.13	14.63	0.50	.115

15 GORDON GRACEFFO, RHP

Born: March 17, 2000. **B-T:** R-R. **HT:** 6-4. **WT:** 210. **Drafted:** Villanova, 2021 (5th round). **Signed by:** Jim Negrych.

TRACK RECORD: Following a freshman season at Villanova split between the bullpen and rotation, Graceffo began working as a starter full-time as a sophomore in the shortened 2020 season and put up a 1.42 ERA in four starts. He sustained that level of excellence over the full 2021 season, posting a 7-2, 1.54 mark with 86 strikeouts and 13 walks in 82 innings. The Cardinals were happy to scoop Graceffo up in the fifth round and sign him to an over-slot $500,000 deal. Graceffo jumped straight to Low-A Palm Beach after signing and posted a 1.73 ERA in 11 appearances (one start).

SCOUTING REPORT: Graceffo started the 2021 season sitting 87-91 mph and touching 93, but by the end of the year his velocity ticked up to sit at 94 mph and was up to 98 in pro ball, and at 6-foot-4, 220 pounds he has some projection left to continue adding velocity. He commands the pitch well, pounding both sides of the strike zone. His best secondary is an upper-70s changeup with fading life and sinking action that is at least average and flashes plus. He rounds out his arsenal with a slider that is an above-average offering and a curveball with two-plane break. He also has the feel and strike-throwing ability to start, and the Cardinals were impressed by the way he constantly got into pitcher's counts.

THE FUTURE: After having no trouble at Low-A Palm Beach, Graceffo could start the 2022 season at High-A Peoria. He projects as a back-end starter thanks to his pitch mix and strike-throwing ability.

Year	Age	Club (Level)	Lge	W	L	ERA	G	GS	IP	H	HR	BB	SO	BB/9	SO/9	WHIP	AVG
2021	21	Palm Beach (LoA)	SEast	1	0	1.73	11	1	26	28	1	9	37	3.1	12.8	1.42	.267
Minor League Totals (1 year)				1	0	1.73	11	1	26	28	1	9	37	3.12	12.81	1.42	.267

16 ANDRE PALLANTE, RHP

Born: Sept. 18, 1998. **B-T:** R-R. **HT:** 6-0. **WT:** 203. **Drafted:** UC Irvine, 2019 (4th round). **Signed by:** Eli Tupuola

TRACK RECORD: A 2019 fourth-rounder out of UC Irvine who was a third-team All-American in 2018, Pallante pitched well in the short-season New York-Penn League after signing, but was not at the Cardinals alternate training site in 2020. He showed no signs of rust at Double-A Springfield this season, posting a 3.82 ERA in 21 starts before earning a late-season promotion to Triple-A Memphis. He finished the season in the Arizona Fall League, striking out 22 batters and allowing just three runs in 21 innings while standing out to opposing scouts.

SCOUTING REPORT: At 6 feet, 203 pounds Pallante isn't an imposing figure on the mound, but his fastball is an intimidating offering. The pitch sat 90-92 mph and touched 94 mph when he was in college, but it averaged 95.2 mph in 2021 and topped out at 98 mph in the fall league. The pitch has cutting action and late life, generating ground balls at a high rate, making it an above-average weapon. His low-80s slider is his best offspeed offering, an above-average pitch, and he also throws a low-80s changeup that grades out as average and a mid-70s, hammer curveball that he struggles to command. Pallante has a high arm slot and a delivery with a plunge in the back, which causes him to sometimes lose his balance on the mound, leading some opposing scouts to believe he best profiles in the bullpen. Pallante struggled at times to throw consistent strikes in 2021, but had shown average control before this season.

THE FUTURE: Pallante should start the 2022 season back at Triple-A Memphis, but he could find himself shuttled back and forth between the big leagues as well.

Year	Age	Club (Level)	Lge	W	L	ERA	G	GS	IP	H	HR	BB	SO	BB/9	SO/9	WHIP	AVG
2021	22	Memphis (AAA)	East	0	0	3.60	2	1	5	7	0	4	4	7.2	7.2	2.20	.304
	22	Springfield (AA)	Cent	4	7	3.82	21	21	94	102	8	42	82	4.0	7.8	1.53	.273
Minor League Totals (3 years)				5	7	3.53	34	31	135.0	136	10	57	124	3.80	8.27	1.43	.259

17 MALCOM NUNEZ, 3B

Born: March 9, 2001. **B-T:** R-R. **HT:** 5-11. **WT:** 205. **Signed:** Cuba, 2018. **Signed by:** Alix Martinez/Angel Ovalles.

TRACK RECORD: Nunez, a star at the 2016 15U World Cup, signed with the Cardinals in 2018 out of Cuba, then won the Dominican Summer League triple crown that same year. His encore performance in 2019 failed to live up to expectations, as he struggled between Rookie ball and Low-A, and he spent the 2020 summer at the alternate training site. He got back on track in 2021, quickly advancing out of High-A before spending 54 games at Double-A Springfield.

SCOUTING REPORT: Nunez is likely to always be a bat-first player, but the Cardinals had him focus on improving his defense at the alternate site while working with infield coordinator Jose Oquendo. The organization was encouraged by the gains he made, but opposing scouts are skeptical he can stay at third base due to his lack of mobility and his maxed out body. He has a strong arm that flashes plus. Nunez has fast bat speed and plus power, but opposing scouts are concerned with his setup due to a hand hitch that causes his hands to go up. He might never be an everyday big leaguer, but his bat gives him value off the bench.

THE FUTURE: Nunez will likely start 2022 back at Double-A Springfield, but he could quickly move up to Triple-A Memphis.

Year	Age	Club (Level)	Lge	AVG	G	AB	R	H	2B	3B	HR	RBI	BB	SO	SB	OBP	SLG
2021	20	Peoria (HiA)	Cent	.285	35	137	18	39	10	2	3	20	11	27	5	.351	.453
	20	Springfield (AA)	Cent	.257	54	202	28	52	5	0	6	19	21	44	2	.330	.371
Minor League Totals (4 years)				.291	191	704	109	205	43	4	24	116	76	147	13	.369	.466

18 EDWIN NUNEZ, RHP

BA GRADE
50 Risk: Extreme

Born: Nov. 5, 2001. **B-T:** R-R. **HT:** 6-3. **WT:** 185. **Signed:** Dominican Republic, 2020. **Signed by:** Alix Martinez.

TRACK RECORD: MLB suspended Nunez a year due to a discrepancy with his age, but he officially signed with the Cardinals for $525,000 in June 2020. It didn't take long for Nunez to make his minor league debut, and he spent the 2021 season at Low-A Palm Beach, showing an elite fastball but bottom-of-the-scale control, walking 56 batters in 53.2 innings while posting a 10.90 ERA.

SCOUTING REPORT: Nunez stands out for a 70-grade fastball that comfortably sits in the upper 90s and touches triple-digits, with sinking life. It's the only pitch he's shown much feel to command, as he struggled mightily to locate his two offspeeds. His slider has slurvy shape with a high spin rate and flashes plus, but he's unable to land it with any consistency. He rounds out his arsenal with a power changeup, but it lacks deception and he doesn't have much feel for throwing it. The Cardinals are taking a patient approach with Nunez, understanding it'll take time for his pitchability and command to catch up to his stuff, but opposing scouts are skeptical he'll ever be able to throw enough strikes. Nunez has a repeatable delivery, lending some hope that he could improve his command and control.

THE FUTURE: After an up-and-down debut, Nunez should find himself at High-A Peoria in 2022. He has the stuff to profile as a late-inning reliever, but he'll have to improve his control and feel for pitching to get to that point.

Year	Age	Club (Level)	Lge	W	L	ERA	G	GS	IP	H	HR	BB	SO	BB/9	SO/9	WHIP	AVG
2021	19	Palm Beach (LoA)	SEast	3	3	10.90	32	2	54	64	7	56	59	9.4	9.9	2.24	.303
Minor League Totals (1 year)				3	3	10.90	32	2	54	64	7	56	59	9.39	9.89	2.24	.303

19 KODI WHITLEY, RHP

BA GRADE
40 Risk: Medium

Born: Feb. 21, 1995. **B-T:** R-R. **HT:** 6-4. **WT:** 220. **Drafted:** Mount Olive (N.C.), 2017 (27th round). **Signed by:** T.C. Calhoun.

TRACK RECORD: Drafted in the 27th round in 2017 out of Mount Olive (N.C.), Whitley quickly showed he was a valuable late-round pick, posting a 2.51 ERA at Low-A in 2018, breezing from High-A to Triple-A in 2019 while posting a 1.60 ERA in 50 appearances and making the team's alternate training site in 2020. Whitley, who made his big league debut in 2020, impressed out of the Cardinals bullpen in 2021 with a 2.49 ERA while proving to be one of the team's more reliable relievers.

SCOUTING REPORT: Whitley leads his arsenal with an above-average fastball that has reached 97-98 mph at times, but averaged 93.7 mph at the big league level in 2021. The pitch has carry up in the zone and induced a 25% whiff rate. His best secondary is a mid-80s slider, an above-average offering that had a 42.9% whiff rate against MLB hitters, and he rounds out his arsenal with a mid-80s changeup. Whitley has a repeatable delivery and has no trouble working north and south in the strike zone. He has above-average control.

THE FUTURE: Whitley should make the Cardinals Opening Day roster in 2022. He has the upside of a medium-leverage reliever.

Year	Age	Club (Level)	Lge	W	L	ERA	G	GS	IP	H	HR	BB	SO	BB/9	SO/9	WHIP	AVG
2021	26	Springfield (AA)	Cent	1	2	13.50	6	1	4	5	1	3	8	5.8	15.4	1.71	.278
	26	Memphis (AAA)	East	3	0	1.69	12	0	16	11	1	7	21	3.9	11.8	1.13	.193
	26	St. Louis (MLB)	NL	0	0	2.49	25	0	25	15	1	12	27	4.3	9.6	1.07	.172
Major League Totals (2 years)				0	0	2.40	29	0	30	17	2	13	32	3.90	9.60	1.00	.165
Minor League Totals (4 years)				11	8	2.28	122	3	177	152	7	59	197	2.99	10.00	1.19	.230

20 ANGEL RONDON, RHP

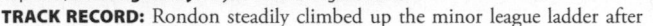

BA GRADE	
45	Risk: High

Born: Dec. 1, 1997. **B-T:** R-R. **HT:** 6-2. **WT:** 185. **Signed:** Dominican Republic, 2016. **Signed by:** Raymi Dicent/Angel Ovalles.

TRACK RECORD: Rondon steadily climbed up the minor league ladder after signing with the Cardinals in 2016 out of the Dominican Republic, making his full-season debut in 2018. He reached the upper minors in 2019, spent the 2020 summer at the alternate training site and reached Triple-A in 2021. He put up middling numbers at Memphis, and made his major league debut in June, striking out National League Rookie of the Year Jonathan India in his first appearance.

SCOUTING REPORT: Rondon doesn't have a flashy arsenal, but he's put up solid or better numbers at every level of the minor leagues, with a 3.29 career ERA in 424 innings. Rondon stands out for his confidence in his four-pitch mix, as he's unafraid to throw all four of his pitches in any count. His fastball, which averaged 93.1 mph in the big leagues, sits in the low 90s, and he rounds out his arsenal with a slider, curveball and changeup. The slider is an above-average offering, with his curveball projecting as average and his changeup projecting as below-average. Rondon stands out to opposing scouts for his pitchability, but others are skeptical that he'll make an impact in the big leagues due to his lack of a plus offering.

THE FUTURE: Although Rondon split time as a starter and reliever at Triple-A, he's likely best suited for a bullpen role in the big leagues, where he could help the Cardinals as a middle reliever in 2022.

Year	Age	Club (Level)	Lge	W	L	ERA	G	GS	IP	H	HR	BB	SO	BB/9	SO/9	WHIP	AVG
2021	23	Memphis (AAA)	East	6	4	4.58	19	13	76	85	15	22	68	2.6	8.0	1.40	.275
	23	St. Louis (MLB)	NL	0	0	0.00	2	0	2	1	0	1	1	4.5	4.5	1.00	.167
Major League Totals (1 year)				0	0	0.00	2	0	2	1	0	1	1	4.50	4.50	1.00	.167
Minor League Totals (6 years)				25	23	3.29	90	74	424	383	43	141	409	2.99	8.68	1.24	.238

21 DIONYS RODRIGUEZ, RHP

BA GRADE	
45	Risk: High

Born: Sept. 3, 2000. **B-T:** L-R. **HT:** 6-0. **WT:** 188. **Signed:** Dominican Republic, 2018. **Signed by:** Braly Guzman/Angel Ovalles

TRACK RECORD: Signed out of the Dominican Republic in 2018, Rodriguez spent his first two seasons in the Dominican Summer League in 2018 and 2019, putting up uninspiring numbers while working exclusively out of the bullpen. Rodriguez, who wasn't at the Cardinals alternate training site in 2020, started the 2021 campaign back in the bullpen for Low-A Palm Beach, but quickly transitioned to the rotation after dominating hitters in June. He made 12 starts to close out the season, finishing with a 4-5, 3.36 mark and 11.4 strikeouts per nine innings.

SCOUTING REPORT: When Rodriguez signed he topped out at just 89-90 mph, but since then he's filled out some and added strength, with his fastball reaching 97 mph out of the bullpen and sitting 92-94 mph as a starter. The fastball misses bats at an above-average rate. He has a good feel for pitching and solid command of his arsenal, especially his cutter, which opposing scouts feel projects as a plus pitch. Rodriguez rounds out his arsenal with a changeup, although it's a clear third pitch currently. Rodriguez throws consistent strikes, projecting for average control, and is competitive on the mound. Some opposing scouts are skeptical he can remain a starter without a quality third pitch.

THE FUTURE: Rodriguez will look to repeat upon his impressive season at Low-A Palm Beach when he moves to High-A Peoria in 2022. He's likely to end up in the bullpen, where his fastball and cutter give him two quality weapons.

Year	Age	Club (Level)	Lge	W	L	ERA	G	GS	IP	H	HR	BB	SO	BB/9	SO/9	WHIP	AVG
2021	20	Palm Beach (LoA)	SEast	4	5	3.36	22	12	69	52	5	22	88	2.8	11.4	1.06	.201
Minor League Totals (3 years)				10	6	4.73	58	12	120	91	7	73	146	5.48	10.95	1.37	.204

22 TRE FLETCHER, OF

BA GRADE	
50	Risk: Extreme

Born: April 30, 2001. **B-T:** R-R. **HT:** 6-2. **WT:** 200. **Drafted:** HS—Portland, Maine, 2019 (2nd round). **Signed by:** Jim Negrych.

TRACK RECORD: Fletcher was originally a member of the 2020 draft class but reclassified to the 2019 class six months before the draft. Fletcher played 43 games in Rookie ball after getting drafted in the second round, and was added to the team's alternate training site in 2020. He played in just seven games this season in the Florida Complex League.

SCOUTING REPORT: Fletcher is extremely athletic, has plus-plus speed and projects to be a plus defender in center field with more refinement, with a plus arm as well. He has fast bat speed and plus raw power, but with a pull-oriented approach. He's overaggressive at the plate, which leads to swing and miss, and he struggles to hit offspeed pitches. After playing just seven games in two years the Cardinals had Fletcher working with their performance staff in the offseason to get him ready for 2022.

THE FUTURE: Fletcher has tools to dream on, but he's yet to make his full-season debut and is still a raw talent. He'll likely start 2022 at Low-A Palm Beach.

Year	Age	Club (Level)	Lge	AVG	G	AB	R	H	2B	3B	HR	RBI	BB	SO	SB	OBP	SLG
2021	20	Cardinals (R)	FCL	.222	7	27	3	6	2	0	1	2	2	11	0	.276	.407
Minor League Totals (3 years)				.241	50	187	18	45	9	1	5	28	13	87	7	.289	.380

23 ALEC WILLIS, RHP

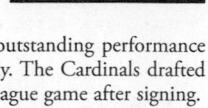

BA GRADE

50 Risk: Extreme

Born: March 30, 2003. **B-T:** R-R. **HT:** 6-5. **WT:** 220. **Drafted:** HS—Aurora, Colo., 2021 (7th round). **Signed by:** Mauricio Rubio

TRACK RECORD: After missing the 2020 summer showcase campaign due to ulnar decompression that led to surgery, Willis shot on to the scene with an outstanding performance during his senior high school season that led his draft stock to rise significantly. The Cardinals drafted him in the seventh round in 2021, and he appeared in one Florida Complex League game after signing.

SCOUTING REPORT: Willis has a powerful build at 6-foot-5, 220 pounds with projection remaining for him to gain additional velocity to a fastball that sits in the low 90s and tops out at 96 mph. He pairs his fastball with a trio of secondary pitches that all project to be average or better. His low-80s slider is the best of the three, a future plus pitch. He also throws a mid-70s curveball and a mid-80s changeup, which is a clear fourth offering. Willis projects for solid-average control, and he has good arm speed and a smooth, balanced delivery.

THE FUTURE: Willis has the upside of a future big league starter, but he's years away from that point. He'll make his full-season debut in 2022.

Year	Age	Club (Level)	Lge	W	L	ERA	G	GS	IP	H	HR	BB	SO	BB/9	SO/9	WHIP	AVG
2021	18	Cardinals (R)	FCL	0	0	0.00	1	1	1	0	0	0	1	0.0	9.0	0.00	.000
Minor League Totals (1 year)				0	0	0.00	1	1	1	0	0	0	1	0.00	9.00	0.00	.000

24 JAKE WALSH, RHP

BA GRADE

40 Risk: High

Born: July 20, 1995. **B-T:** R-R. **HT:** 6-1. **WT:** 192. **Drafted:** Florida Southern, 2017 (16th round). **Signed by:** Mike DiBiase

TRACK RECORD: Walsh has pitched well at every level he's encountered, working as a starter in 2018 and posting a sub-3.00 ERA between the Class A levels before missing the majority of the 2019 season after having Tommy John surgery. He returned in 2021 as a full-time reliever, posting a 1.50 ERA in 13 appearances at Double-A Springfield before a late-season promotion to Triple-A Memphis. He finished the season in the Arizona Fall League, where he struggled in 11 appearances.

SCOUTING REPORT: Walsh overpowered hitters at the Double-A level with a fastball that sat 96 mph and touched 100 mph. The pitch has riding life up in the zone and he threw it for a strike 69% of the time in 2021. He pairs the pitch with a big, downer curveball, a swing-and-miss weapon that projects as above-average. There's some stiffness in Walsh's operation, and some opposing scouts weren't convinced by his feel for pitching, though he is a solid strike thrower. The Cardinals stated their confidence in Walsh by adding him to the 40-man roster after the season ended.

THE FUTURE: Thanks to his two-pitch mix, Walsh profiles as a solid middle reliever. He'll likely make his big league debut in 2022.

Year	Age	Club (Level)	Lge	W	L	ERA	G	GS	IP	H	HR	BB	SO	BB/9	SO/9	WHIP	AVG
2021	25	Springfield (AA)	Cent	2	1	1.50	13	0	18	11	0	5	25	2.5	12.5	0.89	.169
	25	Memphis (AAA)	East	0	1	9.00	4	0	4	2	2	3	9	6.8	20.3	1.25	.143
Minor League Totals (5 years)				16	7	2.39	60	25	192	138	14	55	193	2.58	9.06	1.01	.199

25 DELVIN PEREZ, SS

BA GRADE

40 Risk: High

Born: Nov. 24, 1998. **B-T:** R-R. **HT:** 6-3. **WT:** 175. **Drafted:** HS—Ceiba, P.R., 2016 (1st round). **Signed by:** Mike Dibiase/Juan Ramos.

TRACK RECORD: After getting selected by the Cardinals in the first round in 2016, Perez struggled over his first two seasons in short-season ball before making his full-season debut in 2019 at Low-A Peoria, where he put up solid numbers albeit with little power. He impressed in spring training in 2021, then spent the season at Double-A Springfield, hitting .265/.322/.339 with 17 extra-base hits while providing steady defense at shortstop. Perez was not added to the 40-man roster following the 2021 season.

SCOUTING REPORT: Perez never had much power coming into the 2021 season, but he added muscle and his frame filled out to allow him to hit the ball harder. The Cardinals were pleased with the improvement of his hard-hit ability, but he still managed just four home runs while playing half his games at hitter-friendly Springfield, and he projects for well below-average power. Perez needs to improve his plate recognition and bat-to-ball skills, which are both below-average currently. He is overaggressive at the plate, with a pull-happy approach. Perez's value comes from his defense at shortstop, where he's an above-average defender, a plus-plus runner who has above-average range and a plus arm, and he's learned to play more under control.

THE FUTURE: Perez will likely never be an everyday big leaguer, but he provides value thanks to his defense and speed on the basepaths. He'll likely start 2022 at Triple-A Memphis.

Year	Age	Club (Level)	Lge	AVG	G	AB	R	H	2B	3B	HR	RBI	BB	SO	SB	OBP	SLG
2021	22	Springfield (AA)	Cent	.265	98	389	62	103	9	4	4	23	28	98	24	.322	.339
Minor League Totals (6 years)				.255	357	1367	181	349	41	17	6	102	112	321	71	.323	.323

26 ZANE MILLS, RHP

BA GRADE

40 Risk: High

Born: July 4, 2000. **B-T:** R-R. **HT:** 6-4. **WT:** 220. **Drafted:** Washington State, 2021 (4th round). **Signed by:** Chris Rodriguez.

TRACK RECORD: Undrafted out of high school, Mills struggled in his first season at Washington State in 2019, had an encouraging showing in the West Coast League the following summer, broke out in 2020 and posted solid, if unspectacular, numbers in 2021 before being selected by the Cardinals in the fourth round. Mills made seven appearances in the Florida Complex League after signing, striking out nine and walking none in 7.2 innings.

SCOUTING REPORT: Mills has good size at 6-foot-4, 220 pounds from the right side with projection remaining and a smooth, easy delivery. His fastball sits 89-92 mph with two-seam action, and he pairs it with a slider. While neither pitch projects to be more than average, he has plus command of each offering. He does a good job of mixing his pitches and attacking both sides of the plate. He rounds out his arsenal with a solid-average changeup. What Mills doesn't offer in stuff, he makes up for in his feel for pitching and strike-throwing ability. Scouts who watched him in college were impressed by his pitchability and polish, which should allow him to continue starting at the professional level.

THE FUTURE: Mills should make his full-season debut in 2022, and it wouldn't be surprising to see the Cardinals aggressively push him through the system given his polish. He projects as a back-end starter.

Year	Age	Club (Level)	Lge	W	L	ERA	G	GS	IP	H	HR	BB	SO	BB/9	SO/9	WHIP	AVG
2021	20	Cardinals (R)	FCL	0	0	1.17	7	0	8	4	0	0	9	0.0	10.6	0.52	.154
Minor League Totals (1 year)				0	0	1.17	7	0	8	4	0	0	9	0.00	10.57	0.52	.154

27 JULIO RODRIGUEZ, C

BA GRADE

40 Risk: High

Born: June 11, 1997. **B-T:** R-R. **HT:** 6-0. **WT:** 245. **Signed:** Dominican Republic, 2016. **Signed by:** Braly Guzman/Angel Ovalles.

TRACK RECORD: An under-the-radar signing out of the Dominican Republic in 2016, Rodriguez put up back-to-back solid seasons in the Dominican Summer League in 2016 and the Rookie-level Appalachian League in 2017, then spent the 2018 season at Low-A Peoria. Rodriguez hit well at High-A in 2019 and briefly made his upper minors debut, setting the stage for an anticipated 2021 encore performance. But he dealt with a wrist injury, missed two months and struggled with the bat in 29 games at Double-A Springfield.

SCOUTING REPORT: Rated the best defensive catcher in the Cardinals system in 2020, 2021 and 2022, Rodriguez stands out for his receiving, blocking and game-calling ability, profiling as an above-average defender. He has an average, accurate arm and a swift transfer. Rodriguez has the defensive ability to become a backup at the big league level, but he may never hit enough to get to that point. He has a short swing and solid bat-to-ball skills, but pairs that with below-average power.

THE FUTURE: Rodriguez could head back to Double-A to attempt to improve upon his 2021 struggles before making his Triple-A debut.

Year	Age	Club (Level)	Lge	AVG	G	AB	R	H	2B	3B	HR	RBI	BB	SO	SB	OBP	SLG
2021	24	Cardinals (R)	FCL	.286	7	14	2	4	0	0	0	2	5	3	0	.500	.286
	24	Springfield (AA)	Cent	.196	29	107	10	21	2	0	3	10	7	23	1	.252	.299
Minor League Totals (6 years)				.267	285	1053	126	281	56	6	31	170	79	204	1	.321	.420

28 CONNOR THOMAS, LHP

Born: May 29, 1998. **B-T:** L-L. **HT:** 5-11. **WT:** 173. **Drafted:** Georgia Tech, 2019 (5th round). **Signed by:** Charles Peterson

BA GRADE
40 Risk: High

TRACK RECORD: The 2019 fifth-rounder from Georgia Tech arrived in the short-season New York-Penn League after signing, making five appearances (two starts) before a promotion to Low-A Peoria. He spent the 2020 shutdown at home and made his upper minors debut in 2021. Thomas made four starts at Double-A Springfield before the Cardinals sent him to Triple-A Memphis, where he pitched to a 6-4, 3.10 mark while showing impressive command of his three-pitch mix.

SCOUTING REPORT: Thomas won't wow anyone with his arsenal, which includes two fastball variations that sit 90-91 mph. One is a below-average offering, while the other has natural sinking life and is an average pitch. His plus command allows his stuff to play up. Thomas pairs his fastballs with a plus slider and an above-average changeup. He induces ground balls with all of his pitches, with a 50% or higher groundball rate on each offering. Coming out of college there were concerns that Thomas' modest arsenal would cause him to struggle against better competition, but he's pitched well at every stop in the minor leagues. In addition to having plus command, Thomas has above-average control.

THE FUTURE: Thomas could be in line to make his major league debut after conquering Triple-A in 2021. He'll likely never be a full-time starter, but he provides value as a long reliever and spot starter.

Year	Age	Club (Level)	Lge	W	L	ERA	G	GS	IP	H	HR	BB	SO	BB/9	SO/9	WHIP	AVG
2021	23	Springfield (AA)	Cent	0	2	4.87	4	4	20	26	5	3	24	1.3	10.6	1.43	.321
	23	Memphis (AAA)	East	6	4	3.10	22	14	101	108	11	30	92	2.7	8.1	1.36	.269
Minor League Totals (3 years)				10	7	3.49	41	22	165	176	18	43	152	2.35	8.29	1.33	.272

29 JOSE DAVILA, RHP

Born: Nov. 9, 2002. **B-T:** R-R. **HT:** 6-3. **WT:** 177. **Signed:** Venezuela, 2019. **Signed by:** Adel Granadillo/Jose Gonzalez.

BA GRADE
45 Risk: Extreme

TRACK RECORD: Signed by the Cardinals in July 2019 out of Venezuela, Davila didn't make his pro debut after agreeing to a deal and watched as the 2020 season was shut down due to the coronavirus pandemic. He started the 2021 season at Low-A Palm Beach, struggling in four outings before heading to the Florida Complex League. There he posted 49 strikeouts in 45.1 innings and had a 3.77 ERA in 11 appearances (nine starts).

SCOUTING REPORT: Davila has a lean build at 6-foot-3, 177 pounds with some projection remaining to add velocity to his fastball. The pitch sits 92-93 mph currently, but has topped out at 95 mph from the right side. He pairs the pitch with a curveball, which he has feel to spin. Davila has the traits of a starter, but showed below-average control in 2021.

THE FUTURE: Davila should head back to Low-A Palm Beach to start the 2022 season.

Year	Age	Club (Level)	Lge	W	L	ERA	G	GS	IP	H	HR	BB	SO	BB/9	SO/9	WHIP	AVG
2021	18	Cardinals (R)	FCL	1	3	3.77	11	9	45	33	1	24	49	4.8	9.7	1.26	.201
	18	Palm Beach (LoA)	SEast	0	1	10.80	4	0	8	12	0	10	5	10.8	5.4	2.64	.375
Minor League Totals (1 year)				1	4	4.86	15	9	54	45	1	34	54	5.70	9.06	1.47	.230

30 JHON TORRES, OF

Born: March 29, 2000. **B-T:** R-R. **HT:** 6-4. **WT:** 199. **Signed:** Colombia, 2016. **Signed by:** Domingo Toribio/Felix Nivar/Koby Perez (Indians).

BA GRADE
40 Risk: High

TRACK RECORD: Acquired by the Cardinals in July 2018 from Cleveland as part of the return for outfielder Oscar Mercado, Torres spent the 2019 season between the advanced Rookie-level Appalachian League and Low-A. He was not at the alternate training site in 2020 and struggled with a 2021 assignment at High-A Peoria, hitting .238/.302/.366 with six home runs in 97 games.

SCOUTING REPORT: Torres is a good athlete with some power potential, but he struggles to make contact due to timing issues and length in his swing. He needs to improve his plate discipline and pitch recognition skills, which are below-average. Torres is an average runner and an average defender in the corner outfield with an average arm, but scouts are concerned with his ability to hit enough to profile there.

THE FUTURE: Torres was not added to the Cardinals 40-man roster following the 2021 season. He's in line to make his upper-minors debut in 2022, but his time in the organization could be running out.

Year	Age	Club (Level)	Lge	AVG	G	AB	R	H	2B	3B	HR	RBI	BB	SO	SB	OBP	SLG
2021	21	Peoria (HiA)	Cent	.238	97	383	47	91	25	3	6	32	27	98	3	.302	.366
Minor League Totals (5 years)				.257	249	907	127	233	53	6	25	122	100	241	11	.341	.411

MORE PROSPECTS TO KNOW

31 INOHAN PANIAGUA, RHP   SLEEPER

Paniagua has a pair of intriguing offerings in his above-average fastball that tops out at 96 mph and an upper-70s curveball that flashes plus. He fared well in his full-season debut in 2021 at Low-A Palm Beach.

32 FREDDY PACHECO, RHP

Pacheco rose from High-A to Triple-A while stifling hitters with his fastball and hard breaking ball, and is on the verge of making his big league debut. The Cardinals added him to the 40-man roster after the season.

33 CARLOS CARMONA, OF

Carmona, who made his pro debut in the DSL in 2021, is a toolsy, athletic center fielder with a hit-over-power bat.

34 RYAN HOLGATE, OF

Holgate has all-fields power that is plus or better, but his below-average hit tool led to a high swing-and-miss rate in his pro debut.

35 TOMMY PARSONS, RHP

None of Parsons' four pitches grade better than average, but he has plus control and stands out for his feel for pitching.

36 JEREMY RIVAS, SS

Rivas stood out within the organization thanks to his instincts and understanding of the game. He put up solid numbers in the Florida Complex League, but it's his plus defense that leads the way. He'll make his full-season debut in 2022.

37 IAN BEDELL, RHP

Bedell in 2021 went down with a torn UCL in his pitching elbow that led to Tommy John surgery. When healthy he's shown plus control, a changeup that flashes above-average, a low-90s fastball and a pair of breaking balls.

38 LUKEN BAKER, 1B

Baker has plus-plus raw power, but struggles to regularly access it due to a high swing-and-miss rate. He's a below-average defender at first who profiles as a designated hitter.

39 ALVARO SEIJAS, RHP

Seijas dealt with an arm injury in 2021 and struggled mightily to throw strikes when he was healthy, but a mid-90s fastball gives him a chance to make an impact in the bullpen.

40 KRAMER ROBERTSON, SS

Likely nothing more than a defensive replacement at the next level, Robertson is a strong defender at shortstop and second base.

TOP PROSPECTS OF THE DECADE

Year	Player, Pos	2021 Org
2012	Shelby Miller, RHP	Pirates
2013	Oscar Taveras, OF	Deceased
2014	Oscar Taveras, OF	Deceased
2015	Marco Gonzales, LHP	Mariners
2016	Alex Reyes, RHP	Cardinals
2017	Alex Reyes, RHP	Cardinals
2018	Alex Reyes, RHP	Cardinals
2019	Alex Reyes, RHP	Cardinals
2020	Dylan Carlson, OF	Cardinals
2021	Dylan Carlson, OF	Cardinals

TOP DRAFT PICKS OF THE DECADE

Year	Player, Pos	2021 Org
2012	Michael Wacha, RHP	Rays
2013	Marco Gonzales, LHP	Mariners
2014	Luke Weaver, RHP	D-backs
2015	Nick Plummer, OF	Cardinals
2016	Delvin Perez, SS	Cardinals
2017	Scott Hurst, OF (3rd round)	Cardinals
2018	Nolan Gorman, 3B	Cardinals
2019	Zack Thompson, LHP	Cardinals
2020	Jordan Walker, 3B	Cardinals
2021	Michael McGreevy, RHP	Cardinals

San Diego Padres

BY JEFF SANDERS

With Fernando Tatis Jr. and Manny Machado manning the left side of the infield and general manager A.J. Preller's frenetic overhaul of the rotation, the Padres were a chic pick to build on 2020's playoff run—the franchise's first since 2006—and perhaps push the Dodgers for the National League West division title.

Instead, after sending five players to the All-Star Game, the Padres fell flat in the second half and finished 79-83, a collapse that reverberated throughout the organization.

Manager Jayce Tingler was fired after just two seasons and replaced by Bob Melvin. Preller jettisoned farm director Sam Geaney to promote Ryley Westman from within the organization. Scouting director Mark Conner was reassigned and international scouting director Chris Kemp was assigned to oversee the draft.

For all the failings at the major league level—from injuries tearing through the rotation to the lineup's power outage to the specter of Tatis' repeated shoulder injuries—there was plenty of head-scratching over how little the farm system supported the MLB product.

Much of that had to do with Preller trading away dozens of prospects to acquire the likes of Yu Darvish, Blake Snell, Mike Clevinger, Joe Musgrove and Austin Nola, among others, over the previous two years.

Beyond those moves, shortstop CJ Abrams—the Padres' top position player prospect—was lost for the year after he suffered a fractured left tibia in late June and catcher Luis Campusano was not ready to contribute when injuries forced Nola to start the year on the injured list.

While rookie lefthander Ryan Weathers was a boon early in the season, his effectiveness evaporated in the second half as he topped 100 innings for the first time. Most problematic of all was lefthander MacKenzie Gore—once the top pitching prospect in the game—spending a good chunk of the summer reworking his mechanics in extended spring training, far from consideration for an MLB rotation spot.

Instead of forging a second straight playoff berth, the Padres watched the Giants leapfrog the Dodgers to claim the NL West. The Padres, meanwhile, are left to ponder a path forward after so much went wrong in 2021.

Darvish, Snell and Chris Paddack all are question marks after finishing inconsistent seasons on the injured list. Clevinger and Adrian Morejon also face uncertainty as they return from Tommy John surgeries, leaving the Padres again contemplating

Even in a year that ended poorly for the Padres, Fernando Tatis Jr. was one of the game's best.

PROJECTED 2025 LINEUP

Catcher	Luis Campusano	26
First Base	Jake Cronenworth	31
Second Base	CJ Abrams	24
Third Base	Manny Machado	32
Shortstop	Fernando Tatis Jr.	26
Left Field	James Wood	22
Center Field	Trent Grisham	28
Right Field	Robert Hassell III	23
Designated Hitter	Joshua Mears	24
No. 1 Starter	Blake Snell	32
No. 2 Starter	Joe Musgrove	32
No. 3 Starter	MacKenzie Gore	26
No. 4 Starter	Chris Paddack	29
No. 5 Starter	Ryan Weathers	25
Closer	Dinelson Lamet	32

pitching depth while being bogged down by the contracts of Eric Hosmer and Wil Myers.

The hope is the strides Gore took toward the end of the year put him in position to help the rotation in 2022. The Padres also remain high on Weathers, Abrams and Campusano, but many of their potential impact prospects—from 2020 first-rounder Robert Hassell III to 2021 international signees Victor Acosta, Samuel Zavala and Daniel Montesino—have yet to play above Class A.

Still, with Tatis locked up for the next 13 years, Machado still in his prime and ownership committed to winning, the Padres remain as healthy as ever, even with significant challenges on the horizon as they try to keep up in the NL West. ■

SAN DIEGO PADRES

TOP 2022 ROOKIES	RANK
MacKenzie Gore, LHP	4
Robert Suarez, RHP	13
Kevin Kopps, RHP	14
BREAKOUT PROSPECTS	**RANK**
Victor Acosta, SS	11
Jairo Iriarte, RHP	26

SOURCE OF TOP 30 TALENT			
Homegrown	**26**	**Acquired**	**4**
College	5	Trade	3
Junior college	0	Rule 5 draft	0
High school	9	Independent league	0
Nondrafted free agent	0	Free agent/waivers	1
International	12		

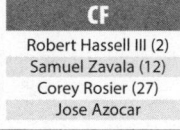

LF
James Wood (5)
Esteury Ruiz
Jorge Oña

CF
Robert Hassell III (2)
Samuel Zavala (12)
Corey Rosier (27)
Jose Azocar

RF
Joshua Mears (8)
Tirso Ornelas
Agustin Ruiz

3B
Eguy Rosario (17)

SS
CJ Abrams (1)
Jackson Merrill (7)
Victor Acosta (11)
Justin Lopez

2B
Euribiel Angeles (10)
Nerwilian Cedeno (28)

1B
Daniel Montesino (29)
Taylor Kohlwey

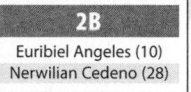
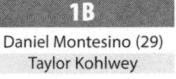

C
Luis Campusano (3)
Brandon Valenzuela (22)
Jonny Homza

LHP

LHSP	LHRP
MacKenzie Gore (4)	Ray Kerr (20)
Adrián Morejón (6)	Tom Cosgrove
Robert Gasser (9)	Osvaldo Hernandez
Ethan Elliott (23)	Mason Feole
Noel Vela (25)	
Aaron Leasher	

RHP

RHSP	RHRP
Victor Lizarraga (15)	Robert Suarez (13)
Justin Lange (16)	Kevin Kopps (14)
Reiss Knehr (18)	Steven Wilson (21)
Adrián Martinez (19)	Jose Quezada
Efrain Contreras (24)	Luke Boyd
Jairo Iriarte (26)	Chase Walter
Matt Waldron (30)	Evan Miller
Michel Báez	Lake Bachar
Reggie Lawson	
Moises Lugo	
Pedro Avila	

1 CJ ABRAMS, SS

Born: Oct. 3, 2000. **B-T:** L-R. **HT:** 6-1. **WT:** 179.
Drafted: HS—Roswell, Ga, 2019 (1st round).
Signed by: Tyler Stubblefield.

EDDIE KELLY/PROLOOK PHOTOS

TRACK RECORD: Abrams long stood out as one of the best and most athletic players for his age in high school and made a big impression when he took over center field for USA Baseball's 18U National Team and made the position look easy despite never playing it before. He followed with a sensational senior spring, and the Padres were thrilled when he fell to them at the sixth overall pick in 2019. They lured him away from an Alabama commitment with a $5.2 million signing bonus, and by the end of that first pro summer, Abrams had won the Rookie-level Arizona League's MVP award after batting .401 and earned a promotion to Low-A Fort Wayne. That assignment, however, was halted after just two games due to a shoulder injury. Abrams spent 2020 at the Padres' alternate training site and made his full-season debut at Double-A San Antonio in 2021, where he got off to a hot start before fracturing his left tibia and spraining his left MCL in a collision with second baseman Eguy Rosario in late June, ending his season. Abrams recovered in time to get back on the field in instructional league but bruised his left shoulder while sliding into a base, an injury that prevented him from participating in the Arizona Fall League.

SCOUTING REPORT: When he is on the field, Abrams stands out for all the right reasons. He has a flat, fluid swing and elite hand-eye coordination—thanks in large part to the various contraptions his dad devised during his youth—that allow him to hit any type of pitch no matter where it's located. He expanded the strike zone a bit much in his first stint at San Antonio, which is not all that surprising given that he was essentially jumping from rookie ball all the way to Double-A. At his best, he has a keen eye for the zone and takes borderline pitches like a seasoned veteran. Abrams' frame is long and lean, but he's no slap hitter. He makes loud contact off the barrel and can drive the ball out to all fields. It's not out of the question for him to develop 20-home run power as he matures. Abrams' 80-grade speed allows him to regularly beat out infield singles and will make him an elite base-stealing threat once he learns pitchers' tendencies. Defensively, Abrams has plus range at shortstop. He doesn't always show off his above-average arm, but he has a plus internal clock and tends to save his bullets for when they're needed. He has gotten more reliable at making the routine plays and will make the occasional highlight-reel

BA GRADE	SCOUTING GRADES
65 Risk: High	Hit: 70. Power: 50. Run: 80. Field: 60. Arm: 55.

Projected future grades on 20-80 scouting scale

BEST TOOLS

Best Hitter for Average	CJ Abrams
Best Power Hitter	Joshua Mears
Best Strike-Zone Discipline	Robert Hassell III
Fastest Baserunner	CJ Abrams
Best Athlete	CJ Abrams
Best Fastball	MacKenzie Gore
Best Curveball	Adrian Morejon
Best Slider	Kevin Kopps
Best Changeup	Adrián Martinez
Best Control	Ethan Elliott
Best Defensive Catcher	Luis Campusano
Best Defensive Infielder	CJ Abrams
Best Infield Arm	Eguy Rosario
Best Defensive Outfielder	Robert Hassell III
Best Outfield Arm	Robert Hassell III

play. While it's easy to compare Abrams to the last shortstop to rise quickly through the Padres' system, the similarities are few. Where Fernando Tatis Jr. seems to play with his hair on fire, Abrams is a low-motor player whose actions often appear effortless. Tatis' presence means Abrams is likely destined for a position change. He has the athleticism and aptitude to make the transition to second base or center field when the time comes.

THE FUTURE: For all his talent, Abrams has just 348 plate appearances in three seasons and needs at-bats. If he can stay healthy, he should become a dynamic table-setter in front of Tatis and Manny Machado in the Padres' lineup. ■

Year	Age	Club (Level)	Lge	AVG	G	AB	R	H	2B	3B	HR	RBI	BB	SO	SB	OBP	SLG
2021	20	San Antonio (AA)	Cent	.296	42	162	26	48	14	0	2	23	15	36	13	.363	.420
Minor League Totals (3 years)				.343	76	312	67	107	27	8	5	45	26	50	28	.398	.529

2 ROBERT HASSELL III, OF

Born: Aug. 15, 2001. **B-T:** L-L. **HT:** 6-2. **WT:** 182. **Drafted:** HS—Thompson's Station., Tenn., 2020 (1st round). **Signed by:** Tyler Stubblefield.

TRACK RECORD: Hassell starred in the Little League World Series and led USA Baseball's 18U national team to a silver medal at the 2019 World Cup with a .514 batting average. The Padres drafted him eighth overall in 2020 and signed him away from a Vanderbilt commitment for $4.3 million. Hassell reported to the alternate training site after signing and got at-bats in big league spring training games in 2021 before making his official pro debut. He lived up to his reputation as a premium hitter by batting .323/.415/.482 at Low-A Lake Elsinore and received a late promotion to High-A Fort Wayne.

SCOUTING REPORT: Hassell's loose, all-fields swing is already perfectly geared for contact. He's a consensus plus hitter who controls the strike zone, covers the entire plate and hangs in well against lefties in a way that is rare for a young lefthanded hitter. With a thin, 6-foot-2, 182-pound frame, Hassell has endured questions about his power potential for years, but he is learning to backspin the ball and pull the appropriate pitches. Until his average power manifests in games more consistently, the Padres are content to hit him atop the order, where he's an on-base machine and a stolen base threat with his above-average speed. Hassell is a natural center fielder who is light on his feet and has the above-average arm strength to play any outfield position. He plays with a chip on his shoulder and isn't afraid to voice it.

THE FUTURE: Hassell is on the fast track and could reach Double-A as a 20-year-old in 2022. He's an all-star in the making if he unlocks his 15-20 homer potential.

BA GRADE
60 Risk: High

SCOUTING GRADES:	Hitting: 60	Power: 45	Running: 55	Fielding: 55	Arm: 55

Year	Age	Club (Level)	Lge	AVG	G	AB	R	H	2B	3B	HR	RBI	BB	SO	SB	OBP	SLG
2021	19	Lake Elsinore (LoA)	West	.323	92	365	77	118	31	3	7	65	57	74	31	.415	.482
	19	Fort Wayne (HiA)	Cent	.205	18	78	10	16	2	1	4	11	9	25	3	.287	.410
Minor League Totals (2 years)				.302	110	443	87	134	33	4	11	76	66	99	34	.393	.470

3 LUIS CAMPUSANO, C

Born: Sept. 29, 1998. **B-T:** R-R. **HT:** 5-11. **WT:** 211. **Drafted:** HS—Augusta, Ga., 2017 (2nd round). **Signed by:** Tyler Stubblefield.

TRACK RECORD: The first catcher selected in the 2017 draft, Campusano overcame a pair of early concussions to win co-MVP honors in the High-A California League in 2019. A year later, Campusano hit his way from the alternate training site to the majors and homered in his debut, but a wrist injury quickly ended that stint. Austin Nola's broken finger pushed Campusano onto the Opening Day roster in 2021, but struggles at the became a drain on his playing time and ultimately pushed him back to Triple-A El Paso. He had 15 homers and a .906 OPS in 81 games for the Chihuahuas before an oblique injury ended his season.

SCOUTING REPORT: Campusano's bat remains his calling card. He is an immensely strong hitter who makes loud contact from foul pole to foul pole and projects as a middle-of-the-order threat who hits for both average and power. He has demonstrated excellent strike-zone control at his best, although he's been too aggressive during his time in the majors. Defensively, Campusano is an athletic backstop who's improved his blocking significantly since joining the system. Improving his framing has long been a point of emphasis, but Padres officials were pleased with the strides he made last year. He has above-average arm strength, although accuracy remains inconsistent. Something of an introvert, Campusano has to work to assert himself in game-planning alongside fellow pitchers. Maturity questions also persist following a 2020 arrest for felony marijuana possession, although prosecutors ultimately dropped the charges.

THE FUTURE: With Nola under team control through 2025, Campusano has time on his side to develop into the Padres' long-term answer at catcher. He'll try to force his way into the team's plans in 2022.

BA GRADE
55 Risk: Medium

SCOUTING GRADES:	Hitting: 50	Power: 55	Running: 30	Fielding: 50	Arm: 55

Year	Age	Club (Level)	Lge	AVG	G	AB	R	H	2B	3B	HR	RBI	BB	SO	SB	OBP	SLG
2021	22	El Paso (AAA)	West	.295	81	292	47	86	21	3	15	45	27	66	1	.365	.541
	22	San Diego (MLB)	NL	.088	11	34	0	3	0	0	0	1	4	11	0	.184	.088
Major League Totals (2 years)				.108	12	37	2	4	0	0	1	2	4	13	0	.214	.189
Minor League Totals (4 years)				.301	298	1108	144	334	67	4	37	191	113	191	1	.370	.469

4 MacKENZIE GORE, LHP

Born: Feb. 24, 1999. **B-T:** L-L. **HT:** 6-2. **WT:** 199. **Drafted:** HS—Whiteville, N.C., 2017 (1st round). **Signed by:** Nick Brannon.

TRACK RECORD: The top pitching prospect in the game heading into 2020, Gore has seen his stock fall as far as anyone's since the start of the coronavirus pandemic. His mechanics fell out of sync at the alternate training site in 2020 and he looked like a shell of himself in 2021 at Triple-A El Paso, where he posted a 5.85 ERA in six starts before being demoted to extended spring training. Gore spent two months at the Padres' complex in Peoria, Ariz. addressing his mechanical deficiencies and finished the season on an upswing, but he was still hit and miss in the Arizona Fall League with a 6.35 ERA in three starts.

SCOUTING REPORT: A plus fastball has always allowed Gore's secondaries to play up. Without that pitch in prime shape, his game fell apart. His arm was late, his elbow was dipping below his shoulder upon release, his velocity was down and his secondaries—a mid-80s slider, a 1-to-7 curveball and a sinking changeup, all of which have flashed plus—backed up. Gore resurfaced in mid August with the athleticism and quickness back in his signature leg kick and quieted some of the upper body movement in his windup. The result was his fastball again sitting in the mid 90s and touching 98, which in turn helped his secondaries. Gore's command remains inconsistent and he still battles his mechanics at times, but his misses off the plate were much smaller after he returned.

THE FUTURE: The Padres still believe Gore is a potential front-of-the-rotation starter, but he'll have to improve his command to approach that ceiling. He was added to the 40-man roster in November and is in position to make his big league debut in 2022.

BA GRADE
55 Risk: Extreme

SCOUTING GRADES:	Fastball: 60	Slider: 60	Curveball: 55	Changeup: 55	Control: 45

Year	Age	Club (Level)	Lge	W	L	ERA	G	GS	IP	H	HR	BB	SO	BB/9	SO/9	WHIP	AVG
2021	22	Padres (R)	ACL	1	0	1.65	3	3	16	13	0	4	22	2.2	12.1	1.04	.220
	22	Fort Wayne (HiA)	Cent	0	1	5.40	1	1	5	3	0	4	5	7.2	9.0	1.40	.176
	22	San Antonio (AA)	Cent	0	0	3.00	2	2	9	6	0	8	16	8.0	16.0	1.56	.182
	22	El Paso (AAA)	West	0	2	5.85	6	6	20	24	3	12	18	5.4	8.1	1.80	.289
Minor League Totals (5 years)				12	11	2.85	55	55	233	177	15	81	304	3.1	11.7	1.11	.209

5 JAMES WOOD, OF

Born: Sept. 17, 2002. **B-T:** L-R. **HT:** 6-7. **WT:** 240. **Drafted:** HS—Bradenton, Fla., 2021 (2nd round). **Signed by:** John Martin.

TRACK RECORD: Wood grew up in Maryland before moving to Florida to hone his baseball skills at IMG Academy. Elevated strikeout totals as a senior sank his draft stock, but the Padres still viewed him as one of the biggest upside plays in the draft. They selected him in the second round, No. 62 overall, and gave him a $2.6 million signing bonus—nearly double the recommended slot amount— to lure him away from a Mississippi State commitment. Wood rewarded their faith with a standout showing in the Rookie-level Arizona Complex League in his pro debut, batting .372/.465/.535 and showing a dynamic combination of power and athleticism.

SCOUTING REPORT: The son of former college basketball standout Kenny Wood, Wood is a uniquely gifted and coordinated athlete for a 6-foot-7 teenager. He generates easy plus-plus raw power from a swing that isn't as long as you'd expect from a big man. He is still prone to striking out, but after the Padres widened his stance and asked him to stand more upright in the box, his bat path flattened out and his swings and misses went down substantially. He has a chance to be an average hitter who gets to his power in games as long as he maintains his adjustments. Wood is a surprisingly smooth runner in center field. He'll remain there as long as he proves he can handle the position, but he'll likely end up in right field, where he projects to be an average defender with an average arm.

THE FUTURE: Wood will head to Low-A Lake Elsinore in 2022. He has 30-35 home run potential and has a chance to be a prototypical middle-of-the-order threat.

BA GRADE
55 Risk: Extreme

BILL MITCHELL

SCOUTING GRADES:	Hitting: 45	Power: 65	Running: 55	Fielding: 50	Arm: 50

Year	Age	Club (Level)	Lge	AVG	G	AB	R	H	2B	3B	HR	RBI	BB	SO	SB	OBP	SLG
2021	18	Padres (R)	ACL	.372	26	86	18	32	5	0	3	22	13	32	10	.465	.535
Minor League Totals (1 year)				.372	26	86	18	32	5	0	3	22	13	32	10	.465	.535

6 ADRIAN MOREJON, LHP

Born: Feb. 27, 1999. **B-T:** L-L. **HT:** 5-11. **WT:** 222. **Signed:** Cuba, 2016.
Signed by: Chris Kemp/Trevor Schumm/Felix Feliz.

TRACK RECORD: The Padres' biggest prize from their 2016-17 international spending spree, Morejon became a prospect to watch on Cuba's junior national team and signed with the Padres for a franchise-record $11 million. Various injuries have since limited him to 196.1 innings over five years as a pro, including an elbow injury that required Tommy John surgery last April after he opened the year in the Padres' starting rotation.

SCOUTING REPORT: Morejon has premium stuff from the left side that includes a 94-96 mph fastball that can touch 99 with ease, albeit with scattershot command. Morejon pairs that offering with a sweeping, 79-82 mph curveball, two variations of a changeup—a traditional one with sink and run and a diving knuckle-change that gets swings and misses—an emerging slider and a sinker he began throwing in 2021. Morejon has spent most of his big league time in the Padres bullpen, which might be his ultimate landing spot if he can't shake the durability concerns that have dogged him since he signed. He has now spent time on the injured list with injuries to his forearm, triceps, elbow and shoulder at various points and has yet to pitch more than 65 innings in a season.

THE FUTURE: Morejon will be slow-played as he returns from surgery and is tentatively slated to return to the mound in the second half of the 2022 season. The Padres continue to dream of developing him as a starter, but that goal is a long way off.

BA GRADE
55 Risk: Extreme

SCOUTING GRADES:	Fastball: 60	Slider: 45	Curveball: 60	Changeup: 55	Control: 40

Year	Age	Club (Level)	Lge	W	L	ERA	G	GS	IP	H	HR	BB	SO	BB/9	SO/9	WHIP	AVG
2021	22	San Diego (MLB)	NL	0	0	3.86	2	2	4	5	2	2	3	3.9	5.8	1.50	.278
Major League Totals (3 years)				2	2	5.91	16	8	32	40	10	9	37	2.53	10.41	1.53	.303
Minor League Totals (5 years)				7	13	3.78	43	43	164	153	13	55	176	3.01	9.64	1.27	.245

7 JACKSON MERRILL, SS

Born: April 19, 2003. **B-T:** L-R. **HT:** 6-3. **WT:** 195. **Drafted:** HS—Severna Park, Md., 2021 (1st round). **Signed by:** Danny Sader.

TRACK RECORD: Merrill didn't attend many of the top showcase events during the summer of 2020 and was subsequently viewed as a popup prospect when he emerged last spring. The Padres, however, were on Merrill well before he tied a school record with 13 homers and were happy to select him 27th overall. Merrill signed for a below-slot $1.8 million to forgo a Kentucky commitment and held his own during his pro debut in the Rookie-level Arizona Complex League until a minor hip flexor injury ended his season. He returned healthy in time to participate in instructional league.

SCOUTING REPORT: Merrill had a huge growth spurt and added nearly 30 pounds in the months leading up to the draft. The added strength gave him plus raw power, which is now his main selling point. Merrill's solid bat speed and feel for hitting intrigued the Padres over multiple workouts, where they tested him against the type of high-velocity pitching he did not see regularly in Maryland's prep circuit. He is still rather raw against spin and will need to learn to turn on pitches to unlock his power potential, but he has the raw ingredients to hit for both average and power. Merrill could very well outgrow shortstop, but he has the average speed, soft hands and above-average arm strength to at least start his career at the position.

THE FUTURE: Merrill will make his full-season debut at Low-A Elsinore in 2022. At worst, the Padres see him developing into a multi-positional, lefthanded hitter in the mold of D-backs utilityman Josh Rojas.

BILL MITCHELL

BA GRADE
55 Risk: Extreme

SCOUTING GRADES:	Hitting: 55	Power: 55	Running: 50	Fielding: 45	Arm: 55

Year	Age	Club (Level)	Lge	AVG	G	AB	R	H	2B	3B	HR	RBI	BB	SO	SB	OBP	SLG
2021	18	Padres (R)	ACL	.280	31	107	19	30	7	2	0	10	10	27	5	.339	.383
Minor League Totals (1 year)				.280	31	107	19	30	7	2	0	10	10	27	5	.339	.383

8 JOSHUA MEARS, OF

Born: Feb. 21, 2001. **B-T:** R-R. **HT:** 6-3. **WT:** 242. **Drafted:** HS—Federal Way, Wash., 2019 (2nd round). **Signed by:** Justin Baughman.

TRACK RECORD: A relative unknown until a breakout senior year of high school, Mears went viral during 2021 spring training with a 117 mph home run off Rockies reliever Carlos Estevez in a Cactus League game. While he was overmatched for much of his stay in big league camp, Mears' power continued to play at Low-A Lake Elsinore for his first full professional season, at least when he was in the lineup. Mears missed time with a shoulder injury, a concussion and also spent time on the Covid-19 injured list. Even his push to make up for lost time at instructional league was halted when he fouled a bunt attempt off his face and broke his nose.

SCOUTING REPORT: Checking in at a chiseled 6-foot-3, 242 pounds, Mears has 80-grade raw power and hits titanic home runs with remarkably little effort. The question is whether he will make enough contact to get to his power. Mears struck out in 39% of his plate appearances at Lake Elsinore with a lot of swings and misses in the strike zone, although he doesn't chase much and draws enough walks to be valuable even as a low-average hitter. Mears has surprising speed for a big man, prompting the Padres to give him exploratory looks in center field last year. His long-term landing spot is likely right field, where he projects to be an average defender with an average arm.

THE FUTURE: Mears has the build, bat speed and plus-plus raw power that are easy to dream on. He'll head to High-A Fort Wayne in 2022 to see if he can stay healthy and get to his power in games against better pitching.

BA GRADE	
50	Risk: Very High

SCOUTING GRADES:	Hitting: 30	Power: 70	Running: 45	Fielding: 45	Arm: 50

Year	Age	Club (Level)	Lge	AVG	G	AB	R	H	2B	3B	HR	RBI	BB	SO	SB	OBP	SLG
2021	20	Lake Elsinore (LoA)	West	.244	71	242	45	59	10	4	17	48	36	114	10	.368	.529
Minor League Totals (3 years)				.248	114	408	75	101	14	7	24	72	59	173	19	.362	.493

9 ROBERT GASSER, LHP

Born: May 31, 1999. **B-T:** L-L. **HT:** 6-1. **WT:** 190. **Drafted:** Houston, 2021 (2nd round). **Signed by:** Kevin Ham.

TRACK RECORD: A lefty with an 88-91 mph fastball in Houston's bullpen in 2020, Gasser hit the weights hard during the coronavirus shutdown and returned in 2021 throwing harder to emerge as the Cougars' staff ace. He logged a 2.63 ERA with 105 strikeouts in 85.2 innings to transform himself from a draft afterthought into a fast-riser, and the Padres drafted him 71st overall and signed him for $884,200. Gasser quickly moved to Low-A Lake Elsinore after signing and hit the ground running with a 1.20 ERA in 15 innings pitched.

SCOUTING REPORT: Gasser's weight room gains improved his entire arsenal. His fastball now sits 90-93 mph with late run and can bump up to 95 when needed. His newly-sharpened slider is now an above-average pitch he can bury for swings and misses and he spots his average changeup well to give him a third quality offering. He is also developing a curveball, but it's more of a show-me pitch at this point. Gasser's best attribute is his plus control. He's able to spot his four-seam fastball up in the zone and can put his secondary pitches where he needs to get swings and misses. His stuff further plays up with a pause in his delivery he devised to throw off hitters' timing.

THE FUTURE: Without overwhelming velocity or an imposing stature, Gasser could be a No. 4 or No. 5 starter. Because he's a polished lefty with pitchability, he's also a fair bet to reach that ceiling. He is set to open the 2022 season at High-A Fort Wayne and could pitch his way to Double-A San Antonio.

MIKE JANES/FOUR SEAM IMAGES

BA GRADE	
45	Risk: High

SCOUTING GRADES:	Fastball: 50	Slider: 55	Curveball: 30	Changeup: 50	Control: 60

Year	Age	Club (Level)	Lge	W	L	ERA	G	GS	IP	H	HR	BB	SO	BB/9	SO/9	WHIP	AVG
2021	22	Padres (R)	ACL	0	0	0.00	1	1	1	0	0	0	1	0.0	9.0	0.00	.000
	22	Lake Elsinore (LoA)	West	0	0	1.29	5	5	14	11	1	2	13	1.3	8.4	0.93	.224
Minor League Totals (1 year)				0	0	1.20	6	6	15	11	1	2	14	1.20	8.40	0.87	.212

10 EURIBIEL ANGELES, SS/2B

Born: May 11, 2002. **B-T:** R-R. **HT:** 5-11. **WT:** 175. **Signed:** Dominican Republic, 2018. **Signed by:** Alvin Duran/Jake Koenig/Chris Kemp.

TRACK RECORD: Because the Padres spent more than $80 million during the 2016-17 international signing period, they were barred from spending more than $300,000 on any prospect the following two years. Among the gems they uncovered at that price was Angeles, who showcased his above-average bat-to-ball skills and raw power with a two-homer game in a tryout for the Padres. Angeles hit .301 in his pro debut in the Dominican Summer League and, despite losing 2020 to the coronavirus pandemic, didn't miss a beat in his stateside debut in 2021. He hit .343 to win the Low-A West batting title at Lake Elsinore and received a late-season promotion to High-A Fort Wayne.

SCOUTING REPORT: Angeles is a natural-born hitter. He has the quick hands to turn around any fastball, stays back on breaking balls and frequently finds the center of the barrel to spray balls from gap to gap. Angeles can make contact with any type of pitch in any part of the strike zone, but in part because he knows he can hit almost anything, he is extremely aggressive and will swing at pitches he can't drive. The Padres believe Angeles will hit the ball with more authority as he cuts down his chase rate, although his swing path will always make him more of a line-drive hitter. Angeles has fringy speed but is an efficient base-stealer with his advanced instincts. He's an instinctive, reliable defender at shortstop, but his speed and average arm make second base his best position long-term.

THE FUTURE: Angeles could develop into an everyday second baseman if he tightens his plate discipline. If not, a utility infielder capable of playing third base, second base and shortstop is a reasonable outcome.

BA GRADE
45 Risk: High

SCOUTING GRADES:	Hitting: 55	Power: 30	Running: 45	Fielding: 55	Arm: 50

Year	Age	Club (Level)	Lge	AVG	G	AB	R	H	2B	3B	HR	RBI	BB	SO	SB	OBP	SLG
2021	19	Lake Elsinore (LoA)	West	.343	87	362	65	124	22	6	3	56	32	61	18	.397	.461
	19	Fort Wayne (HiA)	Cent	.264	18	72	12	19	4	0	1	8	8	16	1	.369	.361
Minor League Totals (2 years)				.321	149	607	105	195	35	8	4	90	55	96	36	.382	.425

11 VICTOR ACOSTA, SS

BA GRADE
50 Risk: Extreme

Born: June 10, 2004. **B-T:** B-R. **HT:** 5-11. **WT:** 170. **Signed:** Dominican Republic, 2021. **Signed by:** Alvin Duran/Trevor Schumm/Chris Kemp.

TRACK RECORD: Acosta ranked as one of the top shortstops in the 2020-21 international signing class and signed with the Padres for $1.8 million, the highest bonus the club awarded that year. Acosta made his pro debut in the Dominican Summer League and made a strong first impression, finishing in the top 10 in the league in runs (45), triples (5), stolen bases (26) and on-base percentage (.431).

SCOUTING REPORT: Acosta has a loud mix of tools and athleticism to dream on. Though he's 5-foot-11, he has plenty of twitch and strength in his compact build. The switch-hitter has fastball bat speed and natural loft in his lefthanded swing that produces surprising power for a player his size. His slashing, righthanded slashing swing is beginning to catch up to his lefthanded swing, giving him the potential to be an above-average hitter with above-average power. Acosta is a plus runner and plays with energy. He has a nose for the ball and is both quick and graceful at shortstop. His plus arm plays anywhere on the infield.

THE FUTURE: Acosta is a projectable offensive talent who the Padres believe can stay at shortstop. He will make his stateside debut in the Arizona Complex League in 2022.

Year	Age	Club (Level)	Lge	AVG	G	AB	R	H	2B	3B	HR	RBI	BB	SO	SB	OBP	SLG
2021	17	Padres (R)	DSL	.285	56	186	45	53	12	5	5	31	38	45	26	.431	.484
Minor League Totals (1 year)				.285	56	186	45	53	12	5	5	31	38	45	26	.431	.484

12 SAMUEL ZAVALA, OF

BA GRADE
50 Risk: Extreme

Born: July 15, 2004. **B-T:** L-L. **HT:** 6-1. **WT:** 175. **Signed:** Venezuela, 2021. **Signed by:** Luis Prieto/Trevor Schumm/Chris Kemp.

TRACK RECORD: Zavala was regarded as one of the best pure hitters in the 2020-21 international signing class and signed with the Padres out of Venezuela for $1.2 million. Zavala made his pro debut in the Dominican Summer League after signing and did not disappoint, hitting for both average (.287) and power (25 extra-base hits in 55 games) while showing remarkable plate discipline for his age with nearly as many walks (32) as strikeouts (36).

SCOUTING REPORT: Zavala has long possessed a knack for finding the barrel with a smooth, whip-like swing. He doesn't have the brute strength of some other teenagers, but he has added more power and loft to his swing as he's matured physically and could wind up with average power to go with his above-average hitting ability tools. Zavala is bilingual and a heady player, leading the Padres to believe he will adjust quickly as he faces more advanced pitching. Zavala is only an average runner, but his advanced instincts help compensate for his speed and the Padres view him as a true center fielder. His above-average arm strength allows him to play all three outfield positions.

THE FUTURE: Zavala will make his U.S. debut in the Arizona Complex League in 2022. He and Victor Acosta give the Padres two, low-level prospects who could blossom into everyday regulars, if not more.

Year	Age	Club (Level)	Lge	AVG	G	AB	R	H	2B	3B	HR	RBI	BB	SO	SB	OBP	SLG
2021	16	Padres (R)	DSL	.297	55	195	44	58	16	6	3	40	32	36	11	.400	.487
Minor League Totals (1 year)				**.297**	**55**	**195**	**44**	**58**	**16**	**6**	**3**	**40**	**32**	**36**	**11**	**.400**	**.487**

13 ROBERT SUAREZ, RHP

BA GRADE
40 Risk: Medium

Born: March 1, 1991. **B-T:** R-R. **HT:** 6-2. **WT:** 200. **Signed:** Japan, 2021.
Signed by: A.J. Preller.

TRACK RECORD: Suarez posted 1.71 ERA in 47.1 innings in the Mexican League in 2015 but had never been part of an MLB organization when he signed with Softbank in Japan after the season. He missed all of 2017 after having Tommy John surgery and moved on to Hanshin, where he had a 1.16 ERA and 45 saves in 2021 and did not allow a home run in 62.1 innings. Suarez exercised his option to become a free agent and signed a two-year, $11 million contract with the Padres right before the lockout began in December.

SCOUTING REPORT: Suarez has an imposing presence on the mound and aggressively goes after hitters with his plus-plus fastball. His fastball lives at 96-97 mph and touches 101 with late explosion and ride, and he throws it in all quadrants of the strike zone. Suarez developed an 88-92 mph split-changeup in Japan that flashes plus and has become his go-to secondary offering. He relied on a short, tilting slider early in his career, but it's now mostly a chase pitch. Suarez attacks the strike zone with plus control and posted a career-low walk rate of 1.2 per nine innings in 2021.

THE FUTURE: Suarez will step right into the Padres' bullpen in 2022. He has a chance to emerge as a high-leverage option quickly.

Year	Age	Club (Level)	Lge	W	L	ERA	G	GS	IP	H	HR	BB	SO	BB/9	SO/9	WHIP	AVG
2021	30	Hanshin (CL)	JPN	1	1	1.16	62	0	62	40	0	8	58	1.2	8.4	0.77	—
Japanese League Totals (5 years)				**7**	**13**	**2.81**	**191**	**0**	**205**	**168**	**14**	**70**	**209**	**3.1**	**9.2**	**1.16**	**—**

14 KEVIN KOPPS, RHP

BA GRADE
45 Risk: High

Born: March 2, 1997. **B-T:** R-R. **HT:** 6-0. **WT:** 200. **Drafted:** Arkansas, 2021 (3rd round). **Signed by:** Steve Moritz.

TRACK RECORD: Kopps missed all of 2018 at Arkansas after having Tommy John surgery and struggled during the shortened 2020 season, but he rebounded with a historic season for the Razorbacks in 2021. He went 12-1 with 11 saves, 131 strikeouts and an NCAA-best 0.90 ERA in 89.2 innings as a super reliever and won the Golden Spikes Award. As a sixth-year senior who was already 24 years old, Kopps fell to the Padres in the third round of the draft. He signed for a below-slot $300,000 and finished the year in Double-A San Antonio's bullpen.

SCOUTING REPORT: Kopps relies overwhelmingly on one pitch: a gyro-like cutter/slider in the mid-80s with downward break. He throws nearly 75% of the time and batters still struggle to hit it even when they know it is coming. Kopps locates the pitch extremely well and batters have trouble identifying it with the way it tunnels off of his 88-82 mph fastball. Kopps occasionally mixes in a below-average curveball that sits in the mid-70s and has toyed with a fringe-average changeup, but his slider is what determines his success.

THE FUTURE: Kopps will turn 25 before Opening Day and doesn't have much development left. He'll likely start the year in the upper levels and could crack the Padres bullpen by the end of the season.

Year	Age	Club (Level)	Lge	W	L	ERA	G	GS	IP	H	HR	BB	SO	BB/9	SO/9	WHIP	AVG
2021	24	Padres (R)	ACL	0	0	1.93	4	0	4	3	0	1	10	1.9	19.3	0.86	.176
	24	Fort Wayne (HiA)	Cent	1	0	0.00	8	0	8	2	0	4	10	4.5	11.3	0.75	.080
	24	San Antonio (AA)	Cent	0	0	0.00	2	0	2	0	0	1	2	4.5	9.0	0.50	.000
Minor League Totals (1 year)				**1**	**0**	**0.61**	**14**	**0**	**15**	**5**	**0**	**6**	**22**	**3.68**	**13.50**	**0.75**	**.104**

15 VICTOR LIZARRAGA, RHP

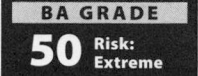

BA GRADE
50 Risk: Extreme

Born: Nov. 30, 2003. **B-T:** R-R. **HT:** 6-3. **WT:** 180. **Signed:** Mexico, 2021.
Signed by: Bill McLaughlin/Emmanuel Rangel/Trevor Schumm/Chris Kemp.

TRACK RECORD: Lizarraga ranked as Mexico's best pitching prospect in the 2020-21 international class and signed with the Padres for $1 million. His advanced feel for pitching led the Padres to challenge him with an assignment to the Arizona Complex League where, at age 17, he was the second-youngest player in the circuit. Lizarraga finished the season on an impressive run—11.1 innings, one run, six walks, 18 strikeouts—after a three-week reset following two deaths in his family just days apart.

SCOUTING REPORT: Long, lean and athletic, Lizarraga is a projectable teenage righthander who is a good bet to add strength and velocity as he fills out. His fastball presently sits 90-94 mph and he pairs it with an upper-70s curveball that has average potential. He rounds out his arsenal with a fading changeup he throws with conviction and confidence to give it above-average potential. Lizarraga walked more batters than expected in his pro debut, but the Padres expect his control to improve to average in pro ball.

THE FUTURE: Lizarraga was essentially a high school junior when the Padres jumped him over the Dominican Summer League to start his career in the U.S. His career can break a lot of different ways, but his three-pitch mix gives him the foundation to stick in a starting rotation.

Year	Age	Club (Level)	Lge	W	L	ERA	G	GS	IP	H	HR	BB	SO	BB/9	SO/9	WHIP	AVG
2021	17	Padres (R)	ACL	0	4	5.10	11	11	30	25	5	15	35	4.5	10.5	1.33	.223
Minor League Totals (1 year)				0	4	5.10	11	11	30	25	5	15	35	4.50	10.50	1.33	.223

16 JUSTIN LANGE, RHP

BA GRADE
50 Risk: Extreme

Born: Sept. 11, 2001. **B-T:** R-R. **HT:** 6-4. **WT:** 207. **Drafted:** HS—Llano, Texas, 2020 (1st round supplemental). **Signed by:** Kevin Ham.

TRACK RECORD: Lange originally committed to Dallas Baptist as an infielder with plus-plus speed, but a huge velocity increase his senior year pushed him up draft boards as a pitcher. The Padres selected him 34th overall in 2020 and signed him for an above-slot $2 million bonus. Lange reported to the alternate training site and instructional league after he signed but was limited by shoulder fatigue. An injury again hindered him in 2021 as a knee issue limited him to just 22 innings in the Arizona Complex League in his official pro debut.

SCOUTING REPORT: Lange is a long-term project with very real but very raw arm strength. His fastball has exceptional carry and sits 95-98 mph when he's healthy, although his balky knee sapped him of velocity over the summer. His work-in-progress secondaries include a potentially above-average slider that sits in the mid-to-high 80s and a seldomly-used change-up. Lange's command of his secondaries have a long way to go for him to make good on the Padres' investment. His control is well below-average overall, largely because of his inability to throw his secondary pitches for strikes.

THE FUTURE: Lange remains a lottery ticket with a wide range of potential outcomes. Getting healthy and improving his command of his secondaries are his most important steps in 2022.

Year	Age	Club (Level)	Lge	W	L	ERA	G	GS	IP	H	HR	BB	SO	BB/9	SO/9	WHIP	AVG
2021	19	Padres (R)	ACL	0	3	6.95	9	9	22	18	1	15	29	6.1	11.9	1.50	.217
Minor League Totals (2 years)				0	3	6.95	9	9	22	18	1	15	29	6.14	11.86	1.50	.217

17 EGUY ROSARIO, 2B/3B

BA GRADE
45 Risk: High

Born: Aug. 25, 1999. **B-T:** R-R. **HT:** 5-9. **WT:** 204. **Signed:** Dominican Republic, 2015. **Signed by:** Felix Felix/Trevor Schumm/Chris Kemp.

TRACK RECORD: Rosario signed with the Padres for $300,000 on his 16th birthday and has generally been among the youngest players in his league every year. As such, he was overmatched in his early years, but he showed signs of life in the High-A California League in 2019 and had a breakout year at Double-A San Antonio in 2021. He led Double-A Central in doubles (31), tied for second in hits (118) and finished fifth in stolen bases (30), leading the Padres to add him to the 40-man roster after the season.

SCOUTING REPORT: Rosario is surprisingly twitchy and athletic despite his round, stocky build. He has a short, quick righthanded swing and is best when his approach is aimed at shooting balls from gap to gap. He showed off his strength gains with the first double-digit homer campaign in 2021, but he is susceptible to pulling off balls when he tries to generate power. Rosario is an above-average runner who has improved his ability to put that speed to good use on the bases. He is playable at shortstop, but his range and actions fit better at second base or even third, where he can show off his nearly plus-plus arm.

THE FUTURE: Rosario best profiles as a utility infielder. He'll start 2022 at Triple-A El Paso.

Year	Age	Club (Level)	Lge	AVG	G	AB	R	H	2B	3B	HR	RBI	BB	SO	SB	OBP	SLG
2021	21	San Antonio (AA)	Cent	.281	114	420	65	118	31	3	12	61	49	109	30	.360	.455
Minor League Totals (6 years)				.270	520	1952	283	527	127	22	30	251	195	468	116	.343	.404

18 REISS KNEHR, RHP

BA GRADE

40 Risk: Medium

Born: Nov. 3, 1996. **B-T:** L-R. **HT:** 6-3 **WT:** 231. **Drafted:** Fordham, 2018 (20th round). **Signed by:** Jake Koenig.

TRACK RECORD: A two-way player at Fordham, Knehr intrigued the Padres as a pitcher and signed for $80,000 after they selected him in the 20th round in 2018. While inconsistent in his full-season, Knehr was the darling of the Padres' 2020 instructional league and pitched his way to the majors in 2021. He appeared both in the rotation and out of the bullpen for the Padres' injury-ravaged staff and logged a 4.97 ERA in 29 innings.

SCOUTING REPORT: Knehr packs a dangerous 1-2 punch with a high-spin, 93-95 mph fastball and an upper-80s changeup with horizontal break that has improved to become a plus pitch. He is still figuring out his mound presence and pitch usage, however. Lauded in the minors for an aggressive, bulldog mentality, Knehr spent much of his big-league time nibbling around the strike zone and was too reliant on his upper-80s cutter, the worst pitch in his arsenal. His changeup gets hit when he overcooks it, so he is working to choke off a bit more velocity. Knehr has tinkered with a curveball to add a bit more differential in his pitch speeds. His control has long been fringy.

THE FUTURE: Knehr will likely open 2022 in Triple-A El Paso's rotation. He projects to be a long reliever or spot starter and will again be in the callup mix in 2022.

Year	Age	Club (Level)	Lge	W	L	ERA	G	GS	IP	H	HR	BB	SO	BB/9	SO/9	WHIP	AVG
2021	24	San Antonio (AA)	Cent	6	1	3.90	11	11	55	41	4	22	46	3.6	7.5	1.14	.209
	24	El Paso (AAA)	West	0	2	2.66	8	5	20	15	3	9	20	4.0	8.9	1.18	.211
	24	San Diego (MLB)	NL	1	2	4.97	12	5	29	23	2	20	20	6.2	6.2	1.48	.221
Major League Totals (1 year)				1	2	4.97	12	5	29	23	2	20	20	6.21	6.21	1.48	.221
Minor League Totals (4 years)				12	9	4.23	56	29	177	153	21	74	194	3.77	9.88	1.28	.231

19 ADRIAN MARTINEZ, RHP

BA GRADE

40 Risk: High

Born: Dec. 10, 1996. **B-T:** R-R. **HT:** 6-2 **WT:** 195. **Signed:** Mexico, 2015. **Signed by:** Chris Kemp.

TRACK RECORD: The Padres purchased Martinez's rights from the Mexican League's Mexico City franchise in 2015, the same year they purchased Andres Muñoz from the team. Martinez missed all of the following season after having Tommy John surgery, but he used the down time to bulk up and broke out at the Class A levels in 2019. Martinez began 2021 at Double-A San Antonio and pushed his way to Triple-A El Paso by the end of the season. He struggled with a tighter strike zone at Triple-A, but the Padres still added him to the 40-man roster after the season.

SCOUTING REPORT: Martinez officially has three pitches in his arsenal but really only throws his fastball and changeup. His four-seam fastball sits 91-92 mph and touches 95 with fade and run. He holds his velocity late in games, although his fastball command is scattered. Martinez's main weapon is a nearly plus-plus changeup that has excellent separation from his fastball in the low 80s and has screwball-like action that dives down and away from lefties. It's a "disgusting" pitch in one evaluator's words and a true out pitch. Martinez rarely throws his below-average slider and is a reverse-splits pitcher more effective against lefties than righties.

THE FUTURE: Martinez projects to be a middle reliever with his fastball and changeup combination. His major league debut should come in 2022.

Year	Age	Club (Level)	Lge	W	L	ERA	G	GS	IP	H	HR	BB	SO	BB/9	SO/9	WHIP	AVG
2021	24	San Antonio (AA)	Cent	7	3	2.34	17	13	80	64	4	24	83	2.7	9.3	1.09	.215
	24	El Paso (AAA)	West	1	2	5.28	9	9	44	50	6	17	39	3.5	7.9	1.51	.291
Minor League Totals (7 years)				21	18	4.30	100	48	327	350	25	100	332	2.76	9.15	1.38	.272

20 RAY KERR, LHP

BA GRADE

40 Risk: High

Born: Sept. 10, 1994. **B-T:** B-R. **HT:** 5-11. **WT:** 183. **Signed:** Lassen (Calif.) JC, 2017 (NDFA). **Signed by:** Jordan Bley (Mariners)

TRACK RECORD: Kerr pitched Lassen (Calif.) JC to the verge of a conference title in 2017 and followed with a star turn in the Alaska Baseball League. He led the summer league with

a 1.13 ERA and finished third with 48 strikeouts while touching 93 mph from the left side, leading the Mariners to sign him as an undrafted free agent for $5,000. Kerr initially worked as a starter, but he moved to the bullpen full-time in 2021 and vaulted to Triple-A. The Padres acquired him after the season as one of two prospects for Adam Frazier.

SCOUTING REPORT: Kerr's stuff ticked up in relief to make him one of the minors' hardest-throwing lefthanders. His fastball averages 97 mph and touches 101 mph out a low arm slot that makes for a tough angle on hitters. The ball gets on batters quicker than they expect out of his low-effort delivery, resulting in late swings and misses. Kerr's sweeping 80-84 mph slider flashes average with late downward bite and is effective against lefties, while his changeup is a well below-average pitch he rarely uses. Kerr is an excellent athlete who throws down vicious dunks on a basketball court, but his control is just fringy.

THE FUTURE: Kerr is on track to be a hard-throwing, lefthanded middle reliever. He should make his major league debut in 2022.

Year	Age	Club (Level)	Lge	W	L	ERA	G	GS	IP	H	HR	BB	SO	BB/9	SO/9	WHIP	AVG
2021	26	Arkansas (AA)	Cent	2	1	2.83	24	0	28	18	2	10	43	3.1	13.5	0.98	.176
	26	Tacoma (AAA)	West	0	0	4.09	12	1	11	8	0	6	17	4.9	13.9	1.27	.205
Minor League Totals (5 years)				11	19	3.91	98	36	244	228	17	110	258	4.06	9.52	1.39	.248

21 STEVEN WILSON, RHP

Born: Aug. 24, 1994. **B-T:** R-R. **HT:** 6-4. **WT:** 213. **Drafted:** Santa Clara, 2018 (8th round). **Signed by:** Tim Reynolds.

BA GRADE
40 Risk: High

TRACK RECORD: A 35th-round pick of the Phillies out of high school, Wilson missed his freshman year at Santa Clara with a shoulder injury and his senior year after having Tommy John surgery. Granted a sixth-year of eligibility, he emerged as the Broncos' best starter and signed with the Padres for $5,000 as an eighth-round pick in 2018. Wilson moved to the bullpen as a professional and raced to Triple-A in his first full season, but he's since been sidetracked by injuries, including a right oblique strain and a sprained right foot in 2021. He was lights-out in 10 scoreless appearances for Escogido in the Dominican League after the season and was added to the 40-man roster.

SCOUTING REPORT: Wilson dominates on the mound when he's healthy. His fastball sits 93-96 mph with late movement and carry at the top of the strike zone. He pairs it with an average mid-80s slider that he commands well. Both pitches get swings and misses and he relies on them heavily, but he will also flash an average changeup that neutralizes lefties. An intelligent pitcher who was working toward a masters degree in business analytics when he signed, Wilson's ability to out-think a hitter is also a strength.

THE FUTURE: Wilson is a low-cost replacement option to fill one of multiple openings in the Padres bullpen in 2022. That's provided he remains healthy.

Year	Age	Club (Level)	Lge	W	L	ERA	G	GS	IP	H	HR	BB	SO	BB/9	SO/9	WHIP	AVG
2021	26	Padres (R)	ACL	0	0	0.00	2	0	2	1	0	0	8	0.0	27.0	0.38	.111
	26	El Paso (AAA)	West	4	0	3.43	28	0	39	22	7	14	63	3.2	14.4	0.92	.157
Minor League Totals (4 years)				8	3	3.24	77	0	114	80	16	44	165	3.47	13.03	1.09	.196

22 BRANDON VALENZUELA, C

Born: Oct. 2, 2000. **B-T:** S-R. **HT:** 6-0. **WT:** 230. **Signed:** Mexico, 2017. **Signed by:** Bill McLaughlin/Trevor Schumm/Chris Kemp.

BA GRADE
40 Risk: High

TRACK RECORD: Valenzuela enjoyed a growth spurt after the Padres purchased his rights from the Mexican's League's Mexico City franchise for $100,000 and rose up the organizational depth chart after the Padres traded away most of their catching depth. Long thought of as a defense-first backstop, Valenzuela showed he could swing the bat too in his full-season debut in 2021. He hit .307/.389/.444 while showing increased power at Low-A Lake Elsinore and earned a late promotion to High-A Fort Wayne.

SCOUTING REPORT: As a catcher, Valenzuela is heads and shoulders above his peer group in his ability to call a game, learn hitters' tendencies and manage a pitching staff. He has an innate ability to know who needs a pep talk and who needs a kick in the pants. He's an elite receiver and blocker with an above-average arm. Valenzuela's feet are not particularly quick, however, and there are questions about his conditioning. Getting in better shape could improve what he lacks in quick-twitch and help him at the plate, too. He has a strong eye for the strike zone and sprays the ball to all fields with a short, sound swing, but his bat speed is below-average and his power potential is fringy.

THE FUTURE: Valenzuela profiles nicely as a backup catcher. He'll need to increase his bat speed to hit enough to start.

Year	Age	Club (Level)	Lge	AVG	G	AB	R	H	2B	3B	HR	RBI	BB	SO	SB	OBP	SLG
2021	20	Lake Elsinore (LoA)	West	.307	82	329	50	101	21	3	6	62	44	80	3	.389	.444
	20	Fort Wayne (HiA)	Cent	.245	15	49	4	12	1	0	1	7	15	20	1	.415	.327
Minor League Totals (4 years)				.276	193	721	109	199	33	6	8	116	132	191	6	.390	.372

23 ETHAN ELLIOTT, LHP

BA GRADE
40 Risk: High

Born: April 28, 1997. **B-T:** L-L. **HT:** 6-3. **WT:** 186. **Drafted:** Lincoln Memorial (Tenn.), 2019 (10th round). **Signed by:** Tyler Stubblefield.

TRACK RECORD: Lightly recruited out of high school, Elliott landed at Division II Lincoln Memorial (Tenn.) and set program records for ERA, wins, strikeouts and innings pitched in a decorated four-year career. The Padres drafted him in the 10th round in 2019 and signed him for $10,000. Elliott began to receive buzz at instructional league in 2020 and had a breakout 2021 that included an immaculate inning on Opening Day at High-A Fort Wayne and a mid-season promotion to Double-A San Antonio. He made just three starts for the Missions before shoulder soreness ended his season in July.

SCOUTING REPORT: On the surface, Elliott's four-seam fastball is a below-average pitch at 88-90 mph that he spots well to both sides of the plate. His fastball gets on hitters quickly, though, due his elite extension out of his three-quarters arm slot and plays up well beyond its velocity. Elliott uses a fastball-heavy attack and keeps hitters off balance with a low-80s, above-average changeup as his main secondary. He is working to tighten his mid-70s slider to make it an average pitch. Elliott throws plenty of strikes with above-average control, but the Padres want to see him up his tempo on the mound. They also hope he can fill out his lanky 6-foot-3 frame and unlock more velocity with more time in the gym.

THE FUTURE: Elliott's fastball-changeup combination is effective enough to play as a bulk reliever in the majors. A bump in velocity would raise his ceiling considerably.

Year	Age	Club (Level)	Lge	W	L	ERA	G	GS	IP	H	HR	BB	SO	BB/9	SO/9	WHIP	AVG
2021	24	Fort Wayne (HiA)	Cent	2	1	2.95	12	12	58	43	13	13	71	2.0	11.0	0.97	.204
	24	San Antonio (AA)	Cent	0	1	3.55	3	3	12	16	1	6	16	4.3	11.4	1.74	.308
Minor League Totals (3 years)				2	2	2.62	27	27	106	86	17	23	125	1.95	10.58	1.03	.218

24 EFRAIN CONTRERAS, RHP

BA GRADE
45 Risk: Extreme

Born: Jan. 2, 2000. **B-T:** R-R. **HT:** 5-10. **WT:** 185. **Signed:** Mexico, 2017. **Signed by:** Emmanuel Rangel/Bill McLaughlin.

TRACK RECORD: The Padres purchased Contreras' rights from the Mexican League's Veracruz franchise for $50,000 in 2017 and quickly realized they had a steal. Contreras finished eighth in the Low-A Midwest League in strikeouts in his pro debut in 2019 and drew high praise from general manager A.J. Preller at instructional league in 2020, but he walked off the mound at the end of instructs with an elbow injury that required Tommy John surgery. Despite not pitching in an official game in two years, Contreras was added to the 40-man roster in November.

SCOUTING REPORT: A stout, stocky righthander with an advanced feel for pitching, Contreras was trending toward becoming a back of the rotation starter before his elbow injury. He locates three pitches for strikes in his 92-95 mph fastball, average downer curveball and fading, above-average changeup in the mid 80s. While none of his pitches are plus, they all play up with how he mixes and commands them. His fastball gets carry up in the zone and his curveball breaks sharply downward, giving him the north-south profile teams covet.

THE FUTURE: Contreras was progressing through his throwing program over the winter in hopes of returning to games in 2022. He'll be just 22 on Opening Day and has time to recapture his momentum.

Year	Age	Club (Level)	Lge	W	L	ERA	G	GS	IP	H	HR	BB	SO	BB/9	SO/9	WHIP	AVG
2021	21	Did not play—Injured															
Minor League Totals (3 years)				8	9	3.03	41	30	178	146	16	46	197	2.33	9.96	1.08	.223

25 NOEL VELA, LHP

BA GRADE
45 Risk: Extreme

Born: Dec. 21, 1998. **B-T:** L-L. **HT:** 6-1. **WT:** 175. **Drafted:** HS—Mission, Texas, 2017 (28th round). **Signed by:** Kevin Ham.

TRACK RECORD: Vela drew little attention in high school and was committed to Texas-Rio Grande Valley, but the Padres took a chance on him in the 28th round in 2017. The late-blooming Vela spent his first two professional seasons in the Rookie levels and came back from the coronavirus shutdown in tip-top shape. Finally sent out to full-season ball in 2021, Vela posted a 3.90

ERA and averaged 11 strikeouts per nine innings as he climbed from Low-A to High-A.

SCOUTING REPORT: Vela's fastball has ticked up from the added strength gains to become an above-average weapon. His four-seamer now sits 91-95 mph and plays up with carry at the top of the strike zone. His fastball command is still raw, but he gets swings and misses when he locates it. Vela's curveball with 1-to-7 break flashes plus and is among the best curves in the system, while others prefer his deceptive, side-spinning changeup that shows above-average potential. Even with below-average control, Vela's arsenal plays against hitters on both sides of the plate. He limited lefties to a .135 batting average and righties to a .216 average in his full-season debut.

THE FUTURE: Vela is likely to settle into a middle relief role, but the Padres are in no hurry to pigeonhole him. He'll see Double-A San Antonio in 2022.

Year	Age	Club (Level)	Lge	W	L	ERA	G	GS	IP	H	HR	BB	SO	BB/9	SO/9	WHIP	AVG
2021	22	Lake Elsinore (LoA)	West	1	8	3.98	13	13	54	42	5	30	63	5.0	10.4	1.33	.202
	22	Fort Wayne (HiA)	Cent	0	3	3.78	8	8	33	31	2	16	44	4.3	11.9	1.41	.244
Minor League Totals (5 years)				4	18	4.40	46	32	145	140	11	94	178	5.82	11.02	1.61	.247

26 JAIRO IRIARTE, RHP

BA GRADE
45 Risk: Extreme

Born: Dec. 15, 2001. **B-T:** R-R. **HT:** 6-5. **WT:** 200. **Signed:** Venezuela, 2018. **Signed by:** Luis Prieto/Chris Kemp.

TRACK RECORD: Iriarte stood 6-foot-2 and weighed 160 pounds when he signed with the Padres for $75,000 in 2018 out of Venezuela. He had a growth spurt and packed on muscle after signing and now stands an imposing 6-foot-5, 200 pounds. Iriarte showed well in the Dominican Summer League after he signed and was pitching in the Arizona Complex League in 2021 when the Padres pushed him to Low-A Lake Elsinore after the Storm lost multiple players to Covid-19 protocols. Iriarte wasn't ready for the assignment and got hit hard, but still showed enough to emerge as a sleeper.

SCOUTING REPORT: Iriarte's fastball sat 85-87 mph when he signed but now sits 95-97 after his explosive growth spurt. His fastball plays up with carry through the top of the strike zone and his 86-87 mph changeup with late fade has the makings of a future plus pitch. Iriarte's 83-85 mph slider could become above-average and gives him the three-pitch mix to be a starter. Iriarte's stuff is mostly potential at this point and he is still very raw as a pitcher. He got shelled for 25 hits and 27 earned runs in nine innings at Lake Elsinore and has a long way to go. His control is fringy and needs work.

THE FUTURE: The Padres see Iriarte as a starting pitching prospect who just needs reps. His stuff could make him a hard-throwing reliever if his control doesn't come.

Year	Age	Club (Level)	Lge	W	L	ERA	G	GS	IP	H	HR	BB	SO	BB/9	SO/9	WHIP	AVG
2021	19	Padres (R)	ACL	0	1	4.71	8	3	21	18	1	7	25	3.0	10.7	1.19	.237
	19	Lake Elsinore (LoA)	West	0	4	27.00	4	3	9	25	5	6	9	6.0	9.0	3.44	.490
Minor League Totals (2 years)				1	7	7.03	24	11	65	78	10	27	55	3.72	7.58	1.61	.298

27 COREY ROSIER, OF

BA GRADE
40 Risk: High

Born: Sept 7, 1999. **B-T:** L-R. **HT:** 5-10. **WT:** 184.
Drafted: UNC Greensboro, 2021 (12th round). **Signed by:** Ty Holub (Mariners).

TRACK RECORD: Rosier led the Southern Conference in hits and triples and tied for the conference lead in runs and RBIs as a third-year sophomore in 2021. He also enjoyed a power surge with 12 home runs after hitting just three in his first 166 collegiate plate appearances. The Mariners drafted Rosier in the 12th round and signed him for $125,000, and he quickly hit his way to Low-A Modesto in a loud pro debut. The Padres were among the teams to take notice and acquired Rosier as one of two prospects for Adam Frazier after the season.

SCOUTING REPORT: Rosier is a contact-oriented hitter with a simple approach and setup and a fluid lefthanded swing. He shows solid control of the strike zone and had nearly as many walks (18) nearly as strikeouts (22) with Modesto. Rosier's home runs were mostly to the pull-side in college and he could develop more pop, but he's a contact hitter first. Rosier's plus-plus speed is his best tool. He uses it efficiently to steal bases and covers ample ground in center field. He is an above-average defender in center and has plus arm strength that keeps runners from taking extra bases.

THE FUTURE: Rosier is a solid bet to become at least an extra outfielder. He'll make his organizational debut at High-A Fort Wayne in 2022.

Year	Age	Club (Level)	Lge	AVG	G	AB	R	H	2B	3B	HR	RBI	BB	SO	SB	OBP	SLG
2021	21	Mariners (R)	ACL	.000	1	3	0	0	0	0	0	0	0	2	0	.000	.000
	21	Modesto (LoA)	West	.390	31	118	31	46	8	3	3	23	18	20	13	.461	.585
Minor League Totals (1 year)				.380	32	121	31	46	8	3	3	23	18	22	13	.451	.570

28 NERWILIAN CEDEÑO, 3B/2B

BA GRADE
45 Risk: Extreme

Born: March 16, 2002. **B-T:** B-R. **HT:** 5-11. **WT:** 175. **Signed:** Venezuela, 2018. **Signed by:** Trevor Schumm/Luis Prieto.

TRACK RECORD: Cedeño signed with the Padres for $300,000 out of Venezuela in 2018 and quickly emerged as a favored low-level sleeper candidate. Many believed Cedeño was primed for a breakout season in 2021, but he suffered a meniscus tear before spring training and didn't get on the field until late August. He hit .241/.354/.537 with 11 extra-base hits in 19 games in the Arizona Complex League after he returned and was a full participant in instructional league.

SCOUTING REPORT: Cedeño boasts a line-drive approach and solid bat-to-ball skills as a young switch-hitter. He's a better hitter from the left side and does a solid job of not chasing out of the strike zone, although he swings and misses in the zone a bit much. Cedeño's strong forearms have the Padres believing he'll develop more power as he matures. He is an average runner with an average arm and has the potential to be an average defender across the infield. He primarily plays shortstop now but figures to settle in as a third baseman or an offensive-minded second baseman

THE FUTURE: Cedeño will still be young for the league when he makes his way to Low-A in 2022.

Year	Age	Club (Level)	Lge	AVG	G	AB	R	H	2B	3B	HR	RBI	BB	SO	SB	OBP	SLG
2021	19	Padres (R)	ACL	.241	18	54	8	13	8	1	2	7	9	20	2	.354	.537
Minor League Totals (2 years)				.205	65	220	34	45	14	2	2	28	49	63	6	.353	.314

29 DANIEL MONTESINO, OF/1B

BA GRADE
45 Risk: Extreme

Born: Feb. 12, 2004. **B-T:** L-L. **HT:** 6-0. **WT:** 195. **Signed:** Venezuela, 2021. **Signed by:** Luis Prieto/Trevor Schumm/Chris Kemp.

TRACK RECORD: Montesino signed with the Padres for $1 million out of Venezuela when the 2020-21 international signing period opened, one of four players the Padres gave a seven-figure bonus. He made his pro debut in the Dominican Summer League after signing and was the Padres' most productive hitter on the team.

SCOUTING REPORT: A left-handed hitter with a hanging leg kick, Montesino has a loose swing with good bat control and an all-fields approach. He has advanced pitch recognition for his age, giving him the early foundation to be a potentially above-average hitter. Montesino's broad shoulders stoke belief that he will develop plus power as he matures, although that requires a lot of physical projection. Montesino is firmly a bat-first prospect. He's a below-average runner and is likely headed to first base if he can't improve his reads and jumps in the outfield corners. He's less athletic than most of his peers.

THE FUTURE: The Padres see Montesino as a middle-of-the-order threat, but he will have to take care not to lose his athleticism and bat speed as he matures. He'll make his stateside debut in 2022.

Year	Age	Club (Level)	Lge	AVG	G	AB	R	H	2B	3B	HR	RBI	BB	SO	SB	OBP	SLG
2021	17	Padres (R)	DSL	.316	56	190	37	60	13	4	4	48	43	53	8	.444	.489
Minor League Totals (1 year)				.316	56	190	37	60	13	4	4	48	43	53	8	.444	.489

30 MATT WALDRON, RHP

BA GRADE
40 Risk: High

Born: Sept. 26, 1997. **B-T:** R-R. **HT:** 6-2. **WT:** 205. **Drafted:** Nebraska-Lincoln, 2019 (18th round). **Signed by:** Kyle Bamberger (Cleveland).

TRACK RECORD: Cleveland drafted Waldron in the 18th round in 2019 and signed him for $5,000 before trading him to the Padres in the 2020 deal that sent Mike Clevinger to San Diego. Waldron started toying with a knuckleball during 2021 spring training and the low-spin floater intrigued the Padres, who convinced him to feature the weapon. Waldron rode the knuckler to a solid early showing at High-A Fort Wayne and a promotion to Double-A San Antonio before shoulder soreness sidelined him in August. He returned in the Arizona Fall League.

SCOUTING REPORT: Previously, Waldron's repertoire was rather nondescript for a minor league right-hander: a 92-94 mph fastball with a fringy slider and a fringy changeup. The introduction of his knuckle-ball, however, gives Waldron a chance to stand out. He throws two varieties of the floater, a low-80s one and a low-70s version. He moved to throwing his knuckleball 80% of the time as the season progressed. His control of his knuckleball is fringy, and the pitch tends to get hit as it flattens out late in games.

THE FUTURE: Waldron should return to Double-A to start 2022.

Year	Age	Club (Level)	Lge	W	L	ERA	G	GS	IP	H	HR	BB	SO	BB/9	SO/9	WHIP	AVG
2021	24	Fort Wayne (HiA)	Cent	3	4	3.24	13	13	72	69	6	19	72	2.4	9.0	1.22	.256
	24	San Antonio (AA)	Cent	0	4	6.61	7	7	31	35	2	16	31	4.6	8.9	1.63	.282
Minor League Totals (3 years)				7	8	3.86	34	21	149	136	11	39	160	2.35	9.64	1.17	.242

MORE PROSPECTS TO KNOW

31 JOSE AZOCAR, OF

SLEEPER

A minor league free agent signee, the 25-year-old Azocar led Triple-A West in triples and stole 32 bases in 2021. He rivals Robert Hassell III for the Padres' best defensive outfielder.

32 TIRSO ORNELAS, OF

Opinions are split on whether Ornelas will indeed fulfill his potential as a power-hitting right fielder. He led High-A Central with 31 doubles but still slugged only .389 in a repeat year at the level.

33 ESTEURY RUIZ, OF

Acquired from the Royals in 2017, the 22-year-old Ruiz is now a full-time outfielder after beginning his career as a second baseman. He stole 36 bases in 2021 but still struggles with making contact.

34 JORGE OÑA, OF

Oña turned 25 in December and has been limited to 237 games in four minor league seasons due to various injuries, including an elbow and leg injuries in 2021. The Padres removed him from the 40-man roster after the season.

35 MICHEL BAEZ, RHP

Baez had Tommy John surgery before the start of the 2021 season and is set to return in 2022. Once a Top 100 Prospect, he has been slowed by injuries and an inability to replicate the control he showed earlier in his career.

36 REGGIE LAWSON, RHP

Lawson made just four starts in his return from Tommy John surgery before shoulder soreness ended his season. The former supplemental second-round pick has pitched more than 75 innings only once in five seasons and was removed from the 40-man roster in November.

37 JOSE QUEZADA, RHP

The 26-year-old led the Padres system with 18 saves on the strength of hard changeup with 10 inches of horizontal break. He pairs that offering with a mid-90s fastball and mid-80s slider.

38 MOISES LUGO, RHP

Lugo's stuff ticked up after a move to the bullpen late in the 2021 season, particularly his slider. He finished the year at Double-A San Antonio and could be a callup option for the Padres in 2022.

39 TAYLOR KOHLWEY, 1B/OF

Kohlwey hit .319/.381/.456 in 97 games at Triple-A El Paso and earned high praise from coaches. He's a versatile lefthanded hitter who profiles as a bench option that can hold down first base, left field or right field.

40 TOM COSGROVE, LHP

A 12th-round pick out of Manhattan in 2017, Cosgrove rode his hammer curveball to immense success out of the bullpen at Double-A San Antonio in 2021. He's a potential callup option for the Padres bullpen in 2022.

TOP PROSPECTS OF THE DECADE

Year	Player, Pos	2021 Org
2012	Anthony Rizzo, 1B	Yankees
2013	Casey Kelly, RHP	LG (Korea)
2014	Austin Hedges, C	Guardians
2015	Matt Wisler, RHP	Rays
2016	Javier Guerra, SS	Padres
2017	Anderson Espinoza, RHP	Padres
2018	Fernando Tatis Jr., SS	Padres
2019	Fernando Tatis Jr., SS	Padres
2020	MacKenzie Gore, LHP	Padres
2021	MacKenzie Gore, LHP	Padres

TOP DRAFT PICKS OF THE DECADE

Year	Player, Pos	2021 Org
2012	Max Fried, LHP	Braves
2013	Hunter Renfroe, OF	Red Sox
2014	Trea Turner, SS	Dodgers
2015	Austin Smith, RHP (2nd round)	Padres
2016	Cal Quantrill, RHP	Guardians
2017	MacKenzie Gore, LHP	Padres
2018	Ryan Weathers, LHP	Padres
2019	CJ Abrams, SS	Padres
2020	Robert Hassell III, OF	Padres
2021	Jackson Merrill, SS	Padres

San Francisco Giants

BY JOSH NORRIS

Entering 2021, most prognosticators saw the National League West as a two-horse race between the Dodgers and the Padres. The Giants had other ideas.

San Francisco and its stable of coaches assembled a group of hitters who bludgeoned fastballs and a group of pitchers who simultaneously put together career seasons.

The former category included relatively anonymous players like Darin Ruf, LaMonte Wade Jr., Austin Slater and Steven Duggar. The latter included rotation pieces Kevin Gausman, Anthony DeSclafani and Logan Webb.

Together, the Giants combined to win 107 games and the division. Their progress was stopped by the Dodgers in the Division Series, however, putting the champagne on ice for another season. Come 2022, they'll be down one of the most influential players in franchise history. That would be catcher Buster Posey, who announced his retirement after the season.

With Posey gone, there's a hole open at catcher in San Francisco for Joey Bart, one of the system's top prospects, to make his own name in the big leagues. Bart has seen major league action in each of the past two seasons, but spent most of 2021 at Triple-A Sacramento getting back on a more normal development track.

Bart could be closely followed by outfielder Heliot Ramos, who appeared in his third consecutive Futures Game and spent the season adding polish to his game. Those are the two top prospects in the system at the upper levels, but the wave coming behind them could be much greater.

Low-A San Jose and High-A Eugene—which each claimed their league's championship in 2021—hold most of the keys to the Giants' future. San Jose's group was helmed by four of the system's top 10 prospects: shortstop Marco Luciano (No. 1), outfielder Luis Matos (3), lefthander Kyle Harrison (5) and outfielder Jairo Pomares (8). Each player put up excellent numbers and graded out well for evaluators both in and out of the organization. For his part, Harrison used a powerful arsenal to strike out 157 batters in 98.2 innings in his pro debut and was one of three pitchers in the system with more than 150 strikeouts in 2021.

Eugene's final roster also included one of the system's breakout stars in righthander Ryan Murphy, whose 164 strikeouts were the third-most in the minor leagues—but second-most in the system behind Carson Ragsdale. Murphy was the Giants' fifth-round pick in the shortened 2020 draft, out of the same Division II Le Moyne (N.Y.) program that produced Nationals righthander Josiah Gray.

Brandon Crawford was one of several Giants regulars in their 30s who had a resurgent 2021.

PROJECTED 2025 LINEUP

Catcher	Patrick Bailey	26
First Base	Joey Bart	28
Second Base	Will Wilson	26
Third Base	Aeverson Arteaga	22
Shortstop	Marco Luciano	23
Left Field	LaMonte Wade Jr.	31
Center Field	Luis Matos	23
Right Field	Heliot Ramos	25
Designated Hitter	Mike Yastrzemski	34
No. 1 Starter	Logan Webb	28
No. 2 Starter	Kyle Harrison	23
No. 3 Starter	Will Bednar	24
No. 4 Starter	Anthony DeSclafani	35
No. 5 Starter	Matt Mikulski	26
Closer	Camilo Doval	28

The Giants also added another glut of potentially high-end arms to their system through the 2021 draft when they selected Mississippi State righthander Will Bednar—fresh off helping his team to its first College World Series title—in the first round. They doubled up a pick later when they selected flamethrowing Fordham lefthander Matt Mikulski. Bednar and Mikulski trail only Harrison in terms of upside among Giants pitching prospects.

The Giants' system has been refurbished over the past few seasons, and the results are starting to show up in the majors. After 107 wins in 2021, the team could be ready to take the next step in 2022. After all, it is an even year. ∎

DEPTH CHART

SAN FRANCISCO GIANTS

TOP 2022 ROOKIES	RANK
Joey Bart, C	2
Heliot Ramos, OF	4
BREAKOUT PROSPECTS	**RANK**
Nick Swiney, LHP	13
RJ Dabovich, RHP	17

SOURCE OF TOP 30 TALENT

Homegrown	26	Acquired	4
College	12	Trade	3
Junior college	0	Rule 5 draft	0
High school	3	Independent league	0
Nondrafted free agent	0	Free agent/waivers	1
International	11		

LF
Jairo Pomares (8)
Hunter Bishop (16)

CF
Luis Matos (3)
Heliot Ramos (4)
Ismael Munguia

RF
Alexander Suarez
Diego Rincones

3B
Marco Luciano (1)
Casey Schmitt (11)
Luis Toribio (26)
David Villar
Jason Vosler

SS
Aeverson Arteaga (9)
Diego Velasquez (23)
Tyler Fitzgerald
Jimmy Glowenke

2B
Will Wilson (14)

1B
Logan Wyatt
Sean Roby
Garrett Frechette

C
Joey Bart (2)
Patrick Bailey (15)
Adrian Sugastey (21)
Ricardo Genoves (24)

LHP

LHSP	LHRP
Kyle Harrison (5)	Chris Wright (27)
Matt Mikulski (7)	Sonny Vargas
Nick Swiney (13)	Seth Lonsway
Sammy Long (19)	
Rohan Handa	
Seth Corry	
Esmerlin Vinicio	

RHP

RHSP	RHRP
Will Bednar (6)	Camilo Doval (12)
Ryan Murphy (10)	RJ Dabovich (17)
Sean Hjelle (20)	Kervin Castro (18)
Eric Silva (22)	Randy Rodriguez (28)
Carson Ragsdale (25)	Prelander Berroa (29)
Tristan Beck (30)	Hunter Harvey
Manuel Mercedes	Cole Waites
Kai-Wei Teng	Austin Reich
Mason Black	Gregory Santos
	Yunior Marte

1 MARCO LUCIANO, SS

Born: Sept. 10, 2001. **B-T:** R-R. **HT:** 6-1. **WT:** 198.
Signed: Dominican Republic, 2018.
Signed by: Jonathan Bautista.

BILL MITCHELL

TRACK RECORD: For the two seasons prior to Luciano's signing, the Giants weren't allowed to sign any international prospect for $300,000. When the restrictions expired, the team opened its wallet and signed a star-studded class that included Luciano as well as outfielders Luis Matos and Jairo Pomares. The Giants skipped Luciano over the DSL and immediately to the Rookie-level Arizona League, where he thrived and ranked as the league's No. 2 prospect behind only the Padres' CJ Abrams. He finished the year with a cameo at short-season Eugene. In 2020, Luciano was invited to San Francisco's alternate training site. He was the youngest player in camp, and the assignment was especially significant because spots were finite and he had no real chance to contribute to the big league team. Luciano started slowly in 2021 before catching fire at Low-A San Jose, where he ranked as the league's No. 2 prospect behind Oakland's Tyler Soderstrom. He scuffled somewhat after a promotion to High-A and then again during a stint in the Arizona Fall League.

SCOUTING REPORT: Luciano has developed a reputation as a bit of a slow starter, but once he gets going it's easy to see why he's valued so highly. He has a strong ability to make a game plan at the plate, and if he gets a pitch in his zone he's going to crush it. His raw power is easily double-plus, and he's capable of hitting balls out to any part of the park. That said, plenty of refinement is needed before he reaches his ceiling. Though Luciano can recognize breaking balls, he will sometimes get over-eager and chase out of the zone. There are some moving parts in his load that can cause his timing to get out of whack, but he has the hand speed to catch up to even the best fastballs. His 90.1 mph average and 115 mph maximum exit velocities in 2021 show a player capable of doing plenty of damage when he connects. Defensively, Luciano has roughly a coin flip's shot of staying at shortstop. He has the arm strength for the left side, but his internal clock leaves much to be desired. His feet don't often catch up with his body, either, leaving him in awkward positions to make throws across the diamond. Rival managers in the Low-A West saw plenty of athleticism and ability in the field, but those traits still need to be honed into consistent, usable skills. None of this is unexpected for a player who didn't turn 20 until season's end and missed out on a key year of in-game devel-opment because of the coronavirus pandemic. Luciano isn't the speediest runner and grades out as below-average at his best. If he does have to move off of shortstop, third base is the likeliest destination because of his arm strength and the way his power is likely to profile at the position.

THE FUTURE: After ending 2021 in High-A, Luciano is likely to return to the level to begin 2022. He'll look to make his play more consistent and show more frequent peeks at the perennial all-star-caliber player he can be when everything is working the way it did during most of his time at San Jose. ∎

BA GRADE	SCOUTING GRADES
65 Risk: V. High	Hit: 60. Power: 60. Run: 40. Field: 50. Arm: 60.

Projected future grades on 20-80 scouting scale

BEST TOOLS

Best Hitter for Average	Luis Matos
Best Power Hitter	Marco Luciano
Best Strike-Zone Discipline	Logan Wyatt
Fastest Baserunner	Simon Whiteman
Best Athlete	Hunter Bishop
Best Fastball	Cole Waites
Best Curveball	Nick Swiney
Best Slider	Kyle Harrison
Best Changeup	Nick Swiney
Best Control	Ryan Murphy
Best Defensive Catcher	Patrick Bailey
Best Defensive Infielder	Casey Schmitt
Best Infield Arm	Casey Schmitt
Best Defensive Outfielder	Alexander Suarez
Best Outfield Arm	Franklin Labour

Year	Age	Club (Level)	Lge	AVG	G	AB	R	H	2B	3B	HR	RBI	BB	SO	SB	OBP	SLG
2021	19	San Jose (LoA)	West	.278	70	266	52	74	14	3	18	57	38	68	5	.373	.556
	19	Eugene (HiA)	West	.217	36	129	16	28	3	2	1	14	10	54	1	.283	.295
Minor League Totals (3 years)				.272	153	574	120	156	30	7	29	113	80	167	15	.368	.500

2 JOEY BART, C

Born: Dec. 15, 1996. **B-T:** R-R. **HT:** 6-2. **WT:** 238. **Drafted:** Georgia Tech, 2018 (1st round). **Signed by:** Luke Murton.

TRACK RECORD: After dealing with a pair of broken bones in his hands in 2019, Bart, whom the Giants chose with the second overall pick in 2018, was invited to the team's alternate training site in 2020 and made his big league debut ahead of schedule while the team tried to fill the hole left by stalwart catcher Buster Posey opting out of the season during the pandemic. Bart returned to the big leagues briefly in 2021 but otherwise spent the season at Triple-A, where he attempted to get back on a normal development track.

SCOUTING REPORT: One of the problematic parts of Bart's game revolved around closing a hole on the inside part of the plate. He made strides in that regard this season, hitting .280 on pitches on the inner third. That's a steep drop from the numbers he produced on balls on the outer third, but a respectable number nonetheless. He shows plenty of impact potential when he connects and is likely to be a power-over-hit player once he reaches San Francisco for good. Evaluators both internally and externally saw improvement from Bart on defense, especially when it came to receiving. He allowed just six passed balls all season and caught 32.6% of attempted basestealers. Opposing evaluators noted he could stand to show better leadership qualities and body language behind the plate.

THE FUTURE: With Posey retired, Bart's pathway to the big leagues is wide open. He should compete for the starting job on Opening Day.

BA GRADE
55 Risk: High

SCOUTING GRADES:	Hitting: 40	Power: 60	Running: 40	Fielding: 50	Arm: 60

Year	Age	Club (Level)	Lge	AVG	G	AB	R	H	2B	3B	HR	RBI	BB	SO	SB	OBP	SLG
2021	24	Sacramento (AAA)	West	.294	67	252	37	74	15	0	10	46	21	82	0	.358	.472
	24	San Francisco (MLB)	NL	.333	2	6	1	2	0	0	0	1	0	2	0	.333	.333
Major League Totals (2 years)				.239	35	109	16	26	5	2	0	8	3	43	0	.291	.321
Minor League Totals (3 years)				.287	197	769	121	221	44	6	39	134	55	200	7	.348	.512

3 LUIS MATOS, OF

Born: Jan. 28, 2002. **B-T:** R-R. **HT:** 6-0. **WT:** 186. **Signed:** Venezuela, 2018. **Signed by:** Edgar Fernandez.

TRACK RECORD: After shining in the Dominican Summer League in 2019, Matos' stateside debut was scuttled by the coronavirus pandemic. Like most Venezuelan players, he was stuck in the U.S. because of travel restrictions in his home country, meaning he spent most of the shutdown at the team hotel in Arizona. Since returning, Matos has been extremely impressive, first at 2020 instructional league, and then again over a season in the Low-A West, where he ranked as the league's No. 6 prospect.

SCOUTING REPORT: Matos has huge upside as a hitter, and he showed an enticing blend of contact and impact in his full-season debut. He was the only player in the minor leagues who hit better than .300 while striking out fewer than 70 times over the course of 450 or more at-bats. He was also one of just

BA GRADE
55 Risk: High

five players with 20 or more doubles, 15 or more homers and 20 or more stolen bases. He struck out just 61 times, though part of that could be explained by a highly aggressive approach that led him to see just 3.2 pitches per plate appearance. He's got lightning-quick hands, an innate ability to find the barrel and produced a maximum exit velocity of 111 mph. For now, Matos will stay in center field, and there's a small chance he can stick there in the long run if he improves his routes and jumps on balls hit his way. He's more likely to move to a corner, however, where he could be an above-average defender thanks to above-average speed coupled with an above-average arm.

THE FUTURE: After a tremendous season with San Jose, Matos' next step will be High-A Eugene, where he will face a host of more advanced pitchers. He has a very high ceiling and should be part of the Giants' long-term outfield picture.

SCOUTING GRADES:	Hitting: 60	Power: 55	Running: 55	Fielding: 55	Arm: 55

Year	Age	Club (Level)	Lge	AVG	G	AB	R	H	2B	3B	HR	RBI	BB	SO	SB	OBP	SLG
2021	19	San Jose (LoA)	West	.313	109	451	84	141	35	1	15	86	28	61	21	.358	.494
Minor League Totals (3 years)				.332	169	702	149	233	60	3	22	134	48	92	42	.388	.520

4 HELIOT RAMOS, OF

Born: Sept. 7, 1999. **B-T:** R-R. **HT:** 6-1. **WT:** 188. **Drafted:** HS—Guaynabo, P.R., 2017 (1st round). **Signed by:** Junior Roman.

TRACK RECORD: Ramos was the Giants' first-round selection out of high school in Puerto Rico in 2017 and has performed well during his climb through the minor leagues, usually as one of the younger players at every stop. Ramos has also been named to each of the last three Futures Games, including the 2021 version in Denver. Ramos closed 2019 at Double-A and returned there to begin 2021. By season's end he'd reached Triple-A, where he got to play games against his brother, Henry, a journeyman who was playing for Triple-A Reno in the D-backs' system.

BA GRADE

55 Risk: High

SCOUTING REPORT: After a strong showing at big league spring training, Ramos returned to Double-A to continue learning how to use the entire field. Previously, Ramos tended to work mostly toward his pull side, so in the regular season he focused more on going the opposite way. All the ingredients—bat speed, raw power, command of the strike zone—are there for Ramos to be an excellent offensive player once he reaches the big leagues. The bigger question is where he winds up playing. Despite a thicker body, it's hard to find an evaluator who's totally out on the idea of Ramos playing center field. He's athletic and surprisingly quick for his size, but he'll have to work hard to make sure those traits stay intact. If he does have to move to a corner, his bat would easily profile. His above-average arm would fit nicely in right field.

THE FUTURE: Ramos is likely headed back to Triple-A in 2022, but the Giants' roster has little in the way of cornerstone outfielders, so there should be plenty of chances for him to hit his way to the majors.

SCOUTING GRADES:	Hitting: 50	Power: 55	Running: 50	Fielding: 55	Arm: 55

Year	Age	Club (Level)	Lge	AVG	G	AB	R	H	2B	3B	HR	RBI	BB	SO	SB	OBP	SLG
2021	21	Richmond (AA)	NEast	.237	62	236	36	56	14	1	10	26	27	73	7	.323	.432
	21	Sacramento (AAA)	West	.272	54	213	30	58	11	2	4	30	15	65	8	.323	.399
Minor League Totals (5 years)				.270	377	1461	224	394	84	18	47	190	129	440	41	.340	.448

5 KYLE HARRISON, LHP

Born: Aug. 12, 2001. **B-T:** L-L. **HT:** 6-2. **WT:** 200. **Drafted:** HS—Concord, Calif., 2020 (3rd round). **Signed by:** Keith Snider.

TRACK RECORD: Harrison had first-round talent but lasted until the third round of the 2020 draft because of a high price tag and perceived strong commitment to UCLA. The Giants lured him away from college with a bonus of $2,497,500, then watched as he dominated at instructional league in 2020 and posted a strong first season as a pro at Low-A San Jose.

SCOUTING REPORT: In terms of pure stuff, Harrison is easily the best pitching prospect in the Giants' system. His four-seam fastball sits at 94 mph and touches 98 while also showing well in terms of horizontal break and vertical approach angle. Together, those qualities helped Harrison get swings and misses at a 35% rate with his fastball in 2021. Harrison's offspeed offerings—a

BA GRADE

55 Risk: Very High

slider and a changeup—are even more impressive. Harrison's slider averages 83 mph and shows dynamic two-plane break while getting swings and misses 43% of the time. He rounds out his mix with a low-80s changeup which averages about 10 mph of separation from his fastball. His changeup's movement is inconsistent but shows strong fading life at its best. The biggest concern for Harrison right now is working to iron out his command and control. His arm is loose and whippy and easily produces velocity and deception from a low slot and cross-body finish, but he doesn't repeat it well enough yet to throw strikes consistently. That issue cropped up both in his walk rate and his efficiency, which caused him to go less than five innings in 14 of his 23 starts.

THE FUTURE: After an excellent debut season, Harrison will move in 2022 to High-A Eugene. If he can iron out his control, he has the look of a mid-rotation starter with the upside for more.

SCOUTING GRADES:	Fastball: 60	Slider: 60	Changeup: 50	Control: 40

Year	Age	Club (Level)	Lge	W	L	ERA	G	GS	IP	H	HR	BB	SO	BB/9	SO/9	WHIP	AVG
2021	19	San Jose (LoA)	West	4	3	3.19	23	23	99	86	3	52	157	4.7	14.3	1.40	.232
Minor League Totals (2 years)				4	3	3.19	23	23	99	86	3	52	157	4.74	14.32	1.40	.232

6 WILL BEDNAR, RHP

Born: June 13, 2000. **B-T:** R-R. **HT:** 6-2. **WT:** 229. **Drafted:** Mississippi State, 2021 (1st round). **Signed by:** Jeff Wood.

TRACK RECORD: Bednar, whose brother David is a reliever with the Pirates, got his moment in the sun in June, when Mississippi State won the College World Series. Bednar pitched six hitless innings in the clincher over Vanderbilt and was named the tournament's Most Outstanding Player. The Giants drafted him with their first-round selection and signed him for $3,647,500. Although he didn't pitch in the series, Bednar added a second championship ring when his San Jose club won the Low-A West title.

SCOUTING REPORT: Bednar makes his bones on an outstanding three-pitch mix fronted by a dynamic fastball-slider combination. His fastball typically sits around 92-94 mph but has touched as high as 97 and plays well when thrown up in the strike zone. Bednar's mid-80s slider shows excellent downer action and is his primary weapon to get swings and misses. He rounds out the mix with a changeup that comes in around the mid 80s and shows armside run at its best. Bednar used the changeup sparingly in college and will have to rely on it more in pro ball in order to establish himself as a potential rotation option. He projects to have average control and issued just one walk in seven innings as a pro.

THE FUTURE: After getting his feet wet in 2021, Bednar will get his first full test as a pro in 2022, likely at High-A Eugene. He has a ceiling of a mid-rotation starter.

BA GRADE
50 Risk: High

LACHLAN CUNNINGHAM/GETTY IMAGES

SCOUTING GRADES:	Fastball: 60	Slider: 60	Changeup: 50	Control: 50

Year	Age	Club (Level)	Lge	W	L	ERA	G	GS	IP	H	HR	BB	SO	BB/9	SO/9	WHIP	AVG
2021	21	Giants Orange (R)	ACL	0	0	0.00	2	2	2	0	0	1	3	4.5	13.5	0.50	.000
	21	San Jose (LoA)	West	0	0	1.80	2	2	5	6	0	0	3	0.0	5.4	1.20	.273
Minor League Totals (1 year)				0	0	1.29	4	4	7	6	0	1	6	1.29	7.71	1.00	.214

7 MATT MIKULSKI, LHP

Born: May 8, 1999. **B-T:** L-L. **HT:** 6-4. **WT:** 205. **Drafted:** Fordham, 2021 (2nd round). **Signed by:** John DiCarlo.

TRACK RECORD: After going unpicked in the shortened 2020 draft, Mikulski returned to Fordham and saw his stock rise astronomically thanks to mechanical changes that led his stuff to tick way up. His 1.45 ERA and 124 strikeouts were each the best in the Atlantic 10 Conference, and the Giants were excited enough to make him their second-round choice. Mikulski signed for $1,197,500 and made four starts at the Rookie-level Arizona Complex League in his pro debut.

SCOUTING REPORT: The mechanical changes Mikulski made were key to his breakout. The lefthander shortened his arm action, and the new path helped create even more deception. With the changes, the ball now appears to come from behind his ear in his delivery and is extremely hard for batters to pick

BA GRADE
50 Risk: High

BILL MITCHELL

up. His fastball velocity also ticked up to average 93 mph and touched the upper 90s. Mikulski showed no clear favorite among his offspeed pitches while in college, throwing his slider, curveball and changeup each between 11% and 14% of the time. His changeup is the most promising of the three because of the deception in his delivery and velocity separation from his fastball. The pitch is thrown in the 83-86 mph range and got whiffs 70% of the time hitters swung. Mikulski's mid-80s slider flashes average, and his curveball is good mostly for an early-count strike. Mikulski's delivery helped him raise his draft stock, but it also doesn't lend itself to precise control and could eventually be the reason he moves to the bullpen.

THE FUTURE: After a few games in the ACL, Mikulski's first full season as a pro should begin at one of the Class A levels in 2022. He could fit toward the back of a rotation or as a power reliever late in games.

SCOUTING GRADES:	Fastball: 60	Slider: 50	Curveball: 40	Changeup: 55	Control: 50

Year	Age	Club (Level)	Lge	W	L	ERA	G	GS	IP	H	HR	BB	SO	BB/9	SO/9	WHIP	AVG
2021	22	Giants Black (R)	ACL	0	0	1.80	4	4	5	4	0	3	5	5.4	9.0	1.40	.235
Minor League Totals (1 year)				0	0	1.80	4	4	5	4	0	3	5	5.40	9.00	1.40	.235

8 JAIRO POMARES, OF

Born: Aug. 4, 2000. **B-T:** L-R. **HT:** 6-1. **WT:** 185. **Signed:** Cuba, 2018.
Signed by: Jonathan Bautista/Gabriel Elias.

TRACK RECORD: The Giants' 2018 international class looks like it will be incredibly fruitful once it's all said and done. The group includes shortstop Marco Luciano and outfielder Luis Matos, two of the team's three best offensive prospects. Visa issues kept Pomares from reaching the U.S. for 2020, but he did get some development time at the team's instructional camp in the Dominican Republic. Pomares split his 2021 season between both Class A levels and hit 20 home runs, tied with David Villar for the most in the Giants system.

BA GRADE
50 Risk: High

SCOUTING REPORT: First and foremost, Pomares hits the daylights out of the ball. His average exit velocity of 92.4 mph was the highest in the system among players with more than 150 plate appearances, and he maxed out at 115.5 mph. His swing is rhythmic and his mechanics allow him to get into a good hitting position early, which helps him prepare for both righties and lefties. Pomares' approach could stand to be refined. Currently, he swings at as many bad balls as he does meatballs, but when he connects the contact is usually loud. Pomares has made strides on defense, including with first-step reactions and quickness, but he's still a below-average defender overall. His average arm is strong and accurate, and he spent a near-equal amount of time at both left and right field.

THE FUTURE: Pomares' power surge was among the biggest surprises in the Giants system in 2021. He'll likely return to High-A Eugene in 2022 to continue working on his defense and honing his approach. He has a ceiling as a powerful corner outfielder.

SCOUTING GRADES:	Hitting: 45		Power: 55		Running: 45			Fielding: 40		Arm: 50			

Year	Age	Club (Level)	Lge	AVG	G	AB	R	H	2B	3B	HR	RBI	BB	SO	SB	OBP	SLG
2021	20	San Jose (LoA)	West	.372	51	199	45	74	22	0	14	44	15	54	0	.429	.693
	20	Eugene (HiA)	West	.262	26	103	13	27	5	1	6	15	1	33	1	.269	.505
Minor League Totals (3 years)				.330	128	515	82	170	40	5	23	96	27	130	6	.372	.561

9 AEVERSON ARTEAGA, SS

Born: March 16, 2003. **B-T:** R-R. **HT:** 6-0. **WT:** 174. **Signed:** Venezuela, 2019.
Signed by: Edgar Fernandez.

TRACK RECORD: Arteaga's $1 million bonus was the largest the Giants paid to any member of their 2019 international class. Like other players from Venezuela, Arteaga was stuck during the coronavirus pandemic at the team's spring training complex in Arizona, where he stayed until instructional league. Arteaga spent his first season as a pro in the Arizona Complex League, where he ranked as the circuit's No. 7 prospect. His 43 RBIs led the league, and his nine home runs placed him third.

BA GRADE
55 Risk: Extreme

SCOUTING REPORT: Defensively, Arteaga is one of the surest bets in the Giants system to stick at shortstop. He has quick hands, smooth actions, excellent range, a strong internal clock and plus arm strength. Despite not hitting the ball particularly hard—his average exit velocity was around 84 mph in his pro debut—Arteaga's initial offensive showing was stronger than expected. He has excellent bat speed and better bat-to-ball skills than his 30% strikeout rate would suggest, but there is plenty of work to be done. He needs to cut down on his swings and misses and has to work hard to improve the way he recognizes breaking balls. The Giants are comforted by Arteaga's makeup and see a player who will identify flaws and work his hardest to fix them.

THE FUTURE: Arteaga should move up to Low-A San Jose in 2022, where he will work to increase his offensive abilities in an effort to make himself an impact player on both sides of the ball.

SCOUTING GRADES:	Hitting: 50		Power: 40		Running: 50			Fielding: 60		Arm: 60			

Year	Age	Club (Level)	Lge	AVG	G	AB	R	H	2B	3B	HR	RBI	BB	SO	SB	OBP	SLG
2021	18	Giants Orange (R)	ACL	.294	56	197	42	58	12	1	9	43	23	69	8	.367	.503
	18	San Jose (LoA)	West	.000	1	3	0	0	0	0	0	0	0	1	0	.000	.000
Minor League Totals (1 year)				.290	57	200	42	58	12	1	9	43	23	70	8	.362	.495

10 RYAN MURPHY, RHP

Born: Oct. 8, 1999. **B-T:** R-R. **HT:** 6-1. **WT:** 190. **Drafted:** Le Moyne (N.Y.), 2020 (5th round). **Signed by:** Ray Callari.

TRACK RECORD: Murphy's emergence was one of the best stories of the Giants' season in the minors. The fifth-rounder out of Division II Le Moyne (N.Y)—the same program that produced Nationals righthander Josiah Gray—rushed his way through both levels of Class A and put himself on the map in a big way. His 164 strikeouts were the third-most in the minors (but second in his own system behind Carson Ragsdale) despite the fact he missed time toward season's end with a minor injury.

SCOUTING REPORT: None of Murphy's pitches is a knockout by any means, but his ability to command them in and out of the strike zone while relentlessly attacking hitters allows his whole arsenal to play up. Murphy works with a full four-pitch complement, fronted by a low-90s fastball that peaks at 95 mph. His fastball shows above-average spin, above-average to plus break in both directions and is thrown at a deceptive angle. Murphy's primary offspeed is a low-80s slider which plays well analytically in terms of both horizontal and vertical break. He rounds out the arsenal with a mid-80s changeup and a low-80s curveball with excellent depth. Murphy also gets some deception from an unorthodox delivery. All of his pitches play up because of his plus control and strong command in all quadrants of the strike zone.

THE FUTURE: Despite his success, Murphy still faces skepticism because of a lack of a true standout pitch. He'll be tested in 2022 at Double-A Richmond, which will help make his ceiling clearer.

BA GRADE: 50 Risk: High

SCOUTING GRADES:	Fastball: 55	Slider: 45	Curveball: 60	Changeup: 50	Control: 60

Year	Age	Club (Level)	Lge	W	L	ERA	G	GS	IP	H	HR	BB	SO	BB/9	SO/9	WHIP	AVG
2021	21	San Jose (LoA)	West	4	2	2.96	15	15	76	59	11	18	116	2.1	13.7	1.01	.215
	21	Eugene (HiA)	West	2	2	1.44	6	6	31	13	1	8	48	2.3	13.8	0.67	.124
Minor League Totals (2 years)				6	4	2.52	21	21	107	72	12	26	164	2.18	13.75	0.91	.189

11 CASEY SCHMITT, 3B

BA GRADE: 50 Risk: High

Born: March 1, 1999. **B-T:** R-R. **HT:** 6-2. **WT:** 215. **Drafted:** San Diego State, 2020 (2nd round). **Signed by:** Brad Cameron.

TRACK RECORD: Schmitt made a name for himself both at San Diego State and in the Cape Cod League, where he starred as both a pitcher and a hitter. He finished his stint on the Cape by closing the game and hitting two home runs to help win the championship for Cotuit, where he was teammates with future Giants system-mate Nick Swiney. Schmitt showed well in his final season at SDSU before the pandemic cut things short, and the Giants selected him with the 47th pick. His pro debut started slowly at Low-A, but he put together a pair of solid months in the middle of the season.

SCOUTING REPORT: Exemplary defensive work is the hallmark of Schmitt's game. He's a natural third baseman with quick reflexes and the strong arm to stick at the position in the long-term, though some question whether his hands might need a little work. Schmitt got off to a much rockier start at the plate than one would expect for a player with a college pedigree making his debut at Low-A. He often looked like he was pressing, and as a result would let his hips fly open and stride too far while selling out for power. That left him with holes on the outside part of the plate and against breaking balls from righthanders. When he stayed within himself, he had more success.

THE FUTURE: Schmitt will move in 2022 to High-A Eugene, where he'll get tested by advanced pitching. If he shows the same form as he did in the middle of his first season, he has the ceiling of an everyday third baseman who plays outstanding defense.

Year	Age	Club (Level)	Lge	AVG	G	AB	R	H	2B	3B	HR	RBI	BB	SO	SB	OBP	SLG
2021	22	San Jose (LoA)	West	.247	64	251	36	62	14	1	8	29	22	44	2	.318	.406
Minor League Totals (2 years)				.247	64	251	36	62	14	1	8	29	22	44	2	.318	.406

12 CAMILO DOVAL, RHP

BA GRADE: 50 Risk: High

Born: July 4, 1997. **B-T:** R-R. **HT:** 6-2. **WT:** 185. **Signed:** Dominican Republic, 2015. **Signed by:** Gabriel Elias.

TRACK RECORD: Doval wound slowly through the minors after signing, but he increased his pace once he moved to the bullpen. He came close to making his big league debut in 2020, when he was part of the Giants' taxi squad, but ultimately didn't get his first shot until April 18,

2021. He worked himself into a high-leverage role by season's end and was a part of the team's roster in the playoffs. After being recalled on Sept. 5, Doval went 17 consecutive appearances without allowing a run.
SCOUTING REPORT: Doval operates with two pitches, an upper-90s fastball and a low-80s slider, which he used to strike out 37 hitters in 27 innings in the regular season. Though he walked seven hitters per nine innings at Triple-A in 2021, his control was much better in the big leagues. His arsenal is amplified by a funky low arm slot that adds a level of deception. The biggest key to Doval's jump to the big leagues was simply working tirelessly to improve his command and control. He tinkered with varying finger pressures at the alternate site in 2020 and added the final pieces of the puzzle throughout the 2021 season in the minor leagues.
THE FUTURE: Doval has the stuff to close games in the major leagues, especially if he can maintain the improvements to his command and control. If not, he still fits nicely as a late-inning reliever in high-leverage situations.

Year	Age	Club (Level)	Lge	W	L	ERA	G	GS	IP	H	HR	BB	SO	BB/9	SO/9	WHIP	AVG
2021	23	Sacramento (AAA)	West	3	0	4.99	28	0	30	28	3	24	44	7.0	12.9	1.70	.241
	23	San Francisco (MLB)	NL	5	1	3.00	29	0	27	19	4	9	37	3.0	12.3	1.04	.192
Major League Totals (1 year)				5	1	3.00	29	0	27	19	4	9	37	3.00	12.33	1.04	.192
Minor League Totals (6 years)				9	10	3.57	146	0	194	145	7	109	277	5.06	12.85	1.31	.206

13 NICK SWINEY, LHP

BA GRADE
50 Risk: High

Born: Feb. 12, 1999. **B-T:** R-L. **HT:** 6-3. **WT:** 185. **Drafted:** North Carolina State, 2020 (2nd round supplemental). **Signed by:** Mark O'Sullivan.
TRACK RECORD: Swiney was supposed to use the 2020 season at North Carolina State to stretch himself into a starter's role after spending his first two years working out of the bullpen. Alas, the pandemic happened and Swiney was limited to just four starts. Nevertheless, the Giants were tempted enough by his potential to draft him in the supplemental second round and sign him for $1,197,500. Swiney's official pro debut was delayed by a concussion in the season's first week that kept him out until mid July and limited him to just 12 starts.
SCOUTING REPORT: Swiney's best pitch is an outstanding changeup thrown in the high 70s with roughly 13 mph of separation from his fastball. He threw his changeup more than 45% of the time in his pro debut, and for good reason. He can land his changeup for called strikes or get hitters to chase it out of the zone thanks to a combination of movement patterns and deception in his delivery. Swiney's fastball averages around 92 mph and plays up with its vertical movement, which helps it be effective at the top of the strike zone despite its pedestrian velocity. His third pitch is a deep-breaking curveball in the high 70s with movement patterns that make it more effective. Swiney needs to throw more strikes overall, and the Giants haven't ruled out potentially adding a slider or cutter to his mix.
THE FUTURE: Swiney is likely to head to High-A Eugene in 2022. He could wind up in the back of a rotation.

Year	Age	Club (Level)	Lge	W	L	ERA	G	GS	IP	H	HR	BB	SO	BB/9	SO/9	WHIP	AVG
2021	22	Giants Black (R)	ACL	0	0	1.13	5	5	8	7	0	6	16	6.8	18.0	1.63	.233
	22	San Jose (LoA)	West	0	0	0.74	7	7	24	16	0	12	42	4.4	15.5	1.15	.178
Minor League Totals (2 years)				0	0	0.84	12	12	32	23	0	18	58	5.01	16.14	1.27	.192

14 WILL WILSON, SS

BA GRADE
45 Risk: High

Born: July 21, 1998. **B-T:** R-R. **HT:** 6-0. **WT:** 184. **Drafted:** North Carolina State, 2019 (1st round). **Signed by:** Chris McAlpin (Angels).
TRACK RECORD: Wilson was the Angels' first-round pick in 2019 but was coveted by the Giants as well. San Francisco added Wilson to its system shortly thereafter when it agreed to acquire Zack Cozart while paying the rest of Cozart's salary. Wilson spent 2020 at the alternate training site and instructional league, then spent his first full season as a pro between High-A and Double-A before finishing the year in the Arizona Fall League.
SCOUTING REPORT: Wilson does not have a carrying tool, but he also doesn't have a glaring deficiency. He performed well at High-A Eugene before running into a bit of trouble at the next level. Wilson is particularly vulnerable against spin from righthanders, but his high swing-and-miss rate against fastballs in Double-A was more concerning. Both factors led to a strikeout-to-walk ratio of nearly 3-to-1. Wilson has some raw power but is best suited hitting line drives from gap to gap rather than selling out for home runs. Defensively, Wilson is unlikely to stick at shortstop. He moved around the infield in the regular season and played every position but first base and catcher in the Fall League. His best fits are at second or third base.

THE FUTURE: Wilson will head back to Double-A in 2022, where he'll try to do better against more advanced pitching. He has the potential to be a super-utility infielder.

Year	Age	Club (Level)	Lge	AVG	G	AB	R	H	2B	3B	HR	RBI	BB	SO	SB	OBP	SLG
2021	22	Eugene (HiA)	West	.251	49	195	37	49	14	2	10	26	24	56	7	.339	.497
	22	Richmond (AA)	NEast	.189	51	196	20	37	8	0	5	22	22	81	1	.281	.306
Minor League Totals (3 years)				.238	146	580	80	138	32	5	20	66	60	184	8	.316	.414

15 PATRICK BAILEY, C

BA GRADE

45 Risk: High

Born: May 29, 1999. **B-T:** B-R. **HT:** 6-1. **WT:** 210. **Drafted:** North Carolina State, 2020 (1st round). **Signed by:** Mark O'Sullivan.

TRACK RECORD: Bailey's decorated college career included three seasons as the starting catcher for North Carolina State and two stints with USA Baseball's Collegiate National Team. He established a reputation as a rock-solid defender capable of handling championship-caliber pitching staffs. After the Giants drafted him No. 13 overall in 2020, Bailey immediately reported to the team's alternate training site before finishing at instructional league. His official pro debut was hampered by early-season struggles at High-A Eugene and a back injury that forced him to return to the Giants' minor league complex in Arizona. Once healed, he was sent to Low-A San Jose to finish the season.

SCOUTING REPORT: Bailey struggled to replicate his collegiate success in his pro debut, especially at the plate. Despite decent swing mechanics, he was often late on fastballs and couldn't adjust to breaking pitches. He hit the ball fairly hard—his average exit velocity was 89 mph—but he didn't hit it often enough. Internal evaluators believe he may have been pressing early and trying to impress too much, which led to his poor start before the injury. Bailey performed well enough behind the plate, where quick mechanics made up for just average arm strength. He's a solid receiver and blocker and works well with pitchers, but there were also those during the Arizona Fall League who questioned Bailey's effort level behind the plate.

THE FUTURE: Bailey will look to take a mulligan for his first professional season in 2022 He'll likely start back at High-A Eugene, where he'll look for a fresh start toward reaching his ceiling as an everyday catcher on a second-division club.

Year	Age	Club (Level)	Lge	AVG	G	AB	R	H	2B	3B	HR	RBI	BB	SO	SB	OBP	SLG
2021	22	Giants Black (R)	ACL	.400	2	5	3	2	0	0	0	0	2	1	0	.571	.400
	22	San Jose (LoA)	West	.322	47	177	45	57	16	0	7	24	28	47	1	.415	.531
	22	Eugene (HiA)	West	.185	33	135	13	25	9	0	2	15	18	43	6	.290	.296
Minor League Totals (2 years)				.265	82	317	61	84	25	0	9	39	48	91	7	.366	.429

16 HUNTER BISHOP, OF

BA GRADE

50 Risk: Extreme

Born: June 25, 1998. **B-T:** L-R. **HT:** 6-5. **WT:** 210. **Drafted:** Arizona State, 2019 (1st round). **Signed by:** Chuck Hensley.

TRACK RECORD: Bishop put himself on the map during his junior year at Arizona State by hitting 22 home runs in a breakout season. Though there were still questions about his overall hitting ability, the Giants were intrigued enough by his potential to select him with their first-round pick in 2019 and sign him for $4,097,500. Bishop's pro debut was cut short by injury and he tested positive for Covid-19 in 2020, which limited his development at the alternate training site and instructional league. A shoulder injury limited Bishop to just 16 games during the 2021 season, including just five outside of the Arizona Complex League. He played an additional 14 games in the Arizona Fall League after the season and struck out in 39.2% of his plate appearances.

SCOUTING REPORT: Bishop has a reputation as a player who tinkers with his stances and mechanics often, so it is hard to get a read on what may or may not be working for an extended period of time. There's little doubt about his power potential, but he's far from answering whether he can make enough contact for it to matter. Defensively, Bishop can stand in center field but is not likely an everyday option at the position, especially if he can't improve his well below-average arm.

THE FUTURE: Bishop is likely to return to High-A Eugene in 2022 to take a second crack at a true first full season as a professional. He has the upside of a second-division regular if he can make enough contact.

Year	Age	Club (Level)	Lge	AVG	G	AB	R	H	2B	3B	HR	RBI	BB	SO	SB	OBP	SLG
2021	23	Giants Black (R)	ACL	.160	11	25	5	4	1	0	0	3	5	10	1	.313	.200
	23	San Jose (LoA)	West	.000	2	8	1	0	0	0	0	0	1	7	0	.111	.000
	23	Eugene (HiA)	West	.167	3	12	1	2	1	0	0	1	2	4	0	.333	.250
Minor League Totals (3 years)				.200	48	150	32	30	6	1	5	16	46	61	8	.396	.353

17 RJ DABOVICH, RHP

BA GRADE
45 Risk: High

Born: Jan. 11, 1999. **B-T:** R-R. **HT:** 6-3. **WT:** 215. **Drafted:** Arizona State, 2020 (4th round). **Signed by:** Chuck Hensley.

TRACK RECORD: Dabovich was drafted by the Royals in 2018 out of Central Arizona JC. Instead of signing, he transferred to Arizona State, where he dabbled as a starter but settled into the closer's role during the brief 2020 season. Dabovich has been a relief-only prospect since the Giants drafted him in the fourth round in 2020, but his pitch mix meshes perfectly with the organization's pitching philosophy.

SCOUTING REPORT: Dabovich works with two pitches—a mid-to-upper 90s fastball that peaks at 99 mph and a hard downer curveball in the mid 70s. By using those two pitches in concert, Dabovich creates a perfect north-south attack pattern that helped him rise quickly through the minors and reach Double-A in his pro debut. He also generates deception with a straight overhand delivery. Despite a bit of starting experience in college, Dabovich's aggression and mentality are best suited for the bullpen, where he can go right at hitters for an inning at a time. He was extraordinarily dominant at High-A Eugene, where he allowed just two hits in 12.2 innings while striking out 28.

THE FUTURE: Dabovich finished the year in the Arizona Fall League, where he made up time lost due to back stiffness toward the end of the regular season. He could reach the majors in 2022 and has the ceiling of a hard-throwing setup man trusted with high-leverage situations.

Year	Age	Club (Level)	Lge	W	L	ERA	G	GS	IP	H	HR	BB	SO	BB/9	SO/9	WHIP	AVG
2021	22	Eugene (HiA)	West	0	0	1.42	11	0	12	2	2	6	28	4.3	19.9	0.63	.050
	22	Richmond (AA)	NEast	1	1	3.66	20	0	19	13	1	7	34	3.2	15.6	1.02	.178
Minor League Totals (2 years)				1	1	2.78	31	0	32	15	3	13	62	3.62	17.26	0.87	.133

18 KERVIN CASTRO, RHP

BA GRADE
40 Risk: Medium

Born: Feb. 7, 1999. **B-T:** R-R. **HT:** 6-0. **WT:** 185. **Signed:** Venezuela, 2015. **Signed by:** Edgar Fernandez.

TRACK RECORD: The Giants' 2015 international class has produced two pieces of its big league bullpen so far. In addition to fireballer Camilo Doval, San Francisco shelled out $100,000 for Castro, a converted catcher who had been pitching for just three months when he signed. Thanks to Tommy John surgery that cost him the bulk of two seasons, Castro had only reached short-season ball when he earned a spot on the 40-man roster after the 2019 season. He turned in a dominant showing at Triple-A Sacramento in 2021 and made his big league debut on Sept. 7.

SCOUTING REPORT: Castro's rise from the low minors to the big leagues in such a short time span centered around the improvements he showed at instructional league in 2020. There, his fastball began touching the 96-97 mph range. He sustained that velocity in 2021, when his fastball sat 95 mph and touched 98. Like many pitchers in the Giants system, Castro's pitch mix is equipped to play the north-south game. He pairs his fastball with a low-80s curveball with plenty of downward bite. Castro will mix in the occasional cut fastball, but his approach is mostly predicated on tunneling his curveball off of his four-seamer. He's more of a control over command type of pitcher and isn't likely to fit in high-leverge situations without improvements to his command.

THE FUTURE: Castro will likely enter 2022 in the mix for a spot in the big league bullpen. If he doesn't earn a spot out of camp, he will likely go back and forth between Triple-A Sacramento and San Francisco.

Year	Age	Club (Level)	Lge	W	L	ERA	G	GS	IP	H	HR	BB	SO	BB/9	SO/9	WHIP	AVG
2021	22	Sacramento (AAA)	West	6	1	2.86	30	0	44	31	3	22	60	4.5	12.3	1.20	.197
	22	San Francisco (MLB)	NL	1	1	0.00	10	0	13	13	0	4	13	2.7	8.8	1.28	.260
Major League Totals (1 year)				1	1	0.00	10	0	13	13	0	4	13	2.70	8.78	1.28	.260
Minor League Totals (6 years)				14	5	3.03	58	14	134	100	5	48	148	3.23	9.97	1.11	.208

19 SAMMY LONG, LHP

BA GRADE
40 Risk: Medium

Born: July 8, 1995. **B-T:** L-L. **HT:** 6-1. **WT:** 185. **Drafted:** Sacramento State, 2016 (18th round). **Signed by:** Alan Hull (Rays).

TRACK RECORD: Long pitched through a pair of herniated discs at Sacramento State and impressed enough for the Rays to take a flier on him in the 18th round of the 2016 draft. He was released by Tampa Bay before the 2018 season, then decided to get his EMT certification and train for a possible career in firefighting. The White Sox signed him as a minor league free agent in 2019 but released him after the 2020 season. He caught on with the Giants shortly thereafter and rose quickly through their system to make his big league debut on June 9, 2021.

SCOUTING REPORT: Long works with a three-pitch mix fronted by a low-90s fastball that reaches 97 mph and has excellent vertical break. He complements his fastball with a slow mid-70s curveball with 11-to-5 break and downward bite that he needs to command better in order for it to be more effective. His third pitch is a low-80s changeup which gets roughly 10 mph of separation from his fastball and garners swings and misses at a high rate. His stiffer delivery inhibits his command and control, which limits his ceiling.
THE FUTURE: Long's role in 2022 is likely to be the same as it was in 2021: an emergency arm who bounces back and forth between Triple-A and the big leagues.

Year	Age	Club (Level)	Lge	W	L	ERA	G	GS	IP	H	HR	BB	SO	BB/9	SO/9	WHIP	AVG
2021	25	Richmond (AA)	NEast	0	1	3.00	4	4	15	12	0	4	22	2.4	13.2	1.07	.214
	25	San Jose (LoA)	West	0	0	0.00	1	0	1	1	0	0	2	0.0	18.0	1.00	.250
	25	Sacramento (AAA)	West	1	0	2.05	11	3	26	16	2	9	31	3.1	10.6	0.95	.172
	25	San Francisco (MLB)	NL	2	1	5.53	12	5	41	37	5	15	38	3.3	8.4	1.28	.237
Major League Totals (1 year)				2	1	5.53	12	5	41	37	5	15	38	3.32	8.41	1.28	.237
Minor League Totals (6 years)				11	7	2.82	77	25	198	156	10	68	231	3.09	10.50	1.13	.213

20 SEAN HJELLE, RHP

BA GRADE
45 Risk: High

Born: May 7, 1997. **B-T:** R-R. **HT:** 6-11. **WT:** 230. **Drafted:** Kentucky, 2018 (2nd round). **Signed by:** Kevin Christman.

TRACK RECORD: The Giants drafted Hjelle with their second-round pick in 2018 and watched as he got all the way to Double-A in his first full season as a pro. While most players missed development time in 2020 because of the coronavirus pandemic, Hjelle's case was particularly acute because he was at neither the alternate training site nor instructional league. He returned to the mound in 2021 and pitched well at Double-A before running into trouble at Triple-A.
SCOUTING REPORT: Hjelle performed admirably in his return despite missing time with back spasms. The towering 6-foot-11 righthander works with a mix of four- and two-seam fastballs that average 93 mph and touch 96. His four-seamer earns plus grades for its horizontal breaking action, but he throws his two-seamer a tick more often. Hjelle backs up his fastballs with a slider and changeup. His short, sweepy slider sits 84-88 mph and serves as an effective complement to his sinker, helping him get grounders nearly 66% of the time. His high-80s changeup is a clear third pitch in his arsenal and has been retooled to turn him into a ground ball machine. Hjelle is uniquely coordinated for his height and has average control. He got blasted in Triple-A because his sinker needs more action to be effective.
THE FUTURE: Hjelle was added to the 40-man roster after the season and will begin 2022 back in Triple-A. He has a chance to be a back-of-the-rotation starter who lives on inducing grounders.

Year	Age	Club (Level)	Lge	W	L	ERA	G	GS	IP	H	HR	BB	SO	BB/9	SO/9	WHIP	AVG
2021	24	Sacramento (AAA)	West	2	6	5.74	10	10	53	67	6	29	35	4.9	5.9	1.80	.307
	24	Richmond (AA)	NEast	3	2	3.15	14	14	65	60	8	19	69	2.6	9.5	1.20	.241
Minor League Totals (4 years)				12	17	3.87	64	64	284	303	24	89	265	2.82	8.40	1.38	.272

21 ADRIAN SUGASTEY, C

BA GRADE
50 Risk: Extreme

Born: Oct. 23, 2002. **B-T:** R-R. **HT:** 6-1. **WT:** 170. **Signed:** Panama, 2019. **Signed by:** Rogelio Castillo.

TRACK RECORD: Sugastey signed out of Panama in 2019 for $525,000 as part of an international class that also included shortstop prospect Aeverson Arteaga. He had a well-traveled career as an amateur, playing in tournaments in Japan, Colombia and the United States. His official pro debut was pushed back by the coronavirus pandemic, but he did get time at 2020 instructional league before emerging in 2021 in the Arizona Complex League., where he hit .358/.405/.439.
SCOUTING REPORT: Sugastey's swing is short, quick and geared to hit line drives to both gaps. He showed the potential for above-average power as well, though he'll need to add more strength to reach that ceiling. Sugastey's overall offensive profile would be further amplified by getting the ball in the air more often. Defensively, Sugastey is very flexible behind the plate, sets good targets for his pitchers and does a good job receiving and framing, though he needs to work on his blocking skills. He has a strong arm and caught 30% of runners attempting to steal in the ACL. With further development, he could be a fringe-average defender.
THE FUTURE: After an excellent pro debut, Sugastey will likely head to Low-A San Jose in 2022. He has a chance to be an everyday catcher with a balanced blend of skills, but he has a long way to go.

Year	Age	Club (Level)	Lge	AVG	G	AB	R	H	2B	3B	HR	RBI	BB	SO	SB	OBP	SLG
2021	18	Giants Orange (R)	ACL	.358	43	148	23	53	6	0	2	25	12	26	1	.405	.439
Minor League Totals (1 year)				.358	43	148	23	53	6	0	2	25	12	26	1	.405	.439

22 ERIC SILVA, RHP

BA GRADE
50 Risk: Extreme

Born: Oct. 3, 2002. **B-T:** R-R. **HT:** 6-1. **WT:** 185. **Drafted:** HS—San Juan Capistrano, Calif., 2021 (4th round). **Signed by:** Brad Cameron.

TRACK RECORD: The Giants lured lefthander Kyle Harrison away from a commitment to UCLA in 2020 and watched him carve up Low-A hitters in his pro debut. A year later, they went back to that game plan when they pried Silva from a Bruins commitment with a $1,497,500 bonus, the highest in the fourth round by $500,000. He debuted in the Arizona Complex League.

SCOUTING REPORT: Silva upped his draft stock when he touched 97 mph early in his senior year and continued that run of success throughout his high school sseason. He comfortably sits 90-94 mph and gets to that velocity with very quick arm despite a smaller frame. Silva backs up his fastball with a short slider in the low 80s that could become above-average with further development. Like most high school pitchers, his changeup exists but is underdeveloped. Amateur scouts were believers in Silva's pitchability but skeptical of his durability given his size, with many projecting him to the bullpen as a pro.

THE FUTURE: Silva will likely move to Low-A San Jose in 2022, when his long-term upside will come into clearer view.

Year	Age	Club (Level)	Lge	W	L	ERA	G	GS	IP	H	HR	BB	SO	BB/9	SO/9	WHIP	AVG
2021	18	Giants Orange (R)	ACL	0	1	36.00	2	0	1	4	0	3	2	27.0	18.0	7.00	.571
Minor League Totals (1 year)				0	1	36.00	2	0	1	4	0	3	2	27.00	18.00	7.00	.571

23 DIEGO VELASQUEZ, SS

BA GRADE
50 Risk: Extreme

Born: Oct. 1, 2003. **B-T:** B-R. **HT:** 6-1. **WT:** 162. **Signed:** Venezuela, 2021. **Signed by:** Robert Moron.

TRACK RECORD: The Giants have done well in Latin America in recent years, signing talents like Marco Luciano, Luis Matos and Aeverson Arteaga. Velasquez could be the next in line. He signed with the Giants on Jan. 15 and played in the Arizona Complex League as a 17-year-old.

SCOUTING REPORT: As an amateur, Velasquez was lauded for his athleticism, quick feet and soft hands. All those attributes, evaluators believed, would help him stick at shortstop in the long-term. He has gotten bigger and stronger since signing, though he still needs to add plenty more strength to his frame in order to put a bit more oomph behind his contact. His average exit velocity was just 81.3 mph in the ACL, which is low but to be expected for a player with Velasquez's combination of youth and frame. He's a contact-type of hitter who struck out in just 13.8% of plate appearances in the ACL.

THE FUTURE: Velasquez's development could be a slower burn. It's entirely possible he starts 2022 in extended spring training before moving to Low-A later in the year. He has the upside of an everyday shortstop who hits toward the bottom of an order, but his future will depend on how his body develops.

Year	Age	Club (Level)	Lge	AVG	G	AB	R	H	2B	3B	HR	RBI	BB	SO	SB	OBP	SLG
2021	17	Giants Black (R)	ACL	.213	46	160	19	34	3	0	0	10	13	25	2	.282	.231
Minor League Totals (1 year)				.213	46	160	19	34	3	0	0	10	13	25	2	.282	.231

24 RICARDO GENOVES, C

BA GRADE
40 Risk: High

Born: May 14, 1999. **B-T:** R-R. **HT:** 6-2. **WT:** 254. **Drafted:** Venezuela, 2015. **Signed by:** Jonathan Arraiz.

TRACK RECORD: Genoves advanced a level per season through 2018 before reaching full-season ball in 2019. After spending 2020 at instructional league, Genoves spent most of 2021 at the Class A levels and had early success at Low-A San Jose before hitting a wall at High-A Eugene..

SCOUTING REPORT: Genoves' skill set is perfectly suited for a backup catcher's role. He's a thicker-bodied catcher who needs to improve his blocking and become more mobile—as shown by the 26 passed balls he allowed—and quicker to unwrap his body for throws to second base. His timing is good at the plate, but his bat speed is a little short and he relies on his strength to drive balls to the gaps and over the wall. Genoves' power sometimes gets him into trouble. He often tries to hit home runs, which causes him to sell out for pull-side power when he should be focusing on using the whole field.

THE FUTURE: Genoves is likely to move to Double-A Richmond in 2022. He'll look to improve his blocking and become more consistent at the plate.

Year	Age	Club (Level)	Lge	AVG	G	AB	R	H	2B	3B	HR	RBI	BB	SO	SB	OBP	SLG
2021	22	San Jose (LoA)	West	.338	38	136	30	46	11	0	6	24	22	29	0	.441	.551
	22	Eugene (HiA)	West	.217	65	217	33	47	11	0	7	26	22	73	0	.294	.364
	22	Sacramento (AAA)	West	.455	6	22	4	10	3	0	1	3	1	6	0	.478	.727
Minor League Totals (6 years)				.261	308	1090	161	285	64	2	27	148	110	250	1	.343	.398

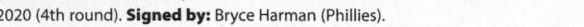

25 CARSON RAGSDALE, RHP

Born: May 25, 1998. **B-T:** R-R. **HT:** 6-8. **WT:** 225. **Drafted:** South Florida, 2020 (4th round). **Signed by:** Bryce Harman (Phillies).

BA GRADE
40 Risk: High

TRACK RECORD: Ragsdale was the Phillies' fourth-round pick in 2020 and was traded to the Giants four months later in the deal that sent reliever Sam Coonrod to Philadelphia. Ragsdale struck out 167 hitters at Low-A San Jose in his pro debut, second-most in the minor leagues.
SCOUTING REPORT: The 6-foot-8 Ragsdale mostly relies on two pitches. He combines a fastball that averages 93 mph and touches 96 with a low-80s curveball. Like many Giants pitching prospects, Ragsdale tunnels those two offerings to work the strike zone from north to south. He's added a cutter to help him get swings and misses down in the zone on something other than his curveball. Despite the gaudy strike-out numbers, the Giants were reluctant to move Ragsdale because of his shaky control. Ragsdale could iron out these issues by working to make sure his arm is on time more often in his delivery and eliminating a hooking action with his wrist, but pitchers his height rarely reach average control.
THE FUTURE: Ragsdale will move to High-A Eugene in 2022. He'll try to improve his control and command while looking toward a ceiling as a depth starter or a low-leverage reliever.

Year	Age	Club (Level)	Lge	W	L	ERA	G	GS	IP	H	HR	BB	SO	BB/9	SO/9	WHIP	AVG
2021	23	San Jose (LoA)	West	8	6	4.43	24	24	114	107	13	45	167	3.6	13.2	1.34	.245
Minor League Totals (2 years)				8	6	4.43	24	24	114	107	13	45	167	3.56	13.22	1.34	.245

26 LUIS TORIBIO, 3B

Born: Sept. 28, 2000. **B-T:** L-R. **HT:** 6-1. **WT:** 213. **Signed:** Dominican Republic, 2017. **Signed by:** Ruddy Moreta.

BA GRADE
40 Risk: High

TRACK RECORD: Toribio signed for $300,000 in 2017 and was impressive at his first two stops. He spent 2020 at the alternate training site, then struggled in 2021 at Low-A San Jose.
SCOUTING REPORT: Toribio's value comes from his bat, so his struggles at San Jose raise more than a few red flags. He has fast hands, a compact swing, a solid bat path and the ability to use the whole field, but his timing gets out of sync and his approach is often lacking. He has a solid idea of the strike zone and takes an excellent batting practice, but the results simply aren't there consistently in games. Defensively, Toribio is not likely to play third base. His body is getting thicker and his reactions are getting slower, and his throws across the diamond aren't always accurate. He can be counted on for the routine plays but not much more. If he shifts positions, his landing spots could be at second base or in the outfield.
THE FUTURE: Toribio will spend 2022 at High-A Eugene, where he'll look to become a more consistent hitter and work toward finding a more firm defensive home.

Year	Age	Club (Level)	Lge	AVG	G	AB	R	H	2B	3B	HR	RBI	BB	SO	SB	OBP	SLG
2021	20	San Jose (LoA)	West	.229	94	340	59	78	20	1	7	39	63	113	2	.351	.356
Minor League Totals (4 years)				.258	212	751	150	194	49	5	20	111	161	234	10	.394	.417

27 CHRIS WRIGHT, LHP

Born: Oct. 14, 1998. **B-T:** L-L. **HT:** 6-1. **WT:** 205. **Drafted:** Bryant, 2019 (12th round). **Signed by:** Ray Callari.

BA GRADE
40 Risk: High

TRACK RECORD: For his first two seasons at Bryant, it appeared Wright's future was as a hard-hitting first baseman. But after a successful stint in the Cape Cod League, his upside on the mound began to show. The Giants drafted him in the 12th round in 2019 and, after waiting out the coronavirus pandemic, Wright spent his first full season in 2021 dominating the Class A levels, primarily as High-A Eugene's closer. He finished the year with a 1.00 ERA and 79 strikeouts in 45 innings.
SCOUTING REPORT: Wright works primarily with two pitches: a low 90s fastball with exceptional movement characteristics and a hammer curveball in the high 70s with deep, powerful break and tilt away from lefties. He also has a cut fastball in the mid 80s he uses sparingly. Wright's fastball-curveball combination helped him strike out 55.6% hitters he faced between both Class A stops. He could stand to tighten up his command and control a little bit, but he's still productive as is. He shows good athleticism on the mound and fields his position well.
THE FUTURE: The Giants view Wright as a fast-moving reliever who thrives on a dynamic two-pitch mix. He should begin 2022 at Double-A and could be a major league option if the need arises.

Year	Age	Club (Level)	Lge	W	L	ERA	G	GS	IP	H	HR	BB	SO	BB/9	SO/9	WHIP	AVG
2021	22	San Jose (LoA)	West	0	0	1.13	6	0	8	4	0	3	17	3.4	19.1	0.88	.143
	22	Eugene (HiA)	West	4	0	0.97	31	0	37	15	2	18	62	4.4	15.1	0.89	.122
Minor League Totals (3 years)				4	0	1.23	45	5	58	34	2	29	87	4.47	13.42	1.08	.168

28 RANDY RODRIGUEZ, RHP

BA GRADE
40 Risk: High

Born: Sept. 5, 1999. **B-T:** R-R. **HT:** 6-0. **WT:** 166. **Signed:** Dominican Republic, 2017. **Signed by:** Gabriel Elias.

TRACK RECORD: Rodriguez has been on a near-exclusive relief track since he signed in 2017 and began blowing away hitters in 2021 at Low-A San Jose. He was one of just four pitchers in the minors to strike out 100 or more hitters in 62 or fewer innings and held opponents to a .193 average. The Giants added him to their 40-man roster after the season.

SCOUTING REPORT: Rodriguez largely works with two pitches: a high-spin fastball thrown in the mid 90s and a dastardly slider in the low 80s. His slider is particularly nasty because of its high spin rate and excellent sweeping life. Rodriguez will also mix in a mid-80s changeup with roughly 10 mph of separation from his fastball. Rodriguez could stand to tighten his control and command, but he shows the makings of an excellent pitch mix.

THE FUTURE: Rodriguez will head to High-A Eugene in 2021, where he'll see how well his impressive arsenal plays against more experienced hitters. He has the ceiling of a middle reliever.

Year	Age	Club (Level)	Lge	W	L	ERA	G	GS	IP	H	HR	BB	SO	BB/9	SO/9	WHIP	AVG
2021	21	San Jose (LoA)	West	6	3	1.74	32	0	62	44	0	23	101	3.3	14.7	1.08	.193
Minor League Totals (4 years)				9	10	3.15	58	2	114	94	2	48	164	3.78	12.91	1.24	.221

29 PRELANDER BERROA, RHP

BA GRADE
40 Risk: High

Born: April 18, 2000. **B-T:** R-R. **HT:** 5-11. **WT:** 170. **Signed:** Dominican Republic, 2016. **Signed by:** Fred Guerrero (Twins).

TRACK RECORD: Berroa originally signed with the Twins in 2016 and was traded to the Giants in 2019 for reliever Sam Dyson. Berroa reached short-season with the Giants after the trade and spent the 2021 season at Low-A San Jose, where he struck out 135 hitters in 98.2 innings.

SCOUTING REPORT: Berroa relies mostly on two pitches: a mid-90s fastball that touches 99 mph with excellent run and ride characteristics through the strike zone and mid-80s slider that gets a good amount of swings and misses. He also sprinkles in a high-80s changeup, but his fastball-slider combo makes up the vast majority of his outings. Berroa's biggest success in 2021 came from developing into more of a pitcher than a thrower. He has started learning how to use his offspeeds in advantage counts and has become more efficient in his outings instead of throwing everything at maximum effort all the time. His command and control need to improve, which can happen if he finds a more consistent release point.

THE FUTURE: The next stop for Berroa is High-A Eugene, where he'll try to build on the gains he made in 2021. If he can do that, he might have a shot at the back of a rotation.

Year	Age	Club (Level)	Lge	W	L	ERA	G	GS	IP	H	HR	BB	SO	BB/9	SO/9	WHIP	AVG
2021	21	San Jose (LoA)	West	5	6	3.56	24	24	98	79	13	53	135	4.8	12.3	1.34	.220
Minor League Totals (5 years)				12	8	4.14	55	46	209	185	19	108	247	4.66	10.65	1.40	.240

30 TRISTAN BECK, RHP

BA GRADE
40 Risk: High

Born: June 24, 1996. **B-T:** R-R. **HT:** 6-4. **WT:** 199. **Drafted:** Stanford, 2018 (4th round). **Signed by:** Jim Blueberg (Braves).

TRACK RECORD: Injuries have followed Beck throughout his career. He dealt with back issues during his sophomore season in college, but the Braves still drafted him in the fourth round the following season. He was traded from Atlanta to San Francisco in the deal for closer Mark Melancon. Beck's 2020 season was spent training remotely until instructional league. He dealt with a herniated disc in 2021 that limited him to 12 appearances and just four above Low-A.

SCOUTING REPORT: When healthy, Beck works with a four-pitch mix fronted by a low-90s fastball that reaches 96 mph with excellent life up in the zone. He primarily backs up his fastball with a curveball and a changeup. The former averages around 80 mph with sharp downer break, and the Giants have challenged him to add more power to his curveball. His changeup is thrown in the low 80s and was his most relied-upon secondary in 2021. Beck has average control when he's right, but he's often rusty after missing time.

THE FUTURE: Beck's workload will have to be managed carefully in 2022. He's likely to start the year at Double-A, where he'll try to stay healthy.

Year	Age	Club (Level)	Lge	W	L	ERA	G	GS	IP	H	HR	BB	SO	BB/9	SO/9	WHIP	AVG
2021	25	Giants Black (R)	ACL	0	3	7.71	6	6	11	17	0	6	17	4.6	13.1	1.97	.333
	25	San Jose (LoA)	West	2	0	4.91	2	0	7	9	1	1	5	1.2	6.1	1.36	.290
	25	Richmond (AA)	NEast	2	2	5.89	4	4	18	20	4	7	17	3.4	8.4	1.47	.274
Minor League Totals (4 years)				9	9	4.52	31	27	123	137	8	47	136	3.43	9.92	1.49	.280

MORE PROSPECTS TO KNOW

31. ALEXANDER SUAREZ, OF   SLEEPER

The 19-year-old Suarez put together a solid season in the Arizona Complex League. He led the league with 60 hits and his .311 average was eighth on the circuit. He plays a decent center field.

32. ROHAN HANDA, LHP

The Giants went all-in on lefties from the Northeast, popping Fordham's Matt Mikulski in the second round and Yale's Handa in the fourth. Handa made tremendous strides during the shutdown, bumping his fastball into the upper 90s and slider into the mid 80s.

33. DAVID VILLAR, 3B

Villar had an outstanding season at Double-A Richmond, where he finished eighth in the Double-A Northeast in home runs. There are questions about his range at third base and scouts have noticed he is particularly susceptible to spin.

34. TYLER FITZGERALD, 2B

The Louisville product brings a lot to the table. He controls the zone and has a smattering of power, albeit with a bit of a pull-heavy approach. He can hack it at all three non-first base spots on the infield without being a standout at any one in particular. He runs well, too, and fits a super-utility mold.

35. MANUEL MERCEDES, RHP

Mercedes is an intriguing young pitcher with a heater that already touches 98 mph and has the horizontal movement teams covet. He backs the fastball up with a mid-80s slider and a nascent changeup.

36. DIEGO RINCONES, OF

Rincones had an excellent season on the surface, but his uber-aggressive approach is likely to get him into trouble at the highest levels. He doesn't show much interest in playing defense, either.

37. ISMAEL MUNGUIA, OF

Munguia had a successful season pairing tons of contact with an extremely aggressive approach. He combined to strike out or walk in just 11% of his plate appearances while manning center field at High-A Eugene. He's a fringe-average runner who can spray the ball from gap to gap.

38. JIMMY GLOWENKE, SS

At Low-A, Glowenke played an adequate shortstop but scouts were concerned about his overall lack of physicality. If he gets stronger, he can up his profile, but as-is he might not have enough thump to hit anywhere but the bottom of a lineup.

39. COLE WAITES, RHP

The Giants' 18th-round pick out of South Alabama in 2019 began the year with surgery to repair a torn meniscus in his knee. Once he got back on the mound, he showed off an electric fastball that ranks as the best in the system. He needs to refine his slider as well as his overall command.

40. KAI-WEI TENG, RHP

Teng was one of three pitchers in the Giants' system to whiff more than 130 hitters in fewer than 100 innings. His is more of a kitchen sink approach than a reliance on one knockout pitch, and his season was sullied by a suspension for 10 games when a foreign substance was discovered on his glove.

TOP PROSPECTS OF THE DECADE

Year	Player, Pos	2021 Org
2012	Gary Brown, OF	Did not play
2013	Kyle Crick, RHP	Pirates
2014	Kyle Crick, RHP	Pirates
2015	Andrew Susac, C	Pirates
2016	Christian Arroyo, SS	Red Sox
2017	Tyler Beede, RHP	Giants
2018	Heliot Ramos, OF	Giants
2019	Joey Bart, C	Giants
2020	Marco Luciano, SS	Giants
2021	Marco Luciano, SS	Giants

TOP DRAFT PICKS OF THE DECADE

Year	Player, Pos	2021 Org
2012	Chris Stratton, RHP	Pirates
2013	Christian Arroyo, SS	Red Sox
2014	Tyler Beede, RHP	Giants
2015	Phil Bickford, RHP	Dodgers
2016	Bryan Reynolds, OF (2nd round)	Pirates
2017	Heliot Ramos, OF	Giants
2018	Joey Bart, C	Giants
2019	Hunter Bishop, OF	Giants
2020	Patrick Bailey, C	Giants
2021	Will Bednar, RHP	Giants

Seattle Mariners

BY KYLE GLASER

Righthander Logan Gilbert could be the first in a line of talented pitchers to reach Seattle.

The Mariners' rebuild landed a year early in 2021. Now the task is to take the next step to end the longest playoff drought in North American professional sports.

The Mariners were the surprise of baseball in 2021, going 90-72 and remaining in playoff contention until the season's final day. It was the franchise's best record in 18 years and wholly unexpected given they are still in the midst of a rebuild.

Outfielder Jarred Kelenic, righthander Logan Gilbert and catcher Cal Raleigh all made their debuts during the season, but it was a cast of 30-and-under veterans like Ty France, J.P. Crawford, Mitch Haniger, Chris Flexen and Marco Gonzales who did most of the heavy lifting. Given the Mariners' success despite reigning American League rookie of the year Kyle Lewis missing most of the season with a knee injury and the club's top prospects still having their best days ahead of them, the outlook in Seattle is brighter than at any time since 2001, the last time the Mariners made the playoffs.

The team's success was even more gratifying given what transpired before the season. In February, a video emerged of team president and CEO Kevin Mather making derogatory comments about former pitcher Hisashi Iwakuma, current top prospect Julio Rodriguez and veteran third baseman Kyle Seager in a speech to the Bellevue (Wash.) Rotary Club and admitted the organization manipulated Kelenic's service time. Mather resigned shortly after the video emerged, but the swift backlash from Major League Baseball, the MLB Players Association, fans and media cast a pall over the organization.

General manager Jerry Dipoto created further discord when he traded closer Kendall Graveman to the division-rival Astros at the trade deadline with Seattle chasing Houston for the division lead. Mariners players told local media they felt "betrayed" by the deal and excoriated Dipoto, with one saying, "He sits up in his suite playing fantasy baseball and rips our team apart without telling us anything."

Despite it all, the Mariners won 90 games and are now primed to reap the fruits of the rebuilding process they began after the 2018 season. The team's top two prospects, Rodriguez and righthanded pitcher George Kirby, each have a case as the best position player prospect and pitching prospect in the minors, respectively, and are in position to make their major league debuts in 2022 after finishing last season in Double-A.

Righthanders Matt Brash, Emerson Hancock and Levi Stoudt and lefthander Brandon Williamson also rose to Double-A in breakthrough

PROJECTED 2025 LINEUP

Catcher	Cal Raleigh	28
First Base	Ty France	30
Second Base	Abraham Toro	28
Third Base	Noelvi Marte	23
Shortstop	J.P. Crawford	30
Left Field	Jarred Kelenic	25
Center Field	Kyle Lewis	29
Right Field	Julio Rodriguez	24
Designated Hitter	Mitch Haniger	34
No. 1 Starter	George Kirby	27
No. 2 Starter	Robbie Ray	33
No. 3 Starter	Logan Gilbert	28
No. 4 Starter	Matt Brash	27
No. 5 Starter	Chris Flexen	30
Closer	Diego Castillo	31

seasons, giving the Mariners arguably the best and most advanced group of pitching prospects in the minors. The lower levels of the system received a boost with the selection of catcher Harry Ford in the first round of the draft and the signing of outfielder Gabriel Gonzalez out of Venezuela, giving the Mariners arguably the most talented collection of prospects in baseball.

With a 90-win team in the majors and one of the game's best farm systems, all the pieces are in place for the Mariners to end their playoff drought and take control of the American League West through the 2020s. As long as Mariners management can avoid further snafus, postseason baseball should return soon to the Emerald City. ■

SEATTLE MARINERS

TOP 2022 ROOKIES	RANK
Julio Rodriguez, OF	1
George Kirby, RHP	2
Matt Brash, RHP	4

BREAKOUT PROSPECTS	RANK
Gabriel Gonzalez, OF	10
Alberto Rodriguez, OF	14

SOURCE OF TOP 30 TALENT

Homegrown	26	Acquired	4
College	11	Trade	3
Junior college	1	Rule 5 draft	0
High school	4	Independent league	0
Nondrafted free agent	1	Free agent/waivers	1
International	9		

LF
Zach DeLoach (12)
Cade Marlowe (28)

CF
Victor Labrada (21)
George Feliz (23)
Jonatan Clase (26)
Luis Bolivar
Jack Larsen

RF
Julio Rodriguez (1)
Gabriel Gonzalez (10)
Alberto Rodriguez (14)

3B
Milkar Perez (16)
Starlin Aguilar (19)
Kevin Padlo (24)
Jose Caballero

SS
Noelvi Marte (3)
Edwin Arroyo (15)

2B
Kaden Polcovich (29)
Donnie Walton
Patrick Frick

1B
Jake Scheiner
Robert Perez

C
Harry Ford (7)
Jose Godoy
Andy Thomas

LHP

LHSP	LHRP
Brandon Williamson (5)	Brayan Perez
Adam Macko (9)	

RHP

RHSP	RHRP
George Kirby (2)	Andres Muñoz (11)
Matt Brash (4)	Connor Phillips (13)
Emerson Hancock (6)	Juan Then (17)
Levi Stoudt (8)	Bryce Miller (22)
Michael Morales (18)	Wyatt Mills (25)
Taylor Dollard (20)	Devin Sweet (27)
Isaiah Campbell	Penn Murfee (30)
Darren McCaughan	Sam Carlson
	Dayeison Arias
	Bryan Woo
	Luis Curvelo
	Travis Kuhn
	Leon Hunter

1 JULIO RODRIGUEZ, OF

Born: Dec. 29, 2000. **B-T:** R-R. **HT:** 6-3. **WT:** 210.
Signed: Dominican Republic, 2017.
Signed by: Eddy Toledo/Tim Kissner.

MIKE JANES/FOUR SEAM IMAGES

TRACK RECORD: Evaluators considered Rodriguez one of the best players in the 2017 international class when he signed with the Mariners for $1.75 million, but he has exceeded even the highest expectations. Rodriguez dominated the Dominican Summer League and both Class A levels in his first two seasons, earning hyperbolic praise from scouts, coaches and opponents. He suffered a hairline fracture in his left wrist diving for a ball in summer camp in 2020, but he returned with no ill effects in 2021. Rodriguez finished second in the minor leagues with a .347 batting average and seventh with a 1.001 OPS while climbing to Double-A, a performance even more impressive given the repeated interruptions to his season. He left twice to play for the Dominican Republic in Olympic qualifiers in Florida and Mexico and helped the Dominicans qualify for the Summer Games. At the Tokyo Olympics, Rodriguez hit .417 as the youngest player in the tournament to lead the Dominican Republic to the bronze medal, the first Olympic baseball medal in the country's history.

SCOUTING REPORT: Rodriguez is a physical presence at 6-foot-3, 210 pounds with the strength and athleticism to take over games. He destroys baseballs with 80-grade raw power and has been known to hit balls out of stadiums. His longest home runs come to his pull side, but he has the strength to drive balls out the other way with shocking ease. Rodriguez has the rare ability to get to his power without sacrificing the ability to hit for average. He is a career .331 hitter in the minors who identifies pitches well and stays short to the ball with a simple approach and direct bat path that allows him to make frequent contact in all parts of the strike zone. His swing occasionally gets too big, but he adjusts quickly within at-bats and doesn't miss the same pitch twice. He is an adept two-strike hitter for a power hitter who stays on tough pitches and rarely strikes out. A plus-plus hitter with plus-plus game power, Rodriguez further enhances his game with his surprising speed. He is an above-average runner who is adept at reading pitchers and stealing bases, and he covers plenty of ground in all directions in right field. He is particularly advanced at ranging back on balls and keeps runners from taking extra bases with his plus, accurate arm. Rodriguez occasionally loses focus on defense, but he's an above-average

BA GRADE	SCOUTING GRADES
75 Risk: Medium	Hit: 70. **Power:** 70. **Run:** 55. Field: 55. **Arm:** 60.

Projected future grades on 20-80 scouting scale

BEST TOOLS

Best Hitter for Average	Julio Rodriguez
Best Power Hitter	Julio Rodriguez
Best Strike-Zone Discipline	Milkar Perez
Fastest Baserunner	Jonatan Clase
Best Athlete	Harry Ford
Best Fastball	George Kirby
Best Curveball	Brandon Williamson
Best Slider	Matt Brash
Best Changeup	Devin Sweet
Best Control	George Kirby
Best Defensive Catcher	Harry Ford
Best Defensive Infielder	Edwin Arroyo
Best Infield Arm	Milkar Perez
Best Defensive Outfielder	Luis Bolivar
Best Outfield Arm	Julio Rodriguez

defender when he's locked in. In addition to his physical skills, Rodriguez is an incredibly charismatic individual and a clubhouse leader. He has been bilingual since he was 18 years old and plays the game with a constant smile on his face, energizing his teammates and lighting up clubhouses with his outgoing, effervescent personality.

THE FUTURE: Rodriguez's talent and personality have him set to be not only the face of the Mariners franchise, but one of the faces of baseball. As long as he stays healthy, he projects to be a perennial all-star and MVP contender who competes for home run titles. ∎

Year	Age	Club (Level)	Lge	AVG	G	AB	R	H	2B	3B	HR	RBI	BB	SO	SB	OBP	SLG
2021	20	Everett (HiA)	West	.325	28	117	29	38	8	2	6	21	14	29	5	.410	.581
	20	Arkansas (AA)	Cent	.362	46	174	35	63	11	0	7	26	29	37	16	.461	.546
Minor League Totals (4 years)				.331	217	838	177	277	58	15	30	152	98	182	32	.412	.543

2 GEORGE KIRBY, RHP

Born: Feb. 4, 1998. **B-T:** R-R. **HT:** 6-4. **WT:** 215. **Drafted:** Elon, 2019 (1st round). **Signed by:** Ty Holub.

TRACK RECORD: Kirby walked six batters in 14 starts his junior year at Elon and posted the best strikeout-to-walk ratio (16.8) in the country. Despite modest stuff, Kirby's elite control and command convinced the Mariners to draft him 20th overall and give him a $3,242,900 signing bonus. Kirby remade his body in 2020 at the alternate training site and re-emerged with vastly improved stuff in 2021. He posted a 2.53 ERA in 15 starts and rose to Double-A, although he missed a month with shoulder tenderness.

SCOUTING REPORT: Kirby's fastball has jumped from 91-94 mph in college to 95-99 as a pro with explosive late life up in the zone. He generates his velocity with little effort and locates his fastball to both sides of the plate with plus-plus command, making it a swing-and-miss pitch even when batters are geared up for it. Kirby complements his fastball with a plus, wipeout slider in the 85-89 mph range that misses bats and an above-average, 79-80 mph curveball with depth and bite. His fading, 85-86 mph changeup has excellent separation from his fastball, but it plays down a tick because his control of it is just average. Despite his long, lanky build, Kirby is a good athlete with excellent body coordination and repeats his delivery for elite control. He has averaged 1.5 walks per nine innings in his minor league career and his misses are very small.

THE FUTURE: Kirby's rare mix of power and precision gives him the potential to be a No. 1 or 2 starter as long as he stays healthy. His major league debut should come in 2022.

BA GRADE
70 Risk: High

| SCOUTING GRADES: | Fastball: 70 | Slider: 60 | Curveball: 55 | Changeup: 50 | Control: 80 |

Year	Age	Club (Level)	Lge	W	L	ERA	G	GS	IP	H	HR	BB	SO	BB/9	SO/9	WHIP	AVG
2021	23	Everett (HiA)	West	4	2	2.38	9	9	41	33	1	8	52	1.7	11.2	0.98	.214
	23	Arkansas (AA)	Cent	1	1	2.77	6	6	26	25	0	7	28	2.4	9.7	1.23	.248
Minor League Totals (3 years)				5	3	2.48	24	23	91	82	2	15	105	1.5	10.4	1.07	.238

3 NOELVI MARTE, SS

Born: Oct. 16, 2001. **B-T:** R-R **HT:** 6-1. **WT:** 195. **Signed:** Dominican Republic, 2018. **Signed by:** Eddy Toledo/Tim Kissner.

TRACK RECORD: Marte set himself apart with his athleticism, tools and performance as an amateur and signed with the Mariners for $1.55 million in 2018. He lived up to his pedigree with a standout debut in the Dominican Summer League and was invited to the Mariners alternate training site in 2020, where he understandably struggled as the youngest player in camp. Marte made his full-season debut in 2021 and finished among the league leaders in hits, runs, doubles, home runs, walks, RBIs and stolen bases at Low-A Modesto, earning a late promotion to High-A Everett.

SCOUTING REPORT: A skinny, projectable teenager when he signed, Marte has grown into a broad-shouldered, physical specimen with explosive power. He generates borderline plus-plus power out of a smooth, easy swing and hits rockets that leave any part of the stadium. He uses his lower half well and has a mechanically sound swing that allows him to project as an above-average hitter who gets to his power in games. Marte occasionally gives away at-bats and gets out of his approach, but at his best he recognizes pitches, stays in the strike zone and adjusts quickly. Marte moves well for his size on the basepaths and is a good athlete at shortstop with twitchy actions, a quick first step and soft hands. He has above-average arm strength but is often careless with his footwork and arm slot, leading to frequent throwing errors.

THE FUTURE: Marte has the potential to be a power-hitting, all-star shortstop if he cleans up his defense. Even if he moves to third base, he still projects to be a middle-of-the-order cornerstone.

BA GRADE
60 Risk: High

| SCOUTING GRADES: | Hitting: 55 | Power: 65 | Running: 50 | Fielding: 50 | Arm: 55 |

Year	Age	Club (Level)	Lge	AVG	G	AB	R	H	2B	3B	HR	RBI	BB	SO	SB	OBP	SLG
2021	19	Modesto (LoA)	West	.271	99	413	87	112	24	2	17	69	58	106	23	.368	.462
	19	Everett (HiA)	West	.290	8	31	4	9	4	0	0	2	2	11	1	.333	.419
Minor League Totals (2 years)				.286	172	706	147	202	46	6	26	125	89	172	41	.368	.479

4 MATT BRASH, RHP

BA GRADE
60 Risk: High

Born: May 12, 1998. **B-T:** R-R. **HT:** 6-1. **WT:** 170. **Drafted:** Niagara, 2019 (4th round). **Signed by:** Jake Koenig (Padres).

TRACK RECORD: A native of Kingston, Ontario, Brash pitched three years in Niagara's rotation and won the Metro Atlantic Athletic Conference's pitcher of the year honors after he set the conference and school records for strikeouts in a single season in 2019. The Padres drafted him in the fourth round and signed him for $512,400, then traded him to the Mariners as the player to be named later for reliever Taylor Williams following the 2020 season. Brash broke out beyond all expectations in 2021. He finished ninth in the minors with 13.1 strikeouts per nine innings and rocketed from High-A to the majors, where he received a callup in the season's final week but didn't pitch.

SCOUTING REPORT: Brash was limited by shoulder tenderness when the Mariners acquired him, but his stuff jumped exponentially with full health. His high-spin, 93-97 mph fastball collects swings and misses in bunches and his dastardly, mid-80s slider with power sweep and sharp dive is a plus-plus pitch that some observers grade an 80. He throws both pitches in any count and can finish batters with either of them. Brash complements his power offerings with an average knuckle curveball he lands for strikes and a changeup that flashes plus, although it is inconsistent. Brash has some effort to his delivery and his control can be scattered, leading to differing opinions whether he projects best as a starter or reliever. He holds his stuff deep into outings and improved his control as last season progressed.

THE FUTURE: Brash's stuff gives him a chance to be a frontline starter if he keeps improving his control. Otherwise, his fastball and slider give him closer potential in relief.

SCOUTING GRADES:	Fastball: 70	Slider: 70	Curveball: 50	Changeup: 55	Control: 45

Year	Age	Club (Level)	Lge	W	L	ERA	G	GS	IP	H	HR	BB	SO	BB/9	SO/9	WHIP	AVG
2021	23	Everett (HiA)	West	3	2	2.55	10	9	42	31	3	25	62	5.3	13.2	1.32	.204
	23	Arkansas (AA)	Cent	3	2	2.13	10	10	55	32	3	23	80	3.8	13.1	1.00	.162
Minor League Totals (3 years)				6	4	2.28	25	20	103	67	6	48	150	4.2	13.2	1.12	.181

5 BRANDON WILLIAMSON, LHP

BA GRADE
55 Risk: High

Born: April 2, 1998. **B-T:** L-L. **HT:** 6-6. **WT:** 210. **Drafted:** Texas Christian, 2019 (2nd round). **Signed by:** Jordan Bley.

TRACK RECORD: Williamson spent two seasons at Northern Iowa JC and was drafted by the Brewers in the 36th round in 2018, but he transferred to Texas Christian rather than sign. He won a spot in the Horned Frogs rotation and pitched well enough for the Mariners to draft him in the second round, No. 59 overall, one year later. Williamson spent 2020 at the alternate training site and made his full-season debut in 2021. He led the Mariners system with 153 strikeouts and rose from High-A to Double-A.

SCOUTING REPORT: Williamson's stuff keeps improving and now ranks among the best in the Mariners' pitching-rich system. A long-limbed, 6-foot-6 lefthander, Williamson sits 90-94 mph and reaches 97 mph on his fastball. The pitch plays up with late life and deception from his delivery and gets on batters faster than they expect with his long extension. Williamson's best pitch is a high-arching, top-to-bottom curveball in the mid 70s with tight spin and sharp, late bite. It gets under the barrels of both lefthanded and righthanded batters and is a borderline plus-plus pitch with his feel for locating it. He also shows feel for an average changeup in the mid 80s and an average slider in the low 80s with tight, horizontal break. Williamson keeps his long limbs in sync and throws plenty of strikes with average control, although he occasionally gets too much of the plate. He threw two immaculate innings last summer.

THE FUTURE: Williamson's build, stuff and control give him a chance to be a No. 3 or 4 starter. He is in line to make his major league debut in 2022.

SCOUTING GRADES:	Fastball: 60	Slider: 50	Curveball: 65	Changeup: 50	Control: 50

Year	Age	Club (Level)	Lge	W	L	ERA	G	GS	IP	H	HR	BB	SO	BB/9	SO/9	WHIP	AVG
2021	23	Everett (HiA)	West	2	1	3.19	6	6	31	21	4	10	59	2.9	17.1	1.00	.189
	23	Arkansas (AA)	Cent	2	5	3.48	13	13	67	62	7	23	94	3.1	12.6	1.26	.244
Minor League Totals (3 years)				4	6	3.25	29	28	114	92	11	38	178	3.0	14.1	1.14	.220

6 EMERSON HANCOCK, RHP

Born: May 31, 1999. **B-T:** R-R. **HT:** 6-4. **WT:** 213. **Drafted:** Georgia, 2020
(1st round). **Signed by:** John Wiedenbauer.

BA GRADE
55 Risk: **Very High**

TRACK RECORD: A 38th-round pick by the D-backs out of high school, Hancock spent three years in Georgia's starting rotation and posted a gaudy 1.99 ERA as a sophomore. He made only four starts his junior year before the coronavirus pandemic canceled the season, but the Mariners still drafted him sixth overall and signed him for $5.7 million. Hancock spent his first professional summer at the alternate training site before making his pro debut in 2021. He posted a 2.62 ERA and advanced to Double-A but was limited to 44.2 innings by recurring shoulder soreness.
SCOUTING REPORT: Known for his advanced control and polished delivery in college, Hancock has become more of a power pitcher as a pro and traded some of that smoothness for increased velocity. He overpowers hitters with a 94-98 mph four-seam fastball that rides up and a 93-96 mph two-seam fastball that sinks down out of his low arm slot, with his two-seamer the better of the two pitches. His sweepy, 79-80 mph slider flashes above-average and his mid-80s changeup is a plus pitch at its best. Hancock's delivery has become more effortful as he's tried to throw harder and his control has regressed to average. He opens up early, costing him deception, and puts a lot of stress on his shoulder with his arm slot, raising concerns about future injuries. He had multiple starts pushed back last season in addition to two separate injured list stints for his shoulder.
THE FUTURE: Hancock has mid-rotation stuff, but his delivery, control and health are all trending toward a bullpen future. He'll try to reverse those trends in 2022.

SCOUTING GRADES:	Fastball: 55		Slider: 55		Changeup: 60		Control: 50		

Year	Age	Club (Level)	Lge	W	L	ERA	G	GS	IP	H	HR	BB	SO	BB/9	SO/9	WHIP	AVG
2021	22	Everett (HiA)	West	2	0	2.32	9	9	31	19	1	13	30	3.8	8.7	1.03	.178
	22	Arkansas (AA)	Cent	1	1	3.29	3	3	13	10	0	4	13	2.6	8.6	1.02	.196
Minor League Totals (2 years)				3	1	2.62	12	12	45	29	1	17	43	3.4	8.7	1.03	.184

7 HARRY FORD, C

Born: Feb. 21, 2003. **B-T:** R-R. **HT:** 5-10. **WT:** 200. **Drafted:** HS—Kennesaw, Ga.
2021 (1st round). **Signed by:** John Wiedenbauer

BA GRADE
55 Risk: **Extreme**

TRACK RECORD: Ford stood out for his premium athleticism at East Coast Pro and solidified his place as the top high school catcher in the 2021 draft class with a strong senior spring. The Mariners considered him one of the top three high school players in the class after he dazzled general manager Jerry Dipoto and other club executives during a private, pre-draft batting practice, and Seattle selected him 12th overall and signed him for $4,366,400 to forgo a Georgia Tech commitment. Ford made his pro debut in the Arizona Complex League and hit .291 with 10 extra-base hits in 19 games, including three homers in his final five games.
SCOUTING REPORT: Ford isn't particularly big at 5-foot-10, 200 pounds, but he packs plenty of bat speed and strength in his compact frame. He consistently squares balls up with his excellent hand-eye coordination and barrel awareness and drives the ball to all fields to project as an above-average hitter. He is a patient hitter who takes an opposite-field approach aimed at lining balls the other way, but he shows surprising plus raw power when he turns on balls. Ford is a plus runner, rare for a catcher, and has the athleticism to play multiple positions. His blocking and receiving need to improve, but his flexibility, strong hands and work ethic give him a chance to be an average defensive catcher in time. His above-average arm strength plays at any position.
THE FUTURE: The Mariners will develop Ford as a catcher and believe he'll stick there. Even if he doesn't, his hitting ability and multi-positional versatility give him plenty of avenues to the majors.

SCOUTING GRADES:	Hitting: 55		Power: 50		Running: 60		Fielding: 50		Arm: 55	

Year	Age	Club (Level)	Lge	AVG	G	AB	R	H	2B	3B	HR	RBI	BB	SO	SB	OBP	SLG
2021	18	Mariners (R)	ACL	.291	19	55	12	16	7	0	3	10	9	14	3	.400	.582
Minor League Totals (1 year)				.291	19	55	12	16	7	0	3	10	9	14	3	.400	.582

8 LEVI STOUDT, RHP

Born: Dec. 4, 1997. **B-T:** R-R. **HT:** 6-1. **WT:** 195. **Drafted:** Lehigh, 2019 (3rd round). **Signed by:** Patrick O'Grady.

TRACK RECORD: Stoudt finished third in Lehigh history with a career 2.69 ERA and showed his stuff played against top competition with a solid summer in the Cape Cod League prior to his junior season. The Mariners drafted him in the third round in 2019 and signed him for $339,000. Stoudt had Tommy John surgery shortly after being drafted and didn't make his pro debut until 2021, but he made up for lost time with a quick ascent. He went 7-3, 3.31 in 15 starts and averaged more than a strikeout per inning while rising from High-A to Double-A.

SCOUTING REPORT: Stoudt got stronger during his rehab and came back throwing harder after surgery. His previously 91-95 mph fastball now ranges from 94-98 mph with good downhill plane. His best pitch is a split-changeup in the low 80s with late dive and run, and the added separation between his fastball and changeup has helped both pitches play up. Both are now consistently above-average pitches and flash plus at their best. Stoudt's slurvy, mid-80s slider is an average pitch that flashes higher, and he has gotten better at separating it from his fringy, mid-70s curveball. Stoudt battled his control at times in his pro debut, but his simple, clean delivery and fluid arm action should yield average control as he moves farther away from surgery. He does have some effort in his delivery and needs to prove his durability after pitching only 81.2 innings last season.

THE FUTURE: Stoudt projects to be a solid, consistent No. 4 starter who isn't flashy but gets the job done. He'll start at Triple-A Tacoma in 2022.

BA GRADE
50 Risk: High

SCOUTING GRADES:	Fastball: 55	Slider: 50	Curveball: 45	Changeup: 55	Control: 50

Year	Age	Club (Level)	Lge	W	L	ERA	G	GS	IP	H	HR	BB	SO	BB/9	SO/9	WHIP	AVG
2021	23	Everett (HiA)	West	6	1	3.52	12	12	64	47	6	29	67	4.1	9.4	1.19	.204
	23	Arkansas (AA)	Cent	1	2	2.55	3	3	17	14	2	8	19	4.1	9.7	1.25	.219
Minor League Totals (3 years)				7	3	3.31	15	15	82	61	8	37	86	4.1	9.5	1.20	.207

9 ADAM MACKO, LHP

Born: Dec. 30, 2000. **B-T:** L-L. **HT:** 6-0. **WT:** 170. **Drafted:** HS—Vauxhall, Alberta, 2019 (7th round). **Signed by:** Les McTavish/Alex Ross.

TRACK RECORD: Born in Slovakia, Macko was introduced to baseball in the first grade when he began hitting balls off a tee at his elementary school. When he was 10, he began watching YouTube videos of Justin Verlander and David Price to teach himself how to pitch. Macko's family moved to Ireland when he was 11 and eventually settled in Canada, where he grew into the country's top high school pitching prospect. The Mariners drafted him in the seventh round in 2019 and signed him for $250,000 to forgo a Purdue commitment. Macko made his full-season debut with Low-A Modesto in 2021 and was limited to 33.1 innings by recurring shoulder tenderness, but he showed electric stuff when healthy.

SCOUTING REPORT: Macko has progressed rapidly given his unconventional background. After sitting in the upper 80s in high school, he now averages 93-94 mph and touches 97-98 with his fastball. His primary weapon is a sweeping, high-spin curveball in the low 70s with late tilt and bite that gets both swings and misses and called strikes on both sides of the plate. He has advanced feel to alter the shape and length of his curveball, making it a consensus plus-plus offering. Macko also has an average low-80s slider and fringy low-80s changeup, although he mostly just dominates with his fastball and curveball. Macko flashes average control but struggles with consistency. He often cruises for a few innings before suddenly unraveling.

THE FUTURE: Macko is frequently requested by other teams in trade discussions. His stuff and projection give him mid-rotation potential if he can stay healthy and tighten his control with more experience.

BA GRADE
55 Risk: Extreme

SCOUTING GRADES:	Fastball: 55	Slider: 50	Curveball: 70	Changeup: 45	Control: 45

Year	Age	Club (Level)	Lge	W	L	ERA	G	GS	IP	H	HR	BB	SO	BB/9	SO/9	WHIP	AVG
2021	20	Modesto (LoA)	West	2	2	4.59	9	9	33	29	1	21	56	5.7	15.1	1.50	.223
Minor League Totals (3 years)				2	5	3.97	18	11	57	48	2	33	88	5.2	13.4	1.43	.223

10 GABRIEL GONZALEZ, OF

Born: Jan. 4, 2004. **B-T:** B-R. **HT:** 5-11. **WT:** 180. **Signed:** Venezuela, 2021. **Signed by:** Luis Martinez.

TRACK RECORD: The Mariners considered Gonzalez one of the top players in the 2020-21 international class and signed him for a $1.3 million bonus out of Venezuela. Gonzalez immediately stood out after signing and carried it over into his official pro debut. He hit .287/.371/.582 and led the Dominican Summer League with 26 extra-base hits, earning reviews as arguably the top player in the league.

SCOUTING REPORT: Gonzalez is only 5-foot-11, but he has a strong, physical frame and surprisingly twitchy athleticism for his muscular build. He rotates quickly with a lot of torque in his swing to generate plus power to all fields. Gonzalez is a power hitter first, but he has a good feel for contact and projects to be an average hitter. He covers the entire plate and has an advanced sense for hunting pitches he can drive. Gonzalez is a slightly above-average runner and has the hands and instincts to play center field. He presently has enough range for the position, but he may move to right field if he loses a step. He has the above-average arm strength to stick in right field if needed.

THE FUTURE: Gonzalez is set to make his stateside debut in the Arizona Complex League in 2022 and will play all season as an 18-year-old.

BA GRADE
55 Risk: Extreme

SCOUTING GRADES:	Hitting: 50	Power: 60	Running: 50	Fielding: 50	Arm: 55

Year	Age	Club (Level)	Lge	AVG	G	AB	R	H	2B	3B	HR	RBI	BB	SO	SB	OBP	SLG
2021	17	Mariners (R)	DSL	.287	54	188	39	54	15	4	7	36	21	35	9	.371	.521
Minor League Totals (1 year)				.287	54	188	39	54	15	4	7	36	21	35	9	.371	.521

11 ANDRES MUÑOZ, RHP

BA GRADE
55 Risk: Extreme

Born: Jan. 16, 1999. **B-T:** R-R. **HT:** 6-2. **WT:** 243 Signed: Mexico, 2015. **Signed by:** Trevor Schumm (Padres)

TRACK RECORD: The Padres purchased Muñoz's rights for $700,000 from the Mexican League in 2015 and watched as he blossomed into one of the hardest-throwing pitchers in baseball. He touched 102 mph by the time he was 19 and reached the majors at 20 before succumbing to Tommy John surgery early in 2020. The Mariners acquired Muñoz in the trade for catcher Austin Nola, and Muñoz returned to make his Mariners debut on the final day of the 2021 season.

SCOUTING REPORT: Muñoz returned from injury with his stuff intact. His fastball sits 99-100 mph and touches 102 with explosive riding life at the top of the zone and late armside movement in the lower quadrants. It's a true 80-grade fastball he dominates with and throws more than two thirds of the time. Muñoz's tight, 81-83 mph slider flashes above-average when he locates it, but it is often a ball out of his hand. He has below-average control overall and is prone to spinning out of his delivery. Muñoz still has to prove he's durable enough to last a full season. He has topped 30 innings only once in six years.

THE FUTURE: Muñoz is ready to move into a setup role for the Mariners in 2022. He could be a closer if he stays healthy.

Year	Age	Club (Level)	Lge	W	L	ERA	G	GS	IP	H	HR	BB	SO	BB/9	SO/9	WHIP	AVG
2021	22	Mariners (R)	ACL	0	0	0.00	1	1	1	0	0	0	3	0.0	27.0	0.00	.000
	22	Tacoma (AAA)	West	0	0	6.75	3	1	2	1	0	1	4	3.4	13.5	0.75	.111
	22	Seattle (MLB)	AL	0	0	0.00	1	0	0	0	0	2	1	27.0	13.5	3.00	.000
Major League Totals (2 years)				1	1	3.80	23	0	24	16	2	13	31	4.94	11.79	1.23	.184
Minor League Totals (6 years)				9	6	3.21	104	3	109	70	7	66	156	5.4	12.8	1.24	.181

12 ZACH DeLOACH, OF

BA GRADE
50 Risk: High

Born: Aug. 18, 1998. **B-T:** L-R. **HT:** 6-1. **WT:** 205. **Drafted:** Texas A&M, 2020 (2nd round). **Signed by:** Derek Miller

TRACK RECORD: DeLoach scuffled his first two seasons at Texas A&M before breaking out in the Cape Cod League prior to his junior year. He carried his success into the following spring and was off to a hot start before the coronavirus pandemic canceled the 2020 college season. The Mariners drafted him in the second round and signed him for $1,729,800. DeLoach continued his upward trend in his pro debut, rising to Double-A and finishing in the top five in the Mariners' organization in hits, runs, doubles, walks and total bases.

SCOUTING REPORT: DeLoach has elite pitch recognition and is rarely fooled. He identifies pitches early, stays in the strike zone and drives the ball with a simple, direct lefthanded swing. He hits both righthanders and lefthanders and projects to be an above-average hitter who draws lots of walks. DeLoach doesn't pack much power, but he has improved at getting the ball in the air and has a chance to reach 14-18 home runs at his peak. He is just a fair athlete and needs to improve his range and reads in the outfield to become an average defender. His average speed and below-average arm strength profile best in left field.
THE FUTURE: DeLoach's ability to get on base gives him a chance to be an everyday player similar to Seth Smith. He'll see Triple-A Tacoma in 2022.

Year	Age	Club (Level)	Lge	AVG	G	AB	R	H	2B	3B	HR	RBI	BB	SO	SB	OBP	SLG
2021	22	Everett (HiA)	West	.313	58	249	56	78	23	2	9	37	32	63	6	.400	.530
	22	Arkansas (AA)	Cent	.227	49	185	28	42	10	2	5	22	28	58	1	.338	.384
Minor League Totals (2 years)				.276	107	434	84	120	33	4	14	59	60	121	7	.373	.468

13 CONNOR PHILLIPS, RHP

BA GRADE
50 Risk: Very High

Born: May 4, 2001. **B-T:** R-R. **HT:** 6-2. **WT:** 190. **Drafted:** McLennan (Texas) JC, 2020 (2nd round supplemental). **Signed by:** Derek Miller.
TRACK RECORD: A 35th-round pick by the Blue Jays out of high school, Phillips was committed to Louisiana State but instead rerouted to McLennan (Texas) JC, where he made six starts before the coronavirus pandemic canceled the 2020 season. The Mariners saw enough to draft him in the second round, No. 64 overall, and sign him for a $1,050,300 bonus. Phillips made his pro debut in 2021 and struck out more than 13 batters per nine innings while moving from Low-A to High-A, but he also walked more than five per nine.
SCOUTING REPORT: Phillips has big stuff but is still learning to harness it. His fastball sits 94-96 mph with late zip and gets swings and misses up in the zone. His mid-80s slider is a second plus pitch with hard, late break away from righthanded batters. His firm, 86-90 mph changeup is a well below-average pitch and leaves him vulnerable against lefties. Phillips dominates with his fastball and slider when he's on, but his control and command vary wildly from game to game. His effortful delivery leads to scattered, below-average control despite his solid athleticism.
THE FUTURE: Phillips' delivery and two plus pitches make him a likely reliever, but the Mariners will keep starting him for now. He is on track to reach Double-A in 2022.

Year	Age	Club (Level)	Lge	W	L	ERA	G	GS	IP	H	HR	BB	SO	BB/9	SO/9	WHIP	AVG
2021	20	Modesto (LoA)	West	7	3	4.75	16	16	72	62	1	44	104	5.5	13.0	1.47	.229
	20	Everett (HiA)	West	0	1	2.25	1	1	4	2	1	2	7	4.5	15.8	1.00	.133
Minor League Totals (2 years)				7	4	4.62	17	17	76	64	2	46	111	5.5	13.1	1.45	.224

14 ALBERTO RODRIGUEZ, OF

BA GRADE
50 Risk: Very High

Born: Oct. 6, 2000. **B-T:** L-L. **HT:** 5-11. **WT:** 180. **Signed:** Dominican Republic, 2017. **Signed by:** Sandy Rosario/Lorenzo Perez/Luciano del Rosario (Blue Jays).
TRACK RECORD: The Blue Jays signed Rodriguez for $500,000 during the 2017 international signing period and traded him to the Mariners for Taijuan Walker at the 2020 deadline. After falling out of shape during the coronavirus shutdown, Rodriguez cleaned up his body during spring training and took off in his first year in the Mariners system. He shook off a slow start at Low-A Modesto to hit .289/.379/.470 with 31 doubles, 10 home runs and 15 stolen bases while advancing to High-A Everett.
SCOUTING REPORT: Rodriguez has exceptional strike-zone recognition and solid bat-to-ball skills from the left side. He was previously too passive, but he started taking a more aggressive approach last summer and began driving balls to all fields. He lays off close pitches, rarely swings and misses and posts high exit velocities to project as an above-average hitter. Rodriguez mostly drives balls from gap to gap, but he does have latent raw power that could translate into 15-20 home runs as he matures. He is an average runner who covers plenty of ground in right field, although his reads and approach on ground balls could use polish. He has an accurate, above-average arm.
THE FUTURE: The Mariners added Rodriguez to the 40-man roster after the season and view him as a potential everyday right fielder. He will begin 2022 at High-A Everett.

Year	Age	Club (Level)	Lge	AVG	G	AB	R	H	2B	3B	HR	RBI	BB	SO	SB	OBP	SLG
2021	20	Modesto (LoA)	West	.295	93	370	75	109	30	5	10	63	51	95	13	.383	.484
	20	Everett (HiA)	West	.208	7	24	5	5	1	0	0	2	2	7	2	.321	.250
Minor League Totals (4 years)				.282	208	795	143	224	53	7	17	128	104	189	49	.368	.430

15 EDWIN ARROYO, SS

Born: Aug. 25, 2003. **B-T:** B-B. **HT:** 6-0. **WT:** 175.
Drafted: HS—Kissimmee, Fla., 2021 (2nd round). **Signed by:** Rob Mummau.

TRACK RECORD: Arroyo was Puerto Rico's top player in the 2021 draft class and raised his stock with an impressive showing at the Perfect Game All-America Classic. He transferred to Central Pointe Christian Academy in Kissimmee, Fla. for his senior year and performed well enough for the Mariners to draft him in the second round and sign him for $1.65 million. Arroyo became famous on social media in his pro debut for his enormous bat flips in the Arizona Complex League, but he hit just .211 with four extra-base hits in 21 games.

SCOUTING REPORT: Arroyo is a rare athlete who is both a switch-hitter and switch-thrower. That athleticism translates to his defense at shortstop, where his fluid actions, quick reads, reliable hands and plus arm strength give him the potential to be a plus-plus defender. He has advanced defensive instincts for his age and gets the ball out of his glove remarkably quickly. Arroyo faces more questions offensively. He has solid hand-eye coordination and surprising power, especially from the left side, but his swing frequently gets too big and doesn't stay in the zone very long. He plays with a lot of flash and flair but at times crosses the line into empty showboating.

THE FUTURE: Arroyo's defense will buy him time to figure out his bat. He'll see Low-A Modesto in 2022.

Year	Age	Club (Level)	Lge	AVG	G	AB	R	H	2B	3B	HR	RBI	BB	SO	SB	OBP	SLG
2021	17	Mariners (R)	ACL	.211	21	71	16	15	2	0	2	10	10	26	4	.337	.324
Minor League Totals (1 year)				.211	21	71	16	15	2	0	2	10	10	26	4	.337	.324

16 MILKAR PEREZ, 3B

Born: Oct. 16, 2001. **B-T:** B-R. **HT:** 5-11. **WT:** 175. **Signed:** Nicaragua, 2018. **Signed by:** Tom Shafer.

TRACK RECORD: Perez starred for Nicaragua's junior national teams as an amateur and made the all-tournament team at the 2018 COPABE 18U Pan American Championships in Panama. The Mariners signed him for $175,000 just before the tournament, the highest bonus given to a Nicaraguan position player in the class. Perez made his U.S. debut in 2021 and excelled against the increased level of competition. He batted .310 with more walks (39) than strikeouts (38) in the Arizona Complex League and received a late promotion to Low-A Modesto.

SCOUTING REPORT: Perez is a patient hitter with uncanny pitch recognition for his age. He quickly separates balls from strikes, stays in the strike zone and makes solid contact on hittable pitches to project as an average hitter. Perez has above-average raw power, but his setup and approach are more geared for contact. He is a passive hitter content to draw walks and has a closed-off stance aimed at hitting low liners up the middle and the opposite way. Perez is a big-bodied third baseman who will have to watch his conditioning to avoid a move to first base. His plus-plus arm strength is an asset at the hot corner.

THE FUTURE: Perez can be an everyday player if he makes adjustments to access his power, but that's a big "if." He'll return to Modesto to start 2022.

Year	Age	Club (Level)	Lge	AVG	G	AB	R	H	2B	3B	HR	RBI	BB	SO	SB	OBP	SLG
2021	19	Mariners (R)	ACL	.310	45	145	33	45	10	0	0	23	39	38	1	.463	.379
	19	Modesto (LoA)	West	.296	6	27	6	8	2	0	0	0	4	4	0	.406	.370
Minor League Totals (2 years)				.289	115	409	77	118	23	2	4	67	80	97	9	.413	.384

17 JUAN THEN, RHP

Born: Feb. 7, 2000. **B-T:** R-R. **HT:** 6-0. **WT:** 178. **Signed:** Dominican Republic, 2016. **Signed by:** Eddy Toledo.

TRACK RECORD: Then signed with the Mariners for $77,000 when he was 16 and quickly emerged as one of the top young prospects in their system. The Mariners traded him to the Yankees in 2017 in a deal for reliever Nick Rumbelow, only to re-acquire him two years later in exchange for Edwin Encarnacion. Then returned from the coronavirus shutdown with a star turn at instructional league, but he struggled at High-A Everett when minor league play resumed in 2021. He went 2-5, 6.46 in 14 starts and was limited to 54.1 innings by shoulder tenderness.

SCOUTING REPORT: Then has plenty of stuff, but the results haven't followed. His lively fastball sits 94-97 mph, touches 99 and plays in the strike zone. His slider is an above-average pitch that is his best secondary at times, and at others his above-average changeup is the better pitch. Then's biggest issue is consistency. He has a hook in the back of his delivery that affects his ability to get to his breaking ball and his below-average control prevents him from effectively navigating a lineup multiple times.

THE FUTURE: Then's pure stuff excites evaluators who think he will be more effective in short stints out of the bullpen. He may make that switch to relief as soon as 2022 at Double-A Arkansas.

Year	Age	Club (Level)	Lge	W	L	ERA	G	GS	IP	H	HR	BB	SO	BB/9	SO/9	WHIP	AVG
2021	21	Everett (HiA)	West	2	5	6.46	14	14	54	68	12	19	59	3.2	9.8	1.60	.300
Minor League Totals (5 years)				5	15	3.70	49	47	214	189	19	58	205	2.4	8.6	1.15	.235

18 MICHAEL MORALES, RHP

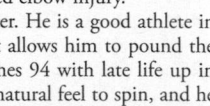

BA GRADE

50 Risk: Extreme

Born: Aug. 13, 2002. **B-T:** R-R. **HT:** 6-2. **WT:** 205. **Drafted:** HS—Enola, Pa., 2021 (3rd round). **Signed by:** Dave Pepe.

TRACK RECORD: Morales stood out for his polished delivery on the summer showcase circuit and followed with a 0.77 ERA for East Pennsboro High his senior spring. The Mariners drafted him in the third round and signed him for an above-slot $1.5 million bonus to forgo a Vanderbilt commitment. He made only one appearance after signing due to an unspecified elbow injury.

SCOUTING REPORT: Morales is a prototypical projectable teenaged righthander. He is a good athlete in his 6-foot-2 frame and has a smooth, repeatable delivery and arm action that allows him to pound the strike zone with three pitches. His fastball ranges from 88-92 mph and touches 94 with late life up in the zone. His best secondary is a sharp, 77-80 mph curveball that he shows a natural feel to spin, and he rounds out his arsenal with a changeup that flashes average but lacks consistency. Morales has room to get stronger and add velocity and power to all his pitches. He is extremely intelligent and has an advanced understanding of pitch design and high-tech training methods.

THE FUTURE: Morales has many years of strength gains ahead, but he has the potential to be a back-of-the-rotation starter if everything clicks. He is expected to be ready for 2022 spring training.

Year	Age	Club (Level)	Lge	W	L	ERA	G	GS	IP	H	HR	BB	SO	BB/9	SO/9	WHIP	AVG
2021	18	Mariners (R)	ACL	0	0	18.00	1	1	1	2	0	1	1	9.0	9.0	3.00	.500
Minor League Totals (1 year)				0	0	18.00	1	1	1	2	0	1	1	9.0	9.0	3.00	.500

19 STARLIN AGUILAR, 3B

BA GRADE

50 Risk: Extreme

Born: Jan. 26, 2004. **B-T:** L-R. **HT:** 5-11. **WT:** 170. **Signed:** Dominican Republic, 2021. **Signed by:** Audo Vicente/Rafael Mateo.

TRACK RECORD: Aguilar was one of the best hitters his age in the Dominican Republic and trained in the same program that produced Red Sox third baseman Rafael Devers and Rays shortstop Wander Franco. The Mariners locked on to Aguilar early and signed him for $1.5 million, the highest bonus they awarded in the 2020-21 international class. Aguilar got off to a slow start in the Dominican Summer League in his pro debut, but he finished strong with a .270 batting average and .413 on-base percentage in September.

SCOUTING REPORT: Like Devers, Aguilar is a big-bodied third baseman with a sweet lefthanded swing. He has a fluid, compact stroke, gets on plane early and stays through the ball. He controls the strike zone and has good hand-eye coordination that allows him to cover the entire plate. Aguilar makes a lot of soft contact and is still learning to pick out pitches he can drive. He has above-average raw power, but his contact-oriented approach limits him from accessing it. Aguilar is a below-average runner who will have to watch his conditioning. He needs to improve his footwork and range to become an average defender.

THE FUTURE: Aguilar's conditioning and power production will determine whether he reaches his everyday potential. He'll make his stateside debut in the Arizona Complex League in 2022.

Year	Age	Club (Level)	Lge	AVG	G	AB	R	H	2B	3B	HR	RBI	BB	SO	SB	OBP	SLG
2021	17	Mariners (R)	DSL	.246	53	183	38	45	13	1	2	21	29	41	0	.359	.361
Minor League Totals (1 year)				.246	53	183	38	45	13	1	2	21	29	41	0	.359	.36

20 TAYLOR DOLLARD, RHP

BA GRADE

45 Risk: High

Born: Feb. 17, 1999. **B-T:** R-R. **HT:** 6-3. **WT:** 195. **Drafted:** Cal Poly, 2020 (5th round). **Signed by:** Ryan Holmes.

TRACK RECORD: Dollard pitched two seasons in relief at Cal Poly before moving into the starting rotation as a junior. He made only four starts before the 2020 season shut down due to the coronavirus pandemic, but the Mariners saw enough to select him in the fifth round and sign him for $406,600. Dollard made his pro debut in 2021 and struggled to a 5.14 ERA across both Class A levels, but he struck out 11.4 batters per nine innings while showing underlying promise on high-performance analytics models.

SCOUTING REPORT: Dollard moves well through his athletic delivery and pounds the strike zone with plus command and control. He is an "elite mover" in the words of one evaluator and has caught the attention of opposing teams who think they can unlock more stuff given his delivery and athleticism. Dollard's stuff is mostly average at present. His fastball sits 91-92 mph and occasionally touches 94, and he has a good feel for using his above-average slider. His curveball and changeup are fringy pitches he'll use to steal a strike or disrupt batters' timing. Dollard has room to get stronger and fill out his frame, but he's likely to always be a control-oriented pitcher.

THE FUTURE: Dollard has a chance to be a back-of-the-rotation starter if his stuff makes the anticipated leap. He'll see Double-A in 2022.

Year	Age	Club (Level)	Lge	W	L	ERA	G	GS	IP	H	HR	BB	SO	BB/9	SO/9	WHIP	AVG
2021	22	Modesto (LoA)	West	3	2	3.35	7	7	37	40	2	10	59	2.4	14.1	1.33	.265
	22	Everett (HiA)	West	6	2	6.15	12	11	67	78	12	14	74	1.9	9.9	1.37	.283
Minor League Totals (2 years)				9	4	5.14	19	18	105	118	14	24	133	2.1	11.4	1.35	.276

21 VICTOR LABRADA, OF

BA GRADE

45 Risk: High

Born: Jan. 16, 2000. **B-T:** L-L. **HT:** 5-9. **WT:** 165. **Signed:** Cuba, 2019.
Signed by: Audo Vicente.

TRACK RECORD: Labrada hit .350 as Cuba's leadoff hitter and team captain at the 2018 Pan-American Championships and briefly played for Industriales in Cuba's major league. He relocated to the Dominican Republic in 2019 to sign with an MLB team and agreed to a $350,000 bonus with the Mariners. After waiting out the coronavirus pandemic, Labrada made his pro debut in 2021 and hit his way out of Low-A Modesto to finish the season at High-A Everett.

SCOUTING REPORT: Labrada is a throwback as an undersized, high-energy center fielder who slaps the ball around and lets his speed work. He has plus-plus speed and always runs hard, including coming on and off the field between innings. He energizes his teams and sets the tone atop the lineup. Labrada can be aggressive at the plate, but he stays in the strike zone and makes a lot of contact with a quick, compact swing from the left side. He has a chance to be an average hitter but gets in trouble when he tries to chase power, which he lacks the strength to generate. Labrada's speed and range allow him to outrun bad reads or jumps in center field. He has a chance to be an above-average defender with below-average arm strength.

THE FUTURE: Labrada projects to be a high-energy fourth outfielder. He'll see Double-A in 2022.

Year	Age	Club (Level)	Lge	AVG	G	AB	R	H	2B	3B	HR	RBI	BB	SO	SB	OBP	SLG
2021	21	Modesto (LoA)	West	.294	50	201	44	59	16	3	1	28	34	60	22	.407	.418
	21	Everett (HiA)	West	.246	49	203	35	50	7	3	6	27	19	63	10	.314	.399
Minor League Totals (1 year)				.270	99	404	79	109	23	6	7	55	53	123	32	.362	.408

22 BRYCE MILLER, RHP

BA GRADE

45 Risk: High

Born: Aug, 23, 1998. **B-T:** R-R. **HT:** 6-2. **WT:** 180. **Drafted:** Texas A&M, 2021 (4th round). **Signed by:** Derek Miller

TRACK RECORD: The Marlins drafted Miller in the 38th round in 2018 out of Blinn (Texas) JC, but he instead transferred to Texas A&M and spent two seasons in the Aggies' bullpen before moving into the rotation as a senior. He finished among the team leaders in wins, innings and strikeouts in 2021, leading the Mariners to draft him in the fourth round and sign him for $400,000. Miller went straight to Low-A Modesto after signing and struck out 15 batters in 9.1 innings, although he also gave up 15 hits.

SCOUTING REPORT: Miller's fastball sits 93-94 mph as a starter and ramps up to 96 with hard ride as a reliever. His average mid-80s slider with hard, late turn misses bats to give him an effective secondary pitch and his low-80s changeup with deception and fade has flashed average, although it was below-average in his pro debut. He also has a fringy curveball. Miller is durable, but he struggles with consistency and is most effective in short spurts. His control is fringy and he relies more on overpowering hitters than hitting his spots.

THE FUTURE: Miller will start for now, but the Mariners acknowledge his future is likely in relief. He has a chance to be a high-leverage, late-game reliever if everything comes together.

Year	Age	Club (Level)	Lge	W	L	ERA	G	GS	IP	H	HR	BB	SO	BB/9	SO/9	WHIP	AVG
2021	22	Modesto (LoA)	West	0	0	4.82	5	3	9	15	0	2	15	1.9	14.5	1.82	.357
Minor League Totals (1 year)				0	0	4.82	5	3	9	15	0	2	15	1.9	14.5	1.82	.357

23 GEORGE FELIZ, OF

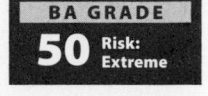

BA GRADE

50 Risk: Extreme

Born: Sept. 21, 2002. **B-T:** R-R. **HT:** 5-11. **WT:** 160. **Signed:** Dominican Republic, 2019. **Signed by:** Audo Vicente/Alfredo Celestin

TRACK RECORD: The Mariners signed Feliz for $900,000 out of the Dominican Republic in 2019, the largest bonus of their international class that year. Feliz's pro debut was delayed by the coronavirus pandemic, but he impressed when minor league play resumed in 2021. He hit .277/.362/.451 in the Dominican Summer League and showcased noteworthy athleticism and tools.

SCOUTING REPORT: Feliz is one of the best pure athletes in the Mariners' system. He is a plus runner who covers plenty of ground in center field to project as an above-average defender, has above-average arm strength and flashes above-average raw power. The question is how much contact he will make. Feliz has plenty of bat speed and strength, but he lacks natural rhythm and timing as a hitter and doesn't use his lower half well in his swing. He has gotten quieter and calmer at the plate and improved at staying balanced and keeping his back foot on the ground, but a fringe-average hitter is his best-case scenario.

THE FUTURE: Feliz needs to prove he can hit, but his tools and athleticism will buy him time. He is set to move to the Arizona Complex League in 2022.

Year	Age	Club (Level)	Lge	AVG	G	AB	R	H	2B	3B	HR	RBI	BB	SO	SB	OBP	SLG
2021	18	Mariners (R)	DSL	.277	46	173	32	48	7	4	5	25	21	46	8	.362	.451
Minor League Totals (1 year)				.277	46	173	32	48	7	4	5	25	21	46	8	.362	.451

24 KEVIN PADLO, 3B

BA GRADE

40 Risk: Medium

Born: July 15, 1996. **B-T:** R-R. **HT:** 6-2. **WT:** 210. **Drafted:** HS—Murrieta, Calif., 2014 (5th round). **Signed by:** Jon Lukens (Rockies).

TRACK RECORD: Padlo starred in both baseball and basketball in high school and was drafted by the Rockies in the fifth round in 2014. Colorado traded him to the Rays two years later in the deal that sent German Marquez to the Rockies. Padlo made his major league debut with the Rays in 2021 before being claimed off waivers by the Mariners in August, and he summarily hit eight homers in 26 games at Triple-A Tacoma.

SCOUTING REPORT: Padlo is a good athlete with plus-plus raw power. He hits towering fly balls to his pull side and has improved at picking out pitches to drive. He posted back-to-back 20-home run seasons in the minors and has the power to do the same in the majors, but that will depend on him getting enough at-bats. Padlo has a pull-heavy approach that leaves a lot of holes in his swing. He's a below-average hitter who relies on making impact on contact. Padlo is an average defender at third base who moves well for his size and has above-average arm strength. He is also experienced playing first base and second base.

THE FUTURE: Padlo's power and infield versatility give him a chance to stick in a reserve or platoon role. He'll return to the majors in 2022.

Year	Age	Club (Level)	Lge	AVG	G	AB	R	H	2B	3B	HR	RBI	BB	SO	SB	OBP	SLG
2021	24	Durham (AAA)	East	.194	69	253	40	49	11	0	12	37	25	93	5	.270	.379
	24	Tacoma (AAA)	West	.298	26	104	22	31	3	2	8	21	16	21	1	.388	.596
	24	Seattle (MLB)	AL	.000	1	1	0	0	0	0	0	0	0	1	0	.000	.000
	24	Tampa Bay (MLB)	AL	.083	9	12	1	1	1	0	0	0	2	8	0	.214	.167
Major League Totals (1 year)				.077	10	13	1	1	1	0	0	0	2	9	0	.200	.154
Minor League Totals (8 years)				.241	649	2242	369	540	148	16	90	372	363	670	83	.351	.442

25 WYATT MILLS, RHP

BA GRADE

40 Risk: Medium

Born: Jan. 25, 1995. **B-T:** R-R. **HT:** 6-4. **WT:** 190. **Drafted:** Gonzaga, 2017 (3rd round). **Signed by:** Alex Ross/Jeff Sakamoto.

TRACK RECORD: A Washington native, Mills finished second in Gonzaga history with 21 saves and was drafted in the third round by the Mariners in 2017. He was solid but unspectacular his first few seasons and was not invited to the Mariners alternate training site in 2020, but he reported to instructional league throwing harder and was added to the 40-man roster after the season. He followed by averaging 16 strikeouts per nine innings at Triple-A Tacoma in 2021 and made his major league debut with 11 appearances for the Mariners.

SCOUTING REPORT: Mills is a classic sidearm reliever who relies on keeping the ball on the ground with his sinker and slider. His sinker sits 92-93 and touches 97 with late armside run that locks up righthanded batters. His average mid-80s slider sweeps horizontally across the plate out of his arm slot that is nearly parallel to the ground. Mills scrapped his changeup to focus on his two best pitches, helping them play up but leaving him vulnerable against lefties. He has average control and relies more on movement and deception than precision.

THE FUTURE: Mills will contend for a spot in the Mariners' bullpen in 2022. He projects to settle in as a middle reliever who matches up against a run of righthanded hitters.

Year	Age	Club (Level)	Lge	W	L	ERA	G	GS	IP	H	HR	BB	SO	BB/9	SO/9	WHIP	AVG
2021	26	Tacoma (AAA)	West	4	2	3.14	23	1	28	19	2	7	51	2.2	16.0	0.91	.179
	26	Seattle (MLB)	AL	0	0	9.95	11	0	13	19	1	7	11	5.0	7.8	2.05	.352
Major League Totals (1 year)				0	0	9.95	11	0	13	19	1	7	11	4.97	7.82	2.05	.352
Minor League Totals (5 years)				14	8	3.49	126	1	155	117	5	46	205	2.7	11.9	1.05	.206

26 JONATAN CLASE, OF

BA GRADE

50 Risk: Extreme

Born: May 23, 2002. **B-T:** B-R. **HT:** 5-9. **WT:** 180. **Signed:** Dominican Republic, 2018. **Signed by:** Audo Vicente.

TRACK RECORD: Clase signed with the Mariners for $35,000 during the 2018 international signing period and quickly emerged as a potential steal. He hit .300 with 21 extra-base hits and 31 stolen bases in his pro debut in the Dominican Summer League, but injuries have sidetracked his development. Clase suffered repeated hamstring and quad strains over the last two years and played only 14 games in the Arizona Complex League in 2021.

SCOUTING REPORT: Clase is a nearly 80-grade runner who gets to top speed quickly and wreaks havoc on the basepaths. He uses his speed to cover wide swaths of ground in center field and has good instincts for the position, helping him project to be at least an above-average defender with an average arm. Clase has excellent strike-zone awareness and began switch-hitting in 2021 after previously batting only lefthanded. He is naturally righthanded and shows the potential to be an average hitter from both sides. He has added strength since signing, but power is not his game. Clase's main challenge is staying healthy. He has played only 77 games in three years and has missed a lot of crucial development time.

THE FUTURE: Clase needs to show he can stay on the field. If he can, his speed, defense and switch-hitting ability make him a potential breakout candidate.

Year	Age	Club (Level)	Lge	AVG	G	AB	R	H	2B	3B	HR	RBI	BB	SO	SB	OBP	SLG
2021	19	Mariners (R)	ACL	.245	14	49	12	12	1	0	2	10	6	15	16	.333	.388
Minor League Totals (2 years)				.290	77	272	76	79	13	7	4	32	57	71	47	.417	.434

27 DEVIN SWEET, RHP

BA GRADE

45 Risk: High

Born: Sept. 6, 1996. **B-T:** L-L. **HT:** 5-11. **WT:** 185. **Signed:** North Carolina Central, 2018 (NDFA). **Signed by:** Ty Holub.

TRACK RECORD: Sweet spent four years in North Carolina Central's rotation and graduated as the program's all-time leader in wins (18) and strikeouts (246) in 2018. He signed with the Mariners as an undrafted free agent for $5,000 and quickly surpassed many of the players picked instead of him. Sweet rose to Double-A in 2021 and struggled with a 5.65 ERA as a starter, but he moved to the bullpen at midseason and dominated with a 0.63 ERA in relief.

SCOUTING REPORT: Sweet's success centers around his changeup, a plus-plus pitch in the 78-80 mph range with late dive and fade. It dies late to get foolish swings and misses out front even when batters are looking for it. Sweet has a good feel for moving his changeup around the strike zone and will throw it against any hitter in any count. Sweet's 92-94 mph fastball serves solely to set up his changeup and he scrapped his below-average curveball once he moved to the bullpen. He has above-average control and limits self-induced mistakes like walks, hit batters and wild pitches.

THE FUTURE: Sweet's changeup alone gives him a chance to be an effective middle reliever. He'll move to Triple-A Tacoma in 2022.

Year	Age	Club (Level)	Lge	W	L	ERA	G	GS	IP	H	HR	BB	SO	BB/9	SO/9	WHIP	AVG
2021	24	Arkansas (AA)	Cent	5	6	4.74	25	13	79	81	18	29	93	3.3	10.5	1.38	.260
Minor League Totals (4 years)				15	12	3.62	74	28	226	214	28	62	269	2.5	10.7	1.22	.249

28 CADE MARLOWE, OF

BA GRADE

45 Risk: High

Born: June 24, 1997. **B-T:** L-R. **HT:** 6-2. **WT:** 220. **Drafted:** West Georgia, 2019 (20th round). **Signed by:** John Wiedenbauer

TRACK RECORD: Marlowe started all four years at Division II West Georgia and set the program's single-season and career stolen base records. The Mariners drafted him in the 20th round in 2019 and signed him for $5,000. Seattle's front office analysts highlighted Marlowe as a break-out candidate before the 2021 season, and he loudly lived up to that prediction. Marlowe led the minor leagues with 107 RBIs as he advanced from Low-A Modesto to High-A Everett and was the only player in the minors to record at least 20 doubles, 10 triples, 20 home runs and 20 stolen bases.

SCOUTING REPORT: Marlowe has plus speed, is an above-average defender in the outfield and has plus raw power he gets to in games. He makes loud contact when he connects and has the combination of speed and strength to rack up extra-base hits. Marlowe has a sound approach and controls the strike zone, but he is prone to swinging and missing in the zone. Some are optimistic he'll make adjustments, but others fear he'll struggle to make contact against better pitching. Marlowe is very smart and has an elite work ethic. He had a 3.87 GPA as a pre-med/biology major and planned to be a doctor before he was drafted.

THE FUTURE: Marlowe will move to Double-A in 2022. It will be a prime chance for him to prove he can hit age-appropriate pitching.

Year	Age	Club (Level)	Lge	AVG	G	AB	R	H	2B	3B	HR	RBI	BB	SO	SB	OBP	SLG
2021	24	Modesto (LoA)	West	.301	34	133	35	40	6	5	6	29	24	40	11	.406	.556
2021	24	Everett (HiA)	West	.259	71	286	52	74	18	5	20	77	36	91	12	.345	.566
	24	Tacoma (AAA)	West	.667	1	3	0	2	1	0	0	1	1	1	1	.750	1.000
Minor League Totals (3 years)				.284	168	641	116	182	40	13	29	137	87	194	34	.369	.523

29 KADEN POLCOVICH, 2B/OF

BA GRADE
40 Risk: High

Born: Feb. 21, 1999. **B-T:** B-R. **HT:** 5-10. **WT:** 185. **Drafted:** Oklahoma State, 2020 (3rd round). **Signed by:** Jordan Bley.

TRACK RECORD: Polcovich, the son of former Pirates infielder Kevin Polcovich, put together a strong summer in the Cape Cod League before his junior year and was off to a hot start for Oklahoma State before the coronavirus pandemic canceled the 2020 college season. The Mariners drafted him in the third round and signed him for $575,000. Polcovich made his pro debut at High-A Everett in 2021 and earned a midseason promotion, but he hit just .133 in 36 games at Double-A.

SCOUTING REPORT: Polcovich's best attribute is his defensive versatility. He is a good athlete and above-average runner who can play second base, third base and all three outfield positions at an average or better level. He has advanced defensive instincts and average arm strength that plays anywhere. Polcovich is a below-average hitter who takes swings that are too big for his 5-foot-10, 185-pound frame and his power is also below-average. A switch-hitter, he has more thump in his bat from the left side.

THE FUTURE: Polcovich's defensive versatility gives him a chance to reach the majors as an up-and-down utility player. He'll see Triple-A in 2022.

Year	Age	Club (Level)	Lge	AVG	G	AB	R	H	2B	3B	HR	RBI	BB	SO	SB	OBP	SLG
2021	22	Everett (HiA)	West	.271	58	214	55	58	12	4	10	47	47	64	16	.415	.505
	22	Arkansas (AA)	Cent	.133	36	128	13	17	4	0	2	14	16	41	4	.242	.211
Minor League Totals (2 years)				.219	94	342	68	75	16	4	12	61	63	105	20	.354	.395

30 PENN MURFEE, RHP

BA GRADE
40 Risk: High

Born: May 2, 1994. **B-T:** R-R. **HT:** 6-2. **WT:** 195. **Drafted:** Santa Clara, 2018 (33rd round). **Signed by:** Jordan Bley.

TRACK RECORD: Murfee spent his first two seasons at Vanderbilt as an infielder before converting to pitching as a junior. He transferred to Santa Clara for his senior season and showed enough for the Mariners to draft him in the 33rd round and sign him for $5,000. Murfee took off and vaulted three levels up to Triple-A in his first full season. He spent 2020 at the alternate training site and returned to the upper levels in 2021, where he went 7-3, 4.23 with 97 strikeouts in 78.2 innings while working effectively as both a starter and reliever.

SCOUTING REPORT: Murfee is older at 27, but he's young in pitching experience and has progressed rapidly in a short time. His low-90s fastball plays up with deception out of his low arm slot and his low-80s slider is a swing and miss pitch with late dive and tilt that gets swings and misses from hitters on both sides of the plate. He throws his slider more frequently than his fastball and can land it for strikes in addition to getting swings and misses. Murfee is an extremely intelligent pitcher who knows how to set hitters up, read their swings and has enough command to hit his spots. He has to work the edges of the plate and will walk batters, but he has average control.

THE FUTURE: Murfee's funk, command and smarts give him a chance to be a low-leverage reliever. He is in position to make his debut in 2022.

Year	Age	Club (Level)	Lge	W	L	ERA	G	GS	IP	H	HR	BB	SO	BB/9	SO/9	WHIP	AVG
2021	27	Arkansas (AA)	Cent	5	2	4.13	10	10	52	50	9	20	62	3.4	10.7	1.34	.250
	27	Tacoma (AAA)	West	2	1	4.44	16	4	26	22	2	15	35	5.1	12.0	1.41	.227
Minor League Totals (4 years)				16	10	4.24	77	34	225	215	23	78	256	3.12	10.24	1.30	.251

MORE PROSPECTS TO KNOW

31 SAM CARLSON, RHP

Carlson went almost four years between starts due to persistent elbow pain that led to Tommy John surgery. He returned in 2021 and showed a low-90s fastball with a slider and changeup that each flashed promise, though he was understandably inconsistent after so much time away.

32 LUIS BOLIVAR, OF

Bolivar signed with the Mariners for $700,000 during the 2021 international signing period. He possesses 80-grade speed, is a plus defender in center field and has above-average raw power, but his ability to make contact is a question mark.

33 DAYEISON ARIAS, RHP

Arias is a late-blooming reliever who rose to Double-A in 2021. His mid-90s fastball, average slider and successful track record have made him a trade target for opposing teams.

34 DONNIE WALTON, SS/2B/OF

Walton has appeared in the majors each of the last three years. He's a bottom-of-the-scale hitter, but his defensive versatility and hard-nosed approach to the game will continue to make him a utility option.

35 DARREN MCCAUGHAN, RHP

McCaughan's below-average stuff limits his upside, but his elite control and pitchability helped him reach the majors last year and make him an option as a spot starter.

36 ISAIAH CAMPBELL, RHP

Campbell made only five appearances at High-A Everett in 2021 before having season-ending surgery to remove loose bodies in his right elbow. When healthy, he flashes a usable three-pitch mix with a 92-93 mph fastball and average slider and curveball.

37 JAKE SCHEINER, 1B

Acquired from the Phillies for Jay Bruce in 2019, Scheiner gets to his power against fastballs and has the plus makeup and work ethic to force his way to the majors. His inability to hit breaking balls and corner-only defense prevents him from being more than an up-and-down option.

38 BRYAN WOO, RHP   SLEEPER

The Mariners drafted Woo in the sixth round out of Cal Poly in 2021 despite the fact he'd just had Tommy John surgery. When healthy, he showed a loose, clean delivery and touched 97 mph in relief with room to project more velocity.

39 BRAYAN PEREZ, LHP

The 20-year-old lefthander showed the ability to be effective as a starter or reliever at Low-A Modesto. He throws a low-90s fastball and promising slider out of a smooth delivery and has some projection left, giving him a chance to rise as a spot starter or long reliever.

40 LUIS CURVELO, RHP

Curvelo struck out 80 batters in 55.1 innings as Low-A Modesto's closer in 2021 and continued to rack up strikeouts as one of the youngest pitchers in the Arizona Fall League. His 94-97 mph fastball and above-average mid-80s slider make him a solid middle relief candidate.

TOP PROSPECTS OF THE DECADE

Year	Player, Pos	2021 Org
2012	Taijuan Walker, RHP	Mets
2013	Mike Zunino, C	Rays
2014	Taijuan Walker, RHP	Mets
2015	Alex Jackson, OF	Marlins
2016	Alex Jackson, OF	Marlins
2017	Kyle Lewis, OF	Mariners
2018	Kyle Lewis, OF	Mariners
2019	Justus Sheffield, LHP	Mariners
2020	Julio Rodriguez, OF	Mariners
2021	Julio Rodriguez, OF	Mariners

TOP DRAFT PICKS OF THE DECADE

Year	Player, Pos	2021 Org
2012	Mike Zunino, C	Rays
2013	D.J. Peterson, 3B	Atlantic League
2014	Alex Jackson, OF	Marlins
2015	Nick Neidert, RHP (2nd round)	Marlins
2016	Kyle Lewis, OF	Mariners
2017	Evan White, 1B	Mariners
2018	Logan Gilbert, RHP	Mariners
2019	George Kirby, RHP	Mariners
2020	Emerson Hancock, RHP	Mariners
2021	Harry Ford, C	Mariners

Tampa Bay Rays

BY J.J. COOPER

In one very important way, the Rays took a step back in 2021.

After winning the American League pennant in 2020, Tampa Bay was eliminated in the American League Division Series in 2021, losing a thrilling series to the Red Sox in four games.

Measured by the most important metric of all, the Rays' season fell short, and the team's goals of winning the organization's first World Series remains unfulfilled.

Looked at from almost any other perspective, this was arguably the best year in organization history. The Rays 100-62 season gave them their first 100-win season. They finished with the American League's best record.

In the minor leagues, the Rays had a season unlike any seen in decades. Four of the five Rays' U.S.-based minor league clubs won their league title and the fifth was defeated in the deciding game of its championship series. Rays minor league teams ranked 1-2-3 in winning percentage among the 120 full-season affiliated minor league teams. The Rays also posted the best record in the Florida Complex League.

Tampa Bay's overall .653 minor league winning percentage not only was the best of any season by any system since the minors reorganized in 1963, but it also saw the organization post an overall winning percentage better than the winning percentage of any other full-season minor league team.

Young talent was key to the Rays' success in the majors and minors. Shortstops Wander Franco and Taylor Walls, outfielder Randy Arozarena, righthanders Luis Patiño, Ryan Thompson and lefthander Shane McClanahan were among significant prospects to graduate to the majors in 2021. They were a key part of the Rays' success. Arozarena and Franco were two of the club's five most productive position players as measured by bWAR and were the team's two best hitters in the playoffs. McClanahan led the Rays' pitchers in strikeouts, and his 3.43 ERA was best among the Rays' starting pitchers.

In the minor leagues, Tampa Bay continues to have a top-tier farm system thanks to solid drafting and international scouting, excellent player development and a front office that continually refreshes its crop.

Baz, the team's No. 1 prospect and a starting pitcher for the team in the playoffs, was acquired as the final piece in a massively lopsided trade that brought Tyler Glasnow and Austin Meadows to Tampa Bay in return for Chris Archer. Curtis Mead, one of the team's breakout stars in 2021, was acquired in a trade when he was playing in the

Wander Franco finished his ascent to Tampa Bay and earned a nine-figure contract extension.

PROJECTED 2025 LINEUP

Catcher	Francisco Mejia	29
First Base	Curtis Mead	24
Second Base	Vidal Brujan	27
Third Base	Wander Franco	24
Shortstop	Taylor Walls	28
Left Field	Brandon Lowe	30
Center Field	Josh Lowe	27
Right Field	Randy Arozarena	30
Designated Hitter	Austin Meadows	30
No. 1 Starter	Shane Baz	25
No. 2 Starter	Shane McClanahan	28
No. 3 Starter	Luis Patiño	25
No. 4 Starter	Taj Bradley	24
No. 5 Starter	J.J. Goss	24
Closer	Seth Johnson	26

Gulf Coast League with the Phillies.

The Rays remain overstuffed with shortstops, middle infielders and center field candidates. That surplus led the team to trade away Willy Adames during the 2021 season. It likely will lead them to make further moves. But that's par for the course for a team that is always looking ahead to its next move.

Anyone expecting Tampa Bay to go all-in to try to make a big final push for a World Series title will likely be disappointed. The Rays have shown time and time again that they want to figure out ways to extend their window. Expect them to do more of the same this offseason, and expect them to remain among the teams to beat in 2022. ∎

TAMPA BAY RAYS

TOP 2022 ROOKIES	RANK
Shane Baz, RHP	1
Josh Lowe, OF	2
Vidal Bruján, 2B/OF	3
BREAKOUT PROSPECTS	**RANK**
Carlos Colmenarez, SS	11
Ian Seymour, LHP	14
Heriberto Hernandez, OF	28

SOURCE OF TOP 30 TALENT

Homegrown	19	Acquired	11
College	8	Trade	11
High School	5	Rule 5 draft	0
Junior College	0	Independent leagues	0
Nondrafted free agent	0	Free agents/waivers	0
International	6		

LF
Heriberto Hernandez (28)
Dru Baker
Jordan Qsar

CF
Josh Lowe (2)
Kameron Misner (23)
Shane Sasaki

RF
Matt Dyer
Mason Auer
Jhonny Piron

3B
Cooper Kinney (16)
Austin Shenton (19)

SS
Greg Jones (6)
Carson Williams (7)
Willy Vasquez (10)
Carlos Colmenarez (11)
Alika Williams (29)
Pedro Martinez
Junior Caminero

2B
Vidal Brujan (3)
Xavier Edwards (8)
Osleivis Basabe (25)
Ryan Spikes
Miles Mastrobuoni

1B
Curtis Mead (5)
Jonathan Aranda (20)
Kyle Manzardo

C
Rene Pinto (22)
Ford Proctor (26)
Blake Hunt (27)

LHP

LHSP	LHRP
Ian Seymour (14)	Patrick Wicklander
Mason Montgomery	Ian Leatherman
Brendan McKay	Ben Brecht
Jacob Lopez	
John Doxakis	

RHP

RHSP	RHRP
Shane Baz (1)	Colby White (15)
Taj Bradley (4)	Calvin Faucher (24)
Cole Wilcox (9)	Tanner Dodson
Seth Johnson (12)	Evan Reifert
Sandy Gaston (13)	Caleb Sampen
JJ Goss (17)	Over Galue
Nick Bitsko (18)	Yoniel Curet
Tommy Romero (21)	
Jayden Murray (30)	
Michael Mercado	

1 SHANE BAZ, RHP

Born: June 17, 1999. **B-T:** R-R. **HT:** 6-2. **WT:** 190.
Drafted: HS—Tomball, Texas, 2017 (1st round).
Signed by: Wayne Mathis (Pirates).

TRACK RECORD: If the Pirates had traded Baz for Chris Archer as a one-for-one deal, the Rays would have reason to be pleased. The fact that Baz was the player to be named in a trade that also included Tyler Glasnow and Austin Meadows makes it one of the most lopsided deals of the 21st century. Baz, whom the Pirates initially drafted 12th overall in 2017, struggled to throw strikes early in his career, was prone to over-throwing and had a pronounced head whack. His delivery has calmed down, as much from improved core strength as any significant tweaks to his delivery. He's allayed concerns that he would be too wild to start by developing into a consistent strike-thrower. After throwing strikes on 59% of his pitches in 2018, Baz upped that figure to 68% in 2021. His 8.7 strikeouts for every walk led all minor league pitchers with 70 or more innings. After pitching for Team USA in the Tokyo Olympics, Baz made his major league debut on Sept. 20. After three regular-season starts, he stepped right into the Rays' playoff rotation.

SCOUTING REPORT: As a Pirates prospect, Baz threw two-seam fastballs and curveballs, which didn't really fit his skillset. Now he blows hitters away with four-seam fastballs and sliders. Baz had both those pitches in high school—he touched 98 at his best in high school and flashed a plus slider—but the Rays made a point of getting him to re-emphasize them. Baz has one of the best fastballs in baseball. He can touch 100 mph and carries 96-97 mph throughout his starts. The life and movement on his four-seam fastball is just as exceptional as its velocity. The vertical movement on his fastball ranked among the most of any MLB starting pitcher. The combination of velocity and life means he can consistently attack hitters in the strike zone, knowing that hitters have trouble squaring him up, especially in the upper third of the strike zone. Baz's mid-80s, plus slider is a relatively tight pitch with lots of gyro spin. It has solid depth but not a lot of tilt. His low-80s fringe-average curveball can be effective, but he almost always throws it as an early-count surprise to steal a strike against hitters not expecting it. Baz's high-80s changeup remains the most important item on his to-do list. It lacks the deception or movement profile to be a true weapon. If he keeps it away from lefties, it can produce foul balls and ground-

BRIAN WESTERHOLT FOUR SEAM IMAGES

BA GRADE	SCOUTING GRADES
65 Risk: Medium	FB: 80. SL: 60. CHG: 50. CB: 45. CTL: 60.

Projected future grades on 20-80 scouting scale

BEST TOOLS

Best Hitter for Average	Xavier Edwards
Best Power Hitter	Curtis Mead
Best Strike-Zone Discipline	Xavier Edwards
Fastest Baserunner	Greg Jones
Best Athlete	Vidal Briján
Best Fastball	Shane Baz
Best Curveball	Calvin Faucher
Best Slider	Shane Baz
Best Changeup	Ian Seymour
Best Control	Tommy Romero
Best Defensive Catcher	Blake Hunt
Best Defensive Infielder	Alika Williams
Best Infield Arm	Carson Williams
Best Defensive Outfielder	Josh Lowe
Best Outfield Arm	Josh Lowe

ers, but if he misses his spot, it can be pounded. Its development may determine whether he works deeper than the fifth or sixth inning.

THE FUTURE: The Rays consistently are slow to promote their prospects, but after Baz earned a spot in the club's postseason rotation, he should be a key part of Tampa Bay's rotation in 2022 and beyond. He has front-of-the-rotation potential and the highest upside of any Rays starting pitching prospect in years thanks to his rare combination of premium stuff and plus control. ∎

Year	Age	Club (Level)	Lge	W	L	ERA	G	GS	IP	H	HR	BB	SO	BB/9	SO/9	WHIP	AVG
2021	22	Montgomery (AA)	South	2	4	2.48	7	7	32	22	3	2	49	0.6	13.5	0.73	.190
	22	Durham (AAA)	East	3	0	1.76	10	10	46	28	6	11	64	2.2	12.5	0.85	.174
	22	Tampa Bay (MLB)	AL	2	0	2.03	3	3	13	6	3	3	18	2.0	12.2	0.68	.130
Major League Totals (1 year)				2	0	2.03	3	3	13	6	3	3	18	2.0	12.2	0.68	.130
Minor League Totals (5 years)				12	14	3.09	56	56	236	195	19	93	278	3.6	10.6	1.22	.223

2 JOSH LOWE, OF

Born: Feb. 2, 1998. **B-T:** L-R. **HT:** 6-4. **WT:** 205. **Drafted:** HS—Marietta, Ga.,
2016 (1st round). **Signed by:** Milt Hill.

TRACK RECORD: In 2016, the Rays snatched Josh Lowe in the first round
before picking his brother Nate in the 13th round. hitting Nate, a first baseman, made it to the majors in 2019, but Josh should have a longer Rays career,
because Nate was quickly traded to the Rangers. Josh made his own major
league debut in 2021 after a breakout season in Triple-A, where he hit .291
with 22 home runs, 78 RBIs, 26 stolen bases and a .916 OPS to lead Durham
to the Triple-A East championship.

SCOUTING REPORT: The Rays and Lowe have benefitted from a patient
development plan. Lowe was one of the most improved hitters in the Rays
organization in 2021. He figured out how to shorten his swing and better use
the whole field when he fell behind in counts without hindering his ability to
drive the ball when he's ahead of the pitcher. Lowe now does a better job of yanking the ball when pitchers try to bust him inside. He still trades some batting average for power, but he has managed to find a
balance and now projects as a fringe-average hitter with plus power. Every other aspect of his game is plus
or better. He plays a plus center field with long gliding strides. He also has a plus arm and has turned into
a threat on the basepaths. His 26 steals came in 26 tries.

THE FUTURE: Lowe's step forward in 2021 should have him poised to play a role for the Rays in 2022.
His opportunities will largely depend on how many of the club's big league outfielders return, but his
power, speed and defense give him the versatility to play any outfield position and also provide options
for a team that always is making moves.

BA GRADE

55 Risk: Medium

SCOUTING GRADES:	Hitting: 45	Power: 60	Running: 70	Fielding: 60	Arm: 60

Year	Age	Club (Level)	Lge	AVG	G	AB	R	H	2B	3B	HR	RBI	BB	SO	SB	OBP	SLG
2021	23	Durham (AAA)	East	.291	111	402	76	117	28	2	22	78	61	123	26	.381	.535
	23	Tampa Bay (MLB)	AL	1.000	2	1	0	1	0	0	0	0	1	0	1	1.000	1.000
Major League Totals (1 year)				1.000	2	1	0	1	0	0	0	0	1	0	1	1.000	1.000
Minor League Totals (6 years)				.261	509	1878	293	490	108	14	59	268	246	575	98	.345	.428

3 VIDAL BRUJÁN, 2B/OF

Born: Feb. 9, 1998. **B-T:** B-R. **HT:** 5-9. **WT:** 180. **Signed:** Dominican Republic,
2014. **Signed by:** Danny Santana.

TRACK RECORD: Brujan signed with the Rays for $15,000 in 2014 and
ascended the minors as a switch-hitting second baseman, but the Rays shifted
his focus toward becoming a utilityman in 2021 at Triple-A Durham. Bruján
played 15 or more games at second base, shortstop and all three outfield spots
in addition to playing six games at third base. His offensive numbers dipped
with his attention on learning a host of new positions, but he still led all of
Triple-A with 44 stolen bases and received his first major league callup in July.

BA GRADE

50 Risk: Medium

SCOUTING REPORT: Bruján's athleticism and versatility are excellent assets,
but they make it hard for him to settle in at any one spot. He has a quick
first step, fluid actions and a plus, accurate arm. His hands are his weakest
attribute, and he will bobble balls at times, but he turns the double play well
in the middle infield and has the range to be an above-average center fielder. Offensively, Bruján made
strides in hitting the ball harder in 2021—he raised his average exit velocity by 1 mph to 87 mph—but
he's unlikely to become a power hitter. He continues to have above-average contact skills and his ability to
drive the ball for doubles makes him a more potent offensive weapon. A switch-hitter, Brujan is a better
pure hitter from the left side and swings and misses more as a righthanded hitter.

THE FUTURE: Bruján's versatility allows him to step in at multiple positions. He's most likely a Swiss
Army knife whose versatility gets him regular at-bats while he plays a little bit of everywhere defensively.

SCOUTING GRADES:	Hitting: 60	Power: 40	Running: 70	Fielding: 55	Arm: 60

Year	Age	Club (Level)	Lge	AVG	G	AB	R	H	2B	3B	HR	RBI	BB	SO	SB	OBP	SLG
2021	23	Durham (AAA)	East	.262	103	389	77	102	31	1	12	56	49	68	44	.345	.440
	23	Tampa Bay (MLB)	AL	.077	10	26	3	2	0	0	0	2	0	8	1	.077	.077
Major League Totals (1 year)				.077	10	26	3	2	0	0	0	2	0	8	1	.077	.077
Minor League Totals (7 years)				.288	502	1943	386	559	109	29	31	197	236	265	195	.371	.422

4 TAJ BRADLEY, RHP

Born: March 20, 2001. **B-T:** R-R. **HT:** 6-2. **WT:** 190. **Drafted:** HS—Stone Mountain, Ga., 2018 (5th round). **Signed by:** Milt Hill.

TRACK RECORD: Bradley mostly played the outfield in his youth and was relatively new to pitching when the Rays drafted him in the fifth round in 2018 and signed him for $747,500 to forgo a South Carolina commitment. His youth, physicality and athleticism made him one of the more intriguing pitchers in the class despite his inexperience, and that potential came to fruition in 2021. In his full-season debut, Bradley led the entire minors in ERA (1.83) and ranked in the top 10 in opponent's batting average (.180) and WHIP (0.93) as he moved from Low-A to High-A.

SCOUTING REPORT: Bradley keeps getting stronger while retaining the athleticism that was so enticing coming out of high school. His fastball now sits in the mid 90s and touches 96-97. In addition to adding 3-5 mph of velocity, Bradley has begun to master a slider that pairs better with his fastball than his curveball did. His slider now regularly flashes plus and he's shown he can both throw it for strikes and get hitters to chase it out of the zone. Bradley's changeup has further to go, but it will flash average at its best. He is an advanced strike-thrower with good tempo to his delivery and an easy arm action that yields above-average control. He's starting to show the ability to self-diagnose when he loses his release point.

THE FUTURE: Bradley appears to be the next in the long line of successful Rays homegrown pitchers. He should spend much of 2022 at Double-A and has a chance to be a mid-rotation starter.

BA GRADE
55 Risk: High

SCOUTING GRADES:	Fastball: 60	Slider: 60	Curveball: 40	Changeup: 50	Control: 55

Year	Age	Club (Level)	Lge	W	L	ERA	G	GS	IP	H	HR	BB	SO	BB/9	SO/9	WHIP	AVG
2021	20	Charleston (LoA)	East	9	3	1.76	15	14	66	37	4	20	81	2.7	10.9	0.86	.165
	20	Bowling Green (HiA)	East	3	0	1.96	8	8	36	28	4	11	42	2.7	10.3	1.06	.207
Minor League Totals (4 years)				15	12	2.64	45	42	177	133	13	62	204	3.15	10.35	1.10	.206

5 CURTIS MEAD, 3B/1B

Born: Oct. 26, 2000. **B-T:** R-R. **HT:** 6-2. **WT:** 171. **Signed:** Australia, 2018.
Signed by: Howard Norsetter/Roberto Aquino/Derrick Chung (Phillies).

TRACK RECORD: Growing up in Australia, Mead seemed destined to be an Australian rules football player. Mead's father Tim had played in the Australian Baseball League, but he believed Curtis had a more promising football career ahead. The younger Mead decided to focus on baseball and quickly earned a spot on the Australian junior national team. He signed with the Phillies for $200,000 and was traded to the Rays for lefthander Cristopher Sanchez after the 2019 season. Mead made his full-season debut in 2021 and had one of the biggest breakout seasons of any prospect, batting .321/.378/.533 and leading the minors in doubles as he soared from Low-A to Triple-A.

SCOUTING REPORT: Mead has the best combination of power, bat-to-ball skills and hitting ability in the Rays' system. He manages to combine some of the best average exit velocities in the system (90 mph average) with the kind of contact-heavy approach (15.5% strikeout rate) the organization covets. His level swing produces more line drives than lofted home runs, but he regularly drills balls into the gaps. Mead still hasn't found a full-time defensive home. He has fringe-average range at third base and playable hands, but his throwing action is long and unorthodox and he can't rifle a throw without getting his feet set. He will most likely slide to first base as he moves up, but he's athletic enough to be a plausible left fielder. He's a below-average runner who likely will slow down further.

THE FUTURE: Mead will only be 21 for the entirety of the 2022 season. He could be ready for Tampa Bay by 2023.

BA GRADE
55 Risk: High

SCOUTING GRADES:	Hitting: 60	Power: 60	Running: 40	Fielding: 45	Arm: 40

Year	Age	Club (Level)	Lge	AVG	G	AB	R	H	2B	3B	HR	RBI	BB	SO	SB	OBP	SLG
2021	20	Charleston (LoA)	East	.356	47	191	36	68	21	1	7	35	15	30	9	.408	.586
	20	Bowling Green (HiA)	East	.282	53	206	38	58	15	1	7	32	19	38	2	.348	.466
	20	Durham (AAA)	East	.429	4	14	3	6	2	0	1	2	0	3	0	.429	.786
Minor League Totals (3 years)				.310	150	575	104	178	50	4	19	88	47	94	15	.368	.510

6 GREG JONES, SS

Born: March 7, 1998. **B-T:** B-R. **HT:** 6-2. **WT:** 175. **Drafted:** UNC Wilmington, 2019 (1st round). **Signed by:** Joe Hastings.

TRACK RECORD: Jones has shown flashes of being a power-speed threat since the Rays selected him 22nd overall in 2019, but he has been hampered by nagging injuries that have slowed his development. A shoulder injury affected his throwing in his draft year, a knee injury slowed him in 2020 and a quad injury kept him from going to the Arizona Fall League in 2021. He's been productive when he's been on the field, however, including batting .270/.366/.482 with 14 home runs, 40 RBIs and 34 stolen bases in only 74 games across High-A and Double-A in 2021.

TONY FARLOW/FOUR SEAM IMAGES

BA GRADE

55 Risk: High

SCOUTING REPORT: Of all the Rays' many minor league shortstops, Jones has the loudest tools. He's a plus-plus runner and also has plus raw power thanks to some of the fastest bat speed in the Rays organization. While he has speed and power, he's prone to chasing pitches and doesn't work counts all that well, limiting him to a potential fringe-average hitter. His level swing isn't necessarily geared for hitting home runs, but he hits the ball hard consistently enough to get to 15-20 per season. Jones' plus arm plays well at shortstop and allows him to make highlight-reel plays other shortstops in the system can't. While Jones often makes the standout play, he'll sometimes botch the routine one, mostly because his hands need to get a little softer.

THE FUTURE: Jones has the highest ceiling of any Rays shortstop prospect because of his speed and developing power. He always has a fallback option of developing into a rangy center fielder. He is ticketed to return to Double-A Montgomery in 2022.

SCOUTING GRADES:	Hitting: 45	Power: 55	Running: 70	Fielding: 55	Arm: 60

Year	Age	Club (Level)	Lge	AVG	G	AB	R	H	2B	3B	HR	RBI	BB	SO	SB	OBP	SLG
2021	23	Bowling Green (HiA)	East	.291	56	220	48	64	7	3	13	38	29	75	27	.389	.527
	23	Montgomery (AA)	South	.185	16	54	8	10	1	1	1	2	4	21	7	.267	.296
Minor League Totals (3 years)				.297	120	465	95	138	21	8	15	64	55	152	53	.385	.473

7 CARSON WILLIAMS, SS

Born: June 24, 2003. **B-T:** R-R. **HT:** 6-2. **WT:** 180. **Drafted:** HS—San Diego, 2021 (1st round). **Signed by:** Jaime Jones.

TRACK RECORD: Williams was seen as a promising pitcher who also played shortstop for much of his high school career, but he began to make people pay attention to his bat when he hit over .400 at the World Wood Bat Association World Championships in Jupiter, Fla. He then was one of the best performers in California all spring, batting hit .506 as a high school senior for Torrey Pines (Calif.) High against top-notch competition in San Diego County. The Rays drafted him 28th overall and signed him for $2,347,500 to forgo a California commitment. Williams had a solid Florida Complex League debut, albeit in limited at-bats because of the Rays' crowded FCL roster.

MIKE JANES/FOUR SEAM IMAGES

BA GRADE

55 Risk: Extreme

SCOUTING REPORT: Williams has developed into a well-rounded shortstop. There are some scouts skeptical about how adjustable his hands are in his swing, but he has a simple setup, load and swing and he's shown an advanced understanding of how to work counts. He's a hitter first, but also has the strength and pop in his bat to hit 18-20 home runs down the road. He's shown he is as comfortable driving the ball to the right-center power alley as he is yanking it down the line. Defensively, Williams has above-average hands, solid body control and a plus arm—his fastball sat 92-95 mph as a pitcher. He sometimes relies on his arm a little too much, and his footwork and first-step quickness will need to be a point of emphasis.

THE FUTURE: The Rays have multiple shortstops ready to head to Low-A Charleston, led by Williams and Willy Vasquez. Williams has the steady heartbeat, solid internal clock and plus arm to stick at short long term, and his bat should handle a slide to third if needed.

SCOUTING GRADES:	Hitting: 50	Power: 55	Running: 50	Fielding: 50	Arm: 60

Year	Age	Club (Level)	Lge	AVG	G	AB	R	H	2B	3B	HR	RBI	BB	SO	SB	OBP	SLG
2021	18	Rays (R)	FCL	.282	11	39	8	11	4	1	0	8	6	13	2	.404	.436
Minor League Totals (1 year)				.282	11	39	8	11	4	1	0	8	6	13	2	.404	.436

8 XAVIER EDWARDS, 2B

Born: Aug. 9, 1999. **B-T:** B-R. **HT:** 5-10. **WT:** 175. **Drafted:** HS—Coconut Creek, Fla., 2018 (1st round supplemental). **Signed by:** Brian Cruz (Padres).

TRACK RECORD: The Rays acquired Edwards with Hunter Renfroe from the Padres in the 2019 trade that sent Tommy Pham and Jake Cronenworth to San Diego. Unless Edwards blossoms, it may end up as one of the rare trades the Rays would like to take back. The 38th overall pick in the 2018 draft, Edwards has hit over .300 at every step of his minor league career and owns a .320 career batting average. He officially has just one career home run, though, although he did add a wall-scraping grand slam for Montgomery in the Double-A South postseason.

SCOUTING REPORT: A scrappy, undersized switch-hitter, Edwards is as comfortable with two strikes as most hitters are when they are ahead in the count because he knows he can connect with almost anything. But Edwards also scares no pitcher because he subsists on a diet of singles—just 17% of his career hits have gone for extra bases. He's a potential plus-plus hitter, but it's unlikely he'll ever hit more than five home runs in a season. Edwards didn't play a game at shortstop in 2021 and now projects as purely a second baseman. He's an above-average defender there thanks to quick hands and feet. Once a top-of-the-scale runner, Edwards now more regularly turns in plus times. He wasn't nearly the threat on the bases he'd been in the past, but an oblique injury may have played a role in that.

THE FUTURE: Edwards' exceptional contact ability, athleticism and speed gives him a role in the majors even if he doesn't get stronger. The difference between him being a useful role player and a David Fletcher/Nick Madrigal-type regular will depend on him adding at least a little thump to his contact-oriented approach.

BA GRADE
50 Risk: High

SCOUTING GRADES:	Hitting: 65	Power: 20	Running: 70	Fielding: 55	Arm: 45

Year	Age	Club (Level)	Lge	AVG	G	AB	R	H	2B	3B	HR	RBI	BB	SO	SB	OBP	SLG
2021	21	Montgomery (AA)	South	.302	79	291	40	88	13	3	0	27	36	42	19	.377	.368
Minor League Totals (4 years)				.320	247	953	156	305	39	12	1	86	111	121	75	.390	.389

9 COLE WILCOX, RHP

Born: July 14, 1999. **B-T:** R-R. **HT:** 6-5. **WT:** 232. **Drafted:** Georgia, 2020 (3rd round). **Signed by:** Tyler Stubblefield (Padres).

TRACK RECORD: Wilcox spent two years in Georgia's rotation and was considered a potential first-round pick in 2020, but he slid because of his bonus demands. The Padres drafted him 80th overall and gave him a $3.3 million bonus, a record for the third round and more than 11 first-rounders received that year. The Rays acquired Wilcox in the deal that sent Blake Snell to San Diego, and he was dominant for the first half of the season at Low-A Charleston before he suffered an elbow injury that he unsuccessfully tried to rehab for two months before having Tommy John surgery in September.

SCOUTING REPORT: Wilcox is a big, powerful pitcher at 6-foot-5, 232 pounds. He pounds the strike zone with a plus, mid-90s fastball that has sink and run and has touched 98-99 mph at his best. Wilcox's fastball sets up a plus, high-80s slider that he commands even better than his fastball. It is a power pitch with tilt and modest depth when he doesn't get on the side of it. His 84-88 mph fringe-average changeup has some sink but isn't as effective or consistent. Wilcox has always had some length in his arm action and he will fly open early in his delivery sporadically, leading to a lack of deception. He has long faced questions about his control, but he walked less than one batter per nine innings in his final college season and first year in pro ball combined.

THE FUTURE: Wilcox will miss all of the 2022 season recovering from Tommy John surgery. If he makes a full recovery, he gives the Rays yet another very promising future starter with a fallback option of being a power reliever.

BA GRADE
55 Risk: Extreme

SCOUTING GRADES:	Fastball: 60	Slider: 60	Changeup: 45	Control: 50

Year	Age	Club (Level)	Lge	W	L	ERA	G	GS	IP	H	HR	BB	SO	BB/9	SO/9	WHIP	AVG
2021	21	Charleston (LoA)	East	1	0	2.03	10	10	44	33	1	5	52	1.0	10.6	0.86	.200
Minor League Totals (2 years)				1	0	2.03	10	10	44	33	1	5	52	1.02	10.56	0.86	.200

10 WILLY VASQUEZ, SS

Born: Sept. 6, 2001. **B-T:** R-R. **HT:** 6-0. **WT:** 191. **Signed:** Dominican Republic, 2019. **Signed by:** Remmy Hernandez/Daniel Santana.

TRACK RECORD: When Vasquez signed with the Rays in 2019, he was expected to be a third baseman in a Rays international class full of shortstops. Two years later, Vasquez is proving to be the most polished shortstop of that signing class. After an excellent pro debut in the Florida Complex League, he was promoted to Low-A Charleston for the playoffs and helped the RiverDogs win their league title by ripping a bases-clearing three-run triple in the deciding game.

MIKE JANES/FOUR SEAM IMAGES

BA GRADE
55 Risk: Extreme

SCOUTING REPORT: Vasquez has the building blocks to be an above-average offensive player. He has above-average bat speed and has shown the ability already to drive a ball at 110-111 mph exit velocities at his best. He had nearly as many walks (20) as strikeouts (27) in the FCL in his pro debut and has a chance to be an above-average hitter with average power. Vasquez could outgrow shortstop, but he shows the body control, range and hands to stick there if he continues to make defensive development a focus. He's gotten bigger and stronger without losing any agility and has the above-average arm strength to make all the throws. Vasquez shows a solid understanding of the game at a young age and has developed into a team leader.

THE FUTURE: Vasquez has one of the best combinations of offensive and defensive potential among the Rays' many shortstop prospects. He should open at Low-A in 2022.

| SCOUTING GRADES: | Hitting: 55 | | Power: 50 | | Running: 50 | | Fielding: 50 | | Arm: 55 | |

Year	Age	Club (Level)	Lge	AVG	G	AB	R	H	2B	3B	HR	RBI	BB	SO	SB	OBP	SLG
2021	19	Rays (R)	FCL	.288	40	146	26	42	6	3	2	31	20	27	14	.382	.411
Minor League Totals (2 years)				.305	51	190	32	58	8	4	2	36	21	31	16	.379	.421

11 CARLOS COLMENAREZ, SS

BA GRADE
55 Risk: Extreme

Born: Nov. 15, 2003. **B-T:** L-R. **HT:** 5-10. **WT:** 185. **Signed:** Dominican Republic, 2021. **Signed by:** Daniel Santana.

TRACK RECORD: Colmenarez was viewed as one of the best players in the 2020-2021 international class. Like the rest of his class, he had to wait until January to sign, meaning he signed as a 17-year-old. Colmenarez's pro debut was somewhat derailed by a hand injury. He missed the first month of the Dominican Summer League season with a fractured hamate, and his power was somewhat lacking upon his return.

SCOUTING REPORT: If everything comes together, Colmenarez could be the Rays' most well-rounded shortstop prospect since Wander Franco. But he had a much more modest debut than Franco, as he struggled in the DSL while Franco jumped straight to the Appalachian League. Colmenarez is a potential plus defender at shortstop. He's a fluid and somewhat flashy shortstop, capable of making the highlight play. His arm is plus and he has a quick release. Offensively, he has a smooth, controlled and compact swing with plenty of bat speed. While he didn't show any power in his pro debut, he projects to have above-average power. He is an above-average runner.

THE FUTURE: Colmenarez's injury-plagued 2021 season doesn't change the fact that he is one of the Rays' best young prospects. He has to prove that his offensive potential will turn into production, but he has a shot to be a well-rounded shortstop who can hit and be a plus defender. He'll come to the Florida Complex League in 2022.

Year	Age	Club (Level)	Lge	AVG	G	AB	R	H	2B	3B	HR	RBI	BB	SO	SB	OBP	SLG
2021	17	Rays1 (R)	DSL	.247	26	97	7	24	2	1	0	12	8	30	7	.319	.289
Minor League Totals (1 year)				.247	26	97	7	24	2	1	0	12	8	30	7	.319	.289

12 SETH JOHNSON, RHP

BA GRADE
50 Risk: High

Born: Sept. 19, 1998. **B-T:** R-R. **HT:** 6-1. **WT:** 200. **Drafted:** Campbell, 2019 (1st round supplemental). **Signed by:** Joe Hastings.

TRACK RECORD: The Rays have long demonstrated that they believe most young pitchers are best on a slow development path. That's been quite apparent with Johnson. The shortstop turned righthander was sent to Low-A Charleston. He was erratic at first, but after posting a 4.62 ERA in his first 12 outings, Johnson posted a 0.84 ERA over his final 11 starts.

SCOUTING REPORT: Johnson's history as a shortstop is still apparent at times when it comes to pitch sequencing, but he's made steady improvement. When he's locked in, he has the look of an athletic mid-rotation starter. Johnson's 84-87 mph power slider earns 70 grades at its best. It has tight, late break. Johnson also can attack hitters with a 94-98 mph four-seam plus fastball. It pairs well with his slider, but it lacks elite movement. Johnson does consistently throw it for strikes. He doesn't command his secondaries as well as his fastball, but he has average control overall. His 71-75 mph curveball is a fringy get-over pitch, and his below-average changeup has a long way to go.

THE FUTURE: Johnson is Rule 5 eligible if not added to the 40-man after the 2022 season. While he'll start at High-A Bowling Green, ideally he needs to move quickly to speed up his development.

Year	Age	Club (Level)	Lge	W	L	ERA	G	GS	IP	H	HR	BB	SO	BB/9	SO/9	WHIP	AVG
2021	22	Charleston (LoA)	East	6	6	2.88	23	16	93	86	7	33	115	3.2	11.1	1.27	.243
Minor League Totals (3 years)				6	7	2.77	32	25	111	103	7	36	131	2.93	10.65	1.26	.245

13 SANDY GASTON, RHP

Born: Dec. 16, 2001. **B-T:** R-R. **HT:** 6-3. **WT:** 200. **Signed:** Cuba, 2018.
Signed by: Carlos Rodriguez/Danny Santana.

BA GRADE
55 Risk: Extreme

TRACK RECORD: A $2.6 million signee out of Cuba in 2018, Gaston was one of the hardest-throwing 16-year-olds anyone had ever seen—he regularly touched 96-97 mph and brushed higher. But Gaston had very poor control, an extremely long arm action and an effortful delivery that finished with plenty of recoil. The Rays have helped him rework his delivery. He now throws with a much shorter arm action and significantly less effort.

SCOUTING REPORT: Gaston has one of the best arms in an organization filled with big arms. He can touch 100 mph as a starter and will sit at 96-98 mph in his best outings. Gaston's fastball has good movement to go with his velocity. What he struggles to do is to get everything synced up, as his extremely fast arm means he has trouble staying in sync with his delivery, which leads to well below-average control. He made strides with turning a slurvy breaking ball into two different pitches. He now throws a cutterish slider and a bigger, downer low-80s power curveball. The curve has a chance to be at least above-average, and his changeup flashes at average as well.

THE FUTURE: Gaston still has a lot of work ahead of him. His control will have to improve by two grades for him to reach his impressive potential, but he's already made significant strides and he's shown his coachability and adaptability.

Year	Age	Club (Level)	Lge	W	L	ERA	G	GS	IP	H	HR	BB	SO	BB/9	SO/9	WHIP	AVG
2021	19	Rays (R)	FCL	1	0	3.20	7	3	19	7	1	13	32	6.0	14.6	1.02	.115
	19	Charleston (LoA)	East	2	1	3.86	7	7	30	22	2	22	38	6.5	11.3	1.45	.206
Minor League Totals (3 years)				4	3	4.44	25	16	77	52	4	62	101	7.3	11.8	1.48	.195

14 IAN SEYMOUR, LHP

Born: Dec. 13, 1998. **B-T:** L-L. **HT:** 6-0. **WT:** 210. **Drafted:** Virginia Tech, 2020 (2nd round). **Signed by:** Landon Lassiter.

BA GRADE
50 Risk: High

TRACK RECORD: Seymour is one of the best pitchers in Virginia Tech history, which just happens to be the alma mater of Rays GM Erik Neander. Seymour likely would have become the Hokies' all-time strikeout leader if not for the shortened 2020 season. The Rays picked him in the second round and saw him blossom in his pro debut in 2021.

SCOUTING REPORT: Seymour is funky. He uses a relatively unique motion, as he begins by taking a simple step back with his right foot that feeds into his hip turn. It's a very rotational delivery with plenty of crossfire and sometimes a head whack. The delivery helps him hide the ball, and his 90-94 mph plus fastball has exceptional carry through the top of the zone as well as a flat approach angle that generates swings and misses. His 79-83 mph plus changeup has solid velocity separation and plenty of deception and fade. Seymour's fringe-average slider comes and goes too much. It needs to develop if he's going to turn over a lineup twice. He also throws a slow, get-over curve. Despite his delivery, Seymour is a strike-thrower with above-average control.

THE FUTURE: Seymour has the stuff to pitch in the majors. If he doesn't develop his breaking ball, he's likely a multi-inning reliever or a bulk-inning pitcher who can go through the lineup once. If he can find a more consistent slider or curve, he could be a back-end starter.

Year	Age	Club (Level)	Lge	W	L	ERA	G	GS	IP	H	HR	BB	SO	BB/9	SO/9	WHIP	AVG
2021	22	Charleston (LoA)	East	2	0	2.55	10	9	35	16	3	13	59	3.3	15.0	0.82	.136
	22	Bowling Green (HiA)	East	1	0	1.80	2	2	10	6	1	2	19	1.8	17.1	0.80	.167
	22	Durham (AAA)	East	1	0	0.00	2	2	10	4	0	4	9	3.6	8.1	0.80	.121
Minor League Totals (2 years)				4	0	1.95	14	13	55	26	4	19	87	3.09	14.2	0.81	.139

15 COLBY WHITE, RHP

BA GRADE

45 Risk: Medium

Born: July 4, 1998. **B-T:** R-R. **HT:** 6-0. **WT:** 210. **Drafted:** Mississippi State, 2019 (6th round). **Signed by:** Rickey Drexler.

TRACK RECORD: While many relievers are converted starters, White has been a reliever since his first day of college baseball. He was the closer for Pearl River (Miss.) JC for two years and then a setup man for Mississippi State. In 2021, he started the season at Low-A, but blistered through four levels of the full-season minors, dominating at every step. His 104 strikeouts were seventh-most among MiLB relievers.

SCOUTING REPORT: Expect White to be one of the next of the Rays' many useful reliever discoveries. His fastball is a plus-plus pitch that should cause hitters problems no matter the level. White has plenty of velocity (94-98 mph) and his fastball has exceptional carry up in the zone. Adding to hitter's issues is his short arm action and an ear-flipping release point that makes it hard for hitters to pick up the ball. He also throws an above-average mid-80s slider that has more depth than tilt. His changeup is a clear third pitch, but it helps ensure he's reasonably effective against lefties. He also toyed with a splitter with forkball-like action late in the year. He has average control.

THE FUTURE: White has less than 100 innings of pro experience, but it's not outlandish to expect him to help the Rays in 2022. His fastball is MLB-ready and his slider isn't far away. He has the potential to get late-inning, high-leverage outs.

Year	Age	Club (Level)	Lge	W	L	ERA	G	GS	IP	H	HR	BB	SO	BB/9	SO/9	WHIP	AVG
2021	22	Charleston (LoA)	East	1	1	0.00	11	0	16	8	1	1	36	0.6	19.8	0.55	.138
	22	Bowling Green (HiA)	East	2	2	2.31	15	1	23	8	3	7	35	2.7	13.5	0.64	.105
	22	Montgomery (AA)	South	0	0	1.38	8	0	13	4	0	3	19	2.1	13.2	0.54	.095
	22	Durham (AAA)	East	1	0	1.86	9	0	9	6	0	4	14	3.7	13.0	1.03	.176
Minor League Totals (3 years)				5	3	1.76	58	1	82	34	7	31	133	3.42	14.66	0.80	.123

16 COOPER KINNEY, 2B/3B

BA GRADE

50 Risk: Very High

Born: Jan. 27, 2003. **B-T:** L-R. **HT:** 6-3. **WT:** 200. **Drafted:** HS—Chattanooga, Tenn., 2021 (1st round supplemental). **Signed by:** Steven Ames.

TRACK RECORD: The Rays like to collect all types of middle infielders. In the past five drafts, they have selected eight middle infielders in the top three rounds. Some, like Taylor Walls and Alika Williams, have great gloves. Kinney fits more in the Brandon Lowe camp as a bat-first middle infielder who will have to figure out a defensive home, but should hit enough to make it worth the effort. The South Carolina signee impressed in his brief pro debut, showing an extremely advanced batting eye in the Florida Complex League.

SCOUTING REPORT: Most young hitters have to learn how to take pitchers' pitches that end up just off the plate. Kinney already spits on those tantalizing sliders and fastballs away, forcing pitchers to come into the zone or give him a walk. His bat control, fluid swing and developing plus power give him a shot to be a well-rounded hitter. Depending on whether he focuses on contact or power, he could be a plus hitter or have plus power. Defensively, Kinney will have to stay on top of his conditioning and work on his flexibility to remain playable at second or third base. He is already a below-average runner and has below-average range, although he fields what's hit to him. He has an average, accurate arm.

THE FUTURE: The bat is the most important tool a position player can have, and Kinney has plenty of offensive potential. He's ready for Low-A Charleston.

Year	Age	Club (Level)	Lge	AVG	G	AB	R	H	2B	3B	HR	RBI	BB	SO	SB	OBP	SLG
2021	18	Rays (R)	FCL	.286	11	35	9	10	1	1	0	5	10	9	2	.468	.371
Minor League Totals (1 year)				.286	11	35	9	10	1	1	0	5	10	9	2	.468	.371

17 JJ GOSS, RHP

BA GRADE

55 Risk: Extreme

Born: Dec. 25, 2000. **B-T:** R-R. **HT:** 6-3. **WT:** 175. **Drafted:** HS—Cypress, Texas, 2019 (1st round supplemental). **Signed by:** Pat Murphy.

TRACK RECORD: An excellent senior season helped push Goss into consideration among the best prep pitchers in the 2019 draft class. Since then, he's barely gotten to pitch. He did throw in the Florida Complex League in 2019, but he lost the 2020 season like most every minor leaguer. Then he was shut down with a shoulder impingement for most of the 2021 season. Goss is Jamey Jr., which is where his JJ nickname comes from.

SCOUTING REPORT: Evaluating Goss, much like fellow prominent prep pick Nick Bitsko, is difficult because he's barely pitched in two full years. Goss did return to the mound for a quartet of outings with the Rays' Florida Complex League team. His stuff was largely back to his pre-injury form (91-95 mph) and he generally threw strikes, but there was also plenty of rust. His fastball didn't show much movement in his brief return to the mound. He has shown feel for spinning a slurve. His changeup, like that of many high school pitchers, has the most development to come.

THE FUTURE: Goss has the potential to be a mid-rotation starter, but he's now a 21-year-old with less than 30 pro innings. He needs to get regular work in 2022, most likely at Low-A Charleston.

Year	Age	Club (Level)	Lge	W	L	ERA	G	GS	IP	H	HR	BB	SO	BB/9	SO/9	WHIP	AVG
2021	20	Rays (R)	FCL	1	0	6.10	4	3	10	15	0	0	12	0.0	10.5	1.45	.341
Minor League Totals (3 years)				2	3	5.93	13	11	27	34	1	2	28	0.66	9.22	1.32	.304

18 NICK BITSKO, RHP

BA GRADE
55 Risk: Extreme

Born: June 16, 2002. **B-T:** R-R. **HT:** 6-4. **WT:** 225. **Drafted:** HS—Doylestown, Pa., 2020 (1st round). **Signed by:** Zach Clark.

TRACK RECORD: Bitsko was expected to be the top prep pitcher in the 2021 class, but he reclassified for the 2020 draft, only to see his final high school season wiped out by the coronavirus pandemic. He didn't get into a game in 2021 either as he was recovering from labrum surgery in Dec. 2020. He'll enter 2022 looking to make his pro debut.

SCOUTING REPORT: Competently evaluating Bitsko at this point is a fool's errand. He hasn't faced hitters in an actual game since 2019. He did get back on the mound for a couple of intrasquad outings late in 2021. In those, his velocity wasn't fully back to normal, but he was throwing free and easy. Before his injury, Bitsko had a potentially plus 92-96 mph fastball and a high-spin, plus power curveball with depth. He hasn't had much of a chance to work on his changeup yet because of his lost time on the mound.

THE FUTURE: Getting a healthy Bitsko back to his pre-injury form is job one in 2022. But it's just as important to get him some much-needed innings—he only threw 33 innings in his high school career, so he's playing catchup.

Year	Age	Club (Level)	Lge	W	L	ERA	G	GS	IP	H	HR	BB	SO	BB/9	SO/9	WHIP	AVG
2021	19	Did not play—Injured															

19 AUSTIN SHENTON, 3B

BA GRADE
45 Risk: Medium

Born: Jan. 28, 1998. **B-T:** R-R. **HT:** 6-0. **WT:** 205. **Drafted:** Florida International, 2019 (5th round). **Signed by:** Dan Rovetto (Mariners).

TRACK RECORD: Shenton has always hit. He hit well over .300 as a freshman at Bellevue (Wash.) JC, in two years at Florida International and in the Cape Cod League. In pro ball, he's hit .295 and .298 in his two seasons. The Rays picked him up along with righthander JT Chargois in a July trade that sent righthander Diego Castillo to Seattle.

SCOUTING REPORT: Shenton's path to the big leagues is based on his feel for the strike zone and his ability to drive the ball when he gets a pitch he likes. Shenton's hands work well, giving him excellent barrel control and the ability to use the whole field. He's also a pest to pitchers because he's a master of the good take, which leads to excellent on-base percentages. He projects as a plus hitter with average power. Shenton is a below-average defender at third, thanks to poor footwork and some stiffness, but there is the hope that he could improve to be playable there. He does have an average arm. He also should be fine at first and runs just well enough (he's a 40 runner) to make left and right field a sporadic option.

THE FUTURE: It will take some creativity to figure out how to get Shenton MLB at-bats because of his defensive limitations, but he hits enough to be worth the effort.

Year	Age	Club (Level)	Lge	AVG	G	AB	R	H	2B	3B	HR	RBI	BB	SO	SB	OBP	SLG
2021	23	Everett (HiA)	West	.295	57	224	55	66	24	3	11	53	41	62	1	.418	.576
	23	Arkansas (AA)	Cent	.326	10	43	6	14	5	0	1	8	4	10	0	.396	.512
	23	Montgomery (AA)	South	.271	13	48	5	13	3	0	2	9	2	15	0	.294	.458
Minor League Totals (3 years)				.296	133	513	95	152	49	5	21	106	66	131	1	.390	.534

20 JONATHAN ARANDA, 2B/1B

BA GRADE
45 Risk: Medium

Born: May 23, 1998. **B-T:** R-R. **HT:** 5-10. **WT:** 175. **Signed:** Mexico, 2015. **Signed by:** Eddie Diaz.

BACKGROUND: The Rays signed Aranda out of Mexico in 2015 and then patiently watched him develop as a hitter. He didn't make it to full-season ball until his fourth pro season and hadn't played above Class A until this season. He had a breakout season in 2021, leading the Double-A South in batting average, on-base and slugging percentage.

SCOUTING REPORT: If hitting ability is the most important tool, Aranda has checked off the biggest box a prospect can check. Scouts are adamant that he can be a useful big league hitter. He works counts, understands what pitchers are trying to do and drives the ball with a short stroke and a modest timing step/leg lift. His .330 average was eighth-best in the minors. Aranda should be a plus hitter with average power. He made a clear attempt to hit the ball harder, and managed to do so without losing his ability to make contact. Aranda's issue is finding a defensive home. Aranda is below-average defensively wherever he plays. He's best at first base, where his lack of range is less noticeable. He has well below-average range at second or third. He also played left field in winter ball in Mexico.

THE FUTURE: The Rays added Aranda to the 40-man roster, knowing he was a big risk to be picked in the Rule 5 draft. Aranda's readiness for Tampa Bay depends on his defensive improvement.

Year	Age	Club (Level)	Lge	AVG	G	AB	R	H	2B	3B	HR	RBI	BB	SO	SB	OBP	SLG
2021	23	Bowling Green (HiA)	East	.351	21	74	20	26	3	0	4	7	9	13	1	.449	.554
	23	Montgomery (AA)	South	.325	79	274	53	89	19	5	10	58	33	63	4	.410	.540
Minor League Totals (6 years)				.290	310	1092	178	317	58	17	19	161	120	204	25	.371	.427

21 TOMMY ROMERO, RHP

BA GRADE	
45	Risk: Medium

Born: July 8, 1997. **B-T:** R-R. **HT:** 6-2. **WT:** 225. **Drafted:** Eastern Florida State JC, 2017 (15th round). **Signed by:** Dan Rovetto (Mariners).

TRACK RECORD: He's not a prominent name, but there have been few more consistently successful minor league pitchers than Romero over the past five years. The Rays acquired Romero in May 2018 in a trade that sent Alex Colome and Denard Span to the Mariners. He's never posted an ERA above 3.00 in any MiLB season.

SCOUTING REPORT: When Romero was drafted, he rarely topped 92-93 mph. Now he can get to 95 mph. Maybe more importantly, his plus fastball has excellent carry. His extreme trunk tilt in his delivery leads to a straight-over-the-top delivery but with a low release point that gives him the flat vertical approach angle that helps a fastball play well at the top of the strike zone. He also has shown he can throw his slider, change and curve for strikes in any count. His average low-90s slider is his best secondary offering, but the change and curve are fringe-average as well. He's one of the best strike-throwers in the minors (68.8% strikes in 2021) with plus-plus control. Because he avoids the heart of the plate, he limits hard contact.

THE FUTURE: Romero can be a bulk-innings reliever or a back-of-the-rotation starter. Added to the 40-man, he should spend most of 2022 at Triple-A Durham, but he'll move up and down as needed.

Year	Age	Club (Level)	Lge	W	L	ERA	G	GS	IP	H	HR	BB	SO	BB/9	SO/9	WHIP	AVG
2021	23	Montgomery (AA)	South	1	0	1.88	11	9	48	36	3	10	75	1.9	14.1	0.96	.202
	23	Durham (AAA)	East	7	2	3.18	12	12	62	39	7	21	70	3.0	10.1	0.96	.178
Minor League Totals (5 years)				37	11	2.52	85	67	407	306	26	135	431	2.99	9.53	1.08	.211

22 RENE PINTO, C

BA GRADE	
45	Risk: Medium

Born: Nov. 2, 1996. **B-T:** R-R. **HT:** 5-10. **WT:** 195. **Signed:** Venezuela, 2013. **Signed by:** William Bergolla/Ronnie Blanco/Marlon Roche.

BACKGROUND: Catching is a family tradition for Rene Pinto. His father Rene was a minor league catcher in the Yankees system from 1994-2000 and ranked as the team's best defensive catcher in 1998. The younger Pinto signed in 2013 for $100,000, but he largely worked in obscurity until this season. He more than doubled his career high in home runs and threw out 37.5% of basestealers.

SCOUTING REPORT: Pinto has been a solid defensive catcher for a few years. He calls a good game, has a plus-plus arm and has steadily improved his receiving to average. Pinto has opened up his stance and adopted a higher hand set. He doesn't hit the ball exceptionally hard, but he hits the ball consistently hard, driving balls over the fence to both power alleys. He's still an aggressive hitter, but with his newfound power, his offensive profile has improved. Now he looks like a .230-.240 hitter, but with the 20-home run power that can make that work as a catcher. Like most catchers, he is a station-to-station runner.

THE FUTURE: The Rays had to add Pinto the 40-man roster both to protect him from the Rule 5 draft and to ensure he couldn't leave as a minor league free agent. Pinto should eventually be a backup catcher with a shot to be a second-division regular.

Year	Age	Club (Level)	Lge	AVG	G	AB	R	H	2B	3B	HR	RBI	BB	SO	SB	OBP	SLG
2021	24	Montgomery (AA)	South	.242	41	153	25	37	9	0	8	25	15	56	2	.322	.458
	24	Durham (AAA)	East	.299	52	201	25	60	11	0	12	35	7	58	2	.327	.532
Minor League Totals (8 years)				.278	448	1639	221	456	106	10	44	245	121	359	16	.332	.436

23 KAMERON MISNER, OF

BA GRADE

45 Risk: High

Born: Jan. 8, 1998. **B-T:** L-L. **HT:** 6-4. **WT:** 219. **Drafted:** Missouri, 2019 (1st round supplemental). **Signed by:** Joe Dunigan (Marlins).

TRACK RECORD: Misner showed an enticing power-speed combination during his time at Missouri, though strikeout issues caught up to him during his draft year. What was to be his first full season was wiped out by the pandemic, so he spent 2021 between High-A Beloit and Double-A Pensacola. He was acquired by the Rays in a 40-man roster-clearing move that sent Joey Wendle to Miami.

SCOUTING REPORT: Misner is a three-true-outcomes player. Of his 658 official plate appearances, 42.4% have ended in either a walk, a home run or a strikeout. The Marlins were working to adjust his swing in order to keep the barrel in the zone longer to add some hittability. They also wanted to correct an issue which saw Misner too often get stuck on the back side of his swing and spin off the ball rather than powering through contact. Misner is an athletic defender with the ability to stick in center field, though he dabbled in right and left field at both of his stops in 2021. He earns above-average grades for both his arm strength and speed on the bases, and has proved to be an extremely efficient basestealer.

THE FUTURE: Misner continued to play to script in the Arizona Fall League, where his seven home runs were tied for the second most, and nearly 60% of his plate appearances were walks, strikeouts or home runs. He's expected to head to Double-A Montgomery in 2022.

Year	Age	Club (Level)	Lge	AVG	G	AB	R	H	2B	3B	HR	RBI	BB	SO	SB	OBP	SLG
2021	23	Beloit (HiA)	Cent	.244	88	340	58	83	22	3	11	56	50	119	24	.350	.424
	23	Pensacola (AA)	South	.309	14	55	12	17	7	0	1	3	7	17	2	.387	.491
Minor League Totals (3 years)				.258	144	558	97	144	38	3	14	83	87	178	37	.365	.412

24 CALVIN FAUCHER, RHP

BA GRADE

45 Risk: High

Born: Sept. 22, 1995. **B-T:** R-R. **HT:** 6-1. **WT:** 190. **Drafted:** UC Irvine, 2017 (10th round). **Signed by:** John Leavitt (Twins).

TRACK RECORD: No team is better at getting a useful throw-in on a trade than the Rays. When acquiring Nelson Cruz from the Twins for righthanders Joe Ryan and Drew Strotman, the Rays also got Faucher added to the trade, even though the former $10,000 senior sign out of UC Irvine had a 7.09 ERA, a .320 opponents average against and a 2.05 WHIP for Double-A Wichita. As a Ray, Faucher dominated at Triple-A and was added to the 40-man roster after the season.

SCOUTING REPORT: Faucher is an analytics darling thanks to his exceptionally high-spin (3,200 rpm) mid-80s plus curveball. It got better as the season wore on, with the kind of late bite that could make hitters look foolish. Faucher has to land his curveball or his harder, cutterish average slider, as his mid-90s average fastball isn't a bat-misser. When Faucher got in trouble early in the season, hitters got into counts where they could hunt fastballs. Faucher has average control, but his breaking ball-heavy approach means he will have plenty of deep counts.

THE FUTURE: Faucher should be ready to at least be an up-and-down reliever for the Rays in 2022, riding the Durham-to-Tampa Bay shuttle like Louis Head did in 2021. His curveball gives him a shot to pitch in high-leverage scenarios eventually, although he doesn't project as a closer.

Year	Age	Club (Level)	Lge	W	L	ERA	G	GS	IP	H	HR	BB	SO	BB/9	SO/9	WHIP	AVG
2021	25	Wichita (AA)	Cent	1	1	7.04	19	0	30	39	6	24	42	7.0	12.3	2.05	.310
	25	Montgomery (AA)	South	0	0	0.00	2	0	4	2	0	0	4	0.0	7.7	0.43	.125
	25	Durham (AAA)	East	0	0	1.77	11	3	20	14	1	7	26	3.1	11.5	1.03	.194
Minor League Totals (5 years)				11	7	4.21	107	3	184	186	15	92	208	4.50	10.17	1.51	.265

25 OSLEIVIS BASABE, 2B/SS

BA GRADE

45 Risk: High

Born: Sept. 13, 2000. **B-T:** R-R. **HT:** 6-1. **WT:** 188. **Signed:** Venezuela, 2017. **Signed by:** Carlos Plaza/Rafic Saab (Rangers).

TRACK RECORD: When the Rangers failed to sign Shohei Ohtani, they turned some of the bonus pool space they had acquired to pursue Ohtani to sign Basabe for $550,000. The Rangers then traded Basabe in the deal that sent Nate Lowe to Texas. Basabe's younger brother Edgar is now a player in the Rangers' system.

SCOUTING REPORT: When Basabe couldn't travel back to Venezuela for the first half of the pandemic he made the best of it by working on getting stronger. Basabe is a pretty pure hitter with a line drive-oriented swing that stays in the zone a long time. He's a premium athlete with plus speed and a plus arm. His swing isn't geared to power right now, but he has the strength to get to average power as he matures if he makes some tweaks. He bounced around the infield because he shared the diamond with Alika Williams, but he's a capable, above-average shortstop and potentially plus at second or third. He was a plus center fielder as an amateur as well.

THE FUTURE: The Rays will be trying to stuff nine to ten infielders into six to eight spots on the Class A teams. That may mean Basabe plays less shortstop and more around the infield at High-A Bowling Green.

Year	Age	Club (Level)	Lge	AVG	G	AB	R	H	2B	3B	HR	RBI	BB	SO	SB	OBP	SLG
2021	20	Charleston (LoA)	East	.284	66	278	51	79	10	6	2	35	26	39	18	.347	.385
	20	Bowling Green (HiA)	East	.250	4	16	2	4	0	0	1	1	2	6	0	.333	.438
Minor League Totals (4 years)				.311	159	647	119	201	28	14	4	102	59	91	37	.368	.416

26 FORD PROCTOR, C/SS

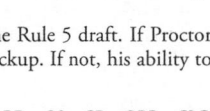

BA GRADE

45 Risk: High

Born: Dec. 4, 1996. **B-T:** L-R. **HT:** 6-1. **WT:** 195. **Drafted:** Rice, 2018 (3rd round). **Signed by:** Pat Murphy.

BACKGROUND: Proctor was Rice's everyday shortstop from virtually his first day on campus, but few MLB teams viewed him as a regular at the position. Buried on the Rays' shortstop depth chart, Proctor took up catching in 2020 and split time between catcher (58 games) and shortstop (28 games) in 2021. He also played some at second and third base.

SCOUTING REPORT: Proctor's move to catcher has given him a much clearer path to a big league role. He's not a polished catcher yet (his 16 passed balls were second most in the minors), but his receiving quickly improved to near-average later in the season and is continually improving. His throwing stroke is a little long behind the plate. He's also a fringe-average defender at shortstop. He makes the plays on balls hit to him with soft hands, but he has modest range and a fringe-average arm. At the plate, Proctor doesn't consistently drive the ball, but his excellent pitch recognition gives him survival skills despite below-average power. He seems most comfortable in deep counts.

THE FUTURE: Proctor was added to the 40-man roster to protect him from the Rule 5 draft. If Proctor continues to develop defensively at catcher, he could end up as a solid MLB backup. If not, his ability to be a No. 3 catcher/middle infield utilityman would still have appeal.

Year	Age	Club (Level)	Lge	AVG	G	AB	R	H	2B	3B	HR	RBI	BB	SO	SB	OBP	SLG
2021	24	Montgomery (AA)	South	.244	97	308	54	75	12	3	12	47	63	100	4	.381	.419
Minor League Totals (3 years)				.268	278	993	166	266	53	7	19	124	164	240	19	.374	.393

27 BLAKE HUNT, C

BA GRADE

45 Risk: High

Born: Nov. 10, 1998. **B-T:** R-R. **HT:** 6-3. **WT:** 215. **Drafted:** HS—Santa Ana, Calif., 2017 (2nd round). **Signed by:** Nick Long (Padres).

BACKGROUND: Hunt seemed destined to head to Pepperdine until a standout senior season vaulted him into the third round. After a strong 2019 season, he was traded to the Rays along with Luis Patiño, Cole Wilcox and Francisco Mejia in the Blake Snell trade in Dec. 2020.

SCOUTING REPORT: Hunt tried to drive the ball more in 2021. He did do more damage when he made contact, but he made a lot less contact. His 32.5% strikeout rate helped sink his batting average, but he also had a career-high nine home runs. Hunt's swing has some length and isn't very adjustable. That and his modest bat speed makes him unlikely to be more than a below-average hitter with below-average power. Defensively, Hunt is an excellent receiver and framer despite his massive 6-foot-5 frame, and he is adept at blocking balls in the dirt. He allowed only two passed balls and a well below-average 29 wild pitches all season.

THE FUTURE: The Rays left Hunt off the 40-man roster, the logic being that it would be hard for a team to carry Hunt's bat on an MLB roster. Hunt has a great glove, but his bat needs to improve a lot.

Year	Age	Club (Level)	Lge	AVG	G	AB	R	H	2B	3B	HR	RBI	BB	SO	SB	OBP	SLG
2021	22	Bowling Green (HiA)	East	.225	59	227	41	51	15	2	9	41	26	79	1	.307	.427
	22	Montgomery (AA)	South	.125	17	56	5	7	2	0	0	0	6	25	0	.210	.161
Minor League Totals (5 years)				.242	251	939	141	227	60	7	19	124	102	269	8	.326	.381

28 HERIBERTO HERNANDEZ, OF

BA GRADE

50 Risk: Extreme

Born: Dec. 16, 1999. **B-T:** R-R. **HT:** 6-1. **WT:** 195. **Signed:** Dominican Republic, 2017. **Signed by:** Willy Espinal (Rangers).

TRACK RECORD: One of three players the Rays acquired from the Rangers for Nate Lowe last offseason (along with Osleivis Basabe and Alexander Ovalles), Hernandez was a low-cost $10,000 signing of the Rangers in 2017. He's far exceeded those expectations since then. He was one of the best players in the Arizona Complex League in 2019. An oblique injury limited him to five games in the Arizona Fall League.

SCOUTING REPORT: Hernandez hits the ball as hard as almost anyone in the system. He consistently tops 110 mph on his hardest-hit balls, although his power numbers haven't fully reflected that plus-plus raw power yet. Hernandez also knows how to work counts and is happy to take a walk. He projects to hit .230-.240, but with plenty of walks and 20+ home runs. The demands on his bat are going to be hefty, because he doesn't do a whole lot else well. Once a catcher, Hernandez is now a well-below-average defender in the outfield corners. His above-average arm plays in right, but his well below-average speed will limit him.

THE FUTURE: Hernandez has excellent bat speed and the chance to get on-base and hit for power. Like several other Rays prospects, his lack of a clear defensive home leads to plenty of questions.

Year	Age	Club (Level)	Lge	AVG	G	AB	R	H	2B	3B	HR	RBI	BB	SO	SB	OBP	SLG
2021	21	Charleston (LoA)	East	.252	73	254	57	64	15	0	12	44	49	90	7	.381	.453
Minor League Totals (4 years)				.293	186	632	159	185	47	9	35	142	131	191	18	.422	.562

29 ALIKA WILLIAMS, SS

BA GRADE	
45	Risk: High

Born: March 12, 1999. **B-T:** R-R. **HT:** 6-2. **WT:** 180. **Drafted:** Arizona State, 2020 (1st round supplemental). **Signed by:** David Hamlett.

TRACK RECORD: As a supplemental first-round pick, Williams was the second-highest drafted Arizona State shortstop of all time, trailing only Red Sox shortstop Deven Marrero (24th overall, 2012). Like Marrero, no one disputes Williams' defensive skills, but there have long been concerns over whether he will hit enough to be a regular.

SCOUTING REPORT: Williams has lived up to the lofty expectations for his plus glove. He's a rangy shortstop who has a good understanding of when to make the highlight play and when to hold the ball. He moves well both to his left and right and has excellent body control. His above-average arm plays even better than that because of a quick release. He's capable of making accurate throws without the need to set his feet. His bat remains the question. He makes plenty of contact (he had an excellent 9% swinging strike rate in 2021), but he's an aggressive hitter who doesn't walk and doesn't drive the ball. He's also an average runner who doesn't swipe bases, so his offensive contribution is largely based on hitting for average. He's a below-average hitter with 5-10 home run power, which means he's best as a bottom-of-the-order bat.

THE FUTURE: Williams is the best pure glove in the Rays' system. He's going to need to either become more patient or get stronger. Otherwise, he's on the Kyle Holder career path.

Year	Age	Club (Level)	Lge	AVG	G	AB	R	H	2B	3B	HR	RBI	BB	SO	SB	OBP	SLG
2021	22	Charleston (LoA)	East	.266	55	237	37	63	13	1	1	34	17	43	5	.317	.342
	22	Bowling Green (HiA)	East	.279	14	61	12	17	3	0	3	9	2	12	1	.302	.475
	22	Durham (AAA)	East	.222	4	9	1	2	0	0	1	3	0	1	0	.250	.556
Minor League Totals (2 years)				.267	73	307	50	82	16	1	5	46	19	56	6	.312	.375

30 JAYDEN MURRAY, RHP

BA GRADE	
45	Risk: High

Born: April 11, 1997. **B-T:** R-R. **HT:** 6-1. **WT:** 190. **Drafted:** Dixie State (Utah), 2019 (23rd round). **Signed by:** David Hamlett.

TRACK RECORD: A $3,000 senior sign out of Dixie State (Utah), Murray set school records for single-season strikeouts (93), strikeout rate (9.9 K/9) and wins (10) as a senior. Murray found High-A unchallenging and didn't flinch at a second-half promotion to Double-A Montgomery. His 2.16 ERA was third best and his 0.71 WHIP was best in the minors among pitchers with 90+ innings.

SCOUTING REPORT: Murray is one of the best pure strike-throwers in the Rays system. He fills the zone with his fastball, slider and changeup. Overall, he threw strikes on 67.5% of all his pitches, ranking in the top 10% of all MiLB pitchers with 90+ innings. Murray is not a soft-tossing command specialist, as his 93-96 mph above-average fastball touched 97 at his best. His sweepy low-80s above-average slider pairs well with it. He also shows confidence in his fringe-average, hard 86-89 mph changeup. Murray's success is largely based on his plus-plus control. His ability to throw all three pitches for strikes in any count makes it hard for hitters to know what is coming.

THE FUTURE: Murray has been a fast-mover so far thanks to his excellent control and command. He should reach Triple-A Durham in 2022. He's a potential No. 4 starter if it all clicks.

Year	Age	Club (Level)	Lge	W	L	ERA	G	GS	IP	H	HR	BB	SO	BB/9	SO/9	WHIP	AVG
2021	24	Bowling Green (HiA)	East	7	1	1.72	12	12	57	30	5	10	53	1.6	8.3	0.69	.149
	24	Montgomery (AA)	South	1	2	2.82	8	8	38	21	6	7	43	1.6	10.1	0.73	.157
Minor League Totals (3 years)				9	5	2.24	32	29	136	82	15	25	143	1.65	9.44	0.78	.170

MORE PROSPECTS TO KNOW

31 MATT DYER, C/OF

Acquired from the Mets in the Rich Hill trade in 2021, Dyer is an unusual prospect as a rangy center fielder who also plays catcher. He hit much better after the trade but did struggle in the Arizona Fall League.

32 RYAN SPIKES, SS

The Rays hoard contact-oriented middle infielders in seemingly every draft. Spikes, the Rays' 2021 third-round pick, should hit for average while playing second base or third base long-term.

33 MASON MONTGOMERY, LHP

SLEEPER

The Rays' sixth-round pick out of Texas Tech dominated the Florida Complex League in his pro debut. He has a 91-95 mph fastball with lots of hop at the top of the zone and improving control.

34 BRENDAN MCKAY, LHP

McKay finished 2019 just one inning short of graduating from prospect status. Since then he's had labrum surgery as well as thoracic outlet syndrome decompression surgery. His brief rehab stint in 2021 was discouraging. The hope is he can return to action and a semblance of his pre-injury form in 2022.

35 KYLE MANZARDO, 1B

Manzardo was one of the best college performers on the West Coast in 2021. He's a lefty hitter who can use the whole field, but with home run power as well.

36 DRU BAKER, OF

A versatile play-everywhere bat at Texas Tech, Baker has never really hit for power, but he makes a ton of contact and hits for average. The Rays have Baker focusing on playing in the outfield.

37 MILES MASTROBUONI, 3B/2B/OF

Mastrobuoni played everywhere but first base and catcher in 2021. He's a versatile and reliable, if range-limited, defender who has shown he can square up a fastball and hit for average while getting on base.

38 JACOB LOPEZ, LHP

Lopez was on his way to an excellent 2021 season thanks to his plus control and above-average slider. Tommy John surgery will sideline him for the entirety of 2022.

39 PEDRO MARTINEZ, SS

Pushed to High-A Bowling Green in 2021, Martinez didn't seem fully comfortable making the jump. He has defensive value at shortstop or second base and has some offensive potential, even if he hit .216 in 2021.

40 JUNIOR CAMINERO, SS

Picked up from the Guardians in the deal that sent RHP Tobias Myers to Cleveland, Caminero has the type of skills the Rays covet: defensive versatility, excellent contact skills and impressive power for a teenager.

TOP PROSPECTS OF THE DECADE

Year	Player, Pos	2021 Org
2012	Matt Moore, LHP	Phillies
2013	Wil Myers, OF	Padres
2014	Jake Odorizzi, RHP	Astros
2015	Willy Adames, SS	Brewers
2016	Blake Snell, LHP	Padres
2017	Willy Adames, SS	Brewers
2018	Brent Honeywell, RHP	Rays
2019	Wander Franco, SS	Rays
2020	Wander Franco, SS	Rays
2021	Wander Franco, SS	Rays

TOP DRAFT PICKS OF THE DECADE

Year	Player, Pos	2021 Org
2012	Richie Shaffer, 3B	Did not play
2013	Nick Ciuffo, C	Orioles
2014	Casey Gillaspie, 1B	American Assoc.
2015	Garrett Whitley, OF	Rays
2016	Josh Lowe, 3B	Rays
2017	Brendan McKay, LHP/1B	Rays
2018	Matthew Liberatore, LHP	Cardinals
2019	Greg Jones, SS	Rays
2020	Nick Bitsko, RHP	Rays
2021	Carson Williams, SS	Rays

Texas Rangers

BY JOSH NORRIS

The most important moments of the Rangers' 2021 season, in which they lost 102 games and finished with the third-worst record in the majors, happened in the draft, a few weeks later at the July trade deadline and in the weeks before baseball went into a lockout.

In July, Texas went into sell mode and began spinning pieces of its big league roster to contenders across the game in an effort to bolster its farm system and make waves toward the future.

To the Yankees went outfielder Joey Gallo and lefty Joely Rodriguez in exchange for a package of three middle infielders—Ezequiel Duran, Josh Smith and Trevor Hauver—and righthander Glenn Otto. To the Phillies went starter Kyle Gibson, closer Ian Kennedy and pitching prospect Hans Crouse in exchange for young starter and former top prospect Spencer Howard as well as minor league righties Kevin Gowdy and Josh Gessner.

All four of the prospects the Rangers received from the Yankees rank among Texas' revamped Top 30, and Gowdy sits just outside.

A few weeks earlier, the Rangers used the No. 2 pick in the draft to select Vanderbilt righthander Jack Leiter—the son of former big leaguer Al Leiter. Leiter formed a one-two punch at the top of the Commodores' rotation with Kumar Rocker and helped lead his team to the finals of the College World Series, which they lost to Mississippi State. His 179 strikeouts tied with Rocker for the most in Division I.

Breakout years from third baseman Josh Jung, righthander Cole Winn and third baseman Dustin Harris further improved the Rangers' system, as did bounceback years from righthander Owen White and Cole Ragans. The latter recovered from two Tommy John surgeries to pitch in the Futures Game along with Winn, who got the start for the American League.

The Rangers' farm is now bursting with middle-infield prospects, including four members of the team's top 10. Yet, once teams were allowed to sign free agents, the Rangers did as they'd been rumored all year and opened their wallets as wide as can be. Before the lockout commenced on Dec. 2, Texas signed Corey Seager and Marcus Semien to contracts totaling half a billion dollars.

The moves set up the Rangers with potential cornerstone pieces for years to come. In doing so, it also turned their farm system's strength into a load of potential firepower to buttress a thin rotation via trades. The Rangers made hay to address that problem as well by signing righthander Jon Gray to a four-year deal for $56 million.

Adolis Garcia went unclaimed on waivers, then led the Rangers with 31 home runs as a rookie.

PROJECTED 2025 LINEUP

Catcher	Sam Huff	27
First Base	Nate Lowe	29
Second Base	Marcus Semien	34
Third Base	Josh Jung	27
Shortstop	Corey Seager	31
Left Field	Ezequiel Duran	26
Center Field	Evan Carter	22
Right Field	Dustin Harris	25
Designated Hitter	Justin Foscue	26
No. 1 Starter	Jon Gray	33
No. 2 Starter	Jack Leiter	25
No. 3 Starter	Cole Winn	25
No. 4 Starter	Owen White	25
No. 5 Starter	Dane Dunning	30
Closer	Joe Barlow	29

After five straight losing seasons, the club simultaneously boosted both their farm system and the major league roster, albeit at significant cost.

Because of the strange arrangement of the 2020 postseason, Texas' new ballpark has already hosted a World Series, albeit one between the Rays and Dodgers that left Rangers executives watching from afar.

With talent infusions from the draft, a series of trades and two massive free agent signings, the team's brass has signaled that it will enter 2022 in a full-on sprint to make sure the next time the Fall Classic passes through Arlington, the Rangers will be competing for a championship for the first time since 2011. ∎

TEXAS RANGERS

TOP 2022 ROOKIES	RANK
Josh Jung, 3B	2
Sam Huff, C	11
BREAKOUT PROSPECTS	
Ricky Vanasco, RHP	13
Tekoah Roby, RHP	14

SOURCE OF TOP 30 TALENT			
Homegrown	**21**	**Acquired**	**9**
College	6	Trade	8
Junior college	0	Rule 5 draft	1
High school	9	Independent league	0
Nondrafted free agent	0	Free agent/waivers	0
International	6		

LF
Ezequiel Duran (4)
Aaron Zavala (12)
Trevor Hauver (22)
Abimelec Ortiz

CF
Evan Carter (8)
Yeison Morrobel (16)
Daniel Mateo
Bubba Thompson
Jonathan Ornelas

RF
Bayron Lora (19)
Steele Walker
Josh Stowers

3B
Josh Jung (2)
Davis Wendzel

SS
Josh Smith (9)
Luisangel Acuña (10)
Maximo Acosta (21)
Cameron Cauley (25)
Danyer Cueva (30)

2B
Justin Foscue (6)
Chris Seise

1B
Dustin Harris (5)
Abimelec Ortiz

C
Sam Huff (11)
Yohel Pozo (28)
Ian Moller
David Garcia
Matt Whatley

LHP

LHSP	LHRP
Avery Weems (18)	Brock Burke
Mitchell Bratt (20)	Tristan Polley
Cody Bradford (23)	Grant Wolfram
Cole Ragans (24)	

RHP

RHSP	RHRP
Jack Leiter (1)	Nick Snyder
Cole Winn (3)	Emiliano Teodo
Owen White (7)	Orceli Gomez
Ricky Vanasco (13)	Kevin Gowdy
Tekoah Roby (14)	Justin Slaten
Glenn Otto (15)	Josh Gessner
Zak Kent (17)	Demarcus Evans
Dane Acker (26)	Yerry Rodriguez
AJ Alexy (27)	Marc Church
Ronny Henriquez (29)	Alex Speas
Mason Englert	

1 JACK LEITER, RHP

Born: April 21, 2000. **B-T:** R-R. **HT:** 6-1. **WT:** 205.
Drafted: Vanderbilt, 2021 (1st round).
Signed by: Derrick Tucker.

TRACK RECORD: Leiter was drafted by the Yankees out of the Delbarton School in New Jersey, where he was teammates with Anthony Volpe, the Yankees' current top prospect. Leiter chose to honor his commitment to Vanderbilt, where he spent the 2021 season as arguably the most dominant pitcher in college baseball. He made national headlines on March 20 when he threw a no-hitter with 16 strikeouts against South Carolina. He followed that performance with seven more hitless innings against Missouri in his next start, cementing his starts as appointment viewing. He finished with 179 strikeouts, tied at the top of the NCAA leaderboard with teammate Kumar Rocker. He and Rocker helped lead the Commodores to the College World Series finals, which they lost to Mississippi State. Come July, Leiter was in the mix for the No. 1 overall pick. He fell to No. 2 overall, but his $7,922,000 bonus was the fourth-highest bonus ever and the largest of the 2021 draft by more than $1 million. The bonus was the second most a pitcher has ever received in the draft, just behind the $8 million Gerrit Cole got in 2011.

SCOUTING REPORT: Leiter has one of the most electric pitch packages of any prospect, led by a fastball that averages 94 mph and touches 99. The velocity, coupled with efficient spin, an elite vertical approach angle, horizontal break and carry through the zone, help the pitch play when he locates it to the upper and lower quadrants. Eventually, the Rangers believe, all those characteristics will combine to form a true plus-plus pitch. Both of Leiter's breaking pitches—a high-70s, downer curveball and a slicing slider in the low 80s—generated plenty of swings and misses in college and project to be at least above-average pitches in pro ball, as well. Leiter completes his arsenal with a mid-80s changeup he threw just 4% of the time in college but still drew whiffs on 39% of swings. Leiter predominantly uses his fastball and curveball, and one of the first bits of his development will be to incorporate his slider and changeup more often so he can more effectively pitch to advanced hitters. The only true knock on Leiter has to do with his smaller stature and ultimate durability. He skipped one start in 2021 due to fatigue, and shorter righthanders—Leiter is listed at 6-foot-1—have long faced questions about whether they can handle the workload required of a big league starter. His height will also generate questions about whether he can generate enough angle on his pitches to avoid becoming

BILL MITCHELL

BA GRADE	SCOUTING GRADES
60 Risk: High	**FB:** 70. **CB:** 60. **SL:** 55. **CHG:** 55. **CTL:** 50.

Projected future grades on 20-80 scouting scale

BEST TOOLS

Best Hitter for Average	Josh Jung
Best Power Hitter	Sam Huff
Best Strike-Zone Discipline	Josh Smith
Fastest Baserunner	Jayce Easley
Best Athlete	Bubba Thompson
Best Fastball	Alex Speas
Best Curveball	AJ Alexy
Best Slider	Cole Winn
Best Changeup	Cole Ragans
Best Control	Cody Bradford
Best Defensive Catcher	Matt Whatley
Best Defensive Infielder	Luisangel Acuña
Best Infield Arm	Chris Seise
Best Defensive Outfielder	Bubba Thompson
Best Outfield Arm	Josh Stowers

homer-prone as a professional, something that was an issue in college. Of the 26 runs Leiter allowed in 2021, 17 came on home runs.

THE FUTURE: Leiter did not pitch either in the regular season or at instructional league, though he was at the team's camp briefly before heading back to Vanderbilt to continue working toward his degree. While there, he continued his workout regimen as if he were going to pitch in a typical college fall ball setting. For his pro debut, the Rangers are strongly considering sending Leiter straight to Double-A Frisco, where he'll work toward achieving his ceiling as a top-end starter who can help lead the Rangers into their new era of contending in the AL West. ■

Year	Age	Club (Level)	Lge	W	L	ERA	G	GS	IP	H	HR	BB	SO	BB/9	SO/9	WHIP	AVG
2021	21	Did not play															

2 JOSH JUNG, 3B

Born: Feb. 12, 1998. **B-T:** R-R. **HT:** 6-2. **WT:** 214. **Drafted:** Texas Tech, 2019 (1st round). **Signed by:** Josh Simpson.

TRACK RECORD: Jung was the Rangers' first-round pick in 2019 out of Texas Tech, where he earned Big 12 conference co-player of the year honors as a junior. He signed for $4.4 million and spent 2020 at the alternate training site before seeing game action in instructional league. Jung's 2021 season was delayed by a broken foot, but he recovered in time to still race up to Triple-A in his pro debut and hit .322 across the minors' highest levels.

SCOUTING REPORT: Jung's offensive profile took a big step forward in 2021. He worked to make contact earlier, and the result was an increase in pull-side power. He has big-time bat speed and plus raw power, which showed up in a 91.1 mph average exit velocity that was nearly the same as big league power brokers Pete Alonso and Jorge Soler. With his natural hitting gifts and approach adjustment, he now projects to be a plus hitter with plus power. Jung has worked hard to improve his defense and shows better first step and pre-pitch anticipation than he did in college. He is a below-average runner and is unlikely to be a standout at third base, but he should reach fringe-average with continued work. He has above-average arm strength and has worked to improve his throwing stroke. Jung is an exceptionally hard worker who used virtual reality to simulate at-bats while he rehabbed his broken foot and would often watch extended spring training games at the team's complex in Arizona.

THE FUTURE: After a standout debut at the upper levels, Jung will likely start 2022 at Triple-A Round Rock and should push for his big league debut. He has the ceiling of a third baseman who fits nicely in the middle of the Rangers' remade lineup.

BA GRADE
55 Risk: Medium

SCOUTING GRADES:	Hitting: 60	Power: 60	Running: 40	Fielding: 45	Arm: 55

Year	Age	Club (Level)	Lge	AVG	G	AB	R	H	2B	3B	HR	RBI	BB	SO	SB	OBP	SLG
2021	23	Frisco (AA)	Cent	.308	43	169	25	52	8	1	10	40	13	42	2	.366	.544
	23	Round Rock (AAA)	West	.348	35	135	29	47	14	0	9	21	18	34	0	.436	.652
Minor League Totals (3 years)				.322	122	478	77	154	36	2	21	89	49	108	6	.394	.538

3 COLE WINN, RHP

Born: Nov. 25, 1999. **B-T:** R-R. **HT:** 6-2. **WT:** 203. **Drafted:** HS—Orange, Calif., 2018 (1st round). **Signed by:** Steve Flores.

TRACK RECORD: Winn was Baseball America's 2018 High School Player of the Year and led his Orange Lutheran team to the championship at the National High School Invitational. He struggled with his control at Low-A in 2019, but after a season at the alternate training site and instructional league, he emerged a much improved pitcher in 2021. He logged a 2.41 ERA in 21 starts across Double-A and Triple-A and started the Futures Game for the American League.

SCOUTING REPORT: With a much tighter, more compact delivery, Winn now shows improved command and control and has started to tap into his massive potential. Winn uses a four-pitch mix fronted by a mid-90 fastball with promising analytic characteristics. The pitch grades out as at least plus in terms of both induced vertical break and vertical approach angle. His most-used secondary pitch is a mid-80s slider which got swings and misses at a roughly 35% clip. His slider pairs nicely with his powerful downer curveball, which has high spin and deep break and remains his signature offspeed offering. Winn worked with pitching coordinator Jomo Arnold to tighten the break on the curveball and turn it into a pitch he could use for early-count strikes as well as chase swings. Winn also focused on sharpening his mid-80s changeup, which has above-average potential.

THE FUTURE: Winn will likely return to Triple-A Round Rock to begin 2022. He has the ceiling of a mid-rotation starter.

BA GRADE
55 Risk: High

SCOUTING GRADES:	Fastball: 60	Slider: 55	Curveball: 60	Changeup: 50	Control: 50

Year	Age	Club (Level)	Lge	W	L	ERA	G	GS	IP	H	HR	BB	SO	BB/9	SO/9	WHIP	AVG
2021	21	Frisco (AA)	Cent	3	3	2.31	19	19	78	38	6	26	97	3.0	11.2	0.82	.144
	21	Round Rock (AAA)	West	1	0	3.38	2	2	8	5	1	5	10	5.6	11.3	1.25	.167
Minor League Totals (4 years)				8	7	3.32	39	39	155	102	12	70	172	4.07	10.01	1.11	.186

4 EZEQUIEL DURAN, 2B/SS

TOM PRIDDY/FOUR SEAM IMAGES

Born: May 22, 1999. **B-T:** R-R. **HT:** 5-11. **WT:** 185. **Signed:** Dominican Republic, 2017. **Signed by:** Juan Rosario/Raymon Sanchez/Victor Mata (Yankees).

TRACK RECORD: The Yankees signed Duran for $10,000 in 2017 and were intrigued by the offensive potential he showed in the first few years of his professional career. He was part of the package Texas received in exchange for Joey Gallo and Joely Rodriguez from the Yankees, and immediately joined the Rangers' glut of middle infield talent.

SCOUTING REPORT: Duran's offense is his calling card, especially his big-time power potential. His 90.8 mph average exit velocity was among the best in the organization, as was his maximum exit velocity of 112 mph. Before the trade, Duran worked hard to improve his contact rates against breaking balls, and the results followed. His ability to hit those pitches improved, as did the confidence he showed when he took them for balls. He now projects to be at least an average hitter and could reach plus power. Defensively, Duran can stand at shortstop, but he's more likely a third baseman. His hands are fine, but his range and internal clock are somewhat limited. He has plenty of arm strength for the position, but his throwing accuracy will need to be addressed.

BA GRADE
50 Risk: High

THE FUTURE: Duran will need to add versatility to his game after the additions of Corey Seager and Marcus Semien. He played second, third and shortstop in the Arizona Fall League and has the upside of an offensive-minded infielder at any spot.

SCOUTING GRADES:	Hitting: 55	Power: 60	Running: 50	Fielding: 45	Arm: 50

Year	Age	Club (Level)	Lge	AVG	G	AB	R	H	2B	3B	HR	RBI	BB	SO	SB	OBP	SLG
2021	22	Hickory (HiA)	East	.229	38	157	25	36	7	0	7	31	12	59	7	.287	.408
	22	Hudson Valley (HiA)	East	.290	67	259	42	75	15	6	12	48	28	71	12	.374	.533
Minor League Totals (5 years)				.257	239	942	162	242	47	16	39	147	77	287	41	.323	.465

5 DUSTIN HARRIS, 1B/3B

Born: July 8, 1999. **B-T:** L-R. **HT:** 6-2. **WT:** 185. **Drafted:** St. Petersburg (Fla.) JC, 2019 (11th round). **Signed by:** Trevor Schaeffer (Athletics).

TRACK RECORD: Harris was Oakland's 11th-round selection in the 2019 draft out of St. Petersburg (Fla.) JC. He made it to short-season ball with the A's before being dealt to Texas as one of two players to be named later in the 2020 deadline deal for Mike Minor. Harris surprised evaluators both inside and outside the Rangers organization in 2021 with his combination of plus contact paired with above-average power, and he finished the year batting .327/.401/.532 across both Class A levels in a breakout campaign.

SCOUTING REPORT: Harris is as pure of a hitter as can be found in the Rangers organization. He was the only player in the minor leagues in 2021 with 20 or more doubles, home runs and stolen bases and fewer than 100 strikeouts. He accomplished those numbers thanks to a short, compact swing,

BA GRADE
50 Risk: High

an innate sense of barrel accuracy and an excellent knowledge of the strike zone. He hits the ball plenty hard, too, with a 90th percentile exit velocity of 101.7 mph. That figure is identical to fellow Top 10 prospect Josh Smith and just a tick below that of Evan Carter. Where Harris plays on defense is a bigger question. He's not going to be a third baseman long term, which gives him a likely home of first base. At instructional league Harris worked some in left field, where some evaluators believe his athleticism will allow him to play.

THE FUTURE: After dominating the Class A levels, Harris will move to Double-A in 2022. If he can dominate there the way he did in 2021, he will rise to the majors quickly.

SCOUTING GRADES:	Hitting: 60	Power: 55	Running: 45	Fielding: 40	Arm: 45

Year	Age	Club (Level)	Lge	AVG	G	AB	R	H	2B	3B	HR	RBI	BB	SO	SB	OBP	SLG
2021	21	Down East (LoA)	East	.301	73	259	54	78	11	3	10	53	34	48	20	.389	.483
	21	Hickory (HiA)	East	.372	37	145	32	54	10	0	10	32	13	25	5	.425	.648
Minor League Totals (3 years)				.326	168	613	119	200	33	4	21	111	72	112	34	.402	.496

6 JUSTIN FOSCUE, 2B

Born: March 2, 1999. **B-T:** R-R. **HT:** 6-0. **WT:** 205. **Drafted:** Mississippi State, 2020 (1st round). **Signed by:** Brian Morrison.

TRACK RECORD: Foscue starred at Mississippi State and earned a spot on USA Baseball's Collegiate National Team during his sophomore season. The Rangers made him their first-round pick in 2020 and signed him to an under-slot bonus of $3.25 million before letting him get his feet wet at the alternate training site and in instructional league. Foscue showed a combination of power and hittability in his 2021 pro debut but scuffled a bit once he got to Double-A. He finished the year with a solid stint in the Arizona Fall League.

SCOUTING REPORT: Foscue's season was interrupted by a pair of injuries to his midsection, but when he was on the field, especially at High-A, he showed the ability to hit for both average and power. The latter was especially clear during a torrid stretch in July when he hit nine home runs in eight games. Foscue got plenty of power from a short swing, but he will fall in love with the home run at times and get out of his approach. Opposing scouts also saw a player with a stiff swing and holes on the outer third of the strike zone, which became somewhat exposed once he got to Double-A. Defensively, Foscue is not a particularly rangy or agile player, but he will make the routine plays and has a fringe-average arm. He's a below-average runner.

THE FUTURE: Foscue is likely to return to Double-A to begin 2022. He will have to shore up his hit tool to reach his ceiling as an offensive-minded second baseman.

BA GRADE
50 Risk: High

SCOUTING GRADES:	Hitting: 50	Power: 55	Running: 40	Fielding: 40	Arm: 45

Year	Age	Club (Level)	Lge	AVG	G	AB	R	H	2B	3B	HR	RBI	BB	SO	SB	OBP	SLG
2021	22	Rangers (R)	ACL	.273	3	11	4	3	1	0	1	3	1	4	1	.385	.636
	22	Hickory (HiA)	East	.296	33	125	34	37	11	1	14	35	16	39	1	.407	.736
	22	Frisco (AA)	Cent	.247	26	93	14	23	7	0	2	13	8	29	0	.317	.387
Minor League Totals (2 years)				.275	62	229	52	63	19	1	17	51	25	72	2	.371	.590

7 OWEN WHITE, RHP

Born: Aug. 9, 1999. **B-T:** R-R. **HT:** 6-3. **WT:** 199. **Drafted:** HS—China Grove, N.C., 2018 (2nd round). **Signed by:** Jay Heafner.

TRACK RECORD: Although White was drafted in 2018, he didn't make his official pro debut until 2021. He was rested post-draft in 2018, missed 2019 while recovering from Tommy John surgery and then lost 2020 to the coronavirus pandemic. His 2021 season was shortened after he broke his hand during the opening start of the season and didn't return until August before shining down the stretch and again in the Arizona Fall League.

SCOUTING REPORT: During his time rehabbing his broken hand, White evolved. He tweaked the grip on his four-seam fastball to give it more true riding action, and the results showed in the data. His mid-90s four-seamer posted a truly elite swing-and-miss rate of nearly 46% and showed strong spin rates and movement patterns. White also throws two-seam and cut fastballs to give him an array of pitches that move in different directions. He backs up the fastballs with a full mix of curveball, slider and changeup. Both breaking balls show promising analytical qualities but still need refinement. He worked this year to throw his high-70s curveball for strikes and chases, and he's trying to become more consistent in general with the way he throws his low-80s slider. His changeup, thrown in the mid 80s, has excellent separation from his fastball and projects as average.

THE FUTURE: White was excellent in the AFL, where he was mostly making up as much lost time as possible. He'll move to High-A next year and is one of the system's most promising pitching prospects.

BA GRADE
50 Risk: High

SCOUTING GRADES:	Fastball: 70	Slider: 55	Curveball: 55	Changeup: 50	Control: 60

Year	Age	Club (Level)	Lge	W	L	ERA	G	GS	IP	H	HR	BB	SO	BB/9	SO/9	WHIP	AVG
2021	21	Rangers (R)	ACL	1	0	0.00	1	0	2	1	0	0	2	0.0	9.0	0.50	.167
	21	Down East (LoA)	East	3	1	3.24	8	8	33	25	2	12	54	3.2	14.6	1.11	.205
Minor League Totals (3 years)				4	1	3.06	9	8	35	26	2	12	56	3.06	14.26	1.08	.203

8 EVAN CARTER, OF

Born: Aug. 29, 2002. **B-T:** L-R. **HT:** 6-4. **WT:** 190. **Drafted:** HS—Elizabethton, Tenn., 2020 (2nd round). **Signed by:** Derrick Tucker/Ryan Coe.

TRACK RECORD: Carter was one of the biggest surprises of the 2020 draft and flew under nearly everybody's radar. The Rangers' amateur scouting department was ecstatic on draft day and have grown even more so with the way Carter has performed as a pro. He opened the year as the youngest position player on a full-season roster but had his year cut short by a hairline fracture in his back.

SCOUTING REPORT: The Rangers were excited by Carter's tools when they drafted him, but the polish he's shown both at instructional league and in his time at Low-A have immediately validated those feelings. He did an excellent job commanding the strike zone and rarely chased pitches out of the zone. When he swung, he hit balls hard. His average exit velocity was just a hair above 91 mph, which is impressive for any player, but especially one so young. He has the speed and instincts to play center field, too, and the average arm to fit in a corner if necessary.

THE FUTURE: Despite the small sample in 2021, Carter should move up to High-A in 2022. He's got one of the bigger upsides in the organization and could become a center fielder who can do a little bit of everything.

BA GRADE
55 Risk: Extreme

SCOUTING GRADES:	Hitting: 55	Power: 50	Running: 55	Fielding: 55	Arm: 50

Year	Age	Club (Level)	Lge	AVG	G	AB	R	H	2B	3B	HR	RBI	BB	SO	SB	OBP	SLG
2021	18	Down East (LoA)	East	.236	32	106	22	25	8	1	2	12	34	28	12	.438	.387
Minor League Totals (2 years)				.236	32	106	22	25	8	1	2	12	34	28	12	.438	.387

9 JOSH SMITH, SS/2B

Born: Aug. 7, 1997. **B-T:** L-R. **HT:** 5-10. **WT:** 172. **Drafted:** Louisiana State, 2019 (2nd round). **Signed by:** Mike Leuzinger (Yankees).

TRACK RECORD: Smith was a standout both at Louisiana State and in the Cape Cod League, where he was teammates with future NL Rookie of the Year Jonathan India and future NFL Offensive Rookie of the Year Kyler Murray. The Yankees selected Smith in the second round of the 2019 draft, then traded him in 2021 to the Rangers as part of the package used to acquire Joey Gallo and Joely Rodriguez.

SCOUTING REPORT: Smith's season was delayed by a few weeks after he dove into a tarp during minor league spring training, but once he got on the field he showed an enticing blend of tools and polish. He did an excellent job working counts to get pitches to drive, then punished balls from gap to gap. He rarely chases, and when he swings at pitches in the zone he almost never misses. Smith hits the ball hard as well, with an average exit velocity of 91.1 mph and a max of 106 mph. Smith is a capable shortstop but likely will begin to move around the diamond to increase his versatility.

BA GRADE
50 Risk: High

THE FUTURE: Now that the Rangers have locked up Corey Seager and Marcus Semien to fill their middle infield spots, Smith likely fits the role of a super-utility player. He could make his big league debut in 2022.

SCOUTING GRADES:	Hitting: 55	Power: 45	Running: 50	Fielding: 50	Arm: 50

Year	Age	Club (Level)	Lge	AVG	G	AB	R	H	2B	3B	HR	RBI	BB	SO	SB	OBP	SLG
2021	23	Tampa (LoA)	SEast	.333	11	39	15	13	0	0	6	15	7	6	5	.480	.795
	23	Hudson Valley (HiA)	East	.320	28	103	29	33	12	3	3	9	16	27	12	.435	.583
	23	Hickory (HiA)	East	.295	9	44	10	13	3	0	1	7	2	9	2	.367	.432
	23	Frisco (AA)	Cent	.294	30	102	12	30	5	0	3	10	18	20	7	.425	.431
Minor League Totals (3 years)				.313	111	399	83	125	26	4	16	56	68	79	32	.435	.519

10 LUISANGEL ACUÑA, SS

Born: March 12, 2002. **B-T:** R-R. **HT:** 5-10. **WT:** 181. **Signed:** Venezuela, 2018. **Signed by:** Rafic Saab.

TRACK RECORD: Ronald Acuña Jr.'s younger brother is starting to create a name for himself. He was signed as one of the headliners of the team's 2018 class and responded by raking in the Dominican Summer League in his first season as a pro. After starring again at instructional league, Acuña had a promising year at Low-A Down East, where he ranked as the league's No. 9 prospect.

SCOUTING REPORT: Acuña's excellent glovework at shortstop nabbed him the organization's defender of the year award. He has smooth, athletic actions in the field and a plus arm to play on the left side of the diamond and the footspeed to move to the outfield. At the plate, Acuña is an aggressive hitter with a quick, whippy swing and the strong hands to drive balls out with authority. His 12 home runs led the Wood Ducks. He's made improvements to the way he understands the strike zone, which will help hit and power tools the Rangers believe are both average or better. He's an above-average runner whose stolen base totals were helped by the rules at Low-A designed to promote movement on the basepaths.

THE FUTURE: Acuña will move to High-A Hickory in 2022. He'll continue to play up the middle but could see some time in the outfield because of the logjam created up the middle by the signings of Corey Seager and Marcus Semien.

BA GRADE
50 Risk: High

SCOUTING GRADES:	Hitting: 55	Power: 50	Running: 55	Fielding: 60	Arm: 60

Year	Age	Club (Level)	Lge	AVG	G	AB	R	H	2B	3B	HR	RBI	BB	SO	SB	OBP	SLG
2021	19	Down East (LoA)	East	.266	111	413	77	110	15	3	12	74	49	110	44	.345	.404
Minor League Totals (2 years)				.291	162	615	138	179	26	6	14	103	83	136	61	.376	.421

11 SAM HUFF, C

BA GRADE
50 Risk: High

Born: Jan. 14, 1998. **B-T:** R-R. **HT:** 6-5. **WT:** 240. **Drafted:** HS—Phoenix, 2016 (7th round). **Signed by:** Josh Simpson.

TRACK RECORD: Huff was the Rangers' seventh-round selection in 2016, then broke on the scene with 28 home runs spread across the Class A levels in 2019. He also won that year's Futures Game MVP award. He reached the big leagues in 2020 and performed well, but dealt with a subluxation in his knee that kept him from catching all season long. The injury flared up again in 2021 and kept him from catching all season long yet again. He was set to make up for lost time in the Arizona Fall League, but left after six games due to precautionary reasons regarding the same injury.

SCOUTING REPORT: Huff's calling card is his truly massive power. Even while he was rehabbing from his injury, he found time to sock a 519-foot home run in the Arizona Complex League. His average (92.3 mph) and maximum (115 mph) exit velocities were both tops in the Texas system. He's improved his pitch-recognition skills over the course of his career and will likely be a below-average hitter with double-plus power. The biggest question remaining is where he'll wind up on defense. Come 2022 he'll get back behind the plate again. He spent time working with Bobby Wilson to get better at the position, but he was fringe-average pre-injury. He's a very large human but has more athleticism than one would expect from someone his size and has a plus throwing arm to boot. When he did get on the field in 2021, he split his time between first base and DH.

THE FUTURE: The Rangers still believe Huff has a shot to catch in the long term, but he had work to do to stick behind the plate even before the injury. He'll try to get back on track in 2022.

Year	Age	Club (Level)	Lge	AVG	G	AB	R	H	2B	3B	HR	RBI	BB	SO	SB	OBP	SLG
2021	23	Rangers (R)	ACL	.276	8	29	6	8	2	0	3	6	3	11	0	.364	.655
	23	Frisco (AA)	Cent	.237	46	173	24	41	5	0	10	23	16	77	0	.309	.439
	23	Round Rock (AAA)	West	.273	7	22	4	6	1	0	3	7	2	9	0	.320	.727
Major League Totals (1 year)				.355	10	31	5	11	3	0	3	4	2	11	0	.394	.742
Minor League Totals (5 years)				.261	383	1408	211	368	71	8	72	211	117	486	18	.327	.477

12 AARON ZAVALA, OF

BA GRADE
50 Risk: High

Born: June 23, 2000. **B-T:** L-R. **HT:** 6-0. **WT:** 193. **Drafted:** Oregon, 2021 (2nd round). **Signed by:** Gary McGraw.

TRACK RECORD: With a standout season at Oregon, Zavala zoomed up draft boards as one of the best lefthanded bats available in the college class. The Rangers popped him in the second round but discovered what they termed a "medical anomaly" and negotiations went down to the wire. Ultimately, he signed for a bonus of $830,000, which was well below slot value.

SCOUTING REPORT: Zavala made big-time noise in the Ducks' regional appearance, including a pair of home runs. That only cemented what Zavala had proved throughout the course of the year. He has a potentially above-average hit tool fueled by a quick swing with a flat path through the zone and burgeoning power that could get to fringe-average. He also has an outstanding knowledge of the strike zone and excellent bat-to-ball skills. Zavala has solid-average speed but a below-average arm, which likely makes left field his future defensive home. He has played second base and third base in the past as well.

THE FUTURE: Zavala made it to Low-A Down East in his debut season. He'll likely move up to High-A Hickory in 2022. He has the ceiling of an everyday left fielder.

Year	Age	Club (Level)	Lge	AVG	G	AB	R	H	2B	3B	HR	RBI	BB	SO	SB	OBP	SLG
2021	21	Rangers (R)	ACL	.273	7	22	5	6	1	0	0	2	3	7	2	.385	.318
	21	Down East (LoA)	East	.302	15	53	13	16	4	0	1	7	10	13	7	.433	.434
Minor League Totals (1 year)				.293	22	75	18	22	5	0	1	9	13	20	9	.419	.400

13 RICKY VANASCO, RHP

Born: Oct. 13, 1998. **B-T:** R-R. **HT:** 6-3. **WT:** 180. **Drafted:** HS—Williston, Fla., 2017 (15th round). **Signed by:** Brett Campbell.

BA GRADE
55 Risk: Extreme

TRACK RECORD: Vanasco upped his draft stock with performances at prep showcases in Florida during his draft season, leading the Rangers to take a flier on him in the 15th round and sign him for $238,000. The gamble quickly proved worth the investment when his fastball jumped way up. He impressed in the short-season Northwest League, where he ranked as the No. 10 prospect in 2019. He was impressive again at the alternate training site in 2020, but had Tommy John surgery and missed all of the 2021 regular season.

SCOUTING REPORT: At his best, Vanasco was bringing his fastball up to 99 mph while sitting in the mid 90s. He'd backed it with a powerful curveball in the mid 80s and a high-80s slider that could get to average with further development. He rounds out the arsenal with a high-80s changeup as well. Control was his biggest question pre-surgery, and he'll need to make up time in 2022 to continue to improve that aspect of his game.

THE FUTURE: Vanasco got on the mound in instructional league, including a start against Texas Christian during the team's barnstorming tour through the Lone Star State. He should move to Double-A in 2022.

Year	Age	Club (Level)	Lge	W	L	ERA	G	GS	IP	H	HR	BB	SO	BB/9	SO/9	WHIP	AVG
2021	22	Did not play—Injured															
Minor League Totals (4 years)				6	5	2.38	28	14	83	61	3	43	116	4.64	12.53	1.25	.210

14 TEKOAH ROBY, RHP

Born: Sept. 18, 2001. **B-T:** R-R. **HT:** 6-1. **WT:** 210. **Drafted:** HS—Pensacola, Fla., 2020 (3rd round). **Signed by:** Brian Morrison.

BA GRADE
55 Risk: Extreme

TRACK RECORD: Roby's stock was rising before his high school season was shut down. The Rangers' area scouts and crosscheckers believed enough in him to draft him with their third-round pick. He was excellent in his pro debut, when he jumped to Low-A Down East and whiffed 35 in 22 innings before an elbow strain ended his season.

SCOUTING REPORT: Roby's pitch mix starts with one of the organization's most electric fastballs. The pitch sits in the low 90s and has touched as high as 97 mph, but its most alluring characteristics show up under the hood. The fastball also showed a double-plus spin rate of 2,540 rpms and similarly elite vertical break. Roby paired the fastball with a high-70s, downer curveball that averaged nearly 2,900 rpms of spin and scored well in plenty of other analytical categories. He finished his mix with an excellent low-80s changeup with nearly 10 mph of separation from his fastball. All told, Roby finished the year with a swinging-strike rate of 17.5%. The Rangers may add a slider or a cutter to Roby's mix in the future, but for now they're very happy with his combination of stuff, strikes and poise.

THE FUTURE: Roby finished the year at instructional league and should move up to High-A Hickory to begin 2022. He's one of the organization's higher upside pitching prospects and could fit in the middle of a rotation.

Year	Age	Club (Level)	Lge	W	L	ERA	G	GS	IP	H	HR	BB	SO	BB/9	SO/9	WHIP	AVG
2021	19	Down East (LoA)	East	2	2	2.45	6	6	22	14	1	7	35	2.9	14.3	0.95	.177
Minor League Totals (2 years)				2	2	2.45	6	6	22	14	1	7	35	2.86	14.32	0.95	.177

15 GLENN OTTO, RHP

BA GRADE
45 Risk: High

Born: March 11, 1996. **B-T:** R-R. **HT:** 6-3. **WT:** 240. **Drafted:** Rice, 2017 (5th round). **Signed by:** Brian Rhees (Yankees).

TRACK RECORD: Otto was the Yankees' fifth-round selection in 2017 and wound his way through the minors until 2021, when he was dealt to the Rangers as part of the deal that sent Joey Gallo and Joely Rodriguez to New York. He saw huge improvements in 2021 and made his big league debut on Aug. 27 and got six starts with Texas.

SCOUTING REPORT: The biggest reason for Otto's success centered around tweaks to his arsenal. Specifically, the Yankees worked with him to add a slider in order to give him weapons to both lefties and righties. The pitch, thrown in the low-to-mid 80s, showed excellent sweepy break and worked as a perfect complement to his downer curveball in the low 80s. Otto rounds out his pitch mix with a high-80s changeup. Before the trade, he also worked to tweak his delivery a little bit in order to improve the timing of his arm stroke. Scouts showed a bit of concern with Otto's inability to command his arsenal to his arm side.

THE FUTURE: Otto will try to win a job in the Rangers' rotation out of spring training. If not, he'll head to Triple-A for more seasoning. He has the ceiling of a No. 4 starter in the big leagues.

Year	Age	Club (Level)	Lge	W	L	ERA	G	GS	IP	H	HR	BB	SO	BB/9	SO/9	WHIP	AVG
2021	25	Somerset (AA)	NEast	6	3	3.17	11	10	65	46	6	14	103	1.9	14.2	0.92	.197
	25	Scranton/W-B (AAA)	East	1	0	4.35	2	2	10	14	0	3	12	2.6	10.5	1.65	.311
	25	Round Rock (AAA)	West	2	1	2.70	4	4	20	13	0	7	19	3.2	8.6	1.00	.188
	25	Texas (MLB)	AL	0	3	9.26	6	6	23	32	2	8	28	3.1	10.8	1.71	.320
Major League Totals (1 year)				0	3	9.26	6	6	23	32	2	8	28	3.09	10.80	1.71	.320
Minor League Totals (5 years)				16	8	3.03	45	36	187	150	8	72	246	3.46	11.82	1.19	.220

16 YEISON MORROBEL, OF

BA GRADE
50 Risk: Extreme

Born: Dec. 8, 2003. **B-T:** L-L. **HT:** 6-2. **WT:** 170. **Signed:** Dominican Republic, 2021. **Signed by:** Willy Espinal.

TRACK RECORD: Morrobel was the jewel of the Rangers' most recent international signing class, which was delayed until Jan. 15 because of the pandemic. He was lauded as an amateur for an athletic frame, a knack for finding the barrel and power that could grow as he matures and gets stronger. He debuted in the Dominican Summer League, where he showed bat-to-ball skills and a knowledge of the strike zone that led to more walks (30) than strikeouts (25).

SCOUTING REPORT: Morrobel's debut season showed the skill set the Rangers coveted. Now it's a matter of letting him develop and add weight and strength to his frame. They also want to tweak his swing a little bit to get the barrel in the zone for a longer period of time. In the long run, they see a player who has an enticing combination of tools, skills and feel for the game in much the same way as fellow Rangers prospect Evan Carter. His average speed could play in center field or be an asset in a corner if his body gets too big to stay up the middle.

THE FUTURE: After a year in the DSL, Morrobel will move stateside in 2022. He'll likely split the year between extended spring training and the Arizona Complex League. His development path is just beginning, but the Rangers like their early returns.

Year	Age	Club (Level)	Lge	AVG	G	AB	R	H	2B	3B	HR	RBI	BB	SO	SB	OBP	SLG
2021	17	Rangers1 (R)	DSL	.270	51	185	33	50	11	6	1	30	30	25	8	.395	.411
Minor League Totals (1 year)				.270	51	185	33	50	11	6	1	30	30	25	8	.395	.411

17 ZAK KENT, RHP

BA GRADE
45 Risk: High

Born: Feb. 24, 1998. **B-T:** R-R. **HT:** 6-3. **WT:** 208. **Drafted:** Virginia Military Institute, 2019 (9th round). **Signed by:** Brian Matthews.

TRACK RECORD: Kent was plucked out of Virginia Military Institute, where he spent three solid seasons. His 132 strikeouts in his junior year were among the most in the country. The Rangers popped him in the ninth round that year and signed him for $140,000. He got his feet wet at the lowest levels of the minor leagues in 2019, then returned to action at 2020 instructional league. His 25 strikeouts were tied with Cody Bradford for the most in Texas' camp.

SCOUTING REPORT: Kent works with a four-pitch mix, but predominantly attacks with a fastball-slider-changeup combination. His heater sits in the low 90s and peaked at 98 this season with High-A and showed excellent spin rates and solid vertical life. He paired the fastball primarily with a similarly high-spin slider in the mid 80s. He leaned on that particularly heavily once he moved to Double-A, where he used the slider roughly 45% of the time. The Rangers added a split-changeup to Kent's repertoire at instructional league in 2020 and saw immediate benefits. The pitch sits in the high 80s and got swings and misses at an above-average clip.

THE FUTURE: Kent will likely return to Double-A in 2022. He ran into some trouble at the level to close 2021 (although a large part of those issues stemmed from two starts at homer-happy Amarillo). He could find a spot toward the back of a rotation.

Year	Age	Club (Level)	Lge	W	L	ERA	G	GS	IP	H	HR	BB	SO	BB/9	SO/9	WHIP	AVG
2021	23	Hickory (HiA)	East	6	2	2.83	14	9	60	46	5	15	78	2.2	11.6	1.01	.206
	23	Frisco (AA)	Cent	0	4	5.34	6	6	28	34	9	9	39	2.8	12.2	1.50	.298
Minor League Totals (3 years)				6	7	3.90	31	22	108	105	16	31	135	2.58	11.22	1.26	.251

18 AVERY WEEMS, LHP

BA GRADE **45** Risk: High

Born: June 6, 1997. **B-T:** R-L. **HT:** 6-2. **WT:** 205. **Drafted:** Arizona, 2019 (6th round). **Signed by:** John Kazanas (White Sox).

TRACK RECORD: Weems was a sixth-round pick of the White Sox out of Arizona in 2019 and spent his first season as a pro with Rookie-level Great Falls. He caught the eye of scouts during instructional league and was eventually used as part of the two-player package that brought starter Lance Lynn to Chicago. He spent 2021 at High-A Hickory, where his 124 strikeouts ranked as the second most in the organization.

SCOUTING REPORT: Weems works with a full four-pitch mix but leans mostly on his fastball and slider. The former sits around 94 mph and has touched up to 98 with excellent horizontal break through the zone. Weems' slider has earned plus grades from scouts and is a high-spin pitch thrown in the high 80s with hints of the lower 90s. He'll mix in a mid-80s changeup and a low-80s curveball, but neither compares to his main two weapons. Internal evaluators are split as to whether he belongs in a rotation or should move to the bullpen, but he'll get a chance to continue down the starter track for the time being.

THE FUTURE: Weems' next stop is Double-A Frisco, where he'll look to sharpen either his curveball or changeup into the third pitch that will give him the best shot to remain a rotation option.

Year	Age	Club (Level)	Lge	W	L	ERA	G	GS	IP	H	HR	BB	SO	BB/9	SO/9	WHIP	AVG
2021	24	Hickory (HiA)	East	4	6	5.06	20	19	85	77	16	27	124	2.9	13.1	1.22	.237
Minor League Totals (3 years)				9	10	3.83	34	33	146	130	17	37	198	2.29	12.23	1.15	.236

19 BAYRON LORA, OF

BA GRADE **50** Risk: Extreme

Born: Sept. 29, 2002. **B-T:** R-R. **HT:** 6-5. **WT:** 240. **Signed:** Dominican Republic, 2019. **Signed by:** Willy Espinal.

TRACK RECORD: Lora was the jewel of the Rangers' 2019 international signing class—which also featured intriguing shortstop prospect Maximo Acosta. He signed for $3.9 million on the strength of some of the best raw power in the class. Lora's pro debut was pushed back because of the pandemic, but he got his feet wet in the Dominican Summer League in 2021 and swatted six home runs.

SCOUTING REPORT: Lora's calling card is his elite raw power—he hit a 500-foot home run in one of his first at-bats in the DSL and posted a maximum exit velocity of 112.5 mph, which was among the best numbers in the Rangers system. Now, it's a matter of getting to it more often. Officials inside the organization would like to see Lora become less passive and make better swing decisions in order to work himself away from a three-true-outcome profile (nearly 65% of his plate appearances ended in a walk, strikeout or home run). Defensively, he's a below-average defender with the plus arm to fit comfortably in right field.

THE FUTURE: After spending his debut in the Dominican, Lora will move stateside in 2022. He has massive upside as a middle-of-the-order bat, but there's a long way to go.

Year	Age	Club (Level)	Lge	AVG	G	AB	R	H	2B	3B	HR	RBI	BB	SO	SB	OBP	SLG
2021	18	Rangers2 (R)	DSL	.218	47	147	34	32	9	0	6	22	48	73	10	.413	.401
Minor League Totals (1 year)				.218	47	147	34	32	9	0	6	22	48	73	10	.413	.401

20 MITCHELL BRATT, LHP

BA GRADE **50** Risk: Extreme

Born: July 3, 2003. **B-T:** L-L. **HT:** 6-1. **WT:** 190. **Drafted:** HS—Statesboro, Ga., 2021 (5th round). **Signed by:** Takeshi Sakurayama.

TRACK RECORD: Bratt was born and raised in Ontario, Canada, but transferred to Georgia Premier Academy during the pandemic in order to be seen by scouts. The move worked. An improvement in his fastball earned Bratt the Rangers' fifth-round pick and the corresponding $850,000, which tied him with the White Sox's Tanner McDougal for the second highest in the round.

He followed his high school season with a stint in the newly formed MLB Draft League, where he whiffed 44 in 28 innings.

SCOUTING REPORT: Bratt works with a three-pitch mix centered around a dynamic fastball-changeup combination. In four appearances in the Arizona Complex League, Bratt showed a low-90s fastball that topped at 94 and combined it primarily with a low-80s changeup thrown with enough arm speed and conviction to get swings and misses. He also throws both a 72-75 mph curveball and a slider with a touch more velo, with the former ahead of the latter in terms of development. His delivery is loose and athletic, giving the Rangers dreams of plenty of upside to come as Bratt gets older and stronger.

THE FUTURE: Bratt is a far-away upside play, but his start in the Arizona Complex League showed hints of good things to come thanks to a combination of strikes and stuff. He could move up to Low-A in 2022.

Year	Age	Club (Level)	Lge	W	L	ERA	G	GS	IP	H	HR	BB	SO	BB/9	SO/9	WHIP	AVG
2021	17	Rangers (R)	ACL	0	0	0.00	4	0	6	4	0	0	13	0.0	19.5	0.67	.174
Minor League Totals (1 year)				0	0	0.00	4	0	6	4	0	0	13	0.00	19.5	0.67	.174

21 MAXIMO ACOSTA, SS

BA GRADE 50 Risk: Extreme

Born: Oct. 29, 2002. **B-T:** R-R. **HT:** 6-1. **WT:** 187. **Signed:** Venezuela, 2019. **Signed by:** Carlos Gonzalez/Jhonny Gomez/Rafic Saab.

TRACK RECORD: Acosta signed with the Rangers for $1.65 million during the 2019 international period, which also netted them powerful outfielder Bayron Lora. His debut season was shelved by the pandemic, but he got on the field during 2020 instructional league. His 2021 season was limited to just 17 games thanks to surgery to alleviate the symptoms of thoracic outlet syndrome.

SCOUTING REPORT: Before the injury, the Rangers were extremely excited about what they'd seen from Acosta. He'd performed extremely well at instructional league in 2020 and carried it over to extended spring training. At his best, Texas expects a player who hits for 50-55 grades in both average and power. Before the surgery, rival scouts saw a player whose body appeared to be nearly maxed out already but had the tools to be a solid everyday shortstop in the big leagues. He's an average runner whose defense plays up because of the way he anticipates, and he has a plus throwing arm.

THE FUTURE: Acosta spent part of his fall and winter at a development camp at the Rangers' spring training complex in Arizona. He should be a full go by next season, when he'll likely start back in extended spring training. His upside is dependent on how he looks post-surgery.

Year	Age	Club (Level)	Lge	AVG	G	AB	R	H	2B	3B	HR	RBI	BB	SO	SB	OBP	SLG
2021	18	Rangers (R)	ACL	.246	17	61	11	15	2	2	1	5	3	15	7	.279	.393
Minor League Totals (1 year)				.246	17	61	11	15	2	2	1	5	3	15	7	.279	.393

22 TREVOR HAUVER, 2B/OF

BA GRADE 45 Risk: High

Born: Nov. 20, 1998. **B-T:** L-R. **HT:** 6-0. **WT:** 205. **Drafted:** Arizona State, 2020 (3rd round). **Signed by:** Troy Afenir (Yankees).

TRACK RECORD: Hauver was the third and final piece of the Yankees draft class in 2020. He was picked out of Arizona State, which saw all four members of its infield get selected despite the draft being just five rounds. Hauver started on fire at Low-A Tampa, where he hit six home runs in the first week of the season. He was part of the package the Yankees used to acquire Joey Gallo and Joely Rodriguez at the trade deadline.

SCOUTING REPORT: Hauver's value is tied near exclusively to his bat. He has a strong knowledge of the strike zone and a swing geared toward loft, leading evaluators to believe he'll post low batting averages but high on-base percentages. That showed up in his pro debut, when he posted a combined .416 OBP between both Class A levels. The Rangers believe he'll blossom into more power as well. He's unlikely to be much more than a below-average defender at either second base or the outfield, with the latter a more likely possibility moving forward because of struggles with throwing accuracy when he played at second or third base. He's a below-average runner.

THE FUTURE: Hauver should move up to Double-A Frisco in 2022, when he'll see if his offense plays at the upper levels. He has the ceiling of a second-division regular in left field.

Year	Age	Club (Level)	Lge	AVG	G	AB	R	H	2B	3B	HR	RBI	BB	SO	SB	OBP	SLG
2021	22	Tampa (LoA)	SEast	.288	66	229	48	66	17	2	9	49	64	78	2	.445	.498
	22	Hickory (HiA)	East	.246	33	122	20	30	4	0	6	21	20	47	0	.357	.426
Minor League Totals (2 years)				.274	99	351	68	96	21	2	15	70	84	125	2	.416	.473

23 CODY BRADFORD, LHP

BA GRADE
45 Risk: High

Born: Feb. 22, 1998. **B-T:** L-L. **HT:** 6-4. **WT:** 197. **Drafted:** Baylor, 2019 (6th round). **Signed by:** Josh Simpson.

TRACK RECORD: Bradford's career at Baylor included a Big 12 Conference pitcher of the year award in 2018, a season when he pitched back-to-back complete game shutouts. In 2019, he had surgery to alleviate the symptoms of thoracic outlet syndrome, which cost him all but three games of his draft year. Nonetheless, the Rangers took him in the sixth round. His 25 strikeouts at instructional league tied him for the top spot in the organization, and he made his official pro debut in 2021.

SCOUTING REPORT: Nothing about Bradford's profile jumps off the page, but his control was tabbed by internal evaluators as the best in the system. His four-seam fastball sits in the low 90s but plays up a touch thanks to its excellent horizontal break. His low-80s changeup is amplified by the extension and deception in his delivery and was his most frequently thrown offspeed pitch. Bradford rounds out his three-pitch mix with a mid-80s slider that grades as fringe-average.

THE FUTURE: Bradford finished 2021 at Double-A Frisco and should begin back there to start 2022. He has the ceiling of a back-end starter but has one of the higher floors among the system's pitching prospects.

Year	Age	Club (Level)	Lge	W	L	ERA	G	GS	IP	H	HR	BB	SO	BB/9	SO/9	WHIP	AVG
2021	23	Hickory (HiA)	East	4	4	4.23	13	13	61	55	9	17	87	2.5	12.7	1.17	.230
	23	Frisco (AA)	Cent	2	0	3.89	7	7	34	41	1	4	41	1.0	10.6	1.30	.293
Minor League Totals (3 years)				6	4	4.11	20	20	96	96	10	21	128	1.96	11.96	1.21	.253

24 COLE RAGANS, LHP

BA GRADE
45 Risk: High

Born: Dec. 12, 1997. **B-T:** L-L. **HT:** 6-4. **WT:** 190.
Drafted: HS—Tallahassee, Fla., 2016 (1st round). **Signed by:** Brett Campbell.

TRACK RECORD: Ragans' season was one of the best stories in the Rangers' system. The 2016 first-rounder missed three seasons of development thanks to the pandemic and two Tommy John surgeries, so simply getting on the mound again was a victory.

SCOUTING REPORT: As ever, Ragans' signature pitch is a nasty changeup in the low 80s with excellent separation from his fastball. The changeup also shows excellent fading action. His fastball sits in the low 90s but peaked at 97 mph and formed a nice tunnel with his changeup. Ragans uses both a curveball and a slider, but neither is a knockout pitch. The slider is the better of the two when he needs a chase and the curveball is best used for early-count strikes. His control waned as the season went on, though some internal sources chalked that up to Ragans understandably tiring down the stretch after three seasons away.

THE FUTURE: Ragans will return to Double-A to begin 2022, when he'll look to build more stamina. He was left off the 40-man roster and therefore was Rule 5 eligible.

Year	Age	Club (Level)	Lge	W	L	ERA	G	GS	IP	H	HR	BB	SO	BB/9	SO/9	WHIP	AVG
2021	23	Hickory (HiA)	East	1	2	3.25	10	10	44	34	4	14	54	2.8	11.0	1.08	.217
	23	Frisco (AA)	Cent	3	1	5.70	9	7	36	39	8	20	33	5.0	8.2	1.62	.275
Minor League Totals (5 years)				7	5	4.08	36	32	146	134	17	75	183	4.63	11.31	1.43	.246

25 CAMERON CAULEY, SS

BA GRADE
50 Risk: Extreme

Born: Feb. 6, 2003. **B-T:** R-R. **HT:** 5-10. **WT:** 170.
Drafted: HS—Mont Belvieu, Texas, 2021 (3rd round). **Signed by:** Josh Simpson.

TRACK RECORD: Cauley is the son of former minor leaguer Chris Cauley, who also is an assistant on Cameron's former team at Barbers Hill High. The Rangers drafted Cauley in the third round and signed him to a bonus of $1 million.

SCOUTING REPORT: As would be expected from a high school wide receiver in Texas, Cauley has athleticism and plus speed. Those traits alone could help him at shortstop but could also facilitate a move to second base or center field if necessary. His average arm strength would also serve him better in the outfield or the right side of the infield. He's a skinnier player whom scouts believe doesn't have a ton of projection remaining, so his offensive profile will depend on his continued ability to make contact and cause havoc on the bases. Scouts saw a player who will have below-average power.

THE FUTURE: Cauley's defensive home will become clearer as he develops, but he has the upside of an everyday player at the top or bottom of a lineup.

Year	Age	Club (Level)	Lge	AVG	G	AB	R	H	2B	3B	HR	RBI	BB	SO	SB	OBP	SLG
2021	18	Rangers (R)	ACL	.255	24	94	20	24	4	4	0	17	8	31	10	.311	.383
Minor League Totals (1 year)				.255	24	94	20	24	4	4	0	17	8	31	10	.311	.383

26 DANE ACKER, RHP

Born: April 1, 1999. **B-T:** R-R. **HT:** 6-2. **WT:** 189. **Drafted:** Oklahoma, 2020 (4th round). **Signed by:** Chris Reilly (Athletics).

BA GRADE

50 Risk: Extreme

TRACK RECORD: Acker was Oakland's fourth-round pick out of Oklahoma in the fourth round of the shortened 2020 draft. Just before the season was shut down by the pandemic, Acker made history by throwing a no-hitter against Louisiana State. He was dealt to the Rangers in February 2021 along with Khris Davis and Jonah Heim as part of the trade that sent Elvis Andrus to Oakland. He made two starts at Low-A Down East, but then was shut down and had Tommy John surgery.

SCOUTING REPORT: At Oklahoma, Acker worked with a heavy low-90s fastball that peaked at 94 mph and a 78-81 mph curveball as his main means of attack. He also showed a fringy slider that sometimes behaved like a cutter as well as a fading changeup that projected to be average. During spring training, the Rangers saw a huge uptick in Acker's stuff. His fastball had jumped into the 95-99 mph range, and his curveball was looking like a potential wipeout pitch. Whether those gains continue will have to wait until he returns from surgery.

THE FUTURE: Once Acker returns from his rehab process, he'll likely be eased back into action. The Rangers were extremely encouraged by what they saw, however, and are excited for his future.

Year	Age	Club (Level)	Lge	W	L	ERA	G	GS	IP	H	HR	BB	SO	BB/9	SO/9	WHIP	AVG
2021	22	Down East (LoA)	East	0	1	2.84	2	2	6	4	0	1	11	1.4	15.6	0.79	.160
Minor League Totals (2 years)				0	1	2.84	2	2	6	4	0	1	11	1.42	15.63	0.79	.160

27 AJ ALEXY, RHP

Born: April 21, 1998. **B-T:** R-R. **HT:** 6-4. **WT:** 195. **Drafted:** HS—Elverson, Pa., 2016 (11th round). **Signed by:** Rich Delucia (Dodgers).

BA GRADE

40 Risk: Medium

TRACK RECORD: Alexy was originally chosen by the Dodgers in the 11th round of the 2016 draft. He was traded to Texas a year later with infielder Brendon Davis in exchange for righthander Yu Darvish. A lat strain limited Alexy to just five games in 2019, and he spent the 2020 season working out in Arizona before getting on the mound at instructional league. He was added to the 40-man roster before the 2021 season and made his big league debut on Aug. 30.

SCOUTING REPORT: The biggest keys to Alexy's success in 2021 were the reshaping and shortening of his arm circle, which led to more consistency in his delivery, and significant weight loss without sacrificing arm strength. Alexy worked primarily with a mid-90s fastball with above-average spin and excellent vertical break. He backed the fastball with his signature high-70s, 12-to-6 curveball as well as a mid-80s changeup. The newest pitch in his arsenal is a slider in the low 80s that showed solid results. He showed improved control in the minors but posted a 1-to-1 strikeout-to-walk ratio in the big leagues.

THE FUTURE: Alexy bounced between starting and relieving in the minors and made four starts in the big leagues. If he is to remain a starter he'll have to significantly improve his control. Otherwise, he fits as a multi-inning reliever.

Year	Age	Club (Level)	Lge	W	L	ERA	G	GS	IP	H	HR	BB	SO	BB/9	SO/9	WHIP	AVG
2021	23	Frisco (AA)	Cent	3	1	1.61	13	7	50	30	4	21	57	3.8	10.2	1.01	.174
	23	Round Rock (AAA)	West	0	0	1.84	3	3	14	9	2	6	19	3.7	11.7	1.02	.176
	23	Texas (MLB)	AL	3	1	4.70	5	4	23	13	4	17	17	6.7	6.7	1.30	.167
Major League Totals (1 year)				3	1	4.70	5	4	23	13	4	17	17	6.65	6.65	1.30	.167
Minor League Totals (6 years)				13	19	3.30	74	62	300	218	20	147	362	4.41	10.85	1.22	.205

28 YOHEL POZO, C

Born: June 14,1997. **B-T:** R-R. **HT:** 6-0. **WT:** 201. **Signed:** Venezuela, 2013. **Signed by:** Jhonny Gomez.

BA GRADE

40 Risk: Medium

TRACK RECORD: Originally signed by the Rangers in 2013, Pozo spent his first six seasons in the minor leagues with Texas before signing with the Padres before the 2020 season, which was ultimately canceled due to the pandemic. The Rangers got Pozo right back when they selected him from San Diego in the minor league phase of the Rule 5 draft. He was one of five minor league Rule 5 picks to make the big leagues in 2021.

SCOUTING REPORT: After not touching the upper levels before this year, Pozo spent the bulk of the year at Triple-A Round Rock, where he hit for average and power. He's an extremely aggressive hitter who feasts on pitches inside and outside the zone and swatted a career-high 23 home runs after hitting just 25 in his six prior seasons. He's earned a reputation as a bad-ball hitter who can use a combination of bat speed and strength to hit pitches anywhere near the plate. Defensively, there's a lot of work to be done. He's worked hard with team catching instructors Bobby Wilson and Brett Hayes, but he's a thicker-bodied player who doesn't move terribly well behind the dish and is more likely a first baseman or DH who dabbles at catcher every now and then.

THE FUTURE: Pozo's role is likely what he did in 2021: A player who can come up and provide a bit of offense every now and then while giving an everyday player a day off. He'll battle in spring training for a spot on the big league roster.

Year	Age	Club (Level)	Lge	AVG	G	AB	R	H	2B	3B	HR	RBI	BB	SO	SB	OBP	SLG
2021	24	Round Rock (AAA)	West	.337	77	315	46	106	17	2	23	74	7	42	0	.352	.622
	24	Texas (MLB)	AL	.284	21	74	8	21	4	0	1	9	3	10	0	.312	.378
Major League Totals (1 year)				.284	21	74	8	21	4	0	1	9	3	10	0	.312	.378
Minor League Totals (8 years)				.288	506	1913	234	550	115	8	48	266	98	184	12	.326	.431

29 RONNY HENRIQUEZ, RHP

BA GRADE
40 Risk: High

Born: June 20, 2000. **B-T:** R-R. **HT:** 5-10. **WT:** 155. **Signed:** Dominican Republic, 2021. **Signed by:** Willy Espinal.

TRACK RECORD: Signed as a 17-year-old in 2017, Henriquez had advanced to Low-A through 2019, then saw action in 2020 at instructional league due to the cancellation of the minor league season in the wake of the pandemic. He made it to Double-A in 2021 but ran into serious trouble keeping the ball in the park. Nonetheless, he was added to the Rangers' 40-man roster after the season.

SCOUTING REPORT: Henriquez's biggest attribute is an electric fastball that sits around 94 mph and has touched up to 97. The pitch plays up thanks to excellent spin rates and horizontal break coupled with a near-elite vertical approach angle. He complements the fastball with a mid-80s slider and a high-80s changeup. Each of his offspeed pitches has its moments, but both need more consistency. The Rangers have confidence that he'll make the necessary improvements because of the innate way he uses his hand to manipulate the baseball. His changeup in particular needs to come along so he has a better chance against lefties.

THE FUTURE: Henriquez will likely head back to Double-A in 2022. If he can improve his slider and changeup, he could fit in the back of the rotation. If only one comes along, he could be a multi-inning reliever.

Year	Age	Club (Level)	Lge	W	L	ERA	G	GS	IP	H	HR	BB	SO	BB/9	SO/9	WHIP	AVG
2021	21	Hickory (HiA)	East	1	3	3.75	5	5	24	13	2	8	27	3.0	10.1	0.88	.153
	21	Frisco (AA)	Cent	4	4	5.04	16	11	69	65	15	17	78	2.2	10.1	1.18	.242
Minor League Totals (4 years)				16	13	3.85	53	46	234	206	25	60	283	2.31	10.90	1.14	.233

30 DANYER CUEVA, SS

BA GRADE
45 Risk: Extreme

Born: May 27, 2004. **B-T:** L-R. **HT:** 6-1. **WT:** 160. **Signed:** Venezuela, 2021. **Signed by:** Jhonny Gomez/Rafic Saab.

TRACK RECORD: Along with outfielder Yeison Morrobel, Cueva was one of the potentially higher-end signings in the Rangers' most recent international class, which was delayed by the pandemic until Jan. 15. He spent the summer in the Dominican Summer League, where he showed hints of his potential. He's the latest in a line of shortstops the Rangers have signed from the international market, including Luisangel Acuña and Maximo Acosta.

SCOUTING REPORT: As an amateur, Cueva showed the signs of being an offensive-minded middle infielder. He's got a smooth, balanced stroke from the left side and the hand-eye coordination to shoot line drives from gap to gap. He worked hard before signing to increase his speed—he is now an above-average runner—in order to increase his chances to stick at shortstop. The Rangers see a potentially powerful player as he gets stronger and fills out his body, especially considering he was one of the younger players in the signing class. Right now, Texas believes Cueva can stick at shortstop but understands his development is just beginning.

THE FUTURE: After a first test of pro ball in the DSL, Cueva will likely move stateside to extended spring training and the Arizona Complex League in 2022. He's got the upside of an everyday, offensive-minded middle infielder.

Year	Age	Club (Level)	Lge	AVG	G	AB	R	H	2B	3B	HR	RBI	BB	SO	SB	OBP	SLG
2021	17	Rangers1 (R)	DSL	.282	49	202	48	57	11	3	1	25	22	48	9	.375	.381
Minor League Totals (1 year)				.282	49	202	48	57	11	3	1	25	22	48	9	.375	.381

MORE PROSPECTS TO KNOW

31 DANIEL MATEO, OF

SLEEPER

Mateo has the tools to be an exceptional defender in center field. He added about 25 pounds of muscle and has begun to tap into raw power. He's got bat-to-ball skills but needs to refine his approach in order to get the most out of his tools.

32 DAVIS WENDZEL, 3B

The Rangers' 2019 supplemental first-rounder has had bad luck with injuries—a hamate injury cost him time in 2021—and has yet to show the power needed to profile at third base.

33 BUBBA THOMPSON, OF

The former first-rounder is still as toolsy as ever and equipped to play center field, but he needs to make more contact to maximize his gifts. He hit 23 doubles and stole 25 bases in 2021 but also produced a strikeout-to-walk ratio of nearly 4-to-1.

34 STEELE WALKER, OF

Walker's profile is that of a classic tweener. He makes plenty of contact but needs to be more selective to maximize that skill. He fits in a corner outfield defensively but might not have the power to profile there.

35 EMILIANO TEODO, RHP

He's a long way away, but Teodo's stuff is some of the filthiest in the organization. The 20-year-old's fastball averaged 98 mph and touched 102 with excellent spin rates. He paired it with a mid-80s curveball that averaged nearly 3,000 rpms of spin.

36 ORCELI GOMEZ, RHP

Gomez pitched just 9.1 innings outside of the complex league, but his fastball sits in the mid 90s and touched 99 mph. He backs it up with a potentially plus changeup and a developing slider and could fit nicely as a reliever if his gains remain.

37 KEVIN GOWDY, RHP

A trade acquisition from the Phillies, Gowdy made some tweaks to his delivery and saw jumps in his stuff. His mid-90s fastball and powerful slider give him a chance to fit in a bullpen.

38 JOSH STOWERS, OF

The twice-traded outfielder might be a few tweaks from a breakout. He hit 20 homers and stole 21 bases in 2021 but still needs to work on his in-zone swing-and-miss rates.

39 DAVID GARCIA, C

Garcia shows hints of his tools on both sides of the ball but has yet to put it together on a consistent basis. He re-signed with the Rangers after electing minor league free agency and could wind up starting back at High-A in 2022.

40 ABIMELEC ORTIZ, OF

The Puerto Rican outfielder might have to move to first base as he develops, but he has big-time power from the left side that should make him intriguing as he develops.

TOP PROSPECTS OF THE DECADE

Year	Player, Pos	2021 Org
2012	Jurickson Profar, SS	Padres
2013	Jurickson Profar, SS/2B	Padres
2014	Rougned Odor, 2B	Yankees
2015	Joey Gallo, 3B	Yankees
2016	Joey Gallo, 3B	Yankees
2017	Leody Taveras ,OF	Rangers
2018	Willie Calhoun, OF	Rangers
2019	Hans Crouse, RHP	Phillies
2020	Josh Jung, 3B	Rangers
2021	Josh Jung, 3B	Rangers

TOP DRAFT PICKS OF THE DECADE

Year	Player, Pos	2021 Org
2012	Lewis Brinson, OF	Marlins
2013	Chi Chi Gonzalez, RHP	Rockies
2014	Luis Ortiz, RHP	Rangers
2015	Dillon Tate, RHP	Orioles
2016	Cole Ragans, LHP	Rangers
2017	Bubba Thompson, OF	Rangers
2018	Cole Winn, RHP	Rangers
2019	Josh Jung, 3B	Rangers
2020	Justin Foscue, 2B	Rangers
2021	Jack Leiter, RHP	Rangers

Toronto Blue Jays

BY BEN BADLER

Vladimir Guerrero Jr. was an MVP finalist in 2021 and is a cornerstone of Toronto's future.

The plan is coming together in Toronto. Vladimir Guerrero Jr. had his breakout season to finish second in the American League MVP vote. Bo Bichette continued to show he's already one of the game's best shortstops at 23. A lineup built around players in their 20s ranked third in the majors in runs scored as the Blue Jays ended the 2021 regular season on a tear, going 22-9 in their final games to finish with 91 wins.

But in the AL East? That was only good enough for fourth place and no postseason appearance. Going forward, the Blue Jays look like one of the game's most dangerous teams, a club that should be consistently in the playoff hunt over the next half decade.

Their farm system, which was No. 4 in last year's Prospect Handbook even after the graduations of Guerrero, Bichette and Lourdes Gurriel Jr., is now more solid than elite, but for all the right reasons. Righthander Alek Manoah graduated to the big leagues and provided a huge boost for a team that needed pitching help, with the makings of a frontline starter. Catcher Alejandro Kirk and infielder Santiago Espinal also graduated, while the Blue Jays used other top prospects—infielder/outfielder Austin Martin and righthander Simeon Woods Richardson—in a trade with the Twins to get righthander Jose Berrios.

Even after those trades and graduations, there are a handful of players at the top of the system with impact potential. Toronto's top prospect now is Gabriel Moreno, a catcher the Blue Jays signed out of Venezuela for $25,000 in 2016. While a broken thumb limited Moreno's playing time in 2021, when healthy he drew effusive praise from scouts for his work at the plate and on defense. He's now one of the game's premier catching prospects. Kirk is a talented hitter, but Moreno appears poised to soon take over as Toronto's catcher of the future.

The Blue Jays' farm system is heavy on infielders and light on outfielders, with shortstop Orelvis Martinez leading the way. His future is likely at third base, with the offensive upside to develop into a plus regular at the position and a chance for 30-home run power if he can keep his strikeouts in check as he moves up the developmental ladder in the coming years.

Righthander Nate Pearson is one of the biggest wild cards among the organization's young players. He's a talented but frustrating player, someone who could end up being a force in their rotation but who has to show better command and more durability.

Lower down the system, shortstop Manuel

PROJECTED 2025 LINEUP

Catcher	Gabriel Moreno	25
First Base	Vladimir Guerrero Jr.	26
Second Base	Santiago Espinal	30
Third Base	Orelvis Martinez	23
Shortstop	Bo Bichette	27
Left Field	Lourdes Gurriel Jr.	31
Center Field	George Springer	35
Right Field	Teoscar Hernandez	32
Designated Hitter	Alejandro Kirk	26
No. 1 Starter	Alek Manoah	27
No. 2 Starter	Jose Berrios	31
No. 3 Starter	Kevin Gausman	34
No. 4 Starter	Nate Pearson	28
No. 5 Starter	Gunnar Hoglund	25
Closer	Jordan Romano	32

Beltre and lefthander Ricky Tiedemann are both breakout candidates who signed in 2021. Beltre, signed from the Dominican Republic, was one of the most polished hitters in his international class with a short, simple swing and good strike-zone judgment. Tiedemann, a third-round pick from Golden West (Calif.) JC, was touching 94 mph before the draft but reached 98 mph after the season at instructional league.

Toronto's international program also remains a strength for the organization. Guerrero, Gurriel and Kirk were all Blue Jays international signings, as are 14 of their top 30 prospects, including their two best position prospects in Moreno and Martinez. ■

DEPTH CHART

TORONTO BLUE JAYS

TOP 2022 ROOKIES	RANK
Gabriel Moreno, C	1
Otto Lopez, 2B/OF/SS	6
Kevin Smith, SS/3B	7

BREAKOUT PROSPECTS	RANK
Estiven Machado, SS	12
Dahian Santos, RHP	22
Yhoangel Aponte, OF	23

SOURCE OF TOP 30 TALENT

Homegrown	28	Acquired	2
College	8	Trade	2
Junior college	2	Rule 5 draft	0
High school	4	Independent league	0
Nondrafted free agent	0	Free agent/waivers	0
International	14		

LF
Gabriel Martinez
J.C. Masson

CF
Yhoangel Aponte (23)
Josh Palacios (30)
Dasan Brown
Chavez Young

RF
Yeuni Muñoz
Will Robertson

3B
Jordan Groshans (4)

SS
Orelvis Martinez (3)
Kevin Smith (7)
Manuel Beltre (8)
Leonardo Jimenez (10)
Estiven Machado (12)
Rikelbin de Castro (28)
Luis Garcia (29)
Addison Barger

2B
Otto Lopez (6)
Samad Taylor (11)
Tanner Morris (19)
Miguel Hiraldo (21)

1B
Spencer Horwitz (15)

C
Gabriel Moreno (1)
Victor Mesia
Phil Clarke

LHP

LHSP	LHRP
Ricky Tiedemann (9)	Adrian Hernandez
Zach Logue (24)	
Kendry Rojas (26)	

RHP

RHSP	RHRP
Nate Pearson (2)	Hagen Danner (27)
Gunnar Hoglund (5)	Graham Spraker
Sem Robberse (13)	
Irv Carter (14)	
C.J. Van Eyk (16)	
Adam Kloffenstein (17)	
Thomas Hatch (18)	
Chad Dallas (21)	
Dahian Santos (22)	
Eric Pardinho (25)	
Bowden Francis	
Fitz Stadler	
Trent Palmer	
Joey Murray	
Yosver Zulueta	

1 GABRIEL MORENO, C

Born: Feb. 14, 2000. **B-T:** R-R. **HT:** 5-11. **WT:** 175.
Signed: Venezuela, 2016.
Signed by: Francisco Plasencia.

TRACK RECORD: Moreno had good hand-eye coordination as an amateur, but he was a lower-profile signing out of Venezuela as a 16-year-old in 2016 for $25,000. He made his debut in 2017 in the Dominican Summer League, where he struck out just five times in 135 plate appearances but also had just five extra-base hits. Moreno's stock rose the following year in the Rookie-level Gulf Coast League, and swing changes helped him tap into more power in 2019 at Low-A Lansing to become one of the game's better catching prospects in the lower levels. In 2021, everything clicked for Moreno. He drew glowing reviews for his well-rounded mix of hitting ability, power, athleticism and defense while crushing Double-A pitching until he missed all of July and August with a broken right thumb that required surgery. He returned in September and finished the season with a strong showing in the Arizona Fall League.

SCOUTING REPORT: Moreno has an elite combination of hitting actions, bat speed, contact skills and quickness in the batter's box. He had just a 15% strikeout rate in 2021 and has been difficult to strike out throughout his career. Moreno's quick, efficient swing and bat-to-ball ability helps him turn around premium velocity on the inner third and counter pitchers who attack at the top of the zone, with a special knack for barreling those pitches. Moreno's swing evolved in the past to incorporate more dynamic, athletic movements, which helped him tap into more power. The last two years, Moreno has maintained that swing while getting significantly stronger, with his maximum exit velocities jumping from the low 100s to 108 mph. The result has been a more complete hitter who makes frequent contact, uses the whole field and has at least average power that he gets to in games. Moreno has always been an aggressive hitter. He chased or swung at borderline pitches too often early in his career, but he has steadily become more selective and posted a 9% walk rate in 2021. Moreno's defense has made significant progress over the years, as well. His lively athleticism helps him move well behind the plate and his arm has improved to a plus tool. That arm strength, along with a quick release, helps him record sub-1.9 second pop times to second base. He also has improved his blocking and receiving, with no passed balls allowed in 29 games behind

BA GRADE	SCOUTING GRADES
65 Risk: Medium	Hit: 70. Power: 50. Run: 40. Field: 55. Arm: 60.

Projected future grades on 20-80 scouting scale

BEST TOOLS

Best Hitter for Average	Gabriel Moreno
Best Power Hitter	Orelvis Martinez
Best Strike-Zone Discipline	Spencer Horwitz
Fastest Baserunner	Dasan Brown
Best Athlete	Dasan Brown
Best Fastball	Nate Pearson
Best Curveball	Sem Robberse
Best Slider	Nate Pearson
Best Changeup	Ricky Tiedemann
Best Control	Eric Pardinho
Best Defensive Catcher	Gabriel Moreno
Best Defensive Infielder	Rikelvin de Castro
Best Infield Arm	Jordan Groshans
Best Defensive Outfielder	Dasan Brown
Best Outfield Arm	Chavez Young

the plate in 2021. Moreno has caught just 139 regular season games, with little of that time coming at the upper levels, so he's still learning the finer points of game-calling.

THE FUTURE: Moreno has a chance to be a perennial all-star as a plus to plus-plus hitter with 20-25 home runs and above-average defense at a premium position. He should be ready to contribute to the Blue Jays at some point in 2022 and eventually become an impact player in their lineup, which continues to stack young, talented players both in the field and the pitching staff. ■

Year	Age	Club (Level)	Lge	AVG	G	AB	R	H	2B	3B	HR	RBI	BB	SO	SB	OBP	SLG
2021	21	Blue Jays (R)	FCL	.750	2	4	1	3	1	0	0	0	0	1	0	.750	1.000
	21	New Hampshire (AA)	NEast	.373	32	126	29	47	9	1	8	45	14	22	1	.441	.651
	21	Buffalo (AAA)	East	.111	3	9	0	1	0	0	0	0	0	2	0	.200	.111
Minor League Totals (5 years)				.308	191	724	110	223	48	9	24	150	49	88	15	.358	.499

2 NATE PEARSON, RHP

Born: Aug. 20, 1996. **B-T:** R-R. **HT:** 6-6. **WT:** 250. **Drafted:** JC of Central Florida, 2017 (1st round). **Signed by:** Matt Bishoff.

TRACK RECORD: Mostly a reliever at Florida International, Pearson became a starter when he transferred to the JC of Central Florida in 2017 and performed well enough to become a first-round pick. Since then, Pearson has teased the Blue Jays with tantalizing upside but also health and command problems. After groin injuries hampered him in spring training in 2021, he struggled with his mechanics through a May 9 start in which he walked five in 2.1 innings. He returned to Triple-A and missed time with a sports hernia, but he came back to the majors in September and pitched exclusively out of the bullpen, striking out 20 and walking seven in 12.2 innings.

BA GRADE
55 Risk: Medium

SCOUTING REPORT: Pearson possesses explosive stuff with a fastball that sits 96-100 mph and touches 102. He complements his fastball with a hard slider in the mid-to-upper 80s that is a plus pitch at times. Pearson has a curveball and changeup that can both be average pitches, but he rarely threw them as a reliever in the majors. Pearson has yet to break through partly because of health but also because he has trouble repeating his delivery, which leads to poor command. The result has been too many walks and hitters geared up for Pearson's fastball because he's too often behind in the count.

THE FUTURE: Pearson has never pitched more than 101.1 innings in a season, so durability concerns remain about whether he can handle a starter's workload. He has the stuff to develop into a high-end starter if he can sync up his mechanics, but the Blue Jays may opt to develop him into a high-leverage reliever.

SCOUTING GRADES:	Fastball: 65	Slider: 60	Curveball: 50	Changeup: 50	Control: 45

Year	Age	Club (Level)	Lge	W	L	ERA	G	GS	IP	H	HR	BB	SO	BB/9	SO/9	WHIP	AVG
2021	24	Buffalo (AAA)	East	1	3	4.40	12	6	30	21	4	13	44	3.8	12.9	1.11	.189
	24	Toronto (MLB)	AL	1	1	4.20	12	1	15	14	2	12	20	7.2	12.0	1.73	.237
Major League Totals (2 years)				2	1	5.18	17	5	33	28	7	25	36	6.82	9.82	1.61	.222
Minor League Totals (4 years)				6	8	2.63	46	40	154	96	13	45	190	2.63	11.10	0.92	.176

3 ORELVIS MARTINEZ, SS/3B

Born: Nov. 19, 2001. **B-T:** R-R. **HT:** 6-1. **WT:** 190. **Signed:** Dominican Republic, 2018. **Signed by:** Alexis de la Cruz/Sandy Rosario.

TRACK RECORD: Martinez signed for $3.51 million in 2018 and starred in his pro debut the following season, ranking as the No. 1 prospect in the Rookie-level Gulf Coast League in 2019. He made his full-season debut in 2021 and led the Low-A Southeast with 19 home runs, a .572 slugging percentage and a .942 OPS despite receiving a promotion to High-A Vancouver for the final month. His highlight of the season came during a memorable stretch in mid July when he hit 10 home runs in 10 games.

BA GRADE
55 Risk: High

SCOUTING REPORT: Martinez has the strong frame, high-end bat speed and plus raw power to be an offensive force. He's an athletic mover in the batter's box who maximizes his whole body to generate a whippy, explosive swing. Martinez has the power to hit the ball out to all fields, but his approach is geared more to pull the ball. His strikeout rate jumped to 25% in 2021 with that pull-heavy approach and increased chase tendencies, especially early in the season against breaking stuff. Martinez became a more selective hitter as the season progressed, but those chase habits reappeared after his promotion and will limit him to an average hitter. Some Blue Jays officials believe Martinez can stick at shortstop, but few others agree. His hands are fine and he has plus arm strength, but he's a below-average runner with heavy feet and will likely continue to lose range as he gets bigger. Third base is his most likely destination.

THE FUTURE: Martinez has the potential to be an all-star if he can make strides with his plate discipline. He'll likely return to High-A to start 2022.

SCOUTING GRADES:	Hitting: 50	Power: 60	Running: 40	Fielding: 45	Arm: 60

Year	Age	Club (Level)	Lge	AVG	G	AB	R	H	2B	3B	HR	RBI	BB	SO	SB	OBP	SLG
2021	19	Dunedin (LoA)	SEast	.279	71	283	49	79	22	2	19	68	33	85	4	.369	.572
	19	Vancouver (HiA)	West	.214	27	112	17	24	4	0	9	19	10	28	0	.282	.491
Minor League Totals (3 years)				.264	138	537	86	142	34	7	35	119	57	142	6	.347	.549

4 JORDAN GROSHANS, SS/3B

Born: July 20, 1998. **B-T:** R-R. **HT:** 6-3. **WT:** 205. **Drafted:** HS—Magnolia, Texas, 2018 (1st round). **Signed by:** Brian Johnston.

TRACK RECORD: A surprise selection with the 12th overall pick in the 2018 draft, Groshans dominated the Low-A Midwest League in his pro debut before a left foot injury ended his season after 23 games. He spent 2020 at the Blue Jays' alternate training site and led the team in home runs, but injuries again limited him in 2021. Groshans played just 75 games at Double-A New Hampshire in between back soreness in May and finishing the year on the injured list. He made a lot of contact when healthy, though without the extra-base impact he showed earlier in his career.

SCOUTING REPORT: Groshans stands out for his feel for hitting. He squares up good fastballs, adjusts to offspeed pitches, has good strike-zone judgement and has an advanced approach that allows him to use the whole field.

BA GRADE	
55	Risk: High

He tightened his swing by condensing some of the bigger movements he had previously, helping him stay more under control. Groshans projects to end up at third base, so he'll need to rediscover his previous power. Optimists believe could hit 20-plus home runs, while others are skeptical his bat speed and approach will ever result in big power numbers. Groshans has plus arm strength and improved defensively in New Hampshire, showing the quickness and range to be an average defender at the hot corner. He has to show he can stay healthy after never making it through a full season.

THE FUTURE: Groshans has the potential to be average or better regular at third base if he can find the right balance of contact and power. He will start 2022 at Triple-A Buffalo and has a chance to reach the majors during the year, provided he stays healthy.

SCOUTING GRADES:	Hitting: 55	Power: 50	Running: 40	Fielding: 45	Arm: 60

Year	Age	Club (Level)	Lge	AVG	G	AB	R	H	2B	3B	HR	RBI	BB	SO	SB	OBP	SLG
2021	21	New Hampshire (AA)	NEast	.291	75	278	46	81	23	0	7	40	34	61	0	.367	.450
Minor League Totals (4 years)				.300	146	547	79	164	42	0	14	96	62	119	1	.372	.453

5 GUNNAR HOGLUND, RHP

EDDIE KELLY/PROLOOK PHOTOS

Born: Dec. 17, 1999. **B-T:** L-R. **HT:** 6-4. **WT:** 220. **Drafted:** Mississippi, 2021 (1st round). **Signed by:** Don Norris.

TRACK RECORD: The Pirates drafted Hoglund out of high school as a supplemental first-round pick in 2018, but the two sides failed to come to an agreement and Hoglund went to Mississippi instead. The decision paid off for Hoglund, who blossomed into one of the top pitchers in the Southeastern Conference and looked like a potential top-10 pick in 2021 before Tommy John surgery ended his season in May. Even with the injury, the Blue Jays drafted Hoglund with the 19th overall pick and signed him for $3,247,500.

SCOUTING REPORT: While elbow surgery adds risk, Hoglund is a high prob-ability bet to remain a starter because of his easy, repeatable delivery, relatively polished strike-throwing and quality three-pitch mix. Hoglund consistently

BA GRADE	
55	Risk: Extreme

pounds the zone and gets ahead of hitters and commands his fastball well to both sides of the plate. His fastball velocity trended up over his time at Ole Miss, sitting at 91-94 mph and touching 96 at its peak. The sharpness of his slider improved to develop into a tick above-average pitch at 80-84 mph, and his slightly above-average changeup keeps lefties off-balance. Hoglund's mix of stuff and ability to locate helped him pile up a 39% strikeout rate in the SEC before he got hurt, and he projects to miss plenty of bats moving forward.

THE FUTURE: Hoglund's rehab means he won't make his pro debut until midway through the 2022 season. If he can stay healthy, he has a chance to be a mid-rotation starter.

SCOUTING GRADES:	Fastball: 70	Slider: 55	Changeup: 55	Control: 70

Year	Age	Club (Level)	Lge	W	L	ERA	G	GS	IP	H	HR	BB	SO	BB/9	SO/9	WHIP	AVG
2021	21	Did not play—Injured															

6 OTTO LOPEZ, 2B/OF/SS

Born: Oct. 1, 1998. **B-T:** R-R. **HT:** 5-10. **WT:** 160. **Signed:** Dominican Republic, 2016. **Signed by:** Sandy Rosario/Lorenzo Perez/Alexis de la Cruz.

TRACK RECORD: Lopez signed out of the Dominican Republic for $60,000 in 2016 and gained attention when he won the Low-A Midwest League batting title in 2019. He wasn't invited to the Blue Jays' alternate training site in 2020, but he performed well enough in instructional league to be added to the 40-man roster after the season. Lopez gained more believers in 2021 when he kept hitting and won another batting title with Double-A New Hampshire. He continued to perform well after a promotion to Triple-A and got one at-bat in the majors when he made his big league debut on Aug. 17.

BA GRADE
50 Risk: High

SCOUTING REPORT: Lopez has long faced skepticism because he is susceptible to stepping in the bucket and pulling off the ball when he swings. His bat control, however, is so strong he projects to be an above-average hitter even with those flaws. Lopez has a penchant for squaring up high-velocity fastballs up in the strike zone, rarely strikes out and takes his walks to post high batting averages and on-base percentages. He has below-average power and a bat path that leads to a lot of balls on the ground, so he doesn't project to ever be much of a home run threat. Lopez is a good athlete who is a plus runner with an average arm. He mostly plays second base and has seen time at shortstop and center field as well, though he's stretched at shortstop.

THE FUTURE: Lopez projects to be in the lineup every day at different positions as a bat-driven utility player. If he adds a bit more power, he could solidify his place as an everyday regular.

SCOUTING GRADES:	Hitting: 55	Power: 40	Running: 60	Fielding: 45	Arm: 50

Year	Age	Club (Level)	Lge	AVG	G	AB	R	H	2B	3B	HR	RBI	BB	SO	SB	OBP	SLG
2021	22	New Hampshire (AA)	NEast	.331	70	278	52	92	24	1	3	39	28	62	7	.398	.457
	22	Buffalo (AAA)	East	.289	43	173	36	50	8	3	2	25	13	26	15	.347	.405
	22	Toronto (MLB)	AL	.000	1	1	0	0	0	0	0	0	0	1	0	.000	.000
Major League Totals (1 year)				.000	1	1	0	0	0	0	0	0	0	1	0	.000	.000
Minor League Totals (5 years)				.312	330	1284	218	400	70	18	14	157	120	200	63	.375	.427

7 KEVIN SMITH, SS/3B

Born: July 4, 1996. **B-T:** R-R. **HT:** 5-11. **WT:** 190. **Drafted:** Maryland, 2017 (4th round). **Signed by:** Doug Witt.

TRACK RECORD: Smith spent his first full season in pro ball posting better numbers than he ever did in college at Maryland. He cratered the following season in 2019 and struck out too much at the alternate training site in 2020 as he battled his swing mechanics. But Smith made a huge turnaround at Triple-A Buffalo in 2021, finishing eighth in on-base percentage and fourth in slugging percentage in Triple-A East. He received his first big league callup in August and appeared in 18 games for the Blue Jays.

BA GRADE
45 Risk: Medium

SCOUTING REPORT: A student of the game, Smith unsuccessfully tinkered with his swing throughout his struggles but finally found a swing and setup that worked for him in 2021. He moved his hands higher to get his barrel more vertical in his setup, which helped him stop dipping his back shoulder and dropping his barrel underneath pitches, which previously led to pitchers beating him with elevated fastballs. The result was a quicker, more efficient swing which, along with a more selective approach, led to more quality at-bats. With his swing adjustments, Smith now projects to be a fringe-average hitter with solid-average raw power and could hit 20-plus home runs over a full season. Smith is an average runner and can handle shortstop, but he has also played third base and can handle second base as well. He projects to be at least an average defender at each spot with above-average arm strength.

THE FUTURE: Smith has been enigmatic, but if his swing and approach adjustments carry over, his power and defensive skill set could allow him to stick around as a utility player.

SCOUTING GRADES:	Hitting: 45	Power: 50	Running: 50	Fielding: 50	Arm: 55

Year	Age	Club (Level)	Lge	AVG	G	AB	R	H	2B	3B	HR	RBI	BB	SO	SB	OBP	SLG
2021	24	Buffalo (AAA)	East	.285	94	355	65	101	27	4	21	69	46	97	18	.370	.561
	24	Toronto (MLB)	AL	.094	18	32	2	3	0	0	1	1	3	11	0	.194	.188
Major League Totals (1 year)				.094	18	32	2	3	0	0	1	1	3	11	0	.194	.188
Minor League Totals (5 years)				.268	400	1570	250	420	105	13	73	266	131	439	67	.328	.490

8 MANUEL BELTRE, SS

Born: June 9, 2004. **B-T:** R-R. **HT:** 5-11. **WT:** 165. **Signed:** Dominican Republic, 2021. **Signed by:** Sandy Rosario/Lorenzo Perez.

TRACK RECORD: Beltre was one of the top international prospects in his class when the Blue Jays signed him for $2.35 million out of the Dominican Republic on Jan. 15, 2021. He spent his pro debut after signing in the Dominican Summer League, where he showed advanced plate discipline and contact skills despite batting just .225.

SCOUTING REPORT: Beltre is a polished player for his age with a high baseball IQ. He manages at-bats with a sharp eye for the strike zone and good bat control, helping him walk more often than he strikes out. Bad luck on balls in play with a lot of hard outs hampered Beltre's overall numbers in his debut. He has started to crack 100 mph on some of his exit velocities, but getting stronger will still be critical for Beltre, who likely will always have a hit-over-power offensive profile. Beltre stood out more for his hitting ability and instincts than his raw tools or athleticism as an amateur, but he significantly increased his chances of sticking at shortstop in his pro debut. He's not the quick-twitch, acrobatic shortstop some teams prefer, but he's a fundamentally sound defender with a quick first step, secure hands and good footwork. He's an average runner and an accurate, efficient thrower, though his arm strength might never be more than average.

THE FUTURE: Beltre has a chance to develop into a steady middle infielder who gets on base at a high clip. He is likely to make his U.S. debut in the Florida Complex League in 2022.

BA GRADE
50 Risk: Extreme

SCOUTING GRADES:	Hitting: 55	Power: 45	Running: 50	Fielding: 50	Arm: 50

Year	Age	Club (Level)	Lge	AVG	G	AB	R	H	2B	3B	HR	RBI	BB	SO	SB	OBP	SLG
2021	17	Blue Jays (R)	DSL	.225	53	182	39	41	10	3	2	29	42	33	10	.391	.346
Minor League Totals (1 year)				.225	53	182	39	41	10	3	2	29	42	33	10	.391	.346

9 RICKY TIEDEMANN, LHP

Born: Aug. 18, 2002. **B-T:** L-L. **HT:** 6-4. **WT:** 220. **Drafted:** Golden West (Calif.) JC, 2021 (3rd round). **Signed by:** Joey Aversa.

TRACK RECORD: Tiedemann emerged as one of the biggest popup prospects in the 2020 draft class at Lakewood (Calif.) High before the coronavirus pandemic canceled the season. Teams weren't willing to meet his bonus demands in the shortened five-round draft, but he made himself eligible for the 2021 draft when he enrolled at Golden West (Calif.) JC instead of sticking with his commitment to San Diego State. The Blue Jays drafted Tiedemann in the third round and signed him for $644,800, then realized they might have gotten a steal when his velocity spiked after he signed.

SCOUTING REPORT: Tiedemann is a good athlete with broad shoulders on a strong, well-proportioned frame. Only 18 on draft day, Tiedemann's youth and physicality led many evaluators to project a velocity increase at some point in his career, but it happened quicker than expected. Tiedemann pitched at 88-93 mph and topped out at 94 in college, but his velocity hit another gear when he reported to the Blue Jays, ranging from 94-98 mph in short bursts. He will probably park below that as a starter, but the jump in his high-end velocity changes his future outlook. Tiedemann flashes a plus changeup he has the confidence to use against both lefties and righties and a hard slider that could develop into an average pitch. His low, three-quarters arm slot wanders at times and has led to inconsistent control and performance, but he dominates when he's on.

THE FUTURE: Tiedemann's velocity increase has made him an even more intriguing starting pitching prospect than he was on draft day. His physical appearance and pitch mix have long earned comparisons to Sean Manaea, and he has similar mid-to-back of the rotation potential.

BA GRADE
50 Risk: Extreme

BILL MITCHELL

SCOUTING GRADES:	Fastball: 60	Slider: 50	Changeup: 60	Control: 50

Year	Age	Club (Level)	Lge	W	L	ERA	G	GS	IP	H	HR	BB	SO	BB/9	SO/9	WHIP	AVG
2021	18	Did Not Play															

10 LEONARDO JIMENEZ, SS/2B

Born: May 17, 2001. **B-T:** R-R. **HT:** 6-0. **WT:** 195. **Signed:** Panama, 2017.
Signed by: Alex Zapata/Sandy Rosario.

TRACK RECORD: Jimenez was Panama's best prospect in the 2017 international class when he signed with the Blue Jays for $825,000. He moved slowly through the system and played his first full season in 2021 at Low-A Dunedin, where he posted a .517 on-base percentage but was limited to 54 games by a dislocated shoulder. The Blue Jays sent Jimenez to the Arizona Fall League to get extra reps after the season, and he posted a .412 on-base percentage.

SCOUTING REPORT: Jimenez has an unusual offensive skill set. He rarely chases pitches and had more walks (54) than strikeouts (36) in 2021, but he also rarely impacts the ball when he swings. Jimenez has added muscle since he signed and puts on impressive batting practice displays, but he's hit only one home run in 154 career games and his game power is minimal. Jimenez's approach is aimed at simply putting the ball in play rather than trying to drive it, even when he's ahead in the count. Some evaluators think Jimenez could access more power with an approach adjustment, but an average hitter with well below-average power may just be who he is. Jimenez is an instinctive, fluid defender in the middle infield. He doesn't have the explosive athleticism some teams prefer at shortstop, but he's steady and reliable with soft hands, loose actions, good body control and a knack for slowing the game down. He's a slightly below-average runner and has average arm strength.

THE FUTURE: Jimenez's on-base skills and defensive ability give him a path to the majors as a utilityman. He'll need to add more power to become an everyday regular.

BA GRADE
45 Risk: High

SCOUTING GRADES:	Hitting: 50	Power: 30	Running: 45	Fielding: 50	Arm: 50

Year	Age	Club (Level)	Lge	AVG	G	AB	R	H	2B	3B	HR	RBI	BB	SO	SB	OBP	SLG
2021	20	Blue Jays (R)	FCL	.385	5	13	6	5	2	0	0	2	3	1	1	.600	.538
	20	Dunedin (LoA)	SEast	.315	54	168	35	53	8	0	1	19	51	35	4	.517	.381
Minor League Totals (4 years)				.292	154	534	88	156	31	4	1	62	91	97	7	.423	.371

11 SAMAD TAYLOR, 2B/OF

BA GRADE
45 Risk: High

Born: July 11, 1998. **B-T:** R-R. **HT:** 5-10. **WT:** 170. **Drafted:** HS—Corona, Calif., 2016 (10th round). **Signed by:** Mike Bradford (Cleveland).

TRACK RECORD: Taylor joined the Blue Jays at the 2017 trade deadline in the deal that sent righthander Joe Smith to Cleveland. Taylor is a springy athlete who had a hard time controlling himself at the plate in 2018 and 2019, but he had a breakthrough in 2021 with Double-A New Hampshire. Despite those steps forward, the Blue Jays left Taylor off their 40-man roster after the season.

SCOUTING REPORT: Taylor is a quick-twitch athlete with plus-plus speed. His explosiveness shows up in his excellent bat speed, but for most of his career Taylor struggled with his timing, often getting jammed. He adjusted his setup, keeping his barrel on his back lat before picking it up and swinging from there, a change that helped him maintain his posture as he moved forward to create a simpler, more repeatable swing. His bat path still doesn't keep his barrel in the zone for long, so he struck out 29% of the time, but he was better able to tap into his average raw power. Taylor is stretched thin at shortstop, and spent most of his time at second base (his best position) but also played third base, center and left field with an average arm.

THE FUTURE: If Taylor can cut down on his strikeouts, he could be a useful utility player in the big leagues, though some scouts are skeptical his bat will translate against big league pitching.

Year	Age	Club (Level)	Lge	AVG	G	AB	R	H	2B	3B	HR	RBI	BB	SO	SB	OBP	SLG
2021	22	New Hampshire (AA)	NEast	.294	87	320	69	94	17	1	16	52	42	110	30	.385	.503
Minor League Totals (6 years)				.256	400	1419	235	363	83	14	39	187	172	388	113	.342	.416

12 ESTIVEN MACHADO, SS

BA GRADE
50 Risk: Extreme

Born: Oct. 4, 2002. **B-T:** B-R. **HT:** 5-10. **WT:** 165. **Signed:** Venezuela, 2019. **Signed by:** Sandy Rosario/Francisco Plasencia.

TRACK RECORD: Machado signed at 16 for $775,000 as one of the top prospects in the 2019 international class. After the pandemic erased the 2020 season, Machado only got one plate appearance in the Rookie-level Florida Complex League before hamstring problems derailed the rest of his 2021 campaign.

SCOUTING REPORT: Machado is one of the best prospects in the system that few people outside the

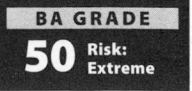

organization have seen much recently. When healthy, Machado has shown a promising blend of quick-twitch athleticism, tools and ability to hit in games. He takes quality at-bats with a good approach for his age and makes frequent contact with a quick, compact swing from both sides of the plate. It's a hit-over-power profile now, but with the bat speed and strength projection to grow into average power. He's an above-average runner who should be able to stick at shortstop, where he has the range for the position with quick first step, good footwork, secure hands and a tick above-average arm.

THE FUTURE: Machado's lack of playing time creates a lot of uncertainty to his forecast, but he's a strong breakout candidate if he can stay healthy in 2022.

Year	Age	Club (Level)	Lge	AVG	G	AB	R	H	2B	3B	HR	RBI	BB	SO	SB	OBP	SLG
2021	18	Blue Jays (R)	FCL	1.000	1	1	0	1	0	0	0	0	0	0	0	1.000	1.000
Minor League Totals (1 year)				1.000	1	1	0	1	0	0	0	0	0	0	0	1.000	1.000

13 SEM ROBBERSE, RHP

BA GRADE
45 Risk: High

Born: Oct. 12, 2001. **B-T:** R-R. **HT:** 6-1. **WT:** 180. **Signed:** Netherlands, 2019. **Signed by:** Andrew Tinnish.

TRACK RECORD: Robberse was a skinny 16-year-old throwing in the mid-80s in the summer of 2018. The next spring, he reached 88 mph before signing with the Blue Jays for $125,000. He went to the United States after signing and touched 90 mph. When the Rookie-level Gulf Coast League started, he was up to 93 mph. He made his full-season debut in 2021, reaching High-A Vancouver as a 19-year-old.

SCOUTING REPORT: Robberse is an easy operator with smooth, fluid mechanics. It's a low-effort delivery with good arm speed, and while Robberse has gotten stronger over the last few years, he still has a lean, lanky build to project more velocity to his 89-94 mph fastball. He shows feel to spin both his hard curveball and mid-80s slider, both average pitches that could still tick up. He throws a firm changeup that isn't much of a factor yet. Robberse's walk rate jumped upon his promotion to High-A, but he's usually a solid strike-thrower with a repeatable delivery.

THE FUTURE: While Robberse's stuff isn't overpowering, the projection indicators are encouraging, with the pitch mix, control and delivery to remain a starter. He likely returns to High-A to begin 2022 but could be in Double-A as a 20-year-old.

Year	Age	Club (Level)	Lge	W	L	ERA	G	GS	IP	H	HR	BB	SO	BB/9	SO/9	WHIP	AVG
2021	19	Dunedin (LoA)	SEast	5	4	3.90	14	12	57	46	4	20	61	3.1	9.5	1.14	.214
	19	Vancouver (HiA)	West	0	3	5.23	7	7	31	39	3	18	29	5.2	8.4	1.84	.305
Minor League Totals (3 years)				7	7	4.00	26	22	99	96	7	38	99	3.45	9.00	1.35	.251

14 IRV CARTER, RHP

BA GRADE
50 Risk: Extreme

Born: Oct. 9, 2002. **B-T:** R-R. **HT:** 6-4. **WT:** 210. **Drafted:** HS—Fort Lauderdale, Fla., 2021 (5th round). **Signed by:** Manny Padron.

TRACK RECORD: Carter teamed up with Phillies first-round pick Andrew Painter at Florida's Calvary Christian to form one of the more fearsome pitching duos in prep baseball. A Miami commit, he was a staple on the summer showcase circuit and one of its fiercest competitors on the mound. The Blue Jays selected Carter in the fifth-round, signing him for a well above-slot bonus of $850,000.

SCOUTING REPORT: Evaluators love Carter's fierce and fiery mentality on the mound, earning the bull-dog label from many. A three-pitch mix led by a low-90s fastball, that's touched 96 mph, with spin rates in the 2,500-2,600 rpm range, Carter mixes in a split-changeup that has gotten plus grades from scouts, and a newly developed slider in the low 80s that has replaced a 12-6 curveball he used as an underclassman. Despite an intriguing pitch mix, Carter comes with question marks around his ability to start due to an extremely high-effort operation that features a pronounced head whack. Despite the explosive violence in his operation, he shows athleticism and control of his big frame often messing with timing, with Johnny Cueto-like pauses.

THE FUTURE: An exciting young arm talent with starting pitcher upside but a very high level of reliever risk. If Carter can iron out his mechanics and continue to throw his three-pitch mix for strikes he has a shot to develop as a starter long-term.

Year	Age	Club (Level)	Lge	W	L	ERA	G	GS	IP	H	HR	BB	SO	BB/9	SO/9	WHIP	AVG
2021	18	Did not play															

15 SPENCER HORWITZ, 1B/OF

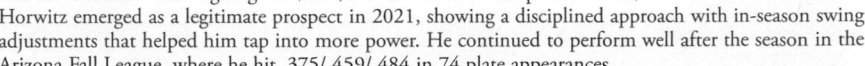

BA GRADE

45 Risk: High

Born: Nov. 14, 1997. **B-T:** L-R. **HT:** 6-0. **WT:** 190. **Drafted:** Radford, 2019 (24th round). **Signed by:** Coulson Barbiche.

TRACK RECORD: After signing for $100,000 as a 24th-round pick in 2019, Horwitz emerged as a legitimate prospect in 2021, showing a disciplined approach with in-season swing adjustments that helped him tap into more power. He continued to perform well after the season in the Arizona Fall League, where he hit .375/.459/.484 in 74 plate appearances.

SCOUTING REPORT: Horwitz has excellent plate discipline. He walked more than he struck out, consistently making good swing decisions. Horwitz never hit for big power in college, but he generated more impact after tweaking his setup during the 2021 season. Horwitz had a bat waggle that didn't allow him to get into a consistently good hitting position, with his hands often getting out away from his body when he started his swing. By midseason, Horwitz held his hands tighter to his body before starting his swing. The result was a quicker stroke that allowed him to drive the ball harder and with loft to his pull side. His average exit velocities jumped, and he went from a peak exit velo of 106 mph before the change to reaching 110 mph after. Defensively, Horwitz is below-average at first base with limited speed and mobility. The Blue Jays gave him more exposure to left field in the Arizona Fall League, but his offensive game will have to carry him.

THE FUTURE: Whether Horwitz will hit for enough power to be a regular at first base is still a question, so how he does at Double-A in 2022 will reveal a lot about how his game translates against upper-level arms.

Year	Age	Club (Level)	Lge	AVG	G	AB	R	H	2B	3B	HR	RBI	BB	SO	SB	OBP	SLG
2021	23	Vancouver (HiA)	West	.290	105	389	65	113	28	1	10	62	70	66	4	.401	.445
	23	New Hampshire (AA)	NEast	.375	4	16	3	6	2	0	2	4	0	2	0	.375	.875
Minor League Totals (3 years)				.299	169	653	105	195	49	2	16	118	94	98	9	.388	.453

16 C.J. VAN EYK, RHP

BA GRADE

45 Risk: High

Born: Sept. 15, 1998. **B-T:** R-R. **HT:** 6-1. **WT:** 205. **Drafted:** Florida State, 2020 (2nd round). **Signed by:** Brandon Bishoff.

TRACK RECORD: Van Eyk signed with the Blue Jays for $1,797,500 out of Florida State as the 42nd overall pick in the 2020 draft. He got off to a rough start in his pro debut though, posting a 5.83 ERA as he struggled to throw strikes in 2021.

SCOUTING REPORT: Van Eyk pitches off a fastball that sits at 91-94 mph with the ability to reach back for 97. He throws a hard curveball that is his go-to offspeed pitch and is solid-average at times, but he had trouble landing it in the zone. He doesn't throw his changeup as often, but it's at least an average pitch that can miss bats with good separation off his fastball. Van Eyk also uses fringe-average cutter in the mid-to-upper 80s. Van Eyk drew praise for his delivery coming out of Florida State, but he battled his mechanics throughout 2021, leading to erratic control.

THE FUTURE: Van Eyk should head to Double-A New Hampshire in 2022, an important year for him to rebound and improve his command.

Year	Age	Club (Level)	Lge	W	L	ERA	G	GS	IP	H	HR	BB	SO	BB/9	SO/9	WHIP	AVG
2021	22	Vancouver (HiA)	West	4	6	5.83	19	19	80	71	9	39	100	4.4	11.2	1.37	.234
Minor League Totals (2 years)				4	6	5.83	19	19	80	71	9	39	100	4.37	11.20	1.37	.234

17 ADAM KLOFFENSTEIN, RHP

BA GRADE

45 Risk: High

Born: Aug. 25, 2000. **B-T:** R-R. **HT:** 6-5. **WT:** 245. **Drafted:** HS—Magnolia, Texas, 2018 (3rd round). **Signed by:** Brian Johnston.

TRACK RECORD: Kloffenstein was one of the top pitching prospects in the short-season Northwest League in 2019 and entered 2021 as one of Toronto's Top 10 prospects. Kloffenstein's stock dropped in 2021 after his first year in a full-season league, and he had trouble throwing strikes with High-A Vancouver.

SCOUTING REPORT: Kloffenstein has an extra-large build at 6-foot-5, 245 pounds and pitches off a mix of four- and two-seam fastballs. The velocity bump from 2020 carried over into 2021, and he sat at 90-93 mph and touching 96. Kloffenstein struggled with his fastball command, however, leading to too much hard contact off his fastball and too many walks. Kloffenstein's slider is his most reliable secondary pitch. The raw spin on both his slider and curveball are a little below-average, but they both flash average overall. Kloffenstein has a mid-80s changeup that's a little firm but has good fade, though it's a pitch he doesn't use much.

THE FUTURE: Kloffenstein lacks a true plus pitch, so he needs to get his delivery in better rhythm to throw more strikes to stick as a starter and regain his stock. Double-A New Hampshire is up next.

Year	Age	Club (Level)	Lge	W	L	ERA	G	GS	IP	H	HR	BB	SO	BB/9	SO/9	WHIP	AVG
2021	20	Vancouver (HiA)	West	7	7	6.22	23	23	101	96	10	61	107	5.4	9.5	1.55	.243
Minor League Totals (3 years)				11	11	4.62	38	38	168	144	14	86	175	4.62	9.39	1.37	.228

18 THOMAS HATCH, RHP

BA GRADE

40 Risk: Medium

Born: Sept. 29, 1994. **B-T:** R-R. **HT:** 6-1. **WT:** 205. **Drafted:** Oklahoma State, 2016 (3rd round). **Signed by:** Ty Nichols (Cubs).

TRACK RECORD: Hatch reached Double-A with the Cubs before they sent him to the Blue Jays in the 2019 trade deadline deal for David Phelps. He made his major league debut as a reliever in 2020, but returned to a starting role in 2021. Hatch opened the year on the injured list with a right elbow impingement and did make three more major league appearances but spent most of the season in Triple-A Buffalo.

SCOUTING REPORT: Hatch is now 27, with a chance he could stick as a back-end starter but might ultimately end up in a relief role. His delivery is smooth and controlled, and he threw plenty of strikes in Triple-A before running into some control issues in the big leagues. His four-seam fastball is a powerful, high-spin pitch that sits at 92-96 mph and can reach 98. He mixes it with a lively two-seamer as well. After Hatch arrived from the Cubs, the Blue Jays encouraged him to throw more of his changeup, which is now his go-to offspeed pitch, grading out plus. He has tight spin on a mid-80s slider that is an average but inconsistent pitch.

THE FUTURE: Hatch has the delivery and repertoire of a starter, but given his age and Toronto's current rotation, he could end up fitting into their bullpen picture in 2022.

Year	Age	Club (Level)	Lge	W	L	ERA	G	GS	IP	H	HR	BB	SO	BB/9	SO/9	WHIP	AVG
2021	26	Buffalo (AAA)	East	2	6	4.04	15	14	64	58	10	19	70	2.6	9.7	1.19	.238
	26	Toronto (MLB)	AL	0	1	6.75	3	2	9	11	2	6	8	5.8	7.7	1.82	.289
Major League Totals (2 years)				3	2	3.79	20	3	36	29	4	19	31	4.79	7.82	1.35	.220
Minor League Totals (4 years)				21	36	4.00	94	93	468	440	46	169	440	3.25	8.46	1.30	.253

19 TANNER MORRIS, 2B/3B/SS

BA GRADE

45 Risk: High

Born: Sept. 13, 1997. **B-T:** L-R. **HT:** 6-2. **WT:** 190. **Drafted:** Virginia, 2019 (5th round). **Signed by:** Coulson Barbiche.

TRACK RECORD: Morris showed strong on-base skills while in college at Virginia and in the Cape Cod League. Signed for $397,500 as draft-eligible sophomore in the fifth round of the 2019 draft, Morris continued to show his disciplined approach with High-A Vancouver in 2021.

SCOUTING REPORT: Morris is an offensive-minded infielder with a hit-over-power profile. He has a good eye for the strike zone, puts together quality at-bats and is comfortable hitting with two strikes. He controls the barrel well, spraying line drives to all fields with a simple lefthanded swing. What holds Morris back offensively is his well below-average power. Entering his age-24 season, he might never develop the strength to drive the ball with much authority. A shortstop at Virginia, Morris has spent time there with the Blue Jays, but he mostly played third base and second in 2021. He has a strong arm that could fit at third base and is reliable on balls he gets to, but his actions aren't the smoothest and his lack of first-step quickness limits his range.

THE FUTURE: Morris has the contact skills and plate discipline to be a high on-base threat, but he will need to get stronger for it to work against more advanced pitching. He will get his first test in the upper minors in 2022 when he opens at Double-A New Hampshire.

Year	Age	Club (Level)	Lge	AVG	G	AB	R	H	2B	3B	HR	RBI	BB	SO	SB	OBP	SLG
2021	23	Vancouver (HiA)	West	.285	103	397	55	113	19	3	7	57	58	90	4	.381	.401
Minor League Totals (3 years)				.270	167	637	92	172	35	4	9	85	107	146	8	.382	.380

20 CHAD DALLAS, RHP

BA GRADE

45 Risk: Very High

Born: June 26, 2000. **B-T:** R-R. **HT:** 5-11. **WT:** 206. **Drafted:** Tennessee, 2021 (4th round). **Signed by:** Nate Murrie.

TRACK RECORD: A standout for Tennessee in the regionals, Dallas started the Volunteers' opening game of the College World Series against Virginia, after leading the team in wins and strikeouts during the 2021 season. His three-year collegiate career spanned a two year stint at Tennessee after spending his freshman season at Panola JC in Carthage, Texas.

SCOUTING REPORT: Dallas is an athletic pitcher, with an up-tempo delivery, and a smooth motion toward the plate despite some effort due to the pace. He delivers the ball from a high three-quarter slot, with a short, fast arm action, a heavy drop and drive operation and a strong leg block, that portends potential velocity gains to be had. Dallas works off of a four pitch mix that features above-average spin. His four-seam fastball has moderate hop, sitting 91-94 mph, touching 96 mph at peak, and is used primarily to set up his trio of secondaries early in counts. His horizontal breaking slider has good velocity sitting in the mid-80s, touching as high as 89 mph, and is his best swing and miss pitch by a wide margin. He shows excellent command of the pitch, and can throw it for strikes or exaggerate the shape to induce chases off the plate glove side. His low-80s curveball is used interchangeably with his slider, featuring 11-5 shape and heavier downward drop than his slider. The pitch is his primary secondary against lefthanded hitters, and is an effective, but not overpowering offering. He throws a low-90s cutter that produced good results in limited 2021 usage.

THE FUTURE: Dallas has all the ingredients of a potential back-end starter, with upside to add more velocity to his fastball. Excellent feel for spin, and command of his secondaries drive his profile.

Year	Age	Club (Level)	Lge	W	L	ERA	G	GS	IP	H	HR	BB	SO	BB/9	SO/9	WHIP	AVG
2021	21	Did not play															

21   MIGUEL HIRALDO, 2B/3B

BA GRADE
45 Risk: Very High

Born: Sept. 5, 2000. **B-T:** R-R. **HT:** 5-11. **WT:** 175. **Signed:** Dominican Republic, 2017. **Signed by:** Luciano del Rosario.

TRACK RECORD: Hiraldo had a reputation as one of the most advanced hitters in the 2017 international class when the Blue Jays signed him for $750,000. He showed why during his first two years in Rookie ball, but the reviews were underwhelming in Hiraldo's first year in a full-season league.

SCOUTING REPORT: Hiraldo has a short, quick swing with good bat speed. He's a good fastball hitter, though his approach can get too aggressive and he isn't as effective against breaking stuff. Hiraldo has average raw power, though he doesn't consistently drive the ball in games, often getting caught in between with his approach. Hiraldo has split time between second and third base. His hands are fine and he has a solid-average arm with adequate range.

THE FUTURE: Hiraldo's bat will drive his value, and he will have to show more—whether it's improving his on-base skills or finding a way to unlock more game power—to develop into a regular. He will head to High-A Vancouver to start 2022.

Year	Age	Club (Level)	Lge	AVG	G	AB	R	H	2B	3B	HR	RBI	BB	SO	SB	OBP	SLG
2021	20	Dunedin (LoA)	SEast	.249	105	390	66	97	26	4	7	52	51	111	29	.338	.390
Minor League Totals (4 years)				.277	226	884	153	245	68	9	16	125	89	189	58	.347	.429

22 DAHIAN SANTOS, RHP

BA GRADE
45 Risk: Extreme

Born: Feb. 23, 2003. **B-T:** R-R. **HT:** 5-11. **WT:** 160. **Signed:** Venezuela, 2019. **Signed by:** Francisco Plasencia/Jose Contreras.

TRACK RECORD: Santos has trended up since the Blue Jays signed him for $150,000 as a 16-year-old out of Venezuela on July 2, 2019. His velocity rose to touch 94 mph that fall, and he made his official debut in 2021 in the Rookie-level Florida Complex League before getting promoted to Low-A Dunedin in September.

SCOUTING REPORT: Santos is a lanky, athletic pitcher who stands out for his touch and feel. He pitches at 89-94 mph with good movement on his fastball from his low three-quarters slot. While Santos has a loose, quick arm and a bit of physical projection remaining in his wiry frame, but his game is more about pitchability than power. He's an advanced strike-thrower for his age with feel for a curveball and a changeup. He has tight spin on his curveball, generally around 2,500-2,600 rpm. Though it can get a bit wide and slurvy at times, it's a slightly above-average pitch. His changeup is inconsistent but he shows feel for that pitch too.

THE FUTURE: Santos isn't that big, but he has a starter look between his three-pitch mix, control and athleticism with an easy delivery. He should start 2022 in the rotation for Low-A Dunedin.

Year	Age	Club (Level)	Lge	W	L	ERA	G	GS	IP	H	HR	BB	SO	BB/9	SO/9	WHIP	AVG
2021	18	Blue Jays (R)	FCL	1	2	4.58	10	7	35	30	5	12	53	3.1	13.5	1.19	.224
	18	Dunedin (LoA)	SEast	0	2	12.60	2	2	5	8	1	4	5	7.2	9.0	2.40	.400
Minor League Totals (1 year)				1	4	5.58	12	9	40	38	6	16	58	3.57	12.94	1.34	.247

23 YHOANGEL APONTE, OF

BA GRADE

45 Risk: Extreme

Born: Feb. 12, 2004. **B-T:** R-R. **HT:** 5-11. **WT:** 190. **Signed:** Venezuela, 2021. **Signed by:** Francisco Plasencia/Jose Contreras.

TRACK RECORD: Aponte signed at 16 for $360,000 on Jan. 15, 2021, and while he wasn't a high-profile player as an amateur, his talent is in line with some of the top international players in the class. He made his pro debut in the Dominican Summer League.

SCOUTING REPORT: Aponte has a chance to develop five average or better tools. It's his instincts that stick out the most, though, especially on the defensive side. Aponte has solid-average speed and arm strength, and while he doesn't have the high-end speed typical of a center fielder, he's a diligent worker when it comes to his defense. That shows up in his first-step reads off the bat and his ability to run efficient routes with good range to both gaps. Aponte has a good eye for the strike zone and a patient approach, and while he hit well in games as an amateur, his 27% strikeout rate in the DSL is a concern. Aponte didn't homer in his pro debut, but he has good bat speed and drove the ball with more impact during instructional league, with multiple balls off the bat over 110 mph.

THE FUTURE: Aponte is still relatively under the radar, but if he can improve his contact rate, he's a good breakout candidate. The Rookie-level Florida Complex League is up next.

Year	Age	Club (Level)	Lge	AVG	G	AB	R	H	2B	3B	HR	RBI	BB	SO	SB	OBP	SLG
2021	17	Blue Jays (R)	DSL	.240	38	129	25	31	9	3	0	18	25	44	5	.393	.357
Minor League Totals (1 year)				.240	38	129	25	31	9	3	0	18	25	44	5	.393	.357

24 ZACH LOGUE, LHP

BA GRADE

40 Risk: Medium

Born: April 23, 1996. **B-T:** R-R. **HT:** 6-0. **WT:** 165. **Drafted:** Kentucky, 2017 (9th round). **Signed by:** Nate Murrie.

TRACK RECORD: Even though Logue posted a 4.97 ERA his junior year at Kentucky in 2017, the Blue Jays drafted him in the ninth round and signed him for $125,000. He didn't do much to distinguish himself as a prospect until 2021, when his stuff ticked up and he pitched well in Triple-A Buffalo as a 25-year-old.

SCOUTING REPORT: Logue was one of the most improved pitchers in the organization in 2021. His velocity went from often sitting in the upper 80s to now sitting in the low 90s and topping at 94 mph. It's not a power fastball, but there's deception to his delivery that helps him generate more empty swings with his fastball than the velocity might suggest. It also pairs well with his changeup, another pitch that improved last year and is an above-average offering with good separation off his heater. Logue mixes a slider and cutter too, with both pitches grading fringe-average. He threw plenty of strikes in 2021, averaging 1.9 BB/9.

THE FUTURE: Logue will be 26 in 2022, so he's on the older end for a prospect, but he has enough ability to throw strikes and change speeds to potentially stick around as a back-end starter.

Year	Age	Club (Level)	Lge	W	L	ERA	G	GS	IP	H	HR	BB	SO	BB/9	SO/9	WHIP	AVG
2021	25	New Hampshire (AA)	NEast	3	1	4.54	7	7	35	33	6	7	51	1.8	12.9	1.12	.246
	25	Buffalo (AAA)	East	9	3	3.32	18	17	89	79	9	20	93	2.0	9.4	1.11	.236
Minor League Totals (5 years)				32	16	3.43	84	73	414	385	46	103	389	2.24	8.45	1.18	.247

25 ERIC PARDINHO, RHP

BA GRADE

45 Risk: Extreme

Born: Jan. 5, 2001. **B-T:** R-R. **HT:** 5-9. **WT:** 200. **Signed:** Brazil, 2017. **Signed by:** Andrew Tinnish/Sandy Rosario.

TRACK RECORD: Pardinho was the top pitching prospect in the 2017 international class when the Blue Jays signed him out of Brazil at 16 for $1.4 million. He was outstanding in his pro debut in 2018, when he picked apart Rookie-level Appalachian League hitters with pitchability beyond his years. Pardinho didn't pitch much due to a sore elbow in 2019, he had Tommy John surgery in 2020 and threw just three innings in 2021 because of setbacks in his rehab.

SCOUTING REPORT: There's little to go off from the last two years with Pardinho because of his health issues, and when he was on the field in 2019, his stuff had dropped off. That could have been because Pardinho was pitching at less than full strength, so there's hope his stuff can return to what he had shown at his best. That version of Pardinho pounded the strike zone with a low-90s fastball that touched 96 mph, flashed a plus curveball, showed a slider that could develop into another swing-and-miss pitch and had feel for a changeup as well.

THE FUTURE: Pardinho has the repertoire and control to start, but his durability issues create a huge amount of doubt about his future and whether he can hold up in that role. The 2022 season will be critical for him to stay healthy and bounce back.

Year	Age	Club (Level)	Lge	W	L	ERA	G	GS	IP	H	HR	BB	SO	BB/9	SO/9	WHIP	AVG
2021	20	Blue Jays (R)	FCL	0	0	0.00	2	2	3	1	0	0	4	0.0	12.0	0.33	.111
Minor League Totals (4 years)				6	4	2.48	21	20	91	68	6	32	103	3.18	10.22	1.10	.208

26 KENDRY ROJAS, LHP

Born: Nov. 26, 2002. **B-T:** L-L. **HT:** 6-2. **WT:** 190. **Signed:** Cuba, 2020.
Signed by: Erick Ramirez/Luis Natera

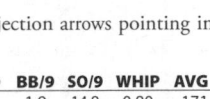

BA GRADE
45 Risk: Extreme

TRACK RECORD: The Blue Jays signed Rojas out of Cuba after the 2020 season. He made his pro debut in 2021 in the Rookie-level Florida Complex League and was one of their best pitchers there, filling the zone and piling up whiffs for a 45% strikeout rate as an 18-year-old.
SCOUTING REPORT: Rojas is one of the most athletic pitchers in the organization. His velocity is below-average, sitting at 88-90 mph and touching 92, but there's arm speed and physical projection for more. Rojas' fastball gets a high swing-and-miss rate because of its life and the way he commands the pitch. Rojas has good feel to spin a slider that's an average pitch at times. Rojas is mainly a two-pitch guy, so developing a changeup will be a focus in 2022.
THE FUTURE: Rojas has a promising mix of polish for his age to go with projection arrows pointing in the right direction. Low-A Dunedin is up next.

Year	Age	Club (Level)	Lge	W	L	ERA	G	GS	IP	H	HR	BB	SO	BB/9	SO/9	WHIP	AVG
2021	18	Blue Jays (R)	FCL	0	0	2.28	8	4	24	14	1	5	39	1.9	14.8	0.80	.171
Minor League Totals (1 year)				0	0	2.28	8	4	24	14	1	5	39	1.9	14.8	0.80	.171

27 HAGEN DANNER, RHP

Born: Sept. 30, 1998. **B-T:** R-R. **HT:** 6-2. **WT:** 210.
Drafted: HS—Huntington Beach, Calif., 2017 (2nd round). **Signed by:** Joey Aversa.

BA GRADE
40 Risk: High

TRACK RECORD: Danner was a legitimate two-way prospect in high school, pitching for USA Baseball's 18U national team for two summers and running his fastball up to 95 mph. Many scouts preferred Danner on the mound, but the Blue Jays drafted him as a catcher with their second-round pick in 2017 and signed him for $1.5 million. It quickly became apparent that Danner's bat was a liability, but he resurrected his prospect status with a move to the mound for the 2021 season, to the point where the Blue Jays added him to the 40-man roster in November.
SCOUTING REPORT: Danner is now a reliever with one of the best fastballs in the organization. He pitches at 95-97 mph and can tickle 100 mph, with good carry up in the zone on his four-seam fastball to blow past barrels. Danner also throws a mid-80s slider that can be an average pitch but is still inconsistent. For a conversion guy, Danner's pitching background was evident in his control with just 3.0 BB/9.
THE FUTURE: If Danner can continue to throw strikes and sharpen his breaking stuff, he should get to the big leagues as a power reliever. He heads to Double-A New Hampshire to start 2022.

Year	Age	Club (Level)	Lge	W	L	ERA	G	GS	IP	H	HR	BB	SO	BB/9	SO/9	WHIP	AVG
2021	22	Vancouver (HiA)	West	2	1	2.02	25	0	35	21	2	12	42	3.0	10.6	0.93	.171
Minor League Totals (1 year)				2	1	2.02	25	0	36.0	21	2	12	42	3.03	10.60	0.93	.171

28 RIKELBIN DE CASTRO, SS

Born: Jan. 23, 2003. **B-T:** R-R. **HT:** 6-0. **WT:** 155. **Signed:** Dominican Republic, 2019. **Signed by:** Sandy Rosario/Lorenzo Perez/Luis Natera.

BA GRADE
45 Risk: Extreme

TRACK RECORD: De Castro received Toronto's top bonus in their 2019-20 international signing class when he got $1.2 million at 16 out of the Dominican Republic. De Castro made his pro debut in 2021 in the Rookie-level Florida Complex League, where he flashed his athleticism at shortstop with a defensive-minded profile.
SCOUTING REPORT: The wiry De Castro draws attention quickly from the way he fields a ground ball. He's a springy, athletic shortstop with quick-twitch actions. He's a high-energy player with a quick first step who moves his feet well, with smooth hands and a solid-average arm. He can make acrobatic plays, though like many young shortstops, he will have to cut down on throwing mistakes. An average runner, de Castro has decent plate patience for his age and quick hands, but his lack of strength shows up both in his well below-average power and his inability to maintain his swing.
THE FUTURE: De Castro has a chance to develop into a plus defender at shortstop but will need to pack on more strength to develop his offensive game, though he might always be limited to a bottom of the

order hitter. He should head to Low-A Dunedin in 2022.

Year	Age	Club (Level)	Lge	AVG	G	AB	R	H	2B	3B	HR	RBI	BB	SO	SB	OBP	SLG
2021	18	Blue Jays (R)	FCL	.238	39	126	19	30	8	3	2	23	24	40	3	.372	.397
Minor League Totals (1 year)				.238	39	126	19	30	8	3	2	23	24	40	3	.372	.397

29 LUIS GARCIA, SS

BA GRADE

45 Risk: Extreme

Born: Sept. 1, 2003. **B-T:** R-R. **HT:** 5-9. **WT:** 160. **Signed:** Venezuela, 2021. **Signed by:** Sandy Rosario/Francisco Plasencia.

TRACK RECORD: Garcia was one of Toronto's prominent 2021 international signings, landing a $520,000 bonus when the signing period opened in January. Known more for his defense as an amateur, Garcia had a promising debut at the plate as a 17-year-old in the Dominican Summer League.

SCOUTING REPORT: Garcia is an athletic shortstop with slick defense, though with a pair of seven-figure signings in Manuel Beltre and Martin Gimenez also on the DSL roster, Garcia played all over the infield. Garcia has the tools to handle shortstop, with quick actions and a solid-average arm. Garcia is also a plus runner who showed good bat control with a 13% strikeout rate. He has minimal power though, with a smaller frame and limited physical projection, so it's unlikely he ever does much extra-base damage.

THE FUTURE: Garcia can stick up the middle, but he will have to get stronger to prove he can drive the ball with more authority. He should make his U.S. debut in the Rookie-level Florida Complex League in 2022.

Year	Age	Club (Level)	Lge	AVG	G	AB	R	H	2B	3B	HR	RBI	BB	SO	SB	OBP	SLG
2021	17	Blue Jays (R)	DSL	.307	36	137	26	42	10	0	0	15	13	20	12	.375	.380
Minor League Totals (1 year)				.307	36	137	26	42	10	0	0	15	13	20	12	.375	.380

30 JOSH PALACIOS, OF

BA GRADE

40 Risk: High

Born: July 30, 1995. **B-T:** L-R. **HT:** 6-1. **WT:** 198. **Drafted:** Auburn, 2016 (4th round). **Signed by:** Don Norris.

TRACK RECORD: Palacios was drafted twice, first in the 31st round of the 2014 draft by Cincinnati following his Freshman season at San Jacinto, and again by the Blue Jays in the fourth round, following a junior campaign with Auburn. A Brooklyn native, Josh is the older brother of Guardians infield prospect Richie Palacios. He made his major league debut on April 9, 2021, but spent a majority of his 2021 season on the Triple-A injury list dealing with an unspecified hand injury.

SCOUTING REPORT: A versatile outfielder with the ability to provide average defense across all three outfield spots. He tracks the ball well off the bat, with above-average closing speed, and an average throwing arm. Palacios dealt with a hand injury for a majority of the year and when he returned he didn't show much impact upon contact. This is to be expected with injuries of that nature, and Palacios wasn't a power hitter to begin with. His game revolves around above-average contact, on-base ability, and speed. Prior to the pandemic, Palacios displayed some intriguing offensive qualities, but it always came with an approach boarding on over-aggressive. The contact and on-base skills came with moderate swing and miss and below-average game power, but enough to drive the gaps and run into a modest number of home runs in the high single-digits. This is unlikely to change without mechanical tweaks to alter his path to the ball.

THE FUTURE: After losing a majority of the last two seasons it's difficult to know where Palacios stands long term. He looks squarely like a reserve outfielder with limited offensive impact.

Year	Age	Club (Level)	Lge	AVG	G	AB	R	H	2B	3B	HR	RBI	BB	SO	SB	OBP	SLG
2021	25	Blue Jays (R)	FCL	.500	2	4	2	2	1	0	0	2	4	0	0	.750	.750
	25	Dunedin (LoA)	SEast	1.000	1	2	0	2	0	0	0	0	0	0	0	1.000	1.000
	25	Buffalo (AAA)	East	.241	16	54	7	13	2	0	0	2	5	16	1	.349	.278
	25	Toronto (MLB)	AL	.200	13	35	7	7	0	0	0	4	3	11	0	.293	.200
Major League Totals (1 year)				.200	13	35	7	7	0	0	0	4	3	11	0	.293	.200
Minor League Totals (6 years)				.288	368	1421	206	409	82	13	17	177	161	317	51	.368	.400

MORE PROSPECTS TO KNOW

31 VICTOR MESIA, C
Mesia performed well in his pro debut in the Rookie-level Florida Complex League as an 18-year-old. He has a simple swing, though he chased too much when he got to Low-A Dunedin and will need to bring along his receiving.

32 BOWDEN FRANCIS, RHP
Acquired from the Brewers in July in the deal that sent Rowdy Tellez to Milwaukee, Francis is a 6-foot-5 starter who had a solid year in Triple-A. He pitches in the low 90s and touched 97 mph with a slider that's an average pitch at times.

33 ADRIAN HERNANDEZ, LHP
SLEEPER

Hernandez is a 5-foot-9 reliever who rose three levels in 2021 to reach Double-A as a 21-year-old, striking out 108 batters in 62.1 innings. He pitches around 90-92 mph and touches 95, with a plus changeup that's his bread-and-butter pitch.

34 FITZ STADLER, RHP
Stadler is a reliever with control issues—he had 6.5 BB/9 between Double-A and Triple-A in 2021—but he's also 6-foot-9 with a fastball up to 100 mph and a power slider.

35 DASAN BROWN, OF
Brown is an elite athlete with premium speed in center field and a quick bat. He is still quite raw at the plate though, as he showed during his 2021 struggles in Low-A.

36 TRENT PALMER, RHP
A third-round pick in 2020 out of Jacksonville, Palmer has good stuff with a fastball up to 96 mph and the ability to miss bats with his slider and splitter, but he also issued 6.0 BB/9 in Low-A.

37 JOEY MURRAY, RHP
Murray generates surprising swing-and-miss for a pitcher who doesn't have a plus pitch, but his deception and life on a fastball that peaks at 94 mph help him miss bats up in the zone.

38 YOSVER ZULUETA, RHP
Zulueta signed for $1 million out of Cuba when he was 21 in July 2019. He had Tommy John surgery soon after, returned with a fastball up to 98 mph, then missed nearly all of 2021 with right knee surgery, leaving a huge amount of uncertainty projecting him.

39 ADDISON BARGER, SS/2B/3B
Barger is a power-hitting infielder with a strong arm and some of the best juice in the system, sending exit velocities up to 113 mph. He also takes a big, aggressive hack that he will have to cut down and be able to control the zone better after posting a 33% strikeout rate in High-A in 2021.

40 RAINER NUÑEZ, 1B
Nuñez repeated the Rookie-level Florida Complex League as a 20-year-old, but he performed well and his plus raw power stacks up among the best in the system with exit velocities up to 114 mph.

TOP PROSPECTS OF THE DECADE

Year	Player, Pos	2021 Org
2012	Travis d'Arnaud, C	Braves
2013	Travis d'Arnaud, C	Braves
2014	Aaron Sanchez, RHP	Giants
2015	Daniel Norris, LHP	Brewers
2016	Anthony Alford, OF	Pirates
2017	Vladimir Guerrero Jr., 3B	Blue Jays
2018	Vladimir Guerrero Jr., 3B	Blue Jays
2019	Vladimir Guerrero Jr., 3B	Blue Jays
2020	Nate Pearson, RHP	Blue Jays
2021	Nate Pearson, RHP	Blue Jays

TOP DRAFT PICKS OF THE DECADE

Year	Player, Pos	2021 Org
2012	D.J. Davis, OF	Did not play
2013	*Phil Bickford, RHP	Dodgers
2014	Jeff Hoffman, RHP	Reds
2015	Jon Harris, RHP	Blue Jays
2016	T.J. Zeuch, RHP	Blue Jays
2017	Logan Warmoth, SS	Blue Jays
2018	Jordan Groshans, SS	Blue Jays
2019	Alek Manoah, RHP	Blue Jays
2020	Austin Martin, SS	Twins
2021	Gunnar Hoglund, RHP	Blue Jays
	* Did not sign	

Washington Nationals

BY JOE HEALY

Just as in 2019 and 2020, the Nationals got off to a slow start in 2021. A 10-12 record in April came before an 11-17 record in May, eventually leading to the team sputtering into the all-star break at 42-47.

But unlike 2019, when a slow start led to a torrid run through the back half of the season and a World Series title, and 2020, when a 60-game season meant there was no time for the Nationals to make up ground, the sluggish start to 2021 pushed the club into a role as a seller at the trade deadline.

In addition to flipping players who were on one-year deals signed the previous offseason like Kyle Schwarber, Brad Hand and Jon Lester, the Nationals dealt franchise cornerstones Max Scherzer and Trea Turner in an effort to kick off the rebuilding process. The sheer volume of moves, and the players involved in said moves, told the story that the Nationals weren't just punting on the 2021 season. They were fully re-tooling with an eye toward assembling its next championship core.

In all, the Nationals traded eight veterans on July 29 and 30 to get back 12 young players, which provided a much-needed infusion of talent for its minor league system, which had fallen behind in recent years largely for the best reason a system could do so, because so many talented players had graduated and helped the big league club win a World Series in 2019.

The upshot of the flurry of activity was not just that the Nationals immediately shifted into rebuilding mode and finished the 2021 season 65-97, but also that the next contending team for the organization might not be as far away as you would assume. Especially for a team that just traded away many of its most productive players and finished 23.5 games back in the division.

Players like Keibert Ruiz, Josiah Gray, Riley Adams, Mason Thompson and Lane Thomas acquired in deadline deals have already made debuts in Washington, and others aren't far behind. The early evidence is also very promising in regards to the top picks in the last couple of drafts. Included among those picks was 2020 first-round pick Cade Cavalli, whose 175 strikeouts led the minor leagues. A pick later, the Nationals selected Louisiana State righty Cole Henry, who was excellent before injury. Their 2021 class led with infielder Brady House, who tore up the Florida Complex League after signing.

One day, Cavalli, Henry and House could complement a roster that already houses Juan Soto, of course, one of the game's premier talents and a shining light in what was a down season.

MICHAEL REAVES/GETTY IMAGES

Even amid a sell-off in 2021, Juan Soto remains a clear franchise cornerstone in Washington.

PROJECTED 2025 LINEUP

Catcher	Keibert Ruiz	26
First Base	Josh Bell	32
Second Base	Luis Garcia	25
Third Base	Carter Kieboom	27
Shortstop	Brady House	21
Left Field	Lane Thomas	29
Center Field	Victor Robles	28
Right Field	Juan Soto	26
Designated Hitter	Yasel Antuna	25
No. 1 Starter	Cade Cavalli	26
No. 2 Starter	Stephen Strasburg	37
No. 3 Starter	Josiah Gray	27
No. 4 Starter	Cole Henry	25
No. 5 Starter	Joan Adon	26
Closer	Gerardo Carrillo	26

Pitching stands out as a particular strength in the Nationals' system. Six of the top 10 players in the system are pitchers, and that doesn't include Gray, who only graduated from being a prospect because he immediately became a member of the team's rotation after joining the Nationals in July in the trade that sent Scherzer and Turner to Los Angeles.

There are likely to be growing pains for the Nationals in the immediate term, but the young talent collected via trade and coming up through the system seems to suggest that the valley for the club won't be as deep as it has been for other rebuilding organizations on the way back to the peak. ■

WASHINGTON NATIONALS

TOP 2022 ROOKIES / **RANK**

Keibert Ruiz, C — 1
Joan Adon, RHP — 7

BREAKOUT PROSPECTS / **RANK**

Aldo Ramirez, RHP — 13
Jackson Cluff, SS — 16

SOURCE OF TOP 30 TALENT			
Homegrown	**22**	**Acquired**	**8**
College	8	Trade	8
Junior college	2	Rule 5 draft	0
High school	4	Independent league	0
Nondrafted free agent	0	Free agent/waivers	0
International	8		

LF
Yasel Antuna (4)
Daylen Lile (18)

CF
Jeremy de la Rosa (14)
Daniel Marte (24)
Ricardo Mendez

RF
Donovan Casey (17)
Roismar Quintana (25)
T.J. White
Gage Canning

3B
Jake Alu
Jose Sanchez
Junior Martina

SS
Brady House (3)
Armando Cruz (9)
Jackson Cluff (16)
Sammy Infante (20)

2B
Jordy Barley (29)
Jake Noll
J.T. Arruda

1B
Drew Mendoza
Branden Boissiere

C
Keibert Ruiz (1)
Riley Adams (12)
Israel Pineda (23)
Tres Barrera (26)
Drew Millas (30)

LHP

LHSP
Tim Cate (19)
Mitchell Parker (21)
Evan Lee (22)
Seth Romero (27)

LHRP
Matt Cronin (15)
Dustin Saenz

RHP

RHSP
Cade Cavalli (2)
Andry Lara (5)
Cole Henry (6)
Joan Adon (7)
Jackson Rutledge (9)
Aldo Ramirez (13)
Mason Denaburg (28)
Seth Shuman
Steven Fuentes
Tyler Dyson
Jake Irvin
Jackson Tetreault
Niomar Gomez

RHRP
Gerardo Carrillo (8)
Mason Thompson (11)
Richard Guasch
Todd Peterson
Zach Brzykcy
Holden Powell
Reid Schaller
Sterling Sharp

1 KEIBERT RUIZ, C

Born: July 20, 1998. **B-T:** B-R. **HT:** 6-0. **WT:** 225.
Signed: Venezuela, 2014.
Signed by: Francisco Cartaya/Pedro Avila (Dodgers).

TRACK RECORD: Ruiz signed with the Dodgers for $140,000 at the age of 16 in 2014 out of the Venezuelan academy run by former big leaguer Carlos Guillen. At the time, he was considered more of a defensive catcher, but that's not the case now. Ruiz's star really began to rise when he reached Double-A at age 19 in 2018. A return to Double-A the next season due to a logjam at catcher in the Dodgers organization slowed his progress, but a promotion to Triple-A later that year seemed to get him going again, at least up until he was sidelined with a fractured finger. Formerly the Dodgers' No. 1 prospect, Ruiz immediately became the top prospect for the Nationals upon being traded to Washington as part of the massive deal that sent Max Scherzer and Trea Turner to Los Angeles at the 2021 trade deadline. After getting a cup of coffee in the big leagues in 2020—including a homer in his first big league at-bat—Ruiz saw more regular playing time down the stretch with the Nationals in 2021 and responded by showing the offensive prowess that has the organization excited about his potential.

SCOUTING REPORT: A switch-hitter, Ruiz has long had a knack for making contact, but up until recently he had faced questions about his ability to impact the baseball. Adjustments made with the Dodgers, including getting more upright in his stance and keeping his hands closer to his body, have helped him make higher-quality contact, a trend that carried over in his small sample with the Nationals. He has also made strides in his approach and hunting for pitches against which he can do damage in the right counts. Traditionally, Ruiz had been more effective from the left side, but recent improvements in his righthanded swing have made him much more of a well-rounded threat at the plate, where he projects to be a plus hitter with near-average power. Ruiz doesn't necessarily have standout tools from a defensive standpoint, but rival evaluators are quick to praise his ability to make it work and have taken note of improvements in game calling and relationship building with his pitching staff. He blocks well and has the potential to be an above-average receiver. His arm strength is fringy, which led to a caught stealing rate of 18% with the Nationals last season.

MITCHELL LAYTON/GETTY IMAGES

BA GRADE	SCOUTING GRADES
60 Risk: Medium	Hit: 60. Power: 45. Run: 30. Field: 55. Arm: 45.

Projected future grades on 20-80 scouting scale

BEST TOOLS

Best Hitter for Average	Yasel Antuña
Best Power Hitter	Brady House
Best Strike-Zone Discipline	Drew Millas
Fastest Baserunner	Jordy Barley
Best Athlete	Donovan Casey
Best Fastball	Cade Cavalli
Best Curveball	Tim Cate
Best Slider	Cade Cavalli
Best Changeup	Steven Fuentes
Best Control	Tim Cate
Best Defensive Catcher	Tres Barrera
Best Defensive Infielder	Jackson Cluff
Best Infield Arm	Jackson Cluff
Best Defensive Outfielder	Cody Wilson
Best Outfield Arm	Daniel Marte

That figure was just below his 20% mark in the minors in 2021.

THE FUTURE: Ruiz is the Nationals' catcher of the future, which is a change from his time with the Dodgers, where he was blocked by Will Smith. After getting a taste of regular playing time in the big leagues and getting hot down the stretch at the end of last season, Ruiz looks poised to make a name for himself in 2022, when he'll be part of a club aiming for a return to prominence. ∎

Year	Age	Club (Level)	Lge	AVG	G	AB	R	H	2B	3B	HR	RBI	BB	SO	SB	OBP	SLG
2021	22	Oklahoma City (AAA)	West	.311	52	206	39	64	18	0	16	45	23	27	0	.381	.631
	22	Rochester (AAA)	East	.308	20	78	11	24	6	0	5	14	7	6	0	.365	.577
	22	Los Angeles (MLB)	NL	.143	6	7	1	1	0	0	1	1	0	5	0	.143	.571
	22	Washington (MLB)	NL	.284	23	81	9	23	3	0	2	14	6	4	0	.348	.395
Major League Totals (2 years)				.271	31	96	11	26	3	0	4	16	6	12	0	.327	.427
Minor League Totals (6 years)				.301	459	1723	238	518	100	6	50	258	134	183	4	.356	.453

2 CADE CAVALLI, RHP

Born: Aug. 14, 1998. **B-T:** R-R. **HT:** 6-4. **WT:** 226. **Drafted:** Oklahoma, 2020 (1st round). **Signed by:** Jerad Head.

TRACK RECORD: As a 2020 draftee, Cavalli's minor league debut was delayed to 2021, though he did impress at the Nationals' alternate training site in 2020 after being drafted 22nd overall out of Oklahoma. Once on the field this year, the righthander wasted no time making a statement, soaring from High-A to Triple-A over the course of the season. Importantly, after battling injuries in college, Cavalli stayed healthy all season and showed his ability to handle a heavy workload. He led the minor leagues with 157 strikeouts.

SCOUTING REPORT: Cavalli's stuff is electric. Over the summer, rival managers in Double-A Northeast voted his the best fastball and breaking ball in the league. His fastball sits 95-97 mph and has touched as high as 100 using an easy, yet powerful delivery. He throws two distinct breaking balls, a power curveball and a slider that is cutterish at times. The latter is used effectively to get off hitters' barrels. He gets good sink on his changeup, but evaluators are less enthused about that offering. He has a sinker in his arsenal, but it's a distant fifth pitch. Don't be fooled by his big frame, either. Cavalli is a plus athlete who fields his position well. He struggled a bit in his short time at Triple-A, but the organization is working with him to get outs in the zone more often, a necessity against mature hitters.

THE FUTURE: The Nationals couldn't have asked for much more out of Cavalli in 2021, and he looks the part of a middle of the rotation starter whose arrival will come sooner rather than later.

BA GRADE
60 Risk: High

SCOUTING GRADES:	Fastball: 70	Slider: 60	Curveball: 55	Changeup: 50	Control: 50

Year	Age	Club (Level)	Lge	W	L	ERA	G	GS	IP	H	HR	BB	SO	BB/9	SO/9	WHIP	AVG
2021	22	Wilmington (HiA)	East	3	1	1.77	7	7	41	24	1	12	71	2.66	15.71	0.89	.171
	22	Harrisburg (AA)	NEast	3	3	2.79	11	11	58	39	2	35	80	5.43	12.41	1.28	.188
	22	Rochester (AAA)	East	1	5	7.30	6	6	25	33	2	13	24	4.74	8.76	1.86	.317
Minor League Totals (2 years)				7	9	3.36	24	24	123	96	5	60	175	4.38	12.77	1.26	.213

3 BRADY HOUSE, SS

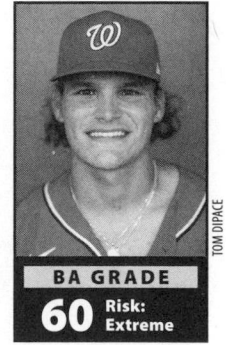

Born: June 4, 2003. **B-T:** R-R. **HT:** 6-4. **WT:** 215. **Drafted:** HS—Winder, Ga., 2021 (1st round). **Signed by:** Eric Robinson.

TRACK RECORD: House was ranked among the best prep prospects in the 2021 draft, and at one point was considered a possible top overall pick, thanks in large part to loud offensive tools. The Nationals selected him 11th overall and signed him for $5 million, the seventh-highest in the class and a little more than $450,000 over the pick value. House shined in the Florida Complex League after signing, hitting .322/.394/.576 and showing an exciting all-around game.

SCOUTING REPORT: Power is House's most noteworthy tool, with some evaluators believing that he could eventually have 70-grade raw power. He also earned high marks in his debut for showing the ability to hit the ball to all fields with authority. Whether he sticks at shortstop is the biggest outstanding question with House, but he showed nothing in the FCL to suggest the Nationals should look to move him anytime soon. He's not the flashiest defender, but he makes all the routine plays look routine, has good hands, an on-time internal clock and more than enough arm for the position.

THE FUTURE: As a player who just turned 18 in June, House has a lengthy climb in front of him. But it also would be impossible for the organization not to be enthused by what they saw in 2021. Testing himself at Low-A is due up next season.

BA GRADE
60 Risk: Extreme

SCOUTING GRADES:	Hitting: 50	Power: 65	Running: 50	Fielding: 55	Arm: 60

Year	Age	Club (Level)	Lge	AVG	G	AB	R	H	2B	3B	HR	RBI	BB	SO	SB	OBP	SLG
2021	18	FCL Nationals (R)	FCL	.322	16	59	14	19	3	0	4	12	7	13	0	.394	.576
Minor League Totals (1 year)				.322	16	59	14	19	3	0	4	12	7	13	0	.394	.576

4 YASEL ANTUNA, OF

Born: Oct. 26, 1999. **B-T:** B-R. **HT:** 6-0. **WT:** 170. **Signed:** Dominican Republic, 2016. **Signed by:** Pablo Arias.

TRACK RECORD: Signed for $3.85 million out of the Dominican Republic in 2016, Antuna had not played much in 2019 or 2020 thanks to injuries and the pandemic, save for a very impressive stint at the alternate training site in 2020. That rust showed in a 4-for-67 start at High-A Wilmington in 2021, but a late-season push in which he hit .315 in July and August helped him finish strong and get back on track. As much as anything else, it was valuable for Antuna to get through a full season healthy and productive.

SCOUTING REPORT: Antuna has one of the most exciting offensive profiles in the Nationals' system. A switch-hitter who is seen as being better from the left side, his bat speed and repeatable swing from both sides help him hit the ball to all fields with authority. A couple of adjustments during the season in 2021, including getting his lower half more involved in his swing and switching from a two-handed finish to a higher one-handed finish are viewed as helping him work back from the extended slump early in the season. He's a plus athlete, but there have always been questions about his viability as a shortstop. To that end, the organization worked with him on transitioning to the outfield corners.

THE FUTURE: Antuna was always destined to be a bat-first prospect, but a move to the outfield provides clarity on his profile. As long as he hits, he will continue to move. Double-A is his next stop.

BA GRADE
55 Risk: Extreme

SCOUTING GRADES:	Hitting: 50	Power: 60	Running: 50	Fielding: 45	Arm: 50

Year	Age	Club (Level)	Lge	AVG	G	AB	R	H	2B	3B	HR	RBI	BB	SO	SB	OBP	SLG
2021	21	Wilmington (HiA)	East	.227	106	405	55	92	26	1	12	65	46	100	4	.307	.385
Minor League Totals (5 years)				.238	244	907	125	216	48	6	19	109	103	209	17	.317	.367

5 ANDRY LARA, RHP

Born: Jan. 6, 2003. **B-T:** R-R. **HT:** 6-5. **WT:** 235. **Signed:** Venezuela, 2019. **Signed by:** Ronald Morillo.

TRACK RECORD: Lara signed for $1.25 million as the top player in the Nationals' 2019 international class, meaning he had the misfortune of having his debut delayed due to the pandemic. After spending 2020 sequestered in a hotel and the team facility in West Palm Beach, Fla., and then battling through struggles at instructional league late in the year, Lara finally debuted in the Florida Complex League in 2021, pitching well enough to earn a promotion to Low-A Fredericksburg near the end of the season.

SCOUTING REPORT: Lara has a smooth, classically beautiful delivery, clean arm action, a physical frame and the stuff to match. He gets good extension on a fastball that has made a recent velocity jump into the mid 90s. His breaking ball is a potential plus pitch down the line, and he flashes a changeup that also projects to be a usable pitch. Given his youth, it's no surprise that Lara is still tapping into his strength, but at the same time, he is given high marks for preternaturally good feel to pitch and for being a leader by example.

THE FUTURE: Lara may be seen as a long way away from the big leagues given his age, and that's true from the standpoint that next season will be his first crack at a full-season league, but he possesses traits that suggest he could move through the system quickly. He has the upside to be a front-end starting pitcher if he continues to progress.

BA GRADE
55 Risk: Extreme

SCOUTING GRADES:	Fastball: 60	Slider: 60	Changeup: 50	Control: 50

Year	Age	Club (Level)	Lge	W	L	ERA	G	GS	IP	H	HR	BB	SO	BB/9	SO/9	WHIP	AVG
2021	18	FCL Nationals (R)	FCL	3	2	4.54	9	7	40	35	5	13	47	2.95	10.66	1.21	.230
	18	Fredericksburg (LoA)	East	0	1	5.19	2	2	9	6	2	8	5	8.31	5.19	1.62	.200
Minor League Totals (1 year)				3	3	4.66	11	9	48	41	7	21	52	3.91	9.68	1.28	.225

6 COLE HENRY, RHP

Born: July 15, 1999. **B-T:** R-R. **HT:** 6-4. **WT:** 214. **Drafted:** Louisiana State, 2020 (2nd round). **Signed by:** Brandon Larson.

TRACK RECORD: In two years at Louisiana State, Henry had a 3.61 ERA and 95 strikeouts in 77.1 innings. As a draft-eligible sophomore, the righthander was selected in the second round at the end of the 2020 season. He debuted in 2021 and was excellent for High-A Wilmington. He missed some time in the middle of the season with elbow soreness, but upon returning, he finished the season as strong as he started.

SCOUTING REPORT: Henry has a power repertoire, including both a four-seam and two-seam fastball that run into the mid 90s, with the four-seam fastball touching the high 90s. His changeup, which features good armside life, is currently his best secondary pitch and tunnels well with his fastball. But his curveball, a short breaker that has been an inconsistent offering for him, tightened up over the course of the season and shows signs of being a plus pitch down the line. In addition to his considerable stuff, Henry goes right after hitters, pitching with moxie and little fear. There is some reliever risk with Henry, because some rival evaluators make note of his reliever arm action.

THE FUTURE: The organization is thrilled with where Henry is after he came back from injury strong. A healthy 2022 season will be key in his development, as it will presumably give him a chance to handle a heavier workload than he has to this point of his career.

BA GRADE

50 Risk: High

MARY DECICCO/MLB PHOTOS VIA GETTY IMAGES

SCOUTING GRADES:			Fastball: 60			Curveball: 50				Changeup: 60			Control: 50		
Year	**Age**	**Club (Level)**	**Lge**	**W**	**L**	**ERA**	**G**	**GS**	**IP**	**H**	**HR**	**BB**	**SO**	**BB/9**	**SO/9**	**WHIP**	**AVG**
2021	21	FCL Nationals (R)	FCL	0	2	6.75	2	2	4	5	0	1	7	2.25	15.75	1.50	.278
	21	Wilmington (HiA)	East	3	3	1.88	9	8	43	23	3	11	63	2.30	13.19	0.79	.158
Minor League Totals (2 years)				3	5	2.30	11	10	47	28	3	12	70	2.30	13.40	0.85	.171

7 JOAN ADON, RHP

Born: Aug. 12, 1998. **B-T:** R-R. **HT:** 6-2. **WT:** 185. **Signed:** Dominican Republic, 2016. **Signed by:** Pablo Arias.

TRACK RECORD: Initially a $50,000 signing, Adon has already far surpassed the expectations set by his relatively modest status as part of the Nationals' 2016 international signing class. The Nationals placed Adon on the 40-man roster after he impressed at the alternate training site in 2020. He validated the confidence the organization showed in him by climbing the ladder through High-A, Double-A and Triple-A in 2021 to make his major league debut in September, throwing 5.1 innings with nine strikeouts against the Red Sox at home.

SCOUTING REPORT: Adon has always had a good fastball, and that pitch averaged 94-96 mph 2021 and touched 97-98. Improvement in both his slider and changeup between his last full season in 2019 and the 2021 season helped him catapult to the big leagues. He gets good depth on an above-average power slider, though some evaluators note that it's more of a chase pitch right now than one he lands consistently for a strike. Command of this offering might be the key to further improvement. His solid-average changeup shows good armside life. Back-to-back seasons of more than 100 innings as a starter has also proven his durability.

THE FUTURE: Adon's experience as a reliever in 2017 and 2018 and lingering concerns about command made many consider him a future reliever. His power stuff would still make him a potentially good fit as a big league bullpen, but his 2021 season allayed many of the concerns about him and opened eyes to the possibility that he sticks as a starter.

BA GRADE

45 Risk: Medium

DECICCO/MLB PHOTOS VIA GETTY IMAGES

SCOUTING GRADES:			Fastball: 60			Slider: 55				Changeup: 50			Control: 45		
Year	**Age**	**Club (Level)**	**Lge**	**W**	**L**	**ERA**	**G**	**GS**	**IP**	**H**	**HR**	**BB**	**SO**	**BB/9**	**SO/9**	**WHIP**	**AVG**
2021	22	Wilmington (HiA)	East	6	4	4.97	17	17	87	77	7	32	91	3.31	9.41	1.25	.235
	22	Harrisburg (AA)	NEast	1	2	6.43	3	3	14	15	1	5	24	3.21	15.43	1.43	.263
	22	Rochester (AAA)	East	0	0	0.00	1	1	4	2	0	3	7	6.75	15.75	1.25	.143
	22	Washington (MLB)	NL	0	0	3.38	1	1	5	6	1	3	9	5.06	15.19	1.69	.300
Major League Totals (1 year)				0	0	3.38	1	1	5	6	1	3	9	5.06	15.19	1.69	.300
Minor League Totals (5 years)				23	11	4.29	76	42	269	244	19	115	283	3.85	9.48	1.34	.241

8 GERARDO CARRILLO, RHP

Born: Sept. 3, 1998. **B-T:** R-R. **HT:** 6-1. **WT:** 180. **Signed:** Mexico, 2016.
Signed by: Mike Brito/Roman Barinas/Juvenal Soto (Dodgers).

TRACK RECORD: Carrillo's velocity made a big jump after he grew three inches and put on 25 pounds soon after signing in 2016, but his quest since then has been to harness his stuff. Formerly buried fairly deep in a loaded Dodgers organization, Carrillo immediately became one of the Nationals' top pitching prospects after coming over in the deal that sent Max Scherzer and Trea Turner to Los Angeles.

SCOUTING REPORT: A great athlete with a lightning-quick arm, Carrillo can pitch east to west with electric stuff. He leads with a fastball that sits 94-97 mph and has touched 99 with massive sink and run. He generates that velocity with relative ease and can hold it deep into his outings. His fastball pairs well with his best secondary pitch, a short, firm slider/cutter hybrid going the other direction in the high 80s to low 90s. He also works with a slurvy curveball and a changeup that are clearly behind the fastball and slider. Well below-average control continues to be a nagging issue for Carrillo, and that limits his upside, but there's hope that improvements still to come in repeating his mechanics and optimizing pitch usage could raise his profile as a potential starter.

THE FUTURE: The command issues that persist for Carrillo as he works his way closer to the big leagues make a future in the bullpen increasingly likely. As a member of the Nationals' 40-man roster and with his fantastic stuff, that future might not be that far away.

BA GRADE	
50	**Risk:** Very High

JENNIFER STEWART/MLB PHOTOS VIA GETTY IMAGES

SCOUTING GRADES:	Fastball: 65	Slider: 60	Curveball: 45	Changeup: 50	Control: 30

Year	Age	Club (Level)	Lge	W	L	ERA	G	GS	IP	H	HR	BB	SO	BB/9	SO/9	WHIP	AVG
2021	22	Tulsa (AA)	Cent	3	2	4.25	15	14	59	49	9	29	70	4.40	10.62	1.31	.221
	22	Harrisburg (AA)	NEast	0	5	5.59	8	8	37	40	5	21	38	5.11	9.24	1.65	.270
Minor League Totals (5 years)				17	19	3.96	73	63	291	261	21	132	276	4.09	8.55	1.35	.237

9 JACKSON RUTLEDGE, RHP

Born: April 1, 1999. **B-T:** R-R. **HT:** 6-8. **WT:** 245. **Drafted:** San Jacinto (Texas) JC, 2019 (1st round). **Signed by:** Brandon Larson.

TRACK RECORD: Leading with a fastball that touched triple digits, Rutledge was dominant in his one season at San Jacinto (Texas) JC, along the way becoming the rare junior college player to be named a semifinalist for the Golden Spikes Award. That performance was enough for the Nationals to draft him 17th overall in 2019. After an excellent debut season in 2019, Rutledge earned some time at the alternate training site in 2020, but he took a step back last season, thanks at least in part to shoulder tightness early in the season and recurring blisters later in the year.

SCOUTING REPORT: Rutledge has a striking 6-foot-8, 245-pound frame on the mound and a mean fastball to match. The pitch is not only a high-90s offering that touches triple digits, but it features good cut and carry. His best secondary pitch is a slider that is at times a wipeout pitch. Currently, he's working on learning how to manipulate his slider to better throw it in the strike zone and to give him a couple of different versions of the pitch. An average curveball and changeup give Rutledge a traditional starter's repertoire, but concerns about consistency have made some wonder if his future is as a high-leverage reliever.

THE FUTURE: As recently as 2020 instructional league, some rival evaluators saw Rutledge as not far off from Cade Cavalli in the prospect pecking order, but Cavalli continued to take off in 2021 while Rutledge faltered. Still, the latter's stuff is some of the best in the system, and having a healthy 2022 season would go a long way toward getting him back on track.

BA GRADE	
50	**Risk:** Very High

MARY DECICCO/MLB PHOTOS VIA GETTY IMAGES

SCOUTING GRADES:	Fastball: 70	Slider: 60	Curveball: 50	Changeup: 50	Control: 45

Year	Age	Club (Level)	Lge	W	L	ERA	G	GS	IP	H	HR	BB	SO	BB/9	SO/9	WHIP	AVG
2021	22	FCL Nationals (R)	FCL	0	1	7.36	2	2	4	3	1	2	5	4.91	12.27	1.36	.214
	22	Fredericksburg (LoA)	East	1	2	5.32	7	7	22	20	1	9	26	3.68	10.64	1.32	.235
	22	Wilmington (HiA)	East	0	3	12.66	4	4	11	17	0	9	10	7.59	8.44	2.44	.370
Minor League Totals (3 years)				3	6	5.38	23	23	74	62	4	35	80	4.28	9.77	1.32	.225

10 ARMANDO CRUZ, SS

Born: Jan. 16, 2004. **B-T:** R-R. **HT:** 5-11. **WT:** 165. **Signed:** Dominican Republic, 2021. **Signed by:** Modesto Ulloa/Ricky Vasquez.

TRACK RECORD: One of the highest-profile international players available in the 2020-21 signing class, Cruz inked a $3.9 million deal with the Nationals one day before his 17th birthday, giving him the largest bonus awarded to a 16-year-old in the class. Cruz got his feet wet in the Dominican Summer League.

SCOUTING REPORT: Cruz is a high-end defensive player who had international scouts raving about his ability prior to his signing. He has great hands, extremely quick feet and a smooth transfer to his above-average arm, which helps him make the flashy play look routine. He charges the ball well using speed that has improved from below-average to slightly above-average in recent years. Though he can dazzle with some of the tricks he can pull fielding the ball in practice, it's not just physical tools that make him a near double-plus shortstop. He also gets fast reads off the bat and is an instinctive player. Offensively, he's very much a work in progress, but the Nationals like his natural bat-to-ball skills and saw improvement at the plate as the summer wore on. He'll undoubtedly add some strength as he matures, but power is not likely to be a part of his game in the end.

THE FUTURE: Cruz's defensive prowess is such that evaluators project him to be a plus defender, with a ceiling as one of the elite defensive shortstops in baseball. That will be his ticket through the Nationals' system, with his offensive value being the icing on the cake should he come into his own in that regard.

BA GRADE
50 Risk: Extreme

SCOUTING GRADES:	Hitting: 50	Power: 40	Running: 55	Fielding: 65	Arm: 55

Year	Age	Club (Level)	Lge	AVG	G	AB	R	H	2B	3B	HR	RBI	BB	SO	SB	OBP	SLG
2021	17	DSL Nationals (R)	DSL	.232	48	177	22	41	8	1	1	17	16	27	11	.292	.305
Minor League Totals (1 year)				.232	48	177	22	41	8	1	1	17	16	27	11	.292	.305

11 MASON THOMPSON, RHP

BA GRADE
40 Risk: Medium

Born: Feb. 20, 1998. **B-T:** R-R. **HT:** 6-7. **WT:** 223. **Drafted:** HS—Round Rock, Texas, 2016 (3rd round). **Signed by:** Matt Schaffner (Padres).

TRACK RECORD: Injuries were a massive part of Thompson's story leading up to last season. He had Tommy John in high school, then faced various shoulder, triceps and elbow issues during the 2017, 2018 and 2019 minor league seasons. He got healthy during the 2020 shutdown and impressed at instructional league the following fall. After coming to Washington in the Daniel Hudson trade in July, Thompson had a 4.15 ERA in 27 appearances as a member of the Nationals' bullpen late in the season.

SCOUTING REPORT: Thompson's fastball sits 94-98 mph, with the ability to really air it out in short stints. His best secondary offering is a slider from 88-90 mph, giving him a true power reliever fastball-slider combination, but he also features a 12-to-6 curveball and a changeup. Righthanded batters hit .358 against Thompson last season, which reversed his minor league trend of handling righties well. The hope for Thompson is that ends up being just small-sample noise in the end.

THE FUTURE: In a healthy 2021 season, Thompson showed his value as a short reliever in a big league bullpen. He'll go into 2022 with a chance to further cement his place as a key piece of the Nationals' bullpen moving forward.

Year	Age	Club (Level)	Lge	W	L	ERA	G	GS	IP	H	HR	BB	SO	BB/9	SO/9	WHIP	AVG
2021	23	El Paso (AAA)	West	3	2	5.74	23	0	27	25	4	8	24	2.7	8.1	1.24	.245
	23	San Diego (MLB)	NL	0	0	3.00	4	0	3	4	0	1	2	3.0	6.0	1.67	.333
	23	Washington (MLB)	NL	1	3	4.15	27	0	22	28	4	14	21	5.82	8.72	1.94	.308
Major League Totals (1 year)				1	3	4.01	31	0	25	32	4	15	23	5.47	8.39	1.91	.311
Minor League Totals (6 years)				11	19	5.18	67	40	186	179	18	84	186	4.06	9.00	1.41	.248

12 RILEY ADAMS, C

BA GRADE
40 Risk: Medium

Born: June 26, 1996. **B-T:** R-R. **HT:** 6-4. **WT:** 225. **Drafted:** San Diego, 2017 (3rd round). **Signed by:** Jim Lentine (Blue Jays).

TRACK RECORD: A third-round pick of the Blue Jays in 2017, Adams steadily hit his way to the big leagues over the course of four years. He debuted with the Blue Jays in June before being sent to Washington for Brad Hand just before the trade deadline. With the Nationals down the stretch, he hit .268/.422/.465 in 35 games.

SCOUTING REPORT: Adams has a power-based skill set, both defensively and at the plate, which matches his physical frame. As a hitter, he has plus or maybe even plus-plus raw power that comes with some swing and miss thanks to length in his swing, but not enough swing and miss that he can't get to power during games. Defensively, he has plus arm strength, but issues in his release keep his arm from being as effective as it could be. In past minor league seasons, he nabbed greater than 40% of would-be base stealers, but those numbers eroded as the competition got better.

THE FUTURE: With the ability to hit the ball out of the ballpark and limit the run game somewhat with his arm, Adams has value as a toolsy backup catcher, and with Keibert Ruiz ahead of him, that's likely his immediate future. However, if he continues to produce as he did in a small sample in 2021, he could also elbow his way into at-bats at other positions.

Year	Age	Club (Level)	Lge	AVG	G	AB	R	H	2B	3B	HR	RBI	BB	SO	SB	OBP	SLG
2021	25	Buffalo (AAA)	East	.239	35	117	20	28	6	1	7	17	16	46	0	.371	.487
	25	Rochester (AAA)	East	.000	1	3	0	0	0	0	0	0	2	0	0	.400	.000
	25	Toronto (MLB)	AL	.107	12	28	2	3	2	0	0	0	2	12	0	.167	.179
	25	Washington (MLB)	NL	.268	35	71	11	19	6	1	2	10	13	28	0	.422	.465
Major League Totals (1 year)				**.222**	**47**	**99**	**13**	**22**	**8**	**1**	**2**	**10**	**15**	**40**	**0**	**.358**	**.384**
Minor League Totals (5 years)				**.262**	**287**	**1024**	**153**	**268**	**66**	**5**	**28**	**146**	**132**	**312**	**8**	**.364**	**.418**

13 ALDO RAMIREZ, RHP

BA GRADE

50 Risk: Extreme

Born: May 6, 2001. **B-T:** R-R. **HT:** 6-0. **WT:** 180. **Signed:** Mexico, 2018. **Signed by:** Sotero Torres/Eddie Romero/Todd Claus (Red Sox).

TRACK RECORD: Ramirez signed with the Red Sox out of the Mexican League for $550,000 in 2018. He continued to pitch well against more mature competition, first in the Dominican Summer League in 2018 and later in the New York-Penn League in 2019. After starting 2021 off strong at Low-A Salem, Ramirez was sidelined with elbow tendonitis in June and was traded to Washington in exchange for Kyle Schwarber in July. After the trade, he made just a handful of appearances in the Florida Complex League.

SCOUTING REPORT: Ramirez has always stood out for the way his stuff plays up due to his good fastball command and feel for his secondary pitches. In recent years, his stuff has ticked up, however, with his fastball now touching 98, all while maintaining feel for a potential plus curveball with impressive movement and depth and a potential average changeup. His numbers in the FCL after the trade weren't pretty, but some in the organization point to Ramirez perhaps trying to do too much in an effort to make a good first impression.

THE FUTURE: Being healthy through a full season workload at Low-A or High-A will be a good next step. If Ramirez can continue his mastery of the finer points of pitching while his stuff ticks up, a future as a back-of-the-rotation starter is in play.

Year	Age	Club (Level)	Lge	W	L	ERA	G	GS	IP	H	HR	BB	SO	BB/9	SO/9	WHIP	AVG
2021	20	FCL Nationals (R)	FCL	1	1	8.22	4	2	8	9	0	4	3	4.7	3.52	1.70	.300
	20	Salem (LoA)	East	1	1	2.03	8	8	31	27	1	8	32	2.32	9.29	1.13	.221
Minor League Totals (4 years)				**5**	**7**	**3.19**	**36**	**28**	**130**	**112**	**8**	**37**	**118**	**2.57**	**8.19**	**1.15**	**.226**

14 JEREMY DE LA ROSA, OF

BA GRADE

45 Risk: Very High

Born: Jan. 16, 2002. **B-T:** L-L. **HT:** 5-11. **WT:** 160. **Signed:** Dominican Republic, 2018. **Signed by:** Modesto Ulloa.

TRACK RECORD: The Nationals signed de la Rosa for $300,000 in 2018 and started him stateside in the Gulf Coast League rather than Dominican Summer League. They continued to push him aggressively by making him part of the 60-man player pool in 2020 and having him compete at the alternate training site. He struggled in his first full minor league season with Fredericksburg, with a .595 OPS and a nearly 40% strikeout rate.

SCOUTING REPORT: De la Rosa has a well-rounded set of tools. He's a plus runner underway, a good athlete, a potential future plus defender in the outfield, even if that future ends up at a corner, and is an intriguing offensive player. There is confidence that he will be at least an average hitter, as he has a preternatural ability to get in a good hitting position and hit the ball on a line with authority, but evaluators are more mixed on his power. He shows plus raw power in spurts, with some assuming a solid hit tool will help him continue to unlock that power as he matures and others unsure that he'll ever have better than below-average power in-game.

THE FUTURE: The Nationals were aggressive in moving de la Rosa early, but he's still a raw prospect. He simply needs to keep compiling at-bats in large numbers.

Year	Age	Club (Level)	Lge	AVG	G	AB	R	H	2B	3B	HR	RBI	BB	SO	SB	OBP	SLG
2021	19	Fredericksburg (LoA)	East	.209	87	326	34	68	12	4	5	22	30	122	7	.279	.316
Minor League Totals (3 years)				.213	113	408	48	87	13	6	7	32	42	151	10	.293	.326

15 MATT CRONIN, LHP

BA GRADE

40 Risk: High

Born: Sept. 20, 1997. **B-T:** L-L. **HT:** 6-2. **WT:** 195. **Drafted:** Arkansas, 2019 (4th round). **Signed by:** Jerad Head.

TRACK RECORD: Cronin put up a 2.77 ERA in 64 relief appearances for powerhouse Arkansas over three college seasons before being drafted in the fourth round in 2019. He dominated in his debut in 2019 in Low-A, and after spending time at the alternate training site in 2020, picked up where he left off in 2021 with mostly dominant outings in the FCL and in High-A, which earned him a promotion to Double-A Harrisburg. He took some lumps and battled his command in his first look at Double-A, but still managed 18 strikeouts in 11.1 innings.

SCOUTING REPORT: There's little ambiguity about Cronin's profile as he moves through the system. He's a reliever, and a good one at that. He works with a high-spin fastball that reaches the mid 90s and a 12-to-6 curveball that has good depth and late break. Both pitches show plus potential. He'll also use a split changeup, but it's a third offering at this point. Cronin has a back-end bullpen mentality and isn't afraid to go after hitters. Some rival evaluators see Cronin as being a Sean Doolittle type of reliever at the big league level.

THE FUTURE: Cronin fits the archetype of the fast-moving college reliever, and with his move all the way up to Double-A in 2021, his big league debut is not that far off in the distance.

Year	Age	Club (Level)	Lge	W	L	ERA	G	GS	IP	H	HR	BB	SO	BB/9	SO/9	WHIP	AVG
2021	23	FCL Nationals (R)	FCL	2	0	2.25	3	0	4	3	0	1	4	2.25	9.0	1.00	.214
	23	Wilmington (HiA)	East	2	0	1.23	10	0	15	8	0	5	28	3.07	17.18	0.89	.163
	23	Harrisburg (AA)	NEast	0	1	5.56	10	0	11	9	2	10	18	7.94	14.29	1.68	.220
Minor League Totals (3 years)				4	1	2.08	40	0	52	31	3	27	91	4.67	15.75	1.12	.176

16 JACKSON CLUFF, SS

BA GRADE

40 Risk: High

Born: Dec. 3, 1996. **B-T:** L-R. **HT:** 6-0. **WT:** 185. **Drafted:** Brigham Young, 2019 (6th round). **Signed by:** Mitch Sokol.

TRACK RECORD: Cluff had just one year, 2019, as a starter at Brigham Young, as he spent the 2017 and 2018 seasons on his Mormon mission, but it was strong enough for him to be selected in the sixth round that year. The Nationals have been aggressive with Cluff. He began at Low-A in 2019, spent time at the alternate training site in 2020 and skipped High-A to spend much of the 2021 season at Double-A Harrisburg.

SCOUTING REPORT: Cluff is a player whose intangibles stand out. The organization raves about his makeup. From a skill standpoint, Cluff is an advanced defender with a strong arm who can handle second base or shortstop. Offensively, he has an aggressive approach at the plate, looking for his pitch early in counts. He uses all fields, he has some pop but isn't a masher, and while he's not a burner, he's a willing base stealer. His performance at the plate in the Arizona Fall League this year turned heads as well.

THE FUTURE: After some growing pains in Harrisburg, Cluff started to get comfortable, only to have injuries slow him. A repeat of that level is likely. His maturity and defense give him a high floor as a utility infielder.

Year	Age	Club (Level)	Lge	AVG	G	AB	R	H	2B	3B	HR	RBI	BB	SO	SB	OBP	SLG
2021	24	FCL Nationals (R)	FCL	.333	5	15	2	5	0	0	0	1	1	5	3	.412	.333
	24	Fredericksburg (LoA)	East	.278	5	18	2	5	1	0	0	0	2	3	1	.409	.333
	24	Harrisburg (AA)	NEast	.190	35	126	14	24	5	0	2	9	9	39	3	.278	.278
Minor League Totals (3 years)				.223	107	399	51	89	14	5	7	29	38	110	18	.315	.336

17 DONOVAN CASEY, OF

BA GRADE

40 Risk: High

Born: Feb. 23, 1996. **B-T:** R-R. **HT:** 6-2. **WT:** 190. **Drafted:** Boston College, 2017 (20th round). **Signed by:** Rich DeLucia (Dodgers).

TRACK RECORD: A 20th-round draft pick out of Boston College in 2017, Casey has already provided outstanding pick value by riding a well-rounded skill set all the way to the upper levels of the minors. After hitting well in a repeat trip to Double-A Tulsa early in 2021, Casey was dealt to Washington as part of the Max Scherzer and Trea Turner blockbuster.

SCOUTING REPORT: After not hitting for much power at Boston College despite having above-average raw power, Casey has had no such problem hitting for power in the minor leagues. He has holes in his swing, which has at times led to a high strikeout rate, peaking at nearly 40% at Triple-A Rochester last season. He's an outstanding defender with a rifle for an arm, excellent athleticism and good speed. While in Tulsa, opposing managers in Double-A Central voted him the best defensive outfielder and best outfield arm in the league.

THE FUTURE: By getting out of a loaded Dodgers system, the path to the big leagues, and regular playing time, has opened up a bit for Casey. He'll be 26 on opening day next season, but he's been productive at every stop so far and he provides tremendous defensive value. A big league debut in 2022 is on the table.

Year	Age	Club (Level)	Lge	AVG	G	AB	R	H	2B	3B	HR	RBI	BB	SO	SB	OBP	SLG
2021	25	Tulsa (AA)	Cent	.296	73	301	51	89	15	1	11	36	26	102	15	.362	.462
	25	Harrisburg (AA)	NEast	.347	12	49	6	17	2	1	3	10	1	9	2	.353	.612
	25	Rochester (AAA)	East	.179	38	134	15	24	9	0	2	9	9	57	5	.245	.291
Minor League Totals (5 years)				.278	355	1395	253	388	65	16	53	199	116	441	52	.338	.462

18 DAYLEN LILE, OF

Born: Nov. 30, 2002. **B-T:** L-R. **HT:** 6-0. **WT:** 195. **Drafted:** HS—Louisville, 2021 (2nd round). **Signed by:** Brian Cleary.

BA GRADE
45 Risk: Extreme

TRACK RECORD: Few high school hitters in the 2021 draft class had a long-term track record of hitting at a high level like Lile's. That earned him a place on the high school All-America team in 2021 and a second-round selection by the Nationals, who were excited to add his polished bat to the system. He signed for $1.75 million, or $169,800 over the pick value. He spent his first season in the Florida Complex League, where he was primarily limited to DH duty due to an arm injury.

SCOUTING REPORT: Lile has a quiet setup at the plate with very little pre-pitch movement. His swing is easy and repeatable, and he leans on his hands to spray line drives to all fields. With a relatively light frame at present, some evaluators are dubious of his future power projection, but internally, there is hope power will come along later. Some evaluators see Lile as a potential center fielder down the line, but more likely, he ends up in left field thanks to fringy arm strength and average speed.

THE FUTURE: Because he doesn't project to add much value defensively and power may never be part of his game, Lile is going to have to hit, hit and hit some more, as he did all throughout his prep days, in order to move up the ladder.

Year	Age	Club (Level)	Lge	AVG	G	AB	R	H	2B	3B	HR	RBI	BB	SO	SB	OBP	SLG
2021	18	FCL Nationals (R)	FCL	.219	19	64	16	14	2	0	0	10	15	20	2	.363	.250
Minor League Totals (1 year)				.219	19	64	16	14	2	0	0	10	15	20	2	.363	.250

19 TIM CATE, LHP

Born: Sept. 30, 1997. **B-T:** L-L. **HT:** 6-0. **WT:** 185. **Drafted:** Connecticut, 2018 (2nd round). **Signed by:** John Malone.

BA GRADE
40 Risk: High

TRACK RECORD: Connecticut's career strikeout leader, Cate was selected in the second round in 2018. He had a big year in 2019, winning the Nationals' minor league pitcher of the year. He spent time at the alternate training site in 2020 before stumbling at Double-A Harrisburg in 2021.

SCOUTING REPORT: Cate does a lot of things well to be effective despite being undersized and having something less than electric stuff across the board. He has an easy delivery, he moves the ball around the zone well and he can locate. His curveball is the one current plus pitch in his arsenal, and it's a true hammer. His changeup shows signs of being a future above-average offering, but he was inconsistent with it in 2021. His fastball has fringy velocity in the high 80s and low 90s, but his ability to cut and sink it helps move it off barrels. Cate is capable of plus-plus command, and the reality is that he needs it, because he gets hit more than most when he misses spots, as was the case in Harrisburg.

THE FUTURE: There's likely a place in the big leagues at some point for Cate just based on his durability, pitchability, moxie and his ability to use his curveball as a weapon at will.

Year	Age	Club (Level)	Lge	W	L	ERA	G	GS	IP	H	HR	BB	SO	BB/9	SO/9	WHIP	AVG
2021	23	Harrisburg (AA)	NEast	2	10	5.31	21	21	97	113	12	37	81	3.44	7.54	1.55	.288
Minor League Totals (4 years)				15	25	4.16	60	59	292	302	23	85	265	2.62	8.16	1.32	.264

20 SAMMY INFANTE

Born: June 22, 2001. **B-T:** R-R. **HT:** 6-1. **WT:** 175. **Drafted:** HS—Miami, 2020 (2nd round supplemental). **Signed by:** Alex Morales.

BA GRADE
45 Risk: Extreme

TRACK RECORD: One of the top shortstops in the 2020 high school class, Infante was drafted 71st overall and signed for an over-slot $1 million bonus to buy him out of his college commitment to Miami. Later that summer, he worked at the Nationals' alternate training site. He got his first taste of the minor leagues in the Florida Complex League in 2021.

SCOUTING REPORT: Infante struggled in his debut season as he learned what it takes to be a pro and the level of consistency that it requires to be successful. His maturity and level-headedness, which were repeatedly mentioned as among his strongest attributes during the draft process and at the alternate site, no doubt helped him push through. He embraced playing second base in the FCL in deference to his teammate Brady House, but he has the strong fundamentals, soft hands and strong arm needed to at least earn a shot to stick at shortstop. Moving forward, Infante will have to cut down on the whiffs, but there is confidence he can be at least an average hitter with occasional power.

THE FUTURE: Given that he will be two years removed the draft, the 2022 season will be big for Infante to take strides forward, even understanding that he's still a long way from the big leagues.

Year	Age	Club (Level)	Lge	AVG	G	AB	R	H	2B	3B	HR	RBI	BB	SO	SB	OBP	SLG
2021	20	FCL Nationals (R)	FCL	.215	37	121	19	26	5	2	3	15	17	43	3	.329	.364
Minor League Totals (2 years)				.215	37	121	19	26	5	2	3	15	17	43	3	.329	.364

21 MITCHELL PARKER, LHP

BA GRADE

40 Risk: High

Born: Sept. 27, 1999. **B-T:** L-L. **HT:** 6-4. **WT:** 195. **Drafted:** San Jacinto (Texas) JC, 2020 (5th round). **Signed by:** Jimmy Gonzales.

TRACK RECORD: A $100,000 signing as a fifth-round pick in 2020, Parker was productive out of the gate in his debut season in 2021. He had a 4.08 ERA and 85 strikeouts in 57.1 innings in Low-A before earning a promotion to High-A, where his 5.89 ERA doesn't fully reflect how effective he was.

SCOUTING REPORT: Parker has a varied repertoire that could help him stick as a starter, even without plus stuff across the board. With a delivery that could use some refinement, his fastball typically sits in the low 90s with elite carry, and he maintains that velocity well into his starts. He also features a low-80s splitter that one rival evaluator described as having "crazy" movement similar to that of a cutter, a changeup with plus sink and a mid-70s curveball with good depth that is better against left-handed hitters than right-handed hitters. None of those pitches are elite, but all have average or better potential. Parker has also proven to be a good competitor in his starts.

THE FUTURE: As long as Parker performs like he did in 2021, expect him to move. Without any setbacks, Double-A in 2022 should be in his sights.

Year	Age	Club (Level)	Lge	W	L	ERA	G	GS	IP	H	HR	BB	SO	BB/9	SO/9	WHIP	AVG
2021	21	Fredericksburg (LoA)	East	3	7	4.08	12	10	57	47	8	21	85	3.3	13.34	1.19	.215
	21	Wilmington (HiA)	East	1	5	5.89	11	11	44	56	4	17	59	3.45	11.98	1.65	.303
Minor League Totals (2 years)				4	12	4.87	23	21	102	103	12	38	144	3.36	12.75	1.39	.255

22 EVAN LEE, LHP

BA GRADE

40 Risk: High

Born: June 18, 1997. **B-T:** L-L. **HT:** 6-1. **WT:** 200. **Drafted:** Arkansas, 2018 (15th round). **Signed by:** Terry Wetzel.

TRACK RECORD: A 15th-round pick out of Arkansas as a draft-eligible sophomore in 2018, Lee has already wildly exceeded his draft position with his performance in the Nationals' system. He excelled in the New York-Penn League in 2019, mostly as a reliever, putting up 2.65 ERA in 34 innings, and followed that up as a starter by striking out 104 batters in 77 innings in High-A in 2021.

SCOUTING REPORT: Lee gets good extension on a fastball that primarily sat 91-93 mph last season but has touched the mid 90s in the past. He also features a potential plus curveball with an 11-to-5 shape that is a real put-away pitch at times, a slider that has cutter-type action and a changeup that subtracts nearly 10 mph off his fastball velocity. Of the four, evaluators are least enthused with the changeup at present.

THE FUTURE: Lee began his time in the system in the bullpen, and perhaps that's where he ends up if his fastball and curveball end up being his only two better-than-average pitches. He excelled as a starter in 2021, however, likely earning himself the chance to continue in that role for now.

Year	Age	Club (Level)	Lge	W	L	ERA	G	GS	IP	H	HR	BB	SO	BB/9	SO/9	WHIP	AVG
2021	24	Wilmington (HiA)	East	4	3	4.32	21	20	77	69	6	32	104	3.74	12.16	1.31	.239
Minor League Totals (4 years)				7	5	3.83	35	23	113	100	8	53	149	4.23	11.90	1.36	.238

23 ISRAEL PINEDA, C

BA GRADE
40 Risk: High

Born: April 3, 2000. **B-T:** R-R. **HT:** 5-11. **WT:** 190. **Signed:** Venezuela, 2016. **Signed by:** German Robles.

TRACK RECORD: Originally a $450,000 signing out of Venezuela in 2016, Pineda impressed in his first two seasons in the system before taking a step back in his first full season in Low-A in 2019. After spending time at the alternate training site and instructional league in 2020, he spent 2021 at High-A, where he hit just .208 but showed off his power with 14 home runs.

SCOUTING REPORT: Offensively, Pineda has a quick swing and impressive raw power, but he has an active setup and appears fidgety at times in the box, as if he's tinkering with his setup in real time. His plate discipline and knowledge of the strike zone is still a work in progress. Defensively, his mobility is sufficient but not exemplary, and he has a strong arm, which has helped him put up caught stealing rates of 40% or better in each of his minor league seasons.

THE FUTURE: Pineda has taken a step back since he was named a New York-Penn League all-star in 2018 as a young player in the league. He has loud tools that give him an intriguing ceiling, but there's refinement to be made for him to reach it.

Year	Age	Club (Level)	Lge	AVG	G	AB	R	H	2B	3B	HR	RBI	BB	SO	SB	OBP	SLG
2021	21	Wilmington (HiA)	East	.208	77	293	35	61	11	0	14	48	18	83	0	.260	.389
Minor League Totals (5 years)				.229	241	891	118	204	35	2	25	119	64	233	1	.287	.357

24 DANIEL MARTE, OF

BA GRADE
45 Risk: Extreme

Born: Jan. 14, 2002. **B-T:** R-R. **HT:** 6-0. **WT:** 180. **Signed:** Dominican Republic, 2018. **Signed by:** Virgilio De Leon.

TRACK RECORD: After signing for $300,000 in 2018, Marte played well in the Dominican Summer League in 2019, at one point putting together a 17-game hitting streak near the end of the season. He continued that momentum by impressing at instructs in 2020. The 2021 season in the Florida Complex League was more of a challenge for him, but he showed enough to keep hopes high for his future.

SCOUTING REPORT: Marte hit just .204 in the FCL in 2021, but some in the organization who observed his play saw him as the most consistent player in the lineup day to day, and he still managed a .363 on-base percentage. From a skill standpoint, he is brimming with plus tools. He's a good runner with an excellent arm, giving him potential plus defensive ability in center field. He also has potential plus power. But plate discipline is a major issue at this point, as he struck out 59 times in 137 at-bats last season, and the holes in his swing got exploited in the FCL schedule, where everyone plays the same small handful of teams repeatedly.

THE FUTURE: Marte has all of the raw tools to be a big leaguer, but the lack of plate discipline threatens to hold him back. That's the development to watch as the 2022 season unfolds.

Year	Age	Club (Level)	Lge	AVG	G	AB	R	H	2B	3B	HR	RBI	BB	SO	SB	OBP	SLG
2021	19	FCL Nationals (R)	FCL	.204	45	137	22	28	4	1	3	20	24	59	10	.363	.314
Minor League Totals (2 years)				.236	100	347	54	82	11	10	8	49	35	126	20	.333	.395

25 ROISMAR QUINTANA, OF

BA GRADE
45 Risk: Extreme

Born: Feb. 6, 2003. **B-T:** R-R. **HT:** 6-1. **WT:** 190. **Signed:** Venezuela, 2019. **Signed by:** Ronald Morillo.

TRACK RECORD: Quintana signed with the Nationals for $820,000 in 2019, and although his debut was delayed by the pandemic, he impressed in instructional league late in 2020. He got on the field in 2021 in the Florida Complex League, but a hamstring injury kept him out of action from early July to early September. He ended up with just 13 at-bats for the season, but he managed three extra-base hits in that small window, two doubles and a home run.

SCOUTING REPORT: Quintana's bat stands out. He has good feel to hit, keeps his barrel in the zone for a long time, and in a testament to the way he has developed his body since signing, plus raw power to all fields from a sturdy frame. He has impressive plate discipline for a player of his age, but at times he's too passive at the plate for a player of his strength. Defensively, Quintana is likely a corner outfielder in the future.

THE FUTURE: Health is paramount for Quintana as he goes into the 2022 season after he missed time at instructs in 2020 and just about all of the 2021 season. In a small sample, he's shown to be one of the most exciting young hitters in the system, but he just hasn't had many chances yet.

Year	Age	Club (Level)	Lge	AVG	G	AB	R	H	2B	3B	HR	RBI	BB	SO	SB	OBP	SLG
2021	18	FCL Nationals (R)	FCL	.308	7	13	3	4	2	0	1	5	6	5	0	.550	.692
Minor League Totals (1 year)				.308	7	13	3	4	2	0	1	5	6	5	0	.550	.692

26 TRES BARRERA, C

Born: Sept. 15, 1994. **B-T:** R-R. **HT:** 6-0. **WT:** 215. **Drafted:** Texas, 2016 (6th round). **Signed by:** Tyler Wilt.

BA GRADE

40 Risk: High

TRACK RECORD: Barrera moved steadily through the Nationals' system, eventually breaking through to the big leagues in 2019. He likely would have graduated from prospect status by now had he not been suspended for 80 games after a positive test for Oral Turinabol, which cost him the 2020 season. That particular drug is controversial in MLB, because Barrera and others who have tested positive for it maintain their innocence and suggest that there are flaws in the testing for it. He returned to Washington in 2021, hitting .264/.374/.385 in 91 at-bats.

SCOUTING REPORT: Barrera checks all the boxes of a solid all-around defensive catcher. He receives well, has a quick release with a strong arm and works well with his pitching staff. He's also a very good athlete. He's not a middle-of-the-order bat, but he hit fairly well in the big leagues in 2021 and he's performed at every stop along the way thanks to sound mechanics and good plate discipline.

THE FUTURE: Barrera has proven himself as a solid backup catcher in MLB, and he has nothing left to prove in the minors. With Keibert Ruiz and Riley Adams both in the organization and on the roster, however, he will have to fight to stay in the big leagues with Washington.

Year	Age	Club (Level)	Lge	AVG	G	AB	R	H	2B	3B	HR	RBI	BB	SO	SB	OBP	SLG
2021	26	Rochester (AAA)	East	.201	54	169	14	34	5	0	3	18	24	43	0	.302	.284
	26	Washington (MLB)	NL	.264	30	91	8	24	3	1	2	10	12	22	0	.374	.385
Major League Totals (2 years)				.258	32	93	8	24	3	1	2	10	12	22	0	.367	.376
Minor League Totals (6 years)				.250	338	1186	139	297	69	2	28	132	120	245	5	.331	.383

27 SETH ROMERO, LHP

Born: April 19, 1996. **B-T:** L-L. **HT:** 6-3. **WT:** 240. **Drafted:** Houston, 2017 (1st round). **Signed by:** Tyler Wilt.

BA GRADE

40 Risk: High

TRACK RECORD: Romero's career got off to a slow start, with just 14 total appearances to his name over his first three seasons in the system, none of them above Low-A, but he made up for lost time in 2020, when he arrived at the Nationals alternate training site and then debuted in the big leagues later that year. A rib injury slowed him for the first few months of 2021, which he spent primarily in Double-A.

SCOUTING REPORT: Romero's fastball sits in the low 90s, touching the mid 90s, and it's easy velocity from the left side. His best offspeed offering is a plus slider that helped make him a natural fit for the big league bullpen in 2020. His changeup is a quality third pitch in his arsenal and he can throw all three pitches for strikes.

THE FUTURE: The rib injury in 2021 was just the latest in a long line of injuries Romero has suffered in his career, which has in part allowed him to throw just 85.2 total innings in five seasons. His brief big league experience is exclusively as a reliever, but the organization wants to continue giving him the chance to prove he can start.

Year	Age	Club (Level)	Lge	W	L	ERA	G	GS	IP	H	HR	BB	SO	BB/9	SO/9	WHIP	AVG
2021	25	FCL Nationals (R)	FCL	0	0	10.80	1	1	2	3	0	2	2	10.8	10.8	3.00	.500
	25	Fredericksburg (LoA)	East	0	0	2.79	3	3	10	15	0	2	14	1.86	13.03	1.76	.349
	25	Harrisburg (AA)	NEast	0	2	5.31	6	6	20	21	2	9	34	3.98	15.05	1.48	.253
	25	Rochester (AAA)	East	0	0	2.25	1	1	4	4	0	2	5	4.5	11.25	1.50	.267
Major League Totals (1 year)				0	0	13.50	3	0	3	5	1	3	5	10.13	16.88	3.00	.333
Minor League Totals (4 years)				0	4	4.45	25	25	83	82	5	31	124	3.36	13.45	1.36	.250

28 MASON DENABURG, RHP

Born: Aug. 8, 1999. **B-T:** R-R. **HT:** 6-4. **WT:** 195. **Drafted:** HS—Merritt Island, Fla., 2018 (1st round). **Signed by:** Alan Marr.

BA GRADE

45 Risk: Extreme

TRACK RECORD: With Denaburg, the trouble is that he doesn't have much track record as a professional due to injuries. Since he was taken 27th overall and signed for $3 million after battling biceps tendonitis as a senior in high school, Denaburg has thrown just 20.1 innings in the system, all in 2019. He had shoulder surgery after the 2019 season and then dealt with tenderness early in 2020 before the pandemic shutdown. In March 2021, he had Tommy John surgery, costing him another season.

SCOUTING REPORT: It remains to be seen what Denaburg will look like when he gets back on the mound, but he typically works with a fastball that touches as high as 97 mph, a high-spin curveball in the upper-70s and a changeup that was making strides toward being an average pitch. In his debut in 2019, he struggled with control, walking 14 in his 20.1 innings, and that will need improvement moving forward. **THE FUTURE:** Step one for Denaburg is getting healthy and back on the mound in games. Everything else is secondary at this point. At 22 years old next opening day, he has some catching up to do, but he still has time to get back on track.

Year	Age	Club (Level)	Lge	W	L	ERA	G	GS	IP	H	HR	BB	SO	BB/9	SO/9	WHIP	AVG
2021	21	Did not play—Injured															
Minor League Totals (2 years)				1	1	7.52	7	4	20	23	1	14	19	6.20	8.41	1.82	.288

29 JORDY BARLEY, SS

Born: Dec. 3, 1999. **B-T:** R-R. **HT:** 6-0. **WT:** 175. **Signed:** Dominican Republic, 2016. **Signed by:** Felix Feliz/Jose Salado (Padres).

BA GRADE
40 Risk: Very High

TRACK RECORD: A $1 million signing for the Padres in 2016, Barley has been inconsistent in his first few seasons as he's worked to turn his readily apparent speed and athleticism into production. He spent all of the 2021 season at Low-A, coming over to the Nationals' system in July as part of the trade that sent Daniel Hudson to San Diego.
SCOUTING REPORT: Barley has an impressive collection of tools but he's not yet a complete player. He has game-breaking speed, and as he's moved up, he's become a more efficient base stealer. He also has power that projects as average down the line. Defensively, he has the hands and arm for shortstop, and he recently made a change to throw from more of a three-quarters slot to improve his accuracy, but he still makes errors in bunches, including 46 miscues last season. Some evaluators have noted that the errors seem to be more of the careless or mental variety rather than physical. He has primarily played shortstop but has also played plenty of second base, and some have seen center field as a potential landing place.
THE FUTURE: Barley has come a long way in his development, but he still has a long way to go. His tools are endlessly intriguing, even if they still require a lot of refinement.

Year	Age	Club (Level)	Lge	AVG	G	AB	R	H	2B	3B	HR	RBI	BB	SO	SB	OBP	SLG
2021	21	Lake Elsinore (LoA)	West	.240	61	242	43	58	8	2	8	28	31	82	33	.333	.388
	21	Fredericksburg (LoA)	East	.205	33	122	17	25	6	0	2	10	17	43	12	.312	.303
Minor League Totals (5 years)				.232	263	1020	169	237	45	16	26	116	96	347	78	.305	.384

30 DREW MILLAS, C

Born: Jan. 15, 1998. **B-T:** B-R. **HT:** 6-2. **WT:** 205. **Drafted:** Missouri State, 2019 (7th round). **Signed by:** Steve Abney (Athletics).

BA GRADE
40 Risk: Very High

TRACK RECORD: Millas' professional career was delayed two seasons, first by a UCL injury and a blood clotting issue after he was drafted in 2019 and later by the pandemic. He finally took the field and was productive at High-A in 2021. He came to Washington in the trade that sent Yan Gomes and Josh Harrison to Oakland in July.
SCOUTING REPORT: Defense is Millas' calling card. An excellent athlete behind the plate, he receives the ball well, is nimble in getting down to block the ball, has an easy plus arm and plays the position with energy. He's athletic and toolsy enough, in fact, that some evaluators see him as a possible fit as a utility player who could also play second and third base. He was productive offensively in 2021, and he has good bat-to-ball skills and excellent plate discipline, but his bat is light in general. He posts below-average exit velocities, and when batting from the left side, he has noticeable length in his load.
THE FUTURE: As an athletic, defense-minded catcher who also takes good at-bats, Millas has a fairly high floor that should help him progress through the system fairly quickly. How well he develops into someone who can impact the baseball would seem to hold the key to unlocking a higher ceiling.

Year	Age	Club (Level)	Lge	AVG	G	AB	R	H	2B	3B	HR	RBI	BB	SO	SB	OBP	SLG
2021	23	Lansing (HiA)	Cent	.255	59	220	34	56	12	1	3	28	41	39	10	.372	.359
	23	Wilmington (HiA)	East	.284	27	102	15	29	4	0	0	20	13	14	5	.373	.324
Minor League Totals (3 years)				.264	86	322	49	85	16	1	3	48	54	53	15	.372	.348

MORE PROSPECTS TO KNOW

31 SETH SHUMAN, RHP

Shuman has a starter's four-pitch repertoire made up of a fastball that sits in the low 90s and touches 94-95 mph, a snappy, above-average slider in the low 80s, an average changeup and a curveball that too often blends with his slider.

32 DREW MENDOZA, 1B

Mendoza has some of the best raw power and plate discipline in the Nationals' system, but he looked lost at the plate all too often at Double-A in 2021. He was consistently behind the fastball and out in front of breaking stuff as he adjusted to being pitched more effectively at a higher level.

33 RICHARD GUASCH, RHP

Acquired alongside Drew Millas and Seth Shuman from Oakland, Guasch features a fastball that touches the mid 90s and a slider that at times looks like a plus-plus offering. His changeup is a distant third pitch, and it's often too firm, but he gets good sink on it.

34 T.J. WHITE, OF

SLEEPER

A fifth-round pick as a 17-year-old high school senior in 2021, White had a successful debut in the Florida Complex League, showing off 65-grade in-game power from both sides of the plate with good on-base skills.

35 BRANDEN BOISSIERE, 1B/OF

A third-round pick in 2021, Boissiere struggled in his debut season at Low-A, but he was a productive pure hitter in college at Arizona over three seasons, and he adds value as a slick defensive first baseman who is also athletic enough to perhaps play the outfield.

36 TODD PETERSON, RHP

Peterson has a fastball that can get up to 97-98 mph and a high-80s slider that he uses effectively. He is a strike-thrower who profiles well as a power reliever as he moves through the system.

37 ZACH BRZYKCY, RHP

With a mid-90s fastball that touches the high 90s with plus carry, a slider with good depth that flashes plus and a changeup, Brzykcy has three potential plus pitches in his repertoire.

38 RICARDO MENDEZ, OF

Mendez has average tools across the board. With a flat bat path and a good approach, he's been a productive hitter all throughout his minor league career. He's made improvements defensively, and ultimately, his value may be tied to his ability to stay in center field.

39 DUSTIN SAENZ, LHP

A fourth-round pick in the 2021 draft, Saenz uses an athletic delivery and above-average control to help make up for a lack of high-end stuff outside of an above-average slider that is clearly his best pitch.

40 HOLDEN POWELL, RHP

A shoulder injury limited Powell to just four appearances in his debut season. When he's healthy, the combination of a fastball that has touched the high 90s, a mid-80s slider and some deception in his delivery gives him the kind of reliever profile that may allow him to move quickly.

TOP PROSPECTS OF THE DECADE

Year	Player, Pos	2021 Org
2012	Bryce Harper, OF	Phillies
2013	Anthony Rendon, 3B	Angels
2014	Lucas Giolito, RHP	White Sox
2015	Lucas Giolito, RHP	White Sox
2016	Lucas Giolito, RHP	White Sox
2017	Victor Robles, OF	Nationals
2018	Victor Robles, OF	Nationals
2019	Victor Robles, OF	Nationals
2020	Carter Kieboom, SS/2B	Nationals
2021	Cade Cavalli, RHP	Nationals

TOP DRAFT PICKS OF THE DECADE

Year	Player, Pos	2021 Org
2012	Lucas Giolito, RHP	White Sox
2013	Jake Johansen, RHP (2nd round)	Did not play
2014	Erick Fedde, RHP	Nationals
2015	Andrew Stevenson, OF (2nd round)	Nationals
2016	Carter Kieboom, SS	Nationals
2017	Seth Romero, LHP	Nationals
2018	Mason Denaburg, RHP	Nationals
2019	Jackson Rutledge, RHP	Nationals
2020	Cade Cavalli, RHP	Nationals
2021	Brady House, SS	Nationals

Seiya Suzuki has all the traits to be a power-hitting, everyday right fielder in the major leagues.

MATT ROBERTS/GETTY IMAGES

Kyle Glaser reported on international professionals who were eligible to sign with MLB teams as the Prospect Handbook went to press. This year, only one notable player is slated to come over from Japan's Nippon Professional Baseball (NPB) or Korea Baseball Organization (KBO).

SEIYA SUZUKI, OF

Age: 27. **Born:** Aug. 18, 1994. **B-T:** R-R. **HT:** 5-11. **WT:** 182.

TRACK RECORD: A second-round pick by Hiroshima out of high school in 2012, Suzuki reached the Japanese major leagues a year later at 18 and grew into one of the country's biggest stars. He became a five-time all-star, won the Central League batting title in 2019 and led Japan to the gold medal at the Tokyo Olympics, including going 2-for-3 in the gold medal game against the United States as Japan's cleanup hitter. After hitting 182 home runs in nine seasons, including a career-high 38 home runs in 2021, he was posted by the Carp in November.

BA GRADE	
55	**Risk: Medium**

SCOUTING REPORT: While many Japanese hitters keep their hands inside and take short, direct swing paths to the ball, Suzuki takes powerful uppercuts more conducive to the modern MLB game. He gets into a launch position and pulls balls hard in the air for long home runs to left and left-center field, as well as driving the occasional shot to right-center. He has plus-plus raw power and above-average game power he should be able to access once he adjusts to major league velocity. Suzuki rarely faced mid-90s fastballs in Japan and opinions are split how effectively he'll adjust to that velocity in MLB. Proponents see the bat speed, hand-eye coordination and feel for the barrel for him to be an average hitter once he settles in. Suzuki gets good jumps and has excellent range in right field, especially going back into the right-center field gap. He is an above-average defender with above-average arm strength and provides defensive value even when he is slumping at the plate. Suzuki has slowed down as he's aged and is no longer a 20-steal threat like he was in his younger years, but he can still swipe an occasional bag and moves fine in the outfield. He has a "grinder" mentality and earns strong reviews for his on-field makeup.

THE FUTURE: Suzuki has all the traits to be a power-hitting, everyday right fielder in the major leagues. He will command a multi-year deal and should compete for a starting job right away.

Year	Age	Club (Level)	Lge	AVG	G	AB	R	H	2B	3B	HR	RBI	BB	SO	SB	OBP	SLG
2021	26	Hiroshima (NPB)	CL	.317	132	435	77	138	26	0	38	88	87	88	9	.433	.639
Japanese League Totals (9 years)				.315	902	2976	548	937	182	16	182	562	486	569	82	.414	.570

2021-22 INTERNATIONAL SIGNING PERIOD: PROJECTED 25 TOP BONUSES

BY BEN BADLER

For the second year in a row, Major League Baseball postponed the start date of the international signing period by six months. Prior to the coronavirus pandemic, the signing period opened each year on July 2.

The 2021-22 signing period officially opens on Jan. 15, 2022. The Prospect Handbook went to press before that date, so the top international prospects who sign in early 2022 won't appear in any of the team Top 30 Prospects rankings in this book.

Still, we know who the big names are and where they're almost certain to sign.

Our ranking presented here is not an assessment of talent. Instead, it's a board of 25 international prospects ranked in order of their expected signing bonuses. Teams often line up commitments from players multiple years in advance of their official signing date, at which point they generally are no longer seen much by other clubs.

While it is premature to provide a talent ranking, this should be a guide to many of the biggest names to know from this year's international signing class.

William Bergolla Jr. is one of the top prospects from Venezuela.

---

1. CRISTIAN VAQUERO, OF   CUBA

Born: Sept. 13, 2004. **B-T:** B-R. **Ht.:** 6-3. **Wt.:** 180.   **Expected Signing Team:** Nationals

The Nationals paid the top bonus for a 16-year-old international prospect last year, when they spent most of their bonus pool money on Dominican shortstop Armando Cruz. It looks like they're going to invest most of their pool space into one player again this year with Vaquero. He is a dynamic center fielder with plus speed, a strong arm and good defensive instincts for his age. At the plate he has a sound lefthanded swing and a chance to grow into plus power, with a lean, projectable frame for his impressive tools to get better as he gets stronger. More recently, Vaquero has also started switch-hitting. He's obviously not as advanced from the right side yet, but he has shown enough that it could continue after signing.

---

2. RODERICK ARIAS, SS   DOMINICAN REPUBLIC

Born: Sept. 9, 2004. **B-T:** B-R. **Ht.:** 6-1. **Wt.:** 175.   **Expected Signing Team:** Yankees

Arias is one of the best all-around players in the class with a promising mix of tools and skills. He's a switch-hitter whose swing is quick, compact and adjustable, with the ability to recognize spin well for his age and good performances against live pitching. He makes hard contact for his age, with more power now from the right side, and a chance to grow into above-average power once he fills out his lean, athletic frame. He's also an above-average runner with the athleticism, hands and footwork to handle shortstop. He has a plus-plus arm. Arias is expected to sign for a bonus in the $4 million neighborhood.

---

3. RICARDO CABRERA, SS   VENEZUELA

Born: Oct. 31, 2004. **B-T:** R-R. **Ht. 6-1. Wt.:** 184.   **Expected Signing Team:** Reds

Cabrera stood out early in the scouting process, when as a 2021 prospect he was one of the top performers on the field playing against 2019 and 2020 players. He has continued to develop into one of the most complete players in the class. Cabrera has a quick, direct swing and good feel for the barrel with a knack for using the whole field. As he has gotten stronger, his power has started to emerge as well. He's also a good athlete with a chance to stick at shortstop with plus speed and a strong arm.

4. DYAN JORGE, SS   CUBA

Born: March 18, 2003. **B-T:** R-R. **Ht.:** 6-2. **Wt.:** 170.   **Expected Signing Team:** Rockies

Jorge was one of the top players in his age group in Cuba before he left the country to train in the Dominican Republic. He's eligible to sign now, but with teams having already spent most or all of their pool space for the current signing period, he's waiting until the 2021-22 signing period opens to sign, with the Rockies expected to pay him close to $3 million. Jorge has a slender, wiry build and is an excellent athlete with plus-plus speed. Scouts highest on Jorge thought he projects to stick at shortstop, where he has easy actions, a good internal clock and a plus arm. Jorge's hitting ability drew a split camp among scouts, but he performed well in Cuba and has generally shown good instincts for the game.

5. OSCAR COLAS, OF   CUBA

Born: Sept. 17, 1998. **B-T:** L-L. **Ht.:** 6-1. **Wt.:** 220.   **Expected Signing Team:** White Sox

One of the least surprising moves of the next international class is that the White Sox are expected to sign Colas, a 22-year-old Cuban outfielder who is eligible to sign now, but with teams mostly tapped out of bonus pool money for the current 2020-21 signing period, he's going to wait to sign when the 2021-22 period opens and the bonus pools reset. Colas has some experience on the mound as well, but his main draw is his big raw power from the left side. He showed that power with home runs in live batting practice sessions and simulated games working out for clubs in the Dominican Republic. Colas has improved his physical conditioning since he got to the Dominican Republic, but his body type, range and athleticism will likely limit him to either left field or first base, with what he does in the batter's box driving his value.

6. LAZARO MONTES, OF/1B   CUBA

Born: Oct. 22, 2004. **B-T:** L-R. **Ht.:** 6-4. **Wt.:** 210.   **Expected Signing Team:** Mariners

Montes trains in the Dominican Republic and is a physically imposing slugger with plus-plus raw power and good bat speed. For a hitter with such a large frame, Montes has a relatively compact swing with good path and leverage that helps him translate that power in games, with the ability to hit home runs to all fields against live pitching. Defensively, he is limited to either a corner outfield spot or possibly first base as he fills out, but the upside is a middle-of-the-lineup slugger. The Mariners are expected to land Montes.

7. DIEGO BENITEZ, SS   VENEZUELA

Born: Nov. 19, 2004.**B-T:** R-R. **Ht.:** 6-0. **Wt.:** 183.   **Expected Signing Team:** Braves

After multiple years of penalties from MLB for their international signing violations, the Braves are entering their first signing period free from those restrictions. Their top target is Benitez, one of the top infielders in Venezuela. He has a large, athletic build with fluid actions both in the box and in the field. His hitting ability stands out the most, with excellent bat speed and a smooth swing that stays through the hitting zone for a long time. He has gap power now with a chance to grow into average or better power as he matures. Benitez is a sound defender, though his range and future size could lead him to third base.

8. WILLIAM BERGOLLA JR., SS   VENEZUELA

Born: Oct. 20, 2004. **B-T:** L-R. **Ht.:** 5-10. **Wt.:** 155.   **Expected Signing Team:** Phillies

William Bergolla was a Reds Top 30 Prospect for five years from 2002 to 2006 and played in 17 big league games for Cincinnati in 2005. The former middle infielder's son, William Bergolla Jr., is now one of the top prospects in Venezuela for the next international signing class. Bergolla Jr. has a sound swing and makes frequent contact in games with a line-drive approach and gap power. He's an instinctive player who projects to stick in the middle infield, with plus speed and an arm that earns 50 to 55 grades on the 20-80 scouting scale.

9. RYAN RECKLEY, SS   BAHAMAS

Born: Sept. 6, 2004. **B-T:** R-R. **Ht.:** 5-10. **Wt.:** 170.   **Expected Signing Team:** Giants

The Bahamas continues to grow as an emerging source of talent for major league clubs, with the Marlins' Jazz Chisholm being the most successful example. The top player in the 2021-22 class from the Bahamas is Reckley, who trains in the Max D Sports Company with Greg Burrows and is expected to sign with the Giants for more than $2 million. Reckley has plus or better speed with quick, athletic actions at shortstop. If everything clicks, he could be a switch-hitting shortstop who hits at the top of a lineup, with a quick stroke that's more efficient from the right side and geared for line drives with gap power.

10. JAVIER OSORIO, SS   VENEZUELA

Born: March 29, 2005. **B-T:** R-R. **Ht.:** 6-0. **Wt.:** 172.   **Expected Signing Team:** Tigers

Osorio was an early standout in the scouting process as one of the most advanced players in the 2021 class. He has high-end bat speed for his age, with quick wrists and an aggressive swing that he snaps through the zone quickly. That bat speed helps him drive the ball with impact and gives him a chance to develop into a power-hitting shortstop as he fills out. Osorio's best tools are on the offensive side, but he has the actions, athleticism and arm strength that could allow him to stay at shortstop. He trains at the Dream Team Academy with Wilfredo Polidor and is expected to sign with the Tigers.

11. LUIS MEZA, C   VENEZUELA

Born: Sept. 11, 2004. **B-T:** R-R. **Ht.:** 5-11. **Wt.:** 185.   **Expected Signing Team:** Blue Jays

Venezuela consistently is home to top international catchers, with Diego Cartaya (Dodgers), Francisco Alvarez (Mets) and Ronnier Quintero (Cubs) in the most recent signing classes. Meza fits into that tier of players as a catcher who projects to stick behind the plate and is one of the better hitters in Venezuela. He has a loose, easy swing with a knack for being on time and strong game performance. He's a high-contact hitter who uses the whole field, with room on his broad-shouldered frame to fill out and drive the ball with more impact as he gets stronger. Meza's catch-and-throw skills are also advanced for his age. The Blue Jays are expected to sign Meza, who trains with Kander Depablos and Reynaldo Gonzalez.

12. TONY BLANCO JR., OF   DOMINICAN REPUBLIC

Born: May 14, 2005. **B-T:** R-R. **Ht.:** 6-5. **Wt.:** 210.   **Expected Signing Team:** Rays

Tony Blanco was a Baseball America Top 100 Prospect two years in a row and played briefly for the Nationals in 2005 before spending several years as a slugger in Japan, including three seasons with 30-plus homers. His son, Tony Blanco Jr., is an even more physically imposing power threat. He's big, strong has high-end bat speed and plus-plus raw power. Some scouts had reservations about his pure hitting ability, but others saw him perform well against live pitching and see him as a potential middle-of-the-order hitter. Blanco has an average arm, but his size limits his defensive value, with a chance he can move around well enough for a corner outfield spot but some first base risk as he gets bigger. Blanco Jr. trains with Ivan Noboa and is expected to sign with the Rays.

13. JONATHAN MEJIA, SS   DOMINICAN REPUBLIC

Born: April 12, 2005. **B-T:** B-R. **Ht.:** 6-0. **Wt.:** 185.   **Expected Signing Team:** Cardinals

Mejia attracted a lot of attention from scouts at Major League Baseball's Trainer Partnership Program showcase in November 2019, where he put on an impressive display in the batter's box. He's a switch-hitter with good bat speed from both sides of the plate, enabling him to drive the ball for damage when he connects. He has a sound swing and generally plays under control in games to make consistent contact. Mejia has a plus arm, and while some he might end up at third base, his improved footwork has helped on the defensive side. The Cardinals are expected to sign Mejia, who trains with Nercy Brito.

14. SIMON JUAN, OF
DOMINICAN REPUBLIC

Born: July 13, 2005. **B-T:** R-R. **Ht.:** 6-2. **Wt.:** 165.　　　　**Expected Signing Team:** Mets

Juan is an athletic center fielder with speed and power. He's on the younger end of the class, but he's already a plus or better runner with an explosive first step that should fit well in center field. He has good bat speed and already drives the ball with impact during batting practice, with a projectable frame that points to more power coming. He doesn't have the cleanest swing, so there is some risk on his pure hitting ability, but if everything clicks he has a chance to be a power/speed threat in the middle of the diamond.

15. NELSON RADA, OF
VENEZUELA

Born: Aug. 24, 2005. **B-T:** L-L. **Ht.:** 6-0. **Wt.:** 168.　　　　**Expected Signing Team:** Angels

If Rada had been born eight days later, he would be in the 2022-23 class instead, so he is one of the younger players in the upcoming 2021-22 class. He was 5-foot-9 early on, but he's the son of a former professional basketball player in Venezuela and has grown a few inches leading up to his signing date. He's an instinctive player, especially in center field, where he gets good reads off the bat with a quick first step and at least solid-average speed. Rada has a fairly short stroke from the left side with a good eye for the strike zone and mostly gap power that has trended up as he's gotten stronger.

16. YASSER MERCEDES, OF
DOMINICAN REPUBLIC

Born: Nov. 16, 2004. **B-T:** R-R. **Ht.:** 6-3. **Wt.:** 180.　　　　**Expected Signing Team:** Twins

Mercedes, who was born in Puerto Rico and has grown up in the Dominican Republic, is one of the best power/speed threats in the class. He's an excellent athlete with a lean, well-proportioned build and flashes of above-average raw power that could tick up as he matures. Mercedes has shown some swing-and-miss risk, but he has also hit big home runs in games with a chance to be a power-hitting center fielder.

17. JARLIN SUSANA, RHP
DOMINICAN REPUBLIC

Born: March 23, 2004. **B-T:** R-R. **Ht.:** 6-5. **Wt.:** 195.　　　　**Expected Signing Team:** Padres

Susana stood out early on when he threw 85-87 mph at 14 at a showcase during the Winter Meetings in Las Vegas in December 2018. At one point, he looked like he would sign with the Cardinals during the 2020-21 signing period, but that never materialized. With MLB's ban on scouting players in person during the pandemic ended in September 2020, Susana emerged showing electric stuff for his age, with a fastball that touched 96 mph along with a sharp breaking ball.

18. BRAYLIN TAVERA, OF
DOMINICAN REPUBLIC

Born: Feb. 19, 2005. **B-T:** R-R. **Ht.:** 6-2. **Wt.:** 175.　　　　**Expected Signing Team:** Orioles

With the Orioles joining the rest of MLB in competing for top players from Latin America, their top expected signing in the upcoming class is expected to be Tavera, likely for a bonus in the $1.5 to $2 million range. Tavera is a center fielder who ran the 60-yard dash in 6.47 seconds at a Dominican Prospect League showcase in October 2019. While he might slow down some as he fills out, he should be able to stay in center. He has a mix of average-ish tools across the rest of his skill set.

19. MARTIN GONZALES, SS
DOMINICAN REPUBLIC

Born: Sept. 28, 2004. **B-T:** R-R. **Ht.:** 5-11. **Wt.:** 160.　　　　**Expected Signing Team:** Mariners

Gonzales is not a speedster, but he is quick and athletic, with the actions and attributes to remain at shortstop. He has a short, level swing plane through the zone, which should lead to a high contact rate. He has mostly been a line-drive hitter with gap power, though he is starting to drive the ball with more impact as he's gained strength over the past year.

20. JOHAN BARRIOS, SS   VENEZUELA

Born: Jan. 8, 2005. **B-T:** R-R. **Ht.:** 6-2. **Wt.:** 170.   **Expected Signing Team:** Brewers

The Brewers have been aggressive in signing top talent from Venezuela in their recent signing classes. That trend should continue in the next class with Barrios, who has a long, projectable frame with a lot of space to fill out. He's quick, athletic and has good body control with a plus arm, giving him a chance to stay at shortstop if he stays lean and agile enough. Scouts highest on Barrios liked his hitting ability as well, with a lot more power to come once he fills out.

21. SAMUEL GIL, SS   VENEZUELA

Born: Nov. 1, 2004. **B-T:** R-R. **Ht.:** 5-9. **Wt.:** 154.   **Expected Signing Team:** Tigers

Gil drew a lot of attention from scouts, more for his in-game skills than his raw tools. He's an instinctive, high-baseball IQ player who puts together consistent quality at-bats with an easy swing, good contact skills and an all-fields approach to get on base frequently. Gil isn't a huge power threat, but he puts a surprising charge into the ball for his smaller, slender size. His game savvy also shows up in the field, where he has a good internal clock, plays under control and has a strong arm.

22. ADAN SANCHEZ, C/3B   PANAMA

Born: May 24, 2005. **B-T:** R-R. **Ht.:** 5-11. **Wt.:** 200.   **Expected Signing Team:** Cubs

Sanchez hit a home run at the Little League World Series with current Cubs manager David Ross on the ESPN broadcast, and it's the Cubs who are expected to land Sanchez. He's an instinctive player who has an advanced offensive approach for his age, which he showed by hitting well against older competition while playing in Panama's youth national league at 14. Sanchez has the attributes to catch, with a strong arm and a high baseball IQ. He has also spent time at third base, where his hands and feet work well.

23. JHONNY SEVERINO, SS   DOMINICAN REPUBLIC

Born: Nov. 8, 2004. **B-T:** B-R. **Ht.:** 6-2. **Wt.:** 175.   **Expected Signing Team:** Brewers

Severino is an offensive-oriented infielder with good bat speed from both sides of the plate. He's a more advanced hitter from the right side and makes hard contact when he connects, with the combination of bat speed and physical upside to potentially grow into above-average power. He has solid hitting instincts for his age and has shown the ability to work his way into favorable counts. Severino is more comfortable in the batter's box than he is on the infield, but he has made progress on the defensive end.

24. MICHAEL ARROYO, SS   COLOMBIA

Born: Nov. 3, 2004. **B-T:** R-R. **Ht.:** 5-10. **Wt.:** 165.   **Expected Signing Team:** Mariners

Arroyo has hit well in games, both at home in Colombia and traveling abroad for different events, including in the U.S. His fast hands allow him to accelerate the barrel into the hitting zone quickly, producing a high contact rate against live pitching. He has a good sense of the strike zone for his age and uses the whole field, with a likely hit-over-power profile and a chance to grow into average pop.

25. YENDRY ROJAS, 3B/2B/OF   CUBA

Born: Jan. 27, 2005. **B-T:** L-R. **Ht.:** 6-0. **Wt.:** 179.   **Expected Signing Team:** Padres

Rojas is one of the better pure hitters in the class. He has a quiet, compact swing that's quick and balanced with an innate ability to manipulate the barrel. Rojas has performed well in games, tracking and recognizing pitches well with the patience to take walks. He can drive the ball for extra-base damage to all fields in games, with a chance for future above-average power. An average runner underway, Rojas is a bat-first prospect who has spent time in both the infield and the outfield.

DRAFT SIGNING BONUSES

2021 DRAFT

TOP THREE ROUNDS

FIRST ROUND

No.	Team: Player, Pos.	Bonus
1.	Pirates: Henry Davis, C	$6,500,000
2.	Rangers: Jack Leiter, RHP	$7,922,000
3.	Tigers: Jackson Jobe, RHP	$6,900,000
4.	Red Sox: Marcelo Mayer, SS	$6,664,000
5.	Orioles: Colton Cowser, OF	$4,900,000
6.	D-backs: Jordan Lawlar, SS	$6,713,300
7.	Royals: Frank Mozzicato, LHP	$3,547,500
8.	Rockies: Benny Montgomery, OF	$5,000,000
9.	Angels: Sam Bachman, RHP	$3,847,500
10.	Mets: Kumar Rocker, RHP	Did not sign
11.	Nationals: Brady House, SS	$5,000,000
12.	Mariners: Harry Ford, C	$4,366,400
13.	Phillies: Andrew Painter, RHP	$3,900,000
14.	Giants: Will Bednar, RHP	$3,647,500
15.	Brewers: Sal Frelick, OF	$4,000,000
16.	Marlins: Kahlil Watson, SS	$4,540,790
17.	Reds: Matt McLain, SS	$4,625,000
18.	Cardinals: Michael McGreevy, RHP	$2,750,000
19.	Blue Jays: Gunnar Hoglund, RHP	$3,247,500
20.	Yankees: Trey Sweeney, SS	$3,000,000
21.	Cubs: Jordan Wicks, LHP	$3,132,300
22.	White Sox: Colson Montgomery, SS	$3,027,000
23.	Guardians: Gavin Williams, RHP	$2,250,000
24.	Braves: Ryan Cusick, RHP	$2,700,000
25.	Athletics: Max Muncy, SS	$2,850,000
26.	Twins: Chase Petty, RHP	$2,500,000
27.	Padres: Jackson Merrill, SS	$1,800,000
28.	Rays: Carson Williams, SS	$2,347,500
29.	Dodgers: Maddux Bruns, LHP	$2,197,500
30.	Reds: Jay Allen, OF	$2,397,500

SUPPLEMENTAL FIRST ROUND

No.	Team: Player, Pos.	Bonus
31.	Marlins: Joe Mack, C	$2,500,000
32.	Tigers: Ty Madden, RHP	$2,500,000
33.	Brewers: Tyler Black, 2B	$2,200,000
34.	Rays: Cooper Kinney, 2B	$2,145,600
35.	Reds: Mat Nelson, C	$2,093,300
36.	Twins: Noah Miller, SS	$1,700,000

SECOND ROUND

No.	Team: Player, Pos.	Bonus
37.	Pirates: Anthony Solometo, LHP	$2,797,500
38.	Rangers: Aaron Zavala, OF	$830,000
39.	Tigers: Izaac Pacheco, SS	$2,750,000
40.	Red Sox: Jud Fabian, OF	Did not sign
41.	Orioles: Connor Norby, 2B	$1,700,000
42.	D-backs: Ryan Bliss, SS	$1,250,000
43.	Royals: Ben Kudrna, RHP	$2,997,500
44.	Rockies: Jaden Hill, RHP	$1,689,500
45.	Angels: Ky Bush, LHP	$1,747,500
46.	Mets: Calvin Ziegler, RHP	$910,000
47.	Nationals: Daylen Lile, OF	$1,750,000
48.	Mariners: Edwin Arroyo, SS	$1,650,000
49.	Phillies: Ethan Wilson, OF	$1,507,600
50.	Giants: Matt Mikulski, LHP	$1,197,500
51.	Brewers: Russell Smith, LHP	$1,000,000
52.	Marlins: Cody Morissette, SS	$1,403,200
53.	Reds: Andrew Abbott, LHP	$1,300,000
54.	Cardinals: Joshua Baez, OF	$2,250,000
55.	Yankees: Brendan Beck, RHP	$1,050,000
56.	Cubs: James Triantos, 3B	$2,100,000
57.	White Sox: Wes Kath, 3B	$1,800,000
58.	Guardians: Doug Nikhazy, LHP	$1,200,000
59.	Braves: Spencer Schwellenbach, RHP	$997,500
60.	Athletics: Zack Gelof, 3B	$1,157,400
61.	Twins: Steve Hajjar, LHP	$1,129,700
62.	Padres: James Wood, OF	$2,600,000
63.	Rays: Kyle Manzardo, 1B	$747,500

SUPPLEMENTAL SECOND ROUND

No.	Team: Player, Pos.	Bonus
64.	Pirates: Lonnie White Jr., OF	$1,500,000
65.	Orioles: Reed Trimble, OF	$800,000
66.	Royals: Peyton Wilson, 2B	$1,000,800
67.	D-backs: Adrian Del Castillo, C	$1,000,000
68.	Rockies: Joe Rock, LHP	$953,100
69.	Guardians: Tommy Mace, RHP	$1,100,000
70.	Cardinals: Ryan Holgate, OF	$875,000
71.	Padres: Robert Gasser, LHP	$884,200

THIRD ROUND

No.	Team: Player, Pos.	Bonus
72.	Pirates: Bubba Chandler, RHP	$3,000,000
73.	Rangers: Cameron Cauley, SS	$1,000,000
74.	Tigers: Dylan Smith, RHP	$1,115,000
75.	Red Sox: Tyler McDonough, 2B	$828,600
76.	Orioles: John Rhodes, OF	$1,375,000
77.	D-backs: Jacob Steinmetz, RHP	$500,000
78.	Royals: Carter Jensen, C	$1,097,500
79.	Rockies: McCade Brown, RHP	$780,400
80.	Angels: Landon Marceaux, RHP	$765,300
81.	Mets: Dominic Hamel, RHP	$755,300
82.	Nationals: Branden Boissiere, OF	$600,000
83.	Mariners: Michael Morales, RHP	$1,500,000
84.	Phillies: Jordan Viars, OF	$747,500
85.	Giants: Mason Black, RHP	$708,200
86.	Brewers: Alex Binelas, 3B	$700,000
87.	Astros: Tyler Whitaker, OF	$1,500,000
88.	Marlins: Jordan McCants, SS	$800,000
89.	Reds: Jose Torres, SS	$622,500
90.	Cardinals: Austin Love, RHP	$600,000
91.	Blue Jays: Ricky Tiedemann, LHP	$644,800
92.	Yankees: Brock Selvidge, LHP	$1,500,000
93.	Cubs: Drew Gray, LHP	$900,000
94.	White Sox: Sean Burke, RHP	$900,000
95.	Guardians: Jake Fox, SS	$850,000
96.	Braves: Dylan Dodd, LHP	$122,500
97.	Athletics: Mason Miller, RHP	$599,100
98.	Twins: Cade Povich, LHP	$500,000
99.	Padres: Kevin Kopps, RHP	$300,000
100.	Rays: Ryan Spikes, SS	$1,097,500
101.	Dodgers: Peter Heubeck, RHP	$1,269,500

DRAFT SIGNING BONUSES

2020 DRAFT

TOP THREE ROUNDS

FIRST ROUND

No. Team: Player, Pos.	Bonus
1. Tigers: Spencer Torkelson, 3B	$8,416,300
2. Orioles: Heston Kjerstad, OF	$5,200,000
3. Marlins: Max Meyer, RHP	$6,700,000
4. Royals: Asa Lacy, LHP	$6,670,000
5. Blue Jays: Austin Martin, SS	$7,000,825
6. Mariners: Emerson Hancock, RHP	$5,700,000
7. Pirates: Nick Gonzales, SS	$5,432,400
8. Padres: Robert Hassell III, OF	$4,300,000
9. Rockies: Zac Veen, OF	$5,000,000
10. Angels: Reid Detmers, LHP	$4,670,000
11. White Sox: Garrett Crochet, LHP	$4,547,500
12. Reds: Austin Hendrick, OF	$4,000,000
13. Giants: Patrick Bailey, C	$3,797,500
14. Rangers: Justin Foscue, 2B	$3,250,000
15. Phillies: Mick Abel, RHP	$4,075,000
16. Cubs: Ed Howard, SS	$3,745,500
17. Red Sox: Nick Yorke, 2B	$2,700,000
18. D-backs: Bryce Jarvis, RHP	$2,650,000
19. Mets: Pete Crow-Armstrong, OF	$3,359,000
20. Brewers: Garrett Mitchell, OF	$3,242,900
21. Cardinals: Jordan Walker, 3B	$2,900,000
22. Nationals: Cade Cavalli, RHP	$3,027,000
23. Indians: Carson Tucker, SS	$2,000,000
24. Rays: Nick Bitsko, RHP	$3,000,000
25. Braves: Jared Shuster, LHP	$2,197,500
26. Athletics: Tyler Soderstrom, C	$3,300,000
27. Twins: Aaron Sabato, 1B	$2,750,000
28. Yankees: Austin Wells, C	$2,500,000
29. Dodgers: Bobby Miller, RHP	$2,197,500

SUPPLEMENTAL FIRST ROUND

No. Team: Player, Pos.	Bonus
30. Orioles: Jordan Westburg, SS	$2,365,500
31. Pirates: Carmen Mlodzinski, RHP	$2,050,000
32. Royals: Nick Loftin, SS	$3,000,000
33. D-backs: Slade Cecconi, RHP	$2,384,900
34. Padres: Justin Lange, RHP	$2,000,000
35. Rockies: Drew Romo, C	$2,095,800
36. Indians: Tanner Burns, RHP	$1,600,000
37. Rays: Alika Williams, SS	$1,850,000

SECOND ROUND

No. Team: Player, Pos.	Bonus
38. Tigers: Dillon Dingler, C	$1,952,300
39. Orioles: Hudson Haskin, OF	$1,906,800
40. Marlins: Dax Fulton, LHP	$2,400,000
41. Royals: Ben Hernandez, RHP	$1,450,000
42. Blue Jays: C.J. Van Eyk, RHP	$1,797,500
43. Mariners: Zach DeLoach, OF	$1,729,800
44. Pirates: Jared Jones, RHP	$2,200,000
45. Padres: Owen Caissie, OF	$1,200,004
46. Rockies: Chris McMahon, RHP	$1,637,400
47. White Sox: Jared Kelley, RHP	$3,000,000
48. Reds: Christian Roa, RHP	$1,543,600
49. Giants: Casey Schmitt, 3B	$1,147,500
50. Rangers: Evan Carter, OF	$1,250,000

No. Team: Player, Pos.	Bonus
51. Cubs: Burl Carraway, LHP	$1,050,000
52. Mets: J.T. Ginn, RHP	$2,900,000
53. Brewers: Freddy Zamora, SS	$1,150,000
54. Cardinals: Masyn Winn, SS/RHP	$2,100,000
55. Nationals: Cole Henry, RHP	$2,000,000
56. Indians: Logan Allen, LHP	$1,125,000
57. Rays: Ian Seymour, LHP	$1,243,600
58. Athletics: Jeff Criswell, RHP	$1,000,000
59. Twins: Alerick Soularie, OF	$900,000
60. Dodgers: Landon Knack, RHP	$712,500

SUPPLEMENTAL SECOND ROUND

No. Team: Player, Pos.	Bonus
61. Marlins: Kyle Nicolas, RHP	$1,129,700
62. Tigers: Daniel Cabrera, OF	$1,210,000
63. Cardinals: Tink Hence, RHP	$1,115,000
64. Mariners: Connor Phillips, RHP	$1,050,300
65. Reds: Jackson Miller, C	$1,290,000
66. Dodgers: Clayton Beeter, RHP	$1,196,500
67. Giants: Nick Swiney, LHP	$1,197,500
68. Giants: Jimmy Glowenke, SS	$597,500
69. Mets: Isaiah Greene, OF	$850,000
70. Cardinals: Alec Burleson, OF	$700,000
71. Nationals: Sammy Infante, SS	$1,000,000
72. Astros: Alex Santos, RHP	$1,250,000

THIRD ROUND

No. Team: Player, Pos.	Bonus
73. Tigers: Trei Cruz, SS	$900,000
74. Orioles: Anthony Servideo, SS	$950,000
75. Marlins: Zach McCambley, RHP	$775,000
76. Royals: Tyler Gentry, OF	$750,000
77. Blue Jays: Trent Palmer, RHP	$847,500
78. Mariners: Kaden Polcovich, 2B	$575,000
79. Pirates: Nick Garcia, RHP	$1,200,000
80. Padres: Cole Wilcox, RHP	$3,300,000
81. Rockies: Sam Weatherly, LHP	$755,300
82. Angels: David Calabrese, OF	$744,200
83. White Sox: Adisyn Coffey, RHP	$50,000
84. Reds: Bryce Bonnin, RHP	$700,000
85. Giants: Kyle Harrison, LHP	$2,497,500
86. Rangers: Tekoah Roby, RHP	$775,000
87. Phillies: Casey Martin, SS	$1,300,000
88. Cubs: Jordan Nwogu, OF	$678,600
89. Red Sox: Blaze Jordan, 3B	$1,750,000
90. D-backs: Liam Norris, LHP	$800,000
91. Mets: Anthony Walters, SS	$20,000
92. Brewers: Zavier Warren, C	$575,000
93. Cardinals: Levi Prater, LHP	$575,000
94. Nationals: Holden Powell, RHP	$500,000
95. Indians: Petey Halpin, OF	$1,525,000
96. Rays: Hunter Barnhart, RHP	$585,000
97. Braves: Jesse Franklin, OF	$497,500
98. Athletics: Michael Guldberg, OF	$300,000
99. Yankees: Trevor Hauver, 2B	$587,400
100. Dodgers: Jake Vogel, OF	$1,622,500
101. Astros: Tyler Brown, RHP	$577,000

TOP 10 PROSPECTS

FROM EVERY MINOR LEAGUE

TRIPLE-A

Triple-A East ★★★★

1. Wander Franco, SS, Durham (Rays)
2. Adley Rutschman, C, Norfolk (Orioles)
3. Bobby Witt Jr., SS, Omaha (Royals)
4. Riley Greene, OF, Toledo (Tigers)
5. Spencer Torkelson, 1B, Toledo (Tigers)
6. Shane Baz, RHP, Durham (Rays)
7. Vidal Brujan, 2B/OF, Durham (Rays)
8. Jose Barrero, SS, Louisville (Reds)
9. Jarren Duran, OF, Worcester (Red Sox)
10. Matthew Liberatore, LHP, Memphis (Cardinals)

Triple-A West ★★★

1. Jarred Kelenic, OF, Tacoma (Mariners)
2. Keibert Ruiz, C, Oklahoma City (Dodgers)
3. Jo Adell, OF, Salt Lake (Angels)
4. Josh Jung, 3B, Round Rock (Rangers)
5. Alek Thomas, OF, Reno (D-backs)
6. Luis Campusano, C, El Paso (Padres)
7. Joey Bart, C, Sacramento (Giants)
8. Jake Meyers, OF, Sugar Land (Astros)
9. Cal Raleigh, C, Tacoma (Mariners)
10. Bryan De La Cruz, OF, Sugar Land (Astros)

DOUBLE-A

Double-A Central ★★★★★

1. Bobby Witt Jr., SS, NW Arkansas (Royals)
2. Julio Rodriguez, OF, Arkansas (Mariners)
3. C.J. Abrams, SS, San Antonio (Padres)
4. M.J. Melendez, C, NW Arkansas (Royals)
5. Alek Thomas, OF, Amarillo (D-backs)
6. Matt Brash, RHP, Arkansas (Mariners)
7. Josh Jung, 3B, Frisco (Rangers)
8. Nolan Gorman, 3B/2B, Springfield (Cardinals)
9. Cole Winn, RHP, Frisco (Rangers)
10. Miguel Vargas, 3B/2B, Tulsa (Dodgers)

Double-A Northeast ★★★★

1. Adley Rutschman, C, Bowie (Orioles)
2. Spencer Torkelson, 1B/3B, Erie (Tigers)
3. Riley Greene, OF, Erie (Tigers)
4. Grayson Rodriguez, RHP, Bowie (Orioles)
5. Gabriel Moreno, C, New Hampshire (Blue Jays)
6. Cade Cavalli, RHP, Harrisburg (Nationals)
7. Oneil Cruz, SS, Altoona (Pirates)
8. Brayan Rocchio, SS, Akron (Guardians)
9. Triston Casas, 1B, Portland (Red Sox)
10. Austin Martin, SS/OF, New Hampshire (Blue Jays)

Double-A South ★

1. Shea Langeliers, C, Mississippi (Braves)
2. Jose Barrero, SS, Chattanooga (Reds)
3. Nick Lodolo, LHP, Chattanooga (Reds)
4. Reid Detmers, LHP, Rocket City (Angels)
5. Hunter Greene, RHP, Chattanooga (Reds)
6. Brennen Davis, OF, Tennessee (Cubs)
7. Jake Eder, LHP, Pensacola (Marlins)
8. Max Meyer, RHP, Pensacola (Marlins)
9. Peyton Burdick, OF, Pensacola (Marlins)
10. Jonathan Aranda, 1B/2B, Montgomery (Rays)

HIGH-A

High-A Central ★★★

1. Spencer Torkelson, 3B/1B, West Michigan (Tigers)
2. Miguel Vargas, 3B, Great Lakes (Dodgers)
3. Jordan Walker, 3B, Peoria (Cardinals)
4. Bobby Miller, RHP, Great Lakes (Dodgers)
5. Andy Pages, OF, Great Lakes (Dodgers)
6. Daniel Espino, RHP, Lake County (Guardians)
7. Brayan Rocchio, SS/2B, Lake County (Guardians)
8. George Valera, OF, Lake County (Guardians)
9. Eddys Leonard, 2B/SS, Great Lakes (Dodgers)
10. Joey Wiemer, OF, Wisconsin (Brewers)

High-A East ★★★★

1. Cade Cavalli, RHP, Wilmington (Nationals)
2. Anthony Volpe, SS, Hudson Valley (Yankees)
3. Francisco Alvarez, C, Brooklyn (Mets)
4. Michael Harris II, OF, Rome (Braves)
5. Ronny Mauricio, SS, Brooklyn (Mets)
6. Oswald Peraza, SS, Hudson Valley (Yankees)
7. Brett Baty, 3B, Brooklyn (Mets)
8. Nick Gonzales, 2B, Greensboro (Pirates)
9. Gunnar Henderson, SS/3B, Aberdeen (Orioles)
10. Liover Peguero, SS, Greensboro (Pirates)

High-A West ★★

1. Julio Rodriguez, OF, Everett (Mariners)
2. George Kirby, RHP, Everett (Mariners)
3. Matt Brash, RHP, Everett (Mariners)
4. Brandon Pfaadt, RHP, Hillsboro (D-backs)
5. Marco Luciano, SS, Eugene (Giants)
6. Orelvis Martinez, SS/3B, Vancouver (Blue Jays)
7. Ezequiel Tovar, SS, Spokane (Rockies)
8. Michael Toglia, 1B, Spokane (Rockies)
9. Levi Stoudt, RHP, Everett (Mariners)
10. Drey Jameson, RHP, Hillsboro (D-backs)

TOP 10 PROSPECTS

LOW-A

Low-A East ★★

1. Gunnar Henderson, SS/3B, Delmarva (Orioles)
2. Nick Yorke, 2B, Salem (Red Sox)
3. Taj Bradley, RHP, Charleston (Rays)
4. Daniel Espino, RHP, Lynchburg (Guardians)
5. Joey Estes, RHP, Augusta (Braves)
6. Dustin Harris, 1B/3B, Down East (Rangers)
7. Curtis Mead, 3B/1B, Charleston (Rays)
8. Colton Cowser, OF, Delmarva (Orioles)
9. Luisangel Acuña, SS, Down East (Rangers)
10. DJ Herz, LHP, Myrtle Beach (Cubs)

Low-A Southeast ★★

1. Anthony Volpe, SS, Tampa (Yankees)
2. Jordan Walker, 3B, PalmBeach (Cardinals)
3. Orelvis Martinez, SS/3B, Dunedin (Blue Jays)
4. Mick Abel, RHP, Clearwater (Phillies)
5. Eury Perez, RHP, Jupiter (Marlins)
6. Elly de la Cruz, 3B/SS, Daytona (Reds)
7. Jasson Dominguez, OF, Tampa (Yankees)
8. Jared Jones, RHP, Bradenton (Pirates)
9. Endy Rodriguez, C/1B, Bradenton (Pirates)
10. Alex Ramirez, OF, St. Lucie (Mets)

Low-A West ★★★★★

1. Tyler Soderstrom, C, Stockton (Athletics)
2. Marco Luciano, SS, San Jose (Giants)
3. Robert Hassell III, OF, Lake Elsinore (Padres)
4. Zac Veen, OF, Fresno (Rockies)
5. Diego Cartaya, C, Rancho Cucamonga (Dodgers)
6. Luis Matos, OF, San Jose (Giants)
7. Noelvi Marte, SS, Modesto (Mariners)
8. Blake Walston, LHP, Visalia (D-backs)
9. Drew Romo, C, Fresno (Rockies)
10. Kyle Harrison, LHP, San Jose (Giants)

ROOKIE

Arizona Complex League ★

1. Elly de la Cruz, 3B/SS, ACL Reds (Reds)
2. James Wood, OF, ACL Padres (Padres)
3. Owen Caissie, OF, ACL Cubs (Cubs)
4. Kevin Alcantara, OF, ACL Cubs (Cubs)
5. Pedro Pineda, OF, ACL Athletics (Athletics)
6. James Triantos, SS/2B, ACL Cubs (Cubs)
7. Aeverson Arteaga, SS, ACL Giants (Giants)
8. Benny Montgomery, OF, ACL Rockies (Rockies)
9. Harry Ford, C, ACL Mariners (Mariners)
10. Jay Allen, OF, ACL Reds (Reds)

Florida Complex League ★★★

1. Marcelo Mayer, SS, FCL Red Sox (Red Sox)
2. Brady House, SS, FCL Nationals (Nationals)
3. Jose Salas, SS, FCL Marlins (Marlins)
4. Coby Mayo, 3B, FCL Orioles (Orioles)
5. Blaze Jordan, 3B, FCL Red Sox (Red Sox)
6. Ian Lewis, 2B, FCL Marlins (Marlins)
7. Joe Mack, C, FCL Marlins (Marlins)
8. Manuel Sequera, SS, FCL Tigers (Tigers)
9. Izaac Pacheco, SS, FCL Tigers (Tigers)
10. Antonio Gomez, C, FCL Yankees (Yankees)